Europe

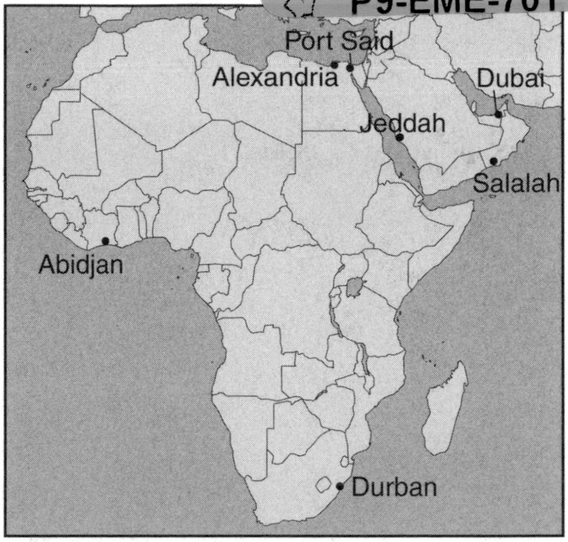

Africa and the Middle East

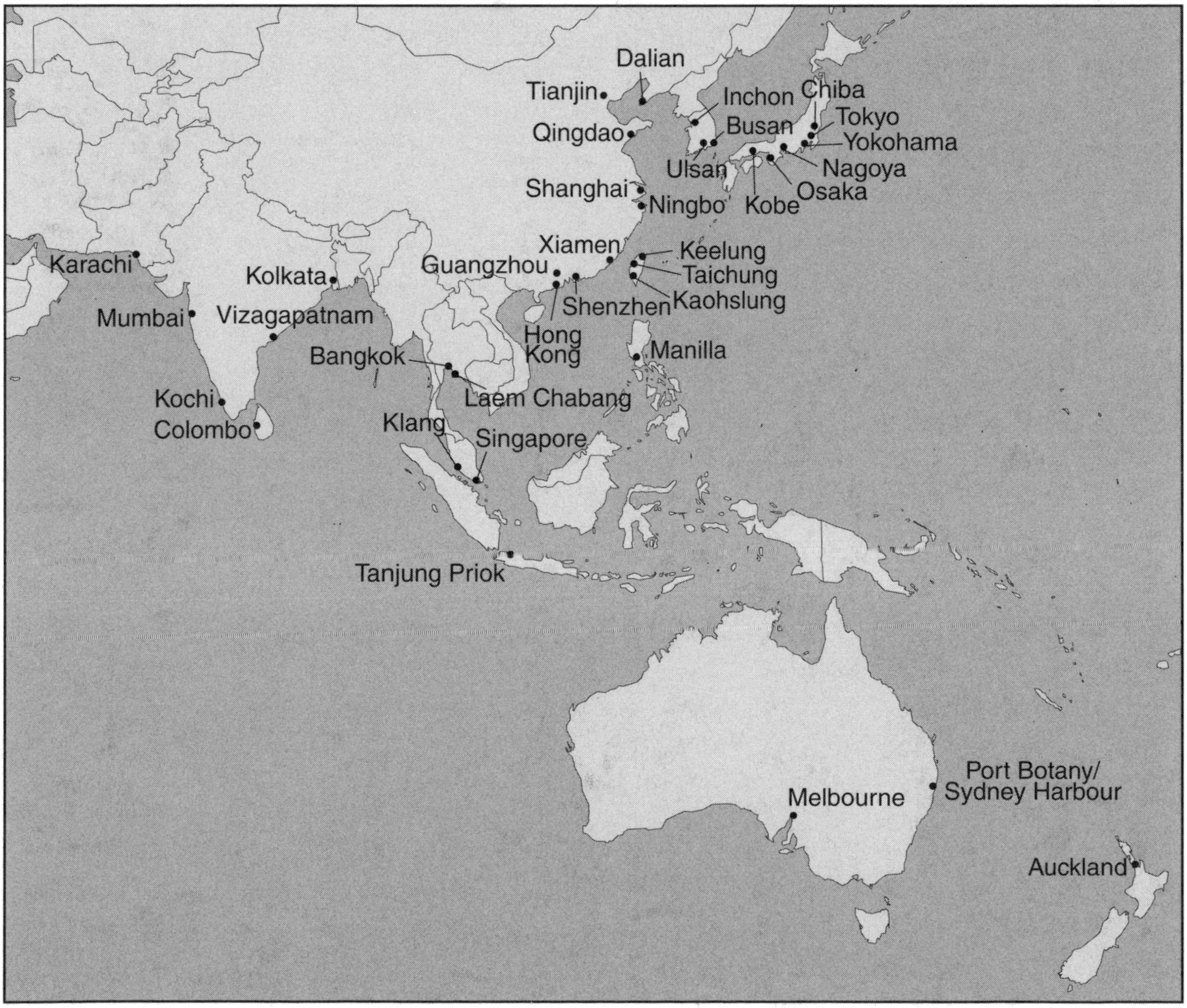

Asia, Australia and the South Pacific region

Seventh Edition

International Business Law and its Environment

Richard Schaffer

Professor Emeritus (Ret.)
Walker College of Business
Appalachian State University

Filiberto Agusti

Senior Partner
Steptoe & Johnson LLP
Attorneys at Law
Washington, DC

Beverley Earle

Professor
Bentley College
McCallum Graduate School of Business

SOUTH-WESTERN
CENGAGE Learning™

Australia • Brazil • Japan • Korea • Mexico • Singapore • Spain • United Kingdom • United States

SOUTH-WESTERN
CENGAGE Learning™

International Business Law and its Environment, 7e

Richard Schaffer, Filiberto Agusti, and Beverly Earle

VP/Editorial Director: Jack W. Calhoun

VP/Editor-in-Chief: Rob Dewey

Acquisitions Editor: Vicky True

Developmental Editor: Kendra Brown

Marketing Manager: Jennifer Garamy

Content Project Manager: Corey Geissler

Production Technology Analyst: Emily Gross

Technology Project Manager: Kristen Meere

Website Project Manager: Brian Courter

Sr. First Print Buyer: Kevin Kluck

Production and Composition: Pre-Press PMG

Senior Art Director: Michelle Kunkler

Internal Designer: Jennifer Lambert/Jen2Design

Cover Designer: Joseph Pagliaro Graphic Design

Cover Image: © Harald Sund/ Photographer's Choice

ISBN-13: 978-0-324-64965-9
ISBN-10: 0-324-64965-7

South-Western Cengage Learning
5191 Natorp Boulevard
Mason, OH 45040
USA

Cengage Learning products are represented in Canada by Nelson Education, Ltd.

For your course and learning solutions, visit **academic.cengage.com**
Purchase any of our products at your local college store or at our preferred online store **www.ichapters.com**

Printed in the United States of America
1 2 3 4 5 6 7 12 11 10 09 08

R. S.

To Avery.

And to John Phillip Reid, Russell D. Niles Professor of Law Emeritus at New York University, dear friend and mentor, whose lectures on the common law and English legal history have influenced my teaching and writing to this day.

F. A.

To my father, Filiberto, and my mother, Maria Luisa, who sacrificed so much that I might be free to write and read as I wish; and to my wife, Susan, and our daughters, Caroline, Olivia, and Jordan, for their patience.

B. E.

To my husband, John, for his support and to our daughter, Molly, for inspiring me with her dedication and hard work.

About the Authors

RICHARD SCHAFFER is Professor Emeritus of Business Law (retired) in the Department of Finance of the Walker College of Business at Appalachian State University. He taught for twenty-five years in the area of business law, international business transactions, and the law of international trade and investment. Professor Schaffer received his J.D. from the University of Mississippi and his LL.M. from New York University. From 1976 through 1982, he assisted United Nations agencies in New York, San Jose, and Vienna with projects related to multinational corporations, corrupt practices, and socioeconomic development, and served as *rapporteur* of international working groups on international economic crime. He also has served as a consultant to business schools, providing advice on the internationalization of the curriculum, and to industry trade groups. Professor Schaffer has extensive experience in business and regularly consults on matters related to the international home textile industry.

FILIBERTO AGUSTI is a partner in the international law firm of Steptoe & Johnson LLP, where he has practiced law since 1978. He represents governments, multinational corporations, manufacturers, and investors in international arbitrations, legal proceedings, and transactional negotiations. His work has included international project finance and privatization transactions, cross-border corporate acquisitions, international joint ventures, and bankruptcy reorganizations. Mr. Agusti has authored articles for the *Harvard Law Review* and other legal publications. He is a frequent speaker at professional seminars around the world and regularly comments on legal issues on camera for Univisión, Telemundo, and CNN en Español. Mr. Agusti was law clerk to the U.S. Court of Appeals for the Second Circuit in 1977–78. He is a graduate of Harvard Law School, where he was a senior editor of the *Harvard Law Review*. He graduated *summa cum laude* with a B.A. from the University of Illinois in 1974.

BEVERLEY EARLE is a professor in the Law, Taxation, and Financial Planning Department and the McCallum Graduate School of Business at Bentley College, Waltham, Massachusetts, where she has been on the faculty since 1983. She teaches international business law at the undergraduate and graduate levels as well as courses on the legal environment of business and law and society. She graduated with a B.A. from the University of Pennsylvania, received a J.D. from Boston University, and is admitted to the practice of law in Massachusetts. Professor Earle has received numerous awards including the Academy of Legal Studies in Business Holmes-Cardozo award (2006), the ALSB Distinguished Proceedings paper (2007), Charles Hewitt Master Teacher Finalist (2006), and the ALSB/Indiana University Center for International Business Education and Research Case Competition (1999). She has been honored as Bentley Scholar of the Year (2001), and has received the Bentley Innovation in Teaching Award and the Bentley Outstanding Scholarly Contribution Award (2007).

Professor Earle has presented papers at numerous conferences including the Cornell Law School Symposium, and her articles have appeared in law reviews including those published at Cornell University, Northwestern University, and the University of California at Berkeley. She taught at Yunnan University in Kunming, China in 1990 and in Strasbourg, France in 1992. She lived in Paris on sabbatical in 1993–1994 and traveled to India on her 2007 sabbatical. She is past president of the International Section of the Academy of Legal Studies in Business. Since 2006, she has been an appointee to the Massachusetts Board of Bar Overseers Hearing Committee on Attorney Discipline.

CONTENTS

Contents in Brief

Table of Cases

Principal cases are in **bold** type. Other cases discussed in the text are in roman type. Cases cited within the principal cases, or other quoted materials are not included.

Table of Treaties

Table of Statutes

Preface

It has been said that America's interest in international education has peaked and ebbed with the changing tide of the American political climate, rising in times of economic expansion and ebbing during periods of political isolation or economic protectionism. Perhaps, however, the cycle has finally been broken, and industry leaders, government policymakers, and educators alike have come to understand the importance of making a permanent commitment to international education.

In the last half of the twentieth century, America faced an increasingly competitive global marketplace and a mounting trade deficit. Rather than seek protection behind often-politicized trade laws, America's leaders committed themselves and the nation to policies of free trade and open investment. American firms realized that they had no choice but to compete aggressively with international competitors, in markets both here and abroad. Witness not only America's great multinational corporations, but also the successes of the many small and medium-sized companies that today do business internationally.

Among nations, the spirit of free trade has become contagious. Examples can be seen everywhere: the rush of nations to join the World Trade Organization, the growth of regional economic integration, privatization of national economies, and the opening of once tightly controlled markets in developing countries and in formerly communist countries as well. The outcome has been the globalization of the world's economy and of world markets for goods and services. It is in this climate that we have seen perhaps the greatest renewal of interest in international business education in America's history.

Trade, Intellectual Property, and Foreign Direct Investment: A Thematic Approach

International Business Law and Its Environment is intended for use in such courses as International Business Law, International Business Transactions, or The Law of International Trade and Investment. Our thematic approach tracks the basic market-entry strategies of most firms as they expand into international markets: trade in goods and services, the protection and licensing of intellectual property rights, and foreign direct investment. Through the study of law, we attempt to provide a comprehensive treatment of each of these market-entry methods—and their variations and combinations—as they fit into the overall strategy of a particular firm. We begin our discussion with trade, which involves the least penetration into the international market, and progress to foreign direct investment, which immerses the firm completely in the social, cultural, and legal systems of its host country. This progression also patterns the life cycle of many firms as they mature and then move more aggressively into new international markets.

Private and Public International Law

International Business Law and Its Environment emphasizes both private and public law. The private law applicable to international business transactions includes the law of international sales, trade finance and letters of credit, distribution agreements, agreements with foreign sales representatives, licensing agreements, and other governing law.

Public international law includes conventions, treaties, and agreements among nations that make up the legal framework within which international business takes place. Customs and tariff laws are good examples, as are laws that open markets to international investors. The treaties of the European Union, the GATT agreements, and NAFTA are prime sources of public international law. Public international law provides the basis for government regulation of international business. It affects the environment within which a firm develops its international business strategies, and establishes the firm's responsibility under national laws and administrative regulations. We also treat general principles of the law of nations, as well as the work of various intergovernmental organizations (such as UN agencies, the WTO, and the OECD), because these are fundamentals needed for study.

International and Comparative Approach

No text can attempt to teach the law of every nation in which a firm might do business, and we have resisted the temptation to merely catalog foreign laws. Instead, we present foreign laws and foreign court decisions throughout the book for comparison purposes, to illustrate differences in legal or economic systems, and to show how business is done in other countries. Where applicable, we compare civil law, common law, socialist law, Islamic law, and concepts from different legal systems. Examples include comparative sales law, labor law, advertising law, and agency law. For instance, our discussion of Chinese law provides U.S. readers with many interesting comparisons, because the United States and China are in different stages of development, with very different political systems. We discuss European law throughout the book. Of course, we treat U.S. law and relevant international agreements, uniform codes, and the decisions of international tribunals in greater detail. Reflecting the importance of international law and comparative law, we rewrote Chapter Two for the seventh edition and gave it a new title: "International Law and the World's Legal Systems."

The Mechanics and Theory of International Business Transactions

International Business Law and Its Environment not only teaches the "hands on" mechanics of international business transactions, but also provides the theory needed for businesspeople to understand the consequences of their actions. Commercial transactions are thoroughly examined and explained. This includes negotiating contracts for the sale of goods and services, negotiating contractual terms of trade, handling shipping contracts and cargo insurance, making agency contracts, dealing with letters of credit and other banking arrangements, considering alternatives for dispute settlement, and much more. Many sample forms and documents are included. Methods for protecting one's intellectual property are closely considered, as are the handling of international investment arrangements, employing persons abroad, and other issues. Similarly, we take readers through many thorny problems of dealing with the government, such as learning how to move goods through U.S. Customs or following a systematic guide to export licensing.

A Business and Managerial Perspective

We begin with the premise that the world of international business is a dangerous place, and that the management of international business is the management of risk. Whether one is developing and implementing an international business strategy, or managing an international business transaction, an understanding of the special risks involved will help ensure a project's success. In keeping with our thematic approach, we examine the risks of trade (for example, managing credit and marine risk); protecting and licensing intellectual property (for example, dealing with gray-market goods and registering foreign patents); handling foreign mergers and acquisitions (for example, coping with unexpected differences in foreign corporate or labor law); and evaluating political risk in less stable regions of the world. We then show how to avoid, reduce, or shift the risk to other parties or intermediaries. The case study approach is excellent for this purpose, as it shows readers the mistakes others have made, and how disputes have been resolved.

We also stress strategic business decision making. For example, our chapter on imports, customs, and tariff law does not view importing as an isolated transaction. Rather, it addresses the importance of customs and tariff law on a firm's global operations, such as the selection of contractors and the location of overseas offices and factories. We have implemented this technique throughout the book.

The Cultural, Political, Social and Economic Environment, and Human Rights Concerns

As with each previous edition, we have made a special effort to discuss the cultural, economic, political, and social aspects of international business as they bear on differences in attitudes toward the law, their impact on trade relations, and how they affect the way we do business in another country.

In discussing trade issues, it is almost impossible to separate politics, foreign policy, and trade. This is evident in our coverage of export controls and trade sanctions imposed for reasons of foreign policy or national security. We have also devoted considerable attention to current events in many countries and their impact on international business there.

Many topics require a historical perspective, such as the *Smoot-Hawley* era of the 1930s, the development of GATT in the 1940s, export controls and the Cold War, the Iranian Revolution of 1979, fifty years of U.S.–Cuba relations, and recent U.S. involvement in Kuwait and Iraq. We often try to draw on the lessons of history, such as the implications of President Carter's grain embargo of the Soviet Union in response to that nation's invasion of Afghanistan, or President Reagan's embargo of U.S. participation in the construction of the Siberian natural gas pipeline to Western Europe.

Throughout the book, we return to focus on U.S.–China relations and the potential impact on U.S. trade, investment, and jobs. Readers are also often asked to consider the impact of world current events on their strategic business decisions, particularly in unstable regions or under hostile political and economic conditions.

We believe that it is impossible to cover the real world of international business without exploring the larger problems of human rights. Thus, we treat the areas of human rights law and international criminal law as global issues of concern to international business. Here we draw on examples from Burma (Myanmar), the Congo, West Africa, the Balkans, and Haiti, to name a few.

Developing Countries

The developing countries of Africa, Asia, Latin America, and the Caribbean present special problems for their richer trading partners. We have tried to paint a realistic picture of trade opportunities, colored by the realities of disease, poverty, and environmental degradation that threaten much of our planet.

Trade and investment issues in developing countries are incorporated in all parts of the book. Examples include the Generalized System of Preferences, the CARICOM *Single Market and Economy Treaty,* the *Doha Development Agenda,* and the recent U.S. trade initiatives for Central America, Latin America, the Middle East, the Caribbean, and Africa. Many special issues related to doing business in the independent republics of the former Soviet Union are covered. The annual UNCTAD *World Investment Report* is discussed, along with the impact of multinational corporations on the developing world.

Ethics and Social Responsibility

Because ethical questions can arise in varying contexts, we have chosen to integrate the subject throughout the book. However, beginning with the seventh edition, we have given a more focused treatment to ethics, social responsibility and corporate codes of conduct in Chapter Two, the chapter on international law. Many chapters also conclude with a hypothetical case problem on ethics, called *Ethical Considerations.* Examples include, among others:

- Codes of conduct
- Bribery and corruption
- Child labor
- Workers' rights
- Protection of the environment and of fish and wildlife

- Prison and forced labor
- Fair trade initiatives
- Human rights issues
- AIDS and other world health issues
- Discrimination issues in foreign countries
- Special issues related to U.S. investment in Mexican *maquiladora* plants
- The ban on asbestos products

To Our International Readers

We are pleased to know that our work is contributing to student learning at universities on virtually every continent and in every region of the world. Naturally, our audience is primarily an American one. We necessarily devote a major portion of the text to American law, U.S. trade relations, and the needs of the American firm. However, we have made every effort to maintain our international perspective and to draw important international comparisons. Cases from countries other than the United States appear throughout the book, as do discussions of foreign codes and practices. Moreover, the increased reliance on uniform rules, harmonized codes, and international standards makes the book suitable for any student interested in international business law.

Key Revisions to the Seventh Edition

The seventh edition is one of our most significant revisions. To begin, several key chapters are completely new. Chapter Two, "International Law and the World's Legal Systems" (formerly "International Law and Organizations") now takes a much broader view of international and comparative law in the modern world, and one that is relevant for students of international business law. The chapter contains a thorough treatment of the following main topics:

- Foundations of international customary law
- Sources and principles of international law
- The law of treaties
- Human rights law and international criminal law
- Principles of international jurisdiction and extraterritoriality
- A comparative analysis of common law, civil law, and Islamic law legal systems, including Islamic case law
- A study of the legal systems in Japan, Saudi Arabia, and Pakistan
- Intergovernmental organizations that affect international business law

We have also included a new, more focused discussion of corporate social responsibility, accountability, and codes of conduct.

Also completely revised is "The Regulation of Exports," which now follows "Imports, Customs, and Tariff Law" (Chapter Twelve). While this chapter takes a straightforward, systematic, transactional approach to export licensing under the Export Administration Regulations, it does not sidestep the larger policy issues behind the control process. To the contrary, the greatest strength of this entirely new chapter is that it now focuses on current foreign policy and national security issues affecting the world since the fall of the Soviet empire and the rise of international terrorism. The chapter gives students a real-life view of the world of international business as it is today. Topics include:

- Export controls to counter terrorism, stop the proliferation of nuclear technology and weapons of mass destruction, and keep technology from America's potential enemies
- The economic and political implications of trade sanctions, using key historical case examples
- The use of organized trade sanctions against states that sponsor terrorism or violate human rights, and an evaluation of their practical effectiveness
- The president's "emergency powers" over financial transactions and foreign assets
- The new threat of foreign industrial espionage in America since the Cold War
- An analysis of the foreign policy and national security issues related to controls on technology, nonproliferation, human rights concerns, multilateral trade sanctions, IEEPA, the *Patriot Act,* and foreign asset regulation
- Arms export controls

The chapter also takes a historical look at export controls during the Cold War, including case studies of the grain embargo on the Soviet invasion of Afghanistan and the U.S. embargo of the Siberian natural gas pipeline, and evaluates their impact on business. Importantly, the chapter approaches the subject from the business law perspective and examines the needs of businesspeople to understand not only the licensing process, but also the policies behind export controls and trade sanctions.

Other chapters have also undergone considerable rewriting and updating. Chapter Fifteen, "The European Union and Other Regional Trade Areas," tackles new EU issues and presents new cases. It addresses privacy issues in Europe and their conflict with U.S. Homeland Security rules, includes new cases on harmonization, discusses the new CARICOM *Single Market and Economy Treaty,* and presents the first case from the new Caribbean Court of Justice, which is the supreme judicial organ of the new Caribbean Community. This builds on the work of the sixth edition, in which Chapter Three, "Resolving International Commercial Disputes," was completely revised. That chapter places a greater emphasis on avoiding disputes and on basic issues related to international arbitration and litigation. It addresses the special problems of international dispute settlement, such as

- Cultural barriers to dispute resolution
- Obtaining jurisdiction over foreign parties in the Internet age
- Cross-border forum shopping
- Foreign judicial assistance

Conflict of laws principles are now introduced in this chapter.

The next section of this preface summarizes topics that are new or significantly revised in this edition.

Part One: The Legal Environment of International Business

As mentioned before, this book contains a completely new Chapter Two, "International Law and the World's Legal System," which presents international and comparative law topics relevant to students of international business law.

Some of the other content that is new to Chapter Two includes:

- Foundations of international law and international customary law, such as *Sosa v. Alvarez-Machain*
- Treaty law, including *Renkel v. U.S.*
- Human rights law, including *Congo v. Belgium* (ICJ), which discusses genocide and extraterritoriality
- International criminal law, international jurisdiction over crimes and terrorist acts, and discussion of *U.S. v. Ramsey Yousef*
- New coverage of cybercrime
- A broader approach to the study of international organizations, focusing on UN agencies and other NGOs that affect business, and the ICJ
- A more focused study of ethics, corruption, corporate social responsibility, and codes of conduct
- A new and thorough treatment of comparative law, including common law, civil law, and Islamic legal systems, their origins, and the modern legal systems of Japan, Saudi Arabia, and Pakistan
- The "Islamic interest cases" decided by the Sharia Appellate Bench of the Pakistani Supreme Court

Other new Chapter Two topics include the ILO conventions, the OECD Code, the *UN Convention Against Corruption,* the *UN Global Contract,* and the *Levi Strauss & Co. Global Sourcing and Operating Guidelines and Country Assessment Guidelines.*

Other major changes to Part One are

- A revised Chapter One that better reflects the many changes in this edition
- Updated trade, investment, and economic data, incorporated into the discussion
- New material on the costs of intellectual property counterfeiting and U.S.–China relations
- Updated material on Russia and Eastern Europe
- Analysis of UNCTAD's latest *World Investment Report* and the impact of multinational corporations on development

- Current political and economic changes in China and developing countries

Part Two: International Sales, Credits, and the Commercial Transaction

Significant changes include the following:

- Revised and rewritten CISG materials, including mutual assent, battle of the forms, performance of contracts, damages, and the historical development of sales law
- Revised coverage of letters of credit to reflect the new UCP 600 (2007)
- Revised COGSA materials
- New coverage of the *Montreal Air Convention* and the liability of air carriers, including new material on jurisdiction and air disaster litigation

Part Three: International and U.S. Trade Law

We have expanded our discussion of presidential powers (inherent authority, emergency powers, etc.) in light of the war on terror, the *PATRIOT Act,* and Bush administration policies. Cases discussed include *Hamdan v. Rumsfeld* and for perspective, *Youngstown Sheet & Tube v. Sawyer.* Other new and revised content includes:

- The controversy over labor and environmental issues affecting trade promotion authority
- Updated WTO materials, including trade relations with Russia, Vietnam, and China
- New coverage of the impact of free trade on cultural diversity
- Updated coverage of agricultural trade and subsidies, including the U.S.–Brazil dispute over cotton subsidies
- Discussion of new rules governing global textile trade
- Revised material on China safeguards and global safeguards
- Changes to the discussion of countervailing duty laws applicable to non-market economy countries, including China
- An updated and clarified rules-of-origin discussion
- An updated U.S.–Mexico cross-border trucking discussion
- Significantly revised production sharing/*maquiladora* materials
- A new approach to the study of the regulatory and licensing process in Chapter Thirteen, "The Regulation of Exports"
- A complete revision of Chapter Fifteen, "The European Union and Other Regional Trade Areas," including new cases

Part Four: Regulation of the International Marketplace

New and updated content includes

- A new comparative look at restrictions on advertising of alcohol and tobacco
- New DOJ and SEC materials on foreign corrupt practices
- Updated WIPO decisions on intellectual property
- *Pasquantino v. U.S.,* the 2005 U.S. Supreme Court decision on the "revenue rule" and the knowing violation of foreign revenue laws by U.S. citizens
- Changes in Venezuela and nationalizations there
- Alien Tort Claims litigation and the *Rio Tinto and Bridgestone/Firestone Rubber Liberia Plantation* decisions
- Updated material on extraterritorial application of U.S. discrimination laws
- Increased focus on child labor standards and working conditions
- New coverage of environmental initiatives and treaties, including the ICJ decision on *Pulp Mills on the River Uruguay,* climate change, and alternative energy
- New coverage of biodiversity, desertification, and other environmental issues
- Expanded and updated competition and antitrust coverage, including the ECJ decision in

Microsoft v. Commission of the European Communities, the *Leegin* decision of the U.S. Supreme Court, and China's new anti-monopoly law

Our Greatest Challenge

Perhaps the greatest challenge in preparing any edition is simply to keep up with the rapid pace of political, economic, and legal changes around the world. We had to make revisions almost daily to keep abreast of current developments. There are countless topics that had to be included or revised at the last moment. Other issues are still outstanding. Will the U.S. Congress extend the president's trade promotion authority? Will the *Doha Development* rounds conclude successfully? Will Russia be admitted to the WTO? Will there be progress toward a free trade area of the Americas? How will the future U.S. response to international terrorism affect U.S. business interests? How will political changes in Venezuela affect the business climate there, and will socialist principles spread in Latin America? How will the end of U.S. quotas on textile imports affect jobs? Will American attitudes toward Chinese imports and illegal immigration affect its attitude toward free trade? How will the 2008 U.S. presidential election affect America's position on trade issues? These and many other questions must await the next edition.

Pedagogical Features of the Seventh Edition

Ethical Considerations provides selected end-of-chapter case studies containing ethical or social responsibility issues. Examples include

- Sewing contractors in India
- Sales commissions on arms sales in the Middle East
- Outsourcing to Mexico
- Exports of outdated pharmaceuticals to Africa
- Letter of credit fraud
- Free trade vs. cultural diversity
- Trade in genetically modified foods
- Chinese dumping: Is low cost selling unfair?
- Fair trade products—will paying a higher price for coffee eradicate poverty?
- Lobbying to decontrol exports of dual-use chemical products and explaining it to your board and shareholders

Other end-of-chapter features include *Managerial Implications,* which provides case problems suitable for extended discussions and end-of-chapter questions based on actual cases (citations provided).

Primary source materials include landmark and cutting-edge cases from U.S. and foreign courts, and decisions of the WTO, NAFTA, ICSID, International Court of Justice, European Court of Justice, Caribbean Court of Justice, and other international judicial and arbitral tribunals.

In addition, we have incorporated

- Business and industry examples, sample documents, and forms
- Current economic data and statistical information
- An expanded list of acronyms frequently used in international business

The *International Business Law and Its Environment* instructor and student supplements are available exclusively on the textbook companion site at *academic.cengage.com/blaw/schaffer*. The Instructor's Manual with Test Bank has been revised and enhanced by Lucien Dhooge of the University of the Pacific at Stockton. The Instructor's Manual provides answers to case questions and problems, end-of-chapter questions, *Managerial Implications,* and *Ethical Considerations.* It also offers teaching summaries, supplemental cases and exercises, teaching suggestions, and class activities. Selected Test Bank chapters have been updated with new essay questions that challenge students to carefully consider both the application and implications of the law.

Chapter PowerPoint slides, updated by Joseph A. Zavaletta of the University of Texas at Brownsville, are also available on the instructor companion Web site. These can be used for lecturing or given to students for studying.

The student companion site also features new interactive chapter quizzes created by Romain

Lorentz of the University of St. Thomas in Minneapolis. Other online resources for students include selected text appendices, Internet activities, links to the organizations and documents referenced in the text as well as relevant international business law and cultural Web sites, and Court Case Updates.

Access to the **South-Western Digital Video Library** is available as an optional package with any of the South-Western Legal Studies in Business textbooks. Featuring over sixty segments on the most important topics in business law, South-Western's Digital Video Library helps students make the connection between the textbook and the business world. Four types of clips are available: *Legal Conflicts in Business* features modern business scenarios, *Ask the Instructor* offers concept review, *Drama of the Law* presents classic legal situations, while *LawFlix* contain clips from many popular Hollywood movies. Together, these clips bring business law to life. Access to the Digital Video Library can be bundled with every new text for no additional cost. For more information, visit *http://academic.cengage.com/blaw/dvl/*.

Instructors can select individual cases from **TextChoice®** to create a customized casebook for their course. Offered through Cengage Learning Custom Solutions, the TextChoice® database offers hundreds of case choices and is searchable by topic or state. Qualified adopters can also receive (10) free hours of **Westlaw®**, an online legal portal with access to over 15,000 databases of information including cases, public records, court dockets, legal forms, research materials and the WestLaw® Directory. Please contact your Cengage Learning sales representative to request access to Westlaw® or to learn more about TextChoice® options.

Acknowledgments

The authors wish to express their gratitude to the following reviewers for their help in preparing this and past editions:

Mark B. Baker
University of Texas—Austin

Michael A. Baker
University of California—Los Angeles

Patricia B. Bartscher
San Francisco State University

Karen Bork
Northwood University

Nivea Castro
Upper Iowa University—Fayette

Sandra J. Defebaugh
Eastern Michigan University

Larry A. Di Matteo
University of Florida

Rafi Efrat
California State University—Northridge

Joan T. A. Gabel
Florida State University—Tallahassee

John M. Garic
University of Central Oklahoma

Christopher Gibson
Suffolk University

Rex D. Glensy
Drexel University

David P. Hanson
Duquesne University

Michael E. Jones
University of Massachusetts—Lowell

Romain M. Lorentz
University of St. Thomas—Minneapolis

F. William McCarty
Western Michigan University

Sean P. Melvin
Elizabethtown College

Carol J. Miller
Southwest Missouri State University

Fred Naffziger
Indiana University—South Bend

Gregory T. Naples
Marquette University

Lynda J. Oswald
University of Michigan

Marisa Anne Pagnattaro
University of Georgia—Athens

Kimberlianne Podlas
University of North Carolina—Greensboro

Emilia Justyna Powell
Georgia Southern University

Bruce L. Rockwood
Bloomsburg University

John C. Ruhnka
University of Colorado—Denver

Martin L. Saradjian
Boston University

Richard Still
Mississippi State University

Clyde D. Stoltenberg
California State University—Long Beach

Michael A. Valenza
Temple University

Susan M. Vance
St. Mary's College

Martha Weisel, Esq.
Hofstra University

John Wrieden
Florida International University

Norman Gregory Young
California State Polytechnic University—Pomona

Our thanks also go to Lucien Dhooge, Joe Zavaletta, and Romain Lorentz for their work on this edition's supplements, and to Stanley Smilack of Steptoe & Johnson LLP.

Each of us would like to express our sincere gratitude to our editors at South-Western Legal Studies in Business, Vicky True, Kendra Brown, Corey Geissler, and Tim Bailey, for their advice, support, and skill as editors and for transforming mere words and thoughts into a valuable tool for learning. We owe a special word of thanks to Susan Smart, who masterfully guided the development of four editions of *International Business Law*, for her dedication to our work during those years and for her kind understanding, patience, and encouragement.

Richard Schaffer
Filiberto Agusti
Beverley Earle

Seventh Edition

International Business Law and its Environment

PART 1 The Legal Environment of International Business

Part One of *International Business Law and Its Environment* provides a framework for understanding both international business and the legal environment in which it operates. The chapters focus on how economic, social, and political forces influence the development of the law and legal institutions. Chapter One provides a conceptual framework for studying international business. The chapter explains the three major forms of international business: trade (importing and exporting); licensing agreements for the transfer and legal protection of patents, copyrights, trademarks, and other intellectual property (including franchising); and active foreign investment through mergers, acquisitions, and joint ventures.

In Chapter One, the reader is also introduced to key trade and investment statistics affecting the United States and its major partners, and their impact. We examine the economic environment of doing business in the developing countries, with special attention to China, Latin America, and countries still transitioning from their once communist pasts. We will also consider the role of multinational corporations in world development, and the special problems they confront in developing countries. At the end of the first chapter, the reader will be asked to consider how the risks of international business differ from the risks of doing business at home. How does a firm deal with the added risks of doing business over great distances, the risks of language and cultural barriers, the risks of miscommunication, currency fluctuations, international hostilities and political interference, the risks of trade controls or restrictions on investment, the risks of foreign litigation, or the risks of nonpayment or breach of contract? By raising these questions, this chapter illustrates that the management of an international business transaction is, in large part, the management of risk. The remainder of the book provides the opportunity for the thoughtful reader to consider how careful business and legal planning can help to avoid or reduce these risks or shift them to another party to the transaction.

Chapter Two provides important foundations for the book. Understand that international business law includes both public law and private law. If the rule of law affects a private (often commercial) transaction between two parties, such as between buyer and seller or shipper and ocean carrier, it is considered private law. If the rule of law determines the rights and responsibilities of nations in relation to one another (such as an agreement to set tariff rates on imports), or places public controls on an otherwise private transaction (such as criminal penalties imposed on an individual or corporation for making a false customs declaration), the law is considered public law. Chapter Two lays a foundation for understanding these basic principles.

Many readers will have little familiarity with international law. Chapter Two explains the nature and sources of international law, including custom, multilateral treaties, international conventions, and other international agreements. We will examine the role of several intergovernmental organizations, including agencies of the United Nations, in developing international standards and legal codes, that become binding on nations that adopt them. Many of these directly affect business operations worldwide. Whether the problem is related to humanitarian issues such as the ethical treatment of labor in developing countries, laundering of drug money through the international banking system, setting standards for the protection of the world's oceans, or developing uniform rules for international sales contracts, international organizations can be useful in bringing individual nations to agreement on difficult issues. Many of the international codes address ethical issues facing businesses operating globally, such as corruption or child labor, and these, too, are examined.

Chapter Two also addresses key doctrines of international law and key U.S. statutes affecting access to U.S. courts for torts and other acts occurring outside U.S. territory.

Chapter Two takes a comparative look at different legal systems, including the common law, civil law, and Islamic law systems, with a special emphasis on China and the Middle East. We will examine several selected legal topics, such as torts and crimes, and see how culturally diverse countries in different regions of the world approach these subjects differently.

Chapter Three discusses how disputes are settled in an international business transaction, including both litigation and arbitration. It addresses issues of jurisdiction and procedural rules for litigating international cases. For instance, the chapter attempts to answer such questions as: If a company does business in a foreign country, can the company be sued there? If a buyer purchases goods from a foreign firm that does not regularly do business in the United States, under what circumstances can the buyer sue that firm in U.S. courts? If a product that is produced in one nation injures a consumer in another nation, where should the injured party's claim be heard? If a firm obtains a court judgment in one country, can the firm enforce it against the defendant's assets held in another country? Finally, because the costs and risks of foreign litigation are substantial, the chapter addresses what the parties can do in advance to provide an alternative to litigation should a dispute result.

CHAPTER 1
INTRODUCTION TO INTERNATIONAL BUSINESS

ECONOMIC INTERDEPENDENCE

Many economists and business experts realize that no business is purely domestic and that even the smallest local firms are affected by global competition and world events. The realities of the modern world make all business international. No longer can an economic or political change in one country occur without causing reverberations throughout world markets. A terrorist event in London, or in the Philippines, is reflected on international stock exchanges and brings entire economies to their knees. War in the Middle East brings international shipping to a standstill. A civil war on the African continent affects the price of commodities in London and New York. A change in interest rates in Germany affects investment flows and currency exchange rates in the United States. Disruption anywhere in the supply chain of today's globally connected manufacturing plants brings distant assembly lines to a halt. The failure of China to safeguard American copyrights on films or software results in the United States imposing retaliatory tariffs and affects the price of Chinese-made clothing in American stores. Terrorist attacks not only affect business operations worldwide, but also affect the ability of managers to travel and live safely in foreign lands.

Perhaps nowhere is global economic interdependence more obvious than in the context of the spread of infectious disease. Whether it be "mad cow" affecting English cattle, or infectious respiratory disease affecting people from Toronto to rural China, the impact of infectious disease can now ripple through the world's economy within days. Indeed, in recent years the effects of terrorism and infectious disease has been felt by international business travel and tourism and affected the global operations of firms on all continents. The world today is more economically interdependent than at any other time in history, and this has led to the globalization of product, service, and capital markets.

Economic interdependence is the result of many factors. Precious natural resources and raw materials are located around the world. Technological advances in travel, shipping and communications, and the Internet have brought people closer together. Nations have moved away from protectionism and increasingly toward free trade, opening markets for goods and services that were once closed to foreign competition. The world has seen a steady movement toward economic integration and the development of free trade areas and "common markets" among nations. Greater political stability in the developing countries has led to increased foreign investment, industrialization, and the integration of those nations into the world economy. Economic interdependence also can be attributed to the sharing of technology and know-how, with patents, copyrights, and trademarks now licensed for use around the globe as freely as goods and services are sold. The interrelatedness of financial markets, the worldwide flow of capital, and the coordination of economic policies between nations have had a tremendous impact on the global economy. Giant multinational corporations now move people, money, and technology across national borders in the blink of an eye.

Political changes in the last two decades have further increased economic interdependence. Throughout the world, countries are moving toward greater political freedom and democracy. The breakup of the Soviet Union in 1991 into independent republics, the largest of which is Russia, opened those countries to opportunities for investment by Western companies. It also freed much of Eastern and Central Europe from communist oppression, leaving them open for foreign investment. As these nations converted from closed communist-dominated governments to a free-market economic system based on private enterprise, they became more economically integrated with the rest of the world. A similar phenomenon is now occurring in Latin America and parts of Asia. Many of these countries that were once ruled by military dictatorships have moved to democracy. This new freedom opens them up to foreign investors and helps to integrate them into the world's economic community.

With interdependence, nations realized the need to reach agreement on important legal issues. This led to the development of widely accepted legal norms and conventions to provide a stable and consistent legal environment for firms doing business across national borders. In summary, the factors that yet hold the greatest promise for change are the growth of democracy, the resurgence of market-oriented economies, and the decline of socialism. Perhaps the greatest challenges are those from international terrorism, entrenched poverty and ignorance, declining natural resources, environmental degradation, and the ever-present risk of widespread infectious disease.

America in International Markets

Americans have long been active in all aspects of international business. U.S. history is rich with stories of the "Yankee trader"—from the colonial period to the present. U.S.–owned trademarks, such as Coca-Cola, McDonald's, Disney, and Microsoft, are recognized in every culture and in every language. U.S. firms have built factories around the globe and shared their technology, know-how, and management capabilities with their foreign partners.

Historically, American involvement in international business has come chiefly from its largest companies. Small- and medium-sized manufacturing firms traditionally shied away from involvement overseas due to a provincial attitude, rooted in America's westward expansion and based on the idea that business could expand infinitely merely by tapping domestic markets. The country had a vast supply of natural resources, and domestic demand exceeded supply, so businesses felt little need to sell products overseas. The presence of vast oceans separating the nation from its trading partners made foreign trade seem even more bothersome. Furthermore, the United States was preoccupied with other matters. First came the movement westward, then the political isolationism and economic protectionism spawned by World War I. New European immigrants of the day quickly sought to forget their pasts, preferring to become Americans and to adopt the language and customs of their new country. It was not until the Great Depression, caused in part by the protectionist policies of the 1920s and 1930s, that Americans realized just how interdependent the world had become.

At the close of World War II, the United States was in a preeminent political and economic position relative to the war-devastated nations of Europe and the Far East. The factories of Europe and Japan lay in rubble, with North America having virtually the only functioning industrialized economy in the world. The United States, to its credit, quickly recognized its responsibility to pull the world out of the ravages of war. It succeeded, in large part, through the creation of a massive industrial economy based on consumer goods that stimulated and strengthened the redevelopment of once-industrial Europe and Japan. The United States also recognized the need for international institutions, such as the UN, the International Monetary Fund, the World Bank, and the global trading organization, GATT, to ensure that the world did not slip back into recession. However, U.S. growth was so strong that many U.S. companies never viewed themselves as a part of a world marketplace and saw little need to sell or manufacture abroad. Most saw the world only as a source for natural resources and cheap labor. Indeed, not until the 1980s, when the effect of mounting U.S. trade deficits began to be felt, when foreign firms gained a greater share of U.S. domestic markets, and when American jobs were lost to foreign workers, did Americans realize that oceans could no longer insulate them from foreign competition.

A Lack of Commitment. In the early part of the last century, managers of many small- and medium-sized U.S. firms simply lacked the commitment to international business. Some, for instance, only began to think of selling their products abroad after domestic orders declined. As a result, many ventures failed. During the time needed to gear up for the export process, which can take months or years, the domestic economic cycles would turn up again, and U.S. companies would soon lose interest in their newfound foreign customers. These same firms would ship products abroad with no thought given to the problems of marketing in foreign cultures or to how they would supply parts or service for the products they sold. Without a long-term commitment, these firms were viewed by foreign buyers as unreliable suppliers. Companies that tried to find foreign buyers or investment partners soon learned that entering international markets required much patience, time, and commitment.

The Education of American Managers. In recent decades, America's small- and medium-sized firms have come to realize the importance of competing in global markets. They have had to learn that selling goods and services abroad can be extremely profitable, but only if senior management makes a long-term commitment to their foreign customers and if they work to maintain their reputation as a valued supplier. They have learned that opportunities abound for sourcing goods and services abroad, but only if they understand how to manage the risks involved. They have learned to do business in more than one currency, to overcome language and cultural barriers, and to recognize that ethnic and religious differences will influence their business dealings overseas. They understand that advertising and marketing strategies must differ from region to region and country to country. They understand that managing people abroad can be enormously different from managing people at home. They have had to learn to do business under foreign laws, to deal with foreign government regulators, to move goods and money across national borders, and to understand and manage the risks of international business.

Forms of International Business

This text classifies international business into three categories: (1) trade, (2) international licensing of technology and intellectual property (trademarks, patents, and copyrights), and (3) foreign direct investment. To the marketer, these broad categories describe three important methods for entering a foreign market. To the international lawyer, they represent three forms of doing business in a foreign country and the legal relationship between parties to an international business transaction. Each form represents a different level of commitment to a foreign market, a different level of involvement in the life of a foreign country, and a different set of managerial challenges. Each form exposes the firm to a different set of business and legal risks. Trade usually represents the least involvement, and thus the least political, economic, and legal risk, especially if the exporting firm is not soliciting business overseas or maintaining sales agents or inventories there. The ownership of a foreign firm carries with it the obligations of corporate citizenship and means the complete involvement in all aspects of life in the foreign country—economic, political, social, cultural, and legal.

Considerable overlap occurs among these different forms of doing business. A business plan for the production and marketing of a single product may contain elements of each form. To illustrate, a U.S. firm might purchase the rights to a trademark for use on an article of high-fashion clothing made from fabric exported from China and assembled in offshore plants in the Caribbean for shipment to the United States and Europe. Here, a business strategy encompasses elements of trade, licensing, and investment. For firms just entering a new foreign market, the method of entry might depend on a host of considerations, including the sophistication of the firm, its overseas experience, the nature of its product or services, its commitment of capital resources, and the amount of risk it is willing to bear.

Trade

Trade consists of the import and export of goods and services. *Exporting* is the shipment of goods out of a country or the rendering of services to a foreign buyer located in a foreign country. *Importing* is the entering of goods into the customs territory of a country or the receipt of services from a foreign provider.

Trade is as old as the oldest civilization. Throughout history, countries traded to obtain needed items that were not readily available in their country. The marketplaces of Europe, Africa, Asia, and the Middle East had been the scene of trade for hundreds of years before seaborne trade became established. By the sixteenth century, the first international sea trade routes were established by the Europeans. With the advent of great naval power, Portugal and Spain opened the Americas, India, and the Pacific to trade. Portuguese was the language of the ocean traders. Portugal purchased textiles from India and China with gold taken from Africa. They traded Chinese porcelain to Spain for gold that Spain had taken from Mexico. By the eighteenth century, the Dutch had created a great trading empire based on pepper and spices, and England relied on America for tobacco, corn, and cotton. For more than three hundred years, trade in horses, weapons, and slaves thrived.

Comparative Advantage. Today the products are different, but the economic concepts are the same. In theoretical terms, the concept of *absolute advantage* states that nations should concentrate their efforts on producing those goods that they can make most efficiently, with a minimum of effort and waste. Any surplus of goods left over after domestic consumption is then traded for goods that another nation has produced under the same circumstances. David Ricardo, a nineteenth-century British economist, stated that a country can gain from trading goods even though it may not have an absolute advantage in producing those goods. This notion formed the basis for the theory of *comparative advantage*. Comparative advantage exists if the costs of production and price received for the goods allow the goods to be sold for a higher price in a foreign country than at home. When countries specialize in producing goods over which they have a comparative advantage, all countries will produce more and consume more, and wealth and employment will increase. An example from the early trading days illustrates how this concept works.

By the sixteenth century, Portugal had already established outposts for trading silk, cloth, and spices throughout the Indian Ocean. The Portuguese had also found ways of trading with faraway China. Portuguese traders discovered that although they could get silk most easily from their outposts in Persia or India, it would be to their benefit to obtain these products from China. China had greater resources and more effective production methods, which made their products less costly and of a better quality than anything that Portugal could obtain elsewhere. China, on the other hand, had a great appetite for the pepper that Portugal could obtain readily from Indian outposts. China could produce its own pepper, but not of the same quantity or quality that the Portuguese traders could provide. Although Portugal had its own source of silk, and China its own pepper, their advantage came from obtaining these goods from one another. Thus, Portugal had a comparative advantage in pepper and China in silk. By focusing their capital and labor on doing what they did best, each country could produce and consume more of both products.

It is important to emphasize that this transaction was not regulated by today's barrage of tariffs, government subsidies to producers, politics, historical events, or other complicating factors. Michael Porter, in *The Competitive Advantage of Nations*, introduced a modification of this earlier concept, advocating that a nation's advantage is determined by the ability of its companies to increase productivity and continuously innovate. In today's world, the politics of protectionism or free trade could turn an economic model inside out. But world trade has developed and become the major commercial activity that it is today based upon this principle of comparative advantage.

Recent Trends in U.S. Trade. Since the 1970s, U.S. imports have increased dramatically, outpacing the growth in exports. This has led to a growing U.S. trade deficit that has continued to worsen to this day. In the early 1980s, the trade deficit was blamed on the high value of the U.S. dollar, which made U.S. goods expensive for export to foreign buyers (who had to exchange their currencies for dollars in order to buy U.S. goods). The decade of the 1980s, however, saw intense international efforts, coordinated by central banks in the United States, Japan, and Europe, to bring the value of the dollar down (to the chagrin of U.S. tourists abroad). In another attempt to boost U.S. exports, the U.S. government initiated a large-scale incentive and public awareness program to encourage small- and medium-sized manufacturers and service companies to enter foreign markets. During the 1980s, reports showed that a mere 250 of the largest U.S. multinational corporations accounted for 85 percent of U.S. exports. The U.S. Department of Commerce believed that a great number of smaller U.S. firms had products suitable for export markets if they would only make the commitment needed to tap those potential customers. To assist these "new-to-export" companies, the Department of Commerce spearheaded a national effort to introduce small firms to the basics of exporting. By the end of the decade, many of these new-to-export companies were contributing significantly to the U.S. export base.

Today, more and more small U.S. companies are entering export markets, fueled in part by the Internet, by cheaper and faster global communications, and by more open access to global supply chains. In 2006, according to the U.S. Department of Commerce *Exporter Database,* there were over 239,000 individual identified companies exporting goods from the United States, up from 112,000 in 1992. Of these, over 97 percent were small- or medium-sized businesses, with fewer than 500 employees. Almost 89 percent of identified exporters had only a single location. These are not the multinational corporations and conglomerates we think of when we think of international business.

Of course, large companies still dominate the total share of U.S. export volume, accounting for 71 percent of total exports in 2005. Yet the success with which more and more small- to medium-sized U.S. firms are entering foreign markets, and their impact on the U.S. economy, is well established.

There is another trend that has worked to increase American exports—investment by foreign firms in the United States. Experience has proven that when a foreign firm opens a subsidiary in the United States, or acquires an existing American company, it often provides its U.S.-based operations with access to new global capital, with export "know-how," and with access to established channels to foreign markets. These foreign-owned U.S. companies are proving to be successful exporters of U.S.-made products. Honda Motor Company, for example, exports sizable numbers of automobiles from its U.S. plants to many countries, including Japan, with its American-made Acura luxury sedans expected to be exported to China. However, the effect reaches companies of all sizes and in all industries. A study of one state, North Carolina, showed that a large percentage—more than 50 percent—of foreign-owned firms operating in that state were exporting their products abroad. As U.S. firms became more competitive, and as economic growth in Europe, Asia, and in the developing countries provided markets for U. S. goods and services, U.S. exports continued to increase.

Trade in Goods: The U.S. Position. Despite the actual increase in U.S. exports, imports of foreign goods into the United States have continued to increase at a faster rate. As a result, the United States has continued to have increasingly large trade deficits. In 2006, the U.S. Department of Commerce reported that the combined U.S. exports of goods and services amounted to a record $1,445.7 billion. (Unless otherwise noted, all figures are reported on a balance of payments basis, seasonally adjusted by the U.S. Bureau of Economic Analysis.) In that year, total U.S. imports of goods and services amounted to more than $2,204.2 billion, for a total trade deficit of $758.5 billion. U.S. exports of goods alone in 2006 were $1,023.1 billion, with imports of goods at $1,861.3 billion, leaving a trade deficit in goods of $838.2 billion. Keep in mind that this last figure includes a $270.9 billion trade deficit in petroleum products alone. America's top trading partner (including both imports and exports) is Canada, followed by Mexico, Japan, China, the United Kingdom (UK), Germany, South Korea, the Netherlands, France, and Taiwan. America's trade deficit was largest with China, Japan, Canada, and Mexico.

According to the World Trade Organization, the U.S. share of world merchandise exports is at 8.7 percent (including intra-EU trade), ranking it just behind Germany as the second leading exporter of merchandise. They are followed by China, Japan, France, the Netherlands, the UK, Italy, and

Canada. Given that China's exports are growing so rapidly, China's merchandise exports may soon exceed that of the United States, indicating that while the United States may be an economic superpower, it is not the only economic superpower.

The importance of trade to the U.S. economy cannot be overstressed. According to the U.S. Department of Commerce, U.S. exports of goods and services account for a substantial portion of real gross domestic product growth. This has been especially important during recessionary periods, when exports continued to fuel growth in the economy. Estimates are that during the last decade, exports accounted for more than half of the new jobs in the United States, and for virtually all of the increase in manufacturing jobs. The Office of the United States Trade Representative estimates that wages paid to U.S. workers in export manufacturing industries are about 17 percent higher than average. In 2006, the top ten U.S. exporting states were California, Texas, New York, Michigan, Washington, Illinois, Ohio, Florida, New Jersey, and Pennsylvania. Specific rankings vary according to industry sector, such as agriculture and merchandise trade.

TRADE IN SERVICES: THE U.S. POSITION. Cross-border trade in services includes business services such as travel (defined as the purchase of goods and services by short-term travelers), passenger fares, shipping, package delivery, banking, insurance, securities brokerage, and royalty payments and license fees resulting from transfers of patents, trademarks, copyrights, and other intellectual property rights. It also includes professional services such as law, accounting, or architecture, and technical services such as waste management, industrial and environmental engineering, software development, and management consulting. In the developed countries of Europe, Japan, Canada, and the United States, business services have actually accounted for the majority of the gross domestic product, jobs, and job growth in recent years. Cross-border trade in services accounts for approximately 20 percent of world trade. According to the World Trade Organization, the top five leading exporters (and also leading importers) of services are the United States, the UK, Germany, France, and Japan, with the United States accounting for over 14 percent of total world exports of services. U.S. exports of services have been rising steadily. The U.S. Department of Commerce reported that in 2006, U.S. exports of services reached $422.5 billion, with imports at $342.8 billion, leaving a trade surplus of $79.7 billion.

Exporting

Exporting is often a firm's first step into international business. Compared to the other forms of international business, exporting is relatively uncomplicated. It may provide the inexperienced or smaller firm with an opportunity to reach new customers and to tap new markets. It usually requires only a modest capital investment, and the risks are generally manageable by most firms. It also permits a firm to explore its foreign market potential before venturing further. For many larger firms, including multinational corporations, exporting may be an important portion of their business operations. The U.S. aircraft industry, for example, relies heavily on exports for significant revenues.

HAVING AN EXPORT PLAN. Although most marketing issues are beyond the scope of this book, it should be noted here that successful exporting requires an *export plan.* Firms that are "new-to-export" should especially consider the following components of such a plan:

- Assessing the firm's readiness for export markets by evaluating its success in domestic markets and its willingness to commit financial resources, human resources, and production output to export markets
- Making a long-term commitment to exporting and to foreign customers on the part of senior management and executives
- Identifying foreign-market potential of the firm's products, including economic, political, cultural, religious, and other factors
- Identifying the risks involved in exporting to that foreign market, including an evaluation of cost-effective shipping arrangements, banking arrangements for getting paid, and political risks
- Evaluating the legal aspects of the firm's export plan for compliance with government rules and

customs regulations, including identifying legal controls on exporting its products out of the United States as well as legal barriers to importing and selling its products in the foreign country, and whether there are any patents, copyrights, or trademarks that have to be protected abroad

- Determining the export readiness and suitability of the firm's products for the export market; whether the products meet the quality standards, technical regulations, and foreign language requirements of foreign countries; and whether any redesign, re-engineering, or re-labeling of products is needed
- Identifying members of the "export team," comprising management, outside advisors, and trade specialists from banking, shipping, and government
- Identifying possible financing arrangements to assist foreign buyers
- Establishing foreign market channels of distribution, including deciding whether to export directly to customers or indirectly through intermediaries, deciding whether to use a sales representative or foreign distributor, identifying potential buyers, and participating in foreign trade shows
- Re-evaluating the firm's export performance over time, reconsidering its export plan, and determining whether the firm should increase its penetration of foreign markets beyond exporting

Firms accept varying levels of responsibility for moving goods and money and for other export functions. The more experienced exporters can take greater responsibility for themselves and are more likely to export directly to their foreign customers. Firms that choose to accept less responsibility in dealing with foreign customers, or in making arrangements for shipping, for example, must delegate many export functions to someone else. As such, exporting is generally divided into two types: direct and indirect.

Direct Exporting. *Direct exporting* refers to a type of exporting where the exporter, often a manufacturer, assumes responsibility for most of the export functions, including marketing, export licensing, shipping, and collecting payment. At first glance, direct exporting seems similar to selling goods to a domestic buyer. A prospective foreign customer may have seen a firm's products at a trade show, located a particular company in an industrial directory, or been recommended by another customer. A firm that receives a request for product and pricing information from a foreign customer may be able to handle it routinely and export directly to the buyer. With some assistance, a firm can overcome most hurdles, get the goods properly packaged and shipped, comply with all legal requirements, and receive payment as anticipated. Although many of these one-time sales are turned into long-term business success stories, many more are not. A successful exporter will develop a regular business relationship with its new foreign customer. However, the problems that can be encountered even in direct exporting are considerable.

Many firms engaged in direct exporting on a regular basis reach the point at which they must hire their own full-time export managers and international sales specialists. These people participate in making export marketing decisions, including product development, pricing, packaging, and labeling for export. They should take primary responsibility for dealing with foreign buyers, for attending foreign trade shows, for complying with government export and import regulations, for shipping, and for handling the movement of goods and money in the transaction. Many direct exporters utilize the services of foreign sales representatives or foreign distributors.

Foreign sales representatives are independent sales agents that solicit orders on behalf of their principals and are compensated on a commission basis. Typically, they sell at the wholesale level to customers for commercial resale. Sales agents do not take ownership or possession of the goods, or bear any risk in the transaction. They simply bring buyer and seller together. They have the advantage of knowing the foreign market, having established customer loyalty, and of carrying a range of complementary products. For instance, they may represent several different manufacturers of U.S. sporting goods in Japan—one that makes baseball bats, another than makes gloves, and a third that makes baseballs.

Direct exporting also can be done through *foreign distributors*. Foreign distributors are independent firms, usually located in the country to which a firm is exporting, that purchase and take delivery of goods for resale to their customers. Foreign distributors are often used when the products involved require service or a local supply of spare parts or are perishable or seasonal. They assume the risks of buying and warehousing goods in their market and provide additional product support services. The distributor usually services the products they sell, thus relieving the exporter of that responsibility. They often train end users to use the product, extend credit to their customers, and bear responsibility for local advertising and promotion.

INDIRECT EXPORTING. *Indirect exporting* is used by companies that do not have the experience, personnel, or capital to tackle a foreign market by themselves. They may be unable to locate foreign buyers or are not yet ready to handle the mechanics of a transaction on their own. By indirect exporting, the firm can use specialized intermediaries that can take on many of the export functions—marketing, sales, finance, and shipping. Two types of intermediary include export trading companies and export management companies.

EXPORT TRADING COMPANIES. *Export trading companies,* commonly called ETCs, are companies that market the products of several manufacturers in foreign markets. They have extensive sales contacts overseas and experience in international finance and shipping. Large Japanese export trading companies are well known for their success in exporting the products of Japanese firms that are competitors in Japanese domestic markets. This has given the Japanese the competitive advantage of being able to penetrate overseas markets with a range of products from companies that are stiff competitors at home, and to do it in a way that takes advantage of economies of scale in exporting. The problem for U.S. firms was that until 1982, such conduct by competitors would have been considered a violation of the U.S. antitrust laws. In 1982, in order to give American exporters the same competitive advantage, Congress passed the U.S. *Export Trading Company Act*. Since then, U.S. export trading companies have been able to apply for and receive a certificate from the U.S. Department of Justice that waives the application of U.S. antitrust laws to their export activities. This waiver makes it lawful for many manufacturers to cooperate in exporting to foreign markets, when such collusion might otherwise be illegal under the antitrust laws of the United States. For example, if two competing firms that manufacture similar products agree to fix prices in the U.S. market, it would be illegal. However, if they are members of an approved ETC, they may jointly establish export prices, enter into joint export marketing arrangements, allocate export territories, and do business in ways that if done with the U.S. market would be illegal. The waiver is issued only if it is shown that it will not lessen competition within the United States, or unreasonably affect domestic prices of the exported products. There are many advantages in selling through an ETC: teaming up to bid on large foreign projects, filling large and complex foreign orders, joint marketing of complementary or competing products, division of foreign territories by competing firms, sharing of marketing and distribution costs, and reducing rivalry between U.S. firms in dealing with foreign customers.

The act permits U.S. banks to have an ownership interest in approved ETCs. This allows ETCs to operate with the assistance and financial backing of large banks, thus making the resources, export know-how, and international contacts of the bank's foreign branches available to the ETC. Export trading companies often take title to the goods and resell them for a profit.

EXPORT MANAGEMENT COMPANIES. *Export management companies,* or EMCs, are independent firms that assume a range of export-related responsibilities for manufacturers, producers, or other exporters. They might do as little as render advice and training on how to export, or they might assume full responsibility for the entire export sales process. Many EMCs specialize in specific industries, products, or foreign markets. They are used by firms that cannot justify their own in-house export departments. They often engage in foreign market research, establish foreign channels of distribution, exhibit goods at foreign trade shows, work with foreign sales agents, prepare documentation for export, and handle language translations and shipping arrangements. As in direct exporting, all

Sogo Sosha

forms of indirect exporting can involve sales through agents or to distributors.

Importing and Global Sourcing

When reading this text, the reader should keep in mind that importing is not to be viewed in the isolated context of a single transaction. True, many importers do import only on a limited or one-time basis. However, in this book importing is presented from the perspective of the global firm for which importing is a regular and necessary part of their business. *Global sourcing* is the term commonly used to describe the process by which a firm attempts to locate and purchase goods or services on a worldwide basis. These goods may include, for example, raw materials for manufacturing, component parts for assembly operations, commodities such as agricultural products or minerals, or merchandise for resale.

Government Controls over Trade: Tariffs and Non-tariff Barriers

Both importing and exporting are governed by the laws and regulations of the countries through which goods or services pass. A central portion of this text will be devoted to understanding why and how nations regulate trade through international trade law. Nations regulate trade in many ways. The most common methods are *tariffs* and *non-tariff barriers.* Tariffs are import duties or taxes imposed on goods entering the customs territory of a nation. Tariffs are imposed for many reasons. They may include (1) the collection of revenue, (2) the protection of domestic industries from foreign competition, (3) retaliation against another country or countries for imposing tariffs higher than agreed or for placing other unfair restrictions on their imports, or (4) to impose political or national security controls. For example, some tariffs provide incentives to import products from politically friendly countries and discourage the importing of products from unfriendly countries. Most tariff rates today are determined by agreement between nations.

NON-TARIFF BARRIERS TO TRADE. Consider this hypothetical: Assume that all automobiles sold in the United States have wheel assemblies with either four or five lug nuts. U.S. tests show that this number is adequate for safety. But the Bureau for the Protection of Wheel Assemblies of the Government of Zimbabwe passes a rule requiring that all wheels be assembled with at least six lug nuts. It just so happens that all Zimbabwean automobile manufacturers already use six nuts. Zimbabwean tests show that six nuts are safer than five. The cost of redesigning, retooling, and testing U.S.–made cars for shipment to Zimbabwe is tens of millions of dollars. Do you think that the U.S. firms can justify the expenditures? Probably not, and Zimbabwean drivers will have to be content with driving Zimbabwean cars. While this may appear to be a perfectly legitimate safety regulation on its face, it also has the effect of being a non-tariff barrier to trade.

Non-tariff barriers are all barriers to importing or exporting other than tariffs. They generally take the form of laws or administrative regulations that have the effect, directly or indirectly, of restricting access of foreign goods or services to a domestic market. These regulations are not necessarily enacted for the explicit purpose of restricting trade—for keeping out foreign goods and services that compete with local firms—but they may have that effect. Many laws and regulations exist to protect the national economic and social well-being of a nation. These include health and safety regulations, environmental regulations, and industrial and agricultural standards, for example.

Here are a few common examples: Some nations may permit the sale of certain genetically modified foods, while other nations may not. One nation may prohibit the sale of a certain pharmaceutical drug, even though it is considered safe and commonly sold in other countries. And virtually all nations require imported goods to be marked with the name of the foreign country of origin and labeled in their local language so that consumers know what they are buying. To the manufacturer with a global marketing strategy, these are examples of direct non-tariff barriers to foreign market entry.

One type of non-tariff barrier, like our Zimbabwean hypothetical above, is the technical barrier to trade. These barriers take the form of technical regulations or standards that mandate how products are to be designed and how they will perform. Examples include safety standards for automobiles and other consumer products, standards for electrical goods, and environmental standards. We are all familiar with standards for the design of infant cribs, car seats, or even food additives. Any of these can be a barrier to trade.

Non-tariff barriers are generally a greater barrier to trade than are tariffs because they are more insidious. Unlike tariffs, which are published and easily understood, non-tariff barriers can be disguised in detailed administrative codes, written in the local language, and not generally made available to foreign firms. It has not been uncommon, especially in some developing countries, for the regulations to be available only to local customs inspectors who use these to deny or delay entry to foreign goods—and then only after the goods have been made, labeled, packaged, and shipped to the foreign market's port of entry. Indeed, most trading nations and businesspeople alike would consider this an unfair method of protecting a domestic market from competition.

Both tariffs and non-tariff barriers have a tremendous influence on how firms make their trade and investment decisions. These decisions, in turn, are reflected in the patterns of world trade and the flows of investment capital. Consider this illustration. In 1992, the European nations virtually eliminated trade barriers among themselves. In the years prior to this event, companies from the United States, Canada, and Japan invested heavily in Europe. They purchased existing firms there and established new ones. If they had stayed on the "outside" and remained content to export to Europe, they would have lost competitiveness to firms within Europe. However, by manufacturing there, they could sell within Europe on the same basis as other European firms. Similar capital investment flows occurred in Mexico in the early 1990s as a result of the creation of a free trade area between Mexico, the United States, and Canada. For example, when Japanese firms learned that Mexican-made products could be shipped to the United States and Canada with few tariffs and non-tariff barriers, companies from Japan quickly sought to establish manufacturing facilities in Mexico to take advantage of changes in trade laws.

QUOTAS, EMBARGOES, AND BOYCOTTS. Other obvious non-tariff barriers include quotas, embargoes, and boycotts. A *quota* is a restriction imposed by law on the numbers or quantities of goods, or of a particular type of good, allowed to be imported. Unlike tariffs, quotas are not internationally accepted as a lawful means of regulating trade except in some special cases.

The term *embargo* is generally used when referring to a total or near-total ban on trade with a foreign country or countries. Embargoes can include restrictions on imports or exports, on financial transactions with the foreign country, or on travel between the countries. Total or partial embargoes are often a response to countries that support terrorism, nuclear proliferation, or severe violations of human rights. Internationally orchestrated embargoes were used against Iraq after its invasion of Kuwait in 1990, and later when it was thought that Iraq was producing weapons of mass destruction. The United States has maintained a near-total embargo on Cuba since the early 1960s. A *boycott* is a refusal to trade or do business with certain firms, usually from a particular country, on political or other grounds. Under certain circumstances, it can be illegal for a private firm or citizen to participate in a boycott. An example is the Arab boycott of Israeli products and firms. It is unlawful for American businesspeople to participate in such a boycott.

EXPORT CONTROLS. An *export control* is a restriction on exports of goods, services, or technology to a country or group of countries imposed for reasons of national security or foreign policy. Export controls in the United States are enforced through an export licensing system administered by the United States Department of Commerce. Licensing requirements can apply to exports of almost any type of goods or technology, although advanced technology items that can contribute to the military capability of a foreign nation are most strictly regulated. In some cases, the mere sharing of technological or scientific information with a foreign national, without an export license, can be illegal. Before signing a contract for the sale of certain products or technical know-how to a foreign customer, U.S. exporters must consider whether they will be able to obtain U.S. licensing for the shipment.

EAR & ITAR

TRADE LIBERALIZATION AND THE WORLD TRADE ORGANIZATION. *Trade liberalization* refers to the efforts of governments to reduce tariffs and non-tariff barriers to trade. In the twentieth century, the most important effort to liberalize trade came with the international acceptance of the *General Agreement on Tariffs and Trade*. This is an agreement between nations, first signed in 1947, and continually expanded since that time, that sets the rules for how nations will regulate international trade in goods and services. In 1995, the Geneva-based *World Trade Organization,* or WTO, was created to administer the rules and to assist in settling trade disputes among its member nations. All WTO nations are entitled to *normal trade relations* with one another. This is sometimes referred to as *most favored nation* trading status. This means that a member country must charge the same tariff on imported goods, and not a higher one, as that charged on the same goods coming from other WTO member countries. Trade liberalization has led to increased economic development and an improved quality of life around the world.

Intellectual Property Rights and International Licensing Agreements

Intellectual property rights (IPRs) are a grant from a government to an individual or firm of the exclusive legal right to use a copyright, patent, or trademark (known as *intellectual property* or IP) for a specified time. They represent ownership rights in intellectual property.

COPYRIGHTS, PATENTS, AND TRADEMARKS. *Copyrights* are legal rights to artistic or written works, including books, software, films, or music, or to such works as the design of a computer chip. *Trademarks* include the legal rights to a name or symbol that identifies a firm or its product. *Patents* are governmental grants to inventors ensuring them the exclusive legal right to produce and sell their inventions for a period of years. Copyrights, trademarks, and patents represent substantial assets of many domestic and international firms. Because of its value, intellectual property can be sold or licensed for use to others through a licensing agreement.

International Licensing Agreements. *Licensing agreements* are contracts by which the holder of intellectual property will grant certain rights in that property to a foreign firm under specified conditions and for a specified time. Licensing agreements represent an important foreign market entry method for firms with marketable intellectual property. For example, a firm might license the right to manufacture and distribute a certain type of computer chip or the right to use a trademark on apparel such as blue jeans or designer clothing. It might license the right to distribute Hollywood movies or to reproduce and market software in a foreign market, or it might license its patent rights to produce and sell a high-tech product or pharmaceutical. U.S. firms have extensively licensed their property around the world, and in recent years have purchased the technology rights of Japanese and other foreign firms.

A firm may choose to license its intellectual property as its market entry method because licensing can provide a greater entrée to the foreign market than is possible through exporting. A firm may realize many advantages in having a foreign company produce and sell products based on its intellectual property instead of simply shipping finished goods to that market. When exporting to a foreign market, the firm must overcome obstacles such as long-distance shipping and the resulting delay in filling orders. Exporting requires a familiarity with the local culture. Redesign of products or technology for the foreign market may be necessary. Importantly, an exporter may have to overcome trade restrictions, such as quotas or tariffs, set by the foreign government. By contrast, licensing to a foreign firm allows the licensor to circumvent trade restrictions by having the products produced locally, and it allows entrance to the foreign market with minimal initial start-up costs. In return, the licensor might choose to receive a guaranteed return based on a percentage of gross revenues. This arrangement ensures payment to the licensor, whether or not the licensee earns a profit.

Even though licensing agreements give the licensor some control over how the licensee utilizes its intellectual property, problems can arise. For instance, the licensor may find that it cannot police the licensee's manufacturing or quality control process. Protecting itself from the unauthorized use or "piracy" of its copyrights, patents, or trademarks by unscrupulous persons not party to the licensing agreement is also a serious concern for the licensor. Such unauthorized use is known as *infringement*. The following case, *First Flight Associates*, illustrates what can happen to a firm that fails to take proper legal steps to protect its trademark rights in a foreign country. Notice how this firm's strategy involved both exporting and licensing.

Rights in intellectual property can be rendered worthless if those rights cannot be protected by law. The protection of intellectual property is often a matter of national law (as in the United States, where it is protected primarily under federal statutes). However, intellectual property rights granted in one nation are not legally recognized and enforceable in another, unless the owner takes certain legal steps to protect those rights under the laws of that foreign country. Most countries have

First Flight Associates v. Professional Golf Co., Inc.

527 F.2d 931 (1975)

United States Court of Appeals (6th Cir.)

BACKGROUND AND FACTS

Pro Golf, a U.S. company, manufactured and sold golf equipment under the brand name "First Flight," which had been registered in the United States and certain other foreign countries. In 1961 Pro Golf negotiated with Robert Wynn to act as their foreign sales representative in Japan. Wynn incorporated First Flight Associates, Inc. (FFA) under Japanese law for the purposes of selling Pro Golf's products there. No formal agency or distributorship agreement was ever entered into by the parties. In 1967 the parties entered into a trademark agreement, whereby FFA was permitted to use Pro Golf's "First Flight" trademark on golf soft goods, such as golf bags and clothing, in return for the payment of a royalty. FFA attempted to sub-license the trademark to another Japanese company, Teito, for a royalty much larger than that paid to Pro Golf. When Pro Golf objected, the company learned that its attempt to register the trademark in Japan had not been completely successful, but that third parties had obtained the right to use the trademark in Japan in marketing certain types of soft goods. Pro Golf terminated the agency ... agreement with FFA, and FFA brought this action for breach of contract.

MARKEY, CHIEF JUDGE

The issue on appeal is whether the district court erred in finding that ... Pro Golf was entitled to terminate the sales representation contract ... and that FFA was not liable under the counterclaims for royalties received from Teito or for Pro Golf's expenditures relating to its trademark rights in Japan....

As to the initial 1961 contract for Japanese sales representation on clubs and balls, we agree with the district court that Pro Golf effectively and lawfully terminated FFA as its representative, the termination being effective as of the end of July 1973. That termination did not breach the contract....

The contract was clearly therefore one for an indefinite period of time. Contracts silent on time of termination are generally terminable at will by either party with reasonable notice....

It is unnecessary to discuss the conduct of Wynn or FFA under the trademark license contract or whether "satisfactory business" was being done under the sales representation contract. The latter contract being terminable at will, Pro Golf was clearly within its rights in terminating it.

Pro Golf contends that royalties paid to FFA by Teito should have been passed through to Pro Golf. That contention is based on Pro Golf's fundamentally unsound characterization of FFA as its agent in entering into the Teito contract. As we have indicated, that contract is a trademark sub-license, wherein FFA conveyed to Teito some or all of its rights to use "First Flight" in Japan as a trademark on "soft goods," which rights FFA had under its license from Pro Golf. Nothing in FFA's trademark license contract with Pro Golf prohibited FFA from granting sub-licenses to others or required FFA to pass along to Pro Golf any royalties FFA might receive from such sub-licenses.

Pro Golf also counterclaimed for damages equal to its expenditures incurred in attempting to perfect its Japanese rights in "First Flight" as applied to

continued

continued

certain golf soft goods. Pro Golf's difficulties stemmed from its own failure to obtain complete registration in Japan of "First Flight" in all of the relevant classes of goods. Under Japanese trademark law, rights are acquired through registration and not through use in commerce as in the United States. Although Pro Golf had exclusive rights in "First Flight" when applied to clubs and balls and to some of the classes of soft goods on which the trademark was being used by FFA, third parties had obtained Japanese registrations of "First Flight" for use on other classes of goods, including other golf soft goods. Pro Golf found it necessary to deal with those third-party registrants in seeking to acquire exclusive rights in "First Flight" as a trademark in Japan for the entire spectrum of golf soft goods. We fully agree with the district court that FFA is not liable for expenditures incurred by reason of Pro Golf's own failure to properly register its trademark in Japan.

Accordingly, the decision of the district court is in all respects affirmed.

Decision. Pro Golf was permitted to terminate its Japanese sales agency relationship with FFA because, under U.S. law, sales agency contracts are terminable at will. However, Pro Golf was not entitled to royalties earned by FFA on soft goods bearing the "First Flight" trademark because Pro Golf had failed to perfect its rights to the use of that trademark under Japanese law.

laws that protect the owners of intellectual property, and they enforce those laws. However, copyrights, patents, and trademarks are widely pirated in China, Russia, Eastern Europe, and the developing countries of Asia, Latin America, Africa, and the Middle East. In these countries, intellectual property protection laws are sometimes nonexistent and often not enforced.

The Costs of Counterfeit Products. Counterfeit, or "bootlegged," products are products sold in violation of the copyright, patent, or trademark of the legitimate owner. Counterfeit products are found in all industries, and not just in films, recordings, and software. The cost of counterfeiting is more than just lost revenue to the rightful owner. Many counterfeit products are inferior and even dangerous. The U.S. Chamber of Commerce has documented cases of fake medicines, exploding cell phone batteries, automotive brake pads made of compressed sawdust, toothpaste containing antifreeze, dangerous baby cribs, and even defective, fake aircraft parts. The Internet has greatly increased the ability of pirates to deliver counterfeit products in digital form. Some counterfeiters have completely infiltrated the global supply lines, selling fake products to unwary customers. Indeed, some developing countries encourage piracy because of the perceived financial gains to their economies. For example, a few developing countries may not protect pharmaceutical and chemical patents at all, believing that some products are so indispensable to the public that low-cost generic versions should be encouraged regardless of IP rights.

Of course, most countries decry the lost tax revenues resulting from counterfeit products. The Organisation for Economic Cooperation and Development (OECD) estimated that counterfeit goods crossing international borders in 2006 cost legitimate producers over $200 billion annually. (The true cost of counterfeiting is unknown, and estimates can vary by hundreds of billions of dollars, depending on whether the report is from a government agency or industry group.) The U.S. Chamber of Commerce estimates that 750,000 American jobs have been lost to counterfeited products and alleges that some proceeds of counterfeiting go to fund international terrorism. A broader perspective was given in a report by business leaders gathered by the International Chamber of Commerce in 2007, which warned that stolen IPRs threatened the very future of the information- and knowledge-based economy of the twenty-first century.

Intellectual Property and U.S.-Chinese Relations. Lost profits and lost royalties to U.S. firms now amount to billions of dollars each year in counterfeited goods sold overseas. This has been a long-standing problem over the past decades, and nowhere is it more visible than in U.S.-Chinese relations. During the 1980s, as China opened its doors and became a member of the world trade community, it passed several new laws for the protection of IPRs. In the decade following, China also joined several international agreements for the protection of IPRs. Despite new legislation, international agreements, and many promises to the United States, China has largely failed to enforce its laws. This led to trade disputes involving many different industries, the most notable of which have been movie production, sound recording, book publishing, pharmaceuticals, software, and consumer goods containing major international brands.

On at least three major occasions during the 1990s, the United States publicly threatened to impose punitive tariffs on Chinese goods. It seemed that "trade wars" were being narrowly averted only as last-minute agreements were reached. It should be pointed out that many Americans did not support U.S. threats to impose tariffs on Chinese-made products. Retailers and consumers in the United States argued that this would increase the cost of their merchandise. U.S. manufacturers feared an increase in the costs of Chinese raw materials and component parts that they used. American exporters, such as U.S. airplane manufacturers and certain agricultural producers, feared losing access to China's growing market. Clearly, a negotiated settlement is usually in the best interests of both nations. In recent years the Chinese government has moved further to improve IPR protection. China has established specialized courts to handle IPR cases and set up a plan for issuing permits to any business wanting to copy software, inspecting businesses for violations, setting up accounting requirements to ensure compliance, and giving Chinese authorities the right to seize and destroy counterfeit goods. The United States is still urging China to use more severe criminal penalties against offenders and to stop exports of counterfeit products. Nevertheless, in a 2006 report, the United States Trade Representative estimated that over 80 percent of imported counterfeit goods entering the United States were coming from China.

International Franchising. *Franchising* is a business arrangement that utilizes an agreement to license, control, and protect the use of the franchiser's patents, trademarks, copyrights, or business know-how, combined with a proven plan of business operation, in return for royalties, fees, or commissions. The most common form of franchising is known as a *business operations franchise* and is usually used in retailing. Under a typical franchising agreement, the franchisee is allowed to use a trade name or trademark in offering goods or services to the public in return for a royalty based on a percentage of sales or other fee structure. The franchisee will usually obtain the franchiser's know-how in operating and managing a profitable business and its other "secrets of success." (Concepts include using a "secret recipe," a store design that has been proven successful, production or accounting methods, and even financing techniques.) Franchising in the United States accounts for a large proportion of total retail sales. When American markets became saturated for franchise opportunities several decades ago, U.S. firms began looking overseas for growth. In foreign markets as well, franchising has been successful in fast-food retailing, hotels, car rental, automobile maintenance, video rentals, educational courses, convenience stores, printing services, and real estate services, to name but a few. U.S. firms have excelled in franchising overseas, making up the majority of new franchise operations worldwide. The prospects for future growth in foreign markets are enormous, especially in China and the developing countries of Asia, the Middle East, and Latin America. According to the U.S. Commercial Service's 2007 *Country Commercial Guide,* Brazil is now the second-largest franchise market in the Western Hemisphere, behind the United States, with over 60,000 outlets for nearly 1,000 different brands. China reports that as of 2007 it had nearly 2,500 franchises in 60 different industries with almost 100,000 locations, and growing rapidly. During the 1990s, franchising extended into the countries of Eastern Europe and the former Soviet Union as a method of introducing private enterprise to their formerly communist-dictated economies.

Some Legal Aspects of Franchising. Franchising is a good vehicle for entering a foreign market because the local franchisee provides capital investment, entrepreneurial commitment, and on-site management to deal with local customs and labor problems. However, many legal requirements affect franchising. Franchising in the United States is regulated primarily by the Federal Trade Commission at the federal level. The agency requires the filing of extensive disclosure statements to protect prospective investors. Other countries have also enacted new franchise disclosure laws. Some developing countries have restrictions on the amount of money that can be removed from the country by the franchiser. Other countries might have restrictions on importing supplies (ketchup, paper products, or whatever) for the operation of the business. These restrictions protect local suppliers. However, developing countries that are more progressive are now abandoning these strict regulations because they want to welcome franchisers, their high-quality consumer products, and their managerial talent to their markets. China eliminated most of its restrictions on franchising in 2004.

The following case, *Dayan v. McDonald's*, illustrates the difficulty in supervising the operations of a franchisee in a distant foreign country. Consider how any U.S. franchiser will allow its franchisees to adapt to the cultural environment in a foreign country while still providing the same consistent quality and service that is expected whenever anyone patronizes one of their establishments anywhere in the world.

Dayan v. McDonald's Corp.

466 N.E.2d 958 (1984)

Appellate Court of Illinois

BACKGROUND AND FACTS

In 1971, Dayan, the plaintiff, received an exclusive franchise to operate McDonald's restaurants in Paris, France. The franchise agreement required that the franchise meet all quality, service, and cleanliness (QSC) standards set by McDonald's. Dayan acknowledged his familiarity with the McDonald's system and with the need for maintaining McDonald's quality standards and controls. The franchise agreement stated that the rationale for maintaining QSC standards was that a "departure of restaurants anywhere in the world from these standards impedes the successful operation of restaurants throughout the world, and injures the value of its [McDonald's] patents, trade-marks, tradename, and property." Dayan agreed to "maintain these standards as they presently existed" and to observe subsequent improvements McDonald's may initiate. Dayan also agreed not to vary from QSC standards without prior written approval. After several years of quality and cleanliness violations, McDonald's sought to terminate the franchise. Dayan brought this action to enjoin the termination. The lower court found that good cause existed for the termination and Dayan appealed.

BUCKLEY, PRESIDING JUSTICE

Dayan also argues that McDonald's was obligated to provide him with the operational assistance necessary to enable him to meet the QSC standards.

... Dayan verbally asked Sollars (a McDonald's manager) for a French-speaking operations person to work in the market for six months. Sollars testified that he told Dayan it would be difficult to find someone with the appropriate background that spoke French but that McDonald's could immediately send him an English-speaking operations man. Sollars further testified that this idea was summarily rejected by Dayan as unworkable even though he had informed Dayan that sending operations personnel who did not speak the language to a foreign country was very common and very successful in McDonald's international system. Nonetheless, Sollars agreed to attempt to locate a qualified person with the requisite language skills for Dayan.

Through Sollars' efforts, Dayan was put in contact with Michael Maycock, a person with McDonald's managerial and operational experience who spoke French. Dayan testified that he hired Maycock some time in October 1977 and placed him in charge of training, operations, quality control, and equipment.

As the trial court correctly realized: "It does not take a McDonald's-trained French-speaking operational man to know that grease dripping from the vents must be stopped and not merely collected in a cup hung from the ceiling, that dogs are not permitted to defecate where food is stored, that insecticide is not blended with chicken breading; that past-dated

continued

continued

products should be discarded; that a potato peeler should be somewhat cleaner than a tire-vulcanizer; and that shortening should not look like crank case oil."

Clearly, Maycock satisfied Dayan's request for a French-speaking operations man to run his training program.... The finding that Dayan refused non-French-speaking operational assistance and that McDonald's fulfilled Dayan's limited request for a French-speaking operational employee is well supported by the record. To suggest, as plaintiff does, that an opposite conclusion is clearly evident is totally without merit. Accordingly, we find McDonald's fulfilled its contractual obligation to provide requested operational assistance to Dayan.

In view of the foregoing reasons, the judgment of the trial court denying plaintiff's request for a permanent injunction and finding that McDonald's properly terminated the franchise agreement is affirmed.

Decision. Judgment was affirmed for McDonald's. McDonald's had fulfilled all of its responsibility under the agreement to assist the plaintiff in complying with the provisions of the license. The plaintiff had violated the provisions of the agreement by not complying with the QSC standards. The plaintiff is permitted to continue operation of his restaurants, but without use of the McDonald's trademarks or name.

Comment. McDonald's has recovered in France from this public relations fiasco.

Foreign Direct Investment

In this text, the term *foreign investment,* or *foreign direct investment* (FDI), refers to the ownership and active control of the productive assets of ongoing business concerns by an investor in a foreign country. This may include investments in manufacturing, mining, farming, assembly operations, and other facilities of production, as well as in service industries. Foreign direct investments are generally made for the long term, and with the expectation of producing a profit. According to *World Investment Report 2007,* issued by the United Nations Conference on Trade and Development, inflows of foreign direct investment worldwide exceeded $1.3 trillion in 2006. Of that, $857 billion was invested in developed countries, $379 billion was invested in developing countries (an increase of 21 percent over 2005), and $69 billion was invested in Russia and the Central Asian republics of the former Soviet Union. The United States attracted the most foreign investment in 2006, followed by the UK, China/Hong Kong, France, Belgium, and Canada. More than twice as much foreign direct investment flowed into service industries in 2006 than in agriculture, mining, and manufacturing combined. Remember, these are only snapshots of investment flows during one year. Throughout this book, a distinction will be made between the home and host countries of the firms involved. The *home country* refers to that country under whose laws the investing corporation was created or is headquartered. For example, the United States is home to multinational corporations such as Ford, Exxon, and Coca-Cola, to name a few, but they operate in *host countries* throughout every region of the world. Of the three forms of international business, foreign investment provides the firm with the greatest opportunity for market penetration, the most involvement, and perhaps the greatest risk of doing business abroad. Investment in a foreign plant is often a result of having had successful experiences in exporting or licensing and of the search for ways to overcome the disadvantages of those other entry methods. For example, by producing its product in a foreign country, instead of exporting, a firm can become more competitive in the host market. It can avoid quotas and tariffs on imported goods, avoid currency fluctuations on the traded goods, provide better product service and spare parts, and more quickly adapt products to local tastes and market trends. Manufacturing overseas for foreign markets can mean taking advantage of local natural resources, labor, and manufacturing economies of scale.

Multinational Corporations

Multinational corporations are firms with significant foreign direct investment assets, comprised of a parent company in the home country and foreign affiliates located in host countries. They are characterized by their ability to derive and transfer capital resources worldwide and to operate facilities of production and penetrate markets in more than one country, usually on a global scale. They can be domiciled in both developed and developing countries. Over the past twenty years, many writers have argued over the best name to use in referring to these companies. *Multinational enterprise* has been a popular term because it reflects the fact that many global firms are not, technically speaking, "corporations," but may have other legal status or even be state-owned. The terms *transnational corporation* and *supranational corporation* are often used within the United Nations system, reflecting that their operations and interests "transcend" national boundaries. This text makes no play on words and places no special meaning on any of the terms used to describe these companies. While most multinational corporations are privately owned, an increasing number of state-owned enterprises, primarily from developing countries, are operating globally.

One significant trend in business during the last half of the twentieth century has been the "globalization" of multinational corporations. At one time, multinational corporations were simply large domestic companies with foreign operations. Today, they are global companies. They typically make decisions and enter strategic alliances with each other without regard to national boundaries. They move factories, technology, and capital to those countries with the most hospitable laws, the lowest tax rates, the most qualified workforce, or abundant natural resources. They see market share and company performance in global and regional terms.

UNCTAD's World Investment Report on Transnational Corporations. The United Nations Conference on Trade and Development (UNCTAD) is a specialized agency of the United Nations dealing with the impact of trade and investment on developing countries. According to the UNCTAD *World Investment Report 2007* there are about 78,000 transnational corporations (or TNCs, the term used by UNCTAD) in the world, with some 780,000 foreign affiliates. The *World Investment Report 2007* gives statistics on the size of the largest of these. It ranks TNCs by their foreign assets, foreign sales, and foreign employment, by the number of foreign affiliates, and by UNCTAD's own *Transnationality Index*. The index is calculated as the average of three ratios: foreign assets to total assets, foreign sales to total sales, and foreign employment to total employment. It was reported for 2005 (the latest year for which TNC data is reported) that of the world's largest 100 non-financial companies (ranked by foreign assets), only about one-quarter were American. Most of the others were based in Western Europe, Japan, Scandinavia, Canada, and Australia, and seven were from developing countries. In terms of foreign assets alone, the ten largest of these companies included (in order) General Electric (U.S.), Vodafone (UK, telecommunications), General Motors (U.S.), British Petroleum (UK), Royal Dutch Shell (the Netherlands/UK), Exxon Mobil (U.S.), Toyota (Japan), Ford (U.S.), Total (France), and Eléctricité de France (France). For the first time in several years, an American company was among the top ten, according to the Transnationality Index. According to this calculation, the ten most "globalized" companies in 2005 (in order) were Thomson (Canada, media/publishing), Liberty Global (U.S., telecommunications), Roche Group (Switzerland, pharmaceuticals), WPP Group PLC (UK, business services), Phillips (the Netherlands, electrical/electronic equipment), Nestle (Switzerland, food/beverage); Cadbury Schweppes (UK, food/beverage), Vodafone (UK, telecommunications), Lafarge (France, non-metallic mineral products), and Sabmiller (UK, consumer goods/brewers). The most globalized industries are motor vehicles, electronics, petroleum, telecommunications, pharmaceuticals, and energy. (It should be noted that changes in these lists from year to year are affected largely by mergers and acquisitions of existing companies.) The foreign sales and employment of the 100 largest non-financial TNCs increased faster than their domestic sales and employment. The largest TNCs from developing countries were from Hong Kong/China, Malaysia, Mexico, Singapore, and Korea.

Transnational Corporations and Development. TNCs have a tremendous impact on the globalization of the world's economy. The UNCTAD report shows that while the output of TNCs makes up

TNC= lowest risk way of creating favorable export situation

only 10 percent of the world's gross domestic product, it accounts for one-third of world exports. It was reported that in 2004 TNCs had employed 62 million workers, and that of those, 9 million were employed in American foreign affiliate companies. This amounts to trillions of dollars in wages and taxes to governments worldwide. Various other reports show that the largest multinationals account for anywhere from one-quarter to one-third of the world's production of goods and services, and perhaps 80 percent of world industrial output. The impact of these companies is huge. They have created jobs and wealth, spawned technology, fostered social development in developing countries, and improved the quality of life of people everywhere. Of course, they are not without their critics, who point to the corporate subversion of national interests, corruption, control over governments, pollution of the environment, destruction of natural resources, and other ills associated with global corporate power. Nevertheless, most modern governments of the world today recognize the benefits of hosting multinational corporations and provide many incentives to attract them.

SUBSIDIARIES, JOINT VENTURES, MERGERS, AND ACQUISITIONS. Multinational corporations wishing to enter a foreign market through direct investment can structure their business arrangements in many different ways. Their options and eventual course of action may depend on many factors, including industry and market conditions, capitalization of the firm and financing, and legal considerations. Some of these options include the start-up of a new foreign subsidiary company, the formation of a joint venture with an existing foreign company, or the acquisition of an existing foreign company by stock purchase. These arrangements are discussed in detail in Part Four of this book. For now, keep in mind that multinational corporations are usually not a single legal entity. They are global enterprises that consist of any number of interrelated corporate entities, connected through extremely complex chains of stock ownership. Stock ownership gives the investing corporation tremendous flexibility when investing abroad.

The *wholly owned foreign subsidiary* is a "foreign" corporation organized under the laws of a foreign host country, but owned and controlled by the parent corporation in the home country. Because the parent company controls all of the stock in the subsidiary, it can control management and financial decision making.

The *joint venture* is a cooperative business arrangement between two or more companies for profit. A joint venture may take the form of a partnership or corporation. Typically, one party will contribute expertise and another will contribute the capital, each bringing its own special resources to the venture. Joint ventures exist in all regions of the world and in all types of industries. Where the laws of a host country require local ownership or require that investing foreign firms have a local partner, the joint venture is an appropriate investment vehicle. *Local participation* refers to the requirement that a share of the business be owned by nationals of the host country. These requirements are gradually being reduced in most countries that, in an effort to attract more investment, are permitting wholly owned subsidiaries. Many American companies do not favor the joint venture as an investment vehicle because they do not want to share technology, expertise, and profits with another company.

Another method of investing abroad is for two companies to *merge* or for one company to purchase another ongoing firm. This option has appeal because it requires less know-how than does a new start-up and can be concluded without disruption of business activity. According to UNCTAD, there were over 6,000 cross-border mergers and acquisitions in 2005, totaling $716 billion, with 141 business deals of over $1 billion each.

United States Foreign Direct Investment

The value of foreign-owned assets in the United States is greater than U.S.–owned assets abroad. According to the U.S. Bureau of Economic Analysis, as of 2005 foreign-owned assets in the United States were valued at $12.7 trillion (cost value), and U.S.–owned assets abroad were valued at $10 trillion. In the past, foreign direct investment in the United States has resulted mainly from foreign firms creating their own U.S. subsidiaries. Today, it results in large part from foreign firms acquiring or merging with existing firms, many of which are publicly owned companies. Most investment is in manufacturing and has come from firms in the United Kingdom, Japan, the Netherlands, Germany, and Canada. Foreign firms have acquired everything from office buildings and movie studios to factories and supermarkets. Some of the best-known companies in the United States are foreign owned, and their impact on the U.S. economy and on employment has been significant.

The United States has supported open investment policies worldwide and encourages foreign investment in this country. This policy is based on the principle of *national treatment*—that foreign investors will be treated the same as domestic firms. There is no need for government approval to invest here, and there are almost no restrictions on foreign exchange, on foreign equity ratios, or on licensing. There are some limitations to the rule, however. For example, under the *Exon-Florio Amendments* to the Defense Production Act, the president can broadly prohibit foreign investment in such industries as atomic energy, transportation, and telecommunications, or in cases involving a potential threat of terrorism or threat to national security. Other restrictions apply to defense-related industries, and to the control of banks and aviation companies (generally, directors of a U.S. bank must be U.S. citizens). There are also restrictions on campaign contributions by foreigners, and some state restrictions over agricultural land.

Conducting Business in Developing and Newly Industrialized Countries

Most of the 192 nations in the world have not reached the same state of economic advance as have the *developed* or *industrialized countries* of the United States, Canada, Japan, and Western Europe. Rather, most countries could be classified as having economies that are either (1) developing, (2) newly industrialized, or (3) least developed. For the purposes of our discussion, we will create a fourth category that includes Russia, the other independent republics of the former Soviet Union, and Eastern Europe, which we will refer to as "countries in transition." These are common terms to describe the socioeconomic status of a country. There is no clear, single definition of these categories by every international organization or writer, because there are so many indicators of socioeconomic development, and because every country is in a different stage of evolution. For example, we commonly consider China, India, Malaysia, Mexico, and Brazil to be among the developing countries, and this text will discuss them generally in that context. However, they are now often classified as newly industrialized countries. China is sometimes referred to as being a part of "emerging Asia." Therefore, for the purposes of our discussion, we will not attempt an economist's precise definition. What we can say with certainty, however, is that these categories differ in culture, geography, language, and religion and in their economic, political, and legal systems as well. Two-thirds of the world's population is located in the least-developed countries—in Africa, Latin America, the Caribbean, parts of Asia and the Pacific Rim, and the Middle East.

The Developing Countries

The "typical" *developing country* is impossible to describe. Most have a large agrarian population, densely populated cities, and a plentiful supply of unskilled labor. Many support high-tech industries. Although some are rich in natural resources, such as Brazil, many others have depleted their natural resources. The protection of the environment has often taken a back seat to industrialization and economic "progress," and so pollution chokes their air and water. Toxic waste dumps threaten entire communities. Widespread violent crimes threaten public security. Kidnappings, once a threat only to the very rich, now threaten all levels of society. Regular business visitors to many developing countries, including Mexico, take security precautions against kidnappings. Economic crimes such as smuggling, hijacking, organized crime, payoffs and corruption, and illicit drug production are major problems. Sanitation and water systems are often inadequate. Education levels are far below that of the developed countries. Poor communication and transportation systems make business difficult. Inadequate distribution systems make it costly to get goods to market. Floods and natural disasters, exacerbated by inappropriate agricultural and industrial policies, have disrupted entire populations. Overpopulation, homelessness, malnutrition, and disease are still common. One example of how disease can affect business is the epidemic of plague that struck India in 1994. It caused workers to flee industrial communities in fear and forced the closing of many factories.

A wide disparity in social and economic classes exists in many developing countries, with great inequality in income and education between the rich and poor. Political systems differ widely in developing countries. Some developing countries have stable, democratic governments; others do not. For instance, Costa Rica has the oldest continuing democracy in Central America, dating back to 1948. Other Central and South American countries have not been stable at all and have experienced varying degrees of freedom, from parliamentary rule to military dictatorship. Tragically, both political and economic stability are threatened by the threat of armed guerrilla groups, terrorists, and other revolutionaries. Examples could include Colombia in Latin America, Sri Lanka in South Asia, and Indonesia in the Pacific Rim region.

The Economic Environment in Developing Countries

Students of economics know that the economies of the developing countries have trailed those of the industrialized countries for many complex reasons, including basic geography, political instability and civil wars, ethnic and religious rivalries, the lack of an educated middle class, government corruption, and for some, the remaining consequences of cold war clashes between the United States and the former Soviet Union. Perhaps the most important factor has been government policies unfavorable to trade and investment. Historically, these governments often imposed high import duties and import licensing requirements to protect local industries from the competition of more efficient foreign firms. This protection allowed local companies to sell inferior products at higher costs than they could have if they had not been insulated from foreign competition. Many developing countries put strict controls over the inflow of capital and technology. These policies were based on the notion that government could best direct how capital and technology should be used, instead of leaving it up to free-market forces. In many cases, socialist policies led to government ownership of businesses and industry. These policies forced many multinational corporations and other investors to stay away.

Latin America is a good example. The economies of Latin America have historically been hampered by excessive government debt to foreign institutions and a basic distrust of the free market and of the influence of large, multinational corporations. Economic health has often been very cyclical, due to fluctuating prices for key commodities, metals, oil, and other raw materials. During the 1970s and 1980s, the region suffered from severe unemployment, declining personal income, financial instability, capital flight, low rates of savings, and high rates of inflation. Inflation was caused partly by the printing of money to cover government spending, and by automatic indexing of wage and price increases. For example, during the 1970s and 1980s, Brazil and Argentina suffered from *hyperinflation*—an inflation rate of several thousand percent per year—that wore away the value of their currency, destroyed the buying power of their consumers, frightened investors, and damaged public confidence in their government's ability to manage its own economy. Governments were forced to cut basic services. Multinational corporations pulled out of the region. Investment in factories, plants, roads, and other infrastructure fell by 30 percent during the 1980s. Inflation was so severe in Latin America that the region's growth rate and living standards during the 1980s actually declined. By the late 1980s, 38 percent of households were living in poverty.

A decade later, by the close of the 1990s, a move toward free-market economics led to an improvement in Latin America. Banking and financial systems were strengthened and fiscal controls instituted. Foreign investment increased, income rose, production and exports were up, and inflation seemed under control. After suffering a severe economic decline in the early 2000s, foreign investment returned in 2004, and by 2007 many Latin American countries were experiencing steady economic growth, an increase in jobs, and a declining poverty rate. Nevertheless, many of the economic ills that existed in Latin America several decades ago still exist. Moreover, several countries are returning to socialist economics. Since 1999, socialist governments have taken office in Venezuela, Ecuador, and Bolivia. Venezuela has the largest oil reserves outside of the Middle East. Its socialist president, Hugo Chavez, was elected in 1999. Since then, he has moved Venezuela away from democratic and free-market principles by converting industries to state control (including oil, electrical power, and telecommunications), turning private farms into worker cooperatives, setting price controls on foods and essential goods, and exerting other economic controls. Food shortages have existed, and the inflation rate has been as high as 20 percent. Marxist curriculum has been introduced in schools. Politically, Chavez pushed through an amendment to Venezuela's Constitution to increase his power to rule by presidential decree, developed close ties to Cuba and Iran, and engaged in a campaign of anti-American rhetoric around the world. This was reflected in the UNCTAD *World Investment Report 2007,* which showed that the Latin American countries continued to attract foreign investment, with the exception of Venezuela and Ecuador.

Availability of Foreign Exchange in Developing Countries. Typically, developing countries have lacked a ready reserve of foreign exchange. Keep in mind that their currencies are not generally accepted for trade around the world like the dollar, euro, yen, or other hard currencies. A *hard currency* is a currency of a nation that is generally accepted worldwide for the payment of obligations and is readily exchangeable into other foreign currencies. A hard currency's value (or price) is determined by what buyers and sellers will pay for it at any given time, as influenced by government intervention, national interest rates, or by other market factors. The currency of most developing countries would be called a "soft currency." A *soft currency* is one that is not readily converted or accepted for payment. Currencies with a *fixed exchange rate* are also called "soft" currencies. The Russian ruble, Indian rupee, and Chinese *renminbi* (or *yuan,* which is the primary unit of Chinese currency) are examples of soft currencies that can only be purchased at the fixed rate established by the government.

A developing country's only access to foreign exchange comes from either receiving foreign payments for the export of raw materials and natural resources, locally made products, foreign direct investment, or foreign aid or loans. Thus, these countries often have not been able to afford to purchase needed products or technologies or to undertake public construction projects like roads, sewage systems, hospitals, utilities, and ports. They also have not had the ability to issue debt to foreigners in their own currency. Indebtedness to foreign banks must be issued in a hard currency. To provide these products and services, and to repay this indebtedness, government banking restrictions were designed to keep as much foreign exchange as possible in the country's central bank. Local companies wanting to import foreign products often could not obtain foreign exchange, or have had to apply to their central bank for authority to make an overseas transfer of foreign funds to their supplier. This was most often the case for the import of luxury or consumer goods or other products that the government deemed non-essential. These restrictions made it risky for a local firm in a developing country to enter into a foreign contract, because there was a chance that money to pay the other party might not be available when needed. Since the 1990s, free-market principles and banking reforms have alleviated many of these restrictions, although the scarcity of foreign currency continues.

Protectionist Policies in Developing Countries. Developing countries do not generally espouse the free-market principles of the United States. They often have high tariffs and other barriers to trade that make it expensive, difficult, and in some cases impossible to import foreign goods and services. For example, governments in developing countries might allow the import of goods and services needed for their own socioeconomic development plans, such as tractors, hydroelectric generators, or machine tools. However, they might ban or discourage the import of goods and services considered non-essential, or that are available from local producers, such as consumer or luxury goods, finished goods, petrochemicals, and agricultural products. Many developing countries (and some developed ones) even restrict the showing of foreign-produced television shows and advertising with foreign content. Developing countries have often used high tariffs or a maze of government regulations, permits, taxes, fees, and paperwork to

some-but-not-all fallacy
most-favored - industry protectionism

render importing expensive or practically impossible. Import of some products can be completely banned. One especially insidious method of barring foreign goods is when government agencies establish regulations and restrictions on imports but fail to publish them or to make them easily available to foreign exporters. Such a lack of "transparency" makes compliance, and thus importing, almost impossible. Moreover, in many developing countries bribery and corruption pose a barrier to trade, even though such practices are illegal and violators are prosecuted.

For example, India still has some of the most severe restrictions in the world. India requires licenses to import foreign motorcycles, and according to the U.S. trade representative, these licenses are almost impossible to obtain (and not available at all to non-Indian citizens).

Like many other developing countries, India also has many restrictions on trade in services. For example, only graduates of Indian universities may engage in professional accounting, and there are strict limitations on the use of trade names and logos by foreign accounting firms. The banking, construction, telecommunications, and insurance sectors are not widely open to foreign firms. A foreign bank may own no more than a 5 percent interest in an Indian bank. Foreign building contractors may not be employed for government projects unless local firms cannot do the work. Agreements to license intellectual property are also restricted. In one extreme example from the 1970s that was cited in popular news articles of the day, Coca-Cola was forced to abandon its efforts to open a bottling operation in India after the Indian government insisted that the company disclose its secret formula for making Coke and required that at least 60 percent of Coke's bottling operations there be Indian owned. (Coke is now bottled in India, but under great criticism from the Indian government and environmental groups.)

Other developing countries with strict barriers to imports include China, Egypt, Indonesia, Malaysia, Pakistan, and the Philippines. They severely limit trade in both goods and services. A few countries, such as Chile in Latin America and newly industrialized Singapore, have a very open trade environment.

Controls on Investment in Developing Countries

Developing countries have also maintained strict controls over investment by foreign firms. Reasons for this vary by country but can include the fear that large foreign firms will disrupt socialist economic planning; the desire to protect local companies; the worry that the government will lose political control over large, foreign multinational corporations; and the fear of technological and industrial dominance by these large firms.

Local Participation Requirements. *Local participation requirements* are government controls prohibiting a foreign firm from owning a 100 percent interest of a local firm. These requirements generally require that any foreign firm wishing to open a local subsidiary, or acquire or merge with a local firm, have a minimum percentage of local ownership, or *local participation.* The goal is to maintain managerial and financial control over the firm by local nationals. These restrictions are most severe in petroleum and energy industries, banking, utilities, agriculture, and transportation. For example, ocean and air freight or package delivery services are often not open to foreign companies. Additionally, in many countries, broadcast and cable television companies cannot be foreign owned.

Restrictions on the Repatriation of Profits. A restriction on the *repatriation of profits* refers to the legal requirement that an investing firm not remove, or *repatriate,* profits from the host country to the home country of the parent company. Where this requirement exists—usually only in developing countries—it is imposed in order to keep capital and foreign exchange within the country. This can be a real disincentive to foreign investment, because few shareholders will put their money into a far-off venture with no hope of seeing a profit on their investment.

Transfer of Technology. The exchange of technology and manufacturing know-how between firms in different countries through arrangements such as licensing agreements is known as the *transfer of technology.* Business arrangements involving transfers of technology and know-how are regulated by the government in some countries. This type of control is common when the licensor is from a highly industrialized country such as the United States and the licensee is located in a developing country such as those in Latin America, the Middle East, or parts of Asia.

Host developing countries have understood that self-sufficiency in technology and production methods is one of the most important engines of social and economic development and key to rapid and continuing modernization. But they have often feared, for historical reasons, that large multinational corporations were operating in their countries for the purpose of exploiting cheap labor and irreplaceable natural resources, without reinvesting in the future of their people. For this reason, some developing countries have required, as a condition of opening a local subsidiary, or of entering into a joint venture or acquiring a local firm, that a foreign company transfer its most advanced technology and products to their subsidiary or partner in the host country, or share them with the subsidiary or partner. This means, for example, that a multinational corporation desiring to build a factory in a developing country might not be permitted to just produce consumer goods for sale there. They might also be required to establish research and development facilities for their more technologically advanced products, operate training centers for local labor and management, or foster educational exchanges in science and technology at the university and industry levels.

Nationalization, Expropriation, and Privatization. An extreme example of government control, although no longer common, occurs when a country seizes private property for its own use. The absolute right of sovereign governments to take private property exists in all countries and is rooted in the ancient "divine right of kings" to all property within their domain. *Expropriation* is the taking by a government of privately owned assets, such as real estate, factories, farms, mines, or oil refineries. One form of legal expropriation in the United States, called *eminent domain,* is the taking of private property for public use with the payment of just compensation. The problem is that in some countries, private property owned by foreign interests has been taken with no or little compensation—and the former foreign owners have been evicted virtually overnight. Cuba is famous for having expropriated American-owned farms, hotels, and real estate during its Marxist-influenced revolution in 1959.

Nationalization refers to the transfer of private-sector firms to government ownership and control, usually with payment to shareholders and pursuant to a larger plan to restructure a national economy. In developing countries, this has often been motivated by political reasons, perhaps resulting from the socialist-inspired belief that the seized assets could best be operated by the government itself for the benefit of the country, rather than for private profit. But nationalization has also been used by Western nations, including the UK, Canada, and even the United States, for reasons such as to save a dying but needed industry. For example, this was done by the UK in 1971 when it purchased Rolls Royce, the critical British maker of aircraft engines. Rolls Royce was not returned to private ownership until 1987.

There are many other policy reasons for nationalizing an industry. For example, after the terrorist attacks in the United States in 2001, the air transportation security industry was taken out of private hands, nationalized, and put under the Department of Homeland Security. Nationalization and expropriation generally no longer are the barrier to foreign investment that they were 20, 30, or 40 years ago.

In the following case, *In re Union Carbide Corporation Gas Plant Disaster at Bhopal,* a U.S. corporation owned the majority of stock in an Indian corporation that operated a chemical plant in Bhopal, India. The company, Union Carbide, delegated responsibility for operating the plant to local managers. The escape of poisonous chemicals resulted in the deaths of thousands of people living near the plant—the worst industrial disaster in history. Union Carbide was placed in the position of defending itself in India. As you read, consider the legal responsibility of a corporation for negligent acts committed by its subsidiaries abroad. Also, consider the risks of a multinational corporation operating in a far-off developing country.

In re Union Carbide Corporation Gas Plant Disaster at Bhopal

809 F.2d 195 (1987)

United States Court of Appeals (2d. Cir.)

BACKGROUND AND FACTS

This case arose out of what has been considered the most devastating industrial disaster in history. The deaths of thousands of persons (estimates range from 2,000 to 4,000) and injuries to several hundred thousand persons were caused by the release of a lethal gas known as methyl isocyanate from a chemical plant operated by Union Carbide India Limited (UCIL) in Bhopal, India, in 1984. The accident occurred on the night of December 2, 1984, when winds blew the deadly gas from the plant operated by UCIL into densely occupied parts of the city of Bhopal. UCIL was incorporated under the laws of India. Fifty-one percent of its stock was owned by Union Carbide Corporation (UCC), a U.S. corporation, 22 percent was owned or controlled by the government of India, and the balance was held by approximately 23,500 Indian citizens. The stock was publicly traded on the Bombay Stock Exchange. The company was engaged in the manufacture of a variety of products, including chemicals, plastics, fertilizers, and insecticides, at 14 plants in India and employed more than 9,000 Indian citizens. Approximately 650 people were employed at the Bhopal plant. It was managed and operated entirely by Indian citizens. All products produced at Bhopal were sold in India. The operations of the plant were regulated by more than two dozen Indian governmental agencies.

Four days after the accident, the first of some 145 actions in federal district courts in the United States was commenced on behalf of victims. In the meantime, India enacted the Bhopal Gas Leak Disaster Act, granting to its government (the Union of India [UOI]) the exclusive right to represent the victims in India or elsewhere. In April 1985, the Indian government filed a complaint in the Southern District of New York on behalf of all of the victims. India's decision to bring suit in the United States was attributed to the fact that although nearly 6,500 lawsuits had been instituted by victims in India against UCIL, the Indian courts did not have jurisdiction over UCC, the parent company. UCC contended that the actions are properly tried in the courts of India on the doctrine of *forum non conveniens; that a court should decline to hear a case if there is another court competent to hear the case in a jurisdiction that is closer to the site where the claims arose and to the parties and witnesses.* The district court dismissed the action on the condition that UCC submit to the jurisdiction of the Indian courts and that UCC agree to satisfy any judgment taken against it in the courts of India.

MANSFIELD, CIRCUIT JUDGE

The plaintiffs seek to prove that the accident was caused by negligence on the part of UCC in originally contributing to the design of the plant and its provision for storage of excessive amounts of the gas at the plant. As Judge Keenan found, however, UCC's participation was limited, and its involvement in plant operations terminated long before the accident.... The preliminary process design information furnished by UCC could not have been used to construct the plant. Construction required the detailed process design and engineering data prepared by hundreds of Indian engineers, process designers, and subcontractors. During the ten years spent constructing the plant, its design and configuration underwent many changes.

The vital parts of the Bhopal plant, including its storage tank, monitoring instrumentation, and vent gas scrubber, were manufactured by Indians in India. Although some 40 UCIL employees were given some safety training at UCC's plant in West Virginia, they represented a small fraction of the Bhopal plant's employees. The vast majority of plant employees were selected and trained by UCIL in Bhopal. The manual for start-up of the Bhopal plant was prepared by Indians employed by UCIL.

In short, the plant has been constructed and managed by Indians in India. No Americans were employed at the plant at the time of the accident. In the five years from 1980 to 1984, although more than 1,000 Indians were employed at the plant, only one American was employed there and he left in 1982. No Americans visited the plant for more than one year prior to the accident, and during the five-year period before the accident the communications between the plant and the United States were almost nonexistent.

The vast majority of material witnesses and documentary proof bearing on causation of and liability for the accident is located in India, not the United

continued

continued

States, and would be more accessible to an Indian court than to a United States court. The records are almost entirely in Hindi or other Indian languages, understandable to an Indian court without translation. The witnesses for the most part do not speak English but Indian languages understood by an Indian court but not by an American court. These witnesses could be required to appear in an Indian court but not in a court of the United States. Although witnesses in the United States could not be subpoenaed to appear in India, they are comparatively few in number and most are employed by UCC, which, as a party, would produce them in India, with lower overall transportation costs than if the parties were to attempt to bring hundreds of Indian witnesses to the United States. Lastly, Judge Keenan properly concluded that an Indian court would be in a better position to direct and supervise a viewing of the Bhopal plant, which was sealed after the accident. Such a viewing could be of help to a court in determining liability issues.

After a thorough review, the district court concluded that the public interest concerns, like the private ones, also weigh heavily in favor of India as the situs for trial and disposition of the cases. The accident and all relevant events occurred in India. The victims, over 200,000 in number, are citizens of India and located there. The witnesses are almost entirely Indian citizens. The Union of India has a greater interest than does the United States in facilitating the trial and adjudication of the victims' claims.

India's interest is increased by the fact that it has for years treated UCIL as an Indian national, subjecting it to intensive regulations and governmental supervision of the construction, development, and operation of the Bhopal plant, its emissions, water and air pollution, and safety precautions. Numerous Indian government officials have regularly conducted on-site inspections of the plant and approved its machinery and equipment, including its facilities for storage of the lethal methyl isocyanate gas that escaped and caused the disaster giving rise to the claims. Thus India has considered the plant to be an Indian one and the disaster to be an Indian problem. It therefore has a deep interest in ensuring compliance with its safety standards. Moreover, plaintiffs have conceded that in view of India's strong interest and its greater contacts with the plant, its operations, its employees, and the victims of the accident, the law of India, as the place where the tort occurred, will undoubtedly govern.

Decision. The district court's dismissal of the actions against Union Carbide Corporation was upheld. The doctrine of *forum non conveniens* is a rule of U.S. law, which states that, to further the administration of justice, where a case is properly heard in more than one court, it should be heard by the one that is most convenient. Given the facts of this case, the courts of India are the more convenient forum.

Comment. In 1989, the Supreme Court of India approved a settlement fund of $470 million to compensate the victims of the disaster.

The Road to Free Markets, Consumer-Based Economics, and Private Ownership

During the last 20 years, the more progressive developing countries, particularly in Latin America, began to give up their isolationist policies and to loosen controls over trade and investment. Today, with some exceptions, they are attracting large sources of new capital for investment, new technologies, new manufacturing techniques and business know-how, improved training for their labor force, and organizational and managerial expertise. For example, developing countries are reducing tariffs on most imported products. They are gradually ending burdensome import licensing schemes and making it easier for local companies and investors to obtain foreign currency. They are reducing many kinds of taxes on business. Some countries are lowering taxes on royalties paid to foreign companies under licensing agreements for modern technology and technical assistance. China, Argentina, and other countries are lifting controls over prices and wages, allowing market mechanisms to work.

Gradually, developing countries are passing new, more progressive laws to protect intellectual property, the environment, consumers, workers, and investors and to increase investment opportunities. Even accounting standards are changing so that investors can receive more information about a company and can better understand its financial health. Government "red tape" is being cut, allowing a faster and easier flow of paperwork through government bureaucracies, which speeds up the application process for investment and eases the way for importers to bring goods into the country.

Developing countries have also instituted new, more prudent fiscal policies. Latin American countries have reduced government borrowing and spending. Several countries, notably Brazil and Argentina, have enacted new regulations to stabilize their exchange rates. These efforts are bringing inflation under control and returning consumer and investor confidence.

Privatization. An important development in these countries is the movement toward privatization. *Privatization,* in a sense, is the opposite of nationalization. It refers to the process by which a government sells or transfers government-owned industries or other assets to the private sector. Since the late 1980s, privatization has occurred in developing countries and throughout the world, including Great Britain and Western Europe, and especially in the Eastern European countries that transitioned from communist societies. The selling of state-owned assets to private investors has caused an infusion of new capital investment, managerial know-how, technological innovation, and entrepreneurial spirit. These issues will be discussed in greater depth in Part Four of this book.

The Results of Reform. Although most developing countries will continue to experience economic instability for many years to come, many have seen improved financial stability and economic growth. Jobs and personal incomes are rising. Modern factories are increasing productivity and turning out products of greater quality. As the quality of products improves, those products are more in demand in world markets, thus increasing export earnings and access to foreign exchange. As the economies of these countries improve, they present important emerging markets for foreign products—industrial equipment, computer and telecommunications technologies, health care, and new agricultural and environmental technologies and chemicals. The developing countries are also vast untapped consumer markets.

Doing business in developing countries is still not like doing business in the United States or Canada, however. Investors have no guarantee that inflation will not skyrocket again, or that an excess of foreign debt and lack of foreign exchange will drag the economy into disaster. Investors cannot be ensured of political stability, or of continued reform toward open markets and democracy. Moreover, developing countries are far behind in education, infrastructure, and public health, and in the least-developed countries the scourges of AIDS and extreme poverty will almost certainly forestall hopes of economic advance.

The People's Republic of China. China has one-quarter of the world's population and one of the world's largest economies despite its communist-dominated government and centrally planned economy. As a communist player in many world markets, China represents a special area of interest to those studying international business. In the modern period, it was not until the 1970s that China began to open its doors to outside trade and investment. Since that time, China has made many changes in its economic and legal systems necessary to doing business with the West. It has opened up opportunities for collectively and privately owned enterprises and made it easier to set up joint ventures with foreign companies. China has increased imports of technology, modernized its banking system and other service industries, encouraged Chinese companies to adopt modern management techniques and international accounting standards, and fostered the development of quality control programs in manufacturing. During the 1990s, China grew to become one of the most attractive markets for foreign direct investment by multinational corporations from around the world. Major investors have come from Chinese Hong Kong, Taiwan, Japan, and the United States. According to the UNCTAD report, over 24 million people are employed in China by foreign-owned companies.

Despite the reforms, China is not a democracy. Rather, it is still a communist country with an economy that is largely centrally regulated and administered by government agencies in Beijing. Its economic and regulatory reforms take place at the government's pace, balancing the need for attracting foreign investment and trade with the need for strict social and economic control. Moreover, China has almost constantly been on the verge of one "trade war" or another with the United States over the course of the past 15 years. One area of dispute has been China's failure to stop the infringement of U.S.–owned copyrights and trademarks. The United States has also threatened to increase duties on Chinese products for political reasons, such as imprisonment of dissidents, the use of prison labor to manufacture consumer goods, and the sale of missiles to hostile countries. China has also been accused of currency manipulations that effectively set the exchange rate between its currency and the dollar so that Chinese products become artificially cheaper in the United States and U.S. products become more expensive in China. Nevertheless, in 1999, the United States completed the political and economic recognition of China that was begun by President Nixon almost three decades earlier. In that year, the United States granted permanent "normal trade relations" status to China, a step that indicates that the United States will treat goods and services coming from China just as it treats similar goods and services coming from any other friendly nation. In 2001, China became a full-fledged member of the world trading community when it joined the World Trade Organization, the international organization that sets the rules for international trade in goods and services.

It has been said that American consumers have become reliant on inexpensive Chinese products. Today, China is America's fourth-largest trading partner, supplying about 15 percent of U.S. imports. In 2006, Americans purchased $232.5 billion more in goods than they sold in return, representing roughly one-quarter of the total U.S. trade deficit. The U.S. trade deficit with China has increased 179 percent since 2000, fueling debate in the United States over its relations with China both economically and politically. The Economic Policy Institute estimates that Wal-Mart alone imported $26 billion in products from China in 2006.

The Newly Industrialized Countries

The *newly industrialized countries* are those countries that are making rapid progress toward becoming an industrialized or technology-based economy. They are located in all regions of the world, including Latin America, the Middle East, and Southern and Southeast Asia. Much of their success in recent years is due to a highly motivated workforce and a stable climate for foreign investment. Some of these countries have largely transitioned from agricultural economies to industrial ones, with burgeoning urban populations. Their manufacturing is export oriented, producing a broad mix of high-quality products, from computers to steel. They are a magnet for foreign investment and have a reserve of foreign exchange. Their success has led to a dramatic rise in per capita gross domestic product and to improvements in jobs, wages, education, health care, living accommodations, and overall quality of life. Other countries outside of Asia that may be described as transitioning to newly industrialized status are Mexico, Turkey, Israel, and South Africa. China is clearly in a state of rapid transition.

The most well known newly industrialized countries are the four "Asian Tigers": Hong Kong, Singapore, Taiwan, and South Korea. Hong Kong is one of the largest banking centers in the world. In 1997, Hong Kong reverted to Chinese control after having been a British colony for 100 years. China considers Hong Kong to be a "special administrative region," and Hong Kong will remain semiautonomous from the government in Beijing until the middle of this century. Hong Kong is a gateway for moving goods, money, and people into and out of China and is important to China's economic future. Many writers consider the four Asian Tigers to now be developed countries.

The Least-Developed Countries

The prospects for business in the *least-developed countries* are not as good as in those regions previously described. The least-developed countries include most countries of sub-Saharan Africa, such as Rwanda, Ethiopia, and Somalia, as well as Haiti in the Caribbean and the countries of Central Asia. They lack many of the basic resources needed for development and require vast amounts of foreign aid from the wealthier nations. Many of these countries have inadequate roads and bridges, inadequate public utilities and telephone systems, poor educational and health-care facilities, a lack of plentiful drinking water, unstable governments, little or no technological base, illiteracy, high infant mortality, AIDS and other diseases, rampant crime, excessive armaments, ethnic and tribal warfare, and weak or nonexistent financial institutions. Their economies are often based on agriculture, mining, some assembly operations, or (to a lesser extent) manufacturing. Their reserves of foreign exchange are limited. Most of these countries lack the type of market-based economy that characterizes the developed world. Business opportunities for trade in consumer goods and for the products and services of most Western companies are limited. Least-developed countries are in need of investments and products that will help them in dealing with these basic problems.

Countries in Transition: Eastern Europe, Russia, and the Newly Independent Republics of the Former Soviet Union

Until its breakup in 1991, the Soviet Union extended from Eastern Europe on the west, across two continents to the Pacific Ocean, and from China and Central Asia on the south to the Arctic Ocean on the north. It was the third most populated nation in the world, after China and India, comprising more than one hundred different ethnic groups. It consisted of the Slavic republics of Russia, Belarus, and Ukraine; the Baltic States of Latvia, Estonia, and Lithuania; the Caucasus region, which includes Armenia and Georgia; and the largely Muslim Central Asian republics that extend geographically from the Caspian Sea to the Mongolian border.

When the Soviet Union collapsed in 1991, it changed the political and economic landscape of Europe and much of Asia. The Soviet republics gained independence. Russia, now officially called the *Russian Federation,* emerged as the largest of these. Eastern Europe, which borders the Soviet Union, was also freed from Soviet and communist domination. In 1989 the Berlin Wall fell, and soon communist East Germany (the former German Democratic Republic) was reunited with democratic West Germany (the Federal Republic of Germany), and Czechoslovakia split into the Czech Republic and the Slovak Republics. Democratically elected governments were installed across Eastern Europe. Many of the Eastern European countries have since joined the European Union; the U.S.–supported North Atlantic Treaty Organization, NATO (over Russia's objection); and the World Trade Organization. As of 2007, Russia had applied for full membership in the World Trade Organization.

The Transition from Communism to Free Markets and Private Enterprise

For more than 70 years the Soviet Union had operated under a socialist economic and political system, dominated by the Communist Party. Following World War II, the communist system was forced on the Soviet-occupied territories of Eastern Europe. The state owned all natural resources, factories, farms, and other means of production. The allocation of resources, as well as production and pricing decisions, were dictated by government agencies based on central economic plans. Because production and the supply of goods were not dictated by demand forces, consumer tastes and preferences became irrelevant. Consumer industries were totally neglected, operating with inefficient, antiquated machinery. Agricultural production was based on centralized planning by government bureaucracies, not market forces. The economy was based on military and defense priorities and on maintaining state security. Illegal "black markets" provided some Western consumer goods to those few who could obtain much-sought-after foreign currency.

As the communist governments fell, the results of seventy years of economic neglect became visible. Roads, bridges, public housing, railroads, and transportation systems were in disrepair. Power plants were deteriorating, and the risk of a serious nuclear disaster was high, even years after the Chernobyl accident. Years of communist rule had caused damaging pollution. Toxic waste had been abandoned near populated communities. Food shortages existed because no modern distribution system existed to harvest crops and bring them to market. It was not uncommon to see long lines of people outside a single store, or sidewalk vendor, hoping to have a chance at purchasing a small arrival of meat or fresh produce. Employment and labor problems remained, particularly evident in rampant absenteeism, lack of motivation, alcoholism, and cronyism. Machinery and equipment in many plants was antiquated. Some factories simply ceased to operate because of a lack of raw materials, constant breakdowns, and an absence of spare parts. After so many years of communism, many workers lacked managerial skills and the understanding of how to run a company in a free market.

Since 1991, Eastern European countries have installed democratically elected governments and freed their economies from years of communist control by liberalizing controls over trade and investment. They rapidly privatized many industries, turning formerly state-owned properties over to private ownership and management. New investors from the United States, Germany, Japan, and other countries are entering joint ventures with Russian and Eastern European firms. Capital, technology, know-how, and entrepreneurial spirit are pouring in. According to UNCTAD, Russia received $28.7 billion in foreign investment in 2006. Local citizens are also investing in their own companies. Inefficient plants from the communist era are modernizing or closing. Russia and Eastern Europe represent enormous potential markets for modern consumer goods, housing, and industrial equipment. Russia has a highly trained technical workforce, including superb engineers, scientists, and technicians. Eastern European cities, once dark and depressed from the communist years, are becoming magnets for Western tourists. Cities like Prague, in the Czech Republic, are quickly re-becoming the pearls of Eastern Europe, blending the history and traditions of Eastern Europe with cultural modernism. Since 1991, Russian business has been plagued by fraud and corruption. Criminals have preyed on unsuspecting and inexperienced foreign investors and on Russian citizens unaccustomed to doing business in a free-market economy. Organized crime and gangs extort "protection money." In what some reporters have described as a "Wild West atmosphere," private businesses have resorted to armed guards to protect their property and expatriate employees.

Laws affecting business and commercial transactions are often contradictory and unreasonably burdensome. Government agencies often invent rules when they feel the need to do so. Even though laws have been passed to protect intellectual property, the government has virtually no way to enforce them. Pirated brand-name goods are sold in stores and on street corners with impunity. Taxes are often imposed arbitrarily and are so high that they discourage investment. The banking system is sometimes unworkable. The Russian currency, the *ruble,* has been unstable, and inflation is high. This instability is making trade and investment difficult and threatens to hold up Russia's entrance into important international economic organizations. Many Western business ventures are not profitable and are losing money.

In the political realm, there is civil unrest among ethnic minorities in the Central Asian republics. Perhaps the greatest threat to economic liberalization is the threat that Russia's leaders could turn away from democratic principles, end privatization of industry, and resume the old Soviet-style foreign expansionism. Many people are still hostile to the United States and private enterprise and would like Russia to be a Soviet empire once again.

Managing the Risks of International Business

Readers need to keep one particular truism in mind throughout this text: The management of international business is the management of risk. No manager can make a strategic business decision or enter into an important business transaction without a full evaluation of the risks involved. Many of the best business plans have been ruined by a miscalculation, a mistake, or an error in judgment that could have been avoided with proper planning. Here we will discuss just three types of international business risks: transaction risk, political risk, and the risk of exposure to foreign laws and courts.

Risk Assessment and the Firm's Foreign Market Entry Strategy

When a firm is considering its entry into or expansion in a foreign market, it must weigh all options and decide on a course of action commensurate with its objectives, capabilities, and willingness to assume risk. As stated earlier, trade generally entails less penetration into a foreign market than licensing, and licensing requires less penetration than foreign investment. To say it another way, selling to a customer in another country results in less risk to the firm than licensing patents, trademarks, and copyrights there. Licensing usually requires less risk than forming a joint venture with a foreign firm to build a factory in China or India, for instance. A firm's global business strategy must take into account the amount of risk that the firm is willing to bear in entering the foreign market.

Consider this real-life example. A U.S. manufacturer of industrial equipment exported products to Europe, but faced growing competition from European firms, higher ocean freight rates, and increased European import restrictions. Moreover, the company experienced some difficulty in servicing its equipment from the United States as well as maintaining a ready supply of spare parts for its European customers. It evaluated its options for overcoming the problems of exporting and for expanding its presence in the European market through a country-by-country analysis of the business climate in Europe. On the basis of labor, tax, and other factors, it determined that its best course of action was to enter the European market through Spain. Prominent in its decision was the presence of an existing firm in Spain that, with the financial and technical assistance of the U.S. firm, would have seemed to make an appropriate joint venture partner. During negotiations, the two firms preliminarily agreed that the U.S. company would take a 40 percent interest in the new business venture, sharing profits with its partner. The Americans had done all of the usual background checks, reviewed credit reports, and made inquiries of others with whom the Spanish company had dealt. Although everything was found to be in order, and despite many trips abroad by management, the U.S. firm wanted their auditors to visit the Spanish company and review its books. During their visit to Spain, the auditors were asked "which set of books and numbers" they wanted to review—the real financial records of the Spanish company or those used to report to Spanish tax authorities. The U.S. company became uneasy about their potential exposure as a minority partner in a foreign investment with this company. Not only were they fearful that their "partner" would mislead them as they had the Spanish government, but they feared liability to Spanish legal and tax authorities for the conduct of their partner, over which they had little or no control.

As a result, they decided not to share ownership of a joint venture with the Spanish company, but instead decided to license their technology and know-how to the Spanish firm. They would obtain patent rights to their products in Europe, license those rights to the Spanish company, provide technical assistance, and in return receive an up-front cash payment and future royalties based on sales. This arrangement would give them the access to the European customers that they needed, without the capital costs and risks of building a plant there. This text will present many such examples of how the risks of international business can affect a firm's strategy for entering a foreign market.

Transaction Risks in Contracts for the Sale of Goods

A major portion of this book focuses on the special risks inherent in international transactions for the purchase and sale of goods. Commercial transactions present special risks because the process of shipping goods and receiving payment between distant countries is riskier than when done within a single country. By identifying some of these risks here, the reader will be better prepared in later chapters to understand the importance of managing these risks. Consider a few examples:

- An importer of camping tents, who thought their products would be subject to the same tariff rate as "sporting goods," found out too late that the U.S. Customs Service considered them to be "miscellaneous textile products" and imposed a much higher import duty.
- The owner of a yacht shipped aboard an ocean carrier from Asia, who failed to declare its real value on the shipping documents, found that when the yacht was destroyed on loading, international law allowed the yacht's owner to collect a mere $500.

- A U.S. exporter shipped goods to a customer on the "irrevocable" promise of a well-known bank to pay for the goods as soon as documents of title were tendered proving the goods were shipped on or before a certain date. When his goods had already gone halfway around the world, the exporter found that he could not get paid as promised, because the goods were loaded on board the ship just one day late.

PLANNING FOR INTERNATIONAL TRANSACTIONS. Planning could have helped to manage the risk in these cases, through inquiry, caution, contract negotiations, insurance, or reliance on professionals. The risks might have been shifted to the other party to the transaction or to some intermediary. For example, the importer of tents could have negotiated a contract for the seller to deliver the goods "duty paid." If that was not possible, why did the importer not rely on the expertise of a licensed customs broker or attorney to have determined the rate of duty sooner? The importer might even have obtained a ruling from U.S. Customs and Border Protection in advance and avoided an unexpected surprise in determining the tariff rate after they were already in the country. The shipper of the yacht might have negotiated different contract terms, requiring the buyer to be responsible for loss or damage during shipment. If not, the shipper could have relied on the advice of its marine insurance company, or even a licensed freight forwarder. If the U.S. exporter was aware that the deadline for shipment could not be met, why did he not attempt to obtain an extension from the buyer's bank? After all, in all of these cases, the risks could have been negotiated, as they are in most international business transactions. Those risks that could not be shifted to the other party could have been minimized by relying on the services of insurers, banks, and professional intermediaries.

PAYMENT OR CREDIT RISK. The risk that a buyer will default on a sales contract and fail to pay for the goods is known as *payment risk,* often called *credit risk*. The consequences of a buyer defaulting on an international contract can be potentially disastrous. Because a company generally incurs greater expense in selling overseas, a failed contract can mean a large loss. Selling overseas adds the costs of travel, foreign marketing and advertising, procuring foreign licenses, retaining counsel overseas, distributor's fees and agent's commissions, packaging and insuring for international shipment, communications expenses, and freight forwarder's fees. One of the major considerations is the expense of international air or ocean freight. Freight costs for ocean cargo, for example, are determined by the greater of weight or volume. Thus, heavy, bulky cargo that cannot be disassembled or have its volume reduced by the removal of air or water prior to shipment is quite expensive to ship. In some cases, the freight costs can equal the value of replacing the goods themselves. One export manager, unable to locate a substitute buyer in a foreign country, had to abandon goods at a foreign port rather than incur the costs of bringing them home!

The buyer's nonpayment or default can occur in a sales transaction for a variety of reasons. Perhaps the buyer found they could obtain the goods more cheaply from another source. Perhaps currency fluctuations destroyed the buyer's anticipated profits on the purchase. Perhaps the buyer became insolvent. Whatever the reason, a seller must plan for these potential risks. If sellers were not able to do so, all world trading would soon come to a grinding halt.

DELIVERY RISK. The transaction risk that a buyer will not receive the goods called for under a contract is called *delivery risk*. It can result from a late shipment, or no shipment at all, or from shipment of goods that do not conform to the contract specifications. It can result from adverse business conditions, labor strikes, disasters at sea, or the actions of an unscrupulous seller. There are many cases of large-scale fraud in international trade. Whatever the cause, buyers must assess the risk of dealing with their foreign suppliers. Business credit reports, trade references, product samples, and visits to their factory are all important in evaluating a vendor. In the words of one experienced purchasing manager for an international firm, "There is no substitute for knowing your seller."

PROPERTY OR MARINE RISK. One special form of delivery risk, known as *property risk* or *marine risk,* is the potential for loss or damage to cargo or freight while in transit over great distances. Between the time that the parties initially enter their agreement and the time that the goods arrive at their destination, any number of unexpected events may cause one or more parties to incur losses under the contract. For example, goods can be damaged by the sea or salt air, ships can sink, planes can crash, refrigeration units in containers can break, food can spoil, grain can become infested with insects, and labor strikes can delay the departure of a vessel. Some of the risks can be quite surprising. Assume that an exporter is shipping goods on an ocean vessel. The ship damages its hull on rocks in the harbor because the captain had negligently left the deck. Imagine the exporter's surprise when it finds out that not only can it not recover from the carrier, but that it must contribute to the ship's owner for the costs of towing the ship to safety, for rescuing the crew, and even for saving cargo that belonged to other shippers!

no fault clause

Pilferage and Containerized Freight. Pilferage and theft has been a problem for international shippers for many years. During the days of *break-bulk* freight, when goods were loaded and unloaded on pallets or in boxes, cargo was relatively easy to steal. However, in the past several decades shipping has changed dramatically. Today, nearly all merchandise is transported in large containers sealed by the shipper and opened only by the buyer or by customs officials. This practice has helped reduce damage and pilferage to shipments. Of course, pilferage is still a tremendous problem, especially in the ports of developing countries. One U.S. shipper of cellular phones to Latin America recently said that his firm could not mark the contents on the outside of the shipping boxes or crates because if they did the phones would never reach their destinations.

Managing Currency and Exchange Rate Risks

Currency risk is a type of transaction risk that a firm is exposed to as a result of buying, selling, or holding a foreign currency or transacting business in a foreign currency. Currency risk includes (1) exchange rate risk and (2) currency control risk. (Other risks, such as inflation risk and interest rate risk, are not the subject of this book.) Most international business transactions involve the use or transfer of foreign currency. Currency risk exists when a firm must convert one currency to the currency of another country before it can be used.

Exchange Rate Risk. *Exchange rate risk* results from the fluctuations in the relative values of foreign currencies against each other when they are bought and sold on international financial markets. Virtually every international business transaction is affected by exchange rate risk. Take a simple example. Assume that a company based in the United States sells goods to a firm in France. In an export/import transaction, one of the parties will be dealing in the currency of the other. The one that deals in the other party's currency will bear the exchange rate risk. If the contract calls for payment in U.S. dollars upon shipment of the goods, which is to take place in 60 days, then the French importer bears the risk during the intervening period. If the French firm does not have a source of income in dollars, it must buy dollars from a French bank at the prevailing rate for dollars at the time it makes the purchase. If the value of the euro declines vis-à-vis the dollar during the same period, then more euros will be needed to purchase the same number of dollars to pay the U.S. firm. Similarly, if the euro appreciates in value against the dollar, then the French firm will find the goods "cheaper" than it had expected. Whichever way the currencies fluctuate, the U.S. exporter will have shifted the exchange rate risk to the French side. The U.S. firm will spend dollars to pay labor, utilities, taxes, and other expenses, and it will receive dollars for the goods sold to France. (Of course, even when dealing in one's own currency, a company still faces "opportunity risk"—if it had sold goods for euros, and the euro had appreciated, then the company might have reaped a windfall profit on the exchange to dollars.) On the other hand, if the U.S. firm prices its goods in euros at the request of its customer (something an exporter often must do for its customers), it will bear the exchange rate risk. As one can see from this example, currency exchange rates can have a tremendous effect on trade and investment decisions made by firms, and thus can affect the flow of money in and out of all countries.

Methods of Managing Exchange Rate Risk. Most international bankers claim that predicting currency fluctuations is more difficult than predicting the stock market. The ability of a firm to manage its currency risk depends on the size, sophistication, and global resources of the firm. A small domestic company might "buy forward" or *hedge*. A firm hedges when it enters into a contract, usually with a bank, for the purchase of a foreign currency to be delivered at a future date at a price agreed upon in the contract.

Multinational corporations also have other, more complex and sophisticated options for managing exchange rate risk. For instance, a multinational corporation's subsidiary units in foreign countries may have excess local currency derived from revenues there. These assets can be transferred to affiliated units owned by the parent company for use anywhere in the world.

Some companies engage in speculative trading of foreign currencies. These risky transactions require experience, skill, and, as traders know, "iron nerves."

Currency Control Risk. Some countries, particularly developing countries in which access to ready foreign reserves is limited, put restrictions on currency transactions. In order to preserve the little foreign exchange that is available for international transactions, such as importing merchandise, these countries restrict the amount of foreign currency that they will sell to private companies. This limitation can cause problems for a U.S. exporter waiting for payment from its foreign customer who cannot obtain the dollars needed to pay for the goods. (The creative exporter may have to weigh alternative methods of payment in these countries, such as bartering.) The most severe form of currency restriction is the *blocked currency*. Blocked currencies, used by the former Soviet bloc countries of Eastern Europe under communism, could not legally be removed from the issuing country at all.

A multinational corporation with income earned in a country with a restricted currency may find restrictions on its freedom to remove, or repatriate, the earnings to its home country. Repatriation of profits or dividends may be limited to a small portion of earnings or taxed at discouragingly high levels. Working in this environment presents one of the greatest creative challenges to a multinational corporation's financial managers. Industrialized countries have only rarely instituted austere currency controls in the past, and then only in times of national monetary crisis.

Managing Distance and Communications

The risks of doing business in a foreign country are different from those encountered at home. A Texas firm, for example, will find doing business in Japan, or even neighboring Mexico, to be different from doing business in Oklahoma. The Texas firm will find Oklahoma City hardly different at all from Austin. Texas and Oklahoma share a common language and customs, a common currency, uniform commercial laws, a seamlessly networked communications system, and so on. The Texas firm would not find these similarities in a foreign country. It would encounter greater distances; problems in communications; language and cultural barriers; differences in ethical, moral, and religious codes; exposure to strange foreign laws and government regulations; and different currencies. All these factors affect the risks of doing business abroad.

Selling Face-to-Face. Parties to an international transaction must find ways of reducing the distance between them. Ask any international sales manager about the importance of face-to-face meetings, and he or she will tell you that you cannot sell your product abroad from the confines of your office. Even though the advent of the Internet and modern communications has brought businesspeople closer to each other than ever before, no one has discovered a substitute for face-to-face meetings. Doing business in Asia may require many trips there and many years of ongoing negotiations in order for the parties to develop trust between them. Face-to-face meetings are essential to negotiations because they enable the parties to better describe their needs, their capabilities, and their products and services. They are better able to communicate and explain their positions and, most importantly, to gauge each other's intentions, attitudes, and integrity. These benefits of face-to-face meetings apply in banking, as well as in other industries. International bankers often travel abroad to meet foreign bankers, foreign government representatives, and foreign customers so they can personally evaluate the risks of lending money or doing other banking business.

ATTENDANCE AT INTERNATIONAL TRADE SHOWS. One opportunity for identifying new customers, renewing old business relationships, and expanding contacts in a given industry is to attend an international trade show, or trade fair. These regularly scheduled exhibitions are common in most industries, including computer hardware and software, home textiles, restaurant products, aircraft, boats, sporting goods, clothing and apparel, paper, and industrial equipment. They are often organized by industry trade associations or convention centers. These shows give sellers from around the world the opportunity to exhibit their products and services, meet prospective buyers, and write orders.

Language and Cultural Differences

As the world's economy moves toward greater globalization, languages and cultural differences become less of a barrier to international business. Even though English is widely used in business all over the world, the language of a given transaction still depends on the type of business one is doing and on the region of the world. In the case of importing and exporting, some truth can be found in the saying that if you're the buyer, the seller will find a way to speak your language; but if you're the seller, you should find a way to communicate with your customer. One corporate CEO argued that he could not possibly know all the languages of all the countries in which he does business. While true, that argument may not be so valid for an international sales manager who does business in one or two primary foreign markets. Some positions require an even greater level of foreign language competency. For certain types of selling or contract negotiations, a mastery of a foreign language will be essential. As a firm moves toward greater penetration of a foreign market, for instance, when negotiating a licensing or investment contract, it will become crucial to use native speakers or nationals of the host country. Contracts such as these will often be written in the languages of both parties, and so the use of foreign lawyers becomes necessary.

In other cases, only social conventions must be observed; you should know how to make introductions, to be courteous, and to show you took the time to learn something about the other country's language and culture. An appreciation for the cultural environment and religious beliefs of a host is essential. When selling in a foreign country, the use of local sales agents and distributors will ease the language and cultural problems. They will also give good advice on handling the cultural differences you might face in their countries. Moreover, many countries are moving toward the use of uniform laws—laws and legal codes that are commonly agreed on and adopted by many countries (and written and made available in many languages). The case of *Gaskin v. Stumm Handel* illustrates what can happen when a party is not able to read and understand a foreign language contract.

Gaskin v. Stumm Handel GMBH

390 F. Supp. 361 (1975)

United States District Court (S.D.N.Y.)

BACKGROUND AND FACTS

The plaintiff, a U.S. citizen, entered into an employment contract with the German firm of Stumm Handel, the defendant. The contract presented to the plaintiff was written entirely in German. Without being able to speak or read German, the plaintiff signed the contract. He never received an English language version. At the time of the signing of the contract, however, the terms of the contract were explained to him in English. One of the terms of the contract, known

continued

continued

as a "forum selection clause," provided that any disputes that might arise between the parties would be settled in the courts of Germany. Later, when the parties reached a disagreement, the plaintiff brought this action against the defendant in the United States, contending that his failure to understand German rendered the forum selection clause invalid.

CANNELLA, DISTRICT JUDGE

With regard to such translation, Gaskin asserts that "I was never informed that by executing the (contract), I was consenting to the Republic of West Germany as the forum within which I must submit all controversies" and that "had I known this, I would not have agreed to the same, as such an obligation is onerous and unconscionable, and a deterrent to bringing any actions whatsoever." ... We find that in making the foregoing assertions, Gaskin flies in the face of well-settled contract law principles and has failed to sustain his burden.

It is a settled proposition of contract law in this state and nation that "the signer of a deed or other instrument, expressive of a jural act, is conclusively bound thereby. That his mind never gave assent to the terms expressed is not material. If the signer could read the instrument, not to have read it was gross negligence; if he could not read it, not to procure it to be read was equally negligent; in either case the writing binds him (citations omitted)...."

While Mr. Gaskin's apparent "blissful ignorance" with regard to the contract under which he was to render his labors to the defendant strikes us as highly incredible as a matter of common sense, we take note of certain facts which are relevant to the disposition of this matter. It must be remembered that Mr. Gaskin is not an ignorant consumer, unlearned in the language of the contract, who has become entangled in the web of a contract of adhesion through the overreaching or other unconscionable practices of the defendant. The contract at bar does not involve the credit sale of a refrigerator or color television set, but rather compensation of some $36,000 per annum for Mr. Gaskin's services as the manager in charge of the defendant's New York operations which were to be conducted under the name Stumm Trading Company. His office (Park Avenue, New York City) is not located in an area which would have precluded his easy access to a competent translation of the involved document. There existed no emergency condition or other exceptional circumstances at the time plaintiff entered into this contract; conditions which might now serve to excuse his present plight. Mr. Gaskin has advanced no evidence to support a finding that the contract sued upon is other than one which was fairly negotiated at arm's length and in a businesslike fashion between the parties and voluntarily entered into by him in the hope of reaping a great economic benefit....

Thus, we find that the instant transaction was a commercial arrangement of a nature which warranted the exercise of care by Mr. Gaskin before his entry into it and that his conduct with regard to this undertaking can only be characterized as negligent, the consequences of which he must now bear....

We, therefore, decline to exercise our jurisdiction over this cause in deference to the contractual forum. An order dismissing this action will be entered.

Decision. The court dismissed the plaintiff's action, holding that the plaintiff's failure to speak or read German was not grounds for invalidating any of the provisions of the contract.

Managing Political Risk

Political risk is generally defined as the risk to a firm's business interests resulting from political instability or civil unrest, political change, war, or terrorism in a country in which the firm is doing business. Political risk is sometimes unpredictable, but not always so, and is greatest in countries undergoing rapid economic or political change. It includes the potentially adverse actions of foreign governments, as well as policies instituted by the firm's home government. For example, a U.S. firm that operates a subsidiary in a Middle Eastern country might find that it has become subject to U.S. restrictions on doing business there because that country has been cited for sponsoring international terrorism. Political risk can affect all aspects of international business—the right to ship goods to a country or own and operate a factory there, or the safety of foreign employees from terrorist acts.

Causes of Political Risk. Political change can lead to a hostile environment for business dealings. Instability is a particular problem in countries that experience rapid changes in government, be they democracies or less-than-democratic developing countries. As governments change, so might their trade, investment, tax, and other economic policies. When the changes result from democratic elections, the impact on business is usually gradual. Italy has undergone a succession of democratically elected governments since World War II, and firms there have had to adjust to changing economic policies. The potential for faster, more dramatic change is greater in the developing countries. Even though foreign business interests may have been welcomed under one government, its successor may take a different view. For many years, a nation may welcome foreign investment, consumer products, and Western culture, and then virtually overnight turn to resent any foreign influence at all. Cuba, Libya, Iran, and Iraq are examples. For most of U.S. history, U.S. firms have had friendly relationships and extensive investments in these countries. Yet after political upheaval, each of these countries became hostile to Americans there.

A change in government can occur because of a popular revolution or military takeover (known as a *coup d'état*). In the 1950s, communist-inspired revolutions forced sudden changes in some governments. Fidel Castro's takeover of Cuba is a good example. U.S. companies in Cuba experienced the seizure of their assets and expulsion from the island.

Changes in some countries have been inspired by religious fundamentalism. The Islamic Revolution in Iran in the late 1970s and the ouster of the Shah of Iran, a dictator himself, resulted in tremendous political instability and economic uncertainty for firms that had done business there for many years. The new Islamic government retaliated against the United States for its support of the Shah of Iran. It seized the U.S. embassy in Tehran, held U.S. citizens hostage, canceled contracts with U.S. firms, and confiscated their assets.

THE RISK OF WAR AND INTERNATIONAL HOSTILITIES. Even the best-laid business plans can be upset when transportation and communications are disrupted by war or revolution. Consider what happened when Egypt blocked the Suez Canal to international shipping during its 1956 war with Israel. Because this important waterway was closed, cargo ships were diverted around the Cape of Good Hope on the southern tip of the African continent, a costly journey of many thousands of miles. The loss fell upon companies that used the canal. In today's world, consider the impact on business of war in the Balkans during the 1990s, of today's civil strife in Africa, and of course, of U.S. actions in the Middle East.

HANDLING POLITICAL RISK. Handling political risk requires planning and vigilance. First, the firm must have an understanding of the domestic affairs of a country. Typical questions might include: Is the country politically stable? Will democracy prevail? Is the country subject to religious or ethnic strife? How are minority groups treated, and how will their treatment be viewed by the more democratic countries of the world? What is the country's economic situation?

The firm must also understand regional politics. Is the region stable? Are neighboring countries in the region hostile? Are border conflicts likely to erupt? These considerations might be especially important in the Middle East. Finally, international affairs must be considered. Is the country abiding by international human rights standards? Is it a member of international organizations? Does it abide by international law?

At a minimum, international managers are well advised to keep abreast of all political affairs that could affect their operations and interests worldwide. Access to the latest information is critical. Good sources include newspapers such as *The Journal of Commerce* and *The Wall Street Journal*. Beyond that, the firm can obtain more sophisticated assessments of the political environment in a foreign country through the process known as *political risk analysis*. Professionally prepared political risk analysis reports are available, giving current assessments and forecasts of future stability. Other resources include political risk consulting firms, insurance industry reports, reports of U.S. government agencies, and informal discussions with experienced international bankers and shipping company representatives. In some cases, *political risk insurance* is available for firms making investments in foreign countries where their exposure is great. A firm engaged in strategic corporate planning should consider this information when developing its global business strategy and when transacting business.

Risks of Exposure to Foreign Laws and Courts

You have heard the expression, "When in Rome, do as the Romans do." Whether you are trying to handle social situations with business colleagues in a foreign culture, devise marketing plans for your products there, or do business without running afoul of local laws, there is considerable truth to this old adage. We are all responsible for conforming our conduct to the laws of the state or country in which we are present. Criminal codes vary from country to country, depending on social, political, cultural, and historical traditions. Many acts that are perfectly legal in one country can be illegal in another. Indeed, most travelers to a foreign country could conceivably break a host of laws and not even be aware of it. The same is true for the law of contracts, employment, competition, torts, and other business laws. It is virtually impossible to catalog all of the differences between these laws from country to country. For example, consider the prohibition against charging interest on a loan under Islamic law in many Middle Eastern countries, something which is taken for granted as an everyday part of Western business. To make matters worse, many foreign laws are not made readily available or understandable to the average foreign guest. Some are unwritten and understood only by the local residents.

Consider the next case. In the United States, no one would even think about the need to apply for a government license before opening a retail store. True, in the United States a sales tax permit is required, but we do not have to seek permission to open a retail store. In the United States, "mom and pop" retail stores, as well as large-scale discount stores, open and close every day. But in many countries, including European countries with a long history of powerful trade unions, shopkeeper unions, and apprenticeships, the attitudes are very different. The 1995 case *DIP SpA v. Commune di Bassano del Grappa,* considered the legality of Italian law that requires applicants to gain permission from local mayors and committees before opening a retail store. American students should consider just how "foreign" this concept really is.

DIP SpA v. Commune di Bassano del Grappa

October 1995

Court of Justice of the European Communities (2nd Chamber)

BACKGROUND AND FACTS

Italian law prohibits the opening of certain retail stores without first obtaining a license from the local authorities. The law requires each municipality to draw up a plan for the development of new businesses in its area. The stated purposes of the licensing scheme are to protect consumers, to achieve a balance between supply and demand, to ensure free competition, and to obtain a balance between different forms of distribution (e.g., permanent stores versus mobile vendors). A license to open a new retail store can be denied if it is believed that the market is adequately served already. The license is granted by the local mayor on the advice of a local committee. The ten- to fifteen-person committees are made up of local government representatives, local merchants, and members of local unions of shopkeepers and workers. This action was brought before the European Court of Justice by three applicants whose licenses to open new retail stores in Italy had been denied. One of the applicants was a subsidiary of a German company. The three applicants wanted to open stores that sold jewelry, hardware, and foodstuffs. The applicants maintain that the Italian retail licensing laws exclude new business, restrict competition, discriminate against non-Italian companies and imported goods, and lead to higher consumer prices. They argued that the Italian law was invalid under the laws of the European Union and the Treaty of Rome.

HIRSCH P.C., PRESIDING

According to the applicants, the Act favours and reinforces anti-competitive practices between existing traders, which is the mechanism through which the Italian retail market is said to be foreclosed.... While the applicants have forcefully stressed what they perceive to be the self-evidently concerted nature of the

continued

continued

activities and common purpose of the distributor and retail representatives on these advisory committees which operate across Italy, they have not referred to any evidence which would be sufficient to justify a conclusion that, as a result of the application of the Act, such a network of collusion either subsists or has been encouraged in Italy....

During the oral hearing the applicants submitted that, because the Act operated effectively to exclude new entrants, many of whom would be non-Italian operators desirous of establishing large-scale and sometimes discount outlets which might sell more non-Italian goods than existing traders, it was likely, either actually or at least potentially, to hinder intra-Community trade.

I believe that this argument must be rejected. [W]hile the Act limits the overall number of trading licences, it does not necessarily produce an overall decrease in the number or value of goods sold on the Italian market nor does it necessarily render more difficult the sale of imports as opposed to domestic goods. I accept the Commission's observation that this type of provision is not capable of hindering intra-Community trade....

Accordingly, I am of the opinion that ...

2. [L]egislation requiring an opinion to be obtained from a collective body, whose members include representatives of traders already operating on the market, both when the plan is drawn up and when new licences are granted, is not contrary to (the competition laws of) either Article 85 or 86 of the *Treaty of Rome.*
3. [S]uch legislation is not capable of hindering intra-European Community trade for the purposes of the application of Article 30 of the *Treaty of Rome* so long as, in law or in fact, it does not distinguish between imports and domestic (Italian) products.

The Italian Act provides that licences are to be issued by the mayor of the municipality concerned, taking into account the criteria laid down in the municipal commercial development plan. The purpose of that plan is to provide the best possible service for consumers and the best possible balance between permanent trading establishments and foreseeable demand from the population.

National rules which require a licence to be obtained before a new shop can be opened and limit the number of shops in the municipality in order to achieve a balance between supply and demand cannot be considered to put individual traders in dominant positions or all the traders established in a municipality in a collective dominant position, a salient feature of which would be that traders did not compete against one another.

On this point, it is sufficient to observe that rules such as those contained in the Italian Act make no distinction according to the origin of the goods distributed by the businesses concerned, that their purpose is not to regulate trade in goods with other Member States and that the restrictive effects which they might have on the free movement of goods are too uncertain and indirect for the obligation which they impose to be regarded as being capable of hindering trade between Member States.

Decision. The Italian law requiring the licensing of new retail stores by local committees is not invalid under the laws of the European Union and the *Treaty of Rome*.

Comment. By 2003, it seemed that supermarkets and mass retailers were changing the face of Italy. Since this decision, the number of supermarkets in Italy almost doubled, and traditional family-owned businesses, with all the character, richness, and history they represent, had sadly declined. But even a country like Italy, where shoppers for generations made daily stops at the meat, produce, or dairy store, seemed to enjoy the new convenience and lower prices.

Settling disputes between companies can be much more difficult in international business than in domestic business. Litigation of a case in a court in a foreign country is both costly and time consuming. In addition, the laws of a foreign country can differ greatly from those laws one is accustomed to at home. There can be differences in the law of contracts, crimes, torts, intellectual property, securities and investment, and more. Language and logistical issues can be problems as well. A firm may need representation by attorneys in their own country *and* in the country of litigation. Frequent court appearances could require great travel expense. International cases also involve complex procedural problems: What country's courts should hear the case? What country's laws should apply? How does a court compel the testimony of witnesses or the production of business records not found in that country? Should the case be submitted to arbitration—perhaps in some "neutral" country? When a firm is negotiating an agreement with a foreign party, such as a contract to sell goods or to franchise a business, both parties will usually want to reach an agreement on these issues, and so the advice of an attorney at this stage in a transaction is extremely important.

Receiving Professional Assistance in Going International

International managers must often rely on professional advice from attorneys, bankers, customs brokers, and others.

The International Attorney. Lawyers who practice in international business can be either in private practice or employed as in-house counsel to a multinational corporation. Their work might include import/export law, customs and tariff law, immigration and nationality law, admiralty law, the licensing of intellectual property, foreign investment contracts, international antitrust law, drafting and negotiating international contracts, and other legal issues. Private practice attorneys who specialize in these areas are usually located in large cities and have associations with other lawyers in foreign countries. Attorneys who are employees of multinational corporations regularly advise management, develop internal corporate policies, work on external government relations at home and abroad, supervise litigation abroad, take responsibility for international tax matters, and coordinate the work of foreign counsel.

Freight Forwarder/Customs Broker. The function of the freight forwarder or customs broker is to expedite the physical transportation of goods and the preparation of shipping or customs documents. The documentation or paperwork required in an export or import shipment is quite extensive. Even though any businessperson needs to understand the legal nature and significance of all documents used to sell goods and transfer money in an international transaction, much of the paperwork is done by the forwarder. Freight forwarders act as the shipper's (the seller's) agent for exporting. In doing so, they help consolidate cargo, arrange for marine insurance policies, book the least costly freight space with a carrier, and occasionally prepare the bank collection documents an exporter needs in order to be paid. When these agents represent U.S. importers, they are called customs brokers. A power of attorney is usually required for them to perform their services and to act for the importer or exporter. Customs brokerage firms are licensed and bonded under the rules of the Federal Maritime Commission and the U.S. Bureau of Customs and Border Protection.

The International Banker. This text devotes considerable study to the role of international banks in all international business transactions. A later chapter, for example, describes how banks move money and shipping documents and, thus, make the international sales contract work. They not only provide important financing, but they also offer a range of specialized international banking and foreign exchange services necessary to any firm going abroad. Some international bankers possess a great wealth of expertise and foreign contacts and are, therefore, able to play an advisory role in international business.

Conclusion

The business environment has changed dramatically since the end of World War II. To be competitive in world markets today, the international manager or world trader needs to be familiar with economics, culture, politics, and law. Multinational firms have adopted business strategies that see the world, and profits, in global terms. Even small- and medium-sized manufacturing and service firms are important competitors in international markets, and will become even more important in the future.

The three basic forms of international business—trade, licensing of intellectual property, and foreign direct investment—are methods of entering foreign markets. They are not mutually exclusive. One joint venture agreement, for instance, can have provisions for the building of a plant and the manufacture of goods, for the licensing of trademarks or patents to the joint venture for a determined period, and for the export or import of those products to other countries of distribution. The methods employed to enter a foreign market must be tailored to the type and size of the firm, the nature of its product or service, and its experience and goals.

The process of managing an international business transaction is the process of managing risk. Nowhere is that risk greater than in the rapidly changing developing world, in Eastern Europe, in the newly independent republics of the former Soviet Union, and in China. The economic and social problems in those regions make experience and caution a prerequisite to tapping the new opportunities that wait there. Through the study of international business law, one can better prepare to identify potential risks and problems and to plan business strategies accordingly.

Chapter Summary

1. The three forms of international business, or methods of entering a foreign market, are trade, the licensing of intellectual property, and foreign direct investment.
2. Trade consists of importing and exporting, including trade in goods and services. The United States has gone from a net exporting nation to a net importing nation in one generation. Despite a trade surplus in services, the U.S. has seen increasing trade deficits. In 2006 the U.S. trade deficit reached $758.5 billion. America's trade deficit was largest with China, Japan, Canada, and Mexico.
3. Today, more and more small- and medium-sized U.S. companies are exporting, with over 239,000 individual identified exporters. Successful exporters make a long-term commitment to their foreign markets and customers and undertake an export plan.
4. The U.S. share of world merchandise exports is at 8.7 percent.
5. Cross-border trade in services includes business services such as travel, passenger fares, shipping, package delivery, banking, insurance, securities brokerage, accounting, management and engineering consulting, and other professional services.
6. Many firms not ready for direct exporting can export indirectly, through export management companies or export trading companies.
7. Importing should not be viewed as an isolated, one-time transaction. Most successful importers have a "global sourcing" strategy.
8. Most tariffs, or import duties, have been reduced to manageable levels. Non-tariff barriers are today the leading barrier to free trade around the world. Many barriers to free trade have been reduced by international agreement at the World Trade Organization in Geneva.
9. Intellectual property rights, also called IPRs, include patents, copyrights, and trademarks. They can be transferred through a licensing agreement in return for a royalty or other compensation arrangement. IPRs can be rendered worthless if they are not protected and infringement occurs. The cost of infringement is estimated at hundreds of billions of dollars annually. International cooperation for the protection of IPRs is essential to the future of a global, information-based economy.
10. Foreign direct investment refers to the long-term ownership and active control of an ongoing business in a foreign "host" country. Flows of foreign direct investment reached over $1.3 trillion in 2006, much of that flowing to developing countries.
11. Multinational corporations are firms with significant foreign direct investment assets. They are becoming increasingly "globalized," meaning that they have the ability to derive and transfer capital resources worldwide and to operate facilities of production and penetrate markets in more than one country, usually on a global scale. Multinational corporations have a tremendous impact on the world's economy and on economic development in developing countries.
12. The management of international business is the management of risk. This includes political risk, such as the risk of war, terrorism, or political instability, as well as commercial or transaction risk. The successful international manager is one who will plan in advance to manage the unique risks of international business.

Questions and Case Problems

1. What factors have influenced the globalization of business?
2. Describe the "investment risk" that a multinational corporation might face in establishing a plant overseas. What were the risks faced by Union Carbide, a Connecticut-based multinational, in the ownership and operation of its plant in Bhopal, India? At the time the investment was being planned, the government of India had made its restrictions clear: Union Carbide's Indian plant would have to have Indian joint ownership, Indian engineers and contractors would be responsible for construction, and Indian citizens would manage and operate the plant. For instance, although Union Carbide provided the basic design for the plant, India insisted that its own firms build it. From 1972 to 1980, the construction was supervised by Indian engineers. During that time, the design was changed many times. Labor and employment policies were set by the Indian government. As the court stated, "more than 1,000 Indians were employed at the plant; only one American was employed there and he left in 1982." The court also notes that plant operations were supervised by more than two dozen Indian government agencies. Evaluate India's policies in this case. Why did they set such strict conditions? Could Indian policies have contributed to the disaster, or was Union Carbide entirely at fault? Why do you think Union Carbide agreed to the terms of the Indian government?
3. How does international business differ from domestic business? Explain how the risks of doing business internationally differ from doing business at home. What factors influence that risk? How do the risks of importing or exporting differ from those of licensing intellectual property or of building a factory abroad?
4. Undertake a study of one country or one region of the world and evaluate its business climate, its attitude toward trade and foreign investment, and the level of political risk. Where would you go for sources of information? How has the breakup of the former Soviet Union affected the business climate in that region?
5. Who are the members of a firm's export team? Describe each of their functions.
6. Plaintiff, a Swiss corporation, entered into contracts to purchase chicken from B.N.S. International Sales Corporation. Defendant was a New York corporation. The English language contracts called for the delivery of "chicken" of various weights. When the birds were shipped to Switzerland, the 2-lb. sizes were not young broiling chickens as the plaintiff had expected, but mature stewing chickens or fowl. The plaintiff protested, claiming that in German the term *chicken* referred to young broiling chickens. The question for the court was: What kind of chicken did the plaintiff order? Was it "broiling chicken," as the plaintiff argued, or any chickens weighing 2 lbs., as the defendant argued? *Frigaliment Importing Co., Ltd. v. B.N.S. International Sales Corp.*, 190 F. Supp 116 (S.D.N.Y. 1960). What could the parties have done to avoid this misunderstanding?
7. Successful international managers agree that success in entering a foreign market comes from planning and commitment. What does this mean? What kind of commitment do you think they are referring to? It is also often said that exporting is not an "elixir" for a company that is failing in its home market and is looking for new sales elsewhere. Evaluate this statement. Do you think it is true?
8. What industries in your state are the leading exporters? Who are the leading export firms? What do you think is the impact of exports on your state's economy? Where would you go for information? What role does your state government play in promoting exports?
9. U.S. firms have been very successful in foreign franchising, particularly in fast food and other retail businesses and service companies. How do you account for this success? Where do you think the best opportunities and hottest markets are for foreign franchising?
10. There are many U.S. government programs to aid American firms in boosting exports. These programs are generally administered by the International Trade Administration and its U.S. Commercial Service, as well as the Small Business Administration. Undertake an Internet search of government resources for small- and medium-sized exporters. What services are offered by the U.S. Commercial Service? What trade statistics are available? Country information? Foreign market information? Export counseling? Matchmaking and trade contact programs?

MANAGERIAL IMPLICATIONS

Your firm, SewTex, Inc., manufactures consumer and industrial sewing machinery. The consumer machines retail for $350 to $1,000 and are sold in the United States through department stores, discount stores, and home sewing stores. The industrial machines range in price from $5,000 to $50,000. The machines contain a unique computer chip that allows them to embroider words and designs on fabric in a choice of four scripts. The firm owns the patent on the machines in the United States. Currently the industrial machines are made in the United States from components made in the United States and Taiwan. The consumer machines are assembled at plants in Texas and in the Caribbean from parts made in Taiwan. The computer chip is manufactured for SewTex by a California firm.

Currently SewTex exports about 5 percent of its production of industrial machines. Of the total exported, the most sophisticated machines go to German and Swiss textile firms. A few earlier-generation models are shipped to India, Pakistan, and Brazil, and market prospects there look excellent.

The president of SewTex is concerned about the decline of the U.S. textile industry. She has asked your opinion on whether the company should consider increasing sales in foreign markets. She feels that some board members might caution against "getting involved overseas," and even she anticipates the U.S. textile market will pick up if the U.S. Congress places higher tariffs on textile imports. But she would like your thoughts. She has asked you to prepare a memorandum on the subject and requests that you address some of the following issues.

1. She feels that she must have the support of the directors for any major overseas venture. What arguments can she offer to explain why SewTex should become active in international markets? She understands that making a commitment is important, but what does that really mean?
2. If SewTex were to consider increasing its export base, what problems might it encounter? What are the advantages and disadvantages of exporting products to Europe? Should SewTex consider direct or indirect exporting in view of its products? If it chooses to continue exporting, how can it offer a repair service and a supply of spare parts to its customers?
3. Should SewTex consider licensing its technology to one of the other textile machinery manufacturers in Europe? Compare the advantages and disadvantages of this method of market entry to those of exporting.
4. The company president would like to know the options available for investment in the European market. Would this be preferable to the other market entry alternatives?
5. The company president recently read that Volkswagen and Mercedes have negotiated the purchase of automobile plants in the Czech Republic. She wonders whether the Czech government might be offering significant incentives to operate one of their mills. She knows that this country split from the Slovak Republic, in what had been Czechoslovakia, and that tension has existed between them over the years. She is concerned about the stability of a democratic government there. What sources can she turn to for more information on investment in the Czech Republic and Eastern Europe? What are the risks inherent in taking over operations there? What are the advantages?
6. SewTex's president is interested in knowing more about its market potential in Latin America for both types of machines. Can you advise her on the best methods for SewTex to penetrate that market? How would your plans for entry into the Latin American market affect SewTex's assembly operations and sales efforts worldwide?
7. Finally, can you advise SewTex on copyright, patent, and trademark issues related to its penetration of foreign markets? What are the major issues and concerns?

ETHICAL CONSIDERATIONS

All of us understand that the law is a floor for judging our behavior, an absolute minimum standard of conduct that one must follow. Anyone doing business in a foreign country understands that he or she must abide by the laws of their host country. But what about the unwritten or informal rules of doing business there—rules based on culture, religious codes, and societal constraints? Sometimes these laws can be very different from those in one's home country or in other countries in which one is working. Pollution may be a crime in one country and tolerated in another; bribery may be a crime in one country and customary in another. What is an accepted practice for employing children in industry in one country may be abhorrent in another, and so on. How does the multinational manager reconcile differences like these? What is the appropriate standard of ethical conduct for a multinational manager—that of his or her home country, the host country, or of some internal personal value system? How will the manager be influenced by the laws, unwritten rules, and cultural values of the host country? How does one balance his or her social responsibility regarding the health, safety, and well-being of the people of the host country with the company's overall objective of maximizing shareholder profit? What can a multinational corporation do to aid its managers in the development of a personal value system that is in keeping with the legal and cultural values of their host countries? Consider some of the legal and ethical issues in the following problems.

1. You have been negotiating with a representative of a government in Africa to sell products to them for a new state building project in their country. The negotiations are finalized during your trip to his offices in Africa. After easily negotiating a fixed price and delivery, he "suggests" that you prepare a price quotation on a "pro forma invoice"—at double the negotiated price. His government will pay the full amount shown on the invoice through a foreign bank, and your firm will pay him the difference as a "commission" in U.S. dollars deposited to his personal bank account in New York. He convincingly argues that this practice is customary in his country. The temptation for you is great; the deal would be a profitable one. Should you make the payment? Does it matter that it is customary in his country? Do you think it is lawful under American law? Does it matter that this is taking place in Africa, far from the United States? Is there a "victim" in this case? Who would be harmed?
2. Your company intends to locate a plant in Mexico to manufacture tires for sale in both Mexico and the United States. If the plant were in the United States, the laws would require expensive safeguards to protect the health and safety of U.S. workers, as well as the added cost of minimum wage rules, social security contributions, health insurance, retirement benefits, and other employee benefits. Assume that Mexican law is not so strict, wages and operating costs are less, and that benefit programs are either nonexistent or far less costly. To what extent should you conform to the legal standards applicable in the United States? Should you comply with American labor rules and environmental rules, even though they are not enforceable in Mexico? After all, should not all workers be safe from harm? Does not polluted air in Mexico travel to the United States? Do you think that any firm operating in a host country should carry with it the ethical codes of its home country? What about competition from firms in Japan or Germany who are operating their plants in Mexico? If they don't comply with American labor and environmental standards in Mexico, how will you compete with them? How does the international manager justify decisions in cross-cultural situations?
3. You are an international manager for a U.S. apparel designer that sells to major U.S. department stores and retailers. Several years ago your firm decided to have clothing sewn in India and Pakistan, which resulted in tremendous cost savings over having the work done in the United States. In making the decision, the firm considered its impact on U.S. families who depend on the income from these jobs. It opted for the cost savings, seeing its responsibility to produce a profit for shareholders as more important than its responsibility to provide jobs in the United States. Now, however, it finds that its contractor in India is overworking and abusing child labor in violation of internationally accepted standards for the treatment of children in the workplace. The Indian government shows little interest in policing its own labor practices. The sad story of the Indian children runs on national television and appears in the national press. What course of action should you take? If you decide to discontinue working with sewing contractors in India, do you do so to protect Indian children, because of the adverse publicity in the United States, or for both reasons? What do you expect the reaction would be from shareholders? From consumers?
4. While your answer to this question may have to wait until the next chapter, do you think that a written corporate code would aid a manager in resolving these conflicts and in making difficult choices? How would a corporation draft such a code and what sources would it draw on?

FOR INTERNET ACTIVITIES, VISIT ACADEMIC.CENGAGE.COM/BLAW/SCHAFFER.

CHAPTER 2
INTERNATIONAL LAW AND THE WORLD'S LEGAL SYSTEMS

INTERNATIONAL LAW

The exact origins of international law, and whether it dates to antiquity or to the Middle Ages, is debatable. The ancient Greeks, Chinese, and Romans all recognized some rudimentary concepts of international law. However, the term *international law* is thought to be derived from the Latin term *jus gentium,* meaning "the law of nations." That term was used in reference to Roman law that governed public and private relations with foreigners or with the rulers of foreign lands.

Many legal historians prefer to date the origins of modern international law to 1645 and the *Treaty of Westphalia,* which followed the Thirty Years' War. For our purposes it is sufficient to recognize that it was the rise of the European nation-state, first ruled by monarchs and later by sovereign governments, that led to the development of modern international law. In the sixteenth and seventeenth centuries, legal scholars from Spain, Italy, and Holland developed the first modern European concepts of international law. In 1625, Hugo Grotius wrote an important work, *On the Law of War and Peace,* which brought together various schools of thought on the nature of law and international obligations. He was a jurist, diplomat, statesman, lawyer for the Dutch East India Company, and respected author on the law of the sea. It was a time of colonialism, trade, and the rise of nations. Grotius wrote that the law of nations was not just divinely given, as was commonly believed in his day, but also that law arose by common agreement, by consensus, and by the accepted practice of nations. He premised these ideas on the idea of national sovereignty and on the recognition that all states are equal. To this day, it is accepted that international law arises not from the work of some supranational legislature, but because nations have agreed to follow customary and accepted rules or norms and to comply with treaties and conventions that they sign. This chapter examines customary international law, the law of treaties, and the role of international organizations in fostering international laws and ideals. We will see how international law addresses human rights, criminal law, and transnational crimes like terrorism. We will also see how international law has indirectly affected standards for corporate social responsibility in international business. Finally, we will take a comparative look at three of the major legal systems in place around the world today, including the common law, civil law, and Islamic legal systems.

Defining International Law

International law can be defined as the body of rules applicable to the conduct of nations in their relationships with other nations, the conduct of nations in their relationships with individuals, and rules for international, or intergovernmental, organizations. It can also include crimes and criminal procedures applicable to genocide, war crimes, and offenses against humanity committed by individuals in an official capacity.

International law has several characteristics that distinguish it from a country's domestic or municipal law. First, instead of being dictated by a legislative body, international law consists of rules that countries agree to follow. It is lawmaking by choice and by consent. Indeed, international law exists because nations agree that it is in their best interests to cooperate and to conform to commonly accepted norms. Second, despite some commonly misunderstood beliefs about the United Nations and other international bodies, there is no global authority for enforcing international law. It is true that international courts and tribunals (such as the International Court of Justice or dispute bodies of the World Trade Organization, for example) do issue judgments against nations. But nations must agree to be a party to these cases, and "hard" enforcement mechanisms do not really exist. There are courts, but no international sheriffs or marshals. International law has only "soft" enforcement mechanisms such as the force of public opinion, diplomacy, the withholding of foreign aid or other assistance, trade and economic sanctions, and political retaliation. Of course, the ultimate sanction against a country for violating international law is war, or at least the threat of it. In certain cases, where individuals are convicted of having committed international crimes, prison sentences and, in rare cases, the death penalty have been used. Later we will see that domestic and international courts do add to the enforcement capabilities of international law.

Public and Private International Law

There are many ways of organizing a discussion of international law. For the purposes of this textbook, we will refer to two broad categories: public international law and private international law. *Public international law* deals with those rules affecting the conduct of nations in their relationships with each other and with individuals. Just as an example, this might include rules for resolving territorial or boundary disputes, for conducting diplomacy or war, and for how nations treat foreign citizens. *Private international law* deals with the rights and responsibilities of private individuals or corporations operating in an international environment. For example, private international law might include international conventions and rules for international business transactions, including sales contracts, international shipping, or the liability of commercial airlines to passengers. There are even private international law rules for administering the wills and trusts of deceased persons who have owned property in more than one country. Private international law also can include laws enacted by national legislatures (i.e., a Congress or Parliament), usually governing international transactions, that are based on a model code prepared by international organizations. This tends to make national laws more uniform and more predictable—something very important if you are doing business in the far corners of the world. This process of making national laws more uniform is known as the *harmonization* of law. Private international law is covered in depth in the remainder of this book.

Sources of International Law

The most frequently cited authority for the sources of international law is the *Statute of the International Court of Justice,* the judicial arm of the United Nations. It sets out both primary and secondary sources of international law. According to Article 38, the *primary sources* of international law are: (1) international treaties and conventions, (2) international custom or customary law, and (3) the general principles of law recognized by civilized nations. *Secondary sources,* which are subsidiary means for the determination of rules of law, include the judicial decisions and teachings of the most highly qualified jurists of the various nations. Secondary sources provide evidence of what international law might be or how it should be interpreted. These include the judicial decisions of international courts and tribunals, scholarly writings, annual surveys published by international law societies in many countries, and publications of the United Nations. In the United States, the Office of the Legal Advisor of the U.S. Department of State publishes an annual *Digest of United States Practice in International Law.* In the United States, *The Restatement of Foreign Relations Law,* published by the American Law Institute, is considered a secondary source of customary law. The first source of international law that we will discuss is customary international law.

Customary International Law

Almost all legal systems, past and present, can trace their laws to some form of custom. Custom ruled primitive societies before there was law. It was, and is, the basis of law in tribal societies. It was the basis of the laws of the Cherokee nation and other tribes in pre-colonial America and included customary rules for dealing with neighboring tribes. It was the law of England prior to the Norman Conquest of 1066. Indeed, the customs of people influenced the early development of English common law. The customs and practices of the early English merchants eventually led to the development of commercial laws—known collectively as the *law merchant*—and the practices of early shipowners and shippers gave rise to the first laws of international shipping and cargo insurance. Custom has always been at the root of legal development, and that includes international law. *Customary international law* includes those commonly accepted rules of conduct that, through a consistent and long-standing practice, nations have followed out of a sense of binding obligation. Examples could include rules for the establishment of diplomatic missions, for the uniform prohibition against state-sponsored piracy on the high seas, or the right to seize the naval vessel of a foreign adversary during wartime. There is little doubt today that customary international law has become a part of the domestic law of virtually every nation. In the landmark American case *Paquette Habana,* the U.S. Supreme Court recognized international law as a part of American law. Notice how the Court discusses the necessity of resorting to "customs and usage" to ascertain international law.

The Paquette Habana

175 U.S. 677 (1900)

United States Supreme Court

BACKGROUND AND FACTS

During the Spanish-American war, the United States Navy seized two commercial fishing ships that were sailing from Havana. The ships were owned by a Spanish citizen living in Cuba and sailed under Spanish flags. The ships were not armed and not engaging in any hostilities. The owners were unaware of the hostilities between the United States and Spain and of the United States blockade of Cuba. The fishing ships were sold by the Navy in Florida as "prizes of war." Their original owner sued for damages in U.S. District Court. The court upheld the seizure and the owner appealed.

JUSTICE GRAY

These are two appeals from decrees of the district court of the United States for the southern district of Florida condemning two fishing vessels and their cargoes as prize of war....

We are then brought to the consideration of the question whether, upon the facts appearing in these records, the fishing smacks were subject to capture by the armed vessels of the United States during the recent war with Spain.

By an ancient usage among civilized nations, beginning centuries ago, and gradually ripening into a rule of international law, coast fishing vessels, pursuing their vocation of catching and bringing in fresh fish, have been recognized as exempt, with their cargoes and crews, from capture as prize of war....

The doctrine which exempts coast fishermen, with their vessels and cargoes, from capture as prize of war, has been familiar to the United States from the time of the War of Independence....

Since the United States became a nation, the only serious interruptions, so far as we are informed, of the general recognition of the exemption of coast fishing vessels from hostile capture, arose out of the mutual suspicions and recriminations of England and France during the wars of the French Revolution....

In the war with Mexico, in 1846, the United States recognized the exemption of coast fishing boats from capture.... International law is part of our law, and must be ascertained and administered by the courts of justice of appropriate jurisdiction as often as questions of right depending upon it are duly presented for their determination. For this purpose, where there is no treaty and no controlling executive

continued

continued

or legislative act or judicial decision, resort must be had to the customs and usages of civilized nations, and, as evidence of these, to the works of jurists and commentators who by years of labor, research, and experience have made themselves peculiarly well acquainted with the subjects of which they treat. Such works are resorted to by judicial tribunals, not for the speculations of their authors concerning what the law ought to be, but for trustworthy evidence of what the law really is....

This review of the precedents and authorities of the subject appears to us abundantly to demonstrate that at the present day, by the general consent of the civilized nations of the world, and independently of any express treaty or other public act, it is an established rule of international law, founded on consideration of humanity to a poor and industrious order of men, and of the mutual convenience of belligerent states, that coast fishing vessels, with their implements and supplies, cargoes and crews, unarmed and honestly pursuing their peaceful calling of catching and bringing in fresh fish, are exempt from capture as prize of war ...

This rule of international law is one which prize courts administering the law of nations are bound to take judicial notice of, and to give effect to, in the absence of any treaty or other public act of their own government in relation to the matter....

Decision. The Supreme Court reversed the district court and said that under an established rule of international law, peaceful fishing vessels are exempt from capture as prizes of war. The Court ordered that the owner receive payment for the loss of the ship, along with damages and costs. The Court acknowledged that it was bound to take judicial notice of international law and that international law is a part of American law.

Recent Issues in International Customary Law: The U.S. Alien Tort Statute. The U.S. *Alien Tort Claims Act* (also known as the *Alien Tort Statute,* or *ATS*) was enacted in 1789. Its plain language gives the federal courts jurisdiction over civil actions for damages brought by non–U.S. citizens for torts committed against them by other non–U.S. citizens outside of the United States in violation of the law of nations. For almost two hundred years, the statute was seldom used. In the 1980s, the statute was interpreted by U.S. courts in a more expansive manner, opening the doors of U.S. courts to more and more civil lawsuits based on violations of the norms of international law. Proponents of human rights, arguing the necessity that human rights cases be heard in the United States, supported this view of the statute. Many executives of U.S. multinational corporations were concerned that they could be sued in the United States by non–U.S. citizens who were accusing them of supporting, or participating in, human rights violations such as unfair or abusive labor practices, environmental damage, or worse (such as aiding and abetting foreign government–sponsored torture). The U.S. government supported this narrow reading of the statute. In the following case, *Sosa v. Alvarez-Machain,* the court addresses the scope of the *Alien Tort Statute* and answers the question of whether an abduction and arbitrary arrest of a Mexican citizen to stand trial in the United States violates a binding norm of customary international law.

The Law of Treaties

Other sources of international law include treaties and other international agreements of nations. A *treaty* is a legally binding (in the "international law" sense) agreement, contract, or *compact* between two or more nations that is recognized and given effect under international law. A treaty between two countries is said to be *bilateral,* and a treaty between three or more countries is *multilateral.* One of the most important principles of treaty law is that of *pacta sunt servanda* ("the pact must be respected"), meaning that treaties are binding upon the parties by consent and must be performed by them in good faith.

A *convention* is a legally binding multilateral treaty on matters of common concern, usually negotiated on a regional or global basis and open to adoption by many nations. Many conventions are negotiated under the auspices of the United Nations, the European Union, or the Council of Europe.

Sosa v. Alvarez-Machain

542 U.S. 692 (2004)

United States Supreme Court

BACKGROUND AND FACTS

Alvarez-Machain (Alvarez), a Mexican physician, was wanted by the U.S. Drug Enforcement Agency for the torture and murder of one of their agents in Mexico in 1985. Alvarez had allegedly administered drugs to the victim over the course of two days to prolong his consciousness during torture. When Mexico would not extradite Alvarez, the agency employed Sosa and several other Mexican citizens to kidnap Alvarez from his home and fly him by private plane to Texas where he was arrested by federal officers. Alvarez was tried and acquitted in a U.S. court. After the acquittal Alvarez returned home and in 1993 brought this civil suit in U.S. District Court against Sosa for damages under the U.S. *Alien Tort Claims Act* (also called the *Alien Tort Statute,* or ATS). The ATS was first enacted in 1789. Today, as amended, it reads: "The district courts shall have original jurisdiction of any civil action by an alien for a tort only, committed in violation of the law of nations or a treaty of the United States." 28 U.S.C. §1350. Alvarez brought this suit on the theory that the abduction and false arrest were a tort committed in violation of customary international law—the law of nations. Alvarez won a judgment against Sosa in District Court, and it was upheld by the U.S. Court of Appeals. Sosa appealed to the U.S. Supreme Court. [Issues related to Alvarez's claim against the government under the *Federal Tort Claims Act* are omitted here.]

JUSTICE SOUTER

* * *

Alvarez says that the ATS was intended ... as authority for the creation of a new cause of action for torts in violation of international law. We think that reading is implausible. As enacted in 1789, the ATS ... bespoke a grant of jurisdiction, not power to mold substantive law. The fact that the ATS was placed in §9 of the *Judiciary Act,* a statute otherwise exclusively concerned with federal-court jurisdiction, is itself support for its strictly jurisdictional nature. * * *

Sosa would have it that the ATS [must have created a right of action] because there could be no claim for relief without a further statute expressly authorizing adoption of causes of action. [The "friend of the court" briefs submitted by several law professors] took a different tack, that federal courts could entertain claims once the jurisdictional grant was on the books, because torts in violation of the law of nations would have been recognized within the common law of the time. We think history and practice give the edge to this latter position. * * *

"When the United States declared their independence, they were bound to receive the law of nations, in its modern state of purity and refinement." *Ware v. Hylton,* 3 Dall. 199 (1796). In the years of the early Republic, this law of nations comprised two principal elements, the first covering the general norms governing the behavior of national states with each other.... There was [also] a sphere in which these rules binding individuals for the benefit of other individuals overlapped with the norms of state relationships. [William Blackstone, in his *Commentaries on the Laws of England* 68 (1769)] ... referred to it when he mentioned three specific offenses against the law of nations addressed by the criminal law of England: violation of safe conducts, infringement of the rights of ambassadors, and piracy. An assault against an ambassador, for example, impinged upon the sovereignty of the foreign nation and if not adequately redressed could rise to an issue of war. It was this narrow set of violations of the law of nations, admitting of a judicial remedy and at the same time threatening serious consequences in international affairs, that was probably on minds of the men who drafted the ATS with its reference to tort. * * *

Still, the history does tend to support two propositions. First, there is every reason to suppose that the First Congress did not pass the ATS as a jurisdictional convenience to be placed on the shelf for use by a future Congress or state legislature that might, someday, authorize the creation of causes of action or itself decide to make some element of the law of nations actionable for the benefit of foreigners. * * * The second inference to be drawn from the history is that Congress intended the ATS to furnish jurisdiction for a relatively modest set of actions alleging violations of the law of nations. Uppermost in the legislative mind appears to have been offenses against ambassadors; violations of safe conduct were probably understood to be actionable, and individual actions arising out of prize captures and piracy may well have also been contemplated. But the common

continued

continued

law appears to have understood only those three of the hybrid variety as definite and actionable, or at any rate, to have assumed only a very limited set of claims. As Blackstone had put it, "offences against this law [of nations] are principally incident to whole states or nations," and not individuals seeking relief in court. 4 *Commentaries* 68. * * *

In sum, although the ATS is a jurisdictional statute creating no new causes of action, the reasonable inference from the historical materials is that the statute was intended to have practical effect the moment it became law. The jurisdictional grant is best read as having been enacted on the understanding that the common law would provide a cause of action for the modest number of international law violations with a potential for personal liability at the time. * * *

We think it is correct, then, to assume that the First Congress understood that the district courts would recognize private causes of action for certain torts in violation of the law of nations, though we have found no basis to suspect Congress had any examples in mind beyond those torts corresponding to Blackstone's three primary offenses: violation of safe conducts, infringement of the rights of ambassadors, and piracy. * * * Congress has not in any relevant way amended ATS §1350 or limited civil common law power by another statute. * * * Accordingly, we think courts should require any claim based on the present-day law of nations to rest on a norm of international character accepted by the civilized world and defined with a specificity comparable to the features of the eighteenth-century paradigms we have recognized. This requirement is fatal to Alvarez's claim. * * *

Since many attempts by federal courts to craft remedies for the violation of new norms of international law would raise risks of adverse foreign policy consequences, they should be undertaken, if at all, with great caution. * * *

We must still, however, derive a standard or set of standards for assessing the particular claim Alvarez raises, and for this action it suffices to look to the historical antecedents. Whatever the ultimate criteria for accepting a cause of action subject to jurisdiction under ATS §1350, we are persuaded that federal courts should not recognize private claims under federal common law for violations of any international law norm with less definite content and acceptance among civilized nations than the historical paradigms familiar when ATS §1350 was enacted. * * *

[Alvarez] attempts to show that prohibition of arbitrary arrest has attained the status of binding customary international law. It is this position that Alvarez takes now: that his arrest was arbitrary and as such forbidden by international law not because it infringed the prerogatives of Mexico, but because no applicable law authorized it Alvarez thus invokes a general prohibition of "arbitrary" detention defined as officially sanctioned action exceeding positive authorization to detain under the domestic law of some government, regardless of the circumstances.... Alvarez cites little authority that a rule so broad has the status of a binding customary norm today. He certainly cites nothing to justify the federal courts in taking his broad rule as the predicate for a federal lawsuit, for its implications would be breathtaking. His rule would support a cause of action in federal court for any arrest, anywhere in the world, unauthorized by the law of the jurisdiction in which it took place, and would create a cause of action for any seizure of an alien in violation of the Fourth Amendment.... Whatever may be said for the broad principle Alvarez advances, in the present, imperfect world, it expresses an aspiration that exceeds any binding customary rule having the specificity we require. It is enough to hold that a single illegal detention of less than a day, followed by the transfer of custody to lawful authorities and a prompt arraignment, violates no norm of customary international law so well defined as to support the creation of a federal remedy. The judgment of the Court of Appeals is reversed.

Decision. The Supreme Court rejected Alvarez's claim, ruling that Alvarez's abduction and transfer to the United States did not violate any norm of customary international law that would create a remedy under the *Alien Tort Statute*. The Court reasoned that the only three offenses recognized at the time of passage of the ATS in 1789 were violations of safe conduct, infringing the rights of ambassadors, and piracy on the seas. Recovery under the ATS should be limited to those situations, or to violations of norms of international law that are accepted by the civilized world and defined with a comparable specificity. The abduction and arrest in this case did not meet that standard.

Comment. Since the *Sosa* decision, there have been a number of cases that have denied the claims of non-U.S. citizens against corporations for wrongful

continued

continued

conduct under the ATS. Citizens of Peru were denied recovery in the United States against a Peruvian mining company that had alleged environmental health problems. Iraqi citizens were denied recovery in the United States against private contractors who provided interpreters that were present during military interrogations where torture was allegedly used. Eleven Indonesian citizens were denied recovery against Exxon-Mobil for aiding and abetting members of the Indonesian army accused of committing civil rights abuses where the soldiers had been hired by Exxon-Mobil to guard their natural gas pipeline.

There are tens of thousands of treaties and conventions in effect worldwide. They touch on every subject affecting humankind, including peace and security, the military use of force and self-defense, nuclear testing and proliferation, chemical weapons, human rights, the condition of refugees, rights of navigation and passage, global climate change, space, taxation, and the issues of international business and trade that are covered in this textbook.

In the United States, treaties must be ratified by a two-thirds majority of the Senate. Treaties of the United States can be found in the U.S. State Department document, *Treaties in Force*. For a discussion of the "treaty power" of the United States under the *U.S. Constitution,* including the functions of the legislative and executive branches of government in making treaties, and the use of executive agreements, see Chapter.

Treaties generally take on the common name of the city in which they were finally agreed and completed. Examples of treaty names include "the Vienna Convention," and "the Montreal Convention." Many treaties discussed in this book were completed in Madrid, Vienna, Geneva, Budapest, Kyoto, Montreal, Paris, Warsaw, and other cities. Therefore, a word of caution is in order when speaking of a treaty in this way. Some cities have been the site of the completion of many treaties. For example, a reference to the "the Vienna Convention" can mean the *Vienna Convention on Diplomatic Relations* or it can mean the *Vienna Convention on Protection of the Ozone Layer*—a big difference. So be careful when abbreviating treaty names by referring only to the city.

Some Other Treaty Terminology. A *protocol* is an agreement that modifies or adds to a treaty or convention, or that deals with matters less significant than those dealt with in treaties. It is usually used to address matters that are ancillary to a main treaty or convention. A treaty or convention is said to have been *adopted* when it is completed in its final form ready for nations to ratify. *Ratification* is the formal expression of a nation's consent to be bound by the treaty terms (ratification in the United States requires the vote of two-thirds of the U.S. Senate). Nations that express their willingness to join a treaty are said to be *signatories.* After the document is adopted by their legislatures or appropriate government bodies, they are said to become *contracting parties.* A treaty becomes effective on the date set out in the treaty for it to "enter into force," which is usually after some minimum number of nations become parties. A *reservation* is an exception to a treaty set out by a signatory country at the time of ratification.

The *Vienna Convention on the Law of Treaties*. The interpretation of treaties is governed by customary international law rules. The *Vienna Convention on the Law of Treaties,* which became effective in 1980 in about half of the countries of the world, codified many of the customary rules. Legal scholars today view it as the summary statement of the law governing treaties and conventions in signatory countries. It covers such issues as when treaties enter into force; how they are interpreted, amended, or terminated; the rights and duties of contracting parties; provisions for dealing with conflicts between treaties (i.e., when two treaties are in conflict on a particular matter, the later treaty prevails), or the effect of a fundamental change in circumstances on treaty obligations. According to Article 53 of the *Vienna Convention on the Law of Treaties,* a treaty is void if it violates a peremptory norm. While the United States is a signatory to the treaty, as of 2007 it had not been ratified by the U.S. Senate. Nevertheless, many U.S. courts apply the treaty's provisions as customary law.

SELF-EXECUTING AND NON-SELF-EXECUTING TREATIES. Treaties can be either *self-executing* or *non-self-executing*. In countries with written constitutions, such as the United States, a self-executing treaty is one that has "domestic law effect." In other words, it needs no further action by a domestic lawmaking body, such as a legislature, in order for it to be binding. It vests legal rights and remedies in private parties, in and of itself. One example is the *Montreal Convention for the Unification of Certain Rules for International Carriage by Air,* which sets out the rights of airlines and airline passengers, and which courts can enforce. On the other hand, a non-self-executing treaty requires some legislative act in order for it to become a part of a country's domestic law. In the United States, the courts cannot enforce rights under a non-self-executing treaty. An example of a non-self-executing treaty in the United States is the *Charter of the United Nations*. In Great Britain, all treaties require legislation to put them into legal effect. In the following case, *Renkel v. United States,* the plaintiff brought an action against the United States alleging rights under the *United Nations Convention against Torture and Other Cruel, Inhuman or Degrading Treatment or Punishment* (*Convention against Torture*). The court was asked to decide if the Convention against Torture is self-executing or not.

Renkel v. United States

456 F.3d 640 (2006)

United States Court of Appeals (6th Cir.)

BACKGROUND AND FACTS

Diana Renkel alleged that she had received substandard medical care while incarcerated in the United States Disciplinary Barracks at Ft. Leavenworth, Kansas. She sued the government, arguing that the government had violated her rights under the *United Nations Convention against Torture and Other Cruel, Inhuman or Degrading Treatment or Punishment* (the *Convention,* or *Convention against Torture*). The district court dismissed her suit, finding that there is no private right of action under the Convention. She appealed to the U.S. Court of Appeals.

McKEAGUE, CIRCUIT JUDGE

Renkel squarely presents us with one issue on appeal: whether she has an actionable claim for relief under the *Convention against Torture.*

Under the federal Constitution, all international treaties in which the United States enters become part of the "supreme Law of the Land." U.S. Const. art. VI, cl. 2. "[T]reaties have the same legal effect as statutes." *United States v. Emuegbunam,* 268 F.3d 377, 389 (6th Cir. 2001). Yet treaties, like some statutes, do not always directly create rights that a private citizen can enforce in court. *Tel-Oren v. Libyan Arab Republic,* 726 F.2d 774, 808 (D.C. Cir. 1984) (Bork, J., concurring). As we explained in *Emuegbunam,* a treaty is primarily a compact between independent nations. It depends for the enforcement of its provisions on the interest and honor of the governments which are parties to it. If these fail, its infraction becomes the subject of international negotiations and reclamation, so far as the injured parties choose to seek redress, which may in the end be enforced by actual war. It is obvious that with all this the judicial courts have nothing to do and can give no redress … see also *Foster v. Neilson,* 27 U.S. (2 Pet.) 253, 307 (1829) ("The judiciary is not that department of the government, to which the assertion of its interests against foreign powers is confided; and its duty commonly is to decide upon individual rights, according to those principles which the political departments of the nation have established.") … "In fact, courts presume that the rights created by an international treaty belong to a state and that a private individual cannot enforce them." *Emuegbunam,* 268 F.3d at 389.

Some treaties may, however, directly provide for private rights of action. "Self-executing treaties" are those treaties which do not require domestic

continued

continued

legislation to give them the full force of law. See *TWA v. Franklin Mint Corp.*, 466 U.S. 243, 252 (1984) [related to the *Warsaw Convention* governing the financial liability of airlines to passengers for injuries or loss of life or property during international flights]; such treaties can create private rights enforceable in court. On the other hand, "non-self-executing" treaties do require domestic legislation to have the force of law. For a non-self-executing treaty, any private claim must be based on a violation of the domestic law implementing the provisions of that treaty. *Raffington v. Cangemi,* 399 F.3d 900, 903 (8th Cir. 2005). In other words, federal courts "are bound to give effect to international law and to international agreements, except that a 'non-self-executing' agreement will not be given effect as law in the absence of necessary authority." *Buell v. Mitchell,* 274 F.3d 337, 372 (6th Cir. 2001) (quoting *Restatement (Third) of Foreign Relations Law* §111 (1987)).

"Whether a treaty is self-executing is an issue for judicial interpretation...." *Frolova v. U.S.S.R.*, 761 F.2d 370, 373 (7th Cir. 1985). In general, we first look to the express terms of the treaty, and then to "the treaty as a whole" to determine whether it evidences an intent to be self-executing and to create a private right of action. See *Tel-Oren,* 726 F.2d at 808 (Bork, J., concurring).

Renkel argues that the government violated her rights under the Convention, and cites several Articles in support, including Articles 1–2 and 13–16. Those Articles are not, however, expressly self-executing. Moreover, in consenting to the treaty's ratification, the United States Senate declared, as recommended by President Reagan, that Articles 1–16 are not self-executing (citing 136 Cong. Rec. S17486-01, S17492 (1990)). Thus, it is clear that it was the intent of both the Senate and the President that Articles 1–16 are not to be self-executing.... As the Articles are not self-executing, they do not create private rights of action; therefore, any private lawsuit seeking to enforce the United States' obligations under the Convention must be based on domestic law.

The domestic law implementing the Convention, however, lends no aid to Renkel. The *Foreign Affairs Reform and Restructuring Act of 1998* ... fulfill(s) the United States' obligations under Article 3 to prohibit the transfer of aliens to countries where they would be tortured. Renkel has no claim related to Article 3. The United States also enacted [a federal statute] to fulfill its obligations under Articles 4 and 5. Yet, those sections criminalize torture outside the United States; they do not provide civil redress for torture within the United States. For the latter, a plaintiff must pursue her claim under [some other federal law] and meet the jurisdictional and substantive requirements for civil relief.

Finally, Renkel argues that the Convention embodies a customary norm of international law against torture. Under certain circumstances, a federal court can imply a private right of action for violations of higher, peremptory norms of international law. Renkel has not shown that the appropriate circumstances exist here.

Decision. Renkel has no cause of action under the *United Nations Convention against Torture* because it is not a self-executing treaty. Nor does Renkel have a cause of action under any domestic law implementing the United States' obligations under the Convention. Judgment for the government is affirmed.

Comment. The U.S. reservations to the Convention declared that it was not self-executing.

Harmonizing Effect of Treaties and Conventions. We said earlier that treaties and conventions often make international business law more uniform and predictable. One example is the *United Nations Convention on Contracts for the International Sale of Goods,* which sets out a uniform code defining the rights of buyers and sellers of goods sold in international commerce. Prior to this convention, buyers and sellers located in different countries could not be certain of how their contract terms would be interpreted by a court, or what their rights would be if a dispute arose. After all, contract law differed widely from country to country and region to region. This convention creates one widely accepted body of sales law governing contracts for the sale of goods between firms located in countries that have adopted the convention. Another example, in this case a non-self-executing treaty, is the *Budapest Convention on Cybercrime.*

Addressing Global Problems: Convention on Cybercrime. This is an excellent example of how a treaty can be used to deal with a global problem that truly "knows no borders"—transnational cybercrime. Without international cooperation, the prevention and prosecution of cybercrime would be nearly impossible. The *Budapest Convention on Cybercrime* (2001), ratified by twenty-one nations as of 2007, calls for signatory countries to cooperate on drafting and enforcing criminal laws dealing with online copyright infringements, computer-related fraud, child pornography, and violations of network security. The convention does not itself criminalize cybercrime or set up an international court. Rather, it puts in place a system for dealing with a global problem that would be impossible for individual nations to stop. The convention was drafted under the aegis of the Council of Europe and included the United States, Canada, Japan, and other countries. It entered into force in the United States in 2007. A protocol to the convention calls for countries to criminalize the publication by computer of racist propaganda or threats (inciting hatred, discrimination, or violence on the basis of race, color, descent, national or ethnic origin, or religion). It also calls for the criminal prosecution of anyone who uses a computer network to deny, grossly minimize, or approve of acts constituting genocide (including the Holocaust) or crimes against humanity as defined by international law.

International Human Rights and Humanitarian Law

No text on international law would be complete without some introduction of human rights. There are many countries, in different regions of the world, whose people suffer from racial, cultural, religious, and ethnic strife, and where discrimination and hatred manifest themselves in crimes of violence against large numbers of people. And there are forms of criminal behavior on a grand scale, some motivated by politics, power, or money, others by ethnic violence or war, that stretch the bounds of our ability to describe them. Reports appear almost daily in the world's press of crimes committed on a mass scale reflecting the worst horrors of humanity. All people, and surely international businesspeople, have an obligation to understand how international law treats these human rights issues.

International Humanitarian Law. *International humanitarian law* refers to those rules for how nations treat combatants, noncombatants, refugees, and other civilians during war or civil conflict. Sources of international humanitarian law include the four *Geneva Conventions* related to the treatment of prisoners and of the wounded and conventions on the use of certain weapons, such as biological and chemical weapons and antipersonnel mines.

International Human Rights Law. *International human rights law* protects individuals and groups from the acts of governments that violate their civil, political, or human rights during times of peace. Examples include the ban on the use of torture in the world's prisons or prohibition of the use of children in military service. Sources of human rights law include the following international conventions. (Parentheses indicate sponsoring organization, United Nations, Council of Europe, or International Labour Organization.)

- 1930 *Convention Concerning Forced or Compulsory Labor* (ILO)
- 1948 *Universal Declaration of Human Rights* (UN)
- 1948 *Convention on the Prevention and Punishment of the Crime of Genocide* (UN)
- 1950 *European Convention for the Protection of Human Rights* (Council of Europe)
- 1966 *International Convention on the Elimination of All Forms of Racial Discrimination* (UN)
- 1966 *International Covenant on Civil and Political Rights* (UN)
- 1966 *International Covenant on Economic, Social and Cultural Rights* (UN)
- 1979 *Convention on Elimination of All Forms of Discrimination against Women* (UN)
- 1984 *Convention against Torture and Other Cruel, Inhuman or Degrading Treatment or Punishment* (UN)
- 1989 *Convention on the Rights of the Child* (UN)
- 1990 *International Convention on the Protection of the Rights of All Migrant Workers* (UN)
- 1998 *Rome Statute of the International Criminal Court* (UN)

- 1998 *Declaration on Fundamental Principles and Rights at Work* (ILO)
- 1999 *Convention on the Worst Forms of Child Labor* (ILO)
- 2003 *Protocol to Prevent, Suppress and Punish Trafficking in Persons, Especially Women and Children* (UN)

Despite lofty objectives, these human rights conventions have not been adopted by all nations. Several have not been ratified by the United States. As of 2007 the United States has not ratified the *Convention on the Rights of the Child.* Ratification has not happened because the convention prohibits sentencing juveniles to the death penalty or to life imprisonment without parole (which can be done in the United States), because of opposition by some private and religious groups in the United States to certain provisions of the convention, and because of certain possible conflicts with U.S. constitutional law. There are other regional human rights conventions from Africa, Asia, and Latin America. Enforcement of human rights standards in some regions is a distant dream, as the world has witnessed in Myanmar, the Balkans, and in Africa in recent years.

International Criminal Law

Another body of public international law closely related to humanitarian and human rights law is *international criminal law.* While international law generally deals with the obligations of nations to other nations, international criminal law deals with the obligations of individuals, who are acting in an official capacity, for crimes committed against other individuals. International criminal law is that body of law and procedure that involves the use criminal sanctions to prosecute individual offenders responsible for genocide, war crimes, and crimes against humanity. While the concept of international criminal law dates back at least to the early part of the last century, it was not popularized until the Tokyo and Nuremberg military trials that followed World War II. The idea of a *permanent* international tribunal to try war criminals existed at least as early as 1951. Since that time, millions of innocent civilians have been killed by genocide and "ethnic cleansing," murders, torture, disappearances, and crimes of sexual violence against women and children. Countries that come to mind are Cambodia under the *Khmer Rouge* regime, which governed Cambodia during the late 1970s, the former Yugoslavia, El Salvador, Uganda, Sudan, Rwanda, and the Democratic Republic of Congo. However, as was stated by José Ayala Lasso, a former United Nations High Commissioner for Human Rights, "A person stands a better chance of being tried and judged for killing one human being than for killing 100,000." This is easy to understand, as many of the worst perpetrators of human rights violations have been military strongmen or heads of government regimes that escaped prosecution in the countries where they held power. In the past few decades, there have been calls from a few legal scholars, internationalists, and human rights groups for a permanent body of international criminal law and the creation of a permanent international criminal court to deal with the most heinous offenses against humankind. During the 1990s, the UN Security Council created temporary tribunals to prosecute war criminals from the former Yugoslavia in Eastern Europe and Rwanda in Africa. This finally revived efforts to create a permanent international criminal court.

THE INTERNATIONAL CRIMINAL COURT. In 1998 the *Rome Statute of the International Criminal Court* (the *Rome Statute)* was adopted (with 105 signatories as of 2007), creating the International Criminal Court, which sits at The Hague, the Netherlands. The court can hear cases where the crime occurs in, or the defendant is a national of, a country that has ratified the treaty, or in limited cases where non-ratifying countries consent to the jurisdiction. All cases must be referred by a national government or by the United Nations Security Council. The court will generally not hear cases that have been heard in national courts. The court does not have exclusive jurisdiction over these crimes, as the right of any nation to prosecute genocide, war crimes, and crimes against humanity still exits under international customary law and domestic law.

JURISDICTION OF THE INTERNATIONAL CRIMINAL COURT. The court has authority to hear three categories of crimes: genocide, crimes against humanity, and war crimes. The crimes of terrorism and drug trafficking are not included. *Genocide* is generally defined as a pattern of conduct intended to destroy a national, ethnic, racial, or religious group by killing or inflicting serious harm, inter-ethnic rape, forcibly preventing births, transferring children from their ethnic group, or similar offenses. *Crimes against humanity* are widespread and systematic attacks against civilians through murder, slavery, forced deportations imprisonment in violation of international law, torture, rape and sexual violence, abductions and disappearances, apartheid, and other persecutions on the grounds of religion, race, ethnicity, national origin, political beliefs, or gender. Historically, *war crimes* have been defined as "grave breaches" of the customs of war, triable in military courts, and have been recognized by international law and by the laws of most nations long before the *Rome Statute*. A war crime is defined under the *Rome Statute* as an offense in violation of the international law of armed conflict, including the wrongful killing, torture, or inhumane treatment of a person protected by the *Geneva Convention of 1949*. It also includes a host of internationally recognized violations of the rules of war, such as intentionally attacking civilians, hospitals, museums, religious buildings, etc.; enlisting children as soldiers; using chemical or biological weapons; rape as a weapon of war; pillaging; denying quarter; and many others. It also includes knowingly causing excessive incidental death or injury to civilians or damage to the natural environment in relation to the overall military objective. It is also a crime to attack those providing humanitarian assistance during a time of civil war. Interestingly, neither terrorism nor drug trafficking were included in the court's jurisdiction because of the widespread magnitude of those problems. While it is intended that the court will have jurisdiction over a country that wages a *war of aggression,* jurisdiction is pending an international agreement on a legal definition of "aggression." Good examples are Hitler's invasion of Poland in 1939 or Saddam Hussein's Iraqi invasion of neighboring Kuwait in 1990, neither of which were based on national self-defense.

The crimes set out in the *Rome Statute of the International Criminal Court* apply regardless of whether they were committed by someone in an official capacity, and even apply to heads of state. Military commanders are responsible for crimes committed by those under them where they knew or should have known of the crimes or did not take reasonable measures to prevent them. Subordinates are not excused from prosecution because they were "just following orders." There is no statute of limitations on these crimes—perpetrators can be apprehended and tried at any time during their lifetime. Penalties include imprisonment and reparations.

Criticisms of the International Criminal Court. The *Rome Statute* has not been ratified by the United States, Russia, China, India, or many other countries. While almost everyone agrees with the motivations for creating the Court, it is not without criticism. Many governments and critics believe that the Court impinges on national sovereignty, that it could subject government and military leaders to prosecutions solely on political grounds, and that it lacks fair procedures and appeal mechanisms. The United States has taken a number of legal and diplomatic steps to ensure that American citizens will not be subject to prosecution before the International Criminal Court.

Basic Principles of International Criminal Jurisdiction

Jurisdiction is a word of many meanings. In the context of this chapter, it means the power of a nation to create laws that proscribe conduct and to act over individuals, corporations, or their property in the application or enforcement of those laws. When used in reference to a court, it is the power of a court to hear a case—to adjudicate. The court must have "subject matter" jurisdiction over that type of case, as well as personal jurisdiction over the parties. Jurisdiction is necessary whenever a court hears any case, whether it is civil or criminal, and regardless of whether it is a domestic case or an international one. While we will deal with jurisdiction in civil cases in the next chapter and later in the book, in this chapter we will focus our discussion on criminal jurisdiction.

The Extraterritorial Reach of Domestic Law. In a world where national political and economic interests span the globe, it has become increasingly important for countries to be able to protect their interests, and the interests of their individual and corporate citizens, wherever they are at risk. One example is combating *transnational crimes*—crimes that typically cross national borders or that are committed by or against a citizen traveling in a foreign country or that are committed from outside a country and harm interests within a country. Examples might include drug smuggling, hijacking, terrorism, counterfeiting, violations of banking laws, bribery of foreign government officials by businesspeople, attacks on computer systems and global information networks, theft of nuclear materials and technology, violations of customs and immigration laws, and on and on.

Consider a few examples:

- A Mexican citizen standing in Mexico along the U.S. border fires a weapon into the United States killing an American citizen. Surely, the perpetrator can be prosecuted in Mexico where the act occurred and the perpetrator is found, but can he or she (also) be prosecuted in the United States where the harm occurred?
- Now consider two conspirators, of Middle Eastern nationality, who attempt to blow up an American passenger aircraft in the Philippines. If captured and returned to the United States, can they be tried in U.S. courts?
- Imagine an American businessperson doing business in, say, Kuwait, who pays a cash bribe to a Kuwaiti government or military official to obtain business. Can the U.S. government arrest and prosecute the American on his or her return home?
- An executive of a Canadian corporation knowingly causes the discharge of a toxic waste into a river that runs into the United States. It poisons most life in the river for miles downstream and renders the water unsuitable for use. Can the business executive be prosecuted in both countries?
- A citizen of Russia, living in London, attacks and disrupts a major computer network in the United States. Where can he be tried?
- A Canadian in Thailand is caught by local authorities in possession of child pornography. In what countries can he be tried?

What would happen in these cases? There are several issues raised here: May a country may pass laws affecting conduct outside its territory? May it exert jurisdiction over individuals or corporations outside its territory? And if so, does this include jurisdiction only over its own citizens who commit crimes abroad, or also over foreign individuals and foreign corporations? The answers to these questions are usually "yes," although it does depend on the facts of the case and the countries involved.

The principle that a nation can project its laws beyond its territorial borders is known as *extraterritoriality*. It applies to both civil and criminal statutes. All countries have different views toward the use of extraterritoriality. Some countries, such as the United States, are more willing to project their laws to individuals in foreign countries than, say, Canada or the countries of Europe. Any attempt by one country to enforce its laws against a citizen of another country might be very controversial and viewed as a violation of a country's sovereignty. For example, China might view the American use of extraterritoriality against Chinese nationals, or even against non-Chinese citizens living and working in China, as a matter of America "sticking its nose" into China's internal affairs. It can even prompt diplomatic or trade retaliation. There are problems of enforcement too. How does one country enforce its laws against foreign citizens unless they can be brought before their own courts? As a result, courts considering the extraterritorial application of a statute often say that there is a general rule that there is a presumption that national laws do not have extraterritorial reach, particularly where they conflict with international law or the laws of another nation. This helps to avoid conflicts in foreign relations. Extraterritoriality is least controversial when it is done by international agreement. For example, there are conventions that approve of the extraterritorial prosecution of many transnational crimes, such as international trafficking in drugs or child pornography, terrorism, slavery and forced prostitution, counterfeiting, aircraft hijacking, the unlawful sale of nuclear or radioactive materials, and piracy (yes, this is still a big, modern-day problem).

In the United States, a number of statutes affecting business have been applied to areas outside U.S. territory, including statutes on discrimination in employment, price-fixing and antitrust violations, bribery and other criminal statutes, and more. It has also been applied to violations of the

Trading with the Enemy Act during a time of war; violations of the *Export Administration Regulations* (regulating exports, particularly of technology or military shipments, to potential adversaries or terrorists); some financial and banking regulations; and others.

It is important to recognize that we are not speaking of any one country becoming the world's police force. No country, under the guise of extraterritoriality, has the right to run roughshod over individual rights, the sovereignty of foreign governments over their people and territory, or principles of international customary law. Extraterritorial jurisdiction does not mean that one nation's law enforcement officials can enter another to make arrests. Normally, it requires a measure of compromise and mutual assistance in law enforcement. All countries agree that extraterritoriality must be based either on a treaty or international agreement, or on one of the five basic principles of jurisdiction:

- *territoriality*
- *nationality*
- *the protective principle*
- *passive personality*
- *universality*

TERRITORIALITY. *Territoriality* or *territorial jurisdiction* refers to jurisdiction over all persons (citizens and noncitizens), places, and property within the territory, airspace, or territorial waters of a country. Jurisdiction over foreign-flag ships within the territorial waters of the United States is generally limited to matters involving the "peace of the port," where the interests of the United States and U.S. citizens are at stake, and with a few possible exceptions, does not apply to the internal operations of the vessel. In the case of jurisdiction for crimes, *subjective territorial jurisdiction* exists where a crime was actually committed within the territory. Subjective territorial jurisdiction is the least controversial form of exerting state power because it does not directly interfere with the sovereignty of other nations. *Objective territorial jurisdiction,* also called the "effects" principle, exists where the act was committed outside a country's territory, but had a substantial effect inside the country. An example of objective territorial jurisdiction in criminal law would be the prosecution of foreign citizens in U.S. courts for attempting to smuggle illegal drugs into the United States aboard a foreign-flag ship in international waters.

NATIONALITY. Under the principle of *nationality jurisdiction,* individual and corporate citizens owe a duty to comply with the laws of their country of nationality no matter where they are in the world. It is considered one of the obligations of citizenship. An American businessperson in Hong Kong must comply with Hong Kong banking laws and with certain banking regulations and executive orders of the President of the United States that might apply to them. For instance, if that executive order states that no funds may be transferred to an account of a party believed to support international terrorism, then the American in Hong Kong is bound just as though he or she were in the United States. Another example of nationality is that a country may tax the income of its citizens earned anywhere in the world, subject of course to certain rules set out in international treaties on income taxation.

Under the principle of nationality, a country may prosecute its citizens for crimes committed anywhere in the world. This includes economic and business crimes as well as crimes such as treason. Virtually all nations accept nationality as a basis for jurisdiction. An extension of this principle permits nations to exert jurisdiction over ships that fly their flag even when they are outside territorial waters. A crime committed aboard a ship anywhere in the world can be prosecuted by the country of the ship's flag. A special U.S. statute gives the United States jurisdiction over U.S. flagged aircraft operating anywhere in the world.

THE PROTECTIVE PRINCIPLE. The *protective* principle allows jurisdiction over noncitizens for acts done abroad on the basis of a country's need to protect its national security, vital economic interests, and governmental functions. *Protective jurisdiction* has been used as a basis of extraterritorial jurisdiction to prosecute terrorism, espionage, counterfeiting, making false statements to customs and immigration officers, and falsifying U.S. government documents (such as passports and visas). In one reported case, it was the basis for prosecuting a foreign citizen who conspired with an American to set up a sham marriage for the sole purpose of gaining entrance to the United States.

PASSIVE PERSONALITY. *Passive personality* jurisdiction can give a country the right to hear cases stemming from crimes committed against their own citizens by foreign citizens outside of their own territory. Passive personality is controversial because the only connection to the prosecuting nation may be the nationality of the victim. This raises the question of whether one nation to should attempt to criminalize and prosecute acts occurring by foreign citizens in foreign countries. Most countries, including the United States, have been reluctant to rely only on passive personality for jurisdiction and are willing to exercise it only in the case of heinous crimes. It could be used, for example, to prosecute a national of a Middle Eastern country for a terrorist attack on an American in London. Of course, crimes other than terrorist acts are also covered, although usually only where there are significant ties to the United States. One case, *United States v. Roberts,* 1 F. Supp. 2d 601 (E.D. La. 1998), involved a sexual assault of an American minor aboard a cruise ship in international waters by a non-U.S. citizen working aboard. The ship was registered in Panama and was flying the flag of Liberia. The court held that there was passive personality jurisdiction because the ship had departed on its cruise from Miami; the ship's corporate officers were located in Miami; the company's stock was traded on the New York Stock Exchange; and a trial in the United States would not infringe the sovereignty of any other nation.

UNIVERSALITY. Finally, the *universality principle* (also called *universal jurisdiction*) permits any country to prosecute perpetrators of the most heinous and universally condemned crimes regardless of where the crimes occurred or the nationality of the perpetrators or victims. One famous case of universality was Israel's 1961 trial of Nazi war criminal Adolf Eichmann for atrocities committed in Europe during World War II. However, in more recent years, universality jurisdiction has not been widely used.

JURISDICTION OVER INTERNATIONAL TERRORISM: *UNITED STATES V. RAMSEY YOUSEF.* One recent case illustrates the application of these principles to fighting international terrorism. In *United States v. Ramsey Yousef,* 327 F.3d 56 (2d Cir. 2003), *cert. den.,* 540 U.S. 933 (2003), the defendant was convicted of conspiracy to bomb American-flag airliners in Southeast Asia (and of the 1993 bombing on the World Trade Center). On appeal, he argued that the U.S. criminal statute on the destruction of aircraft could not be applied to acts outside the United States. The court rejected this argument, stating that jurisdiction is consistent with the United States' obligations under the *Montreal Convention for the Suppression of Unlawful Acts Against the Safety of Civil Aviation* and with three of the five principles of customary international law criminal jurisdiction—objective territorial, protective, and passive personality. The court stated

> First, jurisdiction . . . is consistent with the "passive personality principle" of customary international jurisdiction because [this] involved a plot to bomb United States-flag aircraft that would have been carrying United States citizens and crews and that were destined for cities in the United States. Moreover . . . jurisdiction is appropriate under the "objective territorial principle" because the purpose of the attack was to influence United States foreign policy and the defendants intended their actions to have an effect—in this case, a devastating effect—on and within the United States. Finally, there is no doubt that jurisdiction is proper under the "protective principle" because the planned attacks were intended to affect the United States and to alter its foreign policy.

Yousef was also charged with the bombing of a non-U.S. airliner in the Philippines. It was not flying to or from the United States, and no American citizens were injured or apparent targets. With regard to universality, the court stated

> The historical restriction of universal jurisdiction to piracy, war crimes, and crimes against humanity demonstrates that universal jurisdiction arises under customary international law only where crimes (1) are universally condemned by the community of nations, and (2) by their nature occur either outside of a State or where there is no State capable of punishing, or competent to punish, the crime (as in a time of war). * * * Unlike those offenses supporting universal jurisdiction under customary international law—that is, piracy, war crimes, and crimes against humanity—that now have fairly precise definitions and that have achieved universal condemnation, "terrorism" is a term as loosely deployed as it is powerfully charged. * * * We regrettably are no closer now than eighteen years ago to an international consensus on the definition of terrorism or even its proscription; the mere existence of the phrase "state-sponsored terrorism" proves the absence of agreement on basic terms among a large number of States that terrorism violates public international law. Moreover, there continues to be strenuous disagreement

among States about what actions do or do not constitute terrorism, nor have we shaken ourselves free of the cliché that "one man's terrorist is another man's freedom fighter." We thus conclude that ... terrorism—unlike piracy, war crimes, and crimes against humanity—does not provide a basis for universal jurisdiction.

In 1993, Belgium enacted a law based on universal jurisdiction to prosecute cases of war crimes, genocide, and crimes against humanity. In the following case, *Democratic Republic of the Congo v. Belgium,* Belgium issued an arrest warrant for the foreign minister of the Democratic Republic of the Congo ("Congo" herein refers to the Democratic Republic of the Congo, not its neighbor, Congo-Brazzaville) for crimes against humanity that occurred in the Congo. The judgment of the International Court of Justice addressed universality and other important issues of international criminal law.

Case Concerning the Arrest Warrant of 11 April 2000 (Democratic Republic of the Congo v. Belgium)

[2002] I.C.J. Rep. 3; International Court of Justice (Judgment of 14 Feb. 2002)

BACKGROUND AND FACTS

In 1993 Belgium enacted a statute giving Belgian courts jurisdiction over those who commit crimes against humanity, genocide, and war crimes. The law was based on the principle of universality and extended jurisdiction over those who commit such crimes regardless of their nationality or that of the victims, or of where the crimes were committed, or where the perpetrator may be found. In 2000, a Belgian court issued an international arrest warrant *in absentia* for Yerodia, who was at that time the Minister of Foreign Affairs of the Congo. Yerodia was charged with violations of the Belgian law in that he made various speeches inciting racial hatred and encouraged the population to attack people of the ethnic Tutsi tribes, leading to manhunts, executions, and lynchings. The warrant requested any nation arresting Yerodia to extradite him to Belgium for trial. The brought this action before the International Court of Justice arguing that Yerodia, as foreign minister of a sovereign state, was entitled to diplomatic immunity. The Court's judgment addressed this claim. The validity of Belgian's attempt at universal jurisdiction was not properly raised by the Congo, and not addressed by the Court. An instructive concurring opinion discusses the history and modern status of this principle today.

THE COURT DELIVERS THE FOLLOWING JUDGMENT:

* * *

In customary international law, the immunities accorded to Ministers for Foreign Affairs are not granted for their personal benefit, but to ensure the effective performance of their functions on behalf of their respective States.... He or she is in charge of his or her Government's diplomatic activities and generally acts as its representative in international negotiations and intergovernmental meetings. Ambassadors and other diplomatic agents carry out their duties under his or her authority. His or her acts may bind the State represented, and there is a presumption that a Minister for Foreign Affairs, simply by virtue of that office, has full powers to act on behalf of the State (1969 *Vienna Convention on the Law of Treaties*). In the performance of these functions, he or she is frequently required to travel internationally, and thus must be in a position freely to do so whenever the need should arise. He or she must also be in constant communication with the Government, and with its diplomatic missions around the world, and be capable at any time of communicating with representatives of other States. * * *

The Court accordingly concludes that the functions of a Minister for Foreign Affairs are such that, throughout the duration of his or her office, he or she when abroad enjoys full immunity from criminal jurisdiction and inviolability. That immunity and that inviolability protect the individual concerned against any act of authority of another State which would hinder him or her in the performance of his or her duties.

In this respect, no distinction can be drawn between acts performed by a Minister for Foreign Affairs in an "official" capacity, and those claimed to have been performed in a "private capacity," or, for that matter, between acts performed before the person concerned assumed office as Minister for Foreign

continued

continued

Affairs and acts committed during the period of office. * * *

The Court will now address Belgium's argument that immunities accorded to incumbent Ministers for Foreign Affairs can in no case protect them where they are suspected of having committed war crimes or crimes against humanity. In support of this position, Belgium refers ... to various legal instruments creating international criminal tribunals, to examples from national legislation, and to the jurisprudence of national and international courts. * * * The Court has ... been unable to deduce from this practice that there exists under customary international law any form of exception to the rule according immunity from criminal jurisdiction and inviolability to incumbent Ministers for Foreign Affairs, where they are suspected of having committed war crimes or crimes against humanity. * * *

The Court emphasizes, however, that the *immunity* from jurisdiction enjoyed by incumbent Ministers for Foreign Affairs does not mean that they enjoy *impunity*.... * * * First, such persons enjoy no criminal immunity under international law in their own countries, and may thus be tried by those countries' courts in accordance with the relevant rules of domestic law. Secondly, they will cease to enjoy immunity from foreign jurisdiction if the State which they represent or have represented decides to waive that immunity. Thirdly, after a person ceases to hold the office of Minister for Foreign Affairs, he or she will no longer enjoy all of the immunities accorded by international law in other States. * * * Fourthly, an incumbent or former Minister for Foreign Affairs may be subject to criminal proceedings before certain international criminal courts, where they have jurisdiction. Examples include the International Criminal Tribunal for the former Yugoslavia, and the International Criminal Tribunal for Rwanda, established pursuant to Security Council resolutions under ... the *United Nations Charter,* and the ... International Criminal Court created by the 1998 *Rome Convention.* The latter's Statute expressly provides ... that "[i]mmunities or special procedural rules which may attach to the official capacity of a person, whether under national or international law, shall not bar the Court from exercising its jurisdiction over such a person." * * *

Accordingly, the Court concludes that the circulation of the warrant, whether or not it significantly interfered with Mr. Yerodia's diplomatic activity, constituted a violation of an obligation of Belgium toward the Congo, in that it failed to respect the immunity of the incumbent Minister for Foreign Affairs of the Congo and, more particularly, infringed the immunity from criminal jurisdiction and the inviolability then enjoyed by him under international law.

Separate Opinion of President Judge Guillaume. I fully subscribe to the Judgment rendered by the Court. I believe it useful however to set out my position on one question which the Judgment has not addressed: whether the Belgian judge had [extraterritorial] jurisdiction.... I believe it worthwhile to provide such clarification here.

In order to assess the validity of [Belgium's jurisdiction], the fundamental principles of international law governing States' exercise of their criminal jurisdiction should first be reviewed. The primary aim of the criminal law is to enable punishment in each country of offences committed in the national territory. That territory is where evidence of the offence can most often be gathered. That is where the offence generally produces its effects. Finally, that is where the punishment imposed can most naturally serve as an example. Thus, the Permanent Court of International Justice observed as far back as 1927 that "in all systems of law the principle of the territorial character of criminal law is fundamental" ["Lotus," Judgment No. 9, 1927, P.C.I.J.].

The question has, however, always remained open whether States other than the territorial State have concurrent jurisdiction to prosecute offenders. A wide debate on this subject began as early as the foundation in Europe of the major modern States. Some writers, like Covarruvias and Grotius, pointed out that the presence on the territory of a State of a foreign criminal peacefully enjoying the fruits of his crimes was intolerable. They therefore maintained that it should be possible to prosecute perpetrators of certain particularly serious crimes not only in the State on whose territory the crime was committed but also in the country where they sought refuge. In their view, that country was under an obligation to arrest, followed by extradition or prosecution....

Beginning in the eighteenth century, however, this school of thought favouring universal punishment was challenged by another body of opinion, one opposed to such punishment and exemplified notably by Montesquieu, Voltaire, and Jean-Jacques Rousseau. Their views found expression in terms of

continued

continued

criminal law in the works of Beccaria, who stated in 1764 that "judges are not the avengers of humankind in general.... A crime is punishable only in the country where it was committed." [citations omitted]
* * *

Under the law as classically formulated, a State normally has jurisdiction over an offence committed abroad only if the offender, or at the very least the victim, has the nationality of that State or if the crime threatens its internal or external security. Ordinarily, States are without jurisdiction over crimes committed abroad as between foreigners.

Traditionally, customary international law did, however, recognize one case of universal jurisdiction, that of piracy. In more recent times ... the *Geneva Convention on the High Seas* of 1958 and ... the *Montego Bay Convention* of 1982 have provided [that] universal jurisdiction is accepted in cases of piracy because piracy is carried out on the high seas, outside all State territory. However, even on the high seas, classic international law is highly restrictive, for it recognizes universal jurisdiction only in cases of piracy and not of other comparable crimes ... [unless they are the subject of treaty or international convention].
* * *

A further step was taken in this direction beginning in 1970 in connection with the fight against international terrorism. To that end, States established a novel mechanism: compulsory, albeit subsidiary, universal jurisdiction. This fundamental innovation was effected by *The Hague Convention for the Suppression of Unlawful Seizure of Aircraft* of 16 December 1970. The Convention places an obligation on the State in whose territory the perpetrator of the crime takes refuge to extradite or prosecute him. * * * The system as thus adopted was repeated with some minor variations in a large number of conventions: [the court then cited eleven modern conventions dealing with international terrorism]. Thus, a system corresponding to the doctrines espoused long ago by Grotius was set up by treaty. Whenever the perpetrator of any of the offences covered by these conventions *is found in the territory of a State* [Italics added], that state is under an obligation to arrest him, and then extradite or prosecute. It must have first conferred jurisdiction on its courts to try him if he is not extradited. Thus, universal punishment of the offences in question is assured, as the perpetrators are denied refuge in all States. By contrast, none of these [conventions] has contemplated establishing jurisdiction over offences committed abroad by foreigners against foreigners when the perpetrator is not present in the territory of the State in question. Universal jurisdiction *in absentia* is unknown to international conventional law.

... Belgium cites the development of international criminal courts. But this development was precisely in order to provide a remedy for the deficiencies of national courts, and the rules governing the jurisdiction of international courts as laid down by treaty or by the Security Council of course have no effect upon the jurisdiction of national courts.

[Belgium cannot rely on the custom of states] and I will give some ... examples of this. In France, the *Code of Criminal Procedure provides:* "Pursuant to the international conventions referred to in the following articles, any person, *if present in France* [Italics added], may be prosecuted and tried by the French courts if that person has committed outside the territory of the Republic one of the offences specified in those articles." * * * Numbers of other examples could be given, and the only country whose legislation and jurisprudence appear clearly to go the other way is the State of Israel, which in this field obviously constitutes a very special case.

To conclude ... international law knows only one true case of universal jurisdiction: piracy. Further, a number of international conventions provide for the establishment of subsidiary universal jurisdiction for purposes of the trial of certain offenders arrested on national territory and not extradited to a foreign country. Universal jurisdiction *in absentia* as applied in the present case is unknown to international law.
* * *

Decision. The Court held that the Belgian warrant must be canceled because Yerodia, the Foreign Minister of the Congo, was protected by diplomatic immunity. In a concurring opinion, Judge Guillaume noted that according to history and practice of international customary law, there is no universal jurisdiction over crimes other than piracy on the high seas, unless the prosecuting country has a close connection to the commission of the crimes through territoriality, nationality, or passive personality principles, or unless the crime is the subject of a treaty or international convention granting jurisdiction. Most treaties on terrorism refer to "compulsory" or mandatory jurisdiction. Guillaume is saying that if a signatory country has a terrorist

continued

continued

in custody, it must either extradite him to a country with a closer (jurisdictional) connection to the crime, or try him.

Comment. In 2003, Belgium succumbed to international pressure and clarified its laws on diplomatic immunity. Other amendments to its laws now permit prosecutions of extraterritorial war crimes, genocide, and crimes against humanity only where the crime was committed in Belgium, the perpetrator or victim was a Belgium national, or the perpetrator can be found in Belgium. The perpetrator can be extradited to a state with a closer connection to the crimes. Belgium's extraterritorial jurisdiction is probably less important since the creation of the International Criminal Court.

Today, several treaties confer universal jurisdiction. Examples include United Nations conventions on terrorism and the financing of terrorist organizations, hijacking and other violence aboard aircraft, maritime piracy, slavery, and a few others. The *United Nations Convention against Torture and Other Cruel, Inhuman and Degrading Treatment or Punishment,* in which about three-quarters of the nations of the world have joined, recognizes universality. It calls on member countries to enact laws punishing those who commit torture. It permits countries to take jurisdiction if the victim was their citizen, if the act occurred in their territory, or if the offender is later found in their country (universality). The United States committed only to prohibit "cruel, inhuman and degrading treatment or punishment" if it is a violation of the Fifth, Eighth, or Fourteenth Amendments of the U.S. Constitution (thus avoiding the issue of whether the use of the death penalty in the United States would violate the treaty).

Mutual Legal Assistance and Extradition

Mutual legal assistance treaties are agreements for law enforcement cooperation. They include the powers to summon witnesses, to compel the production of documents and other evidence, to issue search warrants, and to serve process. The United States has over fifty mutual assistance treaties in force. Generally, U.S. courts have ruled that U.S. law enforcement agents investigating traditional crimes in foreign countries must comply with all constitutional protection afforded the accused. However, U.S. courts have not held foreign officers to quite the same standard when they are obtaining evidence in criminal cases for delivery to U.S. law enforcement agents. For instance, foreign officers are not expected to comply with American constitutional standards when searching a suspect's home or office outside of the United States, or when obtaining a voluntary confession, unless they use conduct that "shocks the conscience."

Extradition is where one country surrenders a person to the officials of another country to stand trial in a criminal case. The idea of extradition existed long before there were nations, when society and legal rights revolved around the tribe, clan, or family (such as the early Roman *familias,* the early Anglo-Saxons, and even the first native North Americans). Clan members who committed crimes against other clans could be surrendered for punishment. Ostracized and placed "outside" the protection of their clan, they were the first "outlaws." Today, extradition rights are created by treaty. The United States has extradition treaties with most countries of the world.

Some General Concepts of Public International Law

Three closely related concepts of international law will be briefly introduced here: *comity, sovereign immunity, and act of state.* The one thing that these three concepts have in common is that they have the effect of avoiding conflicts in foreign relations. They will be discussed in more detail in later chapters.

Comity

Comity refers to the willingness of one court or department of government to respect the rules or decisions of another or to grant it some privilege or favor. *International comity* is a judicial doctrine, not an international law, based on the desire for courtesy and reciprocity between countries. It also serves to prevent courts from embroiling themselves in matters of foreign affairs and thereby helps to avoid diplomatic conflicts. Comity allows the courts of one country to recognize the laws and court decrees of another country or to defer hearing a case that is more appropriate for hearing in the courts of another country. Under comity, for example, a court that otherwise might be entitled to hear a case may allow it to be transferred to a court in a foreign country with a greater interest in the case. As an example, assume that there is a breach of contract for the sale of goods between two parties, the buyer residing in the United States and the seller in Japan. Assume that the contract does not mention where disputes should be resolved and that jurisdiction in the case would be appropriate in the courts of either country. If the seller files suit for payment in the courts of Japan, and subsequently the buyer (not wanting to defend the case in a foreign country) files suit in a U.S. court alleging damages for defective goods, the U.S. court will likely dismiss the case on the basis of comity to avoid a conflict with the courts of Japan.

Now assume that the seller wins a money judgment in Japanese courts, but the buyer has no assets there to satisfy the judgment. The seller can take the judgment to U.S. courts to be enforced. (Keep in mind that U.S. courts will only enforce civil judgments from countries who guarantee fair trials and due process. U.S. courts will not enforce foreign tax liens or verdicts in foreign criminal cases.)

THE *CHARMING BETSY*. The *Charming Betsy concept* derives from a U.S. Supreme Court case of the same name, *Murray v. The Schooner Charming Betsy*, 6 U.S. 64 (1804). It is a rule of statutory interpretation. As the Court noted, "an act of Congress ought never to be construed to violate the law of nations if any other possible construction remains." For example, for reasons of comity, a U.S. court will not apply a federal statute to conduct committed outside the territory of the United States unless it is clear that Congress had intended that result. An application of this concept can be seen in *Spector v. Norwegian Cruise Line Ltd.*, 545 U.S. 119 (2005). In that case, a disabled, wheelchair-bound passenger sued a cruise line for inaccessible accommodations aboard a ship. The U.S. Supreme Court ruled that the *Americans with Disabilities Act* applies to foreign-flag cruise ships in U.S. waters, but does not require the removal of physical barriers if it would conflict with a treaty or with other international standards for ship safety.

Sovereign Immunity

Sovereignty is defined as the supreme and absolute power that governs an independent state or nation. Of course, in reality, sovereignty can have a range of meanings. For example, in the United States, sovereignty can be shared between the federal government, the states, and even Native American tribes. In Europe, some national sovereignty had to be sacrificed by countries that joined the European Union. For our purposes, we should recognize that all independent countries are equal with one another and that each has the exclusive right over its citizens, its territory, all property within that territory, and its internal affairs. It follows that the doctrine of *sovereign immunity* states that the courts of one country cannot hear cases brought against the government of another country and that courts cannot involve themselves in the internal affairs of a foreign country. In English law this is derived from the feudal notion that the "king can do no wrong." This principle was firmly established in the United States in *Schooner Exchange v. McFaddon*, 11 U.S. 116 (1812). In that case, an American merchant ship was seized by Emperor Napoleon and pressed into service with the French navy. When the ship docked at Philadelphia, its original owners filed suit to have it returned. The U.S. Supreme Court ruled that under sovereign immunity a warship of a foreign nation was not subject to seizure by U.S. courts. Today, sovereign immunity is recognized by most nations of the world and defined by statute in many.

In the United States, the jurisdiction of U.S. courts over foreign nations is defined by the *Foreign Sovereign Immunities Act of 1976*. This takes a somewhat restrictive view of immunity by creating exceptions to be considered by the courts.

These exceptions generally are waiver (by statute or by agreement in a contract); commercial activity; certain violations of international law such as torture, terrorism, and unlawful expropriation of private property without payment of compensation; and lawsuits for money damages for torts committed within the United States. Examples might include a lawsuit by the victim of state-sponsored terrorism or a lawsuit against a foreign government for negligence in the operation of a motor vehicle within the United States.

COMMERCIAL ACTIVITY EXCEPTION. Sovereign immunity protects foreign governments from suit when they are acting as a political entity. When foreign governments or their agencies enter the commercial field, engaging in business for profit, as would a private company, or engaging in essentially private functions, they can be sued in the courts of a foreign country. When agencies of government buy and sell goods or services, they become liable for damages for breach of contract. An example would be a contract between a private company in the United States and a government-owned company in China for the supply of raw materials. If the Chinese government is acting as a private company in mining, marketing, and selling raw materials, it is liable to suit in the United States (assuming other jurisdictional requirements are met) for delivering materials that do not conform to the contract specifications.

Act of State

The *Act of State* doctrine is a principle of domestic law (not international law) that prohibits the courts of one country from inquiring into the validity of the legislative or executive acts of another country. It was first announced in the United States in the case of *Underhill v. Hernandez,* 168 U.S. 250 (1897) where it was held that "... [T]he courts of one country will not sit in judgment on the acts of the government of another done within its own territory. Redress of grievances by reason of such acts must be obtained through the means open to be availed of by sovereign powers as between themselves."

Many of the U.S. cases discussing the Act of State doctrine involve the confiscation of American-owned property by foreign governments without the payment of compensation, such as occurred with Fidel Castro's communist takeover of Cuba in 1959 and with the Islamic revolution in Iran in 1979. As a general rule, subject to exceptions discussed later in this book, the Act of State doctrine prohibits courts from embroiling themselves in such politically charged issues. The doctrine is based on the idea that courts should not intervene in matters of foreign affairs. These matters are best left to the executive branch, which has the benefit of a diplomatic corps, foreign embassies, and the ability to talk directly to foreign governments. There is also the practical reason that it may very well be impossible for domestic courts to enforce their decisions against foreign governments, as it certainly would have been in the case of both Cuba and Iran. In the latter case, a treaty between the United States and Iran led to the creation of an impartial tribunal in the Netherlands to resolve outstanding claims between U.S. citizens and the Iranian government. The Act of State doctrine is recognized by courts in the United States, the United Kingdom, Germany, France, Italy, Japan, and many other countries.

INTERNATIONAL ORGANIZATIONS

There are a number of international organizations that affect our study of international law. The most important of these is the International Court of Justice. We will also discuss other agencies of the United Nations that directly impact our area of study—the law of international trade, investment, intellectual property, and labor standards. The role of the World Trade Organization and of European organizations will be covered in later chapters. At this point, we will have to leave the discussion of the World Bank and the International Monetary Fund to other texts and courses in the field of international finance.

The Role of the United Nations in International Law

As of 2007, the United Nations had 192 member nations. Most of us are familiar with the work done by the major organs of the UN, including the General Assembly, the Security Council, the Economic and Social Council, and the International Court of

Justice. We are also aware of the UN role in peacekeeping and humanitarian assistance to innocent victims of civil wars and to millions of refugees. Every day we see the work its agencies do in fighting hunger and poverty in developing countries; in fighting AIDS, malaria, and other diseases; and in fighting for the world's children. What we seldom see are the UN efforts in bringing nations together to develop international public and private law. During the last 60 years, the UN has coordinated over five hundred multilateral treaties and international conventions that not only affect world peace and security, but also affect issues like climate change and the protection of the environment; the prevention and control of crime, drug trafficking, and terrorism; rules for Antarctica and the seabeds of the world's oceans; and more. The UN has also been responsible for the development of many areas of international private law that directly affect commerce and business, such as legal rules for the international sale of goods. The UN has also helped to provide standards of conduct for multinational corporations operating in developing countries and around the world. We will examine some of these here. First, we will look at the judicial arm of the UN, the *International Court of Justice.*

International Court of Justice

Earlier in this chapter, you read a decision of the International Court of Justice (ICJ) involving a dispute between Belgium and the Democratic Republic of the Congo. The ICJ, commonly called the World Court, was formed in 1945 as the primary judicial body of the United Nations. The ICJ sits at The Hague, the Netherlands, and bases its work on the *Statute of the International Court of Justice*. The fifteen judges are selected from the leading jurists and scholars of international law on a worldwide basis.

Jurisdiction of the International Court of Justice. The court hears cases brought by nations, against nations. Individuals and private corporations are not parties to cases before the court (although one nation may bring an action against another nation alleging a violation of an individual's rights under international law). The court has jurisdiction over all cases brought by nations under the UN Charter or involving treaties, conventions, international obligations, or questions of international law. Jurisdiction is not compulsory; each nation must agree to submit to the court's jurisdiction. Many treaties and conventions state that the parties agree that the court will hear any disputes that may later arise. The decisions are made public, and there is no appeal. The decisions are binding only on the parties to the case, and not to all nations of the world.

Enforcing Judgments. Judgments of the court are enforced primarily on the basis of world public opinion, diplomatic pressure, and good faith of the countries involved. In a principle established in the *Case Concerning the Factory at* Chorzów (*Poland v. Germany,* PCIJ, 1927), decided by the now-defunct Permanent Court of International Justice, the forerunner of the modern ICJ, any violation of an international obligation requires the payment of financial reparations.

Typical Cases. Typical cases heard by the court have included

- land and maritime boundary disputes (e.g., the dispute between Cameroon and Nigeria over the oil-rich Bakassi peninsula)
- unlawful detaining of diplomats (e.g., Iran holding U.S. diplomats hostage in 1979)
- violations of sovereignty by neighboring armies (e.g., Uganda's plundering of the Democratic Republic of the Congo and the killing and torture of civilians from 1996 to 2001)
- violations of humanitarian law (e.g., Bosnia and Serbia from 1992 to 1995)
- violations of human rights (e.g., the Court's 2003 decision holding that the United States had violated the rights of fifty-one Mexican citizens on death row in the United States by not permitting them to have the assistance of the Mexican embassy in their defense)

Many of these decisions are highly controversial and, as would be expected, subject to criticism from many quarters. Many decisions cannot be enforced. For instance, in the above example, Uganda will probably never pay the $10 billion in reparations that were ordered, and the United States did not overturn the sentences of the Mexican nationals and, indeed, withdrew from the treaty on which the court's decision was based.

The following case, *Liechtenstein v. Guatemala,* illustrates that while only states may be parties before the International Court of Justice, the court can ultimately address individual issues affecting even just one citizen.

UN Agencies Affecting International Business Law

In this part, we will discuss selected UN agencies that directly affect our study of international business law. Although there are many more that are worthy of mention, such as UN agencies working in the areas of environmental protection, world health, and economic development, the following were chosen for their relevance to international business, trade, intellectual property, and foreign investment.

International Labour Organization. The International Labour Organization (or ILO), located in Geneva, was founded in 1919 and became a part of the UN system in 1946. It has 181 member nations. The objectives of the ILO are to bring together government, industry, and labor groups, with a focus on developing countries, to help promote the rights of workers, create decent and beneficial employment opportunities, eliminate child labor, and help foster ideas and the means for the economic and social protection of the poor, the elderly, the unemployable, women, and children. The governing body of the ILO is made up of individual representatives of government, industry, and labor.

Perhaps the most important function of the ILO has been the creation of international labor standards, embodied in 188 conventions and almost two hundred "recommendations" for minimum standards of basic workers' rights. These include the right of workers to freely associate, the right to organize and bargain with employers collectively, abolition of forced labor, and child labor, creation of a safe working environment, protection of migrant workers and workers at sea, elimination of discrimination at work, equality of opportunity and treatment for men and women workers, and other standards addressing workplace health and safety. ILO conventions are legally binding on a member nation only when ratified by its government. Not all countries have ratified all conventions. For example, the United States has ratified fourteen ILO conventions.

ILO "recommendations" are not binding and are not up for ratification. Many of the standards are quite detailed (e.g., standards on night work, minimum wage, protection of mine workers, maternity protection, protection from exposure to hazardous substances, and so on) and are already a part of the laws of virtually all highly industrialized countries. Of course, even those conventions that are not adopted, and those recommendations that do not get implemented, do represent a set of ideals—a moral code—for treating workers, especially by multinational corporations employing labor in developing countries.

UN Commission on International Trade Law. The *UN Commission on International Trade Law* (Vienna), or UNCITRAL, is responsible for coordinating the development several legal codes, embodied in international conventions, which are of great importance to international business. We will study many of them in later chapters. These include codes related to the sale of goods, arbitration of disputes, the movement of money and goods across national borders, and rules for using electronic communications in international business. UNCITRAL also is responsible for developing conventions and codes related to the carriage of goods by sea, the arbitration of disputes, and electronic funds transfer by banks.

UN Conference on Trade and Development. The *UN Conference on Trade and Development* (Geneva), or UNCTAD, is an agency responsible for providing research, policy analysis, coordination, and technical assistance for aiding developing and least-developed countries in their socioeconomic development. Their annual trade and investment reports are widely used for information on the business and economic climate in these areas of the world.

The World Intellectual Property Association. The *World Intellectual Property Association* (Geneva), or WIPO, is a specialized agency of the UN with 184 member nations and almost one thousand employees. Its role is to help foster and protect intellectual property rights in patents,

Liechtenstein v. Guatemala

[1955] I.C.J. Rep. 4

International Court of Justice

BACKGROUND AND FACTS

Nottebohm was born in Germany in 1881. He moved to Guatemala for business reasons in 1905 and lived there until 1943 except for business trips and visits to his brother in Liechtenstein. One month after the start of World War II, while visiting Liechtenstein, Nottebohm applied to be naturalized as a citizen and asked Liechtenstein to waive the 3-year residency requirement. He paid taxes to Liechtenstein and filed the requisite forms, and in 1939 Liechtenstein waived the required time period, swore him in as a citizen, and issued him a passport. In 1943 Guatemala entered World War II, siding with the United States. When Nottebohm returned to Guatemala he was arrested as a German enemy, and turned over to the United States for internment. His property was seized by Guatemala. Nottebohm was released in 1946, but his property was not returned. Liechtenstein filed a "memorial," as the complaint is called, before the International Court of Justice, claiming that Guatemala had violated international law and was obligated to pay damages.

JUDGMENT

Guatemala has referred to a well-established principle of international law, which it expressed in Counter-Memorial, where it is stated that "it is the bond of nationality between the State and the individual which alone confers upon the State the right of diplomatic protection."

... Counsel for Liechtenstein said: "The essential question is whether Mr. Nottebohm, having acquired the nationality of Liechtenstein, that acquisition of nationality is one which must be recognized by other States."

The Court does not propose to go beyond the limited scope of the question which it has to decide, namely, whether the nationality conferred on Nottebohm can be relied upon as against Guatemala in justification of the proceedings instituted before the Court. It must decide this question on the basis of international law.

International arbitrators have ... given their preference to the real and effective nationality, that which accorded with the facts, that based on stronger factual ties between the person concerned and one of the States whose nationality is involved.

The character thus recognized on the international level as pertaining to nationality is in no way inconsistent with the fact that international law leaves it to each State to lay down the rules governing the grant of its own nationality.

At the time of his naturalization, does Nottebohm appear to have been more closely attached by his tradition, his establishment, his interests, his activities, his family ties, his intentions for the near future to Liechtenstein than to any other State?

Naturalization was asked for not so much for the purpose of obtaining a legal recognition of Nottebohm's membership in fact in the population of Liechtenstein, as it was to enable him to substitute for his status as a national of a belligerent State with that of a national of a neutral State, with the sole aim of thus coming within the protection of Liechtenstein but not of becoming wedded to its traditions, its interests, its way of life or of assuming the obligations—other than fiscal obligations—and exercising the rights pertaining to the status thus acquired.

Guatemala is under no obligation to recognize a nationality granted in such circumstances. Liechtenstein consequently is not entitled to extend its protection to Nottebohm vis-à-vis Guatemala, and its claim must, for this reason, be held to be inadmissible.

Decision. The International Court of Justice held that Guatemala was not required to recognize the citizenship granted by Liechtenstein in a way that did not follow well-established principles of international law.

Comment. Under international law an individual may not bring an action against a nation before the International Court of Justice to redress a wrong. This case illustrates that only an individual's country of nationality (in this case Liechtenstein) has the legal right to bring an action before an international tribunal to protect the interests of its citizens. An individual cannot force his or her country to bring such an action.

industrial designs, trademarks, and copyrights. WIPO administers a total of twenty-four treaties, including one on the copyright protection of literary and artistic works and one that works to expedite the process of filing patent applications in more than one country. (There is no single worldwide or international patent on industrial property.) The *Madrid System* facilitates the international registration and protection of trademark rights by providing for the registration of a trademark in all signatory countries by filing in one. A similar system exists for registering industrial designs (referring to the "look and feel" of products ranging from automobiles to watches—think Apple iPOD). There is also a registration for *appellations,* geographical names used in reference to products originating there (such as "Idaho potatoes" or "Scotch whiskey"). WIPO administers a dispute resolution service open to private individuals and corporations (including a service for arbitrating domain name disputes). Many WIPO services to the public are fee-based and paid for by the people and companies who use them.

UN Office on Drugs and Crime. *The UN Office on Drugs and Crime* (Vienna), or UNODC, is responsible for fostering research and providing policy recommendations and technical assistance to UN member countries on dealing with illicit drugs, terrorism, and a range of crime issues—from violent crimes to economic crimes that affect international business. The latter includes work to combat money laundering, organized crime, bribery and corruption, crimes against the environment, cybercrime, and other transnational crimes. For example, the work of the UNODC led to the development of the 2003 *UN Convention against Corruption* (signed by 140 nations and ratified by the United States in 2006). This convention received broad political support because the effects of bribery and corruption can be felt worldwide. In developing countries, corruption breeds contempt for government officials and the rule of law and resentment by the people toward Western business, and has even led to the overthrow of governments whose corrupt leaders had been friendly to Western democracies.

The convention calls for nations to (1) criminalize the offering or giving of a bribe or undue advantage to a public official, including a foreign official, in order to influence his or her official acts or to obtain business; (2) criminalize the "laundering" of money, including passing it through otherwise legitimate businesses or banks in order to disguise its illicit origins and improve enforcement by changing national bank secrecy laws so that the illicit proceeds of crimes can be tracked, identified, and seized; and (3) establish criminal liability for corporations and other legal entities, as well as for individuals.

Since 1977, American citizens have been bound by the U.S. *Foreign Corrupt Practices Act* wherever they are, anywhere in the world. This law makes it illegal to corruptly offer or pay anything of value to a foreign government official in order to obtain business or receive favorable treatment.

Ethics, Social Responsibility, and Corporate Codes of Conduct

In this chapter we have seen how international conventions can form a sort of "Mosaic code" of human rights standards. Many of these establish a moral code for the treatment of labor and create proposals to eliminate bribery and corruption. Therefore, we believe that a chapter on international law is the perfect place to discuss the social responsibility and accountability of multinational corporations. Here we will focus on one of the most widely accepted methods of setting standards for business—the code of conduct.

Corporate Social Responsibility in Developing Countries: A Tale of Two Worlds

While business ethics and social responsibility are of concern to all businesspeople, we ask you to think particularly about the operations and impact of multinational corporations in developing countries. Few areas of international business have been more controversial and politically charged than this. It pits those who view large, powerful corporations as something to be tamed, controlled, and regulated for the benefit of poor countries against those who realize that the investment, productivity, wages, and taxes paid by multinational corporations in developing countries are primary possible with a more *laissez-faire,* pro-business attitude. It pits those who view that the primary responsibility of a multinational business is the maximization of global profit for its shareholders against those who say that multinationals should do more for the people and environment in the poorer countries and take a more active role in promoting social justice there. It pits countries in the Northern Hemisphere, home to many multinationals, against those in the Southern Hemisphere, where many developing countries are located. After all, many policymakers in the developing countries of Latin America and Africa still recall the era of their colonization by European countries, and some still view the presence of multinational corporations as a remnant of that time when colonial powers did exploit labor and natural resources. Keep in mind that many developing countries have a history of socialist economics and even Marxist ideology. So it is, perhaps, to be expected that there would still be some resentment toward the presence of rich multinational corporations in some parts of the world. These arguments came to a head politically during the 1970s, when the social responsibility of corporations was at the forefront of the United Nations agenda. There was an international movement toward greater controls over multinationals by developing countries. However, their demands for regulation gradually calmed in the 1980s when they realized that burdensome regulations would simply drive multinationals away. It was the time of U.S. President Ronald Reagan and British Prime Minister Margaret Thatcher, who promoted free-market principles worldwide. Eventually the communist Soviet Union was gone. Most developing countries quickly realized that multinationals could bring investment, technology, good jobs, and improved living standards.

Today there are still concerns in developing countries about the treatment of workers in farms and factories, global warming, the destruction of forests and pollution of the air and water, and other issues. Industry is seen as both a part of the problem and a part of the solution. Many of these issues are addressed by international conventions and national laws. In recent years, voluntary codes of conduct have become very popular. One can argue whether voluntary regulation is sufficient, or whether it just diverts attention from the real problems.

Codes of Conduct

Today, one of the most widely used means of setting standards for corporate conduct in developing countries is the voluntary *code of conduct.* Various types of codes have been proposed or adopted. Some have been prepared by intergovernmental organizations, by industry trade groups, or by corporations themselves. By studying codes of conduct, we get a sense of some of the most universally accepted values that international businesspeople are expected to have.

The OECD Code of Conduct. The *Organisation for Economic Cooperation and Development* (Paris), or OECD is an intergovernmental organization whose members consist of national governments, with non-governmental organizations joining as observers. The OECD comprises thirty industrialized countries. Members include the United States, Canada, Mexico, Japan, and the European countries. Some of the formerly communist countries of Eastern Europe are members. In 2007, Russia was invited to join. The *OECD Guidelines for Multinational Enterprises* are a set of voluntary recommendations to multinationals encouraging responsible business conduct covering the entire range of business ethics and social responsibility issues. They are not legally enforceable, but are well known and reflect the consensus of many governments. They encourage self-enforcement through accountability, reporting, and internal controls, such as encouraging "whistle blowing" by employees who become aware of corporate violations. The guidelines were first issued in 1976 and revised in 2000. Here are a few representative standards.

Employment—Observe standards of employment and industrial relations no less favorable than those observed in the host country; take adequate steps to ensure occupational health and safety in their operations; to the greatest extent practicable, employ and train local personnel.

Environment—Minimize environmental damage and encourage sustainable development; do not use the lack of full scientific certainty as a reason for postponing measures to prevent or minimize serious damage to the environment.

Bribery—Do not offer, or give in to demands, to pay bribes to public officials.

Consumer Interests—Meet all required standards for consumer health and safety; respect consumer privacy and provide protection for personal data.

Science and Technology—Encourage the diffusion of technology; where practical, perform science and technology development work in host countries as well as employing host country personnel for that purpose.

The OECD is also responsible for having developed the *OECD Convention on Combating Bribery of Foreign Public Officials in International Business Transactions* (1997), adopted by thirty-seven nations. It calls for adopting countries to criminalize the bribery of foreign government officials by individuals and corporations and sets up a method for nations to monitor each other's compliance with the convention. This is discussed in detail in a later chapter.

United Nations Global Compact. During the 1970s and 1980s, the UN attempted to develop a code of conduct for multinational corporations. That effort failed for political reasons, and in 1993, the UN agency charged with developing it was ultimately disbanded. In 1999 then Secretary-General Kofi Annan called for a new initiative—the *UN Global Compact.* Rather than being a purely governmental effort, this is a partnership of international companies, public interest groups, and UN agencies who pledge to support a set of voluntary principles on human rights, labor standards, the environment, and corruption.

The ten core principles are presented in very general terms. For instance, one states that, "Businesses should make sure that they are not complicit [with governments] in human rights abuses." Of course, the *Global Compact* is not without criticism from those who are generally critical of all UN activities. However, the core principles are merely a statement of the most basic, universally recognized principles of environmentalism and corporate social responsibility. According to the UN, as of 2007 there were 3,800 participants, including over 2,900 businesses in 100 countries around the world.

Codes of Conduct from Trade Associations and Private Organizations. Some codes of conduct are developed by trade associations and organizations representing industry, private citizens, or public interest groups. There are industry codes for the oil, apparel, electronic, and chemical industries, to name a few.

The *Coalition for Environmentally Responsible Economies,* or CERES, is a private, mostly American, network of environmental groups, socially conscious investors, and companies committed to following the *CERES Principles* of environmental and social accountability. One provision of the *CERES Principles* requires the appointment of at least one member of senior management and one member of the board of directors to represent environmental interests.

Corporate Codes of Conduct

In recent years, many companies have had an increased interest in enacting their own codes of conduct. There are surely many reasons for a company doing this. It might be seen as good business, in that it creates goodwill with customers and investors. It might be seen as an opportunity to foster an ethical and responsible attitude in their employees. It might be viewed as an opportunity for self-regulation that could forestall the enactment of more restrictive national laws and regulations. In the United States, the guidelines for sentencing corporate offenders allow for reduced fines and sentences if a defendant can show that it has had a code of conduct and compliance program to reduce the likelihood of criminal conduct. Here are a few examples of corporate codes related to international business.

Levi Strauss & Co. Global Sourcing and Operating Guidelines. The *Levi Strauss & Co. Global Sourcing and Operating Guidelines* are discussed here because they are generally recognized as the first code of conduct created by a multinational corporation and made applicable to its foreign suppliers. While they address certain issues important to an apparel company like Levi Strauss, their basic ideas could be applicable to any firm that does business through a global supply chain or with a supplier or contractor in a developing country. These guidelines include the *Business Partner Terms of Engagement*. They represent an effort by Levi Strauss to control the activities of its more than five hundred overseas contractors and suppliers. In the 1990s the company discovered (as did many U.S. apparel and footwear makers) that 25 percent or more of its subcontractors had abused employees in some fashion. One plant in Bangladesh was found to be using child labor. The company not only reacted quickly to stop the practice, but developed guidelines to ensure that its contractors could not do it again. The *Terms of Engagement* sets out, in more than seventy pages, the minimum standards for the protection of the environment and for the fair treatment of workers that must be met by any foreign firm wishing to supply or contract with Levi Strauss. It addresses specifics such as wages, working hours, the use of corporal punishment, and how workers should be treated on the factory floor. For instance, the guidelines state, "Use of child labor is not permissible. Workers can be no less than 14 years of age and not younger than the compulsory age to be in school." Levi Strauss provides its suppliers with manuals and training programs to implement their standards. The company has also developed its *Country Assessment Guidelines*—factors to be considered in deciding in which countries they will do business, including whether the human rights record of the country would be damaging to the Levi Strauss corporate reputation or brand image. The company also makes public its list of all overseas factories producing Levi Strauss products.

Other apparel companies have similar codes. These include The Gap (*Code of Vendor Conduct*), The Limited (*What We Stand For*), Sara Lee (*Global Business Standards* and *Global Standards for Suppliers*), Wal-Mart (*Ethical Standards Program*), and many others. It is generally agreed that for any company's code of conduct to be effective it must be communicated to its employees, become a part of its corporate culture, include disciplinary measures and other methods for ensuring compliance, include a system for measuring its effectiveness, and provide a means of shareholder and public accountability.

Comparative Law: Differences in National Laws and Legal Systems

The study of "comparative law" refers to the study of differences in national laws and legal systems. These differences cover the entire range of law—marriage and family law, business law, liability for wrongful torts, crimes, and more. There are also differences in legal procedures, the role of legislation and case law, the function of judges, the conduct of trials, the use of legal remedies in civil cases, and punishments in criminal cases. These differences are rooted deep in national culture, politics, economics, and especially history and often are the result of centuries of gradual evolution, combined with rapid change caused by wars, revolution, and political turmoil. Even the opening of world markets for commerce and trade—globalization—has influenced the development of law. There is no better example of how legal systems adapt to change than the case of modern Japan.

Modern Japan: An Example of Legal Change. Japan's earliest legal records date back to at least 500 A.D., and for most of its history it was a feudal system whose laws were based on early Confucian and Buddhist principles taken from China. (Recall the image of the Japanese warlord, or *shogun*.) Japan had been largely closed to westerners and Western trade, except for some trade with the Dutch. However, in 1853 Commodore Perry sailed American Navy gunships into Tokyo harbor and demanded safe harbor for American whaling ships and rights to trade with Japan. He also demanded protection for Americans there, by insisting on the extraterritorial application of American law to American citizens. This infuriated and embarrassed the Japanese. Soon other European nations followed. The Japanese recognized that a modern legal system, one on an equal footing with those of the Americans and Europeans, was necessary to trade with them and would enhance their bargaining position in negotiating trade agreements. In response, during the 1860s, the Japanese started a national effort to modernize their legal system. So began a new interest in developing modern legal codes. New law schools opened in Japan, and law professors were exchanged with foreign institutions. Japan sent out legal scholars around the world, primarily to Europe, to study foreign legal codes and to find ways to adapt these to Japan. By the end of the nineteenth century, Japan had remade its legal system largely in the image of the European countries, primarily of Germany. The result was the adaptation of German legal principles to Japanese culture and society. These included written codes in commercial law, real property law, family law, criminal law, and others, as well as procedures for trials and deciding cases.

For the first half of the twentieth century, the influence of German law on Japan continued to mature. Then came World War II. Japan's terms of surrender were dictated by the United States. The United States mandated the rewriting of Japan's constitution, creating a parliamentary democracy and bill of rights, while preserving the symbolic role of the Emperor. The United States also revised many of Japan's business laws. To this day, it is safe to say that Japan's laws are an amalgamation of German civil and criminal law, American constitutional and administrative law, and Japanese cultural values.

We began this section by mentioning some of those forces that influence legal change—war and history, culture, religion, globalization, and international trade. In the case of Japan, we see all of these forces at play.

Modern Legal Systems of the World

While it is obvious that laws can differ from country to country, the differences in legal systems are largely differences in the role of legislatures in enacting statutes or codes, the role of judges and the courts in applying and interpreting the law, and in legal procedures. Let's briefly describe the most widespread modern legal systems found in the world today. These are the common law, civil law, Islamic law, and mixed systems that incorporate characteristics of more than one.

Origins of Civil Law Systems

Civil law systems include most of Eastern and Western Europe, Scandinavia, Latin America, Japan, and Russia. Mixed civil law systems include much of Africa (mixed with tribal law). China's system is largely civil, mixed with principles of socialist economic law and traditional Confucian values.

While the term "civil law" can have several different meanings, the most common meaning to Americans is in reference to the laws affecting private rights and remedies, such as contract law, family or inheritance law, or tort law. However, in this chapter, *civil law* refers to those modern legal systems that are derived from ancient Roman law.

EARLY ROMAN LAW. The early Romans, going back to hundreds of years B.C., had a penchant for writing, or most likely carving, very simple laws into bronze or marble tablets and placing them in public places. These became the earliest written Roman codes. Rome's conquering armies carried Roman law far and wide. Eventually, Rome had amassed thousands of law books containing edicts, rules, and penalties created by generations of emperors. Over the centuries, they had become unwieldy and outdated. By 529 A.D., Rome had long ceased to be the capital of the Roman Empire, and the Emperor Justinian ruled the Eastern Roman Empire from his seat of government in Byzantium (modern Istanbul). In that year, Justinian presided over the rewriting of Roman law, which was condensed and compiled into one code, known as the *Justinian Code.* It classified legal rules and organized them into a logical system that created a "body" of law, in a form that could be learned, understood, and applied. However, Rome had already been overrun by Germanic hordes in the West. The Roman Empire had been lost, and in time, Justinian's code was forgotten—some say lost—almost forever.

THE REVIVAL OF THE JUSTINIAN CODE. Hundreds of years later, around 1100 A.D., copies of Justinian's long-lost code were discovered. Legal scholars from Italy and around the world began to take great interest. They were impressed by how comprehensive it was and how it had arranged legal principles in an orderly and systematic manner. For centuries, Roman law was taught only as an academic discipline, primarily in Italian universities.

Centuries later, the Emperor Napoleon found the clarity and organization of the Roman system

pre-enlightenment law = very disorganized

to be very appealing, and in 1804, he used Roman principles as the basis for consolidating all French law into one code. The *Napoleonic Code* was soon translated into almost every language, and adaptations of it spread throughout Europe and the world. It was the model for the new legal systems of Latin America on their independence from Spain in the years after 1804.

Later in the century, Germany started work on a uniform code, also closely based on the organization of Roman law. In 1900, it enacted its *Bürgerliches Gesetzbuch,* the German civil code, as well as codes of commercial law and criminal law. The *Bürgerliches Gesetzbuch* is still the codified law of Germany to this day, having been amended through the twentieth century, and most recently in 2002. These two codes have been an important influence on the growth of civil law internationally. Earlier we saw the influence of German law on Japan. The German code also influenced the legal systems of China, Portugal, and Brazil. Today, the civil law system is the predominant legal system in the world.

We can still see evidence of Napoleon's work in North America. Louisiana, unlike most of the United States, still owes much of its law to French (as well as Spanish) civil law. Quebec's legal system also draws from French civil law traditions, mixed with common law concepts. Official versions of Quebec's legal codes are written in both French and English. Thanks to the *Napoleonic Code* of two hundred years ago, modern civil codes still have their distant roots in Roman law. It was a Napoleonic victory that has lasted long after his military defeat at Waterloo.

Despite common heritage, there still are many differences in the civil law systems of France, Germany, Switzerland, China, Russia, and other countries. Scotland, South Africa, and the Scandinavian countries have variations of the traditional civil law system.

Origins of Common Law Systems

When most American students are asked about the origins of English law, the answers usually range from the Greeks to the Romans, the Egyptians, or even the Bible. They are always amazed when they learn that the answer is the Normandy region of France. While many English and American legal terms come from French and Latin (after all, the Romans had conquered Gaul and Britain), the revival of Roman law in the eleventh and twelfth centuries that occurred on the European continent completely skipped Britain, which by then was branching off on its own legal track.

The job of describing one thousand years of English legal history in a few paragraphs is not easy. But it is an interesting tale. Anglo-Saxon law governed much of Britain from the fall of the Roman Empire until the Norman Conquest in 1066. Law came partly from the early kings and partly from local custom. By 1066, legal disputes were being heard by Anglo-Saxon courts. (The shire courts were administered by a "shire-reeve," the modern day "sheriff.") There was an early form of trial, but there was no evidence or proof offered. There were no witnesses (which were probably not needed anyway, since most legal acts were performed in public). Trial was by "oath helper." The accused and his "helpers" would all recite a ceremonial oath of the accused's truthfulness. One mistake in reciting the formal oath, one slip of the tongue, and the accused was deemed to have lied, or to be guilty by divine intervention. In some cases, the accused would have had to submit to trial by ordeal—by being submerged in water or placing his hand in fire. Again, by divine intervention, if the hand became infected, he had lied. If it healed, he had told the truth. It was primitive and archaic.

Then, in 1066, the last Saxon king, Harold, was killed when an arrow pierced his eye and his army was defeated at the Battle of Hastings by William, the Duke of Normandy. The course of English law was changed forever. William the Conqueror, as we all know, introduced a political and economic system known as *feudalism.* All land was parceled out to his closest followers, the lords, who in turn gave parcels to subtenants, who in turn did the same. Each took their land with certain rights and in return for certain duties owed to the tenant above, or to their lord. The duties might be farming, knight service, or castle guard, for example. Even the church received land in return for prayers. Indeed, the very first laws developed by William were created to enforce feudal rights in land.

European feudalism no longer exists, although the legal system that William and the kings that followed introduced to England does. They decreed that all justice flowed from the king, and from the King's Court, or *Curia Regis* (the king's closest advisors, sitting at Westminster). Soon traveling judges were sent into the countryside to hold court. Eventually, the king's judges brought with them a new concept, trial by jury.

As one would expect, the popularity of trial by jury over trial by ordeal led to the eventual demise of the old Anglo-Saxon courts. As these itinerant judges decided cases, they wrote down their decisions and shared them with other judges of the king's court. Judges could now justify their decisions by citing the decisions of other judges in similar cases. A "common" body of law resulted. Thus began the common law system that we know today—where the reasoned decisions of judges become the law of the case, a legal precedent that binds judges in deciding similar cases in the future. This is expressed in the common law doctrine of *stare decisis*, meaning that courts should "let the decision stand" unless it is overruled by a higher authority.

The common law spread with the British Empire. Examples of common law countries today include Australia, Canada, Ghana, Great Britain, the United States, and many Caribbean island nations. India has a mixed system that is largely based on the common law. Even many civil law nations have adopted common law principles.

Differences between Modern Civil Law and Common Law Countries

Civil law and common law systems today have many differences and many similarities. Both systems rely on legislative codes, or statutes, as the primary source of law. However, in civil law countries the legal codes are more comprehensive, establishing general principles that are interpreted by judges and applied to the case before them. Where there are gaps in the code law, the judge will draw from the code's principles and doctrine to decide a case. The courts in both systems issue judicial decisions. While civil law judges often cite earlier court decisions that they consider representative of settled law, they are not bound to follow them. Civil law judges do not render opinions that make new law in the form of binding precedent, as do common law judges. It can be said that civil law lawyers are more trained in the interpretation of code law, while common law lawyers are more skilled in using case precedent to develop legal arguments for their clients. It is probably true that researching case law is far more difficult in common law systems, where lawyers must find and piece together common legal principles from unrelated cases and justify the application of those principles to their client's case. Of course, in common law countries, case decisions can always be overridden by statute, as long as the statute does not violate a constitutional doctrine.

The role of judges is also different in civil law countries. The professional judge is schooled for a career as a judge, not a lawyer. In criminal cases, civil law judges take a more inquisitorial role, as do the lawyers for both sides, in an investigative search for the truth. The process is less adversarial than in common law countries. In other legal matters, such as contract or tort cases, civil law judges do the work that both judge and jury would do in common law countries. Unlike common law judges, they can undertake their own investigation of the facts and decide what witnesses are called and what questions are put to them. Much of this is done in writing. In common law countries, the judge is an arbiter between opposing counsel, ruling on what evidence or testimony is admissible, and maintaining a fair trial. By contrast, the use of the jury trial in private damage suits in common law countries is legendary, often resulting in surprisingly high verdicts and punitive damages.

Islamic Law

Over 20 percent of the world's population is of the Muslim religion. They are located in some of the very richest and very poorest countries on earth, in the Middle East, Northern Africa, and Central and Southeast Asia. The largest Muslim populations are in Indonesia, Pakistan, India, Bangladesh, Turkey, Iran, and Egypt. In less than 50 years, the Muslim countries of the Middle East have gone from the age of antiquity to the modern age of information, technology, and oil wealth.

The poorer Muslim countries are undergoing tremendous social and political change. Some have adopted Western practices in business, society, and to a lesser extent, family life. Others have returned to strict Islamic principles. Some Muslim countries give limited rights to women; others abide by strict fundamentalist principles. For example, in Saudi Arabia unmarried women are the wards of their fathers, and widowed women are the ward of their sons.

All Muslim countries seem caught in the political, social, and religious struggle between the Western nations and Islamic fundamentalism. Because of the importance of the Muslim countries today, business students should have some understanding of their basic laws.

Most Muslim countries today have modern legal systems, based on civil law or common law, mixed with principles of Islamic law. Islamic law is known as *Sharia* (or *Shari'ah*), meaning "divine law." It is derived from the Koran (*Qur'an*), and from the *sunna*. The Koran is the main religious book of the Islamic religion that expresses fundamental Islamic values. The *sunna* is the written record of the teachings and actions of the prophet Muhammad. In addition, Islamic jurists and scholars qualified to interpret the scriptural sources have produced opinions known as *fiqh*. An understanding of the *Sharia* requires reference to the *fiqh* for guidance. Islamic judges do not issue written opinions with the force of law, and they are not bound by the precedents of other courts. They are attempting to seek the truth, the divine word of God.

SAUDI ARABIAN LEGAL SYSTEM. An example of a strict Muslim country that is governed by *Sharia* is Saudi Arabia. It is a monarchy and all laws are decreed by the King, in consultation with his highest ministers, in accordance with *Sharia*. All citizens must be Muslim. The basic law sets out very general legal principles. For example, Article 41 states, "Foreign residents in the Kingdom of Saudi Arabia shall abide by its regulations and shall show respect for Saudi social traditions, values, and feelings."

All Saudi citizens must be of the Muslim faith. Serious crimes are punishable by capital punishment, stoning, amputations, or floggings. Rape, theft, the possession or use of alcohol, fornication, and adultery are serious crimes. Drug smuggling can be punishable by death. The *Sharia* courts hear cases involving crimes, family matters, property, and torts. In the last few years, Saudi Arabia has enacted new business regulations on product labeling (2002), insurance (2003), foreign investment (2000), corporate income tax (2004), trademarks (2002), and others. These are considered to supplement Islamic law and must never conflict with it. Commercial and business disputes are heard by special commissions for grievances appointed by the King.

PAKISTANI LEGAL SYSTEM. Other Muslim countries that had been colonized by Western nations in past centuries, such as Pakistan, have closer historical ties to Western legal systems. Pakistan's legal system has been influenced by the British, but is governed by Islamic principles. Today Pakistan has a modern, written constitution, with a bill of rights that has some language that is similar to the American Constitution. It does declare Islam as the state religion.

Pakistan has secular civil and criminal courts, as well as a *Federal Shariat Court,* which has the power to invalidate any public law if it violates Islamic law. Appeals go to the Supreme Court of Pakistan.

The case of *M. Aslam Khaki v. Syed Mohammad Hashim* (2000) illustrates the great differences between banking and finance in Western nations and Islamic law nations. The Muslim countries have both international banks and Islamic banks. Islamic banks abide by *Sharia* law that prohibits the payment of interest on loans and deposits (although they do have alternative forms of compensation that substitute for interest). In its decision, the Supreme Court of Pakistan struck down the use of interest on all loans and bank deposits (including personal loans, commercial and corporate loans, and interest paid by the government on foreign loans). In 2002, the same court reconsidered its opinion, citing errors, and ruled that invalidating the payment of interest to non-Muslims would "pose a high degree of risk to the economic stability and security of Pakistan." As of 2007, the issue was again being considered by Pakistani courts. Given that there are now many purely Islamic banks in the Muslim world that follow Islamic law, cases like this one could have a tremendous effect on international business worldwide.

M. Aslam Khaki v. Syed Mohammad Hashim

Supreme Court of Pakistan (2000)

Shariah *Appellate Bench PLD 2000 SC 225*

BACKGROUND AND FACTS

This case illustrates a classic case of the conflict between Islamic law and modern business. In 1991 the Federal Shariah Court of Pakistan declared the payment of interest (*riba*) by banks on loans and deposits to be contrary to Islamic law. During the 1990s, Pakistani banks adopted many banking techniques to avoid the payment of interest, such as equity investments, profit sharing, and service charges. The government, together with several banks, brought this appeal to the Supreme Court of Pakistan. The court's entire opinion was 1,100 pages long. Below are excerpts from the individual opinion of Maulana Justice Taqi Usmani, an Islamic scholar trained in strict *Sharia* law. As you read, consider the political overtones of the opinion and the economic analysis of interest that would be considered contrary to Western, capitalist economic theory.

MAULANA JUSTICE TAQI USMANI

40. Imam Abubakr Al-Jassas (D.380 AH) in his famous work Ahkamul Qur'an has explained *riba* in the following words: "And the *riba* which was known to and practiced by the Arabs was that they used to advance loan in the form of *Dirham* (silver coin) or *Dinar* (gold coin) for a certain term with an agreed increase on the amount of the principal advanced."

133. Although ... the Holy Qur'an has itself decided what is injustice in a transaction of loan, and it is not necessary that everybody finds out all the elements of injustice in a *riba* transaction, yet the evil consequences of interest were never so evident in the past than they are today. Injustice in a personal consumption loan was restricted to a debtor only, while the injustice brought by the modern interest affects the economy as a whole. A detailed account of the rationale of the prohibition of *riba* would, in fact, require a separate volume....

134. On pure theoretical ground, we would like to focus on two basic issues; firstly on the nature of money and secondly on the nature of a loan transaction.

135. One of the wrong presumptions on which all theories of interest are based is that money has been treated as a commodity. It is, therefore, argued that just as a merchant can sell his commodity for a higher price than his cost, he can also sell his money for a higher price than its face value, or just as he can lease his property and can charge a rent against it, he can also lend his money and can claim interest thereupon.

136. Islamic principles, however, do not subscribe to this presumption. Money and commodity have different characteristics and therefore they are treated differently. * * *

138. Firstly, money (of the same denomination) is not held to be the subject-matter of trade, like other commodities. Its use has been restricted to its basic purpose, i.e., to act as a medium of exchange and a measure of value.

139. Secondly, if for exceptional reasons, money has to be exchanged for money or it is borrowed, the payment on both sides must be equal, so that it is not used for the purpose it is not meant for, i.e., trade in money itself.

140. Imam Al-Ghazzali (d.505 A.H.) the renowned jurist and philosopher of the Islamic history has discussed the nature of money in an early period when the Western theories of money were non-existent. He says: " ... And whoever effects the transactions of interest on money is, in fact, discarding the blessing of Allah and is committing injustice, because money is created for some other things, not for itself. So, the one who has started trading in money itself has made it an objective contrary to the original wisdom behind its creation, because it is injustice to use money for a purpose other than what it was created for.... If it is allowed for him to trade in money itself, money will become his ultimate goal and will remain detained with him like hoarded money. And imprisoning a ruler or restricting a postman from conveying messages is nothing but injustice."

151. This is exactly what Imam Al-Ghazzali had pointed out nine hundred years ago. The evil results of such an unnatural trade have been further explained by him at another place, in the following words: "*Riba* is prohibited because it prevents people from undertaking real economic activities. This is because when a person having money is allowed to earn more money on the basis of interest, either in spot or in deferred transactions, it becomes easy for him to earn without bothering himself to take pains

continued

continued

in real economic activities. This leads to hampering the real interests of the humanity, because the interests of the humanity cannot be safeguarded without real trade skills, industry and construction."

153. Another major difference between the secular capitalist system and the Islamic principles is that under the former system, loans are purely commercial transactions meant to yield a fixed income to the lenders. Islam, on the other hand, does not recognize loans as income-generating transactions. They are meant only for those lenders who do not intend to earn a worldly return through them. They, instead, lend their money either on humanitarian grounds to achieve a reward in the Hereafter, or merely to save their money through a safer hand. So far as investment is concerned, there are several other modes of investment like partnership . . . , which may be used for that purpose. The transactions of loan are not meant for earning income.

158. Thus, financing a business on the basis of interest creates an unbalanced atmosphere which has the potential of bringing injustice to either of the two parties in different situations. That is the wisdom for which the *Shar'iah* did not approve an interest-based loan as a form of financing.

159. Once the interest is banned, the role of "loans" in commercial activities becomes very limited, and the whole financing structure turns out to be equity-based and backed by real assets. In order to limit the use of loans, the *Shar'iah* has permitted to borrow money only in cases of dire need, and has discouraged the practice of incurring debts for living beyond one's means or to grow one's wealth. The well-known event that the Holy Prophet, Sall-Allahu alayhi wa sallam, refused to offer the funeral prayer of a person who died indebted was, in fact, to establish the principle that incurring debt should not be taken as a natural or ordinary phenomenon of life. It should be the last thing to be resorted to in the course of economic activities. * * *

160. Conversely, once the interest is allowed, and advancing loans, in itself, becomes a form of profitable trade, the whole economy turns into a debt-oriented economy which not only dominates over the real economic activities and disturbs its natural functions by creating frequent shocks, but also puts the whole mankind under the slavery of debt. * * *

164. Since in an interest-based system funds are provided on the basis of strong collateral and the end-use of the funds does not constitute the main criterion for financing, it encourages people to live beyond their means. The rich people do not borrow for productive projects only, but also for conspicuous consumption. Similarly, governments borrow money not only for genuine development programs, but also for their lavish expenditure and for projects motivated by their political ambitions rather than being based on sound economic assessment.

204. The basic and foremost characteristic of Islamic financing is that, instead of a fixed rate of interest, it is based on profit and loss sharing. We have already discussed the horrible results produced by the debt-based economy. Realizing the evils brought by this system, many economists, even of the Western world are now advocating in favor of an equity-based financial arrangement.

213. Apart from this, an Islamic economy must create a mentality which believes that any profit earned on money is the reward of bearing risks of the business. * * *

Decision. Interest on the use of money is unjustified and unearned income. A financial system based on the lending of money for interest is unjust and contrary to Islamic law. Equity investments are lawful where all parties share the risk of profit and loss.

Comment. In 2002 this decision was reconsidered by the Supreme Court of Pakistan in *United Bank Limited v. Farooq Brothers and Others* (PLD 2002 SC 800). It held that the decision was based on errors, that it was not feasible to implement, and that the rules against interest could not be made to apply to non-Muslims. As of 2007, a lower court was considering alternative solutions.

Conclusion

Although international law is rooted in centuries of customary law and treaties, it affects modern international relations and international business every day. It affects the movement of people, goods, and money across national borders. Virtually every area of international trade, foreign investment, and intellectual property rights is governed by at least one international convention. International law offers solutions to some of humankind's greatest challenges: human rights abuses by rogue governments, pollution that knows no national boundaries, transnational crimes, international terrorism, and more. However, international solutions depend on the willingness of nations to cooperate, and that is not always politically possible. One can only hope that humankind is up to that challenge.

CHAPTER SUMMARY

1. *International law* includes public and private international law. *Public international law* governs the conduct of nations with other nations or the conduct of nations in their relationships with individuals. It can also include rules for international organizations, such as the *Charter of the United Nations*. *Private international law* governs the rights and responsibilities of private individuals or corporations operating in an international environment, such as international sales contracts or international shipping. International law relies primarily on "soft" enforcement mechanisms: the force of public opinion, trade and diplomatic sanctions, and the withholding of foreign aid. The ultimate sanction is war.
2. *Customary international law* is derived primarily from the widespread and long-standing practices of nations. International law also arises from agreement. A *treaty* is a legally binding agreement between two or more nations that is recognized and given effect under international law. A *convention* is a multilateral treaty on a topic of broad international concern.
3. *International humanitarian law* refers to those rules for how nations treat combatants, noncombatants, refugees, and other civilians during war or civil conflict. Sources of international humanitarian law include the four *Geneva Conventions*. *International human rights law* protects individuals and groups from the acts of governments that violate their civil, political, or human rights during times of peace. Examples include bans on the use of torture in the world's prisons, slavery, forced labor, forced prostitution, and the use of children in military service. All have been widely reported in recent decades.
4. *International criminal law* is that body of law and procedure that involves the use of criminal sanctions to prosecute individual offenders responsible for genocide, war crimes, crimes against humanity, terrorism, and other transnational crimes. The International Criminal Court (the Netherlands) has authority to hear three categories of crimes: genocide, crimes against humanity, and war crimes.
5. *Jurisdiction* is a word of many meanings. Here it means the power of a nation to create laws that proscribe conduct and to act over individuals, corporations, or their property in the application or enforcement of those laws. When used in reference to a court, it is the power of a court to hear a case—to adjudicate. There are five doctrines of international criminal jurisdiction: *territoriality, nationality, the protective principle, passive personality, and universality.*
6. *Comity* refers to the willingness of one court or department of government to respect the rules or decisions of another or to grant it some privilege or favor. *Sovereignty* is the supreme power to govern over an independent state or nation. Sovereign immunity protects foreign governments from lawsuits when they are acting as a political entity, although not when a government agency enters the commercial field to perform essentially private functions. The *Act of State* doctrine is a principle of domestic law (not international law) that prohibits the courts of one country from inquiring into the validity of the legislative or executive acts of another country.
7. The *United Nations* and its agencies have coordinated over five hundred multilateral treaties and international conventions that not only affect world peace and security, but also such important issues as climate change and the protection of the environment; the prevention and control of crime, drug trafficking, and terrorism; rules for Antarctica and the seabeds of the world's oceans; and more.

8. The *International Court of Justice* hears cases brought by nations against other nations. Individuals and private corporations are not parties to cases before the court. The court has jurisdiction over all cases brought by nations under the *UN Charter* or involving treaties, conventions, international obligations, or questions of international law. Jurisdiction is not compulsory; each nation must agree to submit to the court's jurisdiction.
9. In recent decades, there has been a debate over the impact of multinational corporations in developing countries. While it is almost universally accepted that MNCs have contributed greatly to socio-economic development there, a few detractors argue that MNCs exploit developing country natural resources and labor, and return profits to shareholders in their home countries. International standards and voluntary codes of conduct have influenced the role of MNCs in developing countries and the conduct of MNC managers.
10. *Comparative law* refers to the study of differences in national laws and legal systems. These differences cover the entire range of law—marriage and family law, business law, torts, crimes, and more. There are also differences in legal procedures, the role of legislation and case law, the function of judges, the conduct of trials, the use of legal remedies, and punishments in criminal cases. This chapter looked at the development of the common law, civil law, and Islamic law systems.

Questions and Case Problems

1. What is public and private international law? What is international business law?
2. What types of issues lend themselves to international solutions through international law?
3. You overhear someone say, "International law does not exist." What do they mean? What evidence can you provide to persuade them that they are mistaken?
4. Explain how international conventions tend to unify, or harmonize, national laws. Why would this be important to international business?
5. Do you think corporate codes of conduct can have an effect in making firms more socially responsible? Are they a substitute for government regulation or do they complement it?
6. Who are corporations accountable to—the government of their home country, their host country, consumers, investors, or the public? What ideas do you have to set up an accountability system to ensure compliance with codes of conduct and other ethical and social responsibility standards for business?
7. Why do corporations have to be concerned about human rights issues when doing business internationally?
8. The United States and other countries have refused to sign the treaty for the International Criminal Court. Why?
9. Describe the five theories of international criminal jurisdiction. How have these been made applicable to international terrorism? What types of crimes are covered under the principle of universality? Do you think that terrorism should be a universal crime? How would you justify that in terms of legal history of universality? How is universality applied in the *United Nations Convention on Torture*?
10. Do you think the creation of the International Criminal Court will have an effect on the enforcement of human rights law, genocide, or war crimes? Why was terrorism omitted from the jurisdiction of the Court? Do you think the creation of the Court can/should be a substitute for universality jurisdiction?
11. El-Hadad was an accountant and citizen of Egypt working for the government of the United Arab Emirates embassy in Washington, where he was an auditor and supervising accountant in the cultural attaché's office. In 1994, he was promoted and commended for his work. In 1995, his employment was wrongfully terminated. El-Hadad sued the U.A.E. and its Washington embassy for breach of his employment contract and defamation. The defendants claimed that El-Hadad was a government "civil servant" and thus they were immune from suit under the U.S. *Foreign Sovereign Immunities Act*. El-Hadad had supervised eight other accountants. He did not have full civil servant benefits common to other U.A.E. governmental employees. He was not involved in policy-making. Was his employment "commercial" or "governmental?" Was he a "civil servant" or a privately contracted

employee? Does the definition of "civil service" under U.A.E. law matter? Does it matter that he exercised the "powers that can also be exercised by private citizens, as distinct from those powers peculiar to sovereigns?" What else would you like to know about his job functions? For whom do you think judgment was issued was and why? *El-Hadad v. United Arab Emirates,* WL 2141943 (C.A.D.C., 2007).

Managerial Implications

1. You are a vice president of a multinational corporation headquartered in North America. You are asked to visit Latin America to meet with government officials to consider a location for a new factory. On your arrival, you are met at the airport by one of your hosts, who spends some time that day taking you on a tour of the city and getting acquainted. That evening you are invited to his home for dinner with government representatives. After dinner, one of the guests, who works for a key government ministry, asks what you think of your company's role in his country as an employer, taxpayer, and corporate good citizen. He makes it clear that his country is no longer a "puppet" of the North Americans. He asks you to show him that you understand his concerns and to show him that your company will be respectful of his country's culture, environment, natural resources, and local laws. How do you respond?
2. Assume that a Korean company manufacturing critical tail assemblies for commercial aircraft ships several defective assemblies to manufacturers in the United States. The CEO, a Korean national, was not only aware of the defects at the time the assemblies were being made, but was responsible for knowingly using inferior parts. He even threatened an engineer with termination if he leaked the truth. One of the assemblies failed on the American-made plane, leading to the crash of a Canadian-flag passenger airline on takeoff from New York. When the investigation leads to him, he flees Korea for Saudi Arabia, where he lives for several years in luxury. Which countries have jurisdiction to prosecute the Korean citizen, and under what legal principles? You do not need to research any international treaties, but should base your analysis on general principles from this chapter. Subsequently, the U.S. government arranges for his abduction from his home in Saudi Arabia and transport to the United States to stand trial. Does he have the right under the U.S. *Alien Tort Claims Act* to sue the United States for damages resulting from the abduction?
3. Your company in Makonobo uses a number of toxic cleaning solvents to clean manufacturing equipment. You could sell empty solvent containers and make money or pay to have them disposed of in an environmentally safe way. Makonobo has very little environmental regulation, and the first option is legal in Makonobo, but would not be in the United States. What is your decision, and why? Does your answer change if the profit or expenses of each option changes?

Ethical Considerations

We have considered many subjects in this chapter that raise ethical issues—human rights law, international criminal law, international labor standards, bribery and corruption, and others. Here are two cases to consider as food for thought.

Exports of "Unsafe" Pharmaceuticals. Some years ago, it was reported in the world's press that American pharmaceutical companies were selling expired medicines in developing countries that were no longer permitted to be sold in the United States. Assess the validity of the following arguments:

"There are two sides to every debate. We are talking about antibiotics that are lifesaving and in short supply in some developing countries. True, they are expired under federal regulations in the United States, but they will still be effective for some time to come. It is not illegal overseas, and maybe not illegal to export them, so why should I do anything more than just obey the law? After all, we are selling them at reduced prices to the governments of developing countries. They probably have foreign aid money to buy these with. They will sell them, or give them away, to poor people that otherwise would not be able to afford any medicine at all. Why should I destroy them? After all, we are not talking about AIDS, are we? I wonder what the world and big pharmaceutical companies are doing about that problem?"

Bribery as a "Cost of Doing Business." What are the economic, political, and social arguments for and against criminalizing the bribery of foreign government officials in developing countries by employees and representatives of Western companies? Assess the validity of each the following arguments in this statement:

> "I've always thought that bribery is endemic in the developing countries, so 'When in Rome, do as the Romans do.' It's legal there, isn't it? Nothing would happen to me if I get caught there, would it? My government does not have the right to say whether what I do in a foreign country is a crime. They can't tell me what is legal or illegal over there. And I don't have a moral problem either. I see it as a small price to pay—my company just considers this another 'cost of doing business.' We might even try to deduct it on our corporate income tax returns. If I don't offer cash payments or gifts to my customers in government offices overseas, then my competitors from other countries will. Foreign customers will just buy from my competitors. If I don't pay, I'd just be giving my competitors a 'corruption advantage.' And what difference does this make anyway? Why should my country care? I've heard about companies that gave cash payments to the Shah of Iran when he was in power in the 1970s, to his government ministers, even to members of his family. They got contracts worth tens and hundreds of millions of dollars to install everything—telecommunications systems, power plants, and refineries, and most of all, armaments and weapons. I heard he was a brutal dictator, but so what? That's not my problem. I don't see what the problem is."

For Internet Activities, Visit ACADEMIC.CENGAGE.COM/BLAW/SCHAFFER.

CHAPTER 3
Resolving International Commercial Disputes

Avoiding Business Disputes

Long-term business relationships are generally the most profitable ones. Experienced executives and international managers know this, and they work very hard to foster them, at both the personal and organizational levels. Long-term relationships are based on trust. In a world where we do business with people who look, speak, and act differently from ourselves and who live and work oceans away, trust takes on a new and even more important significance. Indeed, it has been said that all of international business is based on trust. Any dispute that threatens the bonds of trust can threaten future business opportunities, do irreparable harm to individual and corporate reputations, and permanently damage long-term relationships. Moreover, when disputes become combative, it can be costly, time consuming, and physically and mentally exhausting for all parties. After all, there is the real possibility that one or both of the parties will have to litigate in a protracted and expensive trial in a foreign court, before a foreign judge, and in a foreign language, and have their rights determined under foreign procedural rules and possibly foreign law. Quite often the parties must retain attorneys in more than one country. So, when disagreements break out, amicable settlements are usually the best outcome and offer the best hope of salvaging a business relationship. It is always helpful if the parties have a reservoir of trust and goodwill that they can draw on to settle the dispute in a friendly way. But, of course, this is not always possible, and the prudent international businessperson, in any contract or any venture, will seek good legal advice and always "hope for the best and plan for the worst."

Nowhere is this more important than in negotiating and drafting business contracts. The contract is the basis of any bargain and its importance cannot be overstated. If and when a dispute arises, the terms of the contract provide the basis for dispute resolution.

Cultural Attitudes toward Disputes

Keep in mind that cultural factors will influence a party's attitude toward how disputes are settled. Americans are notorious litigators, quickly turning to the courts to redress grievances. Their combative stance can result in a "win or lose" mentality. On the other hand, Asians are notable for going to great lengths to seek an amicable settlement. After all, by tradition, it is a virtue to seek harmony and a vice to seek discord. These differences are evident in the way American and Japanese businesspeople approach contract or business negotiations. It is quite common for Americans to include their attorney or corporate counsel as a member of the negotiating team. Indeed, many Western managers and executives would never dream of it being any other way. But to the Japanese, this may seem a little confrontational, a little unnecessary, and a bad omen or a sign that disagreement is inevitable.

All too often, Americans view the negotiating process as something to be gotten out of the way so the deal can be closed, the contract signed, and all can go back home. People of many other cultures, from Asia to Latin America, might see the negotiating process as a time to build a relationship and new friendships. Of course, these attitudes differ throughout the world, and from country to country, and no generalizations should be made. But one thing is certain, and that is that the rest of the world views Americans as confrontational and quick to call in the lawyers. Perhaps the words of the English Lord Denning best sum up the foreign view:

> As the moth drawn to the light, so is a litigant drawn to the United States. If he can only get his case into their courts, he stands to win a fortune. At no cost to himself; and at no risk of having to pay anything to the other side.... The lawyers will charge the litigant nothing for their services but instead they will take forty percent of the damages.... If they lose, the litigant will have nothing to pay to the other side. The courts in the United States have no such cost deterrents as we have. There is also in the United States a right to trial by jury. These are prone to award fabulous damages. They are notoriously sympathetic and know that the lawyers will take their forty percent before the plaintiff gets anything. All this means that the defendant can be readily forced into a settlement. *Smith Kline and French Laboratories v. Bloch,* [1983] 1 W.L.R. 730, 733–4 (Eng. C.A.).

The resolution of disputes between citizens of different countries, with business transactions that span continents and cultures, raises many complicated legal and tactical problems. Consider a dispute involving an American manufacturer that purchases thousands of meters of cloth from a Chinese supplier. The cloth is shipped to Vietnam where the manufacturer contracted to have it embroidered and sewn into pillow shams. When the finished goods arrive in the United States, it is discovered that they are damaged. Apparently the fabric was shipped from China in a defective condition, but the Vietnamese firm failed to inspect for damage as it normally did. The Chinese company claims that the time for bringing the defective fabric to its attention has long passed. The Vietnamese company says it was not its responsibility. Consider all the questions presented. To whom does the manufacturer look for remuneration? Is the relationship between the parties worth keeping, and is the case capable of being settled or should the manufacturer "take the gloves off"? Was there a contract with either party and did it specify the method of resolution, such as mediation, arbitration, or litigation, and if so, where and under what law? If the contract does not specify, what legal rules apply to determine where the case should be heard and what law should govern? (Note that these are two entirely different issues.) Finally, if a judgment is obtained through litigation, how will it be enforced across international borders? These are some of the questions discussed in this chapter.

Methods of Resolution

This chapter presents several alternatives for dispute resolution, including mediation, arbitration, and litigation. Consider a domestic dispute in which a New York supplier tries to sue a Texas distributor. This situation raises several questions: Should the parties settle, mediate, arbitrate, or litigate? Where should the dispute be heard—in New York or Houston? In federal or state court? Which law applies to the transaction—the law of New York, Texas, or some other jurisdiction? Finally, if a resolution is reached (be it a settlement, a verdict, or a judgment), how will it be enforced?

Changing the parties to an American supplier and a foreign distributor adds several dimensions to the problem. Many of the same questions that are relevant to a domestic dispute are equally relevant to an international dispute, but they become infinitely more complex. This chapter examines these questions as they apply to commercial disputes in international business.

Alternate Dispute Resolution

Alternate dispute resolution (ADR) usually offers a faster, cheaper, and more efficient alternative to resolving international commercial disputes than litigation. Unlike litigation, ADR requires that the parties voluntarily submit to the resolution process.

Mediation

Mediation is a voluntary, nonbinding, conciliation process. The parties agree on an impartial mediator who helps them amicably reach a solution. The final decision to settle rests with the parties themselves. It is private, and there are no public

private

court records or glaring articles in the local press to influence local opinion about the firms. The parties reserve all legal rights to resort to binding arbitration or litigation.

Arbitration

can be upheld

Arbitration is a more formalized process resulting in a binding award that will be enforced by courts of law in many countries. The parties must agree to arbitration, but once they do, they may not withdraw. Arbitration is frequently used in international business because it "levels the playing field" since the case may be heard in a more impartial tribunal. First, arbitration permits the resolution of the case in a third "neutral" country, rather than in the country of one of the parties. The parties are generally free to choose a location for arbitration that is mutually convenient. For example, a dispute between an American company and a Russian company might be arbitrated in Paris or Stockholm. Disputes between American companies and Chinese companies are often arbitrated in Hong Kong. (Not only is Hong Kong still considered a neutral site, but its awards are enforceable by the courts of both the United States and China.) Secondly, the arbitrator may be chosen by the parties from a roster of impartial industry experts or distinguished lawyers, who may also be from a third country. Finally, the case may be resolved using the impartial and straightforward arbitration rules of the arbitrating organization, rather than the procedural rules buried in the statutes or rules of court of the country of one of the parties. *Arbitration rules* are the rules of arbitral tribunals that address issues such as the qualification and appointment of arbitrators, the conduct of proceedings, procedures for finding the facts and applying the law, and the making of awards. One major arbitral body published its rules in 12 languages.

There are other advantages to arbitration besides this neutrality. Pretrial discovery is faster and more limited than that available in the United States, resulting in less expense and delay. The process is private and records of proceedings are not publicly available as are court records. Arbitration fees are far less than court fees for litigation, as are attorney fees. The rules for evidence admissibility are more flexible than in many national courts. And finally, a party's right to appeal is more limited.

Although parties can always agree to arbitration, a requirement to submit to arbitration is often set out in many international contracts. Arbitration clauses might be used in contracts for the sale of goods, commodities, or raw materials. They are used in international shipping contracts, employment contracts, international construction contracts, financing agreements, and cruise ship tickets, to name a few, as well as in multimillion- or billion-dollar contracts. Today, arbitration is being used more to resolve disputes over intellectual property and licensing agreements.

Despite its reputation for being less costly than litigation, arbitration is not cheap. The International Chamber of Commerce (ICC) estimates that for a $1 million claim before its International Court of Arbitration in Paris, the average arbitrator's fee would be approximately $32,000, with about $19,000 in administrative expenses, for a total of approximately $49,000 in costs—or about 5 percent. For a $100,000 claim, the costs would be closer to 13 percent.

National Arbitral Laws. Most commercial nations today have laws permitting arbitration and specifying the effect of an arbitral award (see Exhibit 3.1). The *British Arbitration Act* went into effect in 1996. The *Arbitration Law of the People's Republic of China* became effective in

Exhibit 3.1

Some Arbitration Treaties in Force Worldwide

Arab Convention on Commercial Arbitration (1987)
Convention on the Recognition and Enforcement of Foreign Arbitral Awards (New York, 1959)
Convention on the Settlement of Investment Disputes Between States and Nationals of Other States (Washington Convention, 1966)
European Convention Providing a Uniform Law on Arbitration (Strasbourg Convention, 1966)
Geneva Protocol on Arbitration Clauses (1923)
Geneva Convention on the Execution of Foreign Arbitral Awards (1927)
Inter-American Convention on International Commercial Arbitration (Organization of American States, Panama Convention, 1975)

1994 (it provides that arbitrators must have eight years' prior legal experience), and the Russian arbitration law was enacted in 1993. (Notably, it provides that arbitration may be conducted in Russia in any language agreed upon.) The laws of many countries, such as China, Russia, Mexico, and Canada, were patterned after the *1985 Model Law on International Commercial Arbitration* of the UN Commission on International Trade Law (UNCITRAL). The U.S. *Federal Arbitration Act* dates back to 1925, but has been modernized. It applies to both domestic and international arbitration and defers to the specific procedural rules of the arbitral body conducting the arbitration proceedings. Many U.S. states (e.g., California, Connecticut, Illinois, Oregon, and Texas) have enacted statutes on international commercial arbitration, some patterned after the UNCITRAL model.

Arbitration Bodies. There are many organizations worldwide providing arbitral services. The choice is up to the parties, and this is often decided in advance and set out in the terms of the contract. Some of the leading private arbitral organizations for arbitration of commercial disputes are the following:

- China International Economic and Trade Arbitration Commission
- American Arbitration Association
- International Court of Arbitration of the International Chamber of Commerce (ICC)
- London Court of Arbitration
- Arbitration Institute of the Stockholm Chamber of Commerce
- St. Petersburg International Commercial Arbitration Court
- Hong Kong International Arbitration Centre and the HK Mediation Centre
- Singapore International Arbitration Centre
- Japan Commercial Arbitration Association
- World Intellectual Property Organization (WIPO) Arbitration and Mediation Center

Two additional organizations provide dispute resolution between private parties and national governments:

- The *International Centre for Settlement of Investment Disputes* (ICSID), a part of the World Bank group, provides arbitration for the settlement of disputes between member countries and investors who qualify as nationals of other member countries.
- *The Permanent Court of Arbitration at The Hague* provides arbitral services for commercial disputes to states, private parties, and intergovernmental organizations, including handling mass claims and environmental disputes where one of the parties is a national government.

Each of these organizations operates under a different set of procedural rules. The ICC uses its own rules, which are highly respected. Many other arbitral bodies use the widely accepted rules drafted by UNCITAL, which take into account the various legal systems and countries in which they might be used. The UNCITRAL rules, for example, are used by the Hong Kong Arbitration Center, by the WIPO, and by other organizations throughout the world.

Arbitration Clauses. Many contracts contain clauses requiring that disputes be submitted for arbitration because it removes much of the uncertainty in the event of a breach of contract or other dispute. Here is a typical example:

> Any disputes or claims arising out of this contract, or breach thereof, shall be resolved by arbitration before [name of arbitral body], and according to the rules of that body. Any award rendered thereby may be entered in any court of competent jurisdiction.

While the validity of these clauses is now generally accepted, that was not always clear. In the following case, *Scherk v. Alberto-Culver,* the U.S. Supreme Court considered an arbitration clause in an international contract calling for arbitration in Paris.

Enforcement of Arbitration Awards. Arbitral awards are recognized and enforceable by the courts of most nations. In the United States, an arbitral award will usually be enforced if the following conditions are met:

- The award is enforceable under the local law of the country where the award was made
- The defendant was properly subject to the jurisdiction of the arbitral tribunal
- The defendant was given notice of the arbitration proceeding and an opportunity to be heard

Scherk v. Alberto-Culver
417 U.S. 506 (1974)
United States Supreme Court

BACKGROUND AND FACTS

Alberto-Culver Co., a Delaware corporation with its principal office in Illinois, manufactures toiletries and hair products in the United States and abroad. In February 1969, Alberto-Culver signed in Austria a contract to purchase three businesses of Fritz Scherk (a German citizen) that were organized under German and Liechtenstein law, as well as the trademarks to related cosmetics. In the contract, Scherk warranted that he had the sole and unencumbered ownership of these trademarks. The contract also contained a clause that provided that "any controversy or claim [that] shall arise out of this agreement or the breach thereof would be referred to arbitration before the International Chamber of Commerce in Paris, France, and that the laws of Illinois shall govern." One year after the closing, Alberto-Culver discovered that others had claims to Scherk's trademarks. Alberto-Culver tried to rescind the contract; Scherk refused, and Alberto-Culver filed suit in federal court in Illinois claiming that the misrepresentations violated the Securities and Exchange Act, Sec. 10(b), and SEC rule 10b-5. Scherk moved to dismiss or to stay the action pending arbitration. In the U.S. District Court, the motion to dismiss was denied and arbitration was enjoined. The Court of Appeals affirmed. The Supreme Court granted certiorari.

JUSTICE STEWART

The *United States Arbitration Act,* now 9 U.S.C. 1 et seq., reversing centuries of judicial hostility to arbitration agreements, was designed to allow parties to avoid "the costliness and delays of litigation," and to place arbitration agreements "upon the same footing as other contracts. . . ."

Alberto-Culver's contract to purchase the business entities belonging to Scherk was a truly international agreement. Alberto-Culver is an American corporation with its principal place of business and the vast bulk of its activity in this country, while Scherk is a citizen of Germany whose companies were organized under the laws of Germany and Liechtenstein. The negotiations leading to the signing of the contract in Austria and to the closing in Switzerland took place in the United States, England, and Germany, and involved consultations with legal and trademark experts from each of those countries and from Liechtenstein. Finally, and most significantly, the subject matter of the contract concerned the sale of business enterprises organized under the laws of and primarily situated in European countries, whose activities were largely, if not entirely, directed to European markets.

Such a contract involves considerations and policies significantly different from those found controlling in *Wilko v. Swan,* 346 U.S. 427 (1953). In *Wilko,* quite apart from the arbitration provision, there was no question but that the laws of the United States generally, and the federal securities laws in particular, would govern disputes arising out of the stock-purchase agreement. The parties, the negotiations, and the subject matter of the contract were all situated in this country, and no credible claim could have been entertained that any international conflict-of-laws problems would arise. In this case, by contrast, in the absence of the arbitration provision considerable uncertainty existed at the time of the agreement, and still exists, concerning the law applicable to the resolutions of disputes arising out of the contract.

Such uncertainty will almost inevitably exist with respect to any contract touching two or more countries, each with its own substantive laws and conflict-of-laws rules. A contractual provision specifying in advance the forum in which disputes shall be litigated and the law to be applied is, therefore, an almost indispensable precondition to achievement of the orderliness and predictability essential to any international business transaction. Furthermore, such a provision obviates the danger that a dispute under the agreement might be submitted to a forum hostile to the interests of one of the parties or unfamiliar with the problem involved.

A parochial refusal by the courts of one country to enforce an international arbitration agreement would not only frustrate these purposes, but would invite unseemly and mutually destructive jockeying by the parties to secure tactical litigation advantages. In the present case, for example, it is not inconceivable that if Scherk had anticipated that Alberto-Culver would be able in this country to enjoin resort to arbitration he might have sought an order in France or some other country enjoining

continued

continued

Alberto-Culver from proceeding with its litigation in the United States. Whatever recognition the courts of this country might ultimately have granted to the order of the foreign court, the dicey atmosphere of such a legal no-man's-land would surely damage the fabric of international commerce and trade, and imperil the willingness and ability of businessmen to enter into international commercial agreements....

For all these reasons we hold that the agreement of the parties in this case to arbitrate any dispute arising out of their international commercial transaction is to be respected and enforced by the federal courts in accord with the explicit provisions of the Arbitration Act.

Decision. Reversed and remanded.

Comment. The Court understood that an arbitration agreement was the ultimate type of forum selection clause. The Court made reference to national legislation that indicated an acceptance of arbitration (the Arbitration Act, 9 U.S.C 1 et. seq.). Other countries have similar national legislation or are signatories to the *New York Convention* and/or the *European Convention on International Arbitration*.

- Enforcement of the award is not contrary to public policy
- The subject matter of the contract at issue is not unlawful under applicable law
- The contract at issue is not void for reasons of fraud or the incapacity of one of the parties

More than 130 nations have signed the 1958 *United Nations Convention on the Recognition and Enforcement of Foreign Arbitral Awards,* known as the *New York Convention,* further strengthening the ability to enforce awards in those countries.

LITIGATION

Litigation in a court of law is the final alternative for resolving a dispute. It is used more frequently in the United States than in virtually any other country. Many countries have different procedural rules for litigating cases. First, many concepts familiar to American and English students, such as trial by jury and other traditions, may not be used in the civil law countries. While we take jury trials in criminal and civil cases almost for granted in America, the same is not true throughout the world. The role of the judge may be very different; in some countries, the judge is an impartial arbiter of fairness and procedure, while in other countries, he or she may examine witnesses and take an active role in the search for the truth. The *discovery* process, by which the parties attempt to uncover evidence in advance of trial, can also be different. For instance, oral depositions taken under oath outside of court may be routinely done in the United States, while in China and some other countries, their use is prohibited. There are different rules for compensating lawyers; in the United States, for instance, contingent fees are widely used in tort cases, while in other countries, they are barred. The entire issue of damages is frequently handled differently; the United States is famous for its whopping punitive damage awards that serve to punish a losing party for its especially egregious conduct, but in many other countries, such as Japan, punitive damages are not used. Finally, appeals are handled differently in many countries, with some, like the United States, limiting appeals to reconsidering issues of law applied by the trial courts. In other countries, appellate courts will consider new or additional evidence.

There can also be many differences in substantive law ("the law of the case"), although this topic is too broad for this chapter. Suffice it to say that almost every body of law—contracts, torts, crimes, property, business regulation, intellectual property, and so forth—can vary from legal system to legal system and country to country. This will have a tremendous impact on the outcome of litigation. Certainly, parties to a contract can have some control over the choice of substantive law and procedural rules by incorporating *choice of law clauses* and *forum selection clauses* in their contracts. They may also be able to have control over where the litigation takes place.

These are critical issues that must be kept in mind as you read on.

Jurisdiction

Jurisdiction, one of the key concepts of jurisprudence, is the power of a court to hear and decide a case. A court that has jurisdiction is said to be a "competent" court. The term has different meanings depending on how it is used. For example, *territorial jurisdiction* refers to the power of criminal courts to hear cases involving crimes committed within their territory. *In rem* jurisdiction refers to a court's power over property within its geographical boundaries. *Subject matter jurisdiction* refers to the court's authority to hear a certain type of legal matter, such as tort cases or breach of contract. In the United States, for example, federal courts have subject matter jurisdiction over cases involving federal statutes and federal government agencies, constitutional issues, and cases arising between citizens of different states or between citizens of the United States and citizens of foreign countries (where the amount in controversy exceeds $75,000). The latter is known as *diversity of citizenship* jurisdiction. Thus, we see that the term "jurisdiction" can be used in many different ways. But one thing is certain—without it, courts are powerless to act.

***In Personam* Jurisdiction.** *In personam jurisdiction* or "jurisdiction over the person" refers to the court's power over a certain individual or corporation. No party can be made to appear before a court unless that court has personal jurisdiction. If there is no personal jurisdiction, the case will be dismissed. Typically, jurisdiction is obtained by having a summons served on an individual or on the legal agent of a corporation. While the serving of a summons on a party is the best way for a court to obtain jurisdiction over the person, there are many substitute methods, such as those used to summon parties not personally present in the court's territory. (This subject will be discussed later in this chapter.) In certain types of cases, service over those not present in the territory can be done by registered mail or even through publication in the "legal notices" section of approved newspapers. In the United States, the requirement of obtaining service of process on a defendant in a case, and of having jurisdiction over them, is required by the Due Process Clause of the 5th and 14th Amendments. The method used must be authorized by statute and be fundamentally fair.

The basic concept is that one should not be "hauled into court" in some distant state or country unless that person has some connection to that place. Every national legal system has its jurisdictional requirements. For example, the *French Civil Code* states that "a foreigner, even if not residing in France, may be cited before French courts for the execution of obligations by him contracted in France with a citizen of France." In Germany, the presence of property owned by the defendant, whether the property is insignificant or even if it is not related to the case, can still be the basis of jurisdiction. Similarly, in the United States, there are many federal and state statutes that define when a court is competent to hear and decide a case over a defendant.

Requirement for *In Personam* Jurisdiction: Minimum Contacts. At one time in U.S. legal history, the U.S. Supreme Court had interpreted the Due Process Clause to limit personal jurisdiction to people physically present in the court's territory. As the nation grew and as interstate commerce expanded, the concept was broadened to allow jurisdiction over persons who are not present within the court's geographical territory, but who, for reasons of justice and fairness, should be held to answer a complaint there. A modern example is a state "implied consent" statute, by which one operating a motor vehicle on the highways of a state "impliedly consents" to submitting to the jurisdiction of the courts of that state for all suits arising out of the operation of the vehicle there.

The due process requirements for *in personam* jurisdiction over persons absent from a state or territory have been carefully considered by the courts. In the now famous language of U.S. Supreme Court decisions dealing with both interstate and international commerce, "due process requires only that in order to subject a defendant to a judgment *in personam,* if he be not present within the territory of the forum, he have certain minimum contacts with it such that the maintenance of the suit does not offend traditional notions of fair play and substantial justice." *International Shoe Co. v. Washington,* 326 U.S.

310 (1945). Just how much of a connection to a foreign state or country does it take for the courts to require one to defend a case there? The courts have answered the question on a case-by-case basis, looking to see whether it would be fair to ask a nonresident to come to their jurisdiction to defend a case. The courts have looked at many factors, including the extent of the defendant's presence in the state, what business he may have conducted there, the burden on the defendant, fairness to the plaintiff, and the interest of the state in having the case resolved there. Did the defendant have an office, branch location, or salespeople in the territory of the forum? Did any of its employees or agents travel there on business? Did it advertise or otherwise solicit business there? Did it ship goods there? Did it enter into a contract there, or was the contract to be performed there? In *Worldwide Volkswagen Corp. v. Woodson,* 444 U.S. 286 (1980), the U.S. Supreme Court stated that a New York automobile distributor was not required to appear in Oklahoma to defend a products liability suit based on the sale of a vehicle that took place in New York and was later involved in a serious accident in Oklahoma.

> Petitioners carry on no activity whatsoever in Oklahoma. They close no sales and perform no services there. They avail themselves of none of the privileges and benefits of Oklahoma law. They solicit no business there either through salespersons or through advertising reasonably calculated to reach the State. Nor does the record show that they regularly sell cars at wholesale or retail to Oklahoma customers or residents or that they indirectly, through others, serve or seek to serve the Oklahoma market. In short, respondents seek to base jurisdiction on one, isolated occurrence and whatever inferences can be drawn therefrom: the fortuitous circumstance that a single Audi automobile, sold in New York to New York residents, happened to suffer an accident while passing through Oklahoma.

A similar concept exists in the international context. The following case, *Asahi Metal Ind. v. Superior Ct. of California,* 480 U.S. 102 (1987), questions whether a Japanese manufacturing

Asahi Metal Industry, Co. v. Superior Court of California, Solano County

480 U.S. 102 (1987)

United States Supreme Court

BACKGROUND AND FACTS

Asahi Metal Industry, a Japanese corporation, manufactured valve assemblies in Japan and sold them to tire manufacturers including Cheng Shin (a Taiwanese corporation) from 1978 to 1982. Cheng Shin sold tires all over the world, including in California. On September 23, 1978, in Solano County, California, Gary Zurcher was injured riding his motorcycle. His wife was killed. He filed a products liability action against Cheng Shin (Taiwan), the manufacturer of his motorcycle tire, alleging that the tire was defective. Cheng Shin filed a cross-complaint seeking indemnification from Asahi Metal Industry. Cheng Shin settled with Zurcher. However, Cheng Shin (Taiwan) pressed its action against Asahi (Japan), and Asahi petitioned for certiorari to the United States Supreme Court. The case presented the question of whether a dispute between a Taiwanese company and a Japanese company with the above-described relationship to California should be heard by the California courts. In other words, did the California courts have jurisdiction over the matter?

JUSTICE O'CONNOR

The placement of a product into the stream of commerce, without more, is not an act of the defendant purposefully directed toward the forum State. Additional conduct of the defendant may indicate an intent or purpose to serve the market in the forum State, for example, designing the product for the market in the forum State, advertising in the forum State, establishing channels for providing regular advice to customers in the forum State, or marketing the product through a distributor who has agreed to serve as the sales agent in the forum State. But a defendant's awareness that the stream of commerce may or will sweep the product into the forum State does not convert the mere act of placing the product into the stream into an act purposefully directed toward the forum State.

continued

continued

Assuming, *arguendo,* that respondents have established Asahi's awareness that some of the valves sold to Cheng Shin would be incorporated into tire tubes sold in California, respondents have not demonstrated any action by Asahi to purposefully avail itself of the California market. It has no office, agents, employees, or property in California. It does not advertise or otherwise solicit business in California. It did not create, control, or employ the distribution system that brought its valves to California. There is no evidence that Asahi designed its product in anticipation of sales in California. On the basis of these facts, the exertion of personal jurisdiction over Asahi by the Superior Court of California exceeds the limits of due process.

The strictures of the Due Process Clause forbid a state court from exercising personal jurisdiction over Asahi under circumstances that would offend "traditional notions of fair play and substantial justice." *International Shoe Co. v. Washington,* 326 U.S. 310, 316 (1945), quoting *Milliken v. Meyer,* 311 U.S. 457, 463 (1940).

We have previously explained that the determination of the reasonableness of the exercise of jurisdiction in each case will depend on an evaluation of several factors....

Certainly the burden on the defendant in this case is severe. Asahi has been commanded by the Supreme Court of California not only to traverse the distance between Asahi's headquarters in Japan and the Superior Court of California in and for the County of Solano, but also to submit its dispute with Cheng Shin to a foreign nation's judicial system. The unique burdens placed upon one who must defend oneself in a foreign legal system should have significant weight in assessing the reasonableness of stretching the long arm of personal jurisdiction over national borders.

When minimum contacts have been established, often the interests of the plaintiff and the forum in the exercise of jurisdiction will justify even the serious burdens placed on the alien defendant. In the present case, however, the interests of the plaintiff and the forum in California's assertion of jurisdiction over Asahi are slight. All that remains is a claim for indemnification asserted by Cheng Shin, a Taiwanese corporation, against Asahi. The transaction on which the indemnification claim is based took place in Taiwan; Asahi's components were shipped from Japan to Taiwan. Cheng Shin has not demonstrated that it is more convenient for it to litigate its indemnification claim against Asahi in California rather than in Taiwan or Japan.

Because the plaintiff is not a California resident, California's legitimate interests in the dispute have considerably diminished. The Supreme Court of California argued that the State had an interest in "protecting its consumers by ensuring that foreign manufacturers comply with the state's safety standards." ... The State Supreme Court's definition of California's interest, however, was overly broad. The dispute between Cheng Shin and Asahi is primarily about indemnification rather than safety. Moreover, it is not at all clear at this point that California law should govern the question whether a Japanese corporation should indemnify a Taiwanese corporation on the basis of a sale made in Taiwan and a shipment of goods from Japan to Taiwan.

Considering the international context, the heavy burden on the alien defendant, and the slight interests of the plaintiff and the forum State, the exercise of personal jurisdiction by a California court over Asahi in this instance would be unreasonable and unfair.

Because the facts of this case do not establish minimum contacts such that the exercise of personal jurisdiction is consistent with fair play and substantial justice, the judgment of Supreme Court of California is reversed, and the case is remanded for further proceedings not inconsistent with this opinion.

It is so ordered.

Decision. Reversed and remanded. The United States Supreme Court reversed the California Supreme Court and found that there was no jurisdiction. This Supreme Court case is significant because it lists several factors that will be taken into account in determining whether a court will take jurisdiction.

company should be forced to defend a lawsuit in California for an accident that occurred there. As you read, keep in mind that these cases are resolved on a case-by-case basis after a consideration of all of the facts. A decision on jurisdiction may depend on one or more different factors not present in other cases. In other words, it is very difficult for lawyers to counsel whether your actions will or will not subject you to a foreign court's jurisdiction some time in the future. In reading this case, think about what factors, if they had been present, might have forced Asahi to appear in court in California.

JURISDICTION IN THE EUROPEAN COMMUNITY. Jurisdiction in civil and commercial cases between parties domiciled in two or more EU countries is determined by *EU Council Regulation No. 44/2001*. This law became effective in 2002 and replaced the 1968 *Brussels Convention on Jurisdiction and the Enforcement of Judgments in Civil and Commercial Matters* (except in Belgium, for which the *Brussels Convention* is still applicable). The general rule is that jurisdiction is determined by the domicile of the defendant. The regulation states that "persons domiciled in a Member State shall, whatever their nationality, be sued in the courts of that Member State." Corporations are domiciled in the Member State (i.e., member country of the EU) where they are incorporated, where they have their primary administrative offices, or where they have their principal place of business.

There are several exceptions to this general rule. (1) Cases involving commercial contracts for the sale of goods within the EU will be heard in the country where the goods were or should have been delivered. (2) Cases involving a breach of contract for services (other than insurance or employment) within the EU will be heard where the services were or should have been provided. (3) Tort cases, such as an action arising out of an automobile accident, will be heard before the courts in the country where the wrong occurred. (4) In consumer contract cases, a consumer may bring an action against the other party to the contract either in the country in which that party is domiciled or in the country where the consumer is domiciled. Lawsuits against a consumer to enforce the contract can only be brought in the courts of the consumer's country. (5) An employer may sue its employee or former employee only in the employee's place of domicile. However, an employee may bring a lawsuit against an employer either in the country where the employee is domiciled, where the employer is domiciled, or if not domiciled in the EU, where a branch or agent is located, or in the country where the employee regularly or last worked. (6) Where at least one of the parties is domiciled in the EU, by an agreement specifying the courts of a certain EU country, provided that the agreement is in written or electronic form, or in international cases, in a form that the parties should have known amounted to a forum selection. The following decision of the High Commercial Court of Ireland in *General Motors Ireland Limited v. SES-ASA Protection SPA* illustrates jurisdiction between business parties domiciled in the EU.

General Motors Ireland Limited v SES-ASA Protection SPA

[2005] IEHC 223

The High Commercial Court of Ireland

BACKGROUND AND FACTS

General Motors Ireland (GM), a subsidiary of General Motors, Inc., is incorporated in Ireland. At its plant in Galway, GM manufactures instruments used to detect combustible gases and flame. The defendant, SES, is an Italian corporation. In 1999 the parties entered into a "value added reseller" (VAR) agreement setting terms under which GM would sell its products to SES. The agreement addressed issues related to territorial exclusivity, rules for soliciting customers, and advertising and promotion of GM products. It also established prices on products that SES might order. Subsequently, SES placed 22 orders for GM products, which were delivered to SES's forwarding agent in Galway for transport to Italy. This action was brought by GM before the High Court Commercial of Ireland to recover amounts due on several invoices totaling €345,000 and $1 million for goods delivered to SES within the previous 6 years. SES entered an appearance for the purpose of contesting jurisdiction of the Irish court.

JUSTICE FINLAY GEOGHEGAN

Regulation 44/2001 replaces the *Brussels Convention* (1968) on jurisdiction and the enforcement of judgments in civil and commercial matters....

continued

continued

Article 5(1) provides:

A person domiciled in a Member State may, in another Member State, be sued:

1. (a) In matters relating to a contract, in the courts for the place of performance of the obligation in question;
   (b) for the purpose of this provision and unless otherwise agreed, the place of performance of the obligation in question shall be:
   - in the case of the sale of goods, the place in a Member State where, under the contract, the goods were delivered, or should have been delivered.
   - in the case of the provision of services, the place in a Member State where, under the contract, the services were provided or should have been provided.

   (c) if subparagraph (b) does not apply then subparagraph (a) applies. * * *

The defendant submitted that the VAR Agreement of 1999 was the relevant contract between the parties and that this was not a contract for the sale of goods but rather a contract for the supply of services. The VAR Agreement as appears from the terms set out above does not include any agreement to purchase specified goods or even a minimum quantity of identified goods. The VAR Agreement does not impose on the defendant the obligation to pay any of the sums claimed in the summary summons. It cannot therefore be considered that any of the obligations in question at issue in these proceedings arise under a contract which consists exclusively of the VAR Agreement. The obligation on the defendant to pay to the plaintiff any of the amounts claimed in the proceedings did not arise until after the conclusion between the parties of an agreement that the plaintiff would sell to the defendant goods specified in an order from the defendant. The individual contracts for the purchase and sale of specified goods were entered into by the parties pursuant to the VAR Agreement. The price to be paid under the individual contracts was fixed by the terms of the VAR Agreement. Even assuming that certain terms of the VAR Agreement may be implied in the individual contracts for purchase and sale (and I am not so finding) that fact does not alter the conclusion that the obligations in question in these proceedings only came into existence as part of a contract for the purchase and sale of individual goods specified in an order and subsequently, in the relevant invoice. * * * Applying, as I must do an autonomous meaning to a contract for the sale of goods in article (5)(1)(b) of Regulation 44/2001, I am satisfied that the individual contracts for the sale of the goods specified in the invoices come with that meaning. The subject matter of each contract was the sale and purchase of goods.

The final issue is therefore where the goods were delivered or should have been delivered under the terms of each contract for the sale of goods. Mr. Connolly in the affidavit sworn on the 5th October, 2004, on behalf of the plaintiff states that the goods were delivered by the plaintiff to the defendant in Galway by delivering them to the defendant's forwarding agent. He states that the defendant has arranged and paid for shipments of goods from the plaintiff's factory in Galway for over fifteen years. * * * Mr. Connolly exhibits invoices which confirm that dispatches were "via ICS *ex-works*". He also exhibits an order acknowledgment which, as does the invoice, contains an instruction to "deliver to" the defendant at its address in Milan. Mr. Connolly explains this is to specify the ultimate destination of the goods in Italy. None of these facts are disputed.... I have concluded on these facts that the delivery ... took place in Ireland. Hence ... the place of performance of the obligations in question in these proceedings is Ireland and accordingly under article 5(1)(a) the defendant may be sued in the courts of Ireland. There will be an order dismissing the defendant's application to set aside the service of the proceedings herein.

Decision. The Irish court has jurisdiction. Under EU regulations of 2002, a corporate defendant domiciled in an EU country may be sued for non-payment of contracts for the sale of goods in the country where the goods were to be delivered. The relevant contract in this case was not the broader VAR reseller agreement, but the twenty-two individual sales based on orders submitted by the defendant. Those orders were delivered to the defendant's agent in Ireland.

Comment. The Commercial Court of Ireland was created in 2004 as a specialized division of the High Court to ease the heavy burden of commercial cases. It hears disputes involving business documents, insurance, banking and intellectual property, international trade or transport of goods, agency, appeals from regulatory agencies, and other matters.

Jurisdiction in the Internet Age. As electronic commerce brings the world closer together, there will likely be more disputes between parties in distant countries. How will the courts fashion rules for deciding when a party must defend itself against litigation in foreign courts? Just as the meaning of "minimum contacts" adapted to the rise of interstate commerce in the United States over fifty years ago, it is now adapting to the rise of the Internet age. The following case, *Graduate Management Admission Council v. Raju,* involves a situation that many readers may appreciate. In this case, involving several different tort actions including trademark infringement and unfair competition, the Indian defendant must have simply decided not to show up in the United States to answer a complaint against him. Perhaps he thought that the U.S. courts would have no jurisdiction over him if he stayed away. He did not appear and a default judgment was entered against him.

Graduate Management Admission Council v. Raju

241 F. Supp. 2d 589 (2003)

United States District Court (E.D. Va.)

BACKGROUND AND FACTS

Plaintiff GMAC is a nonprofit corporation located in Virginia. It develops and owns all rights to the Graduate Management Admission Test (GMAT), used for admittance to about 1,700 graduate business programs in the United States and elsewhere. The GMAT forms and questions are original, copyrighted materials. GMAC routinely registers its material with the Register of Copyrights and has registered "GMAT" as a trademark with the U.S. Patent and Trademark Office. Defendant Raju is a citizen of India. Raju registered the domain names "gmatplus.com" and "gmatplus.net" in 2000 and operates a Web site under the former name. The Web site sells, for as much as $199, seven books containing "100 percent actual questions" never before published. The books were sold to customers in India, China, Korea, Singapore, France, Australia, Japan, and Taiwan, and to at least two individuals in Virginia. The Web site contained ordering information for customers in the United States. Orders placed on the site were paid for by a money transfer through Western Union or MoneyGram. GMAC filed a complaint against Raju for infringement, cyber piracy, unfair competition, and other torts. The defendant failed to appear, and the court entered a default judgment against him on the basis of having personal jurisdiction over him.

ELLIS, DISTRICT JUDGE

* * *

Under the well-established *International Shoe* formulation, the exercise of personal jurisdiction over a defendant requires that the defendant "have certain minimum contacts with [the forum] such that the maintenance of a suit does not offend 'traditional notions of fair play and substantial justice.'" See *International Shoe Co. v. Washington,* 326 U.S. 310, 316, 66 S. Ct. 154 (1945), *ALS Scan, Inc. v. Digital Service Consultants, Inc.,* 293 F.3d 707, 710 (4th Cir. 2002). Personal jurisdiction can be established under either general or specific jurisdiction. Where, as here, the defendant's contacts with the forum are also the basis for the suit, specific jurisdiction is appropriate. In determining whether specific jurisdiction exists, courts must consider "(1) the extent to which the defendant 'purposefully availed' itself of the privilege of conducting activities in the State; (2) whether the plaintiff's claims arise out of those activities directed at the State; and (3) whether the exercise of personal jurisdiction would be constitutionally 'reasonable.'" *Id.*

As the Fourth Circuit noted in *ALS Scan,* this due process analysis must take account of the modern reality of widespread Internet electronic communications. Accordingly, the Fourth Circuit recently adopted the [*Zippo Manufacturing Co. v. Zippo Dot Com, Inc.,* 952 F. Supp. 1119 (W.D. Pa. 1997)] "sliding-scale" approach for determining whether Internet activity can serve as a basis for personal jurisdiction.

Under the now-familiar *Zippo* test, the likelihood that personal jurisdiction can be constitutionally exercised is determined by focusing on "the nature and the quality of commercial activity that an entity conducts over the Internet." Passive websites, that do "little more" than make information available to users in other jurisdictions, cannot support personal jurisdiction everywhere that information is accessed.

continued

continued

At the other end of the spectrum are situations where a defendant "clearly does business over the Internet," for example through the "knowing and repeated transmission of files over the Internet," which clearly do support personal jurisdiction. In between is the "middle ground" of "interactive Web sites" which are not passive, because they allow a user to exchange information with the host computer, but also do not constitute "clearly doing business over the Internet." To determine whether an "interactive" website is grounds for personal jurisdiction, a court must consider the "level of interactivity and the commercial nature of the exchange of information that occurs on the Web site." * * *

Rule 4(k)(2), *Federal Rules of Civil Procedure* ... provides for personal jurisdiction through nationwide service of process over any defendant provided (i) exercise of jurisdiction is consistent with the Constitution and the laws of the United States, (ii) the claim arises under federal law, and (iii) the defendant is not subject to the jurisdiction of the courts of general jurisdiction of any state. Rule 4(k)(2) was added in 1993 to deal with a gap in federal personal jurisdiction law in situations where a defendant does not reside in the United States, and lacks contacts with a single state sufficient to justify personal jurisdiction, but has enough contacts with the United States as a whole to satisfy the due process requirements. Precisely this situation is presented here. The first element of the Rule 4(k)(2) analysis requires the same minimum contacts due process analysis as is conducted under Rule 4(k)(1)(A), with the significant difference that the relevant forum is the United States as a whole, not an individual State. * * *

In considering Raju's contacts with the United States in this case, the *ALS Scan* test for determining personal jurisdiction based on electronic activities must be adapted for the purpose of national contacts analysis. Substituting the United States as the relevant forum, the test requires a showing in this case (i) that Raju directed his electronic activity into the United States, (ii) that he did so with the manifest intent of engaging in business or other interactions within the United States, and (iii) that his activity creates a potential cause of action in a person within the United States that is cognizable in the United States' courts.

Raju's alleged activity plainly creates a potential cause of action in a person within the United States which is cognizable in federal courts, satisfying the third element of the *ALS Scan* test. GMAC is a Virginia non-profit corporation and thus a "person" within the United States. GMAC's causes of action are based on federal law, and thus are clearly cognizable in federal courts. It is also clear that Raju's intent is to "engage in business," namely the business of selling his GMAT test preparation materials to buyers for a substantial fee. Thus, the second element of the *ALS Scan* test is fulfilled in part. All that remains is a showing that Raju "directed his electronic activity" into the United States, with the intent of engaging in business "within the United States," as required by the first and second elements of the *ALS Scan* test.

The record clearly indicates that Raju directed his activity at the United States market and specifically targeted United States customers. The intended market for business conducted through a website can be determined by considering the apparent focus of the website as a whole. *See Young v. New Haven Advocate,* 315 F.3d 256 (4th Cir. 2002) (Examining the "general thrust and content" of the newspapers' websites, including the local focus of the stories, local advertisements and classifieds, local weather and traffic information, and links to local institutions, in determining that "the overall content of both websites is decidedly local"). The relevant question is whether the website is "designed to attract or serve a [United States] audience." *Id.*

There is ample evidence that Raju targeted the United States market. First, and most significantly, the *GMATplus* site provides specific ordering information for United States customers. The ordering information page directs customers who "live in the United States or Canada" to contact Western Union or MoneyGram, and provides the toll free numbers for use by those customers.... No other countries apart from the United States and Canada are mentioned by name on the ordering information page. Thus, ordering information for customers in the United States (and Canada) is provided first and with more specificity than for customers from other countries. Second, the ordering information page informs customers that materials will "reach most parts of the world (including the US) within 3–5 working days." Third, the prices for the products are listed in dollars, presumably United States dollars. Fourth, three of the six testimonials are purportedly from United States citizens. Fifth, the promotional text on the site suggests that Raju's materials will allow American citizens and others to catch up with test takers from "India, China, Korea, Japan, and Taiwan," who purportedly score

continued

continued

better on the test as a group than "their American or European counterparts ... because most of them have access to 100 percent of unpublished previous questions in these countries." Finally, Raju confirmed his apparent intent to serve United States customers by shipping his materials to the two Virginia residents mentioned in the record.

In sum, it is quite clear upon review of the *GMATplus* website and the record as a whole that while Raju may have aimed his website at the entire, worldwide market of GMAT test takers, he specifically directed his electronic activity at the United States market and did in fact ship materials in the United States. Thus, GMAT has shown under the *ALS Scan* test that Raju "directed his electronic activity into [the United States] with the manifested intent of engaging in business ... within [the United States]," satisfying the remaining elements of the *ALS Scan* test. It follows that the exercise of personal jurisdiction based on nationwide contacts under 4(k)(2) comports with constitutional due process requirements in this case. * * * To find otherwise would not only frustrate GMAC's attempts in this case to vindicate its rights under United States law, by requiring GMAC to turn to foreign courts to vindicate those rights against a likely elusive defendant, it would also provide a blueprint whereby other individuals bent on violating United States trademark and copyright laws could do so without risking suit in a United States court.

Decision. Raju had sufficient minimum contacts with the United States to justify personal jurisdiction over him there under the federal rules. The magistrate judge was directed to take whatever steps deemed necessary to determine the appropriate relief to be awarded GMAC in this matter.

Obtaining Jurisdiction by Service of Process. As we have learned, a court must have personal jurisdiction over individuals or corporate entities before they can be made to appear and defend a civil case. Personal jurisdiction is obtained through lawful service of process. Without proper service, any judgment that might be taken will not be enforceable. This is especially problematic when attempting to enforce a judgment internationally. To illustrate, imagine that an American plaintiff files suit in a U.S. court against a resident of France on a contract that was performed in the United States. Assume that the plaintiff's attorney is able to obtain service of process upon the defendant in France. The French citizen does not appear in the United States and a default judgment is taken. When the American attempts to enforce the U.S. judgment in the courts of France, the defendant will claim that the method of service of process upon him was unsatisfactory under French law. If the French courts agree, the plaintiff's judgment may be worth nothing if the defendant's only assets are in France. Thus, international lawyers trying to obtain jurisdiction over a foreign defendant are advised to consult an attorney in the defendant's country and to follow the requirements of both U.S. and French law to the letter.

double standards must be followed

Making service of process upon a foreign defendant is addressed in *The Hague Convention on the Service Abroad of Judicial and Extra-Judicial Documents in Civil and Commercial Matters,* in force in about seventy-five countries. Authorized methods of service are different even for countries that are members of the treaty. Some countries permit service through the use of registered or certified mail, with a return receipt signed by the defendant being served, although other countries (e.g., Germany, Norway, Egypt, China, and others) do not permit this method. Some countries permit personal service by an agent or attorney of the plaintiff located in the defendant's country who signs an "affidavit of service" at a nearby U.S. embassy affirming that he has served the defendant with notice and a copy of the complaint. Most countries require the complaint to be in the local language as well as in English. Perhaps the safest method, but one that can cause very long delays (up to a year, according to the U.S. State Department), is a formal request for service made through a *letter rogatory* (a "letter of request" sent through diplomatic channels) that results in personal service on the defendant by the courts of the country in which he is found. Defendants located in countries not parties to this convention can also be served with process with a letter rogatory. Letters rogatory are discussed later in this chapter.

Venue

Jurisdiction is often confused with the concept of venue. *Venue* refers to the geographical location of a court of competent jurisdiction where a case can be heard. While the courts of several different states, or countries, may have proper jurisdiction, the concept of venue helps decide which one of these should actually hear the case. For instance, in some civil lawsuits between citizens of different states, we know that the federal courts may have jurisdiction. But in which federal district should it be tried? Imagine an automobile accident in which the passengers of one car are residents of Pennsylvania, while the driver of the other vehicle is a resident of North Carolina, and the accident occurs while they're both on vacation in California. We know that jurisdiction is proper in the federal courts (and it may also be proper in some state courts). But we certainly would not expect that the case could be tried in a federal court located in Montana. Federal rules generally permit the case to be heard either where all of the plaintiffs reside, where all of the defendants reside, or where the cause of action arose. (In complex transnational litigation, it is not unusual that courts in several countries might attempt to exercise jurisdiction over the matter.) While typically the plaintiff will initially choose where to file its suit, it is not unusual for a defendant to request a change of venue, asking that the case be removed to a location that is more convenient and that has a closer connection to the facts of the particular case.

Forum Non Conveniens

The legal doctrine of *forum non conveniens* (meaning "inconvenient forum") refers to the discretionary power of a court to refuse to hear a case, even though it otherwise has proper jurisdiction and venue, because a court in another jurisdiction or location would be more convenient and justice would be better served. According to this doctrine, whenever a case is properly heard in the courts of more than one jurisdiction, it should be heard in the jurisdiction that is more convenient and has the closer connection to the cause of action that led to the case. In deciding on where to hear a case, the courts will examine both "private factors" (factors affecting the convenience of the parties and their ability to pursue their claims) and "public factors" (factors related to the public interest). For example, it may be more convenient to hear a case where the action arose, where witnesses and evidence are located, where the parties reside, or in the state or country whose law applies to the case.

Imagine an airline disaster in the United States, with many plaintiffs and one airline. Venue may be proper in any number of locations, including the airline's principal place of business. But would it not be more convenient to hold the trial where the crash occurred? After all, that is where the wreckage is located, and where the controllers and other witnesses live and work. *Forum non conveniens* is applied by courts in the United States, as well as in many other countries. In the United States, it is applied by the federal courts in determining where to hear lawsuits between citizens of different states. It is also used in determining whether an international case should be heard by U.S. courts or by the courts of some other country. It is not unusual for one of the parties to a case to ask a court to transfer the case to another judicial district or location for reasons of convenience. The factors generally considered were described by the U.S. Supreme Court in *Gulf Oil v. Gilbert,* 330 U.S. 501 (1947).

> Important considerations are the relative ease of access to sources of proof; availability of compulsory process for attendance of unwilling [witnesses] and the cost of obtaining attendance of willing witnesses; ... and all other practical problems that make trial of a case easy, expeditious and inexpensive. There may also be questions as to the enforceability of a judgment if one is obtained.... It is often said that the plaintiff may not, by choice of an inconvenient forum, "vex," "harass," or "oppress" the defendant by inflicting upon him expense or trouble not necessary to his own right to pursue his remedy. But unless the balance is strongly in favor of the defendant, the plaintiff's choice of forum should rarely be disturbed.... There is a local interest in having localized controversies decided at home. There is an appropriateness, too, in having the trial of a diversity case in a forum that is at home with the state law that must govern the case, rather than having a court in some other forum untangle problems in conflict of laws, and in law foreign to itself.

Forum Shopping. It is not unusual that requests to transfer on the basis of *forum non conveniens* are in truth attempts by counsel to "shop around" for a better legal deal. They may be looking for a law that is more favorable to their case or for a jury that might be more sympathetic to their side. After all, in federal lawsuits between residents of different states, such as in tort cases, the federal courts apply the law of the state in which they sit.

Although there are procedural rules that discourage "forum shopping," it still weighs on the minds of most trial lawyers. The same is true, perhaps even more so, in international cases. In the following case, *Iragorri v. United Technologies,* the appellate court had to decide whether a case for wrongful death should be heard in Connecticut or in Cali, Colombia. The plaintiffs wanted the case heard in Connecticut because, as one would expect, the possibility of winning a large damage award was much greater than in Colombia.

In re Union Carbide Gas Plant Disaster at Bhopal. In Chapter One, we read about the Bhopal disaster litigation. After a chemical leak at a plant in India killed almost 2,000 people, Indian citizens filed suit in the United States against Union Carbide. At one point, almost 145 legal actions on behalf of some 200,000 plaintiffs had been consolidated for trial in federal court in New York. However, the case was subsequently dismissed on the basis of *forum non conveniens* in favor of the case being heard in India. The judge

Iragorri v. United Technologies Corp. & Otis Elevator Co.

274 F. 3d 65 (2001)

United States Court of Appeals (2d Cir.)

BACKGROUND AND FACTS

Iragorri and his family had been residents of Florida since 1981, and naturalized citizens of the United States since 1989. In 1993, while visiting his mother in Cali, Colombia, he fell to his death through an open elevator shaft. Iragorri's children had been attending school there as exchange students from their Florida high school. His surviving wife and children brought this action in United States District Court in Connecticut for damages against two American companies, Otis Elevator and its parent corporation, United Technologies. They alleged that employees of International Elevator had negligently wedged a door open with a screwdriver during repairs, leaving the shaft open. International Elevator was a Maine corporation doing business in South America. Both Otis and United had their principal place of business in Connecticut. The complaint alleged that Otis and United were liable because (1) International had acted as their agent in negligently repairing the elevator, and (2) Otis and United were liable under Connecticut's products liability statute for the defective design and manufacture of the elevator which had been sold and installed by their affiliate, Otis of Brazil. Otis and United moved to dismiss the case on the basis of *forum non conveniens,* arguing that it should be heard in the Colombian courts. The District Court dismissed the case, and the plaintiffs brought this appeal.

OPINION BY PIERRE N. LEVAL AND JOSÉ A. CABRANES, CIRCUIT JUDGES FOR THE COURT SITTING *EN BANC*

We regard the Supreme Court's instructions that (1) a plaintiff's choice of her home forum should be given great deference, while (2) a foreign resident's choice of a U.S. forum should receive less consideration, as representing consistent applications of a broader principle under which the degree of deference to be given to a plaintiff's choice of forum moves on a sliding scale depending on several relevant considerations.

The Supreme Court explained in *Piper Aircraft Co. v. Reyno,* 454 U.S. 235, 102 S. Ct. 252 (1981) that the reason we give deference to a plaintiff's choice of her home forum is because it is presumed to be convenient. ("When the home forum has been chosen, it is reasonable to assume that this choice is convenient.") In contrast, when a foreign plaintiff chooses a U.S. forum, it "is much less reasonable" to presume that the choice was made for convenience. In such circumstances, a plausible likelihood exists that the selection was made for forum-shopping reasons, such as the perception that United States courts award higher damages than are common in other countries. Even if the U.S. district was not chosen for such forum-shopping reasons, there is

continued

continued

nonetheless little reason to assume that it is convenient for a foreign plaintiff.

Based on the Supreme Court's guidance, our understanding of how courts should address the degree of deference to be given to a plaintiff's choice of a U.S. forum is essentially as follows: The more it appears that a domestic or foreign plaintiff's choice of forum has been dictated by reasons that the law recognizes as valid, the greater the deference that will be given to the plaintiff's forum choice. Stated differently, the greater the plaintiff's or the lawsuit's bona fide connection to the United States and to the forum of choice and the more it appears that considerations of convenience favor the conduct of the lawsuit in the United States, the more difficult it will be for the defendant to gain dismissal for *forum non conveniens*. Thus, factors that argue against *forum non conveniens* dismissal include the convenience of the plaintiff's residence in relation to the chosen forum, the availability of witnesses or evidence to the forum district, the defendant's amenability to suit in the forum district, the availability of appropriate legal assistance, and other reasons relating to convenience or expense. On the other hand, the more it appears that the plaintiff's choice of a U.S. forum was motivated by forum-shopping reasons—such as attempts to win a tactical advantage resulting from local laws that favor the plaintiff's case, the habitual generosity of juries in the United States or in the forum district, the plaintiff's popularity or the defendant's unpopularity in the region, or the inconvenience and expense to the defendant resulting from litigation in that forum—the less deference the plaintiff's choice commands and, consequently, the easier it becomes for the defendant to succeed on a *forum non conveniens* motion by showing that convenience would be better served by litigating in another country's courts.

* * *

We believe that the District Court in the case before us, lacking the benefit of our most recent opinions concerning *forum non conveniens,* did not accord appropriate deference to the plaintiff's chosen forum. Although the plaintiffs had resided temporarily in Bogota at the time of Mauricio Iragorri's accident, it appears that they had returned to their permanent, long-time domicile in Florida by the time the suit was filed. The fact that the children and their mother had spent a few school terms in Colombia on a foreign exchange program seems to us to present little reason for discrediting the bona fides of their choice of the Connecticut forum. Heightened deference to the plaintiffs' chosen forum usually applies even where a plaintiff has temporarily or intermittently resided in the foreign jurisdiction. So far as the record reveals, there is little indication that the plaintiffs chose the defendants' principal place of business for forum-shopping reasons. Plaintiffs were apparently unable to obtain jurisdiction in Florida over the original third defendant, International, but could obtain jurisdiction over all three in Connecticut. It appears furthermore that witnesses and documentary evidence relevant to plaintiffs' defective design theory are to be found at the defendants' installations in Connecticut. As we have explained, "live testimony of key witnesses is necessary so that the trier of fact can assess the witnesses' demeanor." *Alfadda v. Fenn,* 159 F.3d 41, 48 (2d Cir. 1998). Also, in assessing where the greater convenience lies, the District Court must of course consider how great would be the inconvenience and difficulty imposed on the plaintiffs were they forced to litigate in Cali. Among other factors, plaintiffs claim that they fear for their safety in Cali and that various witnesses on both sides may be unwilling to travel to Cali; if these concerns are warranted, they appear highly relevant to the balancing inquiry that the District Court must conduct.

Decision. Remanded to the District Court for a determination in accordance with this opinion. In deciding whether to hear the case, the District Court should consider the degree of deference to which plaintiffs' choice is entitled, the hardships of litigating in Colombia versus the United States, and the public interest factors involved.

gave many reasons for the decision: The Indian legal system was better able to determine the cause of accident and assign liability; the overwhelming majority of witnesses and evidence were in India; the records of plant design, safety procedures, and training were located in India; most records were not in English and many witnesses did not speak English; the court would be unable to compel witnesses to appear and the cost to transport them to the United States would be prohibitive; visits to the plant might be necessary; there was the likelihood that the U.S. court would have to apply Indian law (the tort law of the jurisdiction where the tort occurred); and the undue burden of this immense litigation would unfairly tax an American tribunal (see Exhibit 3.2). Also considered was the fact that India had a substantial interest in the accident and the outcome of the litigation: The Indian government and Indian citizens owned 49 percent of the plant, with Union Carbide owning the rest. As the judge expressed in the opinion:

> To retain litigation in this forum would be another example of imperialism, another situation in which an established sovereign inflicted its rules, its standards and values on a developing nation. This Court declines to play such a role. The Union of India is a world power in 1986, and its courts have the proven capacity to mete out fair and equal justice. To deprive the Indian judiciary of this opportunity to stand tall before the world and to pass judgment on behalf of its own people would be to revive a history of subservience and subjugation from which India has emerged. India and its people can and must vindicate their claims before the independent and legitimate judiciary created there since the Independence of 1947. This Court defers to the adequacy and ability of the courts of India. Their interest in the sad events ... in the City of Bhopal, State of Madhya Pradesh, Union of India, is not subject to question or challenge. *In re Union Carbide Gas Plant Disaster at Bhopal,* 634 F. Supp. 842 (S.D.N.Y. 1986).

The case was settled in India in 1989 prior to trial when Union Carbide agreed to pay $470 million in compensation, although the government of India is still attempting to assert criminal jurisdiction over former Union Carbide officers.

EXHIBIT 3.2

Why Do Plaintiffs Seek Access to the U.S. Legal System?

- Contingent fee lawyers
- Jury trials in civil cases
- Larger jury awards
- Class action suits permitted
- Discovery process is wide open
- Punitive damages are permitted
- Treble damages in antitrust cases
- Award of attorney fees possible
- Ability to attach property in United States
- Integrity of judicial system

Forum Selection Clauses

Businesspeople and lawyers negotiating international contracts can avoid much of the uncertainty over venue by including a forum selection clause in their contracts. A *forum selection clause* is a provision in a contract that fixes in advance the jurisdiction in which any disputes will be arbitrated or litigated. It provides certainty because the parties know where and how a dispute will be resolved in the event of a breach. One of the major advantages of these clauses is that they eliminate the last-minute attempt by lawyers to go "forum shopping" by filing suits in jurisdictions that offer the best law for their case. The last chance for forum shopping may very well be during contract negotiations. This allows both parties to agree on a forum, perhaps the courts of a certain country, which they find acceptable. Of course, the reality is that these clauses are often not open for negotiation at all—the party to the contract with the greatest bargaining power will simply include a fine print provision calling for disputes to be resolved in the courts of the country where it is located. (This is discussed further in the next chapter when we consider "standard term" contracts.)

Historically, any attempt by private parties to control jurisdiction was viewed with hostility by the courts as an effort to usurp their authority. However, the realities of the international marketplace and the need to reduce uncertainty in a dispute have persuaded many courts to accept forum selection clauses. Today, they are generally accepted as valid provided that the forum chosen has some reasonable connection to the transaction. In the following case, *M/S Bremen v. Zapata,* 407 U.S. 1 (1972), the United States Supreme Court upheld a clause calling for disputes to be resolved before the English courts, noting that U.S. courts can no longer remain geocentric in light of modern-day international trade.

CONFLICT OF LAWS

As a general rule, courts apply the law in force in their jurisdiction to the cases before them. In the

M/S Bremen v. Zapata Off-Shore Co.

407 U.S. 1 (1972)

United States Supreme Court

BACKGROUND AND FACTS

In 1967, Zapata, a Houston-based corporation, entered into a contract with Unterweser, a German corporation, to tow Zapata's drilling rig from Louisiana to Ravenna, Italy. The contract the parties signed contained the clause "Any dispute arising must be heard before the London Court of Justice." During a storm, the rig was damaged, and Zapata instructed Unterweser's tug, the *Bremen,* to tow instead to Tampa, Florida, the nearest port. Immediately thereafter, Zapata filed suit in federal district court in Tampa, Florida, on the basis of admiralty jurisdiction, seeking $3,500,000 damages *in personam* against Unterweser and *in rem* against the *Bremen*. Unterweser moved to dismiss for:

1. Lack of jurisdiction on the basis of the forum clause
2. *Forum non conveniens* (not a convenient forum)
3. A stay of action pending resolution in the London Court of Justice

Unterweser filed suit in London for breach of contract. The U.S. District Court and Court of Appeals had denied the motion to stay, thus allowing the case to proceed in U.S. court despite the forum selection clause. Unterweser filed a petition of certiorari to the Supreme Court.

CHIEF JUSTICE BURGER

We hold, with the six dissenting members of the Court of Appeals, that far too little weight and effect were given to the forum clause in resolving this controversy. For at least two decades we have witnessed an expansion of overseas commercial activities by business enterprises based in the United States. The barrier of distance that once tended to confine a business concern to a modest territory no longer does so. Here we see an American company with special expertise contracting with a foreign company to tow a complex machine thousands of miles across seas and oceans. The expansion of American business and industry will hardly be encouraged if, notwithstanding solemn contracts, we insist on a parochial concept that all disputes must be resolved under our laws and in our courts. Absent a contract forum, the considerations relied on by the Court of Appeals would be persuasive reasons for holding an American forum convenient in the traditional sense, but in an era of expanding world trade and commerce, [prior cases that have decided otherwise] have little place and would be a heavy hand indeed on the future development of international commercial dealings by Americans. We cannot have trade and commerce in world markets and international waters exclusively on our terms, governed by our laws, and resolved in our courts.

Forum-selection clauses have historically not been favored by American courts. Many courts, federal and state, have declined to enforce such clauses on the ground that they were "contrary to public policy," or that their effect was to "oust the jurisdiction" of the court. Although this view apparently still has considerable acceptance, other courts are tending to adopt a more hospitable attitude toward forum-selection clauses. This view, advanced in the well-reasoned dissenting opinion in the instant case, is that such clauses are prima facie valid and should be enforced unless enforcement is shown by the resisting party to be "unreasonable" under the circumstances. We believe this is the correct doctrine to be followed by federal district courts sitting in admiralty....

This approach is substantially what is followed in other common-law countries including England. It is the view advanced by noted scholars and that adopted by the *Restatement of the Conflict of Laws*. It accords with ancient concepts of freedom of contract and reflects an appreciation of the expanding horizons of American contractors who seek business in all parts of the world.... The choice of that forum was made in an arm's length negotiation by experienced and sophisticated businessmen, and absent some compelling and countervailing reason it should be honored by the parties and enforced by the courts.

The elimination of all such uncertainties by agreeing in advance on a forum acceptable to both parties is an indispensable element in international trade, commerce, and contracting. There is strong evidence that the forum clause was a vital part of the agreement, and it would be unrealistic to think that the parties did not conduct their negotiations, including fixing the monetary terms, with the consequences of the forum clause figuring prominently in their calculations.

continued

continued

Thus, in the light of present-day commercial realities and expanding international trade we conclude that the forum clause should control absent a strong showing that it should be set aside. Although their opinions are not altogether explicit, it seems reasonably clear that the District Court and the Court of Appeals placed the burden on Unterweser to show that London would be a more convenient forum than Tampa, although the contract expressly resolved that issue. The correct approach would have been to enforce the forum clause specifically unless Zapata could clearly show that enforcement would be unreasonable and unjust, or that the clause was invalid for such reasons as fraud or overreaching. Accordingly, the case must be remanded for reconsideration.

Decision. Vacated and remanded for proceedings consistent with the opinion. The Court vacated the Court of Appeals judgment stating, "Thus in light of present-day commercial realities and expanding international trade we conclude that the forum clause should control absent a strong showing that it should be set aside."

Comment. The Court noted the possible reasons that a forum selection clause could be unenforceable: (1) if it contravenes strong public policy and (2) if the forum is seriously inconvenient. These reasons still hold today. Other reasons forum selection clauses may be ignored by the courts are because parties are of unequal bargaining power; counsel was not consulted; the clause was written in a foreign language; the clause violates federal law; or circumstances have changed (where the forum is the site of a revolution hostile to one party's country—for example, a forum selection of Iran after the Iranian revolution—could be held invalid). Many other countries also support the validity of forum selection clauses, including Austria, England, France, Germany, Italy, and many Latin American and Scandinavian countries.

United States, state courts usually apply their own state's law. Federal courts hearing diversity of citizenship cases, such as breach of contract or tort actions between residents of different states, generally apply the law of the state in which they sit (unless a federal statute or treaty controls). But these are general rules only, and there are many cases where courts apply the law of another state, or even of a foreign country. The term *conflict of laws* refers to the rules by which courts determine which jurisdiction's laws apply to a case and how differences between laws will be reconciled. In turn, the choice of law will ultimately determine whether a court has jurisdiction, the rights and liabilities of the parties, and how a judgment or monetary award will be enforced.

The *Restatement (Second)* of the Conflict of Laws

Conflict of laws rules are some of the most complex in procedural law, with different jurisdictions following different rules. However, the concepts found in the *Restatement (Second) of the Conflict of Laws,* drafted under the auspices of the American Law Institute in 1971, provide a clear and widely accepted explanation of these rules. As a general rule, courts will apply the law of the state, country, or jurisdiction that has the closest relationship to the action before them. The *Restatement (Second)* addresses different types of actions, including actions for breach of contract and for tort.

Contracts. It has been said that deciding which law governs a contract is like finding its "center of gravity." In other words, in the absence of an agreement by the parties, contracts should be governed by the law of the jurisdiction that has the most significant relationship to the transaction and the parties. The *Restatement (Second)* sets out five factors to be considered: (1) the place of contracting (i.e., where the acceptance took place); (2) the place where the contract was negotiated (particularly if the parties met and negotiated at length); (3) the place where the contract will be performed; (4) the location of the subject matter of the contract; and (5) the domicile, residence, nationality, place of incorporation, and place of business of the parties. If the contract was both negotiated and performed in the same jurisdiction, then the law of that jurisdiction will apply (except for contracts involving real estate or life insurance, which have special rules). Of these, the place of negotiation and performance is often the most important factor, especially if both parties are performing within the same jurisdiction. The place of contracting and the domicile of the parties, while not critical by themselves, are important when supporting other factors.

Torts. Traditionally, the law in the United States and in most countries has been that tort actions, including personal injuries, product liability, wrongful death, fraud, business torts such as libel, and others, should be governed by the law of the place where the injury or damage occurred (known as *lex loci delicti*). In the United States, many courts are adopting the broader view taken by the *Restatement (Second):* that tort liability should be governed by the law of the jurisdiction that has the most significant relationship to the tort and to the parties. The *Restatement (Second)* lists the following factors to be considered: (1) the place where the injury occurred; (2) the place where the conduct causing the injury occurred; (3) the domicile, residence, nationality, place of incorporation, and place of business of the parties; and (4) the place where the relationship between the parties is centered. The courts of New York apply the law of the state or country that has the "greatest interest" in having its law applied.

Choice of Law Clauses

Choice of law clauses are contract provisions that stipulate the country or jurisdiction whose law will apply in interpreting the contract or enforcing its terms. Lawyers are quite aware that laws can be very different from state to state or country to country and will consider this in contract negotiations. Indeed, the choice of law may well become a bargaining point in international contract negotiations. As a general rule, the choice of law selection will be upheld as long as there is a reasonable relationship between the transaction and the jurisdiction chosen. As one court put it, parties today have several choices of law that could apply to their dealings, but they could not choose to have their disputes decided under the ancient *Code of Hammurabi*. For example, imagine a Japanese manufacturer who enters into a contract with a buyer in New York for the shipment of goods to New York. Both parties have offices in California and sign the contract there. A clause making California law applicable to the contract would be valid, because there is a sufficient nexus, or connection, between the contract and the state of California.

The Application of Foreign Law in American Courts

If an American court determines that it should apply foreign law to the case, how does it know what that law is? At one time foreign law was required to be proven in court as fact. Today, in the federal courts, that has changed. Courts are free to determine as a matter of law what the foreign law is. The federal courts will follow the *Federal Rules of Civil Procedure*. Rule 44.1 states that

> A party who intends to raise an issue concerning the law of a foreign country shall give notice by pleadings or other reasonable written notice. The court, in determining foreign law, may consider any relevant material or source, including testimony, whether or not submitted by a party or admissible under the *Federal Rules of Evidence*. The court's determination shall be treated as a ruling on a question of law.

Accordingly, judges may conduct their own research on foreign law, they may request briefs provided by the parties' lawyers, or they may rely on the testimony of foreign lawyers in or out of court. The following case, *Finnish Fur Sales Co., Ltd. v. Juliette Shulof Furs, Inc.,* involves a U.S. court in New York that had to decide a case under the laws of Finland. It offers an explanation of how a choice of law clause works and shows how a U.S. court applies the law of a foreign country to resolve a contract dispute. Notice the interplay of federal and state law and the application of Rule 44.1.

Judicial Assistance: Discovery and the Collection of Evidence

Countries have their own rules governing pretrial discovery, obtaining access to documents and other evidence, and the admissibility of that evidence at trial. In the United States, this is governed by the *Federal Rules of Civil Procedure*. The United States has very liberal rules permitting the pretrial oral deposition of witnesses out of court and the submission of written interrogatories that the parties must answer under oath. The courts have broad subpoena powers over documents and other

China= closed legal system

tangible evidence. When that evidence is located outside the jurisdiction of the court, such as in a foreign country, special problems arise. The *1970 Hague Convention on the Taking of Evidence Abroad in Civil or Commercial Matters* provides methods for collecting foreign evidence via formal requests made by the courts of one country to the courts of another country through diplomatic channels (such as the government Ministry of Justice). Although only thirty countries are party to the convention, most countries cooperate in the collection of civil evidence, some to a greater or lesser degree than others.

Letters Rogatory. When a court in one country wants to make a request of a court in another country for judicial assistance, it does so in writing through a formal request known as *letters rogatory* (letters of request). It can be used to request a deposition, a response to written interrogatories, or the production of documents. Most countries do not have liberal rules of discovery like the United States; for example, many countries do not permit oral depositions to be taken before trial.

Japan and China are notable examples. China has declared that it does not recognize the right of foreign attorneys to take depositions, even of willing witnesses. Any foreigner caught attempting to do so without prior authorization is subject to arrest, detention, or deportation. Moreover, only certain government officials may administer an oath, and anyone else caught doing so is committing a crime. Requests for obtaining evidence from U.S. courts must be addressed in the form of letters rogatory to the Chinese Ministry of

Finnish Fur Sales Co., Ltd. v. Juliette Shulof Furs, Inc.

770 F. Supp. 139 (1991)

United States District Court (S.D.N.Y.)

BACKGROUND AND FACTS

Juliette Shulof Furs (JSF) is a New York corporation that has been in the fur dealing business for 15 years. George Shulof, an officer of JSF, attended two auctions conducted by Finnish Fur Sales (FFS) in Finland in 1987. He purchased more than $1.2 million worth of skins at the auctions. Shulof attended each auction and was the actual bidder. The conditions of sale were listed in the auction catalog in English. JSF paid for the majority of the skins purchased, leaving an unpaid balance of $202,416.85. FFS brought this action to recover the contract price of the skins from Shulof, claiming he is personally liable for payment under Finnish law. Shulof responds that he was acting only as the agent for JSF and that under New York law he is not personally responsible for the contracts of the corporation he represented at the auction.

LEISURE, DISTRICT JUDGE

Section 4 of the *Conditions of Sale* provides:

> Any person bidding at the auction shall stand surety as for his own debt until full payment is made for purchased merchandise. If he has made the bid on behalf of another person, he is jointly and severally liable with the person for the purchase.

George Shulof denies any personal liability on the grounds that the provision is unenforceable under both New York and Finnish law.

Section 15 of the *Conditions of Sale* provides that "[t]hese conditions are governed by Finnish law." Choice of law clauses are routinely enforced by the courts of this Circuit, "if there is a reasonable basis for the choice." *Morgan Guaranty Trust Co. v. Republic of Palau*, 693 F. Supp. 1479, 1494 (S.D.N.Y. 1988). New York courts also generally defer to choice of law clauses if the state or country whose law is thus selected has sufficient contacts with the transaction. Under those circumstances, "New York law requires the court to honor the parties' choice insofar as matters of substance are concerned, so long as fundamental policies of New York law are not thereby violated." *Woodling v. Garrett Corp.*, 813 F.2d 543, 551 (2d Cir. 1987). Finland's contacts with the transactions at issue are substantial, rendering the choice of law clause enforceable unless a strong public policy of New York is impaired by the application of Finnish law. Plaintiff FFS is a Finnish resident, which held

continued

continued

auctions of Finnish-bred furs in Finland. All bids were made in Finnish marks, with payment and delivery to take place in Finland. Mr. Shulof voluntarily traveled to Finland in order to partake in FFS's auctions. Thus, virtually all of the significant events related to these transactions took place in Finland. Finland also has an obvious interest in applying its law to events taking place within its borders relating to an important local industry, and in applying uniform law to numerous transactions with bidders from foreign countries.

Mr. Shulof argues that the choice of Finnish law provision should be held invalid.... According to Mr. Shulof, New York has the following interests in this action: it is the place of business and of incorporation of JSF; FFS has a representative with a New York office who communicated with Mr. Shulof about the fur auctions; and that New York is, allegedly, "the economic and design center for the world's fur industry." Mr. Shulof also argues that, under New York law, Section 4 of the *Conditions of Sale* would be invalid as contravening New York's policy against imposing personal liability on corporate officers....

Under Federal Rule of Civil Procedure 44.1, a court, "in determining foreign law, may consider any relevant material or source, including testimony." Both parties have submitted affidavits of Finnish attorneys on the issue of Mr. Shulof's liability under Finnish law. FFS's expert, Vesa Majamaa, a Doctor of Law and Professor of the Faculty of Law at the University of Helsinki, gives as his opinion that the provision of Section 4 of the *Conditions of Sale* imposing personal liability upon the bidder, regardless of whether he bids on behalf of another, is valid both as a term of the particular auctions at issue and as a general principle of Finnish and Scandinavian auction law. According to Majamaa, it is "commonly accepted in Scandinavia that a bidder, by making a bid, accepts those conditions which have been announced at the auction." Further, he states: According to the Finnish judicial system, no one may use ignorance of the law as a defense.... This same principle is also ... applicable when the matter in question concerns ... terms of trade.... If the buyer is not familiar with the terms observed in an auction, he is obliged to familiarize himself with them. In this respect, failure to inquire will result in a loss for the buyer.... If a businessman who has been and is still active in the fields falls back on his ignorance in a case in which he has been offered an actual opportunity to find out about the terms of the auction, his conduct could be considered to be contrary to equitable business practices [and] the "Principle of Good Faith." ... Majamaa also notes that under Danish law, which he maintains would be applied by a Finnish court in the absence of Finnish decisional or legislative law on point, "It is taken for granted that someone who has bid on merchandise on someone else's account is responsible for the transaction, as he would be for his own obligation, together with his superior.... Hence the auction buyer's responsibility is not secondary, as is, for example, the responsibility of a guarantor." ...

Majamaa also opines that the terms of Section 4 are neither unexpected nor harsh because "the liability has been clearly presented in the terms of the auction," and because the same rule of liability would apply under Finnish law in the absence of any provision.

... [T]he Court concludes that a Finnish court would enforce the provisions of Section 4 and impose personal responsibility upon George Shulof for his auction bids on behalf of JSF.

Moreover, even if a New York court would not enforce such a provision in a transaction to which New York law clearly applied, this Court does not find New York's interest in protecting one of its residents against personal liability as a corporate officer to constitute so fundamental a policy that New York courts would refuse to enforce a contrary rule of foreign law. Indeed, the New York Court of Appeals has held that "foreign-based rights should be enforced unless the judicial enforcement of such a contract would be the approval of a transaction which is inherently vicious, wicked or immoral, and shocking to the prevailing moral sense." *Intercontinental Hotels Corp. v. Golden,* 15 N.Y.2d. 9, 13, 254 N.Y.S.2d 527, 529, 203 N.E.2d 210 (1964). Given the lack of a clear conflict with either New York law or policy, this Court concludes that a New York court would apply Finnish law to the issue before the Court. The Court also notes that a similar result has often been reached under New York conflict rules even in the absence of a contractual choice of law clause. Thus, Mr. Shulof must be held jointly and severally liable with JSF for any damages owed to FFS for the furs purchased.

Decision. Under conflict of law rules, the U.S. court applied Finnish law to hold the defendant Shulof personally liable for the contract debt.

Foreign Affairs. The last time a U.S. party was permitted to take a deposition in China was in 1989.

Japan has a slightly more liberal view. According to the U.S. State Department, Japanese law permits the taking of a deposition of a willing witness for use by a court in the United States, but only if the deposition is presided over by a U.S. consular officer pursuant to a court order and is conducted on U.S. consular premises. It is a violation of Japanese law for anyone to travel to Japan for the purpose of taking a deposition unless they have a special "deposition visa" from a Japanese consulate.

Some countries, on the other hand, such as Canada, are very cooperative with foreign requests for judicial assistance. According to the U.S. State Department, there are no rules in Canada that prohibit taking evidence from a willing person in private civil matters. Parties in a private civil case in the United States may arrange to depose a willing witness in Canada without prior consultation or permission from the Canadian government. The party seeking to take the deposition must arrange for a court reporter or stenographer and facilities in which to take the deposition.

Antisuit Injunctions

U.S. courts have the power to enjoin a party over whom they have jurisdiction from bringing a lawsuit in a foreign country. This is known as an *antisuit injunction*. The purposes are to prevent a party already involved in U.S. litigation from circumventing the American court system and American law, preventing the other party in the dispute from being subjected to undue harassment and expense, and protecting the integrity of American courts. While this may seem to invite a confrontation between U.S. and foreign courts, the injunction is not directed at any foreign court but at the individual involved. A U.S. court may enjoin foreign litigation if at the time it has jurisdiction over the party in a case currently pending before it, if the parties are the same in both cases, and if the issues are so similar that resolution of the domestic case will resolve the issues that could be brought in the foreign case. As of 2003, there was some disagreement between the U.S. Courts of Appeal on how to apply these rules, with some circuits being less willing than others to grant injunctions. A case illustrating the more liberal view is *Kaepa, Inc. v. Achilles Corp.*, 76 F.3d 624 (5th Cir. 1966). Achilles, a Japanese corporation, signed a contract with a provision calling for disputes to be settled in Texas and under Texas law. Achilles then filed suit in Japan. Kaepa requested an antisuit injunction. In permitting the injunction, the appellate court said, "The prosecution of the Japanese action would entail an absurd duplication of effort, and would result in unwarranted inconvenience, expense and vexation. Achilles' belated ploy ... smacks of cynicism, harassment and delay."

Enforcement of Foreign Judgments

At the close of a judicial proceeding, a winning party might obtain a judgment for damages or some other award. Once a judgment is taken against a defendant it must be enforced. If necessary, it can be done through a legal process, including the seizure of the losing party's property. But what if a judgment is won in a state or country where that party has no money or property? This is where some good detective work comes in handy. In the United States, judgments taken against a party by a court of competent jurisdiction in one state will be enforced by all other states under the *Full Faith and Credit Provision* of the U.S. Constitution. This provision, however, does not apply to the recognition of judgments from foreign countries. Nevertheless, as a general rule, the judgments of foreign countries will be recognized by the courts of the United States when the requirements of comity between nations are satisfied.

Many states have statutes specifically permitting the enforcement of foreign judgments. About thirty states have adopted the *Uniform Recognition of Foreign Money Judgments Act*. U.S. courts will usually recognize a foreign judgment based on a full and fair trial on the merits of the case by an impartial tribunal. The foreign court must have had jurisdiction over the subject matter and over the parties or property involved, and the defendant must have been given notice of the action and an opportunity to appear. Judgments will not be enforced where they violate public policy or were procured by fraud, where they contradict an earlier final judgment, where the original proceeding contravened a forum selection clause in the contract, or where the foreign court was a seriously inconvenient forum. (Japan's rules are very similar.)

An example of a U.S. court's refusal to honor a foreign judgment is seen in *Stiftung v. V.E.B. Carl Zeiss*, 433 F.2d 686 (2d Cir. 1970). There, a U.S. court refused to enforce a judgment from (then) communist East Germany because, in the federal judge's view, the procedures were not fair and because the (former) East German judiciary would "orient their judgments according to the wishes of the leaders of the socialist state."

Judgments of U.S. courts will often be enforced by foreign courts on the basis of reciprocity and comity in countries where the losing party or its property can be found. Foreign courts, including several in Europe, have been known to refuse to honor the judgments of American courts where in the view of the foreign court the amount of money awarded was excessive, or for punitive or treble damages, or where in the opinion of the foreign judge the American court extended its net of jurisdiction too widely. To ensure that U.S. judgments will be enforceable in foreign courts, or foreign judgments enforceable in the United States, it is a good idea for the plaintiff's counsel here to coordinate with counsel in the foreign country. That way they can develop some reasonable assurance that the procedures used to obtain the judgment will satisfy the courts of the country in which property is located or it will otherwise be enforced. As of 2002, a European Union regulation requires mutual recognition of court judgments among EU member countries, without requiring any special procedures.

UNIFORM FOREIGN MONEY CLAIMS ACT. As a general rule, courts award money judgments in their own currency. For many years, U.S. courts were only able to award judgments in dollars. This rule was rooted in English law dating back several hundred years. However, it created some problems. If an international contract called for payment in the year 2000 in Japanese yen, and a judgment for a breach of the contract is awarded in 2003 in dollars, fluctuations in currency exchange rates may have distorted the value of the judgment relative to the contract terms. One of the parties may be greatly disadvantaged, while the other may receive a windfall profit. The question of whether or not a foreign money judgment can be awarded is, in the United States, a matter of state law, not federal law. In recent years, about half of the states have enacted the *Uniform Foreign Money Claims Act*. This statute gives state courts the authority to issue a judgment in a foreign currency. Some state courts have permitted foreign money awards by judicial decision, acknowledging the need to make the parties whole. Foreign money awards have been available in Great Britain since 1975. The following case, *Manches & Co. v. Gilby*, considers issues related to foreign money judgments.

Manches & Co. v. Gilby

646 N.E. 2d 86 (1995)

Supreme Judicial Court of Massachusetts

BACKGROUND AND FACTS

On August 20, 1992, the Queen's Bench Division of the High Court of Justice in London entered a default judgment in favor of Manches & Co., a London firm of solicitors, against Suzanne Gilby and Peter Thorton totaling £30,138.35. On November 9, 1992, Manches commenced this action in the Superior Court in Barnstable County to enforce the foreign judgment pursuant to Mass. Gen. Laws ch. 235, § 23A (1992 ed.), the *Uniform Recognition of Foreign Money Judgments Act*. Manches' underlying claim was that the defendants were liable for legal services rendered to Gilby in England following the death of her father.

The principal issue in this appeal concerns the amount of the judgment that should have been entered in Massachusetts in view of changes in the exchange rate between the British pound and the American dollar. It appears that on August 20, 1992,

continued

continued

the date that judgment was entered in London, approximately $58,450 equaled the amount stated in pounds in the English judgment (£30,138.35). On December 13, 1993, the date on which summary judgment was granted in favor of Manches in Barnstable Superior Court, approximately $45,130 would have purchased £30,138.35. Thus, because of the decline in the British pound in relation to the American dollar, the defendants could satisfy their obligation to Manches, expressed in pounds, by paying out considerably fewer dollars in late 1993 than they could have 16 months earlier when the English default judgment was entered.

JUSTICE WILKINS

Because the motion judge entered judgment in dollars using the latter exchange rate (the one more beneficial to the defendants), Manches has appealed. Because the motion judge entered judgment in favor of Manches, the defendants have appealed, arguing that, for various reasons, the English judgment is not worthy of enforcement in Massachusetts. We transferred the cross-appeals to this court on our own motion. If the defendants are correct in their claim that the English judgment is unenforceable, the question of the proper amount of any judgment that should be entered in favor of Manches in Massachusetts is unimportant. Therefore, we shall discuss the defendants' appeal first. We conclude that the English judgment is enforceable in Massachusetts and that the appropriate judgment is one that reflects the exchange rate at the time of the payment of the judgment.

None of the defendants' arguments in opposition to the enforcement of the English judgment has merit. The defendants rely on grounds set forth in G.L. c. 235, § 23A that, if they exist, would deny enforcement of a foreign judgment: lack of jurisdiction over them in England, denial of due process in the English justice system, and a form of *forum non conveniens.*

The English court had jurisdiction over the defendants. Manches received court permission to serve the defendants outside the jurisdiction. The contract for legal services to be rendered in England was governed by English law, and thus under English law the court there had jurisdiction over the parties.

There is no showing that the English system lacked "procedures compatible with the requirements of due process" or that the defendants were denied due process in their attempt to claim an appeal from the default judgment. England was not a "seriously inconvenient forum" and that statutory basis for denial of enforcement of a foreign judgment has no application in any event, because it applied when, unlike this case, jurisdiction in the foreign court was based "only on personal service."

The obligation to pay pounds, expressed in the English judgment, should be enforced by a judgment that orders the defendants at their option either (a) to pay £30,138.35 (with interest) or (b) to pay the equivalent in dollars of £30,138.35 (with interest), determined by the exchange rate in effect on the day of payment (or the day before payment). Manches is entitled to be restored to the position in which it would have been if the defendants had paid their obligations, but it is not entitled to more. The so-called payment day rule achieves this result.

There is no guiding Massachusetts law on this point. The decided cases in this country have adopted various positions. Some have followed the breach day rule, the one Manches advocates, in which the conversion of foreign obligations is made as of the date of breach of the obligation. Others have used the judgment day rule, converting the foreign obligation into dollars based on the exchange rate on the date the judgment is entered. We prefer a third option, the payment day rule.

The Restatement (Third) of Foreign Relations Law advises that the conversion to dollars should be "made at such rate as to make the creditor whole and to avoid rewarding a debtor who has delayed in carrying out the obligation." The Restatement becomes more specific and tentatively adopts the breach day rule if, as here, the foreign currency has depreciated since the breach, and, if the foreign currency has appreciated since the breach, it adopts the exchange rate on the date of judgment or the date of payment. "The court is free, however, to depart from those guidelines when the interests of justice require it."

The *Uniform Foreign Money Claims Act,* which has been enacted in eighteen American jurisdictions (but not in Massachusetts), adopts the payment day rule. It is this rule that, for the circumstances of this case, we apply as a matter of common law. That rule will award Manches in pounds (or the equivalent in dollars on or near the day of payment) the amount it would have recovered had it been able to collect on the judgment in Great Britain. Satisfaction of the judgment in present-day pounds will make Manches whole. In entering judgments, courts do not normally reflect changes in the purchasing power of local currency between the date of a breach and the date of

continued

continued

the award of judgment. As the prefatory note to the Uniform Act states: "The principle of the Act is to restore the aggrieved party to the economic position it would have been in had the wrong not occurred.... Courts should enter judgments in the money customarily used by the injured person." Manches incurred its expenses in England, expected to be compensated in pounds, and sustained its loss in pounds. The payment day rule is fair in this case because its application meets the reasonable expectations of the parties in this case.

Decision. Judgment was entered ordering that Manches & Co. recover from the defendants, at the defendants' option, either (a) the amount of the English judgment (£30,138.35) or (b) the equivalent in dollars of the English judgment determined at the exchange rate in effect on the day of or the day before payment, with interest on that amount (in each instance), payable in pounds or dollars, at the Massachusetts rate of interest from the date of entry of the action until the date of payment.

Commercial Disputes with Nations

This chapter has dealt with commercial disputes between private parties. Of course, governments, too, are players in commercial transactions because they are the largest purchasers of goods and services in the world. Resolving disputes with nations is quite a different matter. In the last part of this book, we will see that when governments act in their capacity as a sovereign, it is very difficult to bring them to answer in court. When they act in a commercial capacity, it is easier. Later in the book, we will examine issues related to the settlement of investment disputes, including the *Convention on the Settlement of Investment Disputes Between States and Nationals of Other States* (*Washington Convention*, 1966) that created the International Centre for the Settlement of Investment Disputes.

Conclusion

When negotiating international transactions, the prudent businessperson or lawyer will hope for the best but always plan for the worst. Planning for disputes in advance is a proper method of minimizing risk in a transaction. This planning includes obtaining expert legal advice in negotiating and drafting business contracts. The importance of the contract cannot be overstated because if and when a dispute arises, the terms of the contract provide the basis for dispute resolution.

Chapter Summary

1. Alternate dispute resolution usually offers a faster, cheaper, and more efficient alternative to litigation. Mediation is a voluntary, non-binding conciliation process. Arbitration is a more formalized process, resulting in a binding award that will be enforced by courts in many countries. The parties must agree to arbitration, but once they do, they cannot withdraw. Most commercial nations today have laws permitting arbitration and recognizing arbitral awards.
2. Litigation is the final step in attempting to resolve a dispute. It is used more frequently in the United States than in virtually any other country. Many litigants from foreign countries seek ways to have their cases heard in American courts. American juries are known for giving larger verdicts, and punitive damage awards are possible.
3. Jurisdiction is the power of a court to hear and decide a case. *In personam* jurisdiction, or "jurisdiction over the person," refers to the court's power over a certain individual or corporation to a suit. No court can enter a judgment against an individual or corporate defendant unless they have jurisdiction over them. When a defendant is not physically present in the state, a court can obtain jurisdiction over them only if the party has had sufficient minimum contacts with the territory of the forum such that it is fair for them to answer in court there. The Internet is leading to new jurisdictional issues.

pre-plan for a dispute, should one arise

4. Jurisdiction is often confused with the concept of venue. Venue refers to the geographical location of a court of competent jurisdiction where a case can be heard. According to the legal doctrine of *forum non conveniens*, whenever a case is properly heard in the courts of more than one jurisdiction, it should be heard in the jurisdiction that is most convenient.
5. The term *conflict of laws* refers to the rules by which courts determine which state or country's laws will apply to a case and how differences between laws will be reconciled. In breach of contract cases, in the absence of an agreement by the parties, contracts are usually governed by the law of the jurisdiction that has the most significant relationship to the transaction and the parties. Tort cases are usually governed by the law of the place where the injury or damage occurred, although today many courts are adopting the broader view that tort liability should be governed by the law of the jurisdiction that has the most significant relationship to the tort and to the parties.
6. A forum selection clause is a provision in a contract that fixes in advance the jurisdiction in which any disputes will be litigated. A choice of law clause is a contract provision that stipulates which country or jurisdiction's law will apply in interpreting the contract or enforcing its terms.
7. As a general rule, the judgments of foreign countries will be honored by the American courts when the requirements of comity between the nations are satisfied and when the foreign judgment was rendered by an impartial tribunal in a fashion that would not offend American notions of fundamental fairness and due process of law.
8. Antisuit injunctions allow U.S. courts to enjoin a party over whom they have jurisdiction from bringing a lawsuit in a foreign country. This prevents a party already involved in U.S. litigation from circumventing the American court system.
9. Judgments of U.S. courts will often be enforced by foreign courts on the basis of reciprocity and comity in countries where the defendant or its property can be found. Some foreign courts have been known to refuse to honor the judgments of American courts where, in the view of the foreign court, the amount of money awarded was excessive.

Questions and Case Problems

1. Explain the concepts of jurisdiction and minimum contacts. What application do they have in international disputes?
2. Should a South Dakota court enforce a Hong Kong court's judgment awarding the plaintiff $98,438 in money damages for failure to pay for shipments of fireworks? What relevance, if any, is it that Hong Kong is formally under mainland China's control? Does it matter that South Dakota is not one of the jurisdictions that has adopted the *Uniform Recognition of Foreign Money Judgments Act*? *Kwongyuen Hagkee Co., Ltd. v. Starr Fireworks Inc.,* 634 N.W.2d 95 (S.D. 2001).
3. In 1992, a picture of George Noonan, a Boston police officer, was used in a Winston cigarette ad in France. Noonan had not given permission. Noonan in fact is an antismoking crusader. The picture was included in a book published by CLB, a British company. CLB sold the rights to the picture to Lintas, a French ad agency, which was working for RJR France. Noonan sued the French ad agency and the tobacco company. Does a U.S. federal court have jurisdiction over this matter? *Noonan v. Winston,* 135 F.3d 85 (1st Cir. 1998).
4. Dickson Marine owned a ship called *Dickson IV*. It needed repairs off the coast of Africa. Panalpina Inc., a N.J. corporation with an office in New Orleans, suggested Air Sea Ltd., which suggested that Panalpina Gabon SA in Gabon could help. Panalpina Gabon subcontracted to do the work. The ship capsized. Panalpina Gabon is a Gabonese corporation and Air Sea is a Swiss corporation. Plaintiff sued them in federal district court. The district court dismissed for lack of personal jurisdiction as to Panalpina and *forum non conveniens* as to Air Sea. How did the court decide? *Dickson v. Panalpina,* 179 F.3d 331 (5th Cir. 1999).
5. What are the risks associated with arbitration? Why might a company prefer to settle disputes by litigation? What are the advantages of arbitration?
6. Why do so many litigants, "like moths to a flame," want to litigate in the United States?

7. Will a U.S. court enforce a Mexican judgment dealing with a loan agreement and collateral on a promissory note if the note violates Texas usury laws? Texas has adopted the *Texas Uniform Foreign Country Money Judgment Recognition Act.* What is the impact of this statute? Discuss the arguments on both sides. What did the court decide? *Southwest Livestock & Trucking Co. v. Ramon,* 169 F.3d 317 (5th Cir. 1999).
8. Compare the different results in *Alfadda v. Fenn,* 966 F. Supp. 1317 (S.D.N.Y. 1997) (U.S. court found French judgment precluded U.S. proceedings) with *Alesayi Beverage Corp. v. Canada Dry Beverage Corp,* 947 F. Supp. 658 (S.D.N.Y. 1996), *affd.* 122 F.3d. 1055 (2nd Cir. 1997) (denying preclusive effect of Saudi judgment in United States). Why do parties initiate such parallel proceedings?
9. A businessman, Mr. Wyser–Pratte, met with Mr. Lederer at the Four Seasons Hotel in New York City. Mr. Lederer made a presentation about a German corporation, Babcock, and its plans to acquire 100 percent of HDW, another corporation. Wyser–Pratte invested $20 million, but shortly thereafter, Babcock sold its 50 percent stake in HDW rather than increasing it. Mr. Lederer left to run HDW and Babcock became insolvent. May Mr. Wyser–Pratte bring suit in New York? Discuss.

Managerial Implications

1. You are CEO of a large publicly traded company. You are negotiating several contracts with foreign governments in Vietnam, India, and Brazil to provide hardware and software to government agencies. Are you interested in including an arbitration clause in the contract? What are the pluses and minuses of such a clause? What alternatives do you have?
   How does your plan change, if at all, if you are dealing with multiple corporations in the same countries? What if you are dealing with one corporation in England and one in New York? Discuss how these variables may affect your decision.
2. You have started a small high-tech company in New York.
   a. You are running an informational Web site. Customers must call your 800 number to place an order. A customer in Alaska is very unhappy with your product. Can they successfully sue you in Alaska?
   b. You decide you want to be clear in all your future dealings, so you insert a choice of forum clause in all of your contracts with your customers that stipulates arbitration in New York under the rules of the American Arbitration Association. Would this be enforceable?
   c. What if the forum clause stated that all disputes would be heard in Tibet?
   d. What ramifications are there to changing your Web site and making it more interactive so that people can place orders there?
   e. What if your competitor is using your trade secrets and your patents without your permission or payment? Would you be interested in arbitrating this dispute? Explain.
   f. What difference would it make if your competitor were a Dutch company?
   g. The CEO has asked you to outline a comprehensive strategy to deal with customers, suppliers, and citizen groups complaining about a myriad of issues as well as employee complaints (both domestic and foreign). Prepare a short memo addressing key principles, major concerns, and suggested actions.

For Internet Activities, Visit ACADEMIC.CENGAGE.COM/BLAW/SCHAFFER.

PART 2 International Sales, Credits, and the Commercial Transaction

Early in this book we said that the management of international business is the management of risk. Nowhere is this adage more relevant than in Part Two, *International Sales, Credits, and the Commercial Transaction.* International business lore is filled with stories about sellers who shipped goods to buyers on the other side of the world, on the basis of a written contract, only to find that that the buyer has refused to take delivery, or has vanished. The risk is equally as great to the unsuspecting buyer who pays in advance, only to find that the seller has delivered an ocean container filled with worthless junk. The risks do not end there. Almost daily, there are reports of cargo being damaged by weather, spoilage, contamination with salt water or chemicals, infestation, inadequate packing and more. It is not uncommon for cargo vessels to go down in storms or to run aground as a result of errors in navigation. Modern day pirates still plow the high seas and dangerous inland waterways, kidnapping crews, plundering cargo, and seizing entire ships for ransom. These are only a few examples of the transaction risks inherent in an international sale. In this part of the book we hope to expose readers to the risks of the international sale, and to suggest methods for dealing with such risks. In doing so, we explore traditional business law topics: contract law, sales law, commercial law and the law applicable to bank collections and letters of credit, aviation and maritime law, and marine insurance law.

In this area, the law is derived from both national and international law. This includes many international conventions, national statutes and the decisions of national courts. The court decisions appearing in this section are composed of both "landmark" cases that explain long-standing and widely accepted legal principles, and those that illustrate common problems faced in international business. Some of the landmark decisions are rooted in the English *Law Merchant* of hundreds of years ago, or early maritime law, although none in this text is so old.

In Chapter Four, *Sales Contracts and Excuses for Nonperformance,* we will study basic principles of international sales law under the *United Nations Convention on Contracts for the International Sale of Goods.* This is the first widely accepted body of international sales law, in force in over seventy nations, that governs two-thirds of world trade in goods. The chapter discusses the validity and formation of contracts, the interpretation of contracts, performance of contracts, remedies for breach of contract, and whether or not events beyond control of the parties (e.g. a fire, storm, or terrorist act) will excuse their performance. Special attention is paid to the development of sales law in the United Kingdom, the United States, and China, and to a few of the major differences in sales law in each of these countries. We close the chapter by examining the cultural influences on contract negotiations, particularly in Japan.

In Chapter Five, *The Documentary Sale and Terms of Trade,* we cover two important transaction risks facing the buyer and seller in an international sale – the seller's credit risk and the buyer's delivery risk, We examine the use of the documentary sale as a secure payment method, and the role of the bill of lading and other negotiable transport documents in facilitating the exchange of goods and money across international borders. We will also look the importance of trade terms in the contract as a means of allocating, as between buyer and seller, the responsibility for arranging the international transportation of goods, as well as for allocating the risk of loss or damage to the goods while in transit. We will also see the crucial role that ocean carriers and international banks play in facilitating the international sale. Chapter Six, *The Carriage of Goods and the Liability of Air and Sea Carriers,* deals with important areas of aviation and maritime law. The first portion of the chapter covers the liability of air carriers for damage or loss to cargo, and for baggage claims and bodily injuries to passengers. Next, the chapter covers the liability of ocean carriers for damage or loss to cargo at sea, as well as important legal issues affecting marine insurance policies. No area of international business has engendered as much litigation in the courts as has the carriage of goods. This is a fascinating and important area of study.

In Chapter Seven, *Bank Collections, Trade Finance, and Letters of Credit,* we build on the material presented in Chapter Five. The chapter gives an overview of the law of negotiable instruments in the context of international trade, and discusses issues related to trade finance. Although the bank letter of credit is widely used in international trade, it is not well understood by most business people. Therefore, we have devoted considerable time to following a typical letter of credit transaction, and to understanding both the law and practice of documentary letters of credit.

CHAPTER 4
SALES CONTRACTS AND EXCUSES FOR NONPERFORMANCE

INTRODUCTION TO CONTRACTS FOR THE INTERNATIONAL SALE OF GOODS

The sales contract is universally recognized as the legal mechanism for conducting trade in goods. The contract for purchase and sale embodies the agreement of the parties, the buyer and seller. It expresses their intention to be bound by its terms, commits them to perform their part of the bargain, and makes them responsible for breach of contract if they do not. The sales contract is essential because it sets out rights and liabilities that may extend well into the future. Any agreement to buy and sell goods, especially an international one, usually takes some time to perform. If buyer and seller could do all that was required at the moment the agreement was reached, or if every seller handed over the goods at the moment the purchase price was paid, there would be far less need for a detailed sales contract. In the real world, however, the risks are usually too great to begin performance without first reaching an agreement on all essential terms, especially when the contract extends well into the future. The contract allows buyer and seller to agree on all essential terms of the contract in advance, and to begin performance, knowing their rights and obligations are understood. The contract might call for shipment at a future date, or for several shipments to be made over many years. The seller might need time to secure raw materials, or to gear up for the engineering and design phase, and for manufacturing. The buyer may want to arrange advance financing for the purchase, to plan future deliveries to meet production schedules, do advance marketing, or plan the introduction of new products. Whatever the case, both buyer and seller can proceed with some confidence, knowing their contract is sealed. During the negotiating process the parties can tend to the details of the contract, air their concerns, and negotiate an agreement on all the terms important to them. After all, there are more details to consider besides quantity and price. There are payment terms, shipping and insurance arrangements, specifications and warranties, remedies on default, and more. There is the question of who will bear the risk of loss if the goods are destroyed in transit. Hopefully, everything will go well and neither party will ever have to pull out the document and read its fine print. Yet if performance breaks down, and a dispute arises, that is the first thing the parties and their attorneys will do. If the case proceeds to litigation and a court must resolve their dispute, it will look to the governing law of sales to interpret and enforce the contract.

The Law of Sales

Sales law, or the *law of sales,* is generally that body of law which governs contracts for the present or future sale of goods. In most countries, the term *sale* means a transfer of the ownership and possession of tangible goods (sometimes referred to simply as "things which are movable" or "tangible personal property") from seller to buyer in return for a price or monetary payment. The "law of sales" does not apply to contracts for the sale of real estate or intangibles, such as stocks, bonds, patents, copyrights, and trademarks. It does not apply to contracts of employment, of insurance, or to the provision of services. The reason for the distinction, as we will see, is that sales law developed out of the practices of merchants and traders who dealt in goods. Generally speaking, courts look to the governing sales law to determine whether a valid and enforceable agreement exists, how to interpret contractual provisions, what remedies are available in the event of a breach, and what damages can be awarded. Sales law is a subcategory of both contract law and commercial law. Today, the sales law of most nations can be found in modern statutes, or codes, supplemented by extensive case decisions. Surprisingly, many countries, particularly developing countries, have newly enacted sales codes that have only recently replaced outdated codes from the nineteenth and early twentieth centuries. Several Latin American countries have only recently modernized their codes, which dated to the mid-1800s. China's modern sales law is less than a decade old.

National Differences in Sales Law and Contractual Uncertainty. In an international contract for the sale of goods, at least one party is likely to have its rights decided under the law of a foreign country. In the last chapter we learned that "conflict of laws" rules determine the country in which a breach of contract case will be heard, and under which country's law will the case be decided. In the absence of a "choice of law" provision in a contract, a court would have to determine which law will govern—and that could be the law of the country where the contract was made, where it was to be performed, where the goods were to be delivered, where the subject matter is located, where either party resides or has its principal place of business, or in some other country with a close connection to the contract. This could lead to some surprising results. Different countries, even with modern codes, often have different rules for interpreting contracts, for remedies and awarding damages, or even for determining if a contract exists at all. This is especially true when buyer and seller come from countries with different legal systems—common law, civil law, or Islamic law. No international businessperson or attorney can possibly know all the laws of every country in which they do business. Attorneys may feel uncertain about negotiating and drafting contracts for their clients that would be governed by foreign codes that are unfamiliar or that are available only in a foreign language. If they do not have foreign legal experience, have not read the foreign case law, and do not have the advice of foreign counsel, then it becomes very difficult for them to advise their clients on the legal ramifications of a contract. Of course, we learned in the last chapter that within some limits the parties are free to negotiate and agree on their choice of national law. However, while it may seem like a freely bargained agreement, the choice is usually that of the party with the greatest bargaining power. It is this unpredictability of foreign law that is the unknown factor in contracting, and that can lead to a tremendous uncertainty in buying and selling goods across national borders.

The ability to predict what will happen in the event of a breach of contract is essential to commerce. For centuries, legal scholars and lawmakers everywhere have realized that no nation can be open for business with the rest of the world without a stable and predictable body of sales law. No nation can expect to attract foreign traders and firms without a modern body of governing law to protect the contract rights of both its own citizens and foreigners alike. Imagine if you had sailed around the world on a merchant ship to a distant land to trade your steel swords and armaments for locally produced cloth, spices, and produce. The exchange goes well, but soon the locals claim that your steel is weak and inferior. You quickly learn that in this country a breach of contract by a foreigner against a local is considered a crime—and your punishment for having delivered defective goods is whipping, flogging, and amputation of a hand. You escape to your ship and flee for home. Doubtless, you and your fellow merchants would not soon return to trade in this foreign land. Soon, all lawmakers, be they warlords, emperors, or feudal kings, realized that a progressive and widely accepted code of commercial law was necessary to the expansion of trade and commerce.

The Unification of Sales Law. The history of legal development in many nations has often coincided with its history of opening to the world through foreign trade. As trade expanded, and as foreigner merchants came to trade, so did nations require a more universally accepted set of laws. In Chapter Two we saw how the English common law spread through the early British Empire, including the American colonies. We saw how the civil law and Napoleonic codes spread through Europe, Latin America, Japan, and even China. This gradual process certainly unified laws, one country at a time. However, as the twentieth century brought the world closer together, there were calls for more organized efforts at unifying the sales laws of diverse countries around the world. The process of making national laws more uniform is known as the *unification of law*. The unification of modern sales law has been ongoing since the early part of the last century. Early efforts were made by the League of Nations, and by private organizations and law societies, although those largely turned out to be unsuccessful. In 1966 the United Nations created a new organization responsible for unifying trade law, the *United Nations Commission on International Trade Law,* or UNCITRAL (Vienna). UNCITRAL's work led to a very successful effort in unifying the law applicable to the international sale of goods and the adoption in 1980 of the *United Nations Convention on Contracts for the International Sale of Goods,* or CISG. The CISG now forms the basis for a widely accepted body of international sales law, now implemented into the national codes and statutes of seventy nations, including the United States and its largest trading partners—Canada, Mexico, China, and most of Europe. The great feat of the United Nations in creating the CISG was that it was able to bring together legal scholars from all regions of the world, representing diverse legal systems. It was able to develop a code acceptable to the common law countries and civil law countries, including both developed and developing countries and as well as the socialist countries of the time. The CISG is the primary subject of this chapter. We will look at contract formation, interpretation, warranties, rights and remedies on default, excuses for nonperformance, and more. We begin, however, by briefly tracing the historical development of sales law at the national level in England, the United States, and in modern China.

The Law Merchant and English Sales Law

In the twelfth century, medieval Europe experienced a renaissance of trade and commerce. Merchants from the cities, many traveling by caravan, met at trade fairs and city markets to exchange goods such as wool, salted fish, cotton cloth, wine, fruit, and oils. Trade routes to the East were opening, with access to silk and new spices. Rudimentary banking systems were founded so that money could be used as payment in long-distance transactions. New legal instruments—the forerunners of today's bank checks—were created. Over time, the merchants developed a set of customs for exchanging goods for money—an unwritten code that protected their word, gave them the benefit of their bargain, and helped foster commerce and trade. For instance, it was custom that if goods were sold by a merchant at an open market—perhaps in the city square—and the buyer subsequently discovered that the merchant had been unwittingly selling stolen goods, then the buyer took ownership of the goods anyway, even if they were claimed by the original owner. This custom protected the integrity of the marketplace by protecting the innocent who did business with merchants. The customs made commerce easier and safer, because everyone knew what was expected of them. Foreigners to the marketplace quickly learned local customs and passed them on to others. These customs became known as the *lex mercatoria* or *law merchant,* and they were "enforced" by the merchants themselves. Similar customs were developing in the maritime trade.

In the centuries to follow, the local courts in both England and continental Europe recognized the *law merchant* and used juries made up of other merchants to decide cases. As trade spanned greater distances, and nations created colonies, merchants took on greater risks, and transactions required more complex legal rules. In England, by the eighteenth century, the *law merchant* became a part of the common law when a famous English judge, Lord Mansfield, ruled that it was up to the English courts to say what the law merchant was and not merely what merchants thought it to be. For his work and influence, Lord Mansfield is heralded as the father of English commercial law. In continental Europe, the *law merchant* gave way early on to more formal legal codes—Napoleonic codes—enacted by legislatures in the nineteenth century, based on legal concepts dating to the Roman period. Those included the French and German civil codes, which eventually spread to much of Latin America, Eastern Europe, China, and Japan.

More than a hundred years after the merger of the law merchant with the common law, England enacted the *English Sale of Goods Act of 1894,* which codified many customary rules, and adapted the common law to business needs of the time. The 1894 act and subsequent legislation were consolidated into the *United Kingdom Sale of Goods Act of 1979.* English sales law was transplanted to most of England's colonies and remains a strong influence around the world to this day. Virtually all common law nations today have modern commercial codes and extensive case law governing the sale of goods. Canadian sales law, for example, borrows principles from both the English common law and from the American *Uniform Commercial Code.*

The American Uniform Commercial Code

In America, the law of sales was originally drawn from the English common law of contracts and the law merchant. In 1906, the *Uniform Sales Act,* codifying the law of sales, was passed in many U.S. states. (It is no longer in effect.) As the business world became more complex, and with the dawn of air travel and worldwide communications, there was a need for a clearer set of modern rules. This led to the creation in 1951 of the *Uniform Commercial Code (UCC),* which has become the primary body of commercial law for domestic transactions in the United States. The UCC has been adopted (with some minor differences) in each of the fifty states plus the District of Columbia. Louisiana has not adopted UCC Article 2 on the Sale of Goods, preferring to follow the rules in its French-influenced Civil Code. The UCC covers many areas of commercial law, including bank deposits and negotiable instruments, as well as the sale of goods, and makes the law uniform throughout the United States. Contracts not governed by the UCC, such as contracts for employment, insurance, and services, the transfer of intellectual property rights, and sales of real property, are governed by the common law.

In 2003, amendments to Article 2 of the UCC were proposed by the National Conference of Commissioners on Uniform State Laws, a drafting and recommending body. The proposals will not be effective until adopted by state legislatures in the United States. Among other things, the amendments include changes that reflect the evolution of electronic commerce.

Contract Law in China

The legal system of the People's Republic of China (China) underwent its first modern change at the dawn of the twentieth century. As in Japan in that period, a civil law system developed, borrowing from the European experience. However, that changed after World War II, with the communist takeover and the introduction of Marxist theory. In the early 1950s, China adopted a system of centrally controlled state planning. There was strong central planning of economic activity, with few market mechanisms regulating the factors of production, the use of natural resources, or pricing. State policy, and not consumer demand, largely dictated how many and what kinds of goods were to be produced. Historically, there was little need for private contracts or for a body of contract law to protect private rights. After all, under Marxist principles, the law was seen as an instrument of class warfare, as a means of establishing state authority and reinforcing socialist market principles. Contracts served only to implement government policy. In other words, domestic contract law ensured that state doctrine was followed and that commitments made to and between state agencies were upheld. Interestingly enough, in sharp contrast to what lawyers in the West were accustomed to, "breach of contract" actions more closely resembled quasi-criminal prosecutions for breaching one's obligation to the state. This difference is reflected in the remedies most commonly used. In the West, when a party breaches a contract, a court typically awards damages to the nonbreaching party as a form of compensation. In China, the focus was on protecting the interests of the state through legal rules that compelled a breaching party to do what it had promised. Penalties and other forms of punishment were also routinely used.

China's business laws changed remarkably in the last quarter of the twentieth century. As China opened its doors to Western business in the late

1970s and early 1980s, it recognized that modern commercial laws were essential to attracting buyers for Chinese-made goods and foreign investors to Chinese industry. Today, its legal system is based on both socialist and Western civil law principles. In the 1980s and 1990s, China enacted many modern codes including codes of banking, joint ventures and investments, company law, copyrights and patents, trademarks, securities, foreign trade regulation, consumer protection, taxation, aviation and transportation, advertising, insurance, and accounting regulations. These helped China demonstrate that it was "open for business," that it deserved to be treated as an equal trading partner by other nations, and that it deserved membership in the World Trade Organization. These laws reflected China's transition from a purely socialist state to a nation with a mixed economy—partially state owned, partially privately owned, albeit with great central state control. During this period, China also enacted two modern codes of contract law. One of these applied exclusively to contracts between domestic individuals or companies and the other applied to contracts involving foreign parties. However, these laws were repealed in 1999 with the enactment of a single, comprehensive *Contract Law for the People's Republic of China* by the National People's Congress, the main legislative body in China.

THE 1999 *CONTRACT* LAW OF CHINA. The *Contract Law for the People's Republic of China* covers many areas traditionally associated with contract law that would be familiar to lawyers from Western countries. It applies not only to the sale of goods, the subject of this chapter, but also to contracts for the sale of electricity, water, and gas; loan agreements; leasing contracts; contracts with independent contractors; construction contracts; contracts for carriage and the transportation of people and cargo; contracts involving the sale or transfer of patents and other technology; warehousing contracts; agency contracts; and brokerage agreements. The law clearly recognizes that contracts may be made through electronic data interchange, the Internet, or e-mail. This is a significant step forward for a nation whose Internet communications are still tightly controlled by the government.

Given the breadth of subjects covered in the Chinese code, its 428 articles seem remarkably short and concise by American law standards, although that is probably in keeping with Chinese thinking. Its provisions would be easily recognized by almost any American lawyer or businessperson. But this is to be expected because the Chinese legal scholars and government representatives who drafted the law spent years studying generally accepted legal principles in the rest of the world and adapted them to the Chinese economic and political systems. Indeed, the Chinese drew on many of the concepts found in the CISG, which will be covered in detail in the next section.

Of course, China does not benefit from the plethora of court decisions found in American or English law that interpret, define, and expand the commercial codes in those countries. In China, the opinions of most judges in deciding cases are not usually publicly reported and do not serve as precedent for future cases, although in 1981, the National People's Congress gave the Supreme Court the power to issue interpretive pronouncements on statutes. Unlike in the United States, where courts only act upon cases brought before them by litigants, the Chinese highest court can issue interpretations of Chinese statutes on its own initiative. The judge's role is to apply the law as written and not to define or expand its principles beyond the case at hand.

THE CONVENTION ON CONTRACTS FOR THE INTERNATIONAL SALE OF GOODS

Throughout most of the twentieth century, international legal scholars envisioned a near-universally accepted, uniform law of sales. In 1980, that work came to fruition in the form of the *UN Convention on Contracts for the International Sale of Goods* (CISG). It was drafted by representatives from many different countries, in all official UN languages, at meetings that took place over many years around the world.

The CISG is now in effect in over seventy countries that account for more than two-thirds of all world trade. It was ratified by the U.S. Senate and became effective in the United States in 1988. The CISG is effective for trade within North America, as it has also been ratified by Canada and Mexico. It has also displaced the Chinese law of contracts for international sales. Interestingly, the United Kingdom, which is so firmly rooted in common law traditions, has not adopted the CISG. As of 2007, it has been adopted by the countries shown in Exhibit 4.1. Translations are available in the official UN languages (Arabic, Chinese, English, French, Russian, and Spanish) and in many others. An edited copy of the CISG appears in the appendix, and students are encouraged to refer to it often while reading this chapter.

EXHIBIT 4.1

Countries that Have Ratified or Acceded to the CISG

Argentina	Latvia
Australia	Lesotho
Austria	Liberia
Belarus	Lithuania
Belgium	Luxembourg
Bosnia and Herzegovina	Macedonia (Republic of)
Bulgaria	Mauritania
Burundi	Mexico
Canada	Moldova
Chile	Mongolia
China	Montenegro
Colombia	Netherlands
Croatia	New Zealand
Cuba	Norway
Cyprus	Paraguay
Czech Republic	Peru
Denmark	Poland
Ecuador	Romania
Egypt	Russian Federation
El Salvador	St. Vincent-Grenadines
Estonia	Serbia
Finland	Singapore
France	Slovakia
Gabon	Slovenia
Georgia	Spain
Germany	Sweden
Greece	Switzerland
Guinea	Syrian Arab Republic
Honduras	Uganda
Hungary	Ukraine
Iceland	United States
Iraq	Uruguay
Israel	Uzbekistan
Italy	Yugoslavia
Korea (Republic of South)	Zambia
Kyrgyzstan	

This chapter examines the following aspects of the CISG: (1) its applicability to international sales, (2) rules for forming and interpreting contracts, (3) performance and nonperformance by the parties, (4) remedies and damages for breach of contract, and (5) excuses for nonperformance of a contract.

Applicability of the CISG to International Sales

The CISG applies if the following conditions are met:

1. The contract is for the commercial sale of goods (the term "goods" is not defined in the CISG).
2. It is between parties whose places of business are in different countries (nationality or citizenship of individuals is not a determining factor).
3. The parties' places of business are located in countries that have ratified the convention.

Assume that a dispute arises over a contract between a buyer whose business is located in the United States and a seller whose business is located in France. Regardless of who initiates the lawsuit or whether it is brought in the United States or France, if no choice of law provision specifies otherwise, their rights will be determined by the CISG—not by the *Uniform Commercial Code* or the *French Civil Code*. Similarly, if the same dispute arises between a U.S. buyer and an English seller whose business is located in the UK, and there is no choice of law provision in the contract, the applicable law is likely to be that of the country with the closest connection to the contract. Here, one of the parties is not located in a country that has ratified the convention—the United Kingdom. Now take another, perhaps more important, example. Assume that American and Chinese firms are in the process of negotiating a contract, but that neither will agree to have a dispute heard under the other's law (and let's say they disagree on the forum as well). There is no arbitration provision. The CISG provides a solution: The contract can be drafted to call for any dispute to be brought before the courts of Hong Kong and to be decided according to the CISG, thus providing a neutral forum and a neutral law.

In the United States, the UCC will continue to apply to purely domestic sales and to sales between firms located in the United States and countries that have not ratified the CISG.

Place of Business Requirement. In the case of buyers or sellers with places of business in more than one country, such as multinational corporations, "place of business" would be considered to be the country that has the closest relation to the contract and where it will be performed. This could mean, at least theoretically, that if two American companies negotiated a contract entirely within the United States, but one of them had a place of business outside of the United States and the contract was to be performed outside the United States (e.g., the contract called for delivery of the goods to a point outside the United States), then the CISG might govern the transaction.

Choice of Law Provisions. Despite the widespread acceptance of the CISG, many attorneys recommend that their clients negotiate a choice of law provision calling for disputes to be decided according to their own national laws. Many American lawyers prefer to have their clients' contracts governed by the more familiar *Uniform Commercial Code.* Article 6 of the CISG allows parties to "exclude the application of this Convention ... or vary from any of its provisions." This is often called the "opting out" provisions of the CISG. Any attempt to "opt out" must be drafted in a contract in clear and unequivocal language and should only be done by attorneys experienced with the CISG.

The following case, *Asante Technologies, Inc. v. PMC-Sierra, Inc.,* discusses three important provisions of the CISG: the place of business requirement, the ability of the parties to "opt out" of the CISG by using a choice of law clause, and the concept that in international transactions the CISG preempts the contract laws of U.S. states.

Asante Technologies, Inc. v. PMC-Sierra, Inc.

164 F. Supp. 2d 1142 (2001)

United States District Court (N.D. Cal.)

BACKGROUND AND FACTS

The plaintiff, Asante, purchased electronic parts from the defendant, PMC, whose offices and factory were in Canada. Asante placed its orders through defendant's authorized distributor, Unique Technologies, located in California. Asante's order stated that the contract "shall be governed by the laws of the state shown on buyer's address on this order." PMC's confirmation stated that the contract "shall be construed according to the laws of Canada." Invoices were sent from Unique, and payment remitted to Unique, either in California or Nevada. Asante claimed that the goods did not meet its specifications and filed suit in California state court to have its claim decided under California law. When the case was transferred to a U.S. federal court, Asante requested that the case be remanded back to state court.

WARE, DISTRICT JUDGE

PLACE OF BUSINESS REQUIREMENT

The *Convention on Contracts for the International Sale of Goods* ("CISG") is an international treaty which has been signed and ratified by the United States and Canada, among other countries.... The CISG applies "to contracts of sale of goods between parties whose places of business are in different States ... when the States are Contracting States." CISG Art. 1 (1) (a). Article 10 of the CISG provides that "if a party has more than one place of business, the place of business is that which has the closest relationship to the contract and its performance." CISG Art. 10....

It is undisputed that plaintiff's place of business is Santa Clara County, California. It is further undisputed that ... defendant's corporate headquarters, inside sales and marketing office, public relations department, principal warehouse, and most of its design and engineering functions were located in Canada. However, plaintiff contends that, pursuant to Article 10 of the CISG, defendant's "place of business" having the closest relationship to the contract at issue is the United States....

Plaintiff asserts that Unique acted in the United States as an agent of defendant, and that plaintiff's contacts with Unique establish defendant's place of

continued

continued

business in the U.S. for the purposes of this contract. Plaintiff has failed to persuade the Court that Unique acted as the agent of defendant.... To the contrary, a distributor of goods for resale is normally not treated as an agent of the manufacturer.... Furthermore, while Unique may distribute defendant's products, plaintiff does not allege that Unique made any representations regarding technical specifications on behalf of defendant.... Plaintiff's dealings with Unique do not establish defendant's place of business in the United States.

Plaintiff's claims concern breaches of representations made by defendant from Canada. Moreover, the products in question are manufactured in Canada, and plaintiff knew that defendant was Canadian, having sent one purchase order directly to defendant in Canada by fax.... Moreover, plaintiff directly corresponded with defendant at defendant's Canadian address.... In contrast, plaintiff has not identified any specific representation or correspondence emanating from defendant's Oregon branch. For these reasons, the Court finds that defendant's place of business that has the closest relationship to the contract and its performance is British Columbia, Canada. Consequently, the contract at issue in this litigation is between parties from two different Contracting States, Canada and the United States. This contract therefore implicates the CISG.

CHOICE OF LAW CLAUSE

Plaintiff next argues that, even if the Parties are from two nations that have adopted the CISG, the choice of law provisions in the [buyer's purchase order and seller's confirmation] reflect the Parties' intent to "opt out" of application of the treaty. The Court finds that the particular choice of law provisions in the "Terms and Conditions" of both parties are inadequate to effectuate an "opt out" of the CISG.

Although selection of a particular choice of law, such as "the California Commercial Code" or the "Uniform Commercial Code" could amount to implied exclusion of the CISG, the choice of law clauses at issue here do not evince a clear intent to opt out of the CISG. For example, defendant's choice of applicable law adopts the law of British Columbia, and it is undisputed that the CISG is the law of British Columbia. Furthermore, even plaintiff's choice of applicable law generally adopts the "laws of" the State of California, and California is bound by the Supremacy Clause to the treaties of the United States. Thus, under general California law, the CISG is applicable to contracts where the contracting parties are from different countries that have adopted the CISG....

FEDERAL PREEMPTION

It appears that the issue of whether or not the CISG preempts state law is a matter of first impression. In the case of federal statutes, "the question of whether a certain action is preempted by federal law is one of congressional intent.... The Court concludes that the expressly stated goal of developing uniform international contract law to promote international trade indicates the intent of the parties to the treaty to have the treaty preempt state law causes of action. The availability of independent state contract law causes of action would frustrate the goals of uniformity and certainty embraced by the CISG. Allowing such avenues for potential liability would subject contracting parties to different states' laws and the very same ambiguities regarding international contracts that the CISG was designed to avoid. As a consequence, parties to international contracts would be unable to predict the applicable law, and the fundamental purpose of the CISG would be undermined.

Finally, plaintiff appears to confuse the matter of exclusive federal jurisdiction with preemption.... Even where federal law completely preempts state law, state courts may have concurrent jurisdiction over the federal claim if the defendant does not remove the case to federal court [citation omitted]. This Court does not hold that it has exclusive jurisdiction over CISG claims.

Decision. The federal court had concurrent jurisdiction over this case (even though the case could also have been heard in state court) because the applicable law was the CISG, an international convention ratified by the United States.

Sales Excluded from the CISG. The following types of sales have been specifically excluded from the convention:

1. Consumer goods sold for personal, family, or household use
2. Goods bought at auction
3. Stocks, securities, negotiable instruments, or money
4. Ships, vessels, or aircraft
5. Electricity

6. Assembly contracts for the supply of goods to be manufactured or produced wherein the buyer provides a "substantial part of the materials necessary for such manufacture or production"
7. Contracts that are in "preponderant part" for the supply of labor or other services
8. Contracts imposing liability on the seller for death or personal injury caused by the goods
9. Contracts where the parties specifically agree to "opt out" of the convention or where they choose to be bound by some other law

In the United States, Article 2 of the UCC applies to both consumer and domestic commercial transactions. Consumer sales were excluded from the CISG because consumer protection laws are so specific to every country that it would have been very difficult to harmonize them. Further, consumer sales are usually domestic in nature.

Validity and Formation of International Sales Contracts

Under the common law, a *valid contract* is an agreement that contains all of the essential elements and meets all the requirements of a binding contract. As students of business law well know, a contract contains a number of elements.

1. It is an agreement between parties entered into by mutual assent and resulting from their words or from conduct that indicates their intention to be bound.
2. It must be supported by consideration (the bargained-for exchange of a legal benefit or incurring of a legal detriment).
3. The parties must have legal capacity (they may not be minors, legally incompetent, or under the influence of drugs or alcohol).
4. The contract must not be for illegal purposes or contrary to public policy.

If a contract is missing any one of these essential elements, under the common law it is a *void contract*. It will not be enforced by the courts.

The CISG only governs the formation of a contract and the rights and obligations of the seller and buyer. The Convention does not provide rules for determining whether a contract is valid, for determining whether a party to a contract is legally competent, nor for determining whether a party is guilty of fraud or misrepresentation. These rules are left to individual state or national laws. Consideration is not mentioned and does not seem to be required under the CISG, although in *Geneva Pharmaceuticals Technology Corp. v. Barr Laboratories Inc.*, 201 F. Supp. 2d 236 (S.D. N.Y. 2002) a U.S. federal court stated that issues of validity, including consideration, were a matter of state law and not governed by the CISG. While the CISG is unclear about consideration in forming a contract, Article 29 seems to state that consideration is not required in order to modify or terminate a contract.

Enforcement of Illegal Contracts

A generally recognized principle of contract law is that, in all legal systems, contracts that violate the laws of a state or nation are void. A void contract is of no legal effect and will not be enforced by a court. As you read the following case, *Tarbert Trading, Ltd. v. Cometals, Inc.*, consider both the legality of the sales contract in question and the ethical behavior of the parties.

The Writing Requirement

The laws of many nations differ as to whether contracts for the sale of goods must be in writing. Under the UCC, American law requires that contracts for the sale of goods of $500 or more be in writing. (Under proposed amendments to the UCC, the requirement would be increased to $5,000 and the requirement of a signed "writing" would be changed to signed "record." See Exhibit 4.2.) Writing requirements in common law countries date back to an act of the English Parliament in 1677. In 1954, however, the United Kingdom repealed its law.

Under CISG Article 11, a contract for the international sale of goods "need not be concluded in or evidenced by writing and is not subject to any other requirement as to form. It may be proved by any means, including witnesses." This is in keeping with a basic concept found in the CISG: that the parties should have flexibility in contracting and as much freedom of contract as possible.

Tarbert Trading, Ltd. v. Cometals, Inc.

663 F. Supp. 561 (1987)

United States District Court (S.D.N.Y.)

BACKGROUND AND FACTS

Cometals purchased Kenyan red beans from Tarbert Trading, an English commodities trading company. Agrimen, a South African company engaged in commodities trading, acted as an agent for Tarbert in connection with the sale. The beans were held in a warehouse in Rotterdam, the Netherlands. Cometals had purchased the beans for resale to a buyer in Colombia. Colombia would only allow the beans to be imported if the seller could provide a certificate of origin (issued by a Chamber of Commerce) proving the beans were a product of a country in the European Economic Community (EEC). Cometals requested that Tarbert supply such a certificate and Tarbert agreed. Both parties understood that it was impossible to honestly furnish the certificate because the Kenyan red beans originated in Africa. Later, the defendant refused the beans claiming that they were of poor quality and the plaintiff sued. Defendant also maintains that the agreement should be declared void and unenforceable because plaintiff could not, except through fraud, supply defendant with an EEC certificate of origin for the beans.

NEWMAN, SENIOR JUDGE

We first address the issue concerning conflict of laws. As to that matter, the court agrees with the contention of Tarbert that the law of New York is applicable in this case rather than the law of the Netherlands, as urged by Cometals. The court has considered various facts: Cometals resides in New York; negotiations took place between Cometals in New York and Agrimen in South Africa; the formal letter agreement was prepared by Cometals in New York; and the physical location of the beans in Rotterdam was not a significant factor in the parties' transaction.... However, in view of the result reached in this case, it is immaterial whether the law of the Netherlands or of New York is applied.

Under the law of the Netherlands a contract that calls for the doing of an illegal or tortious act is absolutely void and unenforceable. See Martindale-Hubbell, *Netherlands Law Digest,* p. 5 (1985).

Insofar as New York law is concerned: *Stone v. Freeman,* 298 N.Y. 268, 271, 82 N.E.2d 571, 572 (1948),

> it is the settled law of this State (and probably of every other State) that a party to an illegal contract cannot ask a court of law to help him carry out his illegal object, nor can such a person plead or prove in any court a case in which he, as a basis for his claim, must show forth his illegal purpose.... For no court should be required to serve as paymaster of the wages of crime, or referee between thieves. Therefore, the law "will not extend its aid to either of the parties" or "listen to their complaints against each other, but will leave them where their own acts have placed them.

Concededly, both Tarbert and Cometals were cognizant of the fact that an EEC certificate of origin stating that the Kenyan beans were of the origin of an EEC member would be false and would be shown to third persons. Simply put, [Cometals] intended to deceive the Colombian customs officials with a false certificate as to the beans' country-of-origin so that they would allow the importation of the beans by Cometals' customer....

Irrespective of the rather incredible explanations of [Tarbert's employees] as to what they understood to be the purport of the requested certificate of origin, they finally and grudgingly conceded that an EEC certificate stating that the goods were of the origin of an EEC member would be understood by anyone reading it to mean that the beans were grown in an EEC country and not simply shipped from such country. Consequently, it is completely understandable why [Agrimen's employees] expressed shock, dismay and disapproval of the oral agreement concerning the EEC certificate between [Cometals and Tarbert].... The fact that the agreement drafted by Cometals duplicitously described the subject commodity simply as "Small red beans, 1982 crop," ... does not avoid the illegality of the contract inasmuch as both parties understood from the prior communications and intended that the Kenyan beans stored in [a Rotterdam] warehouse were the subject of the contract.

It is evident from the Kenyan origin of the beans that it would have been impossible for Tarbert to honestly obtain from a Chamber of Commerce and furnish Cometals with a bona fide EEC certificate of origin stating that the goods were of the origin of a member of the EEC since concededly Kenya is not an EEC member. Thus, the only way in which Tarbert could have complied with the agreement

continued

continued

would have been to convince an official of a Chamber of Commerce to issue a fraudulent certificate or to obtain a forged certificate. Both acts are obviously illegal.

No one shall be permitted to profit by his own fraud, or take advantage of his own wrong, or to found any claim upon his own iniquity, or to acquire property by his own crime. These maxims are dictated by public policy, have their foundation in universal law administered in all civilized countries, and have nowhere been superseded by statutes. Plaintiff maintains that the furnishing of the EEC certificate of origin was a non-essential and separable part of the bargain, and that therefore the court may hold only that portion of the agreement unenforceable. However, the court finds that the illegality is inseparable from and goes to an essential ingredient of the bargain between the parties, because Cometals insisted upon the EEC certificate in the requested form with an eye to its ... surreptitious importation of the beans into Colombia. Plainly, enforcement of the agreement for either party would be contrary to public policy.... [T]he complaint and counterclaim are dismissed.

Decision. Contracts that violate the law are void and will not be enforced by a court. In this case, a contract calling for the delivery of a fraudulent certificate of origin is illegal and contrary to public policy.

Several countries, including Argentina, Chile, Hungary, Russia, and a few others, have elected to omit Article 11 from their version of the CISG. In those countries, foreign sales contracts governed by the CISG must still be in writing. In China, one provision of the 1999 *Contract Law for the People's Republic of China* prevails over CISG Article 11, even for international sales otherwise governed by the CISG. This permits foreign sales contracts to be either written or oral, unless some other statute or administrative regulation requires that they be in writing. That requires knowledge of many different administrative regulations. By practice, almost all foreign trade contracts involving Chinese firms are in writing.

Exhibit 4.2

Requirement of Signed Record under Proposed Amendments to the UCC

UCC §2-201 Formal Requirements; Statute of Frauds (2003 proposed)*

(1) A contract for the sale of goods for the price of $5,000 or more is not enforceable by way of action or defense unless there is some record sufficient to indicate that a contract for sale has been made between the parties and signed by the party against which enforcement is sought or by the party's authorized agent or broker. A record is not insufficient because it omits or incorrectly states a term agreed upon but the contract is not enforceable under this subsection beyond the quantity of goods shown in the record.

(2) Between merchants, if within a reasonable time a record in confirmation of the contract and sufficient against the sender is received and the party receiving it has reason to know its contents, it satisfies the requirements of subsection (1) against the recipient unless notice of objection to its contents is given in a record within 10 days after it is received.

UCC §2-103 Definitions and Index of Definitions

"Record" means information that is inscribed on a tangible medium or that is stored in an electronic or other medium and is retrievable in perceivable form.

*Subject to enactment by state legislatures.

Digital Signatures in Electronic Commerce. As of the year 2000, the United States, Japan, China, and the European countries had enacted laws recognizing the validity of electronic or digital signatures on contracts and legal documents. The U.S. law, the *Electronic Signatures in Global and National Commerce Act,* makes an electronic signature on a contract as legally binding as a handwritten one on a paper document.

Problems of Contract Interpretation

Due to the great distances involved in international business, negotiations are often conducted through a series of conversations, meetings, and communications by mail, package delivery, telephone, fax, e-mail, and sharing of digital files. The parties may make reference to ancillary materials, such as spec sheets and price lists. Samples, models, and prototypes may be exchanged. The negotiations may take place in more than one country and more than one language. The buyer may visit the seller's factory to see the seller's capabilities firsthand. Discussions might take place through "delegations" or negotiating teams of salespeople, technical specialists, agents, and attorneys. Technical discussions are often left to engineers or others experts. Negotiations may be heavily influenced by language barriers and cultural differences, and terminology peculiar to the industry will be used. The parties may have thought that they were close to agreement many times, only to reach an impasse, resuming negotiations at a later time. In the end, the final agreement may be recorded in one written document. On the other hand, it is not unusual for the parties to fail to put their agreement into a complete and final written document. This can happen out of ignorance, a history of past dealings with one another, time constraints, or other reasons. And as we saw, in most countries, contracts for the international sale of goods do not have to be in writing to be enforceable under the CISG. In the event that a dispute ends in court, it might be possible for the court to look at the chain of negotiations and to piece together the intentions of the parties on the basis of the testimony and other evidence. But this can be expensive and lead to an uncertain result. More experienced firms, at the close of negotiations, would be careful to put their complete agreement in writing. If the complete and final agreement has been put into writing, we say that the contract has become "integrated." An *integrated contract* is a written document or documents that evidence the final and complete agreement of the parties. Mere informal notes of one of the parties, or an unsigned document marked "draft," would not be a fully integrated contract.

The Parol Evidence Rule under the Common Law. The common law *parol evidence rule* states that a court may not consider in evidence any written or oral statements that were made by the parties prior to or at the time of concluding a fully integrated written contract if the statements are offered to contradict, vary, or add to the terms of the written contract. The court may not look to prior negotiations, correspondence, or verbal statements offered by one of the parties at trial for the purpose of denying or contradicting the written contract. Parol evidence may be introduced to clarify an ambiguity (but not to contradict the "plain meaning" of a term); to prove fraud, undue influence, or lack of capacity; or to prove the existence of a later agreement that modified or terminated an earlier contract. The parol evidence rule is a common law rule, applicable to all contracts, not just sales contracts. It prevents extrinsic evidence from reaching the ears of a jury and lessens the chance of perjury and unreliable testimony. The civil law systems, which generally do not use jury trials in these cases, do not have the same strict rule against the admissibility of parol evidence in most commercial breach of contract cases.

Parol Evidence under the CISG. The parol evidence rule has not been incorporated into the CISG. Article 8 of the CISG allows a court, when considering the intent of the parties to a contract, to consider "all relevant circumstances of the case, including the negotiations, any practices which the parties have established between themselves, usages, and any subsequent conduct of the parties."

In *MCC-Marble Ceramic Center, Inc. v. Ceramica Nuova D'Agostino, S.P.A.,* 144 F.3d 1384 (11th Cir. 1998), an American had signed a contract for the purchase of Italian ceramic tile while at a trade fair in Bologna. The document consisted of the seller's order form and included preprinted terms on the front and reverse sides. The terms stated that if the goods did not conform to the contract, notice had to be given to the seller within 10 days. When the tile arrived, the buyer believed it was inferior, but never gave notice of this fact to the seller. There was uncontradicted evidence that, at the time of signing the contract, all parties had a verbal understanding that the preprinted terms would not be applicable. The court ruled that parol evidence could be considered to contradict the written terms of the contract. In other words, the trial court could consider the subjective intent of the parties, as well as their verbal understanding at the time of signing the contract, in order to invalidate the preprinted terms. With no preprinted terms, the buyer would be permitted to withhold payment because the goods did not conform to the contract specifications. The case was decided under the CISG.

Customs, Practices, and Trade Usages. It is usually not possible, in an international transaction, for the parties to expressly state or write every single detail into their contract. There are bound to be gaps in most contracts. Firms that have done business in a certain way for many years often expect, and are justified in expecting, that they will continue the same practice. A buyer who has always ordered products and materials of specified quality may not recite that in every order placed with his or her supplier. They may assume that their past dealings will become a part of their future dealings, unless specified. Another issue is that in many industries, it is common to use language and terminology specific to that industry. For example, in purchasing silk from China, a silk buyer in the United States may order "hand-pulled mulberry silk" or "habotai" or "tussah" or "10-momme weight." These are terms that may have very special meanings to merchants but mean nothing to the rest of us.

To fill in these gaps, or to interpret specific contract provisions, the courts of the United States and most other common law countries will look to *trade usages* for guidance. Trade usages are rules derived from the widespread customs of an industry, the practices of merchants in their past dealings, and the usages of trade terminology and language. For example, the Tampa Cigar Co. contracts to buy an ocean container of "Sumatra tobacco" from an independent broker in Mexico City. Tampa Cigar, and indeed most of the industry, believes that Sumatra tobacco is grown on the island of Sumatra. Unless agreed otherwise, this term becomes a part of the contract. If the broker delivers tobacco grown in Honduras from Sumatra seed, he may be in breach of contract if the law recognizes "Sumatra tobacco" as a valid trade usage. Consider another case involving a buyer that sues a seller for delivery of nonconforming goods. The seller points to a guarantee in the contract that the goods "will be of average and acceptable quality for the kind and type of goods sold in the trade." How would a court interpret this provision? It could look to testimony and evidence attesting to what the trade considers "average and acceptable."

Another example of a common trade usage is the practice of using shorthand trade terms to refer to which party is responsible for shipping expenses and the risk of damage or loss to goods during shipment. Companies worldwide utilize trade terms such as F.O.B. or C.I.F. as shorthand expressions of the parties' shipping responsibilities. These are enforceable as a valid trade usage.

In some developing countries, reliance on trade usages is discouraged. This is because of a common belief there that many trade usages were derived from the practices of European powers during their colonial periods. During this time, the European trading companies were able to establish mercantile practices that favored the English, Dutch, and other colonial traders. A good example might be the cocoa trade, which was dominated by London merchants. When they traded in Africa, the Mediterranean, or the Caribbean, these merchants established their trade usages and practices there. Some developing countries still believe that a trade usage derived from European traders and in use by modern Western firms could only be to their disadvantage.

Trade Usages under the CISG. The CISG provisions of Article 9 resemble the way trade usages are handled under American law. The only trade usages that can be used to interpret or fill in the gaps in a contract are (1) those to which the parties have agreed or that they have established between themselves and (2) those usages of which the parties knew or ought to have known, and that are widely known in international trade (or at least in those countries in which both buyer and seller are located) and regularly observed in the industry or trade involved.

Mutual Assent: The Offer

The contract laws of all countries require that the parties reach a mutual agreement and understanding about the essential terms of a contract. This is known as *mutual assent*. The agreement is reached through the bargaining process between offeror and offeree. The offeror, by making the offer, creates in the offeree the power of acceptance, or the power to form a contract. A contract arises upon acceptance by the offeree.

The Intention to Be Bound. Under Article 14 of the CISG, a communication between the parties is considered an offer when (1) it is a proposal for concluding a contract and (2) it is "sufficiently definite and indicates the intention of the offeror to be bound." An offer is considered sufficiently definite if it (1) indicates or describes the goods, (2) expressly or implicitly specifies the quantity, and (3) expressly or implicitly specifies the price for the goods. For example, assume that a manufacturer sends a catalog, samples, and a price quote to a prospective customer. If they are sufficiently definite and meet the requirements of Article 14, then they could be construed as an offer, and the customer would have the power to accept, reject, counteroffer, or do nothing. However, suppose that the manufacturer includes a statement that the materials are not to be construed as an offer, and that no contract can arise until the buyer's order is approved or confirmed by the manufacturer's home office. In that case the manufacturer probably has not made a "proposal for concluding a contract" and has not indicated "the intention to be bound." Here, no power of acceptance has been created in the buyer, and it would be up to the buyer to make an offer and wait for acceptance from the manufacturer's home office. One should not think that just because an item of communication includes a description of the goods, the quantity, and the price, that it always indicates an offer to conclude a contract. In many international contracts involving a great deal of money, no firm would make a commitment without reaching an agreement on many other terms, such as methods of payment, delivery dates, allocation of shipping costs, quality standards, installation and training, warranty, responsibility for duties or taxes, etc. Take the following example. Buyer and seller are negotiating the sale of ten industrial knitting machines for one million euros. The buyer states, "Everything seems agreeable. I'll take the machines." This language probably does not give rise to a contract even though it seems "sufficiently definite." The lack of agreement on other matters that would normally be considered critical in a sale of this magnitude indicates that the parties are still in the negotiating stage. However, in cases where the court does find that the parties had the intention to be bound, it can supply many of the missing terms by looking to their past dealings and to the customs in the trade or industry, or by referring to the applicable provisions of the CISG.

Public Offers. If an offer must express the offeror's intention to be bound, how does the law treat advertisements, brochures, catalogs, and Web sites? Are they offers, inviting acceptance, or are they mere *invitations to deal*—invitations to the public to make an offer? The laws of some nations hold that an offer must be addressed to one or more specific persons. In those countries, an advertisement will not create the power of acceptance in a member of the public who reads the ad. In Germany, for instance, advertisements or price lists addressed to the public in general are mere invitations to deal. Other countries, while treating most advertisements as mere invitations to deal, do recognize that specific advertisements that describe the goods, their quantity, and price may be considered an offer. For example, while under Chinese contract law a price list or advertisement is an invitation to deal, a catalog or advertisement may be considered an offer if the contents are sufficiently detailed and definite.

The CISG takes a middle position by creating a presumption that an advertisement, catalog, price list, or Web site is not an offer. Article 14 states, "A proposal other than one addressed to one or more specific persons is to be considered merely as an invitation to make offers, unless the contrary is clearly indicated by the person making the proposal." Consequently, to be on the safe side, many attorneys recommend that a seller include in all of its price sheets and literature, and on its Web site, a notice that the content does not constitute an offer.

Open Price Terms. In international transactions between companies familiar with their industry or market, it is not unusual that a contract can be concluded without any mention of price. It's not that it was overlooked; it may just have been that they were relying on some external market factor or prior course of dealings to determine price. A contract may even refer to a market price on a date that is months or even years away. For instance, it would not be unusual for a contract to refer to a price on a given date on a specific commodities market. If the price is left "open," is the parties' understanding sufficiently definite to constitute a valid contract? In the United States, most state UCC laws provide that if price is not specified, a "reasonable price" will be presumed. Under this flexible approach, the contract does not fail. On the other hand, such a provision would not be found in a socialist legal system in which prices are dictated by government central planning. Open price terms are not favored in developing countries, either, because they are major exporters of agricultural commodities, minerals, and other raw materials subject to a highly fluctuating market. Even in most civil law nations, such as France, a sales price must be sufficiently definite in order for a contract to be valid. Chinese law takes an approach in keeping with its socialist system. If the price of goods is not stated in the contract, then a market price will be presumed. However, where Chinese law or administrative rulings specify a required or suggested price for the goods in question, then the government-established price must be used.

Although some conflict stems from the language of the CISG regarding open price terms (see Articles 14 and 55), the CISG provisions seem similar to those of U.S. state law. Article 55, found under the section on the obligations of the buyer, states that where price is not fixed, the price will be that charged "for such goods sold under comparable circumstances in the trade concerned." Accordingly, if the buyer and seller fail to specify the price of the goods, a court might look to the trade or to the market price of comparable goods to make its own determination of price, and the contract and all its other provisions will remain in effect.

Firm Offers. As a general rule, an offer may be revoked at any time prior to acceptance. Under the UCC, as between merchants, an offer may not be revoked if it is made in a signed writing that gives assurance that it will remain open for a stated period of time, not to exceed three months. Under the CISG, firm offers are valid even if they are not in writing. Moreover, an offer may not be revoked if the offeree reasonably relies on the offer as being irrevocable and the offeree has acted in reliance on the offer. Consider a buyer who states to a supplier, "Within the next month, I will be placing an order for 100 computers, so please give me your best price." The supplier responds, making no reference as to whether the offer will remain open. If the buyer then quotes a price on the computers for resale to a customer, the offer will be irrevocable during that month. Some civil law countries, such as Germany, France, Italy, and Japan, go even further in limiting the offeror's power to revoke. In civil law countries, the offeror may not revoke during the period of time normally needed for the offeree's acceptance to arrive.

The Pro Forma Invoice. One very common method of offering goods for sale to a foreign buyer is through the pro forma invoice (Exhibit 4.3). The *pro forma invoice* is a formal document addressed to a specified buyer to sell the products described according to certain terms and conditions. Most pro forma invoices are specific and definite enough to meet the requirements of an offer. The pro forma invoice sets out the price for the goods in the currency stated, plus any additional charges payable by the buyer's account, including the cost of packing and crating; the cost of inland freight; the cost of ocean or air freight, freight forwarder's fees, and pier delivery charges; wharfage and warehouse charges; and insurance. (Most exporters rely heavily on their freight forwarders to obtain this cost information in advance and, later, to make these shipping arrangements.) The *pro forma* invoice specifies the mode of shipment, the method of payment, the length of time for which the quoted terms will be valid, and any and all other terms required by the seller as a condition of sale. Sellers usually require the buyer to accept the offer by signing it and returning it to them before shipment. In other cases, a buyer might accept by sending their own purchase order form. *Pro forma* invoices are often required by a buyer's bank or by the customs authority in the buyer's country prior to importation of the goods so that import licenses can be issued in advance.

Exhibit 4.3

Pro Forma Invoice

DownPillow International, Inc.
Pro Forma Invoice
Boone, North Carolina, U.S.A.

Invoice to:	Japanese Retailer Osaka, Japan	Date of pro forma invoice: Oct. 12, 2000
Ship/Consign to:	as per buyer's instructions	This pro forma no. 000044372
Shipment via:	U.S. port to destination Kobe	Terms of Payment:
Notify Party:	Buyer to advise	Cash against documents,
Country-of-Origin:	U.S.A	irrevocable LC payable in U.S. dollars
Total weight (est.):	9405 lbs/4266 kg.	Shipment Date
Shipping volume (est.):	3000 cu.ft./85 cu.m.	45 days after receipt of LC

Quantity	Item Code	Description	Price	Amount
5,000	5WGD-1	Bed pillows of white goose down total fill weight 26 oz./0.74 kg, contents sterilized shell: 100% cotton, with piping size 26" × 26", 66 cm × 66 cm	$32.00	$160,000
		PRICE Ex Works, Domestic packing		$160,000
		Export packing/vacuum pack charges		850
		Cartage/Inland freight charge		1,250
		Pier delivery charge		150
		Freight forwarder's fees		200
		PRICE F.A.S. NC PORT		$162,450
		Ocean freight charges port to port		$3,355
		Container rental charge		450
		Marine insurance charges		640
		PRICE C.I.F. Port of KOBE, Japan		
				$166,895

DownPillow International, Inc.

____________________ ____________________

by, Export Sales Manager Authorized buyer's signature

All terms of sale interpreted by *Incoterms* 2000. This quotation is valid for a period of 60 days from above date. Any changes in the actual cost of shipping, handling, packaging, insurance, or other charges not a part of the actual cost of the goods are buyer's responsibility.

SEE OTHER SIDE FOR ADDITIONAL TERMS AND CONDITIONS

EXHIBIT 4.4

Seller's Terms and Conditions of Sale

(Seller's Order Confirmation—Reverse Side)
Pro Forma Invoice or
TERMS AND CONDITIONS OF SALE

1. Acceptance

This constitutes acceptance by Seller of Buyer's purchase order. This acceptance is expressly made conditional upon Buyer's assent, express or implied, to the terms and conditions set forth herein without modification or addition. Buyer's acceptance of these terms and conditions shall be indicated by any part of the following, whichever first occurs: (a) Buyer's written acknowledgment hereof; (b) Buyer's acceptance of shipment of the goods herein described; (c) Buyer's failure to acknowledge or reject these terms and conditions in writing within five business days after delivery; or (d) any other act or expression of acceptance by the Buyer. Seller's silence or failure to respond to any such subsequent term, condition, or proposal shall not be deemed to be Seller's acceptance or approval thereof.

2. Price and Delivery

The quoted price for the goods may be varied by additions upwards by the Seller according to market conditions at the date of shipment and the Buyer shall pay such additions in addition to the quoted price, including but not limited to increases in the cost of labor, material, operations, and/or transport. Delivery and payment terms shall be made according to this order confirmation. Trade formulas used herein (e.g., CIF, CPT, FAS, or FOB) shall be interpreted according to *Incoterms* (2000). Payment in the currency and at the conditions of this confirmation.

3. Force Majeure

Seller shall not be liable for loss or damage due to delay in manufacture, shipment, or delivery resulting from any cause beyond Seller's direct control or due to compliance with any regulations, orders, acts, instructions, or priority requests of any government authority, acts of God, acts or omissions of the purchaser, fires, floods, epidemics, weather, strikes, factory shutdowns, embargoes, wars, riots, delays in transportation, delay in receiving materials from Seller's usual sources, and any delay resulting from any such cause shall extend shipment or delivery date to the extent caused thereby and Seller shall be reimbursed its additional expenses resulting from such delay. In the case of delay lasting more than eight weeks, Seller has the right to cancel contract. Receipt of merchandise by the Buyer shall constitute a waiver of any claims for delay.

4. Warranties

The Seller makes no representations or warranties with respect to the goods herein. Seller hereby disclaims warranties, express or implied, as to the products, including but not limited to, any implied warranty of quality or merchantability or fitness for any particular purpose, and the Buyer takes the goods on the Buyer's own judgment. Seller is not liable for any damage or loss for a breach of warranty.

5. Limitation of Liability

Seller is not liable for any special, consequential, or incidental damages arising out of this agreement or the goods sold hereunder, including but not limited to damages for lost profits, loss of use, or any damages or sums paid by Buyer to third parties, even if Seller has been advised of the possibility of such damages.

6. Governing Law

In respect of any standard, test, mode of inspection, measurement, or weight, the practice governing the same adopted for use in United States shall prevail. This agreement shall be governed by the Laws of North Carolina and in the event of any dispute arising, whether touching on the interpretation hereof or otherwise, the same shall be resolved before the General Court of Justice of the State of North Carolina.

Pro forma invoices are used in all types of industries, manufacturing firms in particular. The *pro forma* invoice should not be confused with the *commercial invoice,* which is the final bill for the goods that accompanies the request for payment.

Mutual Assent: The Acceptance

A contract is not formed until the offer is accepted by the offeree. The acceptance is the offeree's manifestation of the intention to be bound to the terms silence / implied acceptance

of the offer. Modern legal rules applicable to the sale of goods give great flexibility to the offeree as to the manner and method of accepting—certainly greater flexibility than under the common law. Under the CISG, an acceptance may take the form of a statement or conduct by the offeree that indicates the offeree's intention to be bound to the contract. CISG Article 18 states that "a statement made by or other conduct of the offeree indicating assent to an offer is an acceptance." (UCC 2-206 states that "an offer to make a contract shall be construed as inviting acceptance in any manner and by any medium reasonable in the circumstances.") This rule has day-to-day applicability. It is very common for a prospective buyer to place an order to purchase goods, with the seller responding not with a verbal or written confirmation, or not by initialing the order and returning it to the buyer, but simply by shipping the goods called for. For instance, the seller may be shipping urgently needed replacement parts for a stopped assembly line. Similarly, it is not uncommon for a buyer to accept the delivery of goods by simply remitting payment (as in the case where the seller ships blue widgets instead of the red ones ordered; if the buyer pays for the nonconforming red ones, there is a contract). Both the UCC and the CISG cover these situations. CISG Article 18 states that an offeree may accept by "dispatching the goods or payment of the price, without notice to the offeror" provided that the parties have established this as a practice or it is routinely accepted in the trade, and if the act is performed within the time for acceptance fixed by the offeror or within a reasonable time.

Silence Not an Acceptance. The general rule in most countries is that the offeree's silence or inactivity alone should not be interpreted as an acceptance. If you unexpectedly receive goods that you did not order, you should not have to pay for them (although in most legal systems, you might have to safeguard them until retrieved by the sender). Moreover, it would be unfair if a seller could force you to take goods simply by stating, "If I don't hear from you, I assume you will keep them and pay for them." On the other hand, there are situations where the parties can agree that silence is an acceptance. If seller makes an offer to you, and you reply, "If you do not hear from me by 5:00 p.m., ship the goods," then you have made your silence an acceptance.

Another exception occurs when the parties' previous dealings oblige them to speak up and not remain silent. Consider this case: For the past five years, DownPillow, Inc. has regularly ordered quantities of white goose down from Federhaus GmbH for shipment within three months. At first, Federhaus confirmed all orders. Soon, Federhaus stopped sending written confirmations of orders and just shipped. This time, DownPillow placed the order and Federhaus never shipped. DownPillow suffered damages when it unexpectedly ran out of feathers. It can sue Federhaus for breach of contract on the basis that the established practice of the parties presumed Federhaus's acceptance of DownPillow's order.

When an Acceptance is Effective. Under the common law, and in virtually all legal systems, the offeree may accept at any time until the offer is revoked by the offeror, until the offer expires due to the passage of time, until the original offer is rejected by the offeree, until the offeree makes a counteroffer in return, or until the offer terminates (such as through the death of one of the parties or destruction of the subject matter). Thus, it is often important to know when an acceptance becomes effective because it cuts off the offeror's ability to revoke the offer, and it is at that point in time when contractual rights and obligations arise. Time constraints can be even more critical in international transactions between buyers and sellers located in different time zones and using several different means of communications—next-day letters, e-mail, telephone, and facsimile transmissions.

Under the common law, a contract is formed when the acceptance is dispatched by the offeree. In the case of an acceptance by letter or written document, the time of dispatch is the time the letter is put into the hands of the postal authorities, courier service, or other carrier. This is commonly called the *mailbox rule*. The rule assumes that the correct mode of transmission is used (i.e., one that the offeror specifies or, if none, one that is reasonable under the circumstances) and that it is properly addressed. This assumption makes commercial sense, for if a fax arrives offering to sell fresh roses sitting on the hot tarmac in Colombia, one does not accept by letter and expect a contract to be formed on dispatch. Hence, if a buyer submits an order to a seller, a contract is formed upon the dispatch of the seller's acceptance. The buyer's power to withdraw the offer to purchase ended at the time the contract was formed. While the "mailbox rule" was developed long before the existence of electronic communications, and while it has lost some of its significance in the age of fax machines and e-mail, it is still relevant and applicable.

The CISG follows a somewhat different approach. Under Article 18, an acceptance is not effective upon dispatch, but is effective when it reaches the offeror (or in the case of electronic transmission, appears on the offeror's fax machine or in his or her e-mail inbox). Article 16 protects the offeree by stating that the dispatch of an acceptance cuts off the offeror's right to revoke the offer. Thus, an acceptance may possibly be withdrawn if the withdrawal reaches the offeror before or at the same time as the acceptance does (Article 22). Recall that under the common law, the offeree would not have had the same right because the contract would have been formed at the moment of dispatch. This CISG rule follows the basic rules in effect in China and civil law countries. The following case, *Chateau des Charmes Wines, Ltd. v. Sabaté,* discusses the making of a verbal contract and one party's futile attempt to modify it.

Chateau des Charmes Wines Ltd. v. Sabaté

328 F.3d. 528 (9th Cir. 2003)

United States Court of Appeals (9th Cir.)

BACKGROUND AND FACTS

Sabaté France sold wine corks to Chateau, a winery in Canada. The sale took place through Sabaté's California subsidiary, Sabaté USA. In talks, Sabaté claimed that the corks would not distort the taste of wine. The parties agreed by telephone on the quantity, price, and payment and shipping terms. No other terms were discussed, and the parties had never done business before. After a second order, totaling eleven shipments, a total of 1.2 million corks had been sold. An invoice accompanied each shipment stating that "Any dispute arising under the present contract is under the sole jurisdiction of the Court of Commerce of the City of Perpignan." Chateau took delivery, remitted payment, and after bottling the wine, discovered that the cork had tainted the wine's flavor. When Chateau sued for breach of warranty, Sabaté argued that the forum selection clause required that the case be heard in France. Chateau countered, claiming that a valid and enforceable verbal contract had already existed and that the subsequent forum selection clause was not a part of it. The district court held for Sabaté.

PER CURIAM

The question before us is whether the forum selection clause in Sabaté France's invoices was part of any agreement between the parties. The disputes in this case arise out of an agreement for a sale of goods from a French party and a United States party to a Canadian party. Such international sales contracts are ordinarily governed by a multilateral treaty, the *United Nations Convention on Contracts for the International Sale of Goods* (CISG), which applies to "contracts of sale of goods between parties whose places of business are in different States ... when the States are Contracting States." The United States, Canada, and France are all contracting states to the CISG ... [T]here is no doubt that the CISG is valid and binding federal law....

Under the CISG, it is plain that the forum selection clauses were not part of any agreement between the parties. The Convention sets out a clear regime for analyzing international contracts for the sale of goods: "A contract of sale need not be concluded in or evidenced by writing and is not subject to any other requirement as to form." CISG, art. 11. A proposal is an offer if it is sufficiently definite to "indicate the goods and expressly or implicitly fix or make provision for determining the quantity and the price," *id.*, art. 14, and it demonstrates an intention by the offeror to be bound if the proposal is accepted. In turn, an offer is accepted if the offeree makes a "statement ... or other conduct ... indicating assent to an offer." *Id.*, art. 18. Further, "A contract is concluded at the moment when an acceptance of an offer becomes effective." *Id.*, art. 23. Within such a framework, the oral agreements between Sabaté USA and Chateau as to the kind of cork, the quantity, and the price were sufficient to create complete and binding contracts.

continued

continued

The terms of those agreements did not include any forum selection clause. Indeed, Sabaté France and Sabaté USA do not contend that a forum selection clause was part of their oral agreements, but merely that the clauses in the invoices became part of a binding agreement. The logic of this contention is defective. Under the CISG, a "contract may be modified or terminated by the mere agreement of the parties." *Id.*, art. 29(1). However, the Convention clearly states that "[a]dditional or different terms relating, among other things, to ... the settlement of disputes are considered to alter the terms of the offer materially." *Id.*, art. 19(3). There is no indication that Chateau conducted itself in a manner that evidenced any affirmative assent to the forum selection clauses in the invoices. Rather, Chateau merely performed its obligations under the oral contract.

Nothing in the CISG suggests that the failure to object to a party's unilateral attempt to alter materially the terms of an otherwise valid agreement is an "agreement" within the terms of Article 29. *Cf.* CISG, art. 8(3). ("In determining the intent of a party or the understanding a reasonable person would have had, due consideration is to be given to all relevant circumstances of the case including the negotiations, any practices which the parties have established between themselves, usages and any subsequent conduct of the parties.") Here, no circumstances exist to conclude that Chateau's conduct evidenced an "agreement." We reject the contention that because Sabaté France sent multiple invoices it created an agreement as to the proper forum with Chateau. The parties agreed in two telephone calls to a purchase of corks to be shipped in eleven batches. In such circumstances, a party's multiple attempts to alter an agreement unilaterally do not so effect [citation omitted].

Decision. The verbal contract for the purchase of corks was valid and binding. The attempt by the seller to later include a new and material term (the forum selection clause) in the invoices was not effective. The buyer did not assent to the new term simply by receiving and paying for the goods. Reversed and remanded.

Comment. Here the seller attempted to add a new "surprise" term after the contract had already been formed, and indeed, after the goods had been shipped. This distinguishes this case from cases where the new term is incorporated into the seller's written confirmation sent in reply to a buyer's purchase order form (the typical "battle of the forms" situation).

The Mirror Image Rule. Students of the common law of contracts are very familiar with the *mirror image rule.* The rule requires that an offeree respond to an offer with an acceptance that is definite and unconditional and that matches the terms of the offer exactly and unequivocally. Under the mirror image rule, a purported acceptance that contains different or additional terms, no matter how minor, is considered a counteroffer and, thus, a rejection of the original offer. The principle that an acceptance must be definite and unconditional is found in the civil law countries and in CISG. Article 19(1) states, "A reply to an offer which purports to be an acceptance but contains additions, limitations or other modifications is a rejection of the offer and constitutes a counteroffer." Thus, if the buyer places an order for a quantity of goods of a certain description, for shipment by air no later than "next Tuesday," and the seller replies by promising shipment no later than "next Wednesday morning," there is no contract.

For many contracts this rule works fine, because it prevents contracts from arising when there was actually no mutual assent. It lessens the possibility of contract disputes. However, there are a few situations where strict adherence to the mirror image rule is not commercially practical. One of these situations is where the offeror and offeree, the buyer and seller, are communicating through an exchange of standard business forms, each of which contains extensive "fine print" provisions.

Standard Business Forms and Contract Modifications

Buyers and sellers often use standard business forms for quoting prices, placing orders, and acknowledging receipt of those orders. Two of the most common that we will discuss are the purchase order and the order confirmation. A *purchase order* is a form commonly used by business buyers for placing orders for goods from their vendors. Typically, it includes the description and quantity of the goods ordered, a delivery address, and authorized buyer's signature. It may also recite the prices that the buyer believes to be accurate and current for the goods, a desired shipping date, and any other contractual requirements the buyer may have. The *order confirmation* (also called a "sales acknowledgment") is the seller's formal confirmation of the buyer's order, either accepting the order, rejecting it, or modifying its terms. While formal order confirmations are used in the United States for domestic business, their use in international trade, particularly by European and Asian firms, is customary and expected. Typically, these forms leave room on the front so the parties may insert important contract terms—those that they "bargained for," such as price, quality, or ship date. The reverse side often contains detailed "fine print" provisions or standard clauses, often called *terms and conditions* or *general conditions of sale* (Exhibit 4.4).

They are often drafted by attorneys to limit their client's liability by placing greater responsibility on the other party. Often they are adapted from recommended standard clauses provided by industry or trade associations. For instance, one set of standard clauses might be utilized by the steel industry, another by grain merchants, and yet another by the chemical industry. The parties may not even be aware of the legal significance of these seldom-read fine print provisions. For the most part, a seller would only read the most crucial provisions on the front page of a buyer's purchase order to see what was ordered. A buyer may only glance at the key provisions of the seller's confirmation to see when the goods will be shipped. Usually, the preprinted terms on these forms differ, sometimes in significant ways.

Here are several examples of how they might differ:

- Buyer's purchase order allows the buyer to bring suit for consequential damages if the seller breaches the contract. Seller's confirmation specifically excludes consequential damages.
- Buyer's purchase order calls for disputes to be resolved in the buyer's country. Seller's confirmation calls for disputes to be heard in the courts of the seller's country.
- Buyer's purchase order requires shipment by a certain date named in the order. Seller's confirmation allows a grace period for late shipping or provides for excuses for late shipment.
- Buyer's purchase order is silent about whether the buyer has to notify the seller in the event of problems with the merchandise. Seller's confirmation requires buyer to notify the seller of any problems in the order within seven days.

The potential for conflict is almost endless. When this occurs, lawyers call it a *battle of the forms.* In the following sections, assume that the buyer is the offeror and that the buyer's purchase order is the offer. Assume also that the seller is the offeree and that the seller's confirmation of that order is the (attempted) acceptance. The assumptions serve to simplify the discussion for understanding. Keep in mind that the seller could possibly make an offer first, such as in a *pro forma* invoice, in which case the buyer's purchase order might actually be an attempted acceptance.

The "Battle of the Forms" under the Common Law and Civil Law. If a seller sends a confirmation in response to a buyer's purchase order and the seller's form contains differing or additional terms, no matter how minor, then no contract would exist. The mirror image rule has been violated. Each form or correspondence between them is considered a counteroffer, canceling the previous one. If the parties do not perform (e.g., the seller does not ship the goods), then no contract is formed. Indeed, the buyer cannot force the seller to ship because no contract exists. If the parties do perform—the seller ships the goods—then that action is an acceptance of the terms on the other party's last form. The result usually is that the form sent last in time will prevail as the contract. Consider the following two examples:

- Suppose that a U.S. company, DownPillow International, Inc., sends a purchase order to Federhaus, a German supplier of feathers. Federhaus replies with a confirmation stating that the buyer has only 10 days to notify the seller in the event of a problem with the shipment. DownPillow faxes back that it must have

Minor terms = ok auto modifiers

30 days. With no more said, Federhaus ships. This action is an acceptance—and the contract terms are those in DownPillow's last correspondence. DownPillow has 30 days. If the 10-day provision was important to Federhaus, it should have gotten an affirmative response from DownPillow before shipping.

- Now assume that Federhaus's confirmation states that a charge of 1 percent per month will be applied to outstanding balances if the account is not paid within 30 days. DownPillow does nothing more. If the seller ships, it might not have recourse against DownPillow for refusing the goods—the new term was not a mirror image of the buyer's order, and thus, no contract was formed to protect the seller. On the other hand, if DownPillow accepts the feathers and then fails to pay within 30 days, it will be liable for the interest penalty because the confirmation was a counteroffer that DownPillow accepted by receiving the merchandise. These determinations would be the result if the case were heard in a court that applied the common law or civil law rules. These results are not the case in the United States today.

THE "BATTLE OF THE FORMS" UNDER THE UCC. In the United States the mirror image rule has been modified by statute to deal with modern business practices and to avoid the problems in the preceding examples. Under subsections 1 and 2 of the original UCC 2-207:

1. A written confirmation that is sent within a reasonable time operates as an acceptance even though it states terms additional to or different from those in the purchase order, unless the confirmation "is expressly made conditional on assent to the additional or different terms."
2. If both parties are merchants, any additional terms contained in the seller's confirmation automatically become a part of the contract *unless:*
   a. The buyer's purchase order "expressly limits acceptance" to the terms in that order;
   b. The additional terms in the confirmation "materially alter" the terms of the order; or
   c. The buyer notifies the seller of an objection to the additional terms within a reasonable time after receiving the confirmation containing the new terms.

A careful reading of UCC 2-207 shows that the UCC attempts to uphold the intentions of the parties by keeping the contract in existence where there are only *minor differences* between the forms used by the parties. The UCC states that, between merchants, an acceptance by a confirmation that contains additional terms that reflect only minor changes from the buyer's order will be effective to produce a contract, and the minor terms become a part of it (unless the buyer notifies the seller of an objection to the new term). A minor term might be one that is in usual and customary usage in the trade. Adding a provision that calls for an interest penalty for late payment is an example of a minor term (only because such penalties are common in sales contracts).

Now, reconsider our example under the UCC. DownPillow faxes its purchase order for feathers; its order does not expressly limit the acceptance to the terms of the order. All the "bargained" terms such as price, quality, and ship date are agreed upon. Seller Federhaus's confirmation states, however, that a charge of 1 percent per month will be applied to outstanding balances if the account is not paid within 30 days. DownPillow does nothing more. This time, under the UCC, a contract is formed. The seller is safe in shipping and DownPillow will have breached it if it refuses delivery of the goods. Moreover, if DownPillow is late in paying, interest will run on its open account. DownPillow could have objected to the inclusion of the late payment fee term, but it did not.

The situation is different in the case of new terms in the acceptance that attempt to *materially alter* the offer. A material term is generally considered to be one that is not commonly accepted in the trade and that would result in surprise hardship to one party if unilaterally included in the contract by the party. Such new terms do not become a part of the contract unless accepted by the other party. Suppose that DownPillow sends a purchase order to Federhaus in Germany. The order does not expressly limit an acceptance to the terms of the order. The confirmation is identical as to price, quality, ship date, and other bargained terms. However, the standard clause on the reverse side of the confirmation from Federhaus states that "all disputes are to be resolved in arbitration before the International Chamber of Commerce in Paris." A term that affects the rights of the parties in the event of a breach, such as an arbitration clause like this, is a material term. A contract will be formed without Federhaus's new terms. Sellers who wish to be assured that their order confirmation will comprise the entire agreement should request that the buyer show its acceptance of the new terms by signing the confirmation and returning the completed contract to them.

Proposed amendments to UCC 2-206 and 2-207, if adopted, would simplify the "battle of the forms" problem (Exhibit 4.5).

Confirmation Notices—German Law and the CISG. There are some special rules in effect in many European countries that take into account the formal business practices of European firms. In Germany, for example, manufacturing firms regularly confirm purchase orders with their *Auftragsbestätigung*, or "order confirmation." These documents are given special treatment under German law. If this formal confirmation alters the terms of a buyer's purchase order, the terms of the confirmation prevail unless the buyer specifically rejects them in a prompt and timely fashion. Germany applies this law as a "trade usage" to domestic contracts between parties located in Germany. However, it appears that German courts might not apply the rule in international sales under the CISG unless this is recognized as a trade usage in both buyer's and seller's country or has been an established practice between them. Anyone who does business with manufacturing companies in Germany will tell you that this is an established practice—that every order or modification of an order will be confirmed by an *Auftragsbestätigung*. In any event, any company that receives a formal "order confirmation" at the close of negotiations should promptly reply if all the terms are not as intended.

The Battle of the Forms under the CISG. The CISG rules fall somewhere between the rules set out by the common and civil law and the UCC. In an international sales transaction governed by the CISG, an acceptance containing new terms that do not materially alter the terms of the offer becomes a part of the contract, unless the offeror promptly objects to the change. However, a purported acceptance that contains additional or different terms that do materially alter the terms of the offer would constitute a rejection of the offer and a counteroffer. No contract would arise at all unless the offeror

Exhibit 4.5

Proposed Amendments to UCC 2-206 and 2-207*

§2-206. Offer and Acceptance in Formation of Contract.

(3) A definite and seasonable expression of acceptance in a record operates as an acceptance even if it contains terms additional to or different from the offer.

§2-207. Terms of Contract; Effect of Confirmation.

If (i) conduct by both parties recognizes the existence of a contract although their records do not otherwise establish a contract, (ii) a contract is formed by an offer and acceptance, or (iii) a contract formed in any manner is confirmed by a record that contains terms additional to or different from those in the contract being confirmed, the terms of the contract, subject to Section 2-202, are:

(a) terms that appear in the records of both parties;
(b) terms, whether in a record or not, to which both parties agree; and
(c) terms supplied or incorporated under any provision of this Act.

Preliminary Official Comment

1. This section applies to all contracts for the sale of goods, and it is not limited only to those contracts where there has been a "battle of the forms."

*Subject to enactment by state legislatures.

in return accepted all of the terms of the counteroffer. (Recall that under the UCC a contract would arise, albeit without the new terms.) Continuing the previous example, no contract would be formed between DownPillow and Federhaus under the CISG, and Federhaus's new material terms would amount to no more than a counteroffer.

Under the CISG, an acceptance of the counteroffer may arise by assent or *by performance.* In other words, if the original offeror takes some steps toward performing the contract after having received a counteroffer, the offeror will be deemed to have accepted the counteroffer and a contract will be created on the new terms. So, if DownPillow remits payment for the feathers without having read the fine print provisions of Federhaus's confirmation (a counteroffer), it implies acceptance of Federhaus's terms, including the arbitration terms. By way of example, a draft commentary to Article 19 states:

> For example, an offeree might reply to an offer stating that the offeror has fifty tractors available for sale at a certain price by sending a telegram that accepts the offer but adds "ship immediately." ...
>
> ... [T]he additional or different terms contained in [this] reply would constitute material alteration since the terms "ship immediately" would change the time of delivery (since no shipping date had been specified, a "reasonable time" for shipment would have been presumed under the CISG)....
>
> If the reply contains a material alteration, the reply would not constitute an acceptance but would constitute a counteroffer. If the original offeror responds to this reply by shipping the goods ... a contract may eventually be formed by notice to the original offeree of the shipment....

Unlike the UCC, the CISG states those key elements of a contract that will materially alter a contract: price, payment, quality and quantity of goods, place and time of delivery, extent of one party's liability to the other, and settlement of disputes. This list is so broad that almost any term could conceivably be interpreted as "material." Thus, under the CISG, almost any new or different term in the acceptance could constitute a counteroffer. The effect is that many businesspeople may believe that they are "under contract" when they really are not. Consequently, those businesspeople negotiating an international contract must make certain that all material terms of the contract are understood and agreed upon by the parties.

THE VALIDITY OF STANDARD CONTRACT TERMS: A COMPARISON. Today, so-called "fine print" or standard terms in contracts are widely used. They offer many advantages to businesses by eliminating the need to negotiate all the details of a contract every time goods are sold. For large firms selling to hundreds or thousands of customers around the world, the use of standard forms reduces costs, saves time, and allows the firm's legal department to maintain centralized control over contract terms and negotiations. As the potential for disputes increases with an ever-growing volume of business, the large firm can ensure some control over how those disputes will be resolved. In the United States, standard terms are generally permitted in business-to-business contracts unless in violation of a statute or struck down by the courts for other reasons. However, in some civil law countries, such as China or Germany, to take two examples, the statutes are quite specific about the kinds of standard contract terms that are permissible.

China takes a simplistic, yet clear, legal approach to the validity of standardized terms. Chinese law requires standardized terms to be fair in limiting the rights and liabilities of the parties. The terms must be brought to the attention of the other party, and they must be explained if requested. Caution should be used when using standardized terms in China at all, because if they are not fairly negotiated between both parties they might be declared invalid.

The *German Civil Code* has even more detailed provisions dealing with standard contract terms. The *Standard Contract Terms Act (Gesetz zur Regelung des Rechts der Allgemeinen Geschäftsbedingungen)* provides that standard terms are void if they unreasonably disadvantage the other party to the contract by depriving them of their essential rights under the contract or preventing them from performing their part of the contract. For example, contract terms are deemed invalid if they permit a party to escape all obligations without cause or reason; if they call for the payment of a stated amount of money as damages in the event of a breach (liquidated damage provisions) where the stated damages are unjustified, excessive, or not related to the actual harm suffered; if they permit one party to pass through price or cost increases to the other party for deliveries made within four months of the contract date; or if they release a party from giving notice of receipt of defective goods.

Performance of Contracts

The primary responsibility of the buyer (Articles 53–60) is to pay the price for the goods and take delivery at the time and in the manner promised. The primary responsibility of the seller (Articles 30–35) in performing a contract for the sale of goods is to deliver conforming goods in the manner specified and within the time called for in the contract.

Performance of Seller

One of the primary responsibilities of the seller is to deliver conforming goods. CISG Article 35 states, "The seller must deliver goods which are of the quantity, quality and description required by the contract and which are contained or packaged in the manner required by the contract." Goods that do not conform to the requirements of the contract are said to be nonconforming. This includes all express descriptions, specifications, representations, and warranties set out in the contract. They must also comply with representations implied in the contract by law.

Implied Representations. In the United States, the UCC creates certain implied warranties on goods that become a part of the contract by law (Exhibit 4.6). This includes the warranty of merchantability (drawn from the English common law), the warranty of fitness for a particular purpose in which the buyer relies on the skill and expertise of the seller, and warranty of title. The CISG has similar provisions. Under CISG Article 35, unless otherwise agreed by the parties, the seller must deliver goods that are of the quantity, quality, and description required by the contract and that

1. Are fit for the purposes for which goods of the same description would ordinarily be used (unless at the time of contracting, the buyer knew or could not have been unaware that the goods were unfit; the seller's knowledge in this case is not relevant). This corresponds to the warranty of merchantability under the common law and the UCC and to the implied representation that goods be of "average quality" under European civil law.
2. Are fit for any particular purpose expressly or impliedly made known to the seller at the time of the conclusion of the contract, except where the circumstances show that the buyer did not rely, or that it was unreasonable for him to rely, on the seller's skill and judgment.
3. Possess the qualities of goods which the seller has held out to the buyer as a sample or model.
4. Are contained or packaged in the manner usual for such goods or, where there is no such manner, in a manner adequate to preserve and protect the goods (unless at the time of contracting, the buyer knew or could not have been unaware that the goods were not properly packaged).

The CISG does not prevent parties from waiving these representations. The drafters of the CISG

Exhibit 4.6

UCC Implied Warranties, Merchantability, and Usage of Trade

§2-314(2) Goods to be merchantable must be at least such as

(a) pass without objection in the trade under the contract description; and
(b) in the case of fungible goods, are of fair average quality within the description; and
(c) are fit for the ordinary purposes for which such goods are used; and
(d) run, within the variations permitted by the agreement, of even kind, quality, and quantity within each unit and among all units involved; and
(e) are adequately contained, packaged, and labeled as the agreement may require; and
(f) conform to the promises or affirmations of fact made on the container or label if any.

§2-314(3) (a) Unless excluded or modified other implied warranties may arise from course of dealing or usage of trade.

wanted to give the parties as much freedom of contract as possible, in part because the code does not apply to consumer sales.

Goods Fit for Particular Purpose. In international transactions, goods are often bought for use in manufacturing, assembly, or for resale. Goods must be fit for these purposes if the seller knew or should have known of the intended purpose for which the goods were bought. In *Schmitz-Werke GmbH & Co. v. Rockland Industries, Inc.*, a U.S. court discussed whether fabric sold from the United States to a buyer in Germany was fit for the purposes intended.

Schmitz-Werke GmbH & Co. v. Rockland Industries, Inc.

37 F.Appx 687 (2002)

United States Court of Appeals (4th Cir.)

BACKGROUND AND FACTS

The seller is an American fabric manufacturer that sold "Trevira" drapery fabric to the plaintiff (buyer) in Germany. During negotiations, the seller stated that the fabric was particularly suited to be a printing base for transfer printing. The buyer had another German company, PMD, experiment with printing on a sample. The buyer informed the seller that although they were satisfied with the material, there were some problems. After receiving 15,000 meters of fabric, the buyer noted additional problems but was encouraged by the seller to continue printing. A second shipment of 60,000 meters was received. When PMD complained about problems in printing on the fabric, another German company was asked to inspect the fabric. Their report indicated that over 15 percent of the fabric was lower grade or seconds. The buyer returned the unused portion, and after negotiations broke down, this suit was brought for breach of warranty.

Before Widener and King, Circuit Judges, and Garwood, Sr. Circuit Judge (5th Cir.) sitting by designation.

AFFIRMED BY UNPUBLISHED *PER CURIAM* OPINION

Seller argues that buyer must demonstrate both the existence and the nature of the defect in the fabric before it can recover for breach of warranty—and that to show the nature of that defect, expert testimony is required. Article 35 of the CISG governs the duty of the seller to deliver goods that conform with the contract. Article 35(2) lists various reasons goods may not conform with the contract, including goods which were expressly or impliedly warranted to be fit for a particular purpose. Under Article 35(2)(b) goods are unfit unless they "are fit for any particular purpose expressly or impliedly made known to the seller at the time of the conclusion of the contract, except where the circumstances show that the buyer did not rely, or that it was unreasonable for him to rely, on the seller's skill and judgment." In response, buyer argues that all it need show is that the goods were unfit for the particular purpose warranted—transfer printing—and that it need not show precisely why or how the goods were unfit if it can show that the transfer printing process the goods underwent was performed competently and normally. Seller is correct that buyer did not provide any evidence at trial that would establish the exact nature of the defect in the Trevira fabric. The text of the CISG is silent on this matter.

Under either the CISG or Maryland law, buyer may prevail on a claim that the fabric was unfit for the purpose for which it was expressly warranted (transfer printing) by showing that when the fabric was properly used for the purpose seller warranted, the results were shoddy—even if buyer has introduced no evidence as to just why or how the fabric was unfit. Buyer has shown that the fabric was defective—the fabric's defect was that it was unfit for transfer printing. Seller attempts to counter this argument by claiming that this improperly shifts the burden of proof. Seller's concerns are misplaced—buyer still must prove that the transfer printing process was ordinary and competently performed, and still must prove that the fabric was defective—it just permits buyer to do so without proving the exact nature of the defect.

There was significant evidence regarding PMD's transfer printing process presented at trial.... The district court found that seller warranted its fabric to be fit for transfer printing, that the fabric was transfer printed in a normal and competent way, and that

continued

continued

the resulting printed fabric was unsatisfactory. This is enough to support the district court's factual finding in favor of buyer on the warranty claim—the fabric was not fit for the purpose for which it was warranted....

Seller also argues that even if the court properly found that the Trevira fabric was not particularly well suited for transfer printing as warranted, buyer cannot recover on such a warranty because it did not in fact rely on seller's advice as required under CISG Article 35(2)(b). Seller is correct that Article 35(2)(b) of the CISG requires that the buyer reasonably rely on the representations of the seller before liability attaches for breach of a warranty for fitness for a particular purpose. The district court explicitly found that buyer relied on the statements of seller's representative that the Trevira fabric was particularly well suited for transfer printing. The court also found that buyer continued to print the fabric with the express consent of seller after it discovered and reported problems with the fabric. The district court's finding that buyer relied on seller's statements proclaiming the Trevira fabric's suitability for transfer printing is supported by the evidence and was not clearly erroneous.

Accordingly, the judgment of the district court is affirmed.

Decision. Under the CISG, the fabric was not fit for the purposes for which it was intended. The exact nature of the fabric's defect need not be proved. It was sufficient that the plaintiff prove that it had reasonably relied on the defendant's representations that the fabric was suitable for transfer printing, and that it was not.

Conformance to Laws and Regulation in Buyer's Country. Technical regulations setting standards for product design and performance can vary widely from country to country. This might include safety standards for foods, pharmaceuticals, automobiles, toys, and consumer goods; flammability standards for children's clothing; fire and electrical codes; health codes; environmental standards; and rules for packaging or labeling products. Obviously, these issues are more important in international trade, where the standards are far less uniform, than in domestic commerce. Does Article 35 require the seller to supply goods that conform to the national laws of the buyer's country? The cases seem to depend on the factual situations. The issue often turns on whether the seller knew the uses to which the goods would be put, whether it knew of the regulations in the buyer's country affecting that use, and whether the buyer had relied on the seller's knowledge and expertise. It is usually only then that a court would hold that goods are nonconforming if they do not meet the regulations for sale in the buyer's country.

This issue was addressed by the Federal Supreme Court of Germany in 1995, in the *Case of New Zealand Mussels* (translations available online from the Pace Law School Institute of International Commercial Law or from UNCITRAL). This case dealt with a shipment of mussels from New Zealand to Germany that contained concentrations of cadmium exceeding those recommended by German health authorities. Generally, foodstuffs must be sold in a condition "fit for human consumption." However, the court held that since the mussels were still edible (they are generally not dangerous unless eaten in large quantities) they had conformed to the contract. The court held that the seller was not responsible for complying with the German standards unless it had known of the standards and was aware that this was essential to the buyer, or if similar standards had existed in the exporting country. It did not seem to matter to the German court whether the food safety standards were binding rules or simply "recommended" limits. This should send a warning to international buyers. If it is important that foreign goods meet local standards or regulations, that should be clearly set out in the contract.

In *Medical Marketing International v. Internazionale Medico Scientifica, S.R.L.*, a U.S. court held that an Italian seller was in breach of contract for shipping medical imaging equipment to the United States that did not conform to U.S. government safety standards.

Performance of Buyer, Inspection, and Notice of Nonconformity. We said that the buyer's main responsibility is to "pay the price for the goods and

Medical Marketing International, Inc. v. Internazionale Medico Scientifica, S.R.L.

1999 WL 311945 (1999); United States District Court (E.D. La.)

BACKGROUND AND FACTS

Medical Marketing (MMI), the plaintiff, entered into an exclusive licensing agreement for the U.S. distribution of mammography units manufactured by the defendant (IMS) in Italy. The U.S. Food and Drug Administration seized the equipment because it did not comply with U.S. safety regulations. MMI argued that the defendant was responsible to ensure that its equipment met U.S. standards. When the defendant denied responsibility, MMI declared the contract avoided (terminated) on the grounds of nonconformity of the goods. The dispute was submitted to arbitration, and an award of $357,000 was given to MMI who brought this court action to enforce the award.

DUVAL, DISTRICT J.

The FAA outlines specific situations in which an arbitration decision may be overruled: . . . (4) if the arbitrators exceeded their powers. Instances in which the arbitrators "exceed their powers" may include violations of public policy or awards based on a "manifest disregard of the law." See *W.R. Grace & Co. v. Local Union 759*, 461 U.S. 757, 766, 103 S. Ct. 2177, 2183 (1983).

IMS has alleged that the arbitrators' decision violates public policy of the international global market and that the arbitrators exhibited "manifest disregard of international sales law." Specifically, IMS argues that the arbitrators misapplied the *Convention on Contracts for the International Sale of Goods* (CISG), and that they refused to follow a German Supreme Court case interpreting the CISG.

MMI does not dispute that the CISG applies to the case at hand. Under the CISG, the finder of fact has a duty to regard the "international character" of the convention and to promote uniformity in its application. CISG Article 7. The Convention also provides that in an international contract for goods, goods conform to the contract if they are fit for the purpose for which goods of the same description would ordinarily be used or are fit for any particular purpose expressly or impliedly made known to the seller and relied upon by the buyer. CISG Article 35(2). To avoid a contract based on the nonconformity of goods, the buyer must allege and prove that the seller's breach was "fundamental" in nature. CISG Article 49. A breach is fundamental when it results in such detriment to the party that he or she is substantially deprived of what he or she is entitled to expect under the contract, unless the party in breach did not foresee such a result. CISG Article 25.

At the arbitration, IMS argued that MMI was not entitled to avoid its contract with IMS based on nonconformity under Article 49, because IMS's breach was not "fundamental." IMS argued that the CISG did not require that it furnish MMI with equipment that complied with the United States GMP regulations. To support this proposition, IMS cited a German Supreme Court case, which held that under the CISG Article 35, a seller is generally not obligated to supply goods that conform to public laws and regulations enforced at the buyer's place of business. *Entscheidunger des Bundersgerichtshofs in Zivilsachen* (BGHZ), 129, 75 (8 March 1995). In that case, the court held that this general rule carries with it exceptions in three limited circumstances: (1) if the public laws and regulations of the buyer's state are identical to those enforced in the seller's state; (2) if the buyer informed the seller about those regulations; or (3) if due to "special circumstances," such as the existence of a seller's branch office in the buyer's state, the seller knew or should have known about the regulations at issue.

The arbitration panel decided that under the third exception, the general rule did not apply to this case. The arbitrators held that IMS was, or should have been, aware of the GMP regulations prior to entering into the 1993 agreement, and explained their reasoning at length. IMS now argues that the arbitration panel refused to apply the CISG and the law as articulated by the German Supreme Court. It is clear from the arbitrators' written findings, however, that they carefully considered that decision and found that this case fit the exception and not the rule as articulated in that decision. The arbitrators' decision was neither contrary to public policy nor in manifest disregard of international sales law.

Decision. The arbitration panel did not exceed its authority when it found that the Italian seller was in fundamental breach of contract. As a general rule,

continued

continued

the fitness of goods sold under an international contract will be determined by reference to standards for such goods in the seller's country, unless, as in this case, the seller knew or should have known that the goods would not conform to the standards in the buyer's country.

Comment. The district court's opinion is notable for its discussion of German case law. This seems in keeping with the basic principles of the CISG that state that the convention should be interpreted according to its "international character" and to "promote uniformity in its application."

take delivery of them as required (Article 53). In addition, the buyer has an obligation to inspect the goods and notify the seller of any nonconformity.

The buyer must inspect the goods within "as short a period as is practicable in the circumstances" after they have arrived at their destination (Article 38). Obviously, foodstuffs and perishables must be inspected more quickly than durable goods like machinery. The buyer must then give notice of any defect or nonconformity in the goods within a reasonable time after it is discovered or ought to have been discovered. If the defect can be discovered only upon use, the buyer has a reasonable period from that time to notify the seller. Some defects or other nonconformities may be latent, or hidden, and may take longer to detect. There is no set time limit on discovering these, although the time within which notice must be given to the seller of the nonconformity begins to run at the time that the seller "ought to have discovered" the hidden defect (Article 39). In any event, notice must be given within 2 years from the date on which the goods were "handed over" to the buyer. If the buyer fails to give timely and proper notice, the buyer loses the right to assert the breach against the seller. The parties are free to agree on other inspection and notice requirements and frequently do so in international business.

The notice of nonconformity should specifically, and in necessary detail, state how the goods are nonconforming. This is necessary so a breaching party will be able to send substitute goods or otherwise correct the problem. In one German case, a German fashion retailer purchased clothing from an Italian manufacturer. The buyer refused to pay and notified the seller that the clothes were of "poor workmanship and improper fitting." The German court, applying the CISG, ruled that the buyer had lost his breach of warranty claim because the notice did not precisely say why the goods were defective or nonconforming.

Remedies for Breach of Contract

In the event of a breach of contract, the remedies available to a buyer or seller are set out in the CISG. In principle, these remedies are drawn from both the common law and civil law systems. They are intended to give the parties the benefit of their bargain and to put the parties into the economic position they would have been in had the breach not occurred. The remedies outlined in the CISG include (1) avoidance (cancellation) of the contract, (2) the right to remedy or cure, (3) the setting of an additional time, or extension, for performance, (4) price reduction, (5) money damages, and (6) specific performance. The right to a remedy depends on whether or not the failure of performance amounted to a fundamental breach.

Fundamental Breach

The CISG distinguishes between a serious or fundamental breach of the contract and one that is minor or less than fundamental. Article 25 defines a *fundamental breach* as a breach of contract committed by one of the parties that "results in such detriment to the other party as substantially to deprive him of what he is entitled to expect under the contract, unless the party in breach did not foresee and a reasonable person of the same kind in the same circumstances would not have foreseen such a result."

Assume that the seller has promised to ship 25 tons of corn meal to the buyer, knowing that the buyer will store this for gradual use over a period of several months. Both parties anticipate reorders before the meal is completely used. If the seller ships only 20 tons, then it is safe to assume that this is not a fundamental breach—there is no detriment to the buyer and it did not substantially deprive the buyer of his benefit under the contract. Now assume, in a different case, that a seller is under contract to deliver 400 specially designed gear assemblies to a manufacturer of automotive axles. The seller is only able to ship 200. The buyer has a good argument that it was reasonably foreseeable that the gear assemblies were needed for the assembly of 400 axles and that partial shipment would deprive the buyer of its fundamental benefit under the contract—the ability to resell the axles to an automobile manufacturer. After all, anyone in the automotive industry would know that a breach of a delivery contract could cause an expensive breakdown in the global supply chain feeding manufacturing plants. Thus, it is a fundamental breach if the seller knew, or if it was reasonably foreseeable under the circumstances, that the shipment of less than the full quantity of goods ordered by the buyer would destroy the buyer's fundamental benefit under the contract.

In addition, the seller's shipment of seriously defective goods that cannot be repaired or replaced on time, or that have no value to the buyer under the contract, is probably a fundamental breach. So too would be the seller's failure or refusal to ship at all.

Late shipments are more problematic, because this is so common in international shipping. Most late shipments are not a fundamental breach, and under the CISG sellers are usually given additional time to perform even when they are late. However, in one German case, the court ruled that a late delivery was a fundamental breach because it put the buyer in a position where he would have preferred no delivery at all. A partial shipment may also amount to a fundamental breach if it presents a serious problem for the buyer and one that cannot quickly be remedied. If a buyer knows that the time for delivery is critical, such as where he is awaiting just-in-time inventory deliveries, or that partial shipments are unacceptable, then perhaps the buyer should state in the contract that these are deemed to be a fundamental breach.

A buyer may also be in fundamental breach of a contract. This usually results from the buyer's refusal or inability to live up to its two primary responsibilities—to take delivery and to pay for the goods. As we will see in later chapters, many international sales contracts require buyers to produce advance assurances of payment—in the form of a bank letter of credit. Typically these are sent to the seller well in advance of shipment. If the letter of credit is due on or before a certain date and it does not arrive, most courts would consider that a fundamental breach.

Seller's Right to Remedy

The CISG attempts to encourage the parties to stay in their contract rather than to repudiate it in the event of a dispute. The parties will be more likely to negotiate and, where commercially possible, resolve their dispute in a manner that will keep the contract together and give each of them the benefit of their bargain. It does this by giving the seller (and the buyer) additional time to perform.

Both the UCC and the CISG allow the seller to remedy, or cure, a nonconforming shipment if it can be done within the time for performance called for in the contract. So, if the contract calls for the seller to deliver goods to the buyer by October 1, but defective goods arrive on September 15, then the seller may "cure" by delivering a second shipment of conforming goods by October 1.

***Nachfrist* Period.** Unlike the UCC, civil law systems traditionally grant an extension of time, beyond the date called for in the contract, within which the parties may perform. This grace period is often referred to in French civil law as *mise en demeue* and in German law as *nachfrist,* meaning "the period after." The CISG adopts this civil law rule in Articles 47–49. In the event that the seller has failed to deliver the goods, or has already delivered nonconforming goods, and the time for their shipment or delivery has passed, the seller may request the buyer to grant a reasonable extension of time to perform (or to "cure" the problem), at the seller's own expense, if it can be done without causing the buyer unreasonable inconvenience or the uncertainty of reimbursement of expenses incurred during the extension. If the breach is fundamental and, a "cure" seems impossible, the buyer need not grant the extension. In the case of the delivery of nonconforming goods

extensions

resulting in a breach that is not fundamental, or in the case of a non-delivery that can be cured by the seller within a reasonable time, the buyer may not unreasonably refuse the extension. If the buyer does not respond to the seller's request within a reasonable time, the seller is entitled to the requested extension. If the seller still does not perform within the extension of time, the buyer is then released from the contract whether or not the breach was fundamental. Granting an extension can work to the advantage of the buyer as well as the seller. Assume that a buyer receives nonconforming goods or that the delivery is late. The buyer may not know whether the breach is fundamental—that could always be arguable. But if the buyer does grant the extension, and the seller still does not perform, then the buyer is released from all contractual obligations and may sue for breach of contract regardless of whether the seller's breach was fundamental. The buyer may exercise its rights of "avoidance."

Buyer's Right to Avoidance. When one party fails to perform, the contract does not automatically end. The contract, or certain provisions of it, must be declared to be at an end, or "avoided" by one of the parties. A buyer may declare a contract avoided where the seller's failure to perform any obligation amounts to a fundamental breach (Article 49). It cannot be avoided for an insignificant breach. If the seller requests additional time to cure a fundamental breach, the buyer need not grant it. If the seller takes delivery of goods and learns they are so seriously defective as to amount to a fundamental breach, he must declare avoidance within a reasonable time after he became aware, or should have become aware, of the breach. The buyer need not pay for the goods or find a substitute buyer to take them. After notifying the seller of the avoidance, the buyer may simply return them for a full refund of money paid or institute an action for breach of contract. When the goods can rapidly deteriorate or decay, such as with certain foods, the buyer may notify the seller and then take steps to sell them. These rights are especially important to a buyer in an international transaction because of the hardships associated with having to accept delivery and then reselling or disposing of imported goods in a foreign (i.e., the buyer's) market.

In the case of non-delivery, the buyer may avoid the contract only at the end of the *nachfrist* period—at the end of additional time that the seller was given to perform. The buyer may bring an action for damages against the seller at that time.

Seller's Avoidance. The seller also may avoid a contract. A seller may avoid a contract if a buyer fails to either take delivery or pay the purchase price or otherwise commits a fundamental breach (Article 64). The effect of avoidance is that the seller is released from the contract, need not deliver the goods still in the seller's possession, and may claim their return if they have already been delivered. The seller also may bring a legal action for damages.

Price Reduction

One solution for the buyer in the event that the seller ships defective or nonconforming goods is that of *price reduction* (CISG Article 50). A buyer who would like to retain the goods, even though they are perhaps not the quality or specifications called for, may adjust the amount paid by withholding a part of the purchase price in order to offset the reduced value of the nonconforming goods. If the buyer can repair the goods or bring them up to contract specifications, the buyer may adjust the price paid accordingly. If the goods have already been paid for, the buyer may ask that the seller return a portion of the amount paid. Obviously, the amount of price reduction is far easier to calculate when the seller delivers less than the quantity promised than if the goods are damaged or are of inferior quality. The amount of reduction, then, is within the discretion of the buyer. A buyer who utilized price reduction may still bring suit for damages. A seller who disputes the buyer's calculation can only resort to legal action.

The remedy of price reduction may be used by the buyer whether or not the seller's breach has been fundamental. In the case of fundamental breach, price reduction is an alternative to the buyer's other remedies. In the case of a minor breach (one not fundamental), price reduction is often the buyer's best remedy because the parties can more easily come to an amicable solution. Price reduction is not available if the seller has already delivered substitute goods or if the buyer has refused to accept the seller's attempt to remedy or cure the breach.

Money Damages

In breach of contract cases, the usual remedy granted by common law courts is the awarding of money damages. Damages for breach of contract are addressed in Articles 74–77. The CISG provides that a breaching party, whether buyer or seller, shall be liable for damages in an amount sufficient to make the injured party whole in the event of a breach. Article 74 states that damages to an injured party shall consist of a "sum equal to the loss."

In the event of a breach of contract by either buyer or seller, and the nonbreaching party has exercised their right to avoidance of the contract, the method of measuring money damages depends on whether the nonbreaching party has been able to enter into a substitute transaction. For example, if the seller fails to deliver or delivers nonconforming or worthless goods, and the buyer has been able to purchase substitute goods, the buyer may claim damages if the substitute goods cost more than the contract price. If the buyer has not purchased substitute goods, damages are measured by the difference between the contract price and the current market price or the price of a reasonable substitute. Similarly, if the buyer refuses delivery or fails to pay and the seller has avoided the contract and resold the goods, the seller may recover damages in the amount by which the contract price exceeded the price received in the substitute transaction.

Consequential Damages. The CISG also permits recovery of *consequential damages. Consequential damages* are those special or indirect damages arising as a "reasonably foreseeable" consequence of the breach. They normally result from some special circumstances involving one of the parties to the contract, where those special circumstances were made known, or should have been known, by the other party. For example, assume that the buyer is purchasing the goods in order to resell them at a higher price under a separate contract to a third party. That fact is made known to the seller. If the seller breaches, it may be liable for the buyer's *lost profits* as well as other consequential damages resulting from the buyer's breach to the third party. Consequential damages are limited under Article 74 to those that the parties "foresaw or ought to have foreseen at the time of the conclusion of the contract." A similar rule for consequential damages has been firmly recognized under English common law since 1854. To compare the provisions for consequential damages in the CISG and the UCC, see Exhibit 4.7.

In the following case, *Delchi Carrier SpA v. Rotorex Corp.*, the buyer incurred many

Exhibit 4.7

Comparison of Consequential Damage Provisions of the CISG and the UCC

Convention on Contracts for the International Sale of Goods

Article 74

Damages for breach of contract by one party consist of a sum equal to the loss, including loss of profit, suffered by the other party as a consequence of the breach. Such damages may not exceed the loss which the party in breach foresaw or ought to have foreseen at the time of the conclusion of the contract, in the light of the facts and matters of which he then knew or ought to have known, as a possible consequence of the breach of contract.

UCC 2-715

Buyer's Incidental and Consequential Damages

1. Incidental damages resulting from the seller's breach include expenses reasonably incurred in inspection, receipt, transportation, and care and custody of goods rightfully rejected, and commercially reasonable charges, expenses, or commissions in connection with effecting cover and any other reasonable expense incident to the delay or other breach.
2. Consequential damages resulting from the seller's breach include
   a. any loss resulting from general or particular requirements and needs of which the seller at the time of contracting had reason to know and which could not reasonably be prevented by cover or otherwise; and
   b. injury to person or property proximately resulting from any breach of warranty.

Delchi Carrier, SpA v. Rotorex Corp.

1994 WL 495787 (1994)

United States District Court (N.D.N.Y.)

BACKGROUND AND FACTS

Rotorex, a New York corporation, agreed to sell air compressors to Delchi, an Italian company. The compressors were for use in producing Ariele air conditioners. The first shipment reached Delchi, and Delchi paid $188,000. In preparation Delchi had spent 39 million lire for special tooling, and 27 million lire for special insulation and tubing for use in making Arieles. Delchi expended 18 million lire in shipping and customs duties. Delchi then paid $130,000 to Rotorex for a second shipment. While the second shipment was en route, Delchi discovered that the first lot was nonconforming. It rejected the compressors and canceled the contract. Delchi spent several million lire to replace problem grommets, inspect, repair, and retest the compressors in an effort to make them usable. During this time, Delchi's assembly line shut down, incurring unproductive assembly worker wages. Delchi was able to obtain some substitute compressors from other sources in time for the selling season, which it had to adapt for Ariele units at additional expense. It arranged to have a shipment of Sanyo compressors, which it has previously ordered, sent to it by air freight so that it could fill some orders. Delchi was also unable to fill some orders, amounting to millions of lire in lost profit. Delchi brought this action for damages.

MUNSON, SENIOR DISTRICT JUDGE

The governing law of the instant case is the United Nations Convention on Contracts for the International Sale of Goods ("CISG").

* * *

Rotorex breached its contract with Delchi by failing to supply 10,800 conforming compressors. Under CISG Delchi is entitled to collect monetary damages for Rotorex's breach in "a sum equal to the loss, including loss of profit," although not in excess of the amount reasonably envisioned by the parties. (CISG, article 74). This provision seeks to provide the injured party with the benefit of the bargain, including both its expectation interest and its reliance expenditure.

CONSEQUENTIAL DAMAGES

i. Plaintiff's Attempts to Remedy Nonconformity. Delchi is entitled to recover damages incurred as a result of its attempts to remedy the nonconformity of Rotorex's compressors. These were not anticipated costs of production, but were costs that would not have been incurred without Rotorex's breach. Further, such damages were a foreseeable result of Rotorex's breach. Hence Delchi is entitled to recover for unreimbursed expenses [for repairing the units] ... for labor costs relating to replacing original, problematic grommets with substitutes ... for extraordinary reinspection and testing of units after [repair].

ii. Expedited Shipment of Sanyo Compressors. Once Delchi's attempts to remedy the nonconformity failed, it was entitled to expedite shipment of previously ordered Sanyo compressors to mitigate its damages. Indeed, CISG requires such mitigation. (CISG, article 77): "A party who relies on a breach of contract must take such measures as are reasonable in the circumstances to mitigate the loss." The shipment of previously ordered Sanyo compressors did not constitute cover under CISG article 75, because the Sanyo units were previously ordered, and hence cannot be said to have replaced the nonconforming Rotorex compressors. Nonetheless, Delchi's action in expediting shipment of Sanyo compressors was both commercially reasonable and reasonably foreseeable, and therefore Delchi is entitled to recover ... the net cost of early delivery of Sanyo compressors [the cost of air shipment less the expected cost for ocean shipment].

iii. Handling and Storage of Rejected Compressors. Delchi is further entitled to collect costs incurred for handling and storage of nonconforming compressors....

iv. Lost Profits. CISG permits recovery of lost profit resulting from a diminished volume of sales. In conformity with the common law, to recover a claim for lost profit under CISG, a party must provide the finder of fact with sufficient evidence to estimate the amount of damages with reasonable certainty. Delchi proved with sufficient certainty that it incurred, as a foreseeable and direct result of Rotorex's breach ... a total of 546,377,612 lire in lost profit in Italy. Delchi did not prove with sufficient certainty any lost sales from "indicated [anticipated] orders" in Italy. Delchi's claim of 4,000 additional lost sales in Italy is supported only by the speculative testimony of Italian

continued

continued

sales agents who averred that they would have ordered more Arieles had they been available.... Delchi provides no documentation of additional lost sales in Italy, and no evidence that if any such lost sales did exist, that Delchi's inability to fill those orders was directly attributable to Rotorex's breach. Delchi can not recover on its claim for additional lost profits in Italy because the amount of damages, if any, cannot be established with reasonable certainty.

Delchi is not entitled to recover ... for modification of electrical panels for use with substitute Sanyo compressors. Delchi failed to prove that this cost was directly attributable to Rotorex's breach, and that the cost was not part of the regular cost of production of units with Sanyo compressors.

Decision. The plaintiff was awarded compensatory damages for those expenses incurred in repairing the nonconforming goods and obtaining substitute goods, and for lost profits. Lost profits do not include profits that may arise from anticipated sales that cannot be established by reasonable certainty.

Comment. Although not reprinted in the above excerpt, the District Court denied Delchi's claim for damages based on other expenses, including (i) shipping, customs, and incidentals relating to the two shipments of Rotorex compressors; (ii) the cost of obsolete insulation and tubing that Delchi purchased only for use with Rotorex compressors; (iii) the cost of obsolete tooling purchased only for production of units with Rotorex compressors; and (iv) labor costs for 4 days when Delchi's production line was idle because it had no compressors to install in the air-conditioning units. The court denied an award for these items on the ground that it would lead to a double recovery because "those costs are accounted for in Delchi's recovery on its lost profits claim." On appeal, the Court of Appeals for the Second Circuit disagreed. It held that

> An award for lost profits will not compensate Delchi for the expenses in question.... The expenses incurred by Delchi for shipping, customs, and related matters for the two returned shipments of Rotorex compressors, including storage expenses for the second shipment at Genoa, were clearly foreseeable and recoverable incidental expenses. These are up-front expenses that had to be paid to get the goods to the manufacturing plant for inspection and were thus incurred largely before the nonconformities were detected. To deny reimbursement to Delchi for these incidental damages would effectively cut into the lost profits award. The same is true of unreimbursed tooling expenses and the cost of the useless insulation and tubing materials. These are legitimate consequential damages that in no way duplicate lost profits damages.
>
> The labor expense incurred as a result of the production line shutdown of May 16–19, 1988 is also a reasonably foreseeable result of delivering nonconforming compressors for installation in air conditioners. However, Rotorex argues that the labor costs in question were fixed costs that would have been incurred whether or not there was a breach. The district court labeled the labor costs "fixed costs," but did not explore whether Delchi would have paid these wages regardless of how much it produced. Variable costs are generally those costs that "fluctuate with a firm's output," and typically include labor (but not management) costs. Whether Delchi's labor costs during this four-day period are variable or fixed costs is in large measure a fact question that we cannot answer because we lack factual findings by the district court. We therefore remand to the district court on this issue.

Delchi Carrier SpA v. Rotorex Corp., 71 F.3d 1024 (2nd Cir. 1995), *aff'g in part and rev'g in part,* 1994 WL 495787 (N.D.N.Y. 1994).

expenses because of the seller's delivery of nonconforming goods: repair expenses, storage expenses, assembly line downtime, sourcing substitute merchandise, and lost profits. As you read, consider how the court determines which expenditures are consequential damages and which are not.

The power to avoid a contract is even more important in a fluctuating market for the goods. If the buyer chooses to accept the goods and sues for damages for the seller's breach of contract, the money damages the buyer could collect would be equal to the difference between the value of the nonconforming goods and the contract price. However, if a buyer avoids the contract under Article 49 and refuses to take delivery at all, *and the value of the goods falls greatly in the marketplace,* the buyer may be able to purchase the goods for much less than the amount agreed to under the contract. Alternatively, *if the value of the goods*

commodity price variability

increases in the marketplace, the buyer may still sue for the difference between the contract price and the higher market price at which it purchased substitute goods.

Specific Performance

The usual legal remedy in contract cases in common law countries is an award for money damages. The usual remedy in civil law countries, on the other hand, is that of *specific performance.* Specific performance is used when a court requires a party to the contract to perform, or carry out its part of the bargain. To be sure, courts in the United States and other common law countries hesitate to require parties to specifically perform. It is considered a harsh remedy to be used only where money damages cannot be calculated or are inadequate, which may occur when the subject matter of the contract is unique. For example, in a dispute over the sale of a prized racehorse or a famous work of art, a common law court may specifically require a seller to deliver the item to the buyer because of the "unique" nature of the goods. Money damages would not have been sufficient to remedy the buyer in such a case; the buyer wants the goods contracted for. But in civil law countries, the use of specific performance is not only more common, it is preferred.

Specific Performance under the CISG. The CISG draws strongly on the civil law's acceptance of specific performance as a remedy in contract cases. This is based on the idea that the buyer wants what was ordered and not just the right to sue for those injuries that the seller's non-delivery may have caused. Under Article 46, a court may grant specific performance only if all of the following conditions are met: (1) the buyer has not resorted to another remedy, such as avoidance or price reduction; (2) the seller failed to deliver or, in the case of nonconforming goods, the nonconformity was so serious that it constituted a fundamental breach; (3) the buyer gave timely notice to the seller that the goods were nonconforming; and (4) the buyer made a timely request that the seller provide substitute goods. As in the civil law nations, the court may grant specific performance without regard to whether money damages are inadequate.

The provisions of the CISG probably will not have much effect on the law in common law countries. Article 28 places a limit on the buyer's right to specific performance by providing that a court need not grant specific performance unless "it would do so under its own law." Thus, the CISG will have little effect on the use of specific performance in the United States.

Anticipatory Breach

Anticipatory breach occurs when one party clearly sees that the other party to the contract either will not perform a substantial part of its obligations or will commit a fundamental breach. The breach may occur as a result of one party repudiating the contract and notifying the other that it will not perform, or it may be determined from the conduct of the breaching party.

Right to Suspend Performance. Either party may *suspend performance* under a contract if one party realizes that the other party will not perform a "substantial part" of its obligations. A buyer may suspend payment when aware of evidence that the seller cannot or will not ship. A seller may suspend shipment when the buyer obviously cannot pay or take delivery of the goods. A seller who has already shipped may stop the goods in transit. The right to suspend performance ends when the other party provides adequate assurance that it will perform. If adequate assurance becomes impossible, the other party may then avoid the contract entirely.

Consider this example: Assume that seller is required to deliver goods by March 15. Seller learns that buyer is insolvent and about to declare bankruptcy. On February 1, seller suspends performance and halts shipment. On March 1, buyer provides bank guarantees to seller that it can pay for the goods. The market price of the goods has risen significantly and seller refuses to ship. Seller is correct in suspending performance, but commits a breach of contract by not accepting buyer's assurance of performance.

Right to Avoid for Anticipatory Breach. If, prior to the date of performance, it becomes clear that one of the parties is likely to commit a fundamental breach in the future, the other party may avoid the contract. This is similar to the common law concept of "anticipatory breach." In contrast to the right to suspend, avoidance for anticipatory breach is allowed where one party will *never* be able to perform. For instance, if the seller's plant burns down, or if an embargo in the seller's country makes it legally impossible to ship the contracted goods, then the buyer may avoid the contract.

AVOIDANCE OF INSTALLMENT CONTRACTS. When a contract calls for the delivery of goods by installments, the rules of avoidance apply to each individual delivery. Therefore, a single nonconforming shipment may be refused by a buyer if the seller has committed a fundamental breach. Assume that buyer and seller have a contract for 160,000 pounds of peanuts to be shipped from Georgia to Denmark in twenty shipments over a 5-year period. One shipment arrives in Denmark and is unfit for human consumption. In terms of the entire contract, the one shipment may not amount to a fundamental breach, but because it is an installment contract, the buyer may avoid the contract with respect to this shipment.

Where the breach of one installment indicates strong grounds that a party will breach future installments, the nonbreaching party may declare the contract avoided if done within a reasonable time. So, if a buyer refuses to pay for one or two installments, the seller may avoid the remainder of the contract.

EVENTS BEYOND THE CONTROL OF THE PARTIES: EXCUSES FOR NONPERFORMANCE

Occasionally, a party will find that circumstances make carrying out its part of the contract difficult, unprofitable, or even impossible. As a defense to an action for breach of contract, it may claim that it has been excused because intervening events beyond its control have made performance impossible or financially impracticable. However, it will have a difficult time convincing a court. Courts generally do not allow a party to escape contractual obligations merely because it becomes unable to perform, even though inability to perform was through no fault of its own. When a seller's employees go on strike, when suppliers fail to deliver raw materials on time, when equipment breaks down, when crops are destroyed due to bad weather, or when a party simply becomes financially distressed, its failure to deliver on time will generally not be excused. This common ruling is in keeping with generally accepted legal principles, which hold that contracts are binding. After all, when parties enter into agreements, do they not weigh these contingencies in setting their prices and establishing their terms? Yet, in the real world in which international transactions are conducted, the parties are liable to find many roadblocks in their path to performance.

Whether an intervening event will cause a party to be excused and discharged from its contractual promise depends on the reasoning used by the court. Some courts reason that a party's performance is excused (1) if performance of the contract has been rendered physically or legally impossible, (2) if the underlying purposes of the contract no longer exist, or (3) if a change in circumstances has rendered the contract commercially or financially impracticable.

Impossibility of Performance

Under English law, a court may excuse a party's nonperformance where it becomes *objectively impossible* for it to perform. The courts hold that it must be impossible for *anyone* to perform, not just this particular party, and that the parties did not expressly assume such risk. Impossibility would therefore excuse nonperformance in cases involving the death of one of the parties, the destruction of the specific subject matter of the contract, or when performance of the contract has been rendered illegal or made impossible due to the fault of the other party. Impossibility is usually recognized only where performance becomes a physical impossibility. The inability to pay money is usually never accepted as an excuse.

SUPERVENING ILLEGALITY. A contract becomes impossible to perform and the parties excused when performance becomes illegal or prohibited by supervening government regulation. For instance, suppose that a U.S. company is under contract to ship computers to Iraq. After Iraq's invasion of Kuwait, the U.S. government declared that conducting business with Iraq or shipping goods there was illegal. Because the contract has been rendered illegal, nonperformance is excused.

Frustration of Purpose

Does a contract to purchase a diamond engagement ring from a jeweler become unenforceable because the intended bride jilts her boyfriend? Under the English common law, a party's performance could be excused if some unforeseen event occurred that frustrated the purposes of the contract. This event, called *frustration of purpose,* would have to totally destroy the value of the contract to the party relying on the excuse. Moreover, both parties must have known what the purposes of the contract were. To understand, one might ask the question, "Had this event existed at the time of the contract, would the parties have gone through with it?" In a leading English case, *Knell v. Henry,* 2 K.B. 740 (1903), a party leased a room overlooking the coronation route of the king. When the king took ill and the coronation was canceled, the court ruled that the party was excused from paying rent on the room because the coronation was essential to the purposes of the contract. Although it had been *possible* to perform, the party would have realized no value in doing so.

Frustration of purpose is not widely recognized in the United States today.

This is illustrated in the case of *Coker International v. Burlington Industries,* 935 F.2d 267 (4th Cir. 1991). Coker had contracted to purchase textile looms from Burlington for export to Peru. Subsequently, the government of Peru banned the import of this type of machinery and Coker sued Burlington for a return of its deposit. In denying Coker's claim, the court stated, "The contract is not conditioned on any resale by Coker.... Coker had both the possibility of profit and the risk of loss from resale.... The actions of the government of Peru may have frustrated Coker's intended resale, but it is not the same as the purpose of its contract with Burlington, which was the conveyance of the looms from Burlington to Coker."

Would the case be different if it were the U.S. government prohibiting the export? Probably not. In cases going back at least to 1920, U.S. courts have held that where the buyer's intended purpose was to resell the goods overseas, and it subsequently becomes illegal to export the goods, the contract is not invalid *where the U.S. seller's obligation was to deliver the goods to the buyer within the United States.* The courts reason that the contract only requires delivery of the goods to the buyer within the United States. Where the export provision was never a part of the contract, the buyer will not be let off the hook just because he can no longer make his expected profit on resale outside the country.

Commercial Impracticability

A party to a contract that is prevented from performing may attempt to be excused under the doctrine of *commercial impracticability.* This modern doctrine is used in the United States today. It dates back to 1916 when a court stated, "A thing is impossible in legal contemplation when it is not practicable; and a thing is impracticable when it can be done only at an excessive and unreasonable cost." Today, impracticability in the United States has been codified in the UCC (Exhibit 4.8) and in Article 79 of the CISG. Remember, courts hesitate to excuse parties from contracts. Accordingly, the breaching party will be excused only if performance would result in extreme hardship, difficulty, or unreasonable expense as a result of an unforeseen event.

Extreme Hardship, Difficulty, or an Unreasonable Expense. The courts have experienced some difficulty in determining what is a "hardship" and how much additional cost is "unreasonable." If the cost of performing the contract becomes so excessive that performance is rendered unrealistic and senseless and threatens the viability of the business itself, performance may be excused. Of course, what is a lot of money to one company may be a drop in the bucket to another. Thus, if a large multinational corporation contracts to deliver goods at a contract price and discovers that wage increases or an increase in the price of raw materials will cause it to lose millions of dollars on the deal, the courts still may not release the company from its obligation.

Unforeseen Events. Courts also look to see whether the party claiming the excuse should have foreseen the likelihood of its occurrence. If the

Exhibit 4.8

Excuse by Failure of Presupposed Conditions

Uniform Commercial Code

2-615. Except so far as a seller may have assumed a greater obligation and subject to the preceding section on substituted performance:

a. Delay in delivery or nondelivery (performance or nonperformance, 2003 amendments) in whole or in part by a seller who complies with paragraphs (b) and (c) is not a breach of his duty under a contract for sale if performance as agreed has been made impracticable by the occurrence of a contingency the nonoccurrence of which was a basic assumption on which the contract was made or by compliance in good faith with any applicable foreign or domestic governmental regulation or order whether or not it later proves to be invalid.
b. Where the causes mentioned in paragraph (a) affect only a part of the seller's capacity to perform, the seller must allocate production and deliveries among its customers but may at its option include regular customers not then under contract as well as its own requirements for further manufacture. The seller may so allocate in any manner which is fair and reasonable.
c. The seller must notify the buyer reasonably that there will be delay or nondelivery and, when allocation is required under paragraph (b), of the estimated quota thus made available for the buyer.

general business risks are accepted

event was foreseeable, the nonperforming party will not be released from its obligations. This does not mean that the parties had to foresee the specific event that actually occurred. Rather, the parties *should have* foreseen that an event *of this kind* could occur. Thus, if a party is a sophisticated business, experienced and familiar with the risks of entering into this kind of contract, they might have difficulty in proving that they should not have foreseen a particular risk. Consider the following examples:

- A mining company should foresee the possibility of a cave-in.
- A farming conglomerate should foresee the possibility of bad weather.
- An oil company should foresee the possibility of oil price increases in the Middle East.

The courts generally feel that if a particular risk was foreseeable, then the parties would have provided in their contract that performance would be excused if it occurred. If they did not provide for the excuse in the contract, then they must have intended to bear this risk.

Shortages and Market Price Fluctuations. For the most part, shortages, inflation, and even dramatic fluctuations in market prices are to be anticipated by parties to a contract. Such a result is illustrated by *Eastern Air Lines, Inc. v. Gulf Oil Corp.*, 415 F. Supp. 429 (S.D. Fla. 1975), a case arising out of the oil price increases caused by the Arab oil embargo in 1973. In 1972, Eastern Airlines contracted with Gulf Oil Corporation for a supply of jet aviation fuel. In the following year, the Middle East war and Arab oil embargo of the United States resulted in a 400 percent increase in the price of crude oil. These events caused Gulf to demand a price increase from Eastern and to threaten a cutoff in supply. Eastern brought an action under the UCC to ensure its supply of oil at the contract price. Gulf claimed that the contract as it had been negotiated was commercially impracticable. The court disagreed, noting that not only had Gulf not suffered a sufficient hardship to claim impracticability, but that the actions of the OPEC oil cartel and the resulting energy crisis were reasonably foreseeable by a multinational oil company such as Gulf.

The CISG Exemptions for Impediments Beyond Control

CISG Article 79 provides that a party is not liable for a failure to perform any obligations if (1) it was due to an *impediment beyond control,* (2) the impediment was not reasonably foreseeable at the time the contract was concluded, (3) the impediment was unavoidable and could not be overcome, and (4) notice was given to the other party of the impediment and of its effect on the contract. Unless an impediment renders performance permanently impossible, it does not entirely excuse performance, but merely suspends it during the time that the impediment exists.

Force Majeure Clauses

Courts do not like to release parties from a contract on the basis of an excuse. Under the rule of commercial impracticability, a party will not be excused if the risk was foreseeable, because the party is assumed to have provided for that excuse in the contract itself. As a result, lawyers frequently advise their clients to incorporate a *force majeure* clause into a contract.

The term *force majeure* means "superior force." A *force majeure* clause in a contract excuses a party from failing to perform on the occurrence of one or more specified events. These clauses usually list with specificity those events that will excuse nonperformance. These events might include war, blockades, fire, acts of governments, inability to obtain export licenses, acts of God, acts of public enemies, failure of transportation, quarantine restrictions, and strikes. Of course, such a clause assumes the party claiming the *force majeure* did not cause the event and could not control it. For an example of a *force majeure* clause, see the *Terms and Conditions of Sale,* Exhibit 4.4.

Lawyers advise that *force majeure* clauses should not just provide for standard contingencies such as those listed, but should be tailored to the special nature of the contract and the type of businesses involved. *Force majeure* clauses for the mining industry would not be the same as for the steel or textile industries, for example. A clause in a shipping contract issued by an ocean carrier would be different, too, because the risks differ. In major contracts, the drafting of a *force majeure* clause requires skilled lawyers. Language that is too narrow may not provide sufficient protection, and language that is too broad may leave too many outs in the contract.

In practice, most *force majeure* clauses do not excuse a party's nonperformance entirely, but only suspend it for the duration of the *force majeure.*

Another special type of *force majeure* clause is the *government approval* clause. Because government permission is often needed to transact business across national borders, many companies include a provision in their contract stating that the contract is subject to obtaining government approval or licenses. The *Harriscom Svenska, AB* case illustrates the operation of a *force majeure* clause.

Harriscom Svenska, AB v. Harris Corp.
3 F.3d 576 (1993)
United States Court of Appeals (2d Cir.)

BACKGROUND AND FACTS

RF Systems, a division of Harris Corporation, manufactures radio communications products in New York. It appointed Harriscom, a Swedish firm, as its exclusive distributor to the Islamic Republic of Iran. The contract contained a *force majeure* clause. In 1985 the U.S. Customs Service detained a shipment of radios ordered by Harriscom and bound for Iran. The government prohibited all sales to Iran of goods it categorized as military equipment. In 1986, RF Systems negotiated a compromise under which it agreed to "voluntarily withdraw from all further sales to the Iranian market." Harriscom brought this action for a breach of contract against RF Systems. The District Court granted judgment for the defendants on the basis of commercial impracticability and force majeure, and the plaintiff appealed.

CARDAMONE, CIRCUIT JUDGE

One of the issues before us is whether the manufacturer's refusal to ship the spare parts was a voluntary act on its part, subjecting it to liability to its distributor for damages for breach of contract. We think it a foregone conclusion that a government bureaucracy determined to prevent what it considers military goods from leaving this country and with the will to compel compliance with its directives is an irresistible force, one that cannot reasonably be controlled. The government in these circumstances may be likened to the wife of "Rumpole of the Bailey," John

continued

continued

Mortimer's fictional barrister, who describes his wife as "she who must be obeyed." . . .

What appellant ignores is the overwhelming and uncontradicted evidence that the government would not allow RF Systems to continue sales to Iran. RF Systems established the affirmative defense of commercial impracticability because it complied in good faith with the government's informal requirements. Further, for RF Systems to have failed to comply would have been unusually foolhardy and recalcitrant, for the government had undoubted power to compel compliance. Like commercial impracticability, a force majeure clause in a contract excuses nonperformance when circumstances beyond the control of the parties prevent performance. The contracts between these parties specifically contained force majeure clauses to excuse RF Systems' performance under the present circumstances, namely, "governmental interference."

Decision. Summary judgment for the defendant, RF Systems, was affirmed. The *force majeure* clause in the distributorship agreement excused the manufacturer from performance on the grounds of "government interference."

Cultural Influences on Contract Negotiations

Lawyers and businesspeople in different countries treat their approach to negotiating and drafting contracts quite differently. First, Americans tend to approach contract negotiations in an aggressive, adversarial manner. They often view contracting as a win–lose proposition, taking pride in having driven the hardest bargain. This attitude leads them to attempt to gain legal and business advantages over the other party. Similarly, U.S. lawyers, who are accustomed to practicing in a highly litigious society, press for every legal advantage. They draft their contracts in calculated, technical, and detailed language, setting forth exactly how the parties are to perform and what their legal rights are if the deal falls apart.

Negotiating Contracts in Japan

By contrast, contract negotiations in many countries take a much different form. Japan presents perhaps the best example. The role of a contract in Japanese society is influenced tremendously by three aspects of Japanese culture and ancient Confucian thinking. First, every person must strive to maintain harmony and accord in society. From childhood, individuals are taught to avoid disputes and acrimony in their personal and business relationships with others. Second, the maintenance of harmony and the importance placed on personal dignity stress the importance of not causing others to "lose face" or become embarrassed. The considerable social pressure to avoid dishonor works in all aspects of life, including negotiating contracts and resolving contract disputes. Third, the Japanese attach the utmost importance to the social group to which one belongs, particularly to one's school or company. Thus, Japanese businesspeople may be characterized by their group loyalty and their desire for group harmony and consensus.

These attributes make doing business in Japan, and indeed throughout Asia, different from doing business anywhere else. They also affect the way the Japanese view contractual relationships. A contract is a relationship, and as much a social one as a business one. Therefore, the desire to maintain harmony in society has a dramatic effect on how the Japanese view their business contracts. Instead of the combative approach of U.S. lawyers, Japanese negotiators view the contract as an expression of a common goal and of a desire for a long-lasting business relationship.

These cultural and societal influences affect the manner in which contracts are negotiated and drafted. Because lawyers must do all they can to protect their own clients' interests, they are necessarily adversarial. Japanese firms normally prefer that lawyers not be involved in negotiating, because they feel that lawyers interfere with the parties' concentration on their mutual business interests. Western negotiators also must remember that they must never put the other parties in a situation in which losing face is the only out. One must be careful not to create embarrassment by making demands without offering something in exchange. By avoiding a loss of face, the parties strengthen their business relationships and reduce the likelihood of misunderstanding and contract disputes.

In addition, a Western company must be prepared to carry out negotiations for an extended period. In many cases, the Japanese firm will require a long time to reach a group consensus before a decision can be made. Many U.S. senior managers have gone abroad to negotiate a contract only to face frustration at the other party's apparent refusal or unwillingness to conclude an agreement. The U.S. managers may not realize that, while they have the authority to bind their firm to the agreement, the foreign party does not. The foreign negotiator may require approval from superiors or from a working group. When doing business in Asia, the watchwords are not only "trust" and "respect," but "patience" as well.

When the contract is finally put into writing, it is typically short and written in little detail. The Japanese consider this necessary because a long-term relationship requires a flexible agreement, and one that the parties can easily modify in the future. Many U.S. lawyers are unaccustomed to this Japanese practice.

The desire to maintain social harmony and to avoid the embarrassment of litigation also affects the manner in which contract disputes are resolved. Unlike contracts between Americans, contracts with the Japanese might state that, in the event of a dispute, "the parties will resolve their disagreement harmoniously and in mutual consultation with each other." If the contract breaks down and the parties disagree over an issue, they are more likely to want to settle the matter through private conciliation. Litigation, while on the increase in Japan as elsewhere, is still to be avoided if at all possible.

Another factor that U.S. contract negotiators should be aware of is that foreign firms, more so than U.S. firms, rely on technical experts during contract negotiations. More than one U.S. company has failed to obtain an important order because its negotiating team lacked credibility because it did not include the necessary engineers, specialists, or technicians. This is true not only in Japan, but also in many European countries and much of the rest of the world.

Conclusion

All commerce and trade require a stable and predictable legal environment in which to prosper. In recent years, the international community has agreed on a common body of international sales law, the *UN Convention on Contracts for the International Sale of Goods*. The CISG is important not only because it governs transactions for the trade in goods between parties in those nations that have adopted it, but also because it represents internationally accepted legal principles of sales law. One of its key doctrines is that business parties should have the greatest freedom to contract possible.

The CISG was drafted under the aegis of the United Nations by representatives from countries with diverse political, economic, and legal systems. Thus it draws on common law, civil law, and even socialist law principles. It has already been adopted by countries whose trade volume represents two-thirds of world trade.

This chapter does not purport to cover all aspects of international sales law. For example, the actual mechanics of the transaction—how the contract is carried out by the parties—is yet to be discussed.

The next two chapters look at how goods are shipped and money is exchanged and what happens if the goods are lost at sea. These chapters also examine the responsibility of the carrier for transporting the goods and the carrier's relationship to buyer and seller.

Chapter Summary

1. The *UN Convention on Contracts for the International Sale of Goods* (CISG) was ratified by the United States in 1988 and applies to commercial contracts for the sale of goods between buyers and sellers located in different countries, both of which have ratified the

CISG. The CISG is not applicable to consumer contracts, liability for injury or death caused by defective products, or the sale of services.
2. Under the CISG, contracts for the sale of goods need not be in writing, although most international business transactions are.
3. Evidence as to trade usages is admissible to interpret or fill in the gaps in a contract. It may include those usages derived from past dealings or those that the parties knew of, should have known of, or are regularly observed in their countries in their type of business.
4. An acceptance may take the form of a statement or conduct by the offeree that indicates the offeree's intention to be bound to the contract. An offeree may accept by "dispatching the goods or payment of the price, without notice to the offeror," provided that the parties have established this as a practice or it is routinely accepted in the trade.
5. In an international sales transaction governed by the CISG, a confirmation or other acceptance containing new terms that do not materially alter the terms of the offer becomes a part of the contract, unless the offeror promptly objects to the change. However, a purported acceptance that contains additional or different terms that do materially alter the terms of the offer would constitute a rejection of the offer and a counteroffer.
6. Unless otherwise agreed by the parties, the seller must deliver goods that are fit for the purposes for which goods of the same description would ordinarily be used and fit for any particular purpose expressly or impliedly made known to the seller.
7. Generally, a seller is not responsible for delivering goods that fail to conform to technical regulations and standards in the buyer's country. However, the seller would be responsible if it knew the uses to which the goods would be put, if it knew of regulations in the buyer's country affecting that use and if the buyer had relied on the seller's knowledge and expertise.
8. Unless otherwise agreed in the contract, a buyer must inspect the goods within as short a period as is practicable under the circumstances after the goods have arrived at their destination and notify the seller of any nonconformity within a reasonable time after it is discovered. In no case may the notice be made more than two years from the date the goods were handed over.
9. The remedies outlined in the CISG include (1) avoidance (cancellation) of the contract; (2) the right to remedy or cure; (3) the setting of an additional time, or extension, for performance; (4) price reduction; (5) money damages; and (6) specific performance. The right to a remedy depends on whether or not the failure of performance amounted to a fundamental breach.
10. A *fundamental breach* is one that the seller knew or should have known would result in such detriment to the buyer as substantially deprive him of what he is entitled to under the contract.
11. Performance may be suspended or excused for an impediment beyond the control of the parties that was unavoidable and not reasonably foreseeable at the time the contract was concluded, provided notice was given to the other party. A *force majeure* clause excuses a party from failing to perform on the occurrence of an event specified, such as plant closings or natural disasters.

QUESTIONS AND CASE PROBLEMS

1. Lucent Technologies International, Inc. subcontracted with a Saudi Arabian company, National Group, for work that Lucent was doing as part of a $4 billion telecommunications project for the Saudi government. National Group sued Lucent for damages for terminating the contract. The damages included an amount for lost profits. The contract contained no choice of law provision and Saudi law applied. The U.S. court had to decide if recovery of lost profits was prohibited as *gharar.* After all, *gharar* prohibits gambling, or the sale of the "calf while still in the womb" or of "fish in the sea." What is *gharar,* and how does this Islamic law principle affect calculation of damages for breach of contract under Islamic law? Would this decision have been different under the CISG? *National*

Group for Communications and Computers, Ltd. v. Lucent Technologies International, Inc., 331 F. Supp. 2d 290 (2004).

2. Bende had a contract to sell boots to the government of Ghana for $158,500. Bende promised to deliver the boots "as soon as possible." Bende then contracted with Kiffe, who agreed to make the boots in Korea and to deliver them in Ghana within 60 to 90 days at a price of $95,000. The contract contained no *force majeure* clause. Kiffe knew that Bende was going to resell the boots. Kiffe failed to deliver the boots on the agreed date because a train carrying the boots had derailed in Nebraska. Bende brought this action against Kiffe for breach of contract. *Bende and Sons, Inc. v. Crown Recreation and Kiffe Products*, 548 F. Supp. 1018 (E.D.N.Y. 1982).
   a. Kiffe claims that the contract had been rendered commercially impracticable and that performance was excused. Do you agree? Why or why not? Was the train wreck foreseeable or unforeseeable?
   b. What could Kiffe have done in negotiating the contract to protect itself from this contingency?
   c. If Bende would have incurred an additional $18,815 in freight charges and miscellaneous costs had the breach not occurred, what would be its measure of damages? Is Bende entitled to lost profits? How are damages measured in a case such as this?
   d. In this case, the risk of damage or loss to the boots while in transit remained with the seller, Kiffe. How would the case differ if the parties had agreed that Kiffe would merely ship (not deliver) the goods by a certain date and that Kiffe would bear the risk of loss during transit? (You may have to wait until the next chapter to answer this one.)
3. The defendant purchased sewing machines from a Swiss manufacturer. The contract specified that payment was to be made in Swiss francs. The machines were imported into the United States for sale through distributors. The importer's contract with a distributor contained an "open-price term" that allowed it to pass cost increases in the machines to the distributor. The open-price term worked well until fluctuation in the exchange rate between the U.S. dollar and the Swiss franc became extreme. When the Swiss franc rose in value against the dollar, the importer's profit margin was cut in half. The importer then imposed a 10 percent surcharge to protect itself. The distributor did not feel that this additional "cost" fell under the terms used in the contract. The importer believed that increased costs due to currency fluctuations were covered by the open-price term, and further, that the exchange rate risk had rendered performance under the contract commercially impracticable. The distributor brought this action to have the contract enforced at its original price. Judgment for whom, and why? *Bernina Distributors v. Bernina Sewing Machine Co.*, 646 F.2d 434 (10th Cir. 1981).
4. The CISG contains no provisions that a contract for the sale of goods be supported by consideration. Further, the CISG does not address questions related to the validity of the contract, such as legality, mistake, fraud, duress, or undue influence. How will national courts handle these issues in cases that they might be called upon to decide under the CISG? In common law countries? In civil law countries of Europe? How has this been addressed by courts in the United States?
5. CISG Articles 71–73 contain legal rules on anticipatory breach. Article 77 contains rules on the mitigation of damages. These articles can be found in the appendix. Consider the following case: A contract provided that Mexicana Fabricators, S.A., would deliver 1,000 personal computer housings by December 1 to AES Computer, Inc., in Austin, Texas, for a total price of $50,000. On July 1, Mexicana faxed AES that due to a rise in prices they could not deliver for less than $60,000. AES replied that it would insist that Mexicana deliver at the $50,000 price. From July 1 through September, AES could have bought the housings from other suppliers for $55,000 for December 1 delivery. On December 1, AES covered and purchased the housings for $64,000 for delivery on February 1. Because of the delay until February 1, AES Computer suffered additional damages of $2,000. What is the measure of AES's damages? Was AES under any duty to mitigate damages? Why or why not?
6. An importer of children's toys, Fun 'N Games, Inc., receives a price quotation from a German toy maker offering toy train sets: "KBG train sets. Locomotive. Four cars. Transformers. Thirty pieces of track. Minimum order thirty sets. $7,500 C.I.F. Baltimore." Fun 'N Games, Inc., sends an order stating: "Ship thirty KBG train sets: to include locomotive, four cars, transformer, forty pieces of track," along with a check for $7,500. Was the price quotation from the German toy maker an offer? If it was, how does Fun 'N Games' change in terms—"forty pieces of track"—affect acceptance? If the German toy maker ships the thirty sets with "thirty pieces of track," does a contract exist? Decide the case under the common law, the UCC, and the CISG.
7. A computer printer distributor in Argentina receives an offer by mail from Epson, a U.S. company, in

reply to an inquiry. The offer arrives in Argentina on June 2. On June 12, the Argentinean company sends its acceptance by mail. On June 8, Epson sends a revocation of the offer that was received on June 13 in Argentina. The acceptance from Argentina arrives in the United States on June 17. Did a valid contract arise? When was the offer valid? When was the acceptance valid? When was the revocation valid? Decide the case under the common law and under the CISG.

8. Your company, Acme Widgets, sells its widgets worldwide. Acme has a contract for 250,000 widgets to be shipped to the Czech Republic. The price stated in the offer and acceptance is $1 per widget, C.I.F. Prague. During the production of the widgets, the price of one component increases 250 percent due to a shortage. In addition, these widgets are due for shipment on June 15 and arrival in Prague no later than July 1. On June 15, a stevedores' strike begins, which lasts for 60 days. Are either or both of these factors—the material price increase and the stevedores' strike—an excuse for Acme's nonperformance? What legal theory might Acme use under U.S. common law as an excuse? Under the CISG?

9. A German seller brought a claim against a Russian buyer because the buyer failed to pay for the equipment supplied to the buyer pursuant to their contract. The buyer acknowledged it had received the goods but said its nonpayment should be excused, because it was due to the failure of the bank responsible for the buyer's foreign currency transactions to make payment to the seller. The buyer claimed the fact the bank lacked the available currency resources should be regarded as a *force majeure,* discharging it from liability for nonpayment to the buyer. The contract did include a *force majeure* clause, but it did not refer to the buyer's lack of foreign currency. Do you agree with the buyer? *Tribunal of International Commercial Arbitration at the Russian Federation Chamber of Commerce and Industry 17 October 1995.* (See case law on UNICTRAL texts Abstract No. 142; reproduced with permission on Pace University's CISG Web site.)

10. Barcel, a Mexican company, contracted with Kliff, a citizen of California, to buy 47 million foil "Britney Spears" trading cards to be placed in snack food packaging in direct contact with food. The cards were to be shipped to Mexico. Kliff contracted with Grace Label, Inc. to produce the cards. Grace Label is an Iowa corporation located in Des Moines. Both parties agreed that the cards had to be FDA approved for contact with food. Grace Label did not have any direct communications with Barcel because Kliff did not want Grace Label to be in contact with his customer. Barcel rejected the cards because they were not food compatible. Is this case governed by the CISG? Why or why not? *Grace Label, Inc. v. Kliff,* 355 F. Supp. 2d 965 (S.D. Iowa 2005).

Managerial Implications

You are the vice president of sales for DownPillow International, Inc., a U.S. manufacturer of bed pillows. The raw materials needed for making pillows are all sourced from suppliers overseas. Your firm purchases feathers from exporters in China who maintain large flocks of geese and ducks for breeding. Cotton ticking and other textiles are purchased from mills in Germany. Every year you show your products at the International Bed Show in New York. This year, a delegation of Japanese buyers, representing several well-known Tokyo stores, showed interest in your best quality pillows. The president of your firm expressed interest in these contacts because although Americans use the same old pillow forever, the Japanese are fastidious about their bedding. You followed up with samples, product, and pricing information. After several discussions and months of correspondence, you now expect to be receiving your first overseas orders.

You are to meet with legal counsel next week to discuss this opportunity. What questions might you want to ask about entering a sales contract with a Japanese buyer? If a buyer shows interest in purchasing large quantities, should you consider a visit to their Tokyo office? What would you accomplish? Should your attorney conduct negotiations there for you? If you and your buyer agree to put your agreement in writing, what terms might the document contain? Your customers want assurances that their pillows will be made of the finest white goose down, with less than 10 percent feathers. What assurance will you be able to give them regarding product quality and specifications? What factors might influence the selection of a choice of law clause? Do you think your lawyer will insist on a *force majeure* clause? Can you suggest some of the things DownPillow might want in its clause?

If you anticipate that you may have several accounts in Japan, and each of them will be sending in purchase orders for each order, will you need a confirmation form? Will your attorney recommend that you develop a standard form to use for confirming all export orders? How will this form differ from the form you use for domestic shipments? What kind of provisions should it have?

How might negotiating your supply contracts with the Chinese differ from dealing with German textile mills? You have some concern about making sure that the quality of the down from China remains consistent. How can you be assured that you will receive goose down and not duck down? What other precautions should you take? The German mill has asked that your orders be mailed in or faxed. Your lawyer recommends that certain terms be put into your purchase order form. What might they be? Your purchase order states that the seller is liable for consequential damages for late shipment. The mill's confirmation states that "the liability of the seller is limited to the replacement of returned goods." In the event of a dispute, which will prevail under U.S. law? Under German law? Under the CISG?

Your contract with the Japanese buyer specifies that the CISG is to govern the transaction. Your pillows arrive in Japan and the buyer discovers that they contain only 13 oz. of down instead of the full 16 oz. of down as promised. You admit the error and want to resolve the problem. However, the buyer has just been offered the same quality pillow at considerably lower prices from a firm in Taiwan and wants out. Discuss the rights of each of the parties under the CISG.

FOR INTERNET ACTIVITIES, VISIT ACADEMIC.CENGAGE.COM/BLAW/SCHAFFER.

CHAPTER 5
THE DOCUMENTARY SALE AND TERMS OF TRADE

Imagine that your firm is a manufacturer of specialty cotton yarn, which it sells to domestic knitting and weaving mills. You receive an inquiry from a potential foreign customer expressing an interest in your yarn and requesting a price quote or pro forma invoice showing the price for the goods and two different shipping and cargo insurance options: one if they take delivery of the yarn at a named seaport in your country and arrange ocean transport and insurance themselves, and another if you arrange for all insurance on the goods and their transportation to a seaport near the buyer. This will let them determine if it is more cost-effective for you to arrange and pay the cost of ocean shipping or for them to do it.

They also request your "most favorable payment terms" and supply you with banking and credit information and trade references. Typically, your shipments to established domestic customers are on "open account" terms, and you offer a 30-day credit period for payment. However, you are uncertain about granting the same terms to a new foreign customer because there it is possible that you may never see your money. If they fail to pay, it may be difficult to find a substitute buyer in that part of the world. Moreover, you would like your money as quickly as possible. On the other hand, if you demand cash in advance they may take their business elsewhere. After all, you realize that they probably have no more reason to trust you to ship as promised than you have reason to trust them to pay. Being new to exporting, you begin to do some research and consult several international trade specialists from government, freight forwarding, and banking. You would like to know if there are payment options other than open account or cash in advance.

Evaluating your customer's creditworthiness and deciding on payment terms is not your only concern. You have been asked to quote a price for the yarn using two shipping alternatives. The first requires you to make the goods available to the buyer at a seaport in your country. This means that you have to determine the costs of packing, crating, and ground transportation to the port named by your customer. The second alternative requires you to calculate the costs of ocean transport and marine cargo insurance to a foreign port in your customer's country. You calculate the weight and number of pallets of yarn to be shipped and estimate that it will fill one ocean container. On that basis, you request your freight forwarder to provide land and ocean transportation costs, container fees, dock fees, forwarder's fees, insurance coverage, and other costs.

Now, you are almost ready to produce your pro forma invoice. However, there is one remaining question. You are unsure about your liability for damage to the yarn during shipment. You know the perils of the sea are great. What if the ship went down in a storm or the yarn was stolen or was damaged by saltwater condensation? Which party, buyer or seller, would bear the risk of loss? Even if the insurance did cover the loss, and even if the law permitted a claim against the carrier (the topics of the next chapter), as between buyer and seller, which party would be left trying to recover it? At what moment, or at what place, does the risk of loss shift from the seller to the buyer? Are you free from responsibility when the goods leave your hands, when the goods reach the buyer's mill, or at some point in between? Does it matter which party, buyer or seller, owns the goods at the time they are lost or damaged? You would like to know if there is anything you can do to "negotiate away" the responsibility for damage to the goods as quickly as possible after they leave your hands. Is there any way to put language in the contract that assigns the risks of the ocean voyage to the buyer? We will try to answer these questions in this chapter. In order to do this we will cover several basic subjects:

1. A brief description of the transaction risks facing the buyer and seller
2. The legal nature of documents of title, such as ocean bills of lading, and the significance of their negotiability to international commerce
3. The documentary sale and collection process used in exchanging goods for money
4. The role of ocean carriers and international banks in facilitating the documentary sale
5. An explanation of the difference between "shipment contracts" and "destination contracts"
6. The use of shipping terms and trade terms in sales contracts to assign the shipping responsibilities and the risk of loss between buyer and seller

TRANSACTION RISK

For purposes of this book, the term *transaction risk* refers to the risks facing the buyer and seller when they move money and goods in an international sales transaction. Transaction risks arise from barriers that separate buyer and seller, including distance, oceans, the time that the cargo is out of possession of the parties, communication and language difficulties, cultural differences, national boundaries, interference by local customs authorities, and legal systems.

Two of the most obvious forms of transaction risk are delivery risk and payment risk. *Delivery risk* is the risk to the buyer that the seller will fail to ship the goods as called for in the contract. For instance, the seller might fail to ship the goods at all, or on time, properly packaged, adequately insured, and using the agreed mode of transportation. There is much greater delivery risk in an international sale than in a domestic sale, because the buyer may not know the seller very well. The seller may fail to ship due to any number of business reasons. In addition, the seller may not have the same commitment to its foreign customers as it does to its domestic customers. The seller may even be a cheat and fill the containers with worthless rubbish or ship less than the quantity billed. Indeed, international business can be fraught with peril.

Distance and the use of ocean transport also increase delivery risk. Despite the importance of air transport today, most cargo is still carried by sea. Although all forms of transportation put cargo at risk, ocean cargo can be imperiled by time, moisture, storms, shipwreck, pilferage of ocean containers, and, even today, piracy. In addition, *multimodal transport* (the use of more than one mode of transportation, such as truck plus ocean vessel) places the goods at risk during transfers and at times when they are temporarily warehoused.

Payment risk (also called *credit risk*) is the risk to the seller that the buyer will fail to pay as promised. Payment risk is compounded by the fact that the seller may have difficulty getting a credit history on a foreign customer or obtaining banking and trade information. The buyer's distance, and location in a foreign country with an unfamiliar legal system, means that any attempt to collect payment can be costly and time consuming. If the buyer fails or refuses to pay, the seller might have to resort to litigation in the buyer's country in order to recover the money owed. Even then, recovery might become impossible, if the buyer becomes insolvent or bankrupt. If a foreign buyer refuses delivery, it may not be cost-effective to ship the goods home, and the seller may have difficulty in locating a substitute buyer that far away.

Ideally, if sellers could have their way, they would like to have *cash in advance* from new foreign buyers before the goods leave their hands. That is certainly the most secure form of payment. On the other hand, few buyers would part with their money merely in the hope that the goods they ordered would ever arrive. If the seller is unscrupulous and has already received the cash, he may be tempted to walk away without shipping or to ship goods other than those that were ordered. The seller may have no long-term interest in exporting to a foreign market or may just be dishonest. Cultural and language barriers might make it especially hard to gauge a seller's honesty or intentions. So, cash in advance as a payment option usually will not serve to bring buyer and seller together.

On the other hand, all buyers would like to be able to buy on open credit terms, or on *open account.* With open account terms, the seller grants an extended credit period for the buyer to pay, typically 30 days. In domestic sales, for the seller who has had an opportunity to learn the creditworthiness of the buyer, sales are often made on open account terms. However, few sellers would risk shipping their goods, perhaps halfway around the world, giving up possession, control, and even ownership of the goods to a foreign buyer, without some adequate assurance of payment. Perhaps after a long relationship has developed between them, they may agree to do business this way, but an open account sale is usually not secure enough for most large international transactions. In addition, a seller who agrees to sell on open account in a foreign currency bears the risk that the currency will fall in value during the open credit period. Thus, if cash in advance or open account terms were the only payment options, buyer and seller would be at an impasse. To bring them together, some other form of payment is required. One method that provides assurances to both parties is the documentary sale.

The Documentary Sale

The *documentary sale* is a type of contract for the sale of goods in which possession and ownership of the goods are transferred from seller to buyer through negotiation and delivery of a negotiable document of title issued by an ocean carrier. The seller's obligation is to place the goods in the hands of an ocean carrier within the time called for in the contract, in exchange for a negotiable document of title, and to negotiate the document of title to the buyer in return for either immediate payment or, if an extension of credit is anticipated by the contract, for the buyer's promise to pay at a future date. The buyer's obligation is to "purchase" the document in a timely fashion and to take delivery of the goods. The process of exchanging a document of title in return for money is handled through correspondent banks in the buyer's and seller's countries. It reduces the transaction risks between a buyer and a seller who are great distances apart by ensuring that if one releases the title to the goods, the other will release the money. The documentary sale is a unique method of exchange devised by early traders when their sailing vessels traveled medieval trade routes. The method spread by custom and practice and eventually became recognized in early English law, in the modern common law countries, and in the civil law countries of Europe. Today, the documentary sale is a common type of contract for the sale of goods.

The Document of Title

The first step to understanding the documentary sale is to understand the nature of a negotiable *document of title.* A negotiable document of title is a document that evidences the ownership of goods it represents. It entitles the person who possesses the document to possess the goods. Documents of title are created out of a special "bailment" relationship between the owner of personal property, the *bailor,* and one to whom its possession is entrusted, the *bailee.* A *bailment* is a relationship involving the separation of ownership and possession of personal property. The bailee receives the property on the condition that it will care for and return the property in the condition in which it was given or will transfer or dispose of it in accordance with the terms of the bailee's agreement with the bailor. Bailments are common in everyday life and are treated in more depth in other law classes. One example of a commercial bailment occurs when a bailor places goods in a warehouse for storage. The warehouse operator (the bailee) issues a document of title, known as a *warehouse receipt.* The document serves as a receipt for goods taken into its possession, and also as a document of title. For example, a farmer may place leaf tobacco in a warehouse, receive a warehouse receipt, and either reclaim the tobacco or sell it at auction by delivering the warehouse receipt to the buyer. In international trade, the most commonly used documents of title are bills of lading and multimodal transport documents.

Negotiable Documents of Title. Documents of title may either be negotiable or nonnegotiable.

A *negotiable* document of title is one stating that the goods will be delivered "to the order of" a named person or assigns or "to the bearer." Negotiable documents can be transferred by negotiation from one party to another in return for value or payment. *Negotiation* is the transfer of a document of title by its owner to another in a manner that passes title to the document, title to the goods, and the right to claim the goods from the issuer of the document. Order documents are negotiated by delivery. Bearer documents are negotiated by a signed indorsement and delivery. Documents of title are used to transfer ownership of goods from one party to another without the necessity of transferring physical possession of the goods themselves. When a negotiable document of title is sold in the ordinary course of trade, the seller is said to have made a *constructive delivery* of the goods to the seller. The property can stay in the possession of the bailee while the owner or subsequent owners sell or resell it or pledge it as collateral for a loan. In this chapter, we will discuss just one type of document of title used for moving goods by ocean—the ocean or maritime bill of lading. In a later chapter, we will cover air cargo and the use of air waybills in some detail.

The Bill of Lading

A negotiable ocean *bill of lading* is a document of title issued by an ocean carrier to a shipper upon receiving goods for transport (see Exhibit 5.1). Having first been used in the sixteenth century, the bill of lading has played a vital role in international trade. It has three roles.

1. It is a receipt for the goods from the carrier, indicating any damage to the goods that was visible or apparent at the time of loading.
2. It is the contract of carriage between the shipper and the carrier (i.e., a *transport document*).
3. It is the document of title to the goods described in it.

For the purposes of this chapter, unless otherwise noted, we will refer only to negotiable ocean bills of lading. Later in this chapter, we will describe different types of ocean bills, including nonnegotiable bills, as well negotiable multimodal transport documents. In the United States, the laws governing the negotiability of bills of lading are the *Federal Bills of Lading Act* (for bills originating in the United States for export shipments) and the *Uniform Commercial Code.*

Rights of Purchasers of Documents of Title

Although some readers may be familiar with the rights of parties that purchase *negotiable instruments,* such as checks and promissory notes, the law regarding the transfer and sale of *negotiable documents* is somewhat different because the functions of the two are different. Negotiable instruments serve as a substitute for money, while negotiable documents are used to move goods and to transfer their ownership and possession.

Good-Faith Purchasers of Documents of Title. The legal rights of the purchaser of a document of title in the United States depends on whether the case is governed by Article 7 of the *Uniform Commercial Code* or by the *Federal Bills of Lading Act.* The *Federal Bills of Lading Act* (enacted in 1916) is probably the more important of these, because it applies to all bills of lading issued by any common carrier for the shipment of goods in interstate or international commerce. This discussion generally applies to both laws. In order for negotiable documents of title to be freely accepted in commerce and trade, the law gives special protection to those who purchase negotiable documents under such circumstances as to become holders by due negotiation.

A *holder by due negotiation* (otherwise referred to as a *good-faith purchaser*) is one who purchases a negotiable document (1) for value (and not in settlement of a past debt), (2) in good faith and without any notice of any adverse claim against it, and (3) in the ordinary course of business or financing. If it is an order instrument, then the good-faith purchaser must take it by indorsement.

When a buyer, bank, or other party takes a document as a good-faith purchaser, it not only takes title to the document and to the goods it represents, but it acquires even greater rights in the document and to the goods than were had by the party who negotiated it to the purchaser. The rule is stated as follows: a good-faith purchaser

Exhibit 5.1

Ocean Bill of Lading

OCEAN BILL OF LADING

Shipper/Exporter Shipper's name Address	Export References Invoice or order number (Not negotiable unless consigned to order)
Consignee: (Complete Name and Address) To the order of: Shipper	Forwarding Agent – References Shippers Freight Forwarder Forwarding Agent – References: U.S.A. Forwarding Agent – References
Notify Party (Complete Name and Address) Buyer or buyer's import agent	Domestic Routing/Export Instructions Pre-carriage These commodities licensed by U.S. for ultimate destination Japan and for resale to any destination except North Korea, Iraq, Cambodia, or Cuba.
Pier	Onward Inland Routing / Place of delivery
Ocean Vessel / Flag / Port of Loading	
Port of Discharge / For Transshipment To	

Carrier's Receipt — Particulars Furnished By Shipper

Marks and Numbers	No. of Cont. or Other Pkgs.	Description of Goods	Gross Weight	Measurement
Container No. UP 362459 Seal # 2398112	95	1 x 40' container said to contain down pillows on invoices to be as per proforma invoices nos. 2368714, 2368715 dated April 15, 2008.		
Shipping Marks: Down Bedding		"Shipper Load, Stuff & Count"	1,550 Kg (Net)	
ON BOARD		Clean Shipped on board 5/10/2008 "Freight Prepaid" House to port basis Signed ________ Title of Company Official		

Received in apparent good order and condition except as otherwise noted hereon the goods, containers, or other packages, or units mentioned above for transportation from the place of receipt if named above or (if not named) the port of loading to the port of discharge or place of delivery (as the case may be) subject to exceptions limitations, conditions and liberties hereof and there to be delivered to the consignee or his or their assigns.

(TERMS OF THIS BILL OF LADING CONTINUED ON REVERSE SIDE HEREOF)

Freight Charges	Prepaid	Collect
Land Charges		
Port Charges		
Ocean Charges		
Container Rental		
Total	4850.00	

B/L No.

IN WITNESS WHEREOF, The Master or Agent of said vessel has affirmed to THREE (3) ________ Bills of Lading, all of this tenor and date, one of which being accomplished, the others stand void.

Carrier TAMPA BAY STEAMSHIP JACKSONVILLE, FLA.

By ________
Agent (for the Master) TBS

Dated at Port of Shipment	Mo.	Day	Yr.
	5	10	08

takes a negotiable document of title free from the adverse claims that third parties might have against the goods. For example, a good-faith purchaser of a negotiable document of title, as a general rule, does not have to be concerned that someone else may have a greater right to claim the goods than they do or that a creditor of the seller will claim the goods to satisfy a debt. A good-faith purchaser takes the document free from any claims that other parties might have against either the document or the goods (excluding claims of the carrier for shipping charges or of government customs authorities).

Consider the following case: A entrusts goods to B for storage. B delivers the goods to a carrier, obtains a bill of lading, negotiates the document to C, and absconds with the money. C, who is a good-faith purchaser, takes title to both the document and the goods. A may not reclaim them because C takes *paramount title.* This means that C's rights are superior, even against the original owner, because B was entrusted with the goods and then wrongfully sold them.

There are many cases where the good-faith purchaser takes greater rights than the transferor of the document had. But in certain other instances, a good-faith purchaser might not enjoy greater rights. For instance, if a thief steals goods and obtains a bill of lading, a purchaser of the document does not obtain paramount title over the original owner. In the following case, *Banque de Depots v. Ferroligas,* the court addresses the rights of a party who takes a bill of lading by "due negotiation." Notice how the court attempts to protect the rights of these purchasers of negotiable documents.

Banque de Depots v. Ferroligas

569 So. 2d 40 (1990)

Court of Appeals of Louisiana, 4th Circuit

BACKGROUND AND FACTS

Banque de Depots, a Swiss banker, brought an action against Bozel, a Brazilian exporter, seeking a money judgment because Bozel had allegedly misapplied the bank's funds. The bank obtained an order seizing 1,300 metric tons of calcium silicon located in a Louisiana port. The calcium silicon was shipped under ocean bills of lading by Bozel from Rio de Janeiro to New Orleans for transit to three purchasers, none of whom were domiciled in Louisiana. The documents were still in the hands of the collecting banks and had not yet been negotiated to the buyers. Bozel asked the court to free the goods because he was not the owner of the bills of lading.

LOBRANO, JUDGE

Bozel asserts that ... title to the cargo follows the bills of lading, and once those were transferred to the collecting banks, they [Bozel] were no longer the owner of the cargo.

The Bank asserts that ... only bills of lading which are "duly negotiated" transfer ownership of goods.... They contend that the bills of lading may have been transferred to the collecting banks, but they were not "duly negotiated" ... since there was no value given prior to the attachment....

We agree that Louisiana law governs the ownership of the cargo when it reached Chalmette, La. Article 2 of the UCC has not been adopted in Louisiana, hence the courts must look to the Louisiana Civil Code in determining the ownership of movables....

The holder of a duly negotiated bill of lading acquires title to the document and title to the goods described therein. It is clear that once a carrier has issued a negotiable bill of lading for goods being placed in commerce, the intent of the law is to protect those who subsequently become holders through "due negotiation." Part and parcel of that intent is the protection afforded the [carrier] in relinquishing possession of the goods to the holder of the document. Thus, although goods in the possession of a [carrier] may have been seized, if the document's negotiation has not been enjoined or the document is not in its possession, [Louisiana law] permits the [carrier] to surrender the goods to the duly negotiated holder. The law protects that holder from acquiring goods that are subject to a seizure. Any other conclusion would lead to the absurd result of requiring the holder, prior to

continued

continued

his purchase of the bill of lading, to check every jurisdiction through which the goods passed to determine if it has been seized by judicial process. This would defeat the purpose of our commercial laws.

The record is clear that on May 14, 1990, the date of the seizure, the negotiable bills of lading were outstanding. They were not in the hands of the carrier and their negotiation had not been enjoined. As discussed, the validity of the attachment must be determined as of the date it was issued. The Bank cannot cure this defect by seeking to impound the bills of lading after it obtained the seizure. To hold otherwise would create an impossible contradiction in our commercial laws since the "seized" goods would still be subject to the legal effects of the unimpaired "due negotiation" of the corresponding bills of lading. The legal "capture" of the bills of lading is a prerequisite to the seizure of the goods.

We order that the writ of attachment be dissolved.

Decision. A court-ordered seizure of goods in transit cannot stand when the title to the goods is represented by a bill of lading and the bill of lading itself was not seized by the court order.

Comment. The Swiss bank was attempting to assert jurisdiction over Bozel by seizing its cargo in the United States. Although this attempt failed, the court stated that the bank was free to continue to find other ways to get jurisdiction over Bozel.

Different rules apply to transferees of *nonnegotiable* bills of lading and to transferees of negotiable bills of lading who did not take them by due negotiation or in good faith. In these cases, the holder receives only those rights that the transferor had or that the transferor had the actual authority to convey. Recall the example in which A entrusted goods to B for storage. Now assume that B transfers a nonnegotiable bill of lading to C and absconds with the money. A can reclaim the goods from C.

Carrier's Liability for Misdelivery. The carrier may deliver the goods only to the holder of an original bill of lading. Assume that A entrusts a shipment of goods to an ocean carrier and obtains a bill of lading. The carrier delivers the goods to B without asking B to produce the document. Without knowledge of what has occurred, A sells the bill to C, who takes it for value and in good faith. C is the good-faith purchaser and the owner of the goods and may bring an action to reclaim the goods from B. C also has a cause of action against the carrier for misdelivery of the goods because the carrier violated the terms of the contract of carriage.

Importance of Negotiability to Trade. The negotiability of the bill of lading is what makes it so important to trade. As the document is bought and sold, so too are the goods it represents. Negotiability permits merchants to trade in cargo while it is still afloat. With a bill of lading, goods can be bought and sold, time and again, while they are still on the high seas, with the bill of lading circling the globe from one buyer to the next. This practice is, in fact, quite common. Persian Gulf oil can change hands twenty or thirty times in the 6 weeks that it takes a tanker to reach U.S. waters.

The negotiability of bills of lading was recognized in most European trading centers at least as early as the sixteenth century. Early records of them have been found in many languages. In 1883, Lord Justice Bowen described the bill of lading in this time-honored description from *Sanders Brothers v. Maclean & Co.*, (1883) 11 Q.B.D. 327 at 341.

> The law as to the indorsement of bills of lading is as clear as in my opinion the practice of all European merchants is thoroughly understood. A cargo at sea while in the hands of the carrier is necessarily incapable of physical delivery. During this period of transit and voyage, the bill of lading by the law merchant is universally recognized as its symbol, and the indorsement and delivery of the bill of lading operates as a symbolical delivery of the cargo. Property in the goods passes by such indorsement and delivery of the bill of lading, whenever it is the intention of the parties that the property should pass, just as under similar circumstances the property would pass by an actual delivery of the goods. And for the purpose of passing such property in the goods and completing the title of the indorsee to full possession thereof, the bill of lading, until complete delivery of the cargo has been made on shore to some one rightfully claiming under it, remains in force as a symbol, and carries

BoL = symbolic entity
key to title transfer

> with it not only the full ownership of the goods, but also all rights created by the contract of carriage between the shipper and the shipowner. It is a key which in the hands of a rightful owner is intended to unlock the door of the warehouse, floating or fixed, in which the goods may chance to be.

As the vessel bearing the goods proceeds out of the harbor and onto the open ocean, the seller safely retains the title to the merchandise, literally held in hand. The seller can sell the goods as planned by sending the bill of lading ahead to the buyer, divert the shipment to another buyer around the globe, pledge it for a loan, or bring it home. This unique flexibility has made the documentary sale essential to world trade and the international economy.

DOCUMENTARY COLLECTIONS. The *documentary collection* is the process by which banking institutions serve as intermediaries between seller and buyer to handle the exchange of the bill of lading for payment (see Exhibit 5.2). The documentary collection is an integral part of the documentary sale. It provides a safer alternative for payment than either cash in advance or sale on open account. The parties might indicate their desire for a documentary collection by specifying in the contract that payment terms are "cash against documents" or "documents against payment." (sometimes abbreviated CAD or D/P). Such an indication is not always essential because the collection process is implied in most documentary sales contracts.

EXHIBIT 5.2

The Documentary Sale

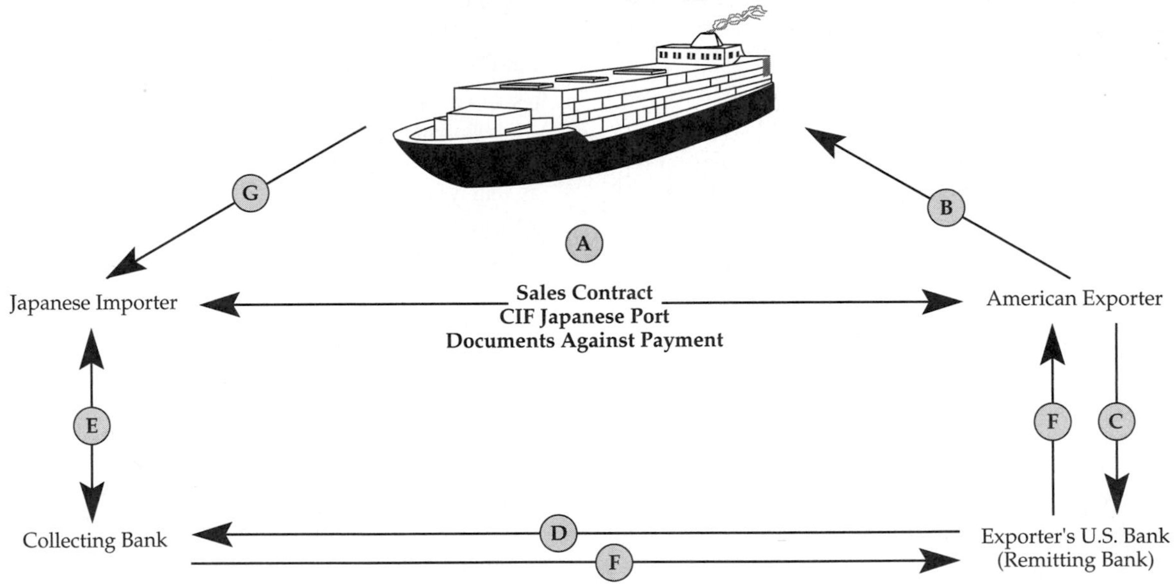

A. Sales contract calls for documentary sale.
B. Documents prepared—export licenses obtained—goods delivered to carrier.
C. Negotiable bill of lading, insurance policy, certificate of origin, invoice with draft attached presented to remitting bank.
D. Documents forwarded for collection through international banking system.
E. Documents presented for negotiation on payment.
F. Payment remitted and exporter's account credited.
G. Importer claims goods and makes entry.

Here is a simplified description of how the documentary collection process works: Seller places the goods in the hands of a carrier and in return receives a negotiable bill of lading or multimodal transport document made to its order or assigns. Seller indorses the bill of lading and presents it to the bank for collection. Along with the bill of lading, the seller will include other essential documents that the contract requires it to submit, such as a *marine insurance* policy on the goods covering the risks of the ocean voyage. A *certificate of origin* may be required by customs regulations in the buyer's country. The seller's *commercial invoice* describing the goods and showing the price to be paid is always required. Finally, a *documentary draft* will be needed to expedite the exchange of money. The draft is a negotiable instrument used to make payment for the invoice and for the bill of lading. As described in a later chapter, the draft is a negotiable "order to pay" made out by the seller, drawn on the buyer for collection, and payable to the order of the seller. Its purpose is to tell the parties how much to pay when purchasing the bill of lading. The draft will also be needed by the bank if financing is to be provided for the sale. Other documents may be required, as well, depending on the needs of the parties or the export-import regulations of their countries.

The seller's bank forwards the draft and documents to a *collecting bank* in the buyer's country, with instructions that the documents be released to the buyer only on payment of the draft. A collecting bank is any bank authorized to collect on an instrument. When the buyer pays the draft, the collecting bank remits the money back to the seller's bank.

If the documents are presented in good order, the collection process should work smoothly, with buyer and seller each getting what they bargained for in the contract. The process may not be so smooth, however, if the documents tendered contain one or more obvious defects. If they appear forged, or if they show that the goods were shipped later than the date called for in the contract, or on an improper vessel, or if the goods are inadequately insured, or if the documents on their face appear fraudulent (e.g., a non-existent shipping line), the buyer may refuse them. The buyer's refusal could come as quite a surprise to the seller, who in good faith shipped and tendered documents to the buyer, only to find that they have been rejected and the draft unpaid, due to some "technicality." Of course, the point of contention may be more than just a technicality to the buyer, who may feel the rejection was based on good cause. Either way, the seller is left with a good deal of exposure while the goods remain in a distant foreign port.

CIF CONTRACTS AND THE ENGLISH COMMON LAW. There are many variations on the documentary sale. However, under one of the oldest and most typical variations, the seller must not only tender a bill of lading to the buyer for payment, but also must provide marine insurance on the goods and prepay the freight charges to the foreign port. These contracts are called *CIF contracts,* which stands for "cost, insurance, and freight." The acronym CIF is a trade term. *Trade terms* are shorthand abbreviations drafted into a contract that assign the risk of loss, freight charges, and other responsibilities to either buyer or seller. CIF and other trade terms, including some not used in documentary sales, are discussed later in the chapter.

In the following English case, the seller in San Francisco tendered documents covering a shipment of hops to the buyer in London. The buyer wanted to inspect the merchandise first and refused to pay until delivery was made. The seller claimed that payment was due immediately upon presentation of the documents, even though the hops were still somewhere aboard ship on the ocean. The Kennedy dissent in *Biddell Brothers* represents a virtually universal view of CIF and other documentary sales contracts today. This rule has been adopted by the UCC, is incorporated into statutes in other countries, and has long been recognized by courts in the United States and throughout the world.

Certificates of Inspection or Analysis

The documentary sales transaction serves to protect not only the seller, but also the buyer. The bill of lading ensure that the goods have been loaded aboard ship for transport on the date shown, and the insurance policy protects against covered marine losses. However, the buyer must take the description of the goods in the bill of lading, and in the invoice that usually accompanies it, at face

mirror-image contract principle

Biddell Brothers v. E. Clemens Horst Co.

1 King's Bench 934 (1911)

Court of Appeal

BACKGROUND AND FACTS

The defendant entered into a contract to sell hops to the plaintiff in London, as follows:

> ... one hundred bales, equal to or better than choice brewing Pacific Coast hops of each of the crops of the years 1905 to 1912 inclusive. The said hops to be shipped to Sunderland. The [buyer] shall pay for the said hops at the rate of ninety shillings sterling per 112 lbs. CIF to London, Liverpool, or Hull. Terms net cash.

The seller wrote to the buyer stating that they were ready to ship and that they expected payment upon presentation of a negotiable bill of lading. The buyer replied that it was prepared to take delivery but insisted that the seller either submit samples for prior inspection or that it be permitted to inspect each bale prior to payment. The buyer was unwilling to accept a certificate of inspection from the San Francisco Merchant's Exchange as assurance of quality. The seller refused to ship and the buyer brought this action. The seller counterclaimed for the buyer's refusal to pay on the documents. The lower court ruled in favor of the defendant buyer. The Court of Appeals affirmed, with Kennedy, L.J., dissenting. On appeal to the House of Lords, the judgment was reversed in favor of the seller.

LORD JUSTICE KENNEDY, DISSENTING

The plaintiffs' case is that the price was not to be paid until they had been given an opportunity of inspecting the shipment, which could not be given until after its arrival in this country. The defendants contend that the plaintiffs' obligation was to pay for the hops, whether they arrived or not, against tender of the shipping documents. The Court, therefore, has in the present case to decide what are the true conditions of the right of the seller to payment under a CIF contract, if that commercial contract is to be performed strictly according to its tenor.

Let us see, step by step, how according to those principles and rules the transactions as in such a CIF contract as that before us is and, I think, must be carried out in order to fulfill its terms.

At the port of shipment—in this case San Francisco—the vendor ships the goods intended for the purchaser under the contract. Under the Sale of Goods Act, 1893, [section] 18, by such shipment the goods are appropriated by the vendor to the fulfillment of the contract, and by virtue of [section] 32 the delivery of the goods to the carrier—whether named by the purchaser or not—for the purpose of transmission to the purchaser is prima facie to be deemed to be a delivery of the goods to the purchaser. Two further legal results arise out of the shipment. The goods are at risk of the purchaser, against which he has protected himself by the stipulation in his CIF contract that the vendor shall, at his own cost, provide him with a proper policy of marine insurance intended to protect the buyer's interest, and available for his use, if the goods should be lost in transit. How is such a tender to be made of goods afloat under a CIF contract? By tender of the bill of lading, accompanied in case the goods have been lost in transit by the policy of insurance. The bill of lading in law and in fact represents the goods. Possession of the bill of lading places the goods at the disposal of the purchaser.... But then I understand it to be objected on behalf of the plaintiffs: "Granted that the purchaser might, if he pleased, take this constructive delivery and pay against it the price of the goods; what is there in the 'cost freight and insurance' contract which compels him to do so? Why may he not insist on an option of waiting for a tender of delivery of the goods themselves after having had an opportunity of examining them after their arrival?"

There are, I think, several sufficient answers to such a proposition. In the first place, an option of a time of payment is not a term which can be inferred, where the contract itself is silent. So far as I am aware, there is no authority for the inference of an option as to times of payment to be found either in the law books or in the Sale of Goods Act. Secondly, if there is a duty on the vendor to tender the bill of lading, there must, it seems to me, be a corresponding duty on the part of the purchaser to pay when such tender is made. For thereunder, as the bill of lading with its accompanying documents comes forward by mail, the purchaser obtains the privilege and absolute power of profitably dealing with the goods days or weeks, or, perhaps, in the case of shipments from a distant port, months, before the arrival of the goods themselves. This is, indeed, the essential and

continued

continued

peculiar advantage which the buyer of imported goods intends to gain under the CIF contract according to the construction which I put upon it.

Finally, let me test the soundness of the plaintiffs' contention that according to the true meaning of this contract their obligation to pay arises only when delivery of the goods has been tendered to them after they have an opportunity of examination, in this way. Suppose the goods to have been shipped, the bill of lading taken, and the insurance for the benefit of the buyer duly effected by the seller, as expressly stipulated in the contract. Suppose the goods then during the ocean transit to have been lost by the perils of the sea. The vendor tenders the bill of lading, with the insurance policy and the other shipping documents (if any) to the purchaser, to whom from the moment of shipment the property has passed, and at whose risk, covered by the insurance, the goods were at the time of loss. Is it, I ask myself, arguable that the purchaser could be heard to say, "I will not pay because I cannot have delivery of and an examination of the goods?" But it is just this which is necessarily involved in the contention of these plaintiffs. The seller's answer, and I think conclusive answer, is, "You have the bill of lading and the policy of insurance."

In my judgment, the judgment of Hamilton, J., was right, and this appeal, so far as relates to the plaintiffs' claim, should be dismissed.

Decision. Under a CIF sales contract, the buyer has no right to inspect the goods but is obligated to pay upon the presentation of the proper documents.

value. If the goods are nonconforming or defective, or if a lesser quantity was shipped, the buyer's only remedy may be an action for breach of contract. In many industries, buyers will require that bills of lading be accompanied by an inspection report of a reputable, independent testing laboratory or inspection service, usually located in the seller's country. These might certify the quantity, quality, or other characteristic of the goods being purchased. Examples include *certificates of inspection, certificates of weight,* or *certificates of analysis.* Inspections are common in the chemical, extraction, and commodities businesses, as well as throughout other types of international trade. For instance, major apparel retailers in the United States typically arrange for pre-shipment inspection of garments for defects in the country of assembly.

In the *Basse and Selve v. Bank of Australasia* case, the buyer claimed that its bank should have

Exhibit 5.3

2003 Amendments to UCC 2-513*

§2-513 Buyer's Right to Inspection of Goods

(1) Unless otherwise agreed and subject to subsection (3), where goods are tendered or delivered or identified to the contract for sale, the buyer has a right before payment or acceptance to inspect them at any reasonable place and time and in any reasonable manner. When the seller is required or authorized to send the goods to the buyer, the inspection may be after their arrival.

(2) Expenses of inspection must be borne by the buyer but may be recovered from the seller if the goods do not conform and are rejected.

(3) Unless otherwise agreed, the buyer is not entitled to inspect the goods before payment of the price when the contract provides
   (a) for delivery on terms that under applicable course of performance, course of dealing, or usage of trade are interpreted to preclude inspection before payment; or
   (b) for payment against documents of title, except where such payment is due only after the goods are to become available for inspection.

*Subject to enactment by state legislatures.

Basse and Selve v. Bank of Australasia

90 Law Times 618 (1904)
King's Bench

BACKGROUND AND FACTS

The plaintiff had purchased ore from Oppenheimer. The plaintiff requested that the defendant bank negotiate documents on its behalf from Oppenheimer covering a shipment of "cobalt ore analysis not less than 5 per cent peroxide." The plaintiff specified that the bill of lading must be accompanied by a policy of insurance and a certificate of analysis from Dr. Helms, a Sydney chemist. Oppenheimer submitted for analysis phony samples of ore to the chemist, who, on the basis of this small sample, issued his certificate indicating the quality to be as described in the bill of lading. In fact, the ore contained in the actual shipment was worthless. The plaintiff brought this action in order to recover amounts paid by the bank against the documents.

JUSTICE BIGHAM

It was no part of their duty to verify the genuineness of the documents; the duty was not cast upon them of making inquiries at the office of the ship's agent as to whether the goods had, in truth, been received on board; nor were they to examine the contents of the packages to see whether they were right; nor were they to communicate with Dr. Helms in order to ascertain whether he had properly made the analysis mentioned in the certificate. The plaintiffs' mandate amounted in business to a representation to the defendants that upon all such matters they might rely on Oppenheimer, and the legal effect of such a representation is now to preclude the plaintiffs from questioning the validity of any apparently regular documents which Oppenheimer might tender. If this is so, then the only question left on this part of the case is whether the documents were apparently regular. It is admitted by the plaintiffs that the bill of lading and the policy of insurance were apparently regular, but an objection is made on this score to Helms's certificate. It is said that it professes to show merely the test of the contents of a sample packet with a mark upon it, and does not purport to show a test of the bill of lading of 100 tons of ore. This, I think, is a fanciful objection. Large quantities of produce are necessarily tested by means of samples. Such samples are drawn either by the servants of the owner of the goods or (as it seems) by the servants of the analyst, and if the samples are carefully and skillfully drawn they generally fairly represent the bulk. But in this case it would be no part of the bank's duty to see to the sampling or to ascertain that it was fairly done. The bank was entitled to assume that it was so just as they were entitled to assume that the analyst had acted skillfully in making the analysis. The certificate is, in my opinion, regular on its face, and comes within the meaning of the mandate under which the bank was acting, and the bank in taking it acted carefully and properly.

Judgment for defendants.

Decision. The court ruled that because the certificate on its face was regular, the bank had acted properly in paying the seller. The bank had no duty to inspect the ore itself.

been more diligent in accepting an inspection certificate that the seller had obtained from a chemist by fraud and trickery.

How Secure Are Documentary Payment Terms?

No reader should be left with the impression that documentary payment terms are appropriate for all parties or for all transactions. They are appropriate for shipments that are of low to moderate value, shipments to repeat customers, and shipments of goods that may cost-effectively be returned home or resold to a substitute buyer if the original buyer rejects the documents. Traders that buy and sell commodities, natural resource materials, or other goods while they are still in transit also use documentary sales.

By establishing a regular course of business on documentary terms, the seller may become more comfortable in advancing to open credit account terms later. However, a documentary sale is not the most secure method of doing business, because it offers no guarantee that the buyer will actually purchase the documents when presented. There is always the possibility that the buyer may become insolvent, find the goods more cheaply from another source, or change their mind.

Even though the seller can maintain possession, ownership, and control of the goods through the bill of lading and can attempt to resell them to a substitute customer, that may not be so easy when the goods are located in a foreign country or if they are custom designed and not readily saleable. Therefore, the seller may want to require some additional security where the goods are of a very high value, specially manufactured, for first-time orders to new customers, or where a seller is uncertain as to the creditworthiness or integrity of a prospective foreign customer. In this case it may be wise to require full or partial payment in advance of shipment. The seller may also want to consider another advance payment alternative that we will study in a later chapter: the use of a "letter of credit" from the buyer's bank wherein the bank irrevocably promises to become primarily responsible for purchasing the documents in lieu of the buyer. This added layer of security substitutes the creditworthiness and integrity of a bank for that of the buyer.

Measuring Damages for Breach of the Documentary Sale

The last chapter discussed the remedies available to a buyer and seller for breach of contract. In the case of the documentary sale, if the buyer sues the seller for nondelivery or other breach of contract, the buyer's damages may be measured by the difference between the contract price for the goods and the cost or fair market value of replacement goods. How is market value determined in a documentary sale? Is it the market value at the time that the goods are shipped, the time of delivery of the goods, or the time of payment?

Under the English view, damages are based on the market value as of the date when the buyer would have paid for the goods had the seller not breached. In *Sharpe & Co., Ltd. v. Nosawa & Co.*, (1917) 2 K.B. 814, a Japanese seller entered into a contract to ship peas to an English buyer under a documentary sale, CIF London. Neither the goods nor the documents were ever sent, and the buyer sued for damages. The question was whether the buyer's damages should have been calculated on the basis of the difference between the contract price (£10.15 sterling per ton) and the market price of peas at the time of the anticipated August delivery (£17.10 sterling per ton), or the difference between the contract price and the market price of peas on July 21, when the documents would have been tendered in London (£12.00 sterling per ton). The court held that the seller's responsibility under this contract would have not been complete until he delivered the shipping documents to the buyer in London, at which time he would have been paid, and that the damages should therefore be measured by the price of peas on that date, July 21.

In a market with rapidly fluctuating prices, this question becomes especially important. *Seaver v. Lindsay Light Co.*, 135 N.E. 329 (N.Y. 1922) illustrates how American courts have diverged from the English rule. The seller and buyer entered a CIF contract for the shipment of thorium from Chicago to London. After the seller refused to ship, the buyer brought an action for breach of contract. Contrary to the English rule, the New York court looked at the nature of a shipment contract and stated,

> Where was the delivery of the thorium in the present case to be made? Was it at Chicago or at the London dock? When the correspondence and cablegrams are all construed together, as they must be, then it seems to me they clearly indicate an intention on the part of both parties that the delivery was to be made at Chicago, and when the defendant delivered to a carrier at that point, paid the freight to point of destination, and forwarded the other necessary documents, he had fully completed his part of the contract.

The court then concluded that damages for breach of a shipment contract should be measured by the market price of the goods *at the port of shipment on that date.*

Types of Ocean Bills of Lading

Bills of lading can take a variety of forms with different functions and usages in trade. The legal significance of each is important to all parties to the document.

Clean Bills of Lading. In addition to being a document of title, the bill of lading is also a receipt for the goods. A *clean bill* is one that contains no notations by the carrier that indicate any visible damage to the goods, packages, drums, or other containers being loaded. Buyers should insist that all contracts call for the seller to provide a clean bill.

A bill of lading that is not clean is *foul.* Normally, this description applies only to the external appearance of the goods. For instance, leaking containers, rust on metal products, and external evidence of infestation by insects must be noted on the bill of lading. As a generally accepted practice, the bill of lading must state the condition of the goods themselves, even if they are not externally observable, if the carrier knows or should have known that the goods are damaged. This type of inspection serves to protect the carrier from responsibility for pre-shipment damage.

A buyer who receives a clean bill still has no assurance that the goods will arrive in good condition. A clean bill of lading means only that the carrier noted no obvious or visible damage to the goods when they were loaded aboard ship. A clean bill of lading is no guarantee as to the quality of the goods or their conformance to the description in the sales contract. Moreover, it is no guarantee that the goods will not be damaged during the voyage.

On-Board Bills of Lading. An *on-board bill of lading,* signed by the ship's master or other agent of the carrier, states that the goods have actually been loaded aboard a certain vessel. In most documentary sales, the buyer would want to specify that payment is conditioned upon receipt of a negotiable, clean on-board bill of lading. This document gives some assurance that the goods described in the bill of lading have actually been loaded on board and are under way to the buyer. It also insulates the exporter from loss of the goods before loading. An importer who buys an on-board bill also has an approximate idea of when the goods will arrive.

Received-for-Shipment Bills of Lading. A *received-for-shipment bill of lading,* on the other hand, is issued by a carrier only upon having received goods for transport. It has limited use in cases of a delay between the delivery of the goods to the carrier and their being loaded aboard ship. Imagine a buyer who is asked to pay for a received-for-shipment bill of lading for bananas being shipped from Honduras to the United States. The buyer has no guarantee that they won't spoil on the sun-parched dock weeks before they are loaded. Most documentary sales contracts will require that sellers tender on-board (and clean) bills of lading.

A received-for-shipment bill of lading can be converted into an on-board bill of lading if the carrier notes the vessel name and date of loading on the face of the bill.

Straight Bills of Lading. The bill of lading used in a documentary sale is negotiable. In nondocumentary sales, a nonnegotiable or *straight bill of lading* (called a "sea waybill" in some countries) will suffice. They are used by ocean carriers only if the seller intends that the goods be delivered directly to a *consignee,* a specific person, named in the bill. The consignee may be the foreign buyer, as in the case of a sale on open account terms. It also may be the buyer's bank or customs agent. The consignee is not required to produce the actual bill in order to receive delivery.

Straight bills of lading are also used when the exporter is shipping to its own agent (or subsidiary company) in the foreign country, with the expectation that the agent will make direct arrangements with the buyer for payment before the goods are turned over. As in the case of negotiable documents, the carrier may deliver only to the party named in the bill. If the carrier delivers the goods to anyone else, it will be liable for misdelivery. Straight bills do not represent transferable title to the goods and cannot be used as the sole collateral for a loan. Thus, the typical use of straight bills of lading is when there is no financing involved.

Other Types of Transport Documents

Many specialized types of transport documents are in use today. The ocean bills of lading just described are only a few of the most common types. Transport documents have specific uses, depending on the type of carrier and the function the document is to perform. Many new types of transport documents have been developed because of modern shipping techniques. The following summary describes the different types of transport documents.

Air Waybills. Most air transport is handled through nonnegotiable *air waybills* issued by air cargo carriers. The carrier will make delivery only to the consignee named in the bill. The importance of negotiability in air transport is not as important as in ocean freight because the goods are not out of the control of the parties for long periods.

The air waybill contains a mechanism by which the seller can guarantee payment, even though the sale is not a documentary sale. The air waybill can name a foreign bank as consignee and specify that the goods be held at the point of destination until payment is guaranteed by the bank or until the bank approves release to the buyer. COD services are also available.

Forwarder's Bills of Lading. Freight forwarders (who usually also act as customs brokers for importers) are federally licensed individuals that act as agents for sellers. They handle their foreign shipments, book transportation, prepare documents and customs forms, and perform other functions. They are excellent sources of information on packing and transporting cargo, evaluating alternative shipping options, and obtaining freight rates. Freight forwarders can issue either straight or order bills of lading. Only certain forms of forwarder's bills are acceptable in a documentary sale. Forwarder's bills allow claims only against the forwarder itself, not the carrier. The carrier is liable only to the forwarder who holds the carrier's bill of lading.

Forwarder's bills must be distinguished from forwarder's receipts, which are mere acknowledgments that the forwarder has received goods for shipment. Such receipts are nonnegotiable and usually will not be accepted for payment under a draft unless specifically allowed.

Multimodal Transport Documents. When goods are transported by only one mode of transportation, the transport is referred to as *unimodal.* If the transport is executed using more than one mode of transportation, the transport is *multimodal. Multimodal transport operators,* sometimes called *combined transport operators,* are firms that arrange for cargo to be sent via several different carriers in one journey—truck, rail, barge, and/or ship. Multimodal transport was made possible by new methods of containerizing freight that replaced "break bulk" cargo for all but the smallest shipments. The *multimodal transport document,* or *combined transport document,* is a single contract between the shipper and the operator, who, in turn, contracts with each of the carriers involved. They are sometimes referred to as "through bills of lading." The operators become responsible for the shipment of goods throughout the time of their transport.

Electronic Data Interchange

Paper transport documents are gradually being replaced by *electronic data interchange* (EDI), whereby shipping data is transmitted over the Internet using one of several standards. Under this practice, trade documents such as bills of lading, letters of credit, and certificates of origin may be filed electronically at a central database.

The electronic transfer of documents has several advantages over paper-based transfers. First, it lets buyers and sellers track goods that are in transit and lets the parties make necessary adjustments when the goods are delayed. Second, the faster transmission of bills of lading and other documents lets the seller get faster payment for goods, which in turn translates into an improved cash flow for the seller. Third, it eliminates the need to prepare multiple copies of documents manually, which reduces redundant paperwork and improves efficiency and accuracy.

The use of EDI raises several issues. A principal concern is security. Traditionally, the buyer has had to present an original signed bill of lading to receive the goods. Although the written signature requirement may be replaced by a "digital signature," such documents may not be protected against unauthorized access. Infrastructure is another issue. Not all geographic regions have reliable telecommunication networks.

Another obstacle to the global paperless system of trade is the lack of standardization. A particular trade document, such as a bill of lading, may have several different formats depending on the country and practices used. In order for a global system to work, the format of trade documents must be standardized.

Allocating Shipping Responsibilities and the Risk of Loss

Earlier in this chapter, and in the *Biddell Brothers* case, we saw that in certain documentary sales the seller is responsible for arranging and paying for ocean transportation and that risk of loss shifts to the buyer when the goods are properly delivered to the carrier at the port of shipment.

In the following sections, we will look at how shipping responsibilities and risk of loss are allocated in general. The material in the following sections applies to all contracts for the sale of goods, not just those with documentary payment terms.

Freight and Transportation Charges

Shipping terms are integral to the price term itself. Because of the high cost of air and ocean freight, a buyer and seller must do more than merely agree on a price for the goods; they must also agree on who is going to pay the transportation and cargo insurance charges. For the price quoted, will the seller deliver the goods to the buyer, put them aboard a ship, or just make them available to a common carrier at the factory door? For instance, a seller might say, "This is the price if you come to my factory and pick up the goods. If you want me to pay to get them to the seaport in my country, or even across the ocean to your country, I will, but this is what the price of the goods will be then."

A seller will frequently present a proposal to a buyer offering a choice of shipping terms. For instance, one proposal may show a price with ocean freight, another without. These choices provide the buyer with a breakdown of the costs and responsibility for those costs within the transaction. Buyers who have an itemized breakdown of the various transportation, handling, and insurance charges from the seller can compare those with the costs of making the shipping arrangements themselves. Furthermore, transportation costs are needed if the buyer is comparing prices from two different foreign suppliers located in different parts of the world.

A buyer who requests all suppliers to quote prices with the same shipping terms can compare "apples to apples." A buyer might also request certain shipping terms because of the nature of their business. A buyer who imports regularly may have buying agents in the seller's country who can handle the details of moving the goods. Similarly, a buyer may take full responsibility for chartering its own ships, as in the case of a developing country making a large purchase of grain. They may want the grain made available to them alongside their ship, and they will pay all expenses and bear all risks from that point. In many cases, a seller that maintains a warehouse in the buyer's country will price the goods for pickup there.

Unless a seller is in such a dominant position in the market that it can dictate terms, it may want to offer more flexible shipping terms in order to make the sale. Even if a competitor offers a lower price, a firm with better shipping terms may get the order. The buyer may be inexperienced at moving cargo or may just not want to deal with arranging transportation in the seller's country.

For instance, imagine a Japanese buyer who attends a trade fair in New York and concludes a contract with a company from Boone, North Carolina. The buyer may not want to bother with getting the goods from "the Boonedocks" to a U.S. seaport and then on to Japan. Rather, the buyer just wants the best price for the goods delivered and unloaded from a ship at a Japanese seaport nearest the buyer's factory.

Allocating the Risk of Loss

The parties to a contract must know when they are responsible for damage or loss to goods and when they are not. Clearly, the seller is responsible if the goods are destroyed by fire during production at the seller's plant. Likewise, if the goods are destroyed after they have been moved into the buyer's warehouse, then the buyer is responsible. But when does the risk pass from one party to the other? In some countries, in the absence of a provision in the contract, the risk of loss is on the party who has "title" to the goods—the party who owns them, or the bill of lading, at that moment. However, because the bill of lading does not move physically with the goods, a determination of who owned the goods at the time of their destruction is often difficult. For example, the bill of lading may have been negotiated to the buyer at 2:12 in the afternoon, but we have no evidence as to what time the ship actually sank. Here, there is no way of determining who actually "owned" the goods at the exact moment of loss. This "title" method has not been employed in the United States for many decades.

Ideally, the seller wants to be free of the risk of loss as soon as the goods leave the back door. The buyer would like to delay it for as long as possible. The ability to negotiate, of course, stems from the relative bargaining position of the parties. If the seller's products contain superior technology or if they are commodities in short supply or patented products that the buyer needs, then the seller may be in a stronger position to shift the risk to the buyer. Similarly, if the buyer is in a dominant economic position, such as by being able to order in large quantities, the buyer may be able to dictate the terms of the contract. For example, the owner of a rare 1927 Rolls-Royce in London may say to a U.S. buyer, "You may purchase my Rolls in London and drive it away, but if you want it shipped to you, you must bear all the risks of the journey from the moment it leaves my door."

Buyer and seller are always free to decide in their contract when the risk of loss will pass from one to the other. However, if the parties fail to do so and a dispute arises, the courts will be forced to decide on the basis of whether the contract is of the shipment type or of the destination type.

Destination Contracts. The question of whether a contract is a shipment or a destination contract will be determined by how the responsibilities of the parties are defined: Who has responsibility for shipping or transporting the goods? Who is paying the freight charges? By what means will the buyer remit payment? If the contract calls for the seller to deliver the goods to a particular destination, such as the buyer's city or place of business, the contract is a *destination contract* (sometimes referred to an "arrival" contract). Under UCC §2-509 (see Exhibit 5.4), the risk of loss in a destination contract passes to the buyer when the goods are tendered to the buyer at the point of destination.

Shipment Contracts. If the contract calls for the seller to ship the goods by carrier but does not require the seller to deliver the goods to a named place, then it is a *shipment contract* (sometimes referred to as a "departure" contract). In a shipment contract, the risk of loss or damage to the goods passes to the buyer when the goods are given to the first carrier—be it truck, airline, or ocean carrier. Shipment contracts are more common in international trade because sellers usually prefer not to be responsible for the goods at sea.

The Risk of Loss in International Sales under the CISG

The *Convention on Contracts for the International Sale of Goods* contains provisions that assign the risk of loss in Articles 66–70, reproduced in Appendix A. The basic rule of Article 66 is that, unless the parties agree otherwise, any loss or damage to the goods occurring after the risk of loss has passed from seller to buyer does not relieve the buyer of his obligation to pay for the goods, unless the loss or damage is the fault of the seller. According to Article 67, if the contract calls for the goods to be handed over to a carrier at a

Exhibit 5.4

2003 Amendments to UCC 2-509*

§2-509 Risk of Loss in the Absence of Breach

(1) Where the contract requires or authorizes the seller to ship the goods by carrier
  (a) if it does not require the seller to deliver them at a particular destination, the risk of loss passes to the buyer when the goods are delivered to the carrier even though the shipment is under reservation (Section 2-505); but
  (b) if it does require the seller to deliver them at a particular destination and the goods are there tendered while in the possession of the carrier, the risk of loss passes to the buyer when the goods are there so tendered as to enable the buyer to take delivery.

* * *

(3) In any case not within subsection (1) or (2), the risk of loss passes to the buyer on the buyer's receipt of the goods.
(4) The provisions of this section are subject to contrary agreement of the parties and to the provisions of this Article on sale on approval (Section 2-327) and on effect of breach on risk of loss (Section 2-510).

*Subject to enactment by state legislatures.

particular place, then the risk passes to the buyer at that place. However, if the seller is simply expected to ship and no particular place is mentioned, the risk passes to the buyer when the goods are handed over to the first carrier for shipment to the buyer. For instance, assume that a company located in Boone, North Carolina, confirms an order for the export of its product to a foreign customer. The contract reads simply "Seller will handle all transportation charges and arrangements." The seller arranges for a trucking company to pick up the goods and deliver them to the air carrier's terminal at the Charlotte airport, 100 miles away. The risk of loss will pass from seller to buyer when the goods are first handed over to the trucking company at the seller's factory or warehouse in Boone. If the goods are damaged from that point forth, on land or in the air (or at sea, in the case of ocean shipment), the loss falls on the buyer. Of course, the seller is responsible for properly packaging and preparing the merchandise for shipment. The buyer would be relieved from any obligation to pay for the goods if the loss was due to an act or omission of the seller (Article 66).

Trade Terms

While it is possible to draft a detailed agreement for allocating shipping and transportation charges between buyer and seller and to specify when the risk of loss shall pass, in most routine cases this is done by using *trade terms*, sometimes called *shipping terms*. Trade terms are usually expressed in the form of abbreviated symbols, such as FOB or CIF. They are a shorthand method that permits the parties to express their agreement quickly, with little confusion, and with few language problems. If the parties use a trade term in their contract, they must define it. If it is not defined in the contract, a court would have to look to the applicable law for its interpretation. The most common method of defining trade terms, however, is to incorporate them into the contract by reference to some independent source or publication.

International Rules for the Interpretation of Trade Terms

The most important set of trade term definitions are the *International Rules for the Interpretation of Trade Terms*, or *Incoterms 2000*, published by the Paris-based *International Chamber of Commerce*.[1] These definitions have the support of important business groups, including manufacturing, shipping, and banking industries worldwide. They are cited by courts and legal scholars in many countries as having the effect of customary law. First published in 1936, the newest revision was released in 2000. The new terms accommodate the changes in air transportation, modern multimodal shipping, containerized cargo, and electronic data interchange.

Incoterms include thirteen trade terms plus variations on them. They are classified into four groups—E, F, C, and D—according to the relative responsibilities of each party and to the point at which the risk of loss passes from seller to buyer. The terms are grouped in Exhibit 5.5. Exhibit 5.5 arranges the terms with the minimum responsibility of the seller and the maximum responsibility of the buyer appearing at the top; the minimum responsibility of the buyer and maximum responsibility of the seller appear at the bottom. International salespeople, export managers, and world traders benefit from a working knowledge of these terms. *Incoterms* are not automatically part of a contract for the sale of goods. To ensure that the *Incoterms* definitions will be applied to their contract, parties should include a clause such as "This contract is to be interpreted in accordance with *Incoterms*."

The following case, *St. Paul Guardian Ins. Co. v. Neuromed Medical Systems & Support, GmbH*, illustrates the wide acceptance of *Incoterms*. Here an American court was called upon to decide who was responsible for goods damaged at sea, the German seller or the U.S. buyer. The contract used a common trade term, CIF (cost, insurance, and freight; see Exhibit 5.5), but did not define CIF. The contract also specified that it was governed by the laws of Germany. The court stated that under German law the CIF term, and thus the rights of the parties, would be defined by *Incoterms*. The court reasoned that *Incoterms* were so commonly used that they had become a trade usage to which the parties were bound in the absence of their agreement to the contrary.

The following section looks at some hypothetical illustrations to see how these terms are used. Keep in mind that the terms were drafted by their authors to reflect how companies actually do

St. Paul Guardian Ins. Co. v. Neuromed Medical Systems & Support, GmbH

WL 465312 (2002); United States District Court (S.D.N.Y.)

BACKGROUND AND FACTS

Shared Imaging, an American company, agreed to purchase an MRI machine from Neuromed, a German seller. The one-page contract of sale stated that the delivery terms were "CIF New York Seaport, the buyer will arrange and pay for customs clearance as well as transport to Calumet City." In addition, under "Disclaimer" it stated, "system including all accessories and options remain the property of Neuromed till complete payment has been received." Payment was to be made when the machine was received in Calumet City. The contract also stated that it was to be governed by the laws of Germany. The MRI was loaded aboard the vessel *Atlantic Carrier* undamaged and in good working order. When it reached its destination of Calumet City, Illinois, it had been damaged and was in need of extensive repair, which led plaintiff to conclude that the MRI had been damaged in transit. Shared Imaging filed its claim for insurance with St. Paul Guardian, who brought this action against Neuromed for damages. Neuromed argues that the case should be dismissed because it is not liable under German law.

STEIN, DISTRICT J.

Neuromed contends that because the delivery terms were "CIF New York Seaport," its contractual obligation, with regard to risk of loss or damage, ended when it delivered the MRI to the vessel at the port of shipment and therefore the action must be dismissed because plaintiff has failed to state a claim for which relief can be granted. Plaintiff responds that the generally accepted definition of the "CIF" term, as defined in *Incoterms 1990,* is inapplicable. Moreover, the plaintiff suggests that other provisions of the contract are inconsistent with the "CIF" term because Neuromed, pursuant to the contract, retained title subsequent to delivery to the vessel at the port of shipment and thus Shared Imaging manifestly retained the risk of loss.

APPLICABLE GERMAN LAW

The parties concede that pursuant to German law, the *U.N. Convention on Contracts for the International Sale of Goods* ("CISG") governs this transaction because (1) both the U.S. and Germany are Contracting States to that Convention, and (2) neither party chose, by express provision in the contract, to opt out of the application of the CISG ... (citations hereinafter omitted). Germany has been a Contracting State since 1991, and the CISG is an integral part of German law. To hold otherwise would undermine the objectives of the Convention which Germany has agreed to uphold.

CISG, INCOTERMS, AND "CIF"

"CIF," which stands for "cost, insurance, and freight," is a commercial trade term that is defined in *Incoterms 1990,* published by the International Chamber of Commerce ("ICC"). The aim of INCOTERMS, which stands for international commercial terms, is "to provide a set of international rules for the interpretation of the most commonly used trade terms in foreign trade...." INCOTERMS are incorporated into the CISG through Article 9(2) which provides that, "The parties are considered, unless otherwise agreed, to have impliedly made applicable to their contract or its formation a usage of which the parties knew or ought to have known and which in international trade is widely known to, and regularly observed by, parties to contracts of the type involved in the particular trade concerned." CISG, art. 9(2).... INCOTERMS defines "CIF" (named port of destination) to mean the seller delivers when the goods pass "the ship's rail at the port of shipment." The seller is responsible for paying the cost, freight and insurance coverage necessary to bring the goods to the named port of destination, but the risk of loss or damage to the goods passes from seller to buyer upon delivery to the port of shipment....

Plaintiff's legal expert contends that INCOTERMS are inapplicable here because the contract fails to specifically incorporate them. Nonetheless, he cites and acknowledges that the German Supreme Court (Bundesgerichtshof)—the court of last resort in the Federal Republic of Germany for civil matters—concluded that a clause "FOB" without specific reference to INCOTERMS was to be interpreted according to INCOTERMS "simply because the INCOTERMS include a clause 'FOB'."

Conceding that commercial practice attains the force of law under section 346 of the German Commercial Code (citing the German Court), plaintiff's

continued

continued

expert concludes that the opinion of the German Court "amounts to saying that the INCOTERMS definitions in Germany have the force of law as trade custom." As encapsulated by defendant's legal expert, "It is accepted under German law that in case a contract refers to CIF-delivery, the parties refer to the INCOTERMS rules ..." Thus, pursuant to CISG art. 9(2), INCOTERMS definitions should be applied to the contract despite the lack of an explicit INCOTERMS reference in the contract.

EFFECT OF TRANSFER OF TITLE CONTRACT PROVISIONS

Plaintiff argues that Neuromed's explicit retention of title in the contract to the MRI machine modified the "CIF" term, such that Neuromed retained title and assumed the risk of loss. INCOTERMS, however, only address passage of risk, not transfer of title. Under the CISG, the passage of risk is ... independent of the transfer of title. Moreover, according to Article 67(1), the passage of risk and transfer of title need not occur at the same time, as the seller's retention of "documents controlling the disposition of the goods does not affect the passage of risk." CISG, art. 67(1).

* * *

EFFECT OF OTHER DELIVERY TERMS

Plaintiff next contends that ... the other terms in the contract are evidence that the parties' intention to supersede and replace the "CIF" term such that Neuromed retained title and the risk of loss. That is incorrect. Citing the "Delivery Terms" clause in the contract, plaintiff posits that had the parties intended to abide by the strictures of INCOTERMS there would have been no need to define the buyer's obligations to pay customs and arrange further transport. Plaintiff's argument, however, is undermined by *Incoterms 1990,* which provides that "[i]t is normally desirable that customs clearance is arranged by the party domiciled in the country where such clearance should take place." The "CIF" term as defined by INCOTERMS only requires the seller to "clear the goods for export" and is silent as to which party bears the obligation to arrange for customs clearance. The parties are therefore left to negotiate these obligations. As such, a clause defining the terms of customs clearance neither alters nor affects the "CIF" clause in the contract.

Plaintiff also cites to the "Payment Terms" clause of the contract, which specified that final payment was not to be made upon seller's delivery of the machine to the port of shipment, but rather, upon buyer's acceptance of the machine in Calumet City. These terms speak to the final disposition of the property, not to the risk for loss or damage. INCOTERMS do not mandate a payment structure, but rather simply establish that the buyer bears an obligation to "[p]ay the price as provided in the contract of sale." Inclusion of the terms of payment in the contract does not modify the "CIF" clause.

The terms of the contract do not modify the "CIF" clause in the contract such that the risk of loss remained with Neuromed. The fact remains that the CISG, INCOTERMS, and German law all distinguish between the passage of the risk of loss and the transfer of title. Thus, because (1) Neuromed's risk of loss of, or damage to, the MRI machine under the contract passed to plaintiff upon delivery of the machine to the carrier at the port of shipment and (2) it is undisputed that the MRI machine was delivered to the carrier undamaged and in good working order, Neuromed's motion to dismiss for failure to state a claim is hereby granted.

Decision. The U.S. court, interpreting German law, held that a delivery term in a sales contract (here CIF) should be defined according to *Incoterms,* in the absence of contractual provisions specifying otherwise. The court reasoned that under the CISG, merchants impliedly agree to trade usages of which they should have known. *Incoterms* are so widely used that they have become a trade usage, or international custom, applicable to this contract. The risk of loss passed to the buyer at the port of shipment.

business. Selecting a term for incorporation in a contract is more than just bargaining over who will pay freight costs or bear the risk of loss. Certain terms may fit better with the needs of the parties. Some are suited for ocean carriage, some for air transport, and others for *multimodal transport.* Some terms are suited for a documentary form of payment; others are suited to open account payment terms. Be sure to study Exhibit 5.5 before reading the following summary. As you read, keep in mind that the following terms are for maritime and inland waterway transport only: FAS, FOB, CFR, CIF, DES, and DEQ. Others are for any mode of transport.

E Terms. *E Terms* place the lowest amount of responsibility on the seller. In the following hypothetical situation, assume a buyer in the Netherlands is placing an order with a supplier in Albany, New York. The buyer states that its U.S. subsidiary will pick up the goods at the Albany plant and arrange export. Therefore, the seller would probably quote its price in terms *EXW Albany factory*. Under this term, the seller need only make the goods available at its factory (or mill, farm, warehouse, or other place of business) and present the buyer with an invoice for payment. The buyer must arrange all transportation and bear all risks and expenses of the journey from that point. The buyer would also have to clear the goods for export by obtaining export licenses from the U.S. government.

This term is most often used when the buyer will pick up the goods by truck or rail. Therefore, for international shipments, EXW terms are common in Europe where goods frequently move across national boundaries by ground transportation. This term is likely to become more popular in trade between Canada, the United States, and Mexico in the future. But unless this term has been requested by the buyer, use of it may show that the seller is not really interested in exporting and is unwilling to accommodate a foreign buyer.

F Terms. The *F terms* are shipment contracts similar to those studied earlier. Under F terms, the seller is required to deliver the goods to the designated point of departure "free" of expense or risk to the buyer. At that point, the risk of loss passes from seller to buyer. The buyer arranges the transportation and pays all freight costs. However, if it is convenient and the parties agree, the seller may pay the freight and add that amount to the invoice price already quoted. F terms are often used when the buyer has contracted for a complete shipload of materials or commodities and thus had reason to assume the responsibility for arranging carriage. F terms may also be used because the buyer feels that it can obtain better freight rates than the seller. Some F terms are for ocean shipment only. Others can be used for all modes of transport.

Assume that the buyer in the Netherlands wants to arrange its own ocean transportation. The seller in Albany would like to deliver the goods to a carrier near it, for transportation to the Port of New York, so different forms of transportation will be required. For instance, the seller might deliver the goods to a barge hauler for a trip down the Hudson, or to a railroad or trucking company. The seller may want to hand over the goods to a multimodal terminal operator nearby and let it handle the goods from there. This inland carrier will then transport the goods to the Port of New York for shipment to the foreign destination. If this inland carrier is in Albany, then the seller should quote prices *FCA Albany*. Here, for the contract price, the seller bears the costs and assumes all risks of getting the goods from its factory to the carrier or terminal in Albany. The seller then has the responsibility to obtain any government export licenses that are required. This term can also be used for air transport. A term *FCA JFK Airport* means that the seller has agreed, for the contract price, to deliver the goods from Albany to the airline in New York for shipment.

Assume now that the Dutch buyer is purchasing a bulk cargo, such as agricultural commodities, and will be chartering a full ship for the overseas voyage—*a voyage charter*—departing from New York to Rotterdam. The buyer may find the voyage charter more convenient and cheaper to arrange than leaving the shipping up to the seller. The buyer would like the seller to place the goods on barges or on the pier alongside the ship, *Queen Anna E,* docked at the Port of New York. The appropriate contract terms would be *FAS Queen Anna E.* (If the name of the vessel is not yet known, the parties can contract on terms *FAS New York.*) The risk of loss passes from seller to buyer at the time the goods are placed alongside the ship. The buyer, having arranged the ocean transport, will pay the separate costs of loading the vessel they have provided or have chosen. The seller must obtain an export license and clear the goods for export. An FAS buyer should also provide the seller with notice of the ship's departure date and loading times. The seller's obligation is to place the goods alongside the vessel within the time called for in the contract.

Under FOB (free on board) contracts, the seller bears slightly more responsibility. In addition to obtaining export clearance, the seller is required to place the goods aboard the ship. Risk of loss passes to the buyer only when the goods cross the ship's rail. Therefore, if the contract were on terms *FOB*

Exhibit 5.5

Explanation of *Incoterms 2000:* ICC Official Rules for the Interpretation of Trade Terms

Group and Type	Term Abbreviation/ In Full	Mode of Transportation	Seller's Responsibilities*	Buyer's Responsibilities*	Passage of Risk
E Group	EXW Ex Works (works: mill, factory, mine, warehouse, etc.)	Up to buyer (all modes)	Have the goods ready for pickup at the location specified in the contract, usually seller's place of business.	Provide vehicle or rail car and load goods. Obtain export licenses. Enter goods through customs.	When the goods are made available by seller at named location.
F Group Shipment Contract	FCA Free Carrier (named place)	Ocean, air, truck, rail, or multimodal (all)	Place the goods in the hands of a carrier (usually inland) named by the buyer at the place specified. Provide export license.	Choose carrier, arrange transport, and pay freight charges. On arrival, enter goods through customs.	When the goods are delivered to the carrier or terminal operator at the named place of shipment.
	FAS Free Alongside Ship (named port of shipment)	Ocean or water only	Place the goods alongside the ship specified by the buyer (on the dock or barge) within the time called for in the contract, ready for loading. Obtain export license.	Choose ocean carrier, arrange transport, and pay freight. Enter goods through customs.	When the goods are delivered alongside the ship specified by buyer.
	FOB Free on Board (named port of shipment)	Ocean or water only	Load the goods on board the ship specified by the buyer within the time called for in the contract. Pay costs of loading. Obtain export license.	Choose ocean carrier and pay freight charges. Enter goods through customs.	When the goods cross the ship's rail at port of shipment.
C Group Shipment Contract	CFR Cost and Freight (named port of destination)	Ocean or water only	Contract for transport and pay freight charges to the named port of destination. Arrange for loading goods on board ship, usually of seller's choice, and pay costs of loading. Obtain export license. Notify buyer of shipment. Documentary sale is assumed. Tender documents to buyer.	Purchase document of title and take delivery from ocean carrier. No date of delivery at buyer's port is implied. Pay import duties. Enter goods through customs.	When the goods cross the ship's rail at port of shipment. Buyer must procure own insurance or else use CIF term.
	CIF Cost, Insurance, and Freight (named port of destination)	Ocean or water only	Same as CFR, with added requirement that seller purchase marine insurance in amount of invoice price plus 10%. Insurance policy is assigned to buyer. Documentary sale is assumed.	Same as CFR, except seller supplies insurance. Buyer may ask for additional insurance coverage at own expense.	When the goods cross ship's rail at port of shipment. If damage or loss, buyer files claim for insurance.

	CPT Carriage Paid To (named place of destination)	Ocean, air, truck, rail, or multimodal (all)	Similar to CFR, but for all modes of transport. Deliver goods to truck, rail, or multimodal carrier, or to ship, and arrange for transport to destination. Freight charges prepaid. Obtain export license. Notify buyer of shipment. Seller need not insure goods. Documentary sale is assumed.	Similar to CFR. Purchase document of title and take delivery of goods from carrier. Enter goods through customs. Pay import duties.	When goods are delivered by the seller to the first carrier. Buyer must procure own insurance or use CIP term.
	CIP Carriage and Insurance Paid To (named place of destination)	Ocean, air, truck, rail, or multimodal (all)	Same as CPT, with added requirement that seller purchase policy of marine insurance in amount of invoice plus 10%. Insurance policy assigned to buyer.	Same as CPT. Purchase document of title and take delivery of goods from carrier. Enter goods through customs. Pay import duties.	When goods are delivered by the seller to the first carrier. If damage or loss, buyer files claim for insurance.
D Group Destination Contract	DAF Delivered at Frontier (named place)	Usually for international rail shipments (can be used for all modes)	Contract for transport and pay freight expenses to the "frontier" point in the country of importation. Buyer clears goods for import by customs authorities.	Pay freight charges from frontier point. Enter goods through customs. Pay import duties.	When the goods are ready to be handed over to the buyer at the named (frontier point) in buyer's country.
	DES Delivered Ex Ship (named port of destination)	Ocean or water only (often used when ship is chartered by seller)	Arrange transport and pay all freight charges to port of foreign destination. Notify buyer of expected arrival date. Place goods at disposal of buyer aboard ship within time called for in contract.	Arrange and pay cost of unloading goods from ship and land transport. Enter goods through customs.	When the goods are ready for unloading by the buyer at port of destination.
	DEQ Delivered Ex Quay, (named port of destination)	Ocean or water only	Contract for transport and pay freight charges to put the goods on the quay (dock) beside the ship at specified port of destination. Notify buyer of arrival date. May be used for documentary sale.	Take delivery of goods at dock and enter goods through customs. Pay import duties. Arrange land transport to buyer's place of business.	When the goods are placed on the dock or in terminal. Seller should insure goods for own protection.
	DDU Delivery Duty Unpaid (named port of destination)	Ocean, air, truck, rail, or multimodal (all)	Similar to DEQ, except used for all modes of transport. Seller usually contracts for carriage to inland port of entry in importing country. May be used for documentary sale.	Purchase document of title if required. Take delivery at specified location and enter goods through customs. Pay import duties.	When goods are delivered at location specified. Seller should insure for own protection.
	DDP Delivery Duty Paid (named place of destination)	Ocean, air, truck, rail, or multimodal (all)	Same as DDU, except that seller obtains import licenses, pays import duties, and clears goods through customs. Place of destination specified is usually buyer's place of business.	Purchase document of title if required. Take delivery of goods at specified location.	When the goods are delivered to buyer at specified location. Seller should insure for own protection.

*In all cases, seller is required to provide goods in conformance with contract; buyer is to pay invoice according to contract. Time for shipment or delivery is determined by contract. Trade term must be stated in contract and reference made therein to *Incoterms 2000* in order for these definitions to apply.

SOURCE: Based on ICC No. 560, *Incoterms 2000*. For more on *Incoterms 2000* or the ICC, visit http://www.iccwbo.org or http://www.iccbooksusa.com.

New York or *FOB Queen Anna E,* the seller would be required to secure export licenses, pay all costs of loading, and deliver the goods over the ship's rail. Notice that under *Incoterms,* the seller's responsibility does not end until the goods have actually passed the ship's rail. Exporters should always use the FOB term as a shipment contract as it was intended. Using it in conjunction with a destination location (e.g., *FOB foreign port*) would contradict the *Incoterms* definition and would shift the risk of the voyage to the exporter.

C Terms. *C terms* are also shipment contracts. The letter *C* indicates that the seller is responsible for certain costs after the goods have been delivered to the carrier. Like the FOB term, however, risk of loss passes to the buyer when the goods cross the ship's rail at the point of shipment. Assume that our Dutch buyer requests pricing information from Albany. As an experienced exporter, the seller might understand that the buyer has little interest in arranging transportation, let alone coming to pick up the goods. The buyer simply wants the goods delivered to the port of entry in its country closest to its company. If ocean shipment is required, the seller will prepare a price quotation *CFR Port of Rotterdam* (formerly called *C & F*) or *CIF Port of Rotterdam.* For the price quoted the seller will deliver the goods to an ocean carrier, arrange shipment, prepay the freight charges to the agreed-upon port of destination, obtain a clean on-board bill of lading marked *freight prepaid,* and forward it along with the invoice to the buyer for payment.

The only difference between CFR and CIF terms is that under CIF terms the seller must also procure and forward to the buyer a policy of marine insurance to cover the risk of loss once it passes to the buyer. (This amount is the minimum coverage; the buyer may want to request additional insurance be purchased for its own protection.) By providing both carriage and insurance coverage, the seller is able to earn additional profit yet retain its rights in the goods until payment is made against documents. Upon presentation of the bill of lading, the Dutch buyer is required to make payment, but once it receives the bill of lading, it can resell the goods, or if the goods are lost, it is entitled to collect the insurance money. However, both *Incoterms* and maritime practice seem to indicate that, if the seller desires, it may forgo its right to collect on the documents, negotiate the bill of lading directly to the buyer, and make other arrangements for payment or credit.

If the seller intends to arrange ocean transportation but will be delivering the goods to a road or rail carrier, inland waterway, or to a multimodal terminal operator for transit to the seaport, the seller may wish to quote *CPT, Port of Rotterdam.* Here, the risk of loss shifts to the buyer when the goods are delivered to the first carrier. CIP terms are the same as under CPT, with the added requirement that the seller procure insurance to cover the buyer's risk of loss.

D Terms. Contracts with *D terms* of sale are destination (or "arrival") contracts. If the seller in Albany is willing to enter into a destination contract, then it must be willing to accept far greater responsibility than under any other terms. For the price stated in the contract, the seller must not only deliver the goods at the port of destination but bear the risk of loss throughout the journey. Thus, if the goods are lost in transit, the Dutch buyer would not be entitled to claim the insurance money although the buyer may have lost profits it was hoping to make on the goods.

DES and DEQ are destination terms used for ocean cargo. If the contract terms are *DES Rotterdam,* the seller must pay the ocean freight to Rotterdam, but the buyer pays the unloading charges at the Rotterdam terminal. Under *DEQ Rotterdam,* the seller will pay the ocean freight, import duties, and unloading charges to place the goods on the *quay* (pronounced "kee," meaning the dock or wharf) in Rotterdam. When specifically stated in the sales contract, the seller may also agree to obtain import licenses from the government of the Netherlands and pay the import duties and taxes at the port of entry. DES and DEQ terms are commonly used with open account payment terms, although the seller may tender a negotiable bill of lading accompanied by all necessary documents to clear the goods through Dutch customs. Clearly, the seller will not want to take on the responsibility and risks of a DEQ shipment unless it is experienced in importing into the Netherlands and familiar with customs regulations and tariff laws there.

Today, destination contracts are actually becoming increasingly popular due to an increasingly competitive and globalized marketplace. Many manufacturers and other shippers find they must do more and more to win and keep customers. In other words, shippers often have to provide credit terms to their customers by shipping on open account and giving the customer time to pay. Shippers are also being forced to take greater responsibility for getting the goods into the customer's hands. For these reasons, more and more shippers are quoting prices on D terms than ever before. Still others are quoting prices on C terms to shift the risk of the voyage but voluntarily forgoing the documentary collection and sending the bill of lading directly to the customer for payment on open account.

Modification of Trade Terms

On occasion, the parties may be tempted to alter the meaning of a trade term in their contract to meet their own business requirements. The International Chamber of Commerce and many experienced lawyers usually recommend that buyer and seller do not attempt to add to, explain, or change the meaning of any trade term without legal advice. This "customizing" only causes needless confusion. The problem usually arises in CIF contract cases. The general rule is that if the additional shipping terms added by the parties to a CIF contract do not contradict the usual terms of a CIF contract, then the contract will still be considered a CIF contract.

On the other hand, if the parties insert additional terms that are contrary to the usual meaning of CIF, then it can destroy the CIF terms. For instance, assume that the parties enter into a contract labeled "CIF." They then add that "payment is not due until the goods are sold by the buyer." A court would then have to decide, looking at all the evidence, whether the contract was on CIF terms. This issue was one discussed by the court in *Kumar Corp. v. Nopal Lines, Ltd.* As you read, notice that the court decides the case on the basis of the seller's failure to obtain insurance on the cargo as required under CIF terms.

Kumar Corp. v. Nopal Lines, Ltd.

462 So. 2d 1178 (1985)

District Court of Appeals of Florida, Third District

BACKGROUND AND FACTS

Kumar sold 700 television sets to one of its largest customers, Nava, in Venezuela. The contract was on CIF terms, Maracaibo. However, they agreed that Nava would not pay Kumar until Nava actually sold the merchandise. Kumar obtained the televisions from its supplier, received them in its Miami warehouse, loaded them on a trailer, delivered the trailer to its freight forwarder, Maduro, in Florida, and obtained the shipping documents. The trailer was stolen from the Maduro lot and found abandoned and empty. Kumar had failed to obtain marine insurance on the cargo. Kumar sued Maduro and the carrier. The defendants argued that, since the risk of loss had passed from Kumar to Nava, Kumar did not have standing to sue. The trial court agreed with the defendants and dismissed Kumar's case. Kumar appealed.

DANIEL S. PEARSON, JUDGE

Kumar's argument that it is the real party in interest proceeds ... from the premise that its agreement to postpone Nava's obligation to pay for the goods modified the ordinary consequence of the CIF contract that the risk of loss shifts to the buyer. A CIF contract is a recognized and established form of contract, the incidents of which are well known. Thus, if a buyer and seller adopt such a contract, "they will be presumed, in the absence of any express term to the contrary, to have adopted all the normal incidents of that type of contract," D. M. Day, *The Law of International Trade,* 4 (1981), one of which is that the buyer, not the seller, bears the risk of loss when the goods are delivered to the carrier and the seller's other contractual obligations are fulfilled. A CIF contract is not a contract "that goods shall arrive, but a contract to ship goods complying with the contract of sale, to obtain, unless the contract otherwise provides, the ordinary contract of carriage to the place of destination, and the ordinary contract of insurance of the goods on that voyage, and to tender these documents against payment of the contract price." C. Schmitthoff,

continued

continued

The Law and Practice of International Trade, 26–27 (7th ed. 1980).

It is clear, however, that parties may vary the terms of a CIF contract to meet their own requirements. But where the agreed-upon variation is such that it removes a vital ingredient of a CIF contract, then the contract ceases to be a CIF contract. Thus, "if according to the intention of the parties the actual delivery of the goods [to the buyer] is an essential condition of performance, the contract is not a CIF contract." C. Schmitthoff, *supra.*

In the present case, Kumar and Nava agreed to payment upon Nava's sale of the goods in Venezuela ... [thereby negating an essential ingredient of the CIF contract].... [T]he use of the term CIF does not ipso facto make the contract a CIF contract if the contract has been altered in a manner that is repugnant to the very nature of a CIF contract. Therefore, because the record before us does not ... conclusively show that the contract remained a true CIF contract despite the agreement between Kumar and Nava concerning the payment for the goods, it was improper for the trial court to conclude as a matter of law that the risk of loss passed to Nava when Kumar delivered the goods to the shipper.

But even assuming, *arguendo,* that we were to conclude, as did the trial court, that the risk of loss passed to Nava merely by virtue of the label CIF on the contract, Kumar must still prevail. Under the CIF contract, Kumar was obliged to procure insurance, and by not doing so, acted, intentionally or unintentionally, as the insurer of the shipment. As the insurer of the shipment, Kumar was obliged to pay Nava, the risk bearer, for the loss when the goods were stolen. Being legally obliged to pay Nava's loss, Kumar would thus be subrogated to Nava's claims against the appellees. Since a subrogee is the real party in interest and may sue in its own name, Kumar would have standing to sue under this theory.

Reversed and remanded for further proceedings.

Decision. The court held that where, under a CIF contract, the seller fails to obtain marine cargo insurance on behalf of the buyer, the risk of loss remains with the seller, who becomes a self-insurer of the property. As such, the seller has standing to sue the carrier for the cargo loss.

Conclusion

Transaction risks can threaten significant costs to doing international business. Contract negotiations represent a good opportunity to address transaction risks in advance. In an international contract for the sale of goods, the terms of sale are as essential to the contract as the quality of the goods themselves. Moving goods around the world is expensive and risky. If a contract does not specify the terms of sale and who bears the risk of loss, the parties may be in for a tremendous surprise. Moreover, because of the risks of nonpayment and nondelivery, the parties may not wish to do business on cash or open account terms until a business relationship is established. Thus, an understanding of the documentary sale, as well as of the most common trade terms, is necessary for any international sales specialist or export manager.

Despite the continued widespread use of the documentary sale, its use has declined somewhat in the past 30 years due to a number of factors. First, the greater reliability of international credit reporting makes open account transactions between foreign parties much safer than in previous years. Second, increasing globalization means closer, long-term relationships between vendors in a global supply chain. Third, many of the same products can be purchased on other terms from domestic sources, such as domestic subsidiaries of foreign manufacturers, or through local distributors. Nevertheless, the documentary sale is often used when the credit risk is significant. It is also used when the goods will be resold while in transit. Common examples are agricultural commodities, oil, and fungible goods. The bill of lading, which serves as a document of title, permits the goods to be bought and sold, time and again, even though they remain aboard ship on the high seas or sitting in a foreign port.

No reader should be left with the impression that the documentary sale eliminates the risk of foreign shipments. The buyer might refuse the documents when they are presented by its bank or be unable to pay. Similarly, the buyer might purchase documents that appear to be in order only to find defective merchandise in the containers—or no merchandise at all. The solution to some of these problems is the subject of the next chapter.

Chapter Summary

1. *Transaction risks* are those risks to buyer and seller resulting from moving money and goods under an international sales contract. Transaction risks arise from barriers that separate buyer and seller, including distance, oceans, the time that the cargo is out of possession of the parties, communication and language difficulties, cultural differences, national boundaries, interference by local customs authorities, and differences in legal systems.
2. The *documentary sale* is one type of contract for the international sale of goods, utilizing ocean transport, in which the buyer is required to pay upon the presentation of a negotiable document of title by the seller. The parties might indicate their desire for a documentary sale by specifying in the contract that payment terms are "cash against documents" or "documents against payment."
3. A *bill of lading* is a document of title issued by an *ocean carrier* to a shipper upon receiving goods for transport. Bills of lading can be negotiable or non-negotiable. Non-negotiable bills are contracts of carriage and receipts for depositing goods with a carrier for shipment. Additionally, negotiable bills of lading serve as a document of title. Only negotiable bills of lading can be used in the documentary sale.
4. The documentary sale is critical to world trade because it allows the holder of the document of title to trade in the goods while they are still at sea. The documents may be bought and sold many times before they reach a final destination.
5. The *documentary collection* is the process by which international banks serve as intermediaries between seller and buyer to handle the exchange of the bill of lading in return for payment.
6. In a documentary sale, the buyer is given no opportunity to inspect the goods. In essence, the buyer is not buying goods, but is buying documents that represent ownership of the goods. The seller's basic obligation is to ship good in accordance with the contract and to tender a clean bill of lading to the buyer. The buyer's obligation is to purchase the bill of lading when presented by a bank in the buyer's country. A "clean" bill is one with no notations from the carrier or carrier's agent indicating that damage to the goods was observable at the time of loading. Cargo insurance is a key component of most documentary sales.
7. Due to the expense of ocean shipment, and the perils of the sea, it is important for the parties to know that they have the freedom to negotiate which of them, buyer or seller, will pay for transportation expenses and insurance, and which of them will bear the risk of loss or damage during transit. This is often done using shorthand *trade term* in the contract. The most commonly used definitions for trade terms are *Incoterms,* published by the International Chamber of Commerce, a private group. If used in a contract, they will be recognized and enforced by courts.
8. *Incoterms* include thirteen trade terms, classified into four groups—E, F, C, and D—according to the relative responsibilities of each party and to the point at which the risk of loss passes from seller to buyer. As Exhibit 5.5 shows, *Incoterms* are arranged in order ranking the responsibility of buyer and seller. The *E term* EXW, or *Ex Works,* represents the maximum responsibility of the buyer and minimum responsibility of the seller. The *D term* DDP, or *Delivery Duty Paid,* represents the maximum responsibility of the seller and the minimum responsibility of the buyer. The *C terms* are shipment contracts. The *D terms* are destination contracts.
9. Some trade terms are appropriate for documentary sales; others can be used for contracts that call for open account or other payment terms.
10. While the documentary sale is still widely used as a safe payment mechanism, experienced parties attempt to forge long term business relationships with flexible payment terms.

Questions and Case Problems

1. Bruitrix held a bill of lading covering a shipment of washing machines that it had purchased. The washing machines were placed into a bonded warehouse operated by the British Transport Commission. Bruitrix pledged the bill of lading to its creditor, Barclay's Bank, as security for an outstanding debt. Two months later, the defendant, the Commissioners of Customs, obtained a judgment against Bruitrix for a delinquent tax. The bank attempted to take possession of the goods in order to satisfy Bruitrix's outstanding debt. On the same day, the Commissioners attempted to take possession of the goods to satisfy their judgment. The bank brought this action claiming that the pledge had transferred title to the goods to it and that as the holder of the bill of lading it was entitled to the goods. Who has a greater right in the property, Barclay's Bank or the Commissioners? Why? How does the bill of lading serve as a financing device? The bill of lading is a contract of carriage. When does the carrier discharge its performance under the contract? *Barclay's Bank, Ltd. v. Commissioners of Customs and Excise,* (1963) 1 Lloyd's 81, Queen's Bench.
2. Colorado Fuel sold caustic soda to a buyer in Bombay under a CIF contract. The soda was fully loaded aboard a ship when a labor strike made it impossible for the vessel to sail. As a result, the soda arrived in Bombay 6 months late. The buyer sued for the late shipment. Was Colorado Fuel liable for damages? Does it matter that Colorado Fuel may have known that a strike was imminent? *Badhwar v. Colorado Fuel and Iron Corp.*, 138 F. Supp. 595 (S.D.N.Y. 1955).
3. Buyer and seller entered into a contract for the sale of sugar from the Philippines to New York on CIF terms. They added language to the contract that delivery was to be "at a customary safe wharf or refinery at New York, Philadelphia, or Baltimore to be designated by the buyer." Before the sugar arrived, the United States placed a quota on sugar imports. The sugar was not allowed to be imported and was placed in a customs warehouse. The buyer refused the documents and the seller sued, claiming that the import restriction was no excuse for the buyer's nonpayment. The buyer argued that the language calling for delivery to a U.S. port converted a shipment contract into a destination contract. Was this a CIF contract or a destination contract? What was the effect of the additional shipping language used by the parties? Why should the parties not attempt to modify a trade term or add other delivery language? *Warner Bros. & Co. v. A.C. Israel,* 101 F.2d 59 (2d Cir. 1939).
4. Phillips contracted to buy naphtha from Tradax for shipment from Algeria to Puerto Rico on C&F terms. Shipment was to be made between September 20 and September 28, 1981. The agreement incorporated the ICC *Incoterms.* It also contained a *force majeure* clause that stated, "In the event of any delay in shipment or delivery of the goods by the seller, the unaffected party may cancel the unfulfilled balance of the contract." On September 16, Tradax shipped on the *Oxy Trader.* While en route, the *Oxy Trader* was detained by maritime authorities at Gibraltar, deemed unsafe, and not allowed to proceed. Tradax informed Phillips, which telexed back on October 1 that October 15 was the last acceptable delivery date. On October 7, its cargo had to be offloaded in Portugal for shipment on another vessel. On October 13, Phillips refused payment of the documents due to the delay. In November, the cargo was sold by Tradax to a third party at a loss. Phillips brought this action in the United States. Tradax claimed that it had ceased to bear responsibility for the goods when it transferred the goods to the carrier for shipment. Phillips maintained that it was excused from performance because the ship's delay constituted *force majeure.* Judgment for whom, and why? *Phillips Puerto Rico Core, Inc. v. Tradax Petroleum Ltd.*, 782 F.2d 314 (2d Cir. 1985).
5. Design Inc., in Newport, Rhode Island, entered into a contract with Buenavista, S.A. in Barcelona, Spain, to buy 1,000 sheets of stained glass. The contract contained a delivery clause that read "FOB Hasta Luego." The contract also stated that it was to be interpreted in accordance with *Incoterms.* While the glass was being loaded onto the ship (*Hasta Luego*), one of the crates slipped from the loading mechanism and landed in the water before it crossed the ship's rail. Who bears the risk of loss of the glass? Would the answer change if the contract was governed by the UCC?
6. The defendant agreed to sell watches to the buyer in Mexico. A notation was printed at the bottom of the contract, which, translated into English, reads as follows: "Please send the merchandise in cardboard boxes duly strapped with metal bands via air parcel post to Chetumal. Documents to Banco de Commercio De Quintana Roo S.A." There were no provisions in the contract that specifically allocated the risk of loss on the goods sold while in the possession

of the carrier. When the goods were lost in transit, the buyer sued for a refund of his purchase price. Judgment was entered for the defendant, and the buyer appealed. Judgment for whom, and why? Was this a shipment or destination contract? When or where did the risk of loss pass? *Pestana v. Karinol Corp.*, 367 So. 2d 1096 (Fla. Dist. Ct. App. 1979).

7. Allied Chemical, a U.S. exporter, shipped chemicals to Banylsa in Brazil under bills of lading showing that the goods were consigned to the order of Banylsa. Allied sent the bill of lading, draft, and invoice to a Brazilian bank for collection, together with a letter of instruction to deliver the documents only on payment of the sight drafts. In the meantime, the goods had arrived in Brazil and were put into a warehouse under the supervision of the port authority. However, in Brazil and in some other Latin American countries, it is customary for goods to be released from a state warehouse to anyone holding either a bill of lading or a *carta declaratoria.* The latter is not a bill of lading, but only a document indicating that Brazilian import fees have been paid. Banylsa obtained a *carta declaratoria* from Lloyd and used it to obtain possession of the goods from the warehouse. Banylsa never purchased the bill of lading and never paid for the goods. Banylsa then became insolvent and filed for receivership in Brazilian civil court. Allied sued Lloyd for misdelivery in New York. Judgment for whom, and why? Explain a bailment. *Allied Chemical International Corp. v. Companhia De Navegacao Lloyd Brasileiro, 775 F.2d 476 (2nd Cir. 1985).*

Managerial Implications

You receive a fax transmittal from Japanese buyers you met in New York. They indicate that they would like to place an order for 5,000 down bed pillows. The pillows must contain no less than 85 percent cluster prime white goose down. In order to make the transportation as cost-effective as possible, they would like to have pricing for a full ocean container. Before placing the order, they have some questions about the details of the sale.

Their fax has indicated that although they would prefer to pay for the pillows on open account terms, they would consider your suggestions for payment options. They have indicated that they are unwilling to purchase against the documents unless they can first inspect the pillows on their arrival in Japan. They want this right of inspection to find out if the quality is what they had ordered and to look for possible freight damage. They feel strongly about this issue and insist on these conditions, unless you can show them that they can be adequately protected. In addition, they also would like to consider the cost of alternative shipping arrangements before they decide whether they want to handle this themselves.

1. Prepare a *pro forma* invoice giving your buyer several options for shipping the pillows. Consider how they will be packed and transported to the closest or best seaport. What facilities are available for handling containerized cargo or for multimodal transport in your region? Utilizing *Incoterms,* present a breakdown of the shipping alternatives and costs involved in the transaction. Contact a freight forwarder and inquire as to what services it can provide. Can it assist you in obtaining the information you need to prepare your *pro forma* invoice?
2. In determining your export price, what other factors must be taken into consideration in addition to freight costs? Do you consider additional communication expenses, port fees, trade show expense, forwarder fees, sales agents, and clerical expenses? Discuss your export pricing with your marketing team and decide on your pricing strategy.
3. Prepare a letter to accompany the *pro forma* invoice explaining why payment by "cash against documents" would be fair to both parties. What can you propose to address their concerns that the goods shipped will conform to their quality specifications? How will they be protected from marine risks?

Ethical Considerations

Your company is expecting a shipment of 10,000 T-shirts from a company in Pakistan. You recently received a call from a nearby bank that it was in possession of a negotiable bill of lading aboard the ship *Jhelum,* and documents from Pakistan covering a shipment of T-shirts, and that they were awaiting your payment. However, you are concerned.

The Pakistani company made the initial contact with your firm via the Internet, locating you through one of several trade directories in which you are listed. The prices quoted for shirts are considerably less than what you are currently paying or able to pay for a comparable quality. You begin to do some research. You find their site on the Internet, with pictures of their mill and textile products. You make inquires through the U.S. Commercial Service. Several days later, you receive an e-mail from their offices in Karachi that indicates that one of their staff officers was not able to locate the mill, but thought that they "were currently exporting from Pakistan."

Recently you have been hearing of many international business scams and are worried about what might really be in the ocean container, and whether or not you should purchase the documents from the bank or refuse them just in case. You look at the documents and see that the bill of lading is dated 1 day later than the date for shipment called for in the contract. You are getting cold feet, and think you might want out. (1) Do you think, under the circumstances, that it is ethical to refuse the documents based on a minor technicality? Why or why not? Do you believe you have enough information to make a fair decision? What are your options? (2) Now assume that you contacted the ocean carrier and they said that they do not have a ship named *Jhelum* currently in the fleet. Does this change your decision? (3) If this were a fraudulent scheme, how could it be perpetrated on an unsuspecting buyer?

Notes

1. For the complete text of *Incoterms 2000,* see *ICC Official Rules for the Interpretation of Trade Terms.* ICC Publishing S.A., ICC Publication No. 560 (1999), available through ICC Publishing Corporation, New York, N.Y.

For Internet Activities, Visit academic.cengage.com/blaw/schaffer.

CHAPTER 6
THE CARRIAGE OF GOODS AND THE LIABILITY OF AIR AND SEA CARRIERS

The last two chapters examined the legal relationship between the seller and buyer in a contract for the international sale of goods. Some basic concepts about the relationship between the seller and the carrier were introduced, such as the function and importance of transport documents. This chapter discusses the liability of air carriers for damages resulting from the death or bodily injury to passengers or to baggage or air cargo; the liability of marine carriers for damage or loss to ocean cargo; the liability of freight forwarders and other transport intermediaries; and finally, selected issues in marine cargo insurance law.

THE LIABILITY OF INTERNATIONAL AIR CARRIERS

The liability of air carriers for loss or damage to baggage and cargo, as well as for bodily injury or death of passengers, is governed by a host of international treaties and national laws. There are few areas of law that have engendered as much litigation as this one. Many cases involve injury to only one plaintiff. Others involve mass litigation resulting from air disasters. All of these cases lead to complex questions as to where the case will be heard and under what law it will be decided. For example, in the United States alone, issues of jurisdiction and liability may turn on whether the injured or deceased passenger was ticketed for domestic or international travel, whether the accident occurred over land or sea, whether it was within 12 nautical miles of the U.S. shoreline, or whether it was over the high seas in "international waters." This section addresses only the liability of air carriers for the injury or death of passengers ticketed for international travel or for damage to baggage or cargo moving in international air transport. The rules are different for domestic travelers or cargo. Also, our discussion only applies to litigation against air carriers brought by passengers, the estates or representatives of deceased passengers, cargo owners, or insurers. There may be additional litigation against other third-party defendants, such as the manufacturer who designed or built the aircraft, service companies that maintained the aircraft, private security companies, terminal operators, retail establishments within a terminal, or others. However, these cases are not likely to be litigated under international law.

The *Warsaw Convention of 1929*

Since 1929, the liability of airlines to passengers engaged in international travel has been governed by a series of international conventions. The first was the *Warsaw Convention of 1929* (still in effect for some purposes), as amended by several protocols adopted during the past 70 years. The Convention standardized procedures for issuing passenger tickets, baggage claim forms, cargo receipts, and other transport documents. It was adopted at a time when the airline industry was in its infancy and the risk of an air disaster was so great that investors feared that their fortunes could be wiped out in one air disaster. Insurance companies also feared insuring the new air carriers. Governments realized that the air industry needed protection from catastrophic loss in order to flourish.

This led to the 1929 *Warsaw Convention,* which protected airlines from liability in the following ways. First, they were not liable if they could prove that they had used "all necessary methods" to avoid the accident. Second, it limited their liability to a specific amount. Until the late 1990s, the limit in the United States for injury or death to passengers was only $75,000 in proven damages, including attorney's fees and costs, and up to $9.07 per pound for luggage or cargo (a figure originally arrived at by pegging the value of a national currency to the value of gold).

In more recent years, many people came to believe that these limits were inequitable and unfair. After all, damages awarded in a wrongful death action against a negligent driver in an automobile accident may amount to hundreds of thousands, if not millions, of dollars. Yet the liability of an airline was limited to what could be recovered under the Convention, and that almost never exceeded $75,000. In fact, a plaintiff could only recover a greater amount by proving that the injury or death was caused by the airline's willful misconduct, and this could rarely be proven. (Willful misconduct was found in the case of Pan Am Flight 103 that went down over Lockerbie, Scotland [where airline security had failed to heed warnings of a bomb], and the case of Korean Airlines Flight 007, which was shot down by the former Soviet Union while in Soviet airspace). In 1997 the airline industry voluntarily raised the monetary limits. In 1999 the *Montreal Convention* was adopted, which gave passengers and shippers even greater rights against airlines.

The *Montreal Convention of 1999*

The most important change to air transportation law in 70 years occurred with the adoption of the *Montreal Convention for the Unification of Certain Rules for International Carriage by Air* (1999), referred to in this chapter as the *Montreal Convention.* It now replaces the outdated *Warsaw Convention* in those countries where ratified (the *Warsaw Convention* remains in effect in others). As of 2007, the *Montreal Convention* had been ratified by seventy-eight countries, including the United States (2003), Canada, Mexico, Japan, China, the European countries, and others. The *Montreal Convention* modernizes the provisions on issuing tickets, baggage claims, and air waybills and provides for the use of electronic documents. It also eases the restrictions on recovering damages from airlines for loss to baggage or cargo, or for bodily injuries or death to passengers, and requires that airlines be adequately insured for such losses. It also includes provisions for compensating passengers for flight delays.

The language of the *Montreal Convention* is patterned after the older *Warsaw Convention.* This was intended by the drafters, so that there could be continuity in its interpretation by courts. The legislative history of the U.S. Senate in considering the ratification of the *Montreal Convention* makes it clear Congress had intended that much of the case law decided by U.S. courts under the earlier convention was to apply to the new convention.

Application to International Carriage. Like the *Warsaw Convention,* the *Montreal Convention* applies only to passengers ticketed for international travel. Specifically, Article 1 states that the Convention applies "to all international carriage of persons, baggage and cargo by aircraft" in which

> [T]he place of departure and the place of destination, whether or not there be a break in the carriage or a transhipment, are situated either within the territories of two States Parties [countries], or within the territory of a single State Party if there is an agreed stopping place within the territory of another State, even if that State is not a State Party. Carriage between two points within the territory of a single State Party without an agreed stopping place within the territory of another State is not international carriage for the purposes of this Convention.
>
> Carriage to be performed by several successive carriers is deemed, for the purposes of this Convention, to be *one undivided carriage* if it has been regarded by the parties as a *single operation,* whether it had been agreed upon under the form of a single contract or of a series of contracts, and it does not lose its international character merely because one contract or a series of contracts is to be performed entirely within the territory of the same State [emphasis added].

The Convention does not apply to a passenger that is ticketed for domestic travel solely within one country or between two countries not party to the Convention. In these cases, state or local law would apply. On the other hand, the Convention does apply to passengers ticketed for flights

EXHIBIT 6.1

International Air Waybill

037– AIRPORT OF DEPARTURE 0226 0123 INTERNATIONAL AIR WAYBILL 037– 0226 0123

SHIPPER'S NAME AND ADDRESS	SHIPPER'S ACCOUNT NUMBER	NOT NEGOTIABLE AIR WAYBILL (AIR CONSIGNMENT NOTE)	US AIR USAir, Inc. NATIONAL AIRPORT, WASHINGTON, D.C. 20001
ABC Company 123 Elm St. Anytown, NC 12345		Copies 1, 2 and 3 of this Air Waybill are originals and have the same validity.	

It is agreed that the goods described herein are accepted in apparent good order and condition (except as noted) for carriage SUBJECT TO THE CONDITIONS OF CONTRACT ON THE REVERSE HEREOF. THE SHIPPER'S ATTENTION IS DRAWN TO THE NOTICE CONCERNING CARRIERS' LIMITATION OF LIABILITY. Shipper may increase such limitation of liability by declaring a higher value for carriage and paying a supplemental charge if required.

TO EXPEDITE MOVEMENT, SHIPMENT MAY BE DIVERTED TO MOTOR OR OTHER CARRIER AS PER TARIFF RULE UNLESS SHIPPER GIVES OTHER INSTRUCTIONS HEREON.

CONSIGNEE'S NAME AND ADDRESS	CONSIGNEE'S ACCOUNT NUMBER
XYZ Corporation 456 Wind St. Anycity, France	

ISSUING CARRIER'S AGENT NAME AND CITY	ALSO NOTIFY NAME AND ADDRESS *(OPTIONAL ACCOUNTING INFORMATION)*
	Foreign Custom Broker 1001 Maple St. Anycity, France

AGENT'S IATA CODE	ACCOUNT NUMBER
1-5678	

AIRPORT OF DEPARTURE (ADDR OF FIRST CARRIER) AND REQUESTED ROUTING: Charlotte

ACCOUNTING INFORMATION (SHIPPER CHECK ONE): XX AIR FREIGHT | AIR EXPRESS | COMAT

ROUTING AND DESTINATION

TO	BY FIRST CARRIER	TO	BY	TO	BY
CDG	US				

CURRENCY	CHGS CODE	WT/VAL PPD	WT/VAL COLL	OTHER PPD	OTHER COLL	DECLARED VALUE FOR CARRIAGE	DECLARED VALUE FOR CUSTOMS
USD			X		X	NVD	5000

AIRPORT OF DESTINATION	FOR CARRIER USE ONLY FLIGHT/DATE	FLIGHT/DATE	AMOUNT OF INSURANCE	INSURANCE– If shipper requests insurance in accordance with conditions on reverse hereof, indicate amount to be insured in figures in box marked amount of insurance.	TC
	US 8/15/08		NIL		

HANDLING INFORMATION These commodities licensed by US for ultimate destination. Diversion contrary to US law is prohibited.

MKD: AS Addr. PO# 0001

NOTIFICATION (PERSON NOTIFIED)	BY
DATE/TIME	DISPOSITION

NO. OF PIECES RCP	GROSS WEIGHT	Kg/lb	RATE CLASS COMMODITY ITEM NO.	CHARGEABLE WEIGHT	RATE/CHARGE	TOTAL	NATURE AND QUANTITY OF GOODS (INCL. DIMENSIONS OR VOLUME)
10	109	K		109	2.10	228.90	Leather aprons

PREPAID / WEIGHT CHARGE / COLLECT	P-UP ZONE / PICK-UP CHARGES	ORIGIN ADVANCE CHARGES	DESCRIPTION OF ORIGIN ADVANCE	ITEMS PREPAID
A. 228.90	B. 25.00	K.		
VALUATION CHARGE D.	DEL ZONE C.	DEST. ADVANCE CHARGES L.	DESCRIPTION OF DESTINATION ADVANCE	ITEMS COLLECT
TAX I.	SHIPPER'S R.F.C. (AMOUNT TO BE ENTERED BY SHIPPER) J.	OTHER CHARGES AND DESCRIPTION F.		

TOTAL OTHER CHARGES DUE AGENT	58.00
TOTAL OTHER CHARGES DUE CARRIER	10.00
I. COD →	CURRENCY
TOTAL PREPAID	TOTAL COLLECT 296.00
CURRENCY CONVERSION RATES	TOTAL COLLECT IN DEST. CURRENCY
FOR CARRIERS USE ONLY AT DESTINATION	CHARGES AT DESTINATION / TOTAL COLLECT CHARGES

SHIPPER CERTIFIES THAT THE PARTICULARS ON THE FACE HEREOF ARE CORRECT AND THAT INSOFAR AS ANY PART OF THE CONSIGNMENT CONTAINS RESTRICTED ARTICLES, SUCH PART IS PROPERLY DESCRIBED BY NAME AND IS IN PROPER CONDITION FOR CARRIAGE BY AIR ACCORDING TO APPLICABLE NATIONAL GOVERNMENT REGULATIONS, AND FOR INTERNATIONAL SHIPMENTS THE CURRENT INTERNATIONAL AIR TRANSPORT ASSOCIATION'S RESTRICTED ARTICLES REGULATIONS.

SIGNATURE OF SHIPPER OR HIS AGENT

EXECUTED ON

(Date) (Time) at (Place) SIGNATURE OF ISSUING CARRIER OR ITS AGENT

CARRIER CERTIFIES GOODS DESCRIBED ABOVE WERE RECEIVED FOR CARRIAGE SUBJECT TO THE CONDITIONS ON THE REVERSE HEREOF, THE GOODS THEN BEING IN APPARENT GOOD ORDER AND CONDITION EXCEPT AS NOTED HEREON.

037– 0226 0123

(ALL COLLECT CHARGES IN DESTINATION CURRENCY)

between two countries that are both party to the Convention. The Convention also governs passengers ticketed for round-trip travel from a country that is party to the Convention, regardless of whether the intermediate destination or stopping place was in a country that had adopted the Convention. It does not matter in which country the damages occurred.

Now consider passengers who are traveling internationally, but whose journey includes a domestic leg. Here, the determining factor is how the passengers were ticketed and whether they were engaged in a continuous international journey. Those passengers on an international journey would be governed by the rules of the Convention. Those aboard the same flight, but ticketed for domestic travel only, are not covered by the Convention. Assume that a passenger is ticketed for round-trip travel from Chicago to Los Angeles, connecting on another flight with a different airline from Los Angeles to Tokyo. Is the domestic portion of the flight considered "international carriage" and governed by the Convention? The answer for that passenger is "yes," if the flight from Chicago to Los Angeles is deemed to be "one undivided carriage" that is part of a "single operation." If all legs of a journey, international and domestic, are booked on the same ticket, then they are presumed to be one undivided carriage. Even where the separate flights are purchased and booked on different tickets, or even on different airlines, they may still be considered one undivided journey if the domestic and international legs may be considered a "single operation."

In *Robertson v. American Airlines, Inc.*, 401 F.3d 499 (D.C. Cir. 2005), the passenger purchased a round-trip ticket on British Airways between London and Denver. Three days later she purchased a round-trip ticket on American Airlines between Denver and Washington, DC. During the flight between Denver and Washington, she was burned by dry ice accidentally given to her by a flight attendant. The court looked at the fact that Robertson had scheduled her connection in Denver so that her flight to Washington would depart within about three hours of her arrival from London. It stated that, "It is unlikely that a layover of that length would even have given her time to leave the airport, and the record confirms that Robertson had no purpose for being in Denver on that day other than to make the plane connection." Because both flights were part of an undivided carriage, according to the court, the 2-year statute of limitations in the *Warsaw Convention* applied, and her case against the airline was dismissed. The decision would probably be the same today under the newer *Montreal Convention.*

Many cases arise when a plaintiff is unsatisfied with their remedies under the *Montreal Convention* and attempt to find some better alternative under state or local law. However, Article 29 provides that

> In the carriage of passengers, baggage and cargo, any action for damages, however founded, whether under this Convention or in contract or in tort or otherwise, can only be brought subject to the conditions and such limits of liabilities as are set out in this Convention without prejudice to the question as to who are the persons who have the right to bring suit and what are their respective rights.

In the following case, *El Al Israel Airlines, Ltd. v. Tseng*, the U.S. Supreme Court ruled that the *Warsaw Convention* provided the exclusive cause of action against an air carrier for injuries incurred during international travel.

Air Carrier's Liability for Death or Bodily Injury

The plaintiff in an air accident is usually the injured passenger or the estate or heirs of a deceased passenger. Article 17 of the Convention states,

> The carrier is liable for damage sustained in case of *death or bodily injury* of a passenger upon condition only that the *accident* which caused the death or injury took place *on board the aircraft or in the course of any of the operations of embarking or disembarking.* [emphasis added]

The sections in italics show the three basic requirements for liability: (1) death or bodily injury of a passenger (2) resulting from an accident (3) on board the aircraft or while embarking or disembarking. There have been thousands of litigated cases on these issues.

Meaning of "Accident." There are many court decisions discussing the meaning of "accident." It generally requires that the injury be caused by

El Al Israel Airlines, Ltd. v. Tseng
525 U.S. 155 (1999)
United States Supreme Court

BACKGROUND AND FACTS

Tseng purchased a ticket on an El Al (Israeli airline) flight from New York to Tel Aviv. Prior to boarding, an El Al security guard questioned her about her travel plans. The guard considered her response "illogical" and ranked her as a security risk. Tseng was taken to a private security room and told to remove her shoes and to lower her blue jeans to mid-hip. A female guard then searched her body outside her clothing by hand. Nothing was found, and she was allowed to board. She did not suffer any bodily injury. Tseng sued El Al in New York state courts for mental injuries for assault and false imprisonment under New York law. El Al removed the case to a federal district court. The district court dismissed, concluding that Tseng's only remedy was under the *Warsaw Convention,* and that Convention precluded recovery unless there was bodily injury. On appeal, the U.S. Court of Appeals held that a plaintiff who did not qualify for relief under the Convention could seek relief under local law for an injury sustained in the course of international air travel. El Al then appealed to the U.S. Supreme Court.

JUSTICE GINSBURG DELIVERED THE OPINION OF THE COURT

[Tseng's] case presents a question of the Convention's exclusivity: When the Convention allows no recovery for the episode-in-suit, does it correspondingly preclude the passenger from maintaining an action for damages under another source of law, in this case, New York tort law? * * * We ... hold that recovery for a personal injury suffered "on board [an] aircraft or in the course of any of the operations of embarking or disembarking," if not allowed under the Convention, is not available at all. Recourse to local law, we are persuaded, would undermine the uniform regulation of international air carrier liability that the *Warsaw Convention* was designed to foster. [citations omitted] * * *

The *Warsaw Convention* ... declares ... that the "[C]onvention shall apply to all international transportation of persons, baggage, or goods performed by aircraft for hire." * * * Article 17 establishes the conditions of liability for personal injury to passengers: "The carrier shall be liable for damage sustained in the event of the death or ... bodily injury suffered by a passenger, if the accident which caused the damage so sustained took place on board the aircraft or in the course of any of the operations of embarking or disembarking." * * *

We accept it as given that *El Al*'s search of Tseng was not an "accident" within the meaning of Article 17, for the parties do not place that Court of Appeals conclusion at issue.... The parties do not dispute that the episode-in-suit occurred in international transportation in the course of embarking. * * *

The cardinal purpose of the *Warsaw Convention,* we have observed, is to "achiev[e] uniformity of rules governing claims arising from international air transportation." *Eastern Airlines, Inc. v. Floyd,* 499 U.S. 530, 111 S.Ct. 1489 (1991). The Convention signatories, in the treaty's preamble, specifically "recognized the advantage of regulating in a uniform manner the conditions of ... the liability of the carrier." To provide the desired uniformity, the Convention sets out an array of liability rules which, the treaty declares, "apply to all international transportation of persons, baggage, or goods performed by aircraft." * * * Given the Convention's comprehensive scheme of liability rules and its textual emphasis on uniformity, we would be hard put to conclude that the delegates at Warsaw meant to subject air carriers to the distinct, nonuniform liability rules of the individual signatory nations. * * *

Construing the Convention, as did the Court of Appeals, to allow passengers to pursue claims under local law when the Convention does not permit recovery could produce several anomalies. Carriers might be exposed to unlimited liability under diverse legal regimes, but would be prevented, under the treaty, from contracting out of such liability. Passengers injured physically in an emergency landing might be subject to the liability caps of the Convention, while those merely traumatized in the same mishap would be free to sue outside of the Convention for potentially unlimited damages. The Court of Appeals' construction of the Convention would encourage artful pleading by plaintiffs seeking to opt out of the Convention's liability scheme when local law promised recovery in excess of that prescribed by the treaty. Such a reading would scarcely advance the predictability that adherence to the treaty has achieved worldwide. * * *

continued

continued

Tseng . . . argues that air carriers will escape liability for their intentional torts if passengers are not permitted to pursue personal injury claims outside of the terms of the Convention. But we have already cautioned that the definition of "accident" under Article 17 is an "unusual event . . . *external to the passenger*," and that "[t]his definition should be flexibly applied." *Air France v. Saks,* 470 U.S. 392, 397, 105 S.Ct. 1338 (1985). In *Saks,* the Court concluded that no "accident" occurred because the injury there—a hearing loss—"indisputably result[ed] from *the passenger's own internal reaction* to the usual, normal, and expected operation of the aircraft." As we earlier noted, Tseng and El Al chose not to pursue in this Court the question whether an "accident" occurred, for an affirmative answer would still leave Tseng unable to recover under the treaty; she sustained no "bodily injury" and could not gain compensation under Article 17 for her solely psychic or psychosomatic injuries. * * *

Both parties agree that . . . the Convention's preemptive effect is clear: The treaty precludes passengers from bringing actions under local law when they cannot establish air carrier liability under the treaty. * * *

Decision. The decision of the Court of Appeals was reversed. Under the *Warsaw Convention* a passenger may not bring an action for personal injury damages under state law when his or her claim does not satisfy the conditions for liability under the Convention.

some event that is a risk peculiar to air travel and "external" to the passenger. This might include injuries resulting from a bomb threat, skyjacking, the spilling of hot coffee on a passenger, air turbulence, or a crash landing.

However, there are many cases where it may not be so clear whether there was an "accident" or not. In the United States, the term was considered by the U.S. Supreme Court in *Air France v. Saks,* 470 U.S. 392 (1985). In that case, Valerie Saks was on a 12-hour flight from Paris to Los Angeles when she felt a severe pressure and pain in her ear during descent. The flight was routine and the plane landed normally. She disembarked without informing the airline of her ailment. Five days later, she consulted a doctor who concluded that she had become permanently deaf in her left ear. The trial court said it was not an accident. The U.S. Court of Appeals reversed, believing that the *Warsaw Convention* imposed absolute liability on airlines for injuries caused by the risks inherent in air travel. The U.S. Supreme Court disagreed and reversed, stating that

> Liability under Article 17 of the *Warsaw Convention* arises only if a passenger's injury is caused by an *unexpected or unusual event or happening that is external to the passenger.* This definition should be flexibly applied after assessment of all the circumstances surrounding a passenger's injuries. . . . In cases where there is contradictory evidence, it is for the trier of fact to decide whether an "accident" as here defined caused the passenger's injury. . . . But when the injury indisputably results from *the passenger's own internal reaction to the usual, normal, and expected operation of the aircraft,* it has not been caused by an accident, and Article 17 of the *Warsaw Convention* cannot apply." [emphasis added]

The court went on to give some examples of accidents from prior cases. These included torts committed by terrorists, a drunken passenger who fell and injured a fellow passenger, and a "sudden dive" that led to pressure change, which caused hearing loss. The general rule of *Air France v. Saks* was accepted by the British House of Lords in 2005 in litigation involving cases of deep vein thrombosis (formation of blood clots in the legs from sitting for long periods during flight). American and British cases have held that blood clots result from a passenger's internal reaction to the usual, normal, and expected operation of an aircraft and thus are not accidents. However, in *Olympic Airways v. Husain*, 540 U.S. 644 (2004) the U.S. Supreme Court arrived at a different conclusion in the case of an asthmatic passenger who died from an allergic reaction to secondhand smoke aboard a passenger aircraft.

Embarking or Disembarking. A carrier is only liable for damages occurring "on board the aircraft or in the course of any of the operations of embarking or disembarking." The question of whether passengers are embarking or disembarking often turns on their proximity to the security or boarding gate, the "imminence of boarding,"

Olympic Airways v. Husain

540 U.S. 644 (2004)

United States Supreme Court

BACKGROUND AND FACTS

Dr. Abid Hanson was traveling aboard an Olympic Airways flight from Athens to New York, returning to the United States from a vacation with his wife and family. He suffered from asthma and was affected by secondhand smoke. They were seated in a non-smoking section, three rows from the smoking section. As Dr. Hanson was struggling to breathe, his wife, Rubina Husain, made three urgent requests that he be moved away from the smoke. Her requests were refused. The flight attendant claimed that the flight was "totally full" (which was not correct) and that she was "too busy." Dr. Hanson walked to the front of the plane for air. He died shortly later, despite attempts to revive him. At trial, the court awarded Mrs. Husain a $1.4 million judgment, which was affirmed by the U.S. Court of Appeals. Olympic Airways (petitioner) appealed to the Supreme Court, arguing that Dr. Hanson's death was the result of his internal reaction to the usual and expected operation of the airplane and thus not the result of an accident.

JUSTICE THOMAS DELIVERED THE OPINION OF THE COURT

Article 17 of the *Warsaw Convention* (Convention) imposes liability on an air carrier for a passenger's death or bodily injury caused by an "accident" that occurred in connection with an international flight. In *Air France v. Saks,* 470 U.S. 392 (1985), the Court explained that the term "accident" in the Convention refers to an "unexpected or unusual event or happening that is external to the passenger," and not to "the passenger's own internal reaction to the usual, normal, and expected operation of the aircraft" [citations omitted]. The issue we must decide is whether the "accident" condition precedent to air carrier liability under Article 17 is satisfied when the carrier's unusual and unexpected refusal to assist a passenger is a link in a chain of causation resulting in a passenger's pre-existing medical condition being aggravated by exposure to a normal condition in the aircraft cabin. We conclude that it is. * * *

Applying Saks' definition of "accident," the Ninth Circuit agreed that the flight attendant's refusal to reseat Dr. Hanson "was clearly external to Dr. Hanson, and it was unexpected and unusual in light of industry standards, Olympic policy, and the simple nature of Dr. Hanson's requested accommodation." We granted certiorari, and now affirm.

Petitioner argues that the "accident" inquiry should focus on the "injury producing event," which, according to petitioner, was the presence of ambient cigarette smoke in the aircraft's cabin. Because the petitioner's policies permitted smoking on international flights, the petitioner contends that Dr. Hanson's death resulted from his own internal reaction—namely, an asthma attack—to the normal operation of the aircraft. The petitioner also argues that the flight attendant's failure to move Dr. Hanson was inaction, whereas Article 17 requires an action that causes the injury. We disagree.* * *

The petitioner's focus on the ambient cigarette smoke as the injury producing event is misplaced. We do not doubt that the presence of ambient cigarette smoke in the aircraft's cabin during an international flight might have been "normal" at the time of the flight in question. But the petitioner's "injury producing event" inquiry—which looks to "the precise factual 'event' that caused the injury"—neglects the reality that there are often multiple interrelated factual events that combine to cause any given injury. In *Saks,* the Court recognized that any one of these factual events or happenings may be a link in the chain of causes and—so long as it is unusual or unexpected—could constitute an "accident" under Article 17. Indeed, the very fact that multiple events will necessarily combine and interrelate to cause any particular injury makes it difficult to define, in any coherent or non-question-begging way, any single event as the "injury producing event."

The petitioner's only claim to the contrary here is to say: "Looking to the purely factual description of relevant events, the aggravating event was Dr. Hanson remaining in his assigned non-smoking seat and being exposed to ambient smoke, which allegedly aggravated his pre-existing asthmatic condition leading to his death," and that the "injury producing event" was "not the flight attendant's failure to act or violation of industry standards." The petitioner ignores the fact that the flight attendant's refusal on three separate occasions to move Dr. Hanson was also a "factual 'event,' "that the District Court correctly found to be a "'link in the chain'" of causes that led

continued

continued

to Dr. Hanson's death. The petitioner's statement that the flight attendant's failure to reseat Dr. Hanson was not the "injury producing event" is nothing more than a bald assertion, unsupported by any law or argument. * * * The exposure to the smoke and the refusal to assist the passenger are happenings that both contributed to the passenger's death.

And the petitioner's argument that the flight attendant's failure to act cannot constitute an "accident" because only affirmative acts are "events or happenings" under *Saks* is unavailing.... The relevant "accident" inquiry under *Saks* is whether there is "an unexpected or unusual event or happening." The rejection of an explicit request for assistance would be an "event" or "happening" under the ordinary and usual definitions of these terms. See *American Heritage Dictionary* 635 (3rd ed. 1992) ("event": "something that takes place; an occurrence"); *Black's Law Dictionary* 554-555 (6th ed. 1990) ("event": "Something that happens"). * * *

For the foregoing reasons, we conclude that the conduct here constitutes an "accident" under Article 17 of the *Warsaw Convention*. Accordingly, the judgment of the Court of Appeals is affirmed.

Decision. Mrs. Husain's verdict for $1.4 million in the trial court was upheld. The flight attendant's "unexpected or unusual" refusal to move the passenger to another seat, contrary to airline policy and industry standards, was an "accident" that was "external to the passenger" within the meaning of Article 17 of the *Montreal Convention*. It was a link in a chain of causation that resulted in the aggravation of a passenger's pre-existing medical condition by exposure to a normal condition (smoking, which was permitted) in the aircraft cabin.

whether their movements were under the control of the airline or security officials, and the activity of the passenger at the time. If they were actually in the process of boarding or exiting the aircraft, then the airline is responsible. However, the airline would generally not be responsible where the passenger is outside of the control of airline employees and moving about the terminal. In one case, an airline was held not responsible where the passenger was injured approximately one-half hour before the flight and several hundred feet from the departure gate, and the passengers had not yet been called to board the flight. Other cases have held the airlines not liable for injuries in corridors and on moving stairs or sidewalks that are under the control of the terminal, not the airline.

In most cases there is no liability for injuries sustained while a passenger is dining or shopping, or at the baggage claim. However, many cases are more complicated. In *Singh v. North American Airlines*, 426 F.Supp.2d 38 (E.D.N.Y. 2006) the passenger was arrested and imprisoned for several months when illegal drugs were discovered in his baggage on arrival in New York on a flight from Guyana. It was later discovered that airline employees had placed Singh's name and identification tags on the bags in order to illegally transport drugs. Singh sued the airline. The District Court ruled that this was "an accident" covered by the Convention because the process of checking baggage in Guyana and obtaining baggage claim tags was a necessary part of the embarkation process there. The court added that it did not matter in this case that the damage arose later, when Singh was imprisoned. It was sufficient, the court believed, that the "accident itself took place on board the aircraft or in the course of any of the operations of embarking or disembarking."

LIMITATIONS ON LIABILITY FOR DEATH OR BODILY INJURIES. The delegates to the original *Warsaw Convention* chose to express the limit on liability as an amount of currency relative to an accepted international standard—the value of gold. The gold system worked until the 1970s when gold was no longer used as the standard value for currencies. Today, the limitation of an air carrier's liability is set in *Special Drawing Rights* (SDRs). SDRs represent an amount equal to a mix of currency values (the euro, Japanese yen, British pound sterling, and U.S. dollar) developed by the International Monetary Fund (IMF). This facilitates an easy conversion from the limits expressed in the Convention into any currency. The value of an SDR on any given day can be found by consulting the IMF (available from the IMF Web site). On January 2, 2008, one SDR was worth approximately $1.58. Under the *Montreal Convention* nations will review the limitations on liability every 5 years and will be able to adjust them upward to account for inflation.

The *Montreal Convention* sets up a two-tiered liability system. First, the carrier is *strictly, or absolutely, liable* for all damages from death or bodily injury that can be proven by the passenger or their representative, in an amount not exceeding 100,000 SDRs per passenger (about $158,000 in early 2008), arising out of an accident. Strict or absolute liability means that the carrier is liable without regard to fault. In addition, the carrier is presumed to be liable for all proven damages above 100,000 SDRs, with no limit on the amount, unless it can show that the damages were not due to its negligence or to the negligence of its employees. The "fault" of the carrier, therefore, is only a factor for damages above the 100,000 SDR level.

Third-Party Suits. The *Montreal Convention* applies only to lawsuits against air carriers. It does not prohibit or govern lawsuits brought against third parties who may be at fault in the accident. This might include the manufacturer of a defectively designed or built airplane, the company that serviced or maintained it, the owners or operators of the airport, private security firms, retailers or vendors operating within airport facilities, or other passengers. These cases would primarily be governed by ordinary tort law of the state or jurisdiction in which the case is heard.

Comparative Negligence of the Passenger or Shipper. The *Montreal Convention* recognizes the carrier's defense of *comparative negligence*. Under this doctrine, a passenger will not be able to recover damages from a carrier to the extent that their own negligence contributed to causing the accident or their own injuries. If the carrier proves that the damage was caused or contributed to by the negligence of the passenger, the carrier will be wholly or partly exonerated from its liability to the extent that such negligence or wrongful act or omission caused or contributed to the damage. Thus, if a passenger is scalded by hot coffee on the seat-back table in front of him because he was not careful while removing his coat, he would most likely be unable to recover anything from the carrier. These issues are questions for the trier of fact, which in the United States is normally the jury.

Compensable Damages. The Convention does not specify what types of damages can be collected by a plaintiff in an air liability case (although, as we will see, it does not permit punitive damages). In personal injury or wrongful death cases that are litigated under state tort law, such as cases arising out of an automobile accident, plaintiffs typically ask for several different types of damages, depending on what is permitted by state law. These might include economic (sometimes called *pecuniary*) and non-economic damages. Pecuniary damages might include medical and other expenses or past and future loss of earnings. Non-economic damages could include pain and suffering, mental anguish (such as for disfigurement or loss of enjoyment of life), loss of consortium or companionship of a spouse, or, occasionally, punitive damages designed to punish and make an example of the wrongdoer. These damages might be typical of those recovered in air liability cases when tried under state law in the United States.

This issue was addressed in a well-known case. In 1983, Korean Air Lines 007 was traveling from New York to Seoul when it was shot down by a Soviet jet fighter for straying into Soviet airspace. All 269 people aboard were killed. In an action by the passengers' families against the airline, the U.S. Supreme Court addressed the question of what types of damages may be awarded in aircraft litigation. In *Zicherman v. Korean Air Lines Co., Ltd.*, 516 U.S. 217 (1996), the Court stated, "The law of the Convention does not affect the substantive questions of who may bring suit and what they may be compensated for. Those questions are to be answered by the domestic law selected by the courts of the contracting states." This means that in virtually all airline injury and disaster cases, the damages that are "compensable" depend on the state or federal law that is applied under conflict-of-laws rules. While in most airline litigation this would be state law, if a lawsuit involves an air disaster on the high seas, it may be governed by a federal statute, the *Death on the High Seas Act*.

The *Death on the High Seas Act*

The U.S. *Death on the High Seas Act* is a federal *admiralty* (maritime) statute that has applicability to airline crashes. Dating back to 1920, the statute originally permitted recovery of damages against a shipowner by a spouse, child, or dependent family member of a seaman killed in international waters. Today it applies also to wrongful death cases arising out of airline disasters over the high seas that occur beyond the 12-nautical miles territorial limit of U.S. waters. The act permits compensation for economic losses as well as for the loss of a deceased family member's "care, comfort, and companionship." Economic losses can include loss of future earnings. Non-economic losses, such as pain and suffering, mental anguish, loss of companionship to the surviving spouse, and punitive damages are not compensable.

Punitive Damages. Punitive damages (also called *exemplary damages*) can never be recovered under the *Montreal Convention.* In another case arising out of the Korean Air Lines 007 litigation, a U.S. Court of Appeals struck down a jury award of $50 million in punitive damages under the Convention.

Mental or Psychological Harm. Where damages for mental anguish or emotional distress are permitted by state or federal law, or by national law in another country, they may only be awarded to a plaintiff under the *Montreal Convention* if they are actually caused by bodily injury. In *Ehrlich v. American Airlines, Inc.,* 360 F.3d 366 (2004), the U.S. Court of Appeals sitting in New York considered a claim by passengers for mental anguish resulting from an emergency evacuation of the aircraft. The passengers testified that they suffered from nightmares and anxiety from the evacuation. In the course of the evacuation, they also sustained knee injuries. The court did not allow recovery for the mental anguish because it was not "caused by" the bodily injury, but merely accompanied it.

In other cases, it has been held that passengers could not recover damages for emotional distress merely because of stolen baggage or because their seat had been downgraded from first class to economy. In a case with a nearly tragic ending, *Eastern Airlines, Inc. v. Floyd,* 499 U.S. 530 (1991), the U.S. Supreme Court considered a passenger's suit for emotional distress resulting when the pilot announced that three engines had failed, that they were losing altitude rapidly, and that they would ditch in the Atlantic Ocean. After a period of descending flight without power, the crew managed to restart an engine and landed the plane safely in Miami. The court concluded that "an air carrier cannot be held liable under Article 17 when an accident has not caused a passenger to suffer death, physical injury, or physical manifestation of injury."

Jurisdiction. Airline disasters often result in lawsuits being filed by many different plaintiffs against several defendants in numerous countries or states. In the United States, some suits may be heard in state court, while others related to the same accident may be heard in federal court. Airline disasters seldom qualify for treatment as *class action* lawsuits—where one litigant brings a lawsuit on their own behalf and on behalf of other potential litigants who are members of the same group that have similar claims—because the issue of damages is specific to each injured or killed passenger. Some actions are consolidated for trial on liability and then separated for trial on the question of individual damages.

Lawsuits governed by the *Montreal Convention* can be brought only in a country that is party to the Convention and only in (1) the country where the tickets were purchased, (2) the country of the passenger's final destination, (3) the country where the air carrier is incorporated or has its principal place of business, or (4) the country of the passenger's "principal and permanent residence," if the carrier operates or conducts business there. (This prevents passengers or their families from having to litigate cases in far-off countries.) But, in the United States, the Convention does not determine whether a case will be heard in federal or state court. That is a question that has to be decided according to the rules of jurisdiction for the federal courts.

Multiparty, Multiforum Trial Jurisdiction Act of 2002. As of 2002 a federal statute (28 U.S.C.A. §1369, popularly called the *Multiparty, Multiforum Trial Jurisdiction Act of 2002*) gives U.S. district courts original jurisdiction over almost all civil actions involving the deaths of seventy-five or more natural persons in a single accident occurring at one location (including a natural disaster such as Hurricane Katrina). The minimum residency (diversity of citizenship) requirement is that at least one plaintiff and one defendant are residents of different states, or one party is a citizen of a foreign country. Other provisions of the act make it likely that many cases that might be filed by plaintiffs in state court will be removed by the defendants to federal court. This means that virtually all airline disaster cases heard in the United States will now be heard in federal court. The federal court must abstain from hearing a case if (1) the substantial majority of all plaintiffs are citizens of a single state of which the primary defendants are also citizens and (2) the claims asserted will be governed primarily by the laws of that state.

Assuming that the case may be heard in federal court, what is the proper *venue* (site) for trial? The act provides that the disaster litigation may be heard in any federal judicial district in which the accident occurred or in which a defendant (usually a corporate defendant) resides.

TIME LIMITATIONS. All legal actions against air carriers for damages must be brought within 2 years of the date of arrival at the destination, or from the date on which the aircraft ought to have arrived, or from the date on which the carriage stopped. Where baggage or cargo are damaged, the carrier must be notified immediately and no later than 7 days from the date of receipt in the case of checked baggage and 14 days from the date of receipt in the case of cargo. Claims for damages for delayed baggage or cargo must be made in writing and at the latest within 21 days from the date on which the baggage or cargo was actually delivered.

Liability for Air Cargo and Baggage Losses

The *Montreal Convention* maintains many of the provisions of the earlier treaties with regard to liability of air carriers for loss to cargo or baggage.

CARGO LOSSES. An air carrier is liable for "damage sustained" to cargo under its control, but not in excess of 17 SDRs per kilogram, unless the shipper has declared a higher value on the air waybill and paid an additional fee if required. This limit does not apply if it can be shown that the damage resulted from an intentional act of the air carrier or its employees or from an act that was done recklessly and with knowledge that damage would probably result from such an act. The carrier is not responsible for damages resulting from an inherent defect or quality of the cargo, defective packing by the shipper or someone other than the carrier, an act of war or armed conflict, or an act of public authority, such as customs authorities.

BAGGAGE LOSSES. The liability of the carrier in the case of loss, damage, or delay to baggage on board an aircraft or under their control is limited to 1,000 SDRs for each passenger, unless the passenger has declared a higher value and paid any additional fees required (but in no case greater than the actual value of the baggage).

DELAY. Travelers will appreciate the new provisions of the *Montreal Convention,* which make airlines liable for delays in transporting passengers, baggage, or cargo. However, the carrier is not liable if it proves that it and its servants and agents took reasonable measures to avoid the damage or that it was impossible for it or them to take such measures. Liability for delays is limited to 4,150 SDRs per passenger.

LIABILITY FOR THE CARRIAGE OF GOODS BY SEA

Oceangoing cargo is constantly at risk. Damage can result from any number of causes, including external forces, the inherent nature of the goods, the passage of time, or any combination of factors. Typical examples of cargo damage include infestation from insects or molds, contamination from chemicals previously held in the ship's hold, rust and other moisture damage from condensation inside the hold, damage from broken refrigeration units and other equipment, storm damage from rain and seawater, losses from fire or the sinking of the ship, damage done to cargo while rescuing the ship from peril, damage resulting from cargo being improperly stowed above deck, losses from theft and modern-day piracy on the seas, damage from acts of war, and so on.

One of the greatest dangers to cargo has traditionally been pilferage and theft. This problem was particularly troublesome during the time when goods were moved by break-bulk freight. With the advent of containerization, particularly in the last 25 years, pilferage has been greatly reduced. The impact of containerization was described by the court in *Matsushita Electric Corp. v. S.S. Aegis Spirit,* 414 F. Supp. 894 (W.D. Wash. 1976):

> The emergent use of these cargo-carrying containers marks a significant technological stride within the maritime industry, and their use seems certain to expand in years to come because of the substantial advantages they provide over conventional modes of ocean carriage for shippers and carriers alike. Their increasing popularity finds its source in the enhanced economy and efficiency they offer in the handling, loading, stowing, and discharge of most types of seagoing cargo. Their value to shippers lies in the greater protection they afford cargo from pilferage, rough handling, and the elements. Use of containers will frequently permit the shipper to substitute lighter, more economical packaging materials without increased risk to the cargo. Furthermore, the shipper can, in most container operations, personally ensure a tight stow and the careful handling of his goods, because he has the responsibility to stuff the containers under the carriage contract. The carrier, for its part, enjoys tremendous savings in labor by eliminating slow, manual handling and stowing of individual packages, and in claim payments by reason of reduced cargo loss and damage. Although shippers and freight forwarders sometimes acquire their own fleet of containers, carriers are the predominant owners of containers used in maritime commerce.

Despite the impact of containerization on international trade, damage and loss to cargo must be anticipated by any international shipper. In the event of a loss, inevitably the owner of the goods or the insurer will look to the carrier for recovery. However, carriers enjoy considerable protection under the law.

History of Carrier Liability

The law governing an ocean carrier's liability for damage or loss to cargo is rooted in the history of transportation and trade. As goods moved across the high seas on sailing ships, they were under the exclusive control of the ship's captain for months at a time. Shippers had no way of proving that goods were lost or destroyed as a result of a natural disaster, the negligence of the carrier, or from the crew's pilferage or theft. As a result, the maritime laws of both England and the United States held carriers to be absolutely liable for all loss or damage to cargo in their possession. Although a few exceptions to this liability were recognized, carriers were virtual insurers of their cargo. With the growth of trade and the advent of steamships, carriers became more economically powerful. They began to include provisions in their bills of lading (which are contracts between the shipper and carrier) that would limit their liability. These limitation-of-liability clauses attempted to free the carrier from all responsibility, including liability for its own negligence or even for providing an unfit vessel. The small shippers were at the mercy of the steamship companies. The result was a period of great uncertainty over the liability of ocean carriers.

THE *HARTER ACT*. In 1892, the U.S. Congress first addressed the problem in the *Harter Act,* a federal law still in effect today. This act set out the liability of a carrier for the care of its cargo and imposed restrictions on the use of exculpatory clauses in bills of lading. Subsequent developments in the law have resulted in the *Harter Act*'s limited application. Today, the *Harter Act* remains applicable to contracts for the carriage of goods only from one U.S. port to another U.S. port. For international shipments, the Harter Act has been superseded by a new statute. The *Harter Act* also applies to the liability of the carrier for caring for the goods before they are loaded and after they are unloaded from the ship (e.g., during warehousing).

THE *HAGUE RULES*. At the end of the first World War, other nations attempted to develop similar rules. The result was the near-universal acceptance of a 1924 international convention on bills of lading known as the *Hague Rules*. These rules represent an international effort to achieve uniformity of bills of lading and were intended to reduce the uncertainties concerning the responsibilities and liabilities of ocean carriers. The *Hague Rules* define the liability of ocean carriers for damage or loss to goods on the seas. Virtually every trading nation of the world today has incorporated them into its national law.

THE *CARRIAGE OF GOODS BY SEA ACT*. The *Hague Rules* were codified in the United States in 1936 in the *Carriage of Goods by Sea Act* or *COGSA*. COGSA is applicable to every bill of lading for the carriage of goods by sea, to or from ports of the

United States in foreign trade. COGSA governs the liability of a carrier from the time goods are loaded onto the ship until the time the cargo is unloaded. COGSA does not apply to losses that occur prior to loading or after discharge from the vessel (during which the Harter Act applies). Thus, it is commonly said that COGSA applies from "tackle to tackle." However, COGSA does permit the shipper and carrier to extend the application of COGSA beyond the "tackle to tackle" period by including a provision to that effect in the bill of lading. Thus, COGSA often applies to damage losses outside the "tackle to tackle" period and to some domestic shipments as well. Because virtually all bills of lading issued in the United States provide that they are controlled by COGSA, the discussion here concentrates on that statute.

Limitations of Liability under COGSA. COGSA invalidates all clauses in the bill of lading that try to exonerate a carrier from liability for damage or loss to cargo or that attempt to lessen a carrier's liability beneath that set by the statute itself. For instance, a carrier is liable under COGSA if refrigeration units are inadequate to prevent spoilage of perishable fruit during a journey. A carrier cannot put a "fine print" provision in a bill of lading that says they are not liable for inadequate refrigeration; such an attempted provision is void.

Forum Selection Clauses. Prior to 1995, U.S. carriers were protected from having to defend themselves in cargo lawsuits filed in foreign countries. In that year, the U.S. Supreme Court decided *Vimar Seguros y Reaseguros, S.A. v. M/V Sky Reefer*, 515 U.S. 528 (1995). The case involved over $1 million in damaged oranges shipped from Morocco to a customer in New York aboard a ship owned by a Japanese company. The bill of lading stated that any dispute would have to be resolved in Japan. In a surprising decision, the Court held that the forum selection clause was valid. The decision threw U.S. shippers into a panic because of the fear of being subjected to lawsuits in foreign countries and under foreign laws. Since then, it has resulted in fewer cargo cases being filed in the United States, because so many foreign carriers include clauses in their bills of lading requiring disputes to be resolved in their countries.

Nautical Liability of the Carrier

The liability of a carrier for damage or loss to oceangoing cargo is strictly defined and limited by COGSA. COGSA provides considerable protection to the carrier for cargo damage resulting from negligence in navigating or managing the ship or from fire or storms. The carrier, however, is liable for its failure to use due diligence in providing a seaworthy ship at the beginning of the voyage.

Establishing the Carrier's Liability. When cargo is found to be damaged upon delivery, COGSA requires that written notice be given to the carrier at the port of discharge. If the damage is visible, the notice must be given before or at the time that the goods are taken from the carrier's custody. If the loss is not visible or apparent, written notice must be given to the carrier within 3 days of delivery. Failure to give notice in writing creates a rebuttable presumption that the goods were delivered in good condition. The statute of limitations for filing claims under COGSA is 1 year.

Proving liability leads to complex litigation and has resulted in untold numbers of cases in the law reports. In the event of a dispute, suits are generally brought by the shipper, owner of the cargo or holder of the bill of lading, or their insurer. The plaintiff must show that the goods were loaded in good condition and unloaded in damaged condition or lost while in the carrier's custody. A clean bill of lading received from the carrier at the time of shipment establishes a rebuttable presumption that the goods were delivered to the carrier in good condition. The plaintiff does not have to prove that the carrier was at fault or explain how the loss occurred. The burden shifts to the carrier to prove that it is not liable.

There is a problem in relying on a clean bill of lading to establish the carrier's liability where goods were shipped in a sealed ocean container. Recall that a clean bill of lading is one that contains no notations from the ship's master that there was visible evidence of damage at the time the goods were turned over to the carrier. If the goods are in closed containers or packages, damage may not be observable, and there may be no way for the carrier to know the condition of the goods inside. Here the clean bill only establishes the external condition of the outer containers.

In these cases, the courts generally require the plaintiff to show more than just a clean bill. The plaintiff must prove the nature and extent of the damage, loss, or shortage and the likelihood that it occurred while in the carrier's custody. Courts generally require the shipper to introduce other evidence, such as inspection certificates or testimony from people who have knowledge of the condition of the goods before or at the time of loading. For example, there might be testimony that the damage was of the type that normally occurs at sea and not on land. In *Allied Signal Technical Services Corp. v. M/V Dagmar Maersk*, 234 F. Supp. 2d 526 (D. Md. 2002), the shipper brought action against the carrier to recover for damages to a space telescope shipped to Italy. Although the court considered the testimony of the plaintiff's insurance investigators, outside experts, and employees, and of independent surveyors who supervised the loading and unloading, it found that the plaintiff's evidence was not sufficient to show that the goods were delivered to the carrier in good condition.

Carrier's Due Diligence. Once the shipper establishes that the goods were turned over to the carrier in good condition and delivered in damaged condition, it becomes the carrier's burden to show that it was not legally responsible for the damage or loss. In the case of losses at sea, the carrier does this by proving one of the following: (1) That the damage was not caused by its failure to use *due diligence* in providing a seaworthy ship at the beginning of the voyage. The term "due diligence" means that the carrier must be prudent and vigilant in investigating the seaworthy condition of the ship and its equipment at the beginning of the voyage; or (2) That the loss occurred from one of the specific exemptions shown in Exhibit 6.2. This exhibit shows the specific exceptions to a carrier's liability set out in COGSA. The carrier is not liable if it can prove that the cargo was damaged as a result of an act of war or terrorism, fire, an error in navigation or management of the ship, an accident, a peril of the sea, or another listed exemption.

Seaworthiness of the Ship. The carrier is liable for damage to cargo resulting from its failure to use due diligence to make the ship seaworthy at the time of its departure on the voyage. This assurance has been called the "warranty of seaworthiness." A vessel is *seaworthy* if it is reasonably fit to carry the cargo it has undertaken to carry on the intended journey. In other words, the carrier must not only use due diligence to inspect the vessel for repair, but it must be sure the vessel is the proper type for carrying this specific type of cargo on this particular voyage. The standard of seaworthiness includes a number of factors, including the type of ship and the condition and suitability of its equipment, the competence of its crew, the type of cargo being carried and the manner in which it is stowed, the weather (e.g., was the ship prepared for the type of weather expected?), and the nature of the voyage. Some courts will recognize a presumption of unseaworthiness at the time of departure if the ship breaks down shortly after departure in clear weather and calm seas.

Exhibit 6.2

Carriage of Goods by Sea Act
Specific Exceptions to Liability

Carriers are not liable for losses resulting from a number of specific causes listed in the statute. These exceptions include the following:

1. Errors in the navigation or in the management of the ship
2. Fire, unless caused by the actual fault of the carrier (the corporate owner of the ship)
3. Perils, dangers, and accidents of the sea
4. An act of God (a natural disaster)
5. An act of war
6. An act of public enemies
7. Legal seizure of the ship
8. Quarantine restrictions
9. An act or omission of the shipper or owner of the goods
10. Labor strikes or lockouts
11. Riots and civil commotions
12. Saving life or property at sea
13. An inherent defect, quality, or vice of the goods that causes wastage in bulk or weight or other damage or loss
14. Insufficiency of packing
15. Inadequate marking of goods or containers
16. Latent defects in ship or equipment (that might render the ship unseaworthy) that were not discoverable by due diligence

The carrier is responsible for properly manning, equipping, and supplying the ship, and making the refrigerating and cooling chambers, and all other parts of the ship in which goods are carried, fit and safe for receiving, carrying, and preserving the goods. The carrier must also properly load, store, and carry the goods. For instance, the cargo holds must not be in such a condition that they cause moisture damage to the goods through condensation. Cargo should not be stowed in a manner that causes it to shift and be crushed. Cargo should not be exposed to rain and seas. Refrigeration units must be in working order, and so forth. The carrier must also properly unload the cargo and hand it over to the party entitled to it.

Errors in Navigation or Mismanagement of the Ship. Exhibit 6.2 shows those situations in which a carrier is not liable for damage to cargo. One of the most important is that the carrier—the corporate ship's owner—is not liable for errors in navigation or mismanagement of the ship caused by the master, mariner, pilot, or a crewmember (except for the crew's negligence in the care and custody of the cargo, such as during loading and unloading, for which the carrier is liable).

Understand that an error in the "navigation and management of the ship" by the crew is a very different thing than when the ship's corporate owner fails to use due diligence in providing a seaworthy ship at the beginning of the voyage. Although carriers are not liable for the former, they are liable for the latter—for failing to provide a seaworthy ship. Thus, some courts have held carriers liable for their crew's negligence by reasoning that a crew that errs in navigating or managing a ship is not competent, and a ship is not seaworthy without a competent crew. As a result, carriers are often held liable despite the protection they receive from this defense.

Damage from Fire aboard Ship. Fire aboard ship has the potential to cause catastrophic losses at sea. Ocean carriers are not liable unless the actual negligence of the carrier—the corporate owner of the ship—caused the fire or prevented it from being extinguished. Although the U.S. federal courts disagree as to how to handle fire cases, they tend to rule that carriers will be liable for fire damage only if the corporate owner of the ship was actually at fault. The negligence of the crew is not enough to make the carrier liable. For instance, the carrier is liable if it allows the ship to leave port with inadequate firefighting equipment or with a crew untrained to fight fires.

In this instance, the *carrier* (the company that owned the ship) would have had control over installation of the equipment or training of the crew in firefighting. Thus, the law holds them responsible. However, once at sea, the corporate owner loses control of the ship—it becomes at the mercy of the elements and the ocean. Here, the corporate owner is not liable for losses due to fire. Once the carrier proves in court that fire damaged the cargo, the burden shifts to the plaintiff (the shipper or cargo owner) to prove that actual negligence of the ship's owner caused the fire or prevented it from being extinguished. In one of the leading fire cases, *Asbestos Corp. Ltd. v. Compagnie de Navigation,* 480 F.2d 669 (2d Cir. 1973), a fire broke out in an engine room where large quantities of hot oil were expected to be present. The firefighting equipment was located in the engine room and thus could not be used to extinguish the fire there. The court ruled that the ship's owner was negligent in installing the equipment at that location and liable for the loss to cargo as a result.

Perils of the Sea. Ships encounter tremendous forces of water and weather on the high seas. COGSA exempts carriers from liability for damage resulting from "perils, dangers, and accidents of the sea." A *peril of the sea* is a fortuitous action of the sea or weather of sufficient force to overcome the strength of a seaworthy ship or the diligence and skill of a good crew. The defense often depends on the severity of the storm and the manner in which the cargo was damaged. The courts will consider the force of the wind, the height of the waves, the foreseeability of the storm when the ship set sail, the ability of the ship to avoid the storm, whether other ships in the same storm suffered damage, the type of damage to the cargo, and other factors. The negligence or lack of competence on behalf of the crew will void the perils of the sea defense. But if the ship was seaworthy when it left port and was operated in a competent manner, the carrier is not liable for cargo damage from a storm so strong that it represents a peril of the sea. In the case that follows, *J. Gerber & Co. v. S.S. Sabine Howaldt,* the court ruled that the carrier had used due diligence to maintain a seaworthy ship and that the damage had resulted from a peril of the sea. As the court notes, just because a ship is seaworthy does not mean that it can withstand every form of violent weather and turbulent sea that oceangoing ships might encounter.

THE Q-CLAUSE DEFENSE. Even if a carrier cannot prove one of the sixteen exceptions shown in Exhibit 6.2, it still may be exonerated from liability under a seventeenth defense, the *Q-clause defense.* This provision states that a carrier is not liable for "any other cause arising without the actual fault and privity of the carrier ... but the burden of proof shall be on the [carrier] to show that neither the actual fault ... nor the fault or neglect of the

J. Gerber & Co. v. S.S. Sabine Howaldt

437 F.2d 580 (1971)

United States Court of Appeals (2d Cir.)

BACKGROUND AND FACTS

The S.S. *Sabine Howaldt,* a small cargo vessel, was chartered for a voyage from Antwerp, Belgium, to Wilmington, Delaware. The ship was carrying a quantity of steel products consigned to the plaintiff. The cargo was in good condition when loaded at Antwerp. On arrival at the port of destination in the United States, however, the steel showed extensive saltwater damage from rust and pitting. In the course of her voyage across the North Atlantic, the *Sabine Howaldt* encountered extremely heavy weather. Water penetrated the ventilators and damaged the cargo. The carrier argued that the damage was caused solely by a peril of the sea and that the ship was not unseaworthy. The trial court found that the ship was unseaworthy due to the negligence of the defendant and that the winds and seas that the vessel encountered did not constitute a peril of the sea.

ANDERSON, CIRCUIT JUDGE

The ship's log records that ... the ship was badly strained in her seams and sea water was breaking over forecastle deck, hatches, and upper works. It was necessary for the vessel to heave to and she so remained for 12 hours. The hull of the *Sabine Howaldt* was twisted and strained in the turbulent cross seas; she rolled from 25 degrees–30 degrees; waves constantly broke over her; and she shuddered and vibrated as she was pounded and wrenched by the heavy seas.... Subsequently it was discovered that during this period of hurricane ... a porthole in the galley was smashed; the catwalk or gangway from the amidships housing aft over the hatches and the well-deck to the poop was destroyed when it was torn loose and landed against a ventilator, which it dented.

The district court not only found that the character and nature of the winds and seas were not sufficiently severe to constitute a peril of the sea in fact, but it also found that the *Sabine Howaldt* was unseaworthy due to the neglect of the defendant carrier. It concluded that the defendant was negligent in permitting the ship to proceed on the voyage with defective hatch covers without tarpaulins over them and also because its ventilators were insufficiently protected....

On arrival at Wilmington, Delaware, on January 3, 1966, the chief officer examined the hatches and found no damage to the hatches, the hatch covers, or their rubber gaskets—all were in good condition.... There was no evidence that there was a customary or usual standard in the exercise of good seamanship that called for the use of canvas tarpaulins over MacGregor hatchcovers. It was quite apparent that the customary practice of most steamship lines was not to use tarpaulins over such hatchcovers.... As there was no evidence in the case that the MacGregor hatchcovers on the *Sabine Howaldt* were not properly maintained and as there was substantial, uncontradicted evidence that they were, it was plain error to hold there was negligence in regard to a failure to cover the hatchcovers with tarpaulins.

The standard of seaworthiness must remain uncertain because of the imponderables of the forces exerted upon a ship by the winds and seas. Ship design and construction over many centuries of experience have evolved to meet the dangers inherent in violent winds and tempestuous seas.

continued

continued

But for the purpose of deciding whether or not they constitute perils of the sea for a particular vessel for the purpose of the statutory exception there is the question of how violent and how tempestuous. These are matters of degree and not amenable to precise definition.... Other indicia are, assuming a seaworthy ship, the nature and extent of the damage to the ship itself, whether or not the ship was buffeted by cross-seas which wrenched and wracked the hull and set up unusual stresses in it and like factors. While the seaworthiness of a ship presupposes that she is designed, built, and equipped to stand up under reasonable expectable conditions, this means no more than the usual bad weather, which is normal for a particular sea area at a particular time. It does not, however, include an unusual combination of the destructive forces of wind and sea which a skilled and experienced ship's master would not expect and which the ship encountered as a stroke of bad luck. Hurricane-force winds and turbulent cross-seas generating unpredictable strains and pressures on a ship's hull are an example.

We are satisfied that the *Sabine Howaldt* was a seaworthy vessel when she left Antwerp on December 15, 1965.... Throughout the voyage she was operated in a good and seamanlike manner. There was no negligence on the part of the carrier. The damage to the cargo was caused by violence of the wind and sea and particularly by the resulting cross-seas which, through wrenching and twisting the vessel, set up torsions within the hull which forced up the hatchcovers and admitted sea water to the holds.

Decision. The Court of Appeals reversed the decision of the trial court. The defendant carrier met its burden of proof that the vessel was seaworthy when it left port, was operated in a seamanlike manner, and the damage to the cargo resulted solely from a peril of the sea.

agents or servants of the carrier contributed to the loss or damage." The carrier must therefore prove that it was free from any fault whatsoever contributing to the loss, damage, or disappearance of the goods entrusted to it, and it must also prove what the actual cause of the loss was. This burden is difficult for the carrier to bear, and relatively few cases in the literature describe carriers that have been successful using this defense.

Shipper's Liability for Hazardous Cargo

Thus far we have been discussing the liability of the ocean carrier. Now consider the liability of a shipper of hazardous cargo for damage caused to a ship at sea. The *M/V Tokyo Senator* was transporting 300 barrels of thiourea from Korea to Norfolk. Thiourea is a white, odorless powder used as a reducing agent and in the bleaching of protein fibers such as paper, paper pulp, and textiles. The chemical spontaneously ignited at sea, damaging the ship. The carrier brought an action against the shipper for damages. The shipper did not know that thiourea was hazardous, and at the time of the shipment, thiourea was considered a stable compound under normal conditions. At trial, the carrier failed to prove the actual cause of the fire or that the shipper was responsible. There was evidence, however, that the combustion was caused by the inherently dangerous nature of the chemical itself. The district court granted summary judgment for the shipper, holding that COGSA does not impose liability on a shipper of inherently dangerous goods unless it can be shown that the shipper actually or constructively knew of the dangerous nature of the cargo prior to shipment and failed to disclose that nature to the carrier. The carrier appealed. In *Senator Linie GmbH & Co. Kg v. Sunway Line, Inc.*, 291 F.3d 145 (2d Cir. 2002), the court reversed, stating:

> We conclude—[as have the British courts]—that COGSA established a rule of strict liability for a shipper of inherently dangerous goods when neither the shipper nor the carrier had actual or constructive pre-shipment knowledge of the danger. This construction of COGSA is consonant with COGSA's goals of fostering international uniformity in sea-carriage rules and allocating risk between shippers and carriers in a manner that is consistent and predictable.... [W]e conclude today that a strict-liability construction will foster fairness and efficiency in the dealings of commercial maritime actors. In contrast to a carrier, which typically is in the position of taking aboard its vessel a large quantity and variety of

cargoes, a shipper can be expected to have greater access to and familiarity with goods and their manufacturers before those goods are placed in maritime commerce. If an unwitting party must suffer, it should be the one that is in a better position to ascertain ahead of time the dangerous nature of shipped goods. That party in many cases will be the shipper.

The case stands as a warning to a shipper of hazardous materials. Be certain that your marine insurance policy covers such losses.

Carrier's Liability for Cargo Shortages

Ocean containers are generally loaded and sealed at the shipper's place of business and not opened until they are in the hands of the consignee. Even so, cargo shortages are a regular occurrence in the maritime trade. The legal problems here are somewhat different from the problems of damaged cargo. As the first step in any litigation, the owner of the cargo or the insurer must establish that a shortage actually occurred while the goods were in the carrier's custody. Then, under the catch-all Q-clause defense that limits the carrier's liability (as discussed in the previous section), the carrier may attempt to prove that the shortage resulted despite its having exercised due care to safeguard the cargo.

A consignee can prove a shortage by showing that the quantity or weight of the cargo at the destination is less than that listed on the bill of lading. This issue can also be problematic, however. Under COGSA, a bill of lading usually lists the number of packages and the quantity or weight of the cargo that the carrier receives for shipment, but the quantity or weight is usually supplied by the shipper. Because shipping containers are sealed at the shipper's place of business, the carrier does not really have the opportunity to physically count the number of packages inside. The carrier will customarily insert a disclaimer in the bill of lading stating that the cargo inside the container is the "shipper's weight, load, and count" (i.e., not weighed, loaded, or counted by the carrier). Thus, carriers claim that they should not be liable for "missing cargo"—for delivering less cargo than described in the bill of lading.

Recent cases have not recognized these disclaimers and, as in the *Westway Coffee* case, are holding carriers liable for shortages in sealed containers where the weight or quantity stated on the bill of lading was verifiable by the shipper. In *Westway Coffee v. M.V. Netuno*, the carrier was held liable for a loss of some 20 tons of coffee in 419 cartons, despite the disclaimer in the bill of lading stating that the weight and quantity were provided by the shipper, because the weight of the sealed container had been verifiable by the carrier. The liability of the carrier in *Westway* stems from the carrier's option of weighing the container when it is received in order to confirm the existence of cargo inside and then weighing it again at its destination in order to prove delivery.

In *Plastique Tags, Inc. v. Asia Trans Line, Inc.*, 83 F.3d 1367 (1996), the 11th Circuit Court of Appeals, citing *Westway Coffee*, held that a carrier was not liable for shortages in a shipment of plastic bags from Korea to the United States in a container sealed by the shipper. The bill of lading recited that the container was the "Shippers Load and Count" and that it was "Said to Contain 5600 boxes/4,437,500 plastic bags." The court apparently believed that because only a number of units was given on the bill of lading, and no weight, that it was impossible for the carrier to verify the accuracy of the shipper's representation.

Westway Coffee Corp. v. M.V. Netuno

528 F. Supp. 113 (1981), aff'd, *675 F.2d 30 (2d Cir. 1982)*

United States District Court (S.D.N.Y.)

BACKGROUND AND FACTS

Westway, the consignee, purchased 1,710 cartons of coffee from Dominium, S.A., of Sao Paulo, Brazil. The cartons were loaded into six cargo containers under the supervision of a government officer who inspected and counted the cartons going into the containers. Dominium sealed and padlocked the containers. The containers were then driven from Sao

continued

continued

Paulo to the port of Santos, where they were stored in a customs bonded warehouse prior to loading onto the *MV Netuno,* a vessel owned by Netumar. Netumar issued an onboard bill of lading listing the serial numbers of the containers, along with the gross weight of the containers filled with coffee and the number of cartons within them. Netumar did not count the cartons. The bill of lading contained disclaimers stating that the containers were "said to contain" a quantity of cargo described by the shipper, that the cargo was the "shipper's load, and count," and that the "contents of packages are shipper's declaration." After the *Netuno's* arrival in New York, the padlocked containers were opened, revealing a shortage of 419 cartons or approximately 20 tons of coffee. Westway purchased the bill of lading and then brought this action against the carrier under the *Carriage of Goods by Sea Act.*

SAND, DISTRICT JUDGE

Plaintiff contends that the weights stated in the bill of lading constitute prima facie evidence of the receipt by the carrier of the goods as therein described; that it was entitled to rely on the weights stated in the bill of lading which was duly negotiated to it; and that Netumar is estopped from claiming that the missing cartons of coffee were not in the containers when Netumar took possession of them.

Defendant contends that plaintiff has failed to prove delivery of the full quantity to the carrier, and thereby has failed to establish a prima facie case; and alternatively, that defendant has established that it exercised proper care, and that plaintiff's estoppel theory does not apply to cases involving sealed containers. These contentions are based largely on the disclaimers contained in the bill of lading, and on the fact that the goods were "hidden" within the containers.

COGSA provides the answer to defendant's contention. Section 1303(3) provides:

> After receiving the goods into his charge the carrier ... shall, on demand of the shipper, issue to the shipper a bill of lading showing among other things,
>
> (b) Either the number of packages or pieces, or the quantity or weight, as the case may be, as furnished in writing by the shipper.
>
> (c) The apparent order and condition of the goods: Provided, that no carrier, master, or agent of the carrier, shall be bound to state or show in the bill of lading any ... quantity, or weight which he has reasonable ground for suspecting not accurately to represent the goods actually received, or which he has had no reasonable means of checking.

As our Court of Appeals has said of this section: "The Act specifically provides a method for avoiding carrier liability for false information given by the shipper, by not stating it in the bill.... The carrier must utilize that method, rather than the quite general reservation attempted here." *Spanish American Skin Co. v. The Ferngulf,* 242 F.2d 551, 553 (2d Cir. 1957). Thus, if defendant has reason to doubt the shipper's weights, it was required to use the method for limiting liability expressly provided by COGSA and cannot now advance the general statement in the bills, "said to weigh," against the consignee. Since plaintiff relied on the weights specified in the bills in purchasing the consignment, defendant is estopped from denying the accuracy of the description contained therein.

We thus find that despite the disclaimers stamped on the bill of lading, the weights recited in the bill established prima facie receipt by the carrier of the entire shipment of coffee.

Plaintiff having satisfied its initial burden, the burden thus shifts to defendant to establish the applicability of a COGSA exception. Defendant contends that it has satisfied this burden by demonstrating that it exercised "proper care," relying on the catchall exception contained in COGSA. Defendant must therefore prove that it was free from negligence. We find the testimony produced by defendant with respect to the loading of the containers on the *Netuno,* their stowage on the ship, and the operation of Pier 36 insufficient to satisfy that burden. We find as a matter of fact that there were significant periods of time when the container could have been pilfered ... most notably during loading and the voyage (which included stops in three other ports), and during discharge. Moreover, we find the testimony with respect to the general security measures taken on Pier 36 insufficient to establish defendant's freedom from negligence, especially in view of the testimony that coffee was an item in high demand on Pier 36 and easily saleable to salvors during this period of time. Finally, the fact that the unnumbered seals and locks were intact when the loss was discovered is not conclusive. First, the seals, which consist of wire and a seal stamped IBC but have no identifying number

continued

continued

or unique characteristic, could be easily duplicated. Second, as the testimony indicated and as other courts have recognized, the locks used on these containers could have been picked.

If defendant had succeeded in showing that the extent of surveillance, fending, internal security measures, and other security measures were such that pilferage could not readily have been accomplished on the pier or during the voyage, we would conclude that, although the precise technique utilized by the thief is still unknown, the defendant had absolved itself of any negligence. But defendant's showing falls far short of this, and the extent of pilferage, especially of coffee, is a matter of record. Since defendant is estopped from denying that the coffee was within the container when it came into its custody, and has not shown that it adopted security measures which would have effectively precluded the inference that the cargo was stolen, plaintiff's prima facie case has not been adequately rebutted, and plaintiff is therefore entitled to recover its damages.

So ordered.

Decision. The District Court ruled that the consignee was entitled to recover for the missing coffee. The carrier was not permitted to relieve itself of liability for the shortage by claiming that the weight or quantity of cargo stated on the bill of lading was the weight or count of the shipper. Further, the court held that the carrier had failed to meet its burden of proof under COGSA that it had used due care in protecting the cargo during shipment.

Comment. This case illustrates the carrier's predicament. If it refuses to put the shipper's quantity or weight on the bill of lading, it runs the risk that a consignee might refuse to purchase it. After all, the buyer wants assurance that the goods are actually in the container. Opening every container to check the shipper's count would be impracticable, costly, and contrary to maritime practice. Thus, the only practical alternative for the carrier might now be to omit all reference on the bill of lading to the shipper's quantity and to simply weigh the container on receipt and on discharge. On appeal, the Second Circuit confirmed that the carrier would have had a defense against a claim for shortage of weight if it had weighed the container at loading, listed that weight on the bill of lading, and then weighed it again at unloading and found the same weight.

The Per-Package Limitation

Imagine that you have traveled to England in search of antiques for sale in your antique store in the United States. You find many pieces from the late eighteenth century. You purchase Regency tables, writing desks, chairs, settees, decorative objects, and other smaller pieces from the George II period. You arrange with a reputable freight forwarder to have everything packaged and shipped to you in the United States. Each item is individually packaged in cardboard and then placed with other items on a wooden pallet, which in turn is wrapped with heavier cardboard and fastened with steel bands. There are 200 pieces of furniture and decorative objects on twenty-six pallets. The forwarder arranges for an ocean carrier to have a steel container delivered to your warehousing agent, where it is loaded. On delivering the container to the carrier, the forwarder receives an ocean bill of lading showing the receipt of "*1 × 40 ft. container STC [said to contain] 26 pallets antique furniture.*" The bill of lading contained no value for the goods, and the forwarder did not object, because the value appeared on other customs documentation. You return to the United States and await delivery. Unfortunately, as your container was being unloaded, it was dropped from the crane and the contents were completely destroyed. You request reimbursement from the carrier in the amount of $100,000, based on the actual value of the antiques. The carrier says that they are only responsible for $13,000 and no more, and they quote the following COGSA provision:

> Neither the carrier nor the ship shall in any event be or become liable for any loss or damage to or in connection with the transportation of goods in an amount exceeding $500 per package lawful money of the United States, or in case of goods not shipped in packages, per customary freight unit, or the equivalent of that sum in other currency, unless the nature and value of such goods have been declared by the shipper before shipment and inserted in the bill of lading. This declaration, if embodied in the bill of lading, shall be prima facie evidence, but shall not be conclusive on the carrier. [COGSA §1304 (5)]

COGSA's Per-Package Liability Limitation. COGSA requires that the shipper be given a "fair opportunity" to declare the "nature and value" of the goods and to state the quantity and description on the bill of lading. Typically, there are blank spaces in columns on the front in which to do this and a notice to the shipper in fine print on the reverse side of its right to do so. The shipper is free to declare any value up to the actual value of the goods, but a higher value may mean a higher freight rate. If no value is stated, the carrier's liability is limited to $500 "per package." The shipper can either accept the $500 per package limit on the carrier's liability in return for a lower rate or declare the higher value and pay an additional fee. In the case of "goods not shipped in packages," the $500 limit applies to a customary freight unit for goods of that type. COGSA does not define the terms "package" or "customary freight unit." One accepted definition of a "package" is that it is a "class of cargo, irrespective of size, shape or weight, to which some packaging preparation for transportation has been made which facilitates handling, but which does not necessarily conceal or completely enclose the goods." *Aluminios Pozuelo, Ltd. v. S.S. Navigator,* 407 F.2d 152 (2d Cir. 1968).

A package can be a box of merchandise, a bale of cotton, a coil of wire, a barrel of oil, or something much larger, as in the following case. *Z.K. Marine, Inc. v. M/V Archigetis* is an excellent example of what can happen to a shipper who fails to understand the significance of the "per package" limitation and who fails to declare an adequate value for its cargo on the bill of lading.

Z.K. V Arch/V Archigetis

776 F. Supp. 1549 (1991)

United States District Court (S.D. Fla.)

BACKGROUND AND FACTS

The plaintiff, Z.K. Marine, is an importer of yachts for sale in the United States. In 1987, five yachts were shipped from Taiwan to the United States aboard the MV *Archigetis*. Each yacht was shipped under a clean negotiable bill of lading. Each of the five bills of lading provided on its face that one unit only was being shipped, that the yacht was being shipped on deck at the shipper's risk, and that the value of the goods could be declared with prior notice. On the back of each bill of lading, the liability for danger or loss was limited to $500 per package or customary freight unit. All five yachts were secured by cradles and shipped on deck. During transit, one yacht was lost and the other four were damaged. The bills of lading were purchased by the plaintiffs while the yachts were in transit. The defendant claims that it is liable only in the amount of $500 per yacht.

HOEVELER, DISTRICT JUDGE

Defendants argue that pursuant to the *Carriage of Goods by Sea Act*, and the explicit provisions of the bills of lading, damages are limited to $500 per package. Because the bills of lading are clearly stamped "one unit," defendants contend that their liability is limited to $500 per yacht. Alternatively, defendants argue that if the yachts are not one package, they are each a customary freight unit—since the freight charges were based upon a customary freight unit and yacht was used as the basis of a single freight charge—and consequently subject to the $500 limitation.

Plaintiffs argue that the terms of the bills of lading should be given no effect because the consignees had no opportunity to declare a higher value for the yachts, they now argue that the carrier cannot now limit its liability. Plaintiffs urge the Court to disregard the explicit limitation because they had no chance to bargain over this clause. Alternatively, plaintiffs argue that the limitation is for $500 per package, not per yacht, and thus the limitation does not apply to this situation. * * *

First, [plaintiffs] argue that there is no opportunity to declare a higher value because the bills of lading themselves provide no space to do so. A cursory inspection of the bills of lading reveals that this is not the case, however. On the face of the bills, in capital letters, it states that the "VALUE OF GOODS MAY

continued

continued

BE DECLARED PROVIDED MERCHANT GIVES PRIOR NOTICE AND AGREES TO PAY GREATER FREIGHT AD VALOREM BASES SEE CL 18 ON BACK HEREOF." Clause 18 limits the value to $500 per package unless a higher value is declared and higher freight paid. Although there is no specific slot for the shipper to write in its higher value, there appears plenty of space on the face of the bills for it to do so, if desired. The bills plainly afford space and, by their terms, opportunity for the shipper to declare a higher value.

Plaintiffs argue in the alternative that even if the bills of lading offer the shipper opportunity to declare a higher value, the plaintiffs, as purchasers of the negotiable bills, had no such opportunity. Therefore, they argue that the limitation provisions should not be enforced. Purchasers of a negotiable bill of lading, however, purchase only those rights which the shipper had. The right to declare a higher value and pay higher freight ended when the goods were delivered on board the ship. Therefore, the purchasers of the bills cannot now complain if a higher value was not declared.

Plaintiffs' next contention is that each yacht is not a package so that the limitation to $500 per package does not apply. Plaintiffs contend that the cradles attached to the yachts for ease in transporting them do not suffice as packaging because the cradles do not enclose the yachts. Plaintiffs are mistaken in this regard. A package is some class of cargo, irrespective of size or weight, which has been prepared for transportation by the addition of some packaging that facilitates handling, but which does not necessarily enclose the goods.... In the instant case, the yachts were all transported on cradles, analogous, for purposes of the package analysis, to skids. Accordingly, this court finds that each yacht constituted a package within the purview of COGSA's liability limitation provisions. Therefore the limitation of $500 per package on the bills of lading applies to limit liability of the carrier to $500 per yacht....

Decision. The court held that each yacht constituted one customary freight unit, or "package," that the shipper had been given a fair opportunity to declare a higher value, and that the carrier's liability was limited to $500 per package. The purchasers of the bills of lading were bound by the terms of the bills of lading, including the limitation provisions.

Comment. COGSA's limitation of liability generally does not apply to goods carried above deck; however, in this case, a provision in the bill of lading stated that it would be governed by COGSA. This type of statement is known as a *clause paramount.* Thus, the court held that the COGSA package limitation applied to these yachts.

THE PER-PACKAGE LIMITATION AND CONTAINERIZED FREIGHT. The meaning of the term "package" became more complicated after the introduction of containerized freight in the 1960s. Carriers have occasionally argued that the ocean shipping container is itself the "package," which makes them liable for only $500 for the entire shipment. Steel ocean containers are 8′ wide by 20′ or 40′ long and are usually stowed one on top of the other, above deck. They are usually provided by the carrier, packed by the shipper, and transported by road or rail to the port for loading. Sometimes they are used to consolidate goods from several different shippers. They might contain thousands of different items valued at up to millions of dollars. The question of whether or not the container is a "package" under COGSA has resulted in many conflicting court opinions over the past 30 years. The most often cited case is *Mitsui & Co. v. American Export Lines,* 636 F.2d 807 (2d Cir. 1980). Armstrong had shipped 1,705 rolls of floor covering to Japan. Each roll was 6 feet long and contained 60 square yards of material wrapped around a hollow cardboard roll and wrapped in brown paper and burlap. The rolls were packed and sealed in thirteen containers at Armstrong's factory. The bill of lading stated the number of rolls and their weights and measurements, but no value. The containers were lost at sea under circumstances where the carrier was held liable. Armstrong claimed damages in excess of $350,000 for the value of the merchandise. The carrier claimed it was liable for only $6,500 ($500 × 13 containers). The court held for Armstrong, because the goods had actually been prepared for shipment in packages, using the "plain and ordinary meaning" of the term "package," and because the quantity and description of the goods on the bill of lading made it clear to the carrier that 1,705 *packages* were being shipped. The court held that the container is like a "detachable stowage compartment of the ship" and that it would not be considered the "package" unless the parties had clearly intended this meaning. That would not happen unless the quantity on the bill of lading was listed only as "*1 container*" and there was absolutely no other indication of the number of packages. Moreover, any ambiguity would be resolved in favor of the shipper.

NUMBER OF PACKAGES NOT SHOWN ON BILL OF LADING. What if the bill of lading does not show the number of packages, but only the number of individual items? *Binladen BSB Landscaping v. The Nedlloyd Rotterdam,* 759 F.2d 1006 (2d Cir. 1985) involved a shipment of potted plants to Saudi Arabia that were stuffed into a container individually, without any prior packing. The bill of lading stated, "*1 × 40 ft. reefer container, said to contain 7,790 live plants.*" The court noted that stating the number of plants was not the same thing as stating the number of packages (or customary freight units). COGSA requires that the number of packages be disclosed. If the carrier only knows the number of individual pieces in the container, without knowing the number of "packages" for which they will be liable, then they have no way of knowing their potential liability and of setting a rate for their services. The court held that if the number of packages cannot be clearly determined from the bill of lading, then the carrier is only liable for $500 per container, irrespective of the contents.

FREIGHT ON PALLETS. One other common problem deals with shipments of cartons strapped to a pallet or skid by steel bands, cardboard, or shrink-wrapping. *Tokio Marine & Fire Ins. Co., Ltd. v. Nippon Express U.S.A.* 155 F. Supp. 2d 1167 (C.D. Cal. 2000) involved a shipment of car radio components shipped in 177 cardboard cartons on thirty-three wooden pallets. Each pallet was wrapped in heavy cardboard and strapped with plastic bands, so that the cartons inside were not visible. The bill of lading showed the quantity as "*1 container STC 33 skids.*" The goods were then described as "*177 pieces, car radio components.*" The court held that each of the 33 skids, and not each of the 177 cartons, was a $500 "package." There seemed to be two reasons. First, the quantity section of the bill of lading clearly specified "33 skids." Second, the smaller cartons could not be seen through the heavy outer cardboard wrapping. The court distinguished this from other cases where the pallets were shrink-wrapped in transparent polyethylene, noting that with shrink-wrapping the carrier could plainly see the number of smaller cartons on each skid and read the markings on each.

GOOD SHIPPING PRACTICES. These cases give due warning that an export sales manager or freight forwarder may need expert advice. Goods should always be prepared and packaged for shipment in a customary and safe manner. The shipper should always be certain that the goods are correctly described, weighed, and counted and that their value is correctly stated on the bill of lading. The number of COGSA packages being shipped, based on the smallest *unit of packaging,* should be declared in the quantity section of the bill of lading (e.g., "*1 × 40 ft. container STC 1,000 cases red table wine*"). Caution should be used when declaring a quantity of goods based on individual unpacked units. For example, declaring the quantity on the bill of lading as "*1 × 40 ft. container STC 12,000 bottles red table wine*" might not give the carrier enough information on which to base its potential liability and may result in only $500 of liability for the entire container. (This outcome may vary from jurisdiction to jurisdiction.) Similarly, if the number of containers is the only thing stated, and the number of packages is not stated at all, then the container would be held to be the package. Shipping cartons fastened to pallets also require special attention.

Where the bill of lading is unclear, courts will sometimes look to other documents, such as the invoice, packing list, or government customs forms for a clarification of the packaging. These should also be consistent with the shipper's intentions. Of course, a shipper must never knowingly or fraudulently misstate the identity of cargo or its value on the bill of lading, or the carrier cannot be held liable for any damage to the goods.

Sometimes the carrier will deliver the bill of lading or amend it after loading or departure. If the shipper issues or amends a bill of lading containing a quantity or description other than what the shipper declared, the shipper should immediately complain to the carrier and have it corrected.

Liability for a Material Deviation

In the nineteenth century, steamships commonly interrupted a voyage and detoured from their customary or shortest route if presented with the opportunity to profit by loading or discharging cargo or passengers. Today, COGSA largely prevents this practice by prohibiting a carrier from deviating from its planned journey unless necessary to save lives or property at sea.

Any material deviation from the terms of the bill of lading can cause the carrier to lose any immunity or protection it may have under the act. For instance, in one case an Israeli-owned vessel was transporting clock movements through the Gulf of Mexico from Israel to Louisville, Mississippi. It was ordered to unload at Mobile and return to Israel in order to join in the war effort. The clocks were left on an unsheltered dock and were damaged. The court held that this action was a material deviation for which the carrier is liable. If the material deviation is unreasonable, the carrier becomes a virtual insurer of the cargo. When a material deviation occurs, most U.S. courts have held that the carrier cannot claim protection of the $500 per package limitation.

Most courts have also held that stowage of cargo *above deck* under a clean bill of lading without the consent of the shipper is deemed to be an unreasonable material deviation from the terms of the bill of lading. Accordingly, goods can generally not be stowed above deck, where they are exposed to the weather and seas, unless the bill of lading specifically allows it, or unless the shipper knew that it was the common practice of the carrier to stow the particular type of goods in question above deck.

Several court cases have distinguished between carrying exposed cargo above deck and stowing it in a sealed ocean container. The courts noted that transporting cargo in a sealed ocean container on the deck of a modern container ship is not an unreasonable deviation because containers stowed on deck are not necessarily subject to greater risks than containers stowed below deck (although as a practical matter, ocean containers are not entirely watertight). The courts also considered the fact that many ships and loading terminals are designed exclusively for handling containerized cargo.

Himalaya Clauses. If a carrier is relieved from liability under COGSA, such as for an error in navigation, can a plaintiff recover against the captain, crew, or other agents of the carrier? Would stevedores be responsible to the owner of cargo for damage caused by the negligent operation of a crane? In many countries, the *Hague Rules,* from which COGSA was derived, do not apply to parties other than the carrier. These countries exclude stevedores, who are generally independent contractors of the carrier. To protect these other parties, carriers include exculpatory clauses in their bills of lading extending the protection of the *Hague Rules* to their agents, employees, and independent contractors. These *Himalaya clauses,* named after a famous case, are recognized in some countries, including the United States, and are invalid in others (e.g., the United Kingdom and Canada).

The *Hamburg Rules*

In 1978, the United Nations completed drafting a new Convention on the *Carriage of Goods by Sea,* known as the *Hamburg Rules*. These rules are different from the *Hague Rules* and COGSA. They do not relieve the carrier for errors in navigation or in the management of the ship, and they make ocean carriers liable for losses resulting from negligence. They also make it easier for cargo owners to win their cases against carriers. These rules were drafted by the United Nations to serve the interests of cargo owners and shippers in developing countries that do not have large carrier fleets. The rules are also supported by shippers in other countries who believe they will reduce insurance costs. As of 2000, only twenty-five countries (mostly developing countries) had sanctioned the new rules, making them legally binding in those countries only. However, higher insurance rates for shipowners who sail to or from these countries are already being charged by international marine insurance pools. The rules are strongly opposed by carriers and insurance companies worldwide, and adoption of the *Hamburg Rules* in the United States and other oceangoing nations seems unlikely.

The *Visby Amendments*

The *Visby Amendments* are amendments to the original 1924 *Hague Rules.* They are already in effect in many countries, including the United Kingdom, Canada, most of Western Europe, Japan, Hong Kong, and Singapore. The *Visby Amendments* raise the per-package limitation of carriers to an amount based on special drawing rights of the IMF, or approximately $1,000, and make them liable for all losses resulting from the carrier's "recklessness" in the operation and navigation of the ship. The carrier is reckless if it knew or should have known that its conduct would be likely to cause damage. The *Visby Amendments* have not been adopted in the United States.

The Liability of Ocean Transportation Intermediaries

Thus far, this chapter has discussed the liability of air and ocean carriers. However, many companies that ship or receive goods internationally often use the services of intermediaries—service companies that handle the cargo, arrange transportation with air or ocean carriers, assist shippers in clearing legal hurdles in moving freight internationally, and provide many other services. These ocean transportation intermediaries include *freight forwarders* and *non-vessel operating common carriers.*

Freight Forwarders

Transporting goods over great distances and across national borders is often costly, complex, and highly susceptible to error and unexpected delays. Most exporters (as well as importers) rely on the services of a professional *freight forwarder* for assistance. *Freight forwarders* are individuals that act as agents for shippers in contracting with air, land, or sea carriers for the transportation of goods to a place of destination. These are some of the functions that forwarders provide to shippers:

- advise shippers on shipping alternatives and cost information
- contract with carriers for transportation of cargo by air, land, and sea
- obtain cargo insurance
- assist in packing, crating, and containerizing cargo
- advise on marking of packages, cartons, and pallets
- assist in consolidating smaller shipments of several different shippers into one container
- arrange warehousing of goods pending shipment or delivery
- prepare shipping and customs documents
- assist in moving goods through customs and across national borders

Many forwarders specialize in moving complex or dangerous cargo, such as explosives. Some have foreign offices and are familiar with foreign import regulations. Freight forwarders that operate in the United States are licensed and regulated by the Federal Maritime Commission and the International Air Transport Association. They must post a bond in order to ensure financial security in handling their customer's money and cargo. States and municipalities in the United States are prohibited from regulating freight forwarders. In order to act on behalf of a customer, a freight forwarder must have a written *power of attorney* form filled out by their customer and kept on file in their offices. This permits them to sign legal documents on their customer's behalf and thus helps to expedite imports and exports. When forwarders receive cargo for shipment, they issue "forwarder's receipts" or "house bills of lading" (called "consignment notes" in some countries). These do not have the same legal effect as an ocean bill of lading and are not negotiable. Most freight forwarders also act as *customs brokers.* A customs broker represents an importer by arranging for the receipt and customs clearance of shipments into a country.

The following case, *Prima U.S. Inc. v. Panalpina, Inc.,* discusses the liability of a freight forwarder for damage to cargo that occurred on the high seas.

Prima U.S. Inc. v. Panalpina, Inc.
233 F.3d 126 (2000)
United States Court of Appeals (2d Cir.)

BACKGROUND AND FACTS
Westinghouse contracted with Panalpina, a freight forwarder, to arrange for the transportation of an electric transformer from the manufacturer in Italy to 3M Corporation in Iowa. Panalpina stated to Westinghouse, "[R]est assured your shipment will receive door to door our close care and supervision...." Westinghouse paid Panalpina $21,785.00 for its services. As was the industry custom, Panalpina did not issue a bill of lading for the shipment.

continued

continued

The standard "Terms & Conditions" listed on the reverse side of its contract stated that Panalpina would use "reasonable care" in the selection of those who would actually carry or handle the goods. The terms also limited Panalpina's liability for losses to $50 per shipment and disclaimed liability for all consequential or special damages in excess of this amount. These were the same terms utilized in the prior 10-year course of dealing involving over 1,000 transactions between Westinghouse and Panalpina.

Panalpina hired an Italian customs broker to coordinate the movement of the transformer through Italy. The Italian broker hired CSM, a local stevedore, to load the transformer aboard the ship for the voyage to the United States. Panalpina never inquired of CSM how the transformer was lashed for the ocean voyage, nor did it supervise the endeavor. CSM improperly secured and lashed the transformer onto a "flat-rack" container for shipment. During the ocean voyage, the ship encountered heavy seas and the transformer broke loose, crushing a laser-cutting machine owned by Prima. Prima sued the owner of the ship, Westinghouse, and Panalpina for damages to the laser. The district court held Panalpina liable, and Panalpina appealed.

MCLAUGHLIN, CIRCUIT JUDGE

The job of a non-vessel operating common carrier ("NVOCC") is to consolidate cargo from numerous shippers into larger groups for shipment by an ocean carrier. An NVOCC—as opposed to the actual ocean carrier transporting the cargo—issues a bill of lading to each shipper. If anything happens to the goods during the voyage the NVOCC is liable to the shipper because of the bill of lading that it issued.

A freight forwarder like Panalpina, on the other hand, simply facilitates the movement of cargo to the ocean vessel. The freight forwarder secures cargo space with a steamship company, gives advice on governmental licensing requirements, proper port of exit and letter of credit intricacies, and arranges to have the cargo reach the seaboard in time to meet the designated vessel. Freight forwarders generally make arrangements for the movement of cargo at the request of clients and are vitally different from carriers, such as vessels, truckers, stevedores or warehouses, which are directly involved in transporting the cargo. Unlike a carrier, a freight forwarder does not issue a bill of lading, and is therefore not liable to a shipper for anything that occurs to the goods being shipped. As long as the freight forwarder limits its role to arranging for transportation, it will not be held liable to the shipper. Panalpina did not issue a bill of lading and it did not consolidate cargo. It was hired by Westinghouse simply as a freight forwarder to arrange for the transportation of a transformer from Italy to Iowa. By analogy, Panalpina was hired to act as a "travel agent" for the transformer: it set things up and made reservations, but did not engage in any hands-on heavy lifting. Admittedly, Panalpina did state that Westinghouse's "shipment [would] receive door to door our close care and supervision ...." However, because of the well settled legal distinction between forwarders and carriers, that statement—mere puffing—cannot transform Panalpina into a carrier, and bestow liability upon it.

Panalpina hired CSM as a stevedore to load and lash the transformer. CSM was the same stevedore that was used by United Arab Shipping, and was the designated official Port of Genoa stevedore. Panalpina clearly acted reasonably in hiring CSM on behalf of Westinghouse, fulfilling its duties as a freight forwarder. Panalpina is not liable to Westinghouse for CSM's negligent actions.

Decision. Judgment reversed for Panalpina. Panalpina was a freight forwarder hired by Westinghouse to arrange for transportation and other services. It was not a carrier and was not liable for the cargo during shipment. Freight forwarders must use due diligence and reasonable care in performing their functions. Panalpina was reasonable in its selection of CSM as stevedore to load the ship.

Non-Vessel Operating Common Carriers

Most international cargo today moves by containerized freight. Shippers who can fill an entire ocean container with goods can receive more favorable shipping rates than those shippers who must move smaller amounts of cargo without a container (a practice known as *break-bulk freight*). *Non-vessel operating common carriers* (commonly referred to as NVOCCs) act as freight consolidators for smaller shippers, permitting them to take advantage of lower freight rates. NVOCCs combine the cargo of several small shippers into one container and book space with an ocean carrier at a lower rate. An NVOCC is a common carrier that functions like an ocean carrier but does not operate the vessels by which transportation is provided. It issues bills of lading and assumes liability for goods due to loss or damage during transport. It also performs many of the same services as a freight forwarder.

The *Ocean Shipping Reform Act of 1998*

Ocean carriers, freight forwarders, and NVOCCs are regulated by the *Ocean Shipping Reform Act of 1998* (OSRA). OSRA represents an attempt by the U.S. Congress to bring sweeping reform to ocean shipping regulation. OSRA amends the *Shipping Act of 1984* by allowing carriers greater flexibility in contracting with shippers and establishing shipping rates.

Prior to OSRA, carriers could only charge their publicly posted freight "tariff" rates and had to offer the same rates to all "similar" carriers. OSRA now permits carriers and shippers to enter confidential "service contracts," with negotiated freight rates and terms. Thus, large shippers, or associations of several shippers, gain lower rates on volume cargo and preferred cargo space. These service contracts serve as a contract of carriage, and so no bill of lading need be issued.

Because these agreements are considered private contracts (with no bill of lading) and the carriers are not acting as "common carriers," they are not subject to COGSA. Instead, the parties are free to negotiate their own liability terms. Exclusive agreements by a shipper to use one carrier in return for reduced rates are no longer illegal. OSRA provides that ocean carriers are not subject to the antitrust laws. Freight rates for regular common carriage need no longer be filed with the Federal Maritime Commission, but may be made publicly available, for instance, on a carrier's Web site. The carriers must treat freight forwarders and NVOCCs, called "Ocean Transportation Intermediaries" in OSRA, just as they would treat shippers under the law.

Carriers may not unreasonably or unjustly refuse to deal or negotiate with shippers and ocean transportation intermediaries. With regard to shipments based on a published tariff under a bill of lading (as opposed to the "service contracts" discussed previously), carriers may not unjustly discriminate against any shipper or ocean transportation intermediary in terms of rates, cargo accommodations, or other services. No person may willfully engage in false billing, false weighing, or otherwise attempt to unjustly obtain a lower freight rate. Civil penalties for violations of OSRA may be as high as $5,000 per day for each violation, unless the violation was willfully and knowingly committed, in which case the penalty may be up to $25,000 per violation.

Marine Cargo Insurance

As is evident from the foregoing discussions, the insuring of cargo is an essential element of international trade. The potential for damage and loss to goods, particularly during ocean shipments, which are lengthier and more hazardous than air shipments, is tremendous. The last chapter demonstrated how the risk of loss can be allocated between buyer and seller, often through the use of trade terms. If loss does occur, the party bearing the risk (perhaps the holder of the bill of lading) will surely seek to shift its financial burden to an insurer. Sellers, buyers, and even banks that finance international sales want to be certain that their interest in the goods is fully insured. If not, the property risks will prove unacceptably high.

Marine Insurance Policies and Certificates

Although policies of insurance are issued to cover individual shipments, many shippers who do large volumes of business overseas maintain *open cargo policies*. An open policy offers the convenience and protection of covering all shipments by the shipper of certain types of goods to certain destinations and over specified routes. With an open policy in effect, the exporter is authorized by the insurance company to issue a certificate of insurance on a form provided by the company. Open cargo policies are often used by exporters shipping on CIF terms. These certificates are negotiable and are transferred along with the bill of lading to the party who purchases and takes title to the goods. The type or form of the certificate is determined by the contract between the parties or by the requirements of the bank that is providing financing for the sale. The insurance company must be notified as soon as possible after shipment under an open policy.

When a sales contract calls for the seller to obtain a marine insurance policy or certificate on behalf of the buyer, the certificate is universally understood to be acceptable. When the parties state only that a contract is CIF, however, and make no reference to insurance, some confusion can arise as to whether a certificate will be accepted.

The English view is that a certificate of insurance will not substitute for an insurance policy. In the 1924 case, *Kunglig Jarnvagsstyrelsen v. Dexter & Carpenter, Inc.*, 299 F. 991 (S.D.N.Y. 1924), a U.S. court rejected the English view. The court based its argument on the fact that insurance certificates are so widely recognized in commerce that they should be recognized in the law. This rule has been incorporated into the UCC.

General Average and FPA Losses

Marine insurance policies cover several different types of loss: (1) total losses of all or part of a shipment, (2) general average losses, and (3) partial or particular average losses.

The term *average* in marine insurance law means loss. A *general average* is a loss that results when extraordinary expenses or losses are incurred in saving the vessel or its cargo from danger at sea. This ancient principle of maritime law, which was developed long before insurance was available, spreads the risk of a disaster at sea by making all parties to the voyage contribute to any loss incurred. Under this rule, if A's cargo is damaged or "sacrificed" in the process of saving the ship, and B's cargo is saved as a result, B or its insurer must contribute to A for the loss. A's claim is a general average. In other words, the owner of the cargo that was sacrificed would have a general average claim for contribution against the owner of the cargo that was saved. For example, when fire threatens an entire ship and certain cargo is damaged by water in putting the fire out, the owners of all of the cargo must contribute to the loss of the cargo that was damaged by the water. The owners of cargo that is thrown overboard to save a sinking ship may have a claim against those whose cargo was thereby saved. General average claims are typically covered by marine insurance.

In order to prove a general average claim, the claimant must show that (1) the ship, cargo, and crew were threatened by a common danger; (2) the danger was real and substantial (the older cases required that the danger also be "imminent"); and (3) either the cargo or ship was voluntarily sacrificed for the benefit of both or extraordinary expenses were incurred to avert a common peril.

THE *YORK-ANTWERP* RULES. The *York-Antwerp Rules* are a set of standardized rules on general average. An effort to develop commonly accepted principles of general average began in England as early as 1860, with work on the rules being completed in 1890. Following World War II, an international effort to achieve universally accepted general average rules resulted in the revised *York-Antwerp Rules* of 1950. The rules have achieved widespread acceptance by the maritime industry; the latest version was agreed to in 1994. The rules are not the subject of treaty or convention and have not been enacted into national laws. They traditionally have become a part of the contract of carriage because their provisions are generally incorporated into all modern bills of lading.

GENERAL AVERAGE CLAIMS BY THE CARRIER. Surprisingly enough, ocean carriers can bring general average claims against the owners of cargo. The principles of general average apply when a carrier incurs extraordinary expenses in rescuing, saving, or repairing an endangered ship.

The results of general average law must have been quite surprising to the plaintiff in *Amerada Hess Corp. v. S/T Mobil Apex*, 602 F.2d 1095 (2d Cir. 1979). Plaintiff shipped gasoline and naphtha. When the cargo was destroyed by an explosion and fire that had been started by sparks from machinery in the engine room, the plaintiff sued the carrier for damages. The carrier counterclaimed for general average losses. The court denied recovery to the cargo owner under COGSA, holding that the carrier was not liable for the fuel because the ship was not unseaworthy. The court then held, much to the chagrin of the plaintiff, that it was actually liable to the carrier for towing and salvage expenses incurred in arresting the fire and saving the ship.

Real and Substantial Danger. Historically, the courts have allowed a general average claim only where the loss occurred as a result of the ship being in imminent peril. Today, that concept has been broadened to include instances of *real and substantial danger*. In *Eagle Terminal Tankers, Inc. v. Insurance Co. of USSR*, 637 F.2d 890 (2d Cir. 1981), the ship had traveled for more than a day with a damaged propeller. It dry-docked, unloaded the cargo, had the damage repaired at a cost of $127,000 (which included the crew's expenses during that time), reloaded, and completed its voyage to Leningrad. The court awarded the carrier the general average claim. It noted that "a ship's master should not be discouraged from taking timely action to avert a disaster," and need not be in actual peril to claim general average.

Particular Average Losses

Although total and general average losses are ordinarily covered up to the policy amount, special problems result from partial or particular average losses. A *particular average loss* is a partial loss to the insured's cargo. Many insurance policies limit the insurer's liability for particular average losses. Because many losses only partially damage the cargo, a shipper must understand the particular average terms of the policy. A policy designed *free of particular average (FPA)* will not cover any partial losses. A policy FPA, followed by certain specified losses, will not pay for any partial or particular average losses of that nature. As such, an "FPA fire" policy will not pay for partial losses to the cargo due to fire.

Types of Coverage

Marine cargo insurance is available for virtually any type of risk, for any cargo, destined for almost any port (see Exhibit 6.3). The only limitations are the willingness of the insurer to undertake the risk and the price. The types of risk covered in a policy are described in the perils clause.

The Perils Clause. The *perils clause* covers the basic risks of an ocean voyage. It generally covers extraordinary and unusual perils that are not expected during a voyage. Examples of perils that are included are bad weather sufficient to overcome a seaworthy vessel, shipwreck, stranding, collision, and hitting rocks or floating objects. (An example of a perils clause follows in the next case.) However, not every event that can damage goods is covered by this clause. Damage due to the unseaworthiness of the vessel is not included in a perils clause; neither is loss from explosion or pilferage, and the clause only covers losses while at sea. Moreover, only *fortuitous losses* are covered. Fortuitous is a concept that runs throughout insurance law. It means that the loss occurred by chance or accident and could not have reasonably have been predicted. For example, damage due to predictable winds or waves are generally *not* held to be fortuitous. Thus, if a ship sinks in calm seas and good weather, it is presumed that the loss was caused by the ship's own unseaworthiness. Only if it is proven that the ship was seaworthy can it then be shown that the loss was due to a fortuitous event. Courts have held that damage from seawater due to improper stowage of goods is not fortuitous.

A shipper who desires additional coverage can purchase it from the insurer at an added charge. This is called a *specially to cover clause.* For instance, damage resulting from explosion is not generally covered in a standard perils clause, but insurance to cover it can be obtained in the form of an explosion clause. Similarly, additional coverage can be purchased to protect against the risks of freshwater damage, moisture damage, and rust or contamination of the cargo from chemicals, oil, or fuel. Many insurers have recently offered specially designed import–export insurance packages for shippers of perishable foodstuffs, tobacco, steel, and other products and commodities.

The *Shaver* case discusses a standard perils clause and several additional types of coverage purchased by the insured. Unfortunately, none of them covered the loss that the plaintiffs had incurred.

All Risks Coverage. An *all risks policy* covers all risks except those specifically excluded in the policy. These policies usually exclude damage from acts of war through a "free of capture and

Exhibit 6.3

Marine Cargo Insurance Policy

CHUBB GROUP
of Insurance Companies
100 William Street, New York, N.Y. 10038

CHUBB

CARGO POLICY OF INSURANCE

Issued by the stock insurance company shown below
FEDERAL INSURANCE COMPANY
Incorporated under the Laws of New Jersey

$ Number

Open Policy No.
In consideration of a premium as agreed, the Company **Does insure (lost or not lost)**
to the amount of Dollars,
on
valued at to be shipped on board of the B/L Date
at and from
to
and it is hereby understood and agreed, that in case of loss, such loss is payable to the order of on surrender of this Policy.

(continued)

Touching the Adventures and Perils which said Assurers are contented to bear, and take upon themselves, in this Voyage, they are of the Seas, Fires, Assailing Thieves, Jettisons, Barratry of the Master and Mariners, and all other like Perils, Losses and Misfortunes that have or shall come to the Hurt, Detriment or Damage of the said Goods and Merchandise, or any part thereof except as may be otherwise provided for herein or endorsed hereon. AND in case of any Loss or Misfortune, it shall be lawful and necessary to and for the Assured, his or their Factors, Servants and Assigns, to sue, labor and travel for, in and about the Defense, Safeguard and Recovery of the said Goods and Merchandise, or any part thereof, without Prejudice to this insurance; nor shall the acts of the Assured or Assurers, in recovering, saving and preserving the property insured, in case of disaster, be considered a waiver or an acceptance of an abandonment; to the charges whereof, the said Assurers will contribute according to the rate and quantity of the sum hereby insured.

In case of loss, such loss to be paid in thirty days after proof of loss and proof of interest in the property hereby insured.

In case the interest hereby insured is covered by other insurance (except as hereinafter provided) the loss shall be collectedfrom the several policies in the order of the date of their attachment, insurance attaching on the same date to be deemed simultaneous and to contribute pro rata; provided, however, that where any fire insurance, or any insurance (including fire) taken out by any carrier or bailee is available to the beneficiary of this policy, or would be so available if this insurance did not exist, then this insurance shall be void to the extent that such other insurance is or would have been available. It is agreed, nevertheless, that where these Assurers are thus relieved of liability because of the existence of other insurance, these Assurers shall receive and retain the premium payable under this policy and, in consideration thereof, shall guarantee the solvency of the companies and/or underwriters this clause, but not exceeding, in any case, the amount which would have been collectible under this policy if such other insurance did not exist.

In all cases of damage caused by perils insured against, the loss shall, as far as practicable, be ascertained by a separation and a sale or appraisement of a damaged portion only of the contents if the packages so damaged and not otherwise.

Losses arising from breakage and/or leakage and/or loss of weight and/or loss of contents are excluded from this insurance unless caused by stranding or collision with another vessel, or unless this insurance has been expressly extended to include such losses.

Warranted free from Particular Average unless the vessel or craft be stranded, sunk or burnt, but notwithstanding this warranty these Assurers are to pay any loss of or damage to the interest insured which may reasonably be attributed to fire, collision or contact of the vessel and/or conveyance with any external substance (ice included) other than water, or to discharge of cargo at port of distress. The foregoing warranty, however, shall not apply where broader terms of average are provided for herein or by endorsement hereon.

If the voyage aforesaid shall have been terminated before the date of this policy, then there shall be no return of premium on account of such termination of the voyage.

Wherever the words "ship", "vessel", "seaworthiness", "ship or vessel owner" appear in this Policy, they are deemed to include also the words "aircraft", "airworthiness", "aircraft owner".

THIS INSURANCE IS SUBJECT TO THE AMERICAN INSTITUTE CARGO CLAUSES (FEB. 1949) (INCLUDING THE WAREHOUSE TO WAREHOUSE CLAUSE), SOUTH AMERICAN 60 DAY CLAUSE WHEN APPLICABLE. ALSO SUBJECT TO THE AMENDED F. C. & S. AND S. R. & C. C. WARRANTIES (OCT. 1959) (*SEE REVERSE*)

(continued)

EXHIBIT 6.3

Marine Cargo Insurance Policy—(*continued*)

Original and Duplicative issued, one of which being accomplished the other to stand null and void

SPECIAL CONDITIONS	**Marks and Numbers**
ON DECK—Merchandise and/or goods shipped on deck to an On Deck Bill of Lading *which must be so specified in this policy* are insured.—Free of particular average unless caused by the vessel being stranded, sunk, burnt, on fire, or in collision, but including jettison and/or washing overboard, irrespective of percentage.	

Where the words "including M. E. C." are typed in the space below at the time the policy is issued, this insurance is subject to the American Institute Marine Extension Clauses.

Where the words "including Strike Risks" are typed in the space below at the time the policy is issued, this insurance is subject to the Current American Institute S. R. & C. C. Clauses.

Where the words "including War Risk" are typed in the space below at the time the policy is issued, this insurance is subject to the Current War Risk Clauses.

In Witness Whereof, the Company issuing this policy has caused this policy to be signed by its authorized officers, but this policy shall not be valid unless signed by a duly authorized representative of the Company.

FEDERAL INSURANCE COMPANY

Date: *Henry G Gubel* Secretary *Henry L. Harlon* President ____________ Authorized Representative

The following Warranties shall be paramount and shall not be modified or superseded by any other provision included herein or stamped or endorsed hereon unless such other provision refers specifically to the risks excluded by these warranties and expressly assumes the said risks.

(A) "Notwithstanding anything herein contained to the contrary, this insurance is warranted free from capture, seizure, arrest, restraint, detainment, confiscation, preemption, requisition or nationalization, and the consequences thereof or any attempt thereat, whether in time of peace or war and whether lawful or otherwise; also warranted free, whether in time of peace or war, from all loss, damage or expense caused by any weapon of war employing atomic or nuclear fission and/or fusion or other reaction or radioactive force or matter or by any mine or torpedo, also warranted free from all consequences of hostilities or warlike operations (whether there be a declaration of war or not), but this warranty shall not exclude collision or contact with aircraft, rockets or similar missiles or with any fixed or floating object (other than a mine or torpedo), stranding heavy weather, fire or explosion unless caused directly (and independently of the nature of the voyage or service which the vessel concerned or, in the case of a collision, any other vessel involved therein, is performing) by a hostile act by or against a belligerent power; and for the purposes of this warranty 'power' includes any authority maintaining naval, military or air forces in association with a power.

Further warranted free from the consequences of civil war, revolution, rebellion, insurrection, or civil strife arising therefrom, or piracy."

(B) Warranted free of loss or damage caused by or resulting from strikes, lockouts, labor disturbances, riots, civil commotions or the acts of any person or persons taking part in any such occurrence or disorder.

NOTE: It is necessary for the assured to give prompt notice to these Assurers when they become aware of an event for which they are "held covered" under this policy and the right to such cover is dependent on compliance with this obligation.

SOURCE: Sample policy provided courtesy of Chubb Group of Insurance Companies.

Shaver Transportation Co. v. The Travelers Indemnity Co.

481 F. Supp. 892 (1979)

United States District Court (D. Or.)

BACKGROUND AND FACTS

Shaver, a barge company, contracted with Weyerhauser, as shipper, to transport caustic soda to a buyer. Shaver arranged for marine cargo insurance with Travelers. Several different types of coverage were discussed. Shaver decided on "free from particular average" and "standard perils" provisions, supplemented with "specially to cover" clauses. Shaver loaded the first shipment of caustic soda on one of its barges and transported it to the buyer. The buyer refused delivery because it had been contaminated with tallow. The contamination occurred as Shaver was loading the caustic soda aboard the barge. The barge had previously carried a load of tallow, and Shaver had not thoroughly cleaned the barge input lines. The barge was returned to Shaver's dock. Shaver and Weyerhauser filed a claim with Travelers. Travelers argued that the contamination did not represent a recoverable loss under the policy. Shaver and Weyerhauser brought this action against Travelers.

SKOPIL, CIRCUIT JUDGE, SITTING BY DESIGNATION

Although the plaintiffs request recovery under several theories, there is only one major issue in the case: Are the losses incurred by the plaintiffs the consequences of an insured event under the marine cargo insurance policy? If the losses are not insured against, no recovery is possible.

RECOVERY UNDER THE PERILS CLAUSE AND FREE FROM PARTICULAR AVERAGE CLAUSE

The perils clause, almost identical to ancient perils provisions dating back several hundred years, defines the risks protected by the policy. In addition to a long list of "perils of the sea," the clause concludes with "and all other perils, losses, and misfortunes, that have, or shall, come to the hurt, detriment, or damage to the said goods and merchandise." Plaintiff argues that the "forced" disposition of the caustic soda was like jettison (an enumerated peril) and is covered by the concluding language of the clause. That language has been interpreted to include only perils that are similar to the enumerated perils.

Whether or not I conclude the forced disposition was a type of jettison, plaintiffs are unable to show an insurable loss due to jettison. The loss contamination of the cargo occurred at the time of loading.... [P]laintiffs cannot recover under the perils clause of the policy. The term "jettison" also appears in the Free from Particular Average clause. If jettison did occur, this clause affords coverage regardless of the amount of cargo damage. However, I find that a jettison did not occur in this instance. Jettison is the act of throwing overboard from a vessel a part of the cargo, in case of extreme danger, to lighten the ship. The orderly unloading and sale of the cargo to a chemical salvage company is not "jettison." Plaintiff cannot recover under the Free from Particular Average clause.

RECOVERY UNDER THE ... SHORE COVERAGE CLAUSE

The shore coverage clause provides coverage for enumerated risks occurring on shore. Plaintiffs argue that contamination while loading is a shore accident. However, since the contamination occurred within the barge's intake lines, the incident arose "on board." Therefore shore coverage does not apply. Even if it were to apply, contamination of cargo is not within the enumerated risks covered by the shore coverage clause....

RECOVERY UNDER THE INCHMAREE CLAUSE

The purpose of the Inchmaree clause is to expand the coverage of the policy beyond the perils provision. Federal law allows a vessel owner to become exempt from liability for fault or error in navigation or management of the ship. In contrast, the shipowner must retain liability for negligence in the care and custody of the cargo. The Inchmaree clause is intended to provide coverage to a cargo owner when a loss is due to error in navigation or management of the vessel since the carrier is exempt from liability. Plaintiffs argue the contamination was the result of an error in management and therefore covered under the Inchmaree clause. Defendant naturally urges the court to find the loss caused by fault in the care and custody of the cargo.

The United States Supreme Court has addressed the distinction between error in management and error in

continued

continued

care of cargo but has not articulated a clear test. The Ninth Circuit, noting that no precise definitions exist, advocates a case-by-case determination using the following test: "If the act in question has the primary purpose of affecting the ship, it is 'in navigation or in management;' but if the primary purpose is to affect the cargo, it is not 'in navigation or in management.'" *Grace Line, Inc. v. Todd Shipyards Corporation,* 500 F.2d 361, 374 (9th Cir. 1974).

Using this test, I find that the contamination of the cargo in this case was caused by fault in the care, custody, and control of the cargo. The Inchmaree clause will not provide coverage for plaintiffs' losses under the facts of this case.

RECOVERY UNDER NEGLIGENCE CLAUSE

The Negligence clause provides coverage against losses due to enumerated perils caused by the unseaworthiness of the vessel.... This unseaworthiness must then cause a loss through one of the enumerated perils: "sinking, stranding, fire, explosion, contact with seawater, or by any other cause of the nature of any of the risks assumed in the policy." ...

Since contamination is not an enumerated peril, plaintiff urges coverage ... by suggesting the barge was in imminent danger of sinking. Although there is evidence that the caustic soda would have eventually corroded through the barge and caused it to sink, the process would have taken three to five years. This possibility is too far removed to find coverage under a provision providing for loss due to sinking. No recovery is possible under the Negligence clause of this policy....

Plaintiffs suggest a number of theories of recovery under the marine cargo insurance policy. None is suited to this case. I am aided in my construction of this policy by one additional fact. Shaver rejected insurance coverage costing more but did not believe contamination was covered under the policy. Plaintiffs' present attempt to include this type of loss within the coverage of the policy is an afterthought.

Judgment shall be entered for the defendant.

Decision. The plaintiffs' loss due to contamination was not covered under any of the clauses of the insurance policy.

Comment. The following clauses were at issue in this case.

THE PERILS CLAUSE

"Touching the adventures and perils which the said Assurers are contended to bear, and take upon themselves, they are of the seas and inland waters, man of war, fires, enemies, pirates, rovers, assailing thieves, jettisons, letters of mart and countermart, reprisals, taking at sea, arrests, restraints and detainments of all kings, princes of people of what nation, condition or quality soever, barratry of the master and mariners, and all other perils, losses, and misfortunes, that have or shall come to the hurt, detriment, or damage to the said goods and merchandise, or any part thereof."

THE SHORE CLAUSE

"Including while on docks, wharves, or elsewhere on shore and/or during land transportation, risks of collision, derailment, fire, lightning, sprinkler leakage, cyclones, hurricanes, earthquakes, floods, the rising of navigable waters, or any accident to the conveyance and/or collapse and/or subsidence of docks and/or structures, and to pay loss or damage caused thereby, even though the insurance be otherwise FPA."

THE INCHMAREE CLAUSE (NAMED AFTER A FAMOUS BRITISH CASE)

"This insurance is also specially to cover any loss of or damage to the interest insured hereunder, through the bursting of boilers, breakage of shafts, or through any latent defect in the machinery, hull, or appurtenances, or from faults or errors in the navigation and/ or management of the vessel by the Master, Mariners, Mates, Engineers, or Pilots; provided, however, that this clause shall not be construed as covering loss arising out of delay, deterioration, or loss of market, unless otherwise provided elsewhere herein."

THE NEGLIGENCE CLAUSE

"... [T]he Assurers agree that in the event unseaworthiness or a wrongful act or misconduct of shipowner, character, their agents or servants, shall, directly or indirectly, cause loss or damage to the cargo insured by sinking, stranding, fire, explosion, contact with seawater, or by any other cause of the nature of any of the risks assumed in the policy, the Assurers will [subject to the terms of average and other conditions of the policy] pay to an innocent Assured the resulting loss."

seizure" clause, damage or loss from delay in reaching the destination, and damage resulting from strikes and civil commotion. Coverage for strikes is available, but only at additional cost.

War Risk. Typically, marine insurance policies do not cover the risks of war. *War risk insurance* is available for ocean shipments. If war risk insurance is desired, the shipper must purchase it separately from the insurer. Under CIF terms, the seller is not expected to provide war risk insurance. If the buyer wants war risk coverage, it will have to agree on the price separately from the marine insurance provisions. The rates for war risk insurance are relatively stable in peacetime, but fluctuate almost daily in times of war.

Conclusion

This chapter began by discussing the liability of air carriers for the death or injury of passengers, for damage to baggage or cargo, and for flight delays affecting international travel and shipments. Airline-related litigation is very common. Some cases involve individual claims for single incidents. Others involve highly publicized major air disasters. Critics of the American legal system are quick to point out that airline litigation is a big business with American law firms and that much of it is frivolous and unnecessary. On the other hand, it would be nearly impossible for victims of air disasters to seek recovery without the benefit of experienced aviation lawyers because of the complexity of aviation law and the technical and engineering knowledge required to handle these cases.

To put that in perspective, according to the U.S. Bureau of Transportation Statistics, in 2006 745 million passengers departed on 10.5 million flights for a total of 797.4 billion miles (one paying passenger carried one mile) in combined scheduled domestic and international travel on U.S. carriers. According to the International Air Transport Association, considering worldwide statistics, 2006 was the safest year on record for air travel. On average, there was only one accident for every 1.5 million flights worldwide.

Air freight, both domestic and international, is the fastest growing method of cargo transportation. Although only a small fraction of goods by weight moves by air, it accounts for much higher percentage when measured by value. This is due to shipments of higher-value goods and perishables and increased package delivery.

The overwhelming portion of the world's trade in goods, over 90 percent, moves on the water. The year 2006 marked the fiftieth anniversary of the beginning of containerized ocean freight. In 1956 the first containers were loaded atop a converted tanker, the *Ideal X*, at the Port of Newark, bound for Houston. They were no more than truck trailer bodies, with the wheels and running gear removed. There were 56 trailers on the *Ideal X*. The largest container ships now carry 5,000 ocean containers or more, and they are getting larger. There are several million ocean containers in transit at any given time. No one knows for sure the number of containers lost at sea each year, or their value. Although it is a relatively small percentage of total ocean freight, by all estimates, it runs into the tens of thousands of containers and billions of dollars annually. There is perhaps no other single area of international business that has engendered as much litigation as ocean cargo losses. It is incumbent on anyone shipping goods to understand the risks involved and what can be done in advance to protect against them.

Chapter Summary

1. The 1999 *Montreal Convention* (MC) is the most important change in air transportation law since 1929. It replaces the *Warsaw Convention* in those countries that ratify it.
2. The MC makes the carrier strictly liable for the death or injury of a passenger ticketed for international travel, or for damages to baggage or cargo, up to an amount equal to 100,000 Special Drawing Rights. In addition, the carrier is liable for all proven damages above that unless the carrier can show that it or its employees were not at fault.
3. The MC does not apply to passengers ticketed solely for domestic travel. It applies only where the place of departure and the place of destination shown on the ticket are situated within the territories of two states parties to the MC or are situated within the territory of one state party to the Convention and there is an agreed stopping place within the territory of another state. Travel on a domestic flight is

included, if it is a part of one continuous international journey.

4. If the MC applies, then it provides the exclusive cause of action against air carriers. Suits may not be brought under state or local law.
5. An air carrier is liable for damage sustained in case of death or bodily injury of a passenger only if the accident that caused the death or injury took place on board the aircraft or in the course of any of the operations of embarking or disembarking. An "accident" is an unexpected or unusual event or happening that is external to the passenger. It is not an accident if death or injury is caused by the passenger's own internal reaction to the usual, normal, and expected operation of the aircraft.
6. The carrier is not liable to the extent that the passenger's own negligence contributed to the accident or to his or her loss. Injuries for mental harm or emotional distress are only permitted if they were caused by a bodily injury. Punitive damages are not permitted under the MC.
7. In most nations of the world, the liability of a carrier for damage or loss to oceangoing goods is governed by the *Hague Rules,* adopted in the United States as the *Carriage of Goods by Sea Act* (COGSA).
8. COGSA provides many limitations on the liability of shipowners. The carrier's primary obligation is to use due diligence to provide a seaworthy ship at the beginning of the voyage. A vessel is *seaworthy* if it is reasonably fit to carry the cargo it has undertaken to carry on the intended journey. Carriers are generally not liable for damage to cargo resulting from errors in navigation, mismanagement of the ship, acts of god, acts of war or public enemies, labor strikes, damage resulting from saving lives at sea, inherent defects in the goods, or perils of the sea. Liability for damage due to fire aboard ship is limited to fires caused by the actual fault of the ship's owner.
9. In the United States, COGSA also provides that carriers are not liable in amounts in excess of $500 "per package" or "customary freight unit" unless the shipper has indicated a higher amount on the bill of lading. If the number of "packages" can be clearly determined from the bill of lading, and if those packages involved some preparation of the cargo that facilitated handling during transportation, then the $500 per package limitation applies to each package and not to the number of ocean containers.
10. Maritime and marine insurance law is a complicated and specialized area of the law, with concepts dating back to the days of the ancient mariners. Under the law of general average, a carrier can assert a general average claim against the owners of cargo demanding that they (or their insurers) contribute to expenses incurred in saving a vessel from a common peril on the seas.

Questions and Case Problems

1. In 2004, Ellen Kruger was boarding a flight from San Francisco to Seattle, on her way home from Australia, when she was struck on the head with a backpack swung by another passenger. During the flight she became ill, vomited, and remained unconscious for much of the flight. She sued the airline for pain and suffering, emotional distress, and punitive damages. Her husband also sued for loss of consortium and companionship of his wife. United Airlines argued that these were not compensable damages under the *Montreal Convention.* Does the *Montreal Convention* specify what types of damages are recoverable or whether the husband may bring an action? How is this decided? *Kruger v. United Airlines, Inc.* 481 F. Supp. 2d 1005 (N.D. Cal. 2007.) How would this case be decided if the injuries were the result of the aircraft plunging into the middle of the Pacific Ocean?
2. Fishman shipped a container of boys' pants on a ship owned by Tropical. The container was lost at sea due to improper storage. The pants were packed into bundles of twelve each and placed into what was known in the industry as a "big pack." A "big pack" is similar to a 4′ × 4′ pallet, partially enclosed in corrugated cardboard, with a base and cover made of plastic. The bill of lading stated, "*1 × 40 ft. [container] STC [said to contain] 39 Big Pack Containing 27,908 units boy's pants.*" Fishman maintains that carrier is liable for an amount up to $500 for each of the 2,325 bundles. If the carrier is liable for up to $500 per "package," what is the limit of the carrier's liability?

Fishman & Tobin, Inc. v. Tropical Shipping & Const. Co., Ltd., 240 F.3d 956 (11th Cir. 2001).

3. Sony Corp. packed a shipment of videocassette tapes into a 40-foot ocean container for transport to England. Sony put the tapes into 1,320 cardboard cartons, then strapped the cartons onto fifty-two wooden pallets. The pallets were put into one shipment container. The bill of lading stated "1 × 40 ft. container: 1,320 ctns. magnetic tape." The value of the tapes shown on the export certificate was $400,000. On loading, the ship's deck crane dropped the container 60 feet to a concrete deck. Sony claims it can recover the value of the tapes. The ship maintains that under COGSA its liability is limited to fifty-two pallets. How many "packages" were involved here and what do you think should be the outcome? *Sony Magnetic Products Inc. of America v. Merivienti O/Y*, 863 F.2d 1537 (11th Cir. 1989).
4. A shipper of fruits and vegetables delivered a refrigerated van of produce to the S.S. *Bayomon* at the port of Elizabeth, New Jersey, on September 22 for shipment to San Juan, Puerto Rico. The ship was supposed to sail that day but was unable to do so because of repairs needed to correct a boiler problem. The ship sailed on September 25 and arrived in Puerto Rico on September 27. A clause paramount incorporated COGSA into the bill of lading. Upon arrival in Puerto Rico, part of the produce was found to be rotten. The shipper claims that the carrier is liable because the ship was not "seaworthy." COGSA states that the carrier shall not be liable unless it shows a failure to make the ship seaworthy before and at the beginning of the voyage. Does COGSA apply here, considering that the port is domestic rather than foreign? Is the carrier liable for an unseaworthy vessel? What is the outcome? *Squillante & Zimmerman Sales, Inc. v. Puerto Rico Marine Management, Inc.*, 516 F. Supp. 1049 (D. Puerto Rico 1981).
5. Dazo entered the San Jose, California, airport to board a flight to St. Louis, where she was to take a connecting flight to Toronto. At the security checkpoint, then operated by Globe Airport Security Services, she placed her bag on the X-ray machine's conveyor belt. After proceeding through the metal detector, she discovered that her bag had been stolen. She sued Globe and the air carrier for $100,000 worth of jewelry in the bag. The trial court dismissed her suit and she appealed. Was the decision affirmed or reversed on appeal? For the purposes of the *Warsaw* or *Montreal Conventions*, was this an international or domestic flight? Did the theft of the bag occur "during the transportation by air"? If the *Warsaw Convention* caps the limit of liability of an air carrier, does it also cap the liability of Globe? Do you think that Globe is an "agent" of the air carrier? If so, how would this be different now that airport security is handled by the U.S. Transportation Security Administration? What about other types of air carrier agents? *Dazo v. Globe Airport Security Services*, 268 F.3d 671 (9th Cir. 2001).

Managerial Implications

1. Reconsider the hypothetical case presented earlier in this chapter involving English antiques shipped to the United States. Do you think that the $500 per package limitation applies to the container, to each wooden skid, or to each of the individually wrapped pieces of furniture or objects fastened onto the skid? What could have been done differently, if anything, to have avoided the confusion and problems in this case? Discuss the ramifications of this case.
2. You are CEO of a firm that regularly imports consumer electronic devices from plants in Thailand, Malaysia, Indonesia, and the Philippines. They are shipped to you by ocean carrier through the South China Sea. They are sold in the United States and exported to ports in Europe and the Middle East. What kind of information do you need in assessing the risk potential to your cargo passing through these dangerous waters? What will the sources of your information be? What sources are available in your library? Which are commercially available? If part of your job is to keep abreast of developments on a daily basis, where will you obtain that information? What types of information might be available from freight forwarders, steamship companies, local port authorities, and insurers?

For Internet Activities, Visit academic.cengage.com/blaw/schaffer.

CHAPTER 7
Bank Collections, Trade Finance, and Letters of Credit

The previous chapters discussed contracts for the sale of goods, documentary sales, the risk of loss, and the liability of air and sea carriers. This chapter now turns to how the international banking system is used to move money in an international trade transaction. We will see how sellers collect for their shipments and how buyers remit payments for their purchases. We will also learn how sellers are assured of payment for their goods or services through the use of bank letters of credit and will briefly discuss some issues related to financing the sale. Keep in mind that most of the concepts covered here do not just apply to collecting money for the sale of goods but are equally applicable to many different types of international transactions involving the movement of money internationally and the use of banks to provide an assurance of contractual commitments.

The Bill of Exchange

An understanding of how international payments or movements of money are made to fulfill contract obligations requires some basic understanding of the law of negotiable instruments. In general, the law of negotiable instruments is covered in courses on business law. For our purposes, we assume the reader has some limited understanding of this field. Here we are not concerned with their technical requirements, but with their use in international trade. A *negotiable instrument* is a signed writing, containing an unconditional promise or order to pay a fixed sum of money, to order or to bearer, on demand or at a definite time. Common negotiable instruments include promissory notes, which are two-party instruments containing a promise to pay, and drafts, which are three-party instruments containing orders to pay. In this chapter, we are concerned only with drafts. A *draft* is the signed order of the drawer, given to a drawee who is in possession of money to which the drawer is entitled, to pay a sum of money to a third party, the payee, on demand or at a definite time. A common *check* is a special form of draft, which is drawn on a bank and payable on demand. The three parties to a check include the drawer, who gave the order to pay, the drawee bank to whom the order to pay is given, and the payee. The *bill of exchange* is a specialized type of international draft commonly used to expedite foreign money payments in many types of international transactions. A *documentary draft* is used to expedite payment in a documentary sale. The word *draft* is more frequently used in U.S. law and banking practice, while the term *bill of exchange* is more frequently used outside the United States, particularly in England. Generally, the term *draft* is used in this text except when referring specifically to an English bill of exchange. These negotiable instruments can serve two purposes: (1) they act as a substitute for money and (2) they act as a financing or credit device.

Although it is beyond the scope of this text to offer a thorough treatment of the law of negotiable instruments, an understanding of the importance of the draft is essential to anyone engaged in international trade.

The Origin of Bills of Exchange

The origin of the bill of exchange lies in the history of the merchants and traders of fourteenth- and fifteenth-century Europe. As merchants visited the markets of distant cities to buy and sell their wares, they sought a safer means of transferring their gold or money than by carrying it in their caravans. It might have worked like this: Assume Merchant A delivered goods to Merchant B in a distant city, who became indebted to A for the amount of the purchase. Later Merchant A desires to purchase goods from Merchant C. Merchant A could pay Merchant C for the goods with a written piece of paper—an order—addressed by A to B to pay that money to C. Assume further that Merchant B is wealthy and respected in the trade—one whose credit is highly regarded. Merchant C could present the written order to B for payment immediately, or if he wished, he could simply ask B to sign (or "accept") the order for future payment. Thus, the written order to pay became an *acceptance*. With the acceptance in hand, Merchant C could purchase new wares from yet another merchant and use the acceptance in payment. Eventually, merchants turned to wealthy families, Italian banking societies, or medieval bankers spread throughout Europe to transfer money over great distances by issuing payment orders to their correspondents living in distant cities. As merchants recognized that these orders could be bought and sold, the concept of negotiability evolved and negotiable instruments were born. At first, English law did not recognize the validity of negotiable instruments. But merchants accepted them as substitutes for money, and they were enforceable in the merchant's private courts under the Law Merchant. As their importance and use evolved, so did their validity and treatment under the law. They became formally recognized by statute in England in 1822 in the *English Bills of Exchange Act* and in the United States in 1866 in the *Uniform Negotiable Instruments Law*.

Bills of exchange or drafts are today governed in the United States by the *Uniform Commercial Code*, in England by the *Bills of Exchange Act*, and in more than twenty other countries by the 1930 *Convention on Bills of Exchange and Promissory Notes*. Despite their common history, these laws differ in their treatment of the creation and transfer of negotiable instruments, as well as in the rights of the parties should an instrument be dishonored or refused.

Brief Requirements of a Bill of Exchange

The English *Bills of Exchange Act* requires that a bill of exchange be (1) an unconditional order in writing, (2) addressed by one person to another, (3) signed by the person giving it, (4) with a requirement that the person to whom it is addressed pay on demand or at a fixed or determinable future time, (5) a sum certain in money, and (6) to or *to the order of* a specified person, or to bearer. These characteristics are similar to the requirements for a draft set out in the *Uniform Commercial Code* (UCC). (The *Convention on Bills of Exchange* requires that the words "bill of exchange" appear on the instrument, but English and U.S. laws do not.)

Basically, a bill of exchange or international draft is similar to a check, in that it is an unconditional order to pay a sum of money. (Drafts can be made payable in any currency.) In the case of a check, the *drawer* orders its bank, the *drawee*, to pay the amount of the check to the *payee*. However, instead of being drawn against funds held on deposit in a bank (as with a check), an international draft is an order from the seller to the buyer or buyer's bank to pay the seller upon the delivery of goods or the presentation of shipping documents (e.g., an ocean bill of lading or air waybill). Thus, the seller is both the drawer (the one giving the order to pay) and the payee (the one entitled to payment under the instrument). The drawee is either the buyer or its bank, depending on the arrangements made for payment.

NEGOTIATION AND TRANSFER OF NEGOTIABLE INSTRUMENTS. The commercial use of a draft or other negotiable instrument is derived from its negotiability, the quality that allows it to act as a substitute for money. *Negotiation* is the transfer of an instrument from one party to another so that the transferee (called a *holder*) takes legal rights in the instrument. The correct manner of negotiation depends on whether the instrument is a *bearer* or *order* instrument. Most drafts used in international trade are order instruments because they are payable to a named payee. In order to negotiate an order instrument, *indorsement* (by signature) *and delivery* of the instrument to the holder must take place. References to the negotiation of international drafts appear throughout this chapter.

The Documentary Draft and the Bank Collection Process

Drafts come in several different types. A draft that is to be paid upon presentation or demand is known as a *sight draft* because it is payable "on sight." The sight draft is prepared by the seller and is sent to the buyer along with the shipping documents (e.g., the bill of lading) through banking channels, moving from the seller's bank in the country of export to a foreign correspondent bank in the buyer's country and city. The draft is sent "for collection," known as a *documentary collection.* The banks act as agents of the seller for collection purposes. The draft and documents are accompanied by a *collection letter* that provides instructions from the seller on such matters as who is responsible for bank collection charges, what to do in the event the buyer dishonors the draft, and how the proceeds are to be remitted to the seller. Thus, the collection letter may specify that in the event of the buyer's dishonor of the draft, the seller's agent in the buyer's country is to be notified, and that the goods are to be properly warehoused and insured pending resolution of the problem or sale of the goods to another party.

Essentially, documentary collections function like a cash-on-delivery (C.O.D.) transaction. When the sight draft is presented to the buyer at its bank or place of business, it is paid, and the payment is remitted to the seller. Only then does the bank turn over the shipping documents with which the buyer can claim its cargo from the carrier. The transaction is somewhat risky, however, because when presented with documents, there is no guarantee that the buyer will actually pay. Assuming the buyer does pay, the average cycle for completing a documentary collection is approximately three weeks (although most banks offer accelerated schedules). If a sales contract between buyer and seller calls for payment upon presentation of a sight draft, the contract terms commonly call for *cash against documents* (sales contracts with documentary payment terms were covered in Chapter Five).

The SWIFT System. International banking transactions are handled through an industry-owned cooperative, the *Society for Worldwide Interbank Financial Telecommunication,* commonly known as the SWIFT network. Most international letters of credit are transmitted through the SWIFT network. This worldwide telecommunications system has greatly expedited the remission of payments in a documentary collection. SWIFT is a private, high-speed communications network between banks, set up to transfer funds worldwide. It originated through the cooperative efforts of major banks in Europe, the United States, and Canada in the mid-1970s and is now in use in more than fifty nations. Due to its speed and cost-effectiveness, it has largely replaced the use of telex and mail-in fund transfers. Currently, SWIFT is involved in the *Bolero Project,* which is designed to eventually replace the paper-based transfer of trade documents with electronic transmissions on a global scale.

Documentary Drafts Used in Trade Finance

Banks and other financial institutions involved in commercial lending provide a wide range of financing packages for international trade, commonly called *trade finance.* Trade finance not only assists the buyer in financing its purchase, but also provides immediate cash to the seller for the sale and is profitable for the lending institution.

The documentary draft can serve as an important financing or credit device, providing the seller and buyer with a mechanism for financing the international sale. In a competitive marketplace, an exporter must be able to offer its customers credit or other financing for their purchase. Many firms consider their ability to arrange credit a crucial component of their marketing strategy. If an exporter can prearrange financing for the buyer, it has an advantage over a competitor who cannot.

The Use of Time Drafts and Acceptances. The use of the draft in trade finance works like this:

Seller agrees to issue a draft that is due, say, sixty days after shipment of the goods. The draft states that it is due in sixty days or on a future date specified on the instrument. A draft due at a future date or after a specified period is known as a *time draft,* as shown in Exhibit 7.1. The time draft is sent to the buyer for its *acceptance.* Typically, acceptance is done by stamping the date and the word "accepted" across the face of the draft, together with the name and signature of the drawee, because no party is obligated on a draft unless its signature appears on it. Under the UCC, the acceptance "may consist of the drawee's signature alone." The buyer has thus created a *trade acceptance.* The buyer's acceptance indicates the buyer's unconditional obligation to pay the draft on the date due. A draft payable at "sixty days after date" is payable by the drawee sixty days after the original date of the instrument. A draft payable at "sixty days sight" means that it is due to be paid sixty days after the date of the acceptance.

As with a sight draft, a seller usually sends the time draft together with the shipping documents to the buyer through banking channels with instructions to the banks that the shipping documents should be handed over to the buyer only upon acceptance of the draft. The sales contract would have indicated the parties' agreement to this arrangement by calling for "documents against acceptance," or other clear language of similar meaning. After acceptance, the draft is returned through banking channels to the seller. The seller can then hold the draft to maturity or sell it at a discount to a local bank or commercial lending institution for immediate cash. The commercial lender takes the acceptance by negotiation. The greater the creditworthiness of the buyer, the greater the marketability of the trade acceptance. Where the foreign buyer is unquestionably creditworthy, such as a major multinational corporation, the trade acceptance carries little risk and is easily saleable.

EXHIBIT 7.1

Time Draft Drawn under Letter of Credit with Banker's Acceptance

AT SIGHT__________ DATE__________ CITY__________
(INDICATE ABOVE WHETHER PAYABLE ON DEMAND OR OTHER TIME LIMIT)

PAY TO THE ORDER OF __________ U.S.$ __________
(NAME OF EXPORTER, EXPORTER'S BANK OR PAYEE)

__________ U.S. DOLLARS

FOR VALUE RECEIVED AND CHARGED TO THE ACCOUNT OF NATIONAL BANK LETTER OF CREDIT NO. __________

ACCEPTED
Date
National Bank, N.A.
Per Authorized Signature

THE TRANSACTION WHICH GIVES RISE TO THIS INSTRUMENT IS THE:
☐ IMPORT ☐ DOMESTIC SHIPMENT
☐ WAREHOUSING
OF __________
FROM __________ TO __________

TO: NATIONAL BANK, N.A.
ANYTOWN, U.S.A.
(IMPORTER, BUYER OR DRAWEE)

____
DRAWER'S SIGNATURE (EXPORTER)

Banker's Acceptances and Acceptance Financing. A *banker's acceptance* is a negotiable instrument and short-term financing device widely used to finance international (as well as domestic) sales. The purpose of an acceptance is to substitute a bank's credit for that of the buyer in order to finance the sale. A banker's acceptance is a time draft drawn on and accepted by a commercial bank. The bank stamps its name, date, and signature on the face of the draft to create the acceptance and thereby becomes obligated to pay the amount stated to the holder of the instrument on the date specified. The holder of the acceptance can convert it to cash immediately at a discounted rate or hold it until it matures.

Banker's acceptances are flexible instruments, with many creative uses. Acceptance financing can be done by either the buyer's or seller's bank. Importing buyers can use a banker's acceptance for short-term borrowing until they can resell and liquidate the goods being purchased. Sellers to export markets can use a banker's acceptance for short-term, pre-export financing of raw materials and production costs until the goods are sold to the foreign customer and payment received. Exporters can also use acceptances to grant credit terms to foreign customers. For instance, in a sale on open account, an exporter might draw a time draft on its own bank for the amount of its overseas sale. The draft is accepted by the exporter's bank, the discounted amount is paid to the exporter, and the acceptance is negotiated and discounted in the credit markets. When the importer pays the invoice amount to the exporter, the proceeds are used to satisfy the acceptance at maturity. In another arrangement, the exporter's draft may be accepted by the importer's bank, then discounted in the credit markets. In any case, the acceptance is satisfied at maturity through the proceeds of the sale.

In essence, the acceptance financing is self-liquidating because repayment is made from the underlying sales transaction, using credit market monies to finance business. The bank charges the borrower a commission and the discount rate for acceptance financing, which is usually deducted from the face amount of the acceptance when paid to the borrower. Depending on market conditions, acceptance financing is often cheaper for companies than regular credit borrowing.

Banker's acceptances are generally short-term instruments because they must be for a period of six months or less. An *eligible* banker's acceptance is one that qualifies for discount at the U.S. Federal Reserve Bank, which will buy it if it is not sold privately. Acceptances thus serve to finance international trade with outside capital. Because they are created by commercial banks, the use of banker's acceptances is subject to banking laws and Federal Reserve regulations in the United States.

Credit Risk in Trade Finance Programs. Institutions regularly involved in trade lending commonly prearrange these financing terms by agreeing in advance to purchase the trade acceptances of the foreign buyer. They must first perform an analysis and evaluation of the buyer's financial position. Thorough credit checks are done on the buyer, utilizing trade and banking information, the reports of U.S. or foreign credit reporting agencies, and even site visits to the foreign firm. (Although obtaining and verifying credit information is relatively easy in the United States, Canada, Japan, and Western Europe, it is somewhat more difficult, and the information is less reliable, in other regions of the world.) To reduce the credit risk and lower the cost of trade finance, several government agencies in the United States and other countries provide credit guarantees to back trade finance lending by commercial institutions. In the United States, these agencies include Eximbank, the Commodity Credit Corporation, and the Agency for International Development (discussed later in this chapter).

Credit Risk in Acceptance Financing: Rights of the Holder in Due Course. One of the primary reasons for the popularity of the acceptance as a financing device is the protection it provides to the financial institution or other party who purchases it, provided that party is a *holder in due course.* The detailed requirements to become a holder in due course are spelled out in the UCC. A holder in due course is a holder in possession of a negotiable instrument (such as a draft or acceptance) that has been taken: (1) for value, (2) in good faith, (3) without notice that it is overdue or has been dishonored, and (4) without notice that the instrument contains an unauthorized signature or has been altered (UCC 3-302). If all of the requirements for transferring a negotiable instrument are met and the transferee qualifies as a holder in due course, the transferee can take greater rights in the instrument than the transferor had.

According to the *holder in due course rule,* the purchaser of an acceptance, or any negotiable instrument, takes it free from most disputes that might arise between the drawer and drawee—the original parties to the underlying transaction. The most common type of dispute that might arise is breach of contract. For example, assume that DownPillow sells pillows to a Japanese buyer and forwards documents and a draft for acceptance. DownPillow discounts the trade acceptance to a U.S. bank, who then discounts the instrument in the credit markets. If the pillows turn out to be moldy and worthless, the Japanese buyer must still honor and pay the acceptance upon presentation in Japan. It may then assert its separate claim for breach of contract against the seller. This rule ensures the free transferability of commercial paper in international commerce. A financial institution can discount an international draft without fear that it will be caught up in the middle of a breach of contract action between buyer and seller. If drafts did not come with this protection, banks might not be so willing to finance international sales.

Credit Risks in Factoring Accounts Receivable: The Rights of the Assignee

As firms become more globalized and as credit information becomes more widely available, many firms are offering open account terms to their better, long-term foreign customers. These sellers are giving their customers an open credit period, typically from thirty days to several months, to pay for goods received. However, companies engaged in exporting products are not in business to loan money. Thus, banks are providing open account trade finance services, including the factoring of foreign accounts receivable.

An account receivable is no more than a representation of a *contract right* belonging to the seller—the right to collect money owed by the buyer under the contract for goods shipped. Contract rights can be *assigned* to another party. In a typical financing arrangement, the seller (*assignor*) assigns its right to collect the account to the financial institution (*assignee*). This is also called *factoring,* and the *assignee* is sometimes called the *factor.* Under basic contract law, the assignee "steps into the shoes" of the assignor and acquires only those rights under the contract that the assignor had against the other party to the contract (e.g., the buyer of the goods).

Take the following example: Assume that DownPillow ships an ocean container of pillows to Japan and factors the account receivable with a U.S. bank (the assignee). DownPillow now has its money and the bank is awaiting payment directly from Japan. (Of course, it is important for the Japanese buyer to be notified of the assignment and instructed to pay only the assignee bank.) If a dispute later breaks out over the quality of the pillows, the Japanese buyer may legally assert any claims and defenses against collection by the bank that it otherwise would have had against DownPillow. Thus, for example, the buyer can successfully argue that it does not have to pay the bank because of the breach of warranty by DownPillow. DownPillow will have to repay the bank for money received and resolve the breach of contract suit with the buyer. For this reason, banker's acceptance financing offers some advantages over accounts receivable financing. Unlike a factor, a holder in due course of a banker's acceptance is protected by the holder in due course rule. Thus, the fact that the products are defective does not provide a defense against payment to one liable on the negotiable instrument. Some insurance companies today offer commercial *credit insurance* to protect against accounts receivable that become uncollectible bad debts.

The Letter of Credit

We will devote considerable attention to letters of credit issued by commercial banks. These flexible banking instruments are in wide use around the world. As much as $1 trillion in goods is purchased worldwide by letter of credit every year, according to most banking and government sources. In very broad terms, we can say that a letter of credit is an obligation of a bank, usually irrevocable, issued on behalf of their customer and promising to pay a sum of money to a beneficiary upon the happening of a certain event or events. In a sense, it is the substitution of the credit and good name of a bank for that of their customer, permitting the customer to do business with other individuals or firms on terms that otherwise might not be available to them. Letters of credit can be either domestic or international. They can be used in transactions for the sale of goods or services or to guarantee performance of other business obligations. Evidence exists that early forms of letters of credit were used in Renaissance Europe and in ancient Greece and Egypt. Today, almost all large banks can issue a letter of credit, although in practice most are issued by a small fraction of the world's largest banks located in major banking centers of the world. In this chapter we will study two types of credits: the international documentary letter of credit used in the sale of goods and the standby letter of credit used to guarantee performance or payment obligations of the bank's customer.

The Documentary Letter of Credit

Suppose that you are an American manufacturer who has been approached by a buyer in a foreign country. The buyer makes initial inquiries about your products, engineering and manufacturing capabilities, and installation and service after the sale. You do some informal background checking within the industry and determine that they are a serious customer. You receive their credit statement, containing banking and trade references. You may even obtain a credit report on them. You learn that they have been in business for relatively few years, so you are not willing to enter the sale without some security. After all, you would be manufacturing these goods to conform to their specifications and shipping them halfway around the world on the basis of their promise to take delivery and remit payment. In earlier chapters we studied some of your options. The risk is too great to ship the goods on thirty-day open account terms and hope for your money, and if you demand cash in advance the customer is not likely to agree. After all, he may not trust you any more than you trust him.

You could use a documentary sale, quoting prices to the customer as "cash against documents," but even then you might never see payment. If you send the documents to the buyer's bank for collection, it is still possible for them to weasel out of the deal. The buyer might not be able to pay, may have changed his mind, or may even have gone out of business. It is often possible for the buyer to find the same goods for less from another supplier. While probably not an issue in our hypothetical, in cases where substitute goods are freely available (and that might include everything from agricultural commodities to computer chips), a buyer might look for a way out of a contract where there has been a sharp decline in market prices. In any event, your customer could simply disappear, leaving the bank with documents to be returned to you and leaving you with specially manufactured goods in a customs warehouse halfway around the world. Unless you can find another foreign customer, which may be unlikely, you will have to pay the freight costs of returning them to your plant. To add a level of security to the documentary sale, you might propose contract terms calling for the buyer to provide an irrevocable, documentary letter of credit issued by a bank and addressed to you. This substitutes the credit and good name of a bank for that of the buyer and is a fairly good assurance (although nothing is absolute) that if you do your part that will be paid, and paid quickly.

A letter of credit would have another advantage to you in this example. If you ship goods to your customer on open account, you may have to wait several weeks or months to receive your money. By using a letter of credit, you will probably receive payment with a few days. Moreover, because the letter of credit is so secure, it can serve as security, or collateral, for you to obtain a short-term loan to help finance the purchase of materials for manufacturing or other start-up costs.

The Parties to the Transaction. A buyer that has committed in the sales contract to obtain a letter of credit begins by applying to its bank for a letter of credit to be issued "in favor of" or "for the benefit of" the seller. In this arrangement, the buyer is known as the *account party,* the buyer's bank is known as the *issuing bank,* or *issuer,* and the seller is known as the *beneficiary*. A typical documentary sale with a letter of credit is illustrated in Exhibit 7.2.

Exhibit 7.2

The Documentary Sale with a Letter of Credit

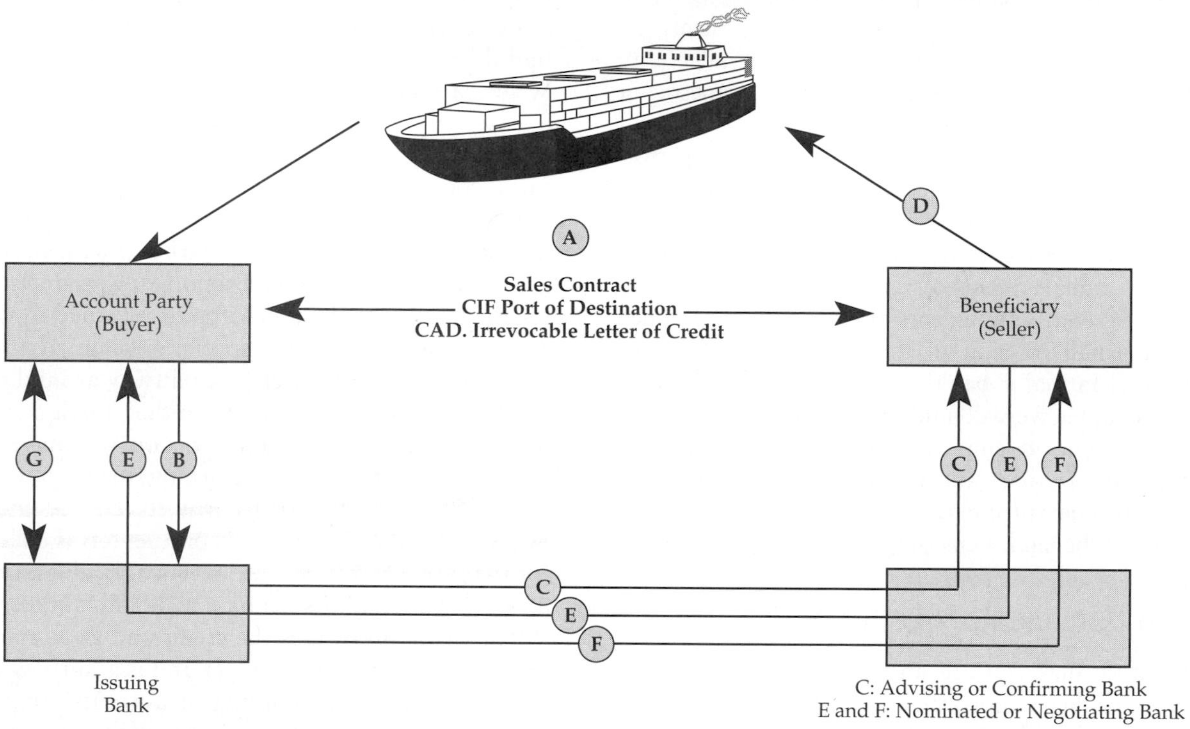

A. Sales contract calls for L/C.
B. Application for L/C.
C. L/C forwarded to beneficiary through advising bank.
D. Documents prepared according to L/C—goods shipped.
E. Documents negotiated for payment through nominated, negotiating or confirming bank.
F. Payment or acceptance of draft after documents checked for discrepancies.
G. Negotiation of documents to buyer for reimbursement.

Documentary Letter of Credit Defined. The *documentary letter of credit* is defined as:

1. The definite undertaking of a bank,
2. issued in accordance with the instructions of their customer,
3. addressed to, or in favor of, the beneficiary,
4. wherein the bank promises to pay a certain sum of money (or to accept or negotiate the beneficiary's drafts up to that sum) in the stated currency,
5. within the prescribed time limits,
6. upon the complying presentation,
7. of the required and conforming documents.

The requirement that the bank will pay the seller only on the presentation of documents is what gives the documentary credit its name. In reality, those documents might differ greatly depending on whether the transaction is a domestic one or an international one; on the needs of the parties; or on the method for shipping the goods. Letters of credit can be used for many different types of shipments, including ocean, air, rail, and road shipments, and with multimodal freight. In reality, they can be used with almost any type of document, from simple invoices to postal receipts. However, we are limiting our discussion to letter of credit transactions involving ocean transport, where the most common documents required by the letter of credit are the ocean bill of lading, the commercial invoice, and the marine insurance policy.

Throughout this chapter we will use the terms "letter of credit," "credit," or "documentary credit" interchangeably, although the latter refers only to credits payable on the presentation of documents.

The Legal Nature of the Letter of Credit. There has long been an academic argument over whether or not the letter of credit is a contract between the issuing bank and the beneficiary. The letter of credit does act like a promise from an issuing bank to a beneficiary, and it seems to be treated at times like a contract and discussed in terms of the principles of contract law. However, the general consensus is that it is not a contract. If you recall the requirements for a contact, a letter of credit does not come about through offer and acceptance or mutual assent, nor is there any requirement for consideration. The basic requirements of a contract are missing. The bank and the beneficiary do not negotiate about anything; in fact, they usually have no contact whatsoever. The letter of credit is not a negotiable instrument, like a check or a promissory note. Nor is it a third-party beneficiary contract because the beneficiary's rights do not derive from the contract between the buyer/account party and its bank. The letter of credit is a legal animal all of its own species; it is created by statute. It gives the beneficiary a statutory right to enforce the letter of credit against the bank that issued it, rather a contract right. Moreover, both the *Uniform Commercial Code* and banking customs refer to the letter of credit as a "definite undertaking" and not as a contract.

Law Applicable to Letters of Credit

Letters of credit are recognized in all legal systems of the world. In the United States, the law governing letters of credit has been codified in Article 5 (1995 revision) of the *Uniform Commercial Code*. In addition, in some states, notably New York, letters of credit are responsible for a great body of case law. Perhaps the most important rules affecting letters of credit are not laws at all, but a privately developed set of guidelines based on the customs and commonly accepted practices of merchants and bankers, known as the *Uniform Customs and Practice for Documentary Credits*.

The Uniform Customs and Practice for Documentary Credits. The *Uniform Customs and Practice for Documentary Credits* (UCP) is a document that international bankers know well. It is a set of standardized rules for issuing and handling letters of credit, drafted and published by the International Chamber of Commerce (which also publishes *Incoterms,* covered in Chapter Five) with the assistance of the international banking community. The UCP establishes the format for letters of credit, sets out rules by which banks process letter of credit transactions, and defines the rights and responsibilities of all parties to the credit. Because banks were the main drafters of the UCP, its provisions tend to protect their rights in any transaction. The UCP was first introduced in the early 1930s, with the latest revision (UCP 600) becoming effective in 2007. The UCP is in use in virtually every nation of the world and applies to most letters of credit issued worldwide.

The International Chamber of Commerce is not a government or lawmaking body, and the UCP is not law. A letter of credit is "governed" by the UCP only to the extent that it states that it is to be "interpreted" according to the UCP (which almost all do). The UCP is used by judges in deciding letter of credit cases, and references to it appear in virtually every reported decision on international letters of credit. The *Uniform Commercial Code,* Article 5 (1995 revision), now defers to the UCP and specifically states that the UCC is *not* applicable to any letter of credit to the extent that it is in conflict with the UCP. As a result, the UCP has a far greater impact on the law of international letters of credit than does the *Uniform Commercial Code.*

Irrevocability of Letters of Credit. Letters of credit issued under UCP 600 are presumed irrevocable unless clear language is used to make them revocable. Nevertheless, most sales contracts recite that the buyer's letter of credit is to be irrevocable. An example of an irrevocable documentary letter of credit is shown in Exhibit 7.3. While revocable credits have some uses, they are not used in documentary sales between unrelated parties.

The Independence Principle of Letters of Credit

The *independence principle* states that the letter of credit is independent of the sales contract between

EXHIBIT 7.3

Irrevocable Documentary Letter of Credit

IMPORTER'S BANK
CONFIRMATION OF BRIEF CABLE

Irrevocable Documentary Letter of Credit

Importer's Bank Charlotte, NC	Date of Issue February 1, 2008	
	Issuing Bank Letter of Credit No. 78346	Advising Bank Letter of Credit No.
Advising Bank German Bank F.R.G.	Applicant Downpillow, Inc. North Carolina	
Beneficiary Federhaus, GMBH F.R.G.	Expiratory Date (For Negotiation) Day: 30 · Month: April · Year: 2008	
Currency: U.S.A.	Amount: 35,000.00	Thirty-Five Thousand Dollars

Gentlemen:
We hereby issue this documentary Letter of Credit in your favor which is available against your draft at sight drawn on Importer's Bank, Charlotte, North Carolina for 100% of the invoice value bearing the clause "Drawn under documentary letter of Credit Number 78346" Accompanied by the following documents:

1. Commercial invoice in triplicate
2. U.S. special customs form #1111 in triplicate
3. Insurance policy/certificate in duplicate covering all risks
4. Certificate of origin "form A" in duplicate
5. Full set 3/3 clean on-board bills of lading issued to the order of Importer's bank, marked "Freight prepaid," notify applicant.

Purporting to cover: 3000 lbs washed white goose down in machine compressed bales, CIF Norfolk, Va.

Shipment from	Partial Shipments	Transshipments
F.R.G. To Norfolk, Va.	Prohibited	Prohibited

Special conditions

Documents must be presented to negotiating bank within 10 days of issuance of shipping documents but within the validity of the credit.
Latest ship date March 15, 2008.

Negotiating bank is authorized to forward all documents to us via airmail. All banking charges outside the United States are for account of the beneficiary.

We hereby engage with the bona fide holders of all drafts under and in compliance with the terms of this letter of credit that such drafts will be duly honored upon presentation to us. The amount of each drawing must be indorsed on the reverse side of this letter of credit by the negotiating bank. B. G. DeWoolfson Authorized Signature	Indications of the Advising Bank Place, Date, Name, and Signature of the Advising Bank

Except so far as otherwise expressly stated this documentary letter of credit is subject to the Uniform Customs and Practices for Documentary Credits (1993 Revision) the International Chamber of Commerce Document No. 500.

buyer and seller, and it is independent of the contract between the buyer and his bank that issued the letter of credit. The issuing bank is not concerned with what the parties had promised to do, or should do, under their contract. The issuing bank is only concerned with the presentation of documents. UCP 600, Article 5, states, "Banks deal with documents and not with goods, services or performance to which the documents may relate." The banks are not concerned with the quality or condition of the goods. They have no obligation to inspect goods or to investigate rumors about them. They do not care if the ship on which they are sailing has gone to the bottom of the sea. The following case, *Maurice O'Meara Co. v. National Park Bank of New York,* is generally considered by scholars in the United States to be the classic statement of the legal nature of letters of credit and the independence principle.

Following a Letter of Credit Transaction

In the following sections we will see how a typical letter of credit transaction works. Some of the topics include the contract between the buyer and the buyer's bank to issue a letter of credit, what the seller should do when the letter of credit arrives, rules for the seller to follow in presenting documents for payment, and the process by which the banks inspect documents and honor or dishonor the seller's request for payment.

THE BUYER'S APPLICATION AND CONTRACT WITH THE ISSUING BANK. Once the buyer has finalized a sales contract calling for payment to the seller under a letter of credit, it is up to the buyer to apply for that letter of credit at a bank. The application for the credit, usually done on the bank's form and accompanied by an initial fee, contains the buyer's instructions and conditions upon which the issuing bank may honor the seller's documents. These instructions are based on the details of the original sales contract between buyer and seller. The application will request the bank to issue a letter of credit to the seller promising to purchase the seller's documents covering a certain quantity and description of goods, with a value up to a certain amount of money, that are insured and shipped on or before a certain date.

The buyer may impose almost any conditions or requirements on the seller's performance, as long as they pertain only to the seller's documents. For example, the buyer could prohibit the bank from taking documents showing a partial shipment, or it could require a document that shows a specific method of shipping, or even name a specific vessel. However, the buyer must remember that this information is based on the buyer's final agreement with the seller.

The buyer's application for the credit, when accepted by the bank, becomes a contract between them. It states what the bank must do on the buyer's behalf. If the bank follows the buyer's instructions, then it is entitled to purchase the seller's documents and obtain reimbursement from the buyer. If it does not, or if it violates any terms of its contract, then the buyer need not take the documents or reimburse the bank that took them contrary to instructions. For instance, if the buyer's application requests the bank to issue a letter of credit calling for the seller to submit documents showing that it shipped "1,000 electric toasters," and the bank, without approval, purchases documents showing that the seller shipped "1,000 toaster ovens," then the bank is not entitled to reimbursement. If the buyer instructs the bank to issue a letter of credit showing that the toasters must ship on or before a certain date, and the bill of lading shows the toasters were shipped after that date, the bank is not entitled to reimbursement. Indeed, banking lore is filled with stories of banks getting "stuck" with cargo like this. So (we say only half jokingly), the next time you are in your bank and you see a sign offering a free toaster oven to anyone opening a new account, you might think of this example and wonder whether it was a marketing decision or a way to unload unwanted cargo. If you choose a career in banking, you might want to remember that banks deal with money and documents. They do not like to deal in goods or to be stuck with them.

The buyer may not make any demands on the issuing bank that are not related to the seller's documents. For example, the application may not attempt to require the bank to inspect goods or to make the letter of credit conditional on an

Maurice O'Meara Co. v. National Park Bank of New York

146 N.E. 636 (1925)

Court of Appeals of New York

BACKGROUND AND FACTS

National Park Bank issued a letter of credit addressed to Ronconi & Millar, beneficiary, at the request of its account party, Sun Herald, "covering the shipment of 1,322 tons of newsprint paper in 72½inch and 36½ inch rolls to test 11–12, 32 lbs. at 8½ cents per pound net weight—delivery to be made in December 1920 and January 1921." The letter of credit did not require that a testing certificate from an independent laboratory accompany the documents. When Ronconi & Millar's invoice and draft were presented to the bank, the documents described the paper as was required in the letter of credit. However, the bank refused payment because it had no opportunity to test the tensile strength of the paper. (Interestingly, the market price of newsprint paper had fallen sharply in the time period between the contract of sale and the presentation of documents, amounting to over $20,000 in this case.) Ronconi & Millar transferred their rights to collect payment to Maurice O'Meara, a financial institution, who brought this action to collect the full amount of the drafts. Maurice O'Meara claims that the issuing bank had no right to test or inspect the paper.

MCLAUGHLIN, JUDGE

[The letter of credit] ... was in no way involved in or connected with, other than the presentation of the documents, the contract for the purchase and sale of the paper mentioned. That was a contract between buyer and seller, which in no way concerned the bank. The bank's obligation was to pay sight drafts when presented if accompanied by genuine documents specified in the letter of credit. If the paper when delivered did not correspond to what had been purchased, either in weight, kind or quality, then the purchaser had his remedy against the seller for damages. Whether the paper was what the purchaser contracted to purchase did not concern the bank and in no way affected its liability. It was under no obligation to ascertain, either by a personal examination or otherwise, whether the paper conformed to the contract between the buyer and seller. The bank was concerned only in the drafts and the documents accompanying them. This was the extent of its interest. If the drafts, when presented, were accompanied by the proper documents, then it was absolutely bound to make the payment under the letter of credit, irrespective of whether it knew, or had reason to believe, that the paper was not of the tensile strength contracted for. This view, I think, is the one generally entertained with reference to a bank's liability under an irrevocable letter of credit of the character of the one here under consideration.

The defendant had no right to insist that a test of the tensile strength of the paper be made before paying the drafts; nor did it even have a right to inspect the paper before payment, to determine whether it in fact corresponded to the description contained in the documents. The letter of credit did not so provide. All that the letter of credit provided was that documents be presented which described the paper shipped as of a certain size, weight, and tensile strength. To hold otherwise is to read into the letter of credit something which is not there, and this the court ought not to do, since it would impose upon a bank a duty which in many cases would defeat the primary purpose of such letters of credit. This primary purpose is an assurance to the seller of merchandise of prompt payment against documents.

It has never been held, so far as I am able to discover, that a bank has the right or is under an obligation to see that the description of the merchandise contained in the documents presented is correct. A provision giving it such right, or imposing such obligation, might, of course, be provided for in the letter of credit. The letter under consideration contains no such provision. If the bank had the right to determine whether the paper was of the tensile strength stated, then it might be pertinent to inquire how much of the paper must it subject to the test. If it had to make a test as to tensile strength, then it was equally obligated to measure and weigh the paper. No such thing was intended by the parties and there was no such obligation upon the bank. The documents presented were sufficient. The only reason stated by defendant in its letter of December 18, 1920, for refusing to pay the draft, was that—"There has arisen a reasonable doubt regarding the quality of the newsprint paper.... Until such time as we can have a test made by an impartial and unprejudiced expert we shall be obliged to defer payment."

This being the sole objection, the only inference to be drawn therefrom is that otherwise the documents presented conformed to the requirements of

continued

continued

the letter of credit. All other objections were thereby waived.

Judgment should be directed in favor of the plaintiff.

Decision. National Park Bank's obligation to pay the beneficiary's drafts submitted under its letter of credit was separate and distinct from the contract of sale between the buyer and seller. Banks deal in documents only. Therefore the defendant, National Park Bank, could not withhold payment of the drafts even if it believed that the paper was not of the weight, kind, or quality ordered by Sun Herald. Defendant also had no right to demand testing of the paper or to inspect it prior to payment.

investigative report of the seller, on a criminal background check, on the buyer's receipt of financing, or on a contract to resell the goods.

The buyer's international banker and customs broker are two good sources of information and advice on what documents a buyer should require from a seller. Buyers would be well warned to heed their advice or consult an attorney experienced in handling international letters of credit.

The willingness of the bank to issue the letter of credit for the buyer—its customer—depends on the buyer's creditworthiness and the banking relationship between them. More than likely, the buyer and its bank have an established history of banking and commercial lending. The buyer will be responsible to the bank for fees and a percentage of the value of the letter of credit, so the buyer should have already considered these additional costs when agreeing to original sales contract.

Advising the Letter of Credit to the Beneficiary. The issuing bank will send the letter of credit to the seller via a foreign *correspondent bank* (a bank with whom the issuing bank has a reciprocal banking relationship) located in the seller's country. This bank is called the *advising bank*. An advising bank merely informs or "advises" the seller that the letter of credit is available to be picked up. An advising bank has no responsibility to honor a draft or purchase the seller's documents. It is not liable on the credit. It provides the service of forwarding the letter of credit to the seller, but it has no obligation to advise the credit and may refuse if it wishes. Its only responsibility is to satisfy itself that the credit is authentic and accurate as received (e.g., that there were no errors in transmission). For example, it might compare the signature on the credit as advised to them with the authorized signature of the banking officer at the issuing bank. Letters of credit are commonly transmitted between banks using the SWIFT network.

Seller's Compliance with the Letter of Credit. Until the seller receives the letter of credit and reads it carefully, he might not want to begin manufacturing, packaging, arranging transportation, or preparing the documents. The letter of credit tells the seller what it must do in order to be paid. It tells him what to ship, how to ship, when to ship, and more. It contains specific terms and conditions drawn from the original sales contract and included in the letter of credit, such as the quantity and description of the goods, shipping dates, the type or amount of insurance, markings on packages, and so on. The letter of credit also tells the seller what documents are needed in addition to the usual ones. For instance, assume a buyer in California wants to import foreign-made beanbag chairs that must meet California's strict flammability standards for upholstered furniture. The letter of credit might call for an inspection certificate showing that the chairs "were tested pursuant to and are compliant with California Technical Bulletin 117." This tells the seller that this test must be performed and the inspection certificate received before the shipping date.

The seller will want to decide if the letter of credit is in keeping with his agreement with the buyer in the underlying contract of sale. If the documents show significant differences, the seller would want to contact the buyer to inquire why. For instance, assume that a sales contract called for shipment of "4,000 lbs. washed white goose down in machine-compressed bales," and the letter of credit reads "3,000 lbs. washed white goose down in machine-compressed bales." The seller must stop and inquire why a difference appears in the quantities expressed. Did the buyer change its mind and decide to purchase only 3,000 lbs. instead of the 4,000 lbs. agreed to? If so, why wasn't the seller contacted to reconfirm the new order? Perhaps the bank erred in transmitting the letter of credit. Whatever the reason, the seller should do nothing until the problem is resolved or until an amended letter of credit is received. If the seller ships 4,000 lbs., its drafts may be refused and it may only get paid for 3,000 lbs.; if it ships 3,000 lbs., it may be losing a sale for the 1,000 lbs. difference.

The seller should examine other conditions of the credit to be certain they can be met. Can the seller acquire materials and manufacture on time for the shipment deadline in the letter of credit or before the expiry date of the credit? Does the credit call for a particular shipping method or route or specify a particular carrier or ship that cannot be used? If an export license is needed in order to export the products from the seller's country, can it be processed and received on time from the government agency?

The seller should also review the credit for accuracy. Is the total amount of the letter of credit sufficient to cover the drafts? Is it in the currency called for in the sales contract? Do the provisions for insurance and the payment of freight charges meet the terms of the contract of sale, and are they agreeable to the seller? Does the letter of credit allow partial shipments?

If the seller is unable to comply with the letter of credit for any reason, the buyer must be contacted immediately, before shipment, so that an amended credit can be issued. In one case, a U.S. furniture manufacturer received a letter of credit from Kuwait calling for the shipment of furniture in "one 40′ ocean container." Only after packaging and loading did the manufacturer realize that some of the furniture would not fit into one container. If the manufacturer's documents had shown two containers, or had it shown less furniture than was called for in the letter of credit, the bank would have rejected the documents. An amended credit had to be issued before it was safe for the furniture to be crated and shipped.

Complying Presentation. A *presentation* is the delivery of the seller's documents and draft to the nominated bank or directly to the issuing bank. A *complying presentation* is one in which

1. The seller delivers all of the required documents,
2. within the time allowed for presentation and prior to the expiry date of the credit,
3. containing no discrepancies, and
4. which complies with all other terms of the letter of credit, the provisions of the UCP, and standard banking practices.

The *nominated bank* is that bank, usually in the seller's country, that has been appointed or "nominated" by the issuing bank to honor the documents. The nominated bank is often the advising bank that originally transmitted the documents to the seller. If no bank is nominated, then the letter of credit is said to be "freely available" and can be negotiated through any bank of the seller's choice.

The UCP requires, in most cases, that presentation be within twenty-one days of the date of shipment (determined by the date of the bill of lading) and before the expiry date stated in the credit. Documents will be refused for late presentment unless waived by the buyer.

Examination of Documents for Discrepancies. If the seller's presentation is complying, the nominating bank will purchase the seller's documents and honor the draft. If the credit calls for payment on sight, the nominated bank will honor and pay the seller's draft on sight. If the credit calls for the draft to be paid at some other time, the nominated bank will honor the draft by acceptance. However, if the seller's documents do not comply with the terms of the letter of credit or if they contain irregularities or discrepancies, the documents will be held pending instructions from the buyer or rejected by the banks. If the banks purchase noncomplying documents, they cannot seek reimbursement from the buyer.

UCP 600 gives banks up to five banking days to inspect the seller's documents for discrepancies or irregularities. A discrepancy exists if the seller's documents, on their face, do not conform to the terms of the letter of credit. The discrepancy may be caused by some wording or data in a document that is not exactly what was required in the credit.

The seller's documents and letter of credit are literally put side by side and compared by a bank's professional document checker. Each term in the documents is matched to the requirement of the letter of credit. For instance, a discrepancy exists if the quantity or description of the goods in the invoice does not match that in the credit, if the bill of lading is dated later than required, if any documents are missing, or if they show signs of fraud, forgery, tampering, or missing signatures.

Banks may not look beyond the letter of credit to see if the documents comply. For example, assume a letter of credit calls for the shipment of "1,000 blood pressure monitoring kits." The shipper's invoice shows the sale and shipment of "1,000 sphygmomanometers and cuffs." The document checker may or may not know if they are the same, nor does it matter. The document checker may not consult dictionary definitions, encyclopedias, medical textbooks, or other outside references. The bank is not responsible for interpreting technical or foreign language. The bank may not telephone the seller and ask what was meant in their invoice. In this case there is a discrepancy, and the documents will be rejected, unless the discrepancy is waived by the buyer. Neither the buyer nor his bank are obligated to take them.

In the following sections, we will look at the most important documents and some common discrepancies. These derive from the UCP, standard international banking practices, and common requirements on letters of credit. The most common discrepancies found in documents are related to descriptions, time, amounts, missing documents, missing signatures, and contradictions among documents. (See Exhibit 7.4). Other documents frequently required in a letter of credit are a packing list, certificate of origin, consular invoice, and many others.

EXHIBIT 7.4

Common Discrepancies Found in Documentation

Bill of Lading /Air Waybill

- Incomplete set of bills (originals missing)
- Onboard notations not dated and signed or initialed
- Time for shipment has expired
- Unclean bill of lading shows damage
- Indorsement missing
- Evidence of forgery or alteration
- Does not show freight prepared if required under the letter of credit
- Description of goods differs substantially from letter of credit
- Name of vessel differs
- Shows partial shipment or transshipment where prohibited by the letter of credit

Commercial Invoice

- Description of goods does not conform to description in letter of credit
- Does not show terms of shipment
- Amount differs from that shown on draft
- Amount exceeds limits of letter of credit
- Weights, measurements, or quantities differ

Draft

- Draft and invoice amounts do not agree
- Draft does not bear reference to letter of credit
- Evidence of forgery or alteration
- Draft not signed
- Maturity dates differ from letter of credit
- Currency differs from letter of credit

Insurance Policy

- Description of goods differs from invoice
- Risks not covered as required by the letter of credit
- Policy dated after date of bill of lading
- Amount of policy insufficient
- Certificate or policy not indorsed
- Certificate presented instead of policy, if required in letter of credit

General Discrepancies

- Letter of credit has expired
- Letter of credit is overdrawn
- Draft and documents presented after time called for in letter of credit
- Incomplete documentation
- Changes in documents not initialed
- Merchandise description and marks not consistent between documents

The Commercial Invoice. The commercial invoice is required by buyers, banks, and customs authorities on every international sale. The commercial invoice must be made out by the seller and addressed to the buyer and be in the same currency as the letter of credit. It need not be signed, notarized, or verified, unless the credit requires. Where a commercial invoice is required, a preliminary "pro forma" invoice will not be accepted.

Perhaps the most important requirement is that the description of the goods in a commercial invoice *must correspond* to that in the credit. Most courts hold that the description must be exactly the same. As we will see in the next section, sellers are encouraged to use the same description in the invoice as the issuing bank used in the letter of credit, misspellings and all. Where bulk items are involved, the invoice should be for the quantity of goods ordered, or within 5 percent of the amount specified in the credit. However, the 5 percent rule does not apply to letters of credit covering a specific number of items or packages. In such a case, the amount of the invoice cannot exceed the amount of the letter of credit. For example, a seller may ship and bill for 5 percent more grain than was ordered, but not for more cases of soft drinks, or tractors.

The Bill of Lading. For ocean freight, the seller must present a bill of lading with the notation "on board," indicating that the goods have been loaded. The seller must present the original bill of lading, but if it was issued in a set of more than one original, then all originals must be presented. The bill of lading must be dated within the time set in the credit for shipping. It must be a "clean" bill—one that has no notations indicating that damage to the goods or packaging was apparent or visible at the time of loading. Under most conditions, the bills of lading must be marked "freight prepaid."

The Insurance Policy. The insurance policy should be of the type and coverage required by the letter of credit, and in the same currency and amount of the invoice, plus 10 percent. It should be effective on or before the date of the bill of lading, to show that the goods were insured during loading. The policy itself should be used; alternatively a certificate of insurance may be used unless a certificate is not permitted by the letter of credit. Declarations are used by companies that have open policies that "float" over many shipments. They must be signed by an agent for the company. Cover letters from agents are not acceptable.

Certificates of Analysis or Inspection. Although these certificates are not required for letter of credit transactions, they are very common and deserve to be mentioned. Frequently, a buyer will require the seller to submit documentary proof of inspection from an independent inspection firm. A seller may require submission of a certificate of inspection for merchandise, a certificate of laboratory analysis, or a certificate of compliance with health, safety, or technical standards from an approved testing lab. Analysis or inspection certificates can be required for almost any product, such as an inspection of the sewing quality of blue jeans, an analysis of the mold content of grain, or a laboratory analysis of the lead content of the paint on children's toys. Sellers should ensure that certificates they include with their documents meet all the terms of the letter of credit.

The Rule of Strict Compliance

The prevailing standard established by the courts for examining documents is found in the *rule of strict compliance*. According to this view, the terms of the documents presented to the issuing bank must strictly conform to the requirements of the letter of credit and the UCP. This rule is as old as letter of credit law itself. It was stated in the famous words of Lord Sumner in *Equitable Trust Co. of New York v. Dawson Partners Ltd.* [1997] 2 Lloyd's Rep 49: "There is no room for documents which are almost the same, or which will do just as well." This does not mean that every "i" must be dotted and every "t" crossed. As one court stated, it's not a discrepancy if Smith is spelled "Smithh." Some typographical errors are excusable, of course. But the thrust of the rule is that every provision of the bill of lading, invoice, insurance policy, and any other required shipping document must match the letter of credit. Even a small discrepancy can cause the bank to reject the documents.

In the following case, *Courtaulds North America, Inc. v. North Carolina National Bank,* the court considered a discrepancy between the description of the goods on the letter of credit and on the invoice.

Courtaulds North America, Inc. v. North Carolina National Bank

528 F.2d 802 (1975)

United States Court of Appeals (4th Cir.)

BACKGROUND AND FACTS

The defendant bank issued an irrevocable letter of credit on behalf of its customer, Adastra Knitting Mills. It promised to honor sixty-day time drafts of Courtaulds for up to $135,000 covering shipments of "100% Acrylic Yarn." Courtaulds presented its draft together with a commercial invoice describing the merchandise as "Imported Acrylic Yarns." The packing lists that were stapled to the invoice contained the following description: "Cartons marked: 100% Acrylic." The bank refused to accept the draft because of the discrepancy between the letter of credit and the commercial invoice. (The buyer had gone into bankruptcy, and the court appointed trustee would not waive the discrepancy.) The documents were returned and the plaintiff brought this action. The lower court held that the bank was liable to the plaintiff for the amount of the draft because the packing lists attached to each carton stated that the cartons contained "100% Acrylic," and the bank appealed.

BRYAN, SENIOR CIRCUIT JUDGE

The defendant denied liability chiefly on the assertion that the draft did not agree with the letter's conditions, viz., that the draft be accompanied by a "Commercial invoice in triplicate stating (inter alia) that it covers ... 100% acrylic yarn"; instead, the accompanying invoices stated that the goods were "Imported Acrylic Yarn."

... [T]he District Court held defendant Bank liable to Courtaulds for the amount of the draft, interest, and costs. It concluded that the draft complied with the letter of credit when each invoice is read together with the packing lists stapled to it, for the lists stated on their faces: "Cartons marked: 100% Acrylic." After considering the insistent rigidity of the law and usage of bank credits and acceptances, we must differ with the District Judge and uphold Bank's position.

In utilizing the rules of construction embodied in the letter of credit—the *Uniform Customs* and state statute—one must constantly recall that the drawee bank is not to be embroiled in disputes between the buyer and the seller, the beneficiary of the credit. The drawee is involved only with documents, not with merchandise. Its involvement is altogether separate and apart from the transaction between the buyer and seller; its duties and liability are governed exclusively by the terms of the letter, not the terms of the parties' contract with each other. Moreover, as the predominant authorities unequivocally declare, the beneficiary must meet the terms of the credit—and precisely—if it is to exact performance of the issuer. Failing such compliance there can be no recovery from the drawee. That is the specific failure of Courtaulds here.

... [T]he letter of credit dictated that each invoice express on its face that it covered 100% acrylic yarn. Nothing less is shown to be tolerated in the trade. No substitution and no equivalent, through interpretation or logic, will serve. Harfield, *Bank Credits and Acceptances* (5th ed. 1974), commends and quotes aptly from an English case: "There is no room for documents which are almost the same, or which will do just as well." Although no pertinent North Carolina decision has been laid before us, in many cases elsewhere, especially in New York, we find the tenet of Harfield to be unshaken.

At trial Courtaulds prevailed on the contention that the invoices in actuality met the specifications of the letter of credit in that the packing lists attached to the invoices disclosed on their faces that the packages contained "cartons marked: 100% acrylic." ... But this argument cannot be accepted.

The district judge's pat statement adeptly puts an end to this contention of Courtaulds: "In dealing with letters of credit, it is a custom and practice of the banking trade for a bank to only treat a document as an invoice which clearly is marked on its face as 'invoice.'" This is not a pharisaical or doctrinaire persistence in the principle, but is altogether realistic in the environs of this case; it is plainly the fair and equitable measure. (The defect in description was not superficial but occurred in the statement of the quality of the yarn, not a frivolous concern.) Bank was not expected to scrutinize the collateral papers, such as the packing lists. Nor was it permitted to read into the instrument the contemplation or intention of the seller and buyer....

Had Bank deviated from the stipulation of the letter and honored the draft, then at once it might have been confronted with the not improbable risk of

continued

continued

the bankruptcy trustee's charge of liability for unwarrantably paying the draft monies to the seller, Courtaulds, and refusal to reimburse Bank for the outlay. Contrarily, it might face a Courtaulds claim that since it had depended upon Bank's assurance of credit in shipping yarn to Adastra, Bank was responsible for the loss. In this situation Bank cannot be condemned for sticking to the letter of the letter.

Nor is this conclusion affected by the amended or substituted invoices which Courtaulds sent to Bank after the refusal of the draft. No precedent is cited to justify retroactive amendment of the invoices or extension of the credit beyond the August 15 expiry of the letter.

For these reasons, we must vacate the decision of the trial court, despite the evident close reasoning and research of the district judge. . . .

Reversed and remanded for final judgment.

Decision. The judgment is reversed for the defendant bank. The description of the goods in the invoice did not match the description of the goods in the credit, and the defect was not cured by a correct description in the packing list.

Apply the strict compliance rule of the *Courtaulds* case to the following situation: Suppose that a seller receives a letter of credit from a foreign buyer covering "1,000 standard-size bed pillows." Seller's export manager completes an invoice for "1,000 bed pillows, size 20 × 26 in." A discrepancy would exist. Bankers are not expected to know that a "standard" bed pillow is 20 × 26 inches, and even if the banker did know, he would still have to refuse the document because of the discrepancy. Assume now that the invoice matches the letter of credit, but that the bill of lading shows shipment of "1,000 pillows." On this point the UCP is very clear: the description in a document other than an invoice may be "in general terms not conflicting with their description in the credit." Here the documents show no discrepancy.

The UCP 600 Rule. The UCP contains its own standards for compliance. Changes in UCP 600 in 2007 seem to indicate that it has moved toward a modified strict compliance rule. Article 14 states "Data in a document ... need not be identical to, but must not conflict with [other data in the same document], any other stipulated document or the credit. In documents other than the commercial invoice, the description of the goods ... may be in general terms not conflicting with their description in the credit." This seems to be more liberal than the former versions of the UCP or earlier case law. However, the rule of strict compliance seems to be retained in Article 18 with regard to the invoice, which states, "The description of the goods, services or performance in a commercial invoice must correspond with that appearing in the credit."

The Functional Standard of Compliance. While the strict compliance rule remains the prevailing view in most jurisdictions, some courts in the United States and in some European countries have used a "functional standard" of compliance, contending that the bank should look at the whole of the documents rather than simply requiring the documents to be the "mirror image" of the letter of credit.

An Ethical Issue in Handling Letters of Credit. In most cases, buyers will waive a minor discrepancy. However, sellers and bankers must beware. If a buyer is looking for a reason to reject the documents (e.g., if the ship has gone down at sea), a discrepancy will give the savvy (or unscrupulous?) buyer a way out. If the buyer is looking for a way to chisel a better price out of the deal, then a discrepancy will give him the leverage. The buyer can reject the documents, and only later reluctantly agree to waive the discrepancy—but only for a huge discount off the contract price! Issuing banks may on occasion want to find discrepancies. If they discover that their customer—the buyer—is going to back out of the deal, they can use the discrepancy to reject the documents. (An old adage states that any banker who cannot find a discrepancy isn't worth his or her salt.) Of course, almost all discrepancies are honest accidents or commercial mistakes and are easily resolved.

PROCEDURES FOR DISHONOR. A bank must follow the UCP guidelines for rejecting or dishonoring a presentation. The first step is to ask the buyer for a waiver. If the buyer decides to refuse the documents, the bank must give notice of its refusal to the presenting bank by telecommunication within five banking days. The notice must inform the presenter whether the documents are being held pending further instructions or are being returned. If the issuing bank fails to do this, it is precluded from claiming that the documents were properly presented.

Enjoining Banks from Purchasing Documents in Cases of Fraud

Earlier in this chapter you read the case of *Maurice O'Meara,* which illustrated the important principle that letters of credit are independent of the underlying sales contract. An issuing bank is responsible only for the seller's documents and is not concerned with the quality of the goods or whether the seller shipped the correct goods. If they are defective or nonconforming, the buyer's remedy is against the seller for breach of contract.

What if the buyer's problem is not that the quality or condition of the goods is defective, but that he or she has fallen victim to a fraud or a scam? What good would a breach of contract suit be against the perpetrator of a fraud who had disappeared with the cash? To address these situations, a partial exception to the independence principle has been created where the letter of credit is fraudulent, or forged, or if *fraud in the transaction* exists in the underlying sales contract. For instance, suppose that the buyer learns, almost too late, that the purported bill of lading is actually a fake and that no carrier exists by that name. Can the buyer stop its bank from honoring the seller's draft? No bank wants to be seen refusing documents without cause (especially where they have already been purchased by a nominated bank that is looking for reimbursement). After all, their international reputation is at stake, and no bank wants to be known for refusing to honor their letters of credit. One "escape hatch" for both buyer and issuing bank is for the buyer to obtain a court injunction stopping the bank from honoring its letter of credit.

The ability of a court to enjoin letters of credit for fraud is found in the case law of several nations and in the *Uniform Commercial Code.* The UCP is silent on the question of fraudulent documents. If an unscrupulous seller tries to present documents for a nonexistent shipment of goods or a container filled with rubbish, the buyer may be about to become a victim of fraud. If a buyer becomes aware that its bank is about to knowingly honor a fraudulent presentation, the buyer may petition a court for an injunction that would prevent the bank from paying on the credit. The court may order the injunction where necessary to protect the buyer from irreparable harm. If the demand for payment is made by a holder in due course, however, then the bank *must* honor the demand for payment.

The following case, *Sztejn v. J. Henry Schroder Banking Corp.*, presents a clear distinction between a mere breach of warranty and fraud. *O'Meara* involved a breach of warranty—the seller shipped newsprint paper of inferior quality. *Sztejn* involves fraud in the transaction—the presentation of documents covering goods and the shipment of bales of worthless rubbish. The *Sztejn* case is one of the most widely cited cases in U.S. letter of credit law.

Compare the rule holding in *Sztejn* regarding fraud in the transaction with the circumstances that arise in the English case *United City Merchants (Investments), Ltd. v. Royal Bank of Canada*. Notice how the English court distinguishes American precedent and narrows the application of the fraud exception.

Fraud in the transaction can take many forms, as illustrated by a common situation. In *Regent Corp., U.S.A. v. Azmat Bangladesh, Ltd.*, 686 N.Y.S.2d 24 (1999), a textile company located in Bangladesh represented to a U.S. buyer that bedsheets and pillowcases were to be manufactured in Bangladesh. In fact, the seller knew that the goods were a product of Pakistan but provided a fake certificate of origin because they were trying to circumvent U.S. import quotas on Bangladeshi linens. The New York court ruled that there was sufficient fraud in the transaction to justify the bank's refusal to honor the draft under the letter of credit.

Sztejn v. J. Henry Schroder Banking Corp.

31 N.Y.S.2d 631 (1941)

Supreme Court, Special Term, New York County

BACKGROUND AND FACTS

The plaintiff contracted to purchase hog bristles from Transea Traders in India. The defendant bank issued an irrevocable letter of credit to Transea covering a shipment of hog bristles and payable upon presentation of the proper documents. Transea filled fifty cases with cow hair and other worthless rubbish in order to obtain an ocean bill of lading from the steamship company showing the shipment of fifty cases of hog bristles. The documents and draft were presented to the defendant bank by The Chartered Bank of India, acting as agent for Transea. The plaintiff brought this action against the issuing bank to restrain it from paying on the letter of credit.

SHIENTAG, JUSTICE

One of the chief purposes of the letter of credit is to furnish the seller with a ready means of obtaining prompt payment for his merchandise. It would be a most unfortunate interference with business transactions if a bank before honoring drafts drawn upon it was obliged or even allowed to go behind the documents, at the request of the buyer and enter into controversies between the buyer and the seller regarding the quality of the merchandise shipped.... Of course, the application of this doctrine presupposes that the documents accompanying the draft are genuine and conform in terms to the requirements of the letter of credit. However, I believe that a different situation is presented in the instant action. This is not a controversy between the buyer and seller concerning a mere breach of warranty regarding the quality of the merchandise; on the present motion, it must be assumed that the seller has intentionally failed to ship any goods ordered by the buyer. In such a situation, where the seller's fraud has been called to the bank's attention before the drafts and documents have been presented for payment, the principle of the independence of the bank's obligation under the letter of credit should not be extended to protect the unscrupulous seller. It is true that even though the documents are forged or fraudulent, if the issuing bank has already paid the draft before receiving notice of the seller's fraud, it will be protected if it exercised reasonable diligence before making such payment. However, in the instant action Schroder has received notice of Transea's active fraud before it accepted or paid the draft....

Although our courts have used broad language to the effect that a letter of credit is independent of the primary contract between the buyer and seller, that language was used in cases concerning alleged breaches of warranty; no case has been brought to my attention on this point involving an intentional fraud on the part of the seller which was brought to the bank's notice with the request that it withhold payment of the draft on this account. The distinction between a breach of warranty and active fraud on the part of the seller is supported by authority and reason. As one court has stated: "Obviously, when the issuer of a letter of credit knows that a document, although correct in form, is, in point of fact, false or illegal, he cannot be called upon to recognize such a document as complying with the terms of a letter of credit."...

While the primary factor in the issuance of the letter of credit is the credit standing of the buyer, the security afforded by the merchandise is also taken into account. In fact, the letter of credit requires a bill of lading made out to the order of the bank and not the buyer. Although the bank is not interested in the exact detailed performance of the sales contract, it is vitally interested in assuring itself that there are some goods represented by the documents.

Accordingly, the defendant's motion to dismiss the supplemental complaint is denied.

Decision. The court held in favor of the plaintiff and enjoined the bank's payment. A court can enjoin an issuing bank from honoring a draft if the bank learns that its customer will suffer irreparable harm as a result of fraud.

Comment. Under the UCC (Section 5-114), a bank "may honor the draft . . . despite notification from the customer (the buyer) of fraud . . . but a court . . . may enjoin such honor." As an interesting note, the California legislature chose to omit the words "but a court ... may enjoin such honor." Therefore, in California, courts have held that no injunction can be issued against a letter of credit for fraud in the transaction.

United City Merchants (Investments), Ltd. v. Royal Bank of Canada

2 Weekly Law Reports 1039

House of Lords, 1982

BACKGROUND AND FACTS

The buyer, a Peruvian company, entered into a contract to purchase glass fibers at a price of $662,082 from an English seller. Payment was to be made under an irrevocable letter of credit confirmed by Royal Bank of Canada. The letter of credit called for a bill of lading dated no later than December 15, 1976. The goods were in fact loaded onto the vessel (the *American Accord*) on December 16, but the loading brokers issued a bill of lading which was dated December 15, 1976. Unaware of the false statement, the sellers submitted documents to Royal Bank, who refused to pay on the credit because it suspected fraud in the documents.

LORD DIPLOCK

If on their face, the documents presented to the confirming bank by the seller conform with the requirements of the credit as notified to him by the conforming bank, that bank is under a contractual obligation to the seller to honour the credit, notwithstanding that the bank has knowledge that the seller at the time of presentation of the conforming documents is alleged by the buyer to have, and in fact has already, committed a breach of his contract with the buyer for the sale of the goods to which the documents appear on their face to relate, that would have entitled the buyer to treat the contract of sale as rescinded and to reject the goods and refuse to pay the seller the purchase price. The whole commercial purpose for which the system of confirmed irrevocable documentary credits has been developed in international trade is to give to the seller an assured right to be paid before he parts with control of the goods that does not permit of any dispute with the buyer as to the performance of the contract of sale being used as a ground for non-payment or reduction or deferment of payment.

To this general statement of principle as to the contractual obligations of the confirming bank to the seller, there is one established exception: that is where the seller, for the purpose of drawing on the credit, fraudulently presents to the confirming bank documents that contain, expressly or by implication, material representations of fact that to his knowledge are untrue.... [*Sztejn v. J. Henry Schroder Banking Corporation* (1941) 31 N.Y.S.2d 631]. This judgment of the New York Court of Appeals was referred to with approval by the English Court of Appeal in *Edward Owen Engineering Ltd. v. Barclays Bank International Ltd.* [1978] Q.B. 159.... The courts will not allow their process to be used by a dishonest person to carry out a fraud.

The instant case, however, does not fall within the fraud exception. [The trial judge] found the sellers to have been unaware of the inaccuracy of Mr. Baker's notation of the date at which the goods were actually on board *American Accord*. They believed that it was true and that the goods had actually been loaded on or before December 15, 1976, as required by the documentary credit.

***

It has so far as I know, never been disputed that as between confirming bank and issuing bank and the buyer, the contractual duty of each bank under a confirmed irrevocable credit is to examine with reasonable care all documents presented in order to ascertain that they appear on their face to be in accordance with the terms and conditions of the credit, and, if they do so appear, to pay to the seller/beneficiary by whom the documents have been presented the sum stipulated by the credit.... It is equally clear, and is so provided by Article 9 of the Uniform Customs, that confirming banks and issuing banks assume no liability or responsibility to one another or to the buyer "for the form, sufficiency, accuracy, genuineness, falsification or legal effect of any documents."

Decision. Confirming banks are not permitted to refuse a demand payment when the documents, on their face, comply with the letter of credit. Under the English view, fraud perpetuated by a third party does not constitute fraud in the transaction so as to permit the confirming bank to deny payment. Here it was not established that the beneficiary had committed or had knowledge of the fraud.

Confirmed Letters of Credit

In most cases, a letter of credit is adequate assurance for payment. In certain instances, however, a seller may want an additional layer of security. Where a seller is uncertain about the soundness of an issuing bank in a foreign country, or of the integrity of the banking system there generally, or the stability of the government, the seller may want to request that the letter of credit be confirmed by a bank in its own country. A *confirmed letter of credit* is one in which a second bank, usually in the seller's country, has agreed to purchase documents and honor drafts on the same terms as the original issuing bank. Suppose a seller is shipping to a country that has a shortage of foreign currency, large foreign debts, and a poor balance of payments record. It is always possible that foreign government currency restrictions, imposed between the time the contract is agreed to and the time the drafts are tendered for payment, could prevent the issuing bank from honoring its letter of credit in dollars. A letter of credit confirmed by a bank in the seller's country will ensure prompt payment regardless of financial or political instability in the country where the issuing bank is located. Additionally, should legal action ever be necessary to collect on a letter of credit, a seller can much more easily sue a U.S. confirming bank in the United States than a foreign bank in foreign courts. Of course, a confirmed credit is far more expensive than one that is unconfirmed because two banks are exposed to the risk of the transaction. These costs must be weighed by the parties in determining the level of acceptable risk in the transaction.

Banks in the United States that confirm foreign letters of credit continuously monitor the economic and political conditions in those foreign countries. If a foreign buyer is unable to have its bank's letter of credit confirmed by a U.S. bank, then that may be a signal that the political and credit risks are too high. After all, if no U.S. bank will confirm a foreign letter of credit, why would the seller want to accept it? In this case, the seller might want to reconsider requesting some amount of cash in advance or other secure arrangement.

Standby Letters of Credit

A *standby letter of credit* (also called a *standby credit,* or simply a *standby)* is one in which the issuer is obligated to pay a beneficiary upon the presentation of documents indicating a default by the account party in the payment of a debt or the performance of an obligation. The documents might be as simple as a notice of default by the account party, signed by the beneficiary, and accompanied by a demand for payment. A standby letter of credit is a backup payment mechanism that the parties hope they will never have to use. It can be used to guarantee performance under a service or construction contract, to guarantee repayment of a loan, or as security for almost any other type of contract. The standby works much like the "performance guarantee" used by banks in other countries (or the "performance bond" in the UK) but is legally different. A standby is subject to the *International Standby Practice* (ISP 98), a set of rules and standards published by the International Chamber of Commerce.

A standby letter of credit is flexible and can be tailored for almost any use. Most are used in large, complex transactions. Assume that a construction firm enters into a contract with a foreign government to construct a public works project. The government wants assurances that the firm will complete the work as promised by being named as beneficiary of a standby credit. The credit could be payable upon the government's presentation of a written demand for payment and a notice of default to the issuing bank stating that the construction firm has failed to complete the required work in the manner and within the time called for in the contract. Like the documentary requirements we have already studied, the language of default must strictly comply with the language used in the standby letter of credit. Documentary requirements will depend on the transaction and the needs of the parties, but could include independent testing reports, architect's reports, court judgments, certified public accounting statements, or a signed statement by the beneficiary or an authorized corporate officer.

In the sale of goods, a standby can be used in lieu of a conventional letter of credit. Assume that a seller agrees to grant thirty-day open account terms to a buyer. In a standby credit, the bank is "standing by" as a backup, ready to purchase the documents if the buyer does not remit payment within thirty days. A standby can also be used to guarantee the *seller's* performance, i.e., that the seller will ship conforming goods within the time called for.

Standby letters of credit can be used to ensure the repayment of a loan. Suppose, for example, that a subsidiary of a U.S. company operating in Latin America borrows money from a local bank. The bank can require a standby letter of credit from a U.S. bank that would allow it to draw against the credit should the subsidiary default on its obligation.

A standby can be used to ensure compliance with almost any obligation. In the Exxon Valdez oil spill that occurred in Alaska in 1989, the court required that Exxon provide a $6 billion standby letter of credit to enssure that they would meet their obligations of environmental cleanup and payment of damages.

Not surprisingly, standby letters of credit have led to a great deal of litigation in the courts. To protect an account party under a standby credit from an "unfair" demand by the beneficiary, many international business lawyers will structure the standby credit to require that the beneficiary's request for payment be accompanied by a written, independent confirmation of the account party's default by a third party.

Middle East Politics and Standby Letters of Credit: The Iranian Claims. The politics of the Middle East have caused a great deal of litigation in this area. Prior to 1979, U.S. companies enjoyed lucrative business contracts with the Imperial Government of Iran, under the rule of the Shah of Iran. Many of these contracts involved the supplying of the latest armaments, consumer goods, and construction projects to this Islamic nation. These contracts had often been obtained using illegal payments to the Shah and his family. At the time of the revolution and the seizing of hostages at the U.S. embassy in Tehran, many U.S. firms had outstanding commitments to the government of Iran that were guaranteed with standby letters of credit. For example, in 1978, five banks alone had $12.6 billion in outstanding standby letters of credit. The following *American Bell* case clearly illustrates that the political risks of international business can even affect letter of credit transactions.

In *KMW International v. Chase Manhattan Bank*, 606 F.2d 10 (2d Cir. 1979), the court held that the unsettled situation in Iran was insufficient reason for releasing the bank from its obligation under a letter of credit. The court in *KMW* gave perhaps the real reason for the decision in the Iranian cases when it stated, "Both in the international business community and in Iran itself, Chase's commercial honor is essentially at stake. Failure to perform on its irrevocable letter of credit would constitute a breach of trust and substantially injure its reputation and perhaps even American credibility in foreign communities. Moreover, it could subject Chase to litigation in connection with not only this matter, but also other banking affairs in Iran."

American Bell International Inc. v. Islamic Republic of Iran

474 F. Supp. 420 (1979)

United States District Court (S.D.N.Y.)

BACKGROUND AND FACTS

In 1978, American Bell International, a subsidiary of AT&T, entered into a contract with the Imperial Government of Iran to provide consulting services and telecommunications equipment. The contract provided that all disputes would be resolved according to the laws of Iran and in Iranian courts. The contract provided for payment to Bell of $280 million, including a down payment of $38 million. Iran had the right to demand return of the down payment at any time and for any reason, with the amount returned to be reduced by 20 percent of the amounts that Bell had invoiced for work done. At the time of this action, about $30 million remained callable. In order to secure the return of the down payment on demand, Bell had been required to arrange for Manufacturers Bank to issue a standby letter of credit to the Bank of Iranshahr, payable on the demand of the Iranian government. However, in 1979, a revolution resulted in the overthrow of the imperial government. The

continued

continued

Shah of Iran fled the country, and a revolutionary council was established to govern the country. The nation was in a state of chaos, and Westerners fled the country. Having been left with unpaid invoices, Bell ceased its operations. Fearing that any monies paid to Iran would never be recouped, Bell brought this action asking the court to enjoin Manufacturers Bank from honoring Iran's demands for payment under the letter of credit.

MACMAHON, JUDGE

Plaintiff has failed to show that irreparable injury may possibly ensue if a preliminary injunction is denied. Bell does not even claim, much less show, that it lacks an adequate remedy at law if Manufacturers makes a payment to Bank Iranshahr in violation of the Letter of Credit. It is too clear for argument that a suit for money damages could be based on any such violation, and surely Manufacturers would be able to pay any money judgment against it....

To be sure, Bell faces substantial hardships upon denial of its motion. Should Manufacturers pay the demand, Bell will immediately become liable to Manufacturers for $30.2 million, with no assurance of recouping those funds from Iran for the services performed. While counsel represented in graphic detail the other losses Bell faces at the hands of the current Iranian government, these would flow regardless of whether we ordered the relief sought. The hardship imposed from a denial of relief is limited to the admittedly substantial sum of $30.2 million.

But Manufacturers would face at least as great a loss, and perhaps a greater one, were we to grant relief. Upon Manufacturers' failure to pay, Bank Iranshahr could initiate a suit on the Letter of Credit and attach $30.2 million of Manufacturers' assets in Iran. In addition, it could seek to hold Manufacturers liable for consequential damages beyond that sum resulting from the failure to make timely payment. Finally, there is no guarantee that Bank Iranshahr or the government, in retaliation for Manufacturers' recalcitrance, will not nationalize additional Manufacturers' assets in Iran in amounts which counsel, at oral argument, represented to be far in excess of the amount in controversy here.

Apart from a greater monetary exposure flowing from an adverse decision, Manufacturers faces a loss of credibility in the international banking community that could result from its failure to make good on a letter of credit.

Bell, a sophisticated multinational enterprise well advised by competent counsel, entered into these arrangements with its corporate eyes open. It knowingly and voluntarily signed a contract allowing the Iranian government to recoup its down payment on demand, without regard to cause. It caused Manufacturers to enter into an arrangement whereby Manufacturers became obligated to pay Bank Iranshahr the unamortized down payment balance upon receipt of conforming documents, again without regard to cause.

Both of these arrangements redounded tangibly to the benefit of Bell. The contract with Iran, with its prospect of designing and installing from scratch a nationwide and international communications system, was certain to bring to Bell both monetary profit and prestige and goodwill in the global communications industry. The agreement to indemnify Manufacturers on its Letter of Credit provided the means by which these benefits could be achieved. One who reaps the rewards of commercial arrangements must also accept their burdens. One such burden in this case, voluntarily accepted by Bell, was the risk that demand might be made without cause on the funds constituting the down payment. To be sure, the sequence of events that led up to that demand may well have been unforeseeable when the contracts were signed. To this extent, both Bell and Manufacturers have been made the unwitting and innocent victims of tumultuous events beyond their control. But, as between two innocents, the party who undertakes by contract the risk of political uncertainty and governmental caprice must bear the consequences when the risk comes home to roost.

So ordered.

Decision. The court refused to issue the injunction. The letter of credit was not enjoined because there was no clear showing of irreparable injury and because the plaintiff had an adequate legal remedy against Iran for the return of the monies that would be paid. Such a rule protects the sanctity of a bank's reputation for honoring its letters of credit. The plaintiff was aware of the risks involved and must bear the consequences.

Other Specialized Uses for Letters of Credit

Many specialized types of letters of credit provide a mechanism for financing a sale or other business transaction. Some of these types are discussed here.

Transferable Credits. *Transferable credits* are usually used by international traders. Traders buy and sell goods in international trade quickly and with no view to actually using the goods themselves. They bear considerable risk every day. Traders operate on little capital, buying merchandise or commodities in one country, taking title through the documents, and then, through their business contacts built up over years of experience, selling at a profit. Some traders specialize in trade with the developing world, often trading commodities for raw materials or merchandise when dollars or hard currency is not available. For instance, assume a Swiss bank issues a letter of credit for the account of an African country in favor of the trader, with a part of the credit transferred to the trader's supplier in the Philippines for the cost of the goods it is supplying to the African country. This letter of credit can be split up among many suppliers around the world, each presenting documents for payment, with the trader taking its profit out of the balance of the credit. Shipments of crude oil are often bought and sold in this fashion.

Red Clauses in Credits. The *red clause* is a financing tool for smaller sellers who need capital to produce the products to be shipped under a letter of credit. A red clause in a letter of credit is a promise (usually written or underlined in red ink) by the issuing bank to reimburse the seller's bank for loans made to the seller. The loan, then, is really an advance on the credit. Loans can be used only for purchasing raw materials or for covering the costs of manufacturing or shipping of the goods described in the credit. Ultimately, the liability will fall on the buyer if the seller defaults on shipment or repayment of the amounts taken under the credit. This form of financing is very risky for the buyer and its bank.

Revolving and Evergreen Credits. When a buyer is planning on purchasing on a regular basis from a foreign seller, a *revolving letter of credit* may be used. Instead of having to use several different credits, one may be used with a maximum amount available during a certain period. As the draws against the credit are paid, the full amount becomes available again and continues until the expiration of the credit. An *evergreen* clause provides for automatic renewal of the letter of credit until the bank gives "clear and unequivocal" notice of its intent not to renew.

Back-to-Back Letter of Credit Financing. A *back-to-back letter of credit* is a special type of financing device. In certain circumstances, an exporter is selling goods to a buyer in one transaction and is buying supplies in another. Under a back-to-back credit, the exporter can use its credit with the buyer to finance the purchase of goods from the supplier. Thus, a back-to-back credit is really two credits, one representing the security for the second. The bank that issues the second credit requires that it be assigned the proceeds of the original credit. Many banks will issue the second credit only if they had opened the first one (known as a *countercredit*). Back-to-back letters of credit are usually used by traders who are not manufacturers or by other intermediaries with minimal capital resources who buy and sell goods for delivery to others.

Electronic Data Interchange and the eUCP

Like funds transfers, letters of credit have been issued and transmitted to advising banks electronically for many years (and from advising bank to beneficiary usually by mail). Now it appears that the use of electronic documentation will soon increase and that beneficiaries in the near future will be presenting documents electronically to banks for payment.

In 2002, the International Chamber of Commerce published the *eUCP,* a set of rules that extends the UCP to electronic documents. When documents are submitted electronically, eUCP rules apply by agreement of the parties. The eUCP addresses the format for electronic documents (the rules are flexible and include signed e-mail attachments or secured transfer), authentication and digital signatures, transmission errors, the manner of presentation, and other issues.

Bolero is a technical infrastructure created by the world's banking and logistics firms for exchanging electronic documents in a common format, including bills of lading, letters of credit, and other bank documents. *Identrus* is a private company founded by a small consortium of the world's largest banks to provide secure "digital identities" or signatures for confidentiality and authentication of financial and legal documents. Both *Identrus* and *Bolero* represent technological innovations necessary to move the centuries-old banking and shipping industries to the paperless age.

Letters of Credit in Trade Finance Programs

Letter of credit financing plays an important role in export financing by government and intergovernmental agencies. U.S. exports are financed by such agencies as the *Agency for International Development* (AID), the *World Bank* (which provides financial and technical assistance to developing countries to stimulate economic growth), the *Commodity Credit Corporation* (which assists with commerce in surplus agricultural products), and the *Export-Import Bank of the United States (Eximbank)*. These agencies often insure payments made to U.S. sellers under letters of credit that are confirmed by U.S. banks using a letter of commitment from the agency to the issuing bank.

AID Financing. A typical AID financing situation might include a letter of credit. A country wishing to import U.S. products, usually to be used in developmental projects such as building roads, power-generating facilities, and the like, applies to AID for financing. AID then issues its commitment to a U.S. bank that issues its letter of credit for the benefit of the U.S. supplier of eligible goods used in the project. The issuing bank receives reimbursement for payments under its letter of credit from AID.

Eximbank Financing. Eximbank is the largest U.S. export financing agency. It can provide guarantees on loans made by commercial banks and insurance on credit extended by U.S. exporters to their foreign customers. It also makes loans directly from Eximbank funds, including fixed-rate loans to foreign buyers of American-made exports. Under another Eximbank loan program, a U.S. bank designated by the foreign buyer opens a letter of credit on behalf of the buyer for the benefit of a U.S. supplier. Eximbank guarantees the issuing bank repayment of sums that it pays out under the credit. Eximbank then receives its payments under the loan agreement worked out in advance between it and the foreign buyer. Despite the importance of the U.S. Eximbank, only a small percentage of U.S. exports are financed by Eximbank. The U.S. air transportation industry received the largest amount of Eximbank support of any industry. Others included oil and gas, power plants, and manufacturing. In 2006, Eximbank authorized over 2,600 export sales for over $12 billion in export loans, guarantees, and export-credit insurance. In the past, Eximbank had been subject to criticism for not having assisted small business U.S. exporters. In 2006, however, about 25 percent of Eximbank support went to aid small business. Eximbank has increased its lending guarantees for U.S. goods going to developing countries. Other countries have export–import banks of their own to assist in financing their exports.

Commodity Credit Corporation. The Commodity Credit Corporation provides payment assurances to U.S. sellers of surplus agricultural products to approved foreign buyers. Standby letters of credit are often used, whereby the seller can draw under the credit for invoices that remain unpaid by the overseas buyer.

Foreign Credit Insurance Association. The Foreign Credit Insurance Association (FCIA) is an association of private insurance companies that insure U.S. exporters from political and commercial risk. It works in partnership with Eximbank. Commercial risk includes losses due to the default of the buyer and the inability of the buyer to pay because of natural disasters. Political covers the confiscation of goods by the government, nonconvertibility of the buyer's currency, war expropriation, and the inability of the buyer to obtain an import license. Typically, the FCIA provides coverage for up to 100 percent of the political risk and 90 percent of the commercial risk. The cost of this insurance is based on an analysis of the country and the foreign importer.

Another benefit to small- and medium-sized exporters is that their foreign accounts receivable are more valuable to commercial banks due to the insurance protection. As such, exports sold on open account to foreign buyers can more readily be sold or assigned to a financial institution. FCIA policies are also available to cover losses under confirmed letters of credit issued in favor of U.S. exporters by U.S. commercial banks.

Conclusion

The letter of credit is a very flexible banking arrangement that can be structured according to the needs of the parties. It is a security device and a tool for financing. It provides enough security for companies to do business safely over great distances. One indirect result of using the letter of credit is that it gives the parties an opportunity to experiment with doing business with each other. It allows them to build trust, which is essential to generating repeat business. If the buyer and seller are both pleased with each other's performance, they may eventually be able to omit the letter of credit from future transactions. The seller may be satisfied by selling on documentary terms alone, and then eventually on open account terms. Each step becomes easier and less expensive for the buyer, and that in turn may translate into additional business for the seller.

Chapter Summary

1. The *bill of exchange* or *international draft* is a specialized type of *negotiable instrument* commonly used to expedite foreign money payments in many types of international transactions.
2. The commercial and financing use of a draft or other negotiable instrument is derived from its *negotiability,* which is the quality that allows it to act as a substitute for money. When a draft is negotiated to a *holder in due course,* that party takes it free from most disputes that might arise between the drawer and drawee (the original parties to the underlying transaction). This protection for the holder in due course allows banks and other parties to purchase or accept drafts without fear of becoming embroiled in litigation over the original contract for which the draft was drawn.
3. A draft that may be paid upon presentation or demand is known as a *sight draft* because it is payable "on sight." The sight draft is prepared by the seller and presented with the shipping documents through banking channels, moving from the seller's bank in the country of export to a foreign correspondent bank in the buyer's country and city. The draft is thereby sent "for collection," a process known as a *documentary collection.*
4. Banks and other financial institutions involved in commercial lending provide a wide range of financing packages for international trade, commonly called *trade finance.* A draft due at a future date or after a specified period of time is known as a *time draft.* The buyer's acceptance indicates the buyer's unconditional obligation to pay the draft on the date due.
5. A *banker's acceptance* is a negotiable instrument and short-term financing device widely used to finance international (as well as domestic) sales.
6. The documentary *letter of credit* is defined as the definite undertaking of a bank, issued in accordance with the instructions of their customer, addressed to, or in favor of, the beneficiary, wherein the bank promises to pay a certain sum of money (or to accept or negotiate the beneficiary's drafts up to that sum), in the stated currency, within the prescribed time limits, upon the complying presentation of the required and conforming documents.
7. The *Uniform Custom and Practice for Documentary Credits* (UCP No. 600, 2007) is a set of standardized rules for issuing and handling letters of credit, drafted and published by the *International Chamber of Commerce.*
8. The letter of credit is a separate transaction and independent from the underlying sales contract on which it was based. Bankers deal in documents and not in goods, so they are not concerned with the quality or condition of goods represented in the credit.

9. The buyer's application for a credit forms a contract between the buyer and the issuing bank.
10. Credits are transmitted to the beneficiary through an *advising bank* (or through a *confirming bank,* in the case of a confirmed letter of credit).
11. The seller must make a *complying presentation* to the *nominated bank* within the time limits of the credit and according to the terms of the credit, the provisions of the UCP, and standard banking practices.
12. Documents containing discrepancies will be rejected and held for the buyer's instructions or returned to the seller. A discrepancy exists if the seller's documents, *on their face,* do not conform to the terms of the letter of credit. The description of the goods in the commercial invoice must correspond exactly to that in the credit. Documents are usually interpreted according to the *strict compliance rule.*
13. Courts have the power in certain cases to enjoin banks from honoring documents that are fraudulent or where there was fraud in the transaction.
14. *Confirmed letters of credit* contain the additional obligation of a second bank, usually in the seller's country, to honor a complying presentation. They are the next best alternative to receiving cash in advance for an international sale.
15. A *standby letter of credit* is one in which the issuer is obligated to pay a beneficiary upon the presentation of documents indicating a default by the account party in the payment of a debt or the performance of an obligation.

Questions and Case Problems

1. Wade entered into a contract to sell irrigation equipment to Ribadalgo, its Ecuadorian distributor. Ribadalgo obtained an irrevocable letter of credit in the amount of $400,000 from Banco General Runinahui, S.A. (Banco), a bank in Quito, Ecuador. The letter of credit provided that Wade was to ship by July 30, 1992. Wade was to present documents for payment "no later than 15 days after shipment, but within the validity of the credit." The expiry date of the letter of credit was August 21, 1992. Partial shipments were acceptable. The letter of credit stated that it was governed by the UCP. Citibank confirmed the letter of credit. Wade shipped a portion of the goods on July 7. On July 21, just before the document presentment deadline, Wade presented the requisite documents to Citibank for payment. Two days later, on July 23, Citibank informed Wade that the documents contained discrepancies and that it therefore would not honor Wade's request for payment. In response, Wade forwarded amended documents to Citibank on July 24 and July 27. Although Citibank conceded the documents as amended contained no discrepancies, it nevertheless rejected them as untimely because they were not received within fifteen days of the July 7 shipment date as required by the credit. On July 17, the Ecuadorian government issued an order freezing all Ribadalgo's assets and precluding payment on any lines of credit made available to Ribadalgo due to alleged drug trafficking. Four days later, Ecuadorian banking authorities entered an order barring Banco from making payment under the letter of credit. In turn, Banco advised Citibank not to honor any request for payment made by Wade thereunder. Is Wade entitled to payment under the letter of credit from Citibank? Wade argues that the documents did not have to be conforming before the presentment deadline, but only before the expiry date of the credit. Is Wade correct? Why do you think Citibank rejected the documents on July 21? *Banco General Runinahui, S.A. v. Citibank,* 97 F.3d 480 (11th Cir. 1996).
2. The rule of strict compliance in New York is best illustrated by *Beyene v. Irving Trust Co.,* 762 F.2d 4 (2d Cir. 1985). The letter of credit specified that payment be made on presentation of a bill of lading naming "Mohammed Sofan" as the party to be notified when the goods arrive. However, the bill of lading submitted to the bank with the demand for payment misspelled the name as "Mohammed Soran." The confirming bank refused payment because of this discrepancy, and the beneficiary sued. Was this a "material" discrepancy, or was it "so insignificant as not to relieve the issuing and confirming bank of its obligation to pay"? The court compared and contrasted the misspelling of "Sofan" as "Soran" to the misspelling of "Smith" as "Smithh." The court stated that the misspelling of "Smith" is not a discrepancy because the meaning is "unmistakably clear despite

what is obviously a typographical error." How did the court decide? Is there a difference between the misspellings of "Smith" and "Sofan"?

3. Hambro Bank, Ltd., an English bank, received a cable from a Danish company, A.O., requesting that an irrevocable letter of credit be opened in favor of J. H. Rayner and Company. A.O. instructed Hambro Bank that the letter of credit be for "... about \P16,975 [pounds] against invoice full straight clean bills of lading ... covering about 1,400 tons Coromandel groundnuts." The bill of lading presented to Hambro by J. H. Rayner stated "... bags machine-shelled groundnut kernels," with the abbreviation "C.R.S." in the margin. Hambro refused to pay on the letter of credit. J. H. Rayner sued Hambro. The custom of trade holds that C.R.S. is short for Coromandel groundnuts. Why did the bank not want to pay on this letter of credit? Was the bank correct in denying payment on this letter of credit? *J. H. Rayner and Co., Ltd. v. Hambro's Bank, Ltd.* [1943] 1 K.B. 36.
4. The seller of goods has a right to proceed judicially against an issuing bank that dishonors its obligation under an irrevocable letter of credit, just as the seller has the right to proceed directly against the buyer. Should the issuing bank also be liable for consequential damages that are reasonably foreseeable? See *Hadley v. Baxendale* [1854] 9 Ex. 341.
5. A South African firm applied for a revolving letter of credit in favor of a German exporter at a branch of Barclays Bank in Johannesburg. The letter of credit was issued covering shipments of pharmaceuticals and was confirmed by Deutsche Bank in Germany. Shipments proceeded with no problem, growing larger and more frequent. Barclays increased the amount of the letter of credit on several occasions to accommodate the growing business. To Barclays' knowledge, their account party had always taken possession of the goods and sold them quickly for a profit. Barclays was pleased with their customer's history and increased their financing. In the last shipment, the largest of all, Deutsche Bank honored the seller's sight draft for the full amount of the letter of credit and presented the documents to Barclays. While Barclays was inspecting the documents, it learned that the South African buyer had ceased business. In the meantime, Deutsche Bank discovered that the seller has ceased business also. On inspection by Barclays, the cargo containers were found to contain only worthless junk. Investigative reports placed both buyer and seller in Brazil. What happened? What are the rights and liabilities of the advising and confirming bank? How do banks handle problems like this?

Managerial Implications

1. Your firm regularly sells to customers in Germany, Poland, Japan, Canada, and Venezuela. How would you evaluate the creditworthiness of firms in each of these countries? How would the credit risk differ in each of these countries? What sources of information would you use? Under what circumstances would you consider selling to firms in these countries without a letter of credit? In which of these countries would you want the buyer's letter of credit to be confirmed by an American bank? Why? What additional protection does the confirmed credit provide?
2. An advising bank presents documents to you for payment. How would you respond to each of the following discrepancies? Explain your answer.
   a. The letter of credit calls for an ocean bill of lading. The seller presents a trucker's bill of lading showing shipment to an ocean port.
   b. The sales contract and the letter of credit call for shipment of "Soda Ash Light." The invoice shows shipment of "Soda Ash Light," but the bill of lading describes the shipment as "Soda Ash."
   c. The letter of credit calls for shipment of 1,000 kilograms. The invoice shows shipment of an equal amount in pounds.
   d. The CIF contract with the letter of credit calls for onboard bill of lading to be dated by December 20. The bill of lading is dated December 20, but the insurance policy is dated December 21.

Ethical Considerations

1. Corby, an experienced tire broker in Wales, offered to sell tires to Chappell, a tire broker in California. Chappell contacted two U.S. tire distributors, Jenkins in Tennessee and Hein in Ohio, and agreed to act as their agent in negotiations with Corby. Corby claimed that he had a large client who had

negotiated an arrangement directly with Michelin to handle all of its overstock blemished tires from France and who could offer 50,000 to 70,000 Michelin tires per quarter at 40 to 60 percent below the U.S. market price on an exclusive and ongoing basis. Corby faxed a list of tires, showing that the tires bore the designation "DA/2C." Chappell faxed the list to Jenkins and Hein. They knew that the "DA" meant "defective appearance." When Chappell asked Corby about the "/2C" he was told that it meant the tires were located at a different warehouse. Chappell told Corby on several occasions that since it was October 1998, the season for selling winter tires was almost over and that he required summer tires as well, to bundle with the winter tires. A second list showed no summer tires and nowhere near the 50,000 tires promised. In November and December, Corby pressured Chappell and Jenkins to open the letter of credit, asserting that if they did not do so the deal would be ended, thus preventing the buyers from being able to procure the requested summer tires. In late December, Jenkins began having reservations regarding the deal because Corby's representations were becoming suspicious. Jenkins requested to speak to Corby's source. Corby put him in touch with Evans, a tire distributor in England. In January, Evans sent the following fax to Jenkins:

> There are large stocks of Michelin summer pattern tyres being made available within the next 7/10 days and we will be pleased to offer these to you when an acceptable Letter of Credit is received for the winter pattern tyres. We will be very happy to work with you on Michelin tyres on a long term basis and give you first option on offers. May we once again stress the urgency of letting us have the Letter of Credit for the Michelin winter tyres so that we can commence business on a long term basis.

Evans faxed a pro forma invoice requesting a letter of credit in favor of PTZ Trading Company in Guernsey as the beneficiary. Evans said that the letter of credit had to be sent immediately. The buyers felt that they had to comply as a show of good faith. An irrevocable credit was issued by an Ohio bank according to the terms of the pro forma invoice and stated:

> Covering shipment of: "14,851 Michelin tyres at usd 34.83 per tire in accordance with seller's pro forma invoice 927-98 dated 11-19-98. Shipping terms: EXWORKS any European location. The credit is subject to UCP Publication 500. Expiry date April 2, 1999. The credit was advised to the sellers through Barclays Bank.

Shortly later, the negotiations broke down over the issue of summer tires, and the parties became hostile. In February, Corby sent a list of summer tires that had fewer units than promised, contained sizes not used in the United States, included various tires not manufactured by Michelin, and specified prices that were often higher than the cost of purchasing the tires one at a time from most dealers in the United States. In March, the buyers discovered that the "DA/2C" designation, attached to many of the tires, actually meant that the U.S. Department of Transportation serial numbers had been buffed off those units, rendering them illegal for import to or sale in the United States. Just before the letter of credit expired, Jenkins was informed by Sievers, a German tire distributor who was shipping the tires for PTZ Trading Co., that the tires were about to ship. Jenkins protested that he had not given permission to ship the tires because there was no agreement on summer tires. He threatened legal action. Sievers responded that he did not need permission and proceeded to ship. Sievers obtained a bill of lading and presented all documents to Barclays Bank for payment. The documents strictly complied with the credit. Jenkins petitioned an Ohio court for a restraining order preventing the issuing bank from honoring the credit. Barclays Bank learned of the order and refused Sievers' presentment. The carrier billed Jenkins for the ocean freight, and the tires remained in a warehouse in Savannah, Georgia. After a hearing in July, the court denied the buyer's petition for the restraining order. The Ohio Court of Appeals reversed, and the buyer appealed to the Ohio Supreme Court. See *Mid-America Tire, Inc. v. PTZ Trading Ltd.*, 768 N.E.2d 619 (2002).

1. What are the buyer's legal arguments supporting their petition for a restraining order? How do the facts support that argument? What precedent can they cite?
2. What are the seller's arguments opposing the petition for a restraining order?
3. What do you think about the way the buyer handled this from the beginning? What does this say about their level of expertise in international business? Explain.
4. If you had been in the buyer's position, what would you have done differently?
5. If the documents had not strictly complied with the credit, would this case have turned out differently?
6. This court's decision only addressed the petition for a restraining order. How will the parties finally resolve the dispute on the underlying sales contract? What do you think will happen to the tires? Who is responsible for their warehousing fees?

2. Your firm has contracted to purchase silk from overseas suppliers on letter of credit terms. After contracting but before presentment of the seller's documents, China expands its production and floods the market with raw silk. The price of silk plummets on world markets. Comment on whether you should try to find a minor discrepancy in the documents to justify rejecting the documents. Is it ethical for a buyer to reject documents presented under a letter of credit that contains only a minor discrepancy between the documents and the credit? Do the reasons matter? Does it matter that the buyer may know that the shipment actually conforms to the requirements of the contract and of the letter of credit? What is meant by the following statement: "Buyers and their banks have on occasion been known to 'invent' discrepancies; to make a 'mountain out of a molehill.'"

FOR INTERNET ACTIVITIES, VISIT ACADEMIC.CENGAGE.COM/BLAW/SCHAFFER.

PART 3 International and U.S. Trade Law

Part Three turns from the study of the private law of international business transactions to a study of the public law of international trade. These are actually two very different areas of the law. As we saw in the preceding chapters, the law of international business transactions is a type of private law that determines the rights and responsibilities of two or more parties in their business relationship. The law of international contracts for the sale of goods was one example. *International trade law,* on the other hand, is a body of public law used to determine the responsibilities that nations have to one another in their trade relations. An agreement between two nations to charge a certain rate of duty on imported goods would be governed by international trade law.

Before one can understand how nations agree upon and implement international trade law, one must first understand the national lawmaking process. Chapter Eight explains how the various branches of the U.S. government share the responsibility for regulating foreign commerce and trade. Once the role of the executive and legislative branches of government in regulating trade activity is explained, the discussion of public law can be extended to international trade relations.

Chapters Nine, Ten, and Eleven cover the basics of international trade law. Chapter Nine examines the *General Agreement on Tariffs and Trade* (GATT) and the *World Trade Organization.* Since its inception in 1947, GATT has provided the framework for regulating most world trade in goods. We will examine in detail the major GATT principles as enacted in 1994 as a result of the *Uruguay Round* trade negotiations and key terminology and concepts of international trade law.

Chapter Ten examines laws that help ensure access to foreign markets. This chapter focuses on how the U.S. government has used its economic and political leverage to force other countries to remove non-tariff barriers to the import of U.S. goods and services. Here, we will have the chance to examine many "sectoral issues," including trade in services, agriculture, textiles, steel, and other industries.

Chapter Eleven looks at special GATT problems involving the issues of free trade versus protectionism and the regulation of import competition. Many of these topics, such as dumping and subsidies, may be familiar to the reader from courses in economics. In this chapter, we will examine the very interesting legal aspects and political ramifications of these issues.

Chapter Twelve examines customs and tariff laws that govern the importing of goods into the United States and the relationship between a U.S. importer and the U.S. government. We will learn how to determine the dutiable status of foreign goods and how to move them into the United States through the "entry process." We will look closely at the role of U.S. Customs and Border Protection, the U.S. agency charged with administering U.S. customs laws. This chapter focuses on importing as an integral part of the global strategy of the firm, in the context of global sourcing and the location of factories and assembly plants in different regions of the world.

Chapter Thirteen discusses controls imposed on the export of goods and technology for reasons of national security and foreign policy. We will examine the use of trade sanctions and other controls to stop the spread of weapons of mass destruction and missile technology, to fight international terrorism, and to further human rights.

Chapter Fourteen covers the *North American Free Trade Agreement* (NAFTA) and trade issues affecting the Western Hemisphere. This subject is covered near the end of this part because it builds upon the principles of global trade covered in the earlier chapters.

Finally, the European Union is covered in Chapter Fifteen, near the end of this part, because it represents one extreme on the continuum of economic integration. Although NAFTA is a "free trade area," the European Union takes the process of economic integration several steps further and is both a "customs union" with common tariff laws and a "monetary union" with a common currency.

CHAPTER 8
National Lawmaking Powers and the Regulation of U.S. Trade

The U.S. Constitution provides for a separation of powers between the executive and legislative branches of government. In the field of international economic affairs, however, the roles of Congress and the president are not clearly defined. We know that Congress has the authority to impose duties, to regulate commerce with foreign nations, to punish offenses against the law of nations, and to declare war. But what of the president? The Constitution tells us that the president appoints ambassadors, negotiates with foreign nations, and is the commander-in-chief of the armed forces. The president also makes treaties, although only with the advice and consent of the Senate.

Even this cursory reading of the Constitution suggests that most of the authority to regulate U.S. commerce and trade with foreign countries rests with Congress and not with the president. Most scholars would agree. After all, the Constitution tells us that Congress "regulates" commerce with foreign nations, while the president merely "negotiates." In practice, it is not so simple. The system of checks and balances between the two branches has taken well over 200 years to develop. One established principle of American government is that Congress, within limits set out by decisions of the Supreme Court interpreting the Constitution, has the authority to delegate aspects of its legislative authority to the executive branch. Congress can enact a statute setting forth the goals to be accomplished and the means by which to achieve them and then authorize the president to carry them out. It can authorize the creation of a regulatory agency and provide funding for its work. As long as the president and the executive branch agencies are complying with the will of Congress, they are acting with the full force of law and usually with a large measure of congressional backing. This applies to the regulation of commerce with foreign nations and the establishment of U.S. trade policies.

In this chapter, we begin by exploring the basic concepts of the separation of powers in a modern context. We will examine congressional power over foreign commerce and foreign relations, the "inherent" authority of the president as chief executive, and delegations of power from Congress to the president. We will see the difference between "treaties" and lesser "executive agreements," both of which are used to implement the trade policies of the nation. We will also see how Congress has enacted statutes giving the president the authority to negotiate foreign trade agreements, including "fast track" trade authority.

The chapter then traces the history of American trade laws from the protectionist days of the *Smoot-Hawley Tariff Act of 1930,* which raised tariffs on imported goods to historic highs, to the free trade mentality that gave birth to the World Trade Organization in 1995. Finally, we will look at the issue of federal–state relations and see the limits placed on state power when it comes to international affairs. This material provides an important background for later chapters.

The Separation of Powers

At the time the Constitution was drafted, people were greatly concerned with how foreign commerce would be regulated. During this period of U.S.

history, each state was interested primarily in its own economic well-being. States imposed regulations on commerce to protect their own local industries, their ports, and their agricultural interests.

To ensure that states would not erect barriers to commerce between them and to guarantee a source of revenue to the federal government in the form of import duties, the drafters of the Constitution placed the power to regulate international commerce in the hands of the federal government. The drafters believed, for example, that economic disintegration could result if states were free to tax exports or if states located along the seacoast could tax imports passing through to states located inland. Moreover, they wanted the United States to be able to deal with foreign nations from a position of political strength and unity. The framers of the Constitution understood that trade relations with foreign nations could not be handled successfully by each state on its own, but only by a strong federal government that could speak for the economic and political interests of the nation as a whole.

The Executive–Legislative Debate

Today, the concept that the power over both foreign affairs and foreign trade rests with the federal government arouses little controversy. Considerable debate has arisen, however, over how the Constitution divides that power between Congress and the president. Indeed, in recent years, both branches of government have sought greater control over international affairs.

One argument in favor of a strong executive branch is that the nation must "speak with one voice" in international affairs. If each senator or representative, perhaps motivated by the local interests of her own constituents, attempted to negotiate agreements with foreign nations on matters such as tariff reductions, trade in agriculture or semiconductors, provisions for military assistance, or even nuclear disarmament, the process would be encumbered by local interests and would be ineffective and potentially disastrous.

The 1970s saw a shift in the balance of power between Congress and the president. Congress began to exercise greater oversight and control over the president's conduct of foreign affairs. Congress and the American people were largely unhappy with the president's use of troops in an unpopular and undeclared war in Vietnam. Abuses of government and political power came to light during the Watergate investigations, leading to the resignation of President Nixon. As a result, Congress began to view the executive branch with suspicion and mistrust.

During the following two decades, Congress continued to keep watch over the presidency and to assert itself though legislation. Then, following the terrorist attacks on the United States in 2001, the balance of power shifted again. With the president's political party controlling Congress and the nation gripped by fear of more terrorist attacks, from anthrax to radioactive bombs, new laws were enacted that gave tremendous power to the president and the executive branch. These laws restructured the government and gave sweeping authority to law enforcement and intelligence agencies to deal with terrorists.

Of course, the relationship between the president and Congress depends on which political party is in power in Congress. After the Republican Party lost control of Congress in President Bush's second term, constitutional scholars and a large segment of the American public viewed the president's powers with more suspicion and constitutional scrutiny.

Legislative Power

Article I of the Constitution confers "all legislative powers" upon Congress, including the power "to regulate commerce with foreign nations, and among the several states" (Section 8, clause 3). In addition, Congress has broad power to pass domestic laws, raise and support armies, provide and maintain a navy, declare war, appropriate monies, and levy and collect taxes. The Senate has the authority to give advice and consent to the president in making treaties with foreign nations and to approve treaties by a two-thirds vote.

Considering these powers as a whole, the U.S. Supreme Court has consistently held that Congress has wide-ranging constitutional power to establish overall economic and trade policy for the United States and to put it into effect through legislation. Congress has recognized, however, that the day-to-day conduct of trade relations with foreign nations is often best accomplished through a strong executive branch. As a result, Congress has delegated authority to the president to carry out the trade policies set by statute.

Presidential or Executive Power

Article II of the Constitution confers executive power on the president. The executive power is not clearly specified, and many court decisions interpret what the Constitution meant to confer. However, both courts and legal scholars have said that the president has greater and wider-reaching power over foreign affairs than over domestic policy. One of the most famous statements about the power of the president over foreign affairs is found in *United States v. Curtiss-Wright Export Co.*, 299 U.S. 304 (1936).

> Not only, as we have shown, is the federal power over external affairs in origin and essential character different from that over internal affairs, but participation in the exercise of the power is significantly limited. In this vast external realm, with its important, complicated, delicate and manifold problems, the President alone has the power to speak or listen as a representative of the nation. He makes treaties with the advice and consent of the Senate; but he alone negotiates. Into the field of negotiation the Senate cannot intrude; and Congress itself is powerless to invade it. As Marshall said in his great argument of March 7, 1800, in the House of Representatives, "The President is the sole organ of the nation in its external relations, and its sole representative with foreign nations." ... It is quite apparent that if, in the maintenance of our international relations, embarrassment—perhaps serious embarrassment—is to be avoided and success for our aims achieved, congressional legislation which is to be made effective through negotiation and inquiry within the international field must often accord to the President a degree of discretion and freedom from statutory restriction which would not be admissible were domestic affairs alone involved. Moreover, he, not Congress, has the better opportunity of knowing the conditions which prevail in foreign countries, and especially is this true in time of war. He has his confidential sources of information. He has his agents in the form of diplomatic, consular and other officials. Secrecy in respect of information gathered by them may be highly necessary, and the premature disclosure of it productive of harmful results.

The president's powers over foreign affairs are derived from (1) inherent executive power, including the power to conduct foreign affairs, appoint ambassadors, receive foreign ambassadors, and act as commander-in-chief of the armed forces; (2) the treaty power; and (3) powers delegated by Congress. Each of these is addressed here in turn, to provide a better understanding of the interplay between the president and Congress in setting trade policies and carrying out trade relations with foreign countries.

Inherent Presidential Power and Its Limitations. The president's inherent executive powers are those that are either expressly granted to the president in the Constitution or found to be there by judicial interpretation. These may be powers necessary to conduct foreign affairs, to appoint ambassadors, to receive foreign ambassadors, or to act as commander in chief of the armed forces. The president may only rely on these inherent powers when Congress has not passed a law directing otherwise. If Congress has passed a statute on a subject, the president's inherent power does not grant "license" to violate that law. Many controversies arise when Congress has failed to address an issue through legislation, and the president acts to "fill the void" by dealing with the issue alone, without the consent of Congress. To this day, one of the most frequently cited cases on the president's inherent power is *Youngstown Sheet & Tube v. Sawyer*. In this case, President Truman had relied on his inherent power as chief executive, and as commander in chief of the armed forces, to force the continued operation of the nation's steel mills during the Korean War in the face of a threatened labor strike. Pay particular attention to Justice Jackson's concurring opinion.

Youngstown Sheet & Tube v. Sawyer

343 U.S. 579 (1952)

United States Supreme Court

BACKGROUND AND FACTS

In the early 1950s, the United States was at war in Korea as part of a United Nations "police action." American steelworkers were threatening to strike over wages and collective bargaining disagreements with steel companies. The president made every

continued

continued

attempt to intervene and to help the parties negotiate an agreement. A strike would have disrupted the supply of steel, leading to a possible shortage of steel during the war effort and an increase in prices in all products made of steel. Despite all efforts, the parties were unable to reach agreement. Just before the steelworkers were to go on strike, President Truman ordered Secretary of Commerce Charles Sawyer to seize the steel mills and keep them in operation. The president based his authority for doing so on Article II of the Constitution and on his power as commander in chief of the armed forces. A district court granted the request of the steel companies for a temporary injunction against the president's order, the Court of Appeals agreed, and the secretary of commerce appealed to the Supreme Court.

DECISION
MR. JUSTICE BLACK DELIVERED THE OPINION OF THE COURT

* * *

The President's power, if any, to issue the order must stem either from an act of Congress or from the Constitution itself. There is no statute that expressly authorizes the President to take possession of property as he did here. Nor is there any act of Congress to which our attention has been directed from which such a power can fairly be implied. Indeed, we do not understand the Government to rely on statutory authorization for this seizure. There are two statutes which do authorize the President to take both personal and real property under certain conditions [the *Selective Service Act* and the *Defense Production Act*]. However, the Government admits that these conditions were not met and that the President's order was not rooted in either of the statutes. The Government refers to the seizure provisions of one of these statutes (§ 201(b) of the *Defense Production Act*) as "much too cumbersome, involved, and time-consuming for the crisis which was at hand."

Moreover, the use of the seizure technique to solve labor disputes in order to prevent work stoppages was not only unauthorized by any congressional enactment; prior to this controversy, Congress had refused to adopt that method of settling labor disputes. When the *Taft-Hartley Act* was under consideration in 1947, Congress rejected an amendment which would have authorized such governmental seizures in cases of emergency. Apparently it was thought that the technique of seizure, like that of compulsory arbitration, would interfere with the process of collective bargaining. * * *

The order cannot properly be sustained as an exercise of the President's military power as Commander in Chief of the Armed Forces. The Government attempts to do so by citing a number of cases upholding broad powers in military commanders engaged in day-to-day fighting in a theater of war. Such cases need not concern us here. Even though "theater of war" be an expanding concept, we cannot with faithfulness to our constitutional system hold that the Commander in Chief of the Armed Forces has the ultimate power as such to take possession of private property in order to keep labor disputes from stopping production. This is a job for the Nation's lawmakers, not for its military authorities.

Nor can the seizure order be sustained because of the several constitutional provisions that grant executive power to the President. In the framework of our Constitution, the President's power to see that the laws are faithfully executed refutes the idea that he is to be a lawmaker. The Constitution limits his functions in the lawmaking process to the recommending of laws he thinks wise and the vetoing of laws he thinks bad. And the Constitution is neither silent nor equivocal about who shall make laws which the President is to execute. The first section of the first article says that "All legislative Powers herein granted shall be vested in a Congress of the United States. * * *" After granting many powers to the Congress, Article I goes on to provide that Congress may "make all Laws which shall be necessary and proper for carrying into Execution the foregoing Powers and all other Powers vested by this Constitution in the Government of the United States, or in any Department or Officer thereof."

The President's order does not direct that a congressional policy be executed in a manner prescribed by Congress—it directs that a presidential policy be executed in a manner prescribed by the President. * * * The power of Congress to adopt such public policies as those proclaimed by the order is beyond question. It can authorize the taking of private property for public use. It can make laws regulating the relationships between employers and employees, prescribing rules designed to settle labor disputes, and fixing wages and working conditions in certain fields of our economy. The Constitution did not subject this law-making power of Congress to presidential or military supervision or control.* * *

The Founders of this Nation entrusted the law making power to the Congress alone in both good and bad times. It would do no good to recall the historical events, the fears of power and the hopes for

continued

continued

freedom that lay behind their choice. Such a review would but confirm our holding that this seizure order cannot stand.

The judgment of the District Court is affirmed.

MR. JUSTICE JACKSON, CONCURRING IN THE JUDGMENT AND OPINION OF THE COURT

* * *

When the President acts pursuant to an express or implied authorization of Congress, his authority is at its maximum, for it includes all that he possesses in his own right plus all that Congress can delegate. In these circumstances, and in these only, may he be said (for what it may be worth), to personify the federal sovereignty. If his act is held unconstitutional under these circumstances, it usually means that the Federal Government as an undivided whole lacks power. A seizure executed by the President pursuant to an Act of Congress would be supported by the strongest of presumptions and the widest latitude of judicial interpretation, and the burden of persuasion would rest heavily upon any who might attack it.

When the President acts in absence of either a congressional grant or denial of authority, he can only rely upon his own independent powers, but there is a zone of twilight in which he and Congress may have concurrent authority, or in which its distribution is uncertain. Therefore, congressional inertia, indifference or quiescence may sometimes, at least as a practical matter, enable, if not invite, measures on independent presidential responsibility. In this area, any actual test of power is likely to depend on the imperatives of events and contemporary imponderables rather than on abstract theories of law.

When the President takes measures incompatible with the expressed or implied will of Congress, his power is at its lowest ebb, for then he can rely only upon his own constitutional powers minus any constitutional powers of Congress over the matter. Courts can sustain exclusive Presidential control in such a case only by disabling the Congress from acting upon the subject. Presidential claim to a power at once so conclusive and preclusive must be scrutinized with caution, for what is at stake is the equilibrium established by our constitutional system. * * *

Into which of these classifications does this executive seizure of the steel industry fit? It is eliminated from the first by admission, for it is conceded that no congressional authorization exists for this seizure. That takes away also the support of the many precedents and declarations which were made in relation, and must be confined, to this category. * * *

Can it then be defended under flexible tests available to the second category? It seems clearly eliminated from that class because Congress has not left seizure of private property an open field but has covered it by three statutory policies inconsistent with this seizure.* * *

The clause on which the Government next relies is that "The President shall be Commander in Chief of the Army and Navy of the United States. * * *" These cryptic words have given rise to some of the most persistent controversies in our constitutional history. Of course, they imply something more than an empty title. But just what authority goes with the name has plagued Presidential advisers who would not waive or narrow it by nonassertion yet cannot say where it begins or ends. It undoubtedly puts the Nation's armed forces under Presidential command. Hence, this loose appellation is sometimes advanced as support for any Presidential action, internal or external, involving use of force, the idea being that it vests power to do anything, anywhere, that can be done with an army or navy.

There are indications that the Constitution did not contemplate that the title Commander-in-Chief of the Army and Navy will constitute him also Commander-in-Chief of the country, its industries and its inhabitants. He has no monopoly of "war powers," whatever they are. While Congress cannot deprive the President of the command of the army and navy, only Congress can provide him an army or navy to command. It is also empowered to make rules for the "Government and Regulation of land and naval forces," by which it may to some unknown extent impinge upon even command functions.

That military powers of the Commander-in-Chief were not to supersede representative government of internal affairs seems obvious from the Constitution and from elementary American history. Time out of mind, and even now in many parts of the world, a military commander can seize private housing to shelter his troops. Not so, however, in the United States, for the Third Amendment says, "No Soldier shall, in time of peace be quartered in any house, without the consent of the Owner, nor in time of war, but in a manner to be prescribed by law." Thus, even in war time, his seizure of needed military housing must be authorized by Congress. It also was expressly left to Congress to "provide for calling forth the Militia to execute the Laws of the Union,

continued

continued

suppress Insurrections and repel Invasions. ***" Such a limitation on the command power, written at a time when the militia rather than a standing army was contemplated as the military weapon of the Republic, underscores the Constitution's policy that Congress, not the Executive, should control utilization of the war power as an instrument of domestic policy. Congress, fulfilling that function, has authorized the President to use the army to enforce certain civil rights. On the other hand, Congress has forbidden him to use the army for the purpose of executing general laws except when expressly authorized by the Constitution or by Act of Congress. * * *

We should not use this occasion to circumscribe, much less to contract, the lawful role of the President as Commander-in-Chief. I should indulge the widest latitude of interpretation to sustain his exclusive function to command the instruments of national force, at least when turned against the outside world for the security of our society. But, when it is turned inward, not because of rebellion but because of a lawful economic struggle between industry and labor, it should have no such indulgence. His command power is not such an absolute as might be implied from that office in a militaristic system but is subject to limitations consistent with a constitutional Republic whose law and policy-making branch is a representative Congress. The purpose of lodging dual titles in one man was to insure that the civilian would control the military, not to enable the military to subordinate the presidential office. No penance would ever expiate the sin against free government of holding that a President can escape control of executive powers by law through assuming his military role. What the power of command may include I do not try to envision, but I think it is not a military prerogative, without support of law, to seize persons or property because they are important or even essential for the military and naval establishment.

In view of the ease, expedition and safety with which Congress can grant and has granted large emergency powers, certainly ample to embrace this crisis, I am quite unimpressed with the argument that we should affirm possession of them without statute. Such power either has no beginning or it has no end. If it exists, it need submit to no legal restraint. I am not alarmed that it would plunge us straightway into dictatorship, but it is at least a step in that wrong direction.

Decision. The lower court's injunction against the president's action was upheld. The president was not acting pursuant to an act of Congress, nor could the seizure of private property during wartime be justified on the basis of his inherent power as president or as commander in chief.

Comment. The concurring opinion by Justice Jackson is one of the most frequently cited opinions in American constitutional history regarding presidential powers. Justice Robert Jackson was America's chief prosecutor of Nazi war criminals at the Nuremberg Trials. Where, as in this case, the president's action is in contradiction to acts of Congress, the president's power is at its "lowest ebb." This case was cited in recent opinions discussing President George W. Bush's actions during the war on terror.

Since 2001, the war on terror has raised new issues regarding the limits on presidential power. After the attacks on the United States in that year, Congress issued a joint resolution authorizing the president to "use all necessary and appropriate force against those nations, organizations, or persons he determines planned, authorized, committed or aided" the attacks of September 11, 2001. President Bush then issued an executive order establishing military commissions at Guantanamo to try military detainees captured during the war on terror. The commissions were not authorized by any act of Congress. Under the commissions' rules, the accused and his or her attorney were not permitted to know the evidence used against them, some sessions were held in private without the accused being present, and there was no limit on the type of evidence that could be presented. Many commentators viewed the actions of President Bush in establishing these military commissions, without the express authority of Congress, as the greatest constitutional challenge to the separation of powers since President Nixon's actions during the Watergate era, or perhaps even since the American Civil War.

In 2001, Salim Hamdan was captured by the U.S. military in Afghanistan. He had been a driver for Osama bin Laden but was unconnected to the terrorist acts or to hostilities in Afghanistan or Iraq. Hamdan was vaguely charged with conspiracy "to commit offenses triable by military commission." He maintained that the commissions had been established in violation of both the *U.S. Code of Military Justice* and the *Geneva Convention.*

In *Hamdan v. Rumsfeld,* 126 S.Ct. 2749 (2006), the Supreme Court agreed and found the establishment of the military commissions to have been an improper exercise of presidential authority. In an opinion by Justice Stevens, the court stated that this case did not involve "the need to accommodate exigencies that may sometimes arise in a theater of war." He noted that this was not a case necessitating the president to respond to an emergency on the battlefield and that there was no reason why the president could not have sought authorization from Congress to establish military tribunals to try terrorists. He concluded his opinion by stating, "It bears emphasizing that Hamdan does not challenge, and we do not today address, the Government's power to detain him for the duration of active hostilities in order to prevent such harm. But in undertaking to try Hamdan and subject him to criminal punishment, the Executive is bound to comply with the Rule of Law that prevails in this jurisdiction."

James Madison wrote in 1788 in the *Federalist Papers* (no. 47) that "The accumulation of all powers, legislative, executive, and judiciary, in the same hands, whether of one, a few, or many, and whether hereditary, self appointed, or elective, may justly be pronounced the very definition of tyranny." This was echoed by Justice Anthony Kennedy in his concurring opinion in *Hamdan v. Rumsfeld,* where he stated "Trial by military commission raises separation-of-powers concerns of the highest order. Located within a single branch, these courts carry the risk that offenses will be defined, prosecuted, and adjudicated by executive officials without independent review. Concentration of power puts personal liberty in peril of arbitrary action by officials, an incursion the Constitution's three-part system is designed to avoid. It is imperative, then, that when military tribunals are established, full and proper authority exists for the presidential directive."

A few months after the *Hamdan* decision, the *Military Commissions Act of 2006* was enacted by Congress and signed by the president. This law sets out more specific guidelines and procedures for the president's creation of military tribunals to try detainees in the war on terror. Given the amount of controversy and politicization of President George W. Bush's handling of the war on terror, there will surely be court challenges to this act in the future.

The Treaty Power

Sovereign governments have been entering into military and trade alliances with one another for thousands of years. As modern nations see the growing need to come to terms with one another on important global issues, these agreements take on an even greater significance. The interdependence of all peoples of the world is expanding. Scientific and technological advances are proceeding more rapidly than ever before. Air and water pollution know no national boundaries. Global warming imperils the entire planet. Toxic waste from one nation is dumped in another. Endangered wildlife slaughtered in one country is sold in another. Illegal drug trafficking, terrorism, and other forms of criminal behavior have taken on multinational dimensions. Products designed and produced in one country cause injuries to consumers in others. All of these problems have one thing in common: Resolving each of them requires the cooperation, understanding, and joint efforts of all nations of the world. In a global economy, in which the economic and financial well-being of all nations is interrelated, economic cooperation thus becomes absolutely necessary.

The primary instrument for implementing foreign political and economic affairs is the *international agreement.* International agreements include treaties and executive agreements. International agreements are either *bilateral* (between two nations) or *multilateral* (between many nations).

According to international law, a *treaty* is an agreement, contract, or *compact* between two or more nations (or between a nation and a public international organization, such as the UN), that is recognized and given effect under international or domestic law. In the United States, a treaty is an international agreement negotiated by the president with the "advice and consent" of the Senate, and which has been approved by a two-thirds vote of the Senate. The *treaty power* of the United States is found in Article II of the Constitution. Treaties can cover almost any subject of mutual concern to nations, from dealing with global warming to eliminating nuclear weapons testing to enhancing the free movement of trade and investment across national borders.

A *convention* is a treaty on matters of common concern, usually negotiated on a regional or global basis and open to adoption by many nations. *Executive agreements,* which are made by the president without resort to the formal treaty process in the Senate, are discussed in the next section.

The Domestic Law Effect of U.S. Treaties

Under the Constitution, a treaty is considered the "law of the land." It is binding on both the federal and state governments with the same force as an act of Congress. Treaties are said to be either *self-executing* or *non-self-executing* (also known as *executory* treaties). The United States is party to both types. In the United States and other countries with written constitutions, a self-executing treaty has a "domestic law effect." This means that once the treaty has been ratified, no further presidential or legislative action is required for it to become binding law. Self-executing treaties therefore provide individuals with specific rights, which the courts will enforce.

An executory or non-self-executing treaty requires an act of Congress or of the President to give it legal effect. (In many other nations, including the United Kingdom, all treaties must be put into force through legislation.) Whether a treaty is self-executing or not depends on how a U.S. court interprets the language of the treaty and the history surrounding its negotiation and approval.

One self-executing treaty is the *Montreal Convention.* This international agreement determines the rights and remedies available to those who are injured or whose property is damaged during travel on commercial aircraft. The Montreal Convention also determines the liability and limitations on liability of the airline. On the other hand, treaties that merely express a nation's desire to cooperate with other nations in achieving broad social, economic, cultural, humanitarian, or political objectives may not be self-executing. *The Charter of the United Nations*, for example, is a non-self-executing international "pledge" to abide by common values for the betterment of humankind and is generally considered by U.S. courts *not* to grant enforceable rights to private parties.

The Equal-Dignity Rule. Self-executing treaties have the same legal effect as statutes passed by both houses of Congress. How, then, do we resolve conflicts between treaties or statutes, the terms of which are inconsistent with one another? In these cases, the rule is that the last in time prevails. A treaty will override an inconsistent prior act of Congress. Similarly, an act of Congress can override an inconsistent prior treaty, provided that Congress had expressed its intention to do so. The rule is easy to understand and is based on the idea that statutes and treaties are of *equal dignity,* meaning they are of equal legal importance.

An Example of Treaties under U.S. Law: FCN Treaties. *Treaties of friendship, commerce, and navigation* (FCN treaties) are important to the business community worldwide and thus provide a good example to see the effect of treaties on U.S. law and U.S. companies. FCN treaties are self-executing bilateral agreements that provide a broad range of protection to foreign nationals doing business in a host country. Although each treaty is different, they all typically state that each country will allow the establishment of foreign branches or subsidiary corporations; the free flow of capital and technology; the equitable and nondiscriminatory treatment of foreign firms, individuals, and products; the right of travel and residence; the payment of just compensation for property taken by the state; the privilege of acquiring and owning real estate; and most-favored-nation trading status for goods.

The self-executing nature of FCN treaties is illustrated in *MacNamara v. Korean Air Lines.* This case involved a conflict between a federal statute that protects workers against discrimination in employment and the FCN treaty between the United States and Korea that allows foreign firms to give preference in hiring their own foreign nationals for executive, managerial, and technical positions.

MacNamara v. Korean Air Lines

863 F.2d 1135 (1988)

United States Court of Appeals (3rd Cir.)

BACKGROUND AND FACTS

MacNamara brought this action against his former employer, Korean Air Lines (KAL), for discrimination under Title VIII of the *Civil Rights Act of 1964* and the *U.S. Age Discrimination in Employment Act.* KAL is a Korean company. MacNamara, an American citizen, was a district sales manager in Philadelphia who had worked for the defendant airline since 1974. In 1982, at age 57, he was dismissed from employment. KAL claimed that his dismissal was part of KAL's reorganization plan, which included merging the Philadelphia and Atlanta offices into one office located in Washington, D.C. KAL had also dismissed six American managers and replaced them with four Korean citizens. The Korean citizen who replaced MacNamara was 42 years old. After exhausting his administrative remedies, MacNamara filed suit claiming that KAL had discriminated against him on the basis of race, national origin, and age. KAL moved to dismiss on the ground that its conduct was protected by the *Treaty of Friendship, Commerce, and Navigation* between the United States and Korea. The motion to dismiss was granted and the plaintiff appealed.

CIRCUIT JUDGE STAPLETON

The Korean FCN treaty is one of a series of friendship, commerce and navigation treaties the United States signed with various countries after World War II. Although initially negotiated primarily for the purpose of encouraging American investment abroad, the treaties secured reciprocal rights and thus granted protection to foreign businesses operating in the United States. The specific provision of the Korean FCN treaty relied upon by KAL in this case provides as follows:

> Nationals and companies of either party shall be permitted to engage, within the territories of the other party, accountants and other technical experts, executive personnel, attorneys, agents, and other specialists of their choice.

We agree with the Courts of Appeals for the Fifth and Sixth Circuits that Article VIII(1) goes beyond securing the right to be treated the same as domestic companies and that its purpose, in part, is to assure foreign corporations that they may have their business in the host country managed by their own nationals if they so desire. We also agree with the conclusion of the Sixth Circuit Court of Appeals that Article VIII(1) was not intended to provide foreign businesses with shelter from any law applicable to personnel decisions other than those that would logically or pragmatically conflict with the right to select one's own nationals as managers because of their citizenship. Insofar as Title VII and the ADEA proscribe intentional discrimination on the basis of race, national origin, and age, we perceive no theoretical or practical conflict between them and the right conferred by Article VIII(1). Thus, for example, we believe that a foreign business may not deliberately undertake to reduce the age of its workforce by replacing older Americans with younger foreign nationals. On the other hand, to the extent Title VII and the ADEA proscribe personnel decisions based on citizenship solely because of their disparate impact on older managers, a particular racial group, or persons whose ancestors are not from the foreign country involved, we perceive a potential conflict and conclude that it must be resolved in favor of Article VIII(1).

Having concluded that KAL cannot purposefully discriminate on the basis of age, race, or national origin, we now turn to the most difficult aspect of this case. To this point we have confined our analysis to liability for intentional discrimination. The reach of Title VII and the ADEA, however, extends beyond intentionally discriminatory employment policies to those practices fair in form, but discriminatory in operation. *Griggs v. Duke Power Co.*, 401 U.S. 424, 91 S.Ct. 849, 28 L.Ed.2d 158 (1971). Accordingly, Title VII and ADEA liability can be found where facially neutral employment practices have a discriminatory effect of "disparate impact" on protected groups, without proof that the employer adopted these practices with a discriminatory motive.

The fact that empirical evidence can satisfy the substantive standard of liability would pose a substantial problem in disparate impact litigation for corporations hailing from countries, including perhaps Korea, whose populations are largely homogeneous. Because a company's requirement that its

continued

continued

employees be citizens of the homogeneous country from which it hails means that almost all of its employees will be of the same national origin and race, the statistical disparity between otherwise qualified noncitizens of a particular race and national origin, and citizens of the foreign country's race and national origin is likely to be substantial. As a result, a foreign business from a country with a homogeneous population, by merely exercising its protected treaty right to prefer its own citizens for management positions, could be held in violation of Title VII. Thus, unlike a disparate treatment case where liability cannot be imposed without an affirmative finding that the employer was not simply exercising its Article VIII(1) right, a disparate impact case can result in liability where the employer did nothing more than exercise that right. For this reason we conclude that disparate impact liability under Title VII and the ADEA for a foreign employer based on its practice of engaging its own nationals as managers cannot be reconciled with Article VIII(1). Accordingly, we hold that such liability may not be imposed.

Decision. The Court of Appeals reversed and remanded for a trial on the question of whether KAL's discriminatory treatment was intentional. The court ruled that the FCN treaty that authorized foreign employers to engage executives and technical specialists "of their choice" granted a limited exemption to U.S. anti-discrimination laws on the basis of citizenship. Although the treaty does not grant foreign employers a blanket exception to the civil rights laws and employers are liable for *intentional* discrimination (disparate treatment) on the basis of race, national origin, or age, the treaty permits foreign employers to retain their own nationals in executive and technical positions even where the effect of such personnel decisions is discriminatory and would otherwise subject the employer to disparate impact liability under the law.

Comment. In a U.S. Supreme Court decision relied upon by the *MacNamara* court, *Sumitomo v. Avagliano,* 457 U.S. 176 (1982), it was held that the FCN treaty between the United States and Japan did not provide immunity to a Japanese trading company for liability under Title VII of the *Civil Rights Act of 1964.* In *Sumitomo* the Court ruled that because the employer was a wholly owned U.S. subsidiary of a Japanese company, incorporated under the laws of the United States, it was not a Japanese company but a U.S. one. Thus, it was not entitled to protection under the treaty.

Other self-executing treaties (in the United States) discussed elsewhere in this text include the *Hague Convention*, the *Convention on Contracts for the International Sale of Goods*, and the *U.N. Convention on Recognition and Enforcement of Foreign Arbitral Awards*. Tax treaties are also considered self-executing in that the provisions of these treaties, like those of the others mentioned, need no further legislation to make them a binding source of law in U.S. courts.

Executive Agreements

Executive agreements are international agreements between the president, representing the United States, and a foreign country, entered into without resort to the treaty process. They are binding obligations of the U.S. government and have the effect of law in the United States. Executive agreements are not provided for in the Constitution, as are treaties. Yet, throughout U.S. history, presidents have utilized executive agreements to conduct foreign affairs. For many practical and political reasons, presidents often favor the executive agreement over the treaty. Since World War II, most international agreements of the United States have not been treaties; they have been executive agreements.

There are two types of executive agreements: sole executive agreements and congressional–executive agreements. A *sole executive agreement* is one that the president can negotiate and put into legal effect on the basis of his inherent authority, without congressional approval. A *congressional–executive agreement* is based on authority granted by Congress to the president in a joint resolution or statute, or by treaty.

Sole Executive Agreements and the President's Inherent Power

The president's authority to enter a sole executive agreement is based on powers inherent in being the chief executive of the nation and commander in chief of the armed forces. Sole executive agreements are usually reserved for agreements with foreign countries that do not affect the broad interests of the nation as a whole. An agreement with a foreign country to lease property for the site of an American embassy could be concluded by a sole executive agreement, without submitting it to Congress. A cease fire agreement during wartime could be concluded with a sole executive agreement under the president's inherent authority. Most sole executive agreements, such as the one in the following case, *Dole v. Carter,* are between two countries on specific matters.

Dole v. Carter

444 F. Supp. 1065 (1977)

United States District Court (D. Kan.)

BACKGROUND AND FACTS

This action was brought by a U.S. senator against the president to enjoin him from returning the Hungarian coronation regalia to the People's Republic of Hungary. The Holy Crown of St. Stephen had been held by the Hungarian people as a treasured symbol of their statehood and nationality for nearly 1,000 years. At the close of World War II, it was entrusted to the United States for safekeeping by Hungarian soldiers. In 1977, the governments of the United States and Hungary entered into an agreement returning the crown to Hungary. Many Hungarians living in the United States were opposed to the return of the crown. The plaintiff filed this action seeking an injunction against delivery of the crown to Hungary on the ground that such action was tantamount to a treaty undertaken by the president without the prior advice and consent of the Senate.

DISTRICT JUDGE O'CONNOR

We turn now to the plaintiff's argument that the agreement to return the coronation regalia to Hungary in and of itself constitutes a treaty which must be ratified by the Senate. It is well established, and even plaintiff admits, that the United States frequently enters into international agreements other than treaties. Indeed, as of January 1, 1972, the United States was a party to 5,306 international agreements, only 947 of which were treaties and 4,359 of which were international agreements other than treaties. These "other agreements" appear to fall into three categories: (1) so-called congressional–executive agreements, executed by the President upon specific authorizing legislation from the Congress; (2) executive agreements pursuant to treaty, executed by the President in accord with specific instructions found in a prior, formal treaty; and (3) executive agreements executed pursuant to the President's own constitutional authority (hereinafter referred to as "executive agreements"). Defendant contends that his agreement to return the coronation regalia to Hungary falls into the latter category, and the court agrees.

Since the *Curtiss-Wright* decision, the Supreme Court has twice upheld the validity of an executive agreement made by President Franklin Roosevelt with the Soviet Union. In the Litvinov Agreement, the President recognized and established diplomatic relations with that nation. In addition, for the purpose of bringing about a final settlement of claims and counterclaims between the Soviet Union and the United States, it was agreed that the Soviet Union would take no steps to enforce claims against American nationals, but all such claims were assigned to the United States with the understanding that the Soviet Union would be notified of all amounts realized by the United States. In speaking for the Court in *United States v. Belmont,* 301 U.S. 324, 57 S.Ct. 758, 81 L.Ed. 1134 (1937), Justice Sutherland, who also authored the majority opinion in *Curtiss-Wright* . . . stated:

> (A)n international compact, as this was, is not always a treaty which requires the participation of the Senate. There are many such compacts, of which a protocol, a *modus vivendi,* a postal convention, and agreements like that now under consideration are illustrations.

continued

continued

The United States enters into approximately 200 executive agreements each year, and it has been observed that the constitutional system "could not last a month" if the President sought Senate or congressional consent for every one of them. *L. Henkin, Foreign Affairs and the Constitution* ... Congress itself recognized this fact in passing P.L. 92–403, 1 U.S.C. §112b, requiring the secretary of state to transmit for merely informational purposes the text of all international agreements other than treaties to which the United States becomes a party. The House Committee on Foreign Affairs stated in recommending passage of that statute that while it wished to be apprised of "all agreements of any significance," "[c]learly the Congress does not want to be inundated with trivia." 1972 *U.S. Code Cong. and Admin. News,* p. 3069. While the President's understanding to return the Hungarian coronation regalia is hardly a "trivial" matter to either the United States or the people of Hungary, the court is yet convinced that the President's agreement in this regard lacks the magnitude of agreements customarily concluded in treaty form. The President's agreement here involves no substantial ongoing commitment on the part of the United States, exposes the United States to no appreciable discernible risks, and contemplates American action of an extremely limited duration in time. The plaintiff presented no evidence that agreements of the kind in question here are traditionally concluded only by treaty, either as a matter of American custom or as a matter of international law. Indeed, while the court has not exhaustively examined all possibly pertinent treaties, the court can hardly imagine that any such examination would lend support to the plaintiff's position. Finally, the agreement here encompasses no substantial reciprocal commitments by the Hungarian government. As a matter of law, the court is therefore persuaded that the President's agreement to return the Hungarian coronation regalia is not a commitment requiring the advice and consent of the Senate under Article II, Section 2, of the Constitution.

Decision. The plaintiff's motion for a preliminary injunction was denied. The agreement to return the coronation regalia was found to be not a treaty requiring ratification by the Senate, but a valid executive agreement based on the president's inherent power.

Congressional-Executive Agreements and the President's Delegated Power

In performing its duties, Congress has broad legislative power to establish policy for the nation. It may, within limits, delegate to the president and the executive branch the responsibility to carry out or enforce those laws. When the president acts pursuant to authority from Congress, he is exercising his *delegated power*.

The *Youngstown* case, which you just read, contained one of the most famous quotes about presidential powers in all American constitutional history. Justice Jackson, in his dissent, described the effect of delegated power.

> When the president acts pursuant to an express or implied authorization of Congress, his authority is at its maximum, for it includes all that he possesses in his own right plus all that Congress can delegate. In these circumstances, and in these only, may he be said (for what it may be worth), to personify the federal sovereignty.

If the president enters into an executive agreement with a foreign country pursuant to this delegated authority, the agreement is valid and has the effect of binding law. These agreements are known as *congressional–executive agreements,* reflecting the dual authority of the legislative and executive branches of government.

Congressional–executive agreements serve much the same purpose as treaties. Their legal nature, however, is different. Unlike treaties, congressional–executive agreements are not described in the Constitution. Their use grew out of the constitutional history of the United States during the present century. For the most part, they were born of the Roosevelt era of the 1930s and 1940s, when the president was seeking new and more flexible ways of dealing with the nation's economic problems during the Great Depression and World War II. By the close of World War II, the House and Senate had informally agreed with the president to provide a substitute process for approving international agreements—one that would not require a two-thirds vote of approval of the Senate, as do treaties. Instead, they agreed on a substitute process permitting international agreements to be approved either by statute or by joint resolutions of both houses of Congress. Statutes and joint resolutions can pass on a *simple majority vote* of both houses. Presidents usually prefer the congressional–executive agreement process to the treaty process because it is often easier for them to obtain congressional approval by majority vote of both houses than by a two-thirds vote of one house. (Thus, the legislature and president become partners in forming international agreements—a type of "balance of power.") Today, congressional–executive agreements, based on the majority vote of both houses of Congress, are recognized as having the same binding legal effect as treaties.

U.S. Trade and Tariff Legislation

The United States has had trade and tariff laws since its founding. In the 1800s, these laws gave little authority to the president other than to collect the tariffs on imported goods according to the tariff rates set by Congress. Today, U.S. trade and tariff laws give far more flexibility and authority to the president to negotiate congressional–executive trade agreements with foreign countries on the basis of objectives set out in the legislation. U.S. trade laws also give the president the authority to prevent foreign unfair trade practices and to retaliate against foreign countries that discriminate against U.S.-made goods or services.

The *Smoot-Hawley Tariff Act of 1930*

The modern era of trade legislation began with the *Smoot-Hawley Tariff Act of 1930*. Shortly after World War I, partially as a result of isolationist sentiments at home, the United States began to increase tariffs on imported goods. In 1930, the U.S. Congress imposed the highest tariff levels in the nation's history when it enacted the *Smoot-Hawley Tariff Act*. The bill was signed by President Herbert Hoover. Under *Smoot-Hawley*, tariffs on more than one thousand items were increased to levels so high that other nations raised their tariffs in retaliation. Some tariff rates reached nearly 100 percent of the cost of the goods. Economic activity declined precipitously. It is generally accepted today that these high tariffs worldwide exacerbated the Great Depression of the 1930s.

President Franklin Roosevelt recognized the immediate need to reduce tariffs and "liberalize" trade. At that time, however, the president simply did not have the legal authority to take any significant action without congressional approval, and the treaty process was too cumbersome. Roosevelt thus worked with Congress to pass the *Reciprocal Trade Agreements Act of 1934*, which provided the president with the authority needed to lower tariffs.

The *Reciprocal Trade Agreements Act of 1934*

Prior to 1934, the president had little or no discretion in setting tariff rates. The *Reciprocal Trade Agreements Act of 1934* provided the president with a mechanism not only for lowering U.S. tariffs, but for encouraging other countries to lower their rates as well. This Act granted the president far more flexible powers to adjust tariffs than under any prior legislation. The president was granted the authority to negotiate tariff reductions on a product-by-product basis with other countries on the basis of *reciprocity*. The United States would reduce a tariff on a foreign product if the foreign country would reciprocate by lowering its tariffs. An agreement to reduce a tariff to a specified level is known as a *tariff concession*. If the United States was to lower an existing tariff on an imported product from, say, France, then France would have to make similar concessions on the same or other products coming from the United States.

The 1934 law also introduced what is known as *unconditional most-favored-nation (MFN) trade*, now commonly referred to as *normal trade relations (NTR)*. It provided that a lower tariff rate negotiated with one nation would automatically be granted to like products imported from all other nations that had signed an MFN agreement with the United States, without any concession being requested from those nations in return. Moreover, if two other nations reached an agreement to lower tariffs on a given product, then that new rate would apply to U.S. products imported into those nations as well. This system served to quicken and expand the process of lowering duties worldwide.

In the following case, *Star-Kist Foods, Inc. v. United States,* the constitutionality of the tariff-setting process of the *Reciprocal Trade Agreements Act* was upheld against a charge that it was an unconstitutional delegation of power by Congress to the president.

Star-Kist Foods, Inc. v. United States

275 F.2d 472 (1959)

United States Court of Customs and Patent Appeals

BACKGROUND AND FACTS

Star-Kist Foods, a U.S. producer of canned tuna, instituted a lawsuit to protest the assessment of duties made by the collector of customs on imported canned tuna. Duty was assessed on the canned tuna at the rate of 12.5 percent pursuant to a trade agreement with Iceland. Prior to the agreement, the tariff rate had been set by Congress in the *Tariff Act of 1930* at 25 percent *ad valorem.* The trade agreement with Iceland, which resulted in lowering the rate of duty, was executed pursuant to the *Reciprocal Trade Agreements Act of 1934.* That act authorized the President to enter into foreign trade agreements for the purpose of expanding foreign markets for the products of the United States by affording corresponding market opportunities for foreign products in the United States. To implement an agreement, the president was then authorized to raise or lower any duty previously set by Congress, but not by more than 50 percent. Star-Kist brought this action, contending that the delegations of authority under the 1934 act and the agreement with Iceland were unconstitutional.

JUDGE MARTIN

A constitutional delegation of powers requires that Congress enunciate a policy or objective or give reasons for seeking the aid of the President. In addition the act must specify when the powers conferred may be utilized by establishing a standard or "intelligible principle" which is sufficient to make it clear when action is proper. And because Congress cannot abdicate its legislative function and confer carte blanche authority on the President, it must circumscribe that power in some manner. This means that Congress must tell the President what he can do by prescribing a standard which confines his discretion and which will guarantee that any authorized action he takes will tend to promote rather than flout the legislative purpose. It is not necessary that the guides be precise or mathematical formulae to be satisfactory in a constitutional sense.

In the act before us the congressional policy is pronounced very clearly. The stated objectives are to expand foreign markets for the products of the United States "by regulating the admission of foreign goods into the United States in accordance with the characteristics and needs of various branches of American production so that foreign markets will be made available to those branches of American production which require and are capable of developing such outlets by affording corresponding market opportunities for foreign products in the United States. . . ."

Pursuant to the 1934 act the presidential power can be invoked "whenever he [the President] finds as a fact that any existing duties or other import restrictions of the United States or any foreign country are unduly burdening or restricting the foreign trade of the United States and that the [purpose of the act] will be promoted." . . .

Under the provisions of the 1934 act the President by proclamation can modify existing duties and other import restrictions but not by more than 50 percent of the specified duties nor can he place articles upon or take them off the free list. Furthermore, he must accomplish the purposes of the act through the medium of foreign trade agreements with other countries. However, he can suspend the operation of such agreements if he discovers discriminatory treatment of American commerce, and he can terminate, in whole or in part, any proclamation at any time. . . .

In view of the Supreme Court's recognition of the necessity of flexibility in the laws affecting foreign relations . . . we are of the opinion that the 1934 act does not grant an unconstitutional delegation of authority to the President.

Decision. The court held in favor of the United States. The congressional delegation of authority under the 1934 statute was constitutional because Congress had provided the president with a sufficiently discernible standard to guide any decisions in carrying out the purposes of the Act.

More Recent U.S. Trade Legislation

The *Reciprocal Trade Agreements Act of 1934* provided the basic system for trade negotiations until 1962. In that year, Congress passed the *Trade Expansion Act of 1962*, which authorized the president to negotiate across-the-board tariff reductions instead of using the tedious product-by-product system set up in 1934. This law also created the *Office of the United States Trade Representative,* empowered to conduct all trade negotiations with foreign countries and international organizations on behalf of the United States.

The *Trade Reform Act of 1974* replaced most provisions of the 1962 law and delegated even more authority to the president. The president was given wide latitude to reduce or eliminate duties (with authority to reduce duties by up to 60 percent and simply end any import duties of less than 5 percent) and to negotiate a reduction of non-tariff barriers during the *Tokyo Round.*

The *Trade Agreements Act of 1979* continued congressional support for expanding free trade by approving the president's trade agreements to reduce non-tariff barriers.

The *Trade and Tariff Act of 1984* authorized the president to negotiate agreements related to high-technology products, trade in services, and barriers to foreign investment. It also authorized the free trade area between the United States and Israel.

The *Omnibus Trade and Competitiveness Act of 1988* extended the president's authority to negotiate trade agreements, including an expansion of the U.S.–Canadian free trade area to include Mexico in the *North American Free Trade Agreement* (NAFTA). It also gave even broader powers to the president to "pry open" foreign markets that have unfair barriers to the entry of U.S. goods and services (through both negotiations and sanctions).

In addition, Congress has also passed a number of trade agreements dealing with specific issues or affecting U.S. trade with specific world regions. For instance, as we will study in later chapters, Congress has passed the *Trade Act of 2002* (which reauthorized an important trade program that promotes imports from developing countries), the *Caribbean Basin Economic Recovery Act of 1983*, the *Andean Trade Program and Drug Eradication Act of 2002*, and the *African Growth and Opportunity Act of 2000*, as well as other important trade laws.

Many of the basic principles and programs established in the 1930s and 1940s are, in a modern form, still in existence today. To this day, every U.S. president has returned to Congress to ask for needed authority to negotiate congressional–executive agreements on trade and investment issues with foreign nations.

Trade Agreements

The United States is a party to many international agreements relevant to the subjects covered in this book. These include trade, tariffs, foreign investment, and the protection of intellectual property. Here we will mention only the most significant trade agreements. Trade *agreements* are executive agreements between countries on matters involving international trade and related issues. They are commonly used to reciprocally reduce tariffs and non-tariff barriers to trade. Trade agreements can be either bilateral or multilateral. The United States' first trade agreement was with France in 1778. Today, the United States participates in many trade agreements, affecting virtually every major industry and sector of the American economy. Companies that import and export these products are directly affected by the trade and tariff regulations outlined in these agreements.

The most important trade agreements are of the congressional–executive type. Some of the most significant trade agreements of the United States since World War II are:

- *General Agreement on Tariffs and Trade,* 1947 (and subsequent GATT agreements)
- *General Agreement on Tariffs and Trade,* 1994 (GATT Uruguay Round Agreement), including the Agreement Establishing the World Trade Organization
- *North American Free Trade Agreement*
- *China Bilateral Market Access Agreement*
- *Central American Free Trade Agreement* (CAFTA-DR), 2006, Costa Rica, El Salvador, Guatemala, Honduras, and Nicaragua and the Dominican Republic
- *Middle Eastern Free Trade Initiative,* 2004–present; currently includes free trade agreements with Jordan, Morocco, and Bahrain; others are pending

In addition, the United States has bilateral free trade agreements with Israel (1985), Chile (2004), Singapore (2004), Australia (2005), and Peru (2007). As of this writing (early 2008) the U.S. Congress was considering approval of trade agreements with Korea, Colombia, and Panama.

According to announcements by the U.S. Trade Representative's office, in recent years, American exports to countries with which the United States has concluded free trade agreements have grown twice as fast as exports to the rest of the world.

The *General Agreement on Tariffs and Trade*

The *General Agreement on Tariffs and Trade*, or GATT, which had the purpose of promoting and expanding trade through multilateral trade negotiations between member nations, became effective in 1947. As the most important trade agreement of the twentieth century, it has provided a global framework for reducing tariffs and non-tariff barriers to trade. Today, more than 150 nations are signatories to one or more of the GATT agreements. The most recent GATT, the *General Agreement on Tariffs and Trade 1994* (commonly called the *Uruguay Round Agreement*), led to the creation of the new *World Trade Organization* (WTO), which is the subject of the next chapter.

THE LEGAL STATUS OF GATT 1947. The original *General Agreement on Tariffs and Trade of 1947* was not a treaty, nor was it a typical congressional–executive agreement. Rather, it was an international agreement adopted only by a proclamation of the president. Despite no explicit congressional approval, GATT 1947 was accepted as a binding agreement of the United States, and its legal status today is completely accepted because GATT 1994 was approved by Congress.

PRESIDENTIAL AUTHORITY FOR GATT MULTILATERAL TRADE NEGOTIATIONS. GATT succeeded in liberalizing trade in this century because it provided a forum for bringing nations together in *multilateral trade negotiations*. GATT negotiations are called "rounds." The most notable GATT rounds were the *Dillon Rounds* (1950s), the *Kennedy Rounds* (1960s), the *Tokyo Rounds* (1970s), and the *Uruguay Rounds* (1980s and 1990s). Each set of rounds resulted in improvements in the world trading environment. The president has sought congressional approval for trade agreements negotiated under GATT, granted under the statutes listed in the preceding sections.

Trade Promotion Authority

Congressional–executive trade agreements require the approval of Congress in order to be legally binding on the United States. However, a foreign nation might be less willing to enter trade negotiations with the president's negotiating team if it thought that any agreement might later be rejected by Congress because of domestic political pressures in the United States. Imagine the U.S. government taking years to negotiate trade agreements with dozens of countries, covering thousands of products affecting hundreds of industries—only to have a senator or representative vote against it because it reduced import duties on foreign products that compete with those made by his or her special interests back home. To avoid this, the *Trade Reform Act of 1974* set up a fast-track process for approving trade agreements, known as the president's *Trade Promotion Authority*. The statute gave the president authority to negotiate trade agreements pursuant to the objectives set out by Congress. During trade negotiations, the president must consult with Congress and notify it of proposed changes to U.S. trade laws. Congress can then comment on the negotiations before there is a final agreement and while there is still time for the president to modify it. At the conclusion of negotiations, Congress must vote by a simple majority to either accept or reject the agreement in its entirety without amendment. This process helped to ensure the passage of trade agreements into U.S. law because it eliminated the possibility that Congress would try to rewrite agreements under pressure from special interests. The fast-track process has been used by every president since 1974 to negotiate many important trade agreements. However, the president's authority expired in mid-2007. At the time of this writing Congress and the president were attempting to reach an agreement on whether the United States should condition U.S. trade agreements with foreign countries on those countries meeting standards for the protection of the environment and worker's rights.

Trade Negotiating Objectives. The objectives of trade promotion authority are:

- reducing tariff and non-tariff barriers to trade in goods, agricultural products, and services on a reciprocal basis
- eliminating trade barriers that decrease market opportunities for U.S. exports
- promoting respect for worker rights and the protection of child labor in light of the standards of the International Labor Organization
- considering the impact of trade on the environment and natural resources and promoting adherence to global environmental standards
- ensuring that trade agreements afford small businesses equal access to international markets and expanded export market opportunities
- reducing barriers to foreign investment by U.S. firms
- protecting intellectual property rights
- prohibiting government officials in foreign countries from accepting bribes or engaging in corrupt practices that affect or distort international trade
- ensuring that global rules for furthering trade apply to electronic commerce

Expanded Powers. Today, the president is authorized not just to reduce duties on products, but also to take a wide range of executive actions to deal with the complexities of the modern business world. This authority is in keeping with the modern notion that the president needs increased flexibility in handling matters related to international trade and foreign affairs. For example, the president has authority to negotiate special trade relations with developing countries; negotiate rules for dealing with agricultural trade problems; coordinate international monetary policies; negotiate better mechanisms for protecting copyrights, patents, and trademarks in foreign countries; negotiate a reduction of barriers to trade in high technology; and ensure equal access to foreign high technology by U.S. firms.

In addition, the president has been given broader powers to deal with a range of complex economic problems. For example, the president may take certain authorized measures (tariffs, quotas, and the like) designed to protect U.S. industry from foreign competition under certain well-defined circumstances, such as when U.S. industry is being injured by increased imports of particular foreign products.

The president has also been granted powers by Congress to respond to international emergencies. The *International Emergency Economic Powers Act* enables the president to block transactions or seize assets of individuals or organizations responsible for terrorism, illegal drug production or drug smuggling, or violations of human rights. These issues are discussed in later chapters.

Federal–State Relations

Thus far our discussion has focused on the relation between the executive and legislative branches of the federal government. But the notion of "federalism" also implies that the United States has two levels of government—state and federal. The Constitution has several provisions that touch upon the relations between the state and federal governments and that determine a state's authority to regulate international (as well as interstate) trade. These include the *Supremacy Clause,* the *Import–Export Clause,* and the *Commerce Clause.*

The *Supremacy Clause*

When a law or regulation of the federal government directly conflicts with those of the state (or local) government, the federal law will still generally prevail when Congress has expressed the intention that the federal law shall prevail or when that intention may be inferred from the legislation or from the circumstances. For example, when Congress enacts a comprehensive scheme of legislation, such as regulations governing commercial aviation, it includes an implication, known as *federal preemption,* that the federal rule will prevail over an inconsistent state rule. The inconsistent state law will be void to the extent it conflicts with the federal scheme.

Burma, Human Rights, and Federal Preemption

Burma (also called Myanmar) is a poor Asian country, about the size of Texas, with a population of about 48 million. Since 1962, a military dictatorship, or *junta,* has ruled Burma with an iron hand. Military rule and mismanagement have resulted in widespread poverty; Burmese citizens have an annual per capita income of less than $300. Burma is known for state monopolization of leading industries, a bloated bureaucracy, arbitrary laws and regulations, corruption, an inadequate infrastructure, a shortage of foreign exchange, and disproportionately large military spending at the expense of social programs. For most Western firms, these problems outweigh Burma's business opportunities.

According to reports from the U.S. State Department and international organizations, the military government uses violence, torture, intimidation, harassment, and fear to remain in power. Harsh prison sentences are handed out, even to foreigners, for unknowingly violating Burmese law. There is no freedom of association or freedom of travel. It is illegal to own or possess an unregistered computer modem, and foreigners entering Burma with a computer are likely to have it confiscated. There are reports of tourists being harassed for taking pictures of men in uniform. U.S. citizens have been detained, arrested, tried, and deported for distributing pro-democracy literature and for visiting the homes and offices of Burmese pro-democracy leaders. In 2007, a crackdown by the military on Buddhist monks and pro-democracy demonstrators resulted in Burma's worldwide condemnation at the United Nations.

Economic Sanctions against Burma. In 1996, the Commonwealth of Massachusetts, several major U.S. cities, and Congress sought to ban U.S. business with Burma. Massachusetts passed a law prohibiting all commonwealth and municipal government agencies from buying goods or services from any person or firm that does business in Burma. Congress took a different strategy. The federal statute banned all economic aid to the Burmese government except for humanitarian assistance, denied U.S. entry visas to Burmese citizens, and authorized the president to prohibit "new investment" in Burma if the Burmese government continued its violent suppression of democracy. The powers delegated to the president were specific and directed him to work with other Asian countries to promote democracy in Burma through diplomatic means. In 1997, the president issued an executive order and imposed further restrictions on new investment as Congress had directed. The president's order was based on both the 1996 statute and the *International Emergency Economic Powers Act.* Criminal penalties for violations ranged from up to 10 years' imprisonment, up to $500,000 in corporate fines, and up to $250,000 in individual fines.

In *Crosby v. National Foreign Trade Council,* 530 U.S. 363 (2000), the U.S. Supreme Court struck down the Massachusetts law on the basis of federal preemption. Justice Souter explained why the state law must give way to the federal statute. He noted the difference between the federal and state sanctions. The Massachusetts sanctions were immediate and direct in prohibiting business in Burma. The federal sanctions were more flexible, gradually allowing the president to increase pressure on Burma as needed and to do so through both specific legal and diplomatic means. The court reasoned, "If the Massachusetts law is enforceable the president has less to offer and less economic and diplomatic leverage as a consequence." Thus, the state law undermined the intended purpose and "natural effect" of the federal act. In deciding that federal law preempted the state statute, the Court repeated that the federal government must "speak with one voice" in foreign policy matters and that Congress had left no room for states or municipalities to become involved.

Many U.S. and European companies—Eddie Bauer, Levi Strauss, Liz Claiborne, Pepsi, and others—have stopped doing business in Burma. Only time will tell whether this economic pressure and international diplomatic efforts aided by U.S. sanctions will help to bring democracy to Burma.

The *Import–Export Clause*

The *Import–Export Clause* prohibits the federal government from taxing exports and prohibits the states from taxing either imports or exports. Historically, three reasons prompted such a provision. First, the federal government needed to be able to "speak with one voice" on matters related to foreign affairs. Second, import duties provided an important source of revenue for the federal government. And third, seaboard states were prevented from imposing burdensome regulations and taxes on "in transit" goods that were destined for inland states.

In *Michelin Tire Corp. v. Wages,* 423 U.S. 276 (1976), the U.S. Supreme Court addressed the issue of the state's power to tax imports. Michelin Tire Corporation imported tires manufactured in France and Nova Scotia, Canada, by Michelin Tires, Ltd. The company maintained a distribution warehouse in Georgia. The state assessed an *ad valorem* property tax against the tires that were held in inventory. The tax was nondiscriminatory in nature in that the same tax was imposed upon all property similarly being held for resale in Georgia. The petitioner filed suit to have the collection of the tax enjoined as unconstitutional under the *Import–Export Clause.* The Supreme Court ruled that the tax was permitted under the *Import–Export Clause* because the tax was imposed on all products for the purpose of supporting the cost of public services, the tax was nondiscriminatory, and it did not interfere with the federal government's regulation of international commerce.

In 1978, the Supreme Court considered the constitutionality of a Washington state tax on stevedoring (the process of loading and unloading cargo on ships). Relying on the *Michelin* decision, the Court in *Department of Revenue of the State of Washington v. Association of Washington Stevedoring Cos.,* 435 U.S. 734 (1978) held that

> the tax does not restrain the ability of the federal government to conduct foreign policy. As a general business tax that applies to virtually all businesses in the state, it has not created any special tariff. The assessments in this case are only upon that business conducted entirely within Washington. No foreign business or vessel is taxed.... The tax merely compensates the state for services and protection extended by Washington to the stevedoring business.

In discussing interstate rivalries, the Court concluded that if it were to strike down the tax, then the state of Washington would be forced to subsidize the commerce of inland consumers. The tax was upheld under the *Import–Export Clause.*

The *Commerce Clause*

As discussed earlier in the chapter, the broadest power of the federal government to regulate business activity is derived from Article I, Section 8 of the Constitution. The *Commerce Clause* vests the federal government with exclusive control over foreign commerce. Conversely, in what is known as the *negative implication doctrine,* state governments may not enact laws that impose a substantial burden on foreign commerce. Where there is an existing federal law governing some aspect of foreign commerce, a conflicting state statute may be invalid (preempted) under the Supremacy Clause.

The *Commerce Clause* and Multiple Taxation. A state's authority to tax a business engaged in foreign commerce is also determined by whether or not the tax imposed results in *multiple taxation.* Multiple taxation occurs when the same service or property is subjected to the same or a similar tax by the governmental authorities of more than one nation. The following case, *Japan Line, Ltd. v. County of Los Angeles,* discusses the problems of multiple taxation.

Japan Line, Ltd. v. County of Los Angeles
441 U.S. 434 (1979)
United States Supreme Court

BACKGROUND AND FACTS

The state of California imposed an *ad valorem* property tax upon cargo containers owned by Japanese companies and temporarily located in California ports. The containers were used exclusively for transporting goods in international commerce. They were based, registered, and subjected to property taxes in Japan. The containers spent, on average, only three weeks a year in California. Japan Lines contended that the tax was invalid because it subjected the containers to multiple taxation in Japan and the United States.

continued

continued

The California Supreme Court upheld the statute and the shipowners appealed.

JUSTICE BLACKMUN

This case presents the question whether a state, consistently with the Commerce Clause of the Constitution, may impose a nondiscriminatory *ad valorem* property tax on foreign-owned instrumentalities (cargo containers) of international commerce. . . .

In order to prevent multiple taxation of commerce, this Court has required that taxes be apportioned among taxing jurisdictions, so that no instrumentality of commerce is subjected to more than one tax on its full value. The corollary of the apportionment principle, of course, is that no jurisdiction may tax the instrumentality in full. "The rule which permits taxation by two or more states on an apportionment basis precludes taxation of all of the property by the state of the domicile. . . . Otherwise there would be multiple taxation of interstate operations." The basis for this Court's approval of apportioned property taxation, in other words, has been its ability to enforce full apportionment by all potential taxing bodies.

Yet neither this Court nor this Nation can ensure full apportionment when one of the taxing entities is a foreign sovereign. If an instrumentality of commerce is domiciled abroad, the country of domicile may have the right, consistently with the custom of nations, to impose a tax on its full value. If a state should seek to tax the same instrumentality on an apportioned basis, multiple taxation inevitably results. Hence, whereas the fact of apportionment in interstate commerce means that "multiple burdens" logically cannot occur, the same conclusion, as to foreign commerce, logically cannot be drawn. Due to the absence of an authoritative tribunal capable of ensuring that the aggregation of taxes is computed on no more than one full value, a state tax, even though "fairly apportioned" to reflect an instrumentality's presence within the state, may subject foreign commerce "to the risk of a double tax burden to which [domestic] commerce is not exposed, and which the commerce clause forbids."

Second, a state tax on the instrumentalities of foreign commerce may impair federal uniformity in an area where federal uniformity is essential. Foreign commerce is preeminently a matter of national concern. "In international relations and with respect to foreign intercourse and trade the people of the United States act through a single government with unified and adequate national power." *Board of Trustees v. United States*. . . .

A state tax on instrumentalities of foreign commerce may frustrate the achievement of federal uniformity in several ways. If the State imposes an apportioned tax, international disputes over reconciling apportionment formulae may arise. If a novel state tax creates an asymmetry in the international tax structure, foreign nations disadvantaged by the levy may retaliate against American-owned instrumentalities present in their jurisdictions. Such retaliation of necessity would be directed at American transportation equipment in general, not just that of the taxing state, so that the Nation as a whole would suffer. . . .

It is stipulated that American-owned containers are not taxed in Japan. California's tax thus creates an asymmetry in international maritime taxation operating to Japan's disadvantage. The risk of retaliation by Japan, under these circumstances, is acute, and such retaliation of necessity would be felt by the Nation as a whole. . . .

We hold the tax, as applied, unconstitutional under the Commerce Clause.

Decision. The Supreme Court reversed, holding that the tax was unconstitutional. The Court ruled that an *ad valorem* property tax applied to cargo containers used exclusively in foreign commerce violates the Commerce Clause because it resulted in multiple taxation of instrumentalities of foreign commerce.

The purpose of restricting multiple taxation is to strengthen the government's ability to foster domestic participation in the international marketplace. By not prejudicing foreign companies operating in the United States, this country does not risk retaliation by foreign governments against U.S. firms operating abroad.

STATE INCOME TAXATION OF MULTINATIONAL CORPORATIONS. The issue of multiple taxation was considered in *Barclays Bank PLC v. Franchise Tax Board of California,* 512 U.S. 298 (1994). This important case upheld the constitutionality of California's "unitary" method of assessing income tax on companies in California that are subsidiaries of foreign multinational corporations.

Barclays Bank of California (Barcal), a California banking institution, was a subsidiary of the Barclays Group, a multinational banking enterprise based in the United Kingdom. The Barclays Group included more than 220 corporations doing business in sixty nations. In 1977, Barcal reported taxable income only from its own operations within California. California claimed that Barcal was a member of a multinational "unitary" business and that the *entire worldwide income* of the unitary business—the income of all of the subsidiaries within the Barclays Group operating anywhere in the world—was taxable in California. Under the unitary method, taxes were assessed on the percentage of worldwide income equal to the average of the proportions of worldwide payroll, property, and sales located in California. Thus, if a multinational corporation had 8 percent of its payroll, 3 percent of its inventory and other property, and 4 percent of its sales in California, the state imposed its tax on 5 percent of the multinational's total income. (The weight given to each category can vary under different formulas.) California used the unitary method because it believed that under traditional methods of tax accounting, conglomerates had the ability to manipulate transactions between affiliated companies so as to shift income to low-tax jurisdictions (although to guard against such manipulation, transactions between affiliated corporations are generally scrutinized to ensure that they are reported on an "arm's-length" basis). Barclays claimed that California's tax resulted in multiple taxation, in violation of the *Commerce Clause*.

Citing its previous decisions, the U.S. Supreme Court upheld the California tax because seven requirements were met: (1) The tax applied to an activity with a substantial connection to California. (2) The tax was "fairly apportioned." (3) The tax did not discriminate against interstate commerce. (4) The tax was fairly related to the services provided by the state. (5) The tax did not result in multiple taxation. (6) The tax did not impair the federal government's ability to "speak with one voice when regulating commercial relations with foreign governments." (7) Compliance with the formula was not so impossible as to deprive the corporation of due process of law.

Even before this case went to court, foreign corporations doing business in California had objected strongly to the unitary tax. Foreign governments also objected, claiming it violated international law.

In response to this outcry, the state of California in 1986 dropped its unitary tax requirement and substituted a *water's edge election* allowing corporations the option of being taxed only on their California income—up to the "water's edge." Nevertheless, the case is important because it stands for the principle that unitary taxation is constitutional. It is still used in a few states.

State Restrictions on Exports. The *Commerce Clause* prohibits state governments from restricting, taxing, or otherwise imposing undue burdens on exports. In *South-Central Timber Development, Inc. v. Wunnicke,* 467 U.S. 82 (1984), the Supreme Court considered a challenge to an Alaska regulation that required that all timber taken from state lands be processed within the state prior to being exported. South-Central was an Alaskan company engaged in purchasing timber and shipping logs overseas. It filed suit claiming that the regulation violated the negative implications of the *Commerce Clause.* Alaska argued that the *Commerce Clause* did not apply because the state was acting as a "market-participant" (a vendor of lumber), not as a regulator. The Court agreed with South-Central.

> The limit of the market-participant doctrine must be that it allows a State to impose burdens on commerce within the market in which it is a participant, but allows it to go no further. The State may not impose conditions, whether by statute, regulation, or contract, that have a substantial regulatory effect outside of that particular market.... [A]lthough the state may be a participant in the timber market, it is using its leverage in that market to exert a regulatory effect in the processing market, in which it is not a participant.
>
> In addressing the *Commerce Clause* question directly, the Court also noted, "In light of the substantial attention given by Congress to the subject of export restrictions on unprocessed timber, it would be peculiarly inappropriate to permit state regulation of the subject."

State Restrictions on Imports. State government restrictions on imports are severely limited. User fees for the use of port facilities are generally permitted. Also, states may impose restrictions directly related to the protection of the public health and safety. For example, Florida could limit, restrict, or ban the import of fruits or vegetables suspected of carrying a disease that could contaminate the local crop. In one case, however, a labeling and licensing statute was invalidated by the courts even though its alleged purpose was the protection of the public health and safety. Tennessee had enacted a statute calling for the licensing of all persons who deal in foreign meat products in the state and the labeling of all foreign meats sold in the state as being of foreign origin. The court, in *Tupman Thurlow Co. v. Moss,* 252 F. Supp 641 (M.D. Tenn. 1961), concluded that "The regulation here involved cannot fairly be construed as a consumer protection measure, and if it should be, it would be interdicted by the *Commerce Clause* because it unreasonably discriminates against foreign products in favor of products of domestic origin."

Federal Agencies Affecting Trade

Thus far, this chapter has discussed the constitutional role of government in regulating international trade. The remainder of the chapter briefly discusses the various agencies and executive branch departments that carry out the functions of government on a daily basis. U.S. government agencies that provide technical and financial assistance for exporters, such as the Small Business Administration, the Export-Import Bank, the Overseas Private Investment Corporation, the Commodity Credit Corporation, the Agency for International Development, the Trade and Development Program, the U.S. Department of Agriculture, and others are discussed elsewhere in the text. The role of the Department of Treasury was, in part, addressed earlier in this chapter. The following agencies are primarily concerned with the establishment of trade policy and the handling of trade disputes.

United States Department of Commerce

The U.S. Department of Commerce has broad authority over many international trade issues. The department's functions include fostering trade and promoting exports of U.S. goods and services (trade promotion), investigating and resolving complaints by U.S. firms that foreign governments are unfairly blocking access to foreign markets (market access), administering U.S. unfair import laws (import administration), issuing export licenses for certain products, developing U.S. international trade statistical information, and many other functions. The *International Trade Administration* (ITA), housed within the department, performs many of the trade promotion, market access, and import administration functions. Within the ITA, the *U.S. Commercial Service* maintains a network of offices at home and abroad to assist U.S. firms in developing export opportunities. The *U.S. Bureau of Industry and Security* regulates the export of sensitive goods and technologies for national security and foreign policy and enforces U.S. export control laws.

United States Department of Homeland Security

The *Department of Homeland Security* was created as an executive department of the federal government in 2003. Its creation was part of the largest reorganization of the American government in over a half-century. The new department brought together many existing government agencies with a common responsibility for protecting the American "homeland." The department is organized into four directorates: Border and Transportation Security, Emergency Preparedness and Response, Science and Technology, and Information Analysis and Infrastructure Protection. Its primary mission is to prevent terrorist attacks within the United States.

Border and Transportation Security. This directorate brings together the major border security and transportation security functions of the department. This includes the following agencies: *U.S. Customs and Border Protection (CBP), U.S. Immigration and Customs Enforcement (ICE), U.S. Citizenship and Immigration Services,* the *Transportation Security Administration,* the *Secret Service,* the *Federal Emergency Management Agency,* and the *U.S. Coast Guard.* Many of the functions of these agencies were previously handled by the Treasury Department, the Justice Department, and the Transportation Department.

The agency with the greatest impact on our reading is the *Bureau of Customs and Border Protection* (CBP). This agency brings together many functions of the former U.S. Customs Service, the Border Patrol, and the Immigration and Naturalization Service. Its functions include preventing suspected terrorists from entering the United States; apprehending individuals attempting to enter the United States illegally; stemming the flow of illegal drugs and other contraband; protecting American agricultural and economic interests from imported pests and diseases; preventing the illegal import of goods in violation of U.S. copyright, patent, and trademark laws; enforcing U.S. import and export laws; and collecting import duties.

The Impact of Homeland Security on American Importers and Exporters. In a free society, the protection of the American homeland from possible terrorist attack or from the smuggling of terrorist weapons requires a balance between maintaining public security and the needs of American companies to move goods swiftly across national borders. Consider that CBP estimates that it takes a team of four inspectors about four hours to search one container. Inspecting every shipment arriving by truck or aircraft and each of the over 6 million ocean containers arriving annually at U.S. ports would be difficult and cause extensive delays at the border. So CBP is implementing several projects to enhance security while speeding delivery of goods. These include advance notice of cargo shipments bound to U.S. ports (the *24-hour rule*); foreign inspections of high-risk containers (*Container Security Initiative*); a CBP program for reviewing security measures in a U.S. importer's foreign supply-chain security (C-TPAT); and FAST, a special cooperative arrangement between the United States and Canada for the expedited clearance of cross-border trade (*Free and Secure Trade*). The war on terrorism will have a tremendous effect in the years to come not only on the movement of goods in international trade, but on the entire world of international business.

United States Trade Representative

The *United States Trade Representative* (USTR) is a cabinet-level post reporting directly to the president. The USTR carries on all bilateral and multilateral trade negotiations on behalf of the United States, serves as the principal adviser on trade matters to the president, represents the United States at all WTO meetings, coordinates the trade agreements program, and coordinates all U.S. trade policies, including those related to agricultural, textile, and commodity trade and unfair trade practices. Much of the responsibility for trade matters once held by the Department of State has been transferred to the USTR.

International Trade Commission

The *International Trade Commission* (ITC), formerly called the U.S. Tariff Commission, is an independent agency of government created by Congress in 1916. The ITC maintains a highly trained cadre of professional economists and researchers who conduct investigations and prepare extensive reports on matters related to international economics and trade for Congress and the president. The role of the ITC (along with that of the International Trade Administration) in investigating unfair trade practices will be thoroughly discussed in future chapters. Because of the highly political nature of many of the investigations related to the impact of imported goods on U.S. domestic industry, the ITC is a bipartisan agency. The members of the commission are appointed by the president from both political parties and are subject to Senate confirmation.

The U.S. Court of International Trade

The *Court of International Trade* (CIT) consists of nine judges who hear cases arising from the trade or tariff laws of the United States. Appeals from U.S. Customs and Border Protection regarding duties assessed on imported goods and appeals from decisions of the ITC in unfair import cases are heard by the CIT. Appeals from the CIT go to the Court of Appeals for the Federal Circuit and, where appropriate, to the U.S. Supreme Court.

The court has exclusive jurisdiction over all civil actions commenced against the United States involving (1) revenue from imports or tonnage; (2) tariffs, duties, fees, or other taxes on importation of merchandise for reasons other than the raising of revenue; (3) embargoes or other quantitative restriction of the importation of merchandise for reasons other than the protection of the public health or safety; and (4) administration or enforcement of the customs laws. The court is located in New York City.

Conclusion

Many students are surprised at the limited powers granted to the president in the Constitution. The president's power is not unlimited and is derived from the treaty power (with the advice and consent of the Senate), the power to conduct foreign affairs, the inherent power under Article II as chief executive and as commander in chief of the armed forces, and the power delegated to the president to enforce and carry out acts of Congress. As Justice Jackson said in his famous concurring opinion in the *Youngstown* case, "When the president takes measures incompatible with the expressed or implied will of Congress, his power is at its lowest ebb, for then he can rely only upon his own constitutional powers minus any constitutional powers of Congress over the matter."

Presidents are given wide latitude in the exercise of their power in foreign affairs, especially during time of war. Virtually every U.S. president in the twentieth century had disputes with Congress over the extent of presidential power. In recent years, President George W. Bush has again tested those limits in the war on terror. While this chapter could do no more than describe the separation of powers, we hope that you now have a better understanding of the limits on presidential power.

Presidents rely on delegations of authority from Congress to negotiate foreign trade agreements. This is known as trade promotion authority. As of mid-2007, Congress had not renewed the president's trade promotion authority. It will be interesting to observe the politics at play in the future as Congress considers this issue.

Chapter Summary

1. U.S. trade law is that body of public law that governs America's trade relations with foreign countries, including the import and export of goods and services. Trade law is used to implement American trade policies as well as American foreign policy and thus can be used to encourage trade with a political ally or to discourage trade with a potential foe. Using trade policy as a tool of foreign policy can lead to many conflicts.
2. Article I of the Constitution confers "all legislative powers" upon Congress, including the power "to regulate commerce with foreign nations, and among the several states." In addition, Congress has broad power to pass domestic laws, raise and support armies, provide and maintain a navy, declare war, appropriate monies, and levy and collect taxes. The Senate has the authority to give advice and consent to the president in making treaties with foreign nations and to approve treaties by a two-thirds vote.
3. The president's powers are derived from two sources: those powers delegated to the president by Congress, and those "inherent" powers set out in Article II of the Constitution. Inherent powers include the treaty power, the power to appoint ambassadors, the power to receive foreign ambassadors, and the power inherent in being commander in chief of the armed forces. Important limits on presidential powers generally, and during time of war in particular, were discussed in *Youngstown Sheet & Tube v. Sawyer* and *Hamdan v. Rumsfeld.*
4. The primary instrument for implementing foreign political and economic affairs is the *international agreement.* International agreements include treaties and executive agreements.
5. Treaties are binding on both the federal and state governments and have the same force as an act of Congress.
6. *Executive agreements* are international agreements between the president and a foreign country, entered into without resort to the treaty process. The two types of executive

agreements are *sole executive agreements* (based on the president's inherent powers) and *congressional–executive agreements* (based on authority delegated by Congress). Sole executive agreements are usually reserved for agreements with foreign countries that do not affect the broad interests of the nation as a whole. Congressional–executive agreements, based on the majority vote of both houses of Congress, are recognized as having the same binding legal effect as treaties.

7. The president's *trade promotion authority* is the authority to negotiate trade congressional–executive trade agreements. The *North American Free Trade Agreement* and many other trade pacts were successfully negotiated under trade promotion authority.
8. The *Smoot-Hawley Tariff Act of 1930* placed the highest tariffs on goods in U.S. history. It was one of the causes of the Great Depression.
9. Beginning with the *Reciprocal Tariff Act of 1934* and continuing to this day, tariff reductions have been negotiated on a reciprocal basis. Today, tariffs are not a major barrier to trade.
10. In the United States, the role of state or local governments in regulating or interfering with trade relations with foreign countries is very limited. States have no authority to regulate imports or exports of foreign goods or services. In case after case, legislation enacted by state or local governments that restricts trade with foreign countries has been ruled unconstitutional under either the Supremacy Clause or the Commerce Clause of the Constitution.

Questions and Case Problems

1. Students interested in examining the relationship between the president and Congress, especially during wartime, are encouraged to read both Justice Stevens' opinion and Justice Kennedy's concurrence in *Hamdan v. Rumsfeld*. In this case, the Court struck down President Bush's establishment, without the approval of Congress, of military tribunals to try military detainees held at Guantanamo during the war on terror. What is your opinion of the *Hamdan* decision? Do you think that the president should have sought authorization from Congress before creating these military commissions? Research the *Military Commissions Act of 2006*. What constitutional objections to the law could be raised by civil libertarians? Why might exceptional powers be needed by the executive branch and the military during time of war?
2. North Carolina, South Carolina, and Georgia produce a large amount of cotton each year. In an effort to protect their farmers from overseas competition, the governors of these three states met and agreed on a uniform "inspection fee" to be imposed on all foreign cotton coming into their states through their ports. They vowed to do their best to get their state legislatures to adopt this fee as law. Would any problem arise with such a fee?
3. From what four sources does the president draw the power to regulate foreign commerce or international trade? Explain each source.
4. The U.S. State Department negotiated directly with European and Japanese steel producers to limit their exports to the United States. This was done because of threats by the president to set import quotas. No foreign government was party to the agreement. Although the president had been granted express authority to limit imports by an act of Congress, this act required that he either hold public hearings through the Tariff Commission about setting import quotas or deal directly with foreign governments about limiting imports. The Consumers Union of U. S., Inc., felt that when Congress gave the president this express power, it preempted any other action by the president. They brought an action against the secretary of state to have the president's agreement with private steel producers in Europe and Japan declared illegal. What should be the result of such an action? *Consumers Union of U.S., Inc. v. Kissinger*, 506 F.2d 136 (D.C. Cir. 1974).
5. The *Trade Expansion Act of 1962* as amended by the *Trade Act of 1974* stated that if the secretary of the treasury finds that an "article is being imported into the United States in such quantities or under such circumstances as to threaten to impair the national security," the president is authorized to "take such action … as he deems necessary to adjust the imports of the article … so that [it] will not threaten to impair the national security." Does this grant of power to the president by Congress allow the president to

establish quotas? If importation of foreign oil were determined to be "a threat to national security," could the president implement a $3- to $4-per-barrel license fee? See *Federal Energy Administration v. Algonquin SNG, Inc.,* 426 U.S. 548 (1976).

6. What is a treaty? Where does the treaty power of the United States come from? What is the difference between a self-executing treaty and a non-self-executing treaty? How does the treaty approval process differ from the approval process for congressional–executive agreements?
7. Future U.S. trade negotiations will focus both on the U.S. trade relationships with the world through the World Trade Organization and on special trade relationships with countries in Latin America. Some leaders of Congress want to use trade negotiations to push Latin American countries to protect worker's rights, conserve tropical forests, and protect the environment. Such issues may dominate U.S. trade relations for most of this decade. As of today, what is the status of the president's fast-track authority? What has Congress required of the president in leading current or future U.S. trade negotiations? To what extent has Congress included side issues such as labor rights or the environment? Research the topic and discuss the pros and cons of linking trade relations to these and other social and political side issues.
8. During the 1940s, the U.S. government instituted a price support system for domestic potatoes. In order to protect the potato market from imported Canadian potatoes, the U.S. secretary of state entered into an executive agreement with the Canadian ambassador in which they agreed that Canada would permit the export of potatoes into the United States only if they were to be used for seed and not for food. The agreement was not submitted to or approved by Congress. The *Agricultural Act of 1948* permitted the president to restrict potato imports by requesting an investigation by the Tariff Commission and considering its recommendations. Guy W. Capps, Inc., the importer, assured the Canadian exporter that the potatoes were destined for planting, but while they were in transit, they were sold to the A&P grocery store chain for resale. The United States brought suit against Guy Capps for damages. The court entered judgment for Guy Capps and the government appealed. Was the U.S.–Canadian agreement valid under the U.S. Constitution? Was the president acting under his inherent constitutional authority, under power delegated from Congress, or neither? What did Congress say the president could do to restrict agricultural imports? See *United States v. Guy W. Capps, Inc.,* 204 F.2d 655 (4th Cir. 1953).
9. Xerox manufactured parts for copy machines in the United States that were shipped to Mexico for assembly. The copiers were designed for sale exclusively in Latin America. All printing on the machines was in Spanish or Portuguese. The copiers operated on a 50-cycle electric current unavailable in the United States. The copiers had been transported by a customs bonded warehouse in Houston, Texas, where they were stored pending their sale to Xerox affiliates in Latin America. The copiers had previously been stored in Panama. Under federal law, goods stored in a customs bonded warehouse are under the supervision of the U.S. Customs Service. Goods may be brought into a warehouse without the payment of import duties and stored for up to 5 years. At any time they may be re-exported duty-free or withdrawn for domestic sale upon the payment of the duty. Harris County and the city of Houston assessed a nondiscriminatory *ad valorem* personal property tax on the copiers. Xerox claimed that the local tax is preempted by the federal legislation. What did the Court decide? Would it have made any difference whether the goods were needed for domestic use or intended for re-export? See *Xerox Corporation v. County of Harris, Texas,* 459 U.S. 145 (1982).
10. The state of Tennessee passed legislation requiring that any person selling or offering for sale in the state of Tennessee any meats that are the products of any foreign country must so identify any such product by labeling it "This meat is of foreign origin." The state law did not require a higher standard of purity and sanitation than that required by the U.S. Department of Agriculture. A New York corporation selling imported meats to customers in Tennessee challenged this state statute in U.S. District Court. The corporation's sales of imported meat to customers in Tennessee were one-half its volume prior to enactment of the statute. What do you think the legal basis was for this challenge to the Tennessee law? What do you think Tennessee's argument was for passing the law? What do you think the court decided? See *Tupman Thurlow Co. v. Moss,* 252 F. Supp. 641 (M.D. Tenn. 1966).
11. Name the federal agencies that deal with the day-to-day functions of U.S. trade.
12. The president's trade promotion authority expired in 2007. What were the issues that led to congressional unwillingness to renew the authority? How has that been resolved? What is the status of the president's authority today?

Managerial Implications

Your firm, Day-O Shoes, Inc., manufactures deck shoes in the Caribbean island country of Haiti. Haiti is the poorest nation in the Western Hemisphere. Your plant there employs more than 400 workers and has always considered itself a good citizen of both Haiti and the United States. Most of the shoes are imported for sale into the United States, where you maintain a 30 percent share of a competitive market. In 1991, the freely elected President of Haiti is removed from office by military officers who install a dictator of their choice. In response, the President of the United States exercises authority under the *International Economic Emergency Powers Act* and issues an executive order imposing a complete embargo on trade with Haiti. The Treasury Department's Office of Foreign Assets Control is charged with enforcing the embargo. Facing the impending embargo, your firm shut down its production operations there one week prior to the date set for the embargo. Feeling some obligation to the unemployed workers, your company's chief executive ships over ten tons of food and clothing to the people who have lost their jobs.

Believing that the United States is serious about the embargo and that it will remain in effect until the rightful president is returned to Haiti, your firm ships its U.S.-made raw materials, such as rubber soles and leather uppers, from Haiti to your other factory in Costa Rica. However, you soon discover, much to your surprise, that your competitors are continuing to produce and stockpile their shoes in Haiti in the belief that the embargo will soon be lifted. Three months after you cease operations, the U.S. government decides to lift the embargo because it has resulted in the loss of 50,000 Haitian jobs. With no inventory of finished shoes and your raw materials en route to Costa Rica, your firm is unable to fill existing orders. Your competitors are ready to ship their shoes from Haiti immediately.

1. Evaluate the course of action taken by Day-O Shoes. How did Day-O Shoes balance its responsibility under U.S. law to comply with the embargo with its need to remain competitive in the industry? What could it have done differently? Evaluate the ethics of Day-O's actions.
2. Was Day-O Shoes required to stop producing in Haiti? Were its competitors violating U.S. law by continuing to produce and stockpile their inventories? Were they violating any moral code or even the "spirit of the law" by continuing to produce there? Evaluate the risks taken by the competitors in continuing their operations in Haiti during the embargo.
3. The embargo was intended to put economic pressure on Haiti to encourage political reform. Is the U.S. government saying that the embargo worked too well? Do you think that the embargo was lifted because of its impact on the Haitian workers or on U.S. firms doing business there? Critics argue that the U.S. government's attempts to use trade policy as a means of conducting foreign policy lead to confusion and uncertainty and are counterproductive. Evaluate this argument.

Ethical Considerations

It is clear that Congress has the authority to require that any trade agreement negotiated by the president take into account environmental and labor issues. At least since 1974, U.S. trade laws have instructed the president to consider foreign worker's rights and workplace conditions in negotiating trade agreements. One U.S. statute, which fosters U.S. trade with developing countries, contains provisions for labor standards. The 1994 *North American Free Trade Agreement* contained specific provisions for protecting worker's rights and the environment. More recently, the *Trade Act of 2002* called for countries entering trade agreements with the United States to abide by the "core labor standards" of the International Labour Organization, including the freedom of association, the right to form unions and to bargain collectively, minimum age requirements and limitations on child labor, and a ban on forced labor.

Some U.S. trade agreements also reflect environmental concerns. They do not set environmental standards, but they call for each nation to enforce its own standards and to ensure that environmental protections are not weakened in order to promote foreign trade.

Do you think that the United States should require foreign countries to address worker's rights and environmental harm in return for trade privileges with the United States? Find out how U.S. trade agreements incorporate concerns over the environment and worker's rights. What has been the policy of presidential administrations in this regard? What are the competing economic and political issues in domestic politics? Should trade be used to accomplish these political and social objectives? How much focus should be placed on human rights? Why or why not?

FOR INTERNET ACTIVITIES, VISIT ACADEMIC.CENGAGE.COM/BLAW/SCHAFFER.

CHAPTER 9
GATT LAW AND THE WORLD TRADE ORGANIZATION: BASIC PRINCIPLES

Our story of the modern era of international trade relations really begins at the close of World War I. After years of a horrible and costly war in Europe, many Americans wanted little to do with the rest of the world. After the troops came home and the 1920s began, the nation entered a period of political isolationism. Political isolationism led to calls for greater economic protectionism. It was in this climate that President Herbert Hoover called for passage of the *U.S. Smoot-Hawley Tariff Act of 1930*, an attempt to protect American firms from foreign competition by imposing the highest tariff rates on imported goods in American history. While scholars still argue to this day whether *Smoot-Hawley* (and the debate that led up to its passage) caused the Great Depression of the 1930s or only exacerbated it, there is no question that other countries responded to punitive American tariffs by imposing high tariff rates of their own. This led to the greatest slowdown of trade and economic activity the world had ever seen. It showed that the world's economies had become interrelated and that actions taken by one country could affect all countries. Further, it showed what can happen when a powerful nation tries to isolate itself economically and politically from the world solely to protect its own economic interests. It was not until the mid-1930s, during the dark days of the Depression, that the U.S. Congress realized that high tariffs were impeding international trade and economic recovery and that *Smoot-Hawley* had not been a good idea. With the passage of the *U.S. Reciprocal Trade Agreements Act of 1934*, the Roosevelt Administration had the authority to negotiate trade agreements with foreign countries—country by country and product by product—to reduce tariffs to pre–Smoot-Hawley levels. But it was a slow process, and before it could be completed the nation entered World War II.

By the close of World War II, a very different picture of America's role in the world had emerged. Unlike the period after World War I, characterized by the failed League of Nations and calls for isolationism, the 1940s were marked by international cooperation and the creation of a host of international organizations, with America at the forefront. Even before the war had ended, the Allied powers had begun planning for a postwar future of economic and political stability. By the close of the war or within a few years afterward, many new international institutions had been created. These included the World Bank, the International Monetary Fund, the *General Agreement on Tariffs and Trade,* and of course, the United Nations. From the economic and industrial ruin of the Great Depression and World War II came a renewed belief in free trade and a new international approach to dealing with common economic problems. Nations learned that their mutual interests could be best served by policies that encouraged free trade in goods, unfettered by high tariffs and other barriers, and by enacting "liberalized" trade rules.

In 1947, the *General Agreement on Tariffs and Trade* (GATT) was created, and the modern global trading system was born. GATT today provides the framework for most multilateral trade negotiations aimed at reducing trade barriers. For sixty years, GATT has functioned to set the rules of international trade and provide a forum for settling international trade disputes. In 1994, a new world trade agreement was reached. The *General Agreement on Tariffs and Trade 1994* enhanced the role of international law in regulating trade and created the *World Trade Organization* (WTO), an international organization charged with administering the GATT world trade system. In this chapter we will study the global trading rules of the GATT agreements and the WTO, and we will examine the WTO process for settling trade disputes between countries. But first, we will look at some basic principles of trade regulation.

As you read this chapter and those following, keep in mind this note about terminology. Technically speaking, the term "GATT agreement" refers to both the original 1947 *General Agreement on Tariffs and Trade* and to the 1994 agreements that resulted from the *Uruguay Rounds,* including the "GATT side agreements" related to specific topics that we will cover in this text. However, as the public becomes increasingly aware of the importance of the WTO, it is becoming common to use the term *WTO agreement* in referring to the GATT agreements effective after 1994. Do not be confused if you see the terms *GATT agreement* and *WTO agreement* used almost interchangeably. Of course, the term *WTO,* when used alone, refers to the World Trade Organization.

Introduction to Trade Regulation

Every country establishes its own trade policies according to its own national interests. Trade policies are heavily influenced by domestic politics. Left to its own devices, any nation would want to protect its industries from foreign competitors by erecting a maze of import trade barriers. These might include high tariffs, quotas, or complex regulations designed to keep out foreign goods and services. A *trade barrier* is any impediment to trade in goods or services. An *import trade barrier* is any impediment, direct or indirect, to the entrance or sale of imported goods or services existing in the country of importation. Typically, trade barriers are tariffs or taxes on imported goods, or laws, government regulations, or national industrial standards, that make importing or selling foreign-made goods or services more difficult or that make imported goods or services more costly to produce, market, or sell.

All countries have trade barriers. Some are very obvious. When a country imposes a tax or tariff on an imported product, both foreign exporters and importers at home know exactly how much that product will cost. A total or partial ban on importation of certain products is also very obvious. Other trade barriers are not so obvious. For example, in recent years the United States has accused China of artificially manipulating the value of its currency, the *yuan* (also called the *renminbi*), so as to undervalue it compared to the dollar. A "cheaper" *yuan* makes China's exports relatively less expensive in the United States, while it makes American and other foreign products relatively more expensive for Chinese consumers. The result contributes to the increasing trade imbalance between the two countries.

Virtually every industrial and agricultural sector has been affected by trade disputes. Notable examples are automobiles, steel, semiconductors, agricultural products, cotton and textiles, and lumber. Although the United States is generally considered a "free trade" nation because it has relatively few barriers to imports compared to some other countries, it still has many trade barriers. The United States has accused Japan of having many unfair barriers to the import of U.S.–made products; however, Japan has responded with similar accusations against the United States. The United States has also accused many developing countries of erecting barriers to U.S. goods and services. Even countries such as Canada and the United States, which have many similar interests, have come to blows over trade. Issues have included restrictions on lumber, television advertising of foreign products, and even beer. When nations are unable to resolve these disputes through negotiated agreements, a *trade war* can erupt.

Reasons for Regulating Imports

Nations impose import trade barriers for many economic and political reasons. Several broad policy reasons prompt the regulation of import or export of goods and services. These include the following:

- *Collection of revenue* (taxing imports)
- *Regulation of import competition* (protection of domestic industry, agriculture, or jobs)

- *Retaliation against foreign government trade barriers*
- *Implementation of foreign policy* (prohibition on import of goods from a country that violates international norms or is a military adversary)
- *Implementation of national economic policies* (preservation of foreign exchange; implementation of industrial policy)
- *Protection of the national defense* (erection of barriers to foreign firms selling defense-related equipment or essential products such as machine tools; protection of strategic national industries such as aerospace or telecommunications)
- *Protection of natural resources or of the environment* (ban on export of scarce minerals; requirement that imported cars be equipped with antipollution devices; ban on import of tuna caught in fishing nets that trap dolphins)
- *Protection of public health, safety, and morals* (to stop the spread of human disease; to ensure safety in consumer goods, pharmaceuticals, construction equipment, etc., or to prevent the import of banned obscene materials)
- *Protection of plant and animal life* (ban on import of disease-carrying fruit or foreign species of wildlife)
- *To ensure uniform compliance with common standards and standard-setting codes* (compliance with electrical codes, fire codes, standards for automotive transportation or aviation; and other technical codes)
- *Protection of local cultural, religious, or ethnic values* (limitations on foreign television programming; prohibition of import of religiously offensive materials in fundamentalist Middle Eastern countries; ban on export of artifacts or antiques)

Import trade barriers can take many different forms and are usually classified as either tariff or non-tariff barriers.

Tariffs

The most common device for regulating imports is the *tariff* or *import duty*. (Note: These terms are used interchangeably in this text.) A tariff is a tax levied on goods by the country of importation. It is usually computed either as a percentage of value (*ad valorem* tariffs) or on the basis of physical units (*specific* or *flat* tariffs). Goods that are fungible (e.g., crude oil, wheat, or standard-size graded lumber) are usually subject to a specific or flat-rate tariff, while goods that vary in value (e.g., chairs, machinery, or specialized steel) are usually subject to an *ad valorem* tariff. Tariffs are generally considered to be one of the least restrictive types of trade barriers.

Non-tariff Barriers to Trade

Non-tariff barriers to trade are broadly defined as any impediment to trade other than tariffs. Non-tariff barriers can be direct or indirect. *Direct non-tariff barriers* include those barriers that specifically limit the import of goods or services, such as embargoes and quotas. *Indirect non-tariff barriers,* discussed in the next section, are those that on their face seem perfectly neutral and nondiscriminatory against foreign-made products, but which in their actual use and application make it difficult or costly to import foreign-made goods.

EMBARGOES. The most restrictive of the direct non-tariff barriers is the *embargo.* An embargo can be either a complete ban on trade with a certain foreign nation (e.g., the United States embargo on trade with Iraq or North Korea) or a ban on the sale or transfer of specific products (such as ivory) or technology (such as nuclear technology or nuclear materials). The embargo can be on both imports from or exports to that nation. Although a quota is used for economic purposes, an embargo is usually reserved for political purposes. This extraordinary remedy is usually used to implement foreign policy objectives, such as to "punish" another country for some offensive conduct in world affairs. In recent years, the United States has imposed embargoes on Afghanistan (under the Taliban), Cuba, Iran, Iraq (under Saddam Hussein), North Korea, Libya, Nicaragua (under the communist Sandinistas), and a few other countries.

QUOTAS. Perhaps the direct non tariff barrier that most people think of first is the *quota.* A quota is a quantitative restriction on imports. It can be based either on the value of goods or on quantity (weight, number of pieces, etc.). A quota can also be expressed as a percentage of the domestic market for that product. Quotas can be placed on all goods of a particular kind coming from all countries, a group of countries, or only one country. Thus, a quota to protect U.S. garment manufacturers could limit imports of men's trousers either to a specified number of pairs of trousers or to a given percentage of the U.S. market for men's trousers.

Global quotas are imposed by an importing nation on a particular product regardless of its country of origin. They are filled on a first-come, first-serve basis. *Bilateral quotas* are placed on a particular product on the basis of its country of origin. A *zero quota* is a complete ban on the import of a product that permits *zero* quantities to be imported.

Quotas are used either to protect domestic industry from foreign competition or as a tool for implementing a nation's economic policy of reducing imports. Governments sometimes prefer quotas to tariffs because quotas can work quickly to protect a domestic industry threatened with increased imports of competing goods. A country that experiences a domestic economic crisis caused by excessive imports (such as during a *balance-of-payments crisis,* when an excessive amount of foreign exchange leaves the country to purchase imported products) can use quotas immediately to restore economic equilibrium.

Because of the ease in administering and applying a quota, it is a more flexible tool for regulating imports than a tariff. It can, therefore, be used to reduce imports on a specific product or commodity to correct short-term market conditions. Also, government policy makers can more easily assess the potential impact of a quota than that of a tariff because no one can predict with absolute certainty what the economic effect of a tariff will be.

Another advantage of quotas is that they can either be applied across the board to all imports from a particular nation or be applied to the products of several nations. These *allocated quotas* can thus serve important foreign policy objectives because the ability to allocate additional quota rights to certain countries can become a powerful economic incentive in world politics. Quotas have been widely used in regulating trade in textiles and agricultural products, although these will soon be phased out by international agreement.

Quotas also have several disadvantages. First, a costly governmental *licensing scheme* is necessary to enforce them. Imports may need to be tracked on the basis of their country of origin, requiring complex record keeping. Second, most quotas provide no revenue to the importing nation. Third, quotas are often politically unpopular because they deprive importers and consumers of the ability to make a choice of products in the marketplace. Fourth, the imposition of quotas often can lead to retaliation by foreign governments whose products have been restricted. Fifth, the complex licensing schemes used to enforce quotas are difficult for many foreign exporters to understand, so they may not know what barriers they will face when their goods reach the foreign country. Sixth, and most importantly, quotas interfere with the *price mechanism* in the marketplace, meaning they affect prices by reducing supply. Firms able to import a product under the quota receive a monopoly profit, which may contribute to considerable price increases to consumers. Indeed, the reduced supply and increased prices attributable to quotas and other restraints on imported products restrict competition and allow the price of competing domestic products to increase correspondingly.

Historically, U.S. presidents have not favored the use of quotas to protect U.S. industry for fear that the foreign nations affected would retaliate, giving rise to trade wars. Import quotas are more likely to be used when increased foreign imports threaten national security. For instance, in the 1980s, quotas were placed on imported machine tools. This quota prompted foreign manufacturers to invest in factories in the United States so they could avoid these restrictions.

Auctioned Quotas. A quota that is sold to the highest bidder is known as an *auctioned quota.* One advantage of auctioned quotas is that they allocate import rights by price, rather than by government restrictions on supply. Moreover, auctioned quotas minimize the cost of relief to the economy by transferring the profits gained from owning quota rights from the foreign producer or importer to the country imposing the quota.

Tariff-Rate Quotas. A *tariff-rate quota* is not really a quota at all, but a tariff that increases according to the quantity of goods imported. It is a limitation or ceiling on the quantity of goods that may be imported into a country at a given tariff rate. Let's use bedspreads as an example. A country that wants to protect its domestic textile industry might impose a tariff rate of, say, 7 percent on the first 500,000 bedspreads to be imported into the country in a given year; 14 percent on the next 500,000; and an even higher rate, perhaps 25 percent, on all bedspreads imported above 1,000,000 pieces. The use of tariff-rate quotas is quite common worldwide.

Indirect Non-tariff Barriers

Indirect non-tariff barriers include laws, administrative regulations, industrial or commercial practices, and even social and cultural forces that have the effect of limiting or discouraging the sale or purchase of foreign goods or services in a domestic market, regardless of whether they were intended to control imports. All countries have indirect non-tariff barriers of some sort. Many indirect barriers are intended to protect domestic industries from foreign competition. Consider some examples.

To restrict imports, countries may impose *monetary and exchange controls* on currencies—regulations or laws that limit the amount of foreign currency available to purchase foreign goods. Foreign *government procurement* policies may encourage government agencies to buy goods and services primarily from domestic suppliers. Foreign administrative regulations can impose *technical barriers to trade,* including performance standards for products, product specifications, or product safety or environmental engineering standards. Examples might include national standards for electrical appliances, health standards for food or cosmetics, safety standards for industrial and consumer goods, and even automotive emission requirements. Unless foreign suppliers of goods can meet these standards in the same fashion as domestic suppliers, they will be frozen out of the foreign market. The refusal to allow the import of beef containing growth hormones would effectively shut down imports of beef from countries in which virtually all beef produced contains such chemicals. Governmental restrictions on the use of food preservatives, such as those that have been imposed by Japan, are another excellent example of a trade barrier in disguise, because foods without preservatives cannot be transported long distances. Other common examples might include requirements that instruction manuals for consumer goods be written in the language of the importing nation, that only metric sizes appear on the product or packaging, or that imported goods be subject to stringent inspections or fees that are not applicable to domestic products. In recent years, U.S. firms such as L.L. Bean and Lands' End have made successful inroads into the Japanese catalog business despite restrictive Japanese postal regulations.

The *Japanese Large-Scale Retail Stores* Law. Another good example of an indirect non-tariff barrier in Japan was the *Japanese Large-Scale Retail Stores Law.* This controversial law, now repealed, protected small "mom and pop" retail stores by limiting the location and operations of large retail stores and supermarkets in Japan. Because large retail chains are high-volume purchasers and large U.S. exporters are set up to sell to high-volume buyers, this law had the effect of limiting U.S. imports. Moreover, it perpetuated the vertically integrated distribution system in Japan and allowed large Japanese manufacturers greater control over the distribution of their products, which were sold through many small retail stores. The effect was to strengthen their market position to the exclusion of foreign firms. The problem was exacerbated because of high land prices in Japan that made it costly for foreign companies to obtain suitable real estate for large-scale retail operations. This law was an excellent example of a non-tariff barrier that on its face was completely neutral. It did not discriminate against products because they were of foreign origin, yet it had the effect of limiting access to the Japanese retail market by American and other foreign discount chains.

The *Japan Large-Scale Retail Stores Law* protected retailers with stores as small as 500 square meters by giving them a voice in determining whether any large stores could come into their locale. The Japanese METI refused to accept a retailer's notification that it planned to open a new store unless there was also a document indicating the terms under which local merchants agreed to the large store's opening. Negotiations between new store owners and local merchants frequently took 7 or 8 years to reach an accord.

Both domestic and international pressure led to changes in the law and in its application in the 1990s. Effective June 1, 2000, the Japanese legislature abolished this law and replaced it with the *Large-Scale Retail Store Location Law*. This law provides that approval of large stores will no longer be based on whether there is a competitive need for additional stores in the local market, but rather on the degree to which a new large store would impact the local environment, particularly traffic, noise, parking, and trash removal. The environmental standards will be developed by the Japanese government and implemented by individual municipalities. Although the United States welcomed the abolition of the original law, the manner in which the new law will be implemented at the local level will determine whether it will really afford greater market access for large stores. The law requires public notification by companies applying to open stores over 1,000 square meters, and a review period during which local residents, businesses, local governments, and others can present their views on the environmental impact of the store. Any firm attempting to open a supermarket, department store, or discount store in Japan will almost certainly face bureaucratic hurdles, local regulations for licensing, taxation, employment, and others and resentment from owners of small stores in the community. Since 2000, large retailers from France, Germany, the United Kingdom, and the United States have all made attempts to enter the Japanese retailing market. American retailers in Japan include Gap, Office Depot, Eddie Bauer, Amazon, Toys "R" Us, and Costco.

Not all stories are successful ones. Wal-Mart entered the Japanese market in 2002 by acquiring a controlling interest in the Japanese retailer Seiyu Ltd, a chain with about four hundred stores. Although it often takes retailers years to reach profitability in a new market, Wal-Mart had an unusually negative experience. After five years in the Japanese market, its Seiyu stores still had increasing losses and employee layoffs, and Seiyu's stock values were declining.

One French company, Carrefour, the largest of all European retailers, has sold its eight stores in Japan and left the Japanese market after experiencing increasing losses there. Most Western general-merchandise retailers find that they must balance their "volume discounting ethic" with the demands of Japanese consumers for quality and freshness, presented in an atmosphere that fits into Japanese cultural expectations. They also find retailing in Japan to be intensely competitive. Despite these issues, large-scale American and European volume discounters have begun to transform retailing in Japan.

Import Licensing Schemes and Customs Procedures as Trade Barriers. Some of the most insidious indirect barriers to trade are import licensing schemes and customs procedures. Some governments require importers to apply for permission to import products, subjecting them to many complex and often discriminatory requirements. The licensing is often expensive and time consuming. For instance, an importer may have to make a deposit of foreign exchange in order to get the license, or the license may be based on a discriminatory quota system.

A host of governmental red tape, administered by entrenched bureaucracies, can also cause delays of days or weeks in bringing goods into a country. Import documentation and inspection requirements, for instance, can be so unreasonable that firms cannot comply without incurring delays and unanticipated expense. Bribery and corruption in a foreign government office can stall an importer's paperwork endlessly. Administrative regulations might be impossible to comply with. For instance, imagine a country that requires all foreign-made jewelry to be marked with the country of origin, but provides no exemption for jewelry too small for engraving. Inspection procedures have also been used to stall shipments. To illustrate, in 1995 the United States accused South Korea of using delaying tactics in the form of "inspections" to hold shipments of U.S.–grown fresh produce on the docks until it rotted. Exporting companies faced with foreign licensing schemes often have to retain local agents and attorneys to advise them on import measures in the foreign market.

Transparency

When a foreign government's import regulations are not made readily available to the public or are hidden or disguised in bureaucratic rules or practices, the regulations are not *transparent*. For instance, government procurement policies *lack transparency* when the requirements for bidding on a project are made available only to select domestic firms. A licensing scheme used to enforce a quota is not transparent when the "rules of the game" are not made known to foreign exporters. When a nation's import regulations or procedures lack transparency, foreign firms cannot easily gain entrance to its markets. Many trade laws today incorporate transparency by requiring nations to publish all regulations that directly or indirectly affect imports.

Impact of Trade Barriers on Managerial Decisions

In making import–export decisions, the international manager needs to assess the impact of trade barriers on a business strategy. For example, the decision to ship goods into a foreign market, or to license or produce goods there, might be made on the basis of government policies that either restrict or promote trade. To the exporter of manufactured goods, regulations of the importing country may determine whether the firm's products can be successfully imported and marketed at all. To the importer, regulations may dictate those countries from which the firm may "source" raw materials, purchase machine parts, or locate finished goods. To the service provider, governmental regulations may determine when and on what terms it can successfully enter the banking, insurance, architectural, or engineering market. And to the investor who is considering building a plant, entering into a joint venture, or forming a subsidiary abroad, governmental regulations and trade barriers may indicate how suitable the economic and political climate is for the enterprise.

The General Agreement on Tariffs and Trade

Most nations have come to realize that trade barriers are damaging to the international economy—and ultimately to their own. Moreover, they have realized that if they restrict the products of their trading partners in order to protect one segment or sector of their economy, another sector will suffer.

Consider a few examples. If the United States (or another major steel-consuming nation) restricts the import of foreign-made steel to protect domestic steel producers, it will add to the cost of materials for domestic automakers and other domestic manufacturers that use steel to produce finished products. This will increase the consumer price of products made from foreign steel and render them less competitive with similar foreign-made products.

In one major trade dispute from 1995, the United States and Japan argued over Japanese regulatory and business practices that made it very difficult to sell U.S.–made automobiles in Japan. After negotiations between the two countries failed to resolve differences, the United States threatened to impose punitive tariffs of 100 percent on Japanese luxury automobiles. Of course, such action would have resulted in the loss of many American jobs related to the sale of Japanese luxury cars and would have likely prompted retaliation by Japan against American products.

Similarly, trade barriers that protect one industry sometimes result in foreign retaliation against another industry. For instance, Korea might put strict quotas on U.S. beef imports, but the United States might respond by placing retaliatory tariffs on Samsung appliances or Hyundai cars. Economists and government policymakers are keenly aware that the double-sided sword of protectionism can cut both ways. Therefore, since World War II, most nations have "agreed to agree" on certain established rules for setting tariffs and reducing trade barriers and for resolving their trade disputes.

Even while World War II was being fought, the United States and its allies were charting a course to rebuild and revitalize the world's economy and to ensure that the economic mistakes of the 1930s would not be repeated. In 1944, the Allied nations met at the *Bretton Woods Conference* in New Hampshire and established several important international economic institutions, including the *International Monetary Fund* and the *International Bank for Reconstruction and Development,* also called the *World Bank*. At that time, a third specialized organization, the International Trade Organization, was planned to promote and stabilize world trade by reducing tariffs. Shortly thereafter, at international meetings held in the United States and in Geneva, Switzerland, in 1947, an agreement was reached that reduced tariffs and set rules to hold countries to their tariff commitments. The International Trade Organization never materialized; one reason was the lack of support in the U.S. Congress for yet another international organization. However, the 1947 agreement, known as the *General Agreement on Tariffs and Trade,* has withstood the test of time.

At the end of World War II, most national leaders stressed a more international view of the world's economy and embraced a policy of trade liberalization. More importantly, they wanted to ensure that the world would never again fall victim to the forces of protectionism that existed in the 1930s. Their efforts to establish new rules for conducting their trade relations resulted in the creation of an international legal system to handle trade matters, complete with laws, dispute settlement mechanisms, and agreed-upon codes for regulating trade. This system is based on the *General Agreement on Tariffs and Trade.* GATT has been the most important multilateral trade agreement for liberalizing trade. It reduced tariffs, opened markets, and set rules promoting freer and fairer trade. The original GATT agreement has continued to govern most of the world's trade in goods since 1947.

Twenty-three nations, including the United States, were the original signatories to GATT in 1947. Although GATT 1947 was never ratified by the U.S. Congress as a treaty, it has consistently been accepted as a binding legal obligation of the United States under international law. Until January 1, 1995, the GATT agreement was administered by *The GATT,* a multilateral trading organization based in Geneva, Switzerland, and composed of countries that were signatories to GATT.

In 1994, after nearly a decade of negotiations, a new *General Agreement on Tariffs and Trade* was adopted that made many changes and additions to the original 1947 agreement. GATT 1994 was a result of the *Uruguay Round* of multilateral negotiations that had begun in 1986. At the close of the *Uruguay Round,* the United States implemented the GATT 1994 agreements in the *U.S. Uruguay Round Agreements Act*, effective January 1, 1995. The United States negotiated and adopted GATT 1994 under "fast-track" negotiating authority as a congressional–executive agreement. The agreement was negotiated over the course of three U.S. presidential administrations and was submitted to Congress by President Clinton. Congress approved the agreement and it became effective on January 1, 1995. As of 2007, 151 nations had signed the GATT agreements.

GATT 1994 establishes rules for regulating trade in goods and services that are broader in scope than those of GATT 1947. It also resulted in the creation of the World Trade Organization, which replaced the original GATT organization that had operated for nearly 50 years. Countries that were signatories to GATT 1947 were called *contracting parties* to reflect that GATT is a contract among nations. Under GATT 1994, signatory nations are called *members.* See appendices B and C online at academic.cengage.com/blaw/schaffer to view selected provisions of GATT 1994 and GATT 1947.

The GATT Framework

The GATT agreements and the WTO provide an organized global structure to improve the economic, political, and legal climate for trade, investment, and development. Their primary goal is to lower tariffs and remove artificial barriers and restrictions imposed by self-serving national governments. The GATT system includes an international legal system with rules, a mechanism for interpreting those rules, and a procedure for resolving disputes under them.

GATT rules are created by international agreement and become guiding principles of international trade law, upon which a WTO member nation's own trade regulations are to be based. In theory, the GATT legal system exists side by side with the domestic legal systems of sovereign nations. The GATT/WTO agreements can only work when national legislatures and government agencies choose to comply with GATT's principles when setting tariffs and regulating imports. For instance, when a nation imposes a tariff or quota on imported products, it must follow guidelines established by GATT. If it does not follow the GATT principles, the offending nation may suffer economic or political sanctions imposed by other GATT members.

Although absolute enforcement of international law is not possible except through war between nations, international trade law is to some extent enforceable because it is in the best economic and political interests of nations to comply with it. In essence, international trade law serves as a check upon the actions of governments that might otherwise severely and unnecessarily restrict the free flow of trade and commerce between nations.

GATT and U.S. Law

The GATT agreement does not provide individual rights and remedies to private parties. It cannot be used by private litigants to assert rights or claims for compensation in lawsuits against the U.S. government or to challenge the legality of a federal statute. For instance, in *Suramerica v. U.S.,* 466 F.2d 660 (Fed. Cir. 1992) the federal appellate court stated, "GATT does not trump domestic legislation." The *U.S. Uruguay Round Agreements Act* says "No state law ... may be declared invalid ... on the ground that the provision or application is inconsistent with any of the Uruguay Round agreements except in an action brought by the United States for the purpose of declaring such law or application invalid."

The *Uruguay Round Agreements Act* also states that "No provision of the Uruguay Round agreements ... that is inconsistent with any law of the United States shall have effect. Nothing in this Act shall be construed to amend or modify any law of the United States relating to the protection of human ... life, the protection of the environment, or worker safety."

If a private firm or industry in the United States believes that its rights under GATT are being violated by a foreign company or foreign government, it may seek redress either with the appropriate federal administrative agency or before the courts on the basis of a U.S. statute, but not under GATT. Of course, it can also communicate its grievance to the U.S. government, which can, at its discretion, negotiate with the foreign government under GATT rules in an attempt to resolve the trade dispute nation to nation.

GATT AGREEMENTS AS A BASIS FOR INTERPRETING U.S. TRADE STATUTES. There may be occasions when a U.S. court is called upon to interpret a U.S. statute whose wording is ambiguous or unclear. If the subject of the statute is addressed in an international treaty to which the United States is a party, the courts of the United States may look to the treaty for guidance in interpreting the statute. Establishing an important rule for interpreting statutes, the U.S. Supreme Court in *Murray v. Schooner Charming Betsy,* 6 U.S. 64 (1804) said, "[A]n act of Congress ought never to be construed to violate the law of nations, if any other possible construction remains...." This rule was recently restated by a lower federal court in a case involving U.S. trade statutes and GATT. *Timken Co. v. United States,* 240 F. Supp. 2d 1228 (Ct. Int'l Trade 2002) involved the dumping of Japanese roller bearings at an unfairly low price in the U.S. market. The plaintiffs argued that the U.S. Department of Commerce's application and interpretation of the antidumping statute was contrary to the *WTO Antidumping Agreement.* In deciding the case, the court examined the U.S. statute and stated, "The interaction between international obligations and domestic law is interesting and complex. While an unambiguous statute will prevail over a conflicting international obligation, an ambiguous statute should be interpreted so as to avoid conflict with international obligations." In this way, GATT and other treaties do sometimes influence the judicial interpretation of U.S. statutory law.

Scope and Coverage of GATT 1947

Before examining the major principles of GATT/WTO law, a reader needs to understand generally the scope and coverage of the GATT agreements. The rules of GATT 1947 applied only to trade in goods. Because most of the major trading nations of the world have been members, GATT has controlled more than 80 percent of the world's trade in goods. GATT 1947 was successful in reducing tariffs and non-tariff barriers to trade worldwide. However, nations encountered many trade issues over which GATT had no responsibility. Trade in services, such as banking or insurance, was specifically excluded from GATT 1947. It also failed to regulate agricultural trade, an area of constant dispute among nations. Trade in textiles and apparel was also not covered because of the politically sensitive nature of these industries. (Trade in textiles and apparel has been regulated by other international agreements between textile-producing and textile-importing nations.) Because GATT 1947 only dealt with trade in goods, it did little or nothing to protect intellectual property rights, such as copyrights and trademarks. GATT 1947 also did not regulate the use of restrictions on foreign investment that interfered with the free movement of goods. GATT 1947 failed to provide adequate standardized rules for nations to deal with "unfair trade" problems. Finally, the dispute settlement process set up under GATT 1947, used to resolve trade conflicts between countries, was filled with loopholes and was often ineffective. Many of these deficiencies were remedied in GATT 1994.

Scope and Coverage of GATT 1994

GATT 1994 is much broader in scope and coverage than the original 1947 agreement and addresses many of the latter agreement's limitations. The two most important agreements included in GATT 1994 are the *WTO Final Act Embodying the Uruguay Round of Multilateral Trade Negotiations* and the *WTO Agreement Establishing the World Trade Organization.* In addition to the original provisions of GATT 1947, GATT 1994 includes the following multilateral trade agreements on specific issues:

- *General Agreement on Tariffs and Trade 1994*
- *Agreement on Agriculture*
- *Agreement on the Application of Sanitary and Phytosanitary Measures*
- *Agreement on Textiles and Clothing*
- *Agreement on Technical Barriers to Trade*
- *Agreement on Trade-Related Investment Measures*
- *Agreement on Implementation of Article VI (Dumping)*
- *Agreement on Implementation of Article VII (Customs Valuation)*
- *Agreement on Preshipment Inspection*
- *Agreement on Rules of Origin*
- *Agreement on Import Licensing Procedures*
- *Agreement on Subsidies and Countervailing Measures*
- *Agreement on Safeguards (Import Relief)*
- *General Agreement on Trade in Services (GATS)*
- *Agreement on Trade-Related Aspects of Intellectual Property Rights*
- *Understanding on Rules and Procedures Governing the Settlement of Disputes*
- *Trade Policy Review Mechanism*
- *Understanding on Commitments in Financial Services*
- *Agreement on Government Procurement, and miscellaneous sectoral trade agreements*
- *Understanding on Balance-of-Payments*

This chapter examines the basic principles of GATT trade and tariff law and the role of the WTO. Most of these principles are applicable to all of the agreements shown above. Later chapters deal with more specific GATT issues, such as those related to agricultural trade, trade in textiles, and trade in services.

The World Trade Organization

As of January 1, 1995, the WTO replaced the original GATT organization. The WTO is an intergovernmental organization that assists nations in regulating trade in manufactured goods, services (including banking, insurance, tourism, and telecommunications), intellectual property, textiles and clothing, and agricultural products. The role of the WTO is to facilitate international cooperation to open markets, provide a forum for future trade negotiations between members, and provide a forum for the settlement of trade disputes. The WTO has a stature equal to that of the IMF or World Bank and will cooperate with those agencies on economic matters. The WTO's membership includes those countries that previously belonged to GATT and is now open to other countries, if their membership is accepted by a two-thirds majority vote of the members. As of 2007, 151 signatory nations were members of the WTO.

Organization of the WTO

The organization of the WTO is shown in Exhibit 9.1. The WTO is overseen by the *Ministerial Conference,* made up of high-ranking representatives from all WTO member countries. They meet at least once every two years to direct

Exhibit 9.1

Structure of the World Trade Organization

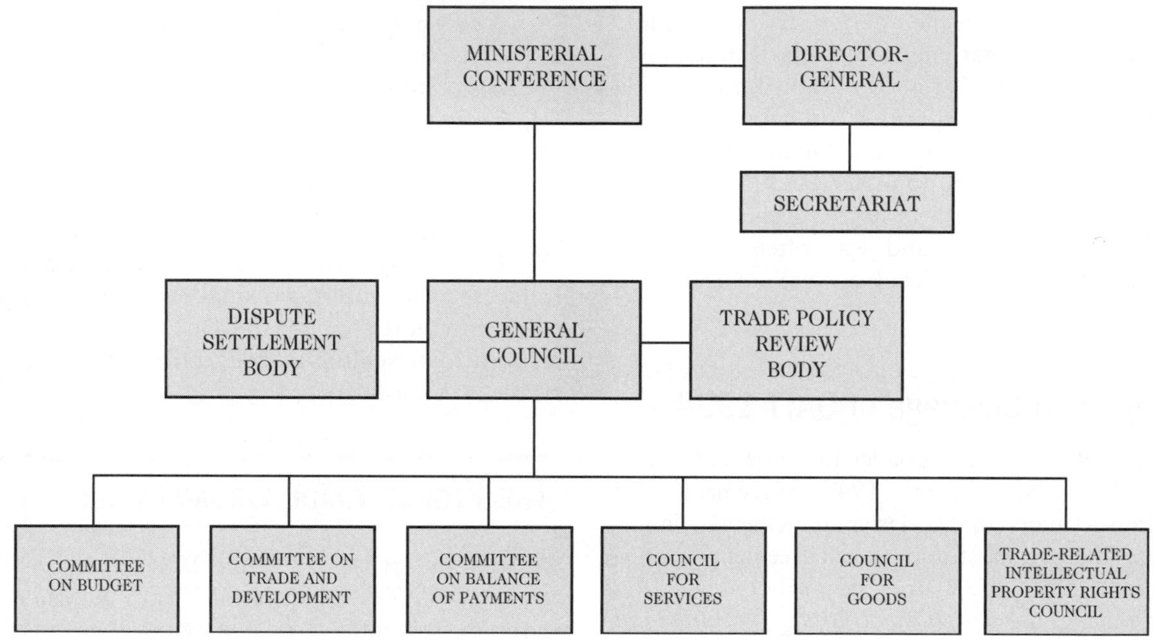

the policies, activities, and future direction of the WTO. The Ministerial Conference appoints the WTO *Director-General* and specifies his duties. The work of the Director-General is supported by the WTO *Secretariat* staff. Beneath the Ministerial Conference is the *WTO General Council,* made up of representatives of each nation and responsible for overall supervision of the WTO's activities. The General Council also oversees the work of the lower councils, which carry out the work of the WTO in specialized areas. As of 2007, the WTO had 625 employees at its headquarters in Geneva, Switzerland, and a budget of 182 million Swiss francs, or about $163 million.

The *WTO Trade Policy Review Body* periodically reviews the trade policies and practices of member countries for transparency and to ensure that member nations adhere to the rules and commitments of GATT. The body is a policy body only and has no enforcement powers. The *WTO Council for Trade in Goods* oversees the functioning and implementation of the multilateral trade agreements. The *WTO Committee on Trade and Development* reviews the treatment received by least-developed countries under GATT, considers their special trade problems, and makes recommendations to the General Council for appropriate action.

Decision making by the WTO is by consensus. If the countries cannot agree by consensus, voting is by majority vote, with each member having one vote. (Each EU country also has one vote.) The Ministerial Conference and the General Council have the authority to adopt interpretations of the GATT agreements. For countries that experience extraordinary circumstances, the Conference may grant a temporary waiver of an obligation imposed under GATT by three-fourths vote of the members.

GATT/WTO Dispute-Settlement Procedures

GATT 1994 envisions that one nation will not take unilateral retaliatory action against another nation in a trade dispute, but that the parties will instead rely on GATT *dispute-settlement procedures* to avert a trade war. GATT's dispute-settlement procedures are a quasi-judicial process for resolving trade disputes when attempts by the countries involved to reach a settlement become deadlocked. This process is intended to resolve conflicts before "trade wars" erupt. For instance, if nation A imposes a "GATT-illegal" quota on nation B's products, then nation B may file a complaint with GATT. In the meantime, nation B is not supposed to unilaterally retaliate with quotas or tariffs on A's products and, in fact, needs GATT approval to do so. Only a government can bring a GATT complaint against another government. Complaints are not filed by or against firms or individuals (although, as a practical matter, GATT cases are often brought by nations upon the instigation of private industry).

WTO Dispute-Settlement Procedures

Under GATT 1947, panel decisions were released only to the countries involved to give them another chance to resolve the issue. Panel decisions did not have the force of international or domestic law. Decisions did not acquire legal effect until they were adopted by the GATT Council of Ministers. Under the rules, valid through 1994, panel decisions were effective only if both sides in the dispute agreed to be bound. Either party could "block" or veto a panel's decision before it was sent to the Council. Many nations chose not to block GATT panel decisions because they did not want to undermine a process for resolving disputes that they might want to use in the future. Furthermore, GATT panel decisions, like WTO decisions today, carried the voice of world opinion and served as an international conscience for determining which trade practices were acceptable and which were not.

Under GATT 1994, the dispute settlement process has been strengthened and the deficiencies remedied. The WTO is given far more authority in handling trade disputes than the former GATT organization had, and individual countries can no longer block panel decisions from going into force. Among the most important changes are new procedures and timetables to ensure prompt handling of disputes. The following provisions are expressed in the *WTO Understanding on Rules and Procedures Governing the Settlement of Disputes,* also known as the *WTO Dispute-Settlement Understanding* (DSU):

- Responsibility for dispute settlement now rests with the WTO's General Council, which oversees the work of the *WTO Dispute Settlement Body*. The Dispute Settlement Body appoints panels, adopts panel decisions, and authorizes the withdrawal or suspension of concessions.
- A complaining party can request *consultations* to seek a solution. If no solution is found within 60 days, the complaining party may request that a panel hear the case. In urgent cases, such as in cases involving perishable goods, members must enter into consultations within 10 days, and if they fail to reach agreement within 20 days thereafter, they may request that a panel be convened. The panel will consist of three to five individuals nominated by the Secretariat, but subject to rejection by a party for compelling reasons.
- Other member nations with a "substantial interest" in the case may make written submissions and an oral argument before the panel. More than one member nation may join in bringing a related complaint to a single panel established by the Dispute Settlement Body.
- A panel must make an objective assessment of the facts of the case and determine whether the terms of a GATT agreement have been violated. It may call on experts for advice on scientific and technical matters. All panel deliberations are confidential. The panel must submit a written report to the parties and to other members within 6 months (3 months in urgent cases). Unless the parties file for an appeal to the Appellate Body, the panel's report will be adopted by the Dispute Settlement Body. However, the Dispute Settlement Body may vote by consensus not to accept the report. Thus, the offending nation in a dispute

settlement case can no longer "block" the decision of the panel without a unanimous vote of all members.

- An *Appellate Body* of three people will hear appeals from a panel case. They may uphold, modify, or reverse a panel decision. People serving on the Appellate Body will be chosen by the Dispute Settlement Body on the basis of their expertise in law and international trade to serve for four-year terms. Other member nations with a substantial interest in the case may file written submissions and appear before the Appellate Body. Appeals are limited to issues of law covered in the panel report and legal interpretations considered by the panel. The appellate report is final unless the Dispute Settlement Body rejects it by consensus vote within thirty days.
- If the panel report finds that the offending party has violated a GATT agreement, the Dispute Settlement Body can recommend ways for the offending party to come into compliance. The offending party has 30 days in which to state how it plans to comply with the panel's ruling. Compliance must be within a reasonable time. If no immediate solution is available, the offending party can voluntarily make compensatory adjustments to the complaining party as a temporary measure.
- If no settlement is reached or if the trade violation is not removed, the panel may authorize the complaining party to impose a retaliatory trade sanction against the offending party by withdrawing or suspending a concession. The sanction should be imposed on the same type of goods imported from the offending nation or on goods from the same type of industry or economic sector. Sanctions should be in an amount equal to the impact that the GATT violation had on the complaining party. Sanctions are to be temporary and remain in force only until the offending party's violation is removed.

The following case, *WTO Report of the Appellate Body on European Communities—Regime for the Importation, Sale and Distribution of Bananas (1997)* involves a long-running trade dispute among the European Community, Latin America, and the United States. It addresses the issue of who may request a WTO panel in a trade dispute.

European Communities—Regime for the Importation, Sale & Distribution of Bananas
WT/DS27/AB/R; September 9, 1997
Report of the Appellate Body of the World Trade Organization

BACKGROUND AND FACTS

In recent years the European Community (EC) has been the world's largest importer of bananas, accounting for 38 percent of world trade in bananas. In 1991, the EC imported over 3.65 million tons, two-thirds of which was grown in Latin America. Almost 19 percent came from developing countries that were once colonies of Britain, Spain, and France, located in Africa, the Caribbean, and the Pacific (known as ACP countries). Growers in the ACP countries could not compete with the highly efficient non-ACP producers, most of which are in Latin America. In order to encourage the import of ACP-grown bananas and to aid in the development of ACP economies, the EC devised a host of tariff and non-tariff barriers aimed at non-ACP bananas. For example, a complex quota scheme was used permitting only a limited quantity of non-ACP bananas to be imported each year. While licenses to import ACP bananas were granted routinely, only importers who met strict requirements could receive licenses to import Latin American and other non-ACP bananas. While most ACP bananas entered duty free, other bananas had a very substantial tariff rate. Several Latin American countries requested consultations, claiming that the EC regulations violated GATT by discriminating against bananas grown in their countries. The United States joined with the Latin American countries in arguing that they too had a substantial interest in the issue. While the United States was not an exporter of bananas, the U.S. government noted that U.S. companies, such as Chiquita Brands and others, conducted a wholesale trade in bananas amounting to hundreds of millions of dollars a year

continued

continued

and would lose market share because of the EC's actions. The EC maintained that the United States had no grounds for complaining about the EC regulations because it was not a producer and grower. A WTO panel was convened, and its decision was appealed to the WTO Appellate Body.

REPORT OF THE APPELLATE BODY

The EC argues that the Panel infringed Article 3.2 of the Dispute Settlement Understanding (DSU) by finding that the United States has a right to advance claims under the GATT 1994. The EC asserts that, as a general principle, in any system of law, including international law, a claimant must normally have a legal right or interest in the claim it is pursuing.... The EC asserts that the United States has no actual or potential trade interest justifying its claim, since its banana production is minimal, it has never exported bananas, and this situation is unlikely to change due to the climatic and economic conditions in the United States. In the view of the EC, the panel fails to explain how the United States has a potential trade interest in bananas, and production alone does not suffice for a potential trade interest. The EC also contends that the United States has no right protected by WTO law to shield its own internal market from the indirect effects of the EC banana regime....

We agree with the Panel that no provision of the DSU contains any explicit requirement that a member must have a "legal interest" as a prerequisite for requesting a panel. We do not accept that the need for a "legal interest" is implied in the DSU or in any other provision of the WTO Agreement.... [We believe] that a member nation has broad discretion in deciding whether to bring a case against another member nation under the DSU....

The participants in this appeal have referred to certain judgments of the International Court of Justice and the Permanent Court of International Justice relating to whether there is a requirement, in international law, of a legal interest to bring a case. We do not read any of these judgments as establishing a general rule that in all international litigation, a complaining party must have a "legal interest" in order to bring a case. Nor do these judgments deny the need to consider the question of standing under the dispute settlement provisions of any multilateral treaty, by referring to the terms of that treaty.

We are satisfied that the United States was justified in bringing its claims under the GATT 1994 in this case. The United States is a producer of bananas, and a potential export interest by the United States cannot be excluded. The internal market of the United States of bananas could be affected by the EC banana regime, in particular, by the effects of that regime on world supplies and world prices of bananas. We also agree with the Panel's statement that: "... with the increased interdependence of the global economy, ... member nations have a greater stake in enforcing WTO rules than in the past since any deviation from the negotiated balance of rights and obligations is more likely than ever to affect them, directly or indirectly."

Accordingly, we believe that a member nation has broad discretion in deciding whether to bring a case against another member under the DSU. The language of Article XXIII:1 of the GATT 1994 and of the DSU suggests, furthermore, that a member is expected to be largely self-regulating in deciding whether any such action would be "fruitful."

Decision. The Appellate Body held that the United States could call for the convening of a WTO panel to question EC import barriers even though its exports were not directly affected.

Comment. The United States sought WTO authorization to "suspend concessions" (i.e., impose retaliatory tariffs) on a wide range of EU products, the value of which was equivalent to the nullification or impairment sustained by the United States. In 1999, the Dispute Settlement Body authorized the United States to impose 100 percent *ad valorem* duties on a list of EU products with an annual trade value of $191.4 million. The range of European products included bath preparations, handbags of plastic, paperboard, lithographs not over 20 years old, cotton bed linens that are printed and do not contain any embroidery or trimming, certain lead-acid batteries, "articles of a kind normally carried in the pocket or handbag, with outer surface of reinforced or laminated plastics," folding cartons of noncorrugated paper, and electric coffeemakers. In 2001, an agreement was reached to end the trade dispute. The EU restrictions were dismantled, and U.S. tariffs were lifted. The "Banana Wars" were the largest trade war to date with tremendous economic and political ramifications. Current information on this and other trade issues is available from the U.S. Trade Representative's Web site.

WTO Reports as Legal Precedent

Do WTO reports carry precedential value for future panels, as judicial decisions do in common-law courts? According to the language of GATT and recent WTO reports, the answer seems to be no. The *WTO Report of the Appellate Body on Japan—Taxes on Alcoholic Beverages* (1996) addressed the status of a report that had been adopted by the Dispute Settlement Body. It said:

> We do not believe that the contracting parties [WTO member nations], in deciding to adopt a panel report, intended that their decision would constitute a definitive interpretation of the provisions of GATT 1947. Nor do we believe that this is contemplated under GATT 1994.... Adopted panel reports can play an important part of the GATT *acquis*. They are often considered by subsequent panels. They create legitimate expectations among WTO members, and, therefore should be taken into account where they are relevant to any dispute. *However, they are not binding....*

This statement is reaffirmed in the actual language of GATT 1994, which states that interpretations of the agreement may only be made by the Ministerial Conference and the General Council. Nevertheless, WTO Appellate Body reports continue to cite prior reports for their precedential value.

In the United States, WTO Panel and Appellate Body decisions are not binding on the courts. However, there are several cases in which the federal courts have cited WTO decisions for their persuasive authority. For example, in *Hyundai Electronics Co., Ltd. v. United States,* 53 F. Supp. 2d 1334 (Ct. Int'l Trade, 1999), the court stated, "Thus, the WTO panel report does not constitute binding precedential authority for the court. Of course, this is not to imply that a panel report serves no purpose in litigation before the court. To the contrary, a panel's reasoning, if sound, may be used to inform the court's decision." In application, this means that a U.S. court cannot strike down a U.S. law or regulation merely because a WTO decision has ruled that it is in violation of an international agreement. For instance, if a WTO panel rules that a U.S. Department of Energy regulation regarding the sale of imported oil is held to be in violation of GATT's nondiscrimination provisions, a U.S. court cannot rely on that decision in striking down the regulation. It would be a matter for the U.S. Congress or the executive branch of government, and not the judiciary, to bring that regulation into compliance with a WTO decision.

GATT 1994: Major Principles of Trade Law

In addition to member nations' commitments to consult with each other over trade differences and to resort to dispute settlement, GATT 1994 reinforces five basic principles of international trade law.

1. *Multilateral trade negotiations:* Nations will meet periodically to reduce tariffs and non-tariff barriers to trade.
2. *Predictability of trade opportunities:* By committing themselves to specific, negotiated tariff rates, or "bindings," nations permit exporters and importers to know the highest tariff rate applicable to that product or commodity. This enhances the stability of the world's trading system.
3. *Nondiscrimination and unconditional most-favored-nation trade:* Members will not give any import advantage or favor to products coming from one member over the goods of another member.
4. *National treatment:* Members will not discriminate in favor of domestically produced goods and against imported goods or treat the two differently under their internal tax laws, regulations, and other national laws.
5. *Elimination of quotas and other non-tariff barriers:* Nations must first "convert" their non-tariff barriers to tariffs (through a process called *tariffication*) and then engage in negotiations to reduce the tariff rates.

In addition, GATT contains provisions to promote trade with developing nations and special rules allowing the establishment of free trade areas and customs unions. Other special rules allow restrictions on imports when necessary to protect the public health and safety or to protect domestic firms from unfair trade practices or increased levels of imports that might cause serious economic injury to domestic industries.

Multilateral Trade Negotiations

Since 1947, the GATT organization has served to bring member nations together to negotiate tariff reductions and the opening of markets. Under the auspices of GATT, the contracting parties have completed eight major *rounds,* or *multilateral negotiating sessions.*

- Geneva, Switzerland, 1947
- Annecy, France, 1948
- Torquay, England, 1950
- Geneva, Switzerland, 1956
- *Dillon Round,* 1960–1961
- *Kennedy Round,* 1964–1967
- *Tokyo Round,* 1973–1979
- *Uruguay Round,* 1986–1994

A ninth round, the *Doha Development Agenda,* 2001, was incomplete as of 2007.

THE *KENNEDY ROUND.* In the early rounds, countries negotiated on a product-by-product basis by presenting lists of tariff reductions that they desired from other countries, which submitted requests for concessions that they wanted in return. These rounds resulted in a lowering of *ad valorem* tariffs from roughly 40 percent in 1945 to approximately 20 percent in 1961. The *Kennedy Round,* which took place from 1964 to 1967, resulted in even larger across-the-board tariff cuts, particularly in manufactured goods, averaging nearly $40 billion in trade. More than sixty nations participated in the *Kennedy Round.* During this period, many developing countries joined GATT.

THE *TOKYO ROUND.* By the 1970s, GATT's efforts had proven so successful that tariffs ceased to be the world's greatest barrier to trade in goods. Indeed, without GATT, decades of bilateral negotiations may have been necessary to achieve the reductions that multilateral negotiations reached within a few years. In the *Tokyo Round,* more than one hundred participating nations agreed to tariff cuts averaging 34 percent and covering $300 billion in trade, which effectively lowered the average level of tariffs to about 5 percent. In addition, the parties established a number of GATT codes that attempted to remove non-tariff barriers. These codes addressed issues such as subsidies, technical barriers to trade, government procurement rules, customs valuation, and dumping (discussed in later chapters).

THE *URUGUAY ROUND.* The *Uruguay Round* negotiations lasted from 1986 to 1994 and resulted in GATT 1994 and the creation of the WTO. Its tariff and market access negotiations resulted in worldwide tariff cuts averaging 35 to 40 percent on merchandise, farm products, and industrial goods and a reduction of non-tariff barriers.

Some products have much greater tariff reductions, which may be as high as 50 to 100 percent on electronic items such as semiconductors and computers. In addition to tariff cuts, tariffs have been *bound,* or capped, at the rate effective at the time of the agreement. A country that raises a bound tariff will violate GATT and will have to withdraw the increase or reach an agreement with the affected countries to lower tariffs on some other product.

THE *DOHA DEVELOPMENT AGENDA.* The trade rounds that began in 2001 are known as the *Doha Development Agenda.* The agenda for the meetings was set by the Doha Declaration, which was drafted by the WTO's Ministerial Conference. The focus of these trade negotiations comprises

- Assisting the developing countries in implementing the trade rules that came out of the *Uruguay Rounds.*
- Reaching an agreement to reduce or end agriculture subsidies (domestic price supports and export incentives) by developed countries (an area of disagreement between the rich and poor countries because they encourage cheap exports of farm products from developed to poorer developing countries).
- Freeing trade in services, such as banking and insurance, to better allow these firms to operate globally.
- Reducing high tariffs on products that countries consider "sensitive imports" and generally limiting them to 15 percent. It also, eliminates "escalating tariffs" in which higher import duties are imposed on semiprocessed products than on raw materials, and higher duties still are imposed on finished products.

- Negotiating a higher level of copyright protection on products with "geographical names," especially wines, meats, and cheeses such as *Champagne, Burgundy, Parma ham,* and *Feta* cheese.
- Trade issues related to investment, government procurement, patent protection, electronic commerce, trade and the environment, foreign investment rules, and other topics.

The world was witness to the failure of two Doha meetings (Seattle, 1999 and Cancun, Mexico, 2003) when televised news reports showed protesters demonstrating against what they perceived as a growing "struggle" of the rich versus the poor, developed versus developing countries, corporations versus consumers and environmentalists, and so on. Indeed, in Cancun, a Korean farmer, the head of the South Korean Federation of Farmers and Fishermen, committed suicide atop a wire barrier in protest over agricultural trade issues. In actuality, the talks failed to reach their goals because of the inability of the rich and poor nations to reach agreement on controversial and highly politically charged trade issues. Agriculture trade and the protection of domestic farmers was one of the main reasons. More recent meetings in 2004 and 2005 were more successful in reaching preliminary agreements.

Tariffication

Tariffication refers to the process by which quotas, licensing schemes, and other non-tariff barriers to trade are "converted" to tariffs. Tariff rates can then be reduced through negotiation and the global economic environment for trade improved. For example, under GATT 1994, quotas on agricultural products will be converted to tariffs and gradually reduced. Tariffication has been a GATT policy since 1947.

Zero-for-Zero Tariff Elimination. During the *Uruguay Round,* the United States adopted a "zero-for-zero" tariff reduction policy. U.S. negotiators sought reciprocal tariff elimination in key industry sectors. The agreement phases out, over periods averaging five years, tariffs in ten product areas: agricultural equipment, medical equipment, construction equipment, beer, distilled spirits, chemicals, furniture, and paper and printed matter. Tariffs on pharmaceuticals and toys were eliminated in 1995. Each nation's tariff schedule, which reflects the new rates, has been deposited with the WTO. Current U.S. legislation grants the president the authority to negotiate additional market access agreements in future WTO negotiations on a zero-for-zero basis.

Tariff Concessions, Bound Rates, and Tariff Schedules

Article II of GATT calls for member nations to cooperate in lowering tariffs through negotiations. In a *tariff concession,* one country promises not to levy a tariff on a given product at a level higher than agreed upon. In essence, each country makes a concession to the products of the other country and receives reciprocal treatment. This process does not set the same tariff rate on a particular product for every nation, but determines a tariff rate that is said to be *bound.* A country may not arbitrarily raise its tariff above its bound rate. The rates are arrived at through compromise, and these concessions are recorded in *tariff schedules,* which are detailed product-by-product listings of all tariff obligations for a particular nation. Tariff schedules for the United States are found in the *Harmonized Tariff Schedule of the United States* (HTSUS). The GATT agreement calls for its members to negotiate reciprocal reductions in tariffs, either on a product-by-product basis or across the board.

The case *GATT Report on European Economic Community—Import Regime for Bananas* (1995) illustrates the importance of countries honoring their tariff rates granted by concession to foreign countries. As the case shows, government and business planners alike rely on access to foreign markets. If an importing nation unexpectedly raises its tariff rate, contrary to its concession, this would cause market disruption and injury to foreign exporters. The GATT Panel ruled that the change in European Economic Community tariff schedules had "nullified and impaired" the rights of foreign banana exporters who should have been able to rely on the existing tariff structure.

European Economic Community—Import Regime for Bananas

34 I.L.M. 177 (1995); Report of the GATT Dispute Settlement Panel (not adopted by the Council)

BACKGROUND AND FACTS

This case was decided in 1995 by a GATT Dispute Settlement Panel prior to GATT 1994 and the creation of the WTO. It resulted from the same "Banana Trade Wars" as a case appearing earlier in this chapter. Since 1963 the European Economic Community (EEC) had negotiated tariff rates with the developing countries that export bananas, and these concessions were bound in the tariff schedules at 20 percent *ad valorem.* In 1993 the EEC took over banana import regulation from the individual countries. The EEC set up uniform rules on quality, marketing standards, and tariffs. Under the EEC regime the tariff rates on bananas from the Latin American countries were increased between 20 and 180 percent. A complex licensing scheme was also set up to limit foreign banana traders (e.g., Chiquita, Dole, and Del Monte) access to sell in the EEC. The Latin American countries claimed that the regulations impaired their Article II tariff concessions and violated Article I, MFN principles, and other GATT provisions.

REPORT OF THE PANEL

Article II—Schedules of Concessions: [Central and South American] banana producers had assessed their competitive position on the basis of the bound tariff level. They had made strategic decisions and investments on that basis; they had cultivated substantially more land specifically for this export trade; and they had pursued marketing ties with European importers. The new tariff quota undermined the legitimate expectations upon which these actions were based and severely disrupted the trade conditions upon which these producers had relied, regardless of the actual protective effect of the new regime.

The Panel noted that Article II required that each contracting party "accord to the commerce of the other contracting parties treatment no less favourable than that provided for in the ... *Schedule of Concessions.*" The Panel then considered whether the introduction of a specific tariff for bananas in place of the *ad valorem* tariff provided for in its *Schedule* constituted "treatment no less favourable" in terms of Article II.... The Panel consequently found that the new specific tariffs led to the levying of a duty on imports of bananas whose *ad valorem* equivalent was, either actually or potentially, higher than 20 percent *ad valorem*....

The Contracting Parties had consistently found that a change from a bound specific to an *ad valorem* rate was a modification of the concession. A working party examining a proposal by Turkey to modify its tariff structure from specific to *ad valorem* had stated: "The obligations of contracting parties are established by the rates of duty appearing in the schedules and any change in the rate such as a change from a specific to an *ad valorem* duty could in some circumstances adversely affect the value of the concessions to other contracting parties. Consequently, any conversion of specific into *ad valorem* rates of duty can be made only under some procedure for the modification of concessions." ...

Decision. The panel held that the EEC had deprived (also called "nullified and impaired") the complaining Latin American countries of the benefits to which they were entitled under the bound tariff schedules.

Nondiscrimination, Most Favored Nation Trade, and National Treatment

The principle of *nondiscrimination* has long been a guiding concept of international economic relations and of trade liberalization. Defined most broadly, nondiscrimination means that in every aspect of economic life, all nations should be treated equally and without discrimination. Nondiscrimination is one of the basic rights of membership in the WTO. It means that every WTO member country must treat the goods and services from all other WTO member countries equally and without discrimination. Simply put, nations should not "play favorites" with each other's goods or services. The principle of nondiscrimination is embodied in two important principles of international trade law: the principle of *unconditional most favored nation trade* and the concept of *national treatment.*

Most Favored Nation Trade

When one country grants "most favored nation" trading status to another country, it is agreeing to accord products imported from that country the most favorable treatment or the lowest tariff rates that it gives to similar products imported from its other MFN trading partners. In the United States, MFN trading status is granted to a foreign country (or "trading partner") by an act of Congress. According to the GATT agreements, all countries that are members of the WTO should automatically be entitled to MFN trading status with other WTO countries (although in reality this may not be the case—Cuba is a WTO member but as of 2007 had not received MFN trading status from the United States). Although MFN trade has been in use for at least three hundred years, it is now a basic principle of GATT law and is found in Article I of the *General Agreement on Tariffs and Trade,* which says

> With respect to customs duties and charges of any kind imposed on or in connection with importation or exportation . . . and with respect to the method of levying such duties and charges, and with respect to all rules and formalities in connection with importation and exportation. . . . Any advantage, favour, privilege, or immunity granted by any other member to any product originating in or destined for any other country shall be accorded immediately and unconditionally to the like product originating in or destined for the territories of all other members.

MFN principles are also applied to trade in services under Article II of the *General Agreement on Trade in Services.*

> With respect to any measure covered by this Agreement, each Member shall accord immediately and unconditionally to services and service suppliers of any other Member treatment no less favourable than that it accords to like services and service suppliers of any other country.

UNCONDITIONAL MFN TRADE. *Unconditional* MFN trade is different from conditional MFN trade. *Conditional* treatment requires that a trading partner give something in return for a tariff concession. Conditional MFN trade was used by the United States in its first trade pact made in 1778 with France and continued through the end of World War I. Then, the United States found out that conditional MFN trade allowed other countries to discriminate against U.S. exports, and the practice was phased out. MFN trade today is unconditional for all WTO members. *Unconditional* MFN trade requires that if a nation negotiates a reduced tariff rate on a certain product imported from one WTO member, that rate of duty *automatically* becomes applicable to like products imported from any and all other WTO members. This means that if nation A negotiates a reduced tariff rate on a particular product imported from WTO nation B, that new rate becomes applicable to like products imported from all WTO member countries. Unconditional treatment is granted because the products from WTO countries are entitled to be treated equally and without discrimination.

MFN treatment for imported goods greatly influences trade flows between nations. If a country's products do not qualify for MFN tariff rates in an importing nation, then it may not be economically practical to import those products at all. For example, assume that a company desires to import products that originated in nation B into nation A. If nation B's goods do not qualify for MFN tariff treatment in nation A, then the transaction may not be profitable because of the high tariff rates. For instance, an MFN rate on a particular product might typically be 5 percent of the value of the import. Without MFN treatment, however, the rate on the same goods might be as high as 90 percent on the value of the import. The importer may actually have to find substitute products in some other country that is an MFN trading partner of nation A.

Most people erroneously think that MFN trade is some "special treatment" applied as a favor to products coming from a foreign country. That is not the case. Actually, under WTO rules, most favored nation treatment is the norm. All WTO member countries must apply MFN tariff rates to products being imported from any and all WTO member countries. Any WTO country that denies MFN treatment to products from another WTO country may be subject to losing MFN status itself. In the United States, all countries are entitled to receive MFN tariff treatment unless specifically exempted.

Exceptions to MFN Trading Status. The WTO agreement includes several exceptions to the MFN requirement. In some special circumstances, countries may impose higher than normal MFN rates on products from certain countries. In other cases they may impose tariff rates lower than the MFN rate. For example, products from some developing countries can be imported into a developed country at tariff rates *even lower* than the MFN rate, as when the United States or the European Union is trying to encourage imports from Africa or the Caribbean. These are known as "preferential" tariff rates, or "tariff preferences." Similarly, some countries' products come into the United States at a rate higher than the MFN rate, as when the United States is restricting trade with a country because of its violations of human rights.

Keep in mind that just because the United States grants MFN trade status to a country, it does not mean that Americans have unrestricted trade with that country. It is possible, as in the case of Syria, that the United States may impose a total embargo on trade with that country for other foreign policy or national security reasons, such as sponsoring terrorism.

Another exception to MFN rules applies to goods traded within free trade areas or common markets. For example, goods traded between the United States, Canada, and Mexico would qualify for better-than-MFN tariff rates, or may pass duty free, under the *North American Free Trade Agreement.* A similar exception would apply for goods traded within the European Union. Smaller trading blocs exist in Latin America, Africa, and Asia.

It should be pointed out that some leading international economists and supporters of the role of the World Trade Organization view regional trading blocs as a threat to further trade liberalization on a global scale. They are concerned that the world will divide into geographic or regional trading blocs and fear that this could become a method of regional protectionism rather than a means of fostering free trade. They encourage the focus of trade liberalization to be through the WTO system.

New Terminology: Normal Trade Relations. In the United States, the term "most favored nation" is now referred to as *normal trade relations,* or NTR. This term has replaced the term "most favored nation" in all U.S. laws because Congress considered it to more accurately describe the "normal" tariff treatment for most countries. The term "most favored nation" is still used in international documents and in other countries, however.

NTR Status and *Jackson-Vanik:* A Remnant of the Cold War

In 1951, at the beginning of the Cold War, the United States passed laws denying MFN/NTR status to communist countries. This applied to China, the Soviet Union, and their satellite communist states in Asia and Eastern Europe. This policy was generally continued under the *U.S. Trade Act of 1974.* At that time the Soviet Union was accused of denying its citizens the right to emigrate and particularly denying the right of Russian Jews to emigrate to Israel. In response, Congress passed the *Jackson-Vanik Amendment* to the *Trade Act of 1974.* Still in effect in 2007, this statute denies NTR status to any communist or nonmarket economy country that deprives its citizens of the freedom or opportunity to emigrate. *Jackson-Vanik* requires the president to review the emigration policies of nonmarket economy countries and to report to Congress on a regular basis. The president is authorized to grant *temporary* NTR status if it is determined that the country is complying with *Jackson-Vanik's* freedom of emigration requirements or if the president finds that NTR status will promote continued advances in the freedom of emigration. NTR status also requires that the United States and the foreign country in question have entered into a bilateral trade agreement on broader issues, including reciprocity of NTR status. Decisions of the president are reviewable by Congress and may be disapproved by a joint resolution of the House and Senate.

As of 2007, the only countries that had not been granted normal trade status by the United States were Cuba and North Korea.

Countries with temporary NTR status can "graduate" to permanent NTR status only if an act of Congress exempts that country from annual review by the president. After the end of the Cold War and the collapse of the Soviet Union in 1989, many of the former republics of the Soviet Union and the formerly communist countries of Eastern Europe and Asia were granted permanent NTR status by the United States. This has normally paved the way for their membership in the World Trade Organization. The granting of permanent NTR status is a very politicized process, as Congress considers both the trade and political implications. Some of the most controversial cases have involved Russia, Vietnam, and China. There have been some calls in Congress for a complete repeal of *Jackson-Vanik*.

NORMALIZATION OF U.S. TRADE RELATIONS WITH RUSSIA. With the collapse of Soviet communism in Russia, the central Asian republics, and in Eastern Europe in the early 1990s, America wanted to assist these countries in their transition to democracy. (Recall that without NTR status, products from these countries would be subject to much higher rates of duty when entering the United States, and many would be rendered prohibitively expensive.) Today, almost all of these formerly communist countries have normal trade status with the United States. For example, the former Soviet republics of Kyrgyzstan, Georgia, Armenia, and Ukraine have received permanent NTR status. However, since 1992 Russia has been granted only temporary NTR status under *Jackson-Vanik*. As of mid-2007, Russia had not been granted permanent NTR status by Congress. Russia has considered this an insult and a "throwback" to its communist days and believes that *Jackson-Vanik* is no longer appropriate. It is likely that the United States will grant permanent NTR status to Russia in the near future.

As of 2007, Russia was attempting to complete its membership in the World Trade Organization. (Russia's neighbors, Ukraine and Belarus, were also in "observer status" at the WTO.) Membership requires a lengthy negotiating process where the applying country must demonstrate that its markets are sufficiently open to goods, services, and investment from other WTO countries and that they will not be subject to discrimination. In 2006, Russia and the United States entered into a bilateral market access agreement, reducing tariffs and non-tariff barriers to the Russian market. The agreement covered goods related to information technology, civil aircraft, chemicals, and capital goods. It eliminated many restrictions on U.S. companies' ownership of Russian service companies, including commercial banks and investment companies, as well as permitting cross-border data processing and credit card services. With Russia purchasing over $1 billion in American agricultural products annually, the agreement commits Russia to agreed tariff rates on imports of U.S. agricultural products. It would seem that Russia's membership in the WTO is certain. All of the formerly communist countries of Eastern Europe (with the exception of the former Yugoslavia) have already been granted membership in the WTO (as well as the European Union).

NORMALIZATION OF TRADE RELATIONS WITH VIETNAM. The scars of the Vietnam War are taking decades to heal. In 1994, the United States ended the trade embargo with Vietnam, and in 1995 it reestablished diplomatic relations. In 2000, President Clinton became the first U.S. president to visit Vietnam since 1969 and the first ever to visit its capitol, Hanoi. Although Vietnam is a socialist country run by a communist government, the signs of American economic capitalism are apparent everywhere. News reports of the president's trip from the Associated Press and CNN showed Ho Chi Minh City crowded with billboard advertising for Coke, American music blaring from sidewalk cafes, and counterfeit Nike and Calvin Klein products being sold on the streets. Obviously, America has had a tremendous and ongoing impact on Vietnamese popular culture. In 2006, the U.S. Congress granted Vietnam permanent NTR status, and in that year, total U.S.–Vietnam trade reached almost $10 billion. In 2007 Vietnam was admitted to the World Trade Organization. The United States has also normalized trade relations with Cambodia and Laos, Vietnam's neighbors in Indochina.

NORMALIZATION OF U.S. TRADE RELATIONS WITH CHINA. In recent years, an important political debate in the United States has surrounded the issue of normalizing trade with the People's Republic of China. China has been ruled by a communist government since shortly after World War II. Although China was an original party to GATT 1947, it withdrew in 1950 as a result of the communist takeover. In 1951 China lost its normal trade status with the United States, resulting in prohibitively high import duties on Chinese goods. From 1974 to 1980, China's human rights record was watched closely under the *Jackson-Vanik*

Amendment. In 1980, China's emigration policies improved, and since that time it has received annual waivers from the *Jackson-Vanik Amendment* that grant temporary normal trade status to Chinese goods entering the United States. Throughout the 1990s, U.S. relations with China improved, and annual renewal of China's normal trade status was "virtually automatic." In 2000, Congress granted permanent normal trade status to China, effective on China's admission to the WTO in December 2001.

The United States and China have strong economic ties, despite many political differences. China has a population of over 1.3 billion people. It represents the largest potential market in the world for U.S. goods and services. There are tremendous opportunities for U.S. exports to China, particularly in electrical equipment, power-generating equipment, aircraft, agriculture, computers, automobiles, financial services, and telecommunications. The United States also relies heavily on Chinese imports. In 2006, China shipped almost $1 trillion in goods to the world. It is sometimes said that U.S. consumers have become "addicted" to inexpensive Chinese products. In 2006, the United States imported $287.8 billion in goods from China and exported $55.2 billion in goods there, leaving a trade deficit in goods of $232.5 billion. The United States had a slight surplus, under $3 billion, in the sale of commercial services to China. In that year, the United States was China's largest export market, and China was the fourth largest export market for U.S. goods (the third largest if you include China and Hong Kong together). U.S. importers spent more purchasing goods from China than from any other country except Canada. More than one-quarter of China's exports are shipped to the United States. As China is a normal trading partner, China's products enter the United States with an average 3 percent import duty. If China did not have normal trade status, import duties on many Chinese goods would exceed 70 percent, resulting in a tremendous cost to U.S. consumers. Thus a continued normal trade relation between the two countries is important to both nations.

Normalization of trade relations with China has always been linked to U.S. foreign policy. China's trade status was called into question in 1989 when the Chinese government used military force to stop pro-democracy demonstrations against the government at Tiananmen Square during which student demonstrators were arrested as political prisoners or killed. Americans who oppose normal trade relations with China make the following arguments: China's human rights record has not improved. It has suppressed religious and other freedoms in Tibet; it does not treat prisoners humanely; it has used forced sterilization and abortion to control population growth; it uses prisoners in forced labor camps to manufacture goods (some of which have been exported to the United States); it has used the Chinese army to manufacture goods sold at unfairly low prices in world markets; it has allowed shipments of textile and apparel products to the United States in violation of U.S. import quotas; and it has allowed violations of U.S.–owned patents, copyrights, and trademarks. In addition, China has been accused of supporting communist North Korea, of exporting nuclear technology in violation of international agreements, and of selling Scud missiles to some Middle Eastern countries.

Arguments for the normalization of relations with China were based on the fact that China had made many economic and political reforms. It had improved its human rights record, released many political prisoners, and permitted greater freedom of travel and emigration. It strengthened its intellectual property laws, reformed its tax laws, opened its borders to foreign direct investment, and made many economic reforms toward a market economy.

Another argument in favor of normal trade relations is that trade is ineffective as a political weapon. Depriving China—or any nondemocratic country—of normal trade status will not effectively change its domestic or foreign policies. By closing the doors to trade with China, the United States would lose its ability to influence the Chinese economically. It would hinder economic development in China, making it harder for China to move from a socialist economy to a free-market economy. Most people agree that trade leads to greater interpersonal contact, more openness in society, and increased democratization. Moreover, history teaches us that if the United States denies normal trade status to China, China will still be able to trade with other nations around the world. The argument, then, is that trade should not be "held hostage to politics" and should not be used as a tool of foreign policy. For these reasons, even many of China's critics support continued normalization of trade relations.

Perhaps the greatest threat to U.S.–Chinese relations is China's claim to the island nation of Taiwan (see the Managerial Implications problem at the end of this chapter). The United States has supported a free and independent Taiwan (called "Chinese Taipei" or the "Separate Customs Territory of Taiwan" in the WTO system) and is pledged to its military defense. There is concern in the United States that a Chinese takeover of Taiwan would give China excessive economic, political, and military influence over Japan and the rest of Asia. China maintains that Taiwan is a "renegade province" and that it is a part of China.

In 2001, just as the U.S. administration was considering weapon sales to Taiwan, a U.S. spy plane and its crew were detained in China. This international incident again called U.S.–Chinese trade relations into question and a few U.S. lawmakers suggested revoking China's normal trade status and imposing economic sanctions. The United States insisted that Taiwan's admission to the WTO be granted simultaneously with that of China.

National Treatment

The *national treatment* provisions of the *General Agreement on Tariffs and Trade* are intended to ensure that imported products will not be subjected to discriminatory treatment under the laws of the importing nation. Under Article III, imported products must not be regulated, taxed, or otherwise treated differently from domestic goods once they enter a nation's stream of commerce. GATT Article III:2 provides that imports shall not be subject to internal taxes or charges in excess of those applied to like domestic products.

> Article III
>
> 1. The contracting parties recognize that internal taxes and other internal charges, and laws, regulations and requirements affecting the internal sale, offering for sale, purchase, transportation, distribution or use of products, and internal quantitative regulations requiring the mixture, processing or use of products in specified amounts or proportions, should not be applied to imported or domestic products so as to afford protection to domestic production.
>
> 2. The products of the territory of any contracting party imported into the territory of any other contracting party shall not be subject, directly or indirectly, to internal taxes or other internal charges of any kind in excess of those applied, directly or indirectly, to *like domestic products*. Moreover, no contracting party shall otherwise apply internal taxes or other internal charges to imported or domestic products in a manner contrary to the principles set forth in paragraph 1.
>
> *Ad* Article III (Annex) to Paragraph 2
>
> A tax conforming to the requirements of the first sentence of paragraph 2 would be considered to be inconsistent with the provisions of the second sentence only in cases where competition was involved between, on the one hand, the taxed product and, on the other hand, a *directly competitive or substitutable product* which was not similarly taxed.

The even broader provisions of Article III:4 state that imported products shall be given "treatment no less favourable than that accorded to like products of national origin in respect of all laws, regulations, and requirements affecting their internal sale." This provision has been interpreted as prohibiting discrimination against imports resulting from a wide range of non-tariff barriers to trade, including discriminatory customs procedures, government procurement policies, and product standards. In the following case, *WTO Report on Japan—Taxes on Alcoholic Beverages (1996)*, the WTO Appellate Body undertook a thorough analysis of the *Japan Liquor Tax Law* and found that the Japanese tax violated GATT Article III. As you read, look not only for its interpretation of national treatment, but also look at the Appellate Body's reflections on GATT as international law.

GATT and the Elimination of Quotas

GATT permits the use of tariffs as the acceptable method of regulating imports, but not quotas or other quantitative restrictions. Since 1947, the agreement has called for countries to give up using quotas. Of course, many countries still utilize them because they are a sure and certain way of keeping

Japan—Taxes on Alcoholic Beverages

WT/DS11/AB/R; October 4, 1996

Report of the Appellate Body of the World Trade Organization

BACKGROUND AND FACTS

The *Japan Liquor Tax Law,* or *Shuzeiho,* taxes liquors sold in Japan based on the type of beverage. There are ten categories of beverage (the categories are *sake, sake* compound, *shochu, mirin,* beer, wine, whiskey/brandy, spirits, liqueurs, and miscellaneous. *Shochu* is distilled from potatoes, buckwheat, or other grains. *Shochu* and vodka share many characteristics. However, vodka and other imported liquors fall in categories with a tax rate that is seven or eight times higher than the category for *shochu.* Foreign spirits account for only 8 percent of the Japanese market, whereas they account for almost 50 percent of the market in other industrialized countries. The United States, the European Union, and Canada called for consultations before the WTO. The panel held that the Japanese tax law violated GATT, and Japan appealed to the Appellate Body.

REPORT OF THE APPELLATE BODY

The WTO Agreement is a treaty—the international equivalent of a contract. It is self-evident that in an exercise of their sovereignty, and in pursuit of their own respective national interests, the Members of the WTO have made a bargain. In exchange for the benefits they expect to derive as Members of the WTO, they have agreed to exercise their sovereignty according to the commitments they have made in the WTO Agreement. One of those commitments is Article III of the GATT 1994, which is entitled *National Treatment on Internal Taxation and Regulation.*

The broad and fundamental purpose of Article III is to avoid protectionism in the application of internal tax and regulatory measures. More specifically, the purpose of Article III is to ensure that internal measures not be applied to imported or domestic products so as to afford protection to domestic production. Toward this end, Article III obliges Members of the WTO to provide equality of competitive conditions for imported products in relation to domestic products. "[T]he intention of the drafters of the Agreement was clearly to treat the imported products in the same way as the like domestic products once they had been cleared through customs. Otherwise indirect protection could be given. Moreover, it is irrelevant that "the trade effects" of the tax differential between imported and domestic products, as reflected in the volumes of imports, are insignificant or even non-existent; Article III protects expectations not of any particular trade volume but rather of the equal competitive relationship between imported and domestic products. Members of the WTO are free to pursue their own domestic goals through internal taxation or regulation so long as they do not do so in a way that violates Article III or any of the other commitments they have made in the WTO Agreement....

[I]f imported products are taxed in excess of like domestic products, then that tax measure is inconsistent with Article III.... [We must determine first] whether the taxed imported and domestic products are "like" and, second, whether the taxes applied to the imported products are "in excess of" those applied to the like domestic products. If the imported and domestic products are "like products," and if the taxes applied to the imported products are "in excess of" those applied to the like domestic products, then the measure is inconsistent with Article III:2.

We agree with the Panel also that the definition of "like products" in Article III:2 should be construed narrowly. How narrowly is a matter that should be determined separately for each tax measure in each case. [A 1970 GATT Report] set out the basic approach for interpreting "like or similar products":

> [T]he interpretation of the term should be examined on a case by case basis. This would allow a fair assessment in each case of the different elements that constitute a "similar" product. Some criteria were suggested for determining, on a case-by-case basis, whether a product is "similar": the product's end-users in a given market; consumers' tastes and habits, which change from country to country; the product's properties, nature and quality.

The concept of "likeness" is a relative one that evokes the image of an accordion. The accordion of "likeness" stretches and squeezes in different places as different provisions of the WTO Agreement are applied. [The definition of "likeness" must be narrowly interpreted.] The Panel determined in this case that *shochu* and vodka are "like products."

continued

continued

A uniform tariff classification of products can be relevant in determining what are "like products." Tariff classification has been used as a criterion for determining "like products" in several previous adopted panel reports.... There are risks in using tariff bindings that are too broad as a measure of product "likeness." ... It is true that there are numerous tariff bindings which are in fact extremely precise with regard to product description and which, therefore, can provide significant guidance as to the identification of "like products." Clearly enough, these determinations need to be made on a case-by-case basis. However, tariff bindings that include a wide range of products are not a reliable criterion for determining or confirming product "likeness" under Article III:2.

The only remaining issue under the first sentence of Article III:2 is whether the taxes on imported products are "in excess of" those on like domestic products. If so, then the Member that has imposed the tax is not in compliance with Article III. Even the smallest amount of "excess" is too much. The prohibition of discriminatory taxes in Article III is not conditional on a "trade effects test" nor is it qualified by a *de minimis* standard.

If imported and domestic products are not "like products" ... those same products may well be among the broader category of "directly competitive or substitutable products" that fall within the domain of the second sentence of Article III:2. How much broader that category of "directly competitive or substitutable products" may be in any given case is a matter for the Panel to determine based on all the relevant facts in that case. In this case, the Panel emphasized the need to look not only at such matters as physical characteristics, common end-uses, and tariff classifications, but also at the "market place." This seems appropriate. The GATT 1994 is a commercial agreement, and the WTO is concerned, after all, with markets. It does not seem inappropriate to look at competition in the relevant markets as one among a number of means of identifying the broader category of products that might be described as "directly competitive or substitutable." Nor does it seem inappropriate to examine elasticity of substitution as one means of examining those relevant markets. In the Panel's view, the decisive criterion in order to determine whether two products are directly competitive or substitutable is whether they have common end-uses, *inter alia,* as shown by elasticity of substitution. We agree.

Our interpretation of Article III is faithful to the "customary rules of interpretation of public international law." WTO rules are reliable, comprehensible and enforceable. WTO rules are not so rigid or so inflexible as not to leave room for reasoned judgements in confronting the endless and ever changing ebb and flow of real facts in real cases in the real world. They will serve the multilateral trading system best if they are interpreted with that in mind. In that way, we will achieve the "security and predictability" sought for the multilateral trading system by the Members of the WTO through the establishment of the dispute settlement system.

Decision. The *Japan Liquor Tax Law* was found to violate the national treatment provisions of GATT Article III. *Shochu* is a "like product" and is "directly competitive and substitutable" with other imported spirits. The imported spirits were taxed higher than the *shochu.* The decision of the panel was upheld and Japan was requested to bring its tax law into compliance with GATT.

Comment. In 1997, the United States was forced to seek binding arbitration when it became apparent that Japan did not intend to bring its liquor tax into WTO compliance within a "reasonable period" as required by WTO rules. The arbitration ruling supported the U.S. position. Japan agreed to revise its tariff system in stages and to eliminate tariffs on all brown spirits (including whiskey and brandy) and on vodka, rum, liqueurs, and gin by April 1, 2002. The U.S. distilled spirits industry reported that, as expected, the change in taxation has increased exports of U.S. distilled spirits to Japan. The United States continues to "monitor" Japan's compliance.

out foreign-made goods. The GATT prohibition of quotas is found in Article XI:

> No prohibitions or restrictions other than duties, taxes, or other charges, whether made effective through quotas, import or export licenses, or other measures, shall be instituted ... on the importation of any product ... or on the exportation or sale for export of any product.

The use of quotas, even where they are permitted by GATT, is subject to the principle of nondiscrimination. GATT Article XIII states that an importing nation may not impose any quantitative restriction on a product unless it imposes the same restriction on all like or similar products coming from all other WTO member nations.

Despite the prohibition on the use of quotas, countries still do use them for many economic and political reasons. Quotas have been used to protect essential industries from foreign competition and to implement national economic policies. They are used by virtually all countries, including (to a lesser extent) the United States. GATT permits the use of quotas to relieve food shortages and to restrict the import of agricultural and fishery products that are subject to governmental price support mechanisms. Quotas are widely used to regulate world trade in textiles and apparel. Quotas are also used as a temporary measure by importing countries facing severe balance-of-payments deficits to preserve needed foreign exchange.

Quantitative Restrictions: The Balance-of-Payments Exception and Developing Countries

From 1947 to this day, the GATT agreements have provided for the special needs of developing countries. One burden that developing countries face is the need for readily acceptable international currency for use in trading in world markets. Historically, many developing countries were agrarian economies, some with only a few "cash crops" that could be sold for export. Others were able to develop basic industries in steel or textiles that provided export revenues. Often this was their only source of scarce foreign exchange, which was needed to purchase essential foreign goods such as medicine, fertilizer, or farm equipment or to repay international debts. After all, dollars, pounds, or yen could be used for trade anywhere on the globe, but usually their local currency could not.

When a nation's payments of foreign exchange exceed receipts, a *balance-of-payments* deficit can arise. Both developed and developing countries can face these crises. However, the problem is usually exacerbated in developing countries because their international transactions are usually done with one of the major currencies, not their own. The fastest way to halt the outflow of foreign exchange by local companies is to place quantitative restrictions on imports of goods and service through quotas or licensing schemes. (Tariffs would take much longer to have the same effect.)

Despite GATT's prohibition of quotas, any nation (including developed nations) may resort to quantitative restrictions in a balance-of-payments crisis. Article XII applies to a developed country "with very low monetary reserves" and allows the use of quantitative restrictions in order to "safeguard its external financial position and its balance-of-payments ... necessary to forestall the imminent threat of, or to stop, a serious decline in its monetary reserves." Article XVIII applies to a developing country that "can only support low standards of living and is in the early stages of development." For a developing country, the rule is more liberal, allowing the use of quantitative restrictions "in order to safeguard its external financial position and to ensure a level of [foreign exchange] reserves adequate for the implementation of its program of economic development." In both cases, the restrictions must be temporary and phase out as economic conditions improve and they are no longer required.

GATT 1994 instituted a new requirement that a WTO member must use the least restrictive means possible for correcting a balance-of-payments emergency, preferably a price-based measure, such as a surcharge or tariff increase, rather than a pure quantitative limit on imports. Restrictions should not be targeted at individual products, but should affect the "general level" of all imports to the country. The restrictions must be transparent and the government must publicly announce its timetable for removing them. Justification for the measure must be given to the WTO *Balance-of-Payments Committee,* and the action is subject to WTO surveillance and periodic review. Exporters who do business in developing countries should pay particular attention to this issue. In the following *WTO Panel Report on India—Quantitative Restrictions on Imports of Agricultural, Textile, & Industrial Products,* the United States sought to have India remove a complex scheme of import restrictions that had existed for almost 50 years.

India—Quantitative Restrictions on Imports of Agricultural, Textile, & Industrial Products
WT/DS90/R (April 6, 1999)
Report of the Panel of the World Trade Organization

BACKGROUND AND FACTS

India is a rapidly developing country of over 1 billion people, one-third of which are under the age of 15. Over 80 percent are of the Hindu religion. Although its per capita GDP is only about $2,500, with almost 25 percent of the population living below the poverty line, during the late 1990s its economy grew at an annual rate of about 6 percent. While its economy is largely agriculture based, it is also strong in the areas of textiles, chemicals, food processing, steel, industrial goods, financial services, technology, and computer software. It has a rapidly growing consumer sector. For the past 50 years, India has placed complex restrictions on the import of agricultural, industrial, and consumer goods from other countries. Goods placed on the "negative list" could only be imported by special license, which was generally only granted to the "actual user," rather than to firms in the normal chain of distribution. Many goods could only be imported by state agencies. The restrictions were, in many cases, applied arbitrarily and in the discretion of Indian government officials on a case-by-case basis. As a result, it was often impossible to know at any given time what goods might be allowed into the country. In 1997, the United States filed a dispute with the WTO against India requesting that restrictions on 2,714 products be removed. India claimed that without restrictions its foreign exchange would leave the country, upsetting its balance of payments and inhibiting its economic development.

REPORT OF THE PANEL

The United States contended that ... persons wishing to import an item on the Negative List had to apply for a license and explain their "justification for import": the authorities provided no explanation of the criteria for judging applications, and no advance notice of the volume or value of imports to be allowed. In fact, licenses were routinely refused on the basis that the import would compete with a domestic producer. The leading item on the Negative List was consumer goods (including many food items), and for many consumer goods inclusion on the Negative List had amounted to an import ban or close to it.

The United States considered that the restrictiveness of India's licensing of consumer goods imports was demonstrated by the trade statistics ... *zero imports for 1995/96,* including meat; fish; cereals; malt and starches; preparations of meat or fish; cocoa, chocolate and cocoa preparations; nuts, canned and pickled vegetables and fruits, and fruit juices; wine, beer, spirits and vinegar; leather articles; matting and baskets; carpets; knitted fabrics; clothing; headgear; umbrellas; and furniture. [Imports of hundreds of other products were allowed in only minute quantities for a population of 1 billion.] Thus, in many cases import licensing amounts to an import ban, or close to it.

The United States noted that ... the "Actual User condition" ruled out any imports by wholesalers or other intermediaries, and itself was a further quantitative restriction on imports.

* * *

Thus, according to the United States, the generally applicable import licensing process was a complete black box for the importer and for the foreign exporter. No information was provided on the Government's sectoral priorities with respect to products or on what its views of "merit" might be. All that the United States knew was that the Indian licensing authority generally refused to grant import licences for "restricted" items when it was considered prejudicial to the state's interest to do so.

The United States added that the broad definition of "consumer goods," and the fact that some goods were *only* restricted if they were consumer goods, created considerable confusion, commercial uncertainty and distortion of trade. * * * The 1996 study on *Liberalisation of Indian Imports of Consumer Durables* by the Export–Import Bank of India had noted that the only two commonly-used consumer durable goods that were freely importable were cameras and nail cutters.

* * *

India said that it needed to use discretionary licensing on a case-by-case basis for the following reasons. India's economy had been almost totally closed to imports barely 15 years ago. Because of the size and structure of the economy, it was impossible for India to estimate precisely the level of demand for imports, the import elasticity of demand for a huge number of products, as well as the elasticity of

continued

continued

substitution of domestic products by consumers, and the effective rate of protection for all these products. Accordingly, India considered recourse to discretionary licensing to be unavoidable. Further, India was progressively phasing out its import restrictions. As part of its autonomously initiated programme of economic liberalization, India had already reduced the number of items on which there were import restrictions to just 2,296 as of 1998, from about 11,000 HS-lines in 1991.

* * *

The United States stated that India's quantitative restrictions and licensing regimes had damaged and continued to damage U.S. trade interests.... In 1996, the United States exported $1.3 billion to India in goods subject to quantitative restrictions. However, while the ASEAN area had a population half the size of India's, U.S. exports to ASEAN were eight times the value of U.S. exports to India. As the panel on *"Japanese Measures on Imports of Leather"* noted, "the fact that the United States was able to export large quantities of leather to other markets [than Japan] ... tended to confirm the assumption that the existence of the restrictions [on leather imports] had adversely affected [the] United States' exports."

The nature and operation of India's import licensing regimes also damaged and continued to damage U.S. trade interests. The uncertainty and limitations imposed by India's licensing regime deterred or prevented exporters from undertaking the investments in planning, promotion and market development necessary to develop and expand markets in India for their products. No exporter would put resources into developing a product's market in India without some assurance that it would be able to export some minimum amount per year, and the Indian system provided no such assurance—only a guarantee of continuing uncertainty—if the product in question was on the Negative List of Imports.

* * *

In light of the foregoing, we note that it is agreed that India's licensing system for goods in the Negative List of Imports is a discretionary import licensing system, in that licences are not granted in all cases, but rather on unspecified "merits." We note also that India concedes this measure is an import restriction under Article XI:1.

* * *

Having determined that the measures at issue are quantitative restrictions within the meaning of Article XI:1 and therefore prohibited, we must examine ... India's defence under the balance-of-payments provisions of GATT 1994.

* * *

In this connection, we recall that the IMF reported that India's reserves as of 21 November 1997 were $25.1 billion and that an adequate level of reserves at that date would have been $16 billion. While the Reserve Bank of India did not specify a precise level of what would constitute adequacy, it concluded only three months earlier in August 1997 that India's reserves were "well above the thumb rule of reserve adequacy" and although the Bank did not accept that thumb rule as the only measure of adequacy, it also found that "[b]y any criteria, the level of foreign exchange reserves appears comfortable." It also stated that "the reserves would be adequate to withstand both cyclical and unanticipated shocks."

* * *

For the reasons outlined ... we find that ... India's monetary reserves of $25.1 billion were not inadequate as that term is used in Article XVIII:9(b) and that India was therefore not entitled to implement balance-of-payments measures to achieve a reasonable rate of growth in its reserves.

* * *

The institution and maintenance of balance-of-payments measures is only justified at the level necessary to address the concern, and cannot be more encompassing. Paragraph 11, in this context, confirms this requirement that the measures be limited to what is necessary and addresses more specifically the conditions of evolution of the measures as balance-of-payments conditions improve: at any given time, the restrictions should not exceed those necessary. This implies that as conditions improve, measures must be relaxed in proportion to the improvements. The logical conclusion of the process is that the measures will be eliminated when conditions no longer justify them.

* * *

In conclusion ... we have found that India's balance-of-payments situation was not such as to allow the maintenance of measures for balance-of-payments purposes under the terms of Article XVIII:9, that India was not justified in maintaining its existing measures under the terms of Article XVIII:11, and that it does not have a right to maintain or phase-out these measures on the basis of other provisions of

continued

continued

Article XVIII:B which it invoked in its defence. We therefore conclude that India's measures are not justified under the terms of Article XVIII:B.

* * *

This panel suggests that a reasonable period of time be granted to India in order to remove the import restrictions which are not justified under Article XVIII:B. Normally, the reasonable period of time to implement a panel recommendation, when determined through arbitration, should not exceed fifteen months from the date of adoption of a panel or Appellate Body report. However, this 15-month period is "a 'guideline for the arbitrator,' not a rule," and ... "that time may be shorter or longer, depending upon the particular circumstances."

* * *

Decision. India's quantitative restrictions and the licensing scheme at issue were no longer justified to preserve its balance of payments and needed to be quickly phased out.

Comment. The panel's decision was upheld by the WTO Appellate Body in its report of August 1999 and adopted by the Dispute Settlement Body in September of that year.

Conclusion

The *General Agreement on Tariffs and Trade* has provided a framework for the international trading system since the close of World War II. It established the principles of international trade law upon which national trade laws are based. The GATT agreement and its principles of trade liberalization prevented reactionary forces from drawing the world back into the isolationism and protectionism of the 1930s. Multilateral trade negotiations have resulted in tariff concessions and a worldwide lowering of duties. Today, tariffs are at reasonable levels compared to the 1930s, and rates no longer act as a barrier to world trade.

Although non-tariff barriers are still an obstacle to free trade, they have been slowly reduced by a number of important WTO agreements and dispute resolutions. Some of the most difficult issues facing global trading nations today are the subsidization of agricultural trade, especially cotton; reducing barriers to trade in services; and finding ways to use trade to promote the economies of the poorest developing countries. Readers are encouraged to follow the work of the WTO and the meetings of the WTO Ministerial Conference as they address these issues.

It seems that all countries, perhaps the United States more than others, use their trade policy as a tool of foreign policy. The United States has linked its trade policies with China and Russia to its foreign policy goals. For example, the United States has used the granting of MFN/NTR tariff rates on imports from these countries as an enticement to encourage these and other countries to move toward democracy, respect for human rights, freedom of emigration, and the development of free-market economies. China received normal trade status with the United States in 2001. As of mid-2007, Russia's trade status was still in question.

Cuba is one of the last remaining countries to not have normal trading relations with the United States. In the next few years, the world will witness the fiftieth anniversary of Cuba's communist revolution. It will be interesting to see whether there will be great political changes in the country or a continuation of past policies; whether the country will move toward democracy; and whether there will be changes in U.S. foreign policy and trade policy toward its island neighbor.

Chapter Summary

1. Nations regulate trade for several important reasons, including collection of revenue, regulation of import competition, retaliation against foreign trade barriers, implementation of foreign policy or national economic policy, national defense, protection of natural resources and the environment, protection of public health and safety, and protection of cultural values or artifacts.

2. The terms *tariff* and *import duty* are used interchangeably. Tariffs are a tax levied on goods by the country of importation. A non-tariff barrier is broadly defined as any impediment to trade other than a tariff. The most severe form of import restriction is the embargo. It is usually used as a drastic measure for reasons of foreign policy or national security.
3. Import licensing schemes are a form of non-tariff barrier to trade that are often hidden in administrative regulations and bureaucratic red tape. Exporters faced with foreign licensing schemes often have to retain local agents and attorneys to advise them on import measures in the foreign market. Import regulations that are not made readily available to foreign exporters are said to lack *transparency*.
4. The *General Agreement on Tariffs and Trade*, or GATT, includes the original 1947 agreement, the 1994 agreement that founded the World Trade Organization, and many side agreements on specific trade issues. The original agreement only covered trade in goods. In 1994 a *General Agreement on Trade in Services* was added.
5. GATT's major principles are a commitment to multilateral trade negotiations, tariff bindings, nondiscrimination, and unconditional MFN trade; national treatment; and the elimination of quotas and other non-tariff barriers.
6. Through multilateral trade negotiations at the WTO, countries agree to reduced tariffs on individual items and become "bound" to those tariff rates. This is found in their "tariff binding," which is kept on record at the WTO. This rate then appears in that country's tariff schedules. The schedules are made available to all exporting and importing countries.
7. WTO dispute settlement procedures provide a legal forum for nations to resolve trade disputes. No single country can veto the decisions of a WTO panel. If a settlement is not reached, the WTO Dispute Settlement Body may authorize one country to impose retaliatory tariffs against another one that has violated a GATT agreement.
8. The principles of most favored nation (MFN) trade mean that a nation must accord products imported from any country with which it has MFN trading status the most favorable treatment or the lowest tariff rates that it gives to similar products imported from other MFN countries. Unconditional MFN treatment means that if a country negotiates a lower tariff rate with one MFN country, that rate is automatically applicable to all MFN countries. The United States applies MFN tariff rates to those countries that qualify for "normal trade relations." The MFN/NTR rate is considered the normal tariff rate for goods coming from most developed countries. Goods imported from developing countries or within free trade areas often qualify for better-than-MFN rates.
9. Under the national treatment provisions of GATT Article III, imported products must not be regulated, taxed, or otherwise treated differently from domestic goods once they enter a nation's stream of commerce.
10. GATT outlaws most quantitative restrictions on imports, such as quotas. Quotas on imported products are permitted only in certain situations, such as when a nation has insufficient foreign exchange to meet its foreign payments obligations.

Questions and Case Problems

1. Visit the Web site of the World Trade Organization (*www.wto.org*). It is a practical, user-friendly guide that offers complete information on the WTO's role and organizational structure as well as access to the GATT legal texts and dispute settlement cases.
   a. As a beginning point, and for an easy-to-understand introduction to the WTO, navigate to the section entitled *Resources* and click *Webcasting.* This page provides access to Webcasts of major world trade events and a series of excellently produced training films. Be sure to watch *Basic Principles of the WTO System* by Pieter Jan Kuijper.
   b. For an interactive training module covering the technical aspects of the WTO, navigate to

Resources and click *WTO Distance Learning*. For an overview, see *Multimedia Presentations*.

c. For links to all GATT/WTO agreements from 1947 to the present, navigate to *Documents* and choose either *Legal Texts* or *Official Documents*, which is a portal to the *Documents Online* database. Accessing WTO materials through the *Legal Texts* page is quick and easy. You can find Web documents either by browsing or searching.

d. For access to WTO trade issues, including trade in goods, services, intellectual property, electronic commerce, investment, government procurement, trade and the environment, and dispute settlement, navigate to *Trade Topics* and choose a subject.

e. The highest decision-making body of the WTO is the Ministerial Conference, which brings together all members of the WTO for meetings every two years. The Ministerial Conference can make decisions on all matters under any of the multilateral trade agreements. Ministerial Conferences have been held in Hong Kong (2005), Cancún (2003), Doha (2001), Seattle (1999), Geneva (1998), and Singapore (1996). From the *Trade Topics* menu, navigate to *Ministerial Conferences*. What is on the current Ministerial agenda?

f. For access to the reports of WTO dispute settlement panels and the Appellate Body, from the home page navigate to *Trade Topics* > *Dispute Settlement* > *The Disputes*. From here you may search either chronologically, by country, or by subject. Notice that disputes are cited as *DS* followed by a number. The numbers are sequential; for example, DS1 designates the first dispute filed in 1995. Citations for panel reports will generally appear as WT/DS#/R, and reports of the Appellate Body will appear as WT/DS#/AB/R.

2. One of the most controversial areas for the WTO and its member governments has been the relationship between trade and the environment. What are the overlapping issues? What impact does trade, or trade negotiations, have on environmental issues? How do these issues affect the developing countries, and what is their position? Explain the relationship between protection of the environment and economic development.

   a. Consider the following major trade-related environmental disputes at the WTO:
      - *U.S.—Standards for Reformulated and Conventional Gasoline* (provisions of the U.S. *Clean Air Act*, DS52)
      - *U.S.—Import Prohibition of Certain Shrimp and Shrimp Products* (selling of shrimp caught in nets without turtle extractors, DS58)
      - *European Communities—Measures Affecting Asbestos and Asbestos-Containing Products* (DS135)
      - *European Communities—Measures Concerning Meat and Meat Products* (containing growth hormones, DS26, DS48, DS39)
      - *European Communities—Measures Affecting the Approval and Marketing of Biotech Products* (genetically engineered foods, DS291)

      Using one of these cases, write a case study on the relationship between trade and environmental issues. Be sure to explore both sides of the debate.

   b. For alternative views on trade and the environment, see the Web sites of Public Citizen and the Sierra Club and a highly educational site offered by the Center for Strategic and International Studies (Washington, D.C.) aptly called Globalization101.org. To learn more about the important Shrimp/Turtle case at the WTO, see the Web site of the National Wildlife Federation.

3. Every year the U.S. Trade Representative issues a report on foreign government trade barriers to U.S. goods and services. Locate these reports and describe the nature of these trade barriers. Which countries are the greatest offenders? What industries are most affected?

4. What is the current trading status of Russia with the United States? Has Russia received permanent NTR status? What are the political issues affecting the granting of permanent NTR status? Which countries of the world do not have normal trade relations with the United States?

5. In 1990, a Korean law established two distinct retail distribution systems for beef: one system for the retail sale of domestic beef and another system for the retail sale of imported beef. A small retailer (not a supermarket or a department store) designated as a "Specialized Imported Beef Store" may sell any beef except domestic beef. Any other small retailer may sell any beef except imported beef. A large retailer (a supermarket or department store) may sell both imported and domestic beef, as long as imported and domestic beef are sold in separate sales areas. A retailer selling imported beef is required to display a sign reading "Specialized Imported Beef Store." The dual retail system resulted in a reduction of beef imports. By 1998, there were approximately 5,000 imported beef shops as compared with approximately 45,000

shops selling domestic beef. Korea claims that stores may choose to sell either domestic or imported beef and that they have total freedom to switch from one to another. Moreover, Korea argues that the dual system is necessary to protect consumers from deception by allowing them to clearly distinguish the origin of the beef purchased. Is the Korean regulation a valid consumer protection law? Do you think this system is necessary to protect consumers from fraudulent misrepresentation of the country of origin of the beef? Does it matter that scientific methods are available to determine the country of origin of beef? How do you think the dual system might affect the prices of imported beef versus domestic beef? Assuming that countries have the right to protect consumers from deception, what other methods might be available to accomplish this goal? *WTO Report on Korea—Measures Affecting Imports of Fresh, Chilled and Frozen Beef,* World Trade Organization Report of the Appellate Body, WT/DS161/AB/R, WT/DS169/AB/R (11 December 2000).

6. One of the central obligations of WTO membership is a limit on tariffs on particular goods according to a nation's tariff commitments. If a member does not abide by its agreement, can another WTO member unilaterally raise its agreed-upon tariff? Explain.
7. The U.S. auto industry has had its problems in the past from foreign competition. If the auto industry lobbied the president and Congress for implementation of a quota on the total number of imported automobiles and trucks, would such a quota be in violation of GATT 1994? Under what circumstances may a country impose a quota?
8. The WTO comprises many nations from all regions of the world. As such, the GATT/WTO system takes a global view of trade liberalization based on nondiscrimination, unconditional MFN, national treatment, tariffication, and multilateral trade negotiations. The GATT agreements recognize that nations may form free trade areas and customs unions. Yet a free trade area only has free trade between the countries that belong to it. How does the concept of a free trade area, such as the *North American Free Trade Agreement* (NAFTA), fit into the GATT/WTO global framework? Do free trade areas violate the principles of nondiscrimination and MFN trade? Evaluate these arguments.

Managerial Implications

Your firm designs, manufactures, and markets children's toys for sale in the United States. Almost 90 percent of your production is done in the People's Republic of China. During the 1990s, U.S. relations with China improved. Even though there were many disagreements between the two countries, the United States granted normal trade status to China and continued to support China's application for membership in the WTO. Your firm invested heavily in China during that time. You have developed close ties to Chinese suppliers and have come to depend greatly on inexpensive Chinese labor and the lower costs of doing business there.

You are now concerned about increasing political tension between China and the United States over a variety of issues. The U.S. president has criticized the Chinese government, arguing that it has supported communist North Korea and sold missile technology to Middle Eastern countries. Most worrisome is China's claim to Taiwan under its "One China" reunification policy. China continues to aim more missiles at Taiwan, accusing the United States of fostering "independence" there. The United States indicates that it may sell the newest navy destroyers and AEGIS radar systems to Taiwan. When China warns that sales of military equipment to Taiwan could lead to "serious danger," the president publicly reaffirms the importance of trade with China.

1. Describe the impact that a trade dispute would have on your firm.
2. Describe the impact on your firm if China were to lose its MFN trading status.
3. What strategic actions might you consider to reduce your firm's exposure to political risk?
4. What are the current areas of agreement or disagreement between the United States and China, and how do you think they will affect future trade relations between the two countries?
5. In the wake of a communist victory in the late 1940s, the nationalist Chinese fled mainland China for the security of the island of Formosa. Today the island is known as Taiwan and has its own independent, multiparty government and popularly elected president. It is industrialized and is considered one of the Asian economic "Tigers." One of the pillars of American foreign policy during the Cold War was that the island of Taiwan should remain independent. But political and economic realities have caused the United States to remain pragmatic in its relationships with both the government

of the People's Republic of China and Taiwan over the last 30 years. Taiwan joined the WTO under the name "Chinese Taipei," encompassing the "separate customs territory of Taiwan, Penghu, Kinmen, and Matsu." Examine the history of Taiwan and its relationship to China. What do you think of U.S. policies toward the region? While both mainland China and Taiwan are "Chinese," doing business in Taiwan differs greatly from doing business in China. Describe that difference. How do business opportunities differ on the mainland versus the island? What do you think of the prospects for reunification, and what would be the impact on firms operating there?

Ethical Considerations

How do you reconcile free trade with the protection of cultural diversity? Free trade in goods and services means that a country will necessarily open itself to foreign influences. Just look at the impact of American fast-food restaurants, hotels, and large retail outlets on the American landscape and particularly on small-town America. Now imagine the influence of American companies and American culture in foreign countries. Consider the long-term impact of American music and film on the indigenous culture of a foreign country. Despite these impacts, free trade agreements mandate the opening of local markets to foreign goods, services, and advertising, including music and film. The French, as well as French-Canadians, are notorious for trying to manipulate trade rules to preserve their French language and French culture. Examples might include limits on foreign advertising, television programming, or films. Consider the *Convention on the Protection and Promotion of the Diversity of Cultural Expressions*, which has been ratified or approved by 69 nations and entered into force in 2007. The Convention states that

> Nations may adopt measures aimed at protecting and promoting the diversity of cultural expressions within its territory. Such measures may include (a) regulatory measures aimed at protecting and promoting diversity of cultural expressions; (b) measures that, in an appropriate manner, provide opportunities for domestic cultural activities, goods and services among all those available within the national territory for the creation, production, dissemination, distribution and enjoyment of such domestic cultural activities, goods and services, including provisions relating to the language used for such activities, goods and services.

In addition, a country may take "all appropriate measures to protect and preserve cultural expressions" that are "at risk of extinction, under serious threat, or otherwise in need of urgent safeguarding."

The United States is not a party to the Convention. In response to the Convention, the U.S. State Department stated, "The United States is a multicultural society that values diversity.... Governments deciding what citizens can read, hear, or see denies individuals the opportunity to make independent choices about what they value."

a. Do you feel that countries should limit the influence of foreign cultures in their communities? How should they do that? Do you think that a country should restrict the foreign content of advertising, television, music, or film?
b. Do you think that this Convention might be used as a means of restricting trade in the guise of protecting cultural expressions and national identity?
c. Reconcile the terms of this convention with principles of free trade. What will be the effect on trade in audiovisual products? How would American industry respond?

For Internet Activities, Visit academic.cengage.com/blaw/schaffer.

CHAPTER 10
Laws Governing Access to Foreign Markets

The process of negotiating open access to foreign markets is the subject of this chapter. Left to their own devices, the natural inclination of most nations is to protect their domestic industrial and agricultural base from foreign competition. National governments are easily tempted by the persuasive voices of trade groups representing powerful industries, political lobbyists, voters, and local politicians, and domestic producers calling for protection from low-cost foreign competitors. That market distortions and inefficiencies are caused by protectionism is one of the most rudimentary principles of modern economics. Most nations today recognize the economic benefits of opening their markets to foreign competition. At the same time, nations realize that many of their domestic firms are also competing for business in foreign markets and facing barriers to market access there. As more and more of their industries become dependent on export sales, they also become vulnerable to protectionist tactics. These nations realize protectionism is a double-edged sword. If they expect their firms to have open access to foreign markets, they must be willing to grant the same privileges to foreign firms in their own markets. Agreeing to concessions that open a market to foreign competition can be a painfully slow process. It can be economically painful, because local firms are finding that they now must either reinvent themselves—retraining employees, retooling their factories, and employing new technologies to become more competitive—or go out of business. And it can be politically painful, because politicians at all levels of government find themselves pressured by local interests to protect the status quo.

This chapter examines specific GATT/WTO agreements that open markets for goods and services in the following areas: (1) technical barriers to trade, including product standards; (2) import licensing procedures; (3) government procurement of goods and services; (4) trade in services, including consulting, engineering, banking and financial services, insurance, telecommunications, and the professions; (5) trade in agricultural products; (6) trade in textiles and apparel; (7) trade-related investment measures; and (8) trade-related aspects of intellectual property rights. The chapter concludes with a look at the U.S. response to foreign trade barriers that deny access to U.S. products and services or that treat U.S. firms unfairly. This includes U.S. laws that permit retaliation against illegal foreign barriers to fair trade.

The General Principle of Least Restrictive Trade

We begin with one of the broadest and most important legal concepts in the body of international trade law: the *principle of least restrictive trade*. The principle states that WTO member countries, in setting otherwise valid restrictions on trade, shall make them no more onerous than necessary to achieve the goals for which they were imposed. For example, if a country requires inspections of foreign fruit arriving from countries affected by a plant disease, the inspection procedures must be no more arduous, rigorous, or expensive than is needed to achieve those ends. They may not be a trade barrier in disguise.

A corollary is that national laws and regulations passed for purely internal purposes, such as the protection of the general health, welfare, and safety, must also pose the fewest barriers to trade as possible. This principle is relevant to all types of regulations: health codes, environmental regulations, worker safety laws, and uniform technical specifications for a wide range of industrial or consumer products. Examples might include laws regulating the sale of alcohol or tobacco or banning the sale of beef containing growth hormones, genetically modified foods, or toxic lead paint. It might include testing requirements for the fire resistance of fabrics or the safety of children's toys or set mandatory standards for the practice of law or medicine. The list is endless; the concept is the same. Countries may protect their citizens to the extent they deem necessary but must choose those methods that do not unduly burden international trade and/or single out foreign goods or service providers for unfair or discriminatory treatment.

The WTO Appellate Body has stated that this is a balancing test: nations must weigh the necessity of protecting the public against restrictions on free trade. The principle of least restrictive trade appears throughout GATT law and applies to most of the discussions in this chapter.

The following case, *Thailand—Restrictions on Importation of Cigarettes (1990),* is an early GATT panel decision that is still cited by the WTO Appellate Body. It considers Thailand's options for reducing tobacco use.

Thailand—Restrictions on Importation of Cigarettes

GATT Basic Instruments and Selected Documents, 37th Supp. 200 (Geneva, 1990)

Report of the Dispute Settlement Panel

BACKGROUND AND FACTS

The Royal Thai government maintains restrictions on imports of cigarettes. The *Tobacco Act of 1966* prohibited the import of all forms of tobacco except by license of the Director-General of the Excise Department. Licenses have only been granted to the government-owned Thai Tobacco Monopoly, which has imported cigarettes only three times since 1966. None had been imported in the 10 years prior to this case. The United States requested the Panel to find that the licensing of imported cigarettes by Thailand was inconsistent with GATT Article XI and could not be justified under Article XX(b) since, as applied by Thailand, the licensing requirements were more restrictive than necessary to protect human health. Thailand argued that cigarette imports were prohibited to control smoking and because chemicals and other additives contained in American cigarettes might make them more harmful than Thai cigarettes.

REPORT OF THE PANEL ADOPTED ON 7 NOVEMBER 1990

The Panel, noting that Thailand had not granted licences for the importation of cigarettes during the past 10 years, found that Thailand had acted inconsistently with Article XI:1, the relevant part of which reads: "No prohibitions or restrictions ... made effective through ... import licenses ... shall be instituted or maintained by any [country] on the importation of any product of the territory of any other [country]." ...

The Panel proceeded to examine whether Thai import measures affecting cigarettes, while contrary to Article XI:1, were justified by Article XX(b), which states in part:

> [N]othing in this Agreement shall be construed to prevent the adoption or enforcement by any [country] of measures: ...
>
> (b) necessary to protect human, animal or plant life or health.

The Panel then defined the issues which arose under this provision.... [The] Panel accepted that smoking constituted a serious risk to human health and that consequently measures designed to reduce the consumption of cigarettes fell within the scope of Article XX(b). The Panel noted that this provision clearly allowed [countries] to give priority to human health over trade liberalization; however, for a measure to be covered by Article XX(b) it had to be "necessary." ...

continued

continued

The Panel concluded from the above that the import restrictions imposed by Thailand could be considered to be "necessary" in terms of Article XX(b) only if there were no alternative measure consistent with the GATT Agreement, or less inconsistent with it, which Thailand could reasonably be expected to employ to achieve its health policy objectives. The Panel noted that [countries] may, in accordance with Article III:4 of the GATT Agreement, impose laws, regulations and requirements affecting the internal sale, offering for sale, purchase, transportation, distribution or use of imported products provided they do not thereby accord treatment to imported products less favourable than that accorded to "like" products of national origin. The United States argued that Thailand could achieve its public health objectives through internal measures consistent with Article III:4 and that the inconsistency with Article XI:1 could therefore not be considered to be "necessary" within the meaning of Article XX(b). The Panel proceeded to examine this issue in detail. . . .

The Panel then examined whether the Thai concerns about the quality of cigarettes consumed in Thailand could be met with measures consistent, or less inconsistent, with the GATT Agreement. It noted that other countries had introduced strict, non-discriminatory labeling and ingredient disclosure regulations which allowed governments to control, and the public to be informed of, the content of cigarettes. A non-discriminatory regulation implemented on a national treatment basis in accordance with Article III:4 requiring complete disclosure of ingredients, coupled with a ban on unhealthy substances, would be an alternative consistent with the GATT Agreement. The Panel considered that Thailand could reasonably be expected to take such measures to address the quality-related policy objectives it now pursues through an import ban on all cigarettes whatever their ingredients.

The Panel then considered whether Thai concerns about the quantity of cigarettes consumed in Thailand could be met by measures reasonably available to it and consistent, or less inconsistent, with the GATT Agreement. The Panel first examined how Thailand might reduce the demand for cigarettes in a manner consistent with the GATT Agreement. The Panel noted the view expressed by the World Health Organization (WHO) that the demand for cigarettes, in particular the initial demand for cigarettes by the young, was influenced by cigarette advertisements and that bans on advertisement could therefore curb such demand. At the Forty-third World Health Assembly a resolution was approved stating that the WHO is: "Encouraged by ... recent information demonstrating the effectiveness of tobacco control strategies, and in particular ... comprehensive legislative bans and other restrictive measures to effectively control the direct and the indirect advertising, promotion and sponsorship of tobacco."

A ban on the advertisement of cigarettes of both domestic and foreign origin would normally meet the requirements of Article III:4. . . . The Panel noted that Thailand had already implemented some non-discriminatory controls on demand, including information programmes, bans on direct and indirect advertising, warnings on cigarette packs, and bans on smoking in certain public places.

The Panel then examined how Thailand might restrict the supply of cigarettes in a manner consistent with the GATT Agreement. The Panel noted that [countries] may maintain governmental monopolies, such as the Thai Tobacco Monopoly, on the importation and domestic sale of products. The Thai Government may use this monopoly to regulate the overall supply of cigarettes, their prices and their retail availability provided it thereby does not accord imported cigarettes less favourable treatment than domestic cigarettes or act inconsistently with any commitments assumed under its Schedule of Concessions. . . .

For these reasons the Panel could not accept the argument of Thailand that competition between imported and domestic cigarettes would necessarily lead to an increase in the total sales of cigarettes and that Thailand therefore had no option but to prohibit cigarette imports.

In sum, the Panel considered that there were various measures consistent with the GATT Agreement which were reasonably available to Thailand to control the quality and quantity of cigarettes smoked and which, taken together, could achieve the health policy goals that the Thai government pursues by restricting the importation of cigarettes inconsistently with Article XI:1. The Panel found therefore that Thailand's practice of permitting the sale of domestic cigarettes while not permitting the importation of foreign cigarettes was an inconsistency with the GATT not "necessary" within the meaning of Article XX(b).

Decision. The licensing system for cigarettes was contrary to Article XI:1 and is not justified by Article XX(b). The Panel recommended that Thailand bring its laws into conformity with its obligations under the GATT.

continued

continued

Comment. GATT Article XVII permits a country to create state agencies and "marketing boards" that have the authority to import and export goods. The Thai Tobacco Monopoly is an example. State trading enterprises are often used in developing countries and usually have the exclusive right to import or export certain classifications of goods. Products traded by state enterprises might include foodstuffs, medicines, liquor, or, as in this case, tobacco. Article XVII requires that state enterprises not discriminate against the purchase of foreign goods, or treat them differently than domestic goods.

Technical Barriers to Trade

A *technical regulation* is a law or regulation affecting a product's characteristics—such as performance, design, construction, chemical composition, materials, packaging, or labeling—that must be met before a product can be sold in a country. A *product standard,* or *standard,* is a voluntary guideline for product characteristics established by a recognized private or administrative body. Technical regulations are mandatory and imposed by government regulations, whereas standards are usually voluntary and issued by either private industry groups or government agencies. Although a standard may be "voluntary," a product may not be accepted by consumers in the marketplace unless it complies with the standard. Technical regulations and standards that apply to imported foreign products, even if they also apply equally to domestic products, are called *technical barriers to trade.*

The Protection of Public Health, Safety, or Welfare

Almost all products are subject to technical regulations or standards set by either government regulators or private standard-setting groups. They are generally imposed for the protection of public health, safety, or welfare to promote uniform design, engineering, and performance standards or to ensure product quality or purity. Examples include standards for the safe design of consumer goods, for automotive safety, vehicle emissions, or fuel economy, for safe foods and pharmaceuticals, standards of weights and measures, or worker safety standards for machinery and industrial equipment. Other standards protect consumers from fraud or deception (such as labels that disclose the product's content or warn of safe uses); impose environmental criteria on appliances and other products (such as by restricting ozone-damaging refrigerants or eliminating dangerous formaldehyde or heavy metals from bed linens, carpeting, or construction materials); set packaging requirements for products such as plastic bottles that aid in recycling or for energy efficiency; require technical specifications standardizing electrical power and telecommunications, building and construction standards (such as common sizes for lumber and building materials), standards for barcodes and barcode readers, and many others. Imagine multinational companies such as Ford, General Electric, Electrolux, or Bosch-Siemens and the incredibly diverse product standards they must meet in each country in which their products are sold.

Product Testing, Inspections, and Certifications for Compliance with Technical Standards and Regulations. Most countries require some type of testing, inspection, or certification of regulated products. There are several different approaches taken with regard to inspections. In some countries, regulated products must be tested or inspected by an approved laboratory, receive a certification of compliance with technical standards, and then receive prior regulatory approval before sale. In other countries, regulated products must be tested or inspected and certified, but that certification remains on file with the manufacturer or importer, and no regulatory approval is needed prior to import or domestic sale. Different countries have different philosophies and thus take different approaches. For instance, in the United States, the *U.S. Flammable Fabrics Act* places technical restrictions on the sale of all bed mattresses. The law is administered through regulations of the *Consumer Products Safety Commission.* Six prototypes of a given mattress are subjected to a controlled cigarette burn test under laboratory conditions to determine whether they meet federal safety requirements. If the length of the char is longer than allowed or if the mattress ignites, then it does not pass. The manufacturer usually arranges to have the test performed by an independent laboratory. They are required to keep photographs and records of the results at their place of business and to make them available to retailers, customers, or agency regulators when requested. Importers are also subject to these regulations; any of their products entering into the United States must meet these standards. If they cannot produce the certification, their goods will be denied entry or removed from stores. Thus, foreign manufacturers and importers alike must be familiar with the regulations of the countries to which their products will be shipped.

Because they often cause delays in getting goods to market, inspection and testing requirements can prove to be a tremendous barrier to trade. This is especially true if the product has a short shelf life, as with produce or other food products, or a short technological life (semiconductors or computer parts). In 1989, the European Community complained that the United States was delaying the inspection of perishable products by making them wait in turn behind nonperishable goods such as steel products, causing the perishables to spoil in the process. Entire shipments of citrus fruit from Spain had to be dumped, and the importer received no compensation.

In the United States, technical regulations and product standards are set by many federal agencies, including the Department of Agriculture, the Consumer Product Safety Commission, the Food and Drug Administration, the Federal Communications Commission, the Department of Energy, and the Department of Transportation. To illustrate, the U.S. Department of Agriculture is required by law to review meat inspection standards in foreign countries to ensure that imported meat products comply with USDA standards. The Federal Communications Commission promulgates uniform standards for telecommunications equipment that apply to foreign products. The Consumer Product Safety Commission's rules apply to all consumer products, regardless of where they are made. In 2007, it was discovered that Chinese-made toys were found to contain dangerous amounts of lead (a known carcinogen, long banned in the United States and other countries), as well as other chemicals that can cause seizures, coma, and death. (In 1994, Chinese crayons had been removed from sale for the same reasons.) Millions upon millions of these toys were found in many countries around the world. The event caused an outcry of public opinion, a reawakening of consumer safety sentiment, a review of consumer legislation in the United States and elsewhere, and a vast change in concern and oversight by the Chinese government.

WHY STANDARDS AND TECHNICAL REGULATIONS ARE BARRIERS TO TRADE. It is obvious that a regulation or standard that applies only to foreign goods and not to domestic goods discriminates against the foreign goods. However, many technical barriers do not discriminate on their face, only in their application. As a result, discrimination may occur even when imported and domestic products are treated the same. A manufacturer whose product meets local regulations may find that building another product specially to meet foreign regulations is cost prohibitive. For instance, if U.S. wallboard manufacturers produce wallboard in compliance with U.S. regulations that is 1/2" thick and Europe requires wallboard to be 2.0 cm thick, then a U.S. exporter would have to produce specially made wallboard for export to Europe. Certainly, the European nations have the right to determine safety standards for construction, but the regulation does not allow the U.S. firm to take advantage of economies of scale and is, thus, an indirect technical barrier to trade. Environmental regulations, in particular, can vary greatly from country to country.

Another problem is that many technical barriers are not readily available to foreign firms. Either they are not published or they are made known only to domestic firms. Moreover, foreign companies are generally not a part of the standard-setting process. Domestic firms are typically invited to participate in developing and writing regulations or standards; foreign firms are not. Thus, they often experience delays in adapting their products for sale in the

A2 vs standard letter size paper

foreign market, causing them to lose competitive advantage to local firms. The U.S. Department of Commerce maintains a collection of international standards so that U.S. exporters will have access to foreign technical regulations and standards applicable to their industries. Another problem is that some countries require the inspection of the factory where a product is made, including foreign factories, or advance approval of certifying laboratories. This makes it extremely difficult and expensive to import these products.

European Union Standards and Technical Regulations

The problem of technical barriers is critical to firms operating in the EU, where national standards vary tremendously. Consider the impact of these barriers on a firm such as Phillips, a Dutch electronics company, which has had to manufacture twenty-nine different types of electrical outlets. Thus, the standards policy of the EU is designed to balance the health and safety interests of member countries with the need for the free flow of goods. Despite decades of work by the EU Commission to reduce technical barriers to trade, thousands of new national standards have arisen. Even after years of debating detailed standards for thousands of products, companies wishing to sell their products in Europe still face a maze of complex regulations, applicable to a wide range of products from beer to hair dryers, automobiles to plywood. However, EU countries understand that uniform standards are essential to achieving a unified market.

The EU's effort to reduce technical barriers is reflected in many opinions of the European Court of Justice. In one case, arising over the sale of liquor made in France and sold in Germany, the Court ruled that an EU member country could not prohibit the sale of a product produced in another EU member country when that product had already met the technical specifications of the producing country.

In decisions handed down in the 1980s, the Court rejected attempts by two EU countries to protect centuries-old industries. Disregarding consumer protection arguments, the Court of Justice struck down Germany's beer purity law, which had kept out foreign beers containing preservatives and required that beer only be made from wheat, barley, hops, and yeast (beer made in other European countries often contains rice and other grains). The Court also struck down Italy's pasta content regulations. In one long-standing dispute with the United States, the EU prohibited the import of beef containing growth hormones. Because these hormones are widely used in the United States, U.S. beef was kept out of European markets.

Most standard setting in the EU takes place through the *European Committee for Standardization,* which sets voluntary standards for nonelectrical products; the *European Committee for Electrotechnical Standardization;* and the *European Telecommunications Standards Institute.* These intergovernmental agencies work with manufacturers, including some European subsidiaries of U.S. firms, and scientists to develop workable product standards. When adopted by directive of the European Council, the standards become legally binding for products sold in Europe (see Exhibit 10.1).

The EU has attempted to increase its standardization through the *CE Mark.* (CE means *Conformité Européene.*) The CE Mark is an internationally recognized symbol for quality and product safety for many different types of products, such as children's toys, gas appliances, machinery, and medical and electrical equipment. European manufacturers seeking the mark are inspected and audited by an EU-authorized body. Their products must be tested by an independent laboratory. Once the mark is received, a European manufacturer may sell its products throughout the EU without undergoing inspections in each individual country. Manufacturers outside the EU may submit their products to an independent laboratory for testing before attaching the CE Mark. The U.S. government estimates that soon half of the U.S. products shipped to Europe will require CE Mark compliance.

Japanese Standards and Technical Regulations

Japan and the United States have had a long history of disputes over Japanese technical barriers to trade. U.S. and other non-Japanese firms have lodged many complaints against Japan's technical barriers, most of which involve unreasonable and

EXHIBIT 10.1

EU Council Directive Concerning the Safety of Toys*

Article 1.1. This Directive shall apply to toys. A "toy" shall mean any product or material designed or clearly intended for use in play by children of less than 14 years of age.

2. Taking account of the period of foreseeable and normal use, a toy must meet the safety and health conditions laid down in this Directive.

Article 5.1. Member states shall presume compliance with the essential requirements referred to in Article 3 in respect of toys bearing the EC mark provided for in Article 11, hereinafter referred to as "EC mark," denoting conformity with the relevant national standards which transpose the harmonized standards the reference numbers of which have been published in the Official Journal of the European Communities.

Article 7.1. Where toys bearing the EC mark are likely to jeopardize the safety and/or health of consumers, it shall withdraw the products from the market.

Article 8.1. Before being placed on the market, toys must have affixed to them the EC mark by which the manufacturer or his authorized representative established within the Community confirms that the toys comply with those standards; . . .

3. The approved [inspection firm] shall carry out the EC type-examination in the manner described below:
-it shall check that the toy would not jeopardize safety and/or health, as provided for in Article 2.
-it shall carry out the appropriate examinations and tests—using as far as possible the harmonized standards referred to in Article 5 (1).

Article 11.1. The EC mark shall as a rule be affixed either to the toy or on the packaging in a visible, easily legible and indelible form.

2. The EC mark shall consist of the symbol "CE."

3. The affixing to toys of marks or inscriptions that are likely to be confused with the EC mark shall be prohibited.

Article 12.1. Member States shall take the necessary measures to ensure that sample checks are carried out on toys which are on their market and may select a sample and take it away for examination and testing.

ANNEX II ESSENTIAL SAFETY REQUIREMENTS FOR TOYS

II. PARTICULAR RISKS

1. Physical and mechanical properties:

(a) Toys must have the mechanical strength to withstand the stresses during use without breaking at the risk of causing physical injury.

(b) Edges, protrusions, cords, cables, and fastenings on toys must be so designed and constructed that the risks of physical injury from contact with them are reduced as far as possible.

. . .

(d) Toys, and their component parts, and any detachable parts of toys which are clearly intended for use by children under thirty-six months must be of such dimensions as to prevent their being swallowed or inhaled.

(e) Toys, and their parts and the packaging in which they are contained for retail sale must not present a risk of strangulation or suffocation.

. . .

(h) Toys conferring mobility on their users must, as far as possible, incorporate a braking system which is suited to the type of toy and is commensurate with the kinetic energy developed by it.

2. Flammability: (a) Toys must not constitute a dangerous flammable element in the child's environment. They must therefore be composed of materials which . . . irrespective of the toy's chemical composition, are treated so as to delay the combustion process.

ANNEX IV WARNINGS AND INDICATIONS OF PRECAUTIONS TO BE TAKEN WHEN USING TOYS

1. Toys which might be dangerous for children under thirty-six months of age shall bear a warning, for example: "Not suitable for children under thirty-six months."

. . .

5. Skates and skateboards for children. If these products are offered for sale as toys, they shall bear the marking: "Warning: protective equipment should be worn."

*Exhibit text was edited for student use by the authors.

Council Directive 88/378/EEC of 3 May 1998 concerning the safety of toys. *Official Journal* I. 187, 16/07/1988, p. 0001–0013; Document 388L0378.

SOURCE: EU Web site.

burdensome inspection procedures or import licensing requirements and the arbitrary enforcement of overly strict standards. Japan has maintained complex technical regulations on thousands of important products, including electrical appliances, telecommunications and medical equipment, lumber, electronic components, pharmaceuticals, and food. The prolific use of technical requirements in Japan is rooted in Japan's protective attitude toward consumers, the historical role of the Japanese government in economic life, and the Japanese people's acceptance of governmental regulation of business. Product standards in Japan have been generally based on *design* characteristics that govern how a product should be designed. U.S. standards, by contrast, are usually based on *performance*. Performance standards describe how a product should function. It is usually more cost-effective for a manufacturer to meet foreign performance standards than design standards. Thus, it is easier for Japanese manufacturers to meet U.S. performance standards than for U.S. manufacturers to meet Japanese design standards. In Japan, products capable of inflicting injury on consumers or products that affect public health are more highly regulated than other products. For example, for many years Japan banned the import of cosmetics containing colorants and preservatives for health reasons, despite the fact that they are approved for use in the United States.

Japanese agencies that enforce technical regulations include the Japanese Ministry of Economy, Trade, and Industry, which has the widest authority, and the ministries that oversee the health, agriculture, and transportation sectors. Many products require testing and prior approval before they can be sold in Japan. For instance, prior to the mid-1980s, foreign products could not be inspected for pre-clearance at the foreign factory, but could only be inspected, shipment by shipment, as they arrived in Japan. Items had to be individually inspected and tested for compliance with the applicable technical regulations or standards. Legal changes have now made it possible for a foreign firm to register with the appropriate regulatory ministry and to obtain advance product approval without going through a Japanese importer or intermediary.

Another problem occurs when Japanese technical regulations and standards lack transparency. Their agencies still generally do not permit foreign input into the drafting of the regulations, although on occasion U.S. industry groups, under pressure, have succeeded in being heard by Japanese standard-setting groups. During the 1980s, new Japanese regulations provided that advance announcements of product standards be made by the Japan External Trade Organization.

The symbol of an approved product in Japan is the government-authorized *Japan Industrial Standards Mark,* or JIS Mark. Its appearance on a product, although voluntary, indicates that the manufacturer has submitted to on-site inspections by the appropriate Japanese ministry and has met accepted standards for quality control, production techniques, and research methods. Because this mark has become widely recognized, foreign products without it are often not competitive in the Japanese market.

Chinese Standards and Technical Regulations

China has a complex regulatory system governing product quality, safety, and other standards and technical regulations. As a socialist country, the enormous bureaucracy dwarfs any similar agencies in Western countries. The laws are administered by China's *General Administration of Quality Supervision, Inspection, and Quarantine,* or AQSIQ. In 2008, AQSIQ had 19 major departments, 15 national institutes and research centers, 35 inspection and quarantine bureaus in 31 provinces, 500 branches and local offices across the country, and over 30,000 employees at Chinese seaports, airports, and other ports of entry. Over 180,000 employees work for provincial or municipal *Bureaus of Technical Quality and Supervision* in developing and enforcing quality and standards laws. These bureaus also have the responsibility for enforcing Chinese laws against counterfeit products. Ten industry trade associations are allied with AQSIQ in setting standards and technical regulations. The most important Chinese laws administered by AQSIQ are:

- The *Law on Product Quality*
- The *Standardization Law*
- The *Law on Metrology* (weights and measures)

- The *Law on Import and Export Commodity Inspection*
- *Food Hygiene Law*
- *Frontier Health and Quarantine Law*
- The *Law on the Entry and Exit Animal and Plant Quarantine*

The two primary AQSIQ agencies that are important to standardization are the Certification and Accreditation Administration and the Standardization Administration. The *Standardization Administration of China* was created in 2001 to coordinate the development of standards at the national and local levels, to coordinate Chinese standards with existing international standards (such as those of the International Electrotechnical Commission for electrical equipment, whose standards cover such diverse items as turbines, electric motors, fiber optics, and household appliances), to disseminate information on standards to industry and the public, to establish administrative rules and propose new standardization laws, and to work with the ISO and the WTO standards committee. Chinese standards are divided into the following hierarchy of categories: (1) national standards; (2) professional standards (i.e., developed by trade association or professional groups); (3) provincial or municipal government standards; and (4) enterprise standards (i.e., developed by a single company). Specific Chinese standards can be either mandatory or voluntary.

The *Certification and Accreditation Administration of China* is the AQSIQ agency charged with enforcement of product quality and standards through compulsory product testing, factory inspections, and certifications and by the accreditation of testing laboratories. The compulsory certification system began in 2003.

China's compulsory certification and inspection system covers products in 132 categories of consumer and industrial equipment in the following industries: electrical, audiovisual, automotive, agricultural, medical, lighting, telecommunications, and information technology. Examples include electrical wire, household appliances, medical devices, and computers. Chinese rules require that covered products receive certification prior to import. Samples must be shipped to an approved laboratory in China for inspection and testing for compliance with Chinese quality, safety, and environmental standards. Chinese inspectors must then visit the foreign plants, whether they be in the United States, Canada, or Europe, that produce goods destined for China. Products that meet the quality and safety requirements for certification may be marked with the *China Compulsory Certification* Mark (CCC). No covered products can be imported into China without the mark. Under the regulations, fines may be imposed for falsification of marks. Anyone who plans to export goods to China should check the AQSIQ and CCC Mark Web sites to determine whether their products are covered by Chinese regulations. The Chinese certification process can be expensive and time consuming. Follow-up supervision and reviews are conducted annually. Many companies wishing to ship to China find that they must employ a consulting firm to manage the certification process.

The *WTO Agreement on Technical Barriers to Trade*

The *WTO Agreement on Technical Barriers to Trade (TBT Agreement)* is one of the 1994 *Uruguay Round* agreements. It governs the use of technical regulations, product standards, testing, and certifications by WTO member countries. The *TBT Agreement* is binding on all WTO member countries. Remember that this agreement does not contain standards of its own. It makes no attempt to say how a product should perform or be designed or when a product is safe or unsafe. These are matters for nations and local governments to decide. But the *TBT Agreement* does prohibit countries from using their regulations or standards to discriminate against the import of foreign goods.

Harmonization, Equivalence, and Mutual Recognition. The primary goal of the *TBT Agreement* is to minimize technical barriers to trade. It sets out three methods of achieving this goal. The first is *harmonization,* by which nations will attempt to bring their standards and technical regulations into harmony with internationally accepted standards. The second is *equivalence,* by which nations agree to accept foreign standards that are functionally equivalent to their own. The third is known as *mutual recognition.* Nations are encouraged to enter into mutual recognition agreements, whereby they recognize the certifications, or *conformity assessments,* of foreign inspection firms and laboratories approved in the country where the article is manufactured. For example, if a manufacturer ships telephones to several different markets, it would be far cheaper if all countries accepted the certification of an inspection firm in the manufacturer's country that the device conforms to the telecommunications standards in the importing country. This avoids the expense of having to perform multiple tests.

MAIN PROVISIONS OF THE *TBT AGREEMENT.* The *WTO Agreement on Technical Barriers to Trade* applies to all products, including agricultural, industrial, and consumer goods. The agreement's main provisions can be outlined as follows:

1. All technical regulations shall be applied on a nondiscriminatory basis, without regard to the national origin of the products.
2. Regulations must not be made or applied to create an unnecessary obstacle to trade, and they must not be more trade restrictive than is necessary to fulfill a legitimate objective such as national security, preventing fraud or deception of consumers, protecting public health or safety, or protecting the environment.
3. Countries should take into account available scientific and technical information in writing their standards. This provision is intended to ensure that standards are not just made to keep out foreign goods, but have some scientific foundation.
4. Wherever possible, product requirements should be based on performance abilities of the product rather than on design or descriptive characteristics. For example, there are several different mechanisms in use to hold automobile doors securely closed. Government regulations that require industry to use a mechanism of a certain type or design are creating a barrier to trade. Instead, the agreement encourages governments to set a performance standard requiring that the door remain securely closed during certain collisions, leaving the design up to the manufacturer.
5. Countries should develop and use internationally accepted standards where they exist. International standards will be presumed to be in compliance with the *TBT Agreement.*
6. Countries should work toward the goals of harmonization of standards and equivalence.
7. Proposed standards must be published and made available to foreign countries, and those countries must be given an opportunity to make written comments prior to adoption.
8. Final regulations must be published a reasonable time before they become effective so that foreign producers have time to adapt their products.
9. Testing and inspection procedures should restrict trade as little as possible and should not discriminate. The agreement encourages on-site factory inspections instead of port-of-entry inspections for foreign goods.
10. Nations should accept the testing reports and certifications from approved foreign inspection firms and laboratories (mutual recognition of conformity assessments).
11. Countries should try to ensure that state and local governments, as well as private standard-setting groups, comply with the agreement.
12. Disputes between countries may be referred to the WTO for negotiation and settlement.

The following case, *WTO Report on the European Communities—Measures Affecting Asbestos & Asbestos-Containing Products* (2001), is considered a landmark case in world trade law. Not only is it the first case to interpret the *WTO Agreement on Technical Barriers to Trade,* but it addresses a country's right to pass laws protecting the public health and safety under this agreement and under general GATT principles.

International Organization for Standardization

The *International Organization for Standardization* (ISO), based in Geneva, is a non-governmental organization comprising the national standards institutes of 157 countries. It has developed over 16,500 product standards for goods and services in many industries. ISO standards are not legally binding, and the organization has no legal authority to enforce them. However, the standards have been accepted by businesses and entire industries worldwide and are legally enforceable in countries

European Communities—Measures Affecting Asbestos & Asbestos-Containing Products
WT/DS135/AB/R (2001)
World Trade Organization Report of the Appellate Body

BACKGROUND AND FACTS

Asbestos is a natural mineral product that has been in use since the 1800s. It is inexpensive, resistant to heat and flame, and has been used in many industrial applications. It has been used in making fireproof materials, fireproof insulation, and brake linings and is used today in construction materials such as asbestos cement boards and pipes. It has been known for some time that exposure to asbestos fibers and particles can cause deadly lung disease, including a form of cancer for which the death rate is 100 percent. Signs of disease may not manifest themselves for 30 years after exposure. Although most uses of asbestos are now banned, it is still used in certain forms. Today, deposits are still mined in Russia, Canada, China, Brazil, and a few other countries. There are substitutes for asbestos whose fibers are not as dangerous, such as glass and cellulose.

The asbestos at issue in this case involved Canadian chrysotile exports to France. Prior to 1997, Canada was exporting up to 40,000 tons of asbestos to France each year. Citing the health risk, France imposed a virtual ban on its manufacture, import, sale, and use, subject to a few limited and temporary exceptions. The Canadian asbestos industry responded that chrysotile fibers could be used without incurring any detectable risk because the fibers become encapsulated in the hardened products into which it is made, such as heat-resistant cement blocks. Canada requested WTO dispute settlement. France claimed that it could restrict asbestos both under GATT Article XX(b) (general provisions that a country may protect public health) and under similar provisions in the *Agreement on Technical Barriers to Trade* (the TBT). The Canadian government argued that the French law was not a "technical regulation" as permitted under the TBT, but a total prohibition. It also argued that under GATT Article III:4 (the general principle of nondiscrimination) a country may not treat imported products differently than "like products" of domestic origin. Canada maintained that the restrictions on asbestos discriminated against other, less-harmful substitute products made of glass or cellulose. Finally, Canada argued that the restrictions went beyond what was "necessary" to protect human health, as set forth in GATT Article XX(b). It claimed that less restrictive measures, such as "controlled use" of the product, were enough to guarantee safety. The Appellate Body report upheld the French law, although for different reasons than those stated by the original panel.

REPORT OF THE APPELLATE BODY

* * *

Are the restrictions on asbestos a technical regulation? [added for understanding]

The heart of the definition of a "technical regulation" is that a "document" must "lay down"—that is, set forth, stipulate or provide—"product characteristics." The word "characteristic" has a number of synonyms that are helpful in understanding the ordinary meaning of that word in this context. Thus, the "characteristics" of a product include, in our view, any objectively definable "features," "qualities," "attributes," or other "distinguishing mark" of a product. Such "characteristics" might relate ... to a product's composition, size, shape, colour, texture, hardness, tensile strength, flammability, conductivity, density, or viscosity.... The definition of a "technical regulation" also states that "compliance" with the "product characteristics" laid down in the "document" must be "mandatory."

* * *

"Product characteristics" may, in our view, be prescribed or imposed with respect to products in either a positive or a negative form. That is, the document may provide, positively, that products must possess certain "characteristics," or the document may require, negatively, that products must not possess certain "characteristics." In both cases, the legal result is the same: the document "lays down" certain binding "characteristics" for products, in one case affirmatively, and in the other by negative implication.

With these considerations in mind, we examine whether the measure at issue is a "technical regulation." [The French law] aims primarily at the regulation of a named product, asbestos [and imposes] a prohibition on asbestos fibers, as such. This prohibition on these fibers does not, in itself, prescribe or impose any "characteristics" on asbestos fibers, but

continued

continued

simply bans them in their natural state. Accordingly, if this measure consisted only of a prohibition on asbestos fibers, it might not constitute a "technical regulation."

There is, however, more to the measure than this prohibition on asbestos fibers.... It is important to note here that, although formulated negatively—products containing asbestos are prohibited—the measure, in this respect, effectively prescribes or imposes certain objective features, qualities or "characteristics" *on all products.* That is, in effect, the measure provides that *all products must not contain* asbestos fibers [emphasis added].... We also observe that compliance with the prohibition against products containing asbestos is mandatory and is, indeed, enforceable through criminal sanctions. * * * For these reasons, we conclude that the measure constitutes a "technical regulation" under the TBT Agreement.

* * *

Do the restrictions on asbestos imports, but not on less harmful domestic substitutes, violate GATT's nondiscrimination provisions? Are they "Like Products"?

We are very much of the view that evidence relating to the health risks associated with a product may be pertinent in an examination of "likeness" under Article III:4 of the GATT 1994. This carcinogenicity, or toxicity, constitutes, as we see it, a defining aspect of the physical properties of chrysotile asbestos fibers. The evidence indicates that [cellulose, glass, and other less harmful fibers] in contrast, do not share these properties, at least to the same extent. We do not see how this highly significant physical difference *cannot* be a consideration in examining the physical properties of a product as part of a determination of "likeness" under Article III:4 [general principles of nondiscrimination] of the GATT 1994.

* * *

We also see it as important to take into account that, since 1977, chrysotile asbestos fibers have been recognized internationally as a known carcinogen.... This carcinogenicity was confirmed by the experts consulted by the Panel, with respect to both lung cancers and mesotheliomas.... "In contrast ... [t]he experts also confirmed, ... that current scientific evidence indicates that [cellulose and glass] do "not present the same risk to health as chrysotile" asbestos fibers. * * * It follows that the evidence relating to properties indicates that, physically, chrysotile asbestos and [its substitutes] are very different....

Is the French law valid under GATT Article XX(b), which provides that a country may adopt measures necessary to protect human life or health, provided that it is not a disguised restriction on trade?

[W]e have examined the seven factors on which Canada relies in asserting that the Panel erred in concluding that there exists a human health risk associated with the manipulation of chrysotile-cement products. We see Canada's appeal on this point as, in reality, a challenge to the Panel's assessment of the credibility and weight to be ascribed to the scientific evidence before it. Canada contests the conclusions that the Panel drew both from the evidence of the scientific experts and from scientific reports before it. As we have noted, we will interfere with the Panel's appreciation of the evidence only when we are "satisfied that the panel has *exceeded the bounds of its discretion,* as the trier of facts, in its appreciation of the evidence." In this case, nothing suggests that the Panel exceeded the bounds of its lawful discretion. To the contrary, all four of the scientific experts consulted by the Panel concurred that chrysotile asbestos fibers, and chrysotile-cement products, constitute a risk to human health, and the Panel's conclusions on this point are faithful to the views expressed by the four scientists. In addition, the Panel noted that the carcinogenic nature of chrysotile asbestos fibers has been acknowledged since 1977 by international bodies, such as the International Agency for Research on Cancer and the World Health Organization. In these circumstances, we find that the Panel remained well within the bounds of its discretion in finding that chrysotile-cement products pose a risk to human life or health. Accordingly, we uphold the Panel's finding that the measure [protects human life or health], within the meaning of Article XX(b) of the GATT 1994.

Does GATT mandate the level of protection necessary to protect life and health or the means of achieving it?

As to Canada's argument, relating to the level of protection, we note that it is undisputed that WTO Members have the right to determine the level of protection of health that they consider appropriate in a given situation. France has determined, and the Panel accepted, that the chosen level of health protection by France is a "halt" to the spread of *asbestos*-related health risks.... Our conclusion is not altered by the fact that [glass and cellulose] fibers might pose a risk to health. The scientific evidence before the Panel indicated that the risk posed by [these substitutes] is,

continued

continued

in any case, *less* than the risk posed by asbestos, although that evidence did *not* indicate that the risk posed by [glass or cellulose substitutes] is non-existent. Accordingly, it seems to us perfectly legitimate for a Member to seek to halt the spread of a highly risky product while allowing the use of a less risky product in its place. In short, we do not agree with Canada's third argument.

Canada asserts that [France could achieve the same level of public safety through a "controlled use" policy instead of a complete prohibition and that this] represents a "reasonably available" measure that would serve the same end. The issue is, thus, whether France could reasonably be expected to employ "controlled use" practices to achieve its chosen level of health protection—a halt in the spread of asbestos-related health risks.

In our view, France could not reasonably be expected to employ *any* alternative measure if that measure would involve a continuation of the very risk that the [French law] seeks to "halt." Such an alternative measure would, in effect, prevent France from achieving its chosen level of health protection. On the basis of the scientific evidence before it, the Panel found that, in general, the efficacy of "controlled use" remains to be demonstrated. Moreover, even in cases where "controlled use" practices are applied "with greater certainty," the scientific evidence suggests that the level of exposure can, in some circumstances, still be high enough for there to be a "significant residual risk of developing asbestos-related diseases." "Controlled use" would, thus, not be an alternative measure that would achieve the end sought by France.

Decision. The French restrictions on asbestos were found to be a valid technical regulation under the *TBT Agreement*. GATT requires that national laws not discriminate between imports and domestic "like products." Asbestos and its less harmful domestic substitutes are not "like products" because their effects on human life and health are very different. This impact on health may be taken into account in determining if the products are "like" each other. The restrictions are permitted both under the *TBT Agreement* and under the general right of a country under Article XX(b) to protect public health. Given the deadly long-term effects of asbestos inhalation, France need not use a less restrictive means of controlling asbestos, but is free to decide the level of health protection for its citizens. Future disputes over the health and safety of other imported products must be considered by panels on a case-by-case basis.

where they have been incorporated into a treaty or under national law. In general, the standards are intended to ensure product quality, safety, efficiency, and interchangeability, although some standards have been adopted to minimize the impact of manufacturing or the use of products on the environment.

These standards also foster international business and trade, because it is easier and cheaper to design and build products that comply with one international standard than to design products that comply with dozens of local standards all over the world. The ISO has developed standards in diverse areas such as the dimensions of screw threads and other fasteners, the size and dimensions of international freight containers, methods of storing data on credit cards, warning and information symbols for signs and labels, ergonomics, computer protocols, food safety management, life vests, and inflatable boats.

The most commonly known ISO standard is ISO 9000. Since 1987, ISO 9000 has become the standard used for ensuring product quality through the product design and manufacturing process. Companies become ISO 9000–certified through a costly and rigorous inspection of their facilities and documentation of their quality control systems. They are audited on a regular basis for compliance. In order to sell in Europe, many U.S. firms have obtained ISO certification. By meeting ISO requirements, the firms no longer have to certify each product individually in every European country.

ISO certification is required under EU law for certain regulated products such as medical devices and construction equipment. Market demands make compliance for other products equally essential. In the United States, a number of firms offer assistance to U.S. companies seeking ISO certification.

Another standard, known as ISO 14000, provides guidelines for environmental management. It does not set criteria for pollution or environmental impact. Rather, it requires that a firm establish a management system for setting its own environmental objectives, complying with national or local environmental laws, and continuing to improve its environmental performance.

Import Licensing Procedures

The case of Thailand's cigarette restrictions earlier in the chapter is an example of how an import licensing scheme can work to block foreign imports.

Article XI does permit a country to use licensing in a nondiscriminatory, MFN, and transparent fashion in order to regulate imports in certain cases. For instance, a country may use licensing to enforce its technical regulations or standards laws. For example, a health department might appropriately permit importation of say, pillows and mattresses only if a license is issued that indicates that the products were made from sterilized materials. Customs officials might request to see this license at the border. Revenues from license fees could go to support the costs of inspection and administering the law.

Import licenses are also used to track the quantities of imported goods subject to a quota. For instance, a few textile products from certain countries still enter the United States under tariff-rate quotas. A textile importer must hand over their license for the given quantity to U.S. Customs. The license must be in the precise format (including typeface and color) that has been agreed upon by the United States and foreign governments so it can be authenticated. After authentication the license information is sent to Washington, where the Customs Service tracks the quantity of each type of textile product that has entered from each foreign country so far in that year.

Imagine if you were trying to ship to a foreign customer in, say, Burkina Faso, Slovenia, or Japan. Suppose that country maintained complex licensing requirements for your products. Imagine now that you and your customer are told that the application and conditions for import are not set out in the local law books or regulations, but are published in some internal "back office" manuals or, even worse, are made up by local government bureaucrats on a case-by-case basis. Both you and your customer might throw up your hands and give up.

This is an example of licensing requirements that lack "transparency." GATT requires that import license procedures be transparent. Under WTO rules, a licensing scheme is *transparent* if the procedures to obtain the license are not unduly complicated and the licensing rules are published and openly available to business parties in all countries. GATT requires that applications for import licenses should be handled within 30 to 60 days.

The *WTO Agreement on Import Licensing Procedures*

The *WTO Agreement on Import Licensing Procedures* (1994) sets guidelines for countries issuing import licenses. It calls for the procedures to be fair, reasonable, and nondiscriminatory and requires application procedures to obtain a license to be as simple as possible. Applications should not be refused because of minor errors in paperwork. In other words, governments should see that clerical workers and bureaucracies do not use the licensing procedures to stand in the way of trade. Where licenses are used to administer quotas, the amount of the quota already used must be published for all importers to see. The *WTO Import Licensing Committee* must be notified if any new products will become subject to licensing requirements.

Trade Facilitation

Anyone experienced in moving goods from one country to another has probably had to suffer through arcane foreign regulations, reams of paperwork, miles of government red tape, and what sometimes seems like endless delays at the border. The WTO estimates that these "hidden" costs can often be greater than the cost of tariffs themselves. *Trade facilitation* refers to the WTO's effort to simplify and standardize government regulations and procedures affecting the movement of goods across national borders. Although many of the specific trade agreements, such as the *WTO Agreement on Import Licensing Procedures,* deal with certain aspects of this problem, trade facilitation is a broader effort to reduce the costs of cross-border shipments and to speed the movement of goods through the use of streamlined procedures, computerization and automation, and increased communication between customs agencies in different countries.

Government Procurement

Governments are among the largest business customers in the world. GATT Article III contains an exception from its national treatment provision for government procurement that allows governments to favor domestic suppliers. Article III, which normally prohibits laws that discriminate against foreign goods, states that

> [T]his article shall not apply to laws, regulations or requirements governing the procurement by governmental agencies of products purchased for governmental purposes and not with a view to commercial resale or with a view to use in the production of goods for commercial sale.

Most nations of the world have laws that require their own government agencies to give some preference to domestically made products. The laws often apply to goods purchased by defense-related agencies or by the military. Other laws might require that the purchased product contain a certain proportion of domestically made component parts or raw materials.

In the United States, the *U.S. Buy American Act* as well as state and local Buy American laws allow preferences for the purchase of domestic goods. The federal government is required to buy domestic products unless such purchases are not in the public interest or the costs are unreasonable. The U.S. Department of Defense must purchase domestic products unless those products are more than 50 percent more expensive than competing foreign goods.

Japan has come under criticism for its discriminatory procurement rules. For the company that is considering bidding on a foreign government procurement contract, knowledge of the specific rules applicable to that bid is essential.

The *WTO Agreement on Government Procurement*

As a general rule, large-scale procurement by governments or government agencies is exempt from the normal WTO rules for trade in goods and services. Instead, most large-scale government procurement is governed by the *WTO Agreement on Government Procurement* (1994), known as AGP. This agreement was revised in 2006 to make it more easily understandable and user-friendly to procuring government agencies and private firms that tender bids on projects. The revisions also address special issues of developing countries and procurement offers by electronic means. The *WTO Revised Agreement on Government Procurement of 2006* will eventually replace the 1994 agreement. It currently is in the process of being adopted by individual countries.

The AGP brought about many changes in procurement practices in the United States and other countries. The purpose of the agreement is to bring competition to world procurement markets. The agreement requires fair, open, and nondiscriminatory procurement practices and sets up uniform procurement procedures to protect suppliers from different countries. It applies to the purchase of goods or services by national governments worth more than 130,000 IMF Special Drawing Rights (approximately $205,000 as of early 2008) and to construction contracts (buildings, dams, power plants, etc.) worth more than 5 million SDRs (approximately $7.9 million as of early 2008). Unlike the other WTO agreements, the AGP applies only to those countries that have signed it. As of 2008, forty nations were participating in the AGP, including the United States, Canada, Japan, and the EU nations.

The signatories have negotiated bilaterally with each other, one on one, as to how the AGP will be applied between them, so the rules can differ depending on the countries involved in a procurement contract. For instance, the AGP says that Japan will not receive the benefit of the agreement if it wants to sell goods or services to NASA because Japan has not treated U.S. companies equally in procuring satellite technology. The ITC estimates that the agreement will open up export markets for U.S. companies worth hundreds of billions of dollars.

Agencies Excluded from the Procurement Rules. The agreement applies to almost ninety U.S. federal agencies, large and small—from the Department of Labor to the American Battle Monuments Commission—and to the executive branch departments. There are several exclusions from the procurement rules, including purchases to be sent to foreign countries as foreign aid; purchases by the Department of Agriculture for food distribution or for farm support programs; and some purchases made by the Federal Aviation Administration, the Department of Energy, and the Department of Defense that are related to national security or to the military. In the United States, thirty-seven states have also agreed to comply, and more will do so in the future. Many states—based on political reasoning—have opted to exclude certain items. For example, New York excluded subway cars and buses, and South Dakota excluded purchases of beef. Thus, state agencies in these states may give preferences to local producers when awarding procurement bids for these products.

Procurement Rules. The AGP reverses the general WTO rules that allow government agencies to favor domestic products. It brings the principles of MFN trade, nondiscrimination, and transparency to government procurement. A procuring agency must treat equally, and no less favorably than if they were from its own country, the products, services, and suppliers that it obtains from all other countries that have signed the agreement. Moreover, a government agency may not discriminate against local suppliers just because they are foreign-owned. The agreement also prohibits a procuring agency from awarding a contract to a foreign firm on the basis of certain conditions, called *offsets.* Examples of offsets might be a condition that the foreign firm awarded the contract use local subcontractors, domestically made materials, or local labor; that the firm agree to license its technology to local firms; that it make local investments; or that it engage in countertrade. Offsets can be complex. For instance, assume that Aeroflop, a U.S. firm, wants to sell several million dollars' worth of airplanes to a government-owned airline in a European country famous for cheese. In order to get the contract it agrees to pay a 5 percent kickback to another U.S. company, Cheezy, if Cheezy agrees to buy all of its cheese from a seller in that European country. If the cheese-producing country requires Aeroflop to make the offset, it violates the AGP.

Other rules state how the country of origin of products sold to a government agency is to be determined. For instance, a supplier that sells a product that is fraudulently labeled with the incorrect country of origin may be subjected to severe penalties under the law of the country involved.

Transparency in Procurement Procedures. To ensure that the procurement rules are applied fairly, the AGP sets up procedures for governments to follow. When a government agency intends to make a purchase by inviting suppliers to "bid on the job," the agency must give adequate notice to potential bidders when the contract is announced and must disclose all the information necessary for them to submit their bid. The agreement requires fairness in qualifying foreign companies to bid (e.g., countries can disqualify companies that are not technically or financially capable of delivering). In the event of a disagreement between a supplier and a procuring agency, a country must allow the supplier to challenge the contract before either an independent administrative review board or the courts.

Administering Government Procurement Rules in the United States

Congress has placed responsibility for implementing the AGP with the president. The president may waive the requirements of the *U.S. Buy American Act* for suppliers from any country that is party to the AGP and complies with the AGP's terms in its own procurement practices. Suppliers from a least-developed country also receive the waiver, which entitles those foreign suppliers to nondiscrimination and equal treatment with U.S. domestic suppliers.

The president must compile an annual report of those countries that have adopted the AGP but do not abide by it. The U.S. Trade Representative (USTR) negotiates with violating countries to get them to end their unfair practices and give equal access to U.S. firms. If no agreement is reached, then the USTR must present the case to the WTO for dispute settlement. If an agreement or resolution is still not reached within 18 months of initiating dispute settlement, then the president must revoke the waiver of the *Buy American Act,* and preferences for domestic suppliers will be allowed.

In certain cases, the president must completely prohibit U.S. government agencies from procuring products from suppliers in a foreign country, such as where the country "maintains a significant and persistent pattern or practice of discrimination against U.S. products or services which results in identifiable harm to U.S. business." The prohibition also applies to a country that has not joined the AGP—but from whom the U.S. government buys significant amounts of goods or services—that fails to provide U.S. firms with equal access to its procurement markets or that permits its agencies to engage in bribery, extortion, or corruption in procuring goods or services. This severe sanction can only be used if the president has first consulted interested U.S. companies and has determined that imposing the sanction will not harm the public interest of the United States or unreasonably restrict competition.

Other Procurement Agreements. The United States has negotiated several other procurement agreements with foreign nations. On behalf of the U.S. telecommunications industry, it entered into an agreement with Japan to help open opportunities for U.S. firms bidding on contracts there. Similarly, a 1993 agreement between the United States and the EU opened up U.S. access to the European market for heavy electrical and power plant equipment. The *North American Free Trade Agreement* contains provisions to guarantee U.S., Canadian, and Mexican firms "equal access" and "equal opportunity" to government contracts over $25,000.

Trade in Services

Trade in services includes areas such as professional services (law, accounting, architecture, engineering, and others); travel, recreation, and tourism; health care; transportation and distribution; finance, banking, and insurance; computer and data processing services; research and development; business services such as advertising, market research, and consulting; education; environmental engineering and waste management; and telecommunications. According to the WTO, world trade in services totaled approximately $2.8 trillion in 2006, or about 20 percent of world trade. Europe was the leading exporter of services, followed by Asia and the United States. In 2006, U.S. exports of services amounted to $422.5 billion, or nearly 30 percent of total U.S. trade volume of goods and services, generating a trade surplus in services of $80 billion. Services account for the majority of the gross domestic product in the United States and most developed countries. Indeed, in 2006, service industries accounted for over 80 percent of U.S. GDP, according to the U.S. Department of Commerce. Although the GATT agreement regulated trade in goods for more than 45 years, it did not regulate trade in services until the *Uruguay Round* agreements. (Also, the *North American Free Trade Agreement* permits a free flow of services between the United States, Canada, and Mexico.)

The *WTO General Agreement on Trade in Services*

Adopted as a result of the 1994 *Uruguay Round,* the *WTO General Agreement on Trade in Services*, or GATS, is the first multilateral, legally enforceable agreement to establish rules for international trade in services. It is a part of the WTO system and is overseen by the *Council for Trade in Services.* The agreement is largely patterned after the concepts that GATT applies to trade in goods. The agreement covers trade in most services, including health services, architecture, engineering and construction, travel and tourism, legal and other professional services, rental and leasing, distribution and courier services, education, management and environmental consulting, market research and advertising consulting, computer services, repair and maintenance, sanitation and disposal, franchising, entertainment, and others. (Two areas, telecommunications and financial services, are treated in separate GATS agreements.) GATS applies to the federal government as well as to state and local governments. GATS defines four different ways of providing an international service:

- services supplied from one country to another (e.g., international telephone calls), officially known as "cross-border supply"

- consumers or firms making use of a service in another country (e.g., tourism), officially known as "consumption abroad"
- a foreign company setting up subsidiaries or branches to provide services in another country (e.g., foreign banks setting up operations in a country), officially known as "commercial presence"
- individuals traveling from their own country to supply services in another (e.g., fashion models or consultants), officially known as "presence of natural persons"

GATS principles are similar to the GATT principles studied in previous chapters. Rules affecting service providers must be transparent and made readily available. Signatory countries to the agreement can place no limit on the number of service providers or on the number of people they may employ. The agreement also prohibits countries from imposing a requirement that local investors own any percentage of the service company (although they may if the parties choose). Like GATT, the GATS agreement also contains MFN trade and national treatment (nondiscrimination) provisions. Countries may not treat foreign service providers less favorably than they treat domestic providers. Laws and regulations must be transparent, reasonable, objective, and impartial. Also, countries may not unreasonably restrict the international transfer of money by service industries or the movement of people across borders for the purpose of providing a service.

GATS contains a set of schedules, or commitments, wherein each country lists its specific commitments for each type of service, which amounts to an exception to the nondiscrimination provision for certain types of services. For example, the United States excluded transportation services from GATS. Japan excluded repair services for certain automobiles and motorcycles, as well as courier services with respect to letters. In Canada, GATS applies to legal services only if they are provided by law firms or attorneys who advise clients on foreign or international law. Many countries exclude printing and publishing services.

A country may not treat foreign services or service providers any less favorably than promised in the schedules. As a result, no new or additional restrictions may be imposed in the future. Countries also are bound to negotiate an eventual elimination of the exceptions made in the schedules.

Recognition of Licensing and Professional Qualifications. GATS also has special provisions governing the qualifications of service providers set by national or local governments. Most governments license certain service providers at some level; in the United States, licensing generally occurs at the state level. Of course, areas such as law, medicine, nursing, engineering, architecture, surveying, and accounting will continue to have more strict professional licensing requirements than, say, management consulting. Countries can continue to license professionals and other service providers as necessary to ensure the quality of the service, provided that licensing is not made overly burdensome just to restrict trade. Licensing must be based on objective criteria, such as education or ability. It must not discriminate on the basis of the person's citizenship. Countries may recognize licenses granted by other countries, but only if they choose to do so.

To illustrate the impact of GATS licensing provisions, in 1999 the Japanese Ministry of Finance held national accreditation examinations for foreign certified public accountants for the first time since 1975. From 1950 through 1975, only seventy-four foreign CPAs had been certified to practice in Japan. Typically, foreign CPAs in Japan only provide auxiliary services to clients in Japan through Japanese CPA offices because of the requirements to register as a member of the Japan Institute of CPAs and laws that allow only Japanese nationals to own and run CPA offices. Since 1999, Japan and other countries have attempted to negotiate mutual recognition agreements for accounting and other professions. Most agreements are still pending.

The *WTO* Agreement on Trade in Financial Services. Over one hundred nations, including the EU and the United States, have joined the *WTO Agreement on Trade in Financial Services*, a part of the GATS agreement. The agreement applies free trade principles to the commercial banking, securities, and insurance industries by opening domestic markets to foreign competition. The agreement is intended to promote efficiency, reduce costs, and provide consumers with a greater choice of service providers, while still permitting countries to regulate these industries for the protection of investors, depositors, and consumers.

THE *WTO* AGREEMENT ON BASIC TELECOMMUNICATIONS. This agreement is also part of the larger GATS agreement. The services included under the *WTO Agreement on Basic Telecommunications* are voice and facsimile telephone systems, data transmission, fixed and mobile satellite systems and services, cellular telephone systems, mobile data services, paging, personal communications systems, and others. The agreement binds eighty-six countries, including the United States, Canada, the EU, and Japan, to MFN trade and to honor their specific commitments to open their telecommunications markets to foreign competitors. Local, long distance, and international communications are included.

TRADE IN AGRICULTURE

Agricultural exports are an important part of world trade. They totaled $852 billion worldwide in 2005, according to the WTO, and accounted for 9 percent of world exports in that year. According to the U.S. Department of Agriculture, the output of about one-third of U.S. crop acreage is exported, accounting for 25 percent of all agricultural revenues. The United States exports almost 20 percent of its agricultural production, worth over $82 billion in 2005, accounting for about 10 percent of world trade in agriculture.

However, agricultural products are among the most heavily protected products traded in the world. No nation wants to be dependent on other nations for its food supply. Also, agriculture represents a politically powerful and important constituency in most countries. To protect farmers, many governments control the domestic pricing structure in order to provide market stability. These agricultural price supports set prices at higher-than-world-market prices and contribute to the buildup of food surpluses. To avoid disrupting their price support systems, many countries impose import restrictions on both raw and processed food products. The United States, Japan, and the EU provide farming subsidies and controls on prices. GATT Article XI, which prohibits quantitative restrictions, contains a loophole allowing quotas on agricultural imports when necessary to protect government price support programs. Thus, prior to 1995, agricultural products effectively escaped control by GATT.

Agricultural price supports in the EU are handled through a *Common Agricultural Policy,* which uses a variable levy to bring the world price of an agricultural import up to the domestic price level. Expenditures for agricultural subsidies and price supports cost billions of dollars each year, constituting nearly three-quarters of the annual total budget of the EU. In the United States, federal legislation (commonly called the *Farm Bill*) provides billions of dollars to subsidize farm exports.

No other single trade issue has created so much international disagreement and controversy as trade in agriculture. The United States has generally demanded that EU farm subsidies, including direct payments to European farmers, be reduced. France, Europe's largest grain exporter, has been unwilling to reduce farm subsidies because French farmers are politically powerful. (Pictures of rioting French farmers setting trucks afire in the early 1990s to contest their government's negotiations with the United States over agricultural subsidies filled TV screens around the world.)

An excellent example of how nations feel about their agricultural trade is Japanese treatment of rice imports. Rice has long been considered the staple food of Japan, and rice farming lies at the center of its agricultural community. Rice is a food that is symbolic of Japanese culture. The Japanese government's objective is to maintain self-sufficiency in rice production by ensuring the economic health of rice farmers. Since World War II Japanese laws have placed strict limitations on rice imports and imposed governmental controls on rice pricing and distribution. As a result, the domestic price of rice in Japan has often been many times higher than the price of rice in international markets. One small but vivid example of protectionism occurred in 1991 when U.S. rice exhibitors at a Japanese trade fair were threatened with arrest for merely exhibiting American-grown rice products there. The American rice had to be removed from the show.

In 1994, in its *Uruguay Round* commitments, Japan promised to deregulate rice imports and to increase target levels for imports of foreign rice. It enacted the *Japanese Food Staple Law*, which permitted regulated competition by foreign rice producers, and began deregulation of government pricing and the rice distribution system. By 2006, Japan had imported $169 million worth of U.S. rice. Although the United States ships rice to Japan today, it is still not treated equally with domestic rice. For example, it is still subject to market regulation and to rigorous testing requirements for quality.

The *WTO Agreement on Agriculture*

The 1994 *Uruguay Round* resulted in many significant changes in government control of agricultural trade. The *WTO Agreement on Agriculture*, effective in 1995, attempts to bring fair trade and competition to the farming sector and to end government programs that distort normal market conditions. The agreement has three main areas: (1) cutting domestic programs that support higher than normal food prices, (2) cutting programs that subsidize exports of farm products, and (3) converting quotas and other non-tariff barriers into tariffs.

Domestic Support Programs. Domestic support programs artificially manipulate farm prices in a way that protects domestic farmers and encourages cheap exports. The agreement prohibits programs that distort farm production, prices, or trade, but permits support for research, disease control, environmental protection, and other national concerns. Cash payments to farmers who have had a loss of income from unexpected emergencies or disasters are permitted. This is a politically sensitive issue in most countries, and any effort to reduce support programs will be difficult.

Agricultural Export Subsidies. Agricultural export subsidies are payments or any other benefits given to farmers that directly encourage, or are conditional upon, the export of food or agricultural products. Even indirect benefits are included, such as where a government subsidizes the cost of shipping food products to foreign customers. Export subsidies were reduced 36 percent in developed countries by 2001 and had been reduced to a lesser extent in developing countries by 2004. Food aid to poorer countries is not considered an export subsidy and will not be affected by the *WTO Agreement on Agriculture*.

Making Export Markets Accessible. An important step in making agricultural markets accessible was to alleviate the quotas, licensing schemes, and non-tariff barriers that existed prior to 1995. The agreement called for this to be done through *tariffication,* the process of converting non-tariff barriers to tariffs, and then gradually negotiating a reduction or elimination of the tariffs. By 2001, developed countries reduced their tariff rates by an average of 36 percent, and developing countries had reduced theirs by 24 percent by 2004.

U.S.–Brazil Dispute over Cotton Subsidies. A dispute between the United States and Brazil over U.S. cotton subsidies illustrates how contentious agricultural trade is. The United States is the world's second largest producer (next to China) and the largest exporter of cotton, with almost 60 percent of production being exported. U.S. cotton farmers are eligible for many different types of subsidies and government assistance, such as cash payments and loan repayment assistance. These subsidies protect them from the ups and downs of economic cycles and provide price stability. However, they also make U.S. cotton cheaper and more competitive in foreign markets. According to the U.S. Department of Agriculture, from 2000 to 2005, subsidies to cotton farmers under the U.S. *Farm Bill* averaged over $3 billion annually.

Despite worldwide negotiations to reduce subsidies that have been ongoing since 1995, U.S. subsidies have increased. In 2004, Brazil, a leading cotton exporter, requested a WTO dispute panel to hear its arguments that the U.S. subsidies had violated international agreements. Other cotton exporting nations joined with Brazil, including Argentina, Australia, Benin, Canada, Chad, China, the European Union, India, New Zealand, Pakistan, Paraguay, Taiwan, and Venezuela. Brazil claimed that the annual increases in U.S. subsidies exceeded U.S. commitments. It also argued that other forms of U.S. assistance to cotton farmers were illegal and "trade distorting." These included direct payments to farmers based on their export performance, payments when cotton prices fell below certain levels, and export loan programs with low interest rates and favorable repayment provisions. Brazil also claimed that the U.S. subsidies caused an overproduction of cotton and a decline of world cotton prices that caused serious injury to Brazilian cotton exporters. The latter argument was especially appealing to developing countries where U.S. subsidies to American farmers were perceived as helping to impoverish farmers in Africa, Asia, and Latin America. A dispute panel issued its final report in 2004, and it was upheld the following year by the WTO Appellate Body in *WTO Report on the United States—Subsidies on Upland Cotton,* WT/DS267/AB/R (2005). The dispute panel and Appellate Body both agreed with Brazil, and their recommendations were adopted by the WTO Dispute Settlement Body. The body ordered the United States to end its prohibited subsidies and approved retaliatory Brazilian tariffs (possibly totaling billions of dollars in tariffs annually on a range of U.S. goods) if the United States failed to do so. The U.S. administration submitted legislation to Congress to comply with the WTO recommendations.

Nevertheless, in 2007, a WTO dispute settlement compliance panel ruled that the United States had not done enough to comply with the prior rulings. As the U.S. government was considering an appeal, Congress was debating the next farm bill, pitting free traders against lawmakers from cotton-producing states. As of mid-2007, Brazil had not imposed any retaliatory tariffs on the United States, in recognition that the United States and Brazil were important trading partners. The effects of the WTO rulings go far beyond the cotton trade, because the United States and other developing countries subsidize production of many different crops and crop-based products such as ethanol. Agricultural subsidies by the United States and other developed countries were still a topic of disagreement at the *Doha Rounds* of trade negotiations during 2007.

Sanitary and Phytosanitary Measures: Food, Animal, and Plant Safety

Trade in agricultural goods has been impeded because some countries use food safety as an excuse for blocking agriculture imports. No one doubts the right of a government to take extraordinary measures to protect its citizens from contagious disease or to protect food or agricultural products from infestation. If a blight, fungus, or insect were found in orange groves in Mexico, no one would argue against the right of the United States to keep out Mexican oranges to protect the U.S. crop. The *WTO Agreement on the Application of Sanitary and Phytosanitary Measures* (known as the SPS agreement) is specifically designed to allow governments to protect human, animal, and plant life from infestations, contaminants, pesticides, toxins, harmful chemicals, or disease-carrying organisms. However, its restrictions may not be used as an excuse to keep out foreign goods.

The SPS agreement opens markets for agricultural exports by requiring that the protective measures taken by nations (1) may not be more trade-restrictive than required and may be applied only to the extent necessary for the protection of human, animal, or plant life; (2) may not be a disguised restriction on trade; (3) must be based on a risk assessment made according to scientific principles and scientific evidence; and (4) may not unjustifiably discriminate between countries where similar threatening conditions prevail. In addition, under the SPS agreement, countries must ensure that inspections or controls are fair and reasonable and are instituted without delay. Consider an example: If an Asian country sets a short shelf life for a food product such as hot dogs, then hot dogs shipped from the United States will be discriminated against because their shelf life has been "used up" in the time it takes to ship them across the Pacific. Under the SPS agreement, however, the shelf life restrictions cannot stand unless they are based on scientific evidence. Another novel example is the strict Japanese law prohibiting thoroughbred racehorses from entering Japan. This prohibition would violate the agreement if the laws were unnecessary, discriminatory toward the United States, or not backed by scientific evidence. Citing the SPS agreement, the U.S. Department of Agriculture in 1995 partially repealed an 81-year-old prohibition against the import of Mexican avocados.

CODEX ALIMENTARIUS. Whenever possible, countries must rely on internationally accepted standards or recommendations for the protection of their plants, animals, and foodstuffs. The most notable are found in the *Codex Alimentarius*. This "food code" for the protection of the world's food supply developed slowly over most of the last century. Today, the *Codex Alimentarius*

Commission develops these important standards on the basis of worldwide scientific studies and disseminates them to government agencies and lawmakers. The commission is based in Rome and is made up of countries that belong to the UN World Health Organization and the UN Food and Agricultural Organization. If a country's national standards are based on the *Codex Alimentarius*, they are deemed to be in compliance with the SPS agreement.

In the following 1997 WTO panel decision, *WTO Report on EC Measures Concerning Meat & Meat Products (Hormones)*, the panel held that the European ban on the sale of beef containing residues of growth hormones violated the SPS agreement.

EC Measures Concerning Meat and Meat Products (Hormones)

WT/DS26/R/USA (1997); Complaint by the United States

World Trade Organization

BACKGROUND AND FACTS

Throughout the 1970s European consumers became more concerned over the use of hormones to speed the growth of livestock. Their fears were in part based on the fact that some people had been injured by the illegal use of certain banned hormones. Some consumer organizations boycotted meats. By 1986 the EC had banned the sale of beef from cattle given growth hormones. The EC maintained that such measures were necessary to protect public health (primarily from hormone-related illnesses and cancer) and necessary to restore confidence in the meat industry. The United States began contesting the hormone ban in 1987 at GATT. In January 1989, the United States introduced retaliatory measures in the form of 100 percent ad valorem duties on a list of products imported from the European Communities. The United States, together with Canada, Australia, and New Zealand, maintained that the ban was unlawful under the 1994 *Agreement on the Application of Sanitary and Phytosanitary Measures* ("SPS Agreement"). The United States argued that the ban was not based on an assessment of risk, not based on scientific principles, more trade-restrictive than necessary, and a disguised restriction on trade. In June 1996, the European Communities requested the establishment of a panel to examine this matter, and the United States terminated its retaliatory action entirely. Prior to the ban U.S. firms had exported hundreds of millions of dollars of goods annually to Europe. After the ban exports plummeted to nearly zero. The European Communities argued that its measures offered equal opportunities of access to the EC market for all third-country animals and meat from animals to which no hormones had been administered for growth promotion purposes. Of the 31 countries that were authorized to export meat to the European Communities, only six apparently allowed the use of some or all of these hormones for growth promotion purposes.

REPORT OF THE PANEL

Article 3.1 requires Members to base their sanitary measures on international standards, guidelines or recommendations [where they exist]. We note, therefore, that even if international standards may not, in their own right, be binding on Members, Article 3.1 requires Members to base their sanitary measures on these standards.... We shall therefore, as a first step, examine whether there are international standards, guidelines or recommendations with respect to the EC measures in dispute and, if so, whether the EC measures are *based on* these standards, guidelines or recommendations in accordance with Article 3.1....

Article 3.1 of the SPS Agreement reads as follows:

> To harmonize sanitary and phytosanitary measures on as wide a basis as possible, Members shall base their sanitary and phytosanitary measures on international standards, guidelines or recommendations, where they exist, except as otherwise provided for in this Agreement....

... For food safety ... the SPS Agreement defines "international standards, guidelines or recommendations" as "the standards, guidelines and

continued

continued

recommendations established by the Codex Alimentarius Commission relating to food additives, *veterinary drug* and pesticide *residues,* contaminants, methods of analysis and sampling, and codes and guidelines of hygienic practice" (emphasis added).... [The Codex Alimentarius Commission is an advisory body to the World Health Organization. The purpose of this programme is to protect the health of consumers and to ensure fair practices in food trade by establishing food standards. These standards, together with notifications received from governments with respect to their acceptance or otherwise of the standards, constitute the *Codex Alimentarius* ... a collection of internationally adopted food standards presented in a uniform manner].... We note that [there are] five Codex standards ... relating to veterinary drug residues ... with respect to five of the six hormones in dispute when these hormones are used for growth promotion purposes.... We find, therefore, that international standards exist with respect to the EC measures in dispute....

The amount of residues of these hormones administered for growth promotion purposes allowed by these Codex standards is ... higher than zero (a maximum level of such residues has not even been prescribed). The EC measures in dispute, on the other hand, do not allow the presence of any residues of these three hormones administered for growth promotion purposes. The level of protection reflected in the EC measures is, therefore, significantly *different* from the level of protection reflected in the Codex standards. The EC measures in dispute are ... therefore, *not based on* existing international standards as specified in Article 3.1....

[For those sanitary measures for which no international standards exist] ... a Member needs to ensure that its sanitary measures are based on an assessment of risks. The obligation to base a sanitary measure on a risk assessment may be viewed as a specific application of the basic obligations contained in Article 2.2 of the SPS Agreement which provides that "Members shall ensure that any sanitary ... measure is *applied only to the extent necessary to protect* human, animal or plant life or health, is *based on scientific principles* and is *not maintained without sufficient scientific evidence* ..." (emphasis added). Articles 5.1 to 5.3 sum up factors a Member needs to take into account in making this assessment of risks.... [A]n assessment of risks is, at least for risks to human life or health, a *scientific* examination of data and factual studies; it is not a policy exercise involving social value judgments made by political bodies....

We recall that under the SPS Agreement a risk assessment should, for the purposes of this dispute, identify the adverse effects on human health arising from the presence of the specific hormones at issue when used as growth promoters in meat or meat products and, if any such adverse effects exist, evaluate the potential or probability of occurrence of these effects. We further recall that a risk assessment should be a scientific examination of data and studies and that the SPS Agreement sets out factors which need to be taken into account in a risk assessment.

[The panel conducted a review of the scientific studies.] All of the scientific studies outlined above came to the conclusion that the use of the hormones at issue for growth promotion purposes is safe; most of these studies adding that this conclusion assumes that good practice is followed. We note that this conclusion has also been confirmed by the scientific experts advising the Panel. Accordingly, the European Communities has not established the existence of any identifiable risk against which the EC measures at issue ... can protect human life or health.

Decision. The EC's ban on the sale of beef containing residues of growth hormones was found to violate the *Agreement on the Application of Sanitary and Phytosanitary Measures.* Where an existing internationally accepted standard permits beef to contain a residue of a certain growth hormone, an EC regulation permitting zero residue is in violation of the agreement. Where no internationally accepted standard exists on the residue of a certain hormone, the EC ban on that hormone is not permitted because it is not based on a risk assessment made using scientifically accepted principles.

Comment. The panel's decision was upheld by the WTO Appellate Body in January 1998. In retaliation, the United States imposed 100 percent duties on a range of European products valued at $116 million per year. In 2004, the EU returned to WTO dispute settlement, arguing that the United States should have removed its retaliatory tariffs since the EC has removed the measures found to be WTO-inconsistent in the first *Hormones* case. As of mid-2007, no decision had yet been reached in that case.

Trade in Textiles and Clothing

Textiles and clothing comprise an important part of total world trade, amounting to over $479 billion in 2005, or 4.7 percent of world exports of total merchandise, according to the WTO. The textile and apparel industries are among the most import-sensitive sectors of the world economy. They are labor intensive, allowing developing countries quickly to become major competitors in world markets. For example, Pakistan's export economy is extremely dependent on textiles, which comprised 44 percent of its total merchandise exports in 2005. China is the world's largest textile and clothing producer, and the United States is the world's largest importer, importing over 10 percent of the world's textile exports and 27 percent of the world's clothing exports in 2005. In 2005, the United States had a trade deficit in textiles of over $80 billion, to the chagrin of U.S. textile workers and politicians in textile-producing states.

History of Textile Import Regulation and Deregulation

Prior to 1995, the textile trade remained outside of the GATT system, allowing strict regulation of textile imports by textile-consuming nations such as the United States. The process of "managing" trade in textiles and apparel began in the early 1960s, when the developed countries were flooded with textile imports from low-wage developing countries such as China, India, Turkey, the Philippines, Egypt, Pakistan, Hong Kong, Indonesia, Korea, Taiwan, and Mexico. Today, countries in Eastern Europe, such as the Czech Republic and Bulgaria, have joined in the export of textile products.

From 1974 through 1994, trade in textiles and textile products was governed by the *Multifiber Arrangement of 1974* (MFA), an international agreement between textile-importing countries and more than forty textile-producing nations. The purpose of the MFA was to promote exports from developing countries, while avoiding market disruption in developed importing countries. The MFA created a system of bilateral agreements between importing and producing countries. It set quotas on a country-by-country basis for each product category (e.g., silk blouses from India, cotton sweaters from Pakistan, down-filled comforters from China). A complex licensing system was established to track shipments and monitor quotas. In the United States, textile negotiations were, and still are, conducted by the *Committee for the Implementation of Textile Agreements* (CITA), an interagency group made up of members from five departments of government.

From 1995 through 2004, trade in textiles and clothing was regulated by the *WTO Agreement on Textiles and Clothing*. This agreement was intended to be a 10-year interim solution giving textile producers in the major textile-consuming nations time to readjust, with minimum economic disruption, and to prepare for global trade in textiles without protection. It required textile-consuming nations to gradually reduce tariffs and other barriers to textile imports. As planned, the agreement came to an end at the beginning of 2005. Since that date, all trade in textiles and clothing between WTO member countries has been governed by the same general rules that apply to trade in goods and general merchandise under the GATT/WTO rules.

Today, trade in textiles and clothing is covered by the basic GATT principles of MFN trade and nondiscrimination. Quotas on textiles have been abolished for trade between WTO countries. A U.S.–China agreement will permit the United States to continue imposing limited special quotas, or "safeguards," on Chinese textiles and clothing through the end of 2008 to further ease the economic shock to the U.S. textile industry.

Although the strict quota systems are gone, textiles are still subject to the WTO "escape clause" on safeguards and unfair trade, a topic covered in Chapter Eleven. As with other goods, an importing country may still impose temporary safeguards consisting of higher tariffs if increased textile imports cause serious injury to a domestic industry making like products.

As expected, textile imports surged almost immediately after the quotas were removed in 2005, and on the request of American textile producers, some safeguard tariffs were imposed on many items of clothing. The politics of regulating textile imports in the United States continues to pit producers, who favor import restraints, against large textile and clothing retailers, who wish to provide cheaper textiles to consumers. Each group is trying to make their case to the U.S. administration.

Trade in textiles and clothing is also governed in the United States by trade agreements and U.S. laws granting special treatment for textile products imported from Africa, the Caribbean, Vietnam, and a few other countries. Readers interested in the textile trade or the status of textile safeguard actions should see the Web site for the Office of Textiles and Apparel of the U.S. International Trade Administration, Department of Commerce.

Other WTO Trade Agreements

Two other agreements that will have an effect on world trade are the *WTO Agreement on Trade-Related Investment Measures* and the *WTO Agreement on Trade-Related Aspects of Intellectual Property Rights*. These issues are mentioned only briefly here because they are discussed more fully in Part Four of this book.

Trade-Related Investment Measures

There is no question today that trade and foreign direct investment are interrelated. To be competitive in a global market, firms must do more than just produce in one country and sell in another. They must be able to supply services or conduct procurement, manufacturing, assembly, and distribution operations on a global scale. This requires the freedom to build foreign factories, open new foreign subsidiaries, or merge with foreign firms. The link between investment and trade becomes even more obvious when looking at the volume of trade between related companies. According to UNCTAD's *World Investment Report 2007,* there are about 77,000 multinational corporations and about 770,000 foreign affiliated companies worldwide. Intracompany trade—trade between foreign affiliated companies or between subsidiaries and their parent companies—accounts for over one-third of world trade. Government controls that hamper the freedom of firms to make these investment decisions will have an adverse effect on trade in goods and services, especially between these multinational affiliates.

The 1994 *Uruguay Round* agreements resulted in the *WTO Agreement on Trade-Related Investment Measures* (commonly called *TRIMS*). The agreement does not set broad rules for local investing, such as rules affecting domestic stock exchanges. It does attempt to reduce restrictions on foreign investment that might restrict cross-border trade in goods and services. It also eliminates discrimination against foreign firms and their goods and services to the extent that those restrictions distort or restrict trade. For example, TRIMS prohibits *trade balancing requirements*—laws that condition a company's right to import foreign goods on the basis of the volume of goods that company exports. TRIMS also prohibits *local content requirements*—regulations that dictate that a foreign company or other producer must use a certain minimum percentage of locally made parts or components in the manufacture of a product. For instance, Argentina may not say to a U.S. multinational corporation,"We will finance the construction of a new automobile factory for you, but only if you guarantee us that 25 percent of the component parts used in assembling cars are made in this country," or "You may only import foreign raw materials on the condition that you export an equal volume of finished goods from our country." These requirements would violate the prohibition of quantitative restrictions of GATT Article XI. Also prohibited are laws that condition the receipt of foreign exchange on the company's foreign exchange revenues. Thus, Argentina may not demand, "Our central bank will only permit you to transfer U.S. dollars out of the country if you have brought into the country an equivalent amount this year in dollars, yen, or other hard currency."

Trade-Related Aspects of Intellectual Property Rights

Intellectual property rights (IPRs) include copyrights, trademarks, and patents. The economic value of an IPR lies in the right of its owner to be the sole user of the IPR or to license its use to someone else; therefore, an IPR only has worth if the owner can prevent its unauthorized use. Because IPRs are not "goods," they did not fall within the bounds of the 1947 GATT agreement. However, IPRs are often attached to, and used to sell, goods. Thus, if IPRs are not protected from unauthorized use, trade in goods and services will suffer as a result. For this reason, the *Uruguay Round* negotiations focused on IPRs and resulted in the *WTO Agreement on Trade-Related Aspects of Intellectual Property Rights*, or TRIPS.

TRIPS sets new, comprehensive standards for the protection of IPRs in all member countries of the WTO. It requires every WTO country to abide by the most important international intellectual property conventions and then calls on countries to grant even greater protection to inventors, authors, and trademark owners. The agreement requires that all domestic and foreign IPR owners, regardless of their citizenship, be treated the same under a country's IPR laws. It prohibits countries from imposing requirements on foreign firms in exchange for being granted a trademark, patent, or copyright. For instance, a WTO country will not be able to condition the award of a patent on the inventor's promise to manufacture the item in that country. Countries must publish all laws, regulations, and administrative rulings that pertain to the availability, application, protection, or enforcement of IPRs. Enforcement efforts will be strengthened worldwide to reduce the billions of dollars, worth of losses every year due to counterfeit and pirated goods (e.g., fake Rolex watches or unauthorized copies of Microsoft software). WTO member countries will bring their IPR laws into compliance with TRIPS, as the United States has already done. For example, in 1995 the United States increased the patent period from 17 years to 20 years to comply with TRIPS' longer period. The TRIPS Council of the WTO monitors compliance with TRIPS. Since the end of 2000, disputes have been settled by the WTO Dispute Settlement Body.

Information Technology Agreement

Seventy nations have signed the 1996 *WTO International Technology Agreement*. The agreement includes the United States, Canada, the EU, Japan, Hong Kong, Singapore, India, China, and other countries that account for virtually all world trade in information technology products. The agreement called for the elimination of tariffs on computers, semiconductors, telecommunications equipment, software, scientific instruments, and other information technology products and component parts by 2005. In 2005, world exports of IT products exceeded $1.4 trillion.

Trade Sanctions and U.S. *Section 301:* The Threat of Retaliation

One of the most important legal weapons in the U.S. arsenal against foreign trade barriers and unfair trade practices is commonly known to businesspeople and lawyers alike as *Section 301*. *Section 301 of the U.S. Trade Act of 1974* has been amended by Congress several times and is still in effect today. The law permits the United States Trade Representative (USTR) to take retaliatory trade action against other countries whose trade policies toward the United States are unjustifiable, unreasonable, or discriminatory and that burden or restrict U.S. commerce.

The purpose of the law is to discourage foreign countries from violating their trade agreements with the United States. If they do, or if they unreasonably restrict access of U.S. goods or services to their markets, they face losing access to the U.S. market. Retaliation would subject their products to punitive tariffs or other trade restrictions upon entering the United States. Even prior to the GATT agreements of the mid-1990s and the founding of the WTO, *Section 301* had already proven to be a significant threat to foreign countries that had discriminated against U.S. goods and services.

After the creation of the WTO in 1995, the United States, like other member countries, became obligated to seek consultations at the WTO and approval from the WTO Dispute Settlement Body before imposing retaliatory measures. For instance, if the European Community imposes a licensing scheme on imports that unfairly discriminates against products from the United States, the United States must first attempt to resolve the matter by negotiations. If this fails, the United States must invoke WTO dispute settlement procedures, seek WTO authorization for retaliation, and gain approval of the amount of punitive tariffs and the types of European goods to which they will apply.

In the 1990s, the EU argued that *Section 301* violated WTO dispute settlement procedures. In the following case, *WTO Report on United States—Sections 301–310 of the Trade Act of*

United States—Sections 301–310 of the Trade Act of 1974

WT/DS152/R (22 December 1999)

World Trade Organization; Report of the Panel

BACKGROUND AND FACTS

The European Communities requested a WTO panel to decide whether U.S. Sections 301–310 [the Act] violated GATT dispute settlement procedures. The Act permits the USTR to investigate possible violations of GATT or other international trade agreements, to negotiate a settlement of the dispute, and to request a WTO dispute settlement panel if necessary. The Act also permits the USTR to impose retaliatory tariffs or other trade sanctions either unilaterally or if authorized by the WTO Dispute Settlement Body. The EC argued that the Act violated WTO rules.

REPORT OF THE PANEL

The European Communities argues that [WTO rules] prohibit unilateralism in the ... dispute settlement procedures. Members must await the adoption of a panel or Appellate Body report by the Dispute Settlement Body, or the rendering of an arbitration decision ... before determining whether rights or benefits accruing to them under a WTO agreement are being denied....

The European Communities ... took the position in the Uruguay Round that a strengthened dispute settlement system must include an explicit ban on any government taking unilateral action to redress what that government judges to be the trade wrongs of others.

The United States argues that nothing in Sections 301–310 requires the US government to act in violation of its WTO obligations. To the contrary, the Act requires the USTR to undertake WTO dispute settlement proceedings when a WTO agreement is involved, and provides that the USTR will rely on the results of those proceedings when determining whether US agreement rights have been denied. Likewise, [the Act] explicitly indicates that the USTR need not take action when the DSB has adopted a report finding no denial of US WTO rights.

Under well-established GATT and WTO jurisprudence and practice which the European Communities appears to accept, a law may be found inconsistent with a Member's WTO obligations only if it precludes a Member from acting consistently with those obligations. The European Communities must therefore demonstrate that Sections 301–310 do not permit the United States government to take action consistent with U.S. WTO obligations—that this legislation in fact mandates WTO-inconsistent action. The European Communities has failed to meet this burden. Its analysis of the language of Sections 301–310 ignores pertinent statutory language and relies on constructions not permitted under U.S. law. Sections 301–310 of the Trade Act of 1974 are fully consistent with U.S. WTO rights and obligations.

* * *

Decision. Sections 301–310 of the *U.S. Trade Act of 1974* were found to be valid under the GATT 1994 agreements. The panel clarified that the United States may impose retaliatory trade sanctions against other WTO members only where the United States strictly followed WTO dispute settlement rules and when authorized by the Dispute Settlement Body.

1974 (1999), a dispute settlement panel held that *Section 301* does not violate U.S. obligations under GATT if it is applied in accordance with WTO dispute settlement provisions.

Section 301 contains several different provisions, including: (1) *Basic Section 301,* (2) *Special 301,* and (3) *Telecommunications 301,* discussed in the following sections. We will also mention a controversial law that was in force from 1988 through 2001, the now repealed *Super 301.*

Basic Section 301

Basic Section 301 sets two different standards for retaliation against different types of foreign trade barriers. The first defines when retaliatory action by the USTR is *discretionary.* The second defines when it is *mandatory.* Discretionary retaliatory action may be taken at the option of the USTR, under the direction of the president, against any foreign country whose policies or actions are found by the USTR to be unreasonable or discriminatory and burden or restrict U.S. commerce. A foreign country acts unreasonably if its policies toward U.S. firms are unfair and inequitable, even if they are not in violation of any international agreement. This includes the unfair restriction of foreign investment, denial of equal access to their markets, failure to protect U.S. intellectual property rights, or the subsidization of a domestic industry. In this case, the USTR determines whether any action is necessary, and if so, what action to take. The USTR also has the discretion to take retaliatory action when a foreign government (1) fails to allow workers the right to organize and bargain collectively; (2) permits forced labor; (3) does not provide a minimum age for the employment of children; or (4) fails to provide standards for minimum wage, hours of work, and the health and safety of workers. This gives the USTR sufficient discretionary authority and flexibility to attack a wide variety of foreign unfair trade practices.

Mandatory retaliatory action is proper if the USTR determines that (1) a foreign country has denied the United States its rights under any trade agreement or (2) a foreign country's actions or policies are *unjustifiable and burden or restrict* U.S. commerce. An act, policy, or practice is unjustifiable if it is in violation of the international legal rights of the United States. Examples of unjustifiable acts or policies include tariffs above the agreed rate, quotas, denial of MFN treatment, illegal import procedures, overly burdensome restrictions on U.S. foreign investment, and IPR violations. In a case of a violation of GATT, the "burden" to U.S. commerce is presumed. Mandatory action is waived if a WTO panel has upheld the foreign government action, if the foreign country has agreed to eliminate the illegal policy, if the USTR believes that a negotiated solution is imminent, or, in extraordinary cases, if the USTR believes that the adverse effects of retaliation on the U.S. economy would exceed the benefits.

SECTION 301 PROCEDURES. A *Section 301* action begins with the filing of a petition by an interested party, such as a U.S. company, or on the initiative of the USTR. The petition asks the USTR to conduct an investigation of the foreign unfair trade practice. The USTR has 45 days in which to decide whether to conduct the investigation. Petitions for investigation are usually granted only when an entire U.S. industry is affected. An opportunity must be provided for interested parties to submit their views in writing, and a hearing must be provided if requested. All petitions and decisions to investigate are published in the *Federal Register*.

Once an investigation is begun, the USTR must also begin negotiations with the foreign government involved. If the petition claims that the foreign government has violated GATT and the dispute is not resolved within 150 days or within the time required in the agreement, then the USTR must invoke the formal WTO dispute settlement procedures. The USTR must complete its investigation and determine whether to impose sanctions within 18 months of having initiated the investigation or within 30 days after the conclusion of WTO dispute procedures, whichever occurs first. When sanctions are authorized by the WTO, *Section 301* is used to carry them out under U.S. law.

SANCTIONS AND RETALIATORY MEASURES. Trade sanctions are imposed for the purpose of ending an illegal foreign practice, not to compensate the petitioning U.S. firm. No benefits accrue directly to the petitioning firm other than those that affect all U.S. companies or industries in a similar position. The most common form of retaliation is the assessment of additional import duties on products from the offending nation in an amount that is equivalent in value to the burden imposed by that country on U.S. firms. The products affected are said to be placed on the USTR's "retaliation list" or "hit list." The USTR may impose sanctions against any type of goods or any industry. If a country puts quotas on U.S. food products, the United States can retaliate against imports of any type, such as electronic parts. For instance, when the United States threatened trade sanctions against Japan for unfairly keeping out U.S. auto parts, the USTR proposed 100 percent import duties on imports of Japanese luxury automobiles. When China refused to protect U.S. copyrights, the United States threatened to impose over $1 billion a year in trade sanctions on all Chinese imports. When the EU refused to comply with a WTO panel decision and lift its ban on U.S. beef containing growth hormones in 1999, the United States imposed 100 percent duties on $117 million in European imports.

The *Trade and Development Act of 2000: The Carousel Law*

Section 407 of the *U.S. Trade and Development Act of 2000* amends *Section 301* by requiring the USTR to periodically review the list of products subject to retaliatory tariffs and to revise them 120 days after their initial effective date and every 180 days thereafter. This has become commonly known as the "*Carousel law,*" referring to the periodic rotation of products on and off the retaliation list. The law was enacted in response to the EU's refusal to comply with WTO rulings to end their restrictions on imports of bananas and on imports of beef from cattle fed growth hormones. The U.S. Congress felt that this law would hasten Europe's compliance with the WTO rulings in those cases. The purpose of regularly changing the list of products subject to retaliatory tariffs every 180 days, instead of simply continuing the tariffs on one group of products, is to "spread the pain" across more companies in the offending country, causing them to put greater political pressure on their governments to conform to WTO requirements. It also eliminates the likelihood that a targeted country could subsidize products kept on the retaliatory list for long periods. The EU has criticized the Carousel law as violating WTO rules. American importers are opposed to the Carousel law because of the uncertainty as to whether their products will unexpectedly end up on the retaliatory list and be subjected to punitive tariffs. For example, in *Gilda Industries, Inc. v. United States,* 446 F.3d 1271 (Fed. Cir. 2006), the Court of Appeals considered the case of an importer of toasted bread from Spain whose products unexpectedly turned up on a retaliation list of products subject to a 100 percent tariff imposed on EU products in retaliation for Europe's refusal to allow imports of U.S. beef from cattle fed beef hormones. (The WTO beef hormones case appeared earlier in this chapter.) The court rejected Gilda's argument that the USTR could not place toasted bread on its retaliation list in a dispute over beef. The court also said that it was in the USTR's discretion whether to terminate the list or remove toasted breads from it.

Special 301

Special 301 is used by the United States against countries that fail to protect U.S. intellectual property rights (IPRs). Each year the USTR must identify foreign countries that deny adequate and effective IPR protection. The worst offenders must be designated as *priority foreign countries,* unless they are making progress in strengthening and enforcing their IPR laws. Designation as a *priority foreign country* requires that the USTR begin a *Section 301* investigation. The USTR has 6 months to decide whether to invoke sanctions according to *Basic Section 301.* In addition, the USTR maintains a *watch list and a priority watch list* of countries that deserve to be monitored for their failure to protect IPRs. Countries on the watch lists are monitored, and can be moved to the list of priority foreign countries. From 2001 through 2005, Ukraine was designated a priority foreign country and was subjected to $75 million per year in trade sanctions. In 2007, the USTR examined intellectual property protection in 79 countries. Twelve countries were placed on the priority watch list: Argentina, Chile, China, Egypt, India, Israel, Lebanon, Russia, Thailand, Turkey, Ukraine, and Venezuela. Thirty countries were on the watch list. Paraguay was also being monitored.

Telecommunications 301

Telecommunications 301 is another special statute that calls for an annual review, by March 31 of each year, of foreign barriers to U.S. telecommunications firms. It requires mandatory retaliation against countries that block access to their markets by U.S. telecommunications companies.

Super 301

The so-called *Super 301* law, no longer in effect as of 2007, was the most controversial piece of trade legislation that the United States ever enacted. It was passed in 1988 by a Congress vowing to "get tough" on trade issues. The law was extended through 2001 by executive orders of President Clinton, but allowed to lapse after that time. It required the USTR to identify and report to Congress those *priority trade practices* and priority countries that posed the greatest barriers to U.S. trade in foreign countries. Within 21 days of the report, the USTR was required to initiate investigations. If a priority country did not remove a trade barrier, then retaliation by the USTR was required. In 2007, some members of Congress called for the renewal of this law.

Assessing the Impact of Unilateral Action. Many experts believe that *Section 301, Special 301,* and *Super 301* have been successful in getting other countries to open their markets to U.S. goods and services. A look at the reports of the USTR and its announcements in the *Federal Register* reveal many cases in which *Section 301* has resulted in increased market access. In the early 1990s, *Section 301* was helpful in getting Japan to reduce its restrictions on the import of citrus products, glass, wood products, medical technology, supercomputers, and satellites. Korea, China, Brazil, Poland, Saudi Arabia, Thailand, and countries in every region of the globe agreed to provide greater protection to IPRs; Taiwan reduced import barriers on foreign tobacco, beer, and wine; Brazil improved market access for the U.S. software industry; and Canada agreed to change its marketing restrictions on the sale of U.S. beer.

Market access has been improved in dozens of countries around the world. Yet the use of trade sanctions in these cases is actually rare. In virtually all cases, trade disputes have been resolved through negotiation or panel decisions. The very existence of the law has provided the USTR with the "negotiating leverage" needed to resolve a dispute and avoid a trade war. The threat of action has prompted other nations to open markets for U.S. products and to protect U.S. IPRs. Many problem areas remain, however. The USTR cites Japanese restrictions inherent in their distribution system that discriminate against foreign suppliers, Japanese standards that discriminate against U.S.–designed products, and Japanese government procurement practices. In terms of product areas, Japan is still criticized by the USTR for unfair treatment of U.S. auto parts, fish, and steel. Europe is criticized for quotas on U.S. television programming, and intellectual property violations continue worldwide. Long-running disputes over Korean restrictions on imports of U.S. products continue.

The use of *Section 301* sanctions against the EU in retaliation for its failure to comply with the WTO ruling on beef hormones subjected European goods to hundreds of millions of dollars in punitive tariffs over many years, at a tremendous cost to American consumers. Yet the tariffs seemed unable to end the long-standing trade dispute. Today it seems certain that *Section 301* will continue to be used in trade disputes and that it will aid in the enforcement of WTO dispute panel decisions.

Conclusion

This chapter discussed the "market access" provisions of international trade law. The laws and cases that you studied represent a worldwide effort, under the auspices of the World Trade Organization, to move from economic protectionism to freer and fairer trade. It is not within the scope of this book to advance the economic and political reasons why a nation might adopt protectionist trade policies versus free trade policies. While it does seem that free trade attitudes are generally supported by most modern economists and by free-thinking politicians, lawmakers, and government leaders, protectionist habits are difficult to break. Nations accustomed to protecting domestic industries from outside competition—in some cases dating to the Smoot-Hawley period of the 1930s—are often politically encumbered by the status quo and by the need to be responsive to the demands of local firms, labor groups, or unemployed workers. Moreover, some countries such as China, Russia, and its former Eastern European allies still retain trade barriers that are remnants of their past, when they were isolated from the world for many decades by their communist governments. Similarly, some Latin American countries that had once been governed according to socialist or Marxist principles still find it difficult to open market access in key industry sectors to competition from firms from the developed countries of the northern hemisphere. Nevertheless, it is probably safe to say that the general trend internationally has been away from protectionism and toward greater open market access for foreign firms.

The United States has generally taken a pro–free trade stance ever since the 1930s. This is despite quite a bit of protectionist talk from lawmakers representing old-industry and organized labor states and from some candidates for public office, a few news commentators, and some think tanks and economists. Every U.S. president has had to balance free trade with domestic political pressure to protect industries at home. However, as U.S. firms became more dependent on export sales, they also became more vulnerable to foreign trade barriers that denied them access to export markets. For this reason, almost all Americans agree with the need to remove foreign trade barriers to the sale of U.S. goods and services abroad. This requires reciprocity—a give and take—with America's trading partners so that all will follow the rules of international trade law for the improvement of the business environment around the world.

Chapter Summary

1. The *Uruguay Round* trade negotiations resulted in many important trade agreements designed to remove trade barriers and improve access to foreign markets, including agreements on technical barriers, import licensing, government procurement, trade in services, agriculture, and textiles.
2. The *WTO Agreement on Technical Barriers to Trade* does not set standards of its own for product performance, design, safety, or efficiency, but it guides nations in the application of their own regulations and standards through legal principles of nondiscrimination, transparency, and MFN trade. The agreement applies broadly to regulations imposed to protect the public health, safety, and welfare, including consumer and environmental protection. Health and safety regulations may not be used unless they are "trade neutral" and restrict trade no more than necessary, according to the principle of least restrictive trade.
3. Governments are some of the largest consumers of goods and services in the world. *The WTO Agreement on Government Procurement* requires that countries "free up" their procurement policies and practices by giving foreign firms equal access to bidding on government contracts and by providing transparent and easily obtained rules for submitting bids.
4. About 20 percent of world trade is in services. The *General Agreement on Trade in Services* (1995) applied basic GATT principles to service industries for the first time since 1947. This agreement has already opened access to foreign markets in construction, engineering, health care, banking, insurance, securities, transportation, and the professions.
5. Trade in agriculture has been distorted by billions of dollars' worth of government subsidies granted to farming interests worldwide that artificially lower the cost of agricultural exports. In turn, importing nations artificially raise the price of agricultural imports with trade restrictions and tariffs. Attempts to limit government support of agriculture have been met by attacks from politically powerful farm groups, particularly in France and other European countries. Negotiations during the Doha Rounds of trade negotiations focus on making agricultural trade freer and fairer.
6. Exports of farm products have suffered because of discriminatory trade barriers imposed under the guise of health standards. Under the *WTO Agreement on Sanitary and Phytosanitary Measures*, countries cannot impose restrictions to protect animal and plant life from pests or contagious diseases unless those restrictions are applied fairly and equally to goods from all countries that present a risk of infection. Restrictions must be supported by scientific evidence and be as unrestrictive of trade as possible. These issues are critical to all humankind, as we face potential scourges like mad cow disease and hoof-and-mouth disease.
7. Textiles are one of the most import-sensitive industries of all. Many jobs in developed countries have been lost to low-wage jobs in textile-producing developing countries. Since 2005, trade in textiles has been governed by ordinary GATT/WTO rules for trade in goods.
8. The *U.S. Trade Act of 1974* (Sections 301–310) provides the United States Trade Representative, under the direction of the president, with the tools needed to retaliate

against foreign government trade barriers that breach trade agreements with the United States or that deny fair and equal access of U.S. goods and services to foreign markets. The United States is committed to only using *Section 301* retaliation after it has unsuccessfully resorted to the dispute settlement process at the WTO.

Questions and Case Problems

1. In 2001, an outbreak of hoof-and-mouth disease threatened the meat supply of Europe. This virus is spread through the air or by contact. To control its spread, millions of cattle, sheep, and pigs were slaughtered and burned; export and transportation of British livestock, meat, and dairy products were halted; and many areas of Great Britain were placed off limits to travelers. Certain areas of the country were quarantined, with "Keep Out" notices posted on the roads. Officials sprayed chemicals to kill the virus on the soles of shoes and automobile tires. The virus quickly spread to continental Europe, and even the United States banned the import of meat from Europe. Explain the application of the *WTO Agreement on Sanitary and Phytosanitary Measures* to this issue. Does the agreement tell countries specifically what actions to take? What action does the agreement permit nations to take to fight a disease like this? Do you think that the agreement gave sufficient latitude to countries to fight the disease? For additional information, see the Web site for the World Organization for Animal Health, a Paris-based government organization comprising 157 nations.
2. Immediately after India was targeted under *Super 301* for restricting market access by U.S. firms, it began a public relations campaign against the United States. Its representatives stated that India would not negotiate "at the point of a gun." Evaluate this statement. Do you agree that unilateral retaliation by the United States has been the best way to improve access to foreign markets and to protect U.S. IPRs?
3. What are the real economic impacts and long-term effects of trade sanctions? Assume that the United States imposes punishingly high tariffs of 100 percent on Japanese cars. Immediate costs might be borne by the Japanese manufacturers, U.S. dealerships, or consumers, but what does such a measure do to the long-term health and competitiveness of the U.S. car industry? Could you see any impact on the U.S. lead in innovation, design, and quality? Discuss.
4. Research the term *managed trade*. Do you agree or disagree that trade can be "managed"? Give examples from the text, and from your reading, of how governments manage trade. Can you cite successful or unsuccessful cases? What is the position of recent U.S. administrations in regard to "managing" trade?
5. Imports of Japanese automobiles in the United States have been a major contributor to the annual U.S. trade deficit. U.S. automobiles and auto parts have not sold very well in Japan either. Access to the Japanese market by U.S. manufacturers has been a key U.S–Japan trade issue for the past several decades. Members of the U.S. auto industry maintain that the Japanese government has not done enough to reduce tariff barriers and to encourage the import of U.S. goods. They further argue that Japan is manipulating the value of its currency to keep it at artificially low levels, making U.S. imports in Japan unfairly expensive. They also argue that Japan's *keiretsu* system of business relationships has resulted in a highly integrated vertical distribution system. *Keiretsu* is the Japanese practice of having interlocking directorships, joint ownership, and other linkages between Japanese companies. *Keiretsu* companies share corporate directors and develop long-term contractual relationships that favor other *keiretsu* members, thus keeping U.S. firms from many business opportunities. The Japanese government has responded by saying that U.S. cars are simply not in demand by Japanese consumers. In a major "trade war" of the mid-1990s, the United States threatened to place 100 percent import duties on Japanese luxury car imports. A 1995 agreement resulted in Japan agreeing to some voluntary goals for U.S. auto imports. In the end, U.S. public opinion saw the Clinton administration as being "tough on Japan." On the other hand, the opinion of many commentators and of the world trade community was that the Japanese commitment was an empty promise. The United States was criticized for resorting to threats and intimidation.

   What have been the key issues affecting trade between the United States and Japan, particularly trade in automobiles and auto parts? How has their relationship been affected by political considerations? What has happened since 1995? Has the U.S. trade deficit in the automobile trade increased or decreased since then? Have there been any further agreements between the United States and Japan over automobiles? What are the current arguments of the U.S. industry against Japan regarding market access for automobiles? Do you think that the United States has been guilty of "Japan-bashing" in the automotive trade? Where would you find information on the current position of the Japanese government on this issue? Where would you find information on the U.S. auto industry's position?

6. At the request of the Canadian owner of a country music channel, Canada removed a Nashville-based country music channel from the air. This effort is only one in a series made by Canada to restrict U.S. programming. Canadians argue that their country is dominated by U.S. culture on television and want it restricted. The U.S. firm petitions the USTR to impose trade sanctions unless the Canadian policy is changed. After an investigation, the USTR threatens the Canadian government with $500 million in punitive tariffs. Discuss whether the USTR should have threatened sanctions before the case is heard by the WTO. See *Initiation of Section 302 Investigation Concerning Certain Discriminatory Communications Practices,* 60 FR 8101 (February 10, 1995).
7. The marketing and sale of beer and alcoholic beverages in Canada are governed by Canadian provincial marketing agencies or "liquor boards." In most of the ten Canadian provinces, these liquor boards not only regulate the marketing of domestic beer in the province, but serve as import monopolies. They also warehouse, distribute, and retail imported beer. Canada imposed restrictions on the number of locations at which imported beer could be sold; authorization from the liquor board was needed to sell a brand of beer in the province; and higher markups were required on the price of foreign beer than on domestic beer sold by the liquor boards. Do the regulations violate the nondiscrimination provisions of GATT? May Canada use state trading monopolies to regulate imports of this kind? Are Canada's provisions valid public health regulations or illegal discrimination? If trade statistics showed that foreign beer sales have actually increased, could an exporting country's rights under GATT still be subject to "nullification and impairment"? Would *Section 301* apply to this case? See 56 FR 60128 (1991). See also *GATT Dispute Settlement Panel Report: Canada Import, Distribution and Sale of Alcoholic Drinks By Canadian Provincial Marketing Agencies* (1988).
8. Each year the United States Trade Representative publishes an annual report to Congress entitled the *National Trade Estimate Report on Foreign Trade Barriers.* In 2007, the report covered the largest export markets for U.S. goods and services, including 58 nations, the European Union, Taiwan, and Hong Kong. Find the report, and select several countries of interest. What is the USTR's position with regard to trade barriers in those countries?

MANAGERIAL IMPLICATIONS

I. Your company is a U.S. multinational corporation with a 40 percent share of the world market for its product. Over the past decade, management has invested more than $100 million dollars trying to get its products into Japanese stores. Despite all of its efforts, the company still has less than a 10 percent share of the Japanese market, and only 15 percent of Japanese stores carry its products. Company investigations show that its major Japanese competitor has a virtual monopoly there and has violated Japanese antitrust laws by fixing prices and refusing to sell to any store that carries your firm's products. Most distributors and retailers are linked to your competitor through *keiretsu* relationships. Management believes that by having the Japanese market all to itself, the competitor is able to maintain sufficiently high prices in Japan to permit them to undersell your company in the United States. Apparently, the Japanese government simply "looks the other way." Moreover, your firm has been effectively restrained by the bureaucracy that administers government procurement contracts in Japan. As a result, management estimates that it has lost several billion dollars in exports since the company first entered the Japanese market. Your competitor responds that it is not the only producer in Japan, that the market there is very competitive, and besides, it also outsells your firm's products in several other Asian countries.

   1. If you petition for a *Section 301* action, do you think the USTR will begin an investigation? What political factors in the United States might

affect the USTR's decision to investigate? What is the attitude of the current U.S. administration toward the use of *Section 301*?

2. Management thinks that the Japanese government should require distributors to agree to import a given quantity of U.S.–made products in a year's period. How would the Japanese government mandate this? Do you think the Japanese distribution system or its *keiretsu* practices can be reformed? What other remedies or sanctions might be appropriate in this case? What is the likelihood that the threat of sanctions by the United States will affect the Japanese position? Given the history of U.S.–Japanese trade relations and the authority of the WTO, what do you think is the likely outcome of this case? Based on your study of the last two chapters, what provisions of the GATT agreement, if any, might apply to this case?
3. Are the market share statistics relevant to your case? What other data or information will be important?

II. The Asian country of Tamoa imports large quantities of down pillows each year. DownPillow, a U.S. company, would like to do more business there, but it has a problem. Tamoa has a number of regulations affecting the importation and sale of down bedding. Consider the following five regulations:

1. Pillows made from down harvested from Tamoan flocks may be labeled as "goose down" even though they contain up to 25 percent duck down. (Down is taken from both geese and ducks, but duck down is considered inferior.) If the pillow is made from foreign down, then a pillow labeled "goose down" may contain no more than 5 percent duck down. U.S. regulations recognize that geese and ducks often get plucked together and therefore permit goose down to contain up to 10 percent duck down. DownPillow believes the 10 percent tolerance is reasonable, but given farming methods in most countries it is not possible to sort out the geese and the ducks any better than that. Tamoa believes that the stricter standard for imported pillows is justified to protect Tamoan consumers from fraud, and because Tamoan farmers do not raise any ducks, the 25 percent domestic standard is irrelevant anyway.
2. Tamoa also requires that the cotton coverings of all pillows be certified to meet certain ecology and human health standards for textiles: they may not contain any harmful chemicals such as formaldehyde or chlorine, and they must be tested according to minimum standards set by the International Organization for Standardization. Certifications are accepted from qualified testing laboratories in any country. U.S. regulations do not require certification.
3. All pillow imports must be inspected on arrival in Tamoa. No inspections are permitted at the foreign factory. Tamoa has only one full-time inspector, who must remove down from at least three pillows from every shipment and subject it to laboratory analysis. Given the current backlog, inspections and analysis are taking up to 4 weeks, during which time the pillows are often damaged by Tamoa's high humidity.
4. Tamoan regulations also require that DownPillow's plant be inspected and that the sterilization process be approved by Tamoan officials. In the United States the down is washed, sanitized, and subjected to hot air heat several hundred degrees in temperature, all under health department supervision. The Tamoan ministry of agriculture refuses to accept the sterilization permits, inspections, and approvals from state health departments in the United States. Tamoa does not pay the overseas travel expenses of its inspectors.
5. Tamoan regulations prohibit pillows and comforters from being compressed or vacuum packed for shipment to ensure the down will not be damaged in shipment. DownPillow ships smaller orders by air freight and larger orders by ocean container.

DownPillow and other U.S. firms are not pleased with these requirements. Evaluate the legality of the regulations and their impact on DownPillow. What course of action should DownPillow take?

Ethical Considerations

Many proponents of environmental safety and public health are concerned about the creation, spread, and potential impact of *genetically modified foods*. The United States, along with Canada and Argentina, is one of the leading producers of genetically modified foods made from bioengineered organisms (GMOs). The U.S. government believes that GMOs are important for the world's food supply because they can boost food production and nutrition and lead to both disease-resistant crops and better-tasting foods. Many respected scientific studies vouch for the safety of GMOs for human and animal consumption and on the earth's environment.

GMOs are important to U.S. agriculture economically. According to the U.S. Department of Agriculture, approximately three-quarters of U.S. soybean and cotton production and over one-third of corn production are genetically modified. However, many consumer groups and countries argue that the dangers to humans, wildlife, and the environment are unknown. Genetically modified corn and soy were approved for sale in the EU prior to 1998, but the European countries ceased new approvals after that time. In addition, the EU and several other countries have adopted regulations requiring the tracing of biotech crops through the chain of distribution, and they imposed strict labeling requirements on all foods and animal feed containing more than 1 percent GMO. European consumers who fear GMO foods will not purchase products with these labels. The United States claims that the requirements are expensive and unnecessary and have cost U.S. farm exporters hundreds of millions of dollars in lost revenues. In 2003, the United States requested a WTO panel to decide whether the moratorium and labeling requirements violate the *WTO Sanitary and Phytosanitary Agreement*. Research the history of the WTO's deliberations. What was the outcome? Can you find any decisions of the European Court of Justice on GMOs? What is the current state of EU legislation on GMOs? What is your opinion? Do you think that GMOs should be permitted, or do you think they present some possible harm to the environment or to public health?

FOR INTERNET ACTIVITIES, VISIT ACADEMIC.CENGAGE.COM/BLAW/SCHAFFER.

CHAPTER 11

REGULATING IMPORT COMPETITION AND UNFAIR TRADE

The last two chapters examined the basic principles of world trade law found in the *General Agreement on Tariffs and Trade,* and in the dispute resolution cases of the World Trade Organization (WTO). The key principles dealt with nondiscrimination, MFN trade, national treatment, and the elimination of quotas and non-tariff barriers. A knowledge of this material is essential here because these concepts are carried throughout this chapter as well as the remainder of the book. Chapter Ten also described how the WTO has become the primary international body for liberalizing trade and how the WTO's dispute-settlement procedures work. Chapter Ten looked at specific GATT agreements related to opening access to foreign markets, particularly those agreements reached in 1994 as a part of the *Uruguay Round* of global trade negotiations. It also examined trade regulation in different sectors, such as agriculture services and textiles.

This chapter covers two main areas: The first is the regulation of import competition through laws that safeguard domestic industries. These laws protect industries that say, "We're doing the best we can to compete, but foreign competitors seem more efficient and more productive. They're shipping ever-greater quantities of products here, and we need time to adjust—to retool our plants and retrain our workers to become more competitive again. Just give us some time!"

The second area covers the regulation of "unfair trade," more specifically, the two most common unfair trade practices of dumping and government subsidies. Here, domestic industries might say, "Foreign firms compete unfairly. They dump their goods in our market at ridiculously low prices. They absorb the losses until they drive us all out of business so they'll have the whole U.S. market to themselves!" Alternatively, "How can we expect to sell our products here at home when we can't match the price of imports? Our overseas competitors are subsidized; they're paid by their own government, with their taxpayers' money, to build products and ship them here. We've got to stop this!"

THE DOUBLE-EDGED SWORD OF IMPORT REGULATION

Trade wars are often depicted in nationalistic terms as an us-against-them problem. Pictures of unemployed factory workers fill the television screens. Politicians call for greater protectionist measures. Of course, these familiar stories have two sides: U.S. autoworkers and manufacturers scream for the president to put high tariffs on imported cars and trucks. Yet the Japanese government claims that the Japanese manufacturers are only producing cars that Americans want. The few remaining U.S. manufacturers of display screens for portable computers call for protection against an onslaught of imports. Yet U.S. computer manufacturers who use the screens threaten to close shop in the United States and move overseas if more duties are placed on the imported screens. U.S. steelmakers want higher tariffs to protect them against imports of cheap imported steel, while U.S. manufacturers of large appliances that use that steel say they cannot pass the higher prices on to U.S. customers. U.S. manufacturers of high-tech products, who are dependent on export markets, fear that if the U.S. government imposes higher tariffs on imports, other countries will retaliate by doing the same to their products. Examples such as these come from every agricultural, industrial, and service sector of the world's economy. Amid the clamor for protection against imports, calls for free trade come from the heads of those firms whose exports might suffer from foreign retaliation and from leaders of consumer groups concerned about the rising price of imported consumer products.

The discussion in this chapter attempts to break through this protectionism-versus-free-trade morass by focusing on how international rules serve as a check on these competing national political interests.

Even purely domestic firms that do not import or export must have an understanding of how governments regulate import competition. Virtually all domestic products compete with products made abroad, and U.S. managers require a knowledge of how U.S. trade policies and trade laws affect their firms' competitive positions. Managers may need to determine whether legal action could forestall a flood of competing imports and on what grounds such a lawsuit could be based. Would an action for relief be brought in the courts or before an administrative agency? Do any government programs exist to provide benefits to workers whose jobs are lost due to import competition? In the United States, many industries have sought protection against foreign competition. Some notable examples include apparel, shoes, gloves, motorcycles, steel, chemicals, foodstuffs, microwave ovens, typewriters, minivans, glass, and automobiles.

Safeguards Against Injury

Economic and political realities often force nations to take temporary corrective action to protect a domestic industry from severe market disruptions and dislocations of the workforce resulting from increased imports. A country takes legal action to protect a domestic industry by granting import relief or adjusting imports, practices commonly known as *safeguards against injury.* Safeguards are generally used to protect a domestic industry from increasing volumes of imported goods (regardless of any wrongdoing or unfair trade practice by a foreign firm or foreign government). These safeguards include temporarily increasing tariffs, imposing quotas, or using some other (lawful) method to restrict or discourage imports. The legal authority for a WTO member nation to safeguard its firms from injury comes from the "escape clause" in the *General Agreement on Tariffs and Trade.*

The GATT Escape Clause

If a nation reduces its tariffs, the result frequently is increased imports and possibly serious market disruption to a domestic industry. *Article XIX of GATT 1947,* known as the *GATT escape clause,* authorizes a country to take temporary corrective action to adjust import levels of a certain product and thus safeguard domestic industry. The escape clause is so named because it temporarily permits a country to "escape" from previous promises (tariff concessions) it may have made to lower tariffs on that product. Article XIX was included in the GATT agreement at the insistence of the United States, which had previously used similar provisions in bilateral treaties. Today, the 1994 *WTO Agreement on Safeguards* establishes additional rules for safeguarding domestic industry and providing import relief.

The WTO 1994 *Agreement on Safeguards*

The *WTO Agreement on Safeguards* provides that a member may apply a temporary safeguard measure (e.g., increase tariffs) to a product only if that product "is being imported in such increased quantities and under such conditions as to cause or threaten to cause serious injury to the domestic industry that produces like or directly competitive products." The term *serious injury* is defined as a "significant overall impairment in the position of a domestic industry." A threat of serious injury must be imminent. The term *domestic industry* means "producers as a whole," as opposed to just one firm within the industry.

In order to apply a safeguard, a country must first undertake an administrative investigation, which includes a public hearing at which importers, exporters, and other interested parties can present evidence and their views of whether the safeguard would be in the public interest. In the United States, investigations are conducted by the International Trade Commission, an independent agency of the federal government. The investigating body is required to evaluate all relevant economic factors bearing on the industry's position, and it must find that the increased imports are the actual cause of the domestic industry's decline. If other factors are shown to be causing injury simultaneously, then the increased imports are not considered to be the cause. Emergency action can be taken without the investigation if clear evidence justifies the safeguards, but any additional tariffs imposed must be lifted within 200 days.

Global Safeguards. Safeguards applicable to WTO member countries are often called *global safeguards*. As the term indicates, the safeguards are imposed on imports of specific products regardless of the country of origin. For example, if increased imports of non-rubber footwear are causing serious injury to a domestic industry, the safeguards must be applied to all imports of non-rubber footwear, regardless of where they are produced. There are also specific safeguards applicable to goods sold within certain free trade areas, such as imports within North America. Most countries also have special safeguards applicable to imports from China.

Limits on the Use of Safeguards. The safeguards agreement places limits on safeguards because they are a temporary remedy to be used only until the problem is resolved. They may not exceed 4 years (with an extension to 8 years). The restrictions on imports must be gradually lifted as conditions warrant. Imposing safeguards on a product can only be done without discrimination, regardless of the product's country of origin, and only as is necessary to prevent or remedy serious injury. WTO Appellate Body reports have ruled that a safeguard "may not be more restrictive than necessary to prevent or remedy a serious injury and to facilitate adjustment." Tariffs are the preferred safeguard. A quota, if used, may not reduce the quantity of imports below the average level of imports of the prior 3 years. Quotas should be allocated among supplying nations based upon their proportion of the total quantity of imports during the preceding years. Governments may not attempt to protect domestic industries by pressuring foreign firms to voluntarily hold back shipments. Although once a popular method of restraining imports, these *voluntary restraint agreements* are no longer permitted under WTO rules. Nations must follow certain limits when imposing safeguards on products from developing countries.

Safeguards can only be applied to imports from developing countries if a particular developing country is supplying more than 3 percent of the total imports of that product.

Trade Compensation. WTO rules from the 1994 GATT agreements encourage a country imposing a safeguard to compensate a supplying nation for the burden the safeguard measure has imposed on it. For instance, if the United States imposes safeguard tariffs on imported bicycles and Taiwan supplies large numbers of bicycles to the United States, then the United States should make *trade compensation* to Taiwan by reducing tariffs on other Taiwanese imports in an equivalent amount. The countries are expected to negotiate trade compensation; if they fail to reach agreement, then the supplying nation may "suspend ... substantially equivalent concessions" or raise tariffs in retaliation.

The WTO Committee on Safeguards. Countries must notify the *WTO Committee on Safeguards* when taking safeguard actions. The Committee reports to the *WTO Council for Trade in Goods*. It monitors compliance with WTO safeguard provisions and assists countries in negotiating trade compensation.

Safeguards against Injury under U.S. Law

The U.S. escape clause is found in *Section 201* of the *Trade Act of 1974* as amended by the *Omnibus Trade and Competitiveness Act of 1988* and the *Uruguay Round Agreements Act*. U.S. law does not follow the guidelines of GATT Article XIX and the *WTO Agreement on Safeguards* completely, but is similar. U.S. law does not refer to the term *safeguards,* but rather to "positive adjustment to import competition" or "import relief."

STANDARD FOR IMPORT RELIEF. Under U.S. law, import relief can be granted when "an article is being imported into the United States in such increased quantities as to be a substantial cause of serious injury or threat thereof to the domestic industry producing an article like or directly competitive with the imported article." The president may make an adjustment to imports (e.g., impose tariffs or quotas) only after an investigation by the U.S. International Trade Commission (ITC) and only if, in the president's discretion, it will "facilitate efforts by the domestic industry to make a positive adjustment to import competition and provide greater economic and social benefits than costs." Because of this discretionary power, a president who adopts free trade or free-market concepts might be reluctant to apply a safeguard remedy at all. Although largely political in nature, a president's decision is usually based on the national interest.

ITC SAFEGUARD INVESTIGATIONS. A petition for relief may be filed with the ITC by any firm, trade association, union, or group of workers, or by Congress or the president, or it may be initiated by the commission itself. The ITC gives public notice in the *Federal Register* of its investigation and hearings. If it finds that the requirements of the law are met, it may advise the president as to what action to take. The commission conducts public hearings at which interested parties may present evidence and make suggestions as to the form of import relief. The ITC prepares a detailed economic analysis of the affected market and then makes its determination. The factors that the commission considers in determining whether increased imports are a substantial cause of serious injury include:

1. A significant idling of productive facilities in the industry.
2. The inability of firms to operate at a reasonable profit.
3. Unemployment or underemployment in the industry.
4. Growing inventories.
5. A decline in sales, market share, production, wages, or employment.
6. A firm's inability to generate capital for plant and equipment modernization or for research and development.
7. An actual increase in imports or in market share held by imports.
8. Other factors that may account for the serious injury to the domestic industry (e.g., incompetent management or lack of technological innovation).

U.S. law defines *substantial cause* as "a cause which is important and not less than any other cause." (Review the requirements for applying a safeguard measure as set out by the WTO Appellate Body in the *Argentina Footwear* case.) The ITC may not consider overall economic trends, such as the impact of a recession on the industry, but must look at the impact of the increased imports. In the ITC report on the U.S. motorcycle industry, Commissioner Eckes found that increased imports of heavyweight motorcycles threatened serious injury to the petitioner, Harley-Davidson, despite the severe impact of a long recession on total sales in the industry.

In the event that a foreign country requests a WTO panel to review a U.S. safeguard decision, the entire investigative process comes under scrutiny. If a WTO panel reviews the fact-finding decisions of the ITC or of an investigative agency in another country, what is the standard of review? Several Appellate Body decisions have addressed this (including the *Argentina Footwear* decision in this chapter) and concluded that Article 11 of the *Dispute Settlement Understanding* obligates a panel to make an "objective assessment" of the facts, not by trying to determine the facts of the case anew, but by looking to see whether domestic agencies have evaluated all relevant facts and have provided an adequate and reasonable explanation about how the facts supported their determinations. This is a practical realization that judges in Geneva cannot gather facts and information from industries around the world.

AVAILABLE REMEDIES UNDER U.S. LAW. Any relief granted by the president must be temporary (limited to 4 years, with an extension to 8 years if

Argentina—Safeguard Measures on Imports of Footwear

WT/DS121/AB/R (14 December 1999)

Report of the Appellate Body of the World Trade Organization

BACKGROUND AND FACTS

In 1997, Argentina initiated a safeguard investigation and determined that increased imports were the cause of serious injury to Argentine producers. Increased import duties were placed on imports of foreign-made footwear greater than those previously bound in Argentine tariff concessions. In effect, the import duty went from the bound rate of 35 percent to 200 percent. The increased duties were imposed on imports of footwear from all countries except those South American countries that were members of the regional MERCOSUR common market. After consultations failed, the European Communities (EC) requested a WTO panel to decide if Argentina had complied with the GATT agreements. The United States joined as a third party. The EC made several arguments: (1) Argentina's administrative safeguard proceedings had failed to show that the surge in imports was the cause of injury to domestic producers and had failed to consider whether the injury to the domestic footwear industry was actually caused by other economic factors; (2) Argentina must impose safeguards without regard to the country of origin, and not solely on non-MERCOSUR countries; and (3) GATT Article XIX required that safeguard measures be imposed only if the increase in imports results from "unforeseen developments."

The EC maintained that because the increases in imports resulted from lowered rates of duty that were freely negotiated between countries as a part of their tariff concessions, the increases could not be "unforeseen." Argentina responded that the 1994 GATT *Agreement on Safeguards* abandoned this requirement. The panel held that the Argentine safeguards had violated the GATT agreements, but expressed its view that there was no requirement that the increases in imports be unforeseeable. Argentina appealed to the WTO Appellate Body.

REPORT OF THE APPELLATE BODY

ARTICLE XIX OF THE GATT 1994 AND "UNFORESEEN DEVELOPMENTS"

The provisions of Article XIX: 1(a) of the *GATT 1994* and Article 2.1 of the *Agreement on Safeguards,* which together set out the conditions for applying a safeguard measure under the *WTO Agreement,* read as follows:

GATT 1994 Article XIX Emergency Action on Imports of Particular Products

1.(a) If, *as a result of unforeseen developments and of the effect of the obligations incurred by a Member under this Agreement, including tariff concessions,* any product is being imported into the territory of that Member in such increased quantities and under such conditions as to cause or threaten serious injury to domestic producers in that territory of like or directly competitive products, the Member shall be free, in respect of such product, and to the extent and for such time as may be necessary to prevent or remedy such injury, to suspend the obligation in whole or in part or to withdraw or modify the concession. (emphasis added)

Agreement on Safeguards Article 2 Conditions

1. A Member may apply a safeguard measure to a product only if that Member has determined, pursuant to the provisions set out below, that such product is being imported into its territory in such increased quantities, absolute or relative to domestic production, and under such conditions as to cause or threaten to cause serious injury to the domestic industry that produces like or directly competitive products.

* * *

As to the meaning of "unforeseen developments," we note that the dictionary definition of "unforeseen," particularly as it relates to the word "developments," is synonymous with "unexpected." "Unforeseeable," on the other hand, is defined in the dictionaries as meaning "unpredictable" or "incapable of being foreseen, foretold or anticipated." Thus, it seems to us that the ordinary meaning of the phrase "as a result of unforeseen developments" requires that the developments which led to a product being imported in such increased quantities and under such conditions as to cause or threaten to cause serious injury to domestic producers must have been "unexpected." With respect to the phrase "of the effect of the obligations incurred by a Member under this Agreement, including tariff concessions ...," we

continued

continued

believe that this phrase simply means that it must be demonstrated, as a matter of fact, that the importing Member has incurred obligations under the GATT 1994, including tariff concessions.

***

In our view, the text of Article XIX:1(a) of the *GATT 1994,* read in its ordinary meaning and in its context, demonstrates that safeguard measures were intended by the drafters of the *GATT* to be matters out of the ordinary, to be matters of urgency, to be, in short, "emergency actions." And, such "emergency actions" are to be invoked only in situations when, as a result of obligations incurred under the *GATT 1994,* a Member finds itself confronted with developments it had not "foreseen" or "expected" when it incurred that obligation.

Imposition of Safeguard Measures by a Member of a Customs Union

Argentina claims on appeal that the Panel erred by "imposing an obligation" on a member of a customs union to apply any safeguard measure on other members of that customs union whenever imports from all sources are taken into account in a safeguards investigation. Article 2 of the *Agreement on Safeguards* provides that "Safeguard measures shall be applied to a product being imported irrespective of its source." On the basis of this reasoning, and on the facts of this case, we find that Argentina's investigation, which evaluated whether serious injury or the threat thereof was caused by imports from *all* sources, could only lead to the imposition of safeguard measures on imports from *all* sources. Therefore, we conclude that Argentina's investigation, in this case, cannot serve as a basis for excluding imports from other MERCOSUR member States from the application of the safeguard measures.

Serious Injury

We agree with the Panel that Articles 2.1 and 4.2(a) of the *Agreement on Safeguards* require a demonstration not merely of *any* increase in imports, but, instead, of imports "in such increased quantities ... and under such conditions as to cause or threaten to cause serious injury."... And this language in both Article 2.1 of the *Agreement on Safeguards* and Article XIX:1(a) of the GATT 1994, *we believe, requires that the increase in imports must have been recent enough, sudden enough, sharp enough, and significant enough, both quantitatively and qualitatively, to cause or threaten to cause "serious injury"* [emphasis added].

With respect to the requirement relating to "serious injury," Article 4.2(a) of the *Agreement on Safeguards* provides, in relevant part:

> In the investigation to determine whether increased imports have caused or are threatening to cause serious injury to a domestic industry under the terms of this Agreement, the competent authorities *shall evaluate all relevant factors of an objective and quantifiable nature having a bearing on the situation of that industry, in particular, ... the share of the domestic market taken by increased imports, changes in the level of sales, production, productivity, capacity utilization, profits and losses, and employment.*

As the Panel found that Argentina had not evaluated two of the listed factors, capacity utilization and productivity, the Panel concluded that Argentina's investigation was not consistent with the requirements of Article 4.2(a).

We agree with the Panel's interpretation that Article 4.2(a) of the *Agreement on Safeguards* requires a demonstration that the competent authorities evaluated, at a minimum, each of the factors listed in Article 4.2(a) as well as all other factors that are relevant to the situation of the industry concerned. Furthermore, we do not dispute the Panel's finding that Argentina did not evaluate all of the listed factors, in particular, capacity utilization and productivity.

Decision. The Appellate Body upheld the Panel's conclusion that Argentina had not shown that the increased imports were the cause of serious harm to the domestic footwear industry. Safeguards, where justified, must be imposed on imports without regard to the country of origin, and only where the increased imports resulted from "unforeseen developments."

the firms in the industry are making needed changes) and designed to allow those firms sufficient time to regain their competitive position in the market. Relief should only provide time to retool, modernize, streamline, recapitalize, improve quality, or take other actions to better meet new competitive conditions in the market. The president's options for adjusting imports

Heavyweight Motorcycles & Engines & Power-Train Subassemblies
Report to the President on Investigation No. TA-201-47
United States International Trade Commission 1983

BACKGROUND AND FACTS

In 1982, the ITC instituted an investigation to determine if motorcycles having engines with displacement more than 700 cubic centimeters were being imported into the United States in such increased quantities as to be a substantial cause of serious injury, or threat thereof, to domestic industry producing like or directly competitive articles. The investigation was in response to a petition for relief filed by Harley-Davidson Motor Co., a U.S. firm. The investigation showed that from 1977 to 1981, U.S. shipments of motorcycles grew by 17 percent, with domestic production capacity increasing by nearly 82 percent (largely as a result of American Honda's increased production in the United States). During that same period the number of U.S. jobs increased by 30 percent. In 1982, however, consumption fell, domestic shipments declined, and employment dropped. In the first 9 months of 1982, domestic shipments fell by 13 percent and inventories rose, leaving large numbers of unsold motorcycles. Production during that period showed a decline of 36 percent, profits were down by 20 percent, and employment was down by 12 percent. Inventories of imported motorcycles doubled in that period, representing a tremendous threat to Harley-Davidson. The country as a whole was in the midst of a recession, and demand for heavyweight motorcycles was depressed.

VIEWS OF CHAIRMAN ALFRED ECKES

* * *

It is evident that inventories of imported motorcycles have increased significantly during the most recent period. These increases exceed growth in consumption and surpass historical shipment trends for importers. The mere presence of such a huge inventory has had and will continue to have a depressing effect on the domestic industry. Also, given the natural desire of consumers for current design and up-to-date performance capabilities, motorcycles cannot be withheld from the market indefinitely. They must be sold. And given the realities of the market place, there is a strong incentive to liquidate these inventories as quickly as possible. The impact of such a massive inventory build-up on the domestic industry is imminent, not remote and conjectural.

I have seen no persuasive evidence that would suggest imports of Japanese heavyweight motorcycles will decline in the near future. Instead, the Japanese motorcycle industry is export oriented—exporting in 1982 some 91 percent of the heavyweight motorcycles produced in Japan. Because motorcycles of more than 750cc, which include the merchandise under investigation here, cannot be sold in Japan under current law, Japanese producers cannot consider domestic sales as a replacement for exports. The other option, which they apparently pursued in 1982, is to push export sales in the face of declining demand in the U.S. market. This tactic helps to maintain output and employment in the producing country but it shifts some of the burden of adjustment to competitors in the importing country. Evidence that the Japanese producers will seek to maintain a high level of export sales to the U.S. is found in an estimate of the Japanese Automobile Manufacturer's Association. This organization estimated that exports of 700cc or over motorcycles to the United States for 1982 and 1983 would average 450,000 units or less for both years combined. That figure results in import levels higher than recent levels.

Finally, imports of finished heavyweight motorcycles pose a "substantial cause" of threat of serious injury. Under section 201(b)(4), a "substantial cause" is a "cause which is important and not less than any other cause." In my view, there is no cause more important than imports threatening injury to the domestic motorcycle industry.

In reaching this conclusion I have considered the significance of the present recession in my analysis. Without a doubt the unusual length and severity of the present recession has created unique problems for the domestic motorcycle industry. Without a doubt the rise in joblessness, particularly among blue-collar workers, who constitute the prime market for heavyweight motorcycles, has had a severe impact on the domestic industry. Nonetheless, if the Commission were to analyze the causation question in this way, it would be impossible in many cases for a cyclical industry experiencing serious injury to obtain relief

continued

continued

under section 201 during a recession. In my opinion Congress could not have intended for the Commission to interpret the law this way.

There are other reasons for doubting the domestic recession is a substantial cause of injury or threat to the U.S. industry. During the current recession, imports from Japan have increased their market share from domestic producers, gaining nearly six percentage points. Imports have taken market share from the domestic facilities of Honda and Kawasaki as well as Harley-Davidson.

Moreover, while the current recession has undoubtedly depressed demand for heavyweight motorcycles, economic conditions are beginning to improve in this country.... As demand responds to this improvement, the domestic industry will be pre-empted from participating in any growth because of the presence of a one-year supply of motorcycles poised and ready to capture market share. Consequently, not the recession, but the inventory of motorcycles coupled with anticipated future imports constitute the greatest threat of injury in the months ahead.

Decision. The commission recommended that incremental duties be imposed for 5 years at the declining rates of 45, 35, 20, 15, and 10 percent, in addition to the existing rate of 4.4 percent *ad valorem.*

Comment. The president followed the commission's recommendations, but added tariff-rate quotas of 5,000 units in order to keep the U.S. market open to European firms that exported to the United States in smaller quantities. The remedy has been considered one of the most successful uses of safeguards. Under protection, Harley-Davidson recapitalized, introduced quality control processes and just-in-time inventory control, and regained its competitiveness. By 2003, Harley was one of the most demanded motorcycles in the world, including in Japan. In that year, Harley exported over 50,000 units worldwide.

include (1) tariff increases, subject to a maximum increase of 50 percent; (2) tariff-rate quotas, which allow a certain number of articles to be imported at one tariff rate, while all excess amounts enter at a higher rate; (3) absolute quotas; (4) quotas administered through the auctioning of import licenses; (5) negotiated agreements with foreign countries that limit their exports to the United States; or (6) trade adjustment assistance for the domestic industry. (Item (5) is not permitted under WTO rules and is no longer used.)

China Safeguards. Increases in imports from China are subject to special rules not applicable to other WTO countries. As a part of China's admission to the WTO, the United States and China agreed that special safeguards would apply to imports from China until 2013. The safeguards were added to U.S. law in the *U.S.–China Relations Act of 2000*, which amended *Section 421 of the Trade Act of 1974*. The statute requires that the president grant import relief (increased duties or other import restrictions) where the ITC finds that increased imports of Chinese goods are causing or threatening to cause market disruption to domestic producers of like or directly competitive products. *Market disruption* occurs whenever increased imports are a significant cause of material injury or threat thereof. [Notice that it is easier to prove a safeguards case against China (by showing that imports are a "significant cause of material injury") than it is to prove a case for global safeguards under *Section 201* (whose standard is a "substantial cause of serious injury")]. The ITC conducts an investigation and issues its report and recommendation to the U.S. Trade Representative, who is required to try and reach an agreement with China. If no agreement is reached, the matter is forwarded to the president. The president must order import relief unless it would be contrary to the national economic interest (having "an adverse impact on the United States economy clearly greater than the benefits of such action") or to national security.

The president's authority to order or deny relief was tested in *Motions Systems Corp. v. Bush*, 437 F.3d 1356 (Fed. Cir. 2006). Motions Systems, a U.S. manufacturer of parts for motorized wheelchairs, initiated a safeguard action against competing products from China. Although the ITC found that market disruption had caused material injury and recommended to the president that quantitative restrictions be placed on imports over a 3-year period, President Bush refused to do so.

He found that safeguards would not benefit U.S. manufacturers, but would only divert imports from China to manufacturers in other foreign countries, and would lead to increased consumer prices. The U.S. Court of Appeals ruled that Motions Systems had no right to judicial review, that the president had not exceeded his authority, and that he had broad discretion to determine that import relief is not in the national economic interest of the United States.

Trade Adjustment Assistance

Workers who become unemployed as a result of increased imports of foreign goods may be entitled to federal *trade adjustment assistance* (TAA). Petitions for TAA are filed with the U.S. Department of Labor. Assistance to workers, in the form of direct cash payments, tax credits, or vouchers, is intended to cover the expenses of job search, retraining and relocation, and health insurance coverage. For workers to be eligible to apply for TAA, the Secretary of Labor must determine that a significant number or group of workers in a firm have become, or are threatened to become, partially or totally separated from their employment; that the firm's sales or production have decreased absolutely; and that increases in like or directly competitive imported products contributed importantly to the separation and to a decline in the firm's sales or production. There are also provisions permitting assistance to workers, irrespective of whether there are increased quantities of foreign imports, whose employer has shifted production to a foreign country that is a party to a free trade agreement with the United States (this includes Mexico, Canada, and countries in the Andean, Caribbean, and African regions). The program is administered by state job agencies. It is not uncommon to see them sponsor announcements in local newspapers asking workers to contact them about assistance if their employer has moved their jobs to foreign factories.

Workers have been certified in many TAA programs. The six industries with the largest concentration of certified workers during the last two decades were automotive equipment, apparel and other finished products made from fabrics and similar materials, primary metal industries, oil and gas production and services, leather and leather products, and electrical and electronic machinery, equipment, and supplies. In 2006, the Department of Labor certified petitions for over 120,000 workers. The *Trade Act of 2002* extended benefits to the farm and fishing industries. That program is administered by the U.S. Department of Agriculture.

FEDERAL ASSISTANCE TO FIRMS. Trade adjustment assistance is not just available for U.S. workers, but also for U.S. companies. This program is administered by the U.S. Department of Commerce through the Economic Development Administration. It is intended to help U.S. companies become more competitive. For a firm to qualify under this law, a certification must be issued that increased imports contributed importantly to a decline in sales and to the unemployment of a significant number of its workers. Twelve assistance centers nationwide help certified companies develop business recovery plans over a 2-year period. The plans include such things as improving production capabilities, marketing, computer systems and Web site development, and standards certification. In order to receive financial assistance, the certified firm must contribute its own matching funds. On average, about 150 firms have been certified annually to receive assistance.

The U.S. Steel Industry: A Case Study in Managed Trade

The U.S. steel industry presents a classic example of the problems and politics of protectionism versus free trade. As is the case in so many industries, tariffs to protect one industry from foreign competition can adversely affect another. Trade remedies such as quotas or retaliatory tariffs may protect a U.S. industry from low-cost imports, but they also raise the price of goods to consumers. In the case of steel, cheaper imported steel benefits steel users and consumers because it lowers the price of everything made from steel—cars, home appliances, bridges, and so on. The modern history of the steel industry has seen steel producers and the steelworkers' union pitted against industry users of steel and consumer groups. Moreover, countries around the world have subsidized steel producers in their countries through an endless scheme of tax breaks and favors, hoping to give them an advantage in world markets. In the United States, lawmakers and presidents from both parties have weighed in. The result is that during the last 30 or 40 years, American steel has benefited from a range of protective actions, to the ire of consumer groups and foreign governments alike.

After World War II, the United States dominated the world steel industry. However, with their steel industries in ruin, Europe and Japan had the opportunity to rebuild with modern plants and techniques. Gradually, developing countries like Taiwan, Korea, India, and Brazil, and later even Russia, also found it easy to spur development by exporting steel. On the other hand, the large American mills did not modernize, and by the late 1960s, they found themselves operating inefficiently and at a competitive disadvantage to the new foreign mills. As foreign plants increased capacity, they ate into former export markets for U.S. steel companies while increasing market share in the United States itself. U.S. companies also faced higher wage rates, as well as loss of market share to plastics, aluminum, and newer technologies.

In the 1960s and 1970s, the steel industry worldwide, including America and Europe, underwent a financial crisis. Since that time, every U.S. president has tried to limit foreign steel to a small percentage of U.S. consumption, generally from 15 to 18 percent. But for decades, it seemed that every time a restriction on steel imports was lifted, imports of foreign steel have surged (sometimes to over one-quarter of U.S. consumption), triggering a string of plant closings, layoffs, and bankruptcies. The steel industry has repeatedly filed for protection under the safeguard laws, antidumping laws, and countervailing duty laws, all the while amassing a tremendous lobbying effort in Washington calling for "toughening" of U.S. unfair trade statutes. Indeed, for the past two decades, the American government has imposed added import duties on foreign steel under its "unfair trade" laws (see the discussion later in this chapter on dumping and subsidies). Critics and consumer groups have long maintained that the decades of protection have resulted in tens of billions of dollars in higher prices for steel products while doing little to encourage steel industry modernization and efficiency.

During these decades, U.S. steel producers maintained that they have attempted to compete in a market that is rigged against them. They have argued that foreign countries are subsidizing the sale of cheap foreign steel in the United States, that foreign firms are dumping steel in the United States at unfairly low prices, and that the additional duties imposed on them are really just necessary to "level the playing field." Unless the U.S. government protects the U.S. steel industry to give it time to modernize, restructure, and compete, they argue, America as a nation will be left without essential steel-producing capabilities. Those opposed to steel industry protection (which includes foreign governments in steel-exporting nations) maintain that competition is not the reason for the decline of the U.S. industry. They point out that America's large, traditional mills (known as "integrated" mills) have become dependent on protection, while America's more competitive "mini-mills," which produce specialty steel products, are very profitable.

By the 1990s, it seemed that the industry was actually becoming more competitive. Those plants that remained were modernizing, corporate mergers and consolidations were improving cost efficiencies, foreign mills were making ownership investment in U.S. mills, and the new "mini-mills" were succeeding in the specialty steel market.

However, in the late 1990s, the Asian financial crisis dried up many markets for steel. With a glut of steel on the world market, foreign producers found it more important than ever to ship to the United States. U.S. steel imports jumped, prices plummeted, high energy prices made manufacturing more costly, tens of thousands of U.S. steelworkers were laid off, and dozens more U.S. steel firms closed or filed for bankruptcy. The Bush administration found itself under tremendous pressure to again protect the industry, and it initiated a *Section 201* safeguard investigation. The ITC found that the imports were "a substantial cause of serious injury or threat thereof" and recommended additional tariffs (on top of those already in place).

In 2002, President Bush imposed tariffs of up to 30 percent on the majority of imported steel coming from all countries except Canada, Mexico, Jordan, and Israel, to be effective for 3 years. In the same year, the European Union, Japan, Korea, China, Switzerland, Norway, New Zealand, and Brazil brought dispute cases to the WTO.

In a 1,000-page report, the panel ruled that (1) the U.S. measures were not a result of "unforeseen developments" as required under the WTO rules (the United States had maintained that the Asian financial crisis was unforeseen); (2) for most steel products, the ITC could not show that the imported quantities have increased; (3) the United States has not shown that the imports caused the serious injury to the U.S. steel industry; and (4) excluding imports from Canada, Mexico, Israel, and Jordan was inconsistent with the non-discrimination WTO rules. The EC claimed a "full victory."

In 2003, the Appellate Body upheld the panel's decision against the United States in *United States—Definitive Safeguard Measures on Imports of Certain Steel Products—Report of the Appellate Body, WT/DS 248/AB/R (10 November 2003).* The EC and Japan had threatened over $2 billion in retaliatory tariffs on U.S. products unless the United States backed down, singling out U.S. products from states key to Bush's 2004 reelection campaign, such as Florida orange juice. Citing his belief that the steel industry was quickly recovering, President Bush lifted the tariffs in December 2003.

Unfair Import Laws: Dumping and Antidumping Duties

In importing, *dumping* is the unfair trade practice of selling products in a foreign country for less than the price charged for the same or comparable goods in the producer's home market. It is a form of price discrimination that causes injury to domestic competitors through artificially low prices against which domestic producers cannot compete at a profitable level. The original GATT agreement has prohibited dumping since 1947, and it has been illegal in the United States since 1916.

Antidumping laws are used more frequently than any other type of trade law in the United States and Europe. Virtually all developed nations have statutes, patterned after the GATT agreement, that permit the importing country to impose antidumping duties on dumped products to offset the unfair low price and to prevent injury to a domestic producer. The United States, the EU, Canada, and Australia all have antidumping laws. China enacted its antidumping law in 1997. In the EU, the antidumping laws are imposed only on trade between a member country and a nonmember country. Japan has similar laws, although they are not widely enforced. Developing countries, such as Mexico, Brazil, Argentina, India, and Korea, also have antidumping codes.

The Economics of Dumping

The theories that explain the economic motivation for dumping fill entire volumes and are certainly beyond the scope of this book. At first glance, one might wonder what is wrong with consumers in one country being able to buy the products of another nation cheaply. As long as the products remain available at a reasonable market price, nothing is wrong. But the lower prices charged in an importing country are often not related to superior efficiencies in production. Rather, dumping is often intended to drive competitors out of business so that the dumping firms will ultimately be free to raise their prices to monopoly levels.

Dumping has become a fairly persistent problem in international trade, often practiced by those firms wishing to sell their excess production capacity at bargain prices to cover fixed costs and to avoid cyclical worker layoffs. As long as dumped products are not sold in the producer's own country, causing price suppression in the producer's home market, then the dumping firm has everything to gain and little to lose. Some economists point out that dumping is not always predatory, but may be related to market conditions. An exporting firm may not be able to command the same prices from foreign buyers as in its domestic market, where it has brand recognition and greater market power.

Critics of antidumping laws claim that they injure consumers by "fixing prices" at high levels. Once the prices rise for imported products, domestic manufacturers follow suit by raising their prices as well. Critics note that antidumping laws are designed to correct an unfair trade practice and not to protect domestic companies. They also maintain that antidumping laws do not require the United States to assess the impact of additional duties on the public interest (i.e., the cost to consumers) and do not provide an exception for goods that are in short supply in the United States.

The *WTO Antidumping Agreement*

The GATT provisions on dumping are found in *GATT 1994 Article VI* and in the *1994 WTO Antidumping Agreement*. The 1994 agreement provides complex rules for determining when dumping has occurred and for resolving dumping disputes.

Every WTO member country is expected to see that its national antidumping laws comply with the WTO rules. These national laws are reported annually to the WTO in Geneva and are easily accessed by anyone interested in a foreign country's dumping laws at the WTO Web site. In the United States, the *Uruguay Round Agreements Act* amended U.S. antidumping laws to reflect the new GATT provisions, which are incorporated into U.S. tariff law generally in Title 19 of the *United States Code*. In this section, our discussions apply generally to both the WTO antidumping agreement and to U.S. antidumping laws. However, laws or procedures specific to the United States are noted as such.

The WTO agreement provides that dumping occurs when foreign goods are imported for sale at a price less than that charged for comparable goods in the exporting or producing country. Antidumping duties may be imposed only when the dumping threatens or causes "material injury" to a domestic industry producing "like products." The agreement requires that an importing country resort to antidumping duties only after conducting a formal investigation to determine both the amount of the dumping and the extent of material injury.

In the United States, there are two federal agencies involved in the investigation. The United States International Trade Administration (ITA) of the U.S. Department of Commerce determines whether the merchandise has been sold in the United States at a price less than its normal value, and the International Trade Commission (ITC) determines whether this has caused, or threatens to cause, a material injury to U.S. producers of like products. Petitions for an investigation may be filed by producers of "like" and competing domestic products, including manufacturers, sellers, or labor groups who produce at least 25 percent of domestic U.S. production. Investigations must be concluded within 18 months.

Calculating the Dumping Margin. Antidumping laws are designed to prevent foreign manufacturers from injuring domestic industries by selling their products in the United States below the prices that they charge for the same products in their home markets. The U.S. statute provides that antidumping duties may be imposed on imported merchandise if that merchandise is sold or likely to be sold in the United States at less than fair value. Contrary to popular belief, dumping does not require that the foreign products be sold for less than the cost to produce them, although a sale at below cost is certainly "less than fair value." In order to determine whether merchandise is sold at less than fair value, the ITA compares the *normal value* of the merchandise, which is the price at which it is first sold for consumption in the exporting or producing country, to the *export price,* meaning the price of the good when sold in or for export to the United States. If the export price is less than the normal value of the product in the home market, then the sale is *below normal value,* or in the language of the U.S. statute, at *less than fair value.* The price differential is known as the *dumping margin.* WTO rules require that the dumping margin use price and value figures that will result in a "fair comparison." When dumping causes or threatens material injury to domestic producers of like products, the importing nation may equalize the price differential by imposing an additional tariff, above the normal tariff charged for that product. These antidumping duties are assessed in an amount equal to the dumping margin and are calculated for each individual exporter. Thus, if a Korean company sells a widget in Korea at $100 and sells the same widget in the United States at $80, then the dumping margin is $20 and an antidumping duty of $20 can be imposed on the imported widget. If the dumping margin is less than 2 percent of the value of the products, the dumping is considered *de minimis* and no duties are imposed.

Calculating the Export Price. The *export price* is the price (usually the *ex factory* price without shipping charges) at which a product is sold to an unaffiliated or unrelated buyer in the importing country. When a price charged for a product does not reflect an "arm's-length" (freely negotiated) transaction, a *constructed export price* must be used. A constructed export price is used when the exporter and importer are affiliated or related companies or the product price is "hidden" in some other type of compensatory arrangement (such as barter). In these cases, the constructed price is deemed to be the price at which the imported product is first resold in its original condition to an independent buyer. An "affiliated buyer" is a U.S. company or corporation in which the foreign seller owns a 5 percent equity ownership or more, or one over which the foreign seller is in a position to control, manage, or direct. This may also include companies where the seller has a degree of control as a result of having an exclusive supplier arrangement or where the same individuals sit on the boards of directors of both companies.

Calculating the Normal Value of Like Products in the Exporting or Producing Country. *Normal value* is the price at which *foreign like products* are sold for consumption in the exporting or producing country in usual commercial quantities and the ordinary course of business, and at the same level of trade—in other words, comparing wholesale sale to wholesale sale, or retail to retail—as the dumped product. If insufficient quantities of like products are sold in the exporting country to permit a fair comparison, then normal value is calculated on the basis of sales to third countries, or on the basis of a *constructed value.* Constructed value is calculated on the basis of what it might actually cost to produce the product in the exporting country, plus an amount for selling, administrative, packaging, and other expenses, and a reasonable profit.

What Is a "Like Product"? One common problem in comparing the price of the dumped product to "like products" sold for normal value in the exporting country is defining what that "like product" is. First, many antidumping actions are taken against an entire category, kind, or classification of merchandise, not just on a single item or product. The ITA will have to determine what products to include in its price analysis and which not to include. Also keep in mind that in many cases the products sold by a manufacturer or producer in one country are not like those sold in foreign countries. For example, the range of qualities, specifications, or dimensions may differ. The goods may be packaged differently or in different quantities and bulk packs. There are endless examples. Steel tubing sold in one country may be different from that sold in another. Building materials may differ according to local construction codes. Electrical standards can require that products be assembled differently or use varying component parts. Consumer preferences often dictate significant changes in products when they are sold for export. All of these factors make it very difficult to compare the export price with the normal value of a "like product" in the exporting country.

Generally speaking, the ITA will look at many factors, including whether the products are identical in physical characteristics, whether they are produced by the same or different firms, whether they are made of the same or similar component materials, whether they are of equal commercial value, and whether they are used for the same purpose. The following case, *Pesquera Mares Australes Ltda. v. United States,* illustrates a typical problem that might face the ITA in determining a "like product." It's actually one of the more readable opinions in this area of the law. (Most cases deal with far more complex industrial product classifications than salmon.) As you read, consider how the agency made its decision and the deference given to that decision by the Court of Appeals for the Federal Circuit.

Adjustments to Value and Price. Calculating the dumping margin requires a *fair comparison* of the price of the dumped product in the export market with the price of a like product sold in the ordinary course of trade in the exporting or producing country (i.e., the normal value). A fair comparison often requires adjustments to either the export price or to normal value to compensate for differences in the sale—comparing "apples to apples." For example, if the German manufacturer of ball bearings must pay a sales commission to sales representatives for ball bearings sold in Germany but does not pay commissions on sales to the United States, then the difference must be accounted for in the calculation. Adjustments can be made for differences in the terms and conditions of sale, for the cost of ocean containers and packaging, for freight and warehouse expenses, customs brokerage fees, insurance on the goods in transit, and

Pesquera Mares Australes Ltda. v. United States (Chilean Salmon)

266 F.3d 1372 (2001)

United States Court of Appeals (Fed. Cir.)

BACKGROUND AND FACTS

Pesquera Mares Australes, a Chilean salmon exporter, was accused of dumping salmon in the U.S. market at less than fair value. An antidumping petition was filed in 1997 by the Coalition for Fair Atlantic Salmon Trade. The U.S. Department of Commerce (ITA) conducted an investigation to compare the price of the salmon sold in the United States with its "normal value" in the home market. Finding no sales of Mares Australes' salmon in Chile during that time, ITA based normal value on the price of the salmon sold in Japan. However, while the salmon sold in the United States was of the "premium" grade, the salmon sold in Japan was of both "premium" and "super-premium" grades. ITA nevertheless found that the salmon sold in Japan and in the United States had "identical physical characteristics" and thus were "like products" as defined by the U.S. statute. ITA then included the price of the super-premium Japanese grade in its determination of normal value. This resulted in the ITA finding a larger dumping margin and imposing higher antidumping duties. The duties were affirmed by the Court of International Trade and Mares Australes appealed to the Court of Appeals for the Federal Circuit.

DYK, CIRCUIT JUDGE

* * *

[T]he antidumping statute specifically defines "foreign like product," as ... merchandise *which is identical in physical characteristics*.... In this case ITA sought to identify salmon sold by Mares Australes to Japan that was "identical in physical characteristics" to salmon exported by that company to the United States. It is ITA's interpretation of the phrase "identical in physical characteristics" that is at issue.

* * *

Mares Australes argued that the super-premium salmon it sold to Japan could not be considered "identical in physical characteristics" to the premium grade salmon it sold to the United States. As evidence of this distinction, the company stressed ... that certain physical defects (such as external lacerations to the salmon) were present in premium but not super-premium salmon; that super-premium salmon enjoyed a darker, redder color than premium salmon; and that its customers in Japan, recognizing these physical and color distinctions, paid higher prices for premium-grade salmon.... But ITA noted that "the record also contains evidence that the distinctions between the two grades were, in practice, nominal...."

As support for its conclusion that super-premium was not a commercially recognized separate grade, ITA also pointed to commercial practice in countries (other than Chile) exporting to Japan, whose salmon industries did "not recognize any grade higher than 'superior'." [In its final determination] ITA stated: "... The Norwegian, Scottish, Canadian, and U.S. salmon industries do not recognize any grade higher than "superior." The "superior" grade is consistent with the premium grade and permits minor defects.... Nonetheless, all salmon in this range are graded equally (*i.e.*, as "superior"/"premium"), and are comparable products in the market place. [*Notice of Final Determination of Sales at Less Than Fair Value: Fresh Atlantic Salmon From Chile,* 63 Fed. Reg. 31411 (June 9, 1998)]. ITA thus determined that "salmon reported as super-premium are in fact of premium grade," and accordingly compared the sales of both super-premium and premium salmon to Japan to corresponding sales of premium salmon only in the United States. The practical consequences of ITA's decision to classify the two grades of salmon as "identical in physical characteristics" was to increase Mares Australes' dumping margin from the de minimis level (1.21%) to a final dumping margin of 2.23%.

* * *

This case requires us to interpret the phrase "identical in physical characteristics" as that phrase appears in the definition of "foreign like product" [U.S. Code]. In order to ascertain the established meaning of a term such as the word "identical," it is appropriate to consult dictionaries. There are a variety of dictionary definitions of "identical." Some require exact identity. *See, e.g., American Heritage Dictionary,* 896 (3d ed. 1996) (defining "identical" as "being the same" and "exactly equal and alike").... Others allow "minor differences" so long as the items are "essentially the same." *See, e.g., The American Heritage Dictionary,* 639 (2d ed. 1991).... We find nothing in the statute to suggest that Congress intended to depart from the

continued

continued

ordinary definition of the term "identical." But that leaves the question of which of the two common usages was intended by Congress: *exactly the same* or *the same with minor differences?*

We conclude that Congress intended the latter usage.... As Coalition for Fair Atlantic Salmon Trade points out, Congress could hardly have intended to require ITA in each and every instance to compare *all* the physical characteristics of the goods. It might not be possible, for example, with certain types of merchandise to "account for every conceivable physical characteristic" of that merchandise.

Despite our conclusion that Congress intended to allow identical merchandise to have minor differences, the phrase "identical in physical characteristics" [as used in the U.S. statute] remains ambiguous, and, as we learn from *Chevron U.S.A., Inc. v. Natural Resources Defense Council, Inc.*, 467 U.S. 837, 104 S.Ct. 2778 (1984), ITA has discretion to define the term.

* * *

ITA has concluded that merchandise should be considered to be identical despite the existence of minor differences in physical characteristics, if those minor differences are not commercially significant. We conclude that this standard adopted by ITA constitutes "a permissible construction of the statute." ... We conclude that this finding is supported by substantial evidence, and that it has been adequately explained.

* * *

Decision. The Chilean salmon exporter (Mares Australes) was found to have violated the antidumping laws of the United States by selling foreign salmon in the United States at less than fair value. The super-premium salmon sold by Mares Australes in Japan was similar enough to the premium grade sold in the United States to be considered a "foreign like product," the price of which should be included in determining the normal value for purposes of calculating the dumping margin.

other expenses. Adjustments should also be made for differences in taxes, advertising and sales commission expenses, quantity discounts, and other factors that might legitimately cause the export price to be lower than normal value. The rules for making adjustments in U.S. dumping cases are spelled out in federal law.

Market Viability Test and Constructed Value. A price comparison between the export price in the foreign market and the normal value of the product in the exporting country only works if the exporting country has a *viable market.* If the exporting country has insufficient sales of a like product, then the *normal value* is difficult to determine. When aggregate sales volume in the exporting country (the "home market") is less than 5 percent of the aggregate sales volume of the dumped product in the U.S. market, the dumping margin is calculated by comparing the dumped product to the price of a like product when it is exported to a third country, provided that this price is representative of a normal value. If sales to a third country are also insufficient, then a constructed value for the product is substituted for normal value and the price of the dumped product is compared to the cost of producing the product in the exporting country plus a reasonable amount for administrative, selling, and other costs and for profits. The amount of profit to be added into constructed value is based on either (1) actual profits in the transaction, (2) average profits on sales of the same product made by other producers, or (3) profits made on different products sold by the same producer.

Sales Below Cost. If substantial quantities of a product are sold in the exporting country (or in a third country if that is used for comparison purposes) at a price below per unit cost of production (including fixed and variable costs plus administrative and selling costs), the below-cost sales may be disregarded in determining a dumped product's normal value. A product is sold in "substantial quantities" if, over the period of one year, 20 percent or more of the sales in question are below cost. Normal value is then calculated on the basis of the remaining above-cost sales.

The Level-of-Trade Problem. A producing firm that sells to its local market at a different level in the chain of distribution than in foreign markets presents a common problem in the evaluation of dumping cases. For example, a higher normal value frequently occurs when the producer sells directly to retailers or to end users in the home country, whereas in the export market the producer may be selling to distributors or to wholesalers. The dumping margin would be attributed to the different costs of sale and different markups required. In a situation such as this, known as a *level-of-trade problem,* the ITA adjusts the price differential so that figures for normal value and export price are comparable.

WTO Dispute Settlement in Dumping Cases

Prior to the WTO agreement in 1994, the original *General Agreement on Tariffs and Trade* (1947) had been criticized for its inability to control dumping or resolve dumping disputes. The 1994 agreement created the *WTO Committee on Antidumping Practices,* which is responsible for assisting countries in implementing the agreement.

Dumping disputes may be taken to the WTO *Dispute Settlement Body* for negotiation or resolution. (The procedures for WTO dispute settlement were discussed in Chapter Nine.) The parties to dispute settlement are the nations involved and not the sellers and buyers of the dumped products—although individual companies often have considerable influence in initiating dumping investigations.

The WTO panel may review a final antidumping order of an administrative agency in the importing country to determine if it is consistent with the *WTO Antidumping Agreement*. The panel can look to see if the agency misinterpreted the provisions of the agreement or whether it properly followed all administrative procedures in an "unbiased and objective" manner. If the panel finds that an antidumping order violates WTO rules, the panel can recommend measures to be taken against the importing country. However, the scope of review of an agency's investigation and antidumping order is limited.

A dispute panel cannot reconsider issues of fact determined during a dumping investigation or overturn an interpretation of the agreement made by the investigating agency. Thus, in reviewing U.S. dumping cases, a panel must accept the facts as found by the ITA and ITC in their investigations and look only to see whether the agencies correctly applied WTO law. This standard of review is similar to the process found in the United States in which courts of law review decisions of administrative agencies.

Dumping and Non-market Economy Countries in Transition

The United States has special rules for calculating the dumping margin of products imported from countries whose political and economic systems rely heavily on government central control, rather than on free-market forces. These *non-market economy countries* (NME) have political and economic systems that are still rooted in the socialist principles of a state-controlled economy. Almost all are in some degree transitioning to a private free-market economy (with a couple of exceptions, of course). Many still have extensive government control over the allocation of resources or the price of raw materials or energy. They can control labor costs or provide transportation, insurance, or other services as an indirect government service to government industries. The governments can set quotas for production output or for export volume. Investment may be heavily regulated and may involve a mixture of government ownership and private interests. Remember, these governments are in a position to see that their exports sell at almost any price they desire. It is impossible to ask a private firm to compete on a level playing field under these circumstances. Thus, in terms of the law of dumping, it is impossible to compare the "normal value" of a product in the NME market to the export price in the United States.

In such a situation, federal law requires the ITA to investigate and to determine a "surrogate" normal value. The *surrogate normal value* is the value of the factors of production, including materials, labor, energy, capital costs and depreciation, packaging, and other general expenses, in a market economy country that is at a level of economic development comparable to that of the NME and that is a significant producer of comparable merchandise. Added to that is an estimated amount for profit. If information is inadequate or not provided, which may be the case if the government does not want it released, surrogate normal value is *the price* at which comparable merchandise produced in market-economy countries that are a level of economic development comparable to that of the NME *is sold in the United States or other countries.* Today, the U.S. government uses the NME method of finding normal value only for China and certain countries of the former Soviet Union.

Market-Oriented Industries. The ITA understands that the transition to free markets cannot happen overnight. Rather, it might take place in steps, with the government freeing certain market sectors to competition or by selling state-owned factories or property through privatization. So, even if the exporting country is an NME, the ITA may look to see if the particular industry producing the dumped products in that country is a market-oriented industry. A *market-oriented industry* is one in which resources (materials, energy, etc.) and labor costs are procured at free-market prices, where there is little government involvement in controlling production and capacity decisions, where prices are set by markets, and where the producers are mostly privately owned. Even where an industry is found not to be market oriented, it is still possible to find that an individual firm or firms are operating freely. In the following case, *Bulk Aspirin from the People's Republic of China,* a French-owned chemical giant with a plant in the United States petitioned the government for antidumping duties against its Chinese competitors. The case will give you a good feel for the administrative process and the combative nature of the proceedings. As you read the case, and especially the comment that follows, consider the ironies in the case, the impact of the antidumping laws on workers and consumers, and the place of dumping laws in the future of the global economy.

Bulk Aspirin from the People's Republic of China

(Notice of Preliminary Determination of Sales at Less Than Fair Value) 65 Fed. Reg. 116 (2000)

International Trade Administration, U.S. Department of Commerce

BACKGROUND AND FACTS

Rhodia Pharma Solutions is one of the world's leading manufacturers of specialty chemicals, including acetylsalicylic acid (bulk aspirin). With corporate headquarters in France, it has about 25,000 employees in offices and manufacturing plants in the United States and throughout the world. In 1999, Rhodia filed a petition with the Department of Commerce ("ITA" herein) alleging that imports from the People's Republic of China (PRC) were being dumped in the United States for less than fair value. Based on industry information, Rhodia believed that their customers were paying less than half of Rhodia's price for the same product. No other firms joined the petition, and Rhodia is apparently the only producer of aspirin in the United States. Rhodia's petition identified several potential Chinese exporters of bulk aspirin. Only two Chinese firms, Jilin and Shandong, responded to the petition. The ITA sent questionnaires to Jilin and Shandong and to the Chinese government, asking that it be forwarded to other Chinese producers. Jilin and Shandong responded with the price and market information requested by the ITA. No other Chinese firms responded. After an investigation, the agency issued this preliminary determination.

PRELIMINARY DETERMINATION

The ITA has treated the PRC as a nonmarket economy ("NME") country in all past antidumping investigations. A designation as an NME remains in effect until it is revoked by the ITA.

Separate Rates: Both Jilin and Shandong have requested separate company-specific rates. These companies have stated that they are privately owned companies with no element of government ownership or control. To establish whether a firm is sufficiently independent from government control to be entitled to a separate rate, the ITA analyzes each exporting entity. Under the separate rates criteria, the ITA assigns separate rates in NME cases only if the respondents can demonstrate the absence of both *de jure* and *de facto* governmental control over export activities.

continued

continued

Absence of De Jure Control ["by law"]: The respondents have placed on the record a number of documents to demonstrate absence of *de jure* government control, including the *Foreign Trade Law of the People's Republic of China* and the *Company Law of the People's Republic of China*. The ITA has analyzed these laws in prior cases and found that they establish an absence of *de jure* control ... over export pricing and marketing decisions of firms.

Absence of De Facto Control ["in fact or reality"]: ... Shandong and Jilin have each asserted the following: (1) They establish their own export prices; (2) they negotiate contracts without guidance from any governmental entities or organizations; (3) they make their own personnel decisions; and (4) they retain the proceeds of their export sales and use profits according to their business needs without any restrictions. Additionally, these two respondents have stated that they do not coordinate or consult with other exporters regarding their pricing. This information supports a preliminary finding that there is no *de facto* governmental control of the export functions of these companies. Consequently, we preliminarily determine that both responding exporters have met the criteria for the application of separate rates.

Use of Facts Available: The PRC-Wide Rate: U.S. import statistics indicate that the total quantity of U.S. imports of aspirin from the PRC is greater than that reported by Jilin and Shandong.... Accordingly, we are applying a single antidumping deposit rate—the PRC-wide rate—to all exporters [other than Jilin and Shandong] based on our presumption that the export activities of the companies that failed to respond to the ITA's questionnaire are controlled by the PRC government. The PRC-wide antidumping rate is based on adverse facts available. The exporters that decided not to respond in any form to the ITA's questionnaire failed to act to the best of their ability in this investigation. Thus ... we are assigning the highest margin in the petition, 144.02 percent, which is higher than any of the calculated margins.

***

Normal Value [NV]: Surrogate Country: Section 773(c)(4) of the Act requires the ITA to value the NME producer's factors of production, to the extent possible, in one or more market economy countries that: (1) Are at a level of economic development comparable to that of the NME, and (2) are significant producers of comparable merchandise. The ITA has determined that India, Pakistan, Sri Lanka, Egypt, Indonesia, and the Philippines are countries comparable to the PRC in terms of overall economic development. We have further determined that India is a significant producer of comparable merchandise. Accordingly, we have calculated NV using mainly Indian values, and in some cases U.S. export values, for the PRC producers' factors of production.

***

Factors of Production: [W]e calculated NV based on factors of production reported by the companies in the PRC which produced aspirin and sold aspirin to the United States. Our NV calculation included amounts for materials, labor, energy, overhead, SG&A, and profit. To calculate NV, the reported unit factor quantities were multiplied by publicly available Indian and U.S. export price values.

Decision. Based on the calculations of normal value, two producers, Jilin and Shandong, were able to show that their export pricing was not under government control and received separate antidumping duty rates based on their individual dumping margins (which ranged from 4 to 42 percent). Bulk aspirin imports from all other Chinese exporters received the PRC-wide rate of 144 percent.

Comment. The final determination of dumping was made in 2000, the same year that the U.S. International Trade Commission found injury to the U.S. producers. In 2001–2002, the Court of International Trade reversed parts of the ITA's methodology of obtaining surrogate values for certain factors of production because it was not based on substantial evidence. The ITA then changed its methods of calculating overhead, labor, and other factors. For example, instead of using a higher weighted average overhead factor, the ITA used figures from the lowest-cost Indian producer. Subsequently, Jilin and Shandong's antidumping duties were cut to zero. In 2003, a Rhodia representative stated in testimony before the U.S. House of Representatives that at first the new duties had helped it regain customers and become profitable again, but when ITA changed its methodology and the antidumping duties disappeared, so did its customers. Rhodia's business in the United States had been devastated. And with that, Rhodia closed the last remaining aspirin plant in America and moved it to—you guessed it—China.

Unfair Import Laws: Subsidies and Countervailing Duties

A second type of unfair trade practice is subsidies. *Subsidies* are financial contributions or benefits conferred by a government to a domestic firm or industry to achieve some economic or social objective. Subsidies might be granted to assist the start-up of new companies, to retire old factories, to help firms meet new environmental regulations, or to protect industries such as steel, aircraft, or agriculture that are essential to national security. They may take many forms, such as low-interest loans, direct cash payments, export financing, credit assistance, or favorable tax treatment. Subsidies are granted by all industrialized nations to virtually all segments of their economies, and not just to manufacturing firms. The EU, the United States, and Japan each spend tens of billions of dollars annually on agricultural subsidies alone, including direct payments to farmers.

Subsidies have long been recognized as damaging to the international economy. Subsidized industries are able to sell their products in foreign markets at prices lower than would otherwise be possible, which distorts trade patterns based on comparative advantage and gives an unfair competitive advantage to subsidized industries. Subsidies also encourage private industries to embark on commercial ventures that, once the subsidy ends, may prove unprofitable or commercially disastrous.

The drawbacks of subsidies are illustrated by the case of the Concorde supersonic aircraft, which was able to fly from Europe to the United States in less than half the time of a regular jet. The aircraft's development by a consortium of European companies was spurred not by demand, but by a host of EU subsidies. In commercial use, the plane turned out to be highly unprofitable. The last Concorde was taken out of service in 2003. Without the subsidy, the plane would have proved too costly to merit production.

WTO Agreement on Subsidies and Countervailing Measures

Subsidies have been regulated by the GATT agreements since 1947. The current law is found in the 1994 GATT agreements: the *WTO Agreement on Subsidies and Countervailing Measures*, negotiated during the *Uruguay Round*. The basic terms of the 1994 agreement have been incorporated into U.S. law in the *Uruguay Round Agreements Act*.

Under the 1994 agreement, subsidies may be dealt with in several ways. First, a WTO member country may appeal to the WTO for dispute resolution. The WTO may recommend that the subsidy be discontinued, that its harmful effects be eliminated, or that some countermeasure be taken by the importing country. Secondly, an importing country may initiate its own administrative proceedings, similar to antidumping proceedings, to impose a countervailing duty on the subsidized goods in order to eliminate their unfair price advantage. A *countervailing duty* (CVD) is a special tariff, in addition to the normal import tariff, imposed on imports of subsidized goods in an amount equal to the amount of the countervailable subsidy. A CVD action may be brought at the same time as the WTO dispute settlement action. However, only one form of relief—either the CVD or a countermeasure approved by the WTO—is available.

Definition of a Subsidy

A subsidy exists if a government confers a benefit on a domestic firm or industry by providing any form of income or price support or provides a financial contribution by

1. Providing funds, grants, or making loans at less than prevailing commercial interest rates or providing loan guarantees that allow the company to receive loans at rates more favorable than nonguaranteed commercial loan rates.
2. Not collecting revenue or taxes otherwise due.
3. Providing investment capital if the investment decision is inconsistent with the usual practices of private investors.
4. Furnishing goods or services other than general infrastructure, such as by building a road or bridge.
5. Purchasing goods from firms at a higher price than would be paid in the marketplace.

GATT 1994 provides for three types of subsidies: prohibited subsidies, domestic or adverse effects subsidies, and nonactionable or socially beneficial subsidies. All three types must meet the preceding definition.

Prohibited Subsidies

Prohibited subsidies include export subsidies or import substitution subsidies. An *export subsidy* is made available to domestic firms upon the export of their product or is contingent upon export performance. An *import substitution subsidy* is a governmental subsidy whose payment is contingent on its recipient using or purchasing domestically made goods over imported goods. Both of these are completely prohibited under WTO rules. An importing country that is a WTO member can request dispute settlement before a WTO panel regardless of whether the subsidy causes injury to any of its firms or industries. WTO dispute resolution should take less than a year to complete. Countervailing duties (CVDs) may be imposed on export subsidies through administrative or legal proceedings in the importing country. In CVD proceedings, export subsidies must be shown to have caused or threatened material injury to a domestic industry producing a like product.

Examples of an export subsidy include money paid on the basis of the number of exported goods, free or subsidized transportation provided for export shipments, rebates of taxes paid on the export of products, export credit guarantees at below market rates, and special tax treatment of income earned through export sales.

In an interesting example of an export subsidy, Germany assisted the development, manufacture, and export of the European Airbus (a jumbo jet that competes with U.S. planes) by providing no-interest loans and currency stabilization guarantees to the manufacturers. These subsidies allowed the manufacturers to enter contracts to sell planes to U.S. airlines without assuming any currency fluctuation risk. In 1992, a GATT (pre-WTO) panel ruled that the German currency stabilization guarantees violated GATT.

Domestic Subsidies

Many subsidies take the form of government programs designed to achieve some greater social or national economic objective, ranging from health care to national defense, and indirectly give firms an advantage in world markets. After all, when a government makes large purchases of overpriced military jets, it subsidizes (and lowers the cost of) passenger aircraft. These purchases generally fall in the category of *domestic subsidies* and must be distinguished from export subsidies. Examples include the provision of capital or low-cost loans for modernizing factories or for buying land on which to build new factories; providing industry with low-cost oil, chemicals, or other raw materials at discount prices from government-owned stockpiles; government defense spending on military aircraft or ships; grants for research and development of medicines; cash payments for apprentice programs or tax deductions to employers that pay college tuition for employees; government-supplied utilities; and tax deductions or tax credits to encourage investment in capital equipment. Domestic subsidies such as these are generally permissible as a part of the legitimate responsibility of government to direct its industrial growth and fund social programs.

REMEDIES FOR ADVERSE EFFECTS OF DOMESTIC SUBSIDIES. Some domestic subsidies give unfair competitive advantage to domestic firms. These are known as *adverse effects subsidies*. They are actionable at the WTO only if they (1) cause injury to a domestic industry of another WTO member country; (2) cause nullification and impairment of rights accruing to a member country under a GATT agreement; or (3) cause serious prejudice to another member. *Serious prejudice* is presumed to exist if the subsidy of a product exceeds 5 percent of its value, if the subsidy covers a firm's operating losses, or if the government forgives a debt owed to it. In addition, serious prejudice may exist if (1) the subsidy impedes world trade in similar products produced in member countries; (2) the subsidy causes lost sales or price undercutting by the subsidized product; or (3) in the case of a subsidy of a primary product or commodity, it causes an increase in the subsidizing country's world market share of that product. In these cases, the WTO may recommend that the subsidizing country remove the prohibited subsidy or that the complaining country take some countermeasures against it.

In a CVD proceeding conducted by an administrative agency in the importing country, as opposed to a WTO panel proceeding, the proof required is different: a complaining party need only show that the domestic subsidy caused or threatens to cause material injury to domestic producers of like products.

What Makes a Subsidy Specific? The second requirement, for both WTO actions and CVD administrative actions, is that the domestic subsidy be "specific." All prohibited (export and import substitution) subsidies are presumed to be specific. All other subsidies are specific if they are limited to helping an enterprise or industry. A government's objective criteria for eligibility for a domestic subsidy is not specific if eligibility is automatic and does not favor one enterprise or industry over another. For instance, suppose that tax authorities allow all taxpayers to deduct $50,000 of the cost of new machinery as an ordinary operating expense in the year of purchase instead of the $25,000 that had been allowed. Because the tax reduction does not favor one industry over another, it is not specific. However, if the companies receiving the subsidy are limited in number, if one firm or industry is the predominant user of the subsidy, or if the subsidy is limited to firms within a certain geographical region, then the subsidy is probably specific. In *Cabot Corp. v. United States,* 620 F. Supp. 722 (Ct. Int'l Trade 1985), the court adopted the "specificity test." The test was enacted into law by Congress in 1988 and subsequently brought to the *Uruguay Round Agreement* by the United States.

Upstream Subsidies. An *upstream subsidy* is one that is granted by a government to a firm or industry that produces raw materials or component parts (input products) that are used in an exported product. For instance, a subsidy on coal might also be considered a subsidy on steel made in furnaces that burn that coal. A subsidy on European wheat might be considered a subsidy upon Italian pasta made from that wheat. Similarly, a subsidy on live swine might be considered an upstream subsidy of unprocessed pork exports. A subsidy of semiconductors would amount to a subsidy of computers in which they are installed. Upstream subsidies are subject to CVDs if the input product is made available at a below-market price and has a significant effect on the cost of manufacturing the final product. Under the U.S. *Uruguay Round Agreements Act,* upstream subsidies include only domestic subsidies and not export subsidies. Upstream subsidies may be countervailed only when they bestow a competitive benefit on the goods in question.

Nonactionable or Socially Beneficial Subsidies

Socially beneficial subsidies are not actionable under WTO rules and are not countervailable if they meet the requirements of the WTO agreement. They include (1) certain subsidies granted to industry or universities for expanding knowledge through research and development, provided they do not directly give an unfair competitive advantage to exported products; (2) certain subsidies to poor, depressed, or underemployed geographic regions—U.S. law requires that per capita GDP or income may not exceed 85 percent of the national average or that unemployment be at least 110 percent of the rate in the subsidizing country; and (3) certain subsidies granted on a one-time basis to help companies meet costly environmental or antipollution regulations, provided the subsidies are limited to 20 percent of the cost of, and made available to all companies that require, the new pollution control equipment or technology. Member countries should notify the WTO Committee on Subsidies and Countervailing Measures in advance of granting a socially beneficial subsidy. A socially beneficial subsidy is not countervailable if the country that granted it has notified the WTO Committee on Subsidies and Countervailing Measures in advance. An importing country's only recourse in this case is the WTO, which uses binding arbitration in these cases.

Subsidies and State-Owned Enterprises

Applying the principles of CVD law to goods exported by state-owned enterprises presents several problems, especially when those enterprises are owned by countries that have a non-market economy. In *Georgetown Steel Corp. v. United States,* 801 F.2d 1308 (Fed. Cir. 1986), the court upheld a policy of the U.S. Department of Commerce of not applying the U.S. CVD statute to imports from non-market countries. The court believed Congress had designed the statute to remedy subsidies that distort the free-market process by altering the market decisions of manufacturers and exporters. In non-market economy countries, the subsidy is, in a sense, made only to the government itself, with no resulting effect on market decision making. In this context, a non-market economy country is defined in U.S. law as "any foreign country [that the U.S. Department of Commerce] determines does not operate on market principles of cost or pricing structures, so that sales of merchandise in such country do not reflect the fair value of the merchandise." The Commerce Department believed that determining a subsidy in this environment would be very difficult.

For over 20 years, the Department of Commerce refused to countervail subsidized goods from China. In 2007, for the first time since 1984, the Department of Commerce reversed its policy and began applying the U.S. CVD law to non-market economy countries, including China. The first cases involved countervailing duties on glossy coated paper from China, which is typically used in catalogs, brochures, and quality full-color magazines. In late 2007, offset duties of 44 percent were imposed, pending a finding by the ITC of material injury. This change in policy was due to the growing influx of Chinese imports to the United States, the increasing privatization of Chinese firms, and demands from members of Congress to stop Chinese subsidies. In 2007 there were several bills before Congress to amend the U.S. countervailing duties statutes applicable to China and non-market countries.

Exports from Newly Privatized Enterprises. What happens when a state-owned enterprise transitions into private ownership? Do the subsidies once provided when the enterprise was government owned continue to benefit the now privately owned firm? Understand that state-owned enterprises exist not just in non-market economies or socialist countries, but also in many countries that we think of as being "free market" or "capitalist." These include Western nations like the UK, Sweden, and France, as well as developing countries such as Mexico, Chile, and Brazil. For example, government ownership of communications or energy industries is not unusual.

Since the late 1980s, there has been a worldwide trend away from government ownership of industry and toward private investment. This is known as privatization. The term *privatization* refers to the process by which a government sells or transfers government-owned industries or other assets to the private sector.

The next case, *United States—Countervailing Measures Concerning Certain Products from the European Communities* (European Steel), sees the largest European steel mills go from their days of

United States—Countervailing Measures Concerning Certain Products from the European Communities (European Steel)

WT/DS212/AB/R (9 December 2002); World Trade Organization Report of the Appellate Body

BACKGROUND AND FACTS

During the 1960s and 1970s, the European steel industry was near financial collapse. With the support of labor groups, the largest firms were kept alive with cash, low-interest loans, and equity investments from European governments. Many mills became government owned. In the early 1980s, the equivalent of tens of billions of dollars of public money was used to keep the mills running. The money financed operations, revitalized equipment, lowered the firms' debt, trained steelworkers, and permitted the export of low-priced steel. The United States responded with a host of trade remedies, including countervailing duties. When the political climate changed in Europe, governments decided to sell off their interests to private investors in free-market stock sales. From 1988 to date, many large steel mills have been privatized. They included British Steel (today Corus), Germany's Saarstahl, France's Usinor, and others. The new privately owned companies continued to sell steel in America.

The U.S. Department of Commerce ("ITA" herein) imposed countervailing duties on European steel

continued

continued

imports despite the fact that the European mills had been privatized. It believed that the benefits endowed by the subsidies while the companies were government owned continued to "pass through" to the same steel companies (arguing that the companies were still the "same legal person") even after the change in ownership. After all, it was assumed, the new shareholders received the modern equipment, trained workers, and other assets paid for by the government. The European Communities maintained that the privatizations took place at arm's length and for fair market value, that the government no longer had any ownership interest or control, and thus that public monies were no longer subsidizing steel production. The EC argued that the U.S. "same person" rule violates the *WTO Agreement on Subsidies and Countervailing Measures [SCM Agreement]*. Consultations between the governments failed, and in 2001, the EC requested that the WTO Dispute Settlement Body convene a dispute panel. After the decision of the panel, the United States appealed to the Appellate Body.

REPORT OF THE APPELLATE BODY

* * *

[W]e find that the Panel erred in concluding that "[p]rivatizations at arm's length and for fair market value *must* lead to the conclusion that the privatized producer paid for what he got and thus did not get any benefit or advantage from the prior financial contribution bestowed upon the state-owned producer." (emphasis added) Privatization at arm's length and for fair market value *may* result in extinguishing the benefit. Indeed, we find that there is a rebuttable presumption that a benefit ceases to exist after such a privatization. Nevertheless, it does not *necessarily* do so. There is no inflexible rule *requiring* that investigating authorities, in future cases, *automatically* determine that a "benefit" derived from pre-privatization financial contributions expires following privatization at arm's length and for fair market value. It depends on the facts of each case.

* * *

With all this in mind, we now turn to the administrative practice of the ITA that is the source and subject of this dispute.... Generally, the ITA applies the "same person" method to countervailing duty determinations following a change in ownership.

* * *

The Panel stated, and the United States agreed before the Panel and on appeal, that the "same person" method *requires* the ITA to "consider that the benefit attributed to the state-owned producer can be automatically attributed to the privatized producer without any examination of the condition of the transaction" when the agency determines the post-privatization entity is not a new legal person. It is only if the ITA finds that a new legal person has been created that the agency will make a determination of whether a benefit exists, and, in such cases, the inquiry will be limited to the subject of whether a *new* subsidy has been provided to the new owners.

Thus, under the "same person" method, when the ITA determines that no new legal person is created as a result of privatization, the ITA will conclude from this determination, *without any further analysis,* and irrespective of the price paid by the new owners for the newly-privatized enterprise, that the newly-privatized enterprise continues to receive the benefit of a previous financial contribution. This approach is contrary to the *SCM Agreement* that the investigating authority must take into account in an administrative review "positive information substantiating the need for a review." Such information could relate to developments with respect to the subsidy, privatization at arm's length and for fair market value, or some other information. The "same person" method impedes the ITA from complying with its obligation to examine whether a countervailable "benefit" continues to exist in a firm subsequent to that firm's change in ownership. Therefore, we find that the "same person" method, *as such,* is inconsistent with ... the *SCM Agreement.*

* * *

Decision. The Appellate Body found that in countervailing duty actions, national administrative agencies must consider a broad range of criteria on a case-by-case basis in determining whether prior subsidies to a former government-owned company have "passed through" to the newly privatized company. The "same person" test used by the U.S. Department of Commerce violated the *SCM Agreement.*

Comment. In 2003, the ITA announced a new rule based on the presumption that a government subsidy can benefit a company over a period of time, corresponding to the useful life of the assets. However, the presumption is rebuttable if it can be shown that the government sold its ownership of all or substantially all of a company or its assets, retaining no control, and that the sale was an arm's-length transaction for fair market value.

near–financial collapse in the late 1960s, through a government bailout and takeover of ownership, to a subsequent return to private hands decades later. The United States believed that the financial contributions made to the firms while they were government owned were benefits that passed through to the newly privatized companies. This, in turn, continued to permit low-cost steel exports to the United States. The issue ultimately reached the WTO Appellate Body in Geneva.

The Controversy over the *Continued Dumping and Subsidy Offset Act of 2000*

Normally, antidumping and countervailing duties collected on imports by the Bureau of Customs and Border Protection are paid to the U.S. Treasury. To toughen U.S. unfair trade laws, in 2000, the U.S. Congress enacted the *Continued Dumping and Subsidy Offset Act*, commonly called the *Byrd Amendment*. In 2003, the WTO Appellate Body ruled that the statute violated WTO subsidies rules, and it was repealed, effective in 2007. It provided that countervailing duties collected by the U.S. government be paid directly to the petitioning companies in the action. From 2001 through 2005, U.S. Customs paid over $1 billion directly to U.S. firms. The industries receiving the largest payments were steel, candles, ball bearings, and computer chips. The law prompted immediate protests by eleven WTO members, including some of America's closest trading partners from across the globe. They argued that the law prompted firms to file unfair import cases and would give them an unfair competitive advantage and that transferring duties to individual firms amounted to the making of subsidy payments, which are not a permitted remedy in unfair import cases under WTO rules. In *United States—Continued Dumping and Subsidy Offset Act of 2000,* Report of the Appellate Body, World Trade Organization, WT/DS217/234/AB/R (16 January 2003), the WTO Dispute Settlement Body recommended that the U.S. law be brought into compliance. The EU, Canada, Japan, and Mexico began trade retaliation in 2005 by imposing new tariffs on U.S. goods. The repeal of the law was supported by industry groups in the United States representing U.S. importers and manufacturers of finished goods, which claimed that the law did little more than provide a windfall for a few large American companies.

Material Injury in Unfair Import Cases

In unfair trade actions between WTO members, the importing country must find that a domestic industry has been materially injured or threatened with material injury or that the establishment of an industry has been materially retarded. This requirement applies to both antidumping actions and CVD actions.

The "material injury" requirement under the antidumping and countervailing duty laws prescribes a finding of less harm than does the "serious injury" requirement in the safeguard actions. *Material injury* has generally been defined as injury that is not inconsequential, immaterial, or unimportant. In determining material injury under the unfair trade laws, the national investigating agency (in the United States, the International Trade Commission) must consider all relevant economic factors. Factors used to determine material injury include (1) the volume of the dumped or subsidized imports (Have dumped imports increased significantly?); (2) the effect of the imports on prices in the domestic market for like products (Have prices been undercut significantly? Have prices been depressed? Are domestic firms unable to raise prices to cover increased costs?); and (3) the impact of the imports on the domestic industry, including all relevant economic data reflecting industry sales, profits, market share, productivity, return on investment, utilization of capacity, cash flow, wages, unemployment, growing inventories, and so on. A finding of material injury must be reviewed every 5 years if the antidumping order is still in effect at that time.

Judicial Review in International Trade Cases

Decisions of the ITA or ITC in both CVD cases and antidumping duty cases are reviewable in the U.S. Court of International Trade if they are final decisions or if they are negative determinations. A *negative determination* is a decision by the agency either to not initiate an investigation or that a material injury does not exist. If an antidumping determination involves Canadian or Mexican goods, appeals may be made to a binational arbitration panel established under NAFTA.

CONCLUSION

Most readers are accustomed to hearing arguments in the news, television, and popular press about free trade versus protectionism. The debates seem to be especially vociferous as national elections approach, whether in the United States or elsewhere in the world. Other readers have had the opportunity to study the issues more academically, perhaps in courses in economics. This chapter, however, looked at the issues of free trade and protectionism from a purely legal perspective. We examined the tools, administrative procedures, and remedies available at the international level, through the WTO, and under American law, for dealing with (1) increased imports that threaten to injure a domestic industry and (2) unfair trade.

Readers interested in knowing more about bringing and handling unfair trade actions in the United States should consult the *Antidumping and Countervailing Duty Handbook,* published by the International Trade Commission (USITC Pub. 3916, April 2007). The text is an excellent summary and informal resource for business. Another excellent source of information is the annual report of the ITC, *The Year in Trade 2006: Operation of the Trade Agreements Program* (USITC Pub. 3927, 58th Report 2007). For statistical data on unfair import cases, see *Import Injury Investigations Case Statistics: 1980–2005* (USITC Office of Investigations, 2006). All three reports are available on the Internet.

According to the latter report, in the period from 1980 through 2005, over 1,500 antidumping and countervailing duty actions were brought before the ITC. In the same 15-year period, most antidumping duty actions in the United States were initiated against producers from China, Japan, Korea, Germany, Taiwan, Canada, Brazil, and India. Of these cases, 42 percent were affirmative determinations. For the same period, most CVD actions in the United States were brought against products from Brazil, France, Italy, Canada, Germany, Korea, and Spain. Of the CVD cases, only 26 percent were affirmative determinations. In dollar terms, the largest cases involved softwood lumber from Canada, minivans from Japan, frozen orange juice from Brazil, steel sheets from Brazil, shrimp from Thailand, and furniture from China.

From 1975 through 2005, only 73 *Section 201* safeguard actions were brought, involving $60 billion in imports. The largest cases in dollar terms involved steel, motor vehicles, footwear, and certain electronic and agricultural products.

According to the World Trade Organization, the United States has reported more countervailing duty investigations than any other country, followed by the European Union, Canada, and South Africa. Worldwide, more CVD actions are brought against products from India than any other country. Now that U.S. countervailing duty laws apply to imports from China, as of 2007, it very well may be that China will become the main target of U.S. CVD actions.

The countries that report the greatest number of antidumping investigations are India, the United States, and the European Union. Worldwide, almost four times as many antidumping actions are brought against producers from China than any other country.

A 2007 report of the International Trade Commission discusses the economic impact of U.S. import restrictions and uses an economic model to estimate what would happen if all significant U.S. trade barriers were removed in the most protected U.S. industries, including beef; canned tuna; dairy products; ethyl alcohol; sugar and sugar-containing products; tobacco; other food and agricultural products; textiles and apparel from China, Vietnam, and certain non-WTO member countries, footwear and leather products; glass; watches; ball and roller bearings; and ceramic wall and floor tile. The ITC concluded that

> [P]ublic and private consumption would increase by about $3.7 billion annually [by 2011] if all of the significant restraints quantified in this report were removed unilaterally. Exports would expand by $13.5 billion and imports by $19.6 billion, while about 60,000 workers would move from contracting sectors to expanding sectors as a result of liberalization. [See *The Economic Effects of Significant U.S. Import Restraints* (USITC Pub. 3906, Fifth Update, February 2007).]

Chapter Summary

1. The terms "safeguard," "import relief," and "adjustments to imports" all refer to the WTO-recognized rights of a nation to protect a domestic industry from increasing foreign imports.
2. The *WTO Agreement on Safeguards* provides that a member may apply a temporary safeguard measure (e.g., increase tariffs) to a product only if that product "is being imported in such increased quantities and under such conditions as to cause or threaten to cause serious injury to the domestic industry that produces like or directly competitive products." WTO safeguards are global safeguards, meaning that they must be applied to imports of specific products without regard to the country of origin.
3. In the United States, safeguard actions are investigated by the International Trade Commission, an independent agency of government, and its recommendations go to the president. The willingness of the president to protect an industry depends on national interests as well as the president's own economic and trade philosophies. Special safeguard actions apply to imports from China.
4. Trade adjustment assistance is available to workers, firms, and farmers whose jobs are lost to foreign imports or by the relocation of factories to foreign countries.
5. Dumping is the unfair trade practice of selling goods in a foreign country for less than the normal value of like products in the home market. It is a form of international price discrimination by exporters. National laws and practices on antidumping must follow the basic framework of the *WTO Agreement on Antidumping*. Antidumping duties can only be imposed on dumped products by the country of import where the dumping causes or threatens material injury to a domestic industry producing like products. Much of the litigation in this area involves determining normal value and the calculation of the dumping margin. In the United States, the International Trade Administration determines the dumping margin, and the International Trade Commission determines if it caused material injury.
6. A *subsidy* is a financial contribution or benefit conferred by a government to a domestic firm or firms, directly or indirectly, to achieve some industrial, economic, or social objective. Subsidies that are prohibited include export subsidies, import substitution subsidies, and adverse effects subsidies. The *WTO Agreement on Subsidies and Countervailing Measures* permits the country of import to impose countervailing duties (CVDs) on illegally subsidized imports to offset the value of the benefit.
7. In 2007, for the first time since 1984, the Department of Commerce reversed its policy and began applying the U.S. CVD law to nonmarket economy countries, including China. This change in policy was due to the growing influx of Chinese imports into the United States, the increasing privatization of Chinese firms, and demands from members of Congress to stop Chinese subsidies.
8. Throughout the area of unfair trade law, the decisions of the WTO Appellate Body in Geneva, Switzerland, are becoming increasingly important. In several cases, the United States has had to reform or repeal its laws and administrative practices to comply with WTO rules.
9. Books and articles on the economics of dumping and subsidies could fill entire libraries. Readers interested in this area should consider furthering their theoretical study of international economics or the economics of international trade.

Questions and Case Problems

1. Consider how *Section 201* (safeguard against injury) has been used in the United States in recent years. Safeguard measures were applied by President Reagan in the *Harley-Davidson* case and by President Bush to protect the U.S. steel industry in 2002. Based on your research, on what other

occasions has a U.S. president imposed safeguard measures to protect an American industry since 1980? Evaluate the government's use of safeguard measures. What are the pros and cons of using safeguards? What are the effects on domestic industry in the short term? How might it affect a firm's competitiveness in the long term? Although the administrative process is handled through a bipartisan, independent commission (the ITC), why is the process still very political?

2. What makes an import practice "unfair"? What remedies are available under U.S. law to protect domestic industries from unfair imports?
3. Describe the different functions of the ITA and the ITC in regulating import competition.
4. The plaintiff, Smith Corona, was the last remaining manufacturer of portable electric typewriters in the United States. An action was brought to challenge the method used by the International Trade Administration to determine whether the Japanese typewriter companies Brother and Silver Seiko had engaged in dumping in the United States. The typewriters in question were sold in Japan (the home market) under different circumstances of sale than in the United States. In Japan, Silver Seiko provided volume rebates to its customers based on total sales of all merchandise sold. Brother incurred advertising expenses in Japan, as well as expenditures for accessories that accompany typewriters sold in Japan but not in the United States. The ITA subtracted these amounts from foreign market value in calculating the dumping margin. Was the ITA correct? See *Smith-Corona Group v. United States,* 713 F.2d 1568 (Fed. Cir. 1983).
5. The American Grape Growers alleged that imports of wine from France and Italy were being subsidized and sold in the United States at less than fair value. The ITC's preliminary review found no reasonable indication that a United States industry was threatened with material injury by reason of those imports. The American growers said the ITC decision did not cumulate the imports from France and Italy as it should have done. It instead had considered the two products different because the French wines were primarily white wines, and the Italian wines were primarily red and effervescent. The growers also said the ITC was wrong to base its decision on whether an injury had been proved, as opposed to whether there was a possibility of injury. Do you agree with the grape growers that the ITC's preliminary decision was wrong?
6. Plaintiff, Cabot Corporation, is contesting the International Trade Administration's finding that the Mexican government's provision of carbon black feedstock and natural gas to Mexican producers at below-market prices did not constitute a countervailable subsidy. Carbon black feedstock and natural gas are used in the production of paints, inks, plastics, and carbon paper. The feedstock is a by-product of crude oil and sold in Mexico through PEMEX, the government-owned oil company. Pursuant to a comprehensive economic development plan, PEMEX supplied the feedstock and natural gas at below-market prices to two Mexican producers of carbon black. The plaintiff, a U.S. producer of carbon black, contends that under U.S. law the actions of the Mexican government amount to a countervailable domestic subsidy. What is the correct legal test to determine if the supply of feedstock to Mexican manufacturers was a countervailable domestic subsidy? *Cabot Corp. v. United States,* 620 F. Supp. 722 (Ct. Int'l Trade 1985).
7. In 2007, the U.S. Department of Commerce announced that it would begin applying the U.S. countervailing duty statute to subsidized imports from China. China filed suit in the United States to contest the announcement, but the U.S. court refused to take jurisdiction. China then requested consultations at the WTO. What is the status of this disagreement at the WTO? Has a resolution been reached? What new CVD investigations have been launched against Chinese imports?

Managerial Implications

Your firm manufactures optic transistors (OTs), which are a component of personal computers. U.S. firms control 60 percent of the U.S. market for OTs. The market has done well overall, but recently, Japanese manufacturers of computers have increased their market share. Over the past two years, the Japanese have been exporting OTs to the United States in larger quantities. You have noticed that in the past two years your firm's share of the U.S. market for OTs has dropped from more than 25 percent to less than 20 percent. In addition, your firm's total sales have declined, its inventories are at their highest levels, and you have had to postpone hiring new employees. You have been informed by one of your better customers that it can purchase imported OTs for \$0.95 each, ex factory, or \$1.00, CIF American port. Your U.S. price has been \$1.20, FOB your factory, with your costs at $0.90. The same OTs are sold to Japanese computer firms at $1.15. Furthermore, you have learned that the Japanese government assists OT manufacturers by rebating the value-added tax normally assessed on all products manufactured in Japan.

To complicate your problems, you have experienced difficulty cracking export markets. You have noticed that countries in which personal computers are now being assembled, such as Brazil, Korea, and Taiwan, have restricted your firm's imports through a maze of complex regulations. These regulations require that you disclose important manufacturing and design techniques before import licenses will be granted. You are also concerned that your design patents will not be protected there, because Korean patent protection laws are not enforced. Korea has imposed quotas on OTs that make it virtually impossible to export to that market.

What remedies are available to your firm under U.S. law? What factors (economic, political, or other) will affect the outcome of the case? Discuss.

Ethical Considerations

Your firm is a paper converter. It converts paperboard into various articles used in homes and restaurants for food preparation, sale, and storage. Its products include pizza boxes, ice cream boxes, bakery and deli boxes, and paper plates as well as boxes and trays used in fast food operations. You have purchased paperboard from both domestic and foreign sources. Recently, a Chinese supplier has begun offering paperboard for sale directly to your firm at extremely low prices—far lower than what you have been paying domestically. One of your colleagues at your firm called the offer "too good to be true." What information do you think you need before committing to a purchase? If it turns out that the products are being "dumped" in the U.S. market, what would be the result? What might be the objective of the exporter in this case? Do you think that it is fair or unfair for an exporter to dump its goods in a foreign market? Evaluate the statement, "Selling at a low price can't be unfair."

For Internet Activities, Visit academic.cengage.com/blaw/schaffer.

CHAPTER 12
IMPORTS, CUSTOMS, AND TARIFF LAW

Importing is the process of entering goods into the customs territory of a country. The study of importing should not be approached from the perspective of an isolated transaction. Rather, importing should be viewed as an integral part of a global company's operations. For instance, a chemical company might find that raw materials can be sourced from foreign suppliers at a net cost far less than if purchased at home. A leading apparel designer might ship garments to the United States that had been assembled in Honduras, from parts of clothing that were cut and sewn at plants in Hong Kong, from fabric that had been woven in China. An automobile company might ship cars to the United States from assembly plants in Mexico that used component parts sourced from Japan or Europe. A Japanese-owned electronics company might assemble televisions in the Caribbean using both Japanese and U.S. parts, with the finished products shipped back to U.S. markets. A large retailer might import foreign-made consumer goods, such as toys or appliances, because they are cheaper from overseas sources. U.S. distributors of Swiss watches, Danish cheese, or French wine might import these foreign brands because customers perceive them to be of superior quality. Each of these companies views the operation of their firm in a global context, and they are aware that their global strategy will be affected by the customs and tariff laws applicable to their products as these goods cross national borders.

Whereas the preceding chapters discussed the process by which nations regulate international trade, this chapter focuses on the specific problems of importing goods into the United States. It examines U.S. regulations governing the admission of goods into the country, the calculation of import duties, tariff preferences for developing countries, the marking requirements for goods, and the use of many duty-saving devices, such as foreign trade zones. The chapter begins with an explanation of how imports into the United States are supervised by the U.S. Bureau of Customs and Border Protection and how the customs and tariff laws are administered.

THE ADMINISTRATION OF CUSTOMS AND TARIFF LAWS

The customs and tariff laws of the United States are enacted by the U.S. Congress and are implemented and enforced by the *U.S. Bureau of Customs and Border Protection,* referred to in this book as U.S. Customs or simply Customs. Customs is an agency within the Department of Homeland Security and is headed by the Commissioner of Customs. The creation of the Department of Homeland Security in 2003 was a part of the largest reorganization of the American government in over fifty years. The Bureau of Customs and Border Protection was created by merging the functions related to border security that had previously been handled by the Department of Agriculture, the Immigration and Naturalization Service, the Border Patrol, and U.S. Customs (formerly a part of the Department of the Treasury). The agency's duties are to prevent terrorists and terrorist weapons from entering the United States, enforce border security, assess and collect the tariff revenue of the United States, enforce the customs laws, which includes regulating the entry of products under quota or embargo, enforce the labeling statutes, supervise exports, administer duty-free zones, and perform other functions. As a law enforcement agency, U.S. Customs combats smuggling of narcotics and contraband and investigates tariff fraud cases. Customs has the authority to bar the entry of goods that violate patent, trademark, or copyright laws. The agency is responsible for the administration of customs laws throughout the customs territory of the United States, which includes Puerto Rico. In addition, U.S. Customs officers are assigned to U.S. embassies in many foreign countries to assist in the administration of U.S. customs laws.

Customs is divided into seven geographic regions, each headed by a regional commissioner. The regions are further divided into districts, each headed by a district director. Customs offices are located at the *ports of entry*, including major seaports, airports, inland ports, and border crossings. Within each district are *field import specialists*, who make initial determinations as to the entry of goods. They can seek advice from *national import specialists*. Some officers are specialists in particular types of products, such as textiles. The district director supervises all imports within the district and makes sure that imported goods are entered in accordance with the rules of the agency and decisions of the courts.

The Formal Entry Process

The *formal entry process* refers to the administrative process required to import goods into the customs territory of a country. Goods have officially "entered" the United States only when the following requirements have been met.

1. The goods have arrived at a U.S. "port of entry."
2. The goods are not of a type that is not permitted entry or from an embargoed country.
3. Delivery is authorized by Customs after inspection and release.
4. Estimated duties have been paid or a customs bond posted.

The process begins upon the arrival of the merchandise at a U.S. port of entry. Goods not processed for entry within fifteen days are sent to a warehouse as "unclaimed freight." The goods may be entered by the owner, purchaser, consignee (the party to whom the goods are shipped or to be delivered), or licensed customs broker. A *customs broker* is an authorized agent, licensed by federal law, to act for and on behalf of importers in making entry of goods. (A broker is not needed to import goods for personal use.) Over 90 percent of all entries are made by customs brokers. A customs broker must possess a written power of attorney from the party making entry. Nonresident individuals and foreign corporations may make entry, but they are bound by much stricter rules. The entry process is not merely transporting the goods into the United States; it includes the filing of customs documents and the payment of duties.

REQUIRED DOCUMENTATION. When goods are entered, the entry documents must be filed within five days. The documents necessary to enter goods generally include the following items:

1. An entry manifest or merchandise release form (see the Entry/Immediate Delivery Form in Exhibit 12.1)
2. U.S. Customs Entry Summary Form (Exhibit 12.2)
3. Proof of the right to make entry (a bill of lading, air waybill, or carrier's certificate)
4. The commercial invoice obtained from the seller (or a pro forma invoice, if the commercial invoice is temporarily delayed by the seller)
5. Packing slips to identify the contents of cartons
6. Other documents required by special regulations (e.g., certificate of origin, quota visa, textile declaration, etc.)

THE COMMERCIAL INVOICE. A seller must provide a separate invoice for each commercial shipment entering the United States. The *commercial invoice* is required for all shipments greater than $500 and intended for sale or commercial use in the United States. The invoice must provide all pertinent information about the shipment, in English, and be signed by the seller. One invoice can be used for installment shipments to the same consignee

Exhibit 12.1

Entry/Immediate Delivery Form

U.S. DEPARTMENT OF HOMELAND SECURITY
Bureau of Customs and Border Protection

Form Approved
OMB No. 1651-0024
Exp. 11/30/2008

ENTRY/IMMEDIATE DELIVERY

19 CFR 142.3, 142.16, 142.22, 142.24

ABI CERTIFIED

1. ARRIVAL DATE 060908	2. ELECTED ENTRY DATE	3. ENTRY TYPE CODE/NAME 01 ABI/S	4. ENTRY NUMBER 669-2242260-6
5. PORT 1512	6. SINGLE TRANS. BOND X 891	7. BROKER/IMPORTER FILE NUMBER 61779SE	
	8. CONSIGNEE NUMBER		9. IMPORTER NUMBER 12-34567
10. ULTIMATE CONSIGNEE NAME Importer's Company Anytown, NC 20000		11. IMPORTER OF RECORD NAME SAME	
12. CARRIER CODE 111	13. VOYAGE/FLIGHT/TRIP 444	14. LOCATION OF GOODS-CODE(S)/NAME(S) L362	
15. VESSEL CODE/NAME LUFTHANSA			
16. U.S. PORT OF UNLADING 1704	17. MANIFEST NUMBER	18. G. O. NUMBER	19. TOTAL VALUE $3331
20. DESCRIPTION OF MERCHANDISE Bedding			

21. IT/BL/ AWB CODE	22. IT/BL/AWB NO.	23. MANIFEST QUANTITY	24. H.S. NUMBER	25. COUNTRY OF ORIGIN	26. MANUFACTURER NO.
I	22069456995		6304.HS.60107	DE	DEBRILRHE4044KRA
M	22069456995				
H	48502287	5			

27. CERTIFICATION

I hereby make application for entry/immediate delivery. I certify that the above information is accurate, the bond is sufficient, valid, and current, and that all requirements of 19 CFR Part 142 have been met.

SIGNATURE OF APPLICANT
X Importer's Custom Broker

PHONE NO.

DATE 6/11/08

29. BROKER OR OTHER GOVT. AGENCY USE

28. CBP USE ONLY

☐ OTHER AGENCY ACTION REQUIRED, NAMELY:

☐ CBP EXAMINATION REQUIRED.

☐ ENTRY REJECTED, BECAUSE:

JUN 12 8.23 AM '08

DELIVERY AUTHORIZED: SIGNATURE WRL DATE 6-12-08

PAPERWORK REDUCTION ACT NOTICE: This information is to determine the admissibility of imports into the United States and to provide the necessary information for the examination of the cargo and to establish the liability for payment of duties and taxes. Your response is necessary. The estimated average burden associated with this collection of information is 15 minutes per respondent depending on individual circumstances. Comments concerning the accuracy of this burden estimate and suggestions for reducing this burden should be directed to Bureau of Customs and Border Protection, Information Services Branch, Washington, DC 20229, and to the Office of Management and Budget, Paperwork Reduction Project (1651-0024), Washington, DC 20503..

CBP Form 3461 (01/89)

Exhibit 12.2

Entry Summary Form

Form Approved OMB No. 1651-0022

DEPARTMENT OF HOMELAND SECURITY
U.S. Customs and Border Protection

ENTRY SUMMARY

1. Filer Code/entry No. 2242260-6	2. Entry Type	3. Summary Date 6/26/08	
4. Surety No. 891	5. Bond Type SEB-9	6. Port Code 1512	7. Entry Date

8. Importing Carrier LUFTHANSA	9. Mode of Transport 40	10. Country of Origin DE	11. Import Date 06/06/08
12. B/L or AWB No. 22069456995	13. Manufacturer ID DEBILRHE4044KRO	14. Exporting Country DE GERMANY	15. Export Date 06/06/08
16. I.T. No. 22069456995 / 17. I.T. Date 06/06/08	18. Missing Docs	19. Foreign Port of Lading Frankfurt	20. U.S. Port of Unlading 1704 ATLANTA
21. Location of Goods/G.O.No. L362	22. Consignee No.	23. Importer No. 12-34567	24. Reference No.

25. Ultimate Consignee Name and Address Importer's Company City Anytown State NC Zip 20000	26. Importer of Record Name and Address Same City State Zip

27. Line No.	28. Description of Merchandise — 29. A. HTSUS No. B. ADA/CVD No. — 30. A. Grossweight B. Manifest Qty. — 31. Net Quantity in HTSUS Units	32. A. Entered Value B. CHGS C. Relationship	33. A. HTSUS Rate B. ADA/CVD Rate C. IRC Rate D. Visa No.	34. Duty and I.R. Tax Dollars Cents
	48502287			
	INV. No. 9999/99/8951			
001	FURN ARTICLES:N/KNIT:WOOL/HAIR			
	6304.9960107 193 193 KG	3331 709	6.4%	213.60
	MERCHANDISE PROCESSING FEE		.17%	5.66
INV	VAL 4039.98			
LESS	NDC 709.00			
	3330.98 US DOLLAR AT 1.00000000			
ENT.	VAL 3330.98 AS 3331 TOTAL			
	5 PCS TOTAL	3331		234.18
	BLOCK 39 SUMMARY:			
MPF	499 21.00			
TOTAL:	21.00 TEV:	3331		

Other Fee Summary for Block 39	35. Total Entered Value $ Total Other Fees $	**CBP USE ONLY** A. LIQ CODE REASON CODE	B. Ascertained Duty C. Ascertained Tax D. Ascertained Other E. Ascertained Total	TOTALS 37. Duty 213.18 38. Tax .00 39. Other 21.00 40. Total 234.18

36. DECLARATION OF IMPORTER OF RECORD (OWNER OR PURCHASER) OR AUTHORIZED AGENT

I declare that I am the ☐ Importer of record and that the actual owner, purchaser, or consignee for CBP purposes is as shown above, OR ☒ owner or purchaser or agent thereof. I further declare that the merchandise ☒ was obtained pursuant to a purchase or agreement to purchase and that the prices set forth in the invoices are true, OR ☐ was not obtained pursuant to a purchase or agreement to purchase and the statements in the invoices as to value or price are true to the best of my knowledge and belief. I also declare that the statements in the documents herein filed fully disclose to the best of my knowledge and belief the true prices, values, quantities, rebates, drawbacks, fees, commissions, and royalties and are true and correct, and that all goods or services provided to the seller of the merchandise either free or at reduced cost are fully disclosed.
I will immediately furnish to the appropriate CBP officer any information showing a different statement of facts.

41. DECLARANT NAME	TITLE	SIGNATURE	DATE
Importer's Broker			6/11/08

42. Broker/Filer Information (Name, address, phone number) Importer's Broker P.O. Box 123 Charlotle, N.C. 28219	43. Broker/Importer File No. 123456ab-6

PaperWork Reduction Act Notice CBP Form 7501 (04/05)

if the shipments arrive within ten days of each other. The invoice must include the following information:

- Names of the port of shipment and the destined port of entry
- Name of buyer and seller or consignee
- Common or trade name for the goods and their detailed description
- Country of origin
- Currency of payment
- Quantity and weight of the goods shipped
- Value of the goods accurately and correctly stated, including a breakdown of all itemized charges such as freight, insurance, packing costs, the costs of containers, and any rebates and commissions paid or payable
- A packing list stating in detail what merchandise is in each individual package
- Special information for certain classes of merchandise (e.g., bedspreads must indicate whether they contain any embroidery, lace, braid, or other trimming)

The Entry Summary and Immediate Delivery Forms. Within ten working days the importer must file these completed documents with Customs at the port of entry. The information on the form is used to determine the amount of duties owed, to gather import statistics, and to determine if the goods conform to other U.S. regulations.

Payment of Duties. If import duties are assessed on the goods by U.S. Customs, the importer must deposit estimated duties with Customs at the time of filing the entry documents or the entry summary form. The duties must be in an amount determined by U.S. Customs, pending a final calculation of the amount actually owed. Payment to a customs broker does not relieve the importer of liability to pay the duties. The liability for duties constitutes a personal debt of the importer, and a lien attaches to the merchandise. In lieu of paying duties immediately, an importer may post a customs bond. This is more convenient for companies needing immediate delivery of their goods. A customs bond can be purchased for a single shipment or for all shipments over the course of a year and up to the amount stated in the bond. The purpose of the bond is to ensure the payment of duties on final calculation. In some cases, goods can be released for transportation or storage *in-bond,* meaning that the payments of duties are suspended until the goods are released for sale or use in the United States. There is no liability for duties on unordered or unclaimed merchandise.

Informal Entries. Personal and some smaller commercial shipments valued at $2,000 or less may be cleared through an *informal entry* process. In this process a bond is not required for entry, and import duties are payable immediately at the time of entry. Informal entries may be processed through the U.S. Postal Service. The letter carrier acts as the agent for U.S. Customs for the purpose of collecting import duties.

This practice has several advantages. Postal rates can be far less for smaller packages than commercial airfreight, and the entry process is quicker and less expensive, with no customs broker needed. The documentation and marking requirements are still strict, however, and the importer should check with the postal service before attempting a postal entry. A commercial invoice must accompany the shipment. In addition, many products have a $250 limit on postal entries; these include furniture, flowers, textiles, leather goods, footwear, toys, games, and many other items. Wool products and wearing apparel from the Pacific Rim countries require a formal customs entry regardless of value. If a mail article is found to contain merchandise subject to an import duty and the article is not accompanied by a customs declaration and invoice, it is subject to seizure and forfeiture.

Electronic Entry Processing. In the late 1990s, Customs instituted a paperless entry process, known as the *Automated Commercial System.* It is designed to reduce costs to business and government and to speed the entry process. The system allows entry documents to be filed electronically through an automated hook-up between importers, customs brokers, and Customs via the *Automated Broker Interface.* Many companies, primarily the largest and more sophisticated importers and brokers, are already filing electronically.

Remote Location Filing. Until recently entry processing had to take place at the port where the goods were located. Thus, importers had to rely on the services of a broker at the port of entry, even if the goods were being entered in a distant location. Large importers who move goods through different ports asked Congress to permit entry processing from remote locations. The Remote Location Filing system allows brokers in all parts of the country to make remote entries at distant ports.

Liquidation and Protest

In a normal import transaction, assuming no errors or penalties are at issue, the entry will be liquidated. *Liquidation* is the final computation and assessment of the applicable duty on entered goods by Customs. This "closes the book," making the entry complete. If Customs accepts the entry as submitted on the importer's documents, liquidation occurs immediately. However, when Customs at the port of entry determines that additional duties are owed, a *notice of adjustment* is sent to the importer. The importer must respond to the notice, or the duty will be assessed as corrected. If a question or dispute arises concerning the goods themselves, as in the case of technical or unusual products, or in complex cases, the case may be referred to an *import specialist* familiar with that type of product. Either the importer or Customs officials may seek internal advice from the agency's headquarters. Officially, the liquidation becomes effective, and the entry is closed, when it is posted at the "customs house" at the port of entry. A courtesy notice is sent to importers advising them of the liquidation, although this notice is not legally effective. If actual duties owed exceed the estimated duties paid at the time of entry, the importer must pay them within fifteen days of the posting of the notice of liquidation.

Time Limits on Liquidation. Liquidation must occur within one year of entry. The time can be extended for good cause. An entry not liquidated within one year is deemed liquidated by operation of law. Under a *deemed liquidation,* the goods are dutied at the rate accepted on the entry summary form. A liquidation can be reopened within two years if there is evidence to suspect that the importer committed fraud.

Protesting Liquidations. An importer that wants to dispute a liquidation made by Customs may file a protest with Customs at the port where the goods were entered within ninety days. An importer may not file a protest where no change was made by Customs to the entry as filed by the importer. Customs has thirty days to respond in cases where the goods have been denied entry; otherwise they have two years to act. Appeals can be made to Customs headquarters in Washington, D.C.

Judicial Review of Protests. If Customs denies a protest—which is what usually happens—the importer may seek judicial review in the Court of International Trade. All duties assessed must first be paid, and the appeal must be filed within 180 days. The Court of International Trade is a specialized federal court located in New York City. Appeals from the Court of International Trade are made to the U.S. Court of Appeals for the Federal Circuit in Washington, D.C.

Enforcement and Penalties

The Bureau of Customs and Border Protection is a law enforcement agency charged with enforcing the tariff laws of the United States. U.S. Customs has broad powers to establish regulations, carry out investigations, and impose penalties. All care must be used in complying with customs requirements, and many experienced importers will tell you that they would no sooner make an error on a customs form than they would on their own tax returns.

The basic enforcement and civil penalty provisions of the customs laws are found in Title 19, Section 1592. The offenses set out here are civil violations calling for civil penalties imposed administratively by Customs. Criminal violations are addressed elsewhere in the U.S. Criminal Code. Section 1592 begins by setting out an importer's basic responsibility: "No person may enter or attempt to enter any merchandise into the United States by means of any written document, electronic transmission of information, oral statement, or other act that is both material and false or which omits any material information affecting the entry."

Making Materially False Statements to Customs. An act or statement is "material" if it refers to the identity, quality, value, source, or country of origin of the merchandise, or if it affects the rate of duty charged or the item's right to be imported into the United States. For instance, falsely stating that cigars of Cuban origin are from Honduras might allow them to illegally pass through customs when they otherwise would be denied entry, and stating that a textile product is decorated with embroidery, when it actually is not, might mean a considerable decrease in the lawful rate of duty.

A false statement or omission can be material even if it doesn't actually cause a change in the rate of duty. Identifying an imported fabric as "100 percent cotton," when in fact it is made of a blend of cotton and silk, would be material even though it may or may not actually result in a change in the rate of duty collected. The statement or omission must also be false. The violation occurs whether the false statement or omission was made intentionally or negligently. There is no violation if the falsity resulted from simple clerical errors or reasonable mistakes of fact outside the control of the importer (such as where a foreign supplier unexpectedly includes merchandise in a sealed container that you were not aware was being shipped to you, and you had no way to find out) as long as the errors are not part of a pattern of negligent conduct. The penalty, however, does depend on whether the offense resulted from negligence, gross negligence, or fraud.

Negligent Violations. A *negligent violation* is one in which the importer fails to use *reasonable care, skill, and competence* to ensure that all customs documents and statements are materially correct and all laws are complied with. It might result because the importer failed to accurately ascertain the facts or information required by Customs when making an entry. It could also result from a misinterpretation of customs regulations or a mistake in completing the customs documents. Negligence penalties can seem pretty severe: If duty has been lost, the penalty can be up to two times the loss of duty, but no more than the value of the goods. If no duty is lost, then the penalty can be as high as 20 percent of the value of the goods, depending on whether there were mitigating or aggravating circumstances.

In the following case, *United States v. Golden Ship Trading Co.*, the importer was found negligent in misstating the country of origin of T-shirts even though she based her information on assurances made by her supplier.

Gross Negligence. An importer commits *gross negligence* if there is "clear and convincing evidence" that the act or omission was done with actual knowledge or reckless disregard for the relevant facts and with disregard for the importer's obligations under the law. The penalty is approximately twice that for negligent violations.

Civil Fraud. Customs fraud is far more serious than negligence. A *fraudulent* violation exists where there is "clear and convincing evidence" that the importer knowingly made a materially false statement or omission while entering or attempting to enter goods into the United States. This might include intentionally giving a phony description of the goods being imported, understating their value by submitting a fake seller's invoice or by concealing money paid to the seller, or altering the country of origin listed on a document. Although the act must have been done knowingly, it does not matter whether the importer intended to evade paying import duties. According to Customs guidelines, the agency will normally seek a penalty equal to 100 percent of the value of the goods, reduced to five to eight times the total loss of duty for mitigating circumstances. Where the fraud did not result in a loss of duty to the government, the minimum penalty sought will be 50 percent of the value of the goods to a maximum of 80 percent. Even greater penalties may be imposed where there has been an egregious violation, a risk to public health or safety, or the presence of aggravating factors. In no case may the penalty exceed the value of the merchandise. In many cases, Customs may seize the merchandise and either have it destroyed or sold at auction.

Crimes. Criminal penalties for customs fraud and smuggling are set out in Title 18, Chapter 27, of the *United States Code* specifies a range of criminal activities, including the use of fraudulent customs documents, making false statements to a Customs officer, smuggling, conspiracy, money laundering, and many other acts. The law provides a maximum sentence of two years' imprisonment, a fine, or both, for each violation. Anyone who

United States v. Golden Ship Trading Co.

2001 WL 65751 (2001)

Court of International Trade

BACKGROUND AND FACTS

J. Wu entered three shipments of T-shirts purchased from Hui, who claimed that he operated a factory in the Dominican Republic. Hui furnished all the relevant information necessary for the importer's custom house broker to prepare the import document and to obtain a visa permit for entry of wearing apparel into the United States. Wu signed the entry papers stating that the country of origin of the T-shirts was the Dominican Republic. Customs discovered that Hui produced the body of the T-shirts in China and shipped them to the Dominican Republic, where sleeves were attached and "Made in Dominican Republic" labels inserted. The finished shirts were then transshipped to the United States. According to law, merely attaching the sleeves did not make the shirts a product of the Dominican Republic. Chinese-made shirts could not have been imported without a textile visa, which Hui may not have been able to obtain. The government alleged that Wu acted without due care in determining the country of origin and sought penalties of $44,000. Wu did not dispute that the country of origin was China but denied that she was negligent and claimed that Hui had duped her.

BARZILAY, J.

Section 1592(e) describes the burden of proof that each side bears in a penalty action based on negligence. The United States bears the burden of establishing that the material false act or omission occurred; the burden then shifts to the defendant to demonstrate that the act did not occur as a result of negligence. See 19 U.S.C. §1592(e)(4). In this action, Customs has adequately demonstrated that the material false act occurred.

Since the court holds that the statements on the entry papers were both material and false, the only remaining issue is whether Ms. Wu has carried her burden that "the act or omission did not occur as a result of negligence." To decide if the mismarking was the result of Ms. Wu's negligence the court must examine the facts and circumstances to determine if Ms. Wu exercised reasonable care under the circumstances.

Ms. Wu admits she relied on the information provided by the exporter and accepted his representations that the Dominican Republic was the country of origin of the tee-shirts because "all the documents that the exporter provided prior to entry stated the country of origin was the Dominican Republic." Further, she claims that she was the victim of the exporter's fraudulent scheme which was so elaborate that even Customs had difficulty discovering it. Ms. Wu points out that the exporter did have a t-shirt factory in the Dominican Republic and that the factory did perform some manufacturing operations on the imported t-shirts. Ms. Wu also claims "figuring out which (t-shirts) qualified as country of origin Dominican Republic and which did not required an entire team of Customs investigators, special agents and import specialists. Obviously, the exporter's fraud in this case was well-concealed." Furthermore, she contends, if Customs had difficulty investigating and uncovering the exporter's falsifications, how could Ms. Wu, with far fewer resources and less expertise, be expected to know that the entry papers falsely reflected the country of origin of the imported t-shirts. Therefore, Ms. Wu claims, she was justified in relying on the exporter's entry information.

The court finds that Ms. Wu failed to exercise reasonable care because she failed to verify the information contained in the entry documents. Under the regulation's definition of reasonable care, Ms. Wu had the responsibility to at least undertake an effort to verify the information on the entry documents. There is a distinct difference between legitimately attempting to verify the entry information and blindly relying on the exporter's assertions. Had Ms. Wu inquired as to the origin of the imported t-shirts or, at minimum, attempted to check the credentials and business operations of the exporter, she could make an argument that she attempted to exercise reasonable care and competence to ensure that the statements on the entry documents were accurate. Instead, Ms. Wu applies circular reasoning to prove she was not negligent. She assumes she would not have been able to discover that the exporter was misrepresenting the county of origin and therefore was not negligent even though she made no attempt to verify. The critical defect with Ms. Wu's argument is

continued

continued

that it removes the reasonable care element from the negligence standard. The exercise of reasonable care may not have guaranteed success, but the failure to attempt any verification undercuts the argument that she would have been unable to determine the truth.

Ms. Wu failed to "exercise" reasonable care because she utterly failed to attempt to verify the exporter's information. Indeed, Ms. Wu admits, and the evidence is uncontraverted, that she relied solely on the word of the exporter.

> Q. What information did you rely on when you signed this document that indicates that the single country of origin of the imported items was the Dominican Republic?
>
> A. I believe [sic] Pedro. He said he sent me all the documents and the documents said it's made in the Dominican Republic so I just signed them.

Furthermore, Ms. Wu openly admits she did not inquire at all about the origin of the imported merchandise.

> Q. Did you discuss with Mr. Hui (the exporter) where the fabrics from the t-shirts were made?
>
> A. I never asked. I don't [sic] know how to ask. I never asked it.

Although it is apparent Ms. Wu did not directly research the authenticity of the exporter's claims, she argues that she employed the services of a licensed customs house broker and relied on the broker's expertise to properly prepare the import documents. However, Ms. Wu did not attempt to verify or ascertain the correctness of the information prepared by the broker.

> Q. Did you discuss with the broker where he got the information from?
>
> A. I did not discuss it with him.

Even though Ms. Wu did not attempt to verify the country of origin, she still signed and certified the accuracy of the information contained in the entry documents. Ms. Wu's reliance on the exporter and the broker does not remove the obligation to exercise reasonable care and competence to ensure that the statements made on the entry documents were correct.

The court finds that Ms. Wu's failure to attempt to verify the entry document information shows she did not act with reasonable care and did, therefore, attempt to negligently introduce merchandise into the commerce of the United States in violation of 19 U.S.C. §1592(a)(1)(A) and, therefore, must pay a civil penalty for her negligence pursuant to 19 U.S.C. §1592(c)(3)(B).

With regard to the amount of the penalty, the court directs the parties to attempt to settle the matter by consultation guided by the court's opinions in *United States v. Complex Machines Works Co.*, 83 F. Supp. 2d 1307 (1999) and *United States v. Modes, Inc.*, 826 F. Supp. 504 (1990) regarding mitigation.

Decision. Wu did not exercise reasonable care because she failed to verify the information contained in the entry documents. Customs could assess a penalty that took into account the mitigating circumstances of the case. Once the government proved the false act occurred, the burden shifted to Ms. Wu to prove that she was *not* negligent.

willfully, and with the intent to defraud the United States, smuggles or attempts to smuggle goods into the country can receive a five-year prison sentence. Special criminal offenses apply to drug smuggling and to travelers entering the United States with merchandise in their baggage or on their person.

Aggravating and Mitigating Circumstances. The following are examples of the types of additional factors that Customs will consider in determining the amount of a penalty.

- *Aggravating Factors:* These include obstructing an investigation, withholding evidence, providing misleading information, prior improper shipments, and illegal transshipments of textiles to hide their actual country of origin.
- *Mitigating Factors:* These include errors committed by Customs itself that contributed to the violation; erroneous advice from a Customs official; cooperation with the investigation; immediate remedial reaction (e.g., payment of the duty voluntarily and immediately, discharge, or retraining of an offending employee); inexperience in importing (except in fraud cases); or a prior good shipment record. In addition, Customs may consider the ability of the importer to pay the penalty.

Enforced and Informed Compliance. Customs and Border Protection takes a two-pronged approach to enforcement of the customs laws: *Enforced compliance* and *informed compliance.* Enforced compliance refers to the active investigation of customs violations and the prosecution of violators. Informed compliance refers to "softer" mechanisms designed to place the burden of voluntary compliance on importers. Compliance with the customs laws is much like compliance with the income tax laws. Unless the majority of U.S. importers, like taxpayers, voluntarily comply with the customs laws, enforcement will be impossible. Congress recognized this when it passed the *Customs Modernization and Informed Compliance Act of 1993* (called the *Mod Act*). It introduced the doctrine of *informed compliance,* which shifted to the importer a major responsibility to comply with all customs laws and regulations. It requires that importers, customs brokers, and carriers use reasonable care in complying with the law, in handling all import transactions, and in preparing all documentation for entered goods. Reasonable care means more than simply being careful. It means that those handling import transactions must be properly trained and that companies must establish internal controls over import operations to ensure compliance. When requirements are not understood, the importer should consult a licensed broker, customs law attorney, or U.S. Customs itself. Importers are expected to have enough information and knowledge to comply with the law. This includes having accurate information about the type of merchandise being imported, its value and origin, the identity of the seller, and so forth. It also requires importers to have a working knowledge of customs statutes, regulations, and rulings and U.S. Customs procedures.

In order to make informed compliance work, Customs recognizes that it has a responsibility to provide information, advice, technical assistance, and clear regulations to importers. Customs works closely with high-volume importers and those in problem or sensitive industries (e.g., textiles, automobiles, and steel) to assist them in developing their own corporate compliance programs.

The Reasonable Care Checklist. In 1997, U.S. Customs published a checklist to give smaller and less experienced importers a better understanding of their obligation to use reasonable care (see Exhibit 12.3). Customs understood that a "black-and-white" definition of reasonable care is impossible because the concept depends on individual circumstances. The checklist is not a law or regulation; it merely helps importers to understand what is expected of them. Importers who fail to meet the reasonable care requirements on the checklist may be subjected to penalties for negligence.

Reporting Errors to Customs before an Investigation. Congress has enacted a statute to encourage importers to voluntarily report their own possible violations of the customs laws. This is called a *prior disclosure.* If an importer admits its mistake and informs Customs of a possible violation *before* learning that it is being investigated, the penalties are limited. The importer must completely disclose the materially false statements or omissions and the circumstances of the violation. Any unpaid duties must be remitted immediately or within thirty days. However, an attorney should be consulted before doing so. Some prior disclosures have reportedly saved companies many millions of dollars in potential fines.

The Statute of Limitations. The government is barred from bringing any action to collect an import duty after five years from the date of the violation involving negligence or gross negligence, or five years from the date of discovery of a violation involving fraud.

Record-Keeping Requirements. Importers are required to keep records of all import transactions for five years from the date of entry and to give Customs access to those documents on demand. The records include all documents "normally kept in the ordinary course of business," including sales contracts, purchase orders, government certificates, letters of credit, internal corporate memoranda, shipping documents, correspondence with suppliers, and any other documents bearing on the entry of the merchandise. It is highly recommended that any corporate importer establish a customs records compliance program to avoid penalties. The willful failure to keep records about the entry is punishable by the lesser of a $100,000 fine or 75 percent of the value of the merchandise. Even negligent record keeping is punishable by

Exhibit 12.3

Just How Informed Do You Have to Be? Reasonable Care Checklist for Importers

1. If you have not retained an expert to assist you in complying with U.S. Customs requirements, do you have access to the *Customs Regulations* (Title 19 of the *Code of Federal Regulations*), the *Harmonized Tariff Schedule of the United States,* and the GPO publication *Customs Bulletin and Decisions*? Do you have access to the *Customs Internet Web site, Customs Electronic Bulletin Board,* or other research service to permit you to establish reliable procedures and facilitate compliance with customs laws and regulations?
2. Have you consulted with a customs "expert" (e.g., lawyer, broker, accountant, or customs consultant) to assist in preparation of documents and the entry of the merchandise?
3. If you use an expert to assist you in complying with U.S. Customs requirements, have you discussed your importations in advance with that person and have you provided that person with full, complete, and accurate information about the import transactions?
4. Has a responsible and knowledgeable individual within your organization reviewed the customs documentation prepared by you or your expert to ensure that it is full, complete, and accurate?
5. Are identical transactions or merchandise handled differently at different ports or customs offices within the same port? If so, have you brought this to the attention of the appropriate customs officials?
6. Have you established reliable procedures within your organization to ensure that you provide complete and accurate documentation to U.S. Customs?
7. Have you obtained a customs ruling regarding the importation of the merchandise?
8. Do you know the merchandise that you are importing and have you provided a detailed and accurate product description and tariff classification of your merchandise to U.S. Customs? Is a laboratory analysis or special procedure necessary for the classification?
9. Have you consulted the tariff schedules, U.S. Customs' informed compliance publications, court cases, or U.S. Customs rulings to assist you in describing and classifying the merchandise?
10. If you are claiming a free or special tariff treatment for your merchandise (e.g., GSP, HTS Item 9802, NAFTA, etc.), have you established a reliable program to ensure that you reported the required value information and obtained any required or necessary documentation to support the claim?
11. Do you know the customs value of the imported products? Do you know the "price actually paid or payable" for your merchandise?
12. Do you know the terms of sale; whether there will be rebates, tie-ins, indirect costs, additional payments; whether "assists" were provided, commissions or royalties paid? Have all costs or payments been reported to U.S. Customs? Are amounts actual or estimated? Are you and the supplier "related parties," and have you disclosed this to U.S. Customs?
13. Have you taken reliable measures to ascertain the correct country of origin for the imported merchandise? Have you consulted with a customs expert regarding the country of origin of the merchandise?
14. Have you accurately communicated the proper country of origin marking requirements to your foreign supplier prior to importation and verified that the merchandise is properly marked upon entry with the correct country of origin?
15. If you are importing textiles or apparel, have you developed reliable procedures to ensure that you have ascertained the correct country of origin and assured yourself that no illegal transshipment (rerouting through a third country for illegal purposes) or false or fraudulent documents or practices were involved? Have you checked the U.S. Treasury's published list of manufacturers, sellers, and other foreign persons who have been found to have illegally imported textiles and apparel products? If you have obtained your textiles from one of these parties have you adequately verified the country of origin of the shipment through independent means?
16. Is your merchandise subject to quota/visa requirements and, if so, have you provided or developed a reliable procedure to provide a correct visa for the goods upon entry?
17. Have you determined or established a reliable procedure to permit you to determine whether your merchandise or its packaging bear or use any trademarks or copyrighted matter or are patented and, if so, that you have a legal right to import those items into, and/or use those items in, the United States?
18. If you are importing goods or packaging which contain registered copyrighted material, have you checked to ensure that it is authorized and genuine? If you are importing sound recordings of live performances, were the recordings authorized?
19. Have you checked to see that your merchandise complies with other government agency requirements (e.g., FDA, EPA/DOT, CPSC, FTC, Department of Agriculture, etc.) prior to or upon entry and procured any necessary licenses or permits?
20. Have you checked to see if your goods are subject to a Commerce Department dumping or countervailing duty determination and reported that to U.S. Customs?

SOURCE: Excerpted and adapted by the authors from TD-97-96 (1997), United States Customs.

fines up to $10,000 or 40 percent of the value of the goods, whichever is less. There is an exception if the records were destroyed by an act of God. Concealment or destruction of records carries an additional $5,000 fine or up to two years' imprisonment or both. U.S. Customs conducts audits to verify business records. Inspections can take place on reasonable notice to the importer. Documents can be seized by court order.

JUDICIAL ENFORCEMENT OF PENALTY ACTIONS. In any action to collect a penalty, U.S. Customs acts as plaintiff in bringing suit in the Court of International Trade. Quite often Customs will ask the court to consider all theories of culpability—negligence, gross negligence, and fraud—hoping to win on one or the other theory. The burden of proof in court depends on the violation. Fraud and gross negligence must be proved by "clear and convincing evidence." In negligence cases, the government must prove only that the act or omission occurred; the burden then shifts to the defendant-importer to show that it did not occur as a result of negligence.

Binding Rulings

Imagine that you have an opportunity to sell imported women's boxer shorts to a leading U.S. department store chain. They would like you to quote "your best price." You learn that some women will wear the boxers as short pants, while others will wear the shorts as underwear. If you underestimate your costs, you'll end up eating your shorts on the deal. The problem is that you are not sure whether Customs will consider the boxers to be "outerwear," which is dutied at almost 18 percent, or "women's slips and briefs," which are dutied at less than 12 percent. Importers faced with a situation like this may make a written request for a *binding ruling,* also called a *ruling letter,* from Customs in advance of an entry. A binding ruling represents the official position of Customs with respect to the specific transaction for which it was issued. It is binding on Customs personnel until revoked. Customs does not publish public notice in advance of a ruling, and there is no opportunity for the public to comment on the issue.

Rulings are important to importers, especially those dealing in new or unusual merchandise that they have not imported before. They relieve them of the uncertainty of how the product will be treated by Customs or how much duty they will have to pay.

Binding rulings can be even more important where companies are considering the tariff consequences of restructuring their global manufacturing operations. Take another simple example. Assume you are trying to choose between Mexico and China as a site to produce bicycles for sale in the United States. The parts will come from many suppliers around the world. Among all the factors to be considered—labor costs, quality control issues, local tax rates, access to the U.S. market—there are also the tariff consequences. Will there be a difference in the tariff rate if you produce bicycles in China and import the completed bicycles into the United States rather than importing the parts into Mexico, assembling the bicycle there, and shipping to customers in the United States? This requires a working knowledge of complex tariff code provisions. Obtaining a ruling letter from Customs in advance will mean one less surprise later on.

A request for a ruling letter should be submitted in writing. It should contain all relevant information, and in some cases—like the boxer shorts case—the importer should send a sample of the article. The ruling is issued only on the basis of the exact facts given and ensures that the products described will be entered according to the terms set out in the letter. The letter applies only to the importer to whom it is addressed. (You can research ruling letters on the Customs Web site.) Most rulings are issued within thirty to sixty days, although especially difficult ones can take up to nine months. Rulings are published in the *Customs Bulletin.*

Judicial Review

The role of the courts in reviewing the decisions and actions of U.S. Customs depends on whether Customs was involved in formal rulemaking applicable to the public at large or whether it was an informal action, such as the issuance of a binding ruling or an action affecting a single shipment of goods belonging to a single importer.

JUDICIAL REVIEW OF FORMAL RULEMAKING. In *United States v. Haggar Apparel Co.,* 526 U.S. 380, 119 S.Ct. 1392 (1999), Haggar shipped U.S.-made fabric to Mexico where it was cut and sewn into pants, then permapressed and returned to the United States for sale. According to U.S statutes (Section 9802 of the U.S. tariff schedules), component parts or materials made in the United States may be shipped to certain foreign plants for assembly and returned to the United States with a partial duty exemption. However, the materials may only be assembled and must not undergo further manufacturing or processing in the foreign country. Customs issued a regulation interpreting the statute, stating that permapressing was an additional step in manufacturing and "not incidental to the assembly process." Customs issued the regulation using a formal rulemaking process (called "notice and comment" rulemaking) so it was applicable to all importers. In other words, as a formal rule it was more than just a ruling regarding a single entry by an individual importer. It was promulgated only after a public comment period, it was published in the *Code of Federal Regulations,* and it had the "force of law."

The Supreme Court held for the government, stating that Customs' decision to define permapressing as "not incidental to the assembly process" was perfectly reasonable. The Supreme Court held that courts must give "judicial deference" to the formal regulations of U.S. Customs where those regulations are a "reasonable interpretation" of an ambiguous statute. This is known as "Chevron deference," taken from the important case of *Chevron U.S.A. Inc. v. Natural Resources Defense Council, Inc.,* 467 U.S. 837, 104 S.Ct. 2778 (1984).

Judicial Review of Binding Rulings. *Haggar* did not address the scope of judicial review of informal decisions such as binding rulings. These and other routine decisions are made on a case-by-case basis every day—thousands every year—by Customs officials around the country. It might be a binding ruling about the tariff classification of imported merchandise or a decision about an entry when the goods arrive at a U.S. port. If an importer seeks review of a Customs decision in the courts, to what extent will the court give deference to Customs' decision? Should the court consider that the agency is an expert on customs matters and simply defer to its original decision? Or should the court undertake its own analysis and reach its own decision independent of the agency's determination? The following U.S. Supreme Court decision, *United States v. Mead,* defines the scope of judicial review of binding rulings, tariff classifications, and other "informal" day-to-day decisions of Customs.

United States v. Mead Corp.

533 U.S. 218 (2001)

United States Supreme Court

BACKGROUND AND FACTS

Mead had imported "day planners" for several years. They had entered duty free under HTSUS 4820.10. The classification covers "[R]egisters, account books, notebooks, order books, receipt books, letter pads, memorandum pads, diaries and similar articles." HTSUS 4820.10 has two subcategories. Items in the first, "[d]iaries, notebooks and address books, bound; memorandum pads, letter pads and similar articles," were subject to a tariff of 4 percent at the time in controversy. Articles in the second, covering "other" items, were free. The planners had been classified in the "other" subcategory. They included a calendar, a section for daily notes, a section for telephone numbers and addresses, and a notepad. The larger models also included a daily planner section, plastic ruler, plastic pouch, credit card holder, and computer diskette holder. A looseleaf ringed binder held the contents, except for the notepad, which fit into the rear flap of the day planner's outer cover. In a binding ruling, Customs changed the classification of the planners to "bound diaries" under the first subcategory, with a 4 percent import duty. Mead argued that the day planners were not diaries and were not bound and that the planners should be classified in an "other" subcategory

continued

continued

that was duty free. After entering the goods and paying the duties, Mead filed a protest. When the protest was denied, Mead appealed. The Court of International Trade issued a summary judgment for the government. The Court of Appeals reversed, holding that the planners were not "bound diaries" on the basis of the dictionary meaning of those words. The court held that it owed no deference to Customs' classification rulings under the *Chevron* and *Haggar* court decisions, but was free to decide the classification issue anew as a matter of law. The court noted that those cases involved formal regulations that carried the force of law, while classification rulings apply only to the specific transaction at issue. The U.S. Supreme Court agreed to hear the case.

JUSTICE SOUTER

We agree that a tariff classification has no claim to judicial deference under *Chevron U.S.A. Inc. v. Natural Resources Defense Council, Inc.,* 467 U.S. 837, 104 S.Ct. 2778, 81 (1984) there being no indication that Congress intended such a ruling to carry the force of law, but we hold that under *Skidmore v. Swift & Co.,* 323 U.S. 134, 65 S.Ct. 161 (1944), the ruling is eligible to claim respect according to its persuasiveness [most citations omitted].

* * *

"[T]he well-reasoned views of the agencies implementing a statute 'constitute a body of experience and informed judgment to which courts and litigants may properly resort for guidance,' *Skidmore,* and [w]e have long recognized that considerable weight should be accorded to an executive department's construction of a statutory scheme it is entrusted to administer . . ." *Chevron.* The fair measure of deference to an agency administering its own statute has been understood to vary with circumstances, and courts have looked to the degree of the agency's care, its consistency, formality, and relative expertness, and to the persuasiveness of the agency's position. . . . Justice Jackson summed things up in *Skidmore:*

> The weight [accorded to an administrative] judgment in a particular case will depend upon the thoroughness evident in its consideration, the validity of its reasoning, its consistency with earlier and later pronouncements, and all those factors which give it power to persuade, if lacking power to control.

* * *

There is room at least to raise a *Skidmore* claim here, where the regulatory scheme is highly detailed, and Customs can bring the benefit of specialized experience to bear on the subtle questions in this case: whether the daily planner with room for brief daily entries falls under "diaries," when diaries are grouped with "notebooks and address books, bound; memorandum pads, letter pads and similar articles," HTSUS subheading 4820.10.20; and whether a planner with a ring binding should qualify as "bound," when a binding may be typified by a book, but also may have "reinforcements or fittings of metal, plastics, etc.," *Harmonized Commodity Description and Coding System Explanatory Notes to Heading 4820.* A classification ruling in this situation may therefore at least seek a respect proportional to its "power to persuade," *Skidmore.* Such a ruling may surely claim the merit of its writer's thoroughness, logic, and expertness, its fit with prior interpretations, and any other sources of weight.

* * *

Since the *Skidmore* assessment called for here ought to be made in the first instance by the Court of Appeals for the Federal Circuit or the CIT, we go no further than to vacate the judgment and remand the case for further proceedings consistent with this opinion. It is so ordered.

Decision. The Court of International Trade and the Court of Appeals for the Federal Circuit must grant a limited degree of deference to the tariff classification ruling letters issued by U.S. Customs, according to the *Skidmore* standard. The degree of deference depends on the agency's thoroughness, the validity of its reasoning, its expertise, and its "power to persuade."

Comment. On remand to the Court of Appeals, the court found Customs' ruling somewhat "unpersuasive" under the *Skidmore* standard. Noting that it was the court's job to determine the meaning of language used in the tariff schedules, the court relied on the dictionary definitions of "bound" and "diary," and, for a second time, entered a judgment for Mead.

Pre-Importation Judicial Review in Emergency Circumstances. Normally, an importer cannot seek court review until a shipment has been entered and a protest denied by Customs. Under limited circumstances, an importer may seek review in the courts prior to entry only where extraordinary circumstances could cause irreparable injury to the importers and severe business disruption and substantial costs would result if a decision were not reached. Other cases have stated that if an importer can show that a Customs ruling threatens to "close the importer's doors," then review will be permitted in advance of entering the goods.

Dutiable Status of Goods

Tariffs, restraints on imports, and other import controls are applied to goods according to the item's *dutiable status*. The dutiable status of goods is determined by (1) the classification of the article (what it is), (2) the customs value of the article, and (3) the country of origin of the article (the country it comes from for purposes of determining the tariff rate or applicability of a quota). An accurate estimate of the duties owed on imports provides information essential for business planning, development of cost estimates, and pricing and marketing decisions.

Determining the dutiable status of an article can require importers to negotiate a maze of regulations. For importers who enter a wide variety of products or materials or who enter them from many different countries, the potential for problems increases significantly. For U.S. exporters trying to enter goods into foreign countries, the regulatory headaches can become nightmarish. Lessons learned from importing into one country are not necessarily transferable when importing into another.

In recent years, worldwide efforts have attempted to make customs procedures and import regulations more uniform, more understandable, and easier to follow. Simplified, uniform rules would make it easier for both importers and their foreign suppliers to plan their transactions in advance and to comply with complicated laws and regulations. These efforts are beginning to result in the development of uniform rules for classifying and valuing imports and for determining their country of origin. These include a standardized system for classifying products (officially known as the *Harmonized Commodity Description and Coding System*), the *WTO Agreement on Customs Valuation* (1994), and the *WTO Agreement on Rules of Origin* (1994).

The *Harmonized Tariff Schedule*

All goods entering the United States are dutiable unless specifically exempted. Duties and restrictions on imports are based on the exact type and classification of goods being imported. Since 1989, goods entering the United States have been classified according to the *Harmonized Tariff Schedule of the United States* (known as HTSUS or HTS). The harmonized system was part of a worldwide effort, spanning nearly two decades, to standardize tariff nomenclature according to the *Harmonized Commodity Description and Coding System*. Under this uniform system, in effect in most trading nations of the world, all goods are classified by their name, description, or use. Goods that fall into a certain classification in one country will be similarly classified in all countries that follow the harmonized system. Thus, a company that knows the classification of its product in the United States, for example, is easily able to determine the classification of its product in most other countries. The harmonized system does not set the tariff rate, and tariff rates are not necessarily uniform between countries. Tariff rates on goods are set by each nation according to the classification of those goods. The harmonized system was developed by the World Customs Organization, an international organization located in Brussels, representing over 170 nations. In the United States, the HTSUS is maintained by the International Trade Commission and is available online directly or through U.S. Customs and Border Protection.

Using the *Harmonized Tariff Schedule*. The HTSUS divides products into approximately 5,000 tariff classifications, ranging from basic commodities and agricultural products to manufactured goods. It is organized into twenty-two sections, covering products from different industries. Sections are broken down into ninety-nine chapters, each covering the commodities, materials, and products of a distinct industry. The chapters are arranged in a progression from crude and natural products such as livestock and agricultural products through advanced manufactured goods such as vehicles and aircraft. The following list provides a few examples:

Chapter 1	Live animals
Chapter 9	Coffee, tea, spices
Chapter 22	Beverages, spirits, vinegar
Chapter 25	Salt, sulfur, earths, and stone
Chapter 30	Pharmaceuticals
Chapter 44	Wood and articles of wood
Chapter 51	Wool, fine or coarse animal hair
Chapter 52	Cotton
Chapter 62	Articles of apparel, accessories not knitted
Chapter 63	Other textile articles, sets, worn clothing
Chapter 76	Aluminum and articles thereof
Chapter 84	Nuclear reactors, boilers, machinery, and mechanical appliances
Chapter 85	Electrical machinery, sound recorders, television image
Chapter 88	Aircraft, spacecraft, parts thereof
Chapter 94	Furniture, bedding, lamps
Chapter 97	Works of art, collectors' pieces
Chapters 98/99	Reserved for special tariff classifications (e.g., imports that enter the United States only temporarily or for service and repair, etc.)

Chapters are broken down into headings, subheadings, and tariff items. Tariff items are denoted by eight-digit codes. In the United States, the schedules break out to ten digits to allow for compiling of statistical data on imports.

Chapter :	first two digits
Heading :	first four digits
Subheading :	first five or six digits
Tariff items :	first eight digits
Statistical break:	ten digits (the ninth and tenth digit)

Consider the example in Exhibit 12.4. Tents made of synthetic fibers—such as nylon—used for backpacking are classified as item 6306.22.10. They are found within subheading 6306.22, for tents of synthetic fibers, heading 6306 for "Tarpaulins, awnings and sunblinds, tents, sails for boats . . ." and chapter 63 for "Other textile articles." Countries that use this international coding system have "harmonized" their classifications to six digits at the subheading level. After the first six digits, each country assigns its own numbers.

After locating the article in the schedule, the importer can determine the tariff rate. The schedule is divided into two columns (see Exhibit 12.4). Column 1 contains a *general rate* applicable to imports from NTR (formerly MFN) nations, and a *special rate* applicable to one or more special tariff programs. The special rate applies to goods coming from developing countries under the *Generalized System of Preferences,* to goods coming from Canada or Mexico under the *North American Free Trade Agreement,* or to goods imported from the Caribbean Basin or Israel. Column 2 rates are the original *Smoot–Hawley* rates applicable to non-NTR countries under the Tariff Act of 1930, although few countries fall in this category today.

Tariffs are imposed on imports either on the basis of *ad valorem,* specific, or compound rates. The most common type of tariff is the *ad valorem* rate, based on a percentage of the value of the materials or articles imported. A specific rate is a specified amount per unit of weight or measure. A compound rate is a combined *ad valorem* and specific rate.

THE CLASSIFICATION OF GOODS. Tariff rates are based on an article's HTS classification. To classify a product, you must know what your product is or how it will be used and where it falls in the tariff schedules. This is not as easy a task as it might seem. The schedules include every kind and category of product on earth. They include consumer goods ranging from "Articles for Christmas festivities and parts thereof" to "Electromechanical domestic appliances;" textile products ranging from "Cotton, not carded or combed, having a staple length under 28.575 mm" to "Men's or boys' suits . . . of worsted wool fabric . . . having an average fiber diameter of 18.5 microns or less;" industrial equipment ranging from "Bookbinding machinery" to "Nuclear reactors;" and electronic products

Exhibit 12.4

Harmonized Tariff Schedule of the United States (2007–Rev. 7)

Annotated for Statistical Reporting Purposes

Heading/ Subheading	Stat. Suf-fix	Article Description	Unit of Quantity	Rates of Duty 1 General	Rates of Duty 1 Special	2
6306		Tarpaulins, awnings and sunblinds; tents; sails for boats, sailboards or landcraft; camping goods:				
		Tarpaulins, awnings and sunblinds:				
6306.11.00	00	Of cotton (369)	kg	8.8%	Free (CA,IL,MX) 4.4% (JO)	90%
6306.12.00	00	Of synthetic fibers (669)	kg	8.9%	Free (CA,IL,MX) 2.3% (JO)	90%
6306.19.00		Of other textile materials		5.2%	Free (CA,E*,IL, MX) 1.3% (JO)	40%
	10	Of artificial fibers (669)	kg			
	20	Other (899)	kg			
		Tents:				
6306.21.00	00	Of cotton	kg	8.8%	Free (CA,IL,MX) 4.4% (JO)	90%
6306.22		Of synthetic fibers:				
6306.22.10	00	Backpacking tents	No. kg	0.5%	Free (A,CA,E,IL, J,MX)	90%
6306.22.90		Other		8.9%	Free (CA,IL,MX) 2.3% (JO)	90%
	10	Screen houses	kg			
	30	Other (669)	kg			
6306.29.00	00	Of other textile materials	kg	3.2%	Free (CA,E*,IL, J*,JO,MX)	40%
		Sails:				
6306.31.00	00	Of synthetic fibers	kg	0.4%	Free (A,CA,E,IL, J,MX)	30%
6306.39.00	00	Of other textile materials	kg	0.4%	Free (A,CA,E,IL, J,MX)	30%
		Pneumatic mattresses:				
6306.41.00	00	Of cotton	kg	3.8%	Free (CA,IL,JO,MX)	25%
6306.49.00	00	Of other textile materials	kg	3.8%	Free (A,CA,E,IL, J*,JO,MX)	25%
		Other:				
6306.91.00	00	Of cotton	kg	3.8%	Free (C AJL,JO,MX)	40%
6306.99.00	00	Of other textile materials	kg	5%	Free (CA,E*,IL, J*,MX) 1.5% (JO)	78.5%

General Notes [edited for student use]

3. *Rates of Duty.* The rates of duty in the "Rates of Duty" columns designated 1 ("General" and "Special") and 2 of the tariff schedule apply to goods imported into the customs territory of the United States as hereinafter provided in this note:
   (a) *Rate of Duty Column 1.*
      (i) Except as provided in subparagraph (iv) of this paragraph, the rates of duty in column 1 are rates which are applicable to all products other than those of countries enumerated in paragraph (b) of this note. Column 1 is divided into two subcolumns, "General" and "Special," which are applicable as provided below.
      (ii) The "General" subcolumn sets forth the general or normal trade relations (NTR) rates which are applicable to products of those countries described in subparagraph (i) above which are not entitled to special tariff treatment as set forth below.
      (iii) The "Special" subcolumn reflects rates of duty under one or more special tariff treatment programs described in paragraph (c) of this note and identified in parentheses immediately following the duty rate specified in such subcolumn. These rates apply to those products which are properly classified under a provision for which a special rate is indicated and for which all of the legal requirements for eligibility for such program or programs have been met. Where a product is eligible for special treatment under more than one program, the lowest rate of duty provided for any applicable program shall be imposed. Where no special rate of duty is provided for a provision or where the country from which a product otherwise eligible for special treatment was imported is

continued

continued

not designated as a beneficiary country under a program appearing with the appropriate provision, the rates of duty in the "General" subcolumn of column 1 shall apply.

(iv) Products of Insular Possessions (omitted)

(v) Products of the West Bank or Gaza Strip (omitted)

(b) *Rate of Duty Column 2.* Notwithstanding any of the foregoing provisions of this note, the rates of duty shown in Column 2 shall apply to products, whether imported directed or indirectly, of the following countries and areas:

Cuba North Korea

(c) *Products Eligible for Special Tariff Treatment.*

(i) Programs under which special tariff treatment may be provided, and the corresponding symbols for such programs as they are indicated in the "Special" subcolumn, are as follows:

United States–Australia Free Trade Agreement	AU
Automotive Products Trade Act	B
United States–Bahrain Free Trade Agreement Implementation Act	BH
Agreement on Trade in Civil Aircraft	C
North American Free Trade Agreement:	
Goods of Canada, under the terms of general note 12 to this schedule.	CA
Goods of Mexico, under the terms of general note 12 to this schedule	MX
United States–Chile Free Trade Agreement	CL
African Growth and Opportunity Act	D
Caribbean Basin Economic Recovery Act.	E or E*
United States–Israel Free Trade Area	IL
Andean Trade Preference Act or Andean Trade Promotion and Drug Eradication Act	J, J* or J+
United States–Jordan Free Trade Area Implementation Act.	JO
Agreement on Trade in Pharmaceutical Products.	K
Dominican Republic–Central America–United States Free Trade Agreement Implementation Act	P or P+
Uruguay Round Concessions on Intermediate Chemicals for Dyes	L
United States–Caribbean Basin Trade Partnership Act.	R
United States–Morocco Free Trade Agreement Implementation Act	MA
United States–Singapore Free Trade Agreement.	SG

from "Ballasts for discharge lamps or tubes" to "Laser imaging assemblies." Finding your product among these is like walking a maze.

The problem is compounded because many products appear to fit into more than one classification. For example, should sleeping bags be classified as "Camping goods," "Sporting goods," or as "Articles of bedding and similar furnishing ... fitted with springs or stuffed"? This is an area where reasonable minds can differ. Naturally, importers will argue that their products should fall into the classification that carries the lowest tariff rate. U.S. Customs, whose job it is to collect the tariff revenue of the United States, will want to classify the products at the highest rate. (Initially, the importer makes the classification by listing it on the entry form filed with Customs, who must then accept or reject the classification. Of course, the importer is bound by the informed compliance standard to use reasonable care in making its classification.) It is especially difficult for importers to classify a product if they are importing it for the first time or if it is a newly designed product. The problem is complicated by the fact that at any time Customs can "change its mind" and decide to reclassify an article, despite having accepted another classification of the same article in the past.

To illustrate how difficult it is to classify an article, consider the following case, *Camel Manufacturing Co. v. United States,* 686 F. Supp. 912 (Ct. Int'l. Trade 1988), involving the import of camping tents. At the time, the tariff schedules had no category specifically for "tents." The importer and Customs disagreed over the other possibilities, which were sporting goods and miscellaneous textiles. Incredibly, the decision turned on the judge's definition of what is a "sport." Although the case was decided under the old schedules (now replaced by the harmonized schedule), it remains one of the authors' favorites. No case better illustrates the unpredictability of customs classifications and the importance of advance planning.

Understanding Tariff Descriptions: The Common Meaning Rule. Articles are described in the tariff schedules in several ways: by common name (known as an *eo nomine* description), by a description of the article's physical characteristics, by a description of its component parts, or by a description of the article's use.

To understand the meaning of terms used in the tariff schedules, the courts look to the common meaning of the articles described. According to the cases, the common or popular meaning of terms used in the tariff schedules applies unless Congress clearly intended a commercial or scientific meaning to apply or unless there is a different commercial meaning that is definite, uniform, and in general use throughout the trade. Courts will often

Camel Manufacturing Co. v. United States
686 F. Supp. 912 (1988)
Court of International Trade

BACKGROUND AND FACTS

The plaintiff imported nylon tents into the United States. The tents were designed to hold up to nine people and weighed over 30 pounds, including carrying bag, stakes, and frames. The floor sizes ranged from 8 feet by 10 feet to 10 feet by 14 feet, and when folded for carrying the tents were approximately 50 inches long. It was undisputed that the tents were used as shelter by people who wish to camp outdoors, either purely for that purpose or for the purpose of engaging in other outdoor activities such as fishing, hunting, and canoeing. The importer entered the tents as "sports equipment" carrying a 10 percent *ad valorem* import duty. U.S. Customs ruled that the tents were properly classifiable as "textile articles not specially provided for" and imposed a duty of 25 cents per pound plus 15 percent *ad valorem.* Upon liquidation, the importer appealed.

JUDGE WATSON

The basic question before the court is whether or not the activity in which the tents are used, which we shall call by the name of "camping out" is a sport, which would then lead to the conclusion that these tents are sporting equipment.

In a previous opinion, *The Newman Importing Co., Inc. v. United States,* 415 F. Supp. 375 (1976), this court decided that certain light tents used in backpacking were sports equipment because the activity of backpacking was found to be a sport. In this action, the court was given a generous range of opinions regarding what it is that makes an activity a sport. Seven witnesses testified on behalf of the plaintiff and two witnesses testified on behalf of the defendant. The witnesses had a wide range of familiarity with the use and manufacture of tents. Although these opinions were extremely interesting, the fact remains that in the end the question of defining the term "sporting equipment" is really one of legal interpretation for the court.

The rationale used in the *Newman Importing* case will not suffice here because these tents are not suitable for backpacking. The court finds that these tents are too heavy for that particular activity and, in fact, are generally used by persons who are camping in the outdoors and are not subject to strict limitations of weight in the tenting equipment which they can take with them. In the absence of persuasive proof regarding any special attributes of these tents which may contribute to their use in backpacking, the court finds it quite reasonable for the

continued

continued

Customs Service to have excluded them from the category of backpacking tents on the basis of their weight and carrying size.

The basic question before the court is whether the general activity of camping out, i.e., taking up temporary residence in the outdoors, is a sport within the meaning of the Tariff Schedules.

The court is unable to expand its view of the term "sports" to include the activity of camping out. To do so would require a definition of the term so loose that it would cover almost any purposeful activity engaged in by humans in a natural setting. If it were simply a question of whether an activity had a certain degree of challenge and skill then the activity of gardening, which has in it a good measure of challenge, skill, and struggle and offers in innumerable ways the "joy of victory and agony of defeat," would also have to be considered a sport. This tells us that as a matter of simple logic and meaning, it does not appear that the term "sport" can be carried past the point which was expressed in the *Newman* case.

It follows that these tents are not "sports equipment" within the meaning of the tariff law.

For the reasons given above, it is the opinion of the court that plaintiff's claim for classification must be denied and judgment must issue dismissing that claim.

Decision. The importer's classification was rejected and the decision of the government upheld. The tents were not properly classifiable as "sporting goods" because the tents were designed for camping out, which was held not to be a sport. Affirmed by the U.S. Court of Appeals for the Federal Circuit, 861 F.3d 1266 (1988).

examine the legislative history of the tariff act and will consult dictionaries and encyclopedias to determine the common meaning of the terms used (e.g., is an *anchovy* commonly understood to be the same thing as a *sardine*?). The courts also rely on scientific authorities and expert witnesses during the trial.

Determining the common meaning is not always so simple. In *Texas Instruments v. United States,* 518 F. Supp. 1341 (Ct. Int'l. Trade 1981), *aff'd.* 673 F.2d 1375 (C.C.P.A. 1982), the court was faced with determining the common meaning of the term "watch movement." The plaintiff, Texas Instruments, Inc., had entered solid state electronic watch modules and electronic watches. The articles consisted of an integrated circuit chip, a capacitor, a quartz crystal, a liquid crystal display for digital readouts, and plastic cases within which the modules were encased. Because digital watches had not yet been invented at the time the tariff schedule was enacted by Congress, the court upheld Customs' determination that the common meaning of "watch movement" in the horological industry did not include these electronic modules. The court believed that Congress could not have intended the term "movement" to include the mere vibration of a quartz crystal in a digital watch. In addressing the impact of technological development on Customs law, the Court of International Trade stated that

> The courts cannot be asked to restructure the tariff schedules by judicial fiat in order to accommodate scientific and engineering innovations which far transcend the vision and intent of the Congress at the time of the enactment of the tariff schedules. It is true ... that it is an established principle of customs law that tariff schedules are written for the future as well as for present application and may embrace merchandise unknown at the time of their enactment. It must be borne in mind, however, that ... in applying a tariff provision to an article, unknown at the time of the enactment thereof, such an article must possess an essential resemblance to the characteristics so described by the applicable tariff provision.

Accordingly, the court ruled that the solid-state electronic module was not a "watch movement."

Dictionary definitions are often used to interpret the tariff schedules. In *C. J. Van Houten & Zoon v. United States,* 664 F. Supp. 514 (Ct. Int'l. Trade 1987), the court ruled that tariff schedule items for "bars or blocks" of chocolate weighing ten pounds or more did not apply to imports of molten, liquid chocolate imported into the United States in tank cars. Rather, the molten chocolate was to be classified as "sweetened chocolate in any other form." After consulting several dictionaries for the common meaning of the terms "bars and blocks," the court concluded that this meant only solid materials.

Determining the Classification of Products: Questions of Law and Fact. Determining an article's tariff classification typically involves two steps. The first step requires you to interpret the common meaning of the terms described in the tariff schedules. Second, you must look at the facts to determine if the imported articles in question fall within the particular category described in the schedules. Courts like to say that the first step in defining tariff language is a "question of law," and the second step is a "question of fact."

Classification by Actual or Principal Use. The tariff schedules describe articles by name, physical characteristics, or by use. When an article is described by both its use and by name, the use provision is generally deemed to be more specific, and often controls. *Principal use* is that use to which articles of the kind being imported are usually put. When an article might have several uses, the principal use controls. Principal use is the use that is greater than any other single use of the article.

An article may be classified according to the actual use intended for the article. To classify according to *actual use,* the product must be used for the purposes listed in the schedule. The actual use must be stated to Customs at the time of entry, and the imported article must actually be used in that manner. Proof of actual use must be furnished to Customs within three years of entry.

Using the General Rules of Interpretation

The *General Rules of Interpretation* (GRI rules) are an integral part of the HTSUS and govern its use. Anyone attempting to locate a product in the schedule must first consult the six required GRI rules. A summary of the rules is given later in this section.

The six rules must be applied in numerical order. To determine how an article is classified, first consult GRI 1. This requires that an article be classified according to the four-digit heading under which it is specifically and completely described or according to any relative section or chapter notes. Most imported goods can be classified according to GRI 1.

Consider Exhibit 12.4. Heading 6306 includes "Tarpaulins, awnings and sunblinds; tents; sails for boats...." If the article is specifically and completely stated in the heading, as are "tents," then you may proceed to look at the six-digit subheading and eight-digit tariff-item levels. Thus, "backpacking tents" would be classified under 6306.22.10.

Notice that GRI 1 also requires that you consult the official notes found at the beginning of each of the twenty-two sections and ninety-nine chapters. The notes define specific terms used in the section or chapter (such as the terms "suit" or "ensemble" when used in reference to sets of apparel). They also list specific goods that are either included or excluded from that section or chapter. For instance, Chapter 94 covers "Furniture, bedding, mattresses, mattress supports, cushions ...," but the notes to Chapter 94 state: "This chapter does not cover ... pneumatic or water mattresses ... dentists' chairs ... toy furniture...."

In the event that the goods cannot be classified solely on the basis of GRI 1, the remaining rules may then be consulted. They must be applied in sequence beginning with GRI 2 and proceeding in order through GRI 6. The rules deal with problems that arise when an article could conceivably be classified under more than one heading and for classifying mixtures and articles made up of component parts.

The following rules have been edited for ease of study. Consult the GRI for the official text. Study them carefully, and be sure you are able to apply them.

> GRI 1. Classification shall be determined according to the terms of the headings and any relative section or chapter notes and, provided such headings or notes do not otherwise require, according to GRI 2–6.
>
> GRI 2. (a) An article described in a four-digit heading includes the completed, finished article as well as one that is incomplete or unfinished, provided that the incomplete or unfinished article has the essential character of the complete or finished article. Articles that are entered unassembled shall be classified as the assembled article. For example, a shipment of an unassembled bicycle will be dutied as a finished bicycle, provided that all of the parts needed to make a completed bicycle arrive in one shipment.

(b) Any reference in a heading to a material or substance shall include mixtures or combinations of that material or substance. Any reference in a heading to goods made from a certain material shall include goods made wholly or partly of that material. Goods consisting of more than one material shall be classified according to GRI 3.

GRI 3. When goods are classifiable under two or more headings, the article shall be classified as follows:

(a) The heading that provides the most specific description shall be preferred to headings that provide more general descriptions. (This is known as the *Rule of Relative Specificity*.)
(b) Mixtures, composite goods consisting of different materials or made up of different components, and goods put up in sets for retail sale, which cannot be classified by referring to 3(a), shall be classified as if they consisted of the material or component that gives them their essential character.
(c) When goods cannot be classified by reference to 3 (a) or (b), they shall be classified under the heading that occurs last in numerical order among those that equally merit consideration.

GRI 4. Goods that cannot be classified according to the above rules shall be classified under the heading for goods to which they are most akin.

GRI 5. In addition to the foregoing, the following rules apply:

(a) Camera cases, musical instrument cases, gun cases ... and similar containers, specially shaped or fitted to contain a specific article, suitable for long-term use and entered with the article for which they are intended, shall be classified with such articles when of a kind normally sold therewith.
(b) Packing materials and containers entered with the goods therein shall be classified with the goods, unless the materials or containers are clearly suitable for repetitive use.

GRI 6. The classification of goods in the subheadings shall be determined according to the terms of the subheading and any related notes, and only subheadings at the same level are comparable.

The Rule of Relative Specificity. Recall that GRI 1 requires us to classify a product according to the four-digit heading. But suppose a product could arguably be classified under more than one heading? The *rule of relative specificity,* found in GRI 3(a), provides that where an article could be classified under more than one heading, it must be classified under the one that most specifically describes the item. Moreover, we must only compare the language of the headings, without reference to any of the subheadings. Only after determining that an article is classifiable under a certain heading can you then proceed to find the proper subheading. For instance, assume you are importing electric toothbrushes. There are two possible classifications. Heading 8509 includes *"electromechanical domestic appliance with self-contained motor"* dutied at 4.5 percent. Heading 9603 includes *"brooms, brushes, including brushes constituting parts of machines,"* which are duty free. Which is the correct classification? The answer is heading 8509 because it more specifically describes the items than does 9603. This is despite the fact that at the eight-digit level, 9603.10.90 includes *"toothbrushes, shaving brushes, hairbrushes. . . ."* We must first determine the most specific four-digit heading, and the description *"electromechanical domestic appliance with self-contained motor"* is more specific than *"brooms, brushes. . . ."* In addition, where items could be classified under more than one heading, a description by name is more specific than a description of a class of merchandise. For example, tools used by a hair stylist would be classified as *"shavers and hair clippers with self-contained electric motor"* under heading 8510 because this description is more specific than *"electromechanical tools for working in the hand with self-contained electric motor"* under 8508.

Classification by Essential Character. Suppose an article is made of two or more different materials or components. There is no heading that specifically and completely describes the entire article, but there are several headings that describe the individual materials or components. If two or more headings each describe only certain materials or components of the article, GRI 3(b) requires that the article be classified under the heading that describes those materials or components that give the article its *essential character* ("essential character" is not defined in the GRI). This method is helpful to determine the classification of mixtures of chemicals, foodstuffs, and other substances or materials blended together, assuming that there is no classification that fits the mixture. The rule also applies to *composite goods.* Composite goods are goods made up of more than one component or material. For instance, imagine a typical notebook computer that also contains a standard AM/FM radio receiver. Should it be classified as "Reception apparatus for radio telephony" under heading 8527 or as an "Automatic data processing machin[e]" under section 8471? If the notebook computer imparts the essential character to this odd contraption, it would probably be classified under 8471.

In *Pillowtex Corp. v. United States,* 171 F.3d 1370 (Fed. Cir. 1999), the court considered the tariff classification of comforters made from a 100 percent cotton shell and filled with white duck down. The court held that the down fill should control the classification because the essential character of the comforters was derived from the insulating ability of the filling, not from the shell. Cases involving the essential-character test are very fact intensive; they turn on a detailed analysis of the facts of the case.

Classification of Items Packaged for Retail Sale as a Set. The essential-character test is also used when "goods are put up in sets" for retail sale. In order for a product to qualify as "goods put up in sets," according to the definition in the *Harmonized Tariff Schedule,* (1) there must be no heading in the tariff schedules providing for the set as a whole; (2) there must be two or more different materials or articles classifiable under different headings; (3) they must be packaged together to meet a particular need or carry out a specific activity; and (4) they must be put up in a manner suitable for retail sale to the user without further repacking. According to this definition, a set of twelve spoons would not be a set (they are not different articles), but different types of food sold as a frozen meal would be a set.

In the following case, *Better Home Plastics Corp. v. United States,* 916 F. Supp. 1265 (Ct. Int'l. Trade 1996), the court had to determine whether a shower curtain set was classified under the heading for "*Curtains*" or under the heading for "*Tableware, kitchenware, other household articles and toilet articles, of plastics ... Other: Curtains and drapes including panels and valances.*" Notice how the court applies the *General Rules of Interpretation* and the essential-character test.

Better Home Plastics Corp. v. United States

916 F. Supp. 1265 (1996)

Court of International Trade

BACKGROUND AND FACTS

Plaintiff, Better Home Plastics Corp., imported shower curtain sets. The shower curtain sets consisted of an outer textile curtain, an inner plastic magnetic liner, and plastic hooks. The plastic liner prevented water from escaping while the shower was in use. The liner was color coordinated to match the outer curtain and added to the set's decorative appearance. The textile curtain was intended to be decorative and did not block the water from getting out on the floor. The curtain was also semi-transparent, permitting the color of the plastic liner to show when the curtain and the liner were drawn. Better Home Plastics sold the sets to budget stores at prices ranging from $5.00 to $6.00, and retailers resold them at prices from $9.00 to $12.00. Customs classified the merchandise under the provision for the set's outer curtain at a duty of 12.8% according to Chapter 63, Subheading 6303.92.0000 of the *Harmonized Tariff Schedule* (HTSUS). Better Home Plastics asserted that classification of the set was properly determined by the set's inner plastic liner under Chapter 39, Subheading 3924.90.1010, HTSUS, at a duty of 3.36% *ad valorem.*

DICARLO, CHIEF JUDGE

The *General Rules of Interpretation* (GRI) govern the classification of the imported shower curtain sets under the HTSUS. GRI 1 establishes the general presumption for classification under the rules. GRI 1 provides that the headings and relative section or chapter notes determine the classification of the imported merchandise, so long as those headings or notes do not require otherwise.

GRI 3 governs where the merchandise at issue consists of more than one material or substance, such

continued

continued

as a textile curtain and an inner plastic liner, as here. GRI 3 mandates that, when "goods are, prima facie, classifiable under two or more headings," the court must classify the merchandise in question pursuant to the heading providing the most specific description. This is known as the *rule of relative specificity*. An exception to this rule exists. When, however, two or more headings each refer ... to only part of the items in a set put up for retail sale, those headings are to be regarded as equally specific ... even if one heading provides a more complete or precise description of the goods. Accordingly, the rule of relative specificity does not apply when two of the headings each refer only to part of the items within the set.

Goods put up in sets for retail sale, which cannot be classified according to the most specific heading, are classified by the "component which gives them their essential character" (the *essential character test*). Better Home Plastics contends the court must apply the essential character test, in classifying the applicable merchandise. Application of the test, Better Home Plastics asserts, would mandate classification of the set on the basis of its inner plastic liner pursuant to Subheading 3924.90.1010, HTSUS....

Defendant contends the essential character of the curtains are embodied in the textile curtain. Defendant raises numerous arguments to support its position, particularly that (1) the plastic liner is replaceable at 1/3 to 1/4 the price of the set; (2) the consumer purchases the set because of the decorative function of the outer curtain, and not for the protection afford by the liner; and (3) the liner is only employed for the limited period that someone is utilizing the shower, whereas the decorative outer curtain is employed, at a minimum, when the bathroom is in use, and as much as 24 hours a day. Defendant also contends Better Home Plastics' invoice description supports Customs' classification. Pursuant to the invoice description, the set is sold as "Fabric Shower Curtain and Liner." Therefore, defendant argues, this description serves as an admission that the curtain provides the essential character of the set.

Although the court agrees that the curtain in the imported set imparts a desirable decorative characteristic, nonetheless, it is the plastic liner that provides the indispensable property of preventing water from escaping the shower enclosure. The liner (1) prevents water from escaping when the shower is in use; (2) protects the fabric curtain from mildew and soap scum; and (3) conceals the shower and provides privacy when the shower is in use. Further, the plastic liner can serve its intended function without the outer curtain and contributes to the overall appearance of the set. The outer curtain, in contrast, merely furthers the set's decorative aspect. The court therefore concludes the essential character of the set is derived from the plastic liner.

Defendant's other contentions are also unpersuasive. The manner in which the set is invoiced does not definitively determine which component provides the essential character of the set. The invoice description is intended to characterize the shipped item; it is not a declaration of the relative importance of its component parts. Finally, while the court takes into consideration the relative cost of the component parts, this point alone is not dispositive, nor very persuasive against the competing arguments.

It is the essential character of the set—derived in part from the plastic's ability to repel water—that denotes the set's utility, purpose, and accordingly, character. Inclusion of the textile curtain within the classification for the plastic liner does little to change the qualities or the basic nature of the set in meeting this purpose.

The court finds Better Home Plastics has overcome the presumption of correctness accorded to Customs, and the shower curtain sets were improperly classified under subheading 6303.92.0000, HTSUS. In addition, the court agrees with Better Home Plastics' proposed classification of the sets under subheading 3924.90.1010, HTSUS.

This decision is limited to its facts, i.e., that the set at issue is at the low end of the shower curtain market. The court does not offer an opinion on the proper classification of sets targeted to a different market segment.

Decision. When articles are made up of component parts, or are in sets, and their parts are referred to in two equally specific headings, then the rule of relative specificity does not apply, and their classification must be determined by which part gives the article its essential character. In this case, the shower liner imparted the essential character to the set.

Comment. Judge DiCarlo's opinion was affirmed by the U.S. Court of Appeals in *Better Home Plastics Corp. v. United States*, 119 F.3d 969 (Fed. Cir. 1997).

Classification at the Subheading Level. Only after an article has been classified at the heading level should the subheadings be consulted. When comparing two or more different subheadings within the same heading, the rules set out in GRI 1–5 (relative specificity, essential character, etc.) must still be followed. Articles must be compared at equal subheading levels, so that only six-digit subheadings are compared to other six-digit subheadings, and so on.

Tariff Engineering. *Tariff engineering* is the process of modifying or engineering your product prior to importation for the purposes of obtaining a lower rate of duty. The general rule established by the U.S. Supreme Court and followed for well over 100 years is that an article is to be classified according to its condition at the time it is imported. Thus, generally, tariff engineering is an acceptable practice. As far back as 1881, the Supreme Court stated that "if the manufacturer uses … bleaching processes in order to make his sugars more saleable, why may he not omit to do so in order to render them less dutiable; nay, why may he not employ an extra quantity of molasses for that purpose?" *Merrit v. Welsh,* 104 U.S. 694 (1881). In *United States v. Citroen,* 223 U.S. 407, 32 S.Ct. 259 (1912), an importer unstrung pearls and then restrung them in the United States, achieving a lower rate of duty. The Court stated:

> The [tariff classification] reads "pearls set or strung." It does not say pearls that can be strung, or that are assorted or matched so as to be suitable for a necklace, but pearls "set or strung." We are not concerned with the reason for the distinction; it is enough that Congress made it. Had these pearls never been strung before importation, no one would be heard to argue … because they could be strung, or had been collected for the purpose of stringing or of being worn as a necklace. Loose pearls—however valuable the collection—however carefully matched or desirable for a necklace—are not "pearls set or strung."

Tariff engineering permits importers to design their products or to enter their goods at any step in the manufacturing or assembly process, in order to obtain a lower rate of duty.

Of course, there are some limits on tariff engineering. There must be no fraud or deception, the goods must be correctly described on the entry documents, and they must be honestly presented to Customs for inspection if requested. In *Heartland By-Products, Inc. v. United States,* 264 F.3d 1126 (Fed. Cir. 2001), the importer added molasses to sugar syrup in Canada and removed it after the syrup was imported into the United States. The syrup with molasses entered free from U.S. tariff-rate quotas on sugar syrup imports. Customs maintained that there was no other purpose for adding molasses except to avoid the quota, that the molasses was a "foreign substance," and that adding it was not a genuine step in the manufacturing process. Since the molasses was later returned to Canada to be reused for the same purpose, Customs maintained that the process was done for "disguise or artifice" to circumvent the customs laws. There was no evidence that Heartland ever falsified or concealed the identity of its sugar syrup, its method of manufacture, or its use. The Court of Appeals yielded to the persuasiveness of Customs' argument and upheld its reclassification of the syrup. The impact of Heartland's imports on the American beet sugar industry and its subsequent loss in this case were widely discussed in the media.

Customs Valuation

The customs value, often called *dutiable value,* of all goods entered into the United States must be established and reported to U.S. Customs at the time of entry. All relevant facts and terms of the contract of sale that affect value must be disclosed. Dutiable value is defined by U.S. law as the *transaction value* of the goods. The transaction value of the merchandise is the price actually paid or payable for the merchandise when sold for exportation to the United States, plus the following amounts if not included in the purchase price: (1) packing costs (including containers, covers, and labor for packing) incurred by the buyer, (2) any selling commission incurred by the buyer, (3) the value of any "assist," (4) any royalty or license fee that the buyer is required to pay as a condition of sale, and (5) the proceeds of any subsequent resale of the merchandise that accrues to the seller. Transaction value does not include international freight charges, insurance or customs brokerage fees, inland freight after importation, charges for assembling or maintaining the goods after importation, or import duties. Charges for transporting the goods in the country of exportation (e.g., from the seller's factory to the port) are also excluded when these charges are identified separately on the seller's invoice. Transaction value is not affected by whether the sales contract called for CIF or FOB payment terms. If the price is expressed as CIF, the freight and insurance will be deducted; if FOB, the freight and insurance were not included anyway.

When a seller provides financing on goods exported to the United States, the interest payments are not included in the transaction value of the goods when the interest is identified separately (rather than as a part of the purchase price), the financing contract or note is in writing, and the interest rate is not unusual.

Importers are often required to pay royalties or license fees to the holders of copyrights, trademarks, or patents for the privilege of importing merchandise subject to those rights. Design and engineering fees may have to be paid to foreign firms separately from payments to the actual producer of the product. Sometimes these payments are made through the seller or exporter of the merchandise. When such payments are made "as a condition of sale of the imported merchandise for exportation to the United States," they are included in transaction value. For instance, if a firm imports blue jeans manufactured in Hong Kong and as a condition of sale makes royalty payments to the designer of the jeans in Paris, the royalty would be included in the transaction value of the merchandise.

The *WTO Agreement on Customs Valuation* (1994) attempts to unify the various nations' methods of calculating dutiable value on the basis of transaction value. It also toughens rules for dealing with importers who fraudulently understate the value of an import. It also helps to assure exporters that their goods will be fairly valued in foreign developing countries according to international principles, rather than being subject to arbitrary rules or the whims of corrupt customs officials.

Agency Commissions. The importance of transacting business through a foreign agent is stressed many times in this text. Agents are used both by sellers attempting to export to foreign markets and by buyers attempting to source materials or goods from foreign suppliers. The terms of the relationship between the importer and the agent can have a distinct impact on the calculation of transaction value. Although commissions paid to a buying agent (an agent of the buyer/importer) are generally not included in transaction value, payments made to or for the benefit of the seller or seller's agent are included. Customs carefully scrutinizes the relationship between U.S. importers and their buying agents to be sure that dutiable value is accurately reported.

In *Monarch Luggage Co. v. United States,* 715 F. Supp. 1115 (Ct. Int'l. Trade 1989), the importer successfully structured a business transaction so that the buying commissions were excluded from transaction value. Although representatives of Monarch traveled to the Far East several times a year to meet with their suppliers, inspect their facilities, and place orders for luggage, they nevertheless maintained a local agent there. Under a written agreement, the agent was to locate the best sources for luggage and visit the suppliers to determine the quality of the luggage, but could place orders only at Monarch's direction. The agent coordinated payment for the luggage and arranged transportation according to Monarch's explicit instructions. The supplier and not the agent absorbed the loss of defective merchandise. The agent bore no risk of loss to the goods and never took title to them. The agreement further stated that "the agent shall never act as a seller in any transaction involving the principal." Most importantly, Monarch made the payments to its agent directly and separately and not as a part of the invoice price paid to the supplier of the luggage. In other words, the agent was in fact a representative of the buyer and not an agent of the seller. The fees paid to the agent were not included in dutiable value.

Assists. Importers will often provide some form of assistance to a foreign manufacturer from whom they are purchasing goods. If this *assist* is provided free of charge or at a reduced cost, for use in the production of or sale of merchandise for export to the United States, the value of the assist is included in transaction value. Assists generally include (1) raw materials and component parts incorporated in or used in the production of the imported merchandise; (2) tools, dies, or molds; and (3) engineering, development, artwork, and design, or plans and sketches performed by a foreign firm or person not domiciled within the United States.

In *Texas Apparel Co. v. United States,* 698 F. Supp. 932 (Ct. Int'l. Trade 1988), the importer provided sewing machines to a Mexican manufacturer and paid the cost of repairs to the machines. The machines were used to produce garments sold to the importer in the United States. The court held that if the machines were supplied to the Mexican firm free of charge or at a reduced cost, then the value of the machines had to be included in the dutiable value of the garments as an assist. In *Salant v. United States,* 86 F. Supp. 2d 1301 (Ct. Int'l. Trade 2000) the importer provided free rolls of fabric to a foreign shirt manufacturer for use in making shirts for sale back to the importer. The court upheld customs regulations under which the value of the assist included the value of the fabric that went into the shirts as well as the value of the scrap fabric discarded as waste because including all of the fabric was more in keeping with "generally accepted accounting principles."

OTHER METHODS OF CALCULATING DUTIABLE VALUE. When the transaction value of imported merchandise cannot be determined, Customs will look to the value of identical merchandise. If identical merchandise cannot be found, then the value of similar merchandise will be used. The identical or similar merchandise used in the comparison must have been recently sold for export to the United States at the same level of trade (manufacturer to distributor, distributor to retailer, for example) and in quantities similar to the entry being valued.

If dutiable value cannot be determined by any of these methods, Customs will utilize the deductive value or computed value methods. *Deductive value* is the resale price of the goods (including packaging costs) in the United States after importation, less international and inland freight, insurance, customs duties, brokerage fees, commissions, and expenses of refining, assembling, or further manufacturing incurred in the United States. The final method for calculating the value of imports gives the computed value. *Computed value* is calculated by adding the costs of raw materials, processing or fabricating, overhead, labor costs, packing costs, the value of any assist, and an amount for profit.

CURRENCY EXCHANGE RATES. If imported products are invoiced in a foreign currency, customs valuation is not based on the actual amount paid to the foreign supplier in U.S. dollars according to the exchange rate obtained by the importer. Rather, the goods will be valued in dollars based on the exchange rate certified by the Federal Reserve Bank of New York on the day of export from the foreign country.

Country-of-Origin Rules

Imagine that it's 1989 and that your trading company has firm commitments from buyers in the United States to take all of the ostrich chicks that you can provide during the next year. After considerable searching and time spent traveling the world, you find an ostrich hatchery in England. You enter into a sales contract with the hatchery, with payment to be made under a confirmed letter of credit. Your bank pays the seller cash on the documents, and the chicks arrive peeping and squawking at a U.S. port of entry. The chicks are entered with their country of origin listed as Great Britain. An astute customs inspector realizes that the chicks could not possibly have "originated" in that country and corrects the country of origin to South Africa where the eggs obviously originated. You agree that the fertilized eggs originated in South Africa but argue that their incubation and hatching in Great Britain amounts to a "substantial transformation" and that Great Britain therefore became the country of origin. U.S. Customs ruled that the processing of the eggs in Great Britain was a natural biological consequence of the initial fertilization of the eggs in South Africa, that the chicks continued to be a product of South Africa, and that they are prohibited from entering the United States under a U.S. law banning the import of products from South Africa. (The ban was lifted in the early 1990s following the end of apartheid and political changes in South Africa.) This not-so-hypothetical case illustrates how critical it is to know the lawful country of origin of imported goods.

DEFINITION AND PURPOSES OF RULES OF ORIGIN. *Rules of origin* are the national laws and regulations of administrative agencies, usually customs authorities, which are used to determine the country of origin of imported products. No importing country will permit goods to be imported unless the country of origin of the goods is properly determined and reported to customs authorities for their review. In the United States, country-of-origin rules are enforced by U.S. Customs and Border Protection. The country of origin is used to determine the following:

- the normal tariff rate on an import
- whether an import is subject to a preferential tariff rate or an increased rate
- whether an import is subject to antidumping or countervailing duties
- whether an import is subject to a quota, embargo, or other trade restriction
- the applicability of government procurement rules
- the proper country-of-origin labeling to be affixed to the product
- statistical information

Difficulty in Determining Rules of Origin. There are few areas of customs law that are so complex and so difficult for importers to understand. One of the reasons for the complexity is that there are many different rules, applicable to imports from different countries. In the United States, there is one set of rules to determine the rate of duty on most imports from most-favored-nation (or normal-trade) countries. There is a separate rule for imports from Canada and Mexico under the *North American Free Trade Agreement,* another for textile and apparel imports, another for government procurement, and another for imports from developing countries that receive trade preferences (reduced rates of duty), in addition to different rules applicable to each of the free trade agreements signed by the United States with nations such as Australia, Bahrain, Chile, Israel, Jordan, Morocco, Singapore, the Caribbean, Africa, the Andean countries, and Central America. There are also special rules applicable to civil aircraft and automobiles. To complicate matters, the rules used to determine the rate of duty on goods is often different from the rules of origin used to determine country-of-origin labeling of those goods. As such, we caution that no reader should rely on the general principles discussed in the following sections, but should seek professional advice or be prepared to carefully research the rules of origin applicable to their specific transactions. The various rules of origin can be found in the harmonized tariff schedules of most countries (in the United States, the HTSUS) and by reference to free trade agreements and to the rules and decisions of customs authorities and courts. In the United States, there are many court decisions interpreting the rules of origin.

The General Rule. The country of origin is not merely the country from which the goods were purchased or from where they were shipped. If that were the case, one could enter Italian leather products into the United States at the lower Mexican tariff rate by simply routing them through Mexico. Where a product is made in one country, entirely from raw materials and components originating there, the country of origin is not difficult to determine. Bananas grown in Honduras and shipped directly to supermarkets in the United States are products of Honduras. Plywood sheets glued and pressed in Brazil, from trees grown in Brazil, are obviously products of Brazil. Men's shirts that were cut and sewn in China, from fabric woven and yarn spun there, that was made completely from cotton grown there, are obviously a product of China. These cases exemplify the general rule of origin applicable to U.S. imports from countries with MFN trading status with the United States (normal trade relations). Here, the general rule is that the country of origin of an imported article is that country where it was wholly and completely produced, manufactured, or obtained entirely from raw materials originating in that country. In these cases, there can be no intermediate steps of processing, production, manufacturing, or assembly in any other country unless an exception exists by statute.

However, few products today are wholly made in one country entirely from materials derived there. More and more products are subjected to manufacturing, processing, and assembly operations on a global scale. Agricultural commodities grown in one country may be processed into food in another. Steel produced in one country may be galvanized, or transformed or processed into wire, steel plates, girders, or automobile parts, in another country. An automobile destined for the United States may be assembled in Latin America or Canada from parts and materials that originated in or were assembled in dozens of countries. Some products can involve hundreds or thousands of component parts that have been manufactured and assembled in plants located on several continents. Nevertheless, importers are expected to accurately track the movement of materials and understand the complex manufacturing or assembly processes, which in turn allow them to accurately know the product's country of origin. Where goods are not wholly and completely produced or manufactured in one country, the country of origin can only be determined by referring to the appropriate rules of origin.

The Substantial Transformation Test. There can be only one country of origin for customs purposes, even for products that undergo manufacturing operations in several different countries. In this case, the generally accepted rule is that the country of origin is that country where a product last underwent a substantial transformation. But there is no easy definition of "substantial transformation." The definition largely depends on the rules of origin applicable to the products and countries involved. In the United States, there are currently four basic sets of rules of origin, each with its own test for what amounts to a substantial transformation. The fifth rule is one currently being developed by the WTO. We will briefly define the rules here and will explain them further in the sections that follow.

1. The *name, character, or use test* is used to determine the country of origin for most goods entering the United States from countries with which the United States has normal trade relations. The rule applies when determining the tariff rate, the applicability of antidumping or countervailing duties, quotas or other trade restrictions, and the country-of-origin marking or labeling requirements. For example, if steel is made in Korea and shipped to Germany (or any other NTR country) where it is turned into fine cutlery, it can enter the United States under the tariff rate for German cutlery and be labeled "Made in Germany" only if the processing in Germany amounted to a substantial transformation that created a new and different article of commerce with a new "name, character, or use" as defined by U.S. law.
2. The rules of origin of the *North American Free Trade Agreement* (NAFTA) between the United States, Canada, and Mexico permit goods that are *wholly produced or obtained* in North America to be sold in North America at favorable NAFTA rates. "Wholly produced or obtained," as some writers have said with a little exaggeration, means that the goods cannot have "one atom" that did not originate in North America. Goods that are made from materials or components that originated outside North America qualify for free trade status only if each and every non-North American material or component (called *inputs*) has undergone a change in tariff classification as described in NAFTA Annex 401. For example, a product manufactured in Canada from raw material inputs originating in Europe can be shipped to the United States as a product of North America (at the tariff rate applicable to Canadian imports and labeled "Made in Canada") only if every single one of the European materials or components underwent a change in tariff classification set out in the NAFTA agreement when they were made into the new product in Canada. This is known as the NAFTA *tariff shift rule.* The United States, Canada, and Mexico each have their own tariff shift rules. Each country's rules are based on the principles of Annex 401 and found in the notes to their national tariff schedules.
3. *Trade-preference rules* are used to determine if goods qualify for favorable tariff treatment (a "preference") as a result of having originated in the Caribbean, Africa, a country with whom the United States has a free trade pact (Israel, Jordan, and Chile are a few examples), or a developing country from some other region that has qualified under U.S. law. For example, if an article originates in China and is sent to a Caribbean processing plant to be made into a finished product destined for customers in the United States, the finished product can be entered under the preferential tariff rates for Caribbean-made products only if the processing that took place in the Caribbean country met the specific "substantial transformation" requirements as defined by the *U.S.–Caribbean*

Basin Economic Recovery Act. Similar laws apply to products of Africa and to developing countries in all regions of the world.

4. *Textile and apparel rules of origin*. Special rules apply to U.S. imports of textile and apparel products.
5. The WTO is currently developing a uniform set of rules of origin under the authority of the *WTO Agreement on Rules of Origin* (1994). These new rules are still several years away from completion, but if they are adopted they will significantly change the rules of origin in the United States and other countries. The rules are similar to the tariff shift rules of NAFTA.

We begin our discussion with the rule of origin that currently has the broadest impact on the customs laws in the United States: the *name, character, or use test*. The other rules will be discussed later in this chapter, except for the NAFTA rules, which are the subject of the next chapter.

Substantial Transformation: The "Name, Character, or Use" Test. For a century, the courts of the United States have held that a substantial transformation occurs when the original article or product loses its identity as such and is transformed into a new and different article of commerce having "a new name, character, or use" different from that of the original item. In 1908, the U.S. Supreme Court ruled that imported cork had not been substantially transformed when it was dried, treated, and cut into smaller sections for use in bottling beer. The Court stated, "Something more is necessary.... There must be a transformation; a new and different article must emerge, having a distinctive name, character or use. This cannot be said of the corks in question. A cork put through the claimant's process is still a cork." *Anheuser-Busch Brewing Association v. United States,* 207 U.S. 556 (1908). Since then, many courts have tried to interpret this phrase and to apply it to many different products and manufacturing operations.

The *name, character, or use test* is used to determine the country of origin for tariff purposes (other than in specialized cases, such as those falling under the *North American Free Trade Agreement*), as well as to determine how foreign-made products are to be marked or labeled. Customs uses the "name, character, or use" test to determine the country of origin for marking and labeling purposes. U.S. law strictly requires that every foreign-made article imported into the United States be marked or labeled in English so as to indicate the country of origin of the article to the *ultimate purchaser*.

Suppose an article is taken from Country A to Country B, where it is subjected to a refining process that combines it with other materials. If the process in Country B amounts to a substantial transformation so that a new product emerges with a new "name, character, or use," then the article may be imported into the United States and marked as "Made in Country B." Similarly, if foreign raw materials are imported into the United States and put through a manufacturing process that substantially transforms them into a product with a new "name, character, or use," the new product need not be marked as of foreign origin when sold to the ultimate purchaser. In other words, through the process the foreign raw materials have been transformed into a product of the United States.

The landmark case *Gibson-Thomsen Co. v. United States,* 27 C.C.P.A. 267 (1940)[BB] involved the application of the name, character, or use test under the marking and labeling laws of the United States. The court ruled that when wooden handles and blocks were imported into the United States from Japan, then drilled with holes into which American bristles were inserted, and with the final product being sold in the United States as toothbrushes and hairbrushes, the imported wooden components had "lost their identity in a tariff sense" and had been transformed into products of the United States. The court took account of the fact that the bristles, which had been of U.S. origin, were a key component of the new product. Because the transformation took place in the United States, the wooden handles did not have to be marked as having originated in Japan. *Gibson-Thomsen* is often cited by courts today.

Since 1940, the courts have interpreted and refined the "name, character, or use" concept. Some courts have looked to see if a "new article of commerce" emerges from the transformation. For instance, in a 1970 case, a court ruled that unfinished furniture chair parts were substantially transformed by the importer into chairs that were new and different articles of commerce. Similarly, wooden sticks imported into the United States and then set into liquid ice cream and frozen have been held to be substantially transformed into a new product having a new name, character, and use. In a 1960 case, a court ruled that the winding of typewriter ribbon onto imported spools resulted in a substantial transformation of the spools because the imported spool became an integral part of the whole product with which it was combined. In 1984, Customs used the same rationale for deciding not to impose country-of-origin marking requirements on the plastic spools and shells in which audiocassette tape is wound. Although many cases look to see if the name commonly given the transformed article has changed, a product's name is generally considered to be only one of several factors to take into account. Greater emphasis is usually placed on whether the *essential character*—sometimes said to be the "essential nature" —of the product or its use has changed.

Many of the modern cases also look to see whether the substantial transformation has resulted in an increase in value, called the *value-added test.* In *National Juice Products Association v. United States,* 628 F. Supp. 978 (Ct. Int'l. Trade 1986), a U.S. company had imported evaporated orange concentrate and blended it with water, orange oils, and fresh juice to make frozen orange concentrate. The blending and processing in the United States had added only a 7 percent value to the orange juice. The court held that the orange juice sold to consumers had to be labeled with the foreign country of origin.

In *Uniroyal, Inc. v. United States,* 542 F. Supp. 1026 (Ct. Int'l. Trade 1982), *aff'd. per curiam,* 702 F.2d 1022 (Fed. Cir. 1983), the court ruled that a substantial transformation had not occurred when the leather upper portion of a shoe was imported and then attached to the preformed rubber sole in the United States and sold as a "Sperry Topsider." The court relied heavily on evidence that the time and cost of producing the leather upper in Indonesia were much greater than the time and cost of attaching it to the rubber sole (called a "minor assembly operation"). The court also considered that the fashioning of the leather uppers in Indonesia required far greater skill than was required to attach the sole in the United States. The court stated that "[I]t would be misleading to allow the public to believe that a shoe is made in the United States when the entire upper—which is the very essence of the completed shoe—is made in Indonesia and the only step in the manufacturing process performed in the United States is the attachment of an outsole." The court noted that unlike the earlier case involving typewriter spools, the upper leather portion of the shoe was not just a vehicle for selling something else, but was the major reason that consumers selected this shoe.

Ferrostaal Metals Corp. v. United States illustrates the difficulty of determining whether a substantial transformation has occurred. As this case shows, the precise definition of substantial transformation is unclear because so many factors can be considered. The courts have recognized that it is difficult to take legal concepts applicable to products such as textiles and apply them to combinations of liquids or the fabrication of steel articles. Faced with complex cases, courts have developed rules on a case-by-case basis. The unpredictable nature of these court rulings increases importers' difficulties in interpreting and applying the rules of origin, as evidenced by the large number of customs cases appealed to the courts.

As you read, consider the actual process of hot-dip galvanizing described here. Would you agree that the operations performed on the steel in New Zealand created a product with a new "name, character, or use"?

WTO *Agreement on Rules of Origin*

Exporters and importers worldwide would benefit greatly from standardized rules of origin, which would let them more accurately determine the country of origin of their shipments in advance. This would help in product labeling as well as in determining the rate of duty and other laws applicable to their products. The *WTO Agreement on Rules of Origin* (1995) called on countries to harmonize and clarify their rules. The agreement resulted from the *Uruguay Round* of trade negotiations, completed in 1994. It is not an easy task for so many countries to agree on such a complex issue as rules of origin. As of this writing, the *WTO Committee on Rules of Origin* was in the process of developing new, uniform rules. These rules will apply to all trade between countries that are members of the WTO. Under the proposed rules, the country of origin is defined as either

Ferrostaal Metals Corp. v. United States

664 F. Supp. 535 (1987)
Court of International Trade

BACKGROUND AND FACTS

Plaintiff attempted to enter steel products at the Port of Seattle. They consisted of unpainted steel sheets that had originated in Japan but had been hot-dip galvanized in New Zealand. Plaintiff's entry documents identified New Zealand as the country of origin. Customs ruled that the country of origin was Japan and that the steel was therefore subject to a voluntary restraint agreement between the United States and Japan. Customs contended that hot-dip galvanizing of Japanese steel sheets in New Zealand was merely a "finishing process" carried out to improve certain performance characteristics of the steel sheets and not a process that results in a substantial transformation so as to change the country of origin. The plaintiff disagreed and brought this action for review.

JUDGE DICARLO

Substantial transformation is a concept of major importance in administering the customs and trade laws. In addition to its role in identifying the country of origin of imported merchandise for purposes of determining dutiable status, or, as in this case, the applicability of a bilateral trade agreement, substantial transformation is the focus of many cases involving country-of-origin markings. . . .

The essence of these cases is that a product cannot be said to originate in the country of exportation if it is not manufactured there. The question, therefore, is whether operations performed on products in the country of exportation are of such a substantial nature to justify the conclusion that the resulting product is a manufacture of that country. "Manufacture implies a change, but every change is not manufacture. . . . There must be transformation; a new and different article must emerge, 'having a distinctive name, character, or use.'" *Anheuser-Busch Brewing Ass'n. v. United States,* 207 U.S. 556, 562, 28 S.Ct. 204, 206 (1908). The criteria of name, character, and use continue to determine when substantial transformation has occurred, and the prior cases of this court and our predecessor and appellate courts provide guidance in the application of this test.

* * *

Whether galvanizing and annealing change the character of the merchandise depends on the nature of these operations and their effect on the properties of the materials. . . . To produce one of the types of imported sheet . . . the sheet must be heated to 1,350 degrees F, at which point recrystallization of the grains of steel occurs. The sheet is then brought down to 880 degrees F, before galvanizing begins. At 880 degrees F, the sheet enters a pot of molten zinc and is dipped. The molten zinc reacts immediately with the solid steel, and begins a process known as "alloying." Alloying constitutes a chemical change in the product, characterized by the formation of iron-zinc alloys at the interface between the steel and the zinc. The galvanized steel sheet emerging from the bath has a mixed zinc-steel surface with an identifiable atomic pattern. The formation of a galvanized surface is an irreversible process which provides electrochemical protection to the sheet. As a result of the galvanic protection, the steel will last up to twenty years, or ten times as long as ungalvanized steel. . . .

The alloy-bonded zinc coating affects the character of the sheet by changing its chemical composition and by providing corrosion resistance. The court also finds that the hot-dip galvanizing process is substantial in terms of the value it adds to full hard cold-rolled steel sheet. The evidence showed that the Japanese product is sold for approximately $350 per ton, while the hot-dipped galvanized product is sold for an average price of $550 to $630.

Taken as a whole, the continuous hot-dip galvanizing process transforms a strong, brittle product which cannot be formed into a durable, corrosion-resistant product which is less hard, but formable for a range of commercial applications. Defendant's witness stated that the imported sheet has a "different character from the standpoint of durability." The court finds that the annealing and galvanizing processes result in a change in character by significantly altering the mechanical properties and chemical composition of the steel sheet.

The court also finds substantial changes in the use of the steel sheet as a result of the continuous hot-dip galvanizing process. Testimony at trial overwhelmingly demonstrated that cold-rolled steel is not

continued

continued

interchangeable with steel of the type imported, nor are there any significant uses of cold-rolled sheet in place of annealed sheet.

The name criterion is generally considered the least compelling of the factors which will support a finding of substantial transformation. Nonetheless, the satisfaction of the name criterion in this case lends support to plaintiffs' claim. The witnesses for both parties testified that the processing of full hard cold-rolled steel sheet results in a product which has a different name, continuous hot-dip galvanized steel sheet.

The court also considers relevant whether the operations underlying the asserted transformation have effected a change in the classification of the merchandise under the Tariff Schedules of the United States. Change in tariff classification may be considered as a factor in the substantial transformation analysis. Here this factor supports a substantial transformation. Full hard cold-rolled steel sheet is classified under item 607.83, TSUS, while continuous hot-dip galvanized steel sheet is classifiable under item 608.13, TSUS. (The TSUS was the forerunner to the *Harmonized Tariff Schedule.*)

Based on the totality of the evidence, showing that the continuous hot-dip galvanizing process effects changes in the name, character, and use of the processed steel sheet, the court holds that the changes constitute a substantial transformation and that hot-dipped galvanized steel sheet is a new and different article of commerce from full hard cold-rolled steel sheet.

Decision. Japanese steel that had been galvanized in New Zealand prior to its importation into the United States was substantially transformed so that it had become a product of New Zealand and thus was not subject to voluntary restraint agreements between the United States and Japan.

Comment. "Voluntary restraint agreements" such as those described in this case to restrict steel imports from Japan are no longer used as a method of limiting imports of foreign goods into America, as they do not fall under the permissible rules of the WTO. Nevertheless, this case serves well to illustrate the use of the substantial transformation test in tariff cases. The case was cited in 2003 by U.S. Customs in a ruling determining the country of origin of fiber-optic cable.

where the article and all of its constituent materials have been wholly obtained or, if the article is produced in more than one country, that country where the article last underwent a specified change in tariff classification. This provision is known as the *tariff shift rule.*

The United States is moving toward the use of the tariff shift rule. Rules of origin based on the tariff shift rule state precisely—for every given category of product in the HTS—what tariff classification changes will result in a substantial transformation. Manufacturers, for example, can look at the tariff schedules and find out what type of changes to imported raw materials or component parts will allow them to sell their finished product as one that originated in their country. The tariff shift rule is more reliable and less vague than many other rules of origin and less subject to argument and court action. This rule is already in effect under *NAFTA* for trade between Canada, Mexico, and the United States, and is used as the rule of origin for most bilateral free trade agreements entered into by the United States. (See Chapter Thirteen for a detailed discussion of North American rules of origin.)

The WTO has agreed on rules covering many non-agricultural products. The goal is to complete a single set of rules of origin covering over 5,500 products in both the agricultural and non-agricultural sectors that would be applied by all WTO member countries.

Special Rules of Origin for Textiles and Apparel

The world's textile and apparel industry operates on a global scale. Textile firms shift the site of spinning, weaving, cutting, sewing, and other operations from country to country and from region to region to take advantage of low-cost labor and materials and to benefit from customs and tariff laws in the country in which the goods will be sold. For instance, cotton might be grown and spun into yarn in China, where it is woven into cloth. The cloth might be sent to Hong Kong, where it is cut to form pieces of garments (e.g., sleeves, collars, etc.), and then sent to Honduras for assembly. Textile and apparel manufacturers must consider the rules of origin in sourcing yarn, fabric, and other raw materials or in locating textile dyeing and finishing operations, cut-and-sew plants, or assembly operations.

Textile and apparel imports to the United States are governed by specialized rules of origin. They are more complex, arcane, and restrictive than rules applicable to other products, which makes it more difficult for firms to import textiles than almost any other product. Many factors determine the country of origin of textile and apparel products: the type of product (e.g., yarn, fabric, clothing and apparel, or textile products for the home), the fiber content (e.g., silk, wool, cotton, etc.), and the steps or processes that take place in the transition from yarn to fabric to final product. The administrative rules of origin for textile and apparel products promulgated by U.S. Customs can be found in 19 CFR 102.21.

Here are a few generalizations: Many textile products are covered by tariff shift rules, under which the country of origin is determined by whether or not the operation (weaving, cutting, assembly, or whatever) causes a specified shift in the tariff classification of a raw material). The country of origin of certain items, including many home textile products, is often the country where the fabric was formed by weaving or some other fabric-making process, regardless of where it was cut and assembled into a finished product. Products that are knitted to shape, such as hosiery, socks, knitted gloves, and mittens, generally originate in the country in which they were knitted. Some articles, such as clothing and apparel, originate in the country where they were wholly assembled, or where the most important assembly or manufacturing process took place. Other items are said to have originated where the fabric from which they were made was dyed and printed (when combined with two or more finishing operations), rather than where they were woven. Cutting fabric into pieces, without more, is not enough to confer country of origin status. Clearly, anyone determining the country of origin of a textile product must understand textile production processes and be able to accurately trace all steps of global operations from beginning to end. Critics of the rules of origin point out that there is no logical method to the rules and many commentators believe they derive primarily from political considerations. For example, prior to 2000, scarves made from Chinese silk entered the United States as products of China, subject to quota limits on Chinese scarves. They had to be labeled "Made in China" despite the fact that they were dyed, printed, and finished in Italy by premier Italian textile converters with exclusive brand names and a reputation for sophisticated designs and quality. It was not until the EU threatened WTO action that the United States changed the rule. Now, scarves and some other items that are made from Chinese silk may be entered as a product of the country in which they were subjected to dyeing and printing plus two other finishing operations. If these criteria are met, the silk scarves may carry the prestigious label "Made in Italy."

To complicate matters, U.S. imports of textiles from Canada or Mexico are treated differently under NAFTA. NAFTA utilizes tariff shift rules to determine origination. For example, assume that fabric is woven and then sewn into unfilled comforter shells in China, then shipped to Canada where the shells are filled with goose down for shipment to the United States. The unfilled comforter shells fall under HTS subheading 6307.90.

They are shipped to Canada to be filled with goose down from China or Europe. Goose down is classified under HTS subheading 0505.10.

On shipment to the United States, the finished comforter, classified under HTS subheading 9404.90, is entered under NAFTA's zero-tariff rate for Canadian comforters, rather than the 12.8 percent tariff rate on comforters from China, and is not subject to any other quotas or restraints on Chinese textiles. The NAFTA rules of origin, based on the tariff shift rule, specifically provide that a transformation of articles from headings 6307 or 0505 to heading 9404 allows the final product to enter the United States at a zero tariff rate and to be marked "Made in Canada."

Textile imports from countries with whom the United States has a free trade agreement, from certain countries in Africa or the Caribbean, or from other developing countries all may be subject to different rules. Moreover, there are separate tariff and marking rules for U.S.–made fabrics that are taken to a foreign country (usually in the Caribbean), where they are processed, cut, and sewn into jeans, T-shirts, and other clothing and returned to the United States for sale.

These contradictory and confusing rules often stymie the most experienced importers. So, textile and apparel manufacturers and importers rely heavily on attorneys and customs brokers that specialize in textile imports. They also frequently obtain binding ruling letters from U.S. Customs in advance of setting up operations to be certain that they comply with the law.

Opportunities for Business Planning. The rules of origin can provide a resourceful importer with significant opportunities for good business planning. With proper legal advice, a firm can structure its global operations to minimize tariffs and take advantage of the favorable trade and tariff treatment granted to goods coming from particular foreign countries. After all, trade and tariff laws are designed in part to either encourage or discourage trade with particular nations. Many firms, particularly multinational corporations, are therefore capable of shifting global resources and production facilities to those countries whose goods receive the most favorable trade and tariff treatment in the United States or other major importing nations. But to do this, the corporation must follow the importing nation's rules of origin meticulously. The tariff savings can be so great that some unscrupulous U.S. importers have been tempted to transship articles through developing countries, repackage or relabel them, and then enter them into the United States at the lower tariff rate. The penalties for furnishing false information to U.S. Customs authorities are quite severe.

Marking and Labeling of Imports

The United States has two key laws that require imports to be labeled with the country of origin: the marking rules of U.S. Customs and the Federal Trade Commission (FTC) rules. The rules of U.S. Customs apply to country-of-origin markings of all imported products sold in the United States. The FTC rules apply primarily to the use of "Made in U.S.A." or similar terms. To be labeled "Made in U.S.A.," a label must meet the requirements of both agencies.

Customs Marking Rules. Every article of foreign origin imported into the United States must be indelibly and permanently marked in English in a conspicuous place and in such a manner as to indicate the name of the country of origin of the article to the *ultimate purchaser* in the United States. The ultimate purchaser is the last person in the United States who receives an article in the form in which it was imported. If an imported article is to be sold at retail in the same form as it was imported, then the retail customer is the "ultimate purchaser."

If the imported article is converted, processed, or combined with other articles or ingredients in the United States so that it undergoes a substantial transformation resulting in a new article of commerce with a new name, character, or use, as defined by the *Gibson-Thomsen* case, then the U.S. firm that transformed the article is considered the ultimate purchaser. As a result, the new product need not be labeled with a foreign country of origin.

Does that mean that it can be labeled "Made in U.S.A."? Perhaps not. As we will see in the next section, the FTC rules take precedence, and they will not allow that claim unless the new product is "all or virtually all" made in America. Because the product was only "transformed" in the United States from foreign materials, it might be labeled "Made in U.S.A. of Imported Materials."

Items Not Requiring Marks. Customs regulations specify many articles by name that are exempt from marking requirements. These are generally objects that are incapable of being marked because of their size or special characteristics. Examples include works of art, unstrung beads, rags, nuts, bolts, screws, cigarettes, eggs, feathers, flowers, cellophane sheets, livestock, bamboo poles, maple sugar, vegetables, and newsprint. In addition, the following general exemptions exist for certain categories of products: (1) products incapable of being marked; (2) products that cannot be marked without injury; (3) crude substances; (4) articles produced more than twenty years prior to importation; (5) products of possessions of the United States; (6) articles imported solely for the use of the importer and not intended for resale (e.g., personal articles purchased abroad by a tourist); (7) products of American fisheries that are entered duty free; and (8) certain products of the United States that are exported and returned. In addition, articles used by an importer as samples in soliciting orders and that are not for sale are exempted from the marking requirements.

When an item is exempt from marking requirements, the container in which it is sold to the consumer must be marked. To illustrate, imported carpentry nails need not be marked, but the box in which they are sold to the consumer must be.

Federal Trade Commission "Made in U.S.A." Rules

In the United States, the FTC and U.S. Customs have overlapping jurisdiction with regard to country-of-origin claims. While Customs oversees foreign country-of-origin marking ("Made in China"), the FTC regulates the use of the term "Made in U.S.A." Customs rules apply only to product marking, while the FTC rules apply to all claims, including those on product labels, catalogs, packaging, and all forms of advertising. Customs rules are more complex and detailed, while the "Made in U.S.A." rules of the FTC are more flexible and are based on whether or not the claims would mislead or cause deception in the minds of the average consumer. The FTC bases its rules on its authority under the *Federal Trade Commission Act* to prevent unfair or deceptive trade practices.

There is no rule that requires a U.S.–made product to be labeled as such. Except for special rules applicable to automobiles and textile and fur products, U.S. content need not be disclosed. However, a seller may not claim that a product is "Made in U.S.A." unless *all or virtually all* of the materials, processing, or component parts are made in the United States and their final assembly or processing took place there. All significant parts and processing that go into the product must be of U.S. origin. That is, the product should contain only negligible foreign content. For instance, the FTC has held that a gas barbecue grill assembled entirely from U.S. parts could be labeled as "Made in U.S.A." despite the fact that the knobs were of foreign origin. The knobs were said to make up a small portion of the product's total cost and an insignificant part of the final product.

The FTC origin rules apply also to other more indirect forms of marketing and promotion that may be deceptive. In one case, a company packaged its Chinese-made product in a package covered with an American flag and eagle. Despite the statement "Made in China," which appeared in small print on the bottom and side panels of the package, the FTC held that the labeling was deceptive.

Partly Made in the U.S.A.? Products that cannot be labeled as "Made in U.S.A." may still bear qualified claims. A qualified claim is one that indicates that the product was partially made or processed in the United States. An example would be a down comforter labeled "Shell made in Germany with filling and further processing in the U.S.A." To use a qualified claim, there must still be a significant amount of U.S. content. A product that is invented in the United States and made in India could *not* claim "Created in U.S.A.," as this would be deceptive. The term "Assembled in U.S.A." may be used only where the product has undergone a substantial transformation in the United States and where the use of the term would not be deceptive. For example, according to the FTC, component parts for computers made in Singapore and assembled in Texas with only a screwdriver and screws may *not* be labeled as "Assembled in U.S.A." Here there was no substantial transformation in the United States and the statement is deceptive.

U.S. Trade Preferences for Developing Countries

A *trade preference* is the granting of preferential access or a trade advantage by a developed country to goods originating in developing countries that is not given to similar goods imported from other developed countries. Trade preferences usually take the form of reduced tariffs or duty-free status. The purpose of trade preferences is to accelerate economic development in poorer or developing countries. Most developed nations, including the United States, Canada, Japan, and the European Union grant trade preferences. Two important U.S. laws that grant trade preferences are the *Generalized System of Preferences* and the *Caribbean Basin Economic Recovery Act.*

The *Generalized System of Preferences*

Under the *Generalized System of Preferences* (GSP), the United States aids in the economic development of certain developing countries by allowing their products to enter the United States at reduced rates of duty, or duty free, until such time as these countries establish their own competitive industries. Such a trade preference is allowed under the terms of GATT and is similar to programs that other industrialized nations offer developing countries (notably the preferences granted by European nations to the products of many African nations). The program was begun in the United States in 1976 and has been renewed regularly by Congress. Mexico no longer qualified for the GSP when it joined NAFTA in 1994. There are approximately 140 countries receiving GSP status. Examples include Brazil and Argentina in South America, India and Thailand in Asia, Indonesia and the Philippines in the Pacific Rim, and Poland and Hungary in Eastern Europe, as well as Russia and most of Africa. In 2007, imports worth over $32 billion entered the United States under the GSP preferences.

Eligibility for GSP Status. In order for a country to be eligible for GSP status, it must be designated a *beneficiary developing country.* Countries are not eligible for GSP status if they (1) have participated in an organized embargo of oil against the United States, (2) do not cooperate with the United States in the enforcement of narcotics laws, (3) aid and abet international terrorism, (4) have unlawfully expropriated the property of U.S. citizens, (5) do not recognize or enforce the arbitral awards of U.S. citizens, or (6) are controlled by communist governments. In addition, the president has wide authority under the GSP statute to deny duty-free treatment on political and economic grounds. For instance, the president can deny GSP status to any country that does not protect the patents, trademarks, and copyrights of U.S. citizens; maintains unreasonable restrictions on U.S. investment; does not grant internationally recognized worker rights to its workers; or whose exports to the United States injure a U.S. industry.

The product must also be eligible for duty-free treatment; over 4,600 products are eligible. Many of the eligible products are agricultural. Other typical products admitted under the GSP include sugar, jewelry, leather shoe uppers, wooden furniture, Christmas tree lighting, and telephones. Certain import-sensitive products, such as textiles, footwear, steel, watches, and some electronic items, are not eligible.

A country may lose GSP benefits for specific products under competitive need limits. *Competitive need* is determined by an annual review process conducted on a product-by-product basis. Usually the duty-free status of a country's product will be terminated when more than half of the total U.S. imports of that product are imported from one GSP country or when imports of that product from the GSP country exceed a level established by Congress. Competitive need limits do not apply to sub-Saharan Africa. U.S. firms, labor unions, and even foreign governments may petition that products be added to or removed from the GSP list.

Once a developing country reaches a per capita gross national product of $8,500, it becomes ineligible for GSP treatment and is considered to have *graduated.* By the close of the 1980s, the four "Asian tigers" of Hong Kong, Singapore, South Korea, and Taiwan had graduated from the GSP.

GSP Rules of Origin. In order for an article to qualify for duty-free treatment, it must meet the following requirements: (1) it must be imported into the United States directly from the beneficiary developing country; (2) it must be the "growth, product, or manufacture" of the beneficiary developing country (or substantially transformed there into a product with a new name, character, and use); and (3) at least 35 percent of the value of materials and the direct cost of processing operations must have been added to the article in a single beneficiary developing country (or in any two or more GSP countries that are members of the same free trade association, such as ASEAN, CARICOM, or the Andean Group). A special rule applies when raw materials are brought to the GSP country from another country and then made into a finished article and shipped to the United States. In this case, the law requires a *dual transformation.* The raw materials brought from another country into the GSP country must first undergo a substantial transformation in the GSP country, resulting in a new and different article of commerce, in order for that article to be included in the 35 percent value content requirement. Then that article must undergo a second transformation into another new and different article of commerce, which is then shipped to the United States.

To better illustrate, consider the following example of a dual transformation adapted from the *Code of Federal Regulations:*

> A raw, perishable skin of an animal grown in a nonbeneficiary country is sent to a beneficiary country where it is tanned to create nonperishable leather. The tanned leather is then cut, sewn, and assembled with a metal buckle imported from a nonbeneficiary country to create a finished belt that is imported directly into the United States. Because the operations performed in the beneficiary country involved both the substantial transformation of the raw skin into a new or different article (tanned leather) and the use of that intermediate article in the production or manufacture of a new or different article imported into the United States, the cost or value of the tanned leather used to make the imported article *may be counted* toward the 35 percent value requirement. The cost or value of the metal buckle imported into the beneficiary country *may not be counted* toward the 35 percent value requirement because the buckle was not substantially transformed in the beneficiary country into a new or different article prior to its incorporation in the finished belt.

Caribbean Basin Economic Recovery Act

America's leading imports from the Caribbean include petroleum products, chemicals, natural gas, textiles and apparel, agricultural products such as coffee and tropical fruits, electrical parts, and many others. According to the U.S. Department of Commerce, total U.S. imports from the Caribbean for 2006 were about $25 billion, of which $9.9 billion received trade preferences under the *Caribbean Basin Economic Recovery Act* (CBERA). CBERA, enacted in 1983, gives the president the authority to grant tariff reductions or duty-free status to imports from eligible countries in order to encourage trade and investment in the Caribbean. The CBERA countries, as of 2007, were those shown in Exhibit 12.5. (Six countries were removed from CBERA when they became a part of a free trade agreement with the United States: Costa Rica, Dominican Republic, El Salvador, Honduras, Guatemala, and Nicaragua. CBERA was part of a larger program, known as the *Caribbean Basin Initiative,* intended to stimulate investment in the Caribbean and to help diversify Caribbean economies. A few of the other products benefiting from CBERA are cigars, cane sugar, communications equipment, electrical and non-electrical machinery, medical appliances, orange juice, bananas, ethyl alcohol, baseballs, and rum. In 2000, preferences were extended to footwear, certain leather goods such as handbags and gloves, luggage, oil, canned tuna, watches, and certain textile products.

Many CBERA countries, but not all, also qualify for benefits under the GSP. However, the criteria are not the same for product eligibility. Unlike the GSP, CBERA has no provisions for graduating Caribbean countries on the basis of any economic criteria. The CBERA applies to a greater variety of products than the GSP, and the competitive need requirements of the GSP are not applicable. CBERA is a permanent program with no date set for expiration of the law.

EXHIBIT 12.5

Caribbean Basin Beneficiary Countries (2007)

Antigua and Barbuda	Haiti
Aruba	Jamaica
Bahamas	Montserrat
Barbados	Netherlands Antilles
Belize	Nicaragua
British Virgin Islands	Panama
Costa Rica	St. Kitts & Nevis
Dominica	St. Lucia
Grenada	St. Vincent & the Grenadines
Guyana	Trinidad & Tobago

CBERA Rules of Origin. CBERA rules of origin are similar to those of the GSP. In addition, CBERA grants duty-free entry into the United States for articles that have been "assembled or processed" in CBERA countries from U.S.–made "components, materials, or ingredients." In other words, U.S.–made parts that have been subjected to minor assembly, finishing, and processing operations in the CBERA country and then shipped back to the United States qualify for duty-free entry. For these products, the substantial transformation requirement has been eliminated.

The Caribbean Basin Trade Partnership Act of 2000. This law significantly increases the trade benefits that the Caribbean countries have had under CBERA. Under the *Caribbean Basin Trade Partnership Act of 2000*, many products formerly excluded from CBERA, such as footwear, luggage, and watches, now receive trade preferences. Apparel made in the Caribbean may now be shipped to the United States both duty and quota free, provided the garments are made from U.S. fabrics woven or knitted from yarn spun in the United States, or are made from fabrics, such as silk or batiste, that are deemed to be in short supply.

To receive the additional benefits, the president of the United States must certify that each of the twenty-four Caribbean countries is adequately recognizing the rights of workers to organize and bargain collectively; prohibiting forced labor; eliminating child labor abuses; setting a minimum age for employing children; setting an acceptable minimum wage; and establishing acceptable hours of work and occupational safety and health standards.

The reason for this is illustrated by the case of Guatemala, where murders of labor organizers have been reported. In 1999, armed thugs kidnapped leaders of a banana workers' union who were protesting the illegal dismissal of 900 workers. The United States pressured Guatemala to recognize the rights of the 900 fired workers, prosecute those responsible, enact changes in its labor laws, and provide adequate law enforcement and legal protection for workers' rights in the future. As of 2003, all fourteen countries have been certified eligible for benefits.

Africa Growth and Opportunity Act of 2000. *The Africa Growth and Opportunity Act of 2000* (AGOA) was intended to aid in the economic growth and the establishment of political freedom in forty-eight poor countries in sub-Saharan Africa where the per capita annual income averages about $500 per year. The law encourages U.S. trade and investment there and improves access for African products to U.S. markets. To qualify for the benefits of the act, the African countries must try to improve their own conditions through progressive economic and social policies. The country must abide by human rights standards, eliminate abuses of child labor, and not support terrorism. Almost forty countries are now eligible. AGOA broadens the GSP for Africa and extends it through 2008. It includes duty-free status for 6,400 eligible products. For certain countries, AGOA removes all quotas on apparel as well.

In order to qualify for AGOA duty-free status, an article must be produced or manufactured in an AGOA country and meet the rules of origin. For most products, the rules are similar to, but more lenient than, the GSP rules with which you are already familiar. African-made apparel generally qualifies for duty-free treatment if it is made from African- or U.S.–made fabric that was woven from U.S.–made yarn and assembled with U.S–made thread or made from fabrics in short supply (linen, silk, batiste, velveteen, and some others). In 2006, U.S. imports from AGOA countries totaled over $36 billion.

Andean Trade Program. The *Andean Trade Preference Act* program is part of an effort by the United States to promote economic development in the Andean countries while combating drug trafficking and encouraging democracy. These countries are Peru, Colombia, Ecuador, and Bolivia, and their major exports are natural gas, minerals, certain metal products (copper, zinc, etc.), jewelry, forest and wood products, coffee, cocoa, fruits and vegetables, cut flowers, sugar, handicrafts, leather accessories, footwear, and textile products, to name a few. The program permits the duty-free import of almost 6,000 different kinds of products into the United States. The program was renewed by the U.S. Congress in the *Andean Trade Promotion and Drug Eradication Act of 2002*. In 2006, the

U.S. imported over $13 billion in Andean goods covered by the program.

United States–Central America–Dominican Republic Free Trade Agreement. In 2005 the United States entered into a free trade agreement known as CAFTA-DR with Costa Rica, El Salvador, Guatemala, Honduras, Nicaragua, and the island nation of the Dominican Republic. Unlike the GSP and other programs just mentioned, CAFTA-DR is not a trade preference program, but a free trade agreement based on reciprocity and mutual agreement. According to the U.S. Department of Commerce, the agreement will result in duty-free status for over 80 percent of U.S. goods shipped there, with remaining tariffs phased out over five to ten years (fifteen years for agricultural products). The agreement also addresses many collateral issues, such as corruption, labor standards, environmental protection, and the protection of intellectual property. CAFTA-DR has its own rules of origin. In 2006, the U.S. imported $18.6 billion worth of products from CAFTA-DR countries, while exporting $19.6 billion to them.

Other Customs Laws Affecting U.S. Imports

This section examines three other laws affecting U.S. imports: drawback provisions allowing a refund of duties paid, the duty-free return of U.S. exports, and foreign trade zones.

Drawbacks

A *drawback* is a refund of duties already paid. The most common type is the *manufacturing drawback,* designed to encourage U.S. manufacturers to export. A manufacturing drawback is a 99 percent refund of duties and taxes paid on merchandise that is imported, subjected to manufacture or production, and then exported within five years. U.S. firms are becoming increasingly sophisticated in using manufacturing drawbacks. For instance, duties paid on imported yarn will be refunded to the importer who exports a finished fabric made from that yarn. Similarly, a poultry farm that imports chicken feed can receive a drawback on duties paid on the imported feed when the chickens are slaughtered and exported. Drawbacks such as these allow the exporter to purchase materials from low-cost foreign suppliers, including non-MFN countries, without having to pay prohibitively high duties. The use of drawbacks in U.S.–Canadian trade was eliminated in 1996. In U.S.–Mexican trade, drawbacks have also been eliminated.

Same-condition drawbacks are utilized when the imported goods are not processed or manufactured, but are reexported in the "same condition" as they were imported. These products are not significantly altered while in the United States (although they may be repackaged, cleaned, tested, or displayed). For example, nuts and bolts can be entered in bulk and sorted and repackaged in packages with foreign-language labeling. On export, the drawback applies. Many trading companies utilize same-condition drawbacks.

In certain cases, an importer may export U.S.–made goods in the substitution of imported goods that are of the "same kind and quality" (i.e., interchangeable) and receive the drawback on the imported items. This practice is known as a *substitution drawback.* In most instances, these substitution drawbacks deal with fungible goods or commodities such as agricultural products. Substitution drawbacks are applicable to both manufacturing and same-condition drawback situations. For instance, assume that a U.S. manufacturer imports semiconductors for use in making computers. The manufacturer may receive a drawback on duties paid if it exports, within three years, products containing U.S.–made semiconductors of the same kind and quality. If the company exports only 40 percent of its production, it can claim a drawback for 40 percent of the duties paid (a manufacturing/substitution situation). To take another example, the importer of soda ash can decide to resell the foreign soda ash in this country and export the same quantity of U.S.–made soda ash to a foreign buyer; the importer then can receive a drawback on duties paid on the imported soda ash (a same-condition/substitution situation).

A drawback of 99 percent is also allowed for imported merchandise that does not conform to specifications or to samples (e.g., zippers that do not zip; receipt of cotton sweaters instead of wool), provided that the error was the fault of the foreign shipper (not the importer) and the merchandise is returned to U.S. Customs within ninety days for inspection and returned to the seller under Customs supervision. A similar drawback is allowed for merchandise shipped to a U.S. firm without its consent. If a U.S. firm imports foreign goods and finds that they are useless and cannot be returned, the importer can receive a drawback on the duties paid on the merchandise, which is subsequently destroyed.

A drawback is essentially a contract with U.S. Customs. Firms wishing to arrange a drawback need competent advice in doing so. The procedures, time limits, documentation, and accounting requirements for obtaining all drawbacks are complex and exact, and many U.S. companies use the services of specialist firms for advice on structuring drawback transactions. Some firms utilize specially developed software to help track and document a drawback transaction. Civil penalties are imposed for violating the provisions of the law. Many firms do not file for drawbacks for fear of being assessed a penalty for clerical errors. The criminal penalties for fraudulently claiming a drawback are severe.

Returns of U.S. Exports

If U.S. exports are returned to the United States, they are dutiable just as though they were foreign products. This rule has three general exceptions: (1) U.S.–made products that were exported and returned to the United States and that were not substantially transformed or advanced in value while outside the United States (e.g., samples sent to a prospective buyer and returned; articles such as equipment leased to a foreign firm and returned at the end of the lease term; or articles subjected to minor processing); (2) articles exported for repair or alteration, which are dutiable on the value of the repair or alteration provided that they were not substantially transformed while outside the United States; and (3) component parts made in the United States and assembled in a foreign country under special provisions of the tariff laws designed to promote economic development in certain developing countries. (This provision is discussed in the next chapter.)

Foreign Trade Zones

Foreign trade zones (FTZs) are legally defined sites within a country that are subject to special customs procedures.. They are monitored by, and under the control of, the customs authorities of that country. Foreign trade zones exist under the laws of most nations, including the United States. In the United States, FTZs operate under a license from the Free Trade Zone Board and according to regulations of the board and of U.S. Customs and Border Protection. Free trade zones must be within a 60-mile radius of a U.S. port of entry. Imported goods may be brought into an FTZ without being subjected to tariffs until such time as the goods are released into the stream of commerce in the United States.

FTZs are operated by state or local governments, airports or seaports, or specially chartered corporations who charge private firms for their use. Originally, FTZs were intended to encourage U.S. firms to participate in international trade by providing a "free port" into which foreign-made goods could be transported, stored, packaged, and then reexported without the payment of import duties. Today, FTZs are used for many different purposes, ranging from warehousing to manufacturing. Goods may be assembled, exhibited, cleaned, manipulated, manufactured, mixed, processed, relabeled, repackaged, repaired, salvaged, sampled, stored, tested, displayed, and destroyed. Manufacturing may result in a change to the tariff classification of the goods only with permission of U.S. Customs. Retail sales are prohibited. The length of time that these goods can be held in a zone is not limited.

The flexibility offered to an importer through the use of FTZs provides many opportunities for creative importing strategies. For example, firms can ship goods to their zone duty free and hold them for later entry and sale in the United States pending buyer's orders or more favorable market conditions. Foreign goods can also be held for exhibition and display in the zone for unlimited periods without the payment of duties. Foreign goods that arrive damaged or defective may be destroyed without the payment of duties. Goods in an FTZ are not subject to quotas and may remain in the FTZ until the quota opens and their entry is permitted. Title to goods held in an FTZ may be transferred to another party without the payment of duties (although not to a retail customer for consumption outside of the FTZ). Opportunities for creative business planning are almost endless. For instance, in certain cases it is possible that foreign component parts can be assembled in an FTZ, making the duties payable when the finished product is sold less than what the duties would have been on the individual components. As another example, if a commodity is dutied by weight, it may be brought into an FTZ for drying; subsequently it may be entered without the excess weight caused by the moisture. But perhaps the most unusual use of an FTZ is the Cape Canaveral Zone in Florida. There, foreign payloads can be imported into the United States, processed and made ready for a space launch, and "exported" to space without the payment of U.S. import duties! Over two hundred general purpose foreign trade zones and more than two hundred and fifty subzones exist in the United States.

In addition to general purpose zones, firms are able to establish their own special purpose *subzones*. Subzones can be placed anywhere in the United States with U.S. Customs approval. Most automotive manufacturers and oil refineries use subzones. They are also widely used in chemicals, pharmaceuticals, computer assembly, electronics, and shipbuilding and as retail distribution centers. The following case, *Nissan Motor Mfg. Corp. U.S.A. v. United States,* arose out of Nissan's importation of equipment into an automotive manufacturing subzone in Tennessee.

Nissan Motor Mfg. Corp., U.S.A. v. United States

884 F.2d 1375 (1989)

United States Court of Appeals (Fed. Cir.)

BACKGROUND AND FACTS

Nissan operates a foreign trade zone subzone at its automotive manufacturing and assembly plant located in Smyrna, Tennessee. Nissan imported production machinery for use in the subzone consisting of industrial robots, automated conveyor systems, and a computerized interface. The machinery was to be assembled and tested in the zone, and if it proved unsatisfactory it was to be replaced, redesigned, or scrapped. Customs ruled that production equipment was not "merchandise" as defined under the FTZ act and was therefore dutiable. Duties were liquidated at $3 million and Nissan filed a protest. On denial, the Court of International Trade ruled that the equipment was dutiable, and this appeal was filed.

CIRCUIT JUDGE ARCHER

The activities performed by Nissan in the foreign trade zone subzone with the imported equipment are not among those permitted by a plain reading of the statute. Section 81c provides that merchandise brought into a foreign trade zone may be "stored, sold, exhibited, broken up, repacked, assembled, distributed, sorted, graded, cleaned, mixed with foreign or domestic merchandise, or otherwise manipulated, or be manufactured. . . ."

The act does not say that imported equipment may be "installed," "used," "operated" or "consumed" in the zone, which are the kinds of operations Nissan performs in the zone with the subject equipment. Alternative operations of a different character should not be implied when Congress has made so exhaustive a list.

Nissan relies upon the case of *Hawaiian Indep. Refinery v. United States,* 460 F. Supp. 1249 (Cust. Ct. 1978), in support of its position. The merchandise there involved was crude oil which was entered into a foreign trade zone for manufacture into fuel oil products. This, of course, is an activity delineated by the act and entry into the zone was exempted from Customs duties. Thereafter, a portion of the crude oil was consumed in the manufacturing process and Customs assessed duty on the theory that there

continued

continued

had been a "constructive" entry into the Customs territory of the United States. In holding that the assessment was improper, the Court of International Trade did not have to deal with the question at issue here of whether the initial entry into the zone was exempt. Clearly, in that case the crude oil was exempt at the time of entry. Thus, the Court of International Trade properly concluded that the *Hawaiian Indep. Refinery* case was not dispositive of this case.

We are convinced that the Court of International Trade correctly determined that the importation by Nissan of the machinery and capital equipment at issue into the foreign trade zone subzone was not for the purpose of being manipulated in one of the ways prescribed by the statute. Instead it was to be used (consumed) in the subzone for the production of motor vehicles. Under the plain language of the 1950 amendment to the act and the legislative history of that amendment, and Customs' published decision interpreting the act as amended, such a use does not entitle the equipment to exemption from Customs duties. Accordingly, the judgment of the Court of International Trade is affirmed.

Decision. The decision of the lower court was affirmed. Machinery entered into a foreign trade zone for use in the manufacture and assembly of automobiles is not "merchandise" under the act and may not be entered duty free.

Conclusion

The Bureau of Customs and Border Protection is responsible for securing America's borders from terrorist threat; interdicting illegal immigration, contraband, and narcotics smuggling collecting tariff revenue; enforcing the customs and tariff laws of the United States; and enforcing the export control laws. The importance of the agency has changed in recent years and will continue to grow as Americans focus more on the issue of illegal immigration, as the terrorist threat continues, and as increases in international trade result in greater amounts of cargo arriving at U.S. ports.

U.S. Customs recognizes its enforcement predicament: it must protect the borders of the United States while considering the needs of American importers and exporters for expedited customs entry and delivery and the impact of cargo delays on the U.S. economy. Given the numbers of ocean containers and international flights arriving at U.S. ports every day, most Americans recognize the immense job the agency has been given. They also recognize that the effective and efficient enforcement of the customs laws and the movement of cargo are largely dependent on their cooperation and partnership with customs officials.

All businesspeople must be concerned about complying with the customs and tariff laws of the countries in which they import or export. In the United States, as in other countries, enforcement actions and penalties for violations can be severe. Individuals and firms must adhere to the concept of informed compliance. This means that importers and exporters must use reasonable care in handling entries and must either be adequately trained or rely on trained professionals.

Finally, customs compliance does not mean that importers should not plan their business strategies to take advantage of opportunities in the customs and tariff laws. To the contrary, tariff laws, like many other types of tax laws, are intended to encourage and reward certain business decisions. Multinational companies that structure their global operations to take advantage of incentives in the customs or tariff laws or that source materials and products made in certain countries that have tariff preferences under U.S. law, for example, are simply taking advantage of business opportunities legally provided by Congress. Customs laws will affect where multinationals build their plants, where they source their materials or component parts, how they move goods from country to country, and how they structure their overall global operations. Careful customs planning is essential to the success of any international business plan.

Chapter Summary

1. The formal entry process is the administrative process required to import goods into the customs territory of a country. The goods may be entered by the owner, purchaser, consignee (the party to whom the goods are shipped or to be delivered), or a licensed customs broker.
2. The *Customs Modernization and Informed Compliance Act* introduced the doctrine of informed compliance, which shifted a major responsibility to comply with all customs laws and regulations to the importer. It requires that importers use reasonable care in complying with the law, in handling all import transactions, and in preparing all documentation for entered goods. Reasonable care means more than simply being careful. It means that those handling import transactions must be properly trained, that companies must establish internal controls over import operations to ensure compliance, and that professional advice must be sought when needed.
3. Binding rulings from the Customs Service are an important tool in properly and safely planning import transactions in advance.
4. Most trading nations of the world utilize the schedules of the *Harmonized Commodity Description and Coding System* for classifying products. In the United States, the *Harmonized Tariff Schedule* is a federal statute that schedules virtually all goods sold in commerce and lists the tariff rate for each according to the country of origin.
5. Tariffs, restraints on imports, and other import controls are applied to goods according to their dutiable status. The dutiable status of goods is determined by the classification of the article, the transaction value of the article, and the country of origin of the article.
6. Goods are classified in the *Harmonized Tariff Schedule* either by name, by description of the article's physical characteristics, by a description of their component parts, or by a description of the article's use. Goods classified by name are defined by the common or popular meaning of the name, unless it is clear that Congress had intended the commercial or scientific name to apply. Anyone attempting to research the classification of an article in the HTSUS must follow the rules set out in the General Rules of Interpretation. Where an article may be classified under more than one heading, it must be classified under the one that most specifically describes the item. If two or more headings each describe only certain materials or components of the article, the article must be classified under the heading that describes those materials or components that give the article its essential character.
7. The dutiable value of the goods is the transaction value. This is the cost of the goods, adjusted for certain elements of cost set out in the statutes and regulations such as packing costs, assists, or royalty fees.
8. Rules of origin are the national laws and regulations of administrative agencies, usually customs authorities, which are used to determine the country of origin of imported products. There are few areas of customs law that are so complex and that are as difficult for importers to understand. One of the reasons for the complexity is that there are so many different rules applicable to imports from different countries. The general rule is that the country of origin of an imported article is that country where it was wholly and completely produced, manufactured, or obtained entirely from raw materials originating in that country. Where goods are not wholly the product of one country, such as goods assembled in more than one country, importers must rely on the substantial transformation test or tariff shift rules set out in the customs statutes and regulations.
9. Tariff preferences are laws that grant lower tariff rates on products imported from certain countries or regions. The most common tariff preference programs in the United States are the *Generalized System of Preferences* for developing countries, and regional programs for imports from the Caribbean, Africa, and the Andean region. Europe and other developed countries also have tariff preference programs.

Questions and Case Problems

1. Visit the Web site of the Bureau of Customs and Border Protection. What resources does it contain for the trade community?
   a. The *Customs Rulings Online Search System* (CROSS) is a searchable database of about 100,000 ruling letters. Try your hand at locating rulings on some of the issues discussed in this chapter. For example, enter "country origin" together with the name of a product or class of products and see what you can find. Remember, these letters are binding only for the individual to whom they are written and only for that transaction. Nevertheless, they are interesting and helpful to importers that use this service frequently.
   b. Go to the "Legal" section of the Web site and look at the *Customs Bulletins and Decisions*. This is a weekly diary of all official acts of the agency. What type of information does it contain, and who might want to follow this on a regular basis?
   c. Go to the Import section and look at the *Container Security Initiative*. Six million ocean containers enter U.S. ports every year. Only a tiny fraction can be inspected by hand. Any one of them could be used to hide a weapon of mass destruction. Look at the *Customs-Trade Partnership Against Terrorism* (C-TPAT), a process for enhancing security between U.S. importers and their foreign supply chains. How do you think the threat of terrorism and Customs' security programs will affect global transportation in the years to come? What is Customs' "24-hour rule" for loading cargo aboard ships destined for the United States?
2. Acquaint yourself with the *Harmonized Tariff Schedules of the United States*. Be sure that you understand how products and commodities are arranged in the schedules and that you know how to use the schedules. The schedules are maintained by the U.S. International Trade Commission and can be found at their Web site or through a link on the Customs site. Be sure to find the full text of the law, which is arranged by chapter. (The schedules will appear in a pop-up box using PDF format files.)
   a. Know how to use the General Rules of Interpretation and the General Notes.
   b. Which countries receive GSP tariff preference treatment?
   c. Which countries qualify for duty-free treatment as "least developed beneficiary developing countries?"
   d. Which countries qualify for the *Andean Trade Preference Act*? The *African Growth and Opportunity Act* preferences?
   e. A good portion of the HTSUS is devoted to the dutiable status of goods moving in North America. NAFTA is the subject of the next chapter. Can you locate the NAFTA rules of origin, known as the "tariff shift" rules, in the schedules?
   f. Choose several products with which you are familiar, and attempt to classify them using the schedules.
3. The primary body of U.S. customs law is found in Title 19 of the *United States Code*. The regulations are found in the *Code of Federal Regulations*. You can access the CFR either through the Web site of the U.S. Customs and Border Protection ("Legal" section) or through the Government Printing Office site. Can you find Customs' record-keeping rules? What are the rules for filing a protest with U.S. Customs? Can you find the rules of origin, including those for textile imports?
4. Inner Secrets entered 2,000 dozen boxer-style shorts from Hong Kong. The boxer shorts were made of cotton flannel in a plaid pattern, with a waistband that was not enclosed or turned over, a side length of 17 inches, and two small nonfunctional buttons on the waistband above the fly. Two seams were sewn horizontally across the fly, dividing the fly opening into thirds. The boxers did not have belt loops, inner or outer pockets or pouches, or button or zipper fly closures. They were marketed under the label "No Excuses." Customs classified the garments as outerwear shorts under HTSUS 6204.62.4055: "Women's or girls' suits, ensembles, suit-type jackets and blazers, dresses, skirts, divided skirts, trousers, bib and brace overalls, breeches and shorts.... Trousers, bib and brace overalls, breeches and shorts ... of cotton ... 17.7%." The Customs Service based its decision on its determination that the boxers will be worn by women as outer clothing. Inner Secrets maintains that the items are not outerwear, as Customs claims, but are actually *underwear* properly classified under HTSUS 6208.91.3010: "Women's or girls' singlets and other undershirts, slips, petticoats, briefs, panties, nightdresses, pajamas, negligees, bathrobes, dressing gowns and similar articles ... of cotton ... 11.9%." Inner Secrets filed a protest with the agency, which was denied. Inner Secrets brought this action with the Court of

International Trade. What is the proper classification of the boxers? How would a camisole worn under a sport jacket or a slip worn as a dress be classified? *Inner Secrets v. United States,* 885 F. Supp. 248 (Ct. Int'l. Trade 1995). *See also St. Eve International v. United States,* 267 F. Supp. 1371 (Ct. Int'l. Trade 2003).

5. Sports Graphics imported soft-sided "Chill" coolers from Taiwan. The coolers consisted of an outer shell of a vinyl-coated nylon material, an insulating core of approximately 1/2-inch-thick polymer-based closed cell foam, a top secured by a zippered interlocking flap, an inner liner of vinyl, a handle or shoulder strap of nylon webbing and plastic fixtures providing a means of carrying the merchandise, and exterior pockets secured by hook-and-loop or zippered closures. Customs classified the merchandise under the luggage provision, which included "Trunks ... satchels, suitcases, overnight bags, traveling bags, knapsacks, and like articles designed to contain ... personal effects during travel ... and brief cases, golf bags, and like containers and cases designed to be carried with the person.... Luggage and handbags, whether or not fitted with bottle, dining, drinking ... or similar sets ... and flat goods ... of laminated plastics ..." at a 20 percent rate of duty. Sports Graphics contended that the imported soft-sided coolers were properly classifiable as "Articles chiefly used for preparing, serving, or storing food or beverages" and were dutiable at a rate of 4 or 3.4 percent *ad valorem.* What is the proper classification? Does the use of this product have a bearing on its classification? *Sports Graphics, Inc. v. United States,* 24 F.3d 1390 (Fed. Cir. 1994).
6. You are in post–September 11th America and the spirit to buy American-made products is high. You enter a large mass-merchandising retail store in your hometown. As you walk down the aisles of clothing, you spy small American flags proudly displayed atop every circular rack of shirts and jackets. You purchase a jacket and take it home, feeling good about your decision. Later, to your surprise, you notice that the jacket is labeled "Made in China." Actually, you had never really thought much about where the jacket was made. Do you feel that the store management should not have allowed the flags to fly in such close proximity to the clothing, or was it just a patriotic gesture? What is your attitude toward purchasing foreign-made products? What do you think the attitude is of most Americans? In 2003, there was wide talk about boycotting French products because of the French lack of support for the U.S. war in Iraq. Do you think consumer boycotts are generally successful?

Managerial Implications

Your firm is one of the last remaining manufacturers of bicycles in the United States. Z-Mart is a U.S. retail chain with nearly 1,000 stores in fifteen countries. Z-Mart has asked you to prepare a proposal for a large number of bicycles to be sold at discount prices under the Z-Mart brand name. They must have a U.S. retail price of no more than $100. Z-Mart would also like to sell these bikes through its stores in France and Italy in order to compete with the European bikes made in that market. You begin to analyze your costs of materials and production. The first step of production is the sourcing of a tubular frame, a major component. You can purchase the bare frames in the United States, Canada, or Taiwan. You must clean and paint the frames before assembly. The high-performance wheels, another major component, are made from an aluminum alloy. The aluminum is made in Japan and shipped in the form of strips and rods to the Philippines, where it is cut into lengths, molded into wheel parts, and assembled. They will arrive at your plant covered in a film of oil to protect them during shipping. The tires are available from companies in Japan or Brazil. Most of the component parts, such as brakes, gears, and chains, are available directly from firms in the United States and Canada.

At a meeting of management, you are asked to prepare a plan for the production of the bicycles that will price them for Z-Mart's discount stores. In doing so, you must give consideration to the following questions. (You may make certain assumptions as to the relative costs of materials and labor if necessary.)

1. Explain how U.S. trade and tariff laws would affect your plans for bicycle production. What influence would U.S. tariff preference laws have on the sourcing of component parts? Explain how the rules of origin might affect the importation of the tubular frame. Would NAFTA have any impact on how you structure your operations?
2. What factors would be taken into consideration in determining whether to assemble the finished bicycles in the United States, Taiwan, or the Philippines? You have heard that U.S. automakers

are assembling cars in Mexico using workers that are paid about $20 a day. What factors would influence your decision to assemble in Mexico? What processes could you do or not do in Mexico in order to obtain the most favorable tariff treatment? What are the advantages and disadvantages of assembling there?

3. Evaluate the potential for using a foreign trade zone. What advantages or disadvantages would your firm experience in this case?
4. Determine the applicability of U.S. marking and labeling requirements with regard to the finished bicycles sold in the United States.

Ethical Considerations

Fair Trade is a worldwide movement based broadly based on the theory that trade between rich and poor should be based on notions of social and economic justice, and which advocates that small farms and farm workers in developing countries receive a fair price in return for their agricultural and handicraft products. Although the fair trade movement dates to the 1940s, it became popular in parts of Europe in the 1960s and more recently has taken hold in the United States. Fair trade is supported by consumers willing to pay a small additional price for goods knowing that the indigenous producers of the goods, living and working under the poorest conditions, received a fair price for their product. Some fair trade farms consist of small cooperatives, with individual families farming only a couple of acres. Typical fair trade products include coffee, tea, bananas, wine, herbs and spices, honey, rice, and cocoa. Standards, minimum prices, inspections, and certifications of producers and traders are the responsibility of private, nonprofit organizations. Fair trade standards also require that certified farms practice sustainable farming techniques, follow rules on the use of pesticides and recycling, refrain from using child labor, and encourage farm children to attend school. These advances are made possible by the higher prices participants receive for their products.

By the early 2000s, labeling standards for fair trade–certified products became standardized, so that consumers could recognize fair trade products in stores. Participants in fair trade include the workers and producers themselves, the brokers and traders who deal in the products, the retailers and vendors in richer countries, and consumers. Some of the most important fair trade organizations are the Fairtrade Labelling Organizations International, the European Fair Trade Association, the International Fair Trade Association, and TransFair USA.

1. Would you be willing to pay a slightly higher price for sugar, coffee, fruits, and basic commodities, knowing that their producers, farmers in Central America or Africa, were paid an internationally established "fair price" for their labors? Do you believe that consumers will make ethical choices in the marketplace, or economic ones?
2. Fair trade is based on the guarantee of a fair price. How is a "fair price" determined? What is the role of independent fair trade organizations in establishing price?
3. Critics suggest that fair trade does not address the root causes of poverty. Some economists argue that low prices for basic commodities, like coffee, result from oversupply. Moreover, fair trade also does not guarantee access to investment or technology. Do you think the fair trade movement can be successful in rooting out poverty?
4. Although fair trade products account for a tiny volume of world trade relative to the total volume, they do focus concern on the plight of poor farmers, farm workers, and producers in agrarian regions. Some of America's largest and best-known retailers are selling fair trade products, including Sam's Club, McDonald's, Dunkin' Donuts, Starbucks, and many grocery chains. Based on your research and outside reading, what do you think the impact of fair trade programs can be?

For Internet Activities, Visit academic.cengage.com/blaw/schaffer.

CHAPTER 13
THE REGULATION OF EXPORTS

Throughout history, every civilization has had to decide whether it will trade with outsiders, and if so, on what terms. After all, there were economic, political, and military interests to protect. There were outlaw tribes and evil princes to punish. What better way than to deprive them of goods and treasures, be they coveted spices, colorful dyes, or prized horses. There were state-of-the-art technological secrets to guard. From the secrets of steelmaking and the fashioning of swords and armor, to the invention of gunpowder and the bow and arrow, to the addition of the lowly stirrup to a horseman's saddle, technology has turned the tide of many battles and the course of history. Empires have been won or lost because of the technological advantage of one warrior, or one army, over another. The warlords and kings of ancient Europe and Asia knew this well and meted out punishments of torture and death to those who disclosed such closely guarded secrets or traded with the enemy. Imagine the diplomatic couriers of the ancient world, or medieval statesmen of later periods, who went out on foot or on horseback to distant kingdoms. They arranged alliances and orchestrated embargoes of common enemies. These were times of secret treaties, encrypted messages, intrigue, and danger.

This could just as well be the story of the modern world. Trade is still used to reward allies and punish outlaw nations. Civilized people still war with barbarians and deny aid and comfort to those who harbor them. Advances in technology are still guarded from foreign enemies. There are, perhaps, a few differences. Today's outlaw nations are violators of human rights; the barbarians are called "terrorists;" the advances in technology involve computers, software for missile guidance systems, stealth technology, and the materials and know-how to destroy entire cities; and secret treaties have been replaced by international conventions and United Nations resolutions.

The primary subject of this chapter is how nations use policy and regulations to control exports to foreign countries for purposes of national security and foreign policy. Our focus will be on the system and methods used by the United States. Much of the discussion would apply equally to Canada or the European Union, although the overarching policies of each nation may be different. In the United States, there are two main, overlapping regulatory systems for controlling exports of goods and technology. The first, which we will study only briefly, is concerned with the control of arms, munitions, and defense systems. This system is primarily administered by the U.S. Department of State. The second, which is the one that we will be most concerned with, is the system of controls over nonmilitary commercial goods, commodities, and technology. These controls, too, can function as tools of national security or foreign policy. (In this chapter, *controlled* goods or technologies are those that require a license for export.) This system is primarily administered by the United States Department of Commerce. In both systems, the lead agencies coordinate with the Department of Defense (for military equipment and defense systems), the Department of Energy (for nuclear technology), the Department of Homeland Security (for customs and border enforcement), and other federal departments and law enforcement agencies.

We will also look at the larger issues of trade policy. Should a nation continue to trade goods and basic commodities, even food, with totalitarian governments that engage in slavery or other human rights abuses, harbor terrorists, or manufacture chemical or biological weapons? Do unilateral controls or multilateral trade sanctions work against rogue nations? How are those controls and sanctions implemented in the United States? How does a U.S. exporter obtain a license to ship controlled goods or technology? What extraordinary powers has Congress given to the president, in war and peacetime, to address perceived international emergencies? What are boycotts, and how do U.S. companies comply with antiboycott laws? Finally, what is business expected to do in terms of internal and external compliance, and what civil and criminal penalties does the government use to enforce the export control laws?

As you read, keep in mind that no person in any country has a guaranteed legal right to export. In the United States, there is no constitutional right to export, although the Constitution protects procedural due process rights. Exporting is considered a privilege that can be granted or revoked according to law.

Trade Controls over Arms, Munitions, and Defense Systems

Advanced nations control the sale of arms, military hardware, weapons and defense systems, and related technologies as means of maintaining military superiority and honoring defense treaty commitments, as well as for strategic reasons. They can deny military technology to their enemies or potential enemies and share it with their friends or military allies. Well-known examples include America's defense commitments to the countries of the North Atlantic Treaty Organization (NATO) and to Israel, Taiwan, Japan, and South Korea. Arms controls are also used to keep weapons from certain war-torn regions of the world and from countries that are experiencing civil war or rebellion, or threatening their neighbors. On the other hand, an arms-exporting country can approve arms sales to countries that cooperate in its foreign policy objectives, such as helping to eradicate and interdict traffic in narcotic drugs or capture terrorists. Most governments strictly regulate these transactions and limit them to registered and licensed firms. Countries also strategically coordinate their export controls over arms, munitions, and weapons systems.

The *Neutrality Acts*

In the United States, the modern system for controlling both exports and imports of armaments derives from a series of statutes enacted in the mid-1930s, known as the *Neutrality Acts.* These statutes were passed by a Congress intent on keeping the United States out of war in Europe by controlling the export of arms and ammunitions. At the time, the government placed arms exports under the direction of a newly created National Munitions Control Board, consisting of five cabinet secretaries and chaired by the secretary of state. Although that board no longer exists, the system established in the 1930s was the direct predecessor of the arms export control system used in the United States today.

The Arms Export Control Act. The *Arms Export Control Act* (AECA) governs the export and import of "defense articles" and "defense services" (including arms, munitions, weapons systems and defense systems, and their technologies) and communication of technical data to foreign persons. The act is administered according to the *International Traffic in Arms Regulations* (ITAR) by the Directorate of Defense Trade Controls, a branch of the U.S. Department of State. These regulations include the *U.S. Munitions List,* which identifies those categories of equipment and technologies subject to export control. To be on the list, an item must be either "specifically designed ... or modified for a military application" and not have "predominant civil applications" or have "significant military or intelligence applications such that control is necessary." The regulations also list countries that are prohibited from receiving U.S. arms or defense technology, such as state sponsors of terrorism and countries subject to United Nations sanctions.

The ITAR regulations require registration by firms and individuals engaged in manufacturing, brokering, importing, or exporting military articles or services. In part, registration is intended to disclose if an applicant company is under foreign ownership or control. License applications for the export of advanced weapons and defense systems go to the Department of Defense for technical review. Congress must be notified in advance in the case of some larger transactions.

The following case, *B-West Imports, Inc. v. United States,* involves an American importer of arms from China whose permits had been unexpectedly revoked on foreign policy grounds. Although the case involves the import of arms, rather than their export, it represents a larger principle: One's right to engage in the import or export of arms, munitions, and other highly regulated products is subject to near-absolute control by government authorities.

National Security and Foreign Policy Issues

Nations restrict exports of goods and technology for many policy reasons. The three most important reasons are to protect national security, to implement foreign policy, and to limit the sale of critical goods and strategic raw materials that are in short supply. Other reasons include regulating the export of fish, wildlife and endangered species, hazardous waste, and nuclear materials intended for energy purposes, preserving antiquities and cultural objects, and promoting other national goals.

B-West Imports, Inc. v. United States

75 F.3d 633

United States Court of Appeals (Fed. Cir. 1996)

BACKGROUND AND FACTS

The U.S. *Arms Export Control Act* (AECA) prohibits the import of arms and munitions from countries on the "proscribed list" without a license. Although China had been on the proscribed list, prior to 1994 exemptions had been made for China and import licenses issued. On May 26, 1994, however, President Clinton announced a ban on the import of arms and munitions from China and imposed other trading sanctions because of "continuing human rights abuses" and other foreign policy reasons. The law was enforced by the U.S. Customs Service and the Bureau of Alcohol, Tobacco, and Firearms (BATF). The agencies detained all shipments of arms from China and revoked all import permits. B-West Imports (the appellants), together with nine other importers, challenged the government's actions in the Court of International Trade. They argued that the AECA does not authorize the president or his delegates to impose an arms embargo and that the revocation of the permits violated the due process and takings clauses of the Fifth Amendment to the Constitution.

BRYSON, CIRCUIT JUDGE

In this court, the appellants renew their argument that the AECA does not authorize an arms embargo. Although the Act, 22 U.S.C. §2778, grants the president the authority to "control" arms imports, the appellants argue that the term "control" limits the president to creating and operating a licensing system for arms importation, and does not allow the president to ban the importation of arms for which import permits have been granted.

The appellant's statutory argument is unconvincing. They concede that the term "control" is broad enough to allow the president to ban imports by denying licenses or permits for future imports. Their contention is thus limited to the assertion that "control" does not include the right to revoke licenses and permits after they are granted.... As the court noted in *South Puerto Rico Sugar Co. v. U.S.*, 167 Ct.Cl. 236, 334 F.2d 622 (1964), presidents acting under broad statutory grants of authority have imposed and lifted embargoes, prohibited and allowed exports, suspended and resumed commercial intercourse with foreign countries. Thus, the broad statutory delegation in the AECA incorporates the historical authority of the president in the fields of foreign commerce and of importation into the country. We therefore agree with the Court of International Trade that the AECA authorizes the president not only to regulate arms importation through a licensing system, but also to prohibit particular

continued

continued

importations altogether when the circumstances warrant....

Finally, the appellants challenge the government's actions as violative of the Takings and Due Process Clauses of the Fifth Amendment. In the *Legal Tender Cases*, 79 U.S. (12 Wall.) 457 (1870), the Supreme Court rejected just such an argument, noting that an embargo would not give rise to a compensable taking or a valid due process claim:

> A new tariff, an embargo, a draft, or a war inevitably bring upon individuals great losses; may, indeed, render valuable property almost valueless. They may destroy the worth of contracts. But whoever supposed that, because of this, a tariff could not be changed, or a non-intercourse act, or an embargo be enacted, or a war be declared.... [W]as it ever imagined this was taking private property without compensation or without due process of law? Id. 79 U.S. (12 Wall.) at 551.

While it is true that takings law has changed significantly since 1870, the principles that the Supreme Court articulated in the *Legal Tender Cases* have remained valid, particularly as they apply to governmental actions in the sphere of foreign relations....

The same principle is directly applicable here. While an individual who obtains a permit to import arms may make commitments in the arms market on the assumption that the permit will not be revoked before the importation is completed, that assumption does not constitute a "reasonable investment backed expectation" of the type necessary to support a takings claim. That is particularly true with respect to importations of arms from a country with which the United States has an arms embargo that is subject to an exemption that could be terminated at any time.

The appellants' due process claim fares no better. They assert that the implementation of the Chinese arms embargo deprived them of property without due process of law by denying them the opportunity to sell in the United States the munitions for which they had obtained permits prior to the announcement of the embargo. As we have discussed, however, the appellants' right to import and sell Chinese arms in the United States was subject at all times to the hazard that their permits would be revoked, pursuant to statute and regulation, on foreign policy grounds or for other reasons. The Due Process Clause does not require the government to stand as a surety against the adverse consequences sometimes suffered by persons who knowingly undertake that kind of commercial risk.

Decision. Judgment affirmed for the United States. Under the *Arms Export Control Act,* the president has wide latitude to enforce this law by prohibiting the import of controlled items. A statute that deprives one of the opportunity to import goods does not violate or "take" one's property under the Fifth Amendment without compensation, nor does it deprive the importer of due process of law.

Trade Controls for Reasons of National Security

In the United States, *national security* controls restrict exports of goods or technology that could make a significant contribution to the military capabilities of any other country and would prove detrimental to the national security of the United States. They are enforced by a licensing system administered by the U.S. Department of Commerce, in cooperation with the Department of Defense, which receives and approves licenses for exports of goods or transfers of technology on a case-by-case basis. License applications are evaluated for compliance with the law based on the product or technology, the end user, and the country of destination.

Trade Controls for Reasons of Foreign Policy

Nations often grant or deny trade privileges to further their foreign policy objectives. Foreign policy controls are the "carrot and stick" of diplomacy. In the United States, foreign policy controls are used for many reasons. Here are a few broad types of reasons:

- to suppress terrorism and to deny aid and assistance to individuals, groups, or nations that sponsor it
- to punish repressive governments for human rights violations and encourage change
- to end regional conflict or civil war
- to fulfill treaty obligations

- to carry out United Nations–sponsored trade sanctions
- to keep crime control and detection equipment out of the hands of repressive regimes
- to encourage countries to eradicate and interdict illegal narcotics
- to stop the proliferation of nuclear technology and weapons of mass destruction
- to prohibit an introduction of strategic goods or technology to a region of the world if that introduction would upset the balance of power among countries in the region
- to limit the spread of missile technology
- to deny aid and assistance to communist governments (less important today than in past decades)

As of 2007, the United States had strict foreign policy trade controls, as well as restrictions on investment and travel, relating to five countries deemed to be "state sponsors of terrorism." These were Cuba, Iran, North Korea, Sudan, and Syria. A sixth country, Libya, recently came off this list, having renounced all attempts to possess weapons of mass destruction and opened its facilities to international inspections.

The Effectiveness of Trade Sanctions

The use of trade controls to accomplish foreign policy objectives has been a subject of great political and economic debate. Proponents of the use of trade sanctions argue that they are often effective, that they bring international attention to important world issues, and that they assert a moral stance. As examples, proponents point out that trade sanctions helped to end the civil war in the former Yugoslavia and drew worldwide attention to the plight of repressed people in Western Africa, funded by the sale of so-called "blood diamonds." They also point out that the imposition on Libya of international and U.S. sanctions (including bans on trade, investments, and travel) for harboring two terrorists accused of shooting down Pan Am flight 103 over Lockerbie, Scotland in 1988, eventually led to Libya handing over the suspects for trial.

Those that argue against the use of trade sanctions say that they are ineffective. They point out that imposing economic sanctions on an already poor country often affects innocent people more than it does those in power. Economic sanctions alone are rarely enough to cause a repressed people to rise up against a brutal military government. Most people would agree that almost fifty years of U.S. restrictions on trade with and travel to communist Cuba have done nothing to remove the Castro government or change its policies. Others argue that the Cuban sanctions did not work because they were not tough enough. Another argument against sanctions is that they are often easy for the targeted country to circumvent. Without universal cooperation, which there seldom is, sanctions quickly lose their effectiveness.

United Nations–Approved Sanctions. Trade sanctions that have broad international participation are more readily enforceable and generally more effective. Trade sanctions under the aegis of the United Nations can be far more effective than unilateral controls by one country. They are harder to circumvent, and more importantly, they carry the backing of international law and the force of international moral opinion. In recent years, the United Nations has backed imposition of economic and/or military sanctions on Afghanistan (under the Taliban), Angola, Cote d'Ivoire, the Democratic Republic of the Congo, Ethiopia and Eritrea, Haiti, Iraq (under Saddam Hussein), Liberia, Libya, Rwanda, Sierra Leone, Somalia, South Africa (under apartheid), Southern Rhodesia (now Zimbabwe), Sudan, and the former Yugoslavia.

The Impact of Export Controls on Business and Trade

The use of export controls and trade sanctions presents a policy dilemma. How does a nation control exports for reasons of national security or foreign policy without harming business, jobs, or economic interests?

This problem has two facets. First, if a nation restricts exports of goods that are widely available in world markets, then that nation's exporters will simply lose the business to foreign competitors. It does not matter whether the goods are semiconductors, agricultural commodities, or something else. Moreover, the controls are unlikely to be effective as trade sanctions.

Second, placing unnecessary restrictions on exports of technology products, beyond those that are necessary to national objectives, could unduly burden a key economic sector. Nations must consider this when trying to keep weapons technology out of the hands of potential foreign enemies, outlaw nations, or terrorists.

Keep in mind the immensity of the problem. We are not just speaking of controlling the export of, say, one ready-to-use nuclear bomb. That is a big enough problem. We are talking about trying to control the thousands of bits of technology, knowledge, critical components, and radioactive fuel that rogue scientists could use to build a bomb. The same issue arises when we think about the fundamental components of outlawed chemical weapons or missile guidance systems. Imagine the thousands of parts that go into advanced military aircraft and other weapons systems, and the thousands of pieces of information one needs to build and run these systems. Having just one more critical component, or one more piece of information, can give a huge advantage to foreign military forces.

The problem is that many arms components are commercially available in the form of dual-use goods from competing suppliers in more than one country. Nations cannot control everything. The answer to the dilemma lies in knowing what to control, what not to control, who to keep it from, and how to control it effectively. This point was clearly expressed in an article, "Policing High Tech Exports," which appeared in the *New York Times* on November 27, 1983.

> The export-control process breeds ironies. Senator Paul E. Tsongas, Democrat of Massachusetts, used to tell the story of how the Ethiopian national airline, seeking to buy the latest model Boeing 767, was thwarted by the United States Government. If Ethiopia were allowed to purchase the plane, with its sophisticated laser gyroscope, the Government's reasoning went, that gyroscope could fall into the hands of the Soviet Union, currently Ethiopia's great friend. So the Ethiopians turned to the French for a new Airbus. The punch line: The American company that manufactures the gyroscope had already sold it to France, an ally, for incorporation into the Air-Bus. "We lose the technology, we lose the foreign business and we become known as an unreliable supplier," Senator Tsongas argued. Ultimately, in this instance, such arguments prevailed: The Commerce Department granted Boeing its license in December 1982.

The fact that the Department of Commerce administers most U.S. export laws covering commercial and dual-use goods and technologies is a recognition that economic and business interests are in play. The United States does not prohibit the foreign sale of all technology, because that would not be practical or commercially possible. Rather, U.S. policy balances security interests with commercial necessity. A good example is the decision made by the U.S. Department of Commerce in 1999 to loosen restrictions on the sale of certain high-speed computer components to China, India, and Russia. High-speed computers can design nuclear weapons and run simulated tests on detonations, design advanced military aircraft and torpedo guidance systems, do three-dimensional modeling, calculate fluid dynamics, and perform other complex functions. In 1999 the *New York Times* reported that at a press briefing in the White House, then–Secretary of Commerce William H. Daley held a Sony Playstation in his hand and said that unless trade controls were eased, the new, more powerful Playstation 2, which was set to be released the following Christmas, would be classified as restricted due to its high-speed computer technology. The event dramatizes how the Department of Commerce must balance national security and commercial interests. To be fair, we should point out that the Clinton administration took a practical view of the problems with enforcing export laws. It changed its policy from using all of its resources, in an almost impossible effort to control the exports of all high-speed computers, which are produced at the rates of tens or hundreds of thousands per month, to controlling just those advanced technologies that it is actually possible to control. In 2002, President George W. Bush continued this policy by doubling the maximum speed of computer chips that could be exported. The effect was to permit export of computers 50 to 100 times faster than a typical home computer. This change recognized that as older technologies become widely available, export controls must keep pace with increasing computer speeds and other changes in technology. Similarly, the Bush administration loosened export controls on certain computer technology and software to take into account the reality that people travel with laptop computers. Strict controls, however, still prohibit export of all types of technology items to "state sponsors of terrorism."

U.S. Agricultural Exports and the Soviet Invasion of Afghanistan. One of the most famous examples of a failed unilateral use of export controls by the United States for foreign policy reasons occurred in 1979. The cold war was ongoing, and the Soviet Union had invaded Afghanistan. In retaliation, President Carter ordered an embargo of U.S. grain sales to the Soviet Union. This policy blocked the sale of millions of tons of American wheat. (In another bold move, he blocked U.S. participation in the 1980 Olympics.) President Carter had not garnered international support for the sanctions, and other countries did not back the United States. Major grain-producing nations, including Canada, Argentina, and Australia, continued to let their farmers sell to the Soviets. They did so and largely neutralized the embargo's impact. The only result of the United States having unilaterally used food exports as a weapon of trade, other than the making of a moral statement, was the devastating economic impact on American farmers who lost a key market. Although President Reagan revoked the embargo, the damage continued for years. American farmers had lost their position as the principal suppliers of grain to the Soviet Union. Subsequent American presidents have been, or should be, far more aware of the importance of getting international support before imposing trade sanctions.

Export Restrictions on Crime Control Equipment. The United States also uses foreign policy controls to prevent exports of crime control and detection equipment to repressive governments and areas of civil disorder. These items can range from handcuffs, polygraphs, and tear gas to mobile crime labs and shotguns. At first glance, one would wonder why the United States would do this. But imagine what would happen if certain products used by law enforcement agencies got into the hands of repressive governments, such as those in Burma (Myanmar) or North Korea. They would become implements of torture. They could also be used to disrupt public demonstrations, arrest protesters, eavesdrop and investigate political opponents, conduct interrogations, and commit other human rights violations. They may also have military applications. In addition to blocking exports to the most egregiously dictatorial governments, in recent years the United States has scrutinized exports of crime control equipment to Saudi Arabia, Russia, and Venezuela. In 2005, the United States approved over 3,000 shipments of crime control items and denied 23.

Trade Controls for Reasons of Short Supply

Another reason why nations control exports is that certain critical goods or strategic raw materials may be in short supply. *Short supply controls* might apply to certain foodstuffs, medicines, or basic metals. For instance, during wartime, a country might limit exports of copper, brass, or steel because it may need these metals for making arms or ammunition. Even during peacetime, short-supply controls are sometimes used to limit inflationary effects on the domestic economy caused by strong foreign demand for scarce resources or materials. U.S. law permits use of short supply controls to protect the U.S. economy from excessive foreign demand for scarce materials. As of 2007, the United States had short supply controls only on petroleum, unprocessed Western red cedar from state and national forest lands, and live horses. In 2005, one U.S. company paid a fine of nearly $500,000 for having exported cedar to Canada for treatment with preservatives and processing.

Trade Controls for the Protection of Wildlife, the Environment, Public Safety, or of Antiquities

There are many other reasons why nations may restrict exports. Many countries of the world prohibit the export of certain wildlife or endangered species. Some countries prohibit the export of artifacts and antiquities. A good example is Egypt, which prohibits the unlicensed export of antiquities found at archaeological sites. Other countries regulate the export of chemicals, hazardous waste, materials for recycling, unsafe products, controlled substances and medicines, medical devices, nuclear material, and other items. Governments often regulate agricultural exports, as well as pesticides, herbicides, and certain fertilizers. Many of these regulations result from international treaty obligations.

History of U.S. Export Control Laws

The Continental Congress passed the very first U.S. export regulations, which restricted trade with Britain, in 1775. Later in America's history, Congress enacted laws that controlled exports to enemies of the United States during time of war. Modern export control laws, however, can be traced to 1949 legislation enacted during the early days of the cold war and the communist threat. During the decades of the cold war, the United States cooperated with its allies in restricting any goods or technologies that could give any economic or military advantage to China, the Soviet Union, or the Eastern European communist countries under Soviet control. In 1962, because of the communist takeover of Cuba and the threat of Soviet influence in the Western Hemisphere, Congress strengthened the export laws. These tough controls reflected the view of the United States and its allies that they could counter the massive military buildup and troop strength by communist countries in the Soviet Bloc, and in Asia, by maintaining an enormous lead in military technology.

In the late 1960s, American export control policy began to take into account the need of American companies to be able to use their technological advantage to boost American exports. In 1969, a new export law relaxed controls in a number of ways. The most important change was that it required the government to consider whether a particular product or technology was already for sale, or available, from sources in a foreign country. It seemed to Congress that the law should not penalize U.S. companies or prohibit them from making a sale if the foreign customer could purchase the items from suppliers in other countries. This concept, known as *foreign availability,* still exists in our export laws today. (Today, the president is required to negotiate with any foreign country that permits the uncontrolled sale or export of sensitive technology to sponsors of terrorism, or to buyers in any other country hostile to American interests, in an effort to get them to control the exports also.)

In 1979, the export control laws were rewritten and enacted as the *Export Administration Act of 1979.* This law forms the basis of current export regulations. Following the Soviet invasion of Afghanistan in 1979 and the election of President Reagan in 1980, the administration embarked on a military buildup to counter what they viewed as Soviet aggression and expansionism. Eastern European communist governments were under Soviet pressure to tighten their political control.

In 1981, Poland declared martial law to suppress demonstrations by the pro-democracy group *Solidarity* and placed factories, mills, and shipyards under military control. In response, President Reagan attempted to tighten export restrictions on the Soviet Union, which he famously termed the "evil empire." He also set out to strengthen international cooperation to keep critical goods, technology, and money away from the Soviet Union.

The Cold War "Cat and Mouse" Game: Spying and Industrial Espionage

During the cold war, communist governments had put all their resources into the development of their military and intelligence apparatus. It was a time of international intrigue, with agents of the Soviet Union, the former East Germany and Czechoslovakia, and other communist countries trying to obtain access to Western goods and technology by any means and at any cost. Spying had become their national obsession. Bribery, threats, and extortion were common tactics. They bought technological secrets wherever they could. In perhaps the most notorious case of the day, one of Japan's largest and best-known companies was implicated in the sale of equipment and technology used to quiet nuclear submarines to the Soviets. This had devastating military consequences for the United States.

The Soviet bloc tried to steal what it could not buy. They planted "moles" in the United States and other Western countries. Women from Eastern Europe were placed in positions where they could meet men from the West, such as by posing as tour guides. They met men who had positions in government, academia, and industry and moved to America or Western Europe, where they could gather technical or industrial reports or information (referred to as soft intelligence). Industrial espionage reached epidemic proportions.

Consider this not-so-hypothetical example: A representative of a Soviet or Eastern European factory is visiting the United States as part of an industry delegation. It is arranged through appropriate U.S. agencies for them to visit an American factory to observe its production techniques. He asks to meet and chat with a lathe operator. Later, after the visit, the foreign visitor gives his shoes to a representative of the Soviet embassy for shipment to Soviet laboratories. The soles of the shoes had secretly been layered with a sticky substance. Soviet intelligence and metallurgists were interested in the company's newly developed metal alloy, and the shavings were lying on the floor for the spy's taking.

Illegal Diversions of Controlled Technology. In export control terminology, a *diversion* is the unlawful transfer, transshipment, rerouting, or reexporting of controlled goods or technology from one destination, to which the goods or technology could legally be shipped, to another destination that has not been lawfully approved to receive the items. During the cold war, operatives from the Soviet Union or its Eastern Bloc allies would use companies (legitimate ones or "dummy" companies set up for this purpose) located in Western countries, perhaps in Europe, the Caribbean, or elsewhere, to place orders for U.S. products containing controlled technology. The goods would then be "diverted" to Soviet authorities or laboratories, where they could be analyzed, reverse engineered, or put to use. The purchasers may have offered to pay more than the asking price for the goods on condition that the American exporter would rush the shipment and forgo the "usual and time consuming" license application process.

In some cases, the American exporter was a complete victim of the scam. They may have gone so far as to obtain an export license. In other cases, the exporter may have been a willing participant in the game. The purchaser may have offered them a higher price for the goods, or even a cash bribe, to rush ship the goods without going through the license application and approval process.

Illegal diversions are still one of the most common, although criminal, methods used to circumvent the export laws and to deliver controlled goods and technology to countries that could be potential foes, or to individuals in those countries who would transfer that technology to international terrorist groups. Examples might include individuals in countries with whom the United States has good relations, such as Pakistan, China, Russia, or friendly Middle Eastern nations, with diversions of controlled technology going from there to countries such as North Korea or Iran.

Changes in the Export Environment since 2001. With the fall of the Berlin Wall in 1989, the collapse of the Soviet Union in 1991, and the end of the cold war came three events that reshaped the political environment for export controls.

First, the rise of international terrorism and the terrorist attacks on the United States in 2001 created a "get tough" political environment in the United States and in other countries affected by terrorism. This led to new laws that gave the president and U.S. law enforcement agencies far-reaching, but controversial, powers to investigate, track down, and prosecute anyone aiding terrorists, and to stop the flow of money to terrorist groups.

Second, renewed concerns and tensions arose over nuclear proliferation, especially in North Korea and Iran. With the fall of the Soviet Union, there is concern that Soviet nuclear technology might have fallen into the hands of terrorists or rogue nations, or those who would sell it to them. There are also documented reports that Pakistani nuclear technology has spread to other countries and groups around the world, sold by unscrupulous scientists and businesspeople.

The third major change is that China has become a global economic powerhouse, and is not satisfied to remain merely the source of cheap labor for the world. It is a major purchaser of U.S. commercial technology and technology products. In 2006, nearly 10 percent of all export licenses issued by the United States were for exports to China. However, China is eager to acquire more then just commercial technology. It is also using any means possible to obtain the latest military and strategic technology for its nuclear forces, missile guidance systems, avionics systems, submarines, and space program.

The *U.S.–China Economic and Security Review Commission,* created by Congress in 2001 to monitor and report on the national security implications of U.S. trade with China, said in a 2007 report that Chinese espionage activities in the United States are so extensive that they comprise the single greatest risk to the security of American technologies. The report also warned of the vulnerability of U.S. companies and institutions to Chinese cyber attack.

Despite dire warnings, U.S. export policy with regard to technology exports to China balances the needs of business for open access to Chinese markets with the needs of national security. In recent years, the United States has loosened some controls on export of high technology to China, while significantly tightening controls and focusing enforcement efforts on those specific items that China could use to modernize its military.

Some Recent Enforcement Actions

The problem of keeping goods and technology away from "the bad guys" is as great or greater today than at any time in the past. More and more developing countries, particularly in the Middle East, the Pacific Rim, and Central Asia, are trying to acquire missile and nuclear technology. These countries may still seek the knowledge and technology to produce chemical or biological weapons, despite international treaties. Some individuals may be acting on behalf of terrorist groups, or sympathize with their causes, while others are trying to acquire technology so they can sell it to the highest bidder. Some governments would gladly turn over their technologies to terrorist groups.

Unfortunately, as statistics on prosecutions and convictions show, many greedy and unscrupulous businesspeople in the United States and around the world are willing to make these technologies available. In 2006, the U.S. government collected more than $13 million in civil penalties, and $3 million in criminal fines, from violators of the export regulations. The Bureau of Industry and Security of the U.S. Department of Commerce, which is the lead agency for administering both national security and foreign policy controls, has released a report of a few of its most significant investigations in 2006. Here are a few examples.

Weapons of Mass Destruction: Nuclear Detonators to Pakistan. In 2005, a South African businessman was sentenced to three years in prison for conspiring to ship electrical switches and components with nuclear weapons applications to Pakistan. He had ordered the switches purportedly for a South African hospital for use in medical equipment, but arranged their shipment to a contact in Pakistan.

Terrorism/State Sponsors of Terror: Night Vision Equipment to Hezbollah. In 2006, a Lebanese-born Canadian citizen was convicted and sentenced to five years in prison and a $100,000 fine for providing material support to a terrorist organization. A sting operation caught him delivering advanced technology night vision goggles and laser sights for military rifles to an FBI agent. The items were to have been shipped to Greece and diverted to Hezbollah, a terrorist organization, in Lebanon.

Diversions to Military Use: National Security Controlled Electronics Equipment to China. In 2006, the Federal government convicted a Chinese resident of Wisconsin of money laundering and shipping $300,000 worth of semiconductors to China without a license. The items could be used in radar, communications, and missile technology. They had been delivered to Chinese institutes that do scientific research for the military. The defendant was sentenced to 60 months in prison, a $50,000 fine, and forfeiture of his Wisconsin home and $329,000 in cash. His wife and two other Chinese citizens were also convicted, imprisoned, and fined for their part in the conspiracy.

Multilateral Cooperation in Controlling Technology

In 1949, the United States, Canada, Japan, Western Europe, and a few of their major cold war allies formed a multilateral organization to cooperate in controlling exports. It was known by its acronym, COCOM. It was much like a basketball game, where one side tried to keep the ball away from the other, except that "the other side" was the Soviet Union and its Eastern Bloc allies. Each country could review licenses issued by other member countries and veto the issuance of a license. This facilitated trade between them, because each country was assured that the other would prevent diversions. COCOM disbanded in 1994.

THE WASSENAAR ARRANGEMENT. In 1996, the *Wassenaar Arrangement* was created. As of 2007, it had forty members, including the United States, Russia, and other former communist countries of Eastern Europe. Unlike COCOM, the countries in this group do not have a common enemy, and no single country has veto power over licenses issued by the others. This is a loose arrangement consisting of recommendations and statements of "best practices," and reflects the lack of consensus about the level of control necessary in today's world and divergent national interests. The lack of an effective international control system over arms and technology is worrisome to many policymakers. They realize that export controls by one nation are ineffective if the same technologies or weapons can be purchased freely on the open market in other countries.

Other Multilateral Export Control Groups. The *Australia Group* is a group of forty-one countries that work together to combat the spread of biological and chemical weapons. They have set up a common list of controlled substances, equipment, and technologies that have weapons applications for nations to use in their licensing programs.

The *Missile Technology Control Regime* is a voluntary association of thirty-four countries committed to keeping missile technology from rogue regimes and terrorist groups that could use it to deliver weapons of mass destruction.

The *Nuclear Suppliers Group* is a group of forty-five nuclear supplier nations that includes the United States, Russia, and China. Its purpose is to share information and to set voluntary guidelines for countries who want to control the export and proliferation of nuclear material, equipment, and technology, especially that used in the enrichment and conversion of nuclear material.

The problem with these multilateral efforts is that they are voluntary and without enforcement powers. Nevertheless, they are an important way for nations to work together to address common terrorist threats.

Export Controls on Commercial and Dual-Use Goods and Technologies

Earlier in the chapter, we studied export controls that apply primarily to arms, munitions, and defense systems. In this section, we are concerned with U.S. export controls and licensing procedures for commercial and dual-use goods and technology, and with compliance and enforcement mechanisms.

Export Administration Act of 1979 and Regulations

The *Export Administration Regulations* (EAR or "regulations") were promulgated under the authority of the *Export Administration Act of 1979* by the *Bureau of Industry and Security* (BIS), U.S. Department of Commerce. In 2001, the act expired and was not renewed by Congress due to political disagreements. However, the regulations remained in effect pursuant to an executive order of the president issued under the authority of another statute, the *International Emergency Economic Powers Act of 1977*. At the close of 2007, the president asked Congress to enact the *Export Enforcement Act of 2007 (proposed)*. The bill, if passed, would renew the 1979 law for five years, but with greatly increased fines and enforcement powers. The Export Administration Regulations are available through the Internet from the BIS or the U.S. Government Printing Office.

Commercial and Dual-Use Goods and Technology. Earlier in this chapter we studied the *Arms Export Control Act*. That law applied primarily to controls on military and defense industry exports. The EAR, on the other hand, applies to the export and reexport of all commercial and dual-use items. (The term "item" is sometimes used to mean both goods and technology that are covered by the regulations.) *Commercial items* are those intended primarily for civilian use and include all goods and technology, not just those considered "high tech." Commercial items might be controlled for foreign policy reasons, perhaps as part of a larger economic embargo (for example, to deprive comfort to nations that sponsor terrorism, seek chemical weapons, or suppress human rights). *Dual-use items* are commercial items that may also have military or "proliferation" uses (relating to the proliferation of nuclear, chemical, or biological weapons). These are usually controlled for military or strategic reasons.

The EAR defines *technology* as "specific information necessary for the development, production, or use of a product." This includes proprietary research, but not research in the basic sciences for academic publication. The information can take the form of technical data (blueprints, models, specifications, etc.) or technical assistance (training, imparting working knowledge, and providing consulting services). The EAR applies to exports of software, encryption technology, and source code.

The following examples of dual-use items are taken from actual cases that resulted in convictions and sentencing for violations of the export control regulations: Night-vision goggles, semiconductors, scopes for sporting rifles, electric cattle prods, thermal imaging cameras, oil drilling equipment, pipe-cutting equipment, high-strength aluminum rods, fingerprinting powder, common chemicals that are precursors of chemical weapons, advanced machine tools, medical and laboratory testing equipment that could be used to develop and test toxins used in biological weapons, parts for diesel engines that could become part of military vehicles or tanks.

Most dual-use goods and technology have commercial, civilian, or industrial applications that would not appear to have military or proliferation consequences. Indeed, in many cases, the engineers that designed them and the people that sold them would never have anticipated possible military uses.

Consider this example: An American firm formulates a new super-hard alloy for use in its advanced drill bits, intended for deep-earth oil drilling. The drill bits are sold to an oil exploration company in a foreign country so that it can tap its deep oil reserves and sell them to the United States. Then, a few years later, to the surprise of the American military, the foreign country rolls out a new tank with advanced armor that is almost impenetrable by ordinary anti-tank weapons. The armor, it turns out, was designed using the same technology that went into the manufacture of the drill bits, and the hardened alloy bits themselves were used to test the penetrability of the new armor.

Consider one more example: An American firm designs and manufactures a device commonly sold to highway engineers to test the depth of hardened road surfaces. A construction company in a foreign country places an order for the device. On further investigation overseas, the "company" turns out to be a front for a foreign government agency that is constructing a military airport runway in a strategic region of the world. They wanted the device in order to build a runway capable of handling their newest generation of military cargo aircraft.

The moral of the story is that American companies cannot rely on their own intuition as to whether their goods or technology are controlled and require government approval for shipment. They must know for certain and follow all procedures for licensing their exports.

What Is an Export and Reexport? The regulations prohibit the export or reexport of controlled items. In this chapter, and for the purposes of export control law, the word *export* is an actual shipment of goods that are subject to the export regulations of the United States. The term also refers to any release of technology or software subject to the regulations in a foreign country, or to a foreign national, whether that person is located in the United States or in a foreign country. The term *reexport* has similar breadth, but it refers to shipment or releases of American technology from one foreign country to another foreign country.

Authority for Prohibiting or Curtailing Exports. Under the regulations, the Department of Commerce may "prohibit or curtail" the export of any goods or technology to any country in order to achieve the specified goals of national security, foreign policy, or the prevention of short supply of domestic materials. The Department of Commerce determines which items to control and places those items on the *Commerce Control List.* The Department of Commerce is required to consult with other executive departments (such as Defense, State, and Agriculture), the intelligence community, and multilateral control or coordinating agencies. The president establishes the list of controlled countries. The three broad goals of control are to maintain national security, implement foreign policy, and (where required) regulate commodities that are in short supply.

National security controls may be used to "prohibit or curtail" the export of goods or technology that would make "a significant contribution to the military potential of any other country or combination of countries which would prove detrimental to the national security of the United States."

Foreign policy controls may be used to "prohibit or curtail" the export of goods or technology, where necessary "to further significantly the foreign policy of the United States or to fulfill its declared international obligations." The president is required to consult with Congress and report on the effectiveness of foreign policy controls. The limitations are that the controls must be likely to achieve their purpose and capable of being enforced. On balance, the detrimental effects on trade, U.S. competitiveness, and the economic well-being of individual U.S. companies must not exceed the benefit to the U.S. foreign policy objectives. Export controls for foreign policy reasons are limited to a period of one year, after which they must be renewed by the president.

The EAR does not authorize banning the sale of medicines or medical supplies, or donations of goods for humanitarian needs (e.g., disaster response or aid to refugees). Exports of food or agricultural commodities may be controlled, but there are limits on the extent to which the president and the Department of Commerce may do this.

Short supply controls may be imposed where necessary to protect the domestic economy from the excessive drain of scarce materials or to reduce the serious inflationary impact of foreign demand.

One important hallmark of the export regulatory system is that the decisions of the president and of the Department of Commerce, including decisions as to which items to put on the Commerce Control List and which countries to sanction, are largely exempt from the usual administrative procedures of public comment and virtually immune from judicial review. In the past, courts have been unwilling to determine what goods or technologies should or should not be placed on the control list, what goods have potential military applications, etc. Judges have also recognized that if different courts around the country were to have different opinions as to what goods may or may not be exported without a license, the entire regulatory scheme would fall apart.

Foreign Availability. Earlier in the chapter, we considered the economic impact of restricting trade for policy reasons. The regulations state that controls shall not be imposed for foreign policy or national security purposes on the export of goods or technology that "are available without restriction from sources outside the United States in sufficient quantities and comparable in quality to those produced in the United States so as to render the controls ineffective in achieving their purposes." The government does not have to consider foreign availability if the president determines that the absence of such controls would be detrimental to foreign policy or national security.

The Export Licensing Process

Export licenses are issued by the Bureau of Industry and Security. According to the bureau's 2006 annual report, in that year the agency processed almost 19,000 export license applications worth approximately \$36 billion. The largest single approval was for a shipment of crude oil worth \$12 billion. The People's Republic of China was the destination for the largest number of approved licenses: over 1,500 individual licenses worth more than \$2.4 billion.

In the following section, we provide a very general overview of how to determine whether a license is needed for your export. Although businesspeople should know how to obtain a license, be sure to get competent professional advice if you are not experienced or have any questions. Civil and criminal penalties for failing to comply with the regulations can be very severe, a point to which we shall return. Never assume that your goods are not covered by the regulations or that their export is not controlled. No matter how innocuous your product may seem, it may require a license. Exporters are encouraged to consult the information and instructional materials available from the Bureau of Industry and Security or through its Web site. Our discussion here applies to all commercial or dual-use goods that the Department of Commerce regulates.

Steps in Determining License Applicability. An inquiry into whether a license is required for an export or reexport can have six possible results:

- A license is required.
- There is an exception to the license requirement.

- The export or reexport is permitted and has *NLR* (no license required) status.
- The export or reexport is not permitted to the country of destination.
- The export or reexport is not permitted to the end user.
- The export or reexport is not permitted for the end use.

The following 10 steps are a basic overview of the licensing process for instructional purposes. Please do not rely on them for use in actual licensing. There is no substitute for reading the Export Administration Regulations and BIS rules. The BIS Web site is an excellent source for additional information and examples.

To begin, you will need the following information in order to determine whether licensing requirements apply to your shipment (1) the classification of the item on the *Commerce Control List;* (2) the ultimate or final destination; (3) the end user (and whether it is someone with whom your transaction may not be permitted); and (4) the end use.

Step 1: Locate your item on the Commerce Control List (CCL). The CCL is available in the supplement to the Export Administration Regulations. There are ten general categories (which are also broken down into product groups):

0. Nuclear materials, facilities, and equipment
1. Materials, chemicals, microorganisms, and toxins
2. Materials processing
3. Electronics
4. Computers
5. Telecommunications and information security
6. Sensors and lasers
7. Navigation and avionics
8. Marine
9. Propulsion systems, space vehicles, and related equipment

Step 2: Using the listings grouped under each category, locate the correct *Export Control Classification Number* (ECCN) for your item by matching its technical characteristics and functions to the correct ECCN. The ECCN is a five-character alphanumeric code that tells the reasons and type of control for your item. If you prefer, you can submit an official request for the correct ECCN to the BIS through the Internet.

Step 3: Identify the "Reason for Control" for that ECCN. The possible reasons for control are listed in the CCL, beginning with the most restrictive (applicable to the most countries), and followed by their respective code: Anti-Terrorism (AT); Chemical & Biological Weapons (CB); Crime Control (CC); Chemical Weapons Convention (CW); Encryption Items (EI); Firearms Convention (FC); Missile Technology (MT); National Security (NS); Nuclear Nonproliferation (NP); Regional Stability (RS); Short Supply (SS); United Nations Embargo (UN); Significant Items (SI); Surreptitious Listening (SL).

Step 4: Consult the *Country Chart,* found in the EAR, for each of the above reasons for control. It lists countries in four groups. The type of control is determined by the reason for control and the country of destination. The fewest controls are over exports to Canada. The most restricted countries are the embargoed countries and those countries designated as supporting terrorism. All exports and reexports to embargoed destinations and to countries designated as supporting terrorism require a license. As of 2007, these countries were Cuba, Iran, North Korea, Sudan, and Syria.

Step 5: Determine if your item is classified as EAR99. The two main reasons for EAR99 classification are (1) the item is not on the CCL and therefore has no ECCN (this usually applies to many commercial goods and consumer goods of low-level technology), or (2) the item is on the CCL, but a license is not required for the destination country. EAR99 items generally do not need a license unless the shipment is going to an embargoed or controlled country or to a suspicious or prohibited customer or end user, or is meant for a prohibited end use (e.g., one related to military uses, etc.). EAR99 items generally ship "no license required" (NLR), although that can change with the circumstances of the shipment.

Step 6: Determine if your item qualifies for a license exception based on the reason for control or the country of destination. If it does, determine the type of license exception, which you will use to prepare your shipping documents.

Step 7: Consult the regulations to determine if the end use of your item is controlled. If you think your item may aid in the proliferation of nuclear, biological, or chemical weapons, or missile technology, stop and inform the BIS. There are special end use and end user requirements in this area.

Step 8: Comply with all *end user regulations.* Regardless of whether your item is on the CCL, or whether you have found an exception, determine if your customer or end user is prohibited from receiving U.S. exports without a license. It is unlawful to release controlled items to anyone on the following lists. Consult these lists carefully.

Entity List: A list originally set up to bar exports or diversions to organizations engaged in activities related to the proliferation of weapons of mass destruction. Today it has been expanded for other reasons. Most end users on this list are in China, Russia, Pakistan, or India.

Specially Designated Nationals and Blocked Persons List: A list maintained by the Department of Treasury, Office of Foreign Assets Control comprising individuals and organizations deemed to represent restricted countries or known to be involved in terrorism and narcotics trafficking.

Unverified List: Firms for which an end use check could not be done in prior transactions. These firms present a "red flag" that exporters have a duty to investigate further. (For other "red flags" that are a warning of a possible illegal attempt to violate U.S. export controls, see Exhibit 13.1)

Denied Persons: A list of persons whose export privileges have been denied or revoked. They may be located abroad or within the United States. If you believe a "denied person" wants to buy your goods in order to export them, you must not make the sale and should report it to the BIS.

Debarred List: This is a list of parties barred from exporting defense articles.

Step 9: Submit your license application on paper or electronically. Do not ship items until you receive the license.

Step 10: Prepare your shipping documents using the correct ECCN and the appropriate symbol (NLR, license exception, or license number and expiration date).

EXHIBIT 13.1

Red Flag Indicators

Things to Look for in Export Transactions

Reprinted from the U.S. Bureau of Industry and Security
These are possible indicators that an unlawful diversion might be planned by your customer:

1. The customer or its address is similar to one of the parties found on the BIS list of denied persons.
2. The customer or purchasing agent is reluctant to offer information about the end-use of the item.
3. The product's capabilities do not fit the buyer's line of business, such as an order for sophisticated computers for a small bakery.
4. The product ordered is incompatible with the technical level of the country to which the product is being shipped, such as semiconductor manufacturing equipment being shipped to a country that has no electronics industry.
5. The customer has little or no business background.
6. The customer is willing to pay cash for a very expensive item when the terms of the sale call for financing.
7. The customer is unfamiliar with the product's performance characteristics but still wants the product.
8. Routine installation, training or maintenance services are declined by the customer.
9. Delivery dates are vague, or deliveries are planned for out-of-the-way destinations.
10. A freight forwarding firm is listed as the product's final destination.
11. The shipping route is abnormal for the product and destination.
12. Packaging is inconsistent with the stated method of shipment or destination.
13. When questioned, the buyer is evasive or unclear about whether the purchased product is for domestic use, for export or for reexport.

Most licenses are good for a period of twenty-four months. (Short supply licenses are good for twelve months.)

Licensing Review Process. The BIS must complete the review of licenses within ninety days or refer it to the president. In 2006, the average time for approval of a license application was only thirty-three days. Many applications go to the Department of Defense for technical review. The BIS also coordinates with the Department of Energy (nuclear issues), the Department of State (arms issues), the Department of the Treasury, the U.S. Treasury's Office of Foreign Assets Control (terrorist groups and state sponsors of terrorism), the Department of Interior (fish and wildlife, endangered species), the Food and Drug Administration, the Arms Control and Disarmament Agency, and with intelligence agencies (regarding end users seeking weapons of mass destruction). Interagency review committees are used if there is the possibility that an item can be used for missile technology or weapons of mass destruction. Interagency disputes lead to a high-level review process, and eventually to the president.

The Destination Control Statement. The destination control statement (DCS) must be entered on the invoice and on the bill of lading, air waybill, and on some other documents that accompany the shipment to the end user abroad. The DCS is generally required for all exports from the United States of items on the Commerce Control List that are not classified as EAR99. At a minimum, the DCS must state: "These commodities, technology or software were exported from the United States in accordance with the Export Administration Regulations. Diversion contrary to U.S. law is prohibited."

Special Comprehensive Licenses. This is a special licensing process for companies that will make multiple shipments over an extended time for special reasons. This might include shipments of spare or replacement parts for items from previously licensed shipments; shipments to the same consignee for use in a major construction project; routine shipments to subsidiary companies, affiliates, or joint venture partners; or recurring shipments to foreign distributors who regularly do business in the exporter's products. A special license requires advance registration with the BIS, approval of the consignee, and approval of a system of internal controls and record keeping to ensure compliance with the export regulations. Both the exporter and foreign consignees are subject to investigations by the BIS. Many controlled items are not eligible for special licensing.

China Validated End User Program. In 2007, the BIS began a test program to simplify procedures and speed shipment to China. It allows qualified exporters to preapprove "trusted customers" and subsidiaries of American companies in China for shipments of certain high-technology, commercial, or dual-use items, without the need for individual export licenses. It is available to companies and end users that have a record of export compliance. It does not apply to any items that might have military or strategic value.

Reexports of U.S. Goods and Technology. U.S. export controls apply to both exports and reexports. The procedures for reexport licensing are similar to the procedures for an export license, although the circumstances requiring a license may be different. A reexport may require a license if the item meets one of the following criteria:

1. It was produced or originated in the United States.
2. It contains more than a specified percentage of U.S.–controlled content.
3. It is foreign made but based on certain U.S.–origin technology or software and is intended for reexport to specified destinations.
4. It was made by a plant located outside the United States if that plant was developed on U.S. technology, and if the item is intended for reexport to specified destinations.

Deemed Exports

Export controls for national security reasons apply to more than just shipments of goods. A *deemed export* is the communication or other transfer by an American citizen of technology, technical data, software, encryption technology, computer source code, or any other controlled information to a foreign national. A *foreign national* is an individual who is neither a U.S. citizen nor a permanent legal resident of the United States. *Deemed reexports* of information from someone licensed to receive it to a third person must also be licensed.

Applying the law is not always easy. Assume a citizen of India is a permanent legal resident of the United Kingdom and is working there. If he consults with an American subsidiary in England or in the United States, communications of controlled technology will be licensed to him just as it would be to a British citizen. Also, if a person has dual citizenship, the country of last citizenship applies.

Deemed exports fall under the export licensing laws. A U.S. company may require a license when communicating controlled technology or information to employees of foreign subsidiary companies, to foreign affiliates, to joint venture partners, to foreign engineers, consultants, or even to foreign customers. This can be a problem whenever U.S. plants, factories, research facilities, or offices, whether located in the United States or in a foreign country, are opened to visiting foreign customers and guests. The communication can be in any form, including a visual inspection or even casual observation of the controlled goods or technology. It also applies to Americans with technical knowledge and experience who could apply that to specific situations or projects in a foreign country without a license. It also applies to universities and research institutions that host foreign scholars and students. Proprietary research, including industrial designs the results of which ordinarily are restricted for corporate or national security reasons, are controlled. However, *fundamental research* (basic or applied) in science and engineering, which is research where the resulting information is ordinarily published and shared broadly with the scientific community, is not controlled or subject to licensing. Most technology companies and research universities have an internal control program to ensure compliance with the law.

The deemed export problem was addressed in a 2006 Report to Congress by the Government Accountability Office, *Exports: Agencies Should Assess Vulnerabilities and Improve Guidance for Protecting Export-Controlled Information at Companies,* (GAO-07-69). The report states in pertinent part,

> In today's global economy, U.S. companies' exchanges of technology and information occur with ease and include the transfer of export-controlled technologies to foreign nationals through routine business practices such as
>
> - transmission of a data file via an e-mail sent from a laptop computer, cell phone, or a personal digital assistant,
> - using company electronic networks to make intra-company transfers of information to overseas subsidiaries or affiliates,
> - visual inspection of U.S. equipment and facilities during company site visits,
> - e-commerce transactions—sales of software over the Internet to overseas customers, and
> - oral exchanges of information when working side-by-side with U.S. citizens.

According to the *Annual Report of the Bureau of Industry and Security for 2006,* in that year the agency processed 865 deemed export license applications. Most cases involved the electronics (semiconductor manufacturing), telecommunications, computer, and aerospace industries. Almost 60 percent involved Chinese nationals working in U.S. companies and universities, followed in descending order by foreign nationals from India (13 percent), Iran (7 percent), Russia (2 percent), Germany (2 percent), and the UK (1 percent).

Extraterritorial Jurisdiction of Export Control Laws

We begin this section with one of the most contentious questions in all of export control law: Should a nation, as a matter of law, be able to extend the power of its export control laws—its *jurisdiction*—over its goods and technology once they have left its territory? Most nations are not willing to say that goods and technology have "nationality" in the same sense that its citizens do. So the legal basis for extending jurisdiction over goods and technology once they leave the nation in which they originated is subject to debate. Most international lawyers reject the idea that one nation, in the absence of a treaty or convention, can control goods and technology within the borders of another nation. Consider a comparison to intellectual property law and the protection of patents, trademarks, and copyrights. We would not expect, for example, the UK to use its police and courts to take action in the United States to enforce a British patent that belongs to a British citizen. Such matters are usually covered by international treaty or convention, handled by local authorities under local law, or negotiated between governments. However, for at least a half century, the United States has attempted to assert the *extraterritorial jurisdiction* of its export control laws over its goods and technology anywhere in the world. The Export Administration Regulations state that they are applicable to "[a]ll U.S. origin items wherever located," including "U.S. origin parts ... or other commodities integrated abroad into foreign-made products." In addition, the reexport provisions attempt to control U.S.–origin items long after they have left the United States. We have also seen this in the "deemed export" rules, under which the United States attempts to control and license the communication or transfer of technology by foreign subsidiaries of U.S. firms to foreign employees in foreign countries. In the example given in the following section, the American attempt to use extraterritorial export controls led to a serious international business crisis.

The Crisis over the Soviet Natural Gas Pipeline to Europe. In the early 1980s, the Soviet Union and European countries agreed to construct a 3,000-mile natural gas pipeline from Siberia, across Russia and communist Eastern Europe, to Western Europe. It was the height of the cold war: The Berlin Wall divided Germany, and U.S. and Soviet tanks faced each other along the border between East and West. President Reagan and the United States stood firmly against construction of the pipeline. The U.S. fear was that it would make America's allies in Western Europe too dependent on the Soviets, which could lead to disastrous consequences if war were to break out in Europe. It also would provide the Soviets with Western "hard currency" from the sale of gas, which would help take economic pressure off the Soviet Union's failing communist economy.

American companies in the United States, as well as their subsidiaries in Europe, produced advanced technology that could be used in drilling and in construction of the pipeline. General Electric produced the most advanced turbines for moving the gas, although less effective alternatives were made by companies in the Soviet Union and elsewhere. Dresser France, S.A., a subsidiary of Dresser Industries of Dallas, Texas, produced gas compressors needed for the project. However, in an attempt to stop the project, President Reagan used the U.S. export control laws to order all American-owned companies and subsidiaries worldwide to refrain from exporting goods or technology for use in the pipeline project. The ban included goods and technology of U.S. origin, as well as those based on U.S. patents and technology licensed to foreign firms by American firms. France, Great Britain, West Germany, Italy, and other countries resented the order and considered it a "slap in the face" to their sovereignty. Their governments responded by making it unlawful for their companies to comply with the U.S. order.

Dresser was in a difficult position. The U.S. government threatened Dresser France, S.A. with sanctions, and possible criminal penalties, if it did not stop its shipment of compressors. The French government threatened to nationalize Dresser France, S.A. if it did. There was a diplomatic impasse. An article published in *TIME* magazine in 1982 quoted John James, Dresser's chairman, as saying, "The laws of the United States are not the laws of the whole world." President Reagan had no support, either at home or abroad. In the end, the Reagan administration's attempt to assert the extraterritorial jurisdiction of U.S. export controls failed, and they were eventually rescinded.

Antiboycott Provisions

For our purposes, a *boycott* is an organized refusal of one or more nations, often backed by economic sanctions, to trade with one or more other nations. Boycotts are often used for political reasons. *Antiboycott* laws are legal responses by governments that make it unlawful for their citizens or companies to participate in a boycott. U.S. export control laws contain antiboycott provisions that make it illegal to "comply ... [with or] support any boycott fostered or imposed by a foreign country against a country which is friendly to the United States." Although the laws apply to any boycott not sponsored by the U.S. government, they primarily target some Middle Eastern countries that have been boycotting Israel for over fifty years. This boycott goes well beyond the Arab refusal to trade directly with Israel. Boycotting countries will not permit the import of any goods or services that have any Israeli components, and they will not do business with firms from anywhere in the world that also do business with Israel or that have ties to Israel. Firms that do business with Israel are "blacklisted."

U.S. antiboycott laws apply to any U.S. person or company located in the United States. They also apply to foreign affiliates of such persons and companies. The laws prohibit participation in the Arab boycott of Israel, refusal to do business with blacklisted companies, or agreements to do so. They also prohibit the furnishing of information relating to the boycott, relationships with or in Israel, or relationships with blacklisted companies. In addition, the laws prohibit discrimination based on, or the furnishing of any information about, the race, religion, sex, national origin, or nationality of another person.

Any request for information related to a boycott, or request to participate in a boycott, must not be answered, but must instead be reported to the Office of Antiboycott Compliance within the Bureau of Industry and Security. Some of these requests are cleverly disguised. For example, a bank letter of credit issued on behalf of a Lebanese buyer for goods being shipped to Lebanon required a "[c]ertificate issued by the shipping company or its agent testifying that the carrying vessel is allowed to enter the Lebanese port...." This was a veiled attempt at enforcing the boycott on Israel, because ships that have carried Israeli goods, or that are Israeli owned, are not permitted to enter Lebanese ports. Violations of the antiboycott regulations by Americans are punishable under the export control laws. In the following case, *Briggs & Stratton Corp. v. Baldridge*, the court addresses a challenge to the U.S. antiboycott regulations.

Compliance and Enforcement

Compliance and enforcement are two sides of the same coin. No government agency, whether it collects taxes or fights water and air pollution, can rely solely on law enforcement to make the system work. Voluntary compliance by regulated companies is essential. Compliance with export

Briggs & Stratton Corp. v. Baldridge

539 F. Supp. 1307 (E.D. Wis. 1982), aff'd 728 F.2d 915 (1984)

United States Court of Appeals (7th Cir.)

BACKGROUND AND FACTS

In December 1954, the League of Arab States called for an economic boycott of Israel. Under the "General Principles" worked out by the Arab states, a firm could be blacklisted if it traded with Israel.

The plaintiff manufactures internal combustion engines. Its products are often used as component parts. Briggs had been blacklisted because of dealings with Israel.

In May of 1977, Briggs received a letter from its Syrian distributor telling it that it had been blacklisted and refused an import license. He also received a questionnaire, which was translated as follows:

1. Has the company now or in the past had main or branch factories in Israel?
2. Has the company now or in the past had general offices in Israel for its regional or international works?
3. Has it granted now or in the past the right of utilizing its name or trademarks or patents to persons or establishments or Israeli works inside or outside Israel?
4. Does it share in or own now or in the past share in Israeli works or establishments inside or outside Israel?
5. Does it now or did it offer in the past any technical assistance to any Israeli work or establishment?
6. Does it represent now or did it represent in the past any Israeli establishment or work inside or outside Israel?
7. What are the companies that it shares in or with, their nationalities, and the size or rate of these shares?

Briggs answered the questions "no," but did not have the questionnaire authenticated because of the new antiboycott regulations. The blacklisting continued, but subsequently the company was

continued

continued

removed from the blacklist. Briggs was unquestionably injured economically by the blacklisting. Briggs brought an action against the officials charged with enforcing the act and regulations, claiming that they violated the First, Fifth, and Ninth Amendments to the U.S. Constitution.

DISTRICT JUDGE GORDON

...The Commerce Department regulations are consistent with this express policy to require persons to refuse to furnish information which would have the effect of furthering a boycott against a nation friendly to the United States. Thus the regulations are not inconsistent with the policies of the act.

I also reject Briggs' argument that the regulations permit a firm to supply information in the absence of a questionnaire that it cannot supply if it gets one. Example (ix) following the intent regulation reads:

> U.S. company A is on boycotting country Y's blacklist. In an attempt to secure its removal from the blacklist, A wishes to supply to Y information which demonstrates that A does at least as much business in Y and other countries engaged in a boycott of X as it does in X. A intends to continue its business in X undiminished and in fact is exploring and intends to continue exploring an expansion of its activities in X without regard to Y's boycott.
>
> A may furnish the information, because in doing so it has no intent to comply with, further, or support Y's boycott. 15 C.F.R. 369.1(e), Examples of Intent.

Briggs' interpretation of this example goes too far. The example merely permits a company on its own initiative to demonstrate non-discriminatory conduct....

Briggs argues that because the regulations cause Briggs to be blacklisted, and thus affect its worldwide sales, the government has totally destroyed Briggs' rights to its foreign trade. Briggs likens the effect to a restriction on private property which "forc[es] some people alone to bear public burdens which, in all fairness and justice, should be borne by the public as a whole."

In *Andrus v. Allard*, the Supreme Court held that the denial of one traditional property right, where the others were not disturbed, did not always amount to a taking. In *Andrus*, there was no physical invasion or restraint on the property in question; the regulation only prohibited the sale of the property. The Court did not find dispositive the fact that the regulations prevented the most profitable use of the property.

> When we review regulation, a reduction in the value of property is not necessarily equated with a taking.... [L]oss of future profits—unaccompanied by any physical property restriction—provides a slender reed upon which to rest a takings claim.

The reed is equally slender here. The regulations apply to all Americans equally. It is possible that they have a somewhat greater impact on Briggs than they do on others, but that does not constitute a taking. Briggs has lost some profits because it has lost some sales, but its property has not been seized or restrained by the government. There is no restriction by the challenged regulation on Briggs' efforts to export its products. In prohibiting Briggs from answering certain questions, the government has not taken Briggs' property in violation of the Fifth Amendment.

Decision. The antiboycott regulations were upheld by the court despite the difficulties of compliance or the economic consequences that may result.

controls is critical to national security. The exporter has the burden of using due diligence to comply with the law. Penalties for noncompliance are onerous.

Export Management System. One of the best ways to ensure compliance is for a company to establish a compliance program, or *export management system*. It should state company compliance policies, use trained personnel or outside specialists to implement the policy, provide for a system of internal audits to prevent and detect violations, and have provisions for notification of the Bureau of Industry and Security in case of irregularity. The policies should cover procedures for internal security; licensing; use of blocked persons lists; screening of foreign customers; investigating end use destinations, foreign travel, Internet, and local area network use; shipping; security at trade shows; and more. The system should also include controls over record keeping and reporting. Technology companies, research and development facilities, and research universities are a few examples of institutions that should have deemed export compliance programs.

Record-Keeping Requirements. Exporters are required to keep records related to all licensed exports for a period of five years. These include all licenses, license applications and supporting documents, bills of lading or transport documents issued by carriers, memoranda, notes, correspondence, contracts, invitations to bid, books of account, financial records, and other records of the transaction. In particular, exporters should keep all formal and informal records related to their investigation into their end users and the end uses of their exports.

Enforcement, Sanctions, and Penalties. Export violations are subject to severe administrative and criminal penalties. The Bureau of Industry and Security (BIS) Office of Export Enforcement carries out investigations and may impose administrative remedies and civil fines. It may detain shipments, issue *temporary denial orders* (orders to prevent imminent illegal shipments), issue warning letters, and monitor compliance with the conditions of individual licenses. The BIS may bring a civil action before an administrative law judge to impose civil fines or other administrative sanctions. Criminal cases are based on willful conduct or *conscious avoidance,* meaning that the exporter purposely avoided learning information (e.g., not asking if the goods will be resold and diverted) that might have had a bearing on his or her license application. Criminal investigations are handled by the BIS, the U.S. Bureau of Customs and Border Protection, the FBI, and often by the Internal Revenue Service, and are prosecuted by the Department of Justice.

It is unlawful to export in violation of the terms of a license, to evade licensing controls, or to buy, use, sell, conceal, or transport any item exported or to be exported from the United States with knowledge that a violation of the export laws has occurred, is about to occur, or is intended to occur in connection with the item. Other violations include soliciting the export of a controlled item; possessing a controlled item with intent to export or reexport it in violation of the law; altering a license; making false statements (usually in a license application, on the Shipper's Export Declaration, or while submitting information electronically via the Automated Export System); failing to comply with a lawful order of the BIS; failing to comply with reporting and record-keeping requirements; and conspiracy. Many investigations also uncover crimes of money laundering.

Penalties Proposed in 2007. Congress has increased civil and criminal penalties several times since the terrorist attacks of 2001. Under the proposed *Export Enforcement Act of 2007*, criminal penalties for individuals would increase to $1 million per violation and/or imprisonment for not more than ten years, for each violation. Corporate fines would increase to a maximum of $5 million or up to ten times the value of the exports involved, whichever is greater, per violation. The civil penalty amounts would increase to a maximum of $500,000 for each violation of the export regulations. For example, an employee of an exporting firm who makes false statements on an application for an export license involving a shipment to a foreign customer worth $1 million could personally be assessed a maximum civil penalty of $500,000 and criminal fines not to exceed $1 million, and receive not more than ten years in prison, per violation. (Many cases involve more than one violation.) In addition, the employer could be subject to a maximum fine of $10 million. Although this bill may never become law, it does illustrate the move toward toughening the export control penalties.

Sentencing factors include the extent of the threat to national security, the number of shipments and their value, and the degree of willfulness and planning, and the experience and sophistication of the exporter. Anyone who makes an "accurate and thorough" voluntary self-disclosure of an export violation is likely to receive a reduced penalty as a result.

Denial of Export Privileges. In addition to fines and imprisonment, individual violators and related parties can be subject to a "denial order" that bars them from exporting for a specified number of years (under the 2007 proposals, not more than twenty-five years). It is unlawful for anyone else to participate in an export transaction with a "denied person."

The President's Emergency Powers During Peace and War

Congress has passed a number of statutes granting the president exceptional powers during times of peace and war. Since the American Civil War era, Congress has granted extraordinary powers to the president to deal with events that could be termed a *national emergency,* such as an international economic, diplomatic, or military crisis. Although originally conceived to allow the president to deal with economic problems that arise during wartime, the concept of national emergency has gradually expanded to include a broad range of situations affecting foreign affairs and international trade during peace or war.

Trading with the Enemy Act

Congress passed the *Trading with the Enemy Act* (TWEA) in 1917 to restrict trade with hostile countries during times of war. In 1933, however, President Roosevelt used this statute during a domestic economic crisis to declare a national banking emergency, close the nation's banks, and prevent the hoarding of gold. Congress ratified the president's actions and expanded the president's emergency powers to include peacetime crises determined by the president to be "national emergencies."

In the 1970s, Congress generally came to believe that the TWEA provided the president with far more sweeping powers to regulate peacetime emergencies than had ever been intended by the law. After all, this was the time of the "undeclared" Vietnam War. The excesses of presidential power were becoming evident as the Watergate disclosures and abuses of public office were made public. Executive actions of the president were considered suspect. In this climate, Congress sought to increase its role in making U.S. foreign policy and to impose new controls on the president's actions during national emergencies. By 1977, Congress had passed new emergency powers statutes, and the TWEA lost its importance during peacetime, with the exception of the provisions that continued to restrict trade with Cuba and North Korea.

National Emergencies Act

In 1976, Congress passed the *National Emergencies Act of 1976* (NEA), which ended four existing states of emergency and established new procedures for declaring new ones. (Ironically, the banking emergency declared by President Roosevelt during the Great Depression had remained in effect until 1976.) Under the NEA, the president can still declare a state of emergency, although the authority to act under it lasts for only one year. At the end of that period, the president must ask Congress to renew authority over that situation. The president must consult with Congress prior to declaring an emergency and report to Congress every six months while the emergency continues. Congress votes every six months on whether to continue the emergency and may terminate a national emergency declared by the president through a joint resolution of both houses of Congress.

Although the procedures for congressional oversight are set out in the *National Emergencies Act,* the powers and the scope of remedies available to the president are set out in the 1977 *International Emergency Economic Powers Act* (IEEPA).

International Emergency Economic Powers Act

This statute provides the current grant of authority to the president to regulate economic and financial transactions and to place restrictions on importing or exporting during a peacetime (or wartime) national emergency. The statute states that the president may declare a national emergency in the event of "any unusual and extraordinary threat, which has its source in whole or substantial part outside the United States, to the national security, foreign policy, or economy of the United States." IEEPA allows the president wide discretion in controlling international financial transactions, including the transfer of monies, goods, and securities to and from the United States. It allows the president to seize foreign assets held in U.S. banks or foreign branches of U.S. banks. The statute also allows the president to impose a trade embargo with a foreign country and to take a wide range of other economic sanctions. The U.S. Treasury often implements the president's policy decisions under IEEPA. Treasury regulations are published in the *Federal Register*.

Economic Sanctions under IEEPA. Since its enactment, IEEPA has been used to impose economic sanctions against countries in every region of the world. Examples from the past few decades include Nicaragua, South Africa, Panama, Libya, Haiti, Serbia, Sudan, Burma (Myanmar), Afghanistan, Iran, and Iraq. Sanctions are usually tailored to the special problems presented in each country. One example was the U.S. ban on imports, financial transactions, and sales of computers, arms, and nuclear equipment to South Africa to punish it for its racist policy of *apartheid* in the decades prior to the 1990s. In the 1980s the United States imposed a ban on air flights between the United States and Nicaragua and a ban on Nicaraguan ships entering U.S. ports as a result of that country's Marxist policies under its *Sandinista* government.

Under IEEPA, the United States imposed sanctions against Libya from the time it was deemed a state sponsor of terrorism in 1979 until 2004, when it renounced weapons of mass destruction and began complete cooperation with international weapons agencies. Presidents Clinton and George W. Bush have used IEEPA as a major weapon in the war on terrorism, using its authority to seize the assets of terrorist groups and cutting off their funding. As of 2007, the United States had ongoing economic and trade restrictions against the following countries for a variety of human rights abuses or for sponsoring terrorism: the Balkans, Belarus, Burma (Myanmar), Côte d'Ivoire (Ivory Coast), the Democratic Republic of the Congo, Cuba, Iran, Syria, Iraq, Liberia, North Korea, Sierra Leone, Sudan, and Zimbabwe.

As of this writing, the U.S. was enforcing other restrictions against certain persons, firms, or governments affiliated with terrorist organizations. These included any country attempting to interfere with the Middle East peace process; certain named individuals and organizations associated with the proliferation of weapons of mass destruction; and certain persons identified by the president as significant foreign drug traffickers under the *Foreign Narcotics Kingpin Designation Act of 1999*.

USA PATRIOT Act

One of the major U.S. legal responses to the terrorist attacks of September 11, 2001, was the enactment of a statute with a rather cumbersome title, *Uniting and Strengthening America by Providing Appropriate Tools Required to Intercept and Obstruct Terrorism (2001)*, commonly called the *USA PATRIOT Act*. The act made significant changes to IEEPA and other U.S. criminal statutes and gave far-reaching powers to law enforcement to deal with the threat of terrorism in America.

The act created new federal crimes and penalties for terrorism. These include new crimes (or increased penalties for existing crimes) for attacks on mass transportation, for harboring terrorists, for possession of biological toxins or weapons, for fraudulent charitable solicitation, and for providing material support to terrorists. The act also modified the immigration laws by giving the government greater freedom to detain and deport noncitizens where the U.S. Attorney General had reasonable grounds to believe that an individual belonged to a terrorist group or jeopardized U.S. national security. The act amended IEEPA to give the government greater flexibility to seize property of those who commit terrorist acts or who provide material support to terrorists. It permitted the president to order the confiscation of foreign property belonging to any individual, group, or country that planned, authorized, aided, or engaged in any attack against the United States. Moreover, it allowed assets of an individual or organization to be frozen pending (rather than following) an IEEPA investigation into its links to terrorists.

The *PATRIOT Act* amended U.S. laws on financial transactions and bank secrecy, so the government can better follow the trail of money supporting terrorists. The act expanded the record-keeping requirements for financial institutions (including banks, brokers, securities dealers, and other financial institutions) and called for greater government scrutiny over international business transactions. Financial institutions were placed in the position of "knowing their customer." By consulting the government's list of "specially designated nationals and blocked persons," they could determine if any transaction included persons or organizations whose assets had been seized under the law. Financial transactions, both inside and outside the United States, were to be tracked and reported to the government whenever there was suspicion of money laundering for terrorist groups. Cash transactions over $10,000 also had to be reported. The law gave enforcement powers to the Department of Treasury, Office of Foreign Assets Control and the Financial Crimes Enforcement Network or FinCen, the Department of Justice, and various other government agencies.

The *PATRIOT Act* also provided law enforcement with greater investigative tools to fight terrorism while requiring less judicial supervision and oversight. It expanded law enforcement's authority to conduct searches, permitted nationwide execution of search warrants against terrorists or those who harbor them, allowed the "roving" electronic surveillance of criminal suspects, permitted monitoring of some e-mail and computer messages without a warrant, and eased restrictions on law enforcement when national security was at stake. The act also expanded the extraterritorial application of federal criminal law to terrorist acts committed against Americans or American property overseas.

While the act was considered crucial in the government's effort to prevent future terrorist attacks in the United States, it has also been criticized by many Americans for its broad and sweeping powers, especially those authorizing electronic eavesdropping, that some believe infringed basic American liberties.

IEEPA and UN Sanctions Against Iraq. In 1990, shortly after the Iraqi invasion of Kuwait, President George H. W. Bush used his authority under IEEPA to impose economic sanctions on Iraq. He also used IEEPA's protective measures to protect American and Kuwaiti interests. In an effort to stop Iraq from seizing and squandering Kuwaiti assets, the Treasury Department used IEEPA to freeze all assets of both countries that were held in U.S.–owned or U.S.–controlled banks and any other property held by U.S. firms. All sales between Iraq and U.S. companies were halted.

The Iraqi case presented a unique situation under IEEPA. The authority for U.S. action against Iraq in 1991 was broadened by international cooperation and by the force of international law. The United States was not acting unilaterally against Iraq; it was, rather, responding to calls from the UN for sanctions against Iraq. This case was also unique in that IEEPA sanctions were used to aid in the protection of foreign assets (those belonging to the government and people of Kuwait), not just to punish an offending country. The sanctions resulted in lost business, disruption of the international oil markets, blocked letter-of-credit transactions, and a regulatory nightmare for U.S. companies doing business in the Middle East. The first Gulf War began when the U.S. administration determined that the sanctions would not be effective. The administration of President George W. Bush lifted the sanctions in 2003 at the end of the second war with Iraq. Trade in arms, stolen cultural artifacts, and transactions with Baath party officials remained prohibited, and blocked Iraqi money was to be used in the rebuilding of Iraq.

Court Challenges to IEEPA

When Libya was implicated in international terrorism in the late 1980s, President Reagan prohibited U.S. citizens from performing any contract in support of commercial, industrial, or governmental projects there. In *Herman Chang v. United States*, 859 F.2d 893 (Fed. Cir. 1988), a group of petroleum engineers brought suit against the United States alleging that the termination of their employment with a Libyan oil company by an executive order under IEEPA violated their constitutional protection against the taking of private property without the payment of just compensation. In upholding the president's order, the court dismissed the argument that the U.S. government may not act in an emergency in a way that causes economic harm to individuals or companies. The court stated,

> A new tariff, an embargo, a [military] draft, or a war may inevitably bring upon individuals great losses; may, indeed, render valuable property almost valueless. They may destroy the worth of a contract. But whoever supposed that, because of this, a tariff could not be changed … or an embargo be enacted, or a war be declared?

IEEPA and the 1979 Iranian Revolution. In the late 1970s, the government of Iran was overthrown during an Islamic revolution. Islamic militants, angry at the United States for its support of the prior government, seized the U.S. embassy in Tehran and held the Americans there hostage for 444 days. At the time, Americans and American firms had considerable business interests and property in Iran. That property was also seized by the new government. In response, President Carter declared a national emergency under IEEPA and froze all Iranian property (worth a total of about $12 billion) held by U.S. banks and corporations, both in the United States and abroad. All trade was halted and travel was restricted between the two countries. In order to free the hostages, the United States and Iran signed the *Algiers Agreement* in 1981, by which the United States agreed to place the blocked Iranian money in trust accounts in British banks pending the settlement of claims by the newly created U.S.–Iranian Claims Tribunal (which sat at The Hague, Netherlands). Chas. T. Main International, Inc., a U.S. engineering firm that had been doing work on an Iranian hydroelectric power plant, brought a legal action of its own in a U.S. court against Iran seeking compensation for its lost property, and a declaration that the *Algiers Agreement* exceeded the president's powers under the Constitution. In *Chas. T. Main International, Inc. v. Khuzestan Water & Power Authority*, 651 F.2d 800 (1st Cir. 1981), the Court of Appeals ruled that the president had the authority to enter an agreement for the settlement of all claims between U.S. firms and Iran. The court further ruled that such an agreement prevailed over all other attempts by Americans to regain their property in courts of law. In ruling that the president had the constitutional power to create a tribunal to settle international claims, the court stated: "This case well illustrates the imperative need to preserve a presidential flexibility sufficient to diffuse an international crisis, in order to prevent the crisis from escalating or even leading to war." Chas. T. Main had to proceed with its claim at The Hague, and it ultimately won an award against Iran there.

The Case of the "American Taliban." In 1999, President Clinton declared a national emergency to deal with the threat posed by the al Qaeda terrorist organization and by the *Taliban* (meaning "student of Islam") government of Afghanistan, where al Qaeda training camps were located. The executive order prohibited the making or receiving of any contribution of funds, goods, or services to or for the benefit of the Taliban. The state of emergency was continued by President George W. Bush and remained in effect until after the successful U.S. military action in Afghanistan. During the war in Afghanistan, an American citizen by the name of John Walker Lindh was captured when it was discovered that he had undergone terrorist training in Pakistan and was fighting with the Taliban. He was charged in the United States with conspiracy to murder Americans, providing material support to foreign terrorist organizations, and violating IEEPA. In the following case, *United States v. Lindh*, the "American Taliban" challenged the *International Emergency Economic Powers Act*.

United States v. Lindh

212 F. Supp. 2d 541 (2002)

United States District Court (E.D. Va.)

BACKGROUND AND FACTS

Beginning in 1995, both Presidents Clinton and Bush issued several executive orders under the *International Emergency Economic Powers Act* (IEEPA) declaring a national emergency in dealing with terrorism. Pursuant to those orders, the Department of the Treasury issued regulations prohibiting transactions with terrorist groups or providing services to them. Al Qaeda was named as a terrorist organization, along with the Taliban government of Afghanistan that supported them. Shortly after September 11, 2001, the United States invaded Afghanistan to locate and

continued

continued

destroy al Qaeda terrorist training camps and to overthrow the Taliban government. During the war, it was discovered that the defendant was an American citizen fighting for the Taliban. He had undergone terrorist training in Pakistan and had allegedly met Osama bin Laden. He was charged in the United States under criminal statutes with conspiracy to murder Americans and with providing material support to foreign terrorist organizations in violation of the president's IEEPA orders. Lindh argued that IEEPA applied only to commercial transactions with terrorist groups and not to his conduct.

ELLIS, DISTRICT JUDGE

* * *

Lindh argues that Counts Six through Nine of the Indictment should be dismissed because they charge violations of regulations that were promulgated in excess of the statutory authority provided by IEEPA. Specifically, these four counts charge Lindh with "Contributing Services to *al Qaeda,* Supplying Services to the Taliban," and conspiracy to do each of these.... Lindh argues that IEEPA cannot be construed to authorize promulgation of any regulations prohibiting his voluntary and noncommercial donation of services to the Taliban and *al Qaeda.*

The IEEPA is a relatively recent addition to this country's arsenal of sanctions to be used against hostile states and organizations in times of national emergency. For much of the twentieth century, this country's sanctions programs were governed by the *Trading with the Enemy Act* (hereafter "TWEA"), enacted in 1917. As amended in 1933, TWEA granted the President broad authority "to investigate, regulate, ... prevent or prohibit ... transactions" in times of war or declared national emergencies. *See Dames & Moore v. Regan*, 453 U.S. 654, 672, 101 S.Ct. 2972, 69 L.Ed.2d 918 (1981). Congress changed this statutory scheme in 1977 to limit TWEA's application to periods of declared wars, but created IEEPA to provide the President similar authority for use during other times of national emergency....

Despite the breadth of the Regulations and Executive Orders issued pursuant to IEEPA, Lindh asserts that IEEPA does nothing more than permit the President to freeze the assets of a foreign state or foreign national and prohibit certain international financial transactions during times of a declared national emergency. Lindh argues, moreover, that neither the plain meaning of IEEPA, nor its legislative history, indicate that it provides a basis for the wide-ranging regulations here in issue. Thus, Lindh argues, the Regulations he is charged with violating exceed IEEPA's statutory grant of power.

The straightforward question presented, therefore, is whether the Regulations are within the scope of IEEPA. As this is a question of statutory construction, analysis must begin "as always with the language of the statute."

The IEEPA language in issue is as follows:

> [T]he President may, under such regulations as he may prescribe, by means of instructions, licenses, or otherwise—
> (A) investigate, regulate, or prohibit—
> (i) any transactions in foreign exchange,
> (ii) transfers of credit or payments between, by, through or to any banking institution, to the extent that such transfers or payments involve any interest of any foreign country or a national thereof,
> (iii) the importing or exporting of currency or securities; and
> (B) investigate, regulate, direct and compel, nullify, void, prevent or prohibit, any acquisition, holding, withholding, use, transfer, withdrawal, transportation, importation or exportation of, or dealing in, or exercising any right, power, or privilege with respect to, or transactions involving, any property in which any foreign country or a national thereof has any interest; by any person, or with respect to any property, subject to the jurisdiction of the United States. 50 U.S.C. §1702.

This language manifestly sweeps broadly, as courts have consistently recognized in according deference to various sanctions programs under IEEPA and TWEA (see ... *United States v. McKeeve*, 131 F.3d 1, 10 (1st Cir. 1997). ("IEEPA codifies Congress's intent to confer broad and flexible power upon the President to impose and enforce economic sanctions against nations that the President deems a threat to national security interests.") See also *United States v. Curtiss-Wright Export Corp.*, 299 U.S. 304, 320, 57 S.Ct. 216, 81 L.Ed. 255 (1936) (noting that generally the President's actions are entitled to greater deference when acting in the fields of foreign affairs or national security). This sweeping language provides ample authority for the issuance of the Regulations and also easily reaches Lindh's alleged conduct. This conduct—which includes, for example, attending Taliban and *al Qaeda* training camps, using and transporting Taliban and *al Qaeda* weapons and ammunition, and using Taliban and *al Qaeda*

continued

continued

transportation and residence facilities—plainly involves "use" of Taliban and *al Qaeda* "property." And, given the breadth of the common dictionary meanings of "use," "dealing," "transactions" and "property," there is similarly no doubt that Lindh's provision of combatant services to the Taliban and *al Qaeda* also falls within the IEEPA and the Regulations.

* * *

Lindh seeks to avoid the result reached here by arguing that IEEPA concerns only commercial or economic conduct. In support, he cites the statute's title and the fact that many cases involving IEEPA and TWEA address solely economic or commercial activity. This argument, while not implausible, is again contradicted by the statute's sweeping broad language. As noted, the plain dictionary meanings of statutory terms like "transaction," "dealing," "use," and "property" do not limit their use to commercial transactions; these terms are sufficiently broad to cover the conduct alleged here, including the donations of combatant services.

Decision. The provisions in the indictment alleging violations of IEEPA were valid. The plain language of IEEPA indicated congressional intent to grant broad powers to the president in times of a declared national emergency. The regulations issued pursuant to IEEPA applied to the rendering of combatant services to the terrorist organizations concerned.

Comment. In 2002, John Walker Lindh, known as the "American Taliban," entered a plea of guilty to the charges and was sentenced to 20 years in prison.

U.S. Sanctions on Trade with Cuba

Prior to 1959, the United States had strong ties to Cuba, an island nation just ninety miles off the coast of Florida. Many Americans had business investments there, and the country was a mecca for tourists from around the world. In 1952, an army general seized power in a military *coup d'état.* Political unrest fermented, culminating with the 1959 overthrow of the government by Fidel Castro's Marxist guerrilla army. Castro set up a communist government, with strong ties to the Soviet Union. Cuba nationalized the assets of American citizens and U.S. firms (including farms, factories, hotels, bank accounts, real estate, etc.) without compensation. Castro began an effort to "export communism" to other countries in Latin America and was a key player in the cold war between the United States and the Soviet Union. So began forty years of anger between the United States and Cuba, beginning with President Kennedy's failed Bay of Pigs invasion in 1963 and the Cuban missile crisis.

In 1963, the United States passed the Cuban Assets Control Regulations, under the authority of the *Trading with the Enemy Act.* The purpose of the law was to isolate Cuba economically and politically. It banned all trade and financial transactions between Cuba and the United States and froze all U.S.–held assets of the Cuban government and of private Cuban citizens. It also prohibited almost all travel to Cuba by U.S. citizens. (Certain researchers, student groups, journalists, athletes, and those traveling to see immediate family members in humanitarian need were excepted.) Although President Carter briefly loosened trade and travel restrictions with Cuba in the late 1970s, that changed with the election of President Reagan in 1980, who reinstituted harsh sanctions. In the following case, *Freedom to Travel Campaign v. Newcomb,* a U.S. court ruled on the constitutionality of the Cuban travel restrictions and the *Trading with the Enemy Act.*

Cuban Sanctions after the Fall of the Soviet Union. In 1989, the Soviet Union stopped supporting the Cuban government financially. No longer did it send billions of dollars of foreign aid annually. Many members of the U.S. Congress saw this as an opportunity to press Cuba for democratic change. First, Congress passed the *Cuban Democracy Act of 1992*, which tightened economic sanctions and travel restrictions by closing most loopholes in the law. The Cuban Democracy Act of 1992 stopped all travel and visits by family members and others, and it banned Cubans in the United States from sending money to their families in Cuba. Then Congress passed the *Cuban Liberty*

Freedom to Travel Campaign (FTC) v. Newcomb
83 F.3d 1431
United States Court of Appeals (9th Cir. 1995)

BACKGROUND AND FACTS

Pursuant to the authority of the *Trading with the Enemy Act* (TWEA), in 1962 President Kennedy announced the Cuban Asset Control Regulations, which prohibited U.S. citizens from engaging in almost any economic activity with communist Cuba without a license. The embargo has lasted through nine U.S. presidents. The regulations at issue also restricted travel to Cuba. Certain persons, such as journalists and government officials, could qualify for a travel license. Permission for all other persons, including tourists, was only considered upon a showing of "compelling need" for reasons such as "educational activities." Traveling to Cuba without a license was a criminal offense, and violators were subject to imprisonment, fine, and property forfeiture. The Freedom to Travel Campaign (FTC) is an organization that organizes educational and other trips to Cuba. It brought this action challenging the regulations. The FTC claimed that (1) the regulations violate the Constitution on the theory that the government lacks sufficient foreign policy reasons to prohibit a person from traveling to a foreign country; and (2) the failure to define "educational activities" for which travel is permitted renders the regulations excessively vague, and therefore void.

HALL, CIRCUIT JUDGE

FTC argues ... that the Regulations' travel ban is unconstitutional because the Government lacks a sufficient foreign policy rationale to inhibit FTC's liberty interest in travel. In substance, this appears to be a substantive due process claim and we will treat it as such. A substantive due process claim involves the balancing of a person's liberty interest against the relevant government interests [most citations omitted]. FTC claims that its freedom to travel is trampled by the Regulations' travel ban. Although the freedom to travel internationally is a liberty interest recognized by the Fifth Amendment, *Kent v. Dulles*, 357 U.S. 116, 127 (1958) ("Freedom to travel abroad is, indeed, an important aspect of the citizen's 'liberty.'"), it is clearly not accorded the same stature as the freedom to travel among the states. Restrictions on international travel are usually granted much greater deference. Given the lesser importance of this freedom to travel abroad, the Government need only advance a rational, or at most an important, reason for imposing the ban.

This the Government can do. The purpose of the travel ban is the same now as it has been since the ban was imposed almost 35 years ago—to restrict the flow of hard currency into Cuba. That goal has been found [by other courts] "important," "substantial," and even "vital." Thus, the Government seems to have satisfied its obligation.

FTC, however, would have us evaluate the foreign policy underlying the embargo. It contends that the President's current reason for the embargo—to pressure the Cuban government into making democratic reforms—is not as compelling a policy for an embargo as were previous justifications that relied on national security concerns. FTC thus invites us to invalidate the ban. This is an invitation we must decline. It is well-settled that "[m]atters relating to the conduct of foreign relations ... are so exclusively entrusted to the political branches of government as to be largely immune from judicial inquiry or interference." See *Regan v. Wald*, 468 U.S. 222 (1984). This immunity manifests itself in a history of judicial deference.

Even were we to second guess the President, this is not a case where the Government has set forth no justifications at all. It has detailed numerous reasons for the embargo. We will look no further. The *Cuban Asset Control Regulations*' travel ban is constitutional.

FTC claims that two provisions [on travel] are void for vagueness and therefore infringe upon its freedom to travel.... FTC correctly states that due process will not tolerate a law restricting the freedom of movement if its enforcement is left to the whim of government officials.... The Treasury Department's recent amendment to the Regulations further cures any vagueness defects. Newly created Regulation 419 now defines "clearly defined educational activities" as (1) those conducted at an international meeting or conference; and (2) those related to undergraduate or graduate studies. Thus, this aspect of Regulation 560(b) is constitutional.

continued

continued

The FTC ... argues that the Regulations' vague language gives Asset Control officials the ability to arbitrarily interfere with its right to gather firsthand information about Cuba, which its members would use to participate in the public debate about the wisdom of the Cuban-American embargo. When a person's right to travel internationally is conditioned on the surrender of his First Amendment expressive or associational rights, the First Amendment is clearly implicated. However, where a person seeks only to gather information, no First Amendment rights are implicated.

Decision. The ban on travel to Cuba imposed by the Cuban Asset Control Regulations was valid. The U.S. government need only have a "rational basis" for prohibiting travel by Americans to foreign countries, such as in this case, where the ban was intended to deprive the communist government of hard currency.

and Democratic Solidarity Act of 1996, commonly called the *Helms–Burton Act*. The law authorized U.S. citizens with claims to confiscated property in Cuba to file private lawsuits in U.S. courts against any person, including a citizen of a foreign country, that *traffics in* (engages in any commercial activity regarding) that property. The most controversial part of the law required the United States to deny an entry visa to any foreign citizen who trafficked in property that was confiscated by Cuba after 1959. This included many Mexican, Canadian, and European businesspeople that did business in Cuba.

The passage of *Helms–Burton* caused a worldwide protest, primarily from Mexico, Canada, and the European Union, who argued that *Helms–Burton* violated international law. A protest was filed with the World Trade Organization by the European Union, but was suspended when the Clinton administration gave assurances that the visa restrictions of *Helms–Burton* would not be enforced against citizens of other countries. *Helms-Burton* calls for sanctions on Cuba to end once Cuba has a democratically elected government, abides by human rights conventions, opens its prisons to international inspection, returns Cuban citizenship to Cuban exiles living in the United States, and makes progress in returning expropriated property to its rightful owners. In 2000, for the first time in four decades, the U.S. government legalized sales of some food and medicines to Cuba. These items must be paid for in cash, and no government financial assistance, credits, or credit guarantees are available to finance Cuba's purchases.

The Effectiveness of Cuban Sanctions. Many people have condemned the Cuban trade and travel sanctions for their harshness. Even the Vatican protested *Helms–Burton,* claiming that it increased the economic suffering of the Cuban people. Many trade groups have argued against the law because they believe that economic engagement promotes freedom in totalitarian countries. United States firms wishing to do business in Cuba also seek an end to U.S. sanctions. Indeed, every year since 1992 virtually every member nation of the UN, except the United States and a few supporters, has passed resolutions calling on the United States to end the sanctions. Ironically, surveys of American public opinion show that the vast majority of Americans also favor ending sanctions and recognizing the communist government. Forty years of communism have left the island nation an economic ruin. However, a lack of necessities and consumer goods has not spurred a democratic uprising. Moreover, a study by the U.S. International Trade Commission released in 2001 revealed that the U.S. embargo has had only a minimal impact on Cuba, noting that the government tends to make trade and investment decisions based on ideology and political factors, not on economic considerations (see USITC Publication 3398, February 2001). Perhaps the argument against modern-day Cuban sanctions was expressed best by Arthur Schlesinger Jr., a noted U.S. historian and close advisor to President Kennedy, when he stated in a letter to the editor of the *New York Times* that "A better policy ... would be to repeal *Helms–Burton,* lift the embargo and drown the [Castro] regime in American tourists, investments, and consumer goods." *New York Times,* February 21, 1997, cited in *Havana Club Holding v. Galleon,* 961 F. Supp. 498 (S.D. N.Y. 1997).

Conclusion

For the United States, the pursuit of both export promotion and control will always be a deliberate balance between economic interests and foreign policy. It might be possible to have a country whose borders are impenetrable, whose technology products never reach the hands of an enemy, and who can stand by moral principles under all circumstances and refuse to do business with military dictators, communist regimes, or other despots. But the economic consequences would be disastrous. These are issues to be debated before Congress and pondered by the president. How can government best maintain America's security in a dangerous world while fostering an environment for trade? Although there are occasional calls for America to "go it alone," history tells us that international cooperation is the least dangerous solution.

Chapter Summary

1. U.S. trade in armaments, munitions, and defense systems is regulated by the *Arms Export Control Act,* administered by the U.S. Department of State.
2. The three primary reasons for control over exports of U.S. goods and technology are national security, foreign policy, and short supply controls to prevent excessive foreign demand on scarce materials.
3. Trade sanctions to achieve foreign policy objectives are generally more effective when done in coordination with other governments or in support of a United Nations resolution.
4. The United States controls the export and reexport of all goods and technology (including software and source code) whether they have commercial (civilian) applications, military applications, or dual-use applications. Dual-use goods and technology are those that have commercial uses, as well as military, intelligence-gathering, or other strategic applications. Nonproliferation controls apply to any goods or technology that can further the spread of weapons of mass destruction or missile technology. Diversion is the illegal transshipment, rerouting, or reexport of controlled goods or technology from a licensed destination to an unlicensed destination.
5. The U.S. Department of Commerce's Bureau of Industry and Security (BIS) is the lead agency for administering the export controls over commercial and dual-use goods.
6. Export licenses are issued according to the item, destination, end user, and end use. All goods and technology on the Commodity Control List require a license for export or reexport, unless it is classified as EAR99 or there is a specific exception.
7. A deemed export is the communication or release, by any means or in any manner, of any technology, technical data, or software to a foreign national, whether done in the United States or in a foreign country.
8. The antiboycott laws prohibit Americans from participating in, or responding to requests for information about, the Arab boycott of Israel.
9. Violations of the export control laws and the antiboycott laws are punishable by civil penalties, denial orders, criminal fines, and imprisonment. Criminal charges can be brought for both willful violations and *conscious avoidance,* which is purposely avoiding learning information about an end user, end use, or destination, in order to evade the export laws. Technology exporters should have a solid corporate compliance plan.
10. The *International Emergency Economic Powers Act* (IEEPA) gives the president authority to impose economic, trade, or financial controls during a declared international emergency. The president may seize assets, cancel contracts, impose export controls, and take a range of extraordinary actions. IEEPA was amended by the *USA PATRIOT Act* to grant exceptional powers against terrorist groups. This is administered by the Department of Treasury, Office of Foreign Assets Control.

QUESTIONS AND CASE PROBLEMS

1. Do goods and technology have "nationality?" What is meant by this statement? Do you think that a nation's laws should apply to its goods and technology after they have left the territory of that nation? What principles of international law permit a nation to extend its jurisdiction over goods and technology that originated there? Can you make arguments for or against the extraterritorial application of export control laws? Does this differ from the extraterritorial application of antitrust law or laws against bribery of foreign government officials?
2. The *International Emergency Economic Powers Act* and the *USA PATRIOT Act* grant exceptional and extraordinary powers to the president to respond to almost any declared international emergency. Since the terrorist attacks of 2001, the United States has used these laws aggressively in the war against terror and against those deemed to be supporters of terrorist groups. Many Americans and civil libertarians view these laws with skepticism because they are easily subject to abuse by a president or law enforcement agencies. Based on your outside reading and knowledge, what are the pros and cons of granting emergency powers to the president for use against terrorism? Do you feel that the law been used overzealously, or has it given the president appropriate law enforcement tools needed to protect the nation? What do you think about their effectiveness against terrorism versus their potential for abuse?
3. Most readers are familiar with the debate over the use of trade sanctions as a means of carrying out foreign policy. President Carter's ban of grain sales to the Soviet Union in response to the Soviet invasion of Afghanistan failed when the Soviets simply started purchasing grain from other countries. Shortly after that, President Reagan angered American allies in Europe, as well as American businesses, by unilaterally imposing controls on the sale of equipment for use by the Soviets in constructing the Trans-Siberian natural gas pipeline. Can you cite any examples where trade sanctions have worked? Under what circumstances do you think that trade sanctions are likely to work?
4. What is a "deemed export"? How can this impact technology companies and research institutions in the United States?
5. Daniel Bernstein, a graduate student, developed a software encryption program called "Snuffle" and wanted to post it on the Internet. The U.S. government said he needed a license. What was the result? How have the export regulations changed since Bernstein's case?
6. Is it ethical to hold a businessperson legally responsible if he or she sells controlled technology to a second party that is then diverted to a prohibited end user? What factors will influence your answer? How does "conscious avoidance" affect one's liability for an export violation?
7. Does the export of electric cattle prods require a license? Why?
8. Determine if and how U.S. export regulations apply to personal shipments made through the U.S. Postal Service or by air couriers such as Federal Express or United Parcel Service.
9. What is the status of the *Export Administration Act of 1979* and the Export Administration Regulations? Has the statute been renewed or replaced since its lapse in 2001? Are the regulations still in force? Have the civil and criminal penalties increased as had been proposed in 2007?

MANAGERIAL IMPLICATIONS

You are in charge of an American subsidiary company in France that manufactures advanced robotics equipment used in the automobile industry. You have engineering and research facilities in both countries. You receive an inquiry about your robotics from someone claiming to represent an upstart Chinese automobile manufacturer. He requests immediate information and explains that the plant is already well beyond the planning and financing stages and that things will soon begin to "move very quickly." Answer the following questions.

1. Do the U.S. export regulations apply to your firm in France? Why?
2. Since this involves a potential sale to a customer, you question whether the U.S. regulations require an export license just to disclose some technical information. Does it? Explain.

3. How do you respond to his request for information? How much information may you give to him without a license? At what point do you have to stop? Explain.
4. You know that if you have to apply for a license, you will need more information about this individual, his company, and its location, the end use of the product, and the ultimate destination. How would you obtain that information? What sources would you use? Are there any industry, government, or banking sources that could help you? What special precautions would you want to take to ensure that his inquiry is legitimate and honest? Explain.
5. You and your prospective customer decide to meet and go over engineering and technical specifications. What steps must you take before the meeting to ensure compliance with the law? Does it matter whether you are meeting in the United States, France, or China?
6. It is some time later, and having worked out all necessary arrangements, you are ready to ship and arrange installation of your first pieces of equipment. In the interim, with no apparent provocation, China refuses to allow a U.S. naval ship to make a prearranged stop in Hong Kong. There are 1,000 sailors aboard who hope to spend Christmas with their family members, who have traveled all the way to Hong Kong for the holidays. You apply for a U.S. license with the BIS, and it is turned down based on a new ban on the sale of certain items to China, including robotics. You exhaust the administrative appeal process. Do you have any rights against the BIS? Are you protected by the U. S. Constitution, since they changed the rule just prior to your shipment date?
7. The French government is very interested in your company making the sale. The President of France considers it a technological *coup d'état*. On learning that the United States blocked your sale, he threatens to fine your company up to five times the value of the shipment and to throw you in a French prison. What do you do? Do you comply with the laws of the United States or the laws of France? What are the alternatives?

Ethical Considerations

1. Your company, Ajax Pharmaceutical, based in New Jersey, is approached by an agent for a company that has offices in Egypt and Jordan about participating in several joint ventures in the Middle East and Asia. The agent inquires about the status of your investment in Israel. You currently have an offer from a newly formed Israeli investment group to purchase your 30 percent share of Drugisco, an Israel-based company. How do you respond? What is your legal obligation? What other information do you need to answer the agent's question?

   He also asks about your ability to ship certain chemicals that are controlled. Do you have any obligation to report this inquiry?

   You initially ship the requested items to Japan. You discover during a late-night meeting in a karaoke bar that these items went to a middleman and are now headed to Sudan. Do you have any legal responsibility? Ethical responsibility? What managerial controls can you implement to reduce the likelihood of this happening in the future?
2. Your company, Enzyme, Inc., manufactures biological and chemical agents that have potential military uses. You understand that Congress is considering the contentious issue of how to revamp the entire export control regimen. Prepare a letter to your state's senators articulating your company's position about decontrol. Do you think your company should take an active role in lobbying for a new law? What are the risks associated with such a position? Will you discuss these issues with your board of directors?

For Internet Activities, Visit academic.cengage.com/blaw/schaffer.

CHAPTER 14 North American Free Trade Law

In previous chapters we discussed principles of international trade law, including the GATT agreements, the role of the World Trade Organization, laws regulating import competition and unfair trade, and laws governing access to foreign markets. We examined how the growth of free trade principles, or *trade liberalization,* has led to increased trade in goods and services and fostered an environment for economic development and globalization. That discussion focused on trade liberalization at the global level. For example, we saw how the principles of most-favored-nation trade are applied globally: if a nation reduces the tariff rate on a product imported from one MFN country, then it must automatically and unconditionally apply that rate to similar products imported from all MFN countries. Safeguards are another example of trade regulation at the global level. Increased tariffs temporarily imposed on a product to protect or safeguard a domestic industry from injury due to a flood of competing imports must be applied globally to imports of similar products coming from all WTO member countries and not just from a select few.

Although the focus of our discussions, up to this point in the book, has been on global trade, many regional trade issues are equally as important. Countries often enter trade agreements with each other that grant lower tariffs and other trade privileges that are more favorable than those granted to the rest of the world. These agreements may create regional free trade areas where goods and services can be bought and sold with few or no tariffs or other trade restrictions. Some free trade areas also have special rules for the cross-border movement of people, for protecting the environment of the region, or for cooperation on workplace health and safety issues. Regional trade areas might be created for economic, political, foreign policy, or security reasons in the region. For example, the United States may enter into a free trade agreement with a Latin American country partially for economic reasons, but also with the hope that it will slow the production of illegal narcotics and drugs.

Other free trade areas tackle even broader issues. There is no better example than Europe. The European countries, over a period spanning fifty years, reduced barriers to trade, investment, and the free movement of people, money, information, and technology. What began in the 1950s as the European Common Market later became the European Economic Community and today is called the European Union. As the name changes signify, each step along the way increased the economic, political, and social ties among European countries.

However, the creation of free trade areas seems inconsistent with the philosophy and objectives of global free trade. After all, is it not protectionist if two or more countries single themselves out for even lower tariffs on goods traded between themselves than on goods imported from countries outside the trading area? Some supporters of global free trade would argue that, indeed, it is protectionist. Others argue that any effort to reduce trade barriers is a positive step, and those efforts will eventually spread to other countries. Moreover, regional agreements can address specific social, economic, and political issues that are incapable of being addressed globally. The right of countries to form free trade areas is recognized in Article 24 of GATT (1947), which states, "[T]he provisions of the Agreement shall not prevent ... the formation of a customs union or of a free trade area...." However, GATT also states, "[T]he purpose of a customs union or of a free trade area should be to facilitate trade between the constituent territories and not to raise barriers to the trade of other [WTO member countries]." Thus, our study of free trade areas should recognize that bilateral or multilateral trade agreements, or the creation of free trade areas, are permitted under GATT only if they do not conflict with broader principles of international trade law.

This chapter examines the North American Free Trade Area among Canada, Mexico, and the United States. These countries have agreed to rules that give the goods and services of each country even more favorable treatment than that given to most other WTO member countries. In addition to customs and tariff regulations, the agreement also addresses many broader issues of common concern, such as cooperation on labor and environmental issues, cross-border trucking, and more.

The North American Free Trade Area

The North American Free Trade Area is comprised of Canada, Mexico, and the United States. They have different economic and political systems as well as different cultures, languages, geographies, and climates. Nevertheless, they have a long history of close economic ties. Together, they encompass the largest free trade area in the world, with a market of about 445 million people and a combined gross domestic product of over $15 trillion. (References to dollars in this chapter refer to U.S. dollars, or their equivalent.) The North American Free Trade Area was created in 1994 after a heated political debate. Its purpose was to spur trade and investment in North America and to improve the standard of living throughout the continent. Proponents in the United States viewed the creation of a free trade area in North America as a means of increasing its exports of goods and services to Mexico, while promoting investment in Mexico, job creation, and economic growth. It was also seen as a means of reinforcing political ties with Mexico, fostering broader participation in democracy there, building a stronger Mexican middle class, stabilizing swings in the Mexican *peso* and Mexican economy, and stemming illegal immigration. It was also hoped that Asian manufacturers would invest in Mexican plants to gain favorable access to markets in the United States and Canada.

Critics claimed that NAFTA would cause a tremendous loss of manufacturing jobs in the United States, as well as hurt American agriculture. Perhaps the best-known critic was former independent presidential candidate Ross Perot, who claimed that on the creation of a free trade area with Mexico, the people of the United States would hear a "giant sucking sound"—the sound of jobs leaving America for Mexico, where wages were lower. It was also feared that American firms would relocate to Mexico to take advantage of reduced operating costs resulting from Mexico's lax labor and environmental laws. Proponents countered that NAFTA included "side agreements" calling for cooperation on labor and environmental issues.

In the United States, there was far greater concern about entering into a free trade area with Mexico than with Canada. While the U.S. and Canadian economies were very similar, and had already been linked by a U.S.–Canadian free trade agreement since 1989, there were vast differences between the United States and Mexico. The United States and Canada are in advanced stages of economic development, with comparable levels of productivity and *per capita* gross domestic product. Canada and the United States are far more similar to each other than to their southern neighbor.

Mexico, on the other hand, is a developing country with a *per capita* GDP that is one-fifth that of the United States and with an unequal distribution of income (20 percent of the population accounts for 55 percent of the income). Also, Mexico has had a history of greater government control over industry, government ownership of key industrial sectors, higher tariffs, and greater barriers to foreign investment than has either the United States or Canada. Despite the controversy, the North American Free Trade Area was created on January 1, 1994, by the *North American Free Trade Agreement* (NAFTA).

Canada-U.S. Trade

Canada and the United States are each other's largest trading partners, with two-way trade in goods totaling about $534 billion in 2006, or almost $1.5 billion a day on a census basis. [All figures in this section are from the U.S. Department of Commerce (Bureau of Economic Analysis/Census Bureau)]. Many people are surprised to learn that in 2006 the United States actually exported slightly more to Canada ($230.6 billion in goods) than to all the countries of the EU combined and about four times as much as to either Japan or China. The United States purchased $302.4 billion in goods from Canada in 2006, more than from any other single country, followed in order by purchases from China, Mexico, and Japan. Of Canada's total imports, about 65 percent come from the United States, while almost 80 percent of Canada's exports are destined for the United States. From the end of 1993, just prior to the creation of the North American Free Trade Area, to 2006, the annual volume of trade between the two countries increased by 150 percent. During that same period, America's trade deficit with Canada increased sevenfold, to $72 billion in 2006. The largest categories of products traded between the countries are automotive products, lumber, agricultural and fishing products, oil and gas products, machinery and industrial goods. Canada has a population of 33 million (compared to 303 million in the United States).

Mexican-U.S. Trade

Mexico is the United States' number-three trading partner (just slightly behind China), with total two-way trade of $332 billion in 2006. From the end of 1993 through 2006, annual two-way trade between the United States and Mexico grew over 300 percent. However, while the United States imports more from China than from Mexico, the United States actually exports almost 250 percent more to Mexico than to China. In 2006, the United States purchased almost 90 percent of Mexico's exports and provided over 50 percent of Mexico's imports. In 2006, the United States sold $134 billion to Mexico and imported $198 billion, leaving a trade deficit of $64 billion. The last year that the United States had a trade surplus with Mexico was in 1994, the year the North American Free Trade Area was created. Today, most Mexican products enter the United States duty free or at a very low tariff rate. Most U.S. goods enter Mexico duty free. Mexico offers U.S. firms low production costs, plentiful labor, easy transportation to the U.S. market, employees who respect and want to work for U.S. firms, and consumers that respect U.S. product brand names. Mexico's population is over 108 million people, with almost three-quarters living in urban areas.

Until the mid-1980s, Mexico had a tightly controlled and protected economy. Its policies restricted imports and discouraged foreign investment. Many key industries were (and some remain) in the hands of government-owned monopolies. Foreign companies that wanted to do business there had to break through a mass of government bureaucracy, red tape, trade barriers, corruption, and an outdated highway, transportation, and telecommunications infrastructure. Hampered by inefficient industries, Mexico during the 1970s and early 1980s suffered low productivity, staggering rates of inflation (as high as several hundred percent a year), and overwhelming foreign debt. Its foreign income was almost totally dependent on exports of oil and petroleum products.

New government policies in the late 1980s and 1990s opened the Mexican economy to trade and private investment. In 2000, Mexico announced that it had signed a trade agreement with the EU allowing European products to enter Mexico at reduced tariff rates. Privatization and deregulation also continued into this decade. Railroads, airports, natural gas transportation, telephone companies, banks, and power generation have all benefited from privatization. Thanks to an influx of foreign capital, technology, and management skills, Mexican companies have become far more efficient than before. Mexican-made products have improved in quality and are now competitive in world markets. By 2000, inflation was down to the single-digit range and unemployment was at an all-time low. As a result, Mexico has become less dependent on oil exports and now has a more broadly based economy. It is safe to say that much of Mexico's economic success since 1993 has been attributable to political and economic reform and to factors other than just NAFTA.

The United States has considerable cross-border investment in both Canada and Mexico. The largest U.S. investors in those countries are General Motors, Ford, and Chrysler, followed by a host of companies in industries including oil, computers, supermarkets, fast food and other franchising, telecommunications, pharmaceuticals, retailing, and beverages. Since 1994, the United States has provided the majority of foreign direct investment in Mexico.

While the topic of U.S. immigration is beyond the scope of this book, it should be noted here that the issue of immigration, particularly illegal immigration, is perhaps the most difficult political and economic issue affecting the relationship between the United States and Mexico.

The *North American Free Trade Agreement*

The *North American Free Trade Agreement* (NAFTA) created a free trade area between Canada, Mexico, and the United States on January 1, 1994. A *free trade area* is a group of two or more sovereign countries in which import duties and other trade barriers are reduced or eliminated.

NAFTA is not a customs union or common market like the European Union. A *customs union* is a free trade area with a common external tariff; the EU goes beyond a free trade area with its common economic and agricultural policies. On trade issues, the EU deals with other countries as outsiders and represents its members in trade negotiations at the WTO. NAFTA does not. NAFTA instead fosters trade and investment among Canada, Mexico, and the United States by reducing tariffs and non-tariff barriers. It also facilitates transportation of goods, provision of services, and financial transactions between the three countries. Each country will generally continue to maintain its own tariff rates applicable to imports from outside the area. (Actually, NAFTA countries adopted a common external tariff on certain computer parts in 2004, but NAFTA is still not considered a customs union.) Each country will continue to establish its own economic policies, and each country will represent itself in the WTO system.

Long before NAFTA existed, many Mexican goods shipped to the United States were already receiving special tariff preferences under the *Generalized System of Preferences* (GSP), which were available to selected products imported from any qualified developing country. Under the GSP, many Mexican products already qualified for either a low tariff or no tariff at all. Canada offered similar preferences for Mexican goods. The purpose of these programs was to encourage trade with developing countries to aid in their economic growth. However, the impact of NAFTA is much broader and much more important than GSP preferences.

Survey of NAFTA's Coverage. Historically, trade agreements focused on the lowering of tariffs, but NAFTA is a trade agreement that does more than just eliminate duties between Canada, Mexico, and the United States. It liberalizes trade in goods and services, contains specific provisions for protecting intellectual property rights, makes cross-border investment easier, and protects the interests of foreign investors from arbitrary government action. It allows easier access for commercial trucks and for business travel between the countries. NAFTA encourages cooperation between governments on antitrust policy dealing with monopolies and unfair methods of competition, worker safety, child labor, and environmental protection. Thus, NAFTA is far broader in scope than most typical trade or investment agreements. Only the EU treaties and perhaps GATT are as broad in scope as NAFTA.

NAFTA Trade and Tariff Provisions

NAFTA's basic trade and tariff provisions pattern the GATT agreements. Many principles are similar, including national treatment, nondiscrimination, tariff reduction, and elimination of non-tariff barriers. NAFTA tariff preferences only apply if the goods are of North American origin, and as we will see in the next section, this requires that you learn how to use the complex rules of origin. NAFTA set a limit of fifteen years for the gradual phasing out of tariffs on goods that originated in North America. On January 1, 2008, all normal tariffs on goods originating and traded between Canada, Mexico, and the United States were eliminated.

National Treatment

NAFTA's *national treatment* principle is similar to that found in GATT. It states that once goods arrive from another NAFTA country, they must be treated without discrimination and no differently than domestically made goods. For example, the United States cannot require that only Mexican-made beer contain a certain alcohol content without setting the same standard for U.S.–brewed beer. Of course, the rule has wide application to all U.S. laws, regulations, and taxes and to a wide range of goods. This provision also applies to regulations of individual U.S. states and Canadian provinces.

Elimination of Non-tariff Barriers. Most quotas, import licenses, and other barriers have been eliminated. Of course, each country may impose import restrictions to protect human, animal, or plant life or the environment. Other special rules permit greater restrictions in key economic sectors, including automobiles, agriculture, energy, and textiles.

NAFTA prohibits new *export taxes* on goods, unless the taxes are also applied to similar goods sold for domestic consumption. *Customs user fees*—fees imposed on importers to help fund the cost of customs enforcement and port services—were eliminated by 1999. NAFTA also addresses issues related to customs administration, the public disclosure of customs regulations, fairness-in-labeling requirements for products, and other barriers to trade. (Mexico does require that all entries valued at more than $2,000 be handled by a Mexican customs broker.)

Continuing Non-tariff Barriers. Mexico, Canada, and the United States have all been accused of maintaining non-tariff barriers despite NAFTA. Here are some examples of trade problems that continue despite NAFTA.

The United States argues that Mexico has still found other ways to block or slow down U.S. imports. Mexico has imposed antidumping duties and safeguards on agriculture and chemical products. It employs burdensome customs procedures that make it difficult for U.S. firms to export to Mexico. U.S. firms complain that regulations change without notice and are applied unfairly toward Americans. Some types of goods can only be entered through certain ports. Goods with counterfeit U.S. trademarks easily pass into Mexico without inspection at the border. Mexico has used the sanitary and phytosanitary provisions to keep out U.S. farm products, even when health and safety were not at stake. For instance, it imposed agricultural inspections at the border, instead of in the United States at the time of packing, resulting in long delays. Some shipments were turned back at the border for mere typographical errors. In 2003, the USTR maintained that Mexico had indirectly imposed a higher rate of income tax on Mexican retailers that sold imported goods.

Similarly, in the *2003 National Trade Estimate Report,* prepared by the USTR, the United States maintained that Canada had raised tariffs on cheese snack foods (to 245 percent!) and that Canada had banned the use of food coloring in margarine and dairy substitutes common in the United States. Many U.S. foods become more expensive in Canada because U.S. manufacturers had to prepare them especially for the Canadian market.

The Canadian government continues to restrict U.S. content in broadcasting media. Broadcasters must still have at least 50 percent Canadian content. Thirty-five percent of music on the radio must be Canadian. There are restrictions on U.S. films that can be shown on certain Canadian stations, and foreign investment in the movie and film industry is largely prohibited or highly regulated.

The *2007 National Trade Estimate Report* tells of other restrictions imposed by Canada. Agricultural products, such as dairy, eggs, and poultry, are subjected to tariff rate quotas. Wheat imports are highly regulated by the Canadian Wheat Board. Many fruits and vegetables cannot be imported or sold in packages larger than the limit, set by the government, without permission. For example, baby food may be sold in jars of only two specified sizes. Because the sizes are not used in the United States, the cost of packaging for the Canadian market becomes excessive. According to the report, the Canadian government has been keeping out U.S. breakfast cereals by prohibiting foods fortified with vitamins and minerals. For instance, in Canada, orange juice with calcium added is considered a drug. Canada even discourages its residents from doing personal shopping in the United States. Canadian residents visiting the United States for less than 24 hours may only return with $50 of U.S. merchandise. In many cases, Canada claims that it is just responding to U.S. barriers on Canadian products.

Rules of Origin

NAFTA tariff rates apply only to articles that originate in Canada, Mexico, or the United States. A foreign product cannot simply be channeled through one North American country for sale in another North American country to avoid the payment of duties. For example, European or Asian products cannot be brought into Canada and then imported duty free into the United States as a product of Canada. In order to know which products qualify for NAFTA's duty-free treatment, one must consult the applicable rule of origin.

Rules of origin were introduced in the last chapter and are a critical issue to importers and exporters. They offer the sole way to determine the rate of duty or even quotas that might apply to the product being bought or sold.

Only goods that qualify under NAFTA's rules of origin can obtain NAFTA tariff rates. The most important general rules are (1) the goods must be *wholly produced or obtained* in Canada, Mexico, or the United States and (2) the goods must contain non-originating inputs (components or raw materials), but meet the regional value content requirements or the tariff shift rules of origin found in Annex 401 of the NAFTA agreement.

Goods Wholly Produced or Obtained in North America

NAFTA applies to goods wholly produced or obtained in North America. These goods may not contain any non–North American parts or materials. NAFTA Article 415 states that the qualifications apply only to minerals mined in North America, vegetables grown in North America, live animals born and raised in North America, fish and fish products, waste, and scrap derived from production in North America. "Produced or obtained" does not mean "purchased." The definition also includes goods produced in North America *exclusively* from the raw materials just mentioned. Thus, NAFTA applies to coal mined in Tennessee, lead mined in Canada, cotton grown in Mississippi, and cattle born in Mexico and raised in Mexico or Texas. It also includes silver jewelry made in Arizona from silver mined in Mexico and taco shells made in Mexico entirely from corn grown in Iowa. The producer, however, must be able to trace *all inputs to raw materials mined, grown, or born in North America.*

Annex 401 Tariff Shift Rule of Origin

Chapter 12 discussed the *substantial transformation test* that is used to determine the country of origin of goods imported into the United States when the goods are produced or assembled in more than one country. This test is difficult to apply, and different courts often come up with different results. The variation in court decisions leads to great uncertainty in applying the test to any given case and complicates importers' sourcing decisions. NAFTA avoids this problem by setting out a simpler rule for when a foreign or non–North American product is "transformed" into a product of North America. NAFTA substitutes a tariff classification change for the vague substantial transformation test. When non–North American goods or materials are brought into a NAFTA country, they can be transformed into a product of North America as long as each non–North American input undergoes a tariff classification change as specified in NAFTA Annex 401. The Annex 401 rules of origin may be based on a *change in tariff classification,* a *regional value-content requirement,* or both, depending on the requirements for that particular product. This is known as the *tariff shift* rule. Annex 401 rules can be found in the *General Notes* of the *Harmonized Tariff Schedules.*

Changes in Tariff Classification. To know if a product imported into the United States has undergone a change in tariff classification, you must refer to the *General Notes* found at the beginning of the *Harmonized Tariff Schedules* of the United States. The following example demonstrates how a product's tariff classification can change.

The harmonized system breaks down product classifications into ten digits, as described in Chapter 12. Countries that have adopted the HTS system have "harmonized" their classification of products internationally at the subheading level. After the first six digits, each country assigns its own numbers. For example, a down-filled comforter (HTS 9404.90.85) is classified in Chapter 94 (which covers a conglomerate of unrelated manufactured articles, including furniture), heading 9404 (covering bedding and similar furnishings, stuffed), subheading 9404.90 (other than sleeping bags), and tariff item 9404.90.85 (down-filled comforters).

To determine the import duty on a North American product, you must know the product's tariff classification at the subheading level. Imagine that you are in the business of making goose down comforters in the United States and Canada. You import unfilled cotton comforter shells from China and goose down fill from Europe. You want to know the U.S. rate of duty on the finished down comforters made at your Canadian plant. You also want to know the correct country-of-origin label to put on the comforter. So, you consult the HTSUS. Your main "non-originating inputs" are the European down (subheading 0505.10) and the cotton shell (subheading 6307.90). You also know that the finished comforter is classified under subheading 9404.90. You find the *General Notes* that contain the NAFTA tariff shift rules and read the following:

> A change to subheading 9404.90 from any other chapter, except from headings 5007, 5111 through 5113, 5208 through 5212, 5408 through 5408 or 5512 through 5516.

Because the non-originating components, the down fill and the unfilled shell, are not in Chapter 94 and are not within any of the exceptions specified, they qualify as having undergone a tariff shift when they are changed to subheading 9494.90. Thus, we have learned that the finished down comforter may be assembled in Canada and shipped to the United States under the rate for Canadian-made comforters and are not subject to any quotas on comforters of Chinese origin (and if we do a little more research we would learn that the comforter can be labeled "Made in Canada"). But suppose we had instead imported Chinese-made cotton fabric and sewed it into an unfilled shell in Canada, filled it with down, and shipped it to the United States. Ironically, the fabric itself falls within subheading 5208 through 5212, and according to the exceptions to the above rule would *not* amount to a qualified tariff shift.

Now, consider pastries that are made in Canada for shipment to the United States. Pastries, breads, cakes, and biscuits fall under subheading 1905.90. Assume their only non–North American input is flour imported from Europe. The rule of origin for pastries in heading 1905 states that the item will be treated as a North American product if it undergoes "A change to heading 1905 from any other chapter." The pastries would qualify for NAFTA tariff treatment because the European-made flour was classified outside of HTS Chapter 19. However, the baker must be careful. If the pastries had been made from a prepared mix (containing flour, shortening, sugar, baking powder, etc.), they would not qualify as a North American product because mixes are classified under Chapter 19, the same chapter as the pastries themselves.

REGIONAL VALUE CONTENT REQUIREMENT. For most products undergoing a transformation in North America, the rule of origin will be based on its tariff classification. In limited cases, NAFTA requires a specified amount of *regional value content* (a similar rule is used for trade in automobiles and parts). For example, a rule might require that at least 50 percent of the value of a finished product be North American. Regional value may be calculated either by *transaction value* or *net cost* methods. Transaction value is the price actually paid for a good. The net cost method removes sales and marketing costs, shipping costs, and certain other expenses from the calculation. The value of non–North American materials is then subtracted from the total cost of the product. Usually the regional value content must be at least 60 percent for transaction value method and at least 50 percent for the net cost method. The value of packaging materials and containers in which a product is packaged for retail sale must be taken into account as either North American or non–North American materials, as the case may be.

Transaction Value Formula

$$RVC = \frac{TV-VNM}{TV} \times 100$$

Nest Cost Formula

$$RVC = \frac{NC-VNM}{NC} \times 100$$

RVC = Percent regional value content
TV = Transaction value of good, FOB basis
VNM = Value of non-originating material
NC = Net cost of good

The importer may generally choose which method it wants to use. (For an example of the calculations, see Exhibit 14.1.) For automobiles and auto parts, however, only the net cost method may be used.

Goods with Minimal Amounts of Non–North American Materials. If the amount of non–North American materials in a finished product is minimal (defined as less than 7 percent of the total cost of the product), the product will still be eligible for NAFTA tariff rates. Thus, if Japanese thread is used to sew together the sleeves on an otherwise 100 percent Mexican-made jacket, and the thread is less than 7 percent of the total cost of the jacket, the finished jacket can be exported to Canada or the United States under NAFTA tariff rates.

Exhibit 14.1

Rules of Origin Example

Product: Wooden Furniture (HS # 9403.50)

Non–North American Inputs: Parts of furniture classified in 9403.90

Rule of Origin:

"A change to subheading 9403.10 through 9403.80 from any other chapter; or

A change to subheading 9403.10 through 9403.80 from subheading 9403.90, provided there is a regional value content of not less than:

a) 60 percent where the transaction value is used, or

b) 50 percent where the net cost method is used."

Explanation: Wooden furniture can qualify for NAFTA tariff preference under two scenarios—a tariff shift, or a combination of a tariff shift and regional value content requirement.

The first option—the tariff shift rule—requires that all non-originating inputs be classified outside of HS Chapter 94 (furniture and bedding). Since the non-originating inputs (furniture parts) are classified in Chapter 94 (subheading 9403.90), then the product cannot qualify based on tariff shift. However, it may still qualify based on the second part of the rule.

The second option has two components—a tariff shift requirement and a regional value content requirement. The tariff shift requirement is satisfied since the non-originating input (furniture parts) is classified in subheading 9403.90 as specified by the rule. The product must meet its regional value content requirement using the transaction value or the net cost methodology.

Given the following values, furniture qualifies for NAFTA tariff preference using the net cost methodology. The calculation is found below, with the following example.

Producer's Net Cost	\$182.00 each (not including shipping, packing royalties, etc.)
Transaction Value	\$200.00 each piece
Value of Non-Originating Parts	\$90.00

Transaction Value Method

$$\frac{(200-90)}{200} \times 100 = 55$$

Good does not qualify under transaction value method because it does not have at least 60 percent regional value content.

Net Cost Method

$$\frac{(182-90)}{182} \times 100 = 50.5$$

Good qualifies under net cost regional value requirement because it has at least a 50 percent regional value content.

SOURCE: U.S. Department of Commerce, 1995.

The NAFTA Certificate of Origin

A NAFTA *certificate of origin,* or CO (see Exhibit 14.2), is required for all shipments moving between the United States, Canada, and Mexico. It certifies that the goods qualify as having originated in North America for purposes of preferential tariff treatment under NAFTA. COs are required for all *commercial* shipments entering the United States where the total line item value for a good (*not* the total shipment value) is more than $2,500 ($1,000 for Mexico, and $1,600 CAD for Canada). For goods below these values, the invoice must state that the goods qualify as an originating good for purposes of preferential tariff treatment under NAFTA. A CO may cover a single shipment or it may be a *blanket certificate* that covers multiple shipments of identical goods. A CO is not required for temporary imports, such as those sent for repair or servicing. COs are not required for noncommercial shipments.

It is the responsibility of the exporter to provide a CO to the importer. The CO may be prepared by the exporter or by the exporter's customs agent with a written power of attorney. Frequently, the exporter is not the actual producer of the goods (as in cases where the exporter is a distributor or other intermediary). In this case, the exporter may complete and sign the certificate only with knowledge that the goods in fact originated in North America or if the producer has provided a written statement to that effect. An exporter that does not want to disclose the producer's identity to the importer may state that the producer's name is "available to Customs on request" (see field 3, Exhibit 14.2). It is unlawful to prepare or present a CO that is known to be false, inaccurate, or incorrect. If the preparer discovers an error in the certificate, it must be corrected within thirty days, with written notice of the corrections sent to all parties. COs may be completed in the language of either the exporting or importing country.

When completing the CO, follow the rules carefully. U.S Customs and Border Protection Form 434 contains instructions on the reverse side (not reproduced here). Field 7 *(Preference Criterion)* requires a letter code indicating the reason why the goods are entitled to NAFTA treatment (i.e., that they have been "wholly obtained or produced" in North America or that they may meet one of the rules of origin). The form looks simple, but it is not intuitive; use caution in preparing it.

U.S. importers must actually be in possession of an original CO before making entry or claiming the NAFTA tariff rate. If the importer does not have the certificate, the claim will be denied and penalties can be assessed. Faxed copies are accepted as originals. An importer who discovers errors in a certificate must notify Customs in writing within thirty days and pay any additional duties owed as a result. The importer must keep the certificate on file for five years.

Standards and Technical Barriers to Trade

All countries can maintain product regulations to protect public health, consumer safety, the environment, and areas of public welfare. However, NAFTA encourages that standards and technical regulations not be used as a non-tariff barrier. For instance, Mexico cannot set unnecessary technical regulations and long, drawn-out approval processes for the sale of telecommunications equipment only to discourage entry to the Mexican market by U.S. or Canadian firms. Technical requirements for telecommunications equipment such as telephones may only require that the equipment not harm the telephone network in order to be approved for use or sale. Standards can be set for energy efficiency in appliances, safety in automobiles, or chemical additives in food. NAFTA requires that each country notify the others when the development of a technical regulation or standard begins, give public notice of the proposed regulations, and provide a sixty-day comment period for interested firms or individuals to submit their arguments and concerns.

Standards and technical regulations in Mexico are called *normas. Normas* are either mandatory—the *Normas Oficiales Mexicanas,* or "official norms"—or voluntary, known simply as *Normas Mexicanas.* They are drafted by dozens of committees operating under the aegis of the Mexican Ministry of the Economy, the *Secretaría de Economía* (formerly the *Secretaría de Comercio y Fomento Industrial). Normas* are published in the *Diario Oficial,* which is similar to the *Federal*

Exhibit 14.2

NAFTA Certificate of Origin

U.S. DEPARTMENT OF HOMELAND SECURITY
Bureau of Customs and Border Protection

OMB No. 1651-0098
See back of form for Paperwork Reduction Act Notice.

NORTH AMERICAN FREE TRADE AGREEMENT
CERTIFICATE OF ORIGIN

Please print or type

19 CFR 181.11, 181.22

Bill of Lading / Air Waybill No. :

1. EXPORTER NAME AND ADDRESS TAX IDENTIFICATION NUMBER:	2. BLANKET PERIOD FROM TO
3. PRODUCER NAME AND ADDRESS TAX IDENTIFICATION NUMBER:	4. IMPORTER NAME AND ADDRESS TAX IDENTIFICATION NUMBER:

5. DESCRIPTION OF GOOD(S)	6. HS TARIFF CLASSIFICATION NUMBER	7. PREFERENCE CRITERION	8. PRODUCER	9. NET COST	10. COUNTRY OF ORIGIN

I CERTIFY THAT:

- THE INFORMATION ON THIS DOCUMENT IS TRUE AND ACCURATE AND I ASSUME THE RESPONSIBILITY FOR PROVING SUCH REPRESENTATIONS. I UNDERSTAND THAT I AM LIABLE FOR ANY FALSE STATEMENTS OR MATERIAL OMISSIONS MADE ON OR IN CONNECTION WITH THIS DOCUMENT;
- I AGREE TO MAINTAIN AND PRESENT UPON REQUEST, DOCUMENTATION NECESSARY TO SUPPORT THIS CERTIFICATE, AND TO INFORM, IN WRITING, ALL PERSONS TO WHOM THE CERTIFICATE WAS GIVEN OF ANY CHANGES THAT COULD AFFECT THE ACCURACY OR VALIDITY OF THIS CERTIFICATE;
- THE GOODS ORIGINATED IN THE TERRITORY OF ONE OR MORE OF THE PARTIES, AND COMPLY WITH THE ORIGIN REQUIREMENTS SPECIFIED FOR THOSE GOODS IN THE NORTH AMERICAN FREE TRADE AGREEMENT AND UNLESS SPECIFICALLY EXEMPTED IN ARTICLE 411 OR ANNEX 401, THERE HAS BEEN NO FURTHER PRODUCTION OR ANY OTHER OPERATION OUTSIDE THE TERRITORIES OF THE PARTIES; AND
- THIS CERTIFICATE CONSISTS OF [ ] PAGES, INCLUDING ALL ATTACHMENTS.

11.			
11a. AUTHORIZED SIGNATURE		11b. COMPANY	
11c. NAME *(Print or Type)*		11d. TITLE	
11e. DATE *(MM/DD/YYYY)*	11f. TELEPHONE NUMBER ▶	*(Voice)*	*(Facsimile)*

CBP Form 434 (04/97)

Register in the United States. Mexico has hundreds of mandatory standards and over 6,000 voluntary ones. Many U.S. exporters argue that these are really used to discourage the sale of their goods in Mexico.

As noted earlier in the chapter, the United States has long complained that Mexican standards and regulations are used as unfair barriers to trade. The United States has cited Mexico's lack of notification to U.S. parties before changing its regulations. For instance, Mexico changed its import requirements on one day and put them into force the next day, leaving no time for companies to comply. The report also cited the inconsistency with which customs agents apply the law. Moreover, the report maintained that Mexico makes U.S. exporters submit their products for testing and certification only to Mexican labs and requires detailed inspections of goods at border checkpoints, tying up shipments for excessively long periods.

Marking and Labeling Rules

The country-of-origin marking and labeling rules are set out in Annex 311 to NAFTA and enacted in the national customs regulations of the United States, Canada, and Mexico. The rules are not uniform among the three countries. As we saw in the last chapter, the country of origin rules for marking and labeling goods are not the same rules that determine the country of origin for tariff purposes. It is actually possible for an item to be deemed a product of a NAFTA country for marking purposes without being eligible for lowered NAFTA tariff rates.

In an important case, the U.S. Court of Appeals held that the *Gibson-Thomsen* "name, character, or use" test is not applicable to NAFTA imports, and only the regulations enacted according to Annex 311 principles apply. *Bestfoods v. United States,* 165 F.3d 1371 (Fed. Cir. 1999). The case was strongly argued by the maker of "Skippy" brand peanut butter, who wanted to be sure that its well-known "all-American" product obtained a "Made in U.S.A." label. The peanut butter was made in the United States from "peanut slurry" imported from Canada. Bestfoods argued that they should be allowed to label "Skippy" as "Made in U.S.A." because the U.S. process substantially transformed the peanut slurry into a product with a "new name, character, or use." However, the court held that NAFTA Annex 311 replaced the old "name, character, or use" test for North American trade. A reading of Annex 311 shows that the processing of Canadian (or Mexican) peanut slurry into peanut butter in the United States does not result in the type of tariff change that would transform the slurry into a U.S. product.

Mexico's marking and labeling requirements have been controversial. The *Normas Oficiales Mexicanas* contains specific labeling requirements for certain products (e.g., appliances, electronics, textiles, and food products). All others fall into the more general requirements for general merchandise. Mexico's labeling requirements are strict and often burdensome to U.S. and Canadian exporters. The cost of compliance is often so difficult that many small exporters cannot afford to sell their products in Mexico. Mexico has dictated the content, form, size, and even the appearance of product labels. The Spanish-language labels must include the generic name of the product, the name and address of the importer and exporter, the contents, and the country of origin. Instructions and warnings as to use and care of the product may be enclosed separately, but an invitation to read them must appear on the label. Product warranties must be clearly stated.

The following incident illustrates the confusion of Mexican labeling laws: The Mexican government announced in the *Diario Oficial* that it would require that all labels be preprinted on the product or package itself, and not on "stickers." Apparently the agency did not want Spanish language labels stuck over English language packaging. After a year of uncertainty and haggling, the *Bureau of National Affairs* reported that the government would probably accept stickers as long as they were as large and "as pretty" as the English language print. Exporters to Mexico need to seek good advice in labeling and marking products to avoid long delays in getting their goods to markets in Mexico.

Items Not Requiring Marks. Annex 301 exempts certain items from marking requirements: items incapable of being marked, items that would be injured by marking, items that cannot be marked except at a cost disproportional to the cost of the goods, items in containers that indicate the country of origin to the ultimate purchaser, crude or bulk materials, personal items for use by the importer and not intended for sale, items produced more than twenty years prior to importation, original works of art, and a few others.

Trade in Goods: Sectoral Issues

Sectoral issues are issues of concern to a particular industrial, agricultural, or service sector of the economy. Examples might be automobile manufacturing and assembly, telecommunications, agriculture, or financial services. NAFTA has specific provisions that reduce tariffs and liberalize trade and investment in these and other sectors. The most important and most controversial industry in North American trade relations is motor vehicles and parts.

Trade in Motor Vehicles and Parts

Perhaps no other sector will be affected by NAFTA as much as the automobile industry. Mexico had long tried to manage its automobile industry through strict trade and investment restrictions. For instance, prior to NAFTA, automobiles sold in Mexico had to contain a minimum of 36 percent Mexican-made parts. Tariffs were 20 percent on cars imported into Mexico and 13.2 percent on automobile parts (as compared to a 2.5 percent tariff on the import of Mexican-made cars into the United States). The result was a Mexican auto parts industry that was largely inefficient and noncompetitive in world markets. Of course, many modern automotive parts and assembly plants in Mexico are owned and operated by U.S., European, and Japanese firms. As discussed later in this chapter, cars assembled there cannot be released for sale into Mexico without meeting Mexican customs regulations and without the payment of duties. Cars assembled there from U.S. parts can only be returned to the United States at lowered tariff rates if they meet the strict requirements of U.S. customs law.

Canada and the United States eliminated duties on each other's automobiles even prior to NAFTA. By 2004, all three countries had eliminated tariffs and restrictions on automobiles, trucks, buses, and automotive parts originating in North America. However, restrictions on the cross-border trade in used cars will continue for many years to come.

Special Rules of Origin for Automobiles. To qualify for duty-free treatment, a motor vehicle that is made or assembled in North America must contain a specified percentage of North American content. For motor vehicles, these rules supersede the regional value content rules for other products, discussed earlier in the chapter.

Beginning in 2002, the content requirement for passenger cars rose to 62.5 percent. The same content requirements apply to engines and transmissions for these vehicles. Compliance with the rules requires complex calculations and the tracing of component parts throughout the supply chain. One of the major purposes of local content rules has been to encourage investment in North America. For example, Japanese manufacturers found it more efficient to build vehicles in North America than in Japan, in order to meet the North American content requirements.

Trade in Textiles and Apparel

The NAFTA textile provisions are of major significance because of the U.S. position as a major textile importer (with a large domestic industry arguing for protection from low-cost imports) and the role of Mexican plants in assembling apparel for sale in the United States. Prior to NAFTA, imports of Mexican textiles and apparel were limited by quotas in the United States and Canada. Mexico also had 20 percent tariffs on U.S. textile products. By 2004, Canada, Mexico, and the United States had phased out all quotas and tariffs on textile and apparel goods that meet the North American rules of origin. Now, textile quotas can only be used as a temporary safeguard in "emergency" situations.

As discussed in the last chapter, there are specific rules of origin covering trade in textiles. They are complex and arcane, based largely on political considerations. Even the most experienced textile manufacturers and importers require an expert customs attorney and customs broker to move textiles and apparel across borders in North America.

With the expiration of the WTO *Agreement on Textiles and Clothing* in 2005 and the end of textile quotas and most trade restrictions at the global level (other than temporary safeguards), Chinese plants have rapidly begun to take the textile and apparel business away from plants in Mexico, the Caribbean, and Central America. China has quickly become the world's leader in low-cost textile production and is the largest supplier of textiles and apparel to the United States, Europe, and Japan. The international textile industry will surely undergo many more changes in the coming years.

Trade in Agriculture

Canada is the largest purchaser of American agricultural products in the world, followed by Mexico. According to the U.S. Department of Agriculture Economic Research Service, in 2006, the United States exported more agricultural products to Canada and Mexico than to China, Japan, and the European Union countries combined. NAFTA is generally attributed to have greatly boosted U.S. agricultural exports to Canada and Mexico since 1994.

Prior to NAFTA, Mexico only permitted the import of U.S. agricultural products under a strict licensing scheme. Agricultural products were also protected by high tariff rates. The most sensitive products were corn, beans, sugar, powdered milk, and corn syrup, among many others. The United States also maintained protection on a variety of Mexican fruits and vegetable products intended to protect American farmers. NAFTA required an end to Mexico's licensing of agricultural imports and a phased-out end to tariffs. All tariffs on agricultural products originating in North America were completely eliminated by January 1, 2008. This has not been without controversy. While large-scale American producers are pleased with open access to Mexican markets, many Mexicans argue that their system of small farms is threatened. Most Mexicans would not want to think that their country would one day not be able to produce its own corn, beans, and customary foods. As the 2008 deadline went into effect, Mexican farmers launched large-scale protests in Mexico City and along the U.S. border against the elimination of tariffs.

Agricultural Rules of Origin. NAFTA tariff preferences apply only to agricultural products that originate in North America. There are special rules of origin covering North American agricultural products. For example, for fresh or frozen juice (all single fruit juices, such as orange juice) to have "originated" in North America, the juice must be made of 100 percent North American fruit. Other bulk commodities, excluding juice, can have up to 7 percent non–North American content. There are other special rules of origin for sugar refining, peanuts, vegetable oils, and dairy products. For example, only North American milk can be used to make butter, cheese, yogurt, or ice cream, traded under NAFTA preferential rates.

Government Procurement

Like many of the topics of this chapter, the basic principles of government procurement were examined in earlier chapters. NAFTA will allow North American companies to compete for contracts for the supply of goods and services to agencies of the three governments. NAFTA's government procurement rules apply to contracts for goods and services greater than $50,000 and construction contracts greater than $6.5 million. The agreement does not cover weapons, equipment, and systems needed for national defense.

When a government agency announces its request for submission of bids, it must publish the technical specifications, qualifications for suppliers, and time limits for submission. Bids from suppliers in all NAFTA countries must be treated without discrimination. Each country has established a bid protest system that allows firms to challenge procurement procedures and awards. Countries will exchange information on bidding procedures to encourage cross-border bidding, particularly from small- and medium-sized firms.

Emergency Action to Protect Domestic Industry (NAFTA Safeguards)

When NAFTA was negotiated, it was clear that increased competition from foreign firms would cause some economic disruption and job loss, particularly to inefficient, uncompetitive, and outdated companies. NAFTA permits the United States, Canada, or Mexico to take very limited *emergency action* to safeguard a domestic industry. Emergency action may be taken only where increased quantities of a particular good are a *substantial cause of serious injury, or threat thereof, to a domestic industry producing a like or directly competitive good* and only with the *consent* of the country from which the goods were exported. Generally, the right to invoke emergency safeguards under NAFTA is more limited than under GATT/WTO rules. For example, the importing country is limited to postponing any further tariff decreases under NAFTA or to increasing the import duty as is needed to remedy the injury, but in no case higher than the MFN level. In addition, the country imposing the safeguard must agree with the exporting NAFTA country on *trade compensation.* Recall from earlier chapters that trade compensation is a temporary reduction of duties on other products from the exporting NAFTA country equivalent in monetary terms to the safeguard action taken. For instance, if the United States seeks to impose higher duties on imports of, say, light bulbs from Mexico, in order to save the U.S. light bulb industry, then it will have to reduce duties on some other Mexican product, such as Mexican beer, in an equal amount.

If a NAFTA country imposes emergency safeguards on certain imported goods arriving from all WTO member countries worldwide, then these *global safeguards* may be applied to the products entering from another NAFTA country only if they comprise a *significant share of the total imports* of that type of good and contribute importantly to the serious injury.

Trade in Services

NAFTA provisions on cross-border services are aimed at facilitating trade in services in North America. The provisions affect a wide range of service providers, including transportation and package delivery, consulting, banking and insurance, and others. The principles of national treatment and MFN trade apply. No NAFTA country may require a North American service provider to have a residence or office within its borders. Each country will be able to continue to certify and license professionals, such as doctors, lawyers, and accountants; however, the countries are working to recognize the foreign credentials of a professional, especially foreign lawyers and engineers. For instance, many professional organizations from NAFTA countries are negotiating *mutual recognition agreements.* Once ratified by state and federal governments, they will permit recognition of professional licenses in all three countries. Citizenship requirements to obtain a professional license have been eliminated.

Financial Services

U.S.–Canadian cross-border investment in financial services was largely opened in 1989. Thus, the most important impact of NAFTA's financial services provisions is that they open Mexican financial service industries to investment by U.S. and Canadian companies. Banks, insurance companies, securities firms, and other financial service providers will now be able to open branches and offices throughout North America. Most restrictions were phased out by 2000, permitting 100 percent foreign ownership of Mexican financial institutions. Similar provisions apply to insurance companies (100 percent U.S. ownership of some Mexican insurance companies was permitted as early as 1996) and other finance companies (commercial credit, real estate lending, leasing, and credit card services).

Transportation

Almost 90 percent of goods sold across the 2,000-mile U.S.–Mexican border—some five million truckloads a year—move by rail or truck transportation. In the past, both U.S. and Mexican truck regulations have severely limited truck access. On the American side, Mexican truckers have been limited to a 25-mile incursion across the border. Typically, carriers on one side of the border have had to hand over their cargo to transfer companies that specialize in moving goods through customs. The trucks and cargo are thoroughly inspected for customs compliance, illegal stowaways, drug smuggling, plants, and invasive insects. After inspection and a short trip across the border, the shipments are then handed over to truckers on the other side, perhaps in San Diego or Laredo for transport to their destination, or held in a warehouse for pickup. The long lines of trucks waiting to cross have caused traffic congestion, idling engines, fuel consumption, pollution, and delays costing millions of dollars every year. Concerns over terrorism have worsened the situation.

NAFTA addresses the issue of cross-border road transportation. The agreement frees up cross-border road transportation by eliminating the intermediate transfer of cargo and eliminating the increased fees, costs, and delays that result. NAFTA does not affect regulations applied to purely domestic truck or bus transportation, and drivers will always be bound by the "rules of the road" in any foreign country in which they operate a vehicle. NAFTA does, however, permit U.S. and Canadian trucking companies to make deliveries and pickups in Mexico and permit Mexican trucking companies to have similar access to their customers north of the border. The three countries are developing common safety standards for vehicles—tires, brakes, truck and cargo weight, etc.—and driver's license certifications, including testing. NAFTA also permits the cross-border ownership of trucking companies. As of 2001, U.S. and Canadian companies were able to own a 51 percent majority interest in Mexican trucking companies and a 100 percent ownership interest after 2004.

No NAFTA provision has been more controversial or more difficult to implement than the open roads provisions. It has pitted the truckers' union, environmentalists, and Americans concerned about the safety of Mexican trucks against the trucking industry, farmers, importers and exporters, and other shippers. During the 1990s, the Clinton administration refused to admit Mexican trucks beyond the border zone until Mexican safety standards were on par with those in the United States and Canada. In the following 2001 decision, a NAFTA arbitral panel ruled that the United States was in violation of NAFTA. As you read, consider the regulatory nightmare of enforcing U.S. safety standards on millions of Mexican trucks arriving in the United States every year.

In the Matter of Cross Border Trucking

No. USA-MEX-98-2008-01 (2001)

(North American Free Trade Agreement Arbitral Panel Established Pursuant to Article 20)

BACKGROUND AND FACTS

To move goods between the United States and Mexico, shippers must typically deal with three trucking firms. Goods are shipped to a storage facility in a border town. The trailer is then detached from the tractor and picked up by a drayage company that moves it across the border, where a truck in that country picks it up to haul it to its final destination. The process is inefficient, and the border delays are a trucker's nightmare. This handing off of cargo is necessary because the United States has prohibited Mexican trucks from carrying goods through to their U.S. destination for safety reasons. According to U.S. government studies, as many as 40 percent of the five million Mexican trucks that entered the United States in 1999 failed to meet U.S. safety requirements. Mexico does not have the same rigorous standards for driver regulation and truck inspections as does the United States, nor does it register or track safety statistics on its carriers. U.S. trucks must undergo periodic safety inspections by qualified personnel employed by the trucking company. Canadian regulations are similar to those in the United States, and Canadian drivers have been permitted on U.S. highways for decades. The United States maintains that because it can inspect less than 1 percent of the Mexican trucks arriving in the United States, it cannot open its border to Mexican trucking companies until Mexico also adopts comprehensive regulatory standards as tough as those in the United States and Canada. Mexico acknowledges that when its trucks operate in the United States they must comply with U.S. standards, but that the United States cannot dictate Mexican regulatory standards. The United States also restricts Mexican investment in U.S. trucking firms. Mexico argues that the United

continued

continued

States does not treat Mexican trucks as favorably as it does trucks from the United States and Canada and that the United States has violated NAFTA open investment rules by prohibiting Mexican ownership of U.S. trucking firms. The United States counters that under NAFTA Mexican trucks must be treated the same as U.S. and Canadian trucks only where there are "like circumstances" and that Mexican regulations are so unlike those in the United States and Canada that more restrictive treatment of Mexican trucks is warranted. An arbitral panel was convened to hear the dispute in 2000.

FINAL REPORT OF THE PANEL

Mexico asserts that no NAFTA provision entitles a party to impose its own laws and regulations on the other. This would be an unacceptable interference in the sovereignty of another state, and certainly not something to which any party to NAFTA has committed. Therefore, Mexico [argues that it] is under no obligation under NAFTA to enforce U.S. standards, despite cooperation between the United States and Mexico to make the regulatory systems compatible [since 1995]. However, according to Mexico, the United States has made adoption of an identical system of motor carrier regulation a condition of NAFTA implementation, even though NAFTA contemplates that harmonization would not be a condition.

According to the United States ... Mexico cannot identify its carriers and drivers so that unsafe conduct can be properly assigned and reviewed. Without such carrier safety performance history, the United States cannot conduct a meaningful safety fitness review of Mexican carriers at the application stage. The United States also contends that it would be futile to try to perform inspections of Mexican carriers in Mexico because "Mexican carriers are not required to keep the types of records that are typically reviewed in these inspections." In contrast to Mexico's system, the United States notes that "Canada's truck safety rules and regulations are highly compatible with those of the United States." Thus, "when Canadian-based commercial trucks cross into the United States, federal and state transportation authorities can have a high level of confidence that those trucks comply with U.S. standards and requirements at least to the same degree as U.S.–based trucks. That confidence level is bolstered by a fully functioning, computerized bilateral data exchange program." Given all of these considerations, the "United States has ... concluded that the 'circumstances' relevant to the treatment of Mexican-based trucking firms for safety purposes are not 'like' those applicable to the treatment of Canadian and U.S. carriers." Accordingly, "the United States maintains that it may apply more favorable treatment to U.S. and Canadian trucking firms than to their Mexican counterparts without running afoul of Chapter Twelve's national treatment or most-favored-nation rules."

Article 1202 [national treatment] provides: *Each Party shall accord to service providers of another Party treatment no less favorable than it accords, in like circumstances, to its own service providers.* Similarly, Article 1203 [most-favored-nation] states: *Each Party shall accord to service providers of another Party treatment no less favorable than it accords, in like circumstances, to service providers of any other Party or of a non-Party.* In its most succinct terms, the disagreement between the United States on the one hand, and Mexico and Canada on the other, is over whether the "in like circumstances" language permits the United States to deny access to all Mexican trucking firms on a blanket basis, regardless of the individual qualifications of particular members of the Mexican industry, unless and until Mexico's own domestic regulatory system meets U.S. approval.

[T]he Panel is of the view that the proper interpretation of Article 1202 [and 1203] requires that differential treatment should be no greater than necessary for legitimate regulatory reasons such as safety.... Similarly, the Panel is mindful that a broad interpretation of the "in like circumstances" language could render Articles 1202 and 1203 meaningless. If, for example, the regulatory systems in two NAFTA countries must be substantially identical before national treatment is granted, relatively few service industry providers could ultimately qualify. Accordingly, the Panel concludes that the U.S. position that the "in like circumstances" language permits continuation of the moratorium on accepting applications for operating authority in the United States from Mexican owned and domiciled carriers is an overly-broad reading of that clause.

The United States claims that Mexico does not even allege that there is any interest on behalf of Mexican nationals to invest in U.S. trucking firms.... [T]he prohibition on allowing Mexican investors to acquire U.S. companies that already have operating authority, on its face, violates ... NAFTA Articles 1102 and 1103 ... even if Mexico cannot identify a particular Mexican national or nationals that have been rejected.

continued

continued

Decision. The panel unanimously held that the U.S. restrictions on the Mexican trucking industry violated NAFTA. The inadequacies of the Mexican safety regulations were not sufficient reason for the United States to refuse applications from Mexican-owned trucking companies to operate on U.S. highways. The ruling preserved the right of the United States to hold Mexican trucks to the same regulations, safety standards, and inspections as any other vehicle on U.S. roads. Mexican drivers can be required to meet the same licensing and performance standards as U.S. drivers and observe all "rules of the road." Under special situations, the United States may establish different procedures to ensure that Mexican trucks and drivers comply with U.S. law, so long as the procedures are in good faith and not more restrictive to trade than necessary. The U.S. restrictions on investment are not valid because investment does not raise a safety issue.

Comment. Was the U.S. position strictly motivated by safety concerns? American truckers and organized labor have generally been opposed to opening the border. Mexican drivers make less than their American counterparts, and the border opening places them in competition with American drivers. Do you think this affected the U.S. government's position in the 1990s?

In response to the arbitral panel decision, the Bush administration made efforts to give Mexican trucks full access to American highways. The Department of Transportation passed regulations to ensure that Mexican trucks complied with the same regulations that apply to American trucks. For example, the regulations require that all trucks comply with safety, environmental, and fuel efficiency standards. Mexican trucks are required to undergo registrations, safety inspections, and equipment checks. Drivers must have a federal license from Mexico and comply with all U.S. safety regulations, including those limiting the number of hours of continuous driving. Mexican trucking companies must implement drug and alcohol testing, maintain insurance, and keep safety-related records. U.S. law enforcement officers can run license checks on Mexican drivers. Mexican trucks may enter only at authorized points of entry when inspectors are present.

In the early 2000s, the truckers' union and environmentalists sought to block implementation of the NAFTA trucking provisions. A lawsuit was brought against the Bush administration, arguing that the administration had failed to comply with U.S. environmental laws. A federal appeals court agreed, but the United States Supreme Court unanimously reversed the decision in favor of the government. In *Department of Transportation v. Public Citizen*, 541 U.S. 752, 124 S. Ct. 2204 (2004), the Court held that the government could implement the NAFTA transportation rules without an environmental impact statement addressing issues such as the effect on increased traffic, fuel consumption, and air pollution. Despite Court approval and the efforts of the Bush administration to ensure truck and driver safety, as of 2007 the U.S. Congress had failed to gather enough support to implement the NAFTA cross-border transportation rules. Most experts, from government, industry, and universities, seem to agree that even with full implementation of the open road rules, Mexican trucks will not likely be running throughout the United States. They argue that Mexican truckers would likely want to load and unload at regional distribution centers in the southern United States, where they could easily pick up return shipments to Mexico.

Telecommunications

NAFTA eliminated all tariffs on telephones, cellular phones, and trade in telecommunications equipment by 2004. Given that the number of telephones per capita in Mexico is only a fraction of the per capita number of phones in the United States, Mexico is considered a giant untapped market for all forms of communications equipment and services. NAFTA provides that Canadian, Mexican, and U.S. telecommunications companies have nondiscriminatory access to all North American public telecommunications networks. They must be granted access to public and private (leased) lines and networks, and only conditions that are reasonable and necessary may be imposed on this access. Access to public telecommunications networks must be at rates related to the cost of operations. Technical standards may be imposed only for safety or to prevent damage to the equipment.

Mexico's telephone system had been operated as a government-owned monopoly from 1972 to 1990, as *Telefonos de Mexico*. Today the company is privately owned and is even traded on the New York Stock Exchange. In the 1990s Mexico developed a telecommunications law that ended the monopoly on telecommunications and opened the Mexican market to foreign investment. Since then, many U.S. and Canadian telecommunications companies teamed up with Mexican companies to take advantage of growing opportunities in the telecommunications market. More recently, the United States and Mexico disagreed over Mexican rules making it more difficult and costly for U.S. firms to connect international calls into Mexico. The United States complained to the World Trade Organization and requested a dispute settlement panel. In 2004 the panel ruled in favor of the United States and held that Mexican regulations discriminated against U.S. firms in violation of the *General Agreement on Trade in Services*.

Cross-Border Investment

Prior to the late 1980s, Mexico had a history of strictly regulating or even prohibiting foreign investment. For instance, Mexico required that foreign investors include local participants—Mexican stockholders or partners—in any new factory or investment venture. If a foreign firm wanted to purchase an interest in a local company, Mexico usually limited them to a minority, non-controlling interest. Mexico, as with many developing countries, has required foreign manufacturing firms located there to export finished goods to other countries for foreign currency. Investors in manufacturing companies were required to use a certain portion of domestic content in the finished goods, thus discouraging imports. Limits were placed on how much money could be transferred out of the country. A common requirement was that foreign investors had to introduce their most advanced technology to the host country.

In the 1980s, Mexico turned away from the philosophy that government control is in the best interest of the country and recognized that the threat of expropriation and nationalization of industries would drive away foreign investors. Mexico became more hospitable toward foreign investment. It still exercises some control over foreign investment, particularly in the energy and petroleum industries, telecommunications, and a few other industries, but not to the extent it did in the past.

NAFTA's Investment Provisions

NAFTA's investment provisions can be summarized as follows:

- NAFTA investors must be treated fairly, equitably, and in full accordance with basic principles of international law.
- NAFTA investors must be granted the basic protections of *most-favored-nation status* (to be treated at least as favorably as investors from outside North America), *nondiscrimination,* and *national treatment* (to be treated no less favorably than a country's own investors or domestically owned firms are treated).
- NAFTA governments must adopt *open investment policies* and eliminate most restrictions on private investment from firms based in other NAFTA countries.
- Private property of a NAFTA investor may not be expropriated by the government without due process of law and the payment of fair compensation.
- Private investors may request an arbitral tribunal to hear an *investor claim* for money damages against a NAFTA country for violating the NAFTA investment provisions. NAFTA countries may invoke other procedures for settling investment disputes between themselves.

NAFTA's Open Investment Policies. Investors from all three countries can now establish new companies and purchase existing ones across North American borders. In addition, NAFTA sets limits on the government regulation of North American–owned companies. (These provisions were largely intended to break down the investment barriers in Mexico.) No NAFTA country can require a minimum level of local participation or ownership by nationals (other than in certain industries in which exceptions to this rule have been reserved). No NAFTA country may place restrictions on the conversion of foreign exchange and transfer of money between accounts in another NAFTA country. Similarly, no country may either require or prohibit a firm from transferring profits earned by a subsidiary in one NAFTA country to another NAFTA country. There can be no *performance requirements* on a NAFTA investor, such as minimum export requirements (where the host government requires foreign-owned firms to export a certain percentage of goods or services produced by the local subsidiary) or domestic content or purchasing requirements (where the host government requires that a minimum percentage of raw materials used in local operations be purchased from local companies). Governments may not require that parent companies in one NAFTA country transfer advanced technology (via patents, licensing, or "know-how" agreements) to a subsidiary in another NAFTA country, and they may not require that senior managers and corporate directors be of any particular nationality.

Environmental Measures Applicable to Investments. Mexico does not have the strict environmental laws that the United States has. For many U.S. firms, compliance with U.S. laws can be costly. When NAFTA was negotiated, heated debate surrounded the issue of whether U.S. companies, especially polluting ones, would flock to open plants in Mexico to avoid U.S. law. As a compromise in the negotiations, NAFTA provides that "it is inappropriate to encourage investment by relaxing domestic health, safety, or environmental measures. Accordingly, a [NAFTA country] should not waive ... such measures as an encouragement for the establishment, acquisition, expansion or retention in its territory of an investment."

Exceptions to the Investment Agreement. Canada reserved the right to review acquisitions of local companies of $150 million (Canadian) or more under the *Investment Canada Act.* Mexico also retained the right to review acquisitions worth $150 million or more. Mexico also may restrict ownership of land, cable television companies, air and land transportation, oil production and refining, and retail sales of gasoline and oil. The United States excluded investments in nuclear power, broadcasting, mining, customs brokerages, and air transportation and may block the takeover of U.S. firms on the basis of national security.

Protecting Investors from Expropriation. The legal requirement that governments must compensate owners of private property whose property is taken for public use is a virtually universal concept. It is based on the notion that at times governments must take private property for public purposes, or for uses like conservation or environmental protection, and that the property owners should not have to shoulder the cost of the public welfare. NAFTA Article 1110 states that no NAFTA country may expropriate property of a NAFTA investor, unless it is done pursuant to internationally accepted rules, that is, that private property may only be taken for a public purpose or for public use on a nondiscriminatory basis, using procedures that are open, fair, and in accordance with due process of law, and fair compensation must be paid according to the market value of the property taken.

The following case, *Metalclad Corp. v. The United Mexican States,* is one of the most interesting and controversial cases to come out of NAFTA. This is a case involving a U.S. firm that attempted to build a hazardous waste landfill in Mexico. It was told that all permits necessary to build the facility had been obtained. After making significant progress to complete the project, the municipality where the landfill was claimed one additional permit was missing and the state issued a decree turning the property into a wildlife refuge. Work was ordered stopped and Metalclad requested that an arbitral tribunal award damages.

Investor Claims and Dispute Settlement Procedures. *Investor claims* are actions for damages brought by a NAFTA investor before an arbitral tribunal against a host NAFTA government for having violated NAFTA investment rules. Investor suits may be brought either under the arbitration rules of the UN Commission on International

Metalclad Corporation v. The United Mexican States

International Centre for the Settlement of Investment Disputes No. ARB(AF)/97/1

Award of the Arbitral Tribunal (August 30, 2000)

BACKGROUND AND FACTS

In 1993, a Mexican firm, Coterin, received a permit from the Mexican government to build a hazardous waste treatment plant in the La Pedrera valley in the state of San Luis Potosi, near the city of Guadalcazar. Metalclad, a U.S. company, was interested in acquiring Coterin. Several Mexican government authorities assured Metalclad that Coterin had obtained all required construction permits for the facility. One month later Metalclad purchased Coterin. In 1994, amid much opposition to the plant from local residents and environmental protestors, the city of Guadalcazar ordered a halt to construction, claiming that no municipal permit had been obtained. Metalclad responded that the Mexican federal government had told it that no further state or municipal permits were needed. Metalclad even promised to create a reserve for native species, create a local scientific advisory council, give discounts for local waste, contribute to local charities, and provide some free medical services to local residents. But, without reason, the city informed Metalclad that it could not begin operation. In 1997, the state governor issued a decree designating the landfill as a protected ecological and wildlife area, putting an end to Metalclad's business there. Having expended $16.5 million on the project, Metalclad requested that a NAFTA arbitral tribunal be convened to resolve the dispute. The company maintained that it had not been given fair and equitable treatment, that the Mexican regulations lacked transparency, and that Mexico had in fact expropriated their property without payment of fair compensation.

AWARD OF THE ARBITRAL TRIBUNAL

For the reasons set out below, the Tribunal finds that Metalclad's investment was not accorded fair and equitable treatment in accordance with international law, and that Mexico has violated NAFTA Article 1105(1).

Prominent in the statement of principles and rules that introduces NAFTA is the reference to "transparency." The Tribunal understands this to include the idea that all relevant legal requirements for the purpose of initiating, completing and successfully operating investments made, or intended to be made, under NAFTA should be capable of being readily known to all affected investors. There should be no room for doubt or uncertainty on such matters.... The absence of a clear rule as to the requirement or not of a municipal construction permit, as well as the absence of any established practice or procedure as to the manner of handling applications for a municipal construction permit, amounts to a failure on the part of Mexico to ensure the transparency required by NAFTA. Metalclad was entitled to rely on the representations of federal officials and to believe that it was entitled to continue its construction of the landfill. Moreover, the permit was denied at a meeting of the Municipal Town Council of which Metalclad received no notice, to which it received no invitation, and at which it was given no opportunity to appear. The Town Council denied the permit for reasons which included, but may not have been limited to, the opposition of the local population, the fact that construction had already begun when the application was submitted ... and the ecological concerns regarding the environmental effect and impact on the site and surrounding communities. None of the reasons included a reference to any problems associated with the physical construction of the landfill or to any physical defects therein. The Tribunal therefore finds that the construction permit was denied without any consideration of, or specific reference to, construction aspects or flaws of the physical facility.

Mexico failed to ensure a transparent and predictable framework for Metalclad's business planning and investment. The totality of these circumstances demonstrates a lack of orderly process and timely disposition in relation to an investor of a Party acting in the expectation that it would be treated fairly and justly in accordance with the NAFTA. The Tribunal therefore holds that Metalclad was not treated fairly or equitably under the NAFTA and succeeds on its claim under Article 1105.

NAFTA provides that "no party shall directly or indirectly ... expropriate an investment ... or take a measure tantamount to ... expropriation ... except: (a) for a public purpose; (b) on a nondiscriminatory basis; (c) in accordance with due process of law and Article 1105(1); and (d) on payment of compensation. Thus, expropriation under NAFTA includes

continued

continued

not only open, deliberate and acknowledged takings of property, such as outright seizure or formal or obligatory transfer of title in favor of the host State, but also covert or incidental interference with the use of property which has the effect of depriving the owner, in whole or in significant part, of the use or reasonably to be expected economic benefit of property even if not necessarily to the obvious benefit of the host State. By permitting or tolerating the conduct of Guadalcazar ... Mexico must be held to have taken a measure tantamount to expropriation in violation of NAFTA.

NAFTA provides for the award of monetary damages and applicable interest where a Party is found to have violated a Chapter 11 provision. With respect to expropriation, NAFTA specifically requires compensation to be equivalent to the fair market value of the expropriated investment immediately before the expropriation took place. However, where the enterprise has not operated for a sufficiently long time to establish a performance record or where it has failed to make a profit, future profits cannot be used to determine going concern or fair market value. Rather, the Tribunal agrees with the parties that fair market value is best arrived at in this case by reference to Metalclad's actual investment in the project. For the reasons stated above, the Tribunal hereby decides that the Respondent shall pay to Metalclad the amount of $16,685,000.

Decision. Through the actions of city, state, and federal officials, Mexico had violated Metalclad's investor rights. The Mexican regulations were not transparent, the procedures were unfair, and Mexico's actions were an indirect expropriation of Metalclad's property. As a U.S. investor in Mexico, Metalclad was not granted fair and equitable treatment.

Trade Law (UNCITRAL) or, as in the *Metalclad* award, the International Centre for the Settlement of Investment Disputes (ICSID). The ICSID is an organization closely allied with the World Bank and is headquartered in Washington, D.C. Investor suits may be brought by either citizens or corporations of another NAFTA country or by investors from other countries that have substantial business activities in a NAFTA country. For example, if a parent company in Sweden owns an incorporated subsidiary company in the United States, then the U.S. subsidiary may make investments in Canada or Mexico according to the open investment policies of NAFTA. Investors may bring suits for monetary damages (no punitive damages are allowed) or restitution of property, but not to force a government to change its laws or policies (as can a WTO panel wherein the cases are brought by complaining governments). There are usually three arbiters, selected by the parties, and their awards are binding on the parties. The awards are effective only for that case and do not establish binding rules that countries must follow in future disputes. NAFTA governments may also bring dispute actions against each other, not for damages, but to compel compliance with NAFTA rules.

Other NAFTA Provisions

In negotiating NAFTA, the United States was able to see the broader implications of free trade and investment in North America. For instance, what if an unscrupulous company in Mexico produces counterfeit software and smuggles it across the border in violation of the copyrights of a U.S. company? Or suppose that a firm emits poisonous gas or pollutants from a smokestack at its Mexican plant, and they are carried by air currents to the United States? What if the top managements of several competing companies meet in Denver or Mexico City and fix consumer prices for a product that they all make? Although these problems undoubtedly occurred before NAFTA and are tremendous issues that no one trade agreement is likely to change, the U.S. negotiators of the agreement used the opportunity to address them openly.

Intellectual Property Rights

Intellectual property rights (IPRs) are generally protected by national law, but as discussed in previous chapters, IPRs are the subject of several international conventions (e.g., the *Berne Convention*) and agreements (e.g., GATT/TRIPS). Intellectual property is covered in greater detail in Part Four of this book. NAFTA adopts the basic tenets of these international agreements and builds upon them. NAFTA's provisions protect the IPRs of North American firms. No country can make citizenship a requirement for IPR protection. Applicants for trademarks, copyrights, and patents must be treated equally and without discrimination. NAFTA guarantees that any IPR is freely transferable by the owner to another party.

Trademarks. Trademarks and service marks are protected under NAFTA for ten years and can be renewed indefinitely. The owner of a registered trademark has the right to prevent others from using identical or similar signs for goods or services if it would result in a *likelihood of confusion* (which is presumed unless the offender can prove otherwise). Specific provisions prohibit the use of the names of geographical regions (e.g., Tennessee Whiskey), unless the products are actually derived from that area. Actual use of a trademark cannot be a condition for filing an application for registration. NAFTA requires fair procedures for obtaining a trademark, including notice and an opportunity to be heard. Registration may be canceled if the trademark is not used for an uninterrupted period of at least two years.

Copyrights. Copyrights are protected equally in all three countries. Computer programs are protected as literary works, and motion pictures and sound recordings are protected for fifty years. (Canada has made some exceptions for "cultural industries.") NAFTA prohibits the importation of copies of a sound recording made without the producers' authorization.

Patents. Patents must be made available for any invention "in all fields of technology" (including pharmaceuticals), whether it is a product or process. It must be new, result from an inventive step (be "nonobvious"), and be capable of industrial application (be "useful"). They are effective for a period of twenty years from the date of application or seventeen years from the date when the patent was granted.

Enforcement and Penalties. NAFTA requires that each country enforce its IPR laws, both internally and at the border to prevent smuggling of counterfeit items. IPR owners will be able to protect their rights through administrative action and judicial relief. Courts will have the authority to order seizure and destruction of infringing items, to issue injunctions against their sale, and to permit lawsuits for damages against infringers. The NAFTA countries must provide criminal penalties for cases in which willful trademark counterfeiting or copyright piracy occurs on a commercial scale. Penalties may include imprisonment or monetary fines or both.

Environmental Cooperation and Enforcement

The *North American Agreement on Environmental Cooperation* (NAAEC) does not set environmental or ecological standards, as does national law, but it does call for the three countries to cooperate in protecting the environment. The countries have promised to enforce their laws more effectively. They also promise to develop environmental emergency procedures and to share information on protecting the environment. They are also working to develop common environmental standards. All countries must notify the others before banning a pesticide or chemical, and afterward, all are urged to prohibit the export of such products to other countries.

The NAAEC created the *North American Commission for Environmental Cooperation* (CEC) to oversee this portion of the agreement. The commission is headed by a council made up of three cabinet-level officers of the three governments. The commission may convene panels to resolve disputes between countries. The arbitral panels can authorize tariff increases against a country that fails to enforce its environmental laws or is otherwise found in violation of the environmental provisions of the agreement, or can impose a monetary penalty (fine).

One of NAFTA's first environmental cases was reported in *The Journal of Commerce* in 1995. The CEC was called upon to investigate the death of 40,000 wild birds in Mexico. The commission acted quickly to determine the cause—apparently the birds died from the industrial dumping of either chromium or red dye—and made recommendations in order to protect other migratory birds that were due to return to the area. Mexico took quick action as a result of the commission's investigation. It was the first time in North America that authorities from other countries investigated an environmental disaster solely within another country. However, no one knows yet how willing Canada, Mexico, and the United States will be in the future to opening these types of incidents to NAFTA investigations.

Labor Cooperation and Worker Rights

Many people worried that NAFTA would cause U.S. companies to move to Mexico to take advantage of cheap labor and weakly enforced labor laws. With this in mind, the United States insisted on a side agreement called the *North American Agreement on Labor Cooperation* (NAALC), intended to make labor policies more uniform by promoting the following basic labor principles in the region:

- Freedom of association and right to organize
- Right to bargain collectively
- Right to strike
- Prohibition of forced labor
- Protection for children and young persons
- Minimum working conditions
- Elimination of employment discrimination
- Equal pay for women and men
- Prevention of accidents and occupational disease and injuries, and compensation to workers
- Protection of migrant workers

NAFTA does not set specific rules or domestic labor standards but requires countries to enforce those standards that they already have. Indeed, Mexico's labor laws meet all international standards. The problems lie in the enforcement of their laws, notably in the *maquiladoras* and factories along the border region. A *North American Labor Commission for Labor Cooperation* was created to oversee the agreement and to promote cooperation in labor issues. The commission is headed by a council consisting of the U.S. Secretary of Labor and labor ministers from the other countries. An arbitral panel may be convened to investigate issues involving worker health or safety, the abuse of child labor, or the failure to enforce minimum wage laws, and it may make recommendations for solutions and impose fines.

There is some criticism of the efficacy of this agreement. One attorney quoted in *The Wall Street Journal* who litigated five cases before the NAO (National Administrative Office) noted:

> Technically speaking in all cases we won. But in all cases workers are left with a piece of paper that says "you were right." Not a single worker was ever reinstated, not a single employer was sanctioned, no union was ever recognized.

At best, the agreement provides a forum to discuss disputes. Many labor groups are poised to push vigorously for new safeguards in any future agreements.

Antitrust and Competition Policy

Antitrust laws, also called *competition laws,* prohibit illegal monopoly control of industries, price fixing, and a range of anticompetitive and unfair business practices. Both the United States and Canada have long had strong antitrust laws. Mexico adopted an antitrust law in 1993. NAFTA countries agreed to cooperate in the enforcement of these antitrust laws, including mutual legal assistance, consultations, and exchange of information. For industries in which the countries permit legal monopolies, such as Mexico's state-owned oil company, NAFTA sets rules to minimize the anticompetitive impact of the monopoly on other industries.

Rights to Temporary Entry

Unlike the European Union, NAFTA does not create a common market in labor. Each country may still determine its own qualifications for employment and its own immigration policies. NAFTA countries, however, have agreed to give businesspeople easy access to their customers, clients, factories, and offices across the borders. NAFTA permits temporary entry in the following cases:

1. Business visitors engaged in international business activities related to research, manufacturing, marketing, sales, and distribution; those who are service providers; and those servicing

products after the sale (repair or maintenance of products after the sale must be done pursuant to a warranty or other service contract on the products)
2. Traders employed by a company in a NAFTA country and those who are buying and selling substantial amounts of goods and services
3. Potential investors
4. Management or executive employees transferred to subsidiary companies in another NAFTA country
5. Qualified professionals (in sixty-three professions, ranging from teachers and lawyers to hotel managers) entering to do business (separate licensing qualifications must also be met if they intend to practice a profession)

Mexico requires these travelers to obtain the FMN card (*Formularia Migratorio* NAFTA), which is valid for thirty days. Special visas are available for periods of stay longer than thirty days. Normal tourist cards are still available.

Administration and Dispute Settlement

NAFTA does not have the type of lawmaking institutions that the EU has. However, an administrative body oversees implementation of the agreement, and a dispute resolution process is available to NAFTA countries. The dispute resolution process is similar to that at the WTO.

NAFTA Fair Trade Commission

The *Fair Trade Commission* supervises the implementation of the agreement and attempts to resolve disputes that may arise regarding its interpretation or application. One cabinet-level official from each of the three governments, supported by an administrative staff and committees, form the commission.

Arbitral Panels. When one NAFTA country accuses another of violating NAFTA's principles, it must first attempt to negotiate a settlement. If a settlement is not reached, then the countries can seek dispute resolution. When the issue falls under both NAFTA and GATT, the countries must agree on whether it will be heard by the NAFTA Fair Trade Commission or the WTO. If they cannot agree on which forum, the case will normally be heard before the Fair Trade Commission. If a settlement is not reached, the commission may convene an *arbitral panel,* which consists of five members who are experts in trade or law. They decide whether one country has violated NAFTA and recommend a solution. If the recommendations of the arbitral panel are not followed and no agreement is reached within thirty days, the complaining country may retaliate by raising tariffs, but no panel has the authority to tell a country to actually change its laws or policies. For example, if a panel rules that a regulation of the U.S. Consumer Product Safety Commission, the National Park Service, or other agency is violating NAFTA, an individual cannot obtain a court order compelling the agency to alter its decision solely on the basis of the panel report.

Antidumping and Countervailing Duty Cases. The Fair Trade Commission also hears cases involving countervailing and antidumping duties. These cases are treated differently from other disputes. Recall that *countervailing duties* are imposed on imported goods that received an unfair price advantage because a part of their cost of production was subsidized by the exporting country. *Antidumping duties* are imposed on "dumped" products. Dumping, another unfair trade practice, is the selling of goods in a foreign market for less than the price charged in the country in which they were produced. Antidumping and countervailing duties are only imposed pursuant to an order of an administrative agency in the importing country.

This practice will continue under NAFTA; however, the appellate process has been changed greatly. In the United States, an appeal of an agency decision in an international trade case normally goes to the U.S. Court of International Trade, but appeals from administrative orders in NAFTA cases now go to NAFTA *binational panels,* not to courts of law. The role of these panels and their standard of review in reviewing agency decisions are limited. Binational panels apply the same standard of review as would a court of law convened in the country where the case originated. Because it is not an appellate court, a panel does not make law in the traditional sense, but applies the existing law of the country from which the case was appealed. This legal process is quite unusual and controversial, because private businesses will be bound by the decision of an intergovernmental panel with no recourse to judicial review. The *Synthetic Baler Twine* case illustrates the appellate function of a binational panel in a dumping case.

Extraordinary Challenge Committees. Appeals of a binational panel decision may be taken only to a NAFTA *Extraordinary Challenge Committee,* and not to courts of law. A challenge committee examines a case only to see if a panelist was biased or guilty of misconduct, or whether the panel departed from a fundamental rule of procedure, or *exceeded its powers, authority, or jurisdiction.* A binational panel must apply the correct standard of review. Under NAFTA, a binational panel that fails to apply the correct standard of review would

Synthetic Baler Twine with a Knot Strength of 200 lbs or Less Originating in or Exported from the United States of America

CDA-94-1904-02; (NAFTA Binational Panel, 1995)

BACKGROUND AND FACTS

Poli-Twine and other Canadian twine manufacturers filed an antidumping complaint in Canada against synthetic baler twine imported from the United States. The Canadian International Trade Tribunal found that the twine was causing material injury to the production of like goods in Canada. Bridon Cordage, a U.S. exporter of twine, challenged the Tribunal's decision on the grounds that the Tribunal committed an error in applying a Canadian statute, the *Special Import Measures Act* (SIMA). A NAFTA Binational Panel was requested. Three aspects of the panel's decision are discussed here: (1) the standard of review; (2) whether the Tribunal properly determined that the dumping had injured Canadian industry; and (3) whether the Tribunal properly determined that the dumped goods are likely to cause injury in the future. The panel applied Canadian law because it was reviewing a decision of a Canadian government agency.

DECISION OF THE PANEL

This Binational Panel was constituted pursuant to Chapter 19 of the North American Free Trade Agreement (NAFTA) to review a finding of the Canadian International Trade Tribunal (the Tribunal). The Tribunal found that the dumping of synthetic baler twine exported from the United States of America had caused and was likely to cause material injury to the production of like goods in Canada.

I. STANDARD OF REVIEW

Binational Panels are directed by NAFTA Article 1904(3) to apply the standard of review set out in the general legal principles that a court of the importing party [Canada] otherwise would apply to a review of a determination of the competent investigating authority. In the case of Canada ... the standard of review is set forth in the [Canadian] *Federal Court Act*.... [The Act] provides that the Tribunal's decisions will be reviewed on the grounds that it: (a) acted without jurisdiction, acted beyond its jurisdiction or refused to exercise its jurisdiction; (b) failed to observe a principle of natural justice, procedural fairness or other procedure that is required by law to observe; (c) erred in law in making a decision or order, whether or not the error appears on the face of the record; (d) based its decision or order on an erroneous finding of fact that it made in a perverse or capricious manner or without regard for the material before it; (e) acted, or failed to act, by reason of fraud or perjured evidence; or (f) acted in any other way that was contrary to law.

Complainants contend that, because binational Panels are themselves expert in international trade, the Tribunal is not entitled to the same degree of deference that ordinarily would be accorded to it by the [Canadian] Federal Court. The Panel disagrees. Pursuant to the NAFTA Binational Panel review replaces judicial review by domestic courts in certain defined circumstances. NAFTA provides: The Panel shall apply the standard of review set out in NAFTA

continued

continued

Annex 1911 and the general legal principles that a court of the importing Party otherwise would apply to a review of a determination of the competent investigating authority. NAFTA Annex 1911 states that the standard of review for Canada means "the grounds set out in subsection 18.1(4) of the Federal Court Act." Under section 18.1(4) the Federal Court is obliged by law to give "considerable deference" to the decisions of the Tribunal. In fulfilling their mandate to "apply the standard of review . . . that a court of the importing Party otherwise would apply" binational Panels are obliged to apply the same standard that would be used by the Federal Court.

The Panel holds that the requirement that Panelists be familiar with international trade law under paragraph 1 of the NAFTA, Annex 1902.2 is not intended to modify the standard of deference that is ordinarily accorded an expert tribunal. The requirement that Panelists be familiar with international trade law assists Panelists to fulfil their mandate by making it easier for them to understand the types of issues that are dealt with by the Tribunal. . . .

II. ERRORS OF LAW AND FACT

Complainants contend that the Tribunal erroneously violated its legal duty under the Special Import Measures Act (SIMA) by failing to [determine all possible factors that could have caused injury to the Canadian twine industry]. This would have essentially required the Tribunal to quantify each and every factor that might be a cause of material injury, not limited to dumped goods from the United States. . . .

It is true that the effects of dumping must be segregated from other causes, and the Tribunal is required under SIMA to determine whether the dumped goods are a cause of material injury. However, neither SIMA, nor the GATT rules as incorporated in SIMA, require that the other causes be calculated or quantified beyond what is necessary to assure that injury from dumped goods is not being attributed to those other causes. . . . Of course, there may be other factors which may have contributed to the injury. As a matter of common sense, it seems to me that there almost always will be. Such matters as efficiency [of Canadian twine producers], quality, cost control, marketing ability, accuracy in forecasting, good luck and a host of others come to mind. It is the function of a specialized tribunal such as the Canadian International Trade Tribunal to weigh and balance those factors and to decide the importance to be given to each.

III. FUTURE INJURY

The amount of evidence required in order to sustain the Tribunal's findings of fact is modest. This, however, does not mean the Tribunal's determination will be upheld in the absence of any evidence in the record to support its conclusions. Such is the situation we find here.

While . . . it may be logical to assume that injury will continue as long as conditions remain the same, we are unwilling to hold that such an assumption is the equivalent of evidence. The Tribunal here based its conclusion on the "belief" that Poli-Twine will [in the future] be faced with the same market conditions as in the recent past . . . and the view that as long as the U.S. has excess production, injury will continue. These assertions may or may not be true, and if so would appear to support a conclusion of future injury, but there are not—on the basis of anything that has been brought to our attention in the briefs or oral argument—in the record as established facts. The references in the record offered in support amount to conjecture, falling short of evidence.

Decision. The Panel affirmed the Canadian Tribunal's determination that the sale of U.S. twine in Canada at unfairly low prices caused past injury to Canadian twine producers. But the Panel held that there was not sufficient evidence to support the Tribunal's conclusion that injury would continue in the future. The case was remanded to the Tribunal to reconsider new evidence on the question of future injury. The Panel applied the same standard of review that a Canadian appellate court would have applied if a court had been reviewing the case.

Comment. When reviewing an order from a U.S. agency, a NAFTA Panel applies U.S. standards for judicial review. In *Live Swine from Canada*, USA-94-1904-01 (May 30, 1995), a NAFTA panel stated that "The Panel steps into the shoes of the Court of International Trade and the Court of Appeals for the Federal Circuit and is to apply the standards and the substantive law that those courts apply when they review a . . . determination by the Department of Commerce. This in turn means that the Panel is to hold unlawful 'any determination, finding or conclusion found . . . to be *unsupported by substantial evidence*.' . . . The Panel is not to substitute its own judgment, and the only question before it is whether the agency's action had appropriate support in fact and/or law."

be considered to have exceeded its powers, authority, or jurisdiction.

Panelists for binational panels and extraordinary challenge committees are chosen from a roster of impartial judges or former judges whenever possible.

Production Sharing: Assembly Plants and the Mexican *Maquiladoras*

The process of spreading manufacturing and assembly operations across international borders is often called *production sharing,* a term coined by business theorist Peter Drucker. One type of production sharing involves the manufacture or fabrication of articles or component parts in one country and their assembly into finished goods in another country. While this is not a part of NAFTA, production sharing is discussed in this chapter because of its importance to industry and trade in North America and the entire Western Hemisphere. Historically, global manufacturing firms have invested in manufacturing operations in developed countries that offered higher-skilled workers, technology, capital investment, research and development, quality control, and state-of-the-art production and management methods, as well as political and economic stability. The manufactured articles were then shipped to "assembly plants" in lower-wage countries for assembly into the final product.

To economists and management theorists, production sharing makes perfect economic sense. It allows countries to specialize in what they do best, be it research and development, highly skilled manufacturing, or low-wage labor. Production sharing also has been a major force for investment, employment, and the transfer of technology and know-how to developing countries. Today, modern production sharing techniques are integral to efficient global manufacturing operations and supply chain management.

Since the mid-1960s, U.S. legislation has encouraged the manufacture of articles in the United States and their assembly in foreign plants. Section 9802 of the *Harmonized Tariff Schedules of the United States* contains a special provision allowing U.S.–made articles or component parts to be shipped to factories in a foreign country where the articles are assembled or joined to other articles and then returned to the United States with duties assessed only on the value of the newly assembled product less the value of the U.S.–made component parts. In essence, import duties are placed only on the low-wage labor and the relatively inexpensive overhead of the foreign plants. For example, a cellular telephone manufacturer can assemble a telephone in a Mexican assembly plant, using parts sourced from North America and from other countries, and then reexport the finished telephone to the United States. Tariffs on the telephone are based on the value of the phone, less the value of the U.S. component parts.

Foreign assembly operations are common in industries that produce electronic goods, home furnishings and appliances, automobiles and automotive parts, textiles and apparel, and many others. Assembly plants can be locally owned or owned by companies from the United States or other countries. They can be located in countries all over the world, although most are located in low-wage countries. Many are located in Mexico. Some of the largest users of assembly plants are Delphi Automotive, General Electric, Ford, General Motors, Siemens, Sony, Whirlpool, Sanyo, Samsung, Motorola, Daewoo, Hyundai, Bose, Mattel, Fisher Price, Toshiba, and Nokia, to name just a few common brand names among hundreds.

During the 1990s, automobile firms from all over the world invested heavily in assembly plants in Japan, Canada, Sweden, Germany, and Mexico, while the electronics and apparel industries invested heavily in Asia, Mexico, and the Caribbean. Production-sharing plants are also called *offshore assembly plants,* or in the case of Mexico, *border plants,* because of their location along the U.S. border. The Spanish term is *maquiladora,* derived from the word *maquilar,* meaning "to process." Production-sharing plants are common not only in Mexico, but also throughout the Caribbean and Central America. Plants in Mexico have the advantage of being located close to the U.S. border, accessible by road and rail transportation. Proximity to the United States means faster shipping, lower inventory requirements, and lower transportation costs. This is particularly important for industries assembling products with short shelf lives, products that can quickly become obsolete, or for managing just-in-time inventory in global manufacturing. Many Asian firms have taken advantage of assembly operations in Mexico, giving them a platform for shipping throughout North America, as well as to Central and South America.

Assembly Plant Tariff Rules

Under Section 9802, the tariff assessed on an assembled article upon re-importation to the United States is calculated on the value of the newly assembled article less the value of the U.S.–made component parts. These tariff savings are available only where the imports were assembled in the foreign plant (1) from U.S.–manufactured or fabricated components (2) that had been exported "ready for assembly without further fabrication" and (3) that have not lost their physical identity and have not been advanced in value or improved in condition abroad except by being assembled and except "by operations incidental to the assembly process" such as cleaning, trimming, calibrating, or lubricating.

Examples of fabricated components that would qualify as being ready for assembly without losing their physical identity include circuit boards, machine parts, semiconductors, precut parts of wearing apparel, lug nuts, and automobile engines or tires. Sending bolts of fabric abroad to be cut into parts of shirts does not qualify as assembly, but sewing two sleeves to the body of a shirt does. It is not "assembly" when lumber, leather, or plastic is sent abroad to be formed into new and different articles that will become components of finished goods. Section 9802 applies only to assembly operations, which include any method of joining two or more solid articles, such as welding, screwing, gluing, or sewing. Combining chemicals, liquids, gases, or food ingredients is not considered assembly. In addition to automobiles and clothing, other representative products include telecommunications and electronic equipment, computers, televisions, sausage casings, mini-blinds, stuffed toys, and almost any product capable of assembly. In *Samsonite Corp. v. United States,* the operations of the plant were held to be a fabrication and not a mere assembly.

Mexican Regulation of *Maquiladoras*. The *maquila* industry is governed by regulations and decrees of the Mexican government. These regulations are intended to promote Mexico's competitiveness in assembly and manufacturing

Samsonite Corp. v. United States
889 F.2d 1074 (1989)
United States Court of Appeals (Fed.Cir.)

BACKGROUND AND FACTS
Samsonite Corporation assembles luggage in Mexico for import into the United States. Many component parts used in the assembly process are made in the United States. Samsonite had shipped steel strips from the United States to Mexico for use as luggage handles. When the strips left the United States, they were five inches long, straight, and bearing a coat of oil. Their value ranged from 95 cents to $1.26. In Mexico, the strips were bent by machine into a form resembling a square-sided letter *C*, cleaned, covered with a vinyl sheath, and riveted to plastic frame assemblies. The assemblies were then placed in, and fastened to, bags of vinyl to make soft luggage. On import into the United States, the Customs Service dutied the luggage, including the value of the steel strips at the rate of 20 percent *ad valorem.* The Court of International Trade upheld the government's contention that the steel strips had not been "exported in a condition ready for assembly" and that the process in Mexico amounted to a fabrication and more than a mere assembly. Samsonite appealed.

SENIOR CIRCUIT JUDGE FRIEDMAN
To obtain a deduction for American-fabricated articles assembled abroad, the components

a. must have been exported from the United States "in condition ready for assembly without further fabrication,"

continued

continued

b. not have lost their physical identity in the articles by change in form, shape, or otherwise, and
c. not have been advanced in value or improved in condition "except by being assembled" and except "by operations incidental to the assembly process such as cleaning, lubricating, and painting."

As the Court of International Trade correctly pointed out, since the "foregoing three conditions for a deduction are set forth in the conjunctive, ... each must be satisfied before a component can qualify for duty-free treatment." We agree with that court that the steel strips involved in this case did not meet those conditions.

The critical inquiry is whether the bending and shaping that the strips underwent constituted "fabrication" or mere assembly and operations incidental to the assembly process. We hold that what was done to the strips in Mexico was fabrication and not mere assembly.

When the steel strips were exported from the United States, they were just that: five-inch strips that could not serve as the frame of the luggage without undergoing a complete change in shape. Prior to assembling the luggage, the strips were bent by machine into a carefully and specially configured rectangular shape that was necessary before the original strip would serve its ultimate function as part of the frame of the luggage.

In short, what emerged after the bending operation was a different object from that which left the United States. The latter was a steel strip, the former was a metal frame for a piece of luggage. The transformation of the strip in this manner into a luggage frame was a fabrication. The strips therefore had not been exported from the United States "in condition ready for assembly without further fabrication."

Samsonite contends, however, that prior decisions of the Court of Customs and Patent Appeals require a contrary conclusion. It relies particularly on *General Instrument Corp. v. United States,* 499 F.2d 1318 (CCPA 1974). That case involved wire wound on spools that had been exported from the United States to Taiwan. There the wire was removed from the spools, formed into a horizontal coil by a winding machine, taped to prevent unraveling, dipped in cement, dried, precision shaped, removed from the spools, and wound around a core. The end product made from the wire was a component of a television set that was imported into the United States.

The Court of Customs and Patent Appeals held that: "The steps performed upon the wire after its exportation to Taiwan are not 'further fabrication' steps, but rather assembly steps within the meaning of [the statute]."

Samsonite argues that far more was done to the wire in *General Instrument* than was done to the steel strips in this case. It argues that if the processing the wire underwent in *General Instrument* was not "fabrication," a fortiori "the one simple-minded act of bending a straight frame into a C was neither a further fabrication nor a nonincidental operation."

The critical inquiry in determining whether fabrication rather than mere assembly took place here, is not the amount of processing that occurred in the two cases, but its nature. In *General Instrument,* the wire, when it left the United States and when it returned as part of a finished product, was a coil. The wire was taken directly from the supply spool on which it was wound and, after processing, was used in assembling the TV set components. The wire underwent no basic change in connection with its incorporation into the television set component.

In contrast, in the present case the steel strips had to undergo a significant change in shape before the actual assembly of luggage could begin. Until the steel strips had been made into C shapes they could not be used as a part of the luggage. Unlike the "assembly" that the court in *General Instrument* held the processing of the wire involved, here "further fabrication" of the steel strips was required in order to change them into frames for luggage, before the assembly of the luggage could take place.

Decision. The Court of Appeals upheld the decision of the lower court. The bending and processing of the steel strips in Mexico was fabrication and not a mere assembly and therefore did not qualify for duty-free treatment under Section 9802.

Comment. In *United States v. Haggar Apparel Co.,* 526 U.S. 380, 119 S. Ct. 1392 (1999), the United States Supreme Court upheld regulations of the U.S. Customs Service (19 C.F.R. 10.16) that permapressing of men's pants was an additional step in manufacturing and not a minor operation incidental to assembly.

and to promote exports by giving tariff and tax incentives to Mexican exporters. *Maquiladoras* are chief beneficiaries of the incentives. The incentives include the elimination or reduction of tariffs on imports of certain component parts or raw materials destined for reexport as finished goods. The duty reductions apply only to products in select industry sectors. In order to qualify for favorable tariff treatment, a Mexican company must meet complex regulatory and tax law requirements that require companies to rely on sophisticated legal and accounting advice.

Mexico's tariff incentives for exporting firms have changed several times in recent years. In large part, the changes are due to changes in NAFTA rules. In 2007, the Mexican Ministry of the Economy merged the *maquila* program with another government export program into the *Maquiladora Manufacturing Industry and Export Services Program*, or IMMEX. The IMMEX law covers eligibility requirements for IMMEX companies and their certification, operation, taxation, inspection, and reporting requirements.

Issues Related to the Mexican Maquila Industry

Mexico has encouraged development in the *maquila* industry since 1965, offering incentives for investment and favorable tariff and tax treatment for *maquiladoras*. Since then, *maquiladoras* have contributed significantly to Mexico's job growth and to its economy generally. For most of that time, *maquiladoras* were used only for low-wage assembly operations, while most capital investment remained in true "manufacturing" plants in the United States. Today, many Mexican plants utilize state-of-the-art production equipment and techniques and employ many more higher-skilled workers than in the past. Many U.S. businesspeople claim that the quality of workmanship in Mexican plants is on par with that anywhere in the world. Some plants are quality certified by the International Standards Organization (ISO). The average hourly wage for direct labor, however, is still only about $2.00 an hour, although ahead of average wages elsewhere in the country.

The success of the *maquila* industry has caused a migration of workers from all over Mexico to the border region. This has led to many social problems that are typical of fast-growing migrant areas. These include overcrowded living conditions, pollution, substandard housing, poor health care, inadequate sanitation and public utilities, poor roads and infrastructure, and many other problems. The electrical power and telecommunications industries are encumbered by a history of government protection and monopoly, and electricity and other utilities are often unreliable and inadequate for industry.

One of the most severe problems in the border region is an epidemic of crime that has spread to both sides of the border, including violent crimes such as kidnapping for ransom, smuggling and drug-related crimes, organized crime, and offenses related to illegal immigration and border crossings. Many foreign companies have to provide personal protective services for their employees.

Other political and societal factors have also detracted from the business climate in Mexico. The government bureaucracy is often encumbered by red tape and corruption, and officials at some levels of government maintain an anti-business attitude.

Still other problems have arisen in the *maquila* workplace. Many accusations of labor abuses have been made by governments, non-governmental organizations, labor activists, and the popular press. These include unsafe or unhealthy working conditions, excessive working hours, sexual harassment, and violations of the right to organize. Although Mexico has enacted sophisticated labor and employment laws related to wages, working hours, and so forth, they are not always adequately enforced. As jobs become harder to find, unskilled workers become more vulnerable to a few unscrupulous supervisors and plant managers who are able to exploit workers desperate for well-paying jobs. Most global brand-name firms that operate *maquiladoras* or that have purchasing and supply arrangements with local plants try to monitor and "police" labor violations, although it is not always an easy task.

No issue is more pressing in the border region than the harm the plants have caused to the environment. In the early 1990s, the governments of the United States and Mexico began negotiations on protecting the Rio Grande and on building municipal sewer systems, water treatment plants, and solid-waste disposal sites. Their greatest concern was how to deal with hazardous waste. The two governments devised methods of tracking hazardous waste and regulating disposal sites. Mexico has reportedly closed hundreds of plants for environmental violations. Complicating the problem are the thousands of trucks that cross the border daily, causing severe air pollution and damage to roads and bridges. Both governments have spent hundreds of millions of dollars to deal with these social and environmental problems.

Recent Trends in the *Maquila* Industry. By the close of the 1990s, *maquiladoras* accounted for half of Mexico's exports and employed over one million people in about 3,500 plants. Since 2001, the *maquila* industry has faced several economic challenges. First, the industry is very dependent on the American economy. In 2001, the *maquila* industry was affected by the American recession. As a result, hundreds of *maquiladoras* closed and hundreds of thousands of Mexican workers were laid off. The declining employment in Mexican *maquiladoras* during that period led many Mexicans to enter the United States illegally, looking for work. By 2007, the industry had recovered somewhat in terms of the number of plants and employees, although not to 2000 levels, and total production output had actually increased over 2000.

A second trend in the *maquila* industry is resulting from China's rise as a force in global production. China has vast labor resources and wage rates even lower than those in Mexico. It is increasing its share of world exports in many industries important to Mexico, such as textiles and electronics. When China joined the WTO in 2001, its exports became subject to normal trade status in the United States and other WTO countries. More recently, the United States removed many restrictions on the import of Chinese textiles and apparel. This could very well lead to a continued shift of production operations from Mexican plants to plants in China. While the 1990s saw many Asian firms moving to Mexico to take advantage of NAFTA tariff rates and Mexico's proximity to the United States and Canada, more recent years have seen the reverse trends, with global firms moving plants to China, Vietnam, and other low-wage Asian countries. Today, China's exports to the United States are increasing far faster than Mexico's. With the passage of CAFTA-DR, plants in Central America and the Dominican Republic will also become more competitive with plants in Mexico.

The Free Trade Area of the Americas

The *Free Trade Area of the Americas* (FTAA) is a proposal, originating at the 1994 Summit of the Americas, to expand NAFTA into a single Western Hemisphere free trade area. Despite continued attempts to work out differences between the United States, Canada, Mexico, and their southern neighbors, the negotiations have not yet been successful. One of the biggest issues is agricultural trade, because countries heavily protect their own farming interests. Given that many Latin American products already enter the United States duty free or at very low rates, it would seem that the FTAA would be a great boon to U.S. exporters that generally face tariff rates in Latin America that are many times higher than American tariffs. It is not known whether the FTAA will ever become a reality or what its provisions might be. However, its impact on international trade and investment in the Western Hemisphere might be tremendous.

Other Western Hemisphere Free Trade Agreements

While the FTAA may still be a few years away, the United States already has succeeded in establishing bilateral and regional trade agreements with countries in Central and South America. The *U.S.–Central American–Dominican Republic Free Trade Agreement* (CAFTA-DR) was concluded in 2005 among Costa Rica, Dominican Republic, El Salvador, Guatemala, Honduras, Nicaragua, and the United States. This agreement grants NAFTA-like treatment for goods and services traded between these countries and provides for national treatment and duty-free treatment for most products. Eligible products must meet the CAFTA-DR rules of origin. CAFTA-DR also addresses labor and environmental issues and promotes investment and the protection of intellectual property.

In addition to CAFTA-DR, the United States concluded a free trade agreement with Peru in 2007. At the beginning of 2008, the U.S. Congress was debating whether to approve free trade agreements that had been negotiated with Colombia and Panama. Like all free trade agreements, these agreements are either supported or opposed by American lawmakers on the basis of economic or political grounds. Many view the agreements as a means of promoting democracy in these countries or of rewarding political allies there. Still others view passage of the free trade agreements as a means of forestalling the populist movement of socialist President Hugo Chavez in neighboring Venezuela. Some critics say that the agreements should be rejected until more progress is made in eradicating drug production there. Other critics of free trade policies in Congress argue against new agreements that could cause a loss of U.S. jobs.

Conclusion

The *North American Free Trade Agreement* was approved by the legislatures of Canada, Mexico, and the United States only after heated debate. Proponents saw it as a means of expanding trade opportunities for North American products, spurring cross-border investment, increasing the number of high-paying jobs in export industries, and bringing greater economic and social stability to Mexico. Opponents argued that it would result in large-scale loss of U.S. and Canadian jobs to low-wage workers in Mexico. Today, the impact of NAFTA is still disputed. NAFTA supporters point to an increase in the volume of trade and investment between the three countries and to an increase in living standards and strengthening of the Mexican middle class. Critics point to an increasing U.S. trade deficit with Mexico, which did not exist in 1993. They argue that NAFTA has caused a loss of U.S. jobs in many industries, particularly manufacturing, and in virtually every U.S. state. These critics maintain that despite an increase in manufacturing jobs in Mexico, real wages have not really increased. Moreover, they point out that many of the new Mexican jobs are in plants along the U.S.–Mexican border, with many people working and living in crowded, slum-like conditions, with inadequate housing, health care, and sanitation. Environmentalists argue that NAFTA and the growth of border factories have created a social and environmental disaster in the region. One thing is certain: arguments over the impact of NAFTA are colored by American attitudes over increased illegal Mexican immigration into the United States. Certainly, the immigration issue has become the hottest topic in U.S.–Mexican relations.

Chapter Summary

1. The *North American Free Trade Agreement* between Canada, Mexico, and the United States went into force in 1994. It created the world's largest free trade area, encompassing a market of about 445 million people and a combined gross domestic product of over $15 trillion.
2. By 2008, all tariffs on goods originating and traded in Canada, Mexico, and the United States were eliminated.
3. NAFTA tariff rates apply only to articles that originate in Canada, Mexico, or the United States. Only goods that qualify under NAFTA's rules of origin can obtain NAFTA tariff rates. Goods originate in a NAFTA country if they are wholly produced or obtained in Canada, Mexico, or the United States. This includes live animals born and raised, minerals mined, and crops grown in these countries. However, if the goods contain non-originating inputs (components or raw materials), they qualify as having originated in a NAFTA country if they meet the regional value content requirements or the tariff shift rules of Annex 401 of the NAFTA agreement.
4. NAFTA's national treatment principle is similar to that found in GATT. It states that once goods arrive from another NAFTA country, they must be treated without discrimination and no differently than domestically made goods. Reports of the United States Trade Representative show that Mexico and Canada still maintain many non-tariff barriers to U.S. goods and services.
5. The country-of-origin marking and labeling rules are set out in Annex 311 to NAFTA and

are enacted in the national customs regulations of the United States, Canada, and Mexico.

6. Canada is the largest purchaser of American agricultural products in the world, followed by Mexico. NAFTA has boosted U.S. agricultural exports to Canada and Mexico since 1994. The total elimination of Mexican tariffs in 2008 on products such as corn and beans has been viewed as a threat by many small Mexican farmers, who fear competition from large-scale American farms. This remains a sensitive political issue in both countries.
7. U.S. and Mexican truck regulations have severely limited cross-border truck access. Shipments must be handed over to transfer companies for customs clearance and transport across the border, where they are turned over to local drivers. NAFTA frees up cross-border road transportation by eliminating the intermediate transfer of cargo and the resulting costs, delays, and air pollution. The three countries are developing common safety standards for vehicles and drivers. However, due to pressure from the truckers' union, environmentalists, and those concerned about the safety of Mexican trucks, as of 2007 the open roads provisions of NAFTA had not yet been implemented by Congress.
8. NAFTA's side agreements on the protection of labor and the environment are also controversial. The *North American Agreement on Environmental Cooperation* does not set environmental or ecological standards, but it does call for the three countries to cooperate in protecting the environment. The *North American Agreement on Labor Cooperation* is intended to make labor policies more uniform by promoting Mexico's enforcement of its labor laws.
9. The Fair Trade Commission supervises the implementation of the agreement and attempts to resolve disputes that may arise among the three governments. If a settlement is not reached, the commission may convene an arbitral panel that can recommend a solution. Panels do not have the authority to tell a country to actually change its laws or policies.
10. The Mexican *maquiladora* industry consists of "production-sharing" factories that assemble U.S. components into finished products for return to the United States. Products include electronics, automobiles, and apparel. This industry allows manufacturers to take advantage of low-cost labor that is located close to the United States. The *maquila* industry is attempting to compete with even lower-cost labor from China, as Chinese imports to the United States grow at faster rates than imports from Mexico. Since 2007, the *maquila* industry has been governed by new Mexican "IMMEX" regulations.

Questions and Case Problems

1. What is the status of the U.S. free trade agreements with Peru, Panama, and Colombia? Have any other free trade agreements between the United States and other Latin American countries been negotiated or passed by Congress? What is the status of negotiations toward the Free Trade Area of the Americas?
2. Consider a study of doing business in Mexico. How do the economic, cultural, social, and political climates affect a business there? Describe Mexico's form of government. How are business relations conducted there? Are they more or less formal than in other Western countries? Describe how Mexico's policies toward trade and investment have changed over the years. Do you believe that Mexico provides a stable climate for trade and investment? What products or industries would seem to do well in the Mexican market?
3. NAFTA and CAFTA-DR contain provisions regarding the fair treatment of labor and the protection of the environment. Evaluate their potential for success. What are the issues, pro and con, for addressing issues in trade agreements? Explain.
4. Your company produces "Big Duster" tires. Your most popular styles are the ones with the raised white lettering on the outside of the tire. You would like to export tires to Mexico but cannot pass the Mexican labeling and marking requirements. Among the many other requirements, to remold the tires in Spanish would be costly. You do not think

the regulations are fair. Do the requirements violate NAFTA? What course of action should you take?

5. Your company distills Kentucky bourbon. A Canadian competitor is selling "Kentucky bourbon" in Ontario, but their bourbon is made in Canada. Canada's liquor control agency has looked the other way and ignored your requests to enjoin the sale. Does the sale violate NAFTA? GATT? Would this action be heard before the NAFTA Free Trade Commission or the WTO? What steps can be taken to force Canada to enjoin the sale? What remedies are available? If the Canadian products are exported to the United States, can they be stopped at the border?
6. Compare and contrast other trade preference programs, such as the GSP and the Caribbean Basin Initiative, with NAFTA. If the Caribbean countries already receive trade preferences under the CBI, why would many of them want admission to NAFTA?
7. How does the function of a NAFTA arbitral panel differ from that of a binational panel? What is the standard of review in binational panel decisions? Describe the role of an extraordinary challenge committee. Why does NAFTA recommend that panelists on binational panels and extraordinary challenge committees be judges or former judges whenever possible, but allow arbitral panelists to be specialists in international business or trade?
8. What is a rule of origin? Why is it important to the operation of a free trade area?
9. Discuss the social responsibility of a Canadian or U.S. manager working in Mexico. If a certain course of action is illegal in the manager's own country but lawful and accepted in Mexico, which standard should the manager follow? Describe the social responsibility of firms operating in Mexico in regard to environmental protection, worker health and safety, and corrupt practices.

Managerial Implications

Consider the following NAFTA management problem in a global business context.

DownPillow, Inc., a small U.S. manufacturer of down comforters and pillows, sells nationally through high-quality retailers. The company is known for its quality of materials and production. Its raw materials include cotton fabric, unfilled cotton shells, and down fills. These materials are not produced in the United States in sufficient quantities to meet the needs of the U.S. market. The HTS classification for unfilled comforter shells is 6307.90. The classification for finished down comforters is HTS 9404.90.

For many years, DownPillow purchased materials from Europe and paid in foreign currency. Gradually, costs rose because European suppliers faced higher labor and overhead costs. A declining U.S. dollar made goods more costly, but as costs rose, the company couldn't pass them on in price increases. When the U.S. market became more competitive in the early 1990s, DownPillow looked to China for cheaper materials. China is the world's leading producer of cotton textiles and down fill. Chinese textiles enter the United States under strict quota limits, enforced by U.S. Customs. Quota category 362 includes unfilled shells, comforters, quilts, bedspreads, and other top-of-the-bed products. DownPillow negotiated with a Chinese manufacturer for low-cost materials priced in dollars. The new products were introduced to U.S. customers in 1993 at competitive prices. The new lower-priced goods quickly became an important part of the company's line.

In the following year the political situation changed. The United States accused China of illegally transshipping textiles through third countries to get around the U.S. quota. In response, the United States reduced the quota on category 362. In 1994, the annual quota closed in early fall. Goods anticipated for shipment during the Christmas season sat in a customs-bonded warehouse at the port until released by U.S. Customs on January 2, 1995. By 1995, the largest U.S. importers of comforters and bedspreads had bought their merchandise early, and the quota closed on March 6. DownPillow was barely able to obtain sufficient unfilled shells for its production needs. When it tried to switch its customers back to the higher-priced merchandise made from European materials, they balked. Many threatened to take their business elsewhere.

1. Management is desperate for a solution. It has learned that Canada will permit the entry of Chinese textiles. They also know that Canadian trade negotiators put a little-known rule of origin in NAFTA providing that a product that undergoes a change from category 6307.90 to category 9404.90 will become a product of North America. (Tariff shifting is not generally available for textile articles, but widely available for many other manufactured and processed goods.) They would like your opinion on answers to the following questions:
   a. May they bring the Chinese cotton shells into Canada, and ship them to the United States

despite the quota? What processes would have to take place in Canada to do this? If they did, what would the tariff rate be? Would they see any net tariff savings?

b. Production in Canada would give ready access to the Canadian home-fashions market. Should the company explore the possibility of investment in a plant in Canada? What are the pros and cons of such a move? How would they be affected by NAFTA investment provisions?

c. Canada is a good supplier of goose down. If DownPillow produces finished comforters in Canada, would it make a difference if they used down from Canada geese, as opposed to down plucked from geese in, say, Poland, and imported into Canada?

d. Every state requires that comforters may only be sold if they are manufactured or imported by licensed bedding manufacturers. Bedding manufacturers are subject to state health codes. Does NAFTA prohibit the application of state health codes to Canadian and Mexican companies or to products made by them?

e. The company also has had some interest from buyers in Mexico. Would any import duties apply on shipments of either its U.S.– or Canadian-made products to Mexico? What would the tariff rate be? What special textile labeling rules are applicable, and how would they affect the company's ability to market there?

f. Management is concerned about meeting foreign health standards applicable to a natural product like down and feathers. Where would they go for information on foreign regulations?

2. Discuss the wisdom of DownPillow's decision to switch its source of supply to China. Describe the impact of customs and tariff law on a North American firm's strategy. Describe how this small company was affected by international political events out of its control. Do you think the company underestimated its customers and its market?

FOR INTERNET ACTIVITIES, VISIT ACADEMIC.CENGAGE.COM/BLAW/SCHAFFER.

CHAPTER 15
THE EUROPEAN UNION AND OTHER REGIONAL TRADE AREAS

Europe's history is long and tumultuous with alliances formed and dissolved over thousands of years. A significant trend in the post–World War II period has been the development of regional economic alliances to facilitate trade, as well as to maintain peace and security. These regional agreements have had significant impact on the conduct of business.

Historical precedents for European economic integration go back to before the Roman Empire. However, the devastation of Europe by World War II and efforts to rebuild were the major forces in bringing the original six European countries—Belgium, France, Italy, Luxembourg, the Netherlands, and West Germany (the western portion of modern Germany)—together to form the *European Common Market* or *European Economic Community*. In January 2007, the number of member states grew to twenty-seven, with three more candidate countries awaiting admission.

The *European Union* (EU) is now the largest single market in the world, surpassing even the United States in its sheer size.

The primary focus of this chapter is to examine the structure and operation of the EU to the extent that it is relevant to business. It also examines the process of gradually greater economic integration within the EU and its impact on business. Finally, the chapter reviews the development of less integrated "free trade areas" and "customs unions" throughout the world, other than the area created by the *North American Free Trade Agreement*, which is discussed in a separate chapter.

THE PHILOSOPHY OF ECONOMIC INTEGRATION

Of the numerous paradigms of economic integration, some involve more comprehensive economic integration, while others are more limited in scope. The economic union created in the United States of America upon enactment of its Constitution in 1790 offers a good starting point for analysis.

Federal Model

The U.S. Constitution is so justly celebrated for its political attributes that its deeply economic character is often overlooked. During the first years of American independence, the states had different currencies and erected barriers against "imports" from other states. The resulting economic calamity inspired the economic provisions of the Constitution, a revolutionary compact among the states through which the states agreed to have their economies managed as a single unit by a strengthened federal government. Under the Constitution's Commerce Clause (Article I, Section 8, Clause 3), the states gave the federal Congress the exclusive power to manage trade among the states and with foreign nations. The federal court system—established by the Constitution's Article III—has interpreted this Clause as striking down any state law that would impede the free interstate movement of goods or people or any state law that would discriminate against businesses based in other states. This effectively created a highly integrated common market: the federal union.

And Congress has used the Commerce Clause to grant the federal government's primacy in the regulation of competition law issues. Article I, Section 8, Clause 5 gives the sole power of issuing currency to the federal government. Congress used that power to create the Federal Reserve System, which centrally controls the nation's monetary supply and monetary policy. Article II of the Constitution gives treaty-making power to the president, with Senate consent, and Article I, Section 10 absolutely forbade the states from entering into treaties. This concentrated all control over commercial policy toward other nations, expressed in international trade and customs treaties, in the hands of the federal government. Article I, Section 8, Clause 4 made even bankruptcy laws the exclusive province of the federal government.

In short, the loosely confederated American states united into a tight customs union and gave the federal government sweeping powers to create and regulate a vast common market encompassing the continent. In the economic arena, states retained control of legal areas in which the fundamental rules came from the states' Anglo-Saxon common law tradition, such as contract and corporate law and the regulation of insurance. Even in those areas, the federal judiciary could review and strike down any state law that impinged on the federal common market.

The American experiment is now over 225 years old and has convincingly proved the economic principle that completely eliminating commercial barriers among political entities, by permitting businesses in each to specialize in areas of competitive advantage and create a larger market for the best products, economically benefits the citizens of all states that join the union. Yet because such change necessarily brings short-term harm to those who cannot compete in the larger pond, and those likely to be harmed inevitably have political power, it has proved quite difficult for other nations to forge economic agreements on the scale of the U.S. Constitution. We will now review the attributes of other, less comprehensive types of economic unions.

Free Trade Area

A *free trade area* (FTA) and a federal system represent the two extreme ends on the continuum of integration. An FTA develops when two or more countries agree to eliminate or phase out customs duties and other barriers to trade among the member countries. Because only products originating in the FTA countries may be shipped duty free, there is no need for the countries to have common commercial policies toward countries outside the FTA. For example, because Korean steel imported into Mexico cannot be re-imported duty free from Mexico to the United States, there is no need for Mexico and the United States to place the same customs duties on Korean steel or have a common commercial policy toward Korea. Free trade agreements vary greatly in the degree to which FTA members have common policies for regulating business in their countries. Nevertheless, as with any system with common norms, an FTA needs a good dispute settlement mechanism to enforce its norms.

Customs Union

A *customs union* is more ambitious in scope than an FTA. In an FTA, there is free trade only in goods produced within the FTA. In a customs union, there is free trade in all goods that come through any of the union members, even imports from outside the customs union. Thus, Brazilian sugar imported into France should move from France into fellow EC member state Germany just as freely as French wine would. By contrast, Brazilian sugar imported into Mexico may not freely move into the United States under NAFTA, whose free trade area applies only to products created in free trade area countries.

Because of this distinction, a customs union can only function if all of its members agree to a common tariff on imports from outside the union. Thus, the EC has a common customs tariff and, under its operating treaties, has the power to negotiate with other countries on behalf of all member states. The United States cannot negotiate with France over tariffs; it can only negotiate with the EC as a whole. This structure ensures that no outsider can gain an advantage by routing its imports through one member state.

In turn, the need of a customs union to have a single tariff policy for products from outside the union means that the members of the union must arrive at other common policies. If they are to impose common tariffs on a specific product, the member states must develop a consistent policy toward that product. For example, European nations have widely divergent interests on free entry of agricultural products, yet they must establish a common policy toward imported beef products from the United States and Australia. Similarly, the need to agree on a common tariff on products from a specific nation requires a common commercial policy toward that nation, even though the union members may have widely divergent views toward the nation's military or political policies.

The following article illustrates the dizzyingly complex dynamics that arise when many different business groups try to negotiate through a single institution that is, in turn, negotiating with many countries.

Common Market

A *common market,* also called an *economic community,* goes further than a customs union. While a customs union ensures the free movement of goods within the union, a common market seeks to further facilitate free competition within a group of nations. To do so it protects the right of all enterprises and persons within the area to do business, invest capital, and sell their services anywhere within the area without discrimination on the basis of national origin.

If they are to achieve free economic competition in a common market, the members of the market must establish certain common rules. If companies can compete everywhere within a market, the member nations must develop common policies and laws on what anticompetitive behavior is and how to curb it. To prevent national governments from unfairly favoring local firms over those from other member states, the members must develop shared rules on using tax dollars to subsidize industries. So that manufacturing concerns will not have a cost advantage in a particular nation, minimum marketwide environmental and consumer protection standards are appropriate.

For policy to be meaningful, it must be transformed into law. Its enforcement needs to be entrusted to a court with jurisdiction and power to enforce its rulings if the member states are to comply effectively with the standards and laws. Without effective enforcement, each member state can continue to operate its own protectionist barriers.

One way to substantially enhance commerce within a multinational market is to eliminate currency risk for businesses within that market. (See the discussion of currency risk in Chapter Eighteen.) This can only be achieved by adoption of a common currency by all actors within the market. Adopting a common currency necessarily implies developing and maintaining a common monetary policy on things like how much of that currency to release into the market and what short-term interest rates to charge financial institutions. In addition, the member states need to agree on an institution that will protect and enforce that policy.

The treaties that govern the EU address all of these issues. In fact, it is theoretically possible for the EU to reach a level of economic integration equal to, or even greater than, that of the United States without creating a political union. After all, even the states within the U.S. have regulatory discretion in many areas affecting business and exercise it differently. From a strictly economic perspective, the United States is no more than a common market with great integration. In actuality, however, the EU market is still far below the level of integration of the U.S. common market. For example, the euro is only the currency in thirteen of the twenty-seven EU countries. As the following case illustrates, many other challenges remain.

Commission of the European Communities v. Italian Republic

Case C-14/00 (2003)

European Court of Justice

BACKGROUND AND FACTS

At the time this case was initiated, Italy required chocolate products manufactured in other member states that contained vegetable fats other than cocoa butter to be sold in Italy as "chocolate substitutes." The Commission claimed that Italy had failed to fulfill its

continued

continued

obligation under Article 30 of the EC treaty (now, after amendment, Article 28). *Council Directive 73/241/ EEC of July 24, 1973*, on the approximation of the laws relating to cocoa and chocolate products, states, in part, "[T]he use of vegetable fats other than cocoa butter in chocolate products is permitted." * * *

Italian Law No. 351 of April 30, 1976, states that [a food preparation containing cocoa] whose "texture, consistency, color, and taste are similar to those of chocolate but whose composition does not correspond to the definition of one of the products listed in the annex to the present law, constitute[s] a 'chocolate substitute.'" The products referred to in that annex do not contain vegetable fats other than cocoa butters.

An Italian Ministry of Health circular of March 15, 1996, ... stated that cocoa and chocolate products containing vegetable fats other than cocoa butter originating in the United Kingdom, Ireland, and Denmark can be marketed within Italian territory only if their composition satisfies the rules of the state of origin and if their sales name corresponds to ... chocolate substitute. The Italian government refused to change its interpretation of the Directive or the Italian law.

* * *

The Commission states that chocolate containing vegetable fats other than cocoa butter up to a maximum of 5 percent of the total weight of the product is manufactured under the name "chocolate" in six member states (Denmark, Ireland, Portugal, Sweden, Finland, and the United Kingdom) and that it is accepted under that name in all member states with the exception of Spain and Italy.

* * *

The Commission considers that it is not possible to claim that the addition of vegetable fats other than cocoa butter to a chocolate product that contains the minimum contents required under *Directive 73/241* substantially changes the nature of the product to the point where the use of the name "chocolate" would create confusion as regards its basic characteristics.

FINDINGS OF THE COURT

First of all, it must be held that the Commission's complaint based on the fact that the Italian legislation is not in compliance with Community law, inasmuch as it places restrictions on the free movement of cocoa and chocolate products containing vegetable fats other than cocoa butter, raises the question of the extent of the harmonisation achieved under *Directive 73/241*.

While the parties agree that the use of such vegetable fats in cocoa and chocolate products was not harmonised by the directive, they disagree as regards the consequences of the fact for the marketing of products which contain such fats.

Since it considers that the absence of harmonisation as regards the use of vegetable fats other than cocoa butter in cocoa and chocolate products cannot exclude the marketing of products containing such fats from the application of the principle of the free movement of goods, the Commission claims that any measures restricting the free movement of those products must be considered in the light of Article 30 of the Treaty.

By contrast, the Italian Government maintains that *Directive 73/241* fully regulates the marketing of the cocoa and chocolate products to which it refers, thereby precluding the application of Article 30 of the Treaty in so far as, first, it sets out the principle that the use of vegetable fats other than cocoa butter is prohibited in the manufacture of cocoa and chocolate products and, secondly, it establishes a system of free movement under the name 'chocolate' only for cocoa and chocolate products which do not contain such vegetable fats.

The Italian Government therefore contends that *Directive 73/241* enables Member States whose national law prohibits the addition of vegetable fats other than cocoa butter to products manufactured within their territory also to prohibit the marketing within their territory, under the name "chocolate", of products whose manufacture does not comply with their national legislation.

* * *

First, as regards the objectives of the provisions in question and the context in which they occur, it is clear that *Directive 73/241* was not intended to regulate definitively the use of vegetable fats other than cocoa butter in the cocoa and chocolate products to which it refers.

* * *

The Community legislature clearly indicated that, in the light of the disparities between Member States' legislation and the insufficient economic and technical data available, it could not, at the time the directive was adopted, take a final position on the use of vegetable fats other than cocoa butter in cocoa and chocolate products.

* * *

It must also be pointed out that, as is made clear by the case-file, the reference in the same recital to certain Member States where the use of those other vegetable fats was at that time not merely permitted but, moreover, extensive, referred to three Member

continued

continued

States which had acceded to the Community shortly before the adoption of *Directive 73/241,* namely the Kingdom of Denmark, Ireland and the United Kingdom, and which traditionally permitted the addition to cocoa and chocolate products manufactured within their territory of such vegetable fats up to a maximum of 5 percent of total weight.

In those circumstances, the Council merely established, for the use of vegetable fats other than cocoa butter, provisional rules which were to be re-examined, in accordance with the second sentence of Article 14(2)(a) of *Directive 73/241,* at the end of a period of three years from its notification.

* * *

... Article 30 of the Treaty prohibits obstacles to the free movement of goods, in the absence of harmonisation of national laws, which are the consequence of applying to goods coming from other Member States, where they are lawfully manufactured and marketed, rules that lay down requirements to be met by those goods (such as those relating to their name, form, size, weight, composition, presentation, labelling and packaging), even if those rules apply to national and imported products alike.

* * *

That is all the more so in view of the fact that the name "chocolate substitute", which the Italian law requires the traders concerned to use, may adversely affect the consumer's perception of the products in question, inasmuch as it denotes substitute, and therefore inferior, products.

* * *

In addition, it must be pointed out that, since *Directive 73/241* explicitly permits Member States to authorise the use, in the manufacture of cocoa and chocolate products, of vegetable fats other than cocoa butter, it cannot be claimed that the products to which those fats have been added, in compliance with that directive, are altered to the point where they no longer fall into the same category as those which do not contain such fats.

Therefore, the addition of vegetable fats other than cocoa butter to cocoa and chocolate products which satisfy the minimum contents required by *Directive 73/241* cannot substantially alter the nature of those products to the point where they are transformed into different products.

It follows that the inclusion in the label of a neutral and objective statement informing consumers of the presence in the product of vegetable fats other than cocoa butter would be sufficient to ensure that consumers are given correct information.

In those circumstances, the obligation to change the sales name of those products which is imposed by the Italian legislation does not appear to be necessary to satisfy the overriding requirement of consumer protection.

It follows that that legislation, to the extent that it requires the name of products which are lawfully manufactured and marketed in other Member States under the sales name "chocolate" to be altered for the sole reason that they contain vegetable fats other than cocoa butter, is incompatible with Article 30 of the Treaty.

In the light of all the foregoing considerations, it must be held that, by prohibiting cocoa and chocolate products which comply with the requirements as to minimum content laid down in point 1.16 of Annex I to *Directive 73/241* to which vegetable fats other than cocoa butter have been added, and which are lawfully manufactured in Member States which authorize the addition of such fats, from being marketed in Italy under the name used in the Member State of production, and by requiring that those products may only be marketed under the name "chocolate substitute", the Italian Republic has failed to fulfill its obligations under Article 30 of the Treaty.

COSTS

Article 69(2) of the Rules of Procedure provides that the unsuccessful party is to be ordered to pay the costs if they have been applied for in the successful party's pleadings. Since the Commission has applied for costs and the Italian Republic has been unsuccessful, the Italian Republic must be ordered to pay the costs.

On those grounds,

THE COURT (Sixth Chamber),

hereby:

1. Declares that, by prohibiting cocoa and chocolate products which comply with the requirements as to minimum content laid down in point 1.16 of Annex I to *Council Directive 73/241/EEC of 24 July 1973* on the approximation of the laws of the Member States relating to cocoa and chocolate products intended for human consumption to which vegetable fats other than cocoa butter have been added, and which are lawfully manufactured in Member States which authorise the addition of such fats, from being

continued

continued

marketed in Italy under the name used in the Member State of production, and by requiring that those products may only be marketed under the name "chocolate substitute", the Italian Republic has failed to fulfil its obligations under Article 30 of the Treaty (now, after amendment, Article 28 EC);

2. Orders the Italian Republic to pay the costs.

Decision and Comment. The court allowed chocolate products containing vegetable fat to be sold as chocolate. This was another victory in the battle against national regulation, which impedes trade and can be construed as protectionist.

Compatibility of Trade Areas with the WTO and GATT

At first glance, the principles underlying the formation of trade areas seem to contradict the basic principles of the WTO and GATT, which require nondiscrimination and reciprocity among all members. How can members of an FTA or customs union treat those members more favorably than other GATT members? Article XXIV of the GATT agreement states:

> [T]he provisions of this Agreement shall not prevent, as between the territories of contracting parties, the formation of a customs union or of a free-trade area ...; Provided that: (a) with respect to a customs union, ... the duties and other regulations of commerce imposed at the institution of any such union ... in respect of trade with contracting parties not parties to such union ... shall not on the whole be higher or more restrictive than the general incidence of the duties and regulations of commerce applicable in the constituent territories prior to the formation of such union....

This section has been used to lower the rates of external tariffs within a trade area for the benefit of non-FTA WTO members. This achieves the goals of GATT for the benefit of WTO members.

The following section looks at the example of the EU, its movement from a customs union to common market, and current uncertainty about future integration efforts.

European Union

The EU of today did not spring forth fully developed in its current form. Rather, it developed over a period of years and with successive modifications. Understanding the present issues requires an examination of the Union's past history.

History

Winston Churchill, former prime minister of Great Britain, stated in 1946 that postwar Europe needed a "... [s]overeign remedy ... to recreate the European family, or as much of it as we can, and provide it with a structure under which it can dwell in peace and safety and freedom. We must build a kind of United States of Europe." Jean Monnet, a French government official considered the founding father of the EU, said that "the states of Europe must form a federation." They hoped this type of partnership would prevent the development of conditions that might result in a third world war.

Although the EU is commonly thought to be a single unit, it is actually three "communities," each created and operating under a separate treaty. The best known is the *European Community*, (EC) formerly known as the European Economic Community, established under the 1957 *Treaty of Rome*. This treaty, like the U.S. Constitution, created a set of marketwide institutions empowered to develop common policies but left the substance of the policies to the new institutions. The second community, the *European Coal and Steel Community* (ECSC) was established in 1952 under the *Treaty of Paris*, which specifically defined the outlines of an agreed common policy. This policy covered combined price and output controls, investment subsidies, tariff protection, and competition rules with respect to coal and steel. The third community, the *European Atomic Energy Community* (Euratom), established on the same day as the EC by a second, separate *Treaty of Rome*, focuses primarily on creating a market for and distributing atomic energy throughout the European states. It also is responsible for selling excess nuclear energy outside member states.

All three of these "communities" exist to this day under the administration of a single institution, the *Commission of the European Communities* (the *Commission*). The continuing existence of all three communities explains why we still call the Commission the "Commission of the European Communities." The fact that three different treaties govern the communities' activities is significant. Because the *EC Treaty* (the first *Treaty of Rome*) went into little substantive detail about policy, the ultimate arbiter of EC policy is the *Council of the European Union* (the *Council*). By contrast, because the ECSC and Euratom policies are well defined in their treaties, the Commission of the European Communities implements ECSC and Euratom policy with little direction from its ostensible superior, the Council of the European Union.

The "European Union" is a concept added by the *Maastricht Agreement*, also known as the *Treaty on European Union*. The Maastricht Agreement did not abolish the Communities, but created the concept of a Union as an expression of the member states' underlying unity, as reflected in the Communities. Maastricht also added goals, to which the member states aspired, that might permit the eventual development of political integration. In practice, the level of political integration is very loose: Member states can and do have very different positions on politico-military, social, and labor questions and make little attempt to coordinate them. The EU has virtually no power to compel agreement in the way that the EU institutions can when they act as the "European Community" in purely economic matters.

Legally, there are today three communities, even if there is only one Council, one Commission, and one Court of Justice. Thus, the somewhat confusing result is that, although the EU is a single set of institutions, each of which we will discuss in depth below, it acts as ECSC on steel and coal matters; it acts as Euratom on atomic energy matters; and when it acts on most other economic matters, it does so as the EC.

One way of understanding it is to envision a holding company that has three subsidiary companies, each with its own corporate purposes, and each operating in a different market, but all owned by one set of shareholders. The same people hold the power, but the scope and substance of their power varies depending upon which company's board meeting they are attending. To simplify the expression, this book, like most general works, refers to this group of nations as the *European Union* or *EU,* although technically the EC takes the actions that we describe as taken by the EU.

Because the general rule is that a "European Community" has only the powers its member states confer upon it in treaties, we will review some of the major treaties in more detail.

Treaty of Rome. The *Treaty of Rome* stated the original objectives of the European Community (see Exhibit 15.1). The *Treaty of Rome* launched the process of establishing a customs union, gradually turning over international trade policy to the Commission. The *Treaty of Rome* also launched internal multinational regulation, as it contained "competition law" calculated to prevent the creation of marketwide private combinations in restraint of trade. As noted in Chapter Twenty-Two, the *Treaty of Rome* is still important in the area of competition law. Notwithstanding the earlier ECSC effort, the *Treaty of Rome* is commonly regarded as the true beginning of European economic integration.

The Single European Act. Notwithstanding the professed goals of the *Treaty of Rome,* progress on economic integration was quite slow. Approaching the thirtieth anniversary of the *Treaty of Rome,* the European Community was still more a loose free trade area than a customs union. It posed significant barriers to imports from other member states, and its divergent approaches on trade policy with non–member states made a customs union untenable. The twelve existing members thus enacted the *Single European Act* (SEA), effective July 1, 1987. The purpose of the SEA was to strengthen the EC institutions and enable them to act to further the goals of the *Treaty of Rome.*

The SEA signaled a dramatic move away from the *Treaty of Rome*'s slow, consensus-based system. The members abandoned the requirement of unanimous consent to move forward and instead adopted the concept of *qualified majority voting.* This change meant that not all the member states had to agree on proposals that related to the internal market. This allowed the Community to make decisions even if there was some objection.

Exhibit 15.1

Treaty of Rome

Article 2

The Community shall have as its task, by establishing a common market and progressively approximating the economic policies of Member States, to promote throughout the Community a harmonious development of economic activities, a continuous and balanced expansion, an increase in stability, an accelerated raising of the standard of living, and closer relations between the States belonging to it.

Article 3

For the purposes set out in Article 2, the activities of the Community shall include, as provided in this Treaty and in accordance with the timetable set out therein.

A. the elimination, as between Member States, of customs duties and of quantitative restrictions on the import and export of goods, and of the other measures having equivalent effect;
B. the establishment of a common customs tariff and of a common commercial policy toward third countries;
C. the abolition, as between Member States, of obstacles to freedom of movement for persons, services, and capital;
D. the adoption of a common policy in the sphere of agriculture;
E. the adoption of a common policy in the sphere of transport;
F. the institution of a system ensuring that competition in the common market is not distorted;
G. the application of procedures by which the economic policies of Member States can be coordinated and disequilibrium in their balances of payments remedied;
H. the approximation of the laws of Member States to the extent required for the proper functioning of the common market;
I. the creation of a European Social Fund in order to improve employment opportunities for workers and to contribute to the raising of their standard of living;
J. the establishment of a European Investment Bank to facilitate the economic expansion of the Community by opening up fresh resources;
K. the association of the overseas countries and territories in order to increase trade and to promote jointly economic and social development.

The *Maastricht Treaty*. After the passage of the SEA, the pace of change within the Community quickened. In 1991, the twelve EC leaders hammered out an agreement at Maastricht, Netherlands, that advanced economic integration and set the stage for a measure of political integration. The European Union concept was established, along with European Union "citizenship," which facilitated movement of labor throughout the Union. It set the stage for a single European currency, the euro, and a European Central Bank to control monetary policy. The agreement also set goals for common policy on internal environmental and other issues important to business. The *Maastricht Treaty* also increased the use of qualified majority voting, which limits the ability of countries to deadlock the Union.

***Treaty of Amsterdam* (1999).** The *Treaty of Amsterdam* primarily advanced the freedom of labor to move among member states. The treaty expanded the European Community's jurisdiction over asylum, immigration, and visa matters, increasing the supranational entity's role in such affairs.

***Treaty Establishing a Constitution for Europe*.** In October 2004, representatives of the member states signed the *Treaty Establishing a Constitution for Europe*, which was subject to ratification by the citizens of the member states. This constitution would have brought together all the previous EU-related treaties and set forth a common set of human rights, akin to the Bill of Rights in the U.S. Constitution, that would have greatly broadened the EU institutions' jurisdiction over national domestic affairs. In May 2005, the French people rejected the constitution, fearing a loss of national control over France's political traditions. In June 2005, the citizens of the Netherlands similarly rejected the constitution, fearing a loss of their political traditions to less tolerant European neighbors. These two firm rebuffs caused other member states to "postpone" referendum votes indefinitely, killing the proposal in its current form. A new intergovernmental conference was called in June 2007 to discuss possible modifications to the constitution that might permit passage. The fate of the rejected constitution illustrates that although Europeans appreciate the benefits of economic integration, they do not trust their political liberties to institutions dominated by people from "foreign" political traditions.

Structure of the European Union

The *Treaty of Rome* allocated power among the Council of the European Union, the Commission of the European Communities, the Assembly or Parliament, and the Court of Justice. This structure largely remains in place today.

THE COUNCIL OF THE EUROPEAN UNION. The *Council of the European Union* (the Council) sits in Brussels, Belgium, the effective "capital" of the European Union. It is composed of one representative from each member state. Each member state has several ministers, each specializing in a different area. A member state will designate a different minister to be its representative on the Council, depending on the subject on the agenda at a given Council meeting. Different areas of specialization include international affairs, finance, agriculture, transportation, etc. The position of president of the Council rotates among the membership every six months. The purpose of the Council is to coordinate economic policies of member states and to make decisions on issues within its jurisdiction, which includes approving legislative directives to the member states and international agreements. The Council shares some legislative power with the Parliament. As noted, on ECSC and Euratom matters, there is less need for the Council to make substantive decisions.

The Council reaches decisions through a complex "qualified majority" voting system. A qualified majority is achieved if (1) a majority of member states (in some cases a two-thirds majority) approve a proposal; (2) member states with a population of at least 62 percent of the total EU population approve it; and (3) a minimum of 255 votes are cast in favor of the proposal, out of a total of 345 votes. The votes are divided as follows:

Votes for each member state	
Germany, France, Italy, United Kingdom	29
Spain, Poland	27
Romania	14
Netherlands	13
Belgium, Czech Republic, Greece, Hungary, Portugal	12
Austria, Bulgaria, Sweden	10
Denmark, Ireland, Lithuania, Slovakia, Finland	7
Cyprus, Estonia, Latvia, Luxembourg, Slovenia	4
Malta	3
TOTAL	345

This multistep system of passage ensures that major member states can prevent major action if they can muster modest support among others. It will be interesting to see what will happen to this voting structure as populations continue to decline in more-prosperous Western European countries while they increase in less-prosperous Eastern European ones.

THE COMMISSION OF THE EUROPEAN COMMUNITIES. The Commission serves as the Union's executive body carrying out the decisions of the Council. It also is the only body that can make legislative proposals for the European Parliament to consider. As a practical matter, however, the Commission proposes whatever the Parliament or the Council requests that it propose. The Commission is headed by the *College of Commissioners*. It consists of one member appointed by each member state, each of whom is theoretically obligated to represent the interests of the Community as a whole rather than the interest of their home member state. One of the commissioners is nominated by the Council to be the Commission's president and the European Parliament elects him or her to a five-year term.

The term *Commission* also refers to the bureaucracy that performs the Commission's day-to-day work: over 25,000 civil servants who serve in the different *Directorates-General,* which are specialized areas of interest of the Commission. For example, *DG-IV* is the part of the Commission responsible for development of its competition law. The actions of the "Commission" discussed in Chapter Twenty-Two are, in fact, actions of DG-IV. Each Commissioner has special responsibilities at a Directorate. There is some overlap among Directorates, and fierce turf battles rage among the bureaucrats. The EU bureaucracy, like bureaucracies everywhere, confuses its proper role of implementing decisions of elected officials with the role-making policy itself. This is particularly acute in the case of the EU bureaucracy which, unlike those in democracies, is not directly commanded by popularly elected officials. This distance from electoral control is one of the primary reasons why European citizens are wary of expanding the Commission's jurisdiction into the political arena. Any foreign investor is well advised to retain Brussels experts to help them maneuver through the powerful EU bureaucracy.

THE COURT OF JUSTICE. The *European Court of Justice* (ECJ) in Luxembourg functions as the final arbiter of EU law. For private parties, its main function is to hear appeals from the European trial court, the *Court of First Instance.* It also has original jurisdiction in cases brought by EU institutions to compel member states to comply with their EU treaty obligations or by member states against EU institutions alleged to have overstepped their powers under the treaties.

Twenty-seven judges are appointed, one by each of the member states, for a renewable term of six years. The judges elect a president of the Court for a renewable term of three years. Unlike most national high courts, the Court may sit as a full court, in a Grand Chamber of thirteen judges, or in smaller chambers of three or five judges. The Court only sits as a full court when the judges determine that a case is of unusual importance, when different small chambers are in conflict, or, in rare cases, to remove a commissioner. The Court of Justice sits in a Grand Chamber in important cases or when petitioned by a member state or an EU institution. The Court hears most cases in chambers of three or five judges, much like the Courts of Appeals in the U.S. federal court system.

The *Court of First Instance* (CFI) is the general trial court of the EU. It has original jurisdiction over lawsuits brought by private parties against acts of EC institutions, such as actions to block mergers, impose fines, or other regulatory actions. It also has original jurisdiction over certain suits brought by the member states against the Commission; suits of member states against the Council in the areas of international trade "dumping" and state subsidies to industry; and suits relating to Community trademarks. The CFI's decisions may be appealed to the Court of Justice.

Like the Court of Justice, the CFI is comprised of twenty-seven judges, one from each member state, who serve renewable six-year terms. A party bringing a suit in the CFI will probably encounter a three-judge chamber. The CFI hears about three-quarters of its cases in this fashion. The judges may also sit in chambers of five judges or, in a few cases, may sit individually. If it feels a case is important enough, the CFI can sit as a Grand Chamber of thirteen judges or as a full court.

The EU courts follow the civil law tradition because all but the British and Irish judges come from this tradition. For example, the court itself calls witnesses, demands the production of documents, and hires necessary experts. The court allows limited cross-examination by the parties and increasingly permits parties to present their own experts on factual disputes.

Several other features serve to distinguish these courts. The decisions of the courts are issued without any dissenting opinions. This practice does not indicate total agreement among the judges; however, the public is not privy to their differences. This is in contrast to the U.S. judicial tradition, where the public, press, and legal scholars examine dissenting opinions to divine the philosophical differences among judges and predict future outcomes on different cases. The rationale for this EU practice is to protect the national judges from pressure within their home states. The practice is under attack, however, and has been called a way to hide the intellectual exchange that gives rise to judicial decisions from the public. Jurists from common-law countries like the United Kingdom have long criticized this aspect of EU court practice. Now, civil lawyers from traditions that include the publication of dissenting opinions have joined their voices to the critique.

National courts are obligated to follow Community law and the ECJ's decisions. An English court recognized this authority in a famous opinion that noted the difference between English and law, but nonetheless followed the controlling EC law. Lord Denning in *Bulmer v. Bollinger* (1974) stated

> The (EC) Treaty is quite unlike any of the enactments to which we have become accustomed.... It lays down general principles. It expresses its aims and purposes. All in sentences of moderate length and commendable style. But it lacks precision. It uses words and phrases without defining what they mean. An English lawyer would look for an interpretation clause, but he would look in vain. There is none. All the way through the Treaty there are gaps and lacunae. These have to be filled in by the judges, or by the regulations or directives. It is the European way.... Seeing these differences, what are the English courts to do when they are faced with a problem of interpretation? They must follow the European pattern. No longer must they argue about the precise grammatical sense. They must divine the spirit of the Treaty and gain inspiration from it. If they find a gap, they must fill it as best they can.... These are the principles as I understand it, on which the European Court acts.

The Court of Justice must also interpret Community law and is the ultimate authority for these conflicts.

The European Parliament. The *European Parliament* (the Parliament) is the only EU institution whose members are elected by European citizens. It has 785 members (*Members of the European Parliament* or MEPs). Each member state elects a different number, based on population. As the following table illustrates, the match between population and representation is not perfect.

Austria	18
Belgium	24
Bulgaria	18
Cyprus	6
Czech Republic	24
Denmark	14
Estonia	6
Finland	14
France	78
Germany	99
Greece	24
Hungary	24
Ireland	13
Italy	78
Latvia	9
Lithuania	13
Luxembourg	6
Malta	5
Netherlands	27
Poland	54
Portugal	24
Romania	35
Slovakia	14
Slovenia	7
Spain	54
Sweden	19
United Kingdom	78
TOTAL	785

The MEPs are elected to five-year terms. Each member state determines the electoral rules for its own candidates. The Parliament comprises members of various political factions that create alliances across national boundaries, including the Socialists, Christian Democrats, European Democrat Alliance, Greens, and other groups.

The Parliament approves the appointment of members of the European Commission and has control over its budget. Although it has legislative power, it cannot initiate legislation, which limits its power.

As previously noted, if the Commission or the Council has power to act under a treaty or a directive, it need not consult with the Parliament. The scope of the Commission's powers vis-à-vis the powers of the Council and the Parliament can sometimes be a hotly debated topic. A marked conflict occurred when the Parliament challenged the power of the EC and the Council to enter agreements with the then–politically unpopular Bush Administration over the privacy of Europeans' personal data.

European Central Bank. Located in Frankfurt, Germany, and founded in 1998, the *European Central Bank's* mission is to "promote price stability" and "to define and implement the monetary policy of the euro zone, conduct foreign exchange operations, issue notes, and promote the smooth operation of payment systems." The European Central Bank is effectively in charge of monetary policy relating to the euro.

European Parliament v. Council of the European Union and Commission of the European Communities; Joined Cases C-317/04 and C-318/04 (30 May 2006)
European Court of Justice (Grand Chamber)

BACKGROUND AND FACTS

After the terrorist attacks of September 11, 2001, the United States passed legislation requiring air carriers operating flights to or from the United States or across U.S. territory to provide the U.S. Customs authorities with electronic access to the data contained in their automated reservation and departure control systems, generally referred to as Passenger Name Records or PNRs. The European Commission informed the United States that the new U.S. law could conflict with EC and member state legislation and Council regulations on data protection. The United States postponed the entry into force of the new provisions but refused to waive its right to impose penalties on airlines that failed to comply. Faced with imminent loss of the massive U.S. market, European air carriers complied with the U.S. requirement although the EU had not yet approved it.

The Commission entered into negotiations with the United States and ultimately entered into an agreement under which the U.S. Department of Homeland Security was to comply with certain procedures to protect data. In 2004, the Commission placed before the Parliament its draft decision on adequacy of the procedure under the Parliament and Council's Directive 95/46/EC on the protection of individuals with regard to the processing and free movement of personal data. The Council sent Parliament a letter in support of the Commission's proposed decision that requested urgent action.

The European Parliament adopted a resolution that set out a number of reservations about the agreement and decision. The Parliament believed that the Commission had exceeded its powers and violated the rights of citizens protected by the directive and asked it to submit a new draft decision. The Parliament also rejected the Council's request for urgent action.

The Commission nonetheless adopted the decision on adequacy, which the Council adopted as its own. The Commission found a basis for its actions in Article 25 of the directive, and the Council relied on its powers under Article 95 of the *EC Treaty.* The European Parliament brought action in the European Court of Justice to annul the Council's agreement and the Commission's decision as inconsistent with the *European Convention for the Protection of Human Rights and Fundamental Freedoms,* the *EC Treaty,* and the directive on data protection.

V. SKOURIS, PRESIDENT; P. JANN, C.W.A. TIMMERMANS, A. ROSAS, AND J. MALENOVSKÝ, PRESIDENTS OF CHAMBERS; N. COLNERIC (RAPPORTEUR), S. VON BAHR, J.N. CUNHA RODRIGUES, R. SILVA DE LAPUERTA, G. ARESTIS, A. BORG BARTHET, M. ILEŠIF, AND J. KLUFKA, JUDGES

* * *

Article 3 of the Directive is worded as follows: 'Scope

1. This Directive shall apply to the processing of personal data wholly or partly by automatic means, and to the processing otherwise than by automatic means of personal data which form part of a filing system or are intended to form part of a filing system.
2. This Directive shall not apply to the processing of personal data:
   —in the course of an activity which falls outside the scope of Community law, such as those provided for by Titles V and VI of the Treaty on European Union and in any case to processing operations concerning public security, defence, State security (including the economic well-being of the State when the processing operation relates to State security matters) and the activities of the State in areas of criminal law . . .

The second sentence of Article 95(1) EC is worded as follows:

> "The Council shall, acting in accordance with the procedure referred to in Article 251 and after consulting the Economic and Social Committee, adopt the measures for the approximation of the provisions laid down by law, regulation or administrative action in Member States which have as their object the establishment and functioning of the internal market." . . .

THE APPLICATION IN CASE C-318/04

The Parliament advances four pleas for annulment, alleging, respectively, *ultra vires* action, breach of the fundamental principles of the Directive, breach of

continued

continued

fundamental rights and breach of the principle of proportionality....

The first indent of Article 3(2) of the Directive excludes from the Directive's scope the processing of personal data in the course of an activity which falls outside the scope of Community law, such as activities provided for by Titles V and VI of the Treaty on European Union, and in any case processing operations concerning public security, defence, State security and the activities of the State in areas of criminal law....

The decision on adequacy concerns only PNR data transferred to [the United States] ... based on a statute.... The [Commission decision] states that PNR data will be used strictly for purposes of preventing and combating terrorism and related crimes, other serious crimes, including organised crime, that are transnational in nature, and flight from warrants or custody for those crimes. It follows that the transfer of PNR data to [the United States] constitutes processing operations concerning public security and the activities of the State in areas of criminal law. While the view may rightly be taken that PNR data are initially collected by airlines in the course of an activity which falls within the scope of Community law, namely sale of an aeroplane ticket which provides entitlement to a supply of services, the data processing which is taken into account in the decision on adequacy is, however, quite different in nature. [T]hat decision concerns not data processing necessary for a supply of services, but data processing regarded as necessary for safeguarding public security and for law-enforcement purposes.... The transfer falls within a framework established by the public authorities that relates to public security. It follows from the foregoing considerations that the decision on adequacy concerns processing of personal data as referred to in the first indent of Article 3(2) of the Directive. That decision therefore does not fall within the scope of the Directive.

Accordingly, the first limb of the first plea, alleging that the first indent of Article 3(2) of the Directive was infringed, is well founded. The decision on adequacy must consequently be annulled and it is not necessary to consider the other limbs of the first plea or the other pleas relied upon by the Parliament.

THE APPLICATION IN CASE C-317/04

The Parliament advances six pleas for annulment, concerning the incorrect choice of Article 95 EC as legal basis for Decision 2004/496 and breach of, respectively, the second subparagraph of Article 300 (3) EC, Article 8 of the ECHR, the principle of proportionality, the requirement to state reasons and the principle of cooperation in good faith....

Article 95 EC, read in conjunction with Article 25 of the Directive, cannot justify Community competence to conclude the Agreement. The Agreement relates to the same transfer of data as the decision on adequacy and therefore to data processing operations which, as has been stated above, are excluded from the scope of the Directive. Consequently, Decision 2004/496 cannot have been validly adopted on the basis of Article 95 EC.

That decision must therefore be annulled and it is not necessary to consider the other pleas relied upon by the Parliament.

Decision. The Court of Justice annulled the Commission's decision and the agreement, but delayed the decision's effective date until September 30, 2006. This gave the Commission a chance to enter into a new interim agreement with the United States that tried to conform to the Parliament's substantive requests in order to obtain its approval. The Commission ultimately reached a permanent agreement with the United States in July 2007.

DISTINCTIONS AMONG INSTITUTIONS. Non-Europeans have some difficulty following developments in the EU because of a lack of clarity about the roles of its various institutions. The Council of the European Union easily can be confused with the *Council of Europe.* The Council of Europe comprises all the EU members plus a number of other countries, including Switzerland. The Council of Europe works to support democracy and human rights and to address the issues facing Europe as a whole. The Council of Europe has a *European Court of Human Rights* that hears complaints about violations of the *European Convention on Human Rights* and the *Anti-Torture Convention.*

Similarly, one should not confuse the EU's Court of Justice, which sits in Luxembourg, with the *International Court of Justice,* a court of final jurisdiction annexed by statute to the *United Nations*

Charter, or the *European Court of Human Rights.* As already discussed in this chapter, the Court of Justice, an EU institution, hears cases dealing with the interpretation of the *Treaty of Rome, the Maastricht Treaty,* and EU legislation and with conflicts between EU and national law.

Harmonization: Directives and Regulations

One of the principal goals of the EU is to harmonize national laws and create a common legal environment for business. The Council, Commission, and Parliament have several avenues open to them to achieve this objective. Article 189 of the *Treaty of Rome* identifies the four principal means:

- A regulation shall have general application. It shall be binding in its entirety and directly applicable in all member states.
- A directive shall be binding as to the result to be achieved upon each member state to which it is addressed but shall leave to the national authorities the choice of form and methods.
- A decision shall be binding in its entirety upon those to whom it is addressed.
- Recommendations and opinions shall have no binding force.

Regulations have a direct impact on the states and circumvent the need to pass legislation on the national level. Many EU regulations exist in the agriculture and competition law areas. (See the discussion of the *Merger Regulation* in Chapter Twenty-Two.) The *Merger Regulation* gave great power to the EU Commissioner in charge of Competition Policy (antitrust). Another example of a regulation is the December 2002 *Regulation 2368/2002,* which aims to block traffic in "blood diamonds."

Directives, in contrast to regulations, require that members bring their laws into harmony with the standard stated in the directive within a stated time period, most often three years. The EU has used this approach in the environmental, products liability, and employment arenas. Directives give member states more autonomy to implement legislative programs in ways that are most consistent with local conditions. The problem with local autonomy, however, is that the national legislation may not really advance the purposes of the directive. If the Commission believes that has happened, the Commission may initiate action in the EU courts to force the member state to comply. The member state will, of course, try to show that its action adequately complied with the directive.

PRIVACY. Many countries in the EU have long cherished privacy. This attitude is reflected in a number of legislative efforts. For example, the EU has a *Directive on Privacy and Electronic Communication (2002/58/EC)* as well as the data protection directive discussed in the *Parliament v. Council* decision. These directives have implications for financial enterprises, as well as for any company that shares customer information with a European counterpart. Indeed, as seen in *Parliament v. Council,* these directives can create complications for the sharing of customer information even with approval of the Commission. The following is a list of a few of the other directives connected to e-commerce and privacy:

- *E-Commerce Directive*
- *Directive on the Harmonization of Certain Aspects of Copyright and Related Rights in the Information Society*
- *Directive on Money Laundering*
- *Directive Concerning Distance Marketing of Consumer Financial Services*
- *Directive Authorization of Electronic Communication Networks and Services*
- *Directive on the Prevention of the Use of Financial Systems for Purpose of Money Laundering*

National legislation implements these directives, which means that there is no uniformity across member countries. These privacy directives impose an economic cost on businesses that must comply with their many requirements.

THE COMMON AGRICULTURAL POLICY. The European Community has committed itself to the establishment of a common agricultural policy (the *CAP*). The CAP has been central to the EU's mission since the EU's inception in 1956. Its goals, which are set forth in Article 39 of the *Treaty of Rome,* are as follows:

1. to increase agricultural productivity
2. to ensure a fair standard of living
3. to stabilize markets

4. to guarantee regular supplies
5. to ensure reasonable prices in supplies to consumers

The EU has implemented these objectives through the CAP, which ensures minimum prices to farmers, imposes import tariff barriers and quotas on agricultural products from non–member states, and pays subsidies to farmers for cultivated land. The CAP has been divisive within the EC because its financial burden falls most heavily on countries that do not directly benefit, particularly the United Kingdom and Germany. The CAP effectively maintains European agricultural firms that otherwise would not be able to withstand competition from lower-cost producers from outside the EC and increases the cost of agricultural products. This does provide the EU with some ability to feed itself in the event of hostilities. However, there is a difference of view between those who benefit from this *de facto* subsidy and those who pay for it as to how much protection the EU should provide.

The EU has agreed to make a few reforms to the system. First, it is slowly changing the subsidy for producing specific crops into a subsidy for land stewardship. This transition should be complete by 2012. Second, after the WTO appellate body upheld an objection by sugar-exporting countries to the EU sugar subsidy program, in February 2006 the EU cut the guaranteed price of sugar by 36 percent. This move is widely expected to reduce the European sugar beet industry significantly. Third, in autumn 2007, the European Commission considered a proposal to limit subsidies to individual landowners. This would allow it to avoid subsidizing wealthy companies and private estates. These moves and proposals are part of a continuing series of attempts to dismantle European trade barriers in the agricultural context. It is a project likely to continue for a long time.

The EU's response to the concern about bovine spongiform encephalopathy (BSE)—more commonly known as mad cow disease—emanating from the UK illustrates some of the problems with the implementation of the single market in the agricultural context. In 1996, the Commission banned exports of beef and other meat products from the UK because of concerns about BSE. In 1998, the ban was lifted but not all countries felt comfortable about British meat exports and France continued to balk at compliance with the court decision in the *National Farmers' Union* case.

National Farmers' Union and Secrétariat général du gouvernement (France)
C-241/01 (2002)

BACKGROUND AND FACTS

Following the discovery of a probable link between a variant of Creutzfeldt Jakob disease, a disease affecting human beings, and bovine spongiform encephalopathy (BSE), which was widespread in the United Kingdom in the mid-1990s, the Commission adopted *Decision 96/239/EC* of 27 March 1996, which contained emergency measures to protect against BSE. This decision prohibited the United Kingdom from exporting certain products, in particular live bovine animals, meat of bovine animals and products obtained from bovine animals, from its territory to the other member states and third countries.

ARTICLE 14

The Commission shall carry out Community inspections on-the-spot in the United Kingdom to verify the application of the provisions of this decision, in particular in relation to the implementation of official controls.

ARTICLE 15

The United Kingdom shall send the Commission every month a report on the application of the protective measures taken against BSE, in accordance with national and Community provisions.

By its third question, the national court seeks to ascertain whether a Member State is justified in invoking Article 30 EC in order to prohibit imports of agricultural products and live animals, inasmuch as *Directives 89/662 and 90/425* cannot be regarded as harmonising the measures needed in order to attain the specific objective of protecting the health and life of humans provided for by that article.

continued

continued

FINDINGS OF THE COURT

According to settled case-law, where Community directives provide for the harmonisation of the measures necessary to ensure the protection of animal and human health and establish Community procedures to check that they are observed, recourse to Article 30 EC is no longer justified and the appropriate checks must be carried out and the measures of protection adopted within the framework outlined by the harmonising directive.

***

The Court has also held that even where a directive does not lay down any Community procedure for monitoring compliance or any penalties in the event of breach of its provisions, a Member State may not unilaterally adopt, on its own authority, corrective or protective measures designed to obviate any breach by another Member State of rules of Community law. . . .

It should indeed be made clear that in the European Community, which is a community based on law, a Member State is bound to comply with the provisions of the Treaty and, in particular, to act within the framework of the procedures provided for by the Treaty and by the applicable legislation.

It is in the light of those various factors that it is necessary to determine whether the French Government was able, at the date of the implicit decisions at issue in the main proceedings, to invoke Article 30 EC in order to maintain the prohibition on imports of beef and veal from the United Kingdom.

Although Regulation No 999/2001 no doubt achieved full harmonisation of the rules relating to the prevention, control and eradication of certain transmissible spongiform encephalopathies, it should be noted, as has the Advocate General in points 91 to 94 of his Opinion, that Decisions 98/256 and 98/692, defining the DBES, laid down the rules necessary for the protection of public health upon the resumption of exports of beef and veal from the United Kingdom to the other Member States.

Those decisions, which are additional to the general legislation already in existence, specify the requirements of eligibility and traceability of animals liable to be used under the DBES, the requirements to be satisfied by slaughterhouses and the conditions specific to the cutting of meat, which are imposed as a supplement to the provisions in force relating to the withdrawal of specific offal.

Moreover, Article 14 of Decision 98/256 as amended provides that Community inspections must be carried out by the Commission in the United Kingdom to verify the application of the provisions of that decision, while Article 15 thereof provides for the United Kingdom to send to the Commission every month a report on the application of the protective measures taken against BSE.

As regards the obligations of the Member States other than the United Kingdom, Article 17 of *Decision 98/256* as amended provides that they are to adopt the necessary measures to comply with that decision and are immediately to inform the Commission thereof.

Furthermore, as was stated in paragraph 38 of this judgment, Article 16 of Decision 98/256 as amended specifies that that decision must be reviewed regularly in the light of new scientific information and that any amendments are to be made in accordance with the procedure laid down in Article 18 of *Directive 89/662*.

Examination of these various provisions show that, in addition to the harmonisation of the measures necessary to ensure the protection of human health, *Decision 98/256* as amended lays down procedures for monitoring compliance with it and specifies, by reference to *Directive 89/662*, the appropriate procedure for making the amendments which might be made essential by the development of scientific knowledge.

As regards the emergency measures liable to be taken by a Member State in the event of a serious hazard to human health, it is important to note that Decision 98/256 was adopted on the basis of *Directives 89/662 and 90/425*, and *Decision 98/692* on the basis of *Directive 89/662* alone.

Directive 89/662 describes, in Article 7, 8 and 9, the measures which may be adopted by a Member State of destination, in particular where its competent authorities establish that the goods imported do not meet the conditions laid down by Community legislation. Article 7 authorises the destruction or return of those goods and Article 9 authorises in particular the adoption, by that Member State, of interim protective measures on serious public-health or animal-health grounds.

It is in accordance with those provisions, which require the measures adopted to be notified without delay to the other Member States and to the Commission and close to collaboration between the

continued

continued

Member States and the Commission, that a Member State must act when faced with a situation endangering the health of its population....

It is moreover the application of the interim protective measures referred to in Article 9 of Directive 89/662 which is envisaged by the 13th recital in the preamble to Decision 98/692 in the event that it is discovered, after the dispatch of products which were believed to fulfil the conditions of the DBES, that those products came from an animal subsequently found to be ineligible under that scheme.

Examination of all these provisions shows that the existing legislation and, in particular, Directive 89/662 and Decisions 98/256 and 98/692 provide for the harmonisation necessary to ensure the protection of public health upon the resumption of exports of beef and veal from the United Kingdom to the other Member States and lay down Community procedures to monitor compliance with them.

It is true that, in paragraph 134 of *Commission v. France*, cited above, the Court noted that there were difficulties in interpreting Decision 98/256 as amended in respect of the Member States' obligations relating to the traceability of products. Suffice it to state, however, that, as paragraph 135 of that judgment shows, those difficulties of interpretation had disappeared by the date of the implicit decisions refusing to lift the ban at issue in the main proceedings.

As regards products subject to the *DBES* which have been cut, processed or rewrapped in another Member State and subsequently exported to France without the affixing of a distinct mark, suffice it to state that the main proceedings do not concern such products and that, in any event, the French Government has never prevented their importation.

It follows from all the foregoing that, since *Directive 89/662* and *Decision 98/256* as amended lay down the rules necessary for the protection of public health upon the resumption of exports of beef and veal from the United Kingdom to the other Member States, lay down a Community procedure to monitor compliance with that decision and a procedure for amending it in the light of new scientific information and provide the appropriate legal framework for the adoption of interim protective measures by a Member State of destination for the purpose of protecting public health, a Member State is not entitled to invoke Article 30 EC in order to prevent the resumption of imports to its territory of beef and veal from the United Kingdom which were carried out in accordance with *Decisions 98/256* as amended and *1999/514*.

Decision and Comment. The UK was allowed to ship beef and veal outside the country. France finally complied in the face of heavy fines.

HARMONIZATION BY ENFORCEMENT OF THE EC TREATY. In addition to its powers to enforce directives and regulations, the Commission can harmonize national laws that, while not expressly addressed in EU directives, are inconsistent with the economic objectives of the EU. Increasingly, the Commission is acting like the U.S. executive branch and federal courts by striking down local legal barriers to the free flow of commerce throughout the union. The following case illustrates the EU analytical framework on such matters.

Commission of the European Communities v. Italian Republic

Case C-134/05 (14 December 2006)

European Court of Justice

BACKGROUND AND FACTS

The European Community sought a declaration that, because of the way in which long-standing Italian law permitted extrajudicial debt recovery self-help by creditors against entities established in other member states, Italy had failed to fulfill its EC Treaty

continued

continued

obligations. The European Union had not passed directly applicable legislation in the area of extrajudicial debt recovery. Italian law provided that, in order to recover debts extrajudicially, a creditor needed to obtain a license from the *Questore* (the local police authority). This license permitted action only in the Italian province where it was issued. Further, the Questore could place such conditions on the grant of a license as it thought appropriate. The license holder needed to display a list of all services provided and their cost on its business premises so that the Questore could confirm that prices for the services did not vary significantly. Further, license holders could not provide banking or credit services. Only banks and financial institutions listed with the ministry of the treasury could provide these services.

The Commission brought an action against Italy, as it considered these requirements to be in restraint of commerce among the member states. The Commission asked the Court of Justice to clarify the degree of discretion that member states retain vis-à-vis the European Commission in inter–member state economic matters.

ADVOCATE GENERAL POIARES MADURO

By its application, the Commission once again asks the Court to clarify the margin of discretion available to the Member States in regulating the pursuit of an economic activity which has not yet been the subject of Community legislation. In that regard, it should be pointed out at the outset that, according to the case-law of the Court, "in the absence of harmonization of a profession, Member States remain, in principle, competent to define the exercise of that profession but must, when exercising their powers in this area, respect the basic freedoms guaranteed by the Treaty".... It is true that the freedoms of movement, such as the rights to freedom of establishment and freedom to provide services, are not intended to liberalize national economies by precluding any legislation by the State which might affect economic and commercial freedom; if they were, they would sound the death knell for the powers of the Member States to legislate in economic matters. They do serve, however, to promote the decompartmentalisation of national markets by making it easier for operators to carry on their activity at a transnational level. To that end, they are intended to cover all transnational situations and to prohibit not only any direct or indirect discrimination on grounds of nationality introduced by the Member States, but also any national measure resulting in the treatment of transnational situations less favourably than purely national ones.... In other words, in accordance with the logic of the internal market, they serve to ensure that discrimination which obstructs the exercise of the freedom of movement will be challenged by legal action.... More specifically, the less favourable treatment of transnational situations which the principle of freedom of movement prohibits may take different forms. It may, of course, be the effect of discrimination advantageous to its own nationals. It may also arise from a restriction on market access, be it that the national rules have the effect of protecting the positions acquired by economic operators established in the national market or that they make the pursuit of a transnational activity or trade between Member States more difficult.

It is in the light of this analytical framework that the relevance of the complaints raised by the Commission should be assessed. As the following analysis will make apparent, those complaints are well founded. This does not mean that a Member State cannot regulate the activity of extrajudicial debt recovery.... However, the conditions which the Italian Republic has attached to the pursuit of that activity are far too restrictive of the freedom of establishment and the freedom to provide services.

A. THE REQUIREMENT OF A LICENCE AND THE ADDITIONAL CONDITIONS GOVERNING THE AWARD OF LICENCES

The Commission first calls into question the condition, which the Italian rules attach to pursuit of the activity of extrajudicial debt recovery, that prior administrative authorisation must be obtained from the local police authority.... In so far as that requirement is also imposed on providers of services established in another Member State, without regard to whether they have complied with any obligations laid down by the rules of the country in which they are established ... those rules infringe the freedom to provide services. This is particularly true given that the Italian rules give the Questore the power to impose requirements additional to those which they expressly lay down....

[I]t is common knowledge that, in keeping with the approach originally adopted with regard to the free movement of goods, the principle of the freedom to provide services has gradually come to be interpreted as prohibiting not only directly or indirectly

continued

continued

discriminatory restrictions, but also obstacles applicable without distinction.... In the light of the foregoing considerations, I therefore propose that the Court should uphold the complaint alleging that Article 49 EC has been infringed by virtue of the fact that the activity of extrajudicial debt recovery is made subject to the grant of a licence.

B. THE TERRITORIAL DELIMITATION OF THE LICENCE

The Commission takes the view that limiting the validity of the licence to the territory of the province in which the Questore that granted it has authority, unless an authorised representative is awarded a contract of agency to pursue the activity in a province for which the operator does not have a licence, constitutes an unjustified restriction on both the freedom to provide services and the freedom of establishment. Since Italy is divided into 103 provinces, that geographical delimitation of the scope of the licence indisputably constitutes a restriction on the exercise of those two fundamental freedoms. An operator who wishes to extend his business throughout much of Italy with a view to operating there on an occasional or stable and continuous basis must submit as many licence applications as there are provinces in the area which he intends to cover, and 103 applications if he intends to carry on his business throughout the Italian territory. Contrary to the Italian Government's submission, it is in this regard also irrelevant that the same requirement is imposed on operators established in Italy because, in any event, indistinctly applicable obstacles to the freedom of establishment are prohibited in the same way as those to the freedom to provide services.

It remains to be determined whether that restriction is appropriate and necessary on the legitimate public security grounds put forward by the defendant, namely to ward off the risk of infiltration by organised crime. In the defendant's view, it is, since the province is the most appropriate territorial level for assessing the impact on public order of the activities of an additional extrajudicial debt recovery operator and supervising existing operators. I am not persuaded by that defence. In my view, the limitation of the territorial scope of the licence is, first of all, an unjustified restriction on the freedom to provide services. If, as I suggested earlier, the general and absolute requirement of a licence infringes the principle of the freedom to provide services, then the same is particularly true of a system under which the number of applications for authorisation which a crossborder service provider must make increases with the size of the geographical area he wishes to cover in the host Member State. Moreover, the Court has already called into question the obligation on an architect to enrol on the professional register of each province in which he plans to provide his services, on the ground that such a delimitation of the territorial scope of registration "further complicates" the exercise of the freedom to provide services, which is already restricted by that obligation in itself.

I therefore propose that the Court should find that, by limiting the validity of the licence to the provincial jurisdiction of the police authority which granted it, and by requiring the operator to award a contract of agency to an authorised representative in order to pursue his activity in a province for which he does not have a licence, the Italian Republic has failed to fulfil its obligations under the principles of the freedom of establishment and the freedom to provide services.

C. MAKING PURSUIT OF THE ACTIVITY SUBJECT TO THE POSSESSION OF PREMISES BY THE OPERATOR

According to the Commission, the contested Italian rules show that there is an obligation to possess premises in which the debt recovery activity is to be carried out, which obligation applies to each province for which the operator has a licence. It argues that such a requirement infringes both the freedom of establishment and the freedom to provide services.... This obligation is therefore closely linked to limiting the validity of the authorisation to the territory of one province: the territorial limitation of the establishment makes it necessary to have multiple establishments. I have already set out the reasons why such a limitation of the geographical scope of the licence infringes the freedom of establishment....

D. LIMITATION OF THE FREEDOM TO FIX SCALES OF CHARGES

The Commission also criticises the Italian Republic for having restricted the freedom of establishment and the freedom to provide services without justification by recommending ... that the Questori control scales of charges by setting objective and uniform parameters, in order to ensure that the prices charged within a single province do not vary too greatly. I concur with the Commission's view that that

continued

continued

recommendation must be regarded as a limitation of the freedom to fix scales of charges, in spite of the denial that that is the case by the Italian authorities, according to which that recommendation simply suggests that the Questori should provide operators with details of price lists based on objective factors (costs, the ratio of supply and demand in relation to services, etc.). However, the fact that those details are binding is apparent from the defendant's own admission that the development of excessive price competition could prompt the law enforcement authority to suspend or even revoke the licences of responsible operators.

Like the Commission, I consider that that limitation of the freedom to fix scales of charges is such as to hinder or make less attractive the exercise of the freedom of establishment and the freedom to provide services and therefore constitutes an obstacle to those two fundamental freedoms. Even if it is not discriminatory, it is such as to restrict access to the Italian market in activities concerned with extrajudicial debt recovery by operators wishing to establish themselves in Italy or provide their services in that State. As the Court made clear in CaixaBank France, price competition is often the best way of attracting customers and thus entering a market, in particular for operators who are not yet present in that market and are therefore unknown to customers. Accordingly, any national measure which has the effect of limiting it constitutes a restriction on the exercise of the right of establishment and the right to provide services....

It is therefore appropriate to uphold the complaint alleging that Articles 43 EC and 49 EC have been infringed by the limitation of the freedom to fix scales of charges.

E. THE PROHIBITION ON THE PURSUIT OF DEBT RECOVERY ACTIVITIES CONCURRENTLY WITH THE PROVISION OF BANKING AND CREDIT SERVICES

Finally, the Commission alleges that the Italian Republic has infringed the freedom of establishment and the freedom to provide services, inasmuch as [Italian law] makes the activity of extrajudicial debt recovery incompatible with the banking and credit services.... In so far as that incompatibility has the effect of prohibiting banking operators from other Member States who are authorised, if they so wish, to pursue both lines of activity concurrently in their country of origin from pursuing debt recovery activities in Italy, it indisputably hinders their right to freedom of establishment and freedom to provide services.

I therefore propose that the Court should also uphold the complaint alleging that Articles 43 EC and 49 EC have been infringed by the incompatibility between the activity of debt recovery and banking and credit services.

Decision. The Advocate General proposed that the Court enter a judgment consistent with his opinion.

The Business Implications of the European Union

The main object of the European Union is to make it easier to do business within Europe. The elimination of intra-EU tariffs means that, once a product enters the EU, an enterprise need not concern itself further with customs duties. Harmonization of laws and standardization of equipment means that companies can manufacture the same product for the entire European market of 500 million people, creating significant economies of scale and streamlining regulatory compliance costs. Companies can centralize or regionalize corporate offices and distribution centers, rather than having a separate office for each country. Firms must still comply with separate national laws, particularly those that regulate health and advertising. However, because such laws must increasingly comply with EU directives, they are less of a hindrance to inter–member state commerce.

Today, the Commission seems relentless in its efforts to impose its economic will on the member states. In 1998, the EU announced a phase-out of tobacco advertising, but in 2000, the Court of Justice in *Imperial Tobacco Ltd. v. European Parliament & Council,* C-74/79 Article 234EC overturned it as attempting to regulate commerce solely within a member state and thus beyond its inter–member state trade powers. Undaunted, in 2003, the European Parliament and Council enacted a new *Tobacco Advertising Directive 2003/33/EC,* which changed its overall ban on tobacco advertising to a ban on ads in the print media, on radio, and over the Internet, on the theory that these media are within inter–member state commerce. The revised ban thus arguably applied only to advertising and sponsorship with a cross-border dimension, but as a practical matter touched virtually all advertising, except ads in cinemas and on billboards. By mid-2006, the European Commission had once more commenced tobacco advertising compliance actions against the Czech Republic, Italy, Hungary, and Spain for failing to enact compliant laws. This example is illustrative of the single-minded persistence of EU officials to regulate all commerce within the Union.

These commercial unification developments particularly benefit competitive European businesses that have a larger duty-free market. They harm marginal European businesses that owe their survival to trade barriers against competition from other member states. Economic theory suggests that ultimately, as more efficient and qualified firms vanquish corporate deadwood, the majority of Europeans will benefit. These developments also benefit competitive firms from non–EU countries. While non–EU concerns must still confront the hurdle of EU tariffs and quotas, once they surmount that barrier, the customs union gives them the same advantages as entities in member states. The dynamic of free internal trade was largely responsible for the economic success of the United States. Today, it appears to be having a similar effect within the European Union.

In many areas, the EU is the principal government regulator. This is particularly true in competition law, where Directorate-General IV has long ruled the roost. As discussed in Chapter Twenty-Two, Sun Microsystems recently succeeded in compelling Microsoft Corporation to modify its licensing practices by enlisting the assistance of the EU Commission. Thus, an American company was able to obtain relief from the practices of another American company which it could not obtain in the United States because both companies had substantial European operations. If a company is in Europe, it is under the jurisdiction of the EU, whose policies can be quite different from those of its home country.

The EU's treaty-making powers also have a direct effect on businesses from non–member states. As noted above, Article 133 of the *Treaty of Rome* gives the EC the exclusive power to conclude trade and tariff agreements with other nations, a necessary precondition to a customs union. (The Commission has treaty-making powers in other areas under Article 300, but those agreements are subject to more onerous review by Council and the Parliament.) Thus, if the EU decides that it needs to protect a particular European industry from non–member state competition, non–member state firms will be directly and adversely affected by EU action. In 2007, it was the EU, and not any single member state, that negotiated with China over possible tariffs on Chinese products, which it wished to impose in retaliation for the artificially low exchange rate of the yuan. In 2007, the EU negotiated with the United States and litigated against it in the WTO with respect to gaming, commercial aircraft, beef hormones, and the U.S. Byrd Amendment. Businesses in those industries who find themselves in the midst of a trade skirmish may either provide or foreclose opportunity. The businessperson from a non–member state must recognize that in modern Europe, the commercial side of foreign policy is largely in the hands of the EU.

Other Regional Trade Areas

The EU and the members of NAFTA (the United States, Canada, and Mexico) are not the only countries that have experimented with economically integrated trade areas. Other countries, attracted by the economic benefits of integration, are accelerating their own integration efforts. The next section looks briefly at some of these efforts.

MERCOSUR

In the early 1990s, Argentina, Brazil, Paraguay, and Uruguay agreed to form a "Southern Common Market" (MERCOSUR), spearheaded by a customs union like that in the EU. The potential of this market is quite significant, because this region has a population of about 230 million. A restricted free trade area was implemented with an initial positive economic effect: the market experienced a 250 percent increase in trade between 1990 and the present.

The importance of MERCOSUR has declined in the first decade of the 21st century. Despite its early ambitions, it has not implemented a true customs union with common tariffs and free movement of goods within the union. In fact, its status as a free trade area degenerated somewhat when the two member countries with over 95 percent of the population encountered difficulties. The Brazilian devaluation of 1999 made Brazilian products cheap in Argentina. This triggered the Argentine economic collapse and devaluation of 2001–2002. After this episode, Argentina took a more aggressive trade posture toward its large neighbor and initiated proceedings against it at the WTO. In doing so, Argentina ignored the availability of the analogous MERCOSUR dispute mechanisms, reflecting its view of MERCOSUR's relative irrelevance. Uruguay and Argentina are now at economic war because investors have been choosing to build facilities in Uruguay rather than Argentina. Argentina has thrown up barriers against Paraguayan bananas. Paraguay is permitting the smuggling of Chinese-made electronic goods into Brazil and Argentina. Although economic activity is again on the upswing in the MERCOSUR countries, the rise in exports has been with non-member countries, while intra-MERCOSUR trade has stagnated. This is a very long way from a "common market."

Despite MERCOSUR's imperfections, its members have sought to expand the dysfunctional trade area to other countries. Chile and Bolivia joined as "associate members" in the late 1990s under terms whereby they would join in the theoretical free trade, but not in the aspiration of a customs union. In 2006, MERCOSUR tentatively accepted Venezuela as a full member, although an increasing distaste for Venezuelan leader Hugo Chavez prevented the Brazilian and Paraguayan legislatures from giving the required approval.

For the present, MERCOSUR appears to be more of a political group than an economic unit. The promise of MERCOSUR has not been realized. It remains to be seen if it ever will.

The DR-Central American Free Trade Area

Hoping to create a free trade area akin to NAFTA, a group of Spanish-speaking Latin American countries in the Caribbean Basin entered into a similar agreement with the United States. In early 2005, these parties signed the *U.S.–Central American–Dominican Republic Free Trade Agreement* (CAFTA-DR). It was subject to ratification by its signatories, the United States, the Dominican Republic, and the Central American countries of Costa Rica, El Salvador, Guatemala, Honduras, and Nicaragua. The U.S. Congress ratified the agreement in mid-2005, triggering a slow process of ratification by the other parties. Costa Rica was the last to ratify it in October 2007.

CAFTA–DR immediately removed the tariffs on roughly 80 percent of U.S. exports to the other signatories and provided for phase-out of the balance over a decade. It provides for similar reductions in U.S. tariffs on imports from those nations.

Andean Community of Nations

The *Andean Community of Nations* (CAN), known until 1996 as the Andean Pact, includes Bolivia, Colombia, Ecuador, and Peru. It was founded in 1969 by the *Cartagena Agreement* and involves an area of some 100 million people. Chile was one of the original members but withdrew in 1977. Venezuela joined in 1973 but withdrew in 2006 to form a trade bloc with Cuba and Bolivia. Through an agreement with MERCOSUR in 2005, MERCOSUR's four members received associate membership in the Andean Community.

Its legal structures include the Commission, Junta, Andean Development Bank and Reserve Fund, and Andean Court of Justice. Initially, the Andean Community's member countries hoped to exclude other countries' products and trade only with one another. This exclusionary aspiration, which has never borne fruit, is really the opposite of free trade. If it had succeeded in excluding more efficient producers from outside the CAN, the population would have paid excessive prices for goods. This aim has been abandoned, however, and the hope now is to create a free trade area.

The CAN has not developed a customs union, but it has taken promising steps in that direction such as approving development of a "Common External Tariff." In 2007, the Andean Community General Secretariat entered negotiations on tariff reductions with the EU on behalf of its four member countries. Thus, it is beginning to act as a single unit. The members, however, retain their independence on a broad number of international trade issues. For example, in 2007, Peru concluded a bilateral free trade agreement with the United States independent of its Andean Community partners. The Andean Community has also made advances toward creating a free trade area among the CAN members. As its members have relatively small economies and do the great bulk of their international trade with countries outside CAN, the free trade bloc is correspondingly less important.

There has been some significant progress in permitting the free movement of people among the CAN member states. Beginning in 2005, citizens from one member country could enter the other member countries without visa. They now need only present a national identity card.

Central American Common Market

Guatemala, El Salvador, Costa Rica, Nicaragua, and Honduras have since 1991 been parties to a trade agreement referred to as the *Central American Common Market* or CACM. The CACM has been successful as a free trade zone, because most local-origin goods move duty-free within the zone. There has been no other significant movement toward a customs union or other economic integration, however. The members' great economic differences—prosperous Costa Rica has a GNP per capita that is more than seven times that of struggling Nicaragua—dampen the more developed nations' desire to integrate.

African Trade Areas

The development of Africa will be important in this century. Ravaged by civil wars and corruption after the end of the colonial period, many African countries are seeking to rebuild their economies. Economic integration would undoubtedly advance that effort.

African Economic Community. The *African Economic Community* has been in existence since 1994 and now counts fifty-one member states. Its founding treaty contemplated a six-phase implementation of economic integration among the members over a twenty-year period. The steps of this integration include:

- establishment of regional trade groups
- eventual legal harmonization among these trade groups
- conversion of regional blocs into free trade areas and customs unions by 2017
- creation of a community-wide customs union and free trade area by 2019
- adoption of standardized economic legislation creating a community-wide common market by 2023
- establishment of a common currency and a central bank to determine its monetary policy by 2028

The African Economic Community has achieved the limited objective of "creating" regional economic blocs. We use the term "created" guardedly because some of these blocs, discussed below, existed prior to the group's inception. To date, however, the African Economic Community has made relatively little progress toward its more ambitious goals.

COMESA: Common Market for Eastern and Southern Africa. The 1982 *Common Market for Eastern and Southern Africa Treaty* has been signed by nineteen African states and creates a "preferential trade area," meaning an area where preferential duties are available to fellow members. The *Common Market for Eastern and Southern Africa* (COMESA) is one of the regional blocs of the African Economic Community. In 2000, nine of COMESA's members created a free trade area for goods originating within the area. It hopes to become an area-wide free trade area and customs union by 2017. This may be difficult to achieve because COMESA's members include several countries racked, variously, by civil war, external invasion, and internal corruption: Congo, Eritrea, Sudan, Uganda, and Zimbabwe.

Southern African Development Community. The *South African Development Community* (SADC), formed in 1992, is another regional bloc under the African Economic Community. It has an overlapping membership with COMESA. Its members are Angola, Botswana, Lesotho, Malawi, Mozambique, Namibia, Swaziland, Tanzania, Zambia, Zimbabwe, Mauritius, and South Africa.

This group has little structure and has accomplished little toward its objectives.

Five members of the group, however—South Africa, Botswana, Lesotho, Swaziland, and Namibia—comprise the *Southern Africa Customs Union,* which is the world's oldest customs union and free trade area. This union, which originated when apartheid South Africa dominated its small neighbors, is a truly functional customs union that has allowed significant economic integration in Africa's southern cone. It is perhaps not surprising that this is also the most affluent area in sub-Saharan Africa. Its success could eventually form the basis for a larger free trade and customs area.

Asia-Pacific Economic Cooperation Group

Founded in 1989, the *Asia-Pacific Economic Cooperation Group* (APEC) is a loose group of twenty-one Pacific Rim countries, including the United States, Japan, Australia, Canada, South Korea, Mexico, China, and Indonesia. Its members comprise over 60 percent of the world's economic output. Although it has a secretariat that arranges periodic meetings and has issued a few hopeful statements, its member nations have no trade agreements of substance. Rather, this famous "group" is little more than another forum where powerful economic actors can discuss trade policy. It has little practical significance for businesspeople.

CARICOM: Caribbean Community

The *Caribbean Community* (CARICOM) comprises fifteen full members and five associate members, all of which are small non-Spanish-speaking Caribbean islands. (Haiti was once a member, but its membership has effectively been suspended.) In 2001, CARICOM's members entered into a revised *Treaty of Chaguaramas* that created a customs union and free trade zone and established a Caribbean Court of Justice. The Caribbean Community is quite similar in structure to the EU. It has a community-wide legislature called the Council and an executive body called the Secretariat. In 2006, its ends progressed even further with the ratification of the *CARICOM Single Market and Economy Treaty.* Under its terms, CARICOM's parties seek to eliminate all barriers, perhaps develop a single currency, and create a single "federal" economy akin to that of the United States. This intense effort at integration is aided by CARICOM's members' common political culture. Most are former English colonies with a common-law tradition, with a few former Dutch colonies. Further, the small size of each member nation makes it critical for its citizens to be able to have the benefits of larger markets and competitive advantage. The Caribbean Community is a trade area whose goals are proceeding apace.

The appellate jurisdiction of the group's highest court, the *Caribbean Court of Justice* (CCJ), is as broad as that of the U.S. Supreme Court, extending to criminal appeals from the appellate courts of the islands. As is illustrated in the following case, the *Caribbean Court of Justice Agreement* effectively abolished the top appellate court of each of the islands and replaced it with the CCJ. The CCJ's jurisdiction, therefore, ranges far beyond international commerce matters.

Barbados Rediffusion Service Limited v. Mirchandani

CCJ Application No. AL 0001 of 2005 (26 October 2005)

Caribbean Court of Justice

BACKGROUND AND FACTS

The plaintiff brought this action against the defendant, the owner of a radio station, in the courts of Barbados. The plaintiff alleged that that the defendant broadcast recordings of three calypso tunes frequently on his radio station during the run-up to the annual "Crop Over Festival" and also broadcast live versions of the songs, which were sung at the semifinals and finals of the calypso competition at the festival. Plaintiff alleged that all three songs

continued

continued

asserted that the plaintiff was selling diseased chickens to the public—chickens that had died of illness rather than being slaughtered. The defendant filed an answer that did not admit the broadcasts and pleaded the defense of justification. The Barbados trial court ordered the defendant to file a list of documents relating to the action by a specified date. When the defendant failed to do so, the Barbados trial court struck the defense and entered judgment against the defendant.

The Barbados Court of Appeal affirmed the trial court's order. Shortly before the defendant radio station owner's appeal came up for hearing, the former high court of Barbados, known as the Judicial Committee of the Privy Council, was replaced by the Caribbean Court of Justice. The defendant ultimately sought leave to appeal to the Caribbean Court of Justice.

PRESIDENT OF THE COURT, THE RT. HON. MR. JUSTICE M. DE LA BASTIDE

This case has the distinction of being the first to reach the Caribbean Court of Justice. It is an application for special leave to appeal to this Court from a decision of the Court of Appeal of Barbados ....

THE JURISDICTION ISSUE

The application to this Court is based on the premise that subject to the applicant obtaining from this Court the special leave which it seeks, it has a right of appeal to this Court. The respondents never sought to challenge the existence of this right and even after the matter was raised by the Court with the applicant's counsel in the course of his oral submissions, counsel for the respondents did not accept the implied invitation to address this issue. Nevertheless, since it is an issue which goes to our jurisdiction, I think we must address it. The question put broadly is whether the legislation by which the Judicial Committee of the Privy Council was replaced by the Caribbean Court of Justice as the final court of appeal for Barbados, has any, and if so, what impact on the applicant's right to pursue an appeal against the Court of Appeal's decision affirming the order of [the trial court].

THE LEGISLATION

The legislation in question consists of two principal Acts. The first is the *Constitution (Amendment) Act, 2003* ("the 2003 Act"). This Act amended the Barbados Constitution firstly by substituting the words "the Caribbean Court of Justice" for the words "Her Majesty in Council" wherever the latter appeared in the Constitution. The 2003 Act also inserted in the Constitution a number of new sections ... dealing with various aspects of the Caribbean Court of Justice.... This Act was assented to by the Governor General on the 24th April, 2003, but was by section 10 to come into effect on a date to be fixed by proclamation.

The second principal Act was the *Caribbean Court of Justice Act* ("the CCJ Act"). This Act provides in section 3 that the Agreement Establishing the Caribbean Court of Justice ("the CCJ") shall have the force of law and in section 4 (1) that the CCJ shall have "appellate jurisdiction provided for in this Act as is conferred on it in accordance with the provisions of Part III of the Agreement."

Section 6 provides for appeals as of right to the CCJ from the decisions of the Court of Appeal in a number of different categories of case, none of which catches the instant case. Section 7 provides for an appeal to this Court with leave of the Court of Appeal inter alia "in any civil proceedings where, in the opinion of the Court of Appeal, the question is one that by reason of its great general or public importance or otherwise, ought to be submitted to the Court".

Section 8 provides: "Subject to section 7, an appeal shall lie to the Court with the special leave of the Court from any decision of the Court of Appeal in any civil or criminal matter".

This Act was assented to on the same day as the 2003 Act and was also to come into effect on a date to be fixed by proclamation. By proclamations contained in Statutory Instruments numbered 44 and 45 respectively of 2005, the 8th April, 2005, was the date appointed for the coming into operation of both the CCJ Act and the 2003 Act.

On the 14th April, 2005, the Acting Governor-General assented to ... *The Caribbean Court of Justice (Amendment) Act, 2005*. [This Act] corrected an omission in that Act by introducing a new section, section 25A, which repealed sections 64 and 65 of the *Supreme Court of Judicature Act*. Section 64 (1) of the *Judicature Act* provided that an appeal should lie from decisions of the Court of Appeal to Her Majesty in Council as of right in certain specified circumstances, and with leave of the Court of Appeal "if, in the opinion of the Court of Appeal, the question involved in the appeal is one that, by reason of its general or public importance, or otherwise, ought to be submitted to Her Majesty in Council for decision."

If one superimposes the legislative time-table on the chronology of these proceedings, what emerges is that the right of appeal to this Court which the applicant is seeking to invoke, first became part of the law of Barbados on the 8th April, 2005 ("the commencement

continued

continued

date"), while the decision against which the applicant seeks to appeal was given by the Court of Appeal on the 20th August, 2004, that is some seven and one-half months earlier. The hearing of the application for leave to appeal to the Privy Council had been completed before the commencement date and all that was outstanding on that date was the delivery of judgment by the Court of Appeal. What appeal then, if any, could the applicant pursue after the commencement date and how could it do so?

We are forced to fall back therefore on general principles of construction to determine the question of jurisdiction in the instant case. First of all, we adopt the view that the substitution of one court of final resort for another is to be regarded as a procedural rather than a substantive change in the law. The proper approach to construction in such cases is formulated in *Bennion on Statutory Interpretation,* 4th edition, page 269, section 98, as follows:

"Because a change made by the legislator in procedural provisions is expected to be for the general benefit of litigants and others, it is presumed that it applies to pending as well as future proceedings. This presumption does not operate where, on the facts of the instant case, to apply it would contravene the principle that persons should not be penalized under a doubtful enactment".

In our view, therefore, the presumption against legislation which changes the substantive law having a retrospective effect has no application here. It cannot be argued therefore that the new legislation should not be interpreted in a way which would affect a right of appeal that had already accrued....

[W]e are satisfied that subject to the applicant obtaining special leave from this Court upon an application made within the relevant time-limit and in compliance with such procedural requirements as may be applicable, the applicant has a right of appeal to this Court. We would have reached the same conclusion even if the Court of Appeal had purported to give him leave to appeal to the Judicial Committee or if he had made no application for leave to appeal to the Court of Appeal, but the time for doing so had not expired before the commencement date. The position of course would be different in the case of a person who on the commencement date had no possibility of pursuing an appeal to the Privy Council. His right of further appeal having died, could not be resurrected on or after the commencement date by the new legislation....

Our function on this application is a very limited one. Our concern is only whether there is some special feature of this case which would warrant our giving special leave to appeal to this Court in these circumstances in which there is no appeal as of right and no basis on which the Court of Appeal could have granted leave to appeal to us. Given our limited function at this stage, it would be quite wrong for us to attempt to come to any conclusion as to whether we are satisfied that there is such a flaw in the exercise of the Judge's discretion as would justify our interfering with it and quashing the order he has made....

It has been said that the Judicial Committee will grant special leave to appeal if there has been either an "egregious" error of law or a substantial miscarriage of justice. In this case there is no egregious error of law involved, but the question does arise whether in the circumstances of this case there exists a real risk that allowing the order barring the applicant from defending this action to stand, without being exposed to further scrutiny by this Court, will result in a serious miscarriage of justice. The sanction imposed on the applicant is a drastic one as it denies it the opportunity to defend the action on its merits. The applicant has always manifested a serious intention to contest liability in this action and there is at least the possibility that if liability is established, the damages in this action will be substantial.

We are certainly not in a position to hold, and do not hold, that the sanction imposed was wrongly imposed. We have, however, come to the conclusion that in the circumstances of this case the possibility that it may have been wrongly or unfairly imposed is significant enough to warrant the issue being fully and finally ventilated before this Court. Obviously we do not wish to say very much at this stage as what we say may be misconstrued as indicative of the likely outcome of the appeal. We would indicate, however, that in concluding that there is a more than negligible risk of a miscarriage of justice, we have a concern whether it was open to the courts below on the evidence before them and in the context of interlocutory proceedings for discovery, to find that there was a contumelious failure by the applicant to comply with the "unless" order.

Because of this concern we have come to the conclusion that we should grant special leave to appeal in order to eliminate the risk that leaving matters as they are, may result in a miscarriage of justice.

Decision. The Caribbean Court of Justice granted leave to appeal. After that consideration, in March 2006, the CCJ affirmed the judgment of the Barbados trial court against the radio station owner.

ASEAN

The *Association of South East Asian Nations* (ASEAN) was formed in 1967 by Indonesia, Malaysia, the Philippines, Singapore, and Thailand, pursuant to the *Bangkok Declaration*. Brunei joined in 1984. In the 1990s, four new members were added: Myanmar, Laos, Cambodia, and Vietnam. Unlike the treaties underlying the EU and CARICOM, the Bangkok Declaration does not set up a legal mechanism to harmonize laws or enforce the rules of a common market.

Nonetheless, on international trade matters, ASEAN's accomplishments have been impressive. In 1993, the ASEAN nations entered into a treaty setting forth the framework for creating an ASEAN Free Trade Area (AFTA), which many hoped would lead to a customs union and free movement of goods and labor. The AFTA was slow to develop into a "free trade" zone, because some member states sought to protect treasured segments of their economy. For example, Malaysia balked at tariff reductions for automobiles, so that it could continue to protect the Malaysian-made Proton car. However, free trade advanced by the gradual expansion of an area-wide *Common Effective Preferential Tariff* (CEPT), which reduced inter–ASEAN tariffs on goods with a minimum of 40 percent ASEAN content. Over time, the CEPT has been gradually lowered, particularly by the older, economically stronger ASEAN nations, to levels in the zero to five percent range for the great majority of products. There are exceptions for goods that a nation believes are important for national security, public health, biodiversity, or other policy reasons. ASEAN nations have pledged zero tariff rates by 2010, with an extension to 2015 for the four newest members. A free trade area is likely to develop in the future.

The ASEAN alliance has not achieved a custom union, but this too is on its way. Today, ASEAN negotiates as a bloc with major economic players for common tariff agreements. In this way, ASEAN has reached free trade agreements with China for goods (2004) and services (2007). As of this writing it was negotiating similar agreements with Japan and the United States.

Commonwealth of Independent States Free Trade Area

In October 1999, twelve former members of the Soviet Union signed the *Commonwealth of Independent States Free Trade Agreement*. The twelve countries—Armenia, Azerbaijan, Belarus, Georgia, Kazakhstan, Kyrgyzstan, Moldova, the Russian Federation, Tajikistan, Turkmenistan, Ukraine, and Uzbekistan—agreed to form an "Economic Union" that would gradually cancel customs duties, eliminate other barriers to the movement of goods and services, jointly coordinate trade policy with non-members, and harmonize legislation so as to create a viable free trade area. Apart from episodic and brief "summits," the group has accomplished very little. In this region, most international trade agreements are accomplished through bilateral negotiations.

Gulf Cooperation Council

The Persian Gulf states of Bahrain, Kuwait, Oman, Qatar, Saudi Arabia, and the United Arab Emirates formed the *Gulf Cooperation Council* (GCC) in 1981. The GCC's activities accelerated at the turn of the 21st century, focusing on standardizing subsidies, unifying rates for eliminating trade barriers, and negotiating with other economic actors, after the model of the EU. In 2003, the GCC created a customs union. It has set a 2010 deadline for the establishment of a common currency. There is an agreement to have a common tariff on most products.

Greater Arab Free Trade Area

In 1997, fourteen Arab countries entered into an agreement that sought to create a *Greater Arab Free Trade Area* (GAFTA). The agreement, which has grown to include all 21 Arab League states, sought to remove tariff and non-tariff barriers to products of which at least 40 percent of the value was added in one of the member states. While the scope of the GAFTA excluded many agricultural products, by 2005, all tariffs on other products were gone.

The agreement has had dramatic effects on trade among member states. From 1997 to 2005, there was an average annual increase in intra-GAFTA exports of over 15 percent. Assisted by the organizational infrastructure of the Arab League, GAFTA has spurred significant economic integration among the GAFTA nations.

Conclusion

The development of integrated trade areas reflects an increasing recognition of the accepted economic principle that free trade maximizes benefits to the whole by allowing each country to specialize in its areas of relative competitive advantage. The United States is a successful model of such an effort. The EU is again demonstrating the advantages of economic integration. Regional trading blocs have risen in recognition of the virtues of this model of economic integration.

In reaction to the EU and NAFTA, other countries have been stimulated to consider cooperative efforts to reduce trade barriers. In every context where free trade has been allowed to proceed, the economic fortunes of the populations have improved. The message is unmistakable: Free trade is the wave of the future.

Chapter Summary

1. The economic provisions of the U.S. Constitution constituted an agreement among the states to have their economies managed as a single unit by the federal government. Under the Constitution's economic provisions, Congress had the exclusive power to manage trade between the states and with foreign nations. The federal court system was empowered to strike down any state law that would impede the free interstate movement of goods or people or discriminate against businesses based in other states. The Constitution gave federal government the sole right to issue currency and determine monetary policy and concentrated all control over commercial policy toward other nations in the federal government.
2. A free trade area (FTA) is created when a group of countries agrees to eliminate or phase out customs duties and other barriers to trade among the member countries as to goods originating in the FTA countries.
3. In a customs union, there is free trade of all goods that come through any of the union's members, even if they made it to a member through importation from outside the customs union. Because of this, a customs union can only function if all of its members agree to a common tariff on imports from outside the union and a common institution to negotiate such tariffs on behalf of the group.
4. A "common market" is a customs union that has reached a further state of integration. In addition to assuring the free movement of goods within the customs union, a common market seeks to further facilitate free competition within the union and protect the right of all enterprises and persons within the area to do business, invest capital, and sell their services within the area without discrimination on the basis of national origin. To achieve free economic competition in a common market, the members of the market establish common rules relating to anti-competitive behavior and subsidization of industry. Further, a court with jurisdiction and power to enforce its rulings is necessary to ensure compliance with the market's norms.
5. The provisions of the *WTO Agreement* do not prevent formation of a customs union or FTA. The WTO treats such a grouping as an economic actor and requires that tariffs against those outside the grouping not be increased as a consequence of the group's formation.
6. The European Union is a concept that represents three "communities," each created and operating under a separate treaty. These are the European Community, formerly known as the European Economic Community; the European Coal and Steel Community; and the European Atomic Energy Community. Although each community is governed by a separate treaty, all treaties are administered by the same institution, the Commission of the European Communities. Because the EC Treaty has little policy substance, the ultimate arbiter of EC policy is the Council of the European Union. By contrast, because the ECSC and Euratom policies are well defined in their treaties, the Commission of the

European Communities implements ECSC and Euratom policy with little direction from the Council of the European Union.

7. The Council of the European Union is composed of one representative from each EU member state. Each member state has several "ministers," each specializing in a different area. A member state will designate a particular minister to be its representative on the Council, depending on the subject to be discussed at a particular Council meeting. Different areas of specialization include international affairs, finance, agriculture, and transportation, among others. The purpose of the Council is to coordinate economic policies of member states and to make decisions on issues within its jurisdiction, which includes approving legislative directives to the member states and international agreements.
8. The Commission of the European Communities is the EU's executive body and it carries out the decisions of the Council of the European Union. It also is the only body that can make legislative proposals for the European Parliament or Council to consider. The Commission is headed by a College of Commissioners. Each member state is entitled to appoint one commissioner. The term "Commission" also refers to the bureaucracy that performs the day-to-day work of the Commission. These civil servants work in the different "Directorates-General," which are specialized areas of interest of the Commission.
9. The Court of Justice and the Court of First Instance hold the judicial power of the European Union. The Court of Justice is comprised of twenty-seven judges. The judges are appointed by the member states for a renewable term of six years. In cases involving private parties, it generally hears appeals of judgments from the Court of First Instance. Unlike most national high courts, the Court of Justice very seldom sits as a unit, but usually sits as a smaller "chamber" of three or five judges. Less frequently, it sits as a Grand Chamber of thirteen judges. The Court of First Instance is the general trial court of the EU. It has original jurisdiction over lawsuits brought by private parties against acts of Community institutions, such as actions to block mergers, impose fines, or other regulatory actions. It also has original jurisdiction over certain suits brought by the member states against the Commission, suits of member states against the Council in the areas of international trade "dumping" and state subsidies to industry, and suits relating to Community trademarks. Like the Court of Justice, the Court of First Instance comprises twenty-seven judges, one from each member state, serving renewable six-year terms. A party that sues in the Court of First Instance will probably go before a three-judge chamber. Both courts follow civil law procedural traditions.
10. Free trade areas and customs unions are developing in many parts of the world. The success of these efforts has varied widely. The most successful have been CARICOM, the Gulf Cooperation Council, and the South African Customs Union, each of which have established customs unions and are moving toward integration as a common market. Approaching this level of success are ASEAN and the Greater Arab Free Trade Area, which have established free trade areas and institutions that will negotiate tariff policy on behalf of all group members. Looser free trade areas have arisen in the DR–Central American Free Trade Area and the Central American Common Market. A number of other country groups have achieved little economic integration to date. These include the African Economic Community, the Andean Community, APEC, COMESA, MERCOSUR, and the South African Development Community.

Questions and Case Problems

1. Rewe, a limited liability company with an office in Germany, imported goods from the EU countries. In 1976, Rewe applied to a German agency for permission to import Cassis de Dijon. The agency responded that spirits needed to contain 32 percent alcohol to be marketed in Germany. (The only exception to this rule was beer.) Cassis had only 15–20 percent spirit content so it could not be

imported. The German court referred the case to the ECJ to deal with conflicts between German law and Article 30 and 37 of the *Treaty of Rome* (see *Commission v. Federal Republic of Germany,* C-178/84, March 12, 1987). The German government argued that it was trying to protect public health and consumers. How did the court rule? Why? Did this settle the issue for the future? See *Rewe–Zentral [Cassis de Dijon],* C-120/78, February 20, 1979.

2. Germany has had laws regulating beer since 1516. For example, Germany had a law that prohibited additives in beer. The Community tried to harmonize its laws on additives and passed several directives on additives. The Commission notified Germany in 1982 that its beer law created barriers to member states that wanted to import beer into Germany: thus Germany's law violated Article 30 and 36 of the *Treaty of Rome.* Germany argued that to sell a beer with additives would mislead consumers and there were resultant public health concerns. How did the Court of Justice rule? Why didn't the *Cassis de Dijon* case (see *Rewe–Zentral [Cassis de Dijon],* C-120/78, February 20, 1979) preclude the necessity of this case? Why did the community need to address such a similar issue nine years after *Rewe*? Does the court still have to address similar issues today? Give an example from your reading. Find a case on the Internet.
3. The UK has not joined the monetary union. How has this decision affected business? Switzerland has also not joined the monetary union. Is the effect of its decision different from a nation with an important financial industry than for a nation with smaller financial importance? What is the reaction of European political leaders? European business leaders? American businesspeople? How workable will a monetary union be without three members?
4. The EU passed the *Electronic Signature Directive* in 2000. It is technology neutral. Germany already had a law that required a specific encrypted form. Was this a conflict? How did this impact business? How does it compare to current U.S. law?
5. Compare the EU and U.S. approaches to privacy. How are they different and similar? What are the ramifications for business of each? Which approach do you prefer?
6. How does the EU's approach to GMOs differ from that of the United States? How does this affect international business? Find some current articles or cases that address the controversy. What role may the WTO play? How interrelated are other trade disputes?
7. May Germany require waste that is shipped to another member state to be disposed of according to Germany's environmental protection laws? See *Daimler Chrysler AG v. Land Baden—Wurttemberg* (C-324/99) (2001). What impact does this ruling have on business? Does the result suggest a need for more Community standards? Why or why not?
8. What is the difference between a directive, a regulation, and a recommendation? Why would the EU choose one over the other? Give examples. What impact does this decision have on businesses?
9. There are a number of developments on the African continent in terms of efforts to build a customs union and establish integrated trade areas. Which ones seem most successful? Why? Do you think a court is essential? Compare these efforts with NAFTA.
10. What progress has the Gulf Cooperation Council made in moving toward the stated goal of a customs union? What impact might that have on the Arab League and neighboring countries? How does this balance with the WTO obligations?
11. Go to the EU Web site and review the *Treaty Establishing a Constitution for Europe*. How does this document compare to the U.S. Constitution? How might it affect business, if at all?

Managerial Implications

1. Your company has an office in Spain. You have hired a worker, Ms. Jimenez, for a fixed term and have renewed her contract twice. Shortly after renewing it for the second time, you discover that she will be giving birth within three months. You send her a notice stating that she is terminated effective in one month (which is two months before her due date). You believe that since she was only on a limited-term contract she cannot expect to be treated like a more permanent employee and given all maternity benefits. Are there any legal concerns here? What impact might this decision have on the advancement of women in employment? How will this affect your hiring practices?

2. You are engaged in the competitive perfume business and decide you want to protect your intellectual property in an aggressive way. You decide to try to register the odor or olfactory mark of a "balsamically fruity scent with a hint of cinnamon" in the EU. You have the chemical formula as well as a description. You argue that *Directive 89/104/EEC of December 21, 1988*, allows registration of "acoustic marks, colors, holograms and other nontraditional marks." Will this be a successful strategy? What else can you do? (See *Ralf Sieckmann v. Deutches Patent-und-Markenamt,* C-273/00, December 12, 2002).
3. Your company is expanding into Europe. You must pick a location for your office and have two locations to choose between.
   a. How will you make this decision?
   b. Will whether the country has adopted the euro have an impact on your decision?
   c. Would you be discouraged from locating to a country that has had a poor record of implementing EU directives?
   d. Would you consider locating an office in one of the countries that plans to join but has not done so yet?
4. Labco is a small manufacturing company that wants to do more exporting to the EU. They discover that the Commission is considering a directive that might limit their ability to do business in those countries.
   a. What can they do? The president of the company has asked you to research this matter and outline a plan of action.
   b. What difference does it make if Labco is a very large, publicly traded corporation?
   c. What are your options if the EU implements a directive or regulation that you believe discriminates against you as a foreign business?
5. Imagine that you are a student intern and will be spending this semester on assignment to the vice president of international sales at a toy firm. Up until now, the firm's primary markets have been in the United States and Canada. The toys are designed in the United States and manufactured by vendor firms in China. At a meeting with the vice president's design and marketing staff, he asks about opening new markets in Europe. He explains that in the United States, the design and sale of children's toys are highly regulated by the U.S. Consumer Products Safety Commission. Indeed, some other companies have had their toys removed from store shelves for noncompliance with federal regulations. He feels there must be some consumer safety regulations in effect in Europe that will act as a barrier to his firm's access to European markets. After all, if the regulations are very different from those in the United States, it may be costly to redesign the toys to comply with European standards. After the meeting, the vice president asks you to find answers to the following questions:
   a. Are there any standards or technical regulations in effect in Europe that govern the sale of toys? Where can he locate the regulations on the design, manufacture, and marketing of children's toys in Europe? Can you give a specific Web address so he can look at them himself?
   b. Do the toys have to meet different requirements in every European country, or is there a single standard that covers all of Europe?
   c. To which toys do the standards apply, and what toys, if any, are exempt?
   d. What are the design and manufacturing standards for toys covered by the regulations, and what is the standard for safety? Are there any specific provisions covering the toys' physical or mechanical properties?
   e. Do the toys have to be tested in advance for compliance with safety regulations?
   f. What are the toy labeling requirements? Is there a certain label or mark that will let consumers know that the toy has been tested for safety?

FOR INTERNET ACTIVITIES, VISIT ACADEMIC.CENGAGE.COM/BLAW/SCHAFFER.

PART 4 Regulation of the International Marketplace

The issues addressed in Parts Two and Three of this text are applicable to any enterprise wishing to export its goods to another country, even if that enterprise does not have operations in the foreign country. Part Two considered international commercial law, which creates a reliable framework assuring exporters and importers in different parts of the world that they will receive money for goods and services. International trade law, discussed in Part Three, involves the framework of barriers and openings to trade among nations. In Part Four, the focus turns to the legal complications that arise when a business actually moves a portion of its enterprise outside its home country.

Many business factors may prompt a business to take this step. First, most businesses—from Madagascar to Minnesota—find that one sells more goods if one employs a local sales representative. A business that wishes to promote sales abroad will be greatly advantaged if it retains the services of an individual abroad to promote sales. If such a retention proves successful, the business may then wish to establish an office in that country. Indeed, the business might eventually generate greater profits from making its product abroad and selling it there—or even exporting it back into the United States.

When a business first establishes a presence abroad, it becomes subject to regulation by the foreign country being "penetrated" and, if it is a U.S. company, to a series of U.S. laws that apply to such "penetrators." As the presence in such a foreign "host country" progresses from a local office phase through a manufacturing plant, the level of host country regulations becomes more intense. For instance, a U.S. company that builds a factory in a foreign nation may become subject to national and provincial norms, such as labor, environmental, and/or tax laws; technology transfer laws; laws governing the appropriate level of foreign ownership of businesses; and laws governing the repatriation of profits to the United States. In addition, the company may encounter possible nationalization by the foreign country, the U.S. *Foreign Corrupt Practices Act* or similar legislation in other nations, and a plethora of U.S. and foreign country antitrust laws.

Part Four treats that immense body of law in a general, thematic way, as the great diversity of local laws governing investment demands. In contrast to international commercial law—in which great consistency has developed over millions of commercial transactions—and to trade law—in which substantial harmonization has emerged through WTO—laws governing foreign investment are peculiarly reflective of local culture and attitudes. Like culture, these laws vary widely among the more than 200 nations of the planet. Further, these laws—like the attitudes they reflect—are constantly evolving. Many countries, including the United States, have fluctuated from the extreme of being aggressively hostile to foreign investment and to a friendlier attitude and back to hostility yet again.

The position of any given country at any given time on this spectrum depends upon mercurial international and domestic political conditions. For instance, from the 1950s through the mid-1970s, many developing countries grew progressively more antagonistic toward foreign investment, reflecting emerging national self-esteem and wariness of former colonial masters. But when anti-foreign investment laws caused those economies to run out of capital resources in the late 1970s and early 1980s, many of the governments reversed course and passed more investment-friendly laws. In the twenty-first century, the pendulum has swung back in many nations to economic nationalism, as recessionary forces have impaired Latin economies.

In short, no one can possibly predict precisely what foreign investment laws will be tomorrow. One can, however, identify different approaches that nations have taken in regulating foreign business penetration. A working knowledge of these approaches provides a framework that a businessperson can employ to analyze different aspects of the legal environment in the country in which investment is considered.

Part Four begins at the least intrusive—and therefore least regulated—foreign presence and moves through increasingly substantial and regulated forms of establishment. Chapter Sixteen reviews issues that arise once the enterprise retains an agent or a representative abroad. Such retention triggers the host country's requirements for agency relationships, as well as its laws relating to advertising and marketing. It also unleashes one of the principal concerns of U.S. business abroad, the U.S. *Foreign Corrupt Practices Act*.

Chapter Seventeen reviews licensing and other arrangements through which a U.S. enterprise is paid for permitting a foreign entity to use its intellectual property. Many host countries closely regulate these arrangements as they wish to capture the intellectual property for their own nationals.

Chapter Eighteen turns to the legal peculiarities of operating in another country—subjecting oneself to the full array of the host country's corporate, currency, and tax laws.

Chapter Nineteen considers the political risk associated with committing capital resources in a foreign country: nationalization or expropriation of one's investment by the foreign sovereign. The end of Chapter Nineteen explores the flip side of nationalization and the emerging process of privatization and reviews the different ways in which formerly public assets are transferred to private hands. Ironically, most assets nationalized in the twentieth century were privatized in the late twentieth century; many are being renationalized today.

Chapter Twenty discusses labor laws, which mirror the broadly varying concepts of the proper relationship between employees and their places of work.

Chapter Twenty-One provides an in-depth treatment of international environmental law, one of the most dynamic legal disciplines in recent years.

Finally, Chapter Twenty-Two addresses the pinnacle of foreign penetration, situations in which U.S. investors become so dominant in the relevant country that they become subject to its antitrust or competition laws.

Confronting foreign law is a bit like taking on Hydra, the many-headed monster of Greek mythology. In the following chapters, the student may find that every time he or she cuts off one of the law monster's heads, this monster—like Hydra—will replace it with two new ones.

CHAPTER 16

INTERNATIONAL MARKETING LAW: SALES REPRESENTATIVES, ADVERTISING, AND ETHICAL ISSUES

As noted in Chapter Five, an American business can sell its goods abroad by simply delivering them FOB a U.S. port to an ocean-bound vessel. If the business sells its products abroad in that fashion and does not otherwise have any contacts with the country to which its goods are bound, it will generally escape regulation by the foreign country. Why then, would a U.S. business place a representative abroad and enmesh itself in foreign regulation?

First, a business can expand its geographic market by expanding the geographic scope of its marketing. If a company advertises popcorn poppers only in Topeka, Kansas, it will sell popcorn poppers only to Zimbabwean buyers who happen by Topeka or who stumble upon its Internet site. If, on the other hand, the company markets in Harare, Zimbabwe, the enterprise will encounter more prospective Zimbabwean buyers. Thus, the enterprise that believes Zimbabwe is a "hot" prospective market for poppers will retain the services of a sales representative in Zimbabwe.

Second, a local presence permits the Topeka enterprise to maintain the popcorn poppers sold abroad. Zimbabweans are more likely to buy a Topeka popper through the Internet if they know they can get it repaired in Harare rather than have to send it back to Topeka for maintenance. If the initial sales efforts bear some fruit, the Topeka enterprise may wish to establish a sales and service facility in Harare.

Before embarking on these initiatives, however, the Topeka enterprise should review the Zimbabwe law affecting representatives of foreign enterprises.

REGULATION OF RELATIONSHIPS WITH REPRESENTATIVES

Relationships with representatives take two basic forms: the agency and the independent contract. An *agency* is a business arrangement in which one party, the *agent,* performs a variety of functions on behalf and at the direction of another party, the *principal.* Most employees of a corporation, for example, are agents of that corporation for one purpose or another.

Independent contractors, often called *independent agents* outside the United States, perform general tasks for the business, but retain substantial discretion and independence in carrying them out. Consultants to a corporation are often viewed as independent contractors. Under U.S. law, a primary importance of the distinction between agents and independent contractors is that third parties can generally sue the principal for acts of an agent, but not for those of an independent contractor. This distinction is important to principals because they wish to avoid paying for their representatives' injuries to third parties. However, the distinction does not change the deal between the agent and principal. The substantive terms of the agreement are those developed between the principal and the agent.

The United States places few restrictions on the substantive terms of the representative–principal relationship. Two sophisticated parties can agree on virtually any compensation they wish, from a few dollars to an ownership interest in the principal's enterprise. They can decide on the extent to which one will indemnify the other. They can expand or restrict the representative's scope of discretion as they mutually deem appropriate. Accordingly, U.S. businesses are accustomed to shaping representative–principal relationships without worrying about governmental intervention. The enterprise assumes it will make its own deal with the agent and further assumes that the government will not alter that arrangement.

Supersession of Agreement with Representative

In many countries, that assumption would be in error. Nations often enact laws calculated to protect local representatives, irrespective of the deal that a particular representative has negotiated. In effect, local law may state that, notwithstanding the written agreement between the principal and the representative, such law will supersede the agreement's language to protect the representative. Stated another way, even if the representative agrees to a 1 percent commission with the U.S. principal, the principal might find that it is obligated under local law to pay the representative no less than 2 percent. Little surprises like this one can greatly affect the profitability of a foreign venture.

This supersession problem is particularly acute when the U.S. business terminates the agency arrangement. No matter what the contract provides, the U.S. principal may need to make a large payment to the representative in order to terminate the arrangement, or may not have a right to terminate the agent at all. For example, a *Voyageur, Representant, et Placier* (VRP)—a type of commercial agent—is entitled to special protection under the French labor code, and every representative is assumed to be a VRP unless the written agreement specifies otherwise. Similarly, under *European Union (EU) Council Directive 86/653,* parties may agree to a fixed-term contract. However, if the parties continue their relationship after the stated term of the contract, it becomes an *evergreen contract*—one that the parties may terminate only by a three-month written notice once the relationship has lasted for three years or more.

The *Puerto Rico Dealer's Act* provides an example of the Spanish-American civil law concerning strictly limiting the termination of an agency. Regardless of whether the parties have reserved the right to terminate in the terms of their agreement, the *Dealer's Act* prohibits the principal from terminating the agreement or from refusing to renew without "just cause." Just cause is often difficult to establish; the Act states that even nonperformance or violation of the contract is not considered just cause unless the principal can prove that the breach affected it in a "substantial manner." Indeed, in the *Waterproofing Systems, Inc. v. Hydro-Stop, Inc.* case in 2007, a federal appellate court with jurisdiction over Puerto Rico found that even continual late payments and alleged fraud involving the distributor retaining the funds from a joint check might be insufficient to constitute "just cause" under the Act. The foreign investor is at a huge disadvantage because the entity that determines whether "just cause" exists is a local court, which naturally may favor a local party.

To American eyes, this web of laws favoring local representatives is viewed as protectionism. However, host countries view such laws quite differently. They regard them as providing a level playing field for local small businesses against multinational giants. In the following case, Paraguay's Supreme Court of Justice stated the rationale for such laws quite capably.

European Union (EU) Council Directive 86/653 on agency requires each EU member state to pass consistent national laws on representatives. These include a few mandatory provisions that may seem odd to Americans. For instance, the directive provides for an *economic conditions alarm:* The principal must notify the agent if it expects that the agent's volume of business—and thus the agent's commission—will be "significantly lower" than what the agent "normally" expects. The directive also requires payment of a commission, not only when a transaction is concluded because of the agent's efforts, but also whenever a transaction is made between the principal and a party that the agent previously acquired as a customer. Further, a *commission override* is included: Whenever a principal makes a sale in a territory or a market sector reserved for the agent, the principal

Electra-Amambay S.R.L. v. Compañía Antártica Paulista Ind. Brasileira de Bebidas E Conexos

Order No. 827 (November 12, 2001); Paraguay Supreme Court of Justice

BACKGROUND AND FACTS

The Paraguayan government has enacted a law that specifically protects Paraguayan representatives of foreign companies. Among other things, the law requires a foreign company to make an extraordinarily large payment to the Paraguayan representative if the representative is terminated for some reason other than "just cause." The Paraguayan statute narrowly defines "just cause." There is no similar law protecting Paraguayan distributors or other representatives of Paraguayan-based enterprises.

Compañía Antártica, a Brazilian firm, terminated Electra-Amambay, its Paraguayan representative. Electra-Amambay argued that the termination was not for good cause and sought its statutory penalty. Compañía Antártica countered by arguing that the Paraguayan statute was an unconstitutional discrimination based on national origin.

JUDGE CARLOS FERNANDEZ GADEA

Compañía Antártica advances the objection that [the] Articles ... of the Law No. 194/93, on which the [Electra-Amambay] bases its lawsuit, is unconstitutional.

* * *

The objection maintains that Articles 1, 4, 5, 6, 7, and 8 constitute an unjust and arbitrary discrimination against foreign manufacturers and companies.... They establish obligations, assumptions, and sanctions only and exclusively against foreign manufacturers and firms, but not against persons domiciled within the country. [The objection is that] this inequality violates Articles 46 and 47, paragraph 2 of the National Constitution.

* * *

This Law, 194/93, is of a special character, regulating the relationships between foreign manufacturers and firms and their representatives, agents, and distributors of their products domiciled in the country. And in the case of the termination of these relationships without a statement of just cause, it sets forth how the amount of damages should be calculated. It is customary that a foreign firm which contracts for the services of physical and legal persons domiciled in Paraguay lays down the ground rules of said relationship, establishing the rights and obligations of both parties. With the promulgation of this law, the parties are placed on an equal footing, establishing the damages that should be paid by the foreign firm in the case of a rupture of the contractual bond without just cause. The firm or persons who find themselves in the country, for the promotion, sale, or placement within the republic of products or services provided by the foreign firm necessarily had to incur expenses in investments so that the referred product would have success in the local market. However, it is necessary to underscore that if there exists just cause, the foreign firm or provider has suitable and appropriate means at its disposal to seek exoneration from liability for the damages.

[Compañía Antártica makes the further point] that Article 2 of the mentioned law ... in defining the different types of contractual relationships, abusively exceeds the intention, will and interest of the manufacturers who simply wish to export their products without creating any contractual relationship other than that of the simple purchase and sale of goods. [Moreover, it notes] Article 9 [of the law] presumes to rise to the level of "public order" [but] in this case, the social order is not implicated. The implicated interests involve a small minority of the population and not the general interest.

* * *

With respect to this point, I believe that it is not logical to think that the foreign manufacturers have an interest only in a simple purchase and sale transaction. The relationship between the parties can go much further than a single transaction. Such a relationship should be found to exist [before the statute applies]. As to Article 9 ... the law was clothed as a matter of "public order" when it was enacted as such by the public legislative power.

* * *

Finally, it is important to emphasize that this law does not reflect an exaggerated protectionism of the State, but rather legal security and equality, bearing in mind that one of the parties (the foreign company) is in better economic condition than its local representative and that the latter finds itself in a unequal state, whether for lack of technical training, economic resources or qualified personnel. It is because of this

continued

continued

that the State intervenes in this relationship, setting forth precise rules with which the parties must comply, especially when the foreign enterprise unilaterally decides to terminate this relationship, without cause. It is in this situation, when the national representative is economically prejudiced, that [the law] compensates for this prejudice in some way by an award of damages.... As has been said, there exist causes that are justifications exempt from the obligation to pay damages through which the foreign enterprise can exonerate itself from this responsibility. These causes are found itemized in the law.

Decision. The court rejected the objection as inadmissible and charged Compañía Antártica with all costs.

must pay the agent a commission, whether or not the agent actually participated in the sale, no matter what the agency agreement provides. Under the directive, these commissions accrue when the customer "should have [executed its part of the transaction] if the principal has executed his part of the transaction." The principal must also pay the commission even if the deal is not consummated.

Tax and Labor Regulation and Principal Liability: The Dependent–Independent Distinction

The retention of a representative often leads to principal liability and triggers tax and labor law requirements. The burdensomeness of these regulations frequently increases upon a finding by the host country that the representative is a *dependent agent* rather than an *independent agent.*

For tax purposes, the principal is often viewed as having opened an office once it hires a dependent agent within the host country. Upon such an office opening, the principal's transactions become subject to the host country's corporate tax laws.

Similarly, a dependent agent is an employee for purposes of the host country's labor laws. As in the United States, having an *employee* subjects a company to pension law, tax withholding, labor laws, and other legal consequences. However, in many countries, such a determination can also affect the control of the U.S. investor's foreign enterprise. For example, as Chapter Twenty explains, in many countries employees may have statutory rights to representation on the company's board of directors.

Finally, if an agent is *dependent,* the principal will be vicariously liable to third parties for the agent's misdeeds. In the context of *product liability*—responsibility to consumers for defects in one's product—the agent–principal relationship is not a critical consideration. As long as the U.S. manufacturer's product enters the foreign market, the manufacturer is likely to be in the "chain of distribution" and subject to suit, whether it does business through a dependent or independent agent. However, it makes a difference if the U.S. manufacturer did not participate in the agent's liability-creating act. If the entrepreneur's Nairobi dependent agent runs over a law student in the agent's delivery truck, the entrepreneur may be liable in Kenya to pay damages equal to a lifetime of lost income. If the agent is independent, the entrepreneur probably has no such liability.

In hiring a representative, a firm should therefore determine whether the arrangement is to be characterized as creating a dependent agency or an independent agency. Unfortunately, this distinction is not based on any single definitive test. Instead, courts review a variety of factors and determine whether, on balance, the parties have created a dependent agency. The more flexibility and discretion the representative has, the more likely the representative is to be considered independent. Representatives who personally organize, pursue, and set the schedule for the marketing program—that is, those who have great discretion in organizing their time and work—are more likely to be considered independent. If, on the other hand, the U.S. principal creates the marketing program in detail and the representatives simply carry it out, the representatives are likely to be dependent. Similarly, agents who have an obligation to follow the specific instructions of the principal are likely to be dependent. In contrast, agents who are given a task to perform, but have no obligation to follow the principal's instructions in carrying out that task, are more likely to be viewed as independent. The *EU Agency Directive,* for example, simply defines an independent agent as someone with "continuing authority to negotiate the sale or purchase of goods" on behalf of the principal. A compensation package that is based solely on commissions, rather than on periodic payments or a fixed salary with reimbursement of overhead expenses, is also indicative of independence. Independent agents typically rent their own office space and hire subagents to carry out the tasks. Finally, representatives who serve more than one principal are more likely to be considered independent. Exhibit 16.1 lays out these considerations in graphic form.

Of course, the U.S. investor may not wish to give an agent the level of discretion required to be an independent agent. The U.S. investor may wish to have a greater level of quality control or a greater share of the entrepreneurial profits in the venture. These benefits of a dependent agent often outweigh the costs of greater regulation. But in weighing the business benefits of retaining a dependent agent, the U.S. investor should thoroughly understand the local legal costs it will incur.

Regulation of Advertising Abroad

If the Topeka enterprise wishes to sell its popcorn poppers to the Zimbabwean public, hiring an agent in Zimbabwe may not be enough. The enterprise will need to determine how best to advertise its poppers to the Zimbabwean consumer. This will require development of marketing strategies attractive to the local culture. Obviously, the soccer-loving Zimbabweans will be unimpressed by endorsements from U.S. football players. Just as cultural differences affect what advertising is attractive to foreign consumers, they affect what advertising is forbidden. Marketing abroad requires sensitivity to the limits that foreign law can place on marketing efforts.

The marketer may not place just anything on the television screens or in the newspapers. These local legal limits do not always correspond with local interests. For instance, a television commercial that features an explicit sexual message might well spur sales both in Denmark and in Saudi Arabia; after all, a significant percentage of individuals in all cultures have an interest in racy things. In Denmark, the authorities would take no interest in such an advertisement. In Saudi Arabia, however, the "religious police" might mete out corporal punishment to one's local representative. An ineffective

Exhibit 16.1

The Distinction Between Independent and Dependent Agents

	Independent	Dependent
Scheduling	Details created by agent within principal's general requirements	Details provided by principal
Work Organization	Principal identifies strategic objectives; agent determines tactics and has continuing authority for achieving objectives	Principal is involved in working out details
Instructions	Principal does not instruct; change in direction causes change in compensation	Agent is always subject to change in instructions
Compensation	Commissions; fixed amount of money	Hourly pay or salary
Expenses	Included in compensation amount	Specific expense reimbursement
Number of Principals	Works for many clients	Works for one client

advertising campaign may simply prove unprofitable, but an illegal advertising campaign may lead someone to an unexpected stay at a local prison.

Truth in Advertising

One of the founding concepts of libertarian capitalism is *caveat emptor* (let the buyer beware). According to this precept, government should not intervene in commercial relations. Buyers should investigate the seller's claims or obtain contractual representations and warranties. If they fail to do so and the seller's claims turn out to be false, the buyer only has him- or herself to blame. Under classic capitalist theory, the invisible hand of the market will eventually ferret out consistently dishonest sellers and consistently careless buyers.

Ultimately, the Ninth Commandment—"thou shalt not bear false witness"—triumphed over caveat emptor in most cultures. Today almost every nation now prohibits false advertising, at least formally. The European Union, for example, specifically excludes fraudulent advertising from its general protection of commercial speech. Even during the late nineteenth century—the high-water mark of libertarian capitalist thought—courts found ways to protect the unwary. Before the United Kingdom enacted consumer protection laws, English courts protected consumers by stretching ancient contract law principles to newspaper advertising. If one promises that one's product can specifically do something, they reasoned, one is liable in contract if the product fails to live up to the promise.

The distaste for deceptive advertising illustrated in *Carbolic Smoke Ball* is shared to varying degrees throughout the world. But some cultures are less tolerant than others of "puffing"—vagueness and exaggeration—in advertising. The Teutonic penchant for accuracy, for example, prevented a

Carlill v. Carbolic Smoke Ball Co.
1 Q.B. 256 (1983)
Queen's Bench

BACKGROUND AND FACTS

The defendant, who made and sold a medical preparation called the "Carbolic Smoke Ball," inserted the following advertisement in the *Pall Mall Gazette* on November 13, 1891:

> £100 reward will be paid by the Carbolic Smoke Ball Company to any person who contracts the increasing epidemic influenza, colds, or any disease caused by taking cold, after having used the ball three times daily for two weeks according to the printed directions supplied with each ball. £1000 is deposited with the Alliance Bank, Regent Street, showing our sincerity in the matter. During the last epidemic of influenza many thousand carbolic smoke balls were sold as preventives against this disease, and in no ascertained case was the disease contracted by those using the carbolic smoke ball.

The plaintiff was a woman who, relying on this advertisement, bought one of the balls at a drugstore and used it as directed, three times a day, from November 20, 1891 to January 17, 1892, when she developed influenza.

LORD JUSTICE LINDLEY

The first observation I will make is that we are not dealing with any inference of fact. We are dealing with an express promise to pay £100 in certain events. Read the advertisement how you will, and twist it about as you will, here is a distinct promise expressed in language which is perfectly unmistakable—"£100 reward will be paid by the Carbolic Smoke Ball Company to any person who contracts the influenza after having used the ball three times daily for two weeks according to the printed directions supplied with each ball."

We must first consider whether this was intended to be a promise at all, or whether it was a mere puff which meant nothing. Was it a mere puff? My answer to that question is No, and I base my answer upon this passage: "£1000 is deposited with the Alliance Bank, showing our sincerity in the matter." Now, for what was that money deposited or that statement made except to negate the suggestion that this was a mere puff and meant nothing at all....

continued

continued

Then it is contended that it is not binding. In the first place, it is said that it is not made with anybody in particular. Now that point is common to the words of this advertisement and to the words of all other advertisements offering rewards. They are offers to anybody who performs the conditions named in the advertisement, and anybody who does perform the condition accepts the offer. . . .

[I]t is said that this advertisement is so vague that you cannot really construe it as a promise—that the vagueness of the language shows that a legal promise was not intended or contemplated. The language is vague and uncertain in some respects, and particularly in this, that the £100 is to be paid to any person who contracts the increasing epidemic after having used the balls three times daily for two weeks. It is said, When are they to be used? According to the language of the advertisement no time is fixed, and, construing the offer most strongly against the person who has made it, one might infer that any time was meant. . . . I do not think that business people or reasonable people would understand the words as meaning that if you took a smoke ball and used it three times daily for two weeks you were to be guaranteed against influenza for the rest of your life, and I think it would be pushing the language of the advertisement too far to construe it as meaning that. . . . [I]t strikes me that there are two, and possibly three, reasonable constructions to be put on this advertisement, any one of which will answer the purpose of the plaintiff. Possibly it may be limited to persons catching the "increasing epidemic" or any colds or diseases caused by taking cold, during the prevalence of the increasing epidemic. That is one suggestion; but it does not commend itself to me. Another suggested meaning is that you are warranted free from catching this epidemic, or colds or other diseases caused by taking cold, whilst you are using this remedy after using it for two weeks. If that is the meaning, the plaintiff is right, for she used the remedy for two weeks and went on using it till she got the epidemic. Another meaning, and the one which I rather prefer, is that the reward is offered to any person who contracts the epidemic or other disease within a reasonable time after having used the smoke ball. . . . What is a reasonable time? It has been suggested that there is no standard of reasonableness; that it depends upon the reasonable time for a germ to develop! I do not feel pressed by that. It strikes me that a reasonable time may be ascertained in a business sense and in a sense satisfactory to a lawyer. . . . It strikes me, I confess, that the true construction of this advertisement is that £100 will be paid to anybody who uses this smoke ball three times daily for two weeks according to the printed directions, and who gets the influenza or cold or other diseases caused by taking cold within a reasonable time after so using it; and if that is the true construction, it is enough for the plaintiff.

Decision. The Queen's Bench found that the advertisement was, in the parlance of contract law, a "definite and operative offer" that the plaintiff had accepted through her performance. It entered judgment of £100 on her behalf.

German snack food marketer from making an unspecific claim that its potato chips contained "40 percent less fat." When a competitor sued, a German court interpreted the ambiguous statement to be a representation that the chips contained 40 percent less fat than *any* existing brand. Finding that the chips did not, the court enjoined the entire advertising program.

The exacting standards of the Japanese are similarly intolerant of exaggeration. In Japan, the Fair Trade Committee prevented PepsiCo, Inc. from advertising its cola drink as "the choice of the next generation" as it did in the United States. Its rationale was that Pepsi was second to Coca-Cola in the Japanese market.

Other nations are far more flexible. In some countries, hucksters have been victimizing others for centuries. While investors are still able to do so, they may wish to take advantage of such greater latitude abroad. But the trend is clear: In most countries, the authorities are catching up to the philosophical descendants of the *Carbolic Smoke Ball* medical science entrepreneurs.

The sanctions for false advertising vary from place to place. The advertising laws in some of the relatively new Eastern European democracies indicate a remaining socialist distrust of capitalist advertising. The Czech Republic bans "hidden seduction" and insists that advertising be based on the "specific features of the goods." And Hungary formerly demanded that the advertiser have sufficient inventories of advertised goods on hand before beginning an advertising campaign. Of particular interest is the South Korean requirement of a public apology. Although to a Westerner such a sanction would be little more than a slap on the wrist, the ignominy of a public apology caused an advertiser to appeal the public apology sentence to the High Court of Seoul. The Seoul court found that the advertiser was guilty of deception, but it also found extenuating circumstances in the case. Therefore, it reversed the sentence of a public apology, finding it too harsh a penalty.

Content-Specific Regulations

Advertising can be unlawful even if its content is perfectly true. Advertising aimed at children, for example, is closely and diversely regulated. More than forty countries prohibit or greatly limit such advertising, reasoning that children cannot intelligently assess the content of commercials. Many of these bans reflect idiosyncratic cultural values.

Language Laws. In some nations, *language laws* can complicate cross-border advertising. The municipal government of Jakarta, Indonesia, worried about cultural invasion by ethnic minorities, bans languages other than Indonesian from billboards and imprisons violators for up three months. The marketing difficulties created by this law become apparent when one considers that, for most of the 207 million people in the Indonesian islands, Indonesian is a second language.

France is famous—or infamous perhaps—for its aggressive policing of language laws. In France, every word used in advertising must be French, even if the French population more commonly uses the English word. For example, although virtually all French businesspeople prefer to use the simple English term *cash flow,* the language law recently required them to reflect the concept in its seldom-used French incarnation of *marge brute d'auto-financement.* If similar laws prevailed in the United States, advertisers would have to refer to *paté* by its less appetizing English name, ground goose liver. Most recently, in October 2003, the French government, in an effort to prevent the use of English, which is the predominant language of technology, banned its civil service from using the term *e-mail,* a term used by people of all languages the world over. All government ministries, Web sites, publications, and documents must now use *courriel*—a shortening of *courrier electronique*—when referring to messages sent via the Internet.

Advertising Restrictions on "Sin" Products: Tobacco and Alcohol. Other advertising regulations target specific types of products deemed to be corrosive to society—"sin" products. As in all advertising, however, regulations reflect the customs of the countries that enact them. With ferocity mindful of its recent totalitarian heritage, Bulgaria has banned all tobacco advertising outside of tobacco shops and threatened violators with a $50,000 fine per violation. The antiauthoritarian British, on the other hand, do not forbid tobacco advertising. Instead, they insist on self-imposed and highly subjective industry guidelines. This approach led to the banning of an ad campaign featuring two overweight, balding, middle-aged men whom the industry watch group deemed "too appealing" to young people. Belgium permits cigarette ads, but only those that focus on the package or on part of its design. A directive by the European Union that would have effectively banned all advertising of tobacco products was annulled in 2000 by the European Court of Justice for being overreaching. [Case C-376/98, Federal Republic of Germany v. European Parliament and Council of the European Union, 2000 E.C.R. I-8419.]

Although the comprehensive European Union ban was annulled, states within the EU have addressed the advertising of tobacco in their own form. Additionally, Japan has instituted its own ban on advertising of tobacco products. Since 2004, Japan has banned outdoor advertising of tobacco and limited newspaper advertising to twelve ads each year, no more than three per month, for each tobacco manufacturer. The World Health Organization's *Framework Convention on Tobacco Control (FCTC)* has a total of 168 signatories and 146 parties. The FCTC institutes a comprehensive ban on tobacco advertising in those states that are signatories to the convention. The minimum requirement is that each party "prohibit all forms of tobacco advertising, promotion and sponsorship that promote a tobacco product by any means that are false misleading or deceptive or are likely to create an erroneous impression."

Alcohol is also considered "sinful" and its advertising is thus regulated, with interesting local peculiarities. Starting in 1993, France banned most liquor advertising—direct or indirect—including sponsorship of sports events. The only exception was French wine. Even more curiously, Belgium generally permits advertising of alcoholic beverages, but bans ads for drinks containing a liquor called *absinthe*. Saudi Arabia, which enforces a strict interpretation of Islamic law, bans alcohol and alcohol advertising altogether. Even the definition of "sinful liquor" can be counterintuitive. In 1995, Iran's spiritual leader forbade foreign soft drinks such as Coca-Cola and Pepsi-Cola because they (somehow) advanced Zionism.

OTHER RESTRICTIONS ON ADVERTISING. At the other end of the spectrum are laws that prohibit advertising of products too important to allow mere marketing to affect their distribution, such as prescription drugs or other medicines. Spain prohibits the advertisement of medicines that may be dispensed only with a prescription, are psychoactive or narcotic drugs, and are part of the National Health System. Similarly, the European Union prohibits the advertising of prescription drugs. However, advertisements for over-the-counter drugs are permitted.

The central point in advertising abroad is that the U.S. enterprise must seek legal advice from local practitioners and fashion local advertising appropriately. Indeed, in many countries, the guiding norms are embodied not in laws but in industry codes observed by the local marketing organizations. The rules in this area are as diverse and arbitrary as human culture itself and as transitory as political opinion. Perhaps the primary general principle is that no useful general principles apply to all cultures.

Marketing Considerations: The Nestlé Infant Formula Case

An enterprise that seeks to market a product in a new nation must be alert to unanticipated risk associated with the product in the new environment. If such risk exists, even if a marketing campaign is technically lawful, the law, public scorn, or both will catch up with the entrepreneur eventually. The Nestlé infant formula case is an excellent illustration of this problem.

Infant formula manufacturers have long provided hospitals with free or low-cost formula as a marketing technique. The concept is that if the mother develops a brand loyalty when her child is a newborn, her loyalty is unlikely to change over time. Formula manufacturers, like all other merchants, have also promoted their products through mass media. Some have argued that these marketing techniques have the effect of discouraging mothers from breast-feeding, which is widely regarded to be superior to feeding infant formulas. This discouragement is said to be particularly influential in the Third World, where mothers are less educated and more impressionable.

Critics argue that in such developing countries, forsaking breast-feeding can have especially grim consequences. Outside hospitals, the water supply may not be sanitary and mothers may not understand formula usage instructions. Improper use can lead to malnutrition, diarrhea, and gastroenteritis.

Nestlé, S.A., a Swiss concern with over 40 percent of the $3 billion baby formula market, became a lightning rod for criticism. Critics charged that Nestlé was luring uneducated Third World mothers away from breast-feeding through its marketing activities. These critics organized a series of boycotts against all Nestlé products throughout developed countries.

In response, Nestlé changed its promotional practices and, in 1976, phased out mass media advertising. But still Nestlé did not escape criticism because it continued to provide free and low-cost formula. The World Health Organization promulgated an "International Code of Marketing of Breast Milk Substitutes," which many countries have implemented as law. Nestlé voluntarily agreed to follow the code in 1982, agreeing to supply formula only upon request by hospital administrators. Third World administrators, however, continued to order formula and give it to virtually all mothers. Accordingly, in 1989, several groups in Britain, Ireland, and Sweden reactivated the boycott because of what they viewed as continued promotion. Finally, in January 1991, Nestlé committed to stop supplying free and low-cost formula completely.

In short, although Nestlé acted in conformance with the law, it still found itself in a vortex of controversy that adversely affected its profitability throughout the world. Marketing often involves understanding that corporations may be held to a higher standard than that mandated by law.

THE *FOREIGN CORRUPT PRACTICES ACT*

In most nations, the government is far more immersed in the day-to-day functioning of commerce than is the government of the United States in its economy. Particularly in emerging nations, favorable government action or inaction is often a prerequisite to concluding a transaction. Government officials have discretion over such government action or inaction, so they have greater influence over commercial transactions than their North American counterparts. Many of these foreign government officials are not above informing their discretion with a bribe. Indeed, in many countries, bribery of public officials has long been a way of life.

This is the case even though almost every nation in the world formally outlaws bribery of its own officials. For example, the Russian Federation has enacted a complex legal framework prohibiting official corruption. Since April 1992, *Presidential Decree 351* has, as a preventive measure, barred civil servants from participating in entrepreneurial activities, managing commercial activities, or accepting foreign business trips paid by commercial entities. Nonetheless, Russia has earned a dubious reputation for omnipresent official corruption that often inhibits foreign investment.

South Korea also has an impressive and strict antibribery legal framework. The Korean *Criminal Code* prohibits not only receipt or solicitation of a bribe, but also "manifestation of a will to deliver" a bribe. In August 1996, two former South Korean presidents were convicted of criminal bribery after they accepted hundreds of millions of dollars from business enterprises. One was sentenced to death, while the other was sentenced to twenty-two years and six months in prison. Yet, in 1998, massive official corruption came to public light, and South Korea experienced a near-collapse of its financial system.

A foreign investor who makes a payoff to a foreign official therefore risks criminal prosecution by the official's country. But in many countries, this risk is not great. For instance, prior to recent events, South Korean prosecutors had enforced bribery laws only against lower-level officials and had exercised their prosecutorial discretion to avoid actions against politically powerful high-level officials. In fact, for the foreign investor, there is often a much greater risk of official persecution if a corrupt payment is not made.

At least thirty-six countries in the world also outlaw payment of bribes by their citizens to public officials in other countries. Because one of those countries is the United States, every American who retains an agent abroad should be familiar with the *Foreign Corrupt Practices Act (FCPA)*.

Origins of the FCPA and Other Antibribery Laws

In the mid-1970s, the press in the United States uncovered a number of instances of U.S.-based corporations making payments to foreign leaders for official favors. For example, an aircraft manufacturer was widely alleged to have made payments to the Japanese prime minister and a Dutch prince in exchange for assistance in obtaining government contracts. At the same time, alleged payments to a number of members of the Italian government caused its president to resign.

Concerned that American industry may be widely engaged in anti-democratic behavior, the U.S. Securities and Exchange Commission (SEC) instituted a voluntary disclosure program to assess the frequency of the phenomenon. Firms were invited to tell of their payoffs abroad under a loose understanding that they would not be prosecuted. The volume of the response was remarkable. More than four hundred U.S. companies revealed that they had bribed foreign public officials. The amounts paid aggregated into the hundreds of millions of dollars. Although corporations based in other countries allegedly engaged in the same practices, no nation had ever publicly confessed to such a massive pattern of corrupt behavior.

The U.S. public was in no mood to condone such frank admissions of immorality. Scarcely a year before, the president of the United States had resigned because of the Watergate cover-up. Nor had any nation ever faced the embarrassment of admitting such an extensive pattern of corrupt activity. Public opinion at home and disdain abroad demanded prompt and decisive action. They got it. By December 1977, Congress had passed and the president had signed the world's first law outlawing citizens' bribes to officials of another nation.

For two decades, the United States was alone in forbidding its citizens from bribing foreign officials. Indeed, some nations permitted tax deductions for such payments. However, the tide finally turned. In February 1999, the *Convention on Combating Bribery of Foreign Public Officials in International Business Transactions* (OECD Convention) became effective. The OECD Convention obligated the member states of the Organization for Economic Cooperation and Development (OECD) to enact a law making the bribery of foreign public officials a criminal act. The OECD Convention mirrors the accounting provisions of the FCPA, which require that public companies' accounting systems detect and report corrupt payments. As of mid-2007, thirty-seven countries had ratified the OECD Convention, including all major European countries and Latin American economic powers such as Argentina, Brazil, Chile, and Mexico. The OECD Convention is particularly significant because the nations that have ratified it are home to virtually all large international corporations. The OECD Convention's restraints are limited to active corruption of foreign public officials and do not include the higher FCPA standards. In most respects, however, the OECD Convention is consistent with the FCPA; indeed, the FCPA was amended in 1998 to harmonize its terms with those of the OECD Convention.

Other international legal efforts are also afoot. In late 2003, the United Nations General Assembly adopted the *UN Convention against Corruption* (UN Convention). The *UN Convention* was formulated through negotiations involving 125 countries, including many less-developed nations. The *UN Convention* entered into force in December 2005, and ninety-five countries had ratified or acceded to it as of mid-2007. Although the *UN Convention* is unlikely to enhance existing enforcement mechanisms, it provides additional international focus on the problem of corruption as a serious obstacle to development.

Separately, the Council of Europe promulgated a *Criminal Law Convention on Corruption* that included a broader definition of corruption than does the *OECD Convention,* one that is closer to that in the FCPA. Like the FCPA, the *Criminal Law Convention on Corruption* covers active and passive bribery and transnational bribes. The *Criminal Law Convention on Corruption* entered into force in January 2002, and thirty-six states had ratified or acceded to it as of August 2007.

The European Union has enacted four treaties and protocols focused on criminalization of transnational bribery. Under the *First Pillar Provisions of Community Law*, the European Commission is trying to promote a comprehensive European Union–wide policy against corruption. Under this policy, all members should join in implementing existing anticorruption treaties, harmonize their legal standards and law enforcement techniques, and properly implement certain audit rules. All members have banned tax deductions for bribes to foreign public officials. The European Council also adopted a decision, known as the *Framework Decision,* which requires members to criminalize private-sector corruption.

In developed countries, the movement against bribery is gathering great force. To understand how these antibribery statutes work, this study now turns in depth to the FCPA, which is the law that applies to U.S. enterprises.

Structure of the FCPA

The *Foreign Corrupt Practices Act* (FCPA) seeks to punish bribery of foreign officials through civil and criminal penalties and to establish internal accounting mechanisms that will prevent such bribery. The law's so-called *antibribery* provisions authorize criminal punishment. The law's prevention function is accomplished through provisions that seek to detect illegal payments by examining the accounting and record-keeping systems of the enterprise.

The Antibribery Provisions. In essence, the FCPA's antibribery provisions prohibit U.S. firms from "corruptly" paying or offering to pay a "foreign official" for assistance in obtaining or retaining business. They also prohibit payments to a person, such as a foreign agent, when the payer had reason to know that a portion of the payment will go to a public official. In light of the increasing importance of multinational organizations, in March 2002, the president signed an executive order designating European Union officials and officials of public international organizations as within the definition of "foreign official."

Violating antibribery provisions is a serious offense. In November 2002, the U.S. Sentencing Commission promulgated amendments making FCPA violations subject to the same sentencing guidelines as domestic bribery cases. Any individual convicted under these provisions can be imprisoned for up to five years and fined up to $100,000, even if that person acted with a reckless disregard of possible bribery but no actual knowledge. An individual may also face a $10,000 civil penalty. Any corporation convicted of a criminal violation can be fined $2 million per violation. Willful criminal violations of the FCPA are subject to even stricter penalties, Individuals may be fined up to $5 million and imprisoned for up to 20 years, and corporations may be fined up to $25 million.

Unfortunately, the law does not clearly define what one has to do to commit these serious offenses. It contains three principal points of ambiguity: the "routine governmental action" exception, the "corruptly" requirement, and the "knowing" requirement.

Congress recognized that in many countries petty graft is so common that to forbid U.S. companies from engaging in it would be tantamount to forbidding them to do business there. Accordingly, Congress excluded from the coverage of the FCPA "any facilitating or expediting payment ... the purpose of which is to expedite or secure the performance of a routine governmental action." Such routine governmental actions must be *nondiscretionary*. In other words, the government official must just be getting paid to do the routine tasks of his or her job: granting qualifications to do business, processing visas, providing police and mail service, or providing basic utilities or transportation services.

The routine governmental action exception (sometimes called the "grease payments" exception) is limited. Few government actions do not involve some discretion, particularly in countries outside the United States. As discussed in other chapters, many national statutes tend to lay out broad, general outlines and allow government officials to fill in the blanks. In short, U.S. executives largely must guess whether the role of any given government official will ultimately be determined by some court to be "routine." If they guess wrong, they can go to prison. Under such circumstances, taking chances is not advisable. Today, businesses in the United States are generally considered more reluctant than those in other countries to make any payments to officials.

In environments where making gratuity payments to customs officials is routine, the U.S. investor must make a careful assessment of its potential FCPA liability vis-à-vis its ability to operate effectively without making such payments. Many U.S. companies have determined that the profits of operating in such countries are not worth the risk. This is one reason why U.S. investment in Russia, for example, has largely vanished.

To violate the antibribery provisions, a payment must also be "corrupt." Although the word *corrupt* is used in a number of criminal statutes, the legal concept of corruption is not well defined. In the case of *Stichting ter Behartiging van de Belangen van Oudaandeelhouders in Het Kapitaal van Saybolt International B.V. v. Schreiber*, the United States Court of Appeals for the Second Circuit, which is the highest federal court for the region that includes New York City, recently found that acting "corruptly" requires "an evil motive or purpose and an intent to induce an official to misuse his position." Someone who is simply negligent in making a payment is not generally considered corrupt. A businessperson who—through lack of sophistication—fails to realize that part of a payment to a local foreign agent is in fact going to a government official may not have the corrupt state of mind required to violate the antibribery provision. (As discussed in the next section, however, such a businessperson might be in violation of the accounting provisions, which have no "corruptness" requirement.) Corruptness requires that the businessperson display a reckless or conscious disregard for the consequences of personal actions. Even if payers do not have actual knowledge that they are making a payment to a government official, they are corrupt if they act as if they do not care whether it is going to a government official.

The corruptness requirement even applies to victims of extortion. If a foreign official is extorting a payment from a U.S. investor—threatening to take action against the investor's business if the payment is not made—the investor is corrupt if it makes the payment. When a U.S. firm is faced with an extortion request in a country in which it already has substantial assets, therefore, the firm must refuse to make the payment and suffer the official's retribution against its assets. This situation, too, suggests that the investor should carefully review the business climate in the foreign country before entering it.

The ambiguities that accompany the "corruptness" concept are similar to those that surround the "knowing" requirement. Although Congress has now made clear that "mere foolishness" is insufficient for liability, the standard is intended to cover "any instance where 'any reasonable person would have realized' the existence of the circumstances or result and the [person] has 'consciously chosen not to ask about what he had reason to believe he would discover.'" The danger is that a foreign agent will ask for a commission that will ultimately end up in the hands of a foreign official. If a firm discovers that its agent made a payment to a government official, U.S. prosecutors would review the circumstances surrounding the payment to the agent to determine whether the firm "knew" of the agent's bribe. Moral: Whenever an agent asks for an unusually large fee or commission, a U.S. investor has reason to be nervous.

THE ACCOUNTING AND RECORD-KEEPING REQUIREMENTS. The FCPA also requires public U.S. companies to "make and keep books, records, and accounts which, in reasonable detail, accurately and fairly reflect the transactions and dispositions of [their] assets." It further requires an investor to "devise and maintain a system of internal accounting controls sufficient to provide reasonable assurances" that all transactions are properly authorized and that access to assets is tracked. These requirements are commonly referred to as the *accounting and record-keeping provisions.* The SEC may bring an enforcement action against any company that knowingly violates the accounting and record-keeping provisions. The *Sarbanes-Oxley Act of 2004* imposed further accounting and record-keeping requirements on companies.

The principal objection to the accounting provisions is that they fail to incorporate any concept of relative importance, known in financial circles as *materiality.* U.S. businesses are not normally expected to unearth every fact in their financial statements because doing so would be impractical and would drown the reader of the financial statements in a sea of detail. Accounting systems are generally geared to track *material* facts—facts of a financial magnitude that a prudent investor in the company should know. A $5,000 problem in a $5 billion company, for instance, would not normally be perceived as material.

By not including a concept of materiality, the accounting provisions of the FCPA require the U.S. company's accounting system to be able to identify bribery irrespective of how small it may be. Although $5,000 might be a great deal of money to an individual, tracking every such problem represents a formidable task for a multibillion-dollar company. Nevertheless, as a technical matter, failing to track even a small problem is a possible violation of the FCPA.

The Department of Justice Review Process

Before entering a transaction that raises a possible FCPA issue, an investor can seek an interpretation of these somewhat ambiguous provisions from the U.S. Department of Justice (DOJ). However, this process is very flawed.

The inquiring firm first must submit all relevant details of the proposed transaction to the DOJ, including appropriate documentation. The DOJ will not respond to hypothetical fact situations. The firm must be willing to risk the confidentiality of the deal. All documents submitted to the DOJ are subject to the *Freedom of Information Act,* which permits any American, including a journalist, to request disclosure of documents in the government's possession. Even in a deal whose specifics receive confidential treatment, the DOJ will issue a release that describes the general nature of the transaction. Because of this, the procedure has the initial disadvantage of subjecting the transaction to the scrutiny of the public at large, including the U.S. firm's competitors, before the transaction closes. In a highly competitive world with near-instant communications, these competitors may be attracted to the opportunity and lure the U.S. firm's proposed business partners away with a more attractive deal.

Disclosure of the deal can have other adverse effects. The public officials involved may resent having their integrity publicly questioned, or such public disclosure might adversely affect the officials' standing in their own home country.

The DOJ will respond in thirty days unless it requires the submission of additional information. If it does require additional information, the DOJ will have an additional thirty days from the time of receipt of that information. At the end of this two-month period, the DOJ will either express an interest to pursue or not to pursue a prosecution under the FCPA, or will decline to state any position. This delay is not very satisfactory in most business transactions. While the parties await a response, market conditions may change and make the deal less attractive or entirely unattractive for one of the parties.

Perhaps because of these problems, the DOJ review procedure is used quite infrequently. Although millions of foreign transactions have occurred since the procedure was instituted in 1980, only a few dozen requests have been made under it. In the overwhelming majority of cases, U.S. firms choose not to avail themselves of the procedure. Nonetheless, one example will help illustrate the process:

Foreign Corrupt Practices Act Review Opinion Procedure Release 07-01
July 24, 2007
United States Department of Justice

The Department has reviewed the FCPA Opinion request of a U.S. company (the "requestor") that was submitted on June 29, 2007. . . .

The requestor proposes to cover the domestic expenses for a trip to the United States by a six-person delegation of the government of an Asian country for an educational and promotional tour of one of the requestor's U.S. operations sites. The stated purpose of the visit is to familiarize the delegates with the nature and extent of the requestor's operations and capabilities and to help establish the requestor's business credibility. The requestor is interested in participating in future operations in the foreign country similar to those it conducts in the United States. The visit will last for four days and will be limited to domestic economy class travel to one U.S. operations site only. The requestor also intends to pay for the domestic lodging, local transport, and meals for the six officials. The foreign government plans to pay the costs of the international airfare. The requestor has asked for a determination of the Department's present enforcement intention under the FCPA.

The requestor has represented, among other things, that:

- it does not currently conduct operations in the foreign country or with the foreign government, although it is interested in pursuing such opportunities in the future;
- it has obtained written assurance, a copy of which has been provided to the Department of Justice, from an established law firm with offices in both the United States and the foreign country that the requestor's sponsorship of the visit and its payment of the expenses described in the request is not contrary to the law of the foreign country;
- it did not select the delegates who will participate in the visit; rather, the foreign government selected the delegates;
- to the requestor's knowledge, the delegates have no direct authority over decisions relating to potential contracts or licenses necessary for operating in the foreign country;
- it will host only officials working for the relevant foreign ministries and one private government consultant;
- it intends to pay all costs directly to the providers; no funds will be paid directly to the foreign government or the delegates;
- it will not pay any expenses for spouses, family, or other guests of the officials;
- any souvenirs that the requestor may provide to the delegates would reflect the requestor's name and/or logo and would be of nominal value;

continued

continued

- apart from meals and receptions connected to meetings, speakers, or events the requestor is planning for the officials, it will not fund, organize, or host any entertainment or leisure activities for the officials, nor will it provide the officials with any stipend or spending money; and
- all costs and expenses incurred by the requestor in connection with the visit will be properly and accurately recorded in the requestor's books and records.

Based upon all of the facts and circumstances, as represented by the requestor, the Department does not presently intend to take any enforcement action with respect to the proposal described in this request. This is because, based on the requestor's representations, consistent with the FCPA's promotional expenses affirmative defense, the expenses contemplated are reasonable under the circumstances and directly relate to "the promotion, demonstration, or explanation of [the requestor's] products or services."

The FCPA Opinion Letter referred to herein, and this release, have no binding application to any party which did not join in the request, and can be relied upon by the requestor only to the extent that the disclosure of facts and circumstances in its request is accurate and complete and continues to accurately and completely reflect such facts and circumstances.

FCPA Enforcement Actions

For over two decades the FCPA was seldom enforced, but this has abruptly changed. Civil and criminal enforcement actions in connection with alleged payments to foreign officials have increased greatly in recent years. From 2003 through the end of June 2007, twenty Securities and Exchange Commission (SEC) enforcement actions and twenty-three DOJ enforcement actions were initiated under the FCPA. There were also about one hundred active FCPA investigations as of July 2007. The largest fines levied against companies under the FCPA have been imposed in the last few years. Titan Corp. was fined $28.5 million in 2005, and Baker Hughes, Inc. was ordered to pay $44 million in 2007.

Prosecution of individuals for FCPA violations has also increased dramatically. In 2006, three individuals pled guilty to FCPA violations. A grand jury indicted another individual in 2001 who was later convicted of agreeing to pay a $1 million bribe to Costa Rican officials to obtain land concessions for a potential development project. He was sentenced to thirty months in prison and fined $60,000. In 2005, two top officers of a rice exporting company were convicted of bribing Haitian officials to reduce customs and sales taxes on the company's rice imports. One defendant was sentenced to three years and one month in prison and fined $1,300; the other defendant was sentenced to five years and three months in prison and fined $1,400.

Some enforcement actions have been ill advised. A 1993 FCPA investigation relating to alleged payments by Northrop Corporation to South Korean officials as persuasion for purchases of F-20 fighter planes was dropped with no action. In 2004 and 2007, significant FCPA charges were dismissed from cases against individuals allegedly involved in a scheme to bribe Azerbaijani officials to allow them to benefit from the privatization of the state oil company. One highly publicized FCPA case has experienced several procedural setbacks since an April 2003 grand jury indictment. In that case, the defendant, a U.S. citizen with a business headquartered in New York, acted as a consultant to the government of Kazakhstan. He allegedly gave $78 million in cash and luxury items like speedboats to Kazakh officials to obtain business for his company.

Foreign Enforcement Actions

Other countries with FCPA-like laws are also stepping up enforcement. Between 2005 and 2007 several countries, including Australia, France, Germany, Italy, Ireland, Switzerland, and the United Kingdom, investigated multiple violations of their transnational bribery laws. Several of these investigations related to the United Nations Oil-for-Food program. In May 2007, a German court convicted two former employees of Siemens AG of bribing officials at an Italian utility to award them contracts for the sale of gas turbines. One received a two-year suspended prison sentence for bribery. The other received a nine-month suspended sentence for aiding the bribery. The court also ordered Siemens to pay 38 million euros ($51.4 million) of the profit from the contracts.

The *Statoil* case, set forth below, is an example of a case in which both the United States and another country, Norway, imposed fines on a company for violating statutes prohibiting bribery of foreign public officials.

In the Matter of Statoil, ASA

Exchange Act Release No. 54,599, SEC Admin. Proc. File No. 3-12453, U.S. District Court (S.D.N.Y), October 13, 2006, Order Instituting Cease-and-Desist Proceedings, Making Findings, and Imposing a Cease-and-Desist Order pursuant to Section 21C of the Securities Exchange Act of 1934

BACKGROUND AND FACTS

Statoil ASA is a Norwegian company listed on the New York Stock Exchange. Statoil was found to have paid bribes to an Iranian government official (the "Iranian Official") in June 2002 and January 2003 to get him to use his influence to (i) assist Statoil in obtaining a contract to develop three phases of the South Pars oil and gas field in Iran (the "South Pars Project") and (ii) open doors to additional projects in the Iranian oil and gas exploration industry. The following order issued by the Securities and Exchange Commission pursuant to Section 21C of the Securities Exchange Act of 1934 approved Statoil's settlement offer.

***

... Statoil agreed to pay the Iranian Official through a consulting contract (the "Contract") with an intermediary company (the "Consulting Company") organized in the Turks and Caicos Islands and nominally owned by a third party located in London, England....

Statoil is an international oil and gas company involved primarily in the exploration for, development, production, and sale of oil and natural gas from the Norwegian Continental Shelf and elsewhere. In late 2000 and early 2001, under its former Chief Executive Officer ("CEO"), Statoil was pursuing opportunities to expand its business internationally....

Statoil identified Iran as a country to focus on to secure operatorships. The Iranian Ministry of Oil, through NIOC and various wholly owned companies, controls the rights to develop the oil and gas resources of Iran.... [In mid-2001, Statoil employees and management met with the influential Iranian Official, who "was an advisor to the Oil Minister."]

THE BRIBERY

In the second half of 2001 and into 2002, the Senior Executive discussed with Statoil's CEO the possibility of entering into a consulting contract to arrange payments to the Iranian Official, and began negotiating the terms with the Iranian Official. In November 2001, Iranian authorities proposed that Statoil consider seeking a participation interest in a subcontract to develop the South Pars Project, under a contract awarded to an Iranian oil and gas development company (the "Development Company") that was indirectly owned and controlled by the Iranian Ministry of Oil.

In December 2001, the Iranian Official sent a sample consulting contract and payment proposal to the Senior Executive, which the Iranian Official represented had previously been used in his dealings with other multinational oil companies. In January 2002, the Senior Executive provided the CEO with a memorandum that described a proposal from the Iranian Official that would have required Statoil to (i) pay a "success fee" payable upon Statoil's being awarded a participation interest in the development of the South Pars Project; (ii) provide money for "charities" of the Iranian Official's choice; and (iii) make payments through an offshore company.

Although the CEO objected to the Iranian Official's proposal, the CEO ultimately approved Statoil's entering into a contract with the Iranian Official in the total amount of $15.2 million to be paid over approximately 11 years. The final Contract was structured as a payment for vaguely defined consulting services through a third-party offshore company. The Iranian Official was not named in the Contract because disclosing Statoil's relationship with the Iranian Official could likely jeopardize Statoil's ability to obtain business in Iran.

In return for the payments, the Iranian Official used his influence to assist Statoil in obtaining business in Iran. For example, the Iranian Official (i) provided Statoil employees in Iran nonpublic information concerning oil and gas projects in Iran and (ii) showed Statoil copies of bid documents of competing

continued

continued

companies that Statoil could not access through appropriate channels. . . .

[The Development Company awarded the South Pars Project to Statoil in October 2002. Statoil expected the project "would yield millions of dollars in profit."]

In late June 2002, Statoil received an invoice from the Consulting Company instructing it to pay $200,000 under the terms of the Contract, and instructing that the money be routed through a United States bank in New York, New York to a bank account in Switzerland held by a company not named in the Contract. Statoil made the payment on June 26, 2002, according to the instructions in the invoice. In December 2002, Statoil received a second invoice from the Consulting Company instructing it to pay $5 million, with payment instructions identical to those in the June 2002 invoice. On January 15, 2003, Statoil paid $5 million pursuant to the instructions in the invoice. [Statoil ended the payments later in 2003 after an internal audit discovered the $5.2 million in payments and determined that they "may have violated Norwegian and U.S. anti-bribery laws." After the contract was disclosed to the press, the Senior Executive, Chairman of the Board, and CEO resigned.]

Statoil violated the anti-bribery provisions of the federal securities laws contained in the Foreign Corrupt Practices Act when it arranged for the payments to the Iranian Official. The payments were intended to (i) induce the Iranian Official to use his influence with NIOC; (ii) influence NIOC's decision about whether to award Statoil a participation interest in the development of the South Pars Project that would net Statoil several millions of dollars; and (iii) secure improper advantage for Statoil by positioning it to obtain future business in Iran, potentially worth hundreds of millions of dollars.

BOOKS AND RECORDS VIOLATIONS

Statoil failed to properly account for the illegal payments and failed to accurately describe the Contract in its books and records. Instead, Statoil improperly characterized the payments it made as legitimate payments for "consulting fees for special consultants and analyses relating to technical, administrative, tax, and financial matters . . . ," and improperly characterized the Contract as an ordinary consulting agreement.

INTERNAL CONTROLS VIOLATIONS

In entering into the Contract, certain Statoil management responsible for the Contract circumvented Statoil's internal controls designed to prevent illegal payments. They concealed the Contract's true nature and true parties, and violated Statoil's procurement policies by directing that the Contract should be entered into and that payments be made under the Contract to parties not named in the Contract. Statoil management responsible for the Contract performed no due diligence concerning the named or unnamed parties to the Contract. Statoil had inadequate systems for review of the Contract and lacked controls sufficient to provide reasonable assurances that the Contract complied with applicable laws. Statoil's lack of sufficient internal controls enabled executives responsible for the Contract to conceal the illegal payments to the Iranian Official.

NORWEGIAN AUTHORITIES' ACTIONS

On September 11, 2003, Norwegian government authorities from the National Authority for Investigation and Prosecution of Economic and Environmental Crime ("Økokrim") seized documents from Statoil's offices as part of an investigation of Statoil. On June 29, 2004, following its investigation, Økokrim issued penalty notices to Statoil in the amount of approximately $3 million and to the Senior Executive in the amount of approximately $30,000, charging them with violating Norway's trading-in-influence statute. Statoil and the Senior Executive agreed to pay the penalties without admitting or denying the violations.

Decision. Because Statoil sold securities in the United States capital markets, the SEC found that it was subject to the FCPA although it was a Norwegian company. The SEC found that Statoil violated the FCPA. Statoil was required to hire an independent compliance consultant to review its internal controls and record-keeping procedures and assess whether they comply with the requirements of the FCPA. Statoil was ordered to "cease and desist from committing or causing any violations and any future violations of" securities laws and to "pay disgorgement of $10,500,000 to the United States Treasury." Under the settlement agreement, Statoil admitted its agents had paid the bribes.

International Refusal to Enforce Contracts Induced by Bribery

Civil and criminal penalties under the FCPA and foreign antibribery statutes are not the only possible legal sanctions for investors who use bribes to induce foreign public officials to award them contracts. In the past few years, international tribunals have refused to enforce contracts based on bribery, leaving the briber out its bribe payment but without the benefit of its wrongdoing. In the 2006 English case *Marlwood Commercial Inc. v. Kozeny*, the Queen's Bench Commercial Court held that English courts will not enforce contracts involving bribery of foreign officials or sale of influence because they are illegal in England and contrary to English public policy. This rule applies even if the bribery is not a crime in the foreign country.

In the 2006 arbitration of *Inceysa Vallisolenta, S.L. v. Republic of El Salvador*, the International Centre for Settlement of Investment Disputes (ICSID) similarly refused to enforce a contract entered into by the Salvadoran government with a contractor who acted fraudulently, in bad faith, and in violation of public policy. The panel's decision includes a careful discussion of some key civil law and international legal principles that protect states from the fraudulent tactics of foreign vendors.

Despite the increased enforcement of the FCPA, the increasing acceptance of the *Convention on Combating Bribery of Foreign Public Officials in International Business Transactions*, and the recent refusal to enforce contracts induced by illegal action, the battle against corruption is far from won.

As we have seen, most other developed countries are now also moving to punish bribe-givers. The OECD and the European Union have each enacted their own anticorruption frameworks. The International Monetary Fund (IMF) has said that IMF officials will press for anticorruption reforms in countries seeking to borrow money. The World Bank has declared that if it finds evidence of corruption in any project it finances, it will cancel the project. Now, the developing world has weighed in through the *UN Convention against*

Inceysa Vallisolenta, S.L. v. Republic of El Salvador

International Centre for Settlement of Investment Disputes (ICSID)

ICSID Case No. ARB/03/26 (AWARD) (August 2, 2006)

BACKGROUND AND FACTS

El Salvador's Ministry of the Environment and Natural Resources (MARN) submitted a bid for a service contract for mechanical vehicle inspection stations. During the bidding process, Inceysa, a Spanish company, submitted false and incorrect information about its financial condition, presented false credentials for the auditor of its financial statements and an expert who verified that Inceysa was capable of rendering vehicle inspection services, misled MARN about the identity and experience of Inceysa's strategic partner, and overstated its own experience with vehicle inspection projects. Inceysa also failed to disclose its close connections to another participant in the bid, Ingeniería, Construcción y Arquitectura del Sur (ICASUR). Based on this false information, MARN awarded exclusive contracts to Inceysa and ICASUR.

However, MARN ultimately hired other companies to perform the services called for in Inceysa's contract. Inceysa brought an ICSID arbitration for $122,532,329, plus interest, costs, and attorneys' fees against El Salvador under the bilateral investment treaty (BIT) between Spain and El Salvador, claiming breach of contract and expropriation. El Salvador argued that ICSID lacked jurisdiction because Inceysa acted fraudulently during the bidding process, and only legitimate contracts not induced by fraud or corruption are protected under the BIT.

continued

continued

ARBITRATOR: RODRIGO OREAMUNO BLANCO (PRESIDENT); BURTON A. LANDY; CLAUS VON WOBESER:

States use multiple mechanisms to limit the scope of application of the agreements for the reciprocal protection of investments signed by them. One of the most commonly used refers to the so-called "accordance with the laws of the host State clause."...

There are various forms by which States establish the "accordance with the laws of the host State clause." Among the mechanisms used to include this limitation is to add it into the definition of *investment* itself, making it clear that for the purposes of that reciprocal protection agreement only those made in accordance with the laws of the host State will be deemed *investments.*

Furthermore, the signatory States may validly exclude from the protection of a **BIT** investments made illegally, precisely in the articles that indicate the scope of protection of the **BIT** in question. In this context, particularly relevant are the indications of the tribunal in the *Salini Costruttori S.P.A. and Italstrade S.P.A v. the Kingdom of Morocco* case in which it was decided that:

> "[...] In envisaging 'the categories of invested assets [...] in accordance with the laws and regulations of the said party,' the provision in question refers to the legality of the investment and not to its definition. It aims in particular to ensure that the bilateral Agreement does not protect investments which it should not, generally because they are illegal." ...
> Having indicated that it is valid and common for States that sign an agreement for reciprocal protection of investments to limit the protection of the agreement to investments made in accordance with the laws of the host State, it is the task of this Arbitral Tribunal to decide whether in the **Agreement** signed between Spain and **El Salvador** these States limited the protection of the **BIT** only to investments made in accordance with the laws of the host State and, consequently, excluded from that protection those made illegally....

In the identification of the will of the Contracting States of the **Agreement**, the *travaux preparatoires* [preparatory briefing] shed light on the intent of the Republic of **El Salvador** and the Kingdom of Spain. In this regard, this Tribunal considers relevant the indications contained in the communications exchanged between **El Salvador** and Spain days before the entry into force of the **Agreement**. In one of these communications, **El Salvador** made certain observations to Spain about the draft text of the **Agreement**. We transcribe below from this letter the following:

"[...] II.- Add to the end of sub-paragraph 5 on the designation of "investments," in paragraph 2 of Article 1, the following language: "... in accordance with the laws in force in each of the Contracting Parties" [...].

The above quote clearly indicates that **El Salvador** had, from the beginning of the negotiations, the intent to limit the protection of the **Agreement** it was about to sign only to investments made in accordance with its laws. Furthermore, it is clear that, by said communication, **El Salvador** tried to include this limitation to its consent in the definition of "*investment.*"

Faced with the request of **El Salvador**, Spain informed El Salvador that it was not necessary to include the limitation requested in the definition of "investment," because it was included in the text of the **Agreement**....

The ... communication indicates, without any doubt, that the will of the parties to the **BIT** was to exclude from the scope of application and protection of the **Agreement** disputes originating from investments which were not made in accordance with the laws of the host State....

So, after analyzing the intent of Spain and **El Salvador** obvious in the *travaux preparatoires* of the **Agreement**, we must look at its own terms. Thus, consistent with what Spain indicated, the conditions imposed on investments are specifically established in other provisions of the **BIT**, specifically in two different articles that refer to the clause of "in accordance with law."

Article III, titled "*Protection,*" indicates that "*Each Contracting Party shall protect in its territory the investments* ***made, in accordance with its legislation*** *...,*" by investors from the other Contracting Party, thus excluding from the protection of the **BIT** investments made illegally....

[Under the BIT, the Tribunal looked to general principles of law to determine whether Inceysa's investment was made illegally.]

Without attempting to define what the general principles of law are, the Tribunal notes that, in general, they have been understood as general rules on which there is international consensus to consider them as universal standards and rules of conduct that must always be applied and which, in

continued

continued

the opinion of important commentators, are rules of law on which the legal systems of the States are based. . . .

A) VIOLATION OF THE PRINCIPLE OF GOOD FAITH

Good faith is a supreme principle, which governs legal relations in all of their aspects and content. . . .

In the contractual field, good faith means absence of deceit and artifice during the negotiation and execution of instruments that gave rise to the investment, as well as loyalty, truth and intent to maintain the equilibrium between the reciprocal performance of the parties. . . .

It is clear to this Tribunal that the investment made by **Inceysa** in the territory of **El Salvador**, which gave rise to the present dispute, **was made in violation of the principle of good faith**. . . .

Among **Inceysa's** violations of the principle of good faith, as demonstrated in chapter IV of this award, the Tribunal emphasizes the following: **(i) Inceysa's** presentation of false financial information as part of the tender made by it to participate in the **bid**; **(ii)** false representations during the bidding process, in connection with the experience and capacity necessary to comply with the terms of the **Contract,** particularly concerning its alleged strategic partner; **(iii)** falsity of the documents by which **Inceysa** sought to prove the professionalism of Mr. Antonio Felipe Martinez Lavado, on whose career in large measure it based its alleged aptness to perform the functions entrusted to it when winning the **bid**; and **(iv)** the fact that it had hidden the existing relationship between **Inceysa** and ICASUR, in clear violation of one of the fundamental pillars of the **bidding** rules. . . .

By falsifying the facts, **Inceysa** violated the principle of good faith from the time it made its investment and, therefore, it did not make it in accordance with Salvadoran law. Faced with this situation, this Tribunal can only declare its incompetence to hear **Inceysa's** complaint, since its investment cannot benefit from the protection of the **BIT**, as established by the parties during the negotiations and the execution of the agreement. . . .

B) VIOLATION OF THE PRINCIPLE *NEMO AUDITUR PROPIAM TURPITUDINEM ALLEGAN* ["NOBODY CAN BENEFIT FROM HIS OWN FRAUD"]

. . . [T]he foreign investor cannot seek to benefit from an investment effectuated by means of one or several illegal acts and, consequently, enjoy the protection granted by the host State, such as access to international arbitration to resolve disputes, because it is evident that its act had a fraudulent origin and, as provided by the legal maxim, "nobody can benefit from his own fraud."

In the dispute brought to this Arbitral Tribunal, there are clear facts and reasons that match the aforementioned supposition, since **Inceysa** acted improperly in order to be awarded the **bid** that made its investment possible and, therefore, it cannot be given the protection granted by the **BIT**. . . .

The clear and obvious evidence of the violations committed by **Inceysa** during the **bidding** process lead this Tribunal to decide that **Inceysa**'s investment cannot, under any circumstances, enjoy the protection of the **BIT**. Allowing **Inceysa** to benefit from an investment made clearly in violation of the rules of the bid in which it originated would be a serious failure of the justice that this Tribunal is obligated to render. No legal system based on rational grounds allows the party that committed a chain of clearly illegal acts to benefit from them.

C) VIOLATION OF INTERNATIONAL PUBLIC POLICY

International public policy consists of a series of fundamental principles that constitute the very essence of the State, and its essential function is to preserve the values of the international legal system against actions contrary to it.

In line with the foregoing, the inclusion of the clause "in accordance with law" in various **BIT** provisions is a clear manifestation of said international public policy, which demonstrates the clear and obvious intent of the signatory States to exclude from its protection investments made in violation of the internal laws of each of them. . . .

It is uncontroversial that respect for the law is a matter of public policy not only in El Salvador, but in any civilized country. If this Tribunal declares itself competent to hear the disputes between the parties, it would completely ignore the fact that, above any claim of an investor, there is a meta-positive provision that prohibits attributing effects to an act done illegally. . . .

In light of the foregoing, not to exclude **Inceysa**'s investment from the protection of the **BIT** would be a violation of **international public policy**, which this Tribunal cannot allow. Consequently, this Arbitral Tribunal decides that **Inceysa**'s investment is not

continued

continued

protected by the **BIT** because it is contrary to international public policy.

D) VIOLATION OF THE PRINCIPLE THAT PROHIBITS UNLAWFUL ENRICHMENT

The acts committed by **Inceysa** during the bidding process are in violation of the legal principle that prohibits **unlawful enrichment.**

The written legal systems of the nations governed by the Civil Law system recognize that, when the cause of the increase in the assets of a certain person is illegal, such enrichment must be sanctioned by preventing its consummation.

Applying the principle discussed above to the case at hand, we note that **Inceysa** resorted to fraud to obtain a benefit that it would not have otherwise obtained. Thus, through actions that violate the legal principles stated above, **Inceysa** tried to enrich itself, signing an administrative contract with MARN, which, without any doubt, would produce considerable profit for it....

Decision. The tribunal concluded that because Inceysa's investment was made in a manner that was clearly illegal, it was not included within the scope of consent expressed by Spain and the Republic of El Salvador in the BIT and, consequently, the disputes arising from it were not subject to the jurisdiction of the Centre. Therefore, the tribunal declared itself incompetent to hear the dispute.

Corruption. As the Adler case below reflects, courts will give no refuge to a bribe-giver, no matter how sympathetic its circumstances.

Prudent Behavior for the U.S. Businessperson

Achieving greater profits for one's company is certainly not worth a prison sentence, improbable as prosecution may be. It is increasingly likely that if any corruption is detected, it will cause multilateral institutions to pull financing and may even void the ill-procured contract, leading to disastrous consequences for the investor. Therefore, the best course of action for the U.S. entrepreneur abroad is to be vigilant against foreign corruption. Here are a few ground rules.

First, avoid making direct payments to government officials, other than payments associated

Adler v. The Federal Republic of Nigeria

219 F.3d 869 (2000)

United States Court of Appeals (9th Cir.)

BACKGROUND AND FACTS

Jaime Adler, a U.S. citizen, and El Surtidor, a Mexican corporation of which Adler was controlling shareholder, brought this action against the Federal Republic of Nigeria, the Central Bank of Nigeria ("CBN"), and seventeen Nigerian officials.

In August 1992, Adler received a letter signed by Chief Abba Ganna. The letter proposed a "business transaction" between Adler, Ganna, and the Chief Accountant of the Nigerian National Petroleum Corporation ("NNPC"). Ganna explained the transaction as follows:

> [D]uring the last civilian regime here in Nigeria, the elected members of the ruling party used their positions and formulated companies and awarded themselves contracts which were fantastically over-invoiced in various government ministries.
>
> On the overthrow of the regime by the present military government, an inquiry was set to this. Findings and recommendations were made to the

continued

continued

> government who has given its blessing for the payment of these contracts half/fully executed. You can now see that there is a good deal for these government officials presently in office hence the ousted notable party stalwarts can not come forward for some of the claims.

Ganna requested that Adler send (1) four signed and stamped copies of El Surtidor letterhead and pro forma invoices and (2) the number of a foreign bank account. In addition, Ganna asked Adler to purchase first-class airplane tickets for Nigerian officials to travel to Mexico to collect their share of the money. In exchange for providing these services, Adler would earn a 40 percent commission. The remaining 60 percent of the funds would be divided between "miscellaneous expenses" (10 percent) and "the government officials" (50 percent). Adler performed as requested.

In September 1992, Adler traveled to Nigeria and visited the home of the Minister of Finance and an office of the CBN where he met with various individuals who identified themselves as Nigerian government officials. Among these "officials" was John Olisa, Deputy Governor of the CBN. Olisa told Adler that the Nigerian government had assigned rights to El Surtidor under a contract between the NNPC and Strabarg Company, another foreign company, for the computerization of Nigerian oil field operations. Olisa also showed Adler a bank draft for $60 million made out to El Surtidor and Jaime Adler, and had Adler sign the assignment. Olisa told Adler that he would give him a copy of the contract after Adler deposited funds to cover the difference in the exchange rate between the U.S. dollar and the Nigerian nira ("shortfall deposit funds").

Beginning with Olisa's request for the shortfall deposit funds, certain individuals, whom Adler believed to be officials of the Nigerian government, repeatedly requested payments from Adler. They described these payments variously as shortfall deposit funds, taxes, processing fees, confirmation fees, surcharges, legal fees, travel expenses, and "gratification." Almost every time someone requested a payment from Adler, that individual told Adler that as soon as he made that payment, the $60 million would be deposited into his account. Adler made payments totaling $5,180,000.

Between August 1992 and July 1994, Adler corresponded, by mail and by telephone, with a variety of individuals who represented themselves as officials of the Nigerian government. In addition, Adler made two more trips to Nigeria prior to filing this lawsuit. In December 1992, he visited Olisa's residence. On the April 1994 trip, Adler met with Paul Ogwuma, Governor of the CBN.

It all turned out to be a fraud perpetrated on Adler by the Nigerian government officials. The promised $60 million never came. Adler ultimately sued in the United States to recover the funds he had advanced the Nigerian government officials.

After trial, the United States District Court for the Southern District of California held, in relevant part, that (1) Adler paid bribes totaling $2.11 million to Nigerian officials in violation of the *Foreign Corrupt Practices Act;* (2) at least one official of the Nigerian government, CBN Governor Paul Ogwuma, participated as a co-conspirator in the fraud against Adler; and (3) the Nigerian government permitted other co-conspirators to use the CBN offices to further the fraud. On these facts, the district court barred Adler from recovering the money he paid to Nigerian government officials because he came to the Court with "unclean hands." Both sides appealed.

HARRY PREGERSON, CIRCUIT JUDGE

We ... affirm the district court's factual findings, and its application of the clean hands defense to bar Adler's recovery.

On appeal, defendants ask us to reverse several of the district court's factual findings. Specifically, defendants challenge the following findings of fact: (1) Adler met CBN Governor Paul Ogwuma and Ogwuma was a co-conspirator in the conspiracy to defraud Adler; (2) Ogwuma sent Adler letters requesting payments; (3) Adler paid Ogwuma $50,000; (4) Adler met the Nigerian Minister of Finance at the Minister's home; (5) Adler met John Olisa and Olisa is a Deputy Governor of the CBN; (6) Adler received a Revenue Collector's Receipt showing payment of $300,000; (7) the Nigerian government required a shortfall payment of $570,000; (8) Adler paid various fees and taxes to the Nigerian government; (9) Brigadier Ball Peters was Unit Commander for the Presidential Task Force on Trade Malpractices of CBN; and (10) Dr. Clement Odozi was the Deputy Governor of the CBN.... We may not reject the district court's "account of the evidence [if it] is plausible in light of the record viewed in its entirety." Here, the district court's factual findings present a plausible account of the evidence, and therefore defendants' challenge fails to satisfy the clear error standard.

On cross-appeal, Adler argues that the district court erred in applying the unclean hands doctrine.

continued

continued

The unclean hands doctrine "closes the doors of a court of equity to one tainted with inequitableness or bad faith relative to the matter in which he seeks relief, however improper may have been the behavior of the defendant...." Under this doctrine, plaintiffs seeking equitable relief must have "acted fairly and without fraud or deceit as to the controversy in issue." ... The district court decided that Adler dirtied his hands by intentionally attempting to aid and abet the Nigerian officials' scheme to steal from the government treasury and by paying bribes....

Nevertheless, Adler puts forth a variety of arguments in an attempt to persuade this court that inequity results from the district court's exercise of discretion. He asserts that he and the Nigerian officials are not equally at fault; that the Nigerian officials will be unjustly enriched if they do not return the funds to Adler; and that this court should grant Adler a remedy because, by doing so, it will discourage Nigerian officials from perpetrating such schemes in the future. Whatever the merits of these arguments, the district court did not abuse its discretion in reaching the opposite conclusion.

First, it is not clear that Adler is any less blameworthy than the Nigerian officials. The Nigerian officials proposed the criminal scheme, but Adler voluntarily participated in it. And while the Nigerian officials successfully defrauded Adler of over five million dollars, Adler attempted to steal sixty million dollars from the Nigerian government. Second, the fact that the defendants will receive a windfall is not an absolute bar to the unclean hands defense.... Finally, it is not clear that justice would be served by compelling the Nigerian government to return the money to Adler. Making a judicial remedy available when the bribe fails to accomplish the intended result would reduce the risk inherent in paying bribes, and encourage individuals such as Adler. In short, public policy favors discouraging frauds such as the one perpetrated on Adler, but it also favors discouraging individuals such as Adler from voluntarily participating in such schemes and paying bribes to bring them to fruition....

Decision. The Ninth Circuit held that the district court properly exercised jurisdiction over this case; the district court's factual findings were not clearly erroneous; and the district court did not abuse its discretion in applying the unclean hands defense to bar Adler's recovery.

with the most ministerial aspects of clearing customs. They should be avoided even if the foreign official threatens to terminate existing contracts with one's firm unless he or she is paid off. The simplest course may be to avoid doing business in nations in which such extortion is known and likely to occur. Such situations put a firm between a rock and a hard place: if it accepts the extortion demand, it risks U.S. criminal conviction; if it refuses the demand, it faces a substantial business loss.

Second, foreign agents should be carefully selected and even more carefully paid. Preferably, one should build an ample "due diligence" file containing the foreign agent's trade references and records of investigations into the person's character. Commissions and other payments should conform to customary rates in that nation. Avoid "premium" transactions in nations with suspect reputations. Make appropriate inquiry with respect to the government officials whose discretion is involved in any given transaction.

Conclusion

If a U.S. enterprise chooses to expand into a foreign nation by hiring an independent agent, it may avoid much of the foreign regulation inherent in establishing a full corporate presence or in cross-border licensing. It will, however, need to take care that its independent agent is recognized as independent. Further, the enterprise will benefit from becoming familiar with the statutory framework of rights that protect the agent—rights that exist irrespective of the terms of its contract with the agent. Once it engages a local agent, the U.S. enterprise must be mindful that its advertising and promotional efforts abroad comply with local regulations and laws and reflect the sensitivities of the local culture. Finally, the enterprise must be particularly careful that its "promotions" do not include payments that are indirectly intended to go to a local official, in violation of national criminal laws and international agreements.

Chapter Summary

1. The United States places few restrictions on the terms of the agent–principal relationship. The principal and the agent each have discretion to agree on appropriate terms, including compensation, exclusivity, and termination of the relationship. Many nations, however, enact laws that supersede contractual arrangements. These laws protect local representatives against enforcement of certain contract terms, no matter what is written in a representative's agreement.
2. For tax purposes, if the principal works through an agent rather than an independent contractor, the principal is often viewed as having opened an office and is subject to taxation. This tends not to occur with independent contractors. In particular, if an investor has a dependent agent in a country, he or she will often be regarded as an employee. This classification may subject the principal to local law regarding pensions, tax withholding, and labor negotiations. Further, if an agent is found to be dependent, the principal will be vicariously liable to third parties for the agent's misdeeds, particularly in the context of product liability.
3. Virtually every country prohibits false advertising, but what is "false" differs according to how exacting the local culture is. What is false advertising in one culture may be acceptable "puffing" in another. In some nations, language laws require that every word in advertising—including technical jargon—be in the local language.
4. Countries tend to impose particularly tight regulations on advertising of products that are considered to be (or lead to) "sin" in the local culture. For example, many countries regulate the advertising of alcoholic beverages or tobacco products. Many countries also restrict the advertising of medicines because such products are too important to allow mere marketing to affect their distribution.
5. Virtually all countries have laws against the bribery of public officials. In many countries, however, the local authorities do not enforce these laws. However, businesspeople must consider the risk of prosecution in their home country for bribing an official in another country. Thirty-six countries, including the United States, have laws that forbid their citizens to bribe foreign public officials. The U.S. *Foreign Corrupt Practices Act* prohibit U.S. citizens from "corruptly" paying or offering to pay a "foreign official" for assistance in obtaining or retaining business. They also prohibit payments to a foreign agent when the payer had reason to know that a portion of the payment will go to a public official.
6. The U.S. *Foreign Corrupt Practices Act* does not prohibit a "facilitating or expediting payment ... the purpose of which is to expedite or secure the performance of a routine governmental action." "Routine governmental actions" are those that are nondiscretionary.
7. The FCPA also requires publicly held U.S. companies to "make and keep books, records, and accounts which, in reasonable detail, accurately and fairly reflect the transactions and dispositions of [their] assets" and requires an investor to "devise and maintain a system of internal accounting controls sufficient to provide reasonable assurances" that all transactions are properly authorized and that access to assets is tracked. These requirements mean that a company may be liable for failing to identify bribery even if the amount would not otherwise be material to the investor company.
8. In recent years, the U.S. Department of Justice has greatly increased its civil and criminal enforcement of the FCPA. From 2003 through the end of June 2007, twenty SEC enforcement actions and twenty-three DOJ enforcement actions were initiated under the FCPA. There were about 100 active FCPA investigations ongoing as of July 2007.
9. Other states, particularly in Western Europe, have begun to greatly increase enforcement of their antibribery of foreign officials law.
10. In the past few years, international tribunals have refused to enforce contracts obtained through bribery, leaving the bribe-givers no way to recapture their investments.

Questions and Case Problems

1. Suppose that Roger Sobodka, a U.S. executive stationed in Paris, wishes to build a support office for his firm's technicians in the Parisian suburb of Asnieres. He enters into an agreement with Francois Demblans, a homebuilder, to do the work for $100,000. Under the agreement, M. Demblans may seek reimbursement of costs attributable to unforeseen circumstances. The agreement further specifies that construction of the office building will be complete in nine months, and that M. Demblans will modify his work upon Mr. Sobodka's reasonable instructions. Assuming that French agency law is consistent with that discussed in this chapter, is M. Demblans a dependent or an independent agent of Mr. Sobodka?
2. After conducting a market survey, Penton Intergalactic, Ltd., a manufacturer of plows, believes that there is pent-up demand for its product in the expanding agricultural economy of Paraguay. Penton retains Saul Ortiz, a Paraguayan who operates a substantial business selling agricultural implements. Penton's New York City advertising agency develops the ad campaign and strategy for introduction of the product, including a rather precise time schedule. Sr. Ortiz is to follow Penton's instructions as the project develops. Sr. Ortiz will use the same employees that he uses in his business operations, except that a few Penton employees will be on-site to assist him. He will receive a commission on each plow sold, plus reimbursement of marketing expenses identifiable as related to the Penton program. Assuming that Paraguayan agency law is consistent with that discussed in this chapter, is Sr. Ortiz a dependent or an independent agent?
3. Jordan Motors, Inc. opens a dealership in Frankfurt, West Germany, selling American cars. In its advertising campaign, Jordan claims that for the next two weeks only, it will beat the price on any comparable German car by 1,000 euros. Faced with this threat to its market share, Hartman Autos, A. G. slashes its prices to cost. Andrea Giebbels comes to Jordan's showroom with a written quote of Hartman's price for its bottom-of-the-line German car and demands that Jordan sell her twenty of its bottom-of-the-line American cars for a substantial loss. Jordan refuses. If Fraulein Giebbels brings an action, will she be able to enforce Jordan's offer? If Hartman sues, can it have Jordan's advertising campaign enjoined?
4. Borges Meat Marketing, Inc., a Nebraska corporation, wishes to establish a network of gourmet butcher shops in India. It has a well-developed introductory advertising campaign that it has employed in establishing similar butcher shops in the United States and does not wish to go to the expense of developing a new one. What should it do?
5. Joseph Supersonic Company, a U.S. jet fighter manufacturer, is eager to sell its aircraft to the state-owned airline of the Republic of Platano and wishes to retain a local representative to assist it. Maria de la Concepcion Casañas y Diaz is reputed to have the best government contracts in Platano; her clients have been successful in garnering contracts a high percentage of the time. Accordingly, she is more in demand than other local representatives, and her fee is the highest in the country. What are the implications of hiring Srta. Casañas y Diaz?
6. Assume the facts in Question 5 and assume further that a reference check has uncovered rumors that Srta. Casañas y Diaz has had intimate relations with Platano's assistant secretary for government procurement, although they have no plans for a more permanent relationship. What are the FCPA implications now?
7. Assume that Joseph retained Srta. Casañas but failed to obtain the contract. To Joseph's chagrin, it subsequently learns that Srta. Casañas y Diaz used part of her fee to make a $10,000 payment to a government official. If Joseph has total assets of $5 billion, should it report the episode on its financial statement?

Managerial Implications

Your firm, Flyboy, Inc. is a successful U.S. manufacturer of aircraft. Flyboy would like to expand its market to Pamonia, a small, oil-rich kingdom that was once an Italian colony. The principal purchaser of aircraft in Pamonia is the government, although some private families have the resources to purchase the product. The same private families are, not coincidentally, also the nobility of the Pamonian kingdom. For a new entrant like Flyboy, breaking into the market without a local representative is not possible. You are also aware that local custom includes "grease payments" and lavish gifts to customers in Pamonia.

1. Prepare a five-page paper considering the pluses and minuses of entering the Pamonian market. Focus on the legal risks inherent in the proposed investment and how Flyboy might avoid them.
2. Describe the arrangements into which you would enter with your Pamonian agent.
3. Evaluate the possibility of using an Italian firm as your distributor in Pamonia. What would be the FCPA implications if Flyboy simply delivered the aircraft FOB Pamonia and had no involvement in marketing? What implications would this have for Flyboy's profit margin?

Ethical Considerations

1. Agent protection laws ostensibly protect small, local entities from powerful foreign companies. It is true that because it is easy for a big company to communicate with and transport people to faraway lands, it can easily displace its local agent after it launches the business. In light of the much greater power of a multinational corporation against even a wealthy local, there may be justification for these laws. Yet, local representatives tend to become extremely wealthy for not doing very much work. Cynics suggest that the political influence of these local elites has more to do with agent protection laws than with any real desire to help "little guys." Furthermore, where such laws are enforced, local consumers typically have to pay more for the same product. Who is right, the countries that enact agent protection laws or the countries that do not?
2. In the summer of 2007, the media revealed that the British defense firm BAE had paid over $2 billion in bribes over twenty years to Prince Bandar, a powerful member of the Saudi royal family. The Prince had delivered a contract under which Saudi Arabia purchased hundreds of British warplanes, spare parts, and training for Saudi pilots. When the British Fraud Office began investigating the transaction, Prime Minister Tony Blair terminated it for "national security" reasons, but the truth came out through the media. Prime Minister Blair ultimately defended the transaction on a national security basis and pointed to the many jobs it provided to the UK economy. The contracts continue today and arms sales to the Middle East typically entail 10–15 percent commissions to "agents" widely reported to channel them to heads of state, generals, and their friends. What is your view as to the Prime Minister's position?

For Internet Activities, Visit academic.cengage.com/blaw/schaffer.

CHAPTER 17
Licensing Agreements and the Protection of Intellectual Property Rights

Reasons for Intellectual Property Transfer Arrangements

The most rapidly growing method of doing business abroad is to transfer *intellectual property rights* (IPRs) to a foreign business in exchange for a fee or other form of remuneration. Intellectual property rights are rights to technological know-how or artistic work. Like the simple engagement of a representative discussed in the preceding chapter, IPR transfers need not involve any capital investment abroad. They usually involve manufacturing or merchandising one's product or service in the foreign country. By engaging a foreign party to do this manufacturing or merchandising, the U.S. investor can avoid the substantial risks and legal entanglements of capital investments abroad, discussed in chapters to follow.

Owners of IPRs transfer them for a variety of reasons. The U.S. firm might, for a fee—sometimes called a *royalty*—grant a *license* to a foreign company. A license is a limited permission to use the U.S. firm's trademarks, copyrights, or know-how in making products for sale in the vicinity of the foreign company's country. Alternatively, the U.S. company might provide the IPR and physical components to a foreign manufacturing plant that will fabricate the product for reexport back to the U.S. concern.

In many cases, the foreign product is itself a component of the U.S. company's ultimate product. Upon receipt, the U.S. company will integrate it into the ultimate product in the United States. In addition, a U.S. firm can use a transfer of technology as its contribution to a joint venture abroad in exchange for a share of the joint venture. The joint venture would use the technology to manufacture and, perhaps, market the product.

A U.S. company typically enters into one of these arrangements because it provides market or other opportunities that the firm otherwise could not exploit efficiently. The firm may already be producing at the full extent of its domestic manufacturing capacity and may not have the resources to expand significantly. Licensing or teaming with a foreign company with adequate capital and perhaps other attractive assets—for instance, a ready marketing network in desired export markets—is a way to expand the company's market without raising substantial additional capital.

Another U.S. firm may have ample funds and a good product, but an inadequate research and development (R&D) capability. If it needs to improve its technology quickly before it is nudged out of market share by competing technologies, such a company may wish to team with a foreign company that has a strong R&D staff in order to expand to new geographic markets in the short term, while developing enhanced products for the future.

Still another company may possess a *utility patent* (one that has a broad range of potential applications), but lack the breadth of management capabilities, developmental resources, or marketing skills to exploit all its applications simultaneously. After such a company reserves for itself the patent applications that seem most consistent with its skills and orientation, the company might license the basic technology to other firms, each of which is authorized to develop a specified product or geographic market.

If labor is substantially cheaper in a foreign country, it may entice an IPR owner to shift production offshore. The U.S. company however, may not, know its way around the foreign country or may fear the risk of nationalization. In such a situation, the U.S. firm might prefer contracting with a local firm for its production requirements, rather than setting up its own factory abroad.

In short, there are many reasons for an IPR owner to transfer its intellectual property. Regardless of the motivation for a transfer, the risk is the same—losing control of one's IPRs and helping to establish a competitor. For example, a small U.S. chemical manufacturer may provide its basic patent to a large French manufacturer through a joint venture in the hope of exploiting the European market and obtaining added R&D capacity. But in doing so, it may give the powerful foreign firm an opportunity to "research around" the patent and develop non-infringing alternatives, or else products whose infringement cannot be proved. With such products, the French firm may come to dominate the European market, as well as pose a threat in the U.S. firm's own home market.

Intellectual Property Rights: Transfer Arrangements

The heart of any IPR transfer is a grant of license that permits the other party to use the relevant right. The conditions of and compensation for that use form the balance of the agreement.

Right to Use and Conditions of Use

The licensor often agrees to provide services to facilitate the anticipated activities, such as assistance in setting up an assembly line or other training and technical support. The licensor generally seeks to restrict the licensee's use of the transferred IPR. One common type of restriction is *geographical limitations*. For example, a licensor of a "name brand" doll may limit the licensee's sale of that doll within a specific nation. *Field of use limitations* restrict the applications for which the licensee may employ the IPR. For example, the licensor of a laser technology might permit one licensee to use the technology only in connection with medical applications, while retaining for itself the right to use the technology for communications applications and other uses. Other potential restrictions include *output or customer restrictions*, especially if the licensor plans to use the licensee as a source of products for the licensor's own distribution requirements.

When the licensor's economic return depends on the licensee's marketing success, the licensor may seek to impose various obligations on the exploitation of the licensed IPR. The licensee usually will be expected to pledge to use its "best efforts" to develop a market for the products manufactured with the IPR. Many licensors go further, demanding that the licensee comply with specific marketing quotas under pain of losing its license.

Competitive Circumstances

When exploitation of the licensed IPR requires significant financial or other resources of the licensee, it will often demand *exclusive rights* in the IPR within some geographic area in order to enhance its chances of earning an adequate return on its investment. The licensor, on the other hand, may not want to "put all of its eggs in one basket." A licensee may fail for many reasons, such as lack of commitment, inability to secure financing, or marketing inadequacies. Meanwhile, competing technologies may come into the market, the licensor's patents may expire, or other events may intrude to reduce the long-term prospects for the venture. Licensors who are concerned about such risks sometimes grant rights to two or more licensees who are willing to compete to develop the target market.

Licensees faced with this situation will probably attempt to negotiate some compensating advantage, such as a reduced royalty obligation. Setting the royalty level for a particular IPR can be a difficult proposition, especially when the degree of market demand for the IPR may not yet be clear. Setting the royalty level too high may boost the total price for the end products to a level that is not competitive with substitute products available in the market. Demand may be high in Dijon for a hamburger sold using McDonald's trademarked materials and quality control practices, justifying a higher price, but at some point, consumers will be happier with a Brand X hamburger produced by someone who does not pay royalties. At that point, sales—and royalties—will decline, hurting licensor and licensee alike. The trick is to identify a royalty level that allows both licensor and licensee to optimize their respective returns.

Confidentiality and Improvements

Another key license provision is the clause that sets forth the licensee's obligation to keep the licensed technology confidential so that third parties cannot exploit the technology. Such provisions are critical when the IPR being licensed is a technology that is protected primarily by trade secret procedures rather than patent law. The licensee often will try to limit the length of time during which it must maintain confidentiality, while the licensor will try to preserve confidentiality for the anticipated useful life of the trade secret. The parties may also bargain over the specific means by which the licensee will be expected to safeguard the confidential technology. For instance, the licensor may demand that the licensee's employees enter into confidentiality and non-exploitation agreements that the licensor can enforce in the event of a breach. The licensor might also demand that only employees who "need to know" the technology be informed of it.

The parties will also usually negotiate over ownership and use rights if the licensee develops improvements in the licensed technology or creates new inventions based on that technology. Reasoning that the licensee would not have had the opportunity to develop these useful technologies without the know-how supplied by the licensor, the licensor may seek a *grant back* to itself of ownership in or, at a minimum, the right to use—often without compensation—such new technology.

Licensors and licensees also haggle about termination issues. These principally focus on the length of time during which the licensee may exploit the licensed IPR; what events may cause the license to terminate early; and what, if any, rights the licensee will have in the IPR after termination. Thus, the licensor will try to be sure that the licensee agrees not to use the IPR in competition with the licensor or to disclose it to a potential competitor. The licensee, on the other hand, will try to keep royalties low and minimize or abbreviate the duration of noncompetition or nondisclosure provisions.

Many of the conflicts discussed here are often at issue during negotiations of IPR transfer agreements, whether domestic or international. The principal difference in the international scenario is that the host government often creates circumstances that favor the local licensee.

International Protection for Patents, Trademarks, and Other Intellectual Property

Host countries regulate transfers of IPRs through a variety of direct and indirect means. Depending upon national policy, governments will be more or less protective of intellectual property. As one might expect, nations that generate intellectual property favor strong protection and those that do not create such property do not. This conflict has been played out in international treaty negotiations where these nations work out common interests.

Whatever differences there may be as to the scope of protection, there is general agreement that some protection is necessary. If not, inventors will not take their innovations to non-protecting states and their commercial development will be disadvantaged.

During the last century, nations struggled to establish a consistent international legal system of intellectual property, with only limited success. The benefits of open trade in IPRs were often outweighed by a desire not to permit foreigners to profit through the sale of mere ideas. Progress was slow when intellectual property was a less important engine of wealth than industrial organization. The personal computing/telecommunications/Internet revolution made intellectual property an increasingly significant source of product value. Not surprisingly, the creators of this new value have moved rapidly to protect it through a comprehensive series of treaties. Nations that formerly opposed such treaties have conceded many issues, recognizing the hopelessness of competing without access to the new technology. These treaties streamline and standardize procedures, expand the geographic scope of protection, and create a much stronger international IPR enforcement network.

Paris Convention

The first international property treaty was the *International Convention for the Protection of Industrial Property,* better known as the *Paris Convention.* The *Paris Convention,* originally prepared in 1883 and since revised many times, guarantees that in each signatory country, foreign trademark and patent applications from other signatory countries will receive the same treatment and priority as those from domestic applicants. "Nationals of each of the [signatory] countries ... shall, as regards the protection of industrial property, enjoy in all the other countries ... the advantages that their respective laws now grant, or may hereafter grant, to nationals...." In other words, no signatory country can give intellectual property protection to its own citizens unless it provides the same protection to the citizens of the other signatories. By implementing this principle of "national treatment"—an animating principle of all intellectual property treaties—the *Paris Convention* targeted discrimination against foreigners in obtaining patents.

The *Paris Convention* also gives a trademark holder in any signatory country a "right of priority." The Convention provides that the date of an applicant's foreign application is deemed to be the same as the date of the applicant's original application on the same invention, so long as the foreign application was filed before the first anniversary of the original application. Because in most countries the first to file is the patent holder, this principle prevented a "race to the patent office" in other countries after the original filing.

There were two main problems with the *Paris Convention* scheme. First, the Convention does not require any minimum substantive standard of patent protection. Thus, if a nation has no pharmaceutical R&D capability, it can decide that it is "immoral" to permit pharmaceutical patents and deny patent protection to pharmaceuticals. Although as a practical matter such a law is aimed at foreigners—because no locals have pharmaceutical patents—it is in compliance with the *Paris Convention.*

A further drawback of the Convention is its lack of an enforcement mechanism. Disputes under the treaty are to be resolved by the International Court of Justice, but most signatory countries either do not recognize the Court's jurisdiction or ignore rulings with which it does not agree. Consequently, there is no real procedure for enforcing verdicts other than voluntary compliance. In the 1990s, the developed nations determined to resolve these two defects of the *Paris Convention.* The result was the *TRIPS Agreement,* discussed later.

Patents

In 1970, *the Patent Cooperation Treaty* (PCT) supplemented the *Paris Convention* by establishing a centralized utility patent application process. The PCT has been signed by 137 states. A PCT application is filed on a standard form with the World Intellectual Property Organization (WIPO). The WIPO, a United Nations agency headquartered in Geneva, Switzerland, processes the common application and forwards it to the countries designated by the applicant. If at least one of the applicants named in the PCT application is a national or resident of a PCT signatory, the PCT gives the application a *priority claim* on that invention in all signatory states. With a priority claim, the applicant business has up to 30 months after filing to begin the administrative processing (prosecution) of the application in the countries in which it wishes to obtain protection. This allows the applicant to lock in an application date while giving it time to raise capital on the basis of the patent filing. If capital cannot be raised—which suggests that there is inadequate commercial interest—the applicant can walk away without having spent needless sums in worldwide patent prosecution.

The only region with a consolidated multinational patent application is the EU. Since 1978, one has been able to obtain protection in all EU countries by filing a single application under the *European Patent Convention.* The Convention is now in force in thirty-two countries. This system was enhanced in December 1989 when the member states signed the *Agreement Relating to Community Patents,* which created a unitary system for the application and grant of European patents and a uniform system for the resolution of litigation concerning patent infringement. Under this system, all persons seeking a European patent complete the same PCT application form and file it with the European Patent Office (EPO), located in Munich, Germany. The EPO's *Revocation*

Division and *Patent Administration Division* grant and revoke patents for the entire EU.

Infringement actions are brought in *Community Patent Courts of First Instance* and *Second Instance,* with all appeals to a single *Common Patent Appeal Court* for the entire EU. As a further bit of streamlining, the EPO filing is coordinated with the PCT process. An applicant can complete the PCT standard filing and designate the EPO as a "country" of origin to obtain both EPO and PCT protection.

The PCT system applies only to "utility" patents. There is a separate but similar treaty system for design patents. The *Hague System for the International Registration of Industrial Designs* first entered into force in 1925. It has been amended and supplemented several times, most recently by the *New Act of the Hague Agreement Concerning the International Registration of Industrial Designs* (better known as the *Geneva Act*), which establishes a single standard application and single design patent filing process. The *Geneva Act* entered into force in December of 2003. The United States is one of twenty-nine countries to sign this Act, but has not yet ratified it. To date, the Act has been ratified or acceded to by only twenty-two countries.

Trademarks

As previously noted, registered trademarks are assured national treatment by the *Paris Convention.* The *Paris Convention* also confers a "right of priority" to a trademark holder if the foreign registrations are made within six months after the original registration. Trademark prosecution, however, is usually based on the law of the country where registration is sought.

One exception to this nation-by-nation process is the EU's single multinational trademark registration system. Since 1996, the *Community Trademark Regulation*, administered by the Office for Harmonization in the Internal Market (OHIM), has allowed a single trademark registration enforceable throughout the EU. The *Trademark Regulation* also provides a unified enforcement authority, the Office for Harmonization in the Internal Market. Infringement in any member state can be prosecuted through this office.

The other exception is the new system established in the 1989 protocol to the *Madrid Agreement Concerning the International Registration of Marks of 1891 (Madrid Protocol).* Like the PCT, the Madrid Protocol provides a centralized filing system on a standard form and a designation of the countries in which trademark registration is sought. The WIPO also administers the prosecution and notifies designated countries. Although seventy-three countries have ratified the Protocol, the United States and many other important nations have not.

Domain Names

It is not clear how trademark law protects Internet domain names. After much international negotiation, in August 1999, the Internet Corporation for Assigned Names and Numbers (ICANN) adopted the *Uniform Domain Name Dispute Resolution Policy* (UDRP). The UDRP set forth general "first to file" rules for domain names, but excepted bad-faith filings. Over time the desire to stop "cybersquatting" led to an expansion of what *bad faith* means in the UDRP context. At common law, bad faith meant intentional wrongful behavior, but in the UDRP, it now includes some negligence without a finding of intent. For example, a negligent failure to conduct prior checks for third-party rights has been held to constitute bad faith.

The UDRP also created an innovative dispute resolution process that submits complaints and replies electronically over the Internet to a WIPO Arbitration and Mediation Center. In January 2000, the first case was decided under the UDRP. The WIPO panel determined that the defendant "cybersquatter" had registered the domain name "worldwrestlingfederation.com" in bad faith and ordered him to cease using it. The new process meted out swift justice: It took only six weeks from submission of the initial complaint to the ultimate decision. In the years since, the UDRP process has continued to provide a refreshingly quick and uncomplicated way of resolving Internet IPR disputes. More than 10,000 complaints have already been filed under the UDRP, concerning more than 18,000 domain names. Ninety-seven percent of these cases have been resolved.

WIPO Arbitration and Mediation Center
Mobile Communication Service Inc. v. WebReg, RN
Administrative Panel Decision (February 24, 2006), Case No. D2005-1304
http://www.wipo.int/amc/en/domains/decisions/html/2005/d2005-1304.html

BACKGROUND AND FACTS

The complainant was Mobile Communication Service Inc., which did business under the name Mobilcom. The domain name in question was "mobilcom.com," which had been registered by respondent WebReg, RN. Mobilcom contended that the domain name consisted entirely of its trademark, that WebReg lacked any rights or legitimate interests in that name, that there was no evidence that WebReg was making a legitimate noncommercial or fair use of the domain name, and that the domain name was registered and is being used in bad faith. Mobilcom noted that WebReg had offered to sell the domain name for $35,000, which they argued was consistent with WebReg's pattern of registering domain names that incorporate the marks of third parties and offering them for sale.

DISCUSSION AND FINDINGS

[T]he burden for Complainant under paragraph 4(a) of [UDRP] is to prove:

(i) that the Domain Name registered by Respondent is identical or confusingly similar to a trademark or service mark in which Complainant has rights; and
(ii) that Respondent has no rights or legitimate interests in respect of the Domain Name; and
(iii) that the Domain Name has been registered and is being used in bad faith.

A. IDENTICAL OR CONFUSINGLY SIMILAR

Complainant alleges that it owns a Pennsylvania trademark registration. State trademark registrations, though, are entitled to minimal weight because they are not examined and thus do not represent persuasive evidence of ownership of a valid, distinctive trademark.... Thus, to prevail under the first factor, Complainant will need to establish common law trademark rights in the MOBILCOM name.... Turning to the evidence in this case, the Panel finds that Complainant has alleged sufficient facts to establish common law trademark rights....

B. RIGHTS OR LEGITIMATE INTERESTS

The website to which the Domain Name resolves is entitled "Tech Buyer.com" and contains links to other sites that offer technology and Internet-related services that appear to compete with those offered by Complainant. This type of use is neither a bona fide offering of goods or services pursuant to paragraph 4(c)(i) of the Policy nor a legitimate non-commercial or fair use pursuant to paragraph 4(c)(iii).... The Panel thus finds that Complainant has satisfied the requirements of paragraph 4(a)(ii) of the Policy.

C. REGISTERED AND USED IN BAD FAITH

As noted above, Internet users who access the website associated with the Domain Name are directed to a website that offers certain services that compete with those offered by Complainant. Using a domain name "to redirect Internet users to websites that host links to external websites, including websites of Complainant's competitors," is evidence of bad faith....

In addition, Respondent offered the Domain Name for sale for $35,000, a sum that is far in excess of the cost of registering a domain name. In the absence of a legitimate interest by Respondent, the offer to sell the Domain Name for a price in excess of registration costs supports an inference that Respondent registered the Domain Name in bad faith, with the primary purpose of selling it in violation of paragraph 4(b)(i) of the Policy....

Finally, Complainant asserts that Respondent is guilty of a pattern of registering domain names to prevent the owners of trademarks from reflecting their marks in the corresponding domain names. [The Panel then summarized seven other UDRP complaints in which WebReg had been found to be in violation of the bad faith standard.] Based on a review of these decisions, it appears that Respondent's business practice includes the registration of domain names containing fanciful trademarks ... trademarks created by the joinder of common or dictionary words ... and [those] that have expired ... followed by efforts to resell those names. Although this Panel has held (including in a number of cases in which Respondent's counsel represented the respondent) that it is not bad faith to resell domain names that incorporate common dictionary terms if the respondent was unaware of complainant's trademark rights at the time of registration ... respondents cannot rely on this precedent to shield their conduct

continued

continued

by closing their eyes to whether domain names they are registering are identical or confusingly similar to trademarks. In other words, where a respondent has registered a domain name consisting of a dictionary term because the respondent has a good faith belief that the domain name's value derives from its generic qualities, that may constitute a legitimate interest and the offer to sell such a domain name is not necessarily a sign of bad faith. Where, in contrast, a respondent registers large swaths of domain names for resale, often through automated programs that snap up domain names as they become available, with no attention whatsoever to whether they may be identical to trademarks, such practices may well support a finding that respondent is engaged in a pattern of conduct that deprives trademark owners of the ability to register domain names reflecting their marks.

On the record of this case, the Panel believes it a fair inference that Respondent's conduct falls into the latter category.... [E]ven a cursory search on search engines like Yahoo! and Google would have shown that MOBILCOM is a trademark. The Panel thus concludes that Respondent has registered this Domain Name to prevent Complainant from reflecting its mark in the corresponding .com Domain Name, and that Respondent is engaged in a pattern of such conduct.

Complainant has therefore satisfied the requirements of paragraph 4(a)(iii) of the Policy.

Decision. For all the foregoing reasons, in accordance with paragraphs 4(i) of the Policy and 15 of the [UDRP], the Panel orders that the Domain Name <mobilcom.com> be transferred to Complainant.

Copyrights

The *Berne Convention for the Protection of Literary and Artistic Works*, better known as the *Berne Convention,* deals with the granting of copyrights among signatory nations. Like the *Paris Convention,* the *Berne Convention* is based on a *national treatment* scheme: Each signatory nation must afford foreigners the same treatment as its own citizens. Unlike the *Paris Convention,* however, the *Berne Convention* requires all 163 signatory nations to enact certain minimum substantive laws. These include prohibitions against copying literary and artistic works and granting authors exclusive rights to adaptations and broadcasts of works. In contrast to the fragmented patent and trademark system, there is no filing requirement. All an author needs to do is affix the symbol (©) and the year of authorship to provide copyright protection throughout the world. The *Berne Convention* signatories agree to grant national treatment to copyright holders from other signatories automatically from the moment of creation rather than the time of filing.

The computer revolution and the growth of the Internet have brought software copyright issues to the forefront. First, there was a significant dispute as to whether computer programs were copyrightable subject matter. This was resolved in late December 1996, when WIPO approved the *Draft Treaty on Certain Questions Concerning the Protection of Literary and Artistic Works,* providing that: "Computer programs are protected as literary works within the meaning of Article 2 of the Berne Convention. Such protection applies to the expression of a computer program in any form." This treaty, also known as the *WIPO Copyright Treaty* or the *Protocol to the Berne Convention,* entered into force in 2002, and sixty-four countries are signatories. It expands the scope of broadcasts that an author must permit to include "any communication to the public of their works, by wire or wireless means, including the making available to the public of their works in such a way that members of the public may access these works from a place and a time individually chosen by them." Naturally, this is carefully crafted to include access through the Internet. Together with the *Performances and Phonograms Treaty,* passed at the same time, the *Protocol to the Berne Convention* sought to tighten international law by requiring signatory nations to provide adequate legal protection against the circumvention of technological security measures, effective remedies against the knowing removal of electronic rights-management information and the related acts of distribution, and necessary measures to permit effective action against any act of infringement of rights covered by the treaties.

The United States wanted to go even further. It sought to cover even temporary reproduction of copyrighted material unless the nation enacted certain minimum standards of protection. Because the Internet works by sending packets of data into a computer's temporary memory, this would have created significant issues as to Internet "browsing." The dispute was resolved through an *Agreed Interpretation of a Treaty* provision, and that interpretation has been implemented in different contexts.

All of these provisions had dubious significance in the context of the *Berne Convention*. Like the *Paris Convention*, it has been very difficult to enforce the *Berne Convention* effectively. This enforcement problem was one of the principal forces that drove negotiations on the *TRIPS Agreement*.

TRIPS

As intellectual property became increasingly valuable, the developed world—which created virtually all such property—increased pressure to cure the defects of the *Paris* and *Berne Convention* systems. These efforts bore fruit in the GATT *Agreement on Trade-Related Aspects of Intellectual Property Rights* (TRIPS), which became effective in most nations on January 1, 2000. TRIPS requires its signatories to enact minimum substantive standards of protection and create a viable enforcement mechanism. In effect, TRIPS has caused developing countries to adopt intellectual property laws that approximate those of Europe and North America and has created a system to enforce them.

TRIPS requires every member of the World Trade Organization (WTO) to abide by the *Paris* and *Berne Conventions*—including the recent protocols to those treaties—and apply the treaties' national treatment requirements so that all foreign IPR owners receive the same protection as local nationals. It establishes fifty-year copyright protection pursuant to the *Berne Convention*. All WTO members must recognize the patent holders' right to assign or license their patents and the term of patent protection must be at least twenty years.

Further, patent protection is now to be available for "any new inventions, whether products or processes, in all fields of technology, provided that they are new, involve an inventive step (*nonobvious*) and are capable of industrial application (*useful*)." TRIPS even established minimum standards for trade secret protection after the model of uniform trade secret statutes in the United States.

TRIPS seeks to remedy some of the acknowledged problems of the *Paris* and *Berne Conventions*. First, unlike the *Paris Convention*, TRIPS sets minimum standards of intellectual property protection. A nation can no longer comply with international intellectual property law if its law provides no effective protection. Second, TRIPS requires signatory countries to

> ensure that enforcement procedures as specified in this Part are available under their laws so as to permit effective action against any act of infringement of intellectual property rights covered by this Agreement, including expeditious remedies to prevent infringements and remedies which constitute a deterrent to further infringements.

If one nation believes that another is out of compliance, it can initiate a dispute proceeding before a WTO panel.

Because most industrialized countries had effective patent, copyright, and trademark systems in place before TRIPS, these countries became compliant with minor adjustments. TRIPS required many emerging nations, however, to enact a wholly new statutory scheme, including an adequate domestic enforcement mechanism. TRIPS was the first WTO agreement to impose "positive" obligations on WTO signatories to adopt new laws; previously, WTO agreements had relied on negative prohibitions.

Although much stronger than previous WTO agreements, TRIPS has a number of drawbacks. The developed nations accepted an "escape clause" to the minimum substantive standards in Article 8 of TRIPS. Signatory nations may

> exclude from patentability inventions, the prevention within their territory of the commercial exploitation of which is necessary to protect *ordre public* or morality, including to protect human, animal or plant life or health or to avoid serious prejudice to the environment.

Though any actions taken under Article 8 must be "consistent with the provisions" of the

TRIPS, Brazil may again refuse to grant pharmaceutical patents if it determines they are at odds with its concept of the *ordre public* (public order).

Developed nations counter that the exception was intended to be narrow, permitting patent infringement only for: (1) noncommercial purposes, (2) research, (3) experimentation for testing or improvement, and (4) educational purposes. Litigation on the issue seems likely, because many emerging countries are not inclined to pay large royalties on certain types of intellectual property, particularly in the area of medicines.

Complaints that a signatory nation is not complying with its obligations under TRIPS are adjudicated through a WTO dispute settlement mechanism. The majority of the complaints filed have been between developed countries. As of this writing, no country had been awarded the power to retaliate in response to the failure of another nation to fulfill its obligations under TRIPS.

Emerging nations fear that high-tech exports protected by intellectual property rights will increase their trade deficits and slow development of their own industries. These fears easily translate into massive domestic political pressure, leading signatory governments to reinterpret their treaty commitments. To the extent these nations seek to comply at all, they do so in the least restrictive way possible.

The Philippines, for example, created a TRIPS-compliant system for patenting and trademarking foreign drugs, but the legislature then took away most of the system's economic value by requiring branded drug manufacturers to produce generic versions of their drugs. Another example of an attempt at reinterpretation is Canada's assault on Article 33, which provides a twenty-year term for patents. In the *Canada 17–20* case, Canada defended its term of seventeen years from grant for certain patents as sufficiently "consistent" with the term of twenty years from filing. Canada contended that seventeen- and twenty-year terms were equivalent and that if Canada's term was shorter in some instances, it was due to circumstances within the control of the applicant. In May 2000, a WTO Panel rejected Canada's position, but the Canadians' willingness to pursue it shows that little is clear in this area. See *Canada—Term of Patent Protection*, WTO Doc. No. 00-1695 (May 5, 2000).

The *Doha Declaration* on TRIPS and Public Health

The effect of TRIPS on the pharmaceutical industry has been extensively debated. Increased protection of drug patents has serious implications for the availability of generic versions of drugs, an area of international concern in light of the exponential increase of HIV/AIDS in emerging nations. Worldwide debate focused on the connection between the cost of pharmaceuticals and the worsening public health of citizens of emerging countries. Emerging nations were concerned that TRIPS was being narrowly interpreted in a way that unduly limited the supply of generic drugs. Responding to these concerns, in November 2001 ministers of WTO member countries agreed to approve what is known as the *Doha Declaration on the TRIPS Agreement and Public Health (Doha Declaration)*. The final text of the *Doha Declaration* recognizes the "gravity of the public health problems afflicting many developing and least-developed countries especially those resulting from HIV/AIDS, tuberculosis, malaria and other epidemics" and the "need for TRIPS to be a wider national and international action to address these problems." The WTO ministers stressed the importance of the implementation and interpretation of TRIPS in a manner that supports public health through improving access to existing medicines and formulating new medicines.

Developed countries were required to comply immediately with the requirements. Countries classified as "developing," such as India, were given ten years from the effective date of TRIPS, or until 2005, to become compliant. The least-developed countries, including many African states, are exempt from providing patent and trade secrets protection for pharmaceuticals until 2016. These least-developed countries were also permitted to retain their right to apply for further extensions.

One key issue that was not resolved at the time of the Doha Ministerial Conference involved the interpretation of Section 31 of TRIPS, which permitted governments to issue compulsory licenses to allow companies to make patented products or use a patented process under license without the consent of the patent owners, but only under certain conditions intended to protect the legitimate interests of the patent holder. Article 31(f) of TRIPS states that products made under compulsory licensing must be "predominantly for the supply of the domestic market." While this section directly applies to countries that have the resources or host companies that have the capability to manufacture these pharmaceuticals, it indirectly affects less developed countries not equipped to manufacture pharmaceuticals by effectively limiting their ability to import cheaper generic drugs from countries that produce pharmaceuticals under the compulsory licensing provisions of TRIPS.

The *Doha Declaration* assigned to the TRIPS Council the task of determining whether to provide additional flexibility so that countries unable to produce pharmaceuticals domestically could import patented drugs made under compulsory licensing. In August 2003, the TRIPS Council decided to allow any WTO member country to export pharmaceuticals made under compulsory licenses. The TRIPS Council decision took the form of an "interim waiver" of Section 31(f) that allowed countries producing generic copies of patented products under compulsory licenses to export the products to eligible importing countries. The waiver is intended to last until the relevant portion of TRIPS is amended. A decision to permanently amend TRIPS to incorporate this waiver was reached in December 2005, and this decision will become part of the agreement when two-thirds of the member states agree to it.

All WTO member countries are permitted to import pharmaceuticals under the TRIPS Council's decision. However, thirty-three developed countries have voluntarily announced that they will not avail themselves of this provision to import pharmaceuticals. Eleven other countries have announced that they will import pharmaceuticals under this provision only in a national emergency.

The War of "Geographical Indications"

Notwithstanding these attempts to standardize the law, a "mark" in one nation may still be a generic name in another. Until the recent attempts to standardize practice take effect, the determination of whether an item is generic requires an analysis of the conditions in the country where a mark is sought. This is particularly well illustrated in the context of "geographical indications" where a product, particularly a wine or liquor, is marketed by reference to a geographic region. For example, there has long been a dispute as to whether it is appropriate to label a sparkling wine made in the style developed in Champagne, France, as "champagne." The following New Zealand case illustrates this "geographic indications" dispute, while underscoring just how narrowly national the focus in trademark law can be.

Comite Interprofessionel du Vin de Champagne v. Wineworths Group, Ltd.

2 N.Z.L.R 432 (1991)

High Court of Wellington

BACKGROUND AND FACTS

An Australian company sought to sell sparkling wine in New Zealand. The wine was made in Australia from grapes grown in Australia, but was packaged in bottles that included the word "champagne" on the label. The *Comite Interprofessionel du Vin de Champagne* (CIVC), a group of champagne producers from the French department of Champagne, sought an injunction to prevent the Australians from "passing off" Australian sparkling wine as wine actually produced in the region of Champagne.

JUDGE JEFFRIES

These proceedings are brought by the plaintiffs to protect their claimed property right in the word "Champagne." As an editorial policy in this judgment I am using the word champagne with a capital when it refers to the district and the wine from the

continued

continued

district. The plaintiffs seek in effect to prevent the defendant from importing into New Zealand sparkling wine from Australia labeled champagne....

Champagne ... is relatively new, having its origin in time at the end of the seventeenth century but its final development was a nineteenth century phenomenon. Dom Perignon of the Benedictine Abbey of Hautvillers near Epernay in the Champagne district is credited with its beginning.... The two features of Champagne of prime importance for its uniqueness are the soil and climate in which the grapes are grown, and the method of manufacture by skilled personnel.... For the production of grapes for Champagne there are strict geographical limitations imposed by law.... By [French] law the wine allowed to carry the appellation Champagne must be produced exclusively within precise zones.... The essence of the methode champenoise is that the process of second fermentation takes place in the bottle in which it is sold....

This proceeding is about New Zealand law and the understanding of its people so it is appropriate to say something of the wine industry and wine drinking by New Zealanders. Viticulture commenced with the first settlers 150 years ago and never abated, but New Zealanders did not early develop a widespread interest in and use of wines either locally made or imported. This was in contrast to Australia where indigenous wine manufacture and drinking became a more integral part of the lifestyle of that country.... New Zealanders' attitude toward wine underwent a marked change commencing from about thirty years ago.... The population became markedly more knowledgeable on wines and the demand for information was met principally by newspaper columns and books on wine.

Champagne has been exported to New Zealand from about the middle of the last century in small quantities until 1979, and increasingly in the 1980s. It is certain there were quite small volume exports of Australian champagne from 1977 onwards.... New Zealand has, apart from the foregoing, no history of material consumption, or manufacture, of sparkling wine prior to 1980.... In about 1981 Montana Wines, Ltd., which is New Zealand's largest maker, launched a sparkling wine produced by methode champenoise and labeled it "Lindauer New Zealand Champagne." Proceedings were issued in 1982 against Montana and after four years were settled by a consent order of the Court issuing an injunction generally restraining the use of the word champagne on that defendant's products.

[In Australia,] [s]parkling wine calling itself champagne made from grapes grown in Australia by the methode champenoise, and by other methods, has been entirely accepted and without direct challenge from the CIVC. The plaintiffs recognize, and although reluctantly accept, for Australia, like Canada and the United States of America, there is no legal protection available to them over the use of the appellation champagne.

The sparkling wine market in New Zealand changed dramatically with the introduction here from Australia in 1986 of Yalumba Angas Brut Champagne. The wine was of good quality and reasonably priced. It was a stunning success and other wine importers began a serious search in Australia for competitors....

It is appropriate here to emphasize the plaintiffs' view of what makes the product and therefore the name of Champagne so special. The product is a quality one and by virtue of the cost of manufacture it is necessarily expensive, which is part of its exclusivity. From the quality product the reputation has developed, which reflects the specialness of the wine itself arising from factors outlined above. Whilst it has developed a reputation as a quality sparkling wine the consumption of it has also become widely associated with certain types of human activity which are mobilized around celebration and joy. Champagne is appropriate as a wine with which to celebrate (a characteristic is that it palpably agitates in the glass) and that is reinforced by exotic origin (for all but the French) and its cost. The plaintiffs say the excellent wine, whose quality is secured by the law of France, is rolled up with its deserved reputation and the name is a valuable right to them as owners....

It is appropriate here to deal with a phenomenon which is occurring in Australia ... whereby [s]parkling wines at the lower end of the price range not made from the classic Champagne grape varieties and using the transfer method are continued to be called champagne but those at the upper end of the price range made by methode champenoise are tending not to be called champagne, but given a brand name with the label showing it was produced by methode champenoise. That trend clearly suggests that the word champagne has been so devalued in the market in Australia that the public now needs a word, or words, that will convey the excitement and

continued

continued

quality surrounding the word champagne say in New Zealand or the United Kingdom.

What the defendant [says] is that the word *champagne* has in New Zealand lost its distinctive significance so as to be properly defined now as a generic term having generic use within the wine market. . . .

The task of the Court is to decide how the adult population of New Zealand as a group perceives the word. One has only to frame the task in that way to demonstrate its immense difficulty.

The Court holds [market research] studies supporting the contention that there is significant evidence that champagne is not a generic word by usage in New Zealand. . . . From the evidence of the wine experts emerged two other observations worth making. If Australian wine interests were able to export sparkling wines to New Zealand it would have overall a deleterious effect by setting back the desirable goal of attainment of the maximum accuracy and fair labeling on wine bottles. . . . The countries who are members of the Common Market strictly adhere to France's proprietary right in the word Champagne. . . . There was a conscious attempt to supply [restaurant wine] lists encompassing a wide range of restaurants from the select and expensive ones downwards . . . the great majority make the distinction between sparkling wines and Champagne. [T]he Court's decision is that the word champagne in New Zealand is not generically used to describe any white sparkling wine.

The word *champagne* does, in my view, have a special impact or impression on ordinary, average New Zealanders for whom wine drinking generally plays no significant part in their lives. This non-expert, phlegmatic, even uninterested representative New Zealander does have a definite response to the word *champagne* over and above noting it to be a white sparkling wine, or one with bubbles in it. That response if pushed to articulation might be, a wine for celebration, expensive, of French origin, special method of manufacture, name of district in France, consumed by a certain social class, a wine ships are launched with or crowds are sprayed with after a major sporting event is won. . . .

The question for the Court is whether importation into New Zealand, as aforesaid by the defendant advertising and selling Seaview Champagne, is deceptive in the way complained of by the plaintiffs. The Court's decision is that it is deceptive. To begin with the finding of the Court is that the word *champagne* is distinctive and that in New Zealand it has not passed into generic territory. Having found it is not generic then to use it in the market previously described is deceptive. . . . By using the word *champagne* on the label the defendant is deceptively encroaching on the reputation and goodwill of the plaintiffs.

Decision. The Court enjoined the Australian defendants from using the word *champagne* in New Zealand.

For a time, these worldwide liquor name wars resulted in an armistice of sorts between the United States and the EU. In a bilateral agreement concluded in 1994, the United States agreed to prevent its companies from labeling U.S.–made liquor as *Scotch whiskey, Irish whiskey, cognac, Armagnac, Calvados,* or *brandy de Jerez.* In exchange, Europeans may not label European-made products as *bourbon* or *Tennessee whiskey.* The debate over trademarks for "geographic indications," however, has recently grown very heated. In October 2003, the WTO agreed to establish a panel to examine *EC Council Regulation 2081/92,* which creates restrictive rules to protect trademarks and geographical indications for geographical products and foodstuffs. Regulation 2081/92 does not allow a nation to register its geographical indications in the EU's Register of Protected Designations of Origin and Protected Geographical Designations (EU's Geographical Designations Register) unless the nations provide the same enhanced protection as the EU. The United States and Australia each complained separately about the Regulation, and in 2003 a single panel was established by the WTO to adjudicate these allegations.

The United States and Australia argued that by not permitting the names of agricultural products from non–EU member countries to be registered without reciprocity in the EU's Geographical Designations Register, the EU violated its national treatment and most favored nation obligations under the GATT and TRIPS. Further, the terms of the Regulation mean that the EU did not grant the advantages that EU products receive to products of non–EU member countries. For example, *EC Council Regulation 2081/92* granted certain monitoring and enforcement benefits to geographical indications of EU members, but does not grant the same benefits to non–EU member countries.

In a report formally issued in early 2005, the WTO panel agreed with some of the arguments made by the United States and by Australia. The panel held that the EC's regulatory system failed to provide national treatment to non–EC nations, but only to the extent that it required non–EC nations to (1) adopt a system of GI protection equivalent to the EC's system and offer reciprocal protection to EC GIs and (2) have applications and objections from citizens of non–EC members examined and transmitted by the governments of those members, and required those governments to operate systems of product inspection equivalent to EC nations. In April of 2006, the EC implemented new regulations which it claimed brought the EC into full compliance with its obligations under TRIPS. The United States and Australia, however, continue to maintain that further reforms are required to fully address the WTO panel requirements. The geographical indications war rages on.

Geographical Indications under the *Doha Development Agenda*

The battle of "geographical indications" is not limited to the developed worlds of North America, Australia, and Europe and, now, is not limited to wines and liquors. The *Development Agenda of the Doha Ministerial Conference* included two issues relating to geographical indications: (a) creating a multi-register for wines and spirits and (b) extending the higher or enhanced level of protection accorded to wines and spirits under TRIPS to other products.

The negotiations for the creation of a multi-register for geographical indications for wines and spirits are required under TRIPS and the *Doha Declaration.*

There are two main arguments in the negotiations. On one hand, countries led by the United States, Argentina, Australia, and Japan propose a voluntary system where notified geographical indications would be registered in a database. Under this proposal, governments choosing to participate would have to consult the database when making decisions on protection in their countries. Countries that do not wish to participate would simply be "encouraged" but not "obliged" to consult the database. In contrast, the so called "EU proposal" suggests that the registration would establish a "presumption" that the geographical indication is to be protected in all countries. The presumption of protection can be challenged on certain grounds, but once a name or term has been registered, a nation can no longer refuse protection to the registered name or term unless the name or term is challenged within eighteen months from registration.

A number of countries, including the EU, China, Thailand, Pakistan, and Nigeria, have requested extending the enhanced protection given to wines and spirits by TRIPS to other products. They argue that a key component of the value of certain agricultural products (such as basmati rice and Parma ham) is the well-established link to the regions where these goods are produced. As in the case of wines and spirits, the demand for these products provides opportunities for producers from those regions. To protect these producers from usurpation, the extension advocates argue that safeguards similar to those of wines and spirits need to be in place.

The opponents of the extension—including the United States, Japan, Canada, Australia, and New Zealand—argue that the existing level of protection under Article 22 of TRIPS is adequate and that providing the enhanced protection would be expensive to enforce. The opponents of enhanced protection also argue that the usurpation claim is flawed, especially since the world has seen a great number of immigrants taking the methods of producing or making these products with them to their new home countries. In July of 2006, the general council of the WTO suspended the Doha Round of negotiations, citing a failure of the parties involved to draw any closer to consensus on the issues before it, including extending the broader protection of Article 23 to all geographical indications. For the present, the dispute seems intractable.

Continuing TRIPS Turmoil on Biodiversity

Beginning in 1999, the TRIPS Council commenced its review of Article 27.3 of TRIPS, which relates to biotechnological inventions. Article 27.3 of TRIPS permits countries to exclude plants, animals, and biological processes from patent protection. (Microorganisms and nonbiological and microbiological processes are eligible for patents.) Article 27.3(b), however, requires member countries to provide for the protection of plant varieties either by patents, through a system created specifically for that purpose (*sui generis*), or by a combination of both.

The TRIPS Council's discussions include a variety of controversial topics. First, how should the existing TRIPS provisions on the patentability or nonpatentability of plant and animal inventions be modified? Second, the Council addressed the interpretation of effective protection for new plant varieties, including a discussion on the effects of other laws such as the *International Union for the Protection of New Variety of Plants*. Third, it focused on the handling of certain moral and ethical issues such as the extent to which invented life forms should be eligible for patent protection. Finally, the Council considered the issue of traditional knowledge and genetic material, and the rights of communities or countries where this knowledge or genetic material originates.

A key topic under consideration by the TRIPS Council is whether TRIPS conflicts with the UN *Convention on Biological Diversity* (CBD). Those who argue that a conflict exists claim that while the CBD appears to grant sovereignty in biological resources to the countries that possess them, TRIPS permits these resources to be patented. Consequently, there is currently a dispute as to whether rights and benefits given to the resource holders under the CBD are taken away by TRIPS.

In November 2001, the *Doha Declaration* linked the issues of biotechnology, biodiversity, and traditional knowledge and declared that further work by the TRIPS Council on these reviews should be guided by the TRIPS objectives and principles and must take development into account.

Since the Doha Ministerial Conference, a number of proposals have been submitted for dealing with these complex subjects on biodiversity. On October 17, 2002, the EU submitted a paper that included a proposal to examine the requirement that patent applicants disclose the origin of genetic material. Switzerland submitted a proposal on May 28, 2003, suggesting an amendment to WIPO's *Patent Cooperation Treaty,* which in essence would require domestic law to ask patent applicants to disclose the origins of genetic resources and traditional knowledge. Under this proposal, a failure to disclose required information could delay the grant of patent protection or affect its validity.

Similar proposals have been submitted by nations that are home to biological resources. A paper submitted by Brazil, Cuba, Ecuador, India, Peru, and Venezuela in June 2003 developed earlier proposals on disclosure of the origins of biological resources. This led to the six nations advancing, in May 2006, a proposal to add a new Article 29bis to the TRIPS agreement. Under this amendment, it would become mandatory to disclose in patent application forms the source of biological resources and associated traditional knowledge to show that authorization has been given for this use and to show that the applicant has entered into a benefit-sharing arrangement with the source of the biological resources. Many EU nations support this suggestion.

Several other developed countries—particularly the United States, the residence of most owners of pharmaceutical IPRs—have opposed these provisions. These countries argue that further legislation on these subjects is not necessary because these issues can be adequately addressed in contractual agreements between the researching entities and the communities that own these genetic materials and traditional knowledge. Private pharmaceutical entrepreneurs are less circumspect: they characterize the proposal as little more than an attempt by Third World elites to profit without making real contributions. Indeed, emerging nations loudly complain about the potential that *biopiracy*—illicit taking of biological resources with medical applications—will develop as pharmaceutical firms take evasive action. The outcome of this conflict remains to be seen.

NONENFORCEMENT OF IPR LAWS

As seen throughout this book, nations' varying attitudes are generally reflected in the text of their laws. In the IPR context, however, TRIPS now mandates what each country's laws must say. Attitudes in this context are now more accurately reflected in how the words of these laws are actually enforced.

It is one thing to enact laws as TRIPS requires and quite another to enforce them. A number of industrialized emerging countries have a panoply of laws designed to protect domestic and foreign IPRs, but fail to enforce the laws or do not have adequate procedures to enable foreign parties to take advantage of the laws. After NAFTA, for example, Mexico adopted most internationally accepted standards with respect to IPRs. To this day, however, Mexico City streets are littered with pirated music CDs and videos because Mexico has not devoted many of its scarce resources to enforcing those laws.

Still other nations enforce their laws in a discriminatory fashion so that foreign parties do not have confidence that their rights will be vindicated against clear infringement. Indeed, some nations tacitly encourage piracy of such IPRs by their citizens. In South Korea, the government once published details of pharmaceutical and pesticide formulations to facilitate their copying by locals.

In China, after a great deal of prodding from developed nations, the Chinese government enacted modern copyright infringement legislation and even created special IPR tribunals. But in the meantime, China allowed construction of twenty-six compact disc plants with the capacity to manufacture over fifty million CDs a year, despite the fact that China had a relatively small number of consumers who can purchase CDs and that virtually no Western companies had licensed the reproduction of their products in China. A particularly flagrant violation occurred in 1994, when a relative of the Chinese premier opened a huge laser disk and compact disc factory with the capacity to manufacture 5.5 million CDs and 1.5 million laser disks a year. Despite open violations of the ostensible IPR protection laws, Chinese authorities refused to permit even an inspection of the facility by Westerners.

This piracy is very big business. The Motion Picture Association of America estimates that the American movie industry alone loses $3.5 billion a year due to piracy; the Recording Industry Association of America reports much higher losses in the CD realm. In recent years, the U.S. government and leaders of its domestic high-tech and entertainment industries have focused a great deal of attention on the interrelation between the quality of foreign intellectual property protection and the vitality of U.S. trade in foreign countries and, indeed, the U.S. domestic market. In 1979, international firms from developed nations joined to form the *International Anti-Counterfeiting Coalition*, a trade group that pressures governments to enforce IPR laws, and the group has grown exponentially in recent years. At the urging of these industry groups, the U.S. government has become active in promoting the adoption and effective enforcement of intellectual property laws by its various trading partners. As noted previously, the TRIPS Agreement requires WTO countries to ensure that IPR laws are enforced and to call for the seizure of goods infringing upon IPR rights. A failure to enforce such laws now can give rise to a WTO trade proceeding. Taiwan, once an internationally notorious haven of piracy, largely eliminated piracy after the United States was on the verge of enacting retaliatory tariffs on Taiwanese products. When the United States threatened to block hundreds of millions of Brazilian products from entering the United States, the government of Brazil agreed to a strict timetable for implementing patent and copyright reforms. U.S. movie industry officials, in partnership with the U.S. government, have used the threat of *Super 301* trade proceedings against Italian products to prod Italian officials into more diligent enforcement of its copyright laws.

In April 2007, the United States filed two complaints with the World Trade Organization against the People's Republic of China for its "unfair trade practices," centering on "deficiencies in China's legal regime for protecting and enforcing copyrights and trademarks." In other words, after years of attempting to persuade the Chinese to police their rampant piracy and counterfeiting of U.S. entertainment products, it decided to initiate hostilities. Indeed, the United States argued, Chinese laws actually impeded the legitimate distribution of such products, further increasing the demand for pirated products. The following case illustrates that this relentless pressure has resulted in some enforcement, even in China.

Walt Disney Co. v. Beijing Publishing Press
Zhongjing zhichu No. 141 (1994)
Beijing First Intermediate Court

BACKGROUND AND FACTS

Beijing Publishing Press, Beijing Children's Publishing Press, and the Beijing Distribution Office of New World Bookstore Distribution Center published and distributed a series of books called *Collection of Disney Moral Tales.* The collection included reproductions of many Disney cartoon characters, although these Chinese firms had not received authorization from the copyright holder, the Walt Disney Company. Disney brought action in Chinese court against the Chinese entities for infringement of copyright.

Beijing Publishing Press and its corporate affiliate, Children's Press, countered that use rights for the cartoon likenesses had been obtained through a "Contract for Assignment of Simplified Versions" executed with Maxwell Communications Corporation plc. Maxwell had since gone bankrupt.

Beijing Publishing Press and Children's Press further relied on an agreement with Maxworld (China) Publishing Corp., Ltd., a joint venture between Children's Press and Maxwell, under certification that the foreign party had confirmed publishing rights to the collection. Beijing Publishing Press and Children's Press took the view that, in light of this latter agreement, they had no obligation to contact the foreign party regarding copyright matters. They brought in Maxwell as a third-party defendant.

Beijing Distribution Office asserted that it was merely a distributor, not a publisher, and was under no obligation to investigate the legality of copyright of books and periodicals.

CHIEF JUDGE SU CHI

[P]rocedures for registration of copyright for the Mickey Mouse likeness were completed ... in the United States, and the copyright belonged to the Disney Company. The Beijing Publishing Press, in each of August 1991, November 1992 and November 1993, printed and published "Bambi," "Dumbo," "101 Dalmatians," "Alice in Wonderland," "Lady and the Tramp," "Sleeping Beauty," "Cinderella," "Snow White," and "Peter Pan" in which the cartoon likeness were exactly the same as those appearing in the original versions provided by the plaintiffs....

The Disney Company and the Maxwell Company signed an agreement on 19 August 1987 which provided: "Disney Company licenses to Maxwell Company exclusive rights to publish and sell within China Chinese-language publications based on Disney World characters. The license granted under this License Agreement may not be assigned by the Licensees to any third party."... [T]he Maxwell Company signed the "Contract for Assignment of Simplified Versions" with the Children's Press on 21 March 1991, which contract provided: "Under authorization from the Disney Company, the Maxwell Company possesses an exclusive right to publish Chinese language versions of Disney children's reading materials and to represent the Disney Company in regard to copyright trading of such publications. Maxwell Company assigns the authorization from the Disney Company to the Children's Press." On the same day, the Children's Press and the Maxworld Company, in order to implement the "Contract for Assignment of Simplified Versions," signed an agreement whereby the Children's Press entrusted the Maxworld Company to finalize, arrange composition of, and make printing plates for and of the text of Disney children's reading materials.... Maxworld also undertook to provide to the Children's Press confirmation by the foreign party of the copyright contract relating to the Disney Collection, which would serve as the legal basis for possession within China of the copyright by the Children's Press. Following this, the Maxworld Company obtained film costs for the Collection in the amount of RMB 69,750 yuan, which, after deducting costs of RMB 59,312.40 yuan, resulted in a profit of RMB 10,437.60 yuan.

On 11 March 1992, the Children's Press delivered the "Contract for Assignment of Simplified Versions" to the Beijing Municipal Copyright Authority for examination and approval. Because no authorization had been issued by the Disney Company, this Authority could not complete registration procedures. No supplemental registration procedures were ever completed by the Children's Press.

[T]he Beijing Publishing Press and the Beijing Distribution Office signed a working agreement on

continued

continued

1 February 1991 which provided ... "Where it publishes foreign products and books, the publishing press shall enter into a publishing contract with the copyright owner and shall register the contract with the Copyright Registration Authority. After obtaining a registration number, the book shall be passed to the Beijing Distribution Office for pre-selling and publication. Failing this, the publishing press shall be responsible for any disputes that may arise regarding publication, distribution, and selling of foreign copyrighted materials. . . ."

After entry into force of the 17 March 1992 Sino–U.S. Memorandum of Understanding, the Beijing Publishing Press published 118,200 volumes of the Collection, of which it published 41,779 volumes on its own, stored 33,341 volumes, and entrusted the Beijing Distribution Office to distribute 43,080 volumes ... gross profits were RMB 5,999.04 yuan. . . .

This Court, based on the provisions of the Sino–U.S. Memorandum of Understanding, concludes that, effective 17 March 1992, products of United States nationals have received the protection of Chinese law. Disney Company, in regard to the cartoon likeness germane to this matter—Mickey Mouse, Cinderella, Snow White, Peter Pan, Bambi, Dumbo, 101 Dalmatians, Alice, Lady, etc.—enjoys copyright protection. Absent authorization by the Disney Company, commercial use of these cartoon likenesses constitutes infringement.

Although the Disney Company had previously authorized the Maxwell Company to publish and print an album of cartoon likenesses in China, it never authorized the Maxwell Company to assign such publishing and printing rights to third parties. Accordingly, assignment by the Maxwell Company of its publishing and printing rights in respect of these products ... to the Children's Press constitutes, on the one hand, an infringement of Disney's rights and, on the other hand, is a fraud on the Children's Press. The Contract by which this assignment was made is void as a matter of law.

From a legal perspective, the Maxwell Company's use of fraudulent means to sign the "Contract for Assignment of Simplified Versions" was the main cause of this infringement of rights. . . . [C]onsidering that the Maxwell Company became bankrupt in July 1993, this Court will not offer any opinion regarding the liability of the Maxwell Company in this matter.

That the Children's Press, without having first investigated whether the Maxwell Company had any right to assign publication rights to the Disney Company products, nonetheless concluded a publishing agreement with it, was extremely reckless. [In a publication of] the State Copyright Administration, ... there is a provision as follows: "Effective 1 March 1988, any unit or individual entering into publishing trading contract with Taiwan, Hong Kong or Macao, and regardless of whether it provides for licensing out of copyrights or for authorizing use or for taking assignment of authorizations, shall be submitted to the Copyright Administration Authority for review and registration. Where a contract has not been reviewed and registered, it shall, prior to 1 March 1990, be submitted to the review and registration authority in accordance with procedures. Contracts not reviewed and registered shall be void."

The Children's Press, after being refused permission by the relevant department of the State Copyright Administration to register this contract on the ground that it could show no legal proof of copyright, did not conduct any inquiry, and did not implement registration procedures in accordance with relevant national legislation, and proceeded to publish picture albums containing likenesses of Disney cartoon characters. That it was aware it was at fault in so doing is clear. Since the Children's Press is not an independent legal person, its liability shall be borne by the Beijing Press. . . . Both of the ... occasions on which the Beijing Publishing Press published the products occur following entry into force of the Sino–U.S. Memorandum of Understanding, and constituted infringement for which the Beijing Publishing Press should assume responsibility.

The Beijing Distribution Office participated in marketing the second and third publications by the Beijing Publishing Press of the Collection. In accordance with ... "Implementing Regulations of the People's Republic of China on the Law of Authorship Rights," marketing, regardless of whether it takes the form of "consignment sales" or "distribution" is a form of publishing. . . . A publisher has a legal responsibility to know whether or not the publications it handles are legally defective. The cooperative agreement signed by the Beijing Distribution Office and the Beijing Publishing Press provides that, where foreign products or books are published, the Beijing Publishing Press and the owner of the copyright shall sign a publishing agreement and register it with the Copyright Administration Authority. . . . In fact, whether or not the Beijing Distribution Office

continued

continued

ever obtained a registration number from the Copyright Administration Authority was not investigated. This demonstrates clearly that the Beijing Distribution Office, at the time it signed the agreement, took notice of the regulations of relevant State departments but did not implement them. We hold that the Beijing Distribution Office was aware of its fault in this regard and that it should accept responsibility for infringement in publishing the infringed books....

This Court is of the view that the profits or losses of actual business operations are not always the same as the illegal benefits it can obtain. Profits, as a legal matter, should be determined based on the total amount made by the Beijing Publishing Press from publication of infringed works minus reasonable costs (of printing and for payment of taxes). At the same time, the amount payable to the plaintiff as compensation should be this amount plus reasonable bank interest and reasonable fees of the plaintiff incurred in the course of prosecuting this lawsuit.

Decision. The Beijing First Intermediate Court entered an order providing, among other things, that (1) Beijing Publishing Press and the Beijing Distribution Office should cease all publication and distribution of the *Collection of Disney Moral Tales* and that all volumes in their possession should be confiscated, along with the colored films thereof; (2) Beijing Publishing Press should make a public apology to the Walt Disney Company in a Chinese newspaper published and printed throughout China; (3) Beijing Publishing Press should make a one-time compensation payment to the Disney Company of RMB 227,094.14 yuan and pay a fine of RMB 50,000 yuan; (4) RMB 5,000.04 yuan in illegal income earned by the Beijing Distribution Office should be confiscated; and (5) the defendants should bear RMB 40,000 yuan of Disney's attorneys' fees.

The Mechanics of IPR Transfer Regulations

Three basic types of regulatory schemes provide the format for IPR transfer agreements. They range from preapproval to notification–registration to no regulation. The third scheme is obviously the most beneficial to the U.S. entrepreneur. Because the absence of law is somewhat uninteresting to legal scholars, however, this text focuses on the preapproval and registration–notification systems in selected countries.

Prior-Approval Schemes

Requiring substantive prior approval from a government agency is the more intrusive type of regulatory scheme. It is indicative of a relatively protectionist government policy. The degree to which such a scheme intrudes on private enterprise depends largely on the attitude and mandate of the relevant regulatory agencies.

Some prior-approval schemes delegate specific types of authority to government entities and contain relatively objective standards. In others, the laws are written in general terms and vest broad interpretive powers in the bureaucracy. Some nations call for the exercise of this discretion by giving government officials a broad range of reasons for disapproving a transfer of technology. As noted earlier, the Royalties Committee in Colombia could refuse to register a technology transfer agreement if the proposed license continued confidentiality obligations after its term or if the term extended for more than three to five years.

Other countries have taken an approach that depends even more on discretion: All transfer-of-technology agreements are prohibited unless a specific reason can be found for them to be permitted. The Japanese *gensoku kinshi* (prohibited in principle) system was a good example. In this system, transactions were presumed to be prohibited, but there were some exemptions. These exemptions were not based on law, but instead reflected an evolving bureaucratic tradition that decided what transactions should be exempt. Therefore, a foreign investor could only obtain key "legal" insights from someone familiar with the personalities who administered the process.

These discretionary systems make it easy for a government to reject requests for technology transfers by mere delay. In its heyday, the Japanese approval mechanism held up for more than four years a request for a technology transfer by Texas Instruments, Inc. to a proposed Texas Instruments subsidiary in Japan. While Texas Instruments was stalemated, Japanese competitors were able to develop technologies that would help them combat the Americans once they arrived. Many other foreign companies that were not as dogged as Texas Instruments were simply driven away by delay.

Delay is also used to deter technology transfers that require a patent. For instance, in some Latin American countries, the patent process sometimes took eight years from start to finish. During that entire period, there was an embargo on all fees payable to the owner of the patent.

Notification–Registration Schemes

A notification–registration system is more open to technological transfer. The Japanese *gensoku kinshi* (prohibited in principle) system transformed over time into the *gensoku jiyu* (free in principle) system. Similar instances may be found in South Korea, Venezuela, and Mexico, where prior-approval schemes have been replaced by a simple registration procedure. Countries with a general system of notification often make exceptions for areas of heightened concern, such as technology agreements between foreign companies and their controlled subsidiaries. Because of the patent inequality in bargaining position in such situations, many countries with a notification–registration system will still require specific approval of technology transfer agreements between such companies.

A danger in notification–registration countries is that some provisions of a registered contract might not be enforceable under a country's laws. License royalties in a given contract might be retroactively ruled excessive and recharacterized as taxable income to the foreign company. For instance, in some Chinese special economic zones, the foreign investor must compensate the local licensee for losses it incurs on sales of products manufactured by the transferred technology.

A significant danger in any approval–notification system is the risk that the government bureaucracy can make an unauthorized disclosure of the foreign party's intellectual property. Some commentators have suggested that, notwithstanding its advanced IPR protection laws, Mexico is not acquiring the most modern industrial technology because foreign investors do not wish to risk piracy of their IPRs. In Japan, foreign investors cast a wary eye on the Japanese government's continuing requirements for specificity in describing transferred technology under its notification system. Although Japanese authorities respond that they need such information for statistical purposes and that any disclosure by a government official could lead to criminal sanctions, foreign investors remain concerned about possible leaks from government ministries to Japanese firms.

A relevant provision of U.S. trade law is Section 337 of the *Tariff Act*, which prohibits, among other things, the importation of articles that infringe a U.S. patent, trademark, or copyright. For example, if someone tries to import fake Rolex watches into the United States from a country that does not enforce its IPR laws, the Rolex trademark holder may seek to exclude the fakes through Section 337. The International Trade Commission (ITC) carries out investigations under this provision upon the filing of a complaint by the trademark holder or by the ITC on its own initiative. If the ITC determines that an article is being imported in violation of Section 337, U.S. Customs may stop the article from entering the United States. If there is a subsequent violation, Customs may seize the property and forfeit it to the U.S. government. Proof of injury is not required in order to block the imported items. After TRIPS was accepted by other nations effective in 1995, Congress amended Section 337 in the *Uruguay Round Agreement Act* to respond to concerns about allegedly discriminating aspects of Section 337.

The Gray Market

As noted earlier, the prospective U.S. licensor fears that the IPR that it licenses abroad may come back into its home market to compete with the licensor's goods. After a license's anti-competition restrictions expire, the licensee might take the product it makes with the IPR and invade the U.S. market. But even before that occurs, a licensor must contemplate the danger that a completely unrelated party with whom the licensor has no anti-competition agreement will purchase the licensed product and import it back into the United States. This importation of merchandise produced and sold abroad and then imported back into the United States for sale in competition with the U.S. trademark owner is referred to as the *gray market* or *parallel trade*. The products imported back are *gray market goods* or *parallel imports*.

The Nature of the Problem

The gray market principally threatens the U.S. licensor if the product is sold at a lower price abroad than in the United States. This can happen for a variety of reasons. The U.S. licensor might have established such a reputation for quality in the U.S. market that it can command a substantial premium for its product there. But until its product builds a similar reputation abroad, the licensor will not be able to charge a similar premium. In the meantime, the gray marketer could purchase the goods abroad more cheaply, transport them back to the United States, and place them in direct competition with the U.S. licensor.

The gray market is also stimulated by international currency fluctuations. Relative currency values vary minute by minute during each business day. Retailers and wholesalers of goods are much slower to react, however. If the Canadian dollar goes down in value relative to the U.S. dollar, a nimble arbitrageur can purchase the U.S. product in Canada at a price that is a bargain in U.S. dollars.

Holders of trademarks oppose the gray marketers. They note that some products sold abroad under their trademarks are actually different from the domestic products. For instance, soft drinks sold in the Far East are sweetened more than their U.S. counterparts. U.S. licensors argue that sale of the foreign product in the United States could have a detrimental impact on the reputation of their domestic product.

U.S. licensors also argue that gray marketers receive a "free ride" on their U.S. marketing efforts. They point out that they make a substantial investment in time, effort, and capital to develop the sort of reputation that commands a premium in the United States market. Consequently, they argue, the gray marketer who comes in without making any payment to the U.S. trademark holder is stealing some of the return on the holder's investment.

Consumers, on the other hand, are generally delighted by the gray market. It often enables them to obtain goods of the same or comparable quality as well-known brands at a lower price. U.S. consumer advocates and merchandise retailers favor the gray market.

Resolution of the Dispute

In this hotly debated area, courts have gone in a variety of directions. National legislatures, including the U.S. Congress, are often called upon to provide assistance to one side or the other in the struggle.

Under one view, the trademark holder has no right to control goods after it sells them in commerce. After such a sale, the trademark holder has exhausted its control, and once its control is exhausted, the trademark holder cannot complain of competition by others. The exhaustion doctrine, if pursued to its logical end, would create a wide-open gray market.

Courts seem to have accepted the proposition, however, that if a gray market product is so different as to call into question the quality of the domestic product, the licensor should be granted relief, especially if the seller of the domestic product has independently developed goodwill in its home country. Justice Oliver Wendell Holmes wrote one of the opinions that formed the foundation for analysis in this area.

In situations with relatively little possibility of confusion, in which the quality of the gray market product is indistinguishable from the domestic product, U.S. courts have not been solicitous of the rights of licensors. In such cases, courts prize the benefits of price competition over concerns about a free ride for the gray marketer. More recent Supreme Court cases confirm this trend, favoring gray market forces where there is little chance of confusion. In *K Mart Corp. v. Cartier, Inc.*, 486 U.S. 281 (1988), the U.S. Supreme Court allowed the entry of gray market imports as long as the foreign manufacturer and the domestic trademark owner were subject to common control.

A. Bourjois & Co. v. Katzel
360 U.S. 689 (1923)
United States Supreme Court

BACKGROUND AND FACTS

A French cosmetic company with a business in the United States sold that business to a U.S. company, A. Bourjois & Co., along with its trademark for face powder. A. Bourjois reregistered the trademark and continued with the face powder business, using the same box and trademark for the product. Katzel bought a quantity of the same powder in France and sold it in the United States in boxes closely resembling the A. Bourjois boxes, but with its own labels. The plaintiff, A. Bourjois, sued for copyright infringement. It sought a preliminary injunction restraining the defendant from infringing its copyrights.

JUSTICE HOLMES

In 1913 A. Bourjois & Cie., E. Wertheimer & Cie., Successeurs, doing business in France and also in the United States, sold the plaintiff for a large sum their business in the United States, with their good will and their trade marks registered in the Patent Office. The latter related particularly to face powder, and included the above words. The plaintiff since its purchase has registered them again and goes on with the business that it bought, using substantially the same form of box and label as its predecessors and importing its face powder from France. It uses care in selecting colors suitable for the American market, in packing and in keeping up the standard, and has spent much money in advertising, so that the business has grown very great and the labels have come to be understood by the public here as meaning goods coming from the plaintiff. The boxes have upon their backs: "Trade Marks Reg. U.S. Pat. Off. Made in France—Packed in the U.S.A. by A. Bourjois & Co., Inc., of New York, Succ'rs. in the U.S. of A. Bourjois & Cie., and E. Wertheimer & Cie."

The defendant, finding that the rate of exchange enabled her to do so at a profit, bought a large quantity of the same powder in France and is selling it here in the French boxes which closely resemble those used by the plaintiff except that they have not the last quoted statement on the backs, and that the label reads, "Poudre de Riz de Java," whereas the plaintiff has found it advisable to strike out the suggestion of rice powder and has "Poudre Java" instead. There is no question that the defendant infringes the plaintiff's rights unless the fact that her boxes and powder are the genuine product of the French concern gives her a right to sell them in the present form.

After the sale the French manufacturers could not have come to the United States and have used their old marks in competition with the plaintiff.... If for the purpose of evading the effect of the transfer, it has arranged with the defendant that she should sell with the old label, we suppose that no one would doubt that the contrivance must fail. There is no such conspiracy here, but, apart from the opening of a door to one, the vendors could not convey their goods free from the restriction to which the vendors were subject.... It deals with a delicate matter that may be of great value but that easily is destroyed, and therefore should be protected with corresponding care. It is said that the trade mark here is that of the French house and truly indicates the origin of the goods. But that is not accurate. It is the trade mark of the plaintiff only in the United States and indicates in law, and, it is found, by public understanding, that the goods come from the plaintiff although not made by it. It was sold and could only be sold with the good will of the business that the plaintiff bought. It takes the reputation of the plaintiff upon the character of the goods.

Decision. The U.S. Supreme Court reversed the decision of the U.S. Court of Appeals not to grant the plaintiff, A. Bourjois, a preliminary injunction.

The European Court of Justice has charted a different course. In the cases of *Sebago Inc. v. GB Unic, SA,* [1999] E.T.M.R. 681 and *Silhouette International Schmied GmbH & Co. KG v. Hartlauer Handelsgesellschaft mbH,* [1999] E.C.R. 1–4799, the ECJ interpreted the EU's Trademark Directive to permit re-import from one Union country to another, but to forbid re-import from other countries into the European Union. This "regional trademark exhaustion" principle was calculated to protect free access to markets within the Union while protecting the integrity of the common market from nonmembers. Other nations, led by Australia, have charted yet another course. Australia advocates the principle of "international exhaustion," meaning free re-import whether or not there is a danger of confusion. The Australians argue that rights to trade are part of the property purchased. Therefore, the purchaser should be free to trade its property regardless of where it finds the buyer.

The parallel import issue was purposefully left open in the TRIPS agreement. The divisions among nations are too wide to permit comprehensive agreement in the foreseeable future. Until the future day when agreement is reached, the exporter must simply inform itself of the law in the area to which it is sending product.

Franchising: Licensing Outside the Technological Context

Franchising seldom involves technological complexity. It is an arrangement in which the licensor permits the licensee to sell certain goods under the licensor's trademark or service mark under a franchising agreement. To prevent devaluation of its trademark, the licensor will typically condition its use on the licensee's observance of certain quality standards. A Muscovite who wishes to open a McDonald's restaurant will contract with McDonald's Corporation for a franchise. A condition of the franchise might be that the franchisee must follow specified processes in cooking hamburgers.

Several observations may be made about franchises. First, although franchising seldom involves significant patent law or other technological issues, many of the considerations noted in other licensing contexts apply with equal force. Often, the franchiser will only keep renewing a franchise if the franchisee meets defined marketing quotas. The franchisee will attempt to obtain exclusive rights within some geographic area, while the franchiser will resist granting such rights or will try to narrow the geographic area. Franchisers must make the same balancing considerations as other licensors in arriving at an appropriate royalty level and duration for the franchise.

Second, although patent law protection is generally not a significant issue in franchising, trademark protection is a big issue. Quite often, the most valuable asset that the franchisee purchases is the right to use the franchiser's good name and trademarks on what are otherwise local products. If trademark protection or enforcement is lax in the local jurisdiction, the value of the franchise accordingly declines.

Third, as we discuss in the next chapter on antitrust and competition laws, the latter have greatly affected a number of these issues. For instance, the European Commission has invalidated franchisers' quality assurance provisions when they were deemed unduly restrictive of the franchisee's ability to compete. Franchisers must also be concerned about the application of competition laws to *tied-purchase* clauses in franchise contracts. These clauses require the franchisee to buy certain goods from the franchiser. Such provisions are sometimes difficult to justify on quality control grounds. Further, courts will deny geographic exclusivity if it unduly restricts competition within the host country.

Fourth, because franchisees typically sell to the local domestic market and generate few exports, franchisers face special difficulties repatriating profits from soft currency countries. This problem is often solved by creating hard currency sections within franchise stores where you can buy the same products for hard currency at relatively favorable exchange rates. Even if hard currency transactions are a small part of the total sales, as long as they are equal to the franchisee's payments due to the franchiser, they can largely relieve the problem.

Another approach has been to make *countertrade* payments to the franchiser with goods instead of hard currency. PepsiCo, Inc. is partially paid for its cola products by its Russian coventurers with mushrooms for the pizzas of PepsiCo's Pizza Hut subsidiary. The potential for countertrade is limited in most soft currency countries, because goods from such nations are often not competitive with those from hard currency countries.

Fifth, a few nations have a number of laws that are specifically directed at the franchising phenomenon. The franchiser must be alert for *franchise tax* laws, which can impose taxes based on the franchiser's worldwide operations even if its local operations fizzle. A business may sometimes avoid such taxes by structuring the franchise agreement in accordance with local preferences.

Sixth, *system* franchisers—those with a prepackaged program of instruction and initiation for prospective franchisees—should be careful to avoid the entanglements of *language politics.* This term describes the situation, found in regions of a few countries, where laws require that companies conduct business in a certain language. A prominent example is in the province of Quebec in Canada, where the law requires that business be done in French. A U.S. franchiser that brings its standard English-language package into such an area may be subject to significant civil penalties.

Finally, some nations impose stringent disclosure requirements on who may be a franchiser and what must be disclosed to prospective franchisees. These restrictions include registration requirements and highly detailed disclosure requirements under which a franchiser must reveal information about its business that it may not wish to make known.

Conclusion

In general, licensing permits a firm with intellectual property to increase the IPR's returns by permitting someone else to exploit it in another market. In the international context, this capability is particularly useful. For example, a U.S. concern with little or no experience in Nepal can contract with someone with such experience to exploit the Nepalese market. In the normal course, licensor and licensee will negotiate over matters such as conditions and extent of use, compensation, and confidentiality. However, negotiations between licensor and licensee are complicated in the international context. Many countries seek to assist local licensees in their efforts to acquire advanced technology. Local legislation may supersede contractual provisions in order to permit host-country nationals to possess the intellectual property more rapidly. Lax enforcement of local legislation may provide a further source of mischief. Under some approval systems, nothing is likely to happen without cooperation of a local licensee.

The TRIPS agreement should greatly standardize and improve the situation. After it is fully implemented, TRIPS should provide minimum standards of intellectual property protection and a reliable worldwide system of enforcement. It will take a while, however, for the parties to work through continuing disagreements on TRIPS implementation.

If all these complications are not bad enough, the U.S. firm that sends goods abroad may find them exported back to its local market. The trend among developed countries has been to permit such increased competition.

Notwithstanding all of these hazards, the logic of efficiency and accelerating technical advances that underlie licensing makes it a rapidly expanding and highly profitable form of doing business abroad. It is, however, an endeavor that must be pursued cautiously.

Chapter Summary

1. Intellectual property rights, or IPRs, are licensed for many business reasons, such as the receipt of royalties or for use in contract manufacturing. IPR licensing agreements are drafted to protect the IPR owner by restricting the licensee's use of the IPR. Common restrictions include geographical limitations, field of use limitations, and output or customer restrictions. The parties will also negotiate on exclusivity of license, royalty levels, confidentiality, rights to IPR improvements, and termination provisions.
2. The first international property treaty was the *International Convention for the Protection of Industrial Property,* known as the *Paris Convention.* It guarantees that in each signatory country, foreign trademark and patent applications from other signatory countries receive the same treatment and priority as those from domestic applicants. The *Paris Convention* has major drawbacks. First, it does not require any minimum substantive standard of patent protection. Second, it lacks an enforcement mechanism. The *Patent Cooperation Treaty (PCT)* supplemented the *Paris Convention* by establishing a centralized utility patent application process.

3. The *European Patent Convention* and the *Agreement Relating to Community Patents* created a unitary system for the application and grant of European patents and a uniform system for the resolution of litigation concerning patent infringement.
4. The international treaty system for design patents is the *Hague System for the International Registration of Industrial Designs.* This System was significantly enhanced by the *Geneva Act,* which established a single standard application and single design patent filing process in 2003.
5. The *Madrid Protocol* provides a centralized filing system on a standard form and a designation of the countries in which trademark registration is sought. The WIPO administers trademark prosecution and notifies designated countries. Many important economic powers, including the United States, have not ratified the Madrid Protocol.
6. The *Internet Corporation for Assigned Names and Numbers* (ICANN), which regulates the Internet, has adopted the *Uniform Domain Name Dispute Resolution Policy* (UDRP). The UDRP set forth general "first to file" rules for domain names, but excepts "bad faith" filings. "Bad faith" under the UDRP is much easier to show than it generally is at law. In the URDP context, it now includes some negligence without a finding of intent.
7. Under the *Berne Convention,* each signatory nation must afford foreigners the same copyright protection as its own citizens. The *Berne Convention* requires all 163 signatory nations to enact certain minimum substantive laws. These laws, known as *minima,* include prohibitions against copying literary and artistic works and grant authors exclusive rights to adaptations and broadcasts of works. There is no filing requirement.
8. The *Draft Treaty on Certain Questions Concerning the Protection of Literary and Artistic Works* provides that computer programs are protected as literary works under the *Berne Convention.*
9. The *GATT Agreement on Trade-Related Aspects of Intellectual Property Rights* (TRIPS), effective since 2000, obligates its signatories to enact minimum substantive standards of protection for intellectual property rights and to create a viable enforcement mechanism. If one nation believes that another is out of compliance, it can initiate a dispute proceeding before a WTO panel. TRIPS has caused the enactment of IPR protection laws in many countries where the prevailing culture and political elites do not support protection. Thus, many countries with extensive IPR protection laws on the books do little to enforce those laws. Under TRIPS, this has resulted in international proceedings regarding non-enforcement of IPR laws.
10. The terms *gray market* and *parallel trade* refer to the importation of merchandise produced and sold abroad and then imported back into the country of origin for sale in competition with the IPR owner.

Questions and Case Problems

1. Hirt Systems Company is a U.S. company that has a strong market in the United States for securing computer terminals. It envelops such terminals with lead to prevent them from emitting microwaves that can be picked up by "spy receivers." The key to Hirt's success is its design know-how. Because the application is labor intensive, models produced abroad are significantly cheaper. Hirt has been affected by these lower-priced models, though it has held its own because its design is superior. As part of its expansion program, Hirt is considering constructing a new assembly plant. Discuss the relative benefits and risks of building it as a Hirt-owned concern in a Third World country under the direction of Hirt's U.S. management and building it in the United States.
2. Assuming the same facts as in Question 1, what would be the advantages and disadvantages of a joint venture with a major foreign company abroad compared to the alternatives discussed in Question 1?

3. David Wise, a U.S. inventor, has developed and patented a revolutionary new running shoe that increases one's speed significantly. His invention has achieved considerable success in his native American Midwest. Two European companies have offered him joint venture packages to take his invention to the track-happy Europeans. Barthelemy Plus Grande, S.A. is a French sportswear giant with a marketing and distribution system that includes every major city in Western Europe and massive capital resources. Pék Társaság, a recently privatized Hungarian firm, offers substantially lower labor costs. Which should Mr. Wise choose as a joint venture partner? Why?
4. Mr. Wise's marketing experts advise him that the Japanese market is hungry for his shoes. Focusing on technology transfer issues, discuss whether he should seek a Japanese joint venture partner or enter through a wholly owned subsidiary.
5. Analyze the same issues raised in Question 4, but assume Mr. Wise is considering entry into a "prior-approval" country.
6. Laffite Enterprises, Inc., a U.S. firm, has purchased the right to use the trademark of Wellington Imperial, Ltd., in the United States for a high-quality line of Napoleonic War reproductions. Wellington has a cheap line of Napoleonic trinkets that it sells in France. Degas Magazines, S.A., a French firm, begins to import the low-priced Wellington line into the United States. If Laffite brings an action against Degas, how would a U.S. court address the policy considerations presented?
7. Geyer Schokolade, A.G. makes the bonbon of choice for the German yuppie. Its product's cachet permits Geyer to charge a hefty premium at home. Geyer expands into the U.S. market, where no one has heard of its bonbons, and charges a more reasonable price to garner market share. Henry Joseph, a U.S. entrepreneur, re-imports the bonbons into Germany and offers them at a substantial savings below Geyer's price. What will be the result of Geyer's attempt to stop Mr. Joseph at the EEC Court of Justice?

MANAGERIAL IMPLICATIONS

1. You work for Wilbur Intergalactic, Ltd., a leading North Carolina processor and purveyor of North Carolina–style pork barbecue. Certain areas of North Carolina centered around Wilson, N.C., are known for producing superior pork barbecue because of the peculiar nature of the soil in which the pigs wallow and because of the method for preparing barbecue developed in that area. Soon, Limited Wilbur and other purveyors begin to promote their barbecue products as "Wilson-Style Barbecue." In 1999, the North Carolina legislature designates Wilson County as a special barbecue area and prohibits anyone from using the designation "Wilson-Style Barbecue" for barbecue not made from Wilson-bred hogs, in Wilson, pursuant to the Wilson method. Soon thereafter, the Professional Committee of Wilson Barbecue secures the U.S. trademark "Wilson-Style Barbecue" for Limited Wilbur and its other members.

   In 2001, Limited Wilbur management learns that at France's Euro Wally World, a French firm has been selling pork barbecue with the words "Method Wilson" on the label. The barbecue is made from local French hogs, but pursuant to the Wilson method of barbecuing. The committee has not secured trademark protection in France.

   a. Explain how a French court would analyze the issue of whether the French barbecuers are infringing upon Limited Wilbur's property rights. In this analysis, discuss whether "Wilson-Style Barbecue" is too generic to receive protection and what Limited Wilbur's rights are under the various intellectual property treaties.
   b. Develop a plan for expanding Limited Wilbur's product marketing to France, giving consideration to steps that it should take to preserve its "Wilson-Style Barbecue" trade name.
2. Undertake a study of the trade war between China and the United States over intellectual property rights. After years of trying to get China to protect American IPRs, an agreement was reached between the two countries in 1992. Reports of copyright and trademark violations continued, and in June 1994, an investigation was initiated under *Special 301*. China was identified as a priority country in July 1994 (59 FR 35558). A determination was made to take action against China on February 7, 1995 (60 FR 7230). The nation's press covered the story daily, describing how it would cost U.S. consumers billions of dollars a year. China embarked on its own public relations campaign, with U.S. television showing bulldozers crushing thousands of bootlegged and counterfeit CDs on

a street in China. A month later, on March 7, 1995, the USTR announced that China had agreed to take the needed action to protect IPRs of U.S. film, recording, and software companies. As reflected in the text of the chapter, however, the United States continues to take the view that China is engaged in massive IPR piracy. In April 2007, the United States initiated two WTO proceedings.

a. What is the annual cost of Chinese IPR violations to U.S. companies? How have IPR violations affected the decision of American companies to do business there? What has been the response of private firms to these violations, and how have they tried to control them?
b. What positive actions has China taken to correct the problem? What new laws have been passed for the protection of IPRs, and how are they enforced?
c. Consider specifically the problems of U.S. software companies in China. Can you find any information about Microsoft's position on doing business in China? What has been their strategy for tapping into the potentially huge Chinese market, while ensuring that their copyrights on software remain protected? If the Chinese government views IPR violations as a legitimate way to make a profit, would bringing the government in as a joint venture partner be one way to get the Chinese to see the need for IPR protection?

3. L'anza Research Inc. manufactures high-quality hair care products in California. Copyrighted labels are attached to all products and packaging. In the United States, L'anza sells exclusively to authorized distributors who resell within limited geographic areas and only to authorized retailers such as hair salons. Exports to foreign distributors are sold at a 40 percent discount. L'anza sold three shipments containing several tons of merchandise to its distributor in the United Kingdom, Quality King, who resold them to a buyer in Malta. L'anza later discovered that the products had been resold to a U.S. buyer for less than the wholesale price and were being sold at discounted prices by unauthorized retailers in California. L'anza complained that because it held the right to the copyrighted language and design of the labels, the unauthorized resale violated U.S. copyright laws. The lower courts agreed. The U.S. Supreme Court reversed, unanimously holding that under the "first sale" doctrine, once a copyright owner places an authentic, copyrighted item in the stream of commerce, it has no further right to control its distribution or reimportation. Thus any lawful purchaser of the products may dispose of them as they please without further obligation. This decision does not apply to counterfeited, pirated, or illegally copied goods shipped into the United States in violation of the copyright or trademark laws. What should L'anza have done to protect itself? Why is a foreign distributorship agreement important? What specific areas of concern should it address? See *Quality King Distributors v. L'anza Research Int'l. Inc.*, 523 U.S. 135 (1998).

FOR INTERNET ACTIVITIES, VISIT ACADEMIC.CENGAGE.COM/BLAW/SCHAFFER.

CHAPTER 18

HOST-COUNTRY REGULATION: CORPORATE LAW, TAXATION, AND CURRENCY RISK

A business that operates in a foreign country must comply with the laws of that country. This rule of international business has significant implications for U.S. business managers. A projected high profit margin may be meaningless if local law prevents repatriation of profits to the foreign investor's home jurisdiction. Low per-hour labor costs will be less attractive if local law dictates that employees control 50 percent of the local board of directors. The anticipated capital cost of building a factory may be grossly in error if the manager fails to consider that he is in an Islamic country in which it is more difficult to arrange short-term financing. These legal differences are not all bad for foreign investors. In fact, many nations attract investment precisely because of less demanding laws.

Foreign law is almost always different from U.S. law. First, as noted in earlier chapters, the U.S. common law system is based on Anglo-Saxon antecedents and is fundamentally different from the legal system in all non-English-speaking nations. Second, these fundamental differences in approach to law are compounded by cultural and political differences that are reflected in law. For instance, the United States strongly favors the free flow of capital in and out of the country, and its laws impose relatively few barriers to that flow. Countries that are concerned about their foreign reserves or that favor central governmental control place many more restrictions on the flow of capital.

Managers trained in the business environment of the United States must become familiar with the legal schemes created by foreign cultures before subjecting their companies to them. This chapter reviews the limits on foreign investment imposed by host-country corporate laws and tax laws.

HOST-COUNTRY CORPORATE LAW AFFECTING FOREIGN INVESTMENT

Nationalization—a government's taking of a private business—once seemed like a quick route for a host government to take control of enterprises operating in its country, but it can have adverse long-term effects. Once a country nationalizes an industry, potential foreign investors stay away and capital resources dry up. Further, because the government that takes over the enterprise lacks the entrepreneurial skills necessary for the business to prosper, the business soon stalls. An economy filled with such moribund businesses goes into limbo. Citizens find themselves without employment, living standards fall, and the government faces a different, more intense pressure.

Accordingly, most countries now focus on preventing a resurgence of foreign economic domination rather than impeding the flow of foreign investment. This is done by regulating the form and substance of foreign investment under a wide assortment of domestic corporate laws. These laws often reflect the nation's preoccupation with foreign economic domination that previously led to nationalization. This concern is particularly visible in strategic industrial sectors.

Those nations that are more apprehensive about foreign economic domination tend to have more restrictive laws against foreign penetration of their economies. Because the massive U.S. economy has relatively little fear of being dominated by outsiders, it has few obstacles to foreign investors. However, developing economies, which can be easily overwhelmed by sophisticated and well-heeled capitalists, place many preconditions on such investment. Within these more restrictive countries, regulation tends to become more stringent as the level of an enterprise's foreign ownership or foreign operational control grows. Nations in transition to entrepreneurial systems remain suspicious of foreign penetration even as they try to enact free-enterprise legal systems.

Corporate control is a principal line of demarcation in studying different schemes of corporate law. This chapter first discusses foreign investment in businesses owned by local nationals, and then turns to those businesses controlled from abroad. In its examination of the former, the text addresses corporate requirements associated with all investments, irrespective of control considerations. In its discussion of the latter, the chapter addresses the additional considerations that arise once foreign ownership exceeds 50 percent of the equity of an enterprise.

Minority Ownership Investments

Among minority investments, it is useful to distinguish between "passive" and "active" investments. For our purposes, a *passive investment* is one in which the investor limits its involvement to providing equity or debt capital to an enterprise managed by another party. The classic passive investment consists of acquiring a noncontrolling amount of stock in, or making a loan to, a company without participating in its management. This is an investment that relies on the managerial efforts of others, not unlike an investor's purchase of stock on a public exchange. With an *active investment,* the investor participates in the management of the enterprise. The prototype of an active minority investment is an international joint venture. Under these circumstances, each investor brings substantial operational experience to the new company along with its capital contribution.

Because passive minority investments create the least risk of foreign control, they are the least regulated type of foreign investments. Active minority ownership investments, on the other hand, begin to raise the specter of "outsider" influence and thus are the subject of greater governmental regulation.

Passive Debt Investments

Perhaps the least intrusive of all investments is the extension of credit. In a loan, the foreign investor analyzes the proposed foreign activity and evaluates its commercial prospects and *political risk* or the risk that the investment value will decline due to political acts. If the activity seems profitable and capable of repaying the loan, the foreign lender will make its advance in exchange for repayment at an agreed-upon interest rate before any equity owners in the enterprise are repaid. Because lenders are *senior* to other investors (meaning that they are entitled to be paid ahead of them), they are willing to accept a fixed, lower return than others and to participate very little in management. In some countries, any significant participation in management can lead to *lender liability,* which is a partial or total forfeiture of the lenders' special status.

Because it is relatively unobtrusive, the international lender faces little government regulation. For the international lender, the principal form of risk apart from *enterprise risk* is *currency risk.* Legal and administrative restrictions on the conversion of local currency into hard currency and on the transfer of hard currency out of the country can endanger loan repayment. Currency fluctuation can also create difficulties. Because international loans are typically made in the currency of the lender's home country, if the value of the local currency is dropping vis-á-vis that of the lender's home currency, the borrower may suddenly be unable to repay the loan even if its business is operating as projected. Issuing the loan in the home currency does not solve this problem from the foreign lender's perspective. While this reduces the risk of borrower default, it shifts currency risk directly to the lender. The lender, after all, obtained the funds it lent from its own home country investors. The lender's depositors, shareholders, and bondholders will expect to be repaid, with appropriate returns on the investment, in hard currency.

To ameliorate this currency fluctuation issue, *currency arbitrageurs* offer *currency swaps* and other "hedges" against currency fluctuation. These devices are discussed in greater detail later in this chapter. Arbitrageurs are intermediaries who limit a party's risk by agreeing—pursuant to standard contracts sanctioned by the International Swap Dealers Association—to deliver a certain amount of a stated currency at a specified future date in exchange for a current payment of another currency. This limits the risk of the purchaser of the swap, transferring it to the arbitrageur. The arbitrageur will then try to find someone who wants to enter into a balancing swap to supply him the currency needed for the first swap. If the arbitrageur does its job properly, it will satisfy matching needs for currency, taking relatively little risk.

In the Islamic world, religious law adds additional complications to the passive foreign lender. The Koran prohibits making money from the lending of money. Because bank financing is necessary for effective business, however, lenders have devised an interesting array of financing techniques that do not violate Islamic scripture.

Passive Equity Investments

The capital markets of the developed world are becoming increasingly unified. Investors from each part of the developed world have increasing confidence in securities issued in other areas. Consequently, "foreign" money has become an important segment of each of these markets. In fact, one can monitor the price quotations of an internationally traded stock on the different stock exchanges in order to seek the best price. As long as the foreign investors do not try to accumulate a block sufficient in size to exert control in the governance of the company, their money is welcome. Through *American Depository Receipts* (*ADR*s)—certificates held by U.S. trust institutions that represent interests in stock held by a bank in a foreign country—many non–U.S. companies have become available to U.S. investors. ADRs permit Americans to invest in foreign firms in very much the same way that they can invest in companies listed on U.S. stock exchanges. Today Americans can do more than just invest abroad; they can now offer their securities to investors abroad by listing their stock in European and other foreign markets. Indeed, the phenomenon of transnational takeovers—mergers between companies in developed economies—has become more common, with European and Japanese investors taking over U.S. concerns and U.S. investors taking over European companies. In Europe, many national firms are merging across borders to form multinational concerns better suited to competing in the continent-wide competitive environment of the EU.

In this world market, a U.S. investor needs to investigate nuances of overseas equity markets. One of the major differences among countries lies in how they regulate trading in securities by people with access to nonpublic information, known as *insider trading*. In the United States, insider trading is a criminal violation. In the infamous corporate scandals of 2001–2002, participation in insider trading resulted in the incarceration of a number of senior corporate officers. In stark contrast, many foreign nations view insider trading as "a mere violation of the rules of ethics," rather than a violation of law. Further, some nations have anti-insider trading laws on the books, but government authorities do not appear to enforce them. Thus, U.S. investors must approach a purchase of securities in certain countries carefully, because the sellers may have adverse nonpublic information about what they are selling.

Because regulated, honest markets tend to attract more investors, however, the international trend is now decisively toward the U.S. "high-disclosure" model of securities regulation. The EU moved aggressively to prod national legislatures to improve uniform standards of investor protection through a series of binding directives: the *Directive on Admission of Securities in the Stock Market,* the *Directive on Prospectuses,* and the *Directive on Semi-Annual Reports.* These directives set the stage for the development of pan-European stock markets with reliable market information. Virtually all Western European nations have now outlawed insider trading.

The EU has also moved to have a community-wide system of securities offering disclosure. The EU has moved to develop a fully integrated EU securities market with the *EU Prospectus Directive* (Directive 2003 (71/EC), which took effect in 2004. The *Prospectus Directive* contains an EU–wide definition of "public offer," requires uniformity in offering documents prepared by EU issuers, embodies a more consistent approach to the approval process for documentation required for listing on Europe's various stock exchanges, and facilitates securities offerings on a pan-European basis. Under the Prospectus Directive, securities prospectuses may only be published with the approval of the competent authority of the issuer's home member state. The *Prospectus Directive,* however, leaves room for intra–EU competition among members, which runs counter to full disclosure.

Although the intention of the *Prospectus Directive* is that the standards of prospectuses and the review process should be consistent in all EU member states, some member states are friendlier than others to issuers. In the wake of the *Prospectus Directive,* some smaller member states have been soliciting issuers, with the hope of replicating Delaware's corporation-friendly role in the United States. Thus, a non–EU issuer should decide which member state it wishes to select as its "home" for securities purposes. The identity of the home member state depends on a number of factors, including whether the securities are debt or equity. An issuer of non–equity securities generally can choose its home member state by either making an offer there or seeking an admission to trading there. The rule is the same for non–EU issuers.

Even infant securities markets such as those in China are seeking to implement regulatory schemes that ensure broad dissemination of information about companies whose shares are publicly traded. This trend toward disclosure is not motivated by a reverence for honesty; it is a calculated realization that, in the long run, honest markets increase capital investment and the wealth of all market participants.

Other peculiarities of foreign equity markets are more subtle. In certain Swiss industries, for instance, a company's capital stock is divided into bearer shares (*inhaberaktien*) and registered shares (*namensaktien*). Although both kinds of shares are publicly traded, only Swiss citizens may purchase registered shares. Because registered shares most often hold the majority of the Swiss company's voting power, this system generally ensures Swiss control.

In some countries, legal structures do not create formal impediments to foreign equity investments. However, a country's traditions can frustrate attempts to convert a passive investment into a more active holding. In Japan, efforts by large minority U.S. stockholders to gain greater influence have been unsuccessful. In the absence of a mutually acceptable joint venture arrangement, minority investment in Japan is often viewed as permanently passive.

Active Investments

For the U.S. investor that wishes to exercise a measure of control over its minority investment, joint ventures are often the vehicle of choice. A foreign investor may enter into a joint venture by combining with a national of the host country to create a new entity or by acquiring a portion of an existing local entity. The four basic forms of a joint venture are (1) a foreign corporation, (2) a foreign partnership, (3) a U.S. corporation with a foreign branch, and (4) a U.S. partnership with a foreign branch.

The precise shape of the joint venture depends largely on the participants' relative treatment under the tax laws of the host country and the United States, and whether the countries have entered into a tax treaty that might affect the application of those laws. In many cases, for instance, remittances from branches may be taxed at higher rates than dividends from a foreign subsidiary. This is because taxes are generally deferred until dividends are declared.

In some strategic sectors of their economies, many nations strictly limit foreign investment. Even in the United States—with the world's largest economy, the most powerful armed forces and presumably the least fear of outside influence—foreign nationals may not hold more than a 25 percent voting interest in an airline or a company that owns an earth station or microwave license. Some of these restrictions led Australian Rupert Murdoch to become a U.S. citizen before completing his acquisition of the Fox television network. Foreigners are also prevented from controlling U.S. defense contractors that own technologies deemed important to the national security.

Countries that are more concerned about overseas domination exclude foreigners from a larger number of sectors. Some nations have historically required prior approval of any investments in defense or national security, electricity, gas, telecommunications, public utilities, radio and television stations, insurance companies, or financial entities. In many of these cases, the government's inability to run these sectors effectively without private initiative, foreign capital, and expertise has ultimately caused restrictive governments to open up these sectors through privatization.

Even if a foreign entity cannot control a joint venture directly by owning a majority of its voting equity, it may control the venture indirectly by entering into one or more key contracts with the venture that obligate the venture to the foreigner in key ways. For example, if the joint venture is to assemble components manufactured in the United States under terms that give the U.S. investor substantial discretion over whether to continue supplying the components, the U.S. investor retains significant control over the venture no matter who nominally owns the venture. Similarly, a U.S. investor can exercise control through supply contracts, marketing agreements, management contracts, and veto powers in the joint venture agreements. Because these contractual means of control can be so effective, some nations require full substantive preapproval procedures for active foreign investments in key sectors of the economy.

The administrative difficulties and expense involved in such a process discourage foreign investment. Because almost all nations covet foreign investment, these approval processes have been substantially simplified and streamlined. For example, in India, as long as the foreign investor limits its equity stake to 51 percent or less in thirty-four formerly closed industries, only the Reserve Bank of India needs to approve the transaction. Many countries in the developing world now have a unified national entity that approves projects. Examples include Egypt's semiautonomous Investment Authority and Kenya's Foreign Investment Agency.

Conversely, many countries give preferences and incentives to certain types of foreign investments, especially by high-technology companies and export-oriented industries. For instance, in India, export-oriented businesses are granted special relief from duties normally imposed on foreign components and are given assistance in obtaining import licenses. The People's Republic of China tries to make up for its poor infrastructure by giving high-technology firms priority access to its public utilities.

Local Assistance

The great variety and complexity of laws and regulations affecting foreign investment make it particularly important for the U.S. investor to retain the assistance of host-country nationals familiar with local law and customs. For example, in Germany, businesses must be members of a *Handelskammer,* which is a society of merchants. Because many registered Handelskammer members have been working together for decades, for practical purposes, an investor cannot conduct business without someone who has an established relationship within that circle. In short, the foreign investor may have to navigate around legal obstacles with substantial cultural overtones. Typically, the only way the investor can do this is by enlisting the assistance of local experts.

Majority Ownership Interests

There are a number of important business reasons why an enterprise would prefer to establish an entity it can control through majority ownership rather than an entity in which it owns a minority interest. For instance, a firm that greatly fears disclosure of its software know-how would be reluctant to enter into any venture that it did not fully control, whether the potential co-venturer was a Mongolian or a Virginian. However, the international context adds an additional layer of complexity to the decision process. For example, certain nations either forbid 100 percent foreign ownership of software manufacturers or impose taxes that make such ownership extremely unattractive. Therefore, taking a minority interest in the new entity may be a foreign enterprise's only option.

Establishing a Foreign Branch or Subsidiary

An enterprise that wishes to establish an entity abroad under its control may create a subsidiary (a separate corporation) or a branch (a division of the main corporation). Neither step is to be taken lightly. Whether the company establishes a subsidiary or a branch, it may waive rights of protection under the bilateral investment protection agreements of the United States. In many cases, the company also subjects itself completely to the foreign nation's corporate tax laws.

Certain differences separate the subsidiary approach from the branch approach. If a company chooses to establish a branch abroad, it faces greater potential vicarious liability. In essence, the foreign company is directly accountable for any liabilities of a branch, but not for those of a subsidiary, which is a separate corporation in the target market. Thus, if the foreign activity involves potential product liability or environmental liability, a subsidiary corporation is indicated. On the other hand, the establishment of a branch rather than a subsidiary may have significant consequences under local tax law and U.S. tax law. Because tax laws often distinguish between different forms of an enterprise, such laws will often dictate the choice of entity: a U.S. branch, a U.S. partnership, a foreign corporation, or a foreign partnership.

Tax Issues Associated with Foreign Branches and Subsidiaries

Tax issues are as varied as local tax laws, the tax treaties between the target market and the investor's home country, and the circumstances of the individual venture. Although nations may enter tax treaties, methods of calculating income, deductions, and depreciation differ significantly from nation to nation. Further complications occur when these different systems are applied to multinational transactions. A general international business law textbook could not possibly address the tax systems of all nations in the world. Indeed, U.S. federal tax law, as embodied in the *Internal Revenue Code*, is the subject of multiple courses in most American law schools. The U.S. investor should, however, be aware of the main provisions of the U.S. tax law that affect international transactions.

Foreign Tax Credits. Under U.S. tax law, corporations are taxed on all income, including income from foreign sources, regardless of where it is earned. The United States, however, does not tax foreign subsidiaries of U.S. companies on the income that they earn abroad; instead, it taxes income that is *repatriated* (sent back to the United States) as a dividend to the U.S. parent. Thus, if the tax systems of different countries were not coordinated to some degree, companies would face double taxation on the same business profits: once by the host country when the foreign subsidiary earns it and a second time by the United States when the parent receives it from the subsidiary as a return on investment.

Because such double taxation discourages international transactions, different nations have developed their own systems for avoiding it. The Netherlands, for example, completely exempts from tax the foreign-source income of domestic firms. This is why many enterprises headquartered in other nations choose to run some or all of their foreign activities through corporations organized in the Netherlands Antilles. The United States uses a tax credit method, allowing a 100 percent credit for foreign income taxes paid. If the foreign tax is lower than the U.S. tax, the U.S. company must pay the difference. If the foreign tax is greater, the U.S. company does not get a refund, but need not pay any U.S. tax on the foreign-source income. On the other hand, if the U.S. company never repatriates the revenue it earns through a foreign-based corporation, it may not need to pay any U.S. taxes on that revenue.

The strength of international pressure to compel cooperation on these tax issues can be decisive. In recent years, the state of California defied international convention by taxing the foreign income of foreign affiliates of companies with a California presence. Because this "worldwide reporting method" did not correspond with the usual taxation of income "where earned," it created a double taxation problem for all foreign firms doing business in California. Accordingly, these firms sent their U.S. lawyers to challenge the constitutionality of the worldwide reporting method. California successfully defended its system against this attack for years, finally winning in the United States Supreme Court in the 1994 case of *Barclays Bank v. Franchise Tax Board of California,* 512 U.S. 298. However, both the British Exchequer and the Organization for Economic Cooperation and Development condemned the California tax system and threatened retaliatory action against California firms. With this threat to California's business community—why would a firm stay in California if it would be substantially disadvantaged in its international business?—California backed down. Its legislature enacted "water's edge" legislation that limited taxation to the activities of a firm within the United States.

One recurring tax issue is the U.S. investor's ability to credit taxes it has paid to a foreign country against taxes payable to the United States. Put simply, with respect to income from foreign sources, a U.S. enterprise receives a credit for certain foreign taxes against its U.S. taxes. Thus, an investor needs to consider the tax rates applicable to a particular form of organization and whether the foreign impositions are creditable taxes for U.S. purposes. The following case illustrates the importance of this issue to an enterprise's investment decision.

Bank of America Nat'l Trust & Savings Assn. v. United States

459 F.2d 513 (1972)

United States Court of Claims

BACKGROUND AND FACTS

Plaintiff Bank of America conducted a general banking business in the Kingdom of Thailand, the Republic of the Philippines, and the Republic of Argentina. With respect to this business, Bank of America paid the three jurisdictions various types of taxes. Bank of America demanded a credit for most of these assessments either on its federal income tax returns or by refund claim.

The Internal Revenue Service disallowed a number of the credits claimed, and Bank of America appealed to a trial commissioner. The trial commissioner held for the Bank of America with respect to the Thailand Business Tax, Type 1 and Type 2; the Philippine Tax of Banks; and the City of Buenos Aires Tax on Profit-Making Activities. Bank of America appealed the matter to the Court of Claims.

JUDGE DAVIS

For a domestic corporation, §901(a) and (b)(1) of the *Internal Revenue Code* ... allows a credit against federal income taxes of "the amount of any income, profits, and excess profits taxes paid or accrued during the taxable year to any foreign country or to any possession of the United States." It is now settled that the question of whether a foreign tax is an "income tax" within §901(b)(1) must be decided under criteria established by our revenue laws and court decisions, and that the foreign tax must be the substantial equivalent of an income tax as the term is understood in the United States....

[T]he Thailand Business Tax ... states that ... persons engaged in business have the duty to pay business tax on the "gross takings" for each tax month at [rates ranging from 2.5 percent to 10.5 percent]. "[G]ross takings" from the business of banking [are] (a) interest, discounts, fees, or service charges, and (b) profit, before the deduction of any expense, from the exchange, purchase, or sale of currency, issuance, purchase, or sale of notes or foreign remittances.

The City of Buenos Aires Tax on Profit-Making Activities ... imposes a tax on the gross receipts of banks, insurance, savings and loan, and security and investment companies, and ... provides that, in the case of banks and other lending institutions, "the taxable amount shall be composed of interest, discounts, profits from nonexempt taxable securities, and other revenue, resulting from profits and remuneration for service received in the course of the last business year."

The Philippines Tax on Banks provides ... that there shall be collected a tax of 5 percent on the gross receipts derived by all banks doing business in the Philippines from interest, discounts, dividends, commission, profits from exchange, royalties, rentals of property, real and personal, and all other items treated as gross.... For none of the three taxes was the taxpayer permitted to deduct from gross income the costs or expenses of its banking business or of producing its net income.

The problem, then, is whether such imposts on gross banking income ... are "income taxes" under the foreign tax credit—"income taxes" as we use that term in the federal system under our own revenue laws.

continued

continued

There is consensus on certain basic principles, in addition to the rule that the United States notion of income taxes furnishes the controlling guide. All are agreed that an income tax is a direct tax on gain or profits, and that gain is a necessary ingredient of income.... Income, including gross income, must be distinguished from gross receipts which can cover returns of capital.... Only an "income tax," not a tax which is truly on gross receipts, is creditable.

[W]e cannot accept the position that all foreign gross income taxes, no matter whether or not they tax or seek to tax profit or net gain, are covered by that provision. [F]rom 1913 on, Congress has always directed the domestic levy at some net gain or profit, and for almost sixty years the concept that the income tax seeks out net gain has been inherent in our system of taxation. That is the "well-understood meaning to be derived from an examination of the [United States] statutes which provide for the laying and collection of income taxes"—the basic test ... for determining whether a foreign tax is an "income tax" under the foreign tax credit.... Where the gross income levy may not, and is not intended to, reach profit (net gain), allowance of the credit would serve only haphazardly to avoid double taxation of net income, since only the United States tax—under the concept followed since 1913—would necessarily fall upon such net gain. There would not then be any significant measure of commensurability between the two imposts (except by chance).

We do not, however, consider it all-decisive whether the foreign income tax is labeled a gross income or a net income tax, or whether it specifically allows the deduction or exclusion of the costs or expenses of realizing the profit. The important thing is whether the other country is attempting to reach some net gain, not the form in which it shapes the income tax or the name it gives. In certain situations a levy can in reality be directed at net gain even though it is imposed squarely on gross income.

For instance, it is almost universally true that a wage or salary employee does not spend more on expenses incident to his job than he earns in pay. A foreign tax upon the gross income of an employee from his work should therefore be creditable by the employee under 901(b)(1) despite the refusal of the other jurisdiction to permit deduction of job-related expenses. The reason is, of course, that in those circumstances the employee would always (or almost always) have some net gain and, accordingly, the tax, though on gross income, would be designed to pinch net gain in the end—and would in fact have that effect. In those circumstances, a loss (excess of expenses over profit) is so improbable, and some net gain is so sure, that the tax can be placed on gross income without any real fear or expectation that there will be no net gain or profit to tax.

Our review of the [law] persuades us that the term "income tax" in 901(b)(1) covers all foreign income taxes designed to fall on some net gain or profit, and includes a gross income tax if, but only if, that impost is almost sure, or very likely, to reach some net gain because costs or expenses will not be so high as to offset the net profit....

Do the three foreign taxes we are now discussing ... meet this test? Each of the taxes is levied on gross income from the banking business and allows no deductions for the costs or expenses of producing the income. Any taxpayer could be liable whether or not it operated at a profit during the year.

The only question is whether it is very unlikely or highly improbable that taxpayers subject to the impost would make no profit or would suffer a loss. Obviously, plaintiff and the other institutions subject to the taxes had substantial costs in their banking business, salaries and rent being the major items. The covered banks must also have had bad debts and defaults, and these would have to be taken into account in calculating annual net gain....

Nor can one say on this record that the three governments felt that net gain would always (or nearly so) be reached by these special banking levies, or that they designed these particular taxes to nip such net profit. Each of the three jurisdictions had a general net income tax (comparable to ours, and admittedly creditable) which the Bank of America and other banks had to pay. That was the impost intended to reach net gain. We cannot say, therefore, that there was only a minimal risk that the combination of a bank's expenses plus its debt experience (and other losses) would outbalance its net gain or profits in any particular year—or that the foreign countries so considered.

Decision. The United States Court of Claims dismissed Bank of America's petition for a tax credit.

Taxation of E-Commerce. Products and services sold over the Internet to a foreign nation are subject to that nation's taxation. For a time, this fact was obscured by the sheer ease with which the Internet crosses borders and the U.S. government's treatment of the Internet as a tax-free zone. The moratorium on taxation of the medium is now over. An e-company marketing abroad has to consider the foreign tax liability incurred in such transactions.

All European Union purchases are subject to a value-added tax, or VAT, that is similar to but much higher than U.S. states' sales taxes on retail goods. Each of the EU member states has its own VAT rate, ranging from 15 percent to 25 percent of the price of the item sold. This application of land-based law to Internet transactions has odd consequences. For example, a U.S. customer who buys a product over the Internet from a European vendor owes no VAT at the time of purchase. If he or she later visits Europe, he or she would owe the VAT upon arrival. If the customer pays it (a big 'if'), he or she will be eligible for reimbursement of the VAT upon leaving European territory. Obviously, authorities are not enforcing VAT against U.S. consumers. The provision was enacted to impose a tax obligation on U.S.–based merchants selling to European consumers. All such suppliers that make over 100,000 euros in sales to an EU nation must file returns and pay VAT on all sales.

More controversially, the EU treats sales of downloadable music or software as services for tax purposes. Because EU member states tax services at higher VAT rates than goods and most music and software downloads originate in the United States, this was clearly a political decision aimed at American business. An immediate international confrontation broke out between the United States and Europe on the issue. They resolved this dispute apolitically. Under VAT rules, services—unlike goods—are taxed at the place where they are provided. Therefore, there was no way for the EU to enforce the law without U.S. government cooperation. The EU recognized that no tax was due on such VAT sales from a non–EU supplier because it was impossible for the EU tax authorities to enforce such transactions. More debates like this are likely to unfold before nations' e-commerce tax systems are coordinated in the same manner as those for income taxation.

Transfer Pricing. Another major recurring international tax issue is generally referred to as *transfer taxes* or the *transfer-pricing* provisions. The transfer-pricing provisions are an attempt by the Internal Revenue Service to prevent U.S. firms from avoiding U.S. taxes. A firm typically tries to avoid taxes by structuring deals with its foreign affiliates so that affiliates in low-tax jurisdictions get most of the profit. When a U.S. corporation enters into a contract with a foreign subsidiary that it controls, it can structure the transaction so that only the subsidiary profits from the deal. If international firms had free rein to do this, they would price their transactions so that they would realize all profit through subsidiaries in low-tax or no-tax jurisdictions, depriving Uncle Sam of his cut of the action.

To prevent this type of tax avoidance, transfer-pricing provisions require that such intercompany transactions be conducted at *arm's-length* prices (prices comparable to those that would have resulted from negotiation between unrelated parties). If the related parties do not transact business at arm's-length prices, the Internal Revenue Service may reconstruct the transaction retroactively for tax purposes at what the arm's-length price should have been and impose penalties based upon that recomputation. Virtually all developed nations have adopted similar transfer-pricing provisions, with the same objective of preventing firms from avoiding taxes by manipulating related-company transactions.

In the *Compaq* case, the U.S. Tax Court delineated the limits of the discretion of the IRS in this area, decisively underscoring the preeminence of market-based transactions over cost-plus methodologies in transfer-pricing cases.

Foreign Sales Corporations. Virtually all nations provide incentives to companies that export. In the United States, tax incentives are provided in part through the "extraterritorial income" provisions of the *Internal Revenue Code*. Under this law, U.S. firms may create a foreign subsidiary, informally called a foreign sales corporation, to handle their export taxation. The U.S. parent may sell goods directly to this entity, which will resell them in export markets, or the parent may export directly overseas and pay a commission to the entity for

Compaq Computer Corp. Subsidiaries v. Commissioner of Internal Revenue

113 T. C. 214; United States Tax Court

BACKGROUND AND FACTS

Petitioner Compaq Computer Corporation manufactures personal computers (PCs). Printed circuit assemblies (PCAs) are the electronic circuitry inside a PC's central processing unit that allows the PC to operate. Compaq set up a PCA manufacturing subsidiary in Singapore. The petitioner purchased PCAs from its Singapore subsidiary at actual market prices based on purchases of similar PCAs from unrelated subcontractors that were primarily located in the United States, with a "turnkey equivalent" adjustment based not on actual transactions, but on industry practice. The Internal Revenue Service took the position that such pricing resulted in too much profit being left in Singapore, a low-tax jurisdiction. The IRS argued that a "cost-plus" approach—which would place more profit in the United States—should have been used. Accordingly, the IRS declared a deficiency in Compaq's consolidated returns. Compaq appealed to the Tax Court.

COHEN, CHIEF JUDGE

The issue addressed in this opinion is whether income relating to printed circuit assemblies (PCA's) should be reallocated ... to petitioner from its Singapore subsidiary for its 1991 and 1992 fiscal years.... Unless otherwise indicated, all section references are to the Internal Revenue Code....

Compaq U.S. bought 3.6 million PCA's worth $597 million on a turnkey equivalent basis from unrelated subcontractors. The PCA's were nearly identical to PCA's sold by Compaq Asia to Compaq U.S. After adjustment for differences in physical property and circumstances of the sales, the prices that Compaq U.S. paid to the unrelated subcontractors for PCA's were comparable to the prices that Compaq U.S. paid to Compaq Asia for PCA's.

The issue that we are considering here is whether the transfer prices for PCA's that were charged between Compaq U.S. and Compaq Asia meet the arm's-length standard.... Petitioner asserts that [the IRS] notice determinations are unacceptable and that comparable transactions between unrelated parties prove that the transfer prices satisfy the arm's-length standard.... [The IRS] asserts that petitioner has not presented comparable uncontrolled prices to prove that its transfer pricing system should be upheld.... [The IRS's] primary argument is that petitioner's turnkey equivalent analysis is not based on actual transactions....

Section 482 gives [the IRS] broad authority to allocate gross income, deductions, credits, or allowances between two related corporations if the allocations are necessary either to prevent evasion of taxes or to reflect clearly the income of the corporations.... The applicable standard is arm's-length dealing between taxpayers unrelated by ownership or control....

> The purpose of section 482 is to prevent the artificial shifting of the net incomes of controlled taxpayers by placing controlled taxpayers on a parity with uncontrolled, unrelated taxpayers.
>
> * * *
>
> [T]he regulations attempt to identify the "true taxable income" of each entity based on the taxable income which would have resulted had the entities been uncontrolled parties dealing at arm's length.* * *

When [the IRS] has determined deficiencies based on section 482, the taxpayer bears the burden of showing that the allocations are arbitrary, capricious, or unreasonable.... [The IRS] section 482 determination must be sustained absent a showing of abuse of discretion.... "Whether respondent has exceeded its discretion is a question of fact."* * * In reviewing the reasonableness of respondent's determination, the Court focuses on the reasonableness of the result, not on the details of the methodology used.

[The IRS] used unrealistic material, labor, and overhead markups in applying its formulas. If markups in the range of industry markups are used, the results of [IRS] analysis bear no recognizable relation to [the IRS] notice amounts. [Compaq's] analysis establishes an arm's-length price for PCA purchases by Compaq U.S. from Compaq Asia that is approximately $232 million greater than [the IRS] determination in the notice. Due to the significant difference in these arm's-length prices and [the IRS] determination in the notice of deficiency, we conclude that [the IRS] allocations lead to an unreasonable result and are thus arbitrary, capricious, and unreasonable.

In addition to proving that the deficiencies set forth in the notice are arbitrary, capricious, or unreasonable, petitioner must also prove that the prices charged by Compaq Asia were consistent with arm's-length pricing.... The regulations set forth

continued

continued

three pricing methods to determine whether there is an appropriate arm's-length price. First, if comparable uncontrolled sales exist, the regulations mandate that the CUP method be used. If there are no comparable uncontrolled sales, the resale price method must be utilized if the standards for its application are met. If the standards for the resale price method are not satisfied, either that method or the cost-plus method may be used, depending upon which method is more feasible and is more likely to result in an accurate estimate of an arm's-length price. Where none of the three methods can be reasonably applied, some other appropriate method may be used.

Under the CUP method, the arm's-length price of a controlled sale is equal to the price paid in comparable uncontrolled sales including necessary adjustments. "Uncontrolled sales" are sales in which the seller and the buyer are not members of the same controlled group.... Uncontrolled sales are considered "comparable" to controlled sales if the physical property and circumstances involved in the uncontrolled sales are identical to the physical property and circumstances involved in the controlled sales or if such properties and circumstances are so nearly identical that differences either have no effect on price or such differences can be reflected by a reasonable number of adjustments to the price of the uncontrolled sales. Adjustments can be made only where such differences have a definite and reasonably ascertainable effect on price. Some of the differences listed in the regulations as possibly affecting price are differences in quality, terms of sale, intangible property associated with the sale, level of the market, and geographic market in which the sales take place. Whether differences render sales noncomparable depends upon the particular circumstances and property involved....

Petitioner has presented substantial evidence of uncontrolled transactions with unrelated subcontractors. Petitioner's CUP analysis is predicated on Compaq U.S. purchases of 3.6 million PCA's from unrelated subcontractors between 1990 and 1993. The aggregate purchase price of these PCA's totaled $597 million on a turnkey equivalent basis and was 93.1 percent of the Compaq U.S. standard cost. In addition, the purchases occurred in the regular course of business and were substantial in both frequency and amount.... Although these transactions were not identical to the controlled transactions involving Compaq Asia, we conclude that they are sufficiently similar to provide a reliable measure of an arm's-length result. Thus, the purchases from unrelated subcontractors identified by petitioner qualify as comparable uncontrolled sales for purposes of application of the CUP method.

Compaq U.S. purchases of PCA's from unrelated subcontractors, however, differ in some respects from the PCA purchases from Compaq Asia. Accordingly, within the context of [tax regulations] and the particular facts in this case, the specific differences between the Compaq U.S. purchase of PCA's from Compaq Asia and unrelated subcontractors must be examined to determine "Whether and to what extent differences in the various properties and circumstances affect price...." The record demonstrates that the only differences in PCA's within each product category were the particular components used on each individual PCA and the time required to process PCA's on the manufacturing line. We are persuaded that these differences can be corrected with adjustments to Compaq U.S. standard costs....

Based on the uncontrolled purchases of 3.6 million PCA's, the turnkey equivalent price of PCA's purchased from unrelated subcontractors was 93.1 percent of the Compaq U.S. standard costs weighted to the Compaq Asia production amount. Compaq Asia turnkey prices were 93.9 percent of the Compaq U.S. standard cost. Thus, the relationship between Compaq Asia prices and unrelated subcontractors prices is definite, and a reasonably accurate adjustment can be made using these ratios....

Ultimately, [the IRS] argues that, because the CUP method cannot be applied, a profits-based fourth method is the appropriate method of determining arm's-length prices in this case. The Court was faced with the same "prices v. profit" argument [in a prior case]. This Court held:

> The fact that B&L Ireland could, through its possession of superior production technology, undercut the market and sell at a lower price is irrelevant. Petitioners have shown that the $7.50 they paid for lenses was a "market price" and have thus "earned the right to be free from section 482 reallocations." * * *

The same is true in the present case. The CUP method establishes arm's-length prices for PCA's that were sold by Compaq Asia, and a large profit margin does not prevent use of the CUP method.

Decision. The Tax Court found that petitioner satisfied its burden of proving that the prices in the intercompany transactions were consistent with arm's-length prices and ordered the IRS to reduce its deficiency notices accordingly.

helping it make the sale. The earnings of the entity are called *extraterritorial income*. Of the extraterritorial income earned, just over one-third is taxable to the entity at regular corporate rates. The earnings can be repatriated to the U.S. parent without incurring further tax liability.

Companies involved in a shared foreign sales corporation can sometimes obtain export trading company immunity from U.S. antitrust laws so that they may divide export territories, use common export marketing plans, share export pricing information, and engage in other joint marketing activities. They do not normally share profits or bear the risks of the sale of each other's products.

U.S. Enforcement of Foreign Tax Laws. Traditionally, each nation was solely in charge of prosecution of its own tax laws. Indeed, there was significant question as to whether one country's prosecutors had any right to enforce the tax laws of another nation. At least in the United States, these questions appeared to end in 2005 when a narrow majority of the Supreme Court, over a spirited dissent, ruled in *Pasquantino v. United States* that the Department of Justice had the power to prosecute Americans for the evasion of foreign tax laws.

David B. Pasquantino, et al. v. United States

544 U.S. 349 (2005)

United States Supreme Court

BACKGROUND AND FACTS

Defendants were convicted of wire fraud in connection with scheme to smuggle liquor into Canada, thereby evading Canadian liquor importation taxes. The U.S. Court of Appeals for the Fourth Circuit affirmed the conviction.

JUSTICE THOMAS:

At common law, the revenue rule generally barred courts from enforcing the tax laws of foreign sovereigns. The question presented in this case is whether a plot to defraud a foreign government of tax revenue violates the federal wire fraud statute.... Because the plain terms of [the wire fraud statute] criminalize such a scheme, and because this construction of the wire fraud statute does not derogate from the common-law revenue rule, we hold that it does....

I

We granted certiorari to resolve a conflict in the Courts of Appeals over whether a scheme to defraud a foreign government of tax revenue violates the wire fraud statute.... The [wire fraud] statute prohibits using interstate wires to effect "any scheme or artifice to defraud, or for obtaining money or property by means of false or fraudulent pretenses, representations, or promises." ... Two elements of this crime, and the only two that petitioners dispute here, are that the defendant engage in a "scheme or artifice to defraud," *ibid.*, and that the "object of the fraud ... be '[money or] property' in the victim's hands," ... Petitioners' smuggling operation satisfies both elements.

Taking the latter element first, Canada's right to uncollected excise taxes on the liquor petitioners imported into Canada is "property" in its hands. This right is an entitlement to collect money from petitioners, the possession of which is "something of value" to the Government of Canada.... Valuable entitlements like these are "property" as that term ordinarily is employed.... Had petitioners complied with this legal obligation, they would have paid money to Canada. Petitioners' tax evasion deprived Canada of that money, inflicting an economic injury no less than had they embezzled funds from the Canadian treasury. The object of petitioners' scheme was to deprive Canada of money legally due, and their scheme thereby had as its object the deprivation of Canada's "property...."

Turning to the second element at issue here, petitioners' plot was a "scheme or artifice to defraud" Canada of its valuable entitlement to tax revenue. The evidence showed that petitioners routinely concealed imported liquor from Canadian officials and

continued

continued

failed to declare those goods on customs forms.... By this conduct, they represented to Canadian customs officials that their drivers had no goods to declare. This, then, was a scheme "designed to defraud by representations," ... and therefore a "scheme or artifice to defraud" Canada of taxes due on the smuggled goods.

Neither the antismuggling statute, ... nor U.S. tax treaties, ... convince us that petitioners' scheme falls outside the terms of the wire fraud statute. Unlike the treaties and the antismuggling statute, the wire fraud statute punishes fraudulent use of domestic wires, whether or not such conduct constitutes smuggling, occurs aboard a vessel, or evades foreign taxes.... Petitioners would be equally liable if they had used interstate wires to defraud Canada not of taxes due, but of money from the Canadian treasury. The wire fraud statute "applies without differentiation" to these two categories of fraud.... To give these same words a different meaning for each category would be to invent a statute rather than interpret one." ... We therefore decline to "interpret [this] criminal statute more narrowly than it is written." ...

We are aware of no common-law revenue rule case decided as of 1952 that held or clearly implied that the revenue rule barred the United States from prosecuting a fraudulent scheme to evade foreign taxes.... We first consider common-law revenue rule jurisprudence as it existed in 1952, the year Congress enacted [the wire fraud statute]. Since the late 19th and early 20th century, courts have treated the common-law revenue rule as a corollary of the rule that, as Chief Justice Marshall put it, "[t]he Courts of no country execute the penal laws of another." *The Antelope*, 10 Wheat. 66, 123, 6 L.Ed. 268 (1825). The rule against the enforcement of foreign penal statutes, in turn, tracked the common-law principle that crimes could only be prosecuted in the country in which they were committed.... The basis for inferring the revenue rule from the rule against foreign penal enforcement was an analogy between foreign revenue laws and penal laws.... Courts first drew that inference in a line of cases prohibiting the enforcement of tax liabilities of one sovereign in the courts of another sovereign, such as a suit to enforce a tax judgment. The revenue rule's grounding in these cases shows that, at its core, it prohibited the collection of tax obligations of foreign nations. Unsurprisingly, then, the revenue rule is often stated as prohibiting the collection of foreign tax claims.

The present prosecution is unlike these classic examples of actions traditionally barred by the revenue rule. It is not a suit that recovers a foreign tax liability, like a suit to enforce a judgment. This is a criminal prosecution brought by the United States in its sovereign capacity to punish domestic criminal conduct.... [N]one of [prior] cases ... involved a domestic sovereign acting pursuant to authority conferred by a criminal statute. The difference is significant. An action by a domestic sovereign enforces the sovereign's own penal law. A prohibition on the enforcement of foreign penal law does not plainly prevent the Government from enforcing a domestic criminal law. Such an extension, to our knowledge, is unprecedented in the long history of either the revenue rule or the rule against enforcement of penal laws....

"While it is doubtless true that this court will not aid a foreign country in the enforcement of its revenue laws, it will not refuse to direct a just and equitable administration of that part of an estate within its jurisdiction merely because such direction would result in the enforcement of such revenue laws...."

It may seem an odd use of the Federal Government's resources to prosecute a U.S. citizen for smuggling cheap liquor into Canada. But the broad language of the wire fraud statute authorizes it to do so, and no canon of statutory construction permits us to read the statute more narrowly.

JUSTICE GINSBURG, WITH WHOM JUSTICE BREYER JOINED, AND WITH WHOM JUSTICES SCALIA AND SOUTER JOINED IN PART, DISSENTING:

* * *

The Government's prosecution of David Pasquantino, Carl Pasquantino, and Arthur Hilts for wire fraud was grounded in Canadian customs and tax laws. The wire fraud statute ... required the Government to allege and prove that the defendants engaged in a scheme to defraud a victim—here, the Canadian Government—of money or property.... To establish the fraudulent nature of the defendants' scheme and the Canadian Government's entitlement to the money withheld by the defendants, the United States offered proof at trial that Canada imposes import duties on liquor, and that the defendants intended to evade those duties.... The defendants' convictions for wire fraud therefore resulted from, and could not have been obtained without proof of, their intent to violate Canadian revenue laws....

continued

continued

Construing [the wire fraud statute] to encompass violations of foreign revenue laws, the Court ignores the absence of anything signaling Congress' intent to give the statute such an extraordinary extraterritorial effect.... The presumption against extraterritoriality, which guides courts in the absence of congressional direction, provides ample cause to conclude that [the wire fraud statute] does not extend to the instant scheme. Moreover, as to foreign customs and tax laws, there is scant room for doubt about Congress' general perspective: Congress has actively indicated, through both domestic legislation and treaties, that it intends "strictly [to] limit the parameters of any assistance given" to foreign nations.

Complementing the principle that courts ordinarily should await congressional instruction before giving our laws extraterritorial thrust, the common-law revenue rule holds that one nation generally does not enforce another's tax laws.... It seems to me unavoidably obvious ... that this prosecution directly implicates the revenue rule. It is equally plain that Congress did not endeavor, by enacting [the wire fraud statute], to displace that rule....

Decision. The Supreme Court affirmed the Fourth Circuit's decision, with four Justices dissenting in whole or in part.

Comment. Because of *Pasquantino,* American companies that knowingly evade the tax laws of foreign jurisdictions may face criminal prosecution back home. Compliance with host country tax law has become very serious indeed.

Laws Prohibiting Foreign Control

Virtually every country prohibits entities in sensitive sectors to be controlled by foreigners. As noted previously, the United States outlaws foreign control in "national security-sensitive" fields such as telecommunications, air transportation, and military procurement. Governments that feel more insecure about foreign domination tend to exclude foreign-controlled investments from even more sectors of their economies. Until NAFTA and the privatizations of the 1990s, Mexico generally prohibited 100 percent foreign investment, permitting it only in thirty-four designated industrial activities. The Mexican government permitted its bureaucracy to add to or subtract from that list, depending on changing conditions. These laws have been modified as Mexico's powerful private sector—as of this writing, the world's richest man was Carlos Slim, a Mexican—made it less concerned about foreign economic domination and more interested in attracting foreign capital. Mexican government officials now have discretion to permit 100 percent foreign ownership in many industries and foreign ownership of majority shares in even more.

Other countries are more restrictive, permitting foreign control only in sectors in which they have the greatest interest in development. India and China, for example, have until recent years generally permitted full foreign ownership only in firms that manufacture exclusively for export. Such firms were tolerated because they earned needed foreign exchange for the host country. India and China also permitted high levels of foreign majority ownership in high-technology firms. In that instance, the overwhelming desire for modernization outweighed distrust of foreign control.

Finally, a few nations such as North Korea have been so xenophobic that they have not permitted foreign majority ownership at all. However, the collapse of the communist system and the extreme unavailability of capital to isolationist nations in the 1990s pushed nearly all countries to accept foreign majority ownership in the early twenty-first century. Nominally communist nations such as Cuba and Vietnam now permit foreigners to own and control investments within their borders. As noted in Chapter Nineteen, however, Venezuela and Bolivia have recently reversed this trend in their economies, effectively re-nationalizing extractive industries. It remains to be seen whether these moves can be sustained.

An example of the evolution in anti-majority ownership laws was seen in the former Soviet Union republics. The joint venture law passed in the Soviet Union in January 1987 limited foreign ownership in a joint venture to 49 percent or less.

Although the law sought to promote foreign investment and was widely publicized and discussed in the West, restrictions on ownership and other barriers to foreign investment continued to limit the number of entrepreneurs willing to risk investing in the Soviet Union. In December 1988, responding to criticisms of its 1987 law, the Soviet Union passed another law that, among other things, eliminated the 49 percent ownership requirement. In the current century, the foreign investment laws of the Russian Federation and most of the former Soviet Republics have become even more accepting of foreign participation in all sectors of the economy.

Effects of Prohibition of Control

As noted above, investors prize control highly. Firms interested in the long-term growth of the joint venture are vitally interested in guiding the venture's progress through its startup period and in holding the reins as the venture matures. Investors that have valuable technology or know-how fear that it could be transferred into unfriendly hands.

Accordingly, investor reaction to legal measures prohibiting control has always been negative. India's enactment of a general 40 percent limitation on foreign ownership, for example, led to a 55 percent drop in foreign investment between 1975 and 1987. Similarly, Mexico's enactment of a 49 percent foreign investment limit—since modified in most industries other than the petroleum sector—led to an abrupt reduction of foreign investment from over 10 percent of all private investment to about 3 percent. In short, the need for foreign capital—which, as we will see in Chapter Nineteen, reversed the trend to nationalization—has reversed the movement to broad prohibition of foreign control.

Controlling Currency Risk

One of the most distinctive aspects of doing business outside one's own country is currency risk. *Currency risk* simply does not exist in domestic transactions. An entrepreneur who makes an investment in a domestic business is principally concerned with its operational profitability. However, if the investment is in an enterprise that will be earning foreign currency, the entrepreneur must also consider the two forms of currency risk: fluctuation risk and inconvertibility risk.

Fluctuation risk is the possibility that the currency of the country in which the U.S. investor has put its money will devalue against the U.S. dollar. For example, in 2000, the pressure of massive imports from Brazil drove the Argentine government suddenly to abandon its ten-year-old policy of pegging the Argentine peso to the U.S. dollar. The Argentine currency abruptly devalued over 50 percent against the U.S. dollar. When a foreign currency devalues against the dollar, the value of the investment's profit declines, and so does the rate of return on the entrepreneur's investment. If the U.S. investor borrowed the U.S. dollars that it invested abroad, a devaluation of the foreign currency may prevent the investment from generating enough U.S. dollars to repay the debt. Thus, a sudden variation in the exchange rate can ruin an operationally successful business investment.

Fluctuation risk can also make a foreign investment better. In the 2006–2007 period, the U.S. dollar dramatically lost value against the currencies of developed economies. The returns from an investment in Canada to a U.S. investor would be worth 30 percent more than it would have two years earlier. Investing abroad, therefore, means taking a substantial gamble on the relative value of currencies, something over which the investor has no control.

Inconvertibility risk is the risk that the government of a country with soft currency will hinder the foreign entrepreneur from trading the foreign currency back into U.S. dollars or another hard currency. A *soft currency* is one that is not freely exchangeable on public markets for currencies of other nations. Generally, this is because its fluctuation risk is viewed as too great. To obtain hard currencies such as the U.S. dollar in soft-currency countries, one must often go through the country's government, which will exchange the local currency for dollars at an "official rate," often very favorable to the government.

In a soft-currency nation, hard currency is in short supply. At the time of the initial investment, the U.S. investor must often hand over its dollars to the local central bank, which will incorporate them into the government's hard currency reserves and exchange them for the local currency. To obtain dollars back for the local soft currency, the U.S. investor must fill out an application and await a response. The government then decides who gets to exchange the local soft currency for its supply of hard currency.

Through a wide variety of diverse and imaginative ceilings, prohibitions, and controls, such governments can limit access to hard currency for foreigners seeking to take profits out of the local economy. For instance, the local country may require central bank approval of all remittances. This permits the bank to place a moratorium on remittances during periods when the government's hard currency needs exceed its resources. The nation may impose a large surtax on out-of-country royalty-fee remittances. It may prohibit remittances on returns on capital for a period of years after the initial investment. Remittances of fees from local subsidiaries to U.S. parent corporations may be limited or proscribed altogether. An effective unofficial technique is for the government to sit on the investor's application indefinitely. Because inconvertibility controls can effectively destroy profit, investors need to understand how to limit this risk.

Minimizing Fluctuation Risk: Currency Swaps

The foreign entrepreneur's principal concern is how to limit the risk posed by the fact that the investment will be earning profits in a currency different from their own. A broad assortment of financial contracts, generically known as *currency swaps,* may be purchased from financial intermediaries to hedge against fluctuation risk. For example, a party who will need dollars in the future can enter into an agreement to deliver a certain number of Argentine pesos in the future to a currency arbitrageur or other financial intermediary. The number of pesos to be delivered to the financial intermediary in the future will implicitly reflect anticipated fluctuation rates and a profit for the intermediary. In other words, the currency swap transfers the risk of fluctuation to the intermediary, leaving the investor with only the risk of the business itself. The intermediary will then seek to "hedge" its risk by a matching transaction with another, unrelated party in which the intermediary agrees to deliver the Argentine pesos it receives in the first transaction for the U.S. dollars the intermediary has agreed to deliver in the first transaction. Done properly, the intermediary matches business parties' needs and takes a spread. To facilitate these transactions, the International Swap Dealers Association has developed a standard form agreement so that all legal terms in these deals are consistent as well. This effectively creates a futures market in each currency, keeping the price of currency hedges at reasonable levels, permitting the foreign investor to limit the currency risk inherent in his investment.

In modern international business, currency swaps are the principal method for controlling currency risk. A number of other approaches can further minimize fluctuation and inconvertibility risks.

Arrangements with the Soft-Currency Country

The most direct way of ensuring access to hard currency is to obtain that access from the government of the soft-currency country. The essential problem in soft-currency countries is the great demand for a limited amount of hard currency. Accordingly, the queue for hard currency is long, and when the investor finally gets to the front of the queue, it receives only its ration of foreign currency.

If the investor proposes bringing a desired industry to the soft-currency nation—a high-technology plant or a hard-currency earner—it can negotiate with the government in advance for preferential access to hard currency. The resulting *currency exchange rights* can help solve the inconvertibility problem for the foreign investor.

If preferential currency exchange rights are not available, the U.S. investor may seek *import substitution rights* from the government. These rights are available when the new venture will manufacture a product in the soft-currency country that the nation had previously imported. Through import substitution rights, the government permits the foreign investor to repatriate profit up to the amount of money the country would have otherwise spent importing what the new venture is providing. Again, however, an investor must reach this agreement before actually committing capital to the soft-currency nation.

Payment and Price Adjustment Approaches

In most situations, the government will not be willing or legally able to provide the foreign investor either currency exchange or import substitution rights. The investor must therefore create legal structures for its investment that will maximize the foreign venture's U.S. dollar resources. One way to protect against currency risk is through the structure of payments back to the foreign investor.

First, whenever possible, the foreign investor should negotiate to receive lump-sum, hard-currency payments as early as possible rather than in a series of future installments, even in situations where one would normally extend installment financing in the domestic context. Thus, even in a royalty deal for intellectual property, the investor may opt for a single payment for the present value of the anticipated income stream. This up-front payment avoids the uncertainty of whether the foreign customer will receive hard-currency allocations in future years, which is dependent not only on the nation's foreign exchange success but also on the investor's political prowess. Hard currency today is the best antidote to fluctuation and inconvertibility risk.

The obvious drawback of this approach is that most foreign customers and foreign investments cannot yield immediate cash. Many foreign ventures are start-up operations and rely on future earnings to pay a return. Further, the approach does not work at all for a U.S. firm that plans to generate revenue by selling its products abroad for foreign currency.

A second approach is to build currency adjustment mechanisms into contractual payment terms through *profit margin preservation* provisions or *unitary index adjustment* factors, explained below. Under the profit margin preservation approach, the price or payment to the foreign investor will be adjusted periodically to maintain the same profit margin. The parties agree by contract to identify a cost structure in the relevant currency and to modify the price as the cost of the cost structure's elements change over time. Profit margin preservation, however, discloses the foreign company's cost structure, which is often valuable information to its competitors and therefore highly confidential.

This serious problem does not exist if the parties provide for formulaic adjustment of payment terms based on an accepted unitary index. This index can be a commonly accepted measure of relative currency value or national inflation. One drawback of indexes is that they are frequently independent of the facts of the transaction. Another is that many public indexes relating to soft-currency values are notoriously unreliable. Finally, neither the profit margin preservation nor the unitary index adjustment approaches address the issue of repatriation. In other words, if your cost structure is stated in zlotys or adjusted to an acceptable index, you may be technically protected against 300 percent devaluation against the dollar, but still have no way of exchanging your zlotys for dollars.

Structuring of Hard-Currency Obligations and Revenues

Another series of methodologies for dealing with currency risk involves structuring transactions so as to conserve U.S. dollar resources. An investor can achieve this type of risk reduction by avoiding obligations denominated in currencies outside of the investment site and by conserving hard currency earned by the venture.

Few investments are funded entirely through contributions of equity from the entrepreneur. In most cases, the entrepreneur borrows a significant portion of the capital necessary to launch the venture. An important rule for avoiding currency risk in a venture that will be generating local currency revenues is to borrow that money, to the greatest extent possible, in local currency. In that way, the local outpost will be able to use its local revenues directly to service its obligations without exposure to the vagaries of the international currency markets or the whims of local authorities who control access to hard currencies.

The Argentine devaluation of the early 2000s illustrates this point. In view of Argentina's decade-long commitment to maintaining fiscal stability by maintaining parity between the peso and the U.S. dollar, many North American entrepreneurs came to regard the peso's exchange rate to the dollar as relatively stable. Many such businesses invested in Argentine power plants and other infrastructure projects, borrowing money through lower-interest U.S. dollar loans. However, when the peso crashed, the pesos the Argentine power plants earned were suddenly worth 50 percent less in dollars. Many ventures could no longer make their debt payments and went into bankruptcy. By contrast, those investors who had borrowed in pesos did not face this financial problem: The peso had dropped in value relative to the dollar, but within Argentina, it still was the unit of exchange. These ventures could continue to use their pesos within Argentina to pay their debts. In fact, because devaluation was accompanied by some inflation, those with fixed-interest-rate debt actually had to devote less of their cash flow to debt service. Of course, the U.S. dollar value of their profits did fall, but many used the excess pesos to focus on the impact on their business of the attendant economic crisis in Argentina, itself no easy task.

The same rule applies with respect to contracts between the venture and *trade creditors,* the entities that sell supplies or services to the venture. To the greatest extent possible, the venture should buy locally so that it can pay for the goods and services in local currency. This again conserves the enterprise's hard-currency resources so that as many of these resources as possible can be available for transfer back to the U.S. investor.

If the investor anticipates that the foreign venture will experience significant hard-currency earnings, it should take steps to prevent the hard currency from reentering the soft-currency country. Instead of transferring payment for the foreign venture's products directly to the venture, it can instruct hard-currency customers to pay the U.S. investor directly. The investor takes what the foreign venture owes it in debt payments, fees, or dividends and transfers the balance to the foreign venture.

Through a related approach, the U.S. investor can "call" a percentage of the foreign venture's production. In other words, the investor finds hard-currency customers, sells the product to them, obtains the payment, takes its agreed-upon share, and transfers the remaining share to the venture. This practice is particularly common in situations in which the foreign venture is the manufacturing or assembling arm of the foreign investor.

Countertrade

Countertrade is another popular way of dealing with currency inconvertibility. *Countertrade* is a reciprocal arrangement between buyer and seller for the sale of goods or services intended to minimize the outflow of foreign exchange from the buyer's country. In countertrade, local currency earnings are used to purchase local products, which are then exported to a hard-currency country for sale. The proceeds of the hard-currency sale are then converted into dollars and returned to the foreign investor. Although there are several main types of countertrade, every countertrade arrangement is unique. The way such arrangements are structured depends largely on the country and industry involved.

COUNTERPURCHASE. The most common type of countertrade is the *counterpurchase agreement.* Counterpurchase involves the sale of goods to a buyer, often a foreign government, who requires as a condition of the sale that the seller buy other goods produced in that country. For example, Vietnam may agree to purchase a firm's machine tools, but require in return that the firm either purchase a quantity of Vietnamese-made products, or find someone who will. These deals are usually structured as two separate contracts where each party is paid in currency when its products are delivered to the other party. Often, the private firm is given a period of several years in which to fulfill its purchase obligation. Usually, the seller will be given a selection of items for export so that if the particular products do not fit into the seller's channels of distribution, the seller can choose other products instead. The goal of a counterpurchase arrangement, however, is for export transactions to offset the "cost" of import transactions.

BARTER. Another form of countertrade is barter. *Barter* is the direct exchange of goods for goods (or services). Unlike counterpurchase transactions, which involve payment in currency, barter transactions are not pegged to market prices. Therefore, it is difficult to determine the value of the goods exchanged. Barter transactions can involve a wide range of items, from pharmaceuticals and aircraft to agricultural commodities, oil, natural resources, and even consumer goods. In one notable case, Pepsi agreed in 1972 to trade products and build bottling plants for Pepsi-Cola in Russia in return for Stolichnaya vodka and other Russian-made products. Some firms that specialize in barter transactions have developed creative schemes for minimizing risks for exporters.

Barter, like all countertrade, can be risky. Many small firms, when first aware of a barter opportunity, believe they can quickly and profitably sell the bartered products. Many of them are disappointed. They find out that they are not familiar with the market for that product and end up selling it at a great loss. If a smaller firm is bartering for products that they can directly use themselves, such as component parts, barter may be appropriate for them. There is also less risk involved in taking commodities whose prices are readily determined by the world's commodity markets. However, for the most part, only experienced countertrade firms should engage in barter transactions.

OFFSETS. *Offsets* are used in the defense industry to require, as a condition of sale of defense equipment to a foreign government, that a portion of the components or subsystems be procured by the manufacturer from firms within the foreign country.

BUY-BACK. A *buy-back agreement* is often associated with the sale of machinery or industrial equipment, or the construction of plants and factories. Here the provider of the equipment or technology will receive, as its payment, a portion of the goods manufactured by that equipment or in that factory. In some countries, buy-back agreements are required by law. One of the problems for firms that enter into buy-back agreements is that they cannot effectively control the quality of the goods taken back. Another problem arises when the firm that provides the equipment also manufactures the same products as those for which the equipment will be used. The goods produced may possibly compete with those that the firm manufactures itself.

Informal Consortia or Parallel Exchanges

In some soft-currency countries, foreign investors form consortia to trade local soft currency. At various times, some members of a consortium would have more of the local currency than they can get rid of, while others may need more than they can earn to develop profitable business. By broadening the base of foreign investors, a private *parallel exchange* is thereby formed in countries without formal currency exchanges.

Parallel exchanges have existed among hard-currency investors in Latin American countries. As Latin American currencies become freely convertible, however, their incidence has declined. The key to participating in these informal exchanges is to be sure that the U.S. investor does not inadvertently violate local currency exchange laws.

Inconvertibility Insurance

A final alternative for the U.S. investor is an *inconvertibility* or *"non-transfer" insurance* policy. Investors can purchase such policies to insure against *hard blockages,* which occur when the foreign government passes a law that prevents conversion or transfer. For a somewhat higher fee, a businessperson may purchase a policy that also protects against *soft blockages,* which are excessive delays in processing a request to convert or transfer by the local government authorities. Protected items can include repatriation of profits, dividends, local repayments, management and royalty fees, technical assistance fees, and any other form of income considered to be earnings or return on capital. *Inconvertibility insurance* is a type of political risk insurance and companies may obtain it in the same manner as other forms of political risk insurance (described in Chapter Nineteen).

CONCLUSION

Companies operating in other countries must abide by those nations' laws. The level of foreign investment regulation in a given country depends on a number of factors, including the amount of foreign currency reserves, whether the government favors central control, and its fear of foreign control. In minority ownership investments (comprising less than 50 percent of the enterprise), an investor can have either an active investment that lets them participate in managing the enterprise, or a passive investment that provides only equity capital to be managed by others. Many countries create a legal structure that limits foreign majority control of businesses. For the more active investor, a joint venture is often the best form of foreign investment. Local traditions, regulations, and tax laws all influence what form of joint venture is most attractive.

Currency risk in cross-border business transactions comes in two forms: fluctuation and inconvertibility. Fluctuation risk for a U.S. investor is the possibility that the value of a given foreign currency will decrease against the value of the U.S. dollar. Inconvertibility risk occurs in soft-currency countries. Governments whose currency is not exchanged in public international markets often lack a supply of hard currency they can use in conducting international business. Because of their low reserves of easily exchangeable currency, these countries often limit repatriation of foreign profits through a wide range of regulations, such as central bank approvals for money transfers, surtaxes, and legal prohibitions.

These risks can be minimized by hedging with a variety of financial instruments, or through legal approaches such as currency swaps, prior arrangements with the soft-currency government, payment and price adjustments, countertrade, consortia or parallel exchanges, and inconvertibility insurance.

Chapter Summary

1. Many host nations, particularly in the developing world, regulate foreign investment in order to prevent foreign economic domination. Passive debt investments are the least regulated, and active equity investments are most closely regulated.
2. Because passive equity investments provide capital without allowing foreign control of management, nations generally facilitate entry by foreigners into equity capital markets. Most developed nations have sought to attract foreign passive equity investment.
3. Most nations limit the types of businesses over which a foreign investor can exercise control. These range from limits on investment in sectors affecting national security—such as those found in the United States—to sweeping limits on majority ownership in all businesses, or on all but those directed at the export market. This type of limit is common in China and many developing countries.
4. Because active foreign investors greatly value the ability to control their enterprises abroad, limits on control tend to reduce the amount of investment into a country. Nations that have imposed such controls have experienced dramatic drops in capital investment in affected industries. Thus, the trend over time has been for nations to remove control limitations as they become more developed and capital needs increase.
5. A foreign investor may operate in another country through a subsidiary/partnership organized in that country or through a branch of its entity. Generally, the foreign branch gives certain tax advantages to the foreign investor, but can subject its entire business to the jurisdiction of the host country regulators and legal liability.
6. Nations generally enter into tax treaties to prevent double taxation of international investors. This is most often achieved by limiting taxation to the "water's edge" and providing credit for analogous taxes on the same activity. There are also tax laws that prevent evasion of tax through artificial transactions such as transfer pricing. Nonetheless, there are a variety of corporate structures that can legitimately reduce the overall tax burden to the enterprise.
7. There are two forms of currency risk: fluctuation risk and inconvertibility risk. Fluctuation risk is the possibility that the value of the currency in the country where one has invested will go down relative to the currency of the foreign investor's home country. Inconvertibility risk is the possibility that the foreign investor will not be able to convert local currency earned by its investor into a hard currency.

8. In modern international business, currency swaps are the principal method for controlling currency fluctuation risk. A financial intermediary agrees to pay the business party if currency rates go over a certain level and the business party agrees to pay the intermediary if it does not, effectively negating fluctuation risk for the operating company. To facilitate these transactions, the International Swap Dealers Association has developed a standard form agreement so that all legal terms in these deals are consistent and parties can easily redistribute the risk inherent in swaps.
9. Inconvertibility risk can be reduced by negotiating with the local government for currency exchange rights that provide preferred access to hard currency reserves or import substitution rights, which are available when the new venture will manufacture a product in the soft-currency country. Foreign investors can also ameliorate inconvertibility risk by structuring transactions correctly. Structuring techniques include requiring lump-sum, hard-currency payments as early as possible; negotiating with local partners for profit margin preservation provisions; or applying unitary index adjustment factors. It is also important, in investments that will be generating local currency revenues, to borrow to the greatest extent possible in local currency and purchase services and supplies from parties who can be paid in the local currency.
10. Countertrade is a way of controlling inconvertibility risk by trading goods. The principal forms are counterpurchase, barter, offsets, and buy-back. In light of the rise of currency swaps and parallel exchanges, the importance of countertrade has declined. A final method for containing inconvertibility risk is to buy insurance against it.

Questions and Case Problems

1. Keefe Energy, Inc., a U.S. firm, enters into a joint venture with Energia Guerra, S.A., a Mexican firm, to build and operate a coal-fired electric-power-generating plant with an estimated useful life of thirty-five years. The building and land will be owned by G/K, S.A., a company 80 percent owned by Guerra and 20 percent owned by Keefe. G/K will enter into an agreement with Keefe under which Keefe is to build and operate the plant and receive 95 percent of the projected profit from the plant for the first twenty years of its operation. Is Keefe making a minority investment? What sort of scrutiny is the joint venture likely to receive from government officials?
2. Assume the same facts as in Question 1, except that the joint venture is to build and operate a computer microcircuit manufacturing plant. What different considerations come into play in government review? What is the likely outcome?
3. What financing alternatives would be available to a U.S. firm that was interested in investing in a proposed manufacturing plant in a small country that recently left the communist bloc and did not wish to invest many of its own resources?
4. If a U.S. company establishes a 100 percent subsidiary in another country, what three general aspects of U.S. income tax law should the company be sure it has addressed?
5. What are the implications for an American who purchases shares in a German company on the basis of inside information?

Managerial Implications

You work for Luree Intergalactic, Inc., a Montana Alpine ski manufacturer. Because of Latvia's attractive relative labor costs, Luree joins forces with Aivars, AG, a Latvian firm, to build a new factory in Riga to serve the European market. Together, Luree and Aivars establish Udris, Ltd., a Latvian joint-stock company that will own the factory and sell products from it. Udris will be free to sells its skis to anyone, but expects to sell most of its initial output to Luree and Aivars. Under an agreement between Luree and Aivars, Luree will purchase skis from Udris for resale in Europe east of Ukraine, and in North and South America, New Zealand, and Japan;

Aivars will market the remaining portion of Udris's production to the rest of the world.

1. Because Luree has greater financial resources than does Aivars, its capital contribution will entitle it to 90 percent ownership of Udris. Aivars also recognizes that it has received the less attractive ski markets. It expects to derive most of its income from a special contract with Udris to test new ski models on mogul runs. Prepare a memorandum that anticipates what principal corporate law concerns will need to be addressed in this arrangement.
2. Aivars suggests that, as compensation for being Udris's first customers, Luree and Aivars receive a discount off the price that Udris charges other purchasers. Analyze the transfer-pricing issues raised by this proposal.

For Internet Activities, Visit academic.cengage.com/blaw/schaffer.

CHAPTER 19

Nationalization, Expropriation, and Privatization

The preceding chapters discussed the gradual progression of commitment by a U.S. investor in a nation—from appointment of a representative, through the transfer of intellectual property rights, to commitment of capital resources abroad. Up to now, the discussion has covered the investor's increasing vulnerability to regulation under the laws of the host country. In a sense, the differences in risk between doing business in the United States and doing business abroad are only of degree and local peculiarity. After all, the United States often has similar regulations to other countries.

Political risk is an altogether different issue. Perhaps the most elementary and important distinction between investment in the United States or Western Europe and investment in other locations is that the foreign government may, through *nationalization*—a taking of an industry by a government—or an *expropriation*—the taking of a foreign entity's assets while a domestic entity's assets in the industry are not taken—simply take one's investment without paying full compensation. Concerns about nationalization and expropriation were paramount through most of the twentieth century. In the early twentieth century, communist and socialist governments aggressively nationalized industries in Europe. In the 1960s and 1970s, emerging and newly independent governments took over foreign-owned enterprises in Latin America, Asia, and Africa. Questions about the level of adequate compensation for such takings were vital.

Then, in the late 1980s, communism died and governments ran nationalized industries into the ground. Suddenly, the government was selling the assets back to the private sector. *Privatization,* the transfer of government-owned assets to the private sector, is simply the reverse of the nationalization–expropriation process. In the first decade of the twenty-first century, many emerging nations encountered economic crises. Populist governments returned to power in Latin America and began taking back what they had recently sold.

The wildly gyrating cycle of nationalization and privatization illustrates vividly that trends in international law, like the political environment that law reflects, are cyclical. This chapter begins with a discussion of the legal issues surrounding nationalization and proceeds through the unwinding of nationalization in the privatization movement.

Theories Relating to Takings of Foreign Property

Nationalization is quite au courant, but Western legal scholars have been debating the propriety of the takings of foreign property for hundreds of years. This anti-nationalization dialectic comprises two major theories: the *traditional* theory and the *modern–traditional* theory.

The Traditional Theory and Modern–Traditional Theory

The traditional theory prohibits all takings of foreign property, while modern–traditional requires prompt, adequate, and effective compensation for such takings. The modern–traditional requirement of adequate compensation has been questioned or rejected in some parts of the world, particularly in socialist countries that adhere to the theory of preeminence of the sovereign rights of the state. In order to understand how to limit risks, the foreign investor must be aware of their extent in all parts of the globe.

The classic doctrine on the taking of the property of foreign citizens was developed in Europe beginning in the seventeenth century. Because the European states were capital exporters during that period, they were jealously protective of foreign investment. Grotius fundamental principle was that foreign investors—unlike local merchants—should be exempt from the sovereign's condemnation rights: "The right of subjects then differs from the right of foreigners in this, that over those who are in no way subject, the power of eminent domain has no control." The local investor was subject to expropriation by the sovereign under the legal doctrine of *eminent domain.* For example, the government could condemn a U.S. citizen's land if it needed the land to build a highway, so long as it compensated that citizen for the fair value of the land. Under the traditional theory, however, foreign investors were exempt from such takings. This made some sense in the context of the pre-twentieth-century international system, in which citizens of the advanced mercantile or industrial countries were considered to be wholly immune from the judicial power of the less-developed host state. Thus, in the nineteenth century, Britain dispatched gunboats to Venezuela to compel restitution for expropriated property of British subjects.

As the sovereign equality of nations became accepted in the twentieth century, the traditional doctrine became indefensible and evolved into the *modern–traditional theory.* This theory recognizes the sovereign's right to nationalize foreign-owned property, but places conditions on the proper exercise of that right. The exercise of the right must be (1) for a public purpose; (2) nondiscriminatory (not directed against a specific foreign person); and (3) accompanied by prompt, adequate, and effective compensation. Thus, a sovereign cannot take foreign property for harassment, personal aggrandizement, or other nonpublic purposes, and cannot target the property of one nationality discriminatorily. Further, compensation must be paid. To modern–traditional thinkers, "adequate" compensation meant fair market value as a going concern, including future earnings and intangibles; "prompt" meant as soon as reasonable, and "effective" meant cash or a commodity immediately available and freely convertible to cash. This modern–traditionalism was eloquently advanced by Secretary of State Cordell Hull in his response to the expropriations triggered by the Mexican Revolution (see Exhibit 19.1).

Modern–traditional theory is accepted as customary international law by the countries that have historically been capital exporters: the North American and Western European nations. In the 1970s and 1980s, arbitrations arising out of the expropriation of foreign petroleum holdings led to pronouncements by the Iran–United States Claims Tribunal in The Hague confirming that modern–traditional theory remains the accepted international standard.

Thus, although an overseas investment is normally subject to the host country's sovereign right to expropriate, in developed countries the investor should be entitled, under customary international law, to full compensation—at least if the investor can obtain arbitration of the dispute. However, the modern–traditional theory has not been accepted everywhere.

Non-Western Theories of Takings

In the nineteenth century, the first intellectual counterpoint to the traditional theory came from Latin America, the most developed of the capital importing regions. The so-called *Calvo Doctrine*—named after the Argentine scholar who first articulated it—placed the sovereign ahead of the foreign investor within the sovereign's territory and challenged any intervention by foreign states in investment disputes as a violation of the territorial jurisdiction of the host country. Calvo proponents argued that nationalization is a legitimate exercise of the sovereign's preeminent right to restructure the economy and is not subject to the law of any other jurisdiction, including international law.

The *Calvo Doctrine* maintained that a sovereign nation should be free to decide whether and how it wishes to provide compensation for a taking. Once it decides, all within its national territory should be subject to that decision. The recourse available to the foreign investor should be no

Exhibit 19.1

Diplomatic Note from the Secretary of State of the United States of America to the Minister of Foreign Affairs of Mexico
July 21, 1938
United States Department of State

Background and Facts

Agrarian expropriations began in Mexico in 1915. As of August 30, 1927, 1,621 moderate-sized properties of American citizens had been taken. Subsequent to 1927, additional properties, chiefly farms of a moderate size, with a value claimed by their owners of $10,132,388, were expropriated by the Mexican government. The claims of their owners were referred to a General Claims Commission established by agreement between the two governments, but as of 1938, when Secretary Hull sent his letter, not a single claim had been adjusted and none had been paid.

Secretary of State Cordell Hull

The taking of property without compensation is not expropriation. It is confiscation. It is no less confiscation because there may be an expressed intent to pay at some time in the future. If it were permissible for a government to take the private property of the citizens of other countries and pay for it as and when, in the judgment of that government, its economic circumstances and its local legislation may perhaps permit, the safeguards which the constitutions of most countries and established international law have sought to provide would be illusory. Governments would be free to take property far beyond their ability or willingness to pay, and the owners thereof would be without recourse. We cannot question the right of a foreign government to treat its own nationals in this fashion if it so desires. This is a matter of domestic concern. But we cannot admit that foreign government may take the property of American nationals in disregard of the rule of compensation under international law. Nor can we admit that any government unilaterally and through its municipal legislation can, as in this instant case, nullify this universally accepted principle of international law, based as it is on reason, equity and justice. . . .

The whole structure of friendly intercourse, of international trade and commerce, and many other vital and mutually desirable relations between nations indispensable to their progress rest upon the single and hitherto solid foundation of respect on the part of governments and of peoples for each other's rights under international justice. The right of prompt and just compensation for expropriated property is a part of this structure. It is a principle to which the government of the United States and most governments of the world have emphatically subscribed and which they have practiced and which must be maintained. It is not a principle which freezes the status quo and denies changes in property rights but a principle that permits any country to expropriate private property within its borders in furtherance of public purposes. It enables orderly change without violating the legitimately acquired interests of the citizens of other countries.

greater than that of any domestic investor: to appeal to the courts or political branches of the sovereign nation that takes the "nationalizing" action. No foreign nation or entity has any right to impose its laws on behalf of an investor that happens to be of foreign origin.

Calvo's emphasis on the primacy of the state corresponded nicely with the concept of state property inaugurated by the Bolshevik Revolution. To communists, the theory that the sovereign state had a right to restructure its own economy was consistent with the expropriations that followed the revolution. Other communist states followed the Soviet example and justified it along Calvo lines.

Finally, when Europe's former Asian and African colonies became politically independent in the years following World War II, they came to view nationalization as a necessary part of economic independence. In their view, as long as foreigners controlled the economy, they effectively controlled the country, irrespective of who operated the political apparatus. These newly emerging states could not begin to pay full compensation for such nationalizations because they lacked the tax base to do so. Hence, the sovereign state countertheories came into vogue there as well.

In short, during the twentieth century, much of the world rejected modern–traditional theory and instead adopted theories that asserted that the state had a right to take foreign property for what purposes it chose and upon payment of less than full compensation. Whatever the intellectual basis for the takings, for the foreign investor, the results were the same: Its property was taken and the investor was paid less than the property was worth.

In the 1980s and 1990s, the number of adherents to sovereign rights theories went into deep decline. When Latin American governments and their nationalized enterprises defaulted on loans made to them by capital exporting nations, capital for their economies dried up. The absence of capital in turn further devastated these economies, leading to the election of governments that were more supportive of private enterprise. In order to attract new capital investment—in many cases for the re-privatization of assets Latin governments had nationalized—the governments were compelled to assure prospective foreign investors that future investments would be treated under the modern–traditional theory. This was accomplished both through domestic legislation and international treaties. Similarly, when the Eastern European communist bloc collapsed in the 1989–1991 period, the new democracies adopted the modern–traditional theory in a series of bilateral treaties and national legislation so they could attract foreign investment. In the 1990s, most former colonies also accepted the modern–traditional theory as a prelude to attracting foreign capital.

However, the sovereign rights theory remains very much alive as an intellectual force and in the first decade of the twenty-first century has staged a robust comeback. This is particularly the case in the Latin American countries of Argentina, Bolivia, Venezuela, Nicaragua, and Ecuador. Bolivia, Nicaragua, and Venezuela have recently announced that they will withdraw from the *ICSID Convention*, thereby withdrawing them once more from the reach of international arbitration. These Latin American governments suggest since ICSID is a branch of the World Bank, ICSID rulings are subject to conflicts of interest between the World Bank as stakeholder and as arbitrator, impartial, shrouded in secrecy, and inconsistent. Thus, they have called for a return to sovereign control of disputes within their borders, rejecting international means of enforcement. Similarly, the energy and infrastructure privatizations that marked previous decades have slowed in Latin America.

Some Latin governments are now assertively re-imposing state control. In recent years, Venezuela has steadily reduced the role of private capital in the oil industry through a series of "offer you can't refuse" buyouts achieved under the express threat of nationalization. On May 1, 2006, Bolivia nationalized the energy industry. Ecuador has reasserted state control over the oil industry, including cancellation of a concession to the nation's largest foreign investor. In Argentina, selective re-nationalization of previously privatized enterprises is proceeding. Whether this recent surge of the sovereign rights theory in Latin America will spread or wane is not certain, but these governments are certainly calling out Calvo's name.

Public Purpose, Nondiscrimination, and the Expropriation-Nationalization Distinction

Sovereign rights proponents like Professor Calvo rejected the modern–traditional theory's prerequisites for takings: public purpose and nondiscrimination. They argue that the right to take foreign property is an attribute of national sovereignty. Therefore, it cannot be conditioned on whether an international tribunal characterizes the taking as discriminatory or as furthering a private purpose. In essence, within their territory, there should be no limit to what a nation's government can do to restructure its economy. The people have a right to take foreign property within their own territory without having outsiders impose preconditions.

Paradoxically, sovereign rights states nevertheless incorporated public purpose concepts in deciding whether a taking is one that merits full compensation—as in an expropriation—or one that merits less compensation—as in nationalization. The classic *expropriation* is a taking of an isolated item of property. The foreign investor is singled out as the target of governmental action in a fashion that might be viewed as discriminatory and not part of a national public plan. By contrast, a *nationalization* is the taking of an entire industry or a natural resource as part of a plan to restructure the nation's economic system. In a nationalization, the values underlying sovereign rights theories are most strongly implicated, and full compensation is not required by those theories.

One of the few nations in recent years that has not been precluded by treaty from espousing sovereign rights theories is the Islamic Republic of Iran. The *INA Corp.* arbitration demonstrated that some jurists still accept sovereign rights concepts.

The approach suggested by the panel in the *INA* case—that less than full compensation could be paid in the event of any large-scale nationalization—remains a distinct minority view.

INA Corp. v. Islamic Republic of Iran

8 Iran–U.S. Cl. Trib. Rep. 373 (1985)

Iran–United States Claims Tribunal

BACKGROUND AND FACTS

On May 3, 1978, a subsidiary of INA Corporation (INA), INA International Insurance Company, Ltd. (INA International), acquired 20 percent of the shares of Bimek Shargh (Shargh), an Iranian insurance company. The proposed investment by INA International was approved by Central Insurance of Iran (CII), the government body responsible for the regulation of insurance activities in Iran, by a letter to Shargh management dated December 27, 1977. INA International paid 20 million rials for the shares of Shargh.

On June 25, 1979, Iran's government enacted the *Law of Nationalization of Insurance and Credit Enterprises.* Article 1 provided as follows:

> To protect the rights of the insured, to expand the insurance industry and the entire State and to place it at the service of the people, from the date of this law, all insurance enterprises in Iran are proclaimed nationalized with acceptance of the principle of legitimate ownership.

INA sued for what it alleged to be the going value of its Shargh shares, together with interest and legal costs.

JUDGE LAGERGREN

The essence of the dispute between the Parties lies not in the fact of nationalization having taken place, which is agreed, but in the determination of the level of compensation, if any, which should be paid to the shareholders of Shargh as a consequence. No compensation has been paid to date, INA argues for compensation that is "prompt, adequate and effective," on the basis both of general principles of international law and the Treaty of Amity, Economic Relations, and Consular Rights of 15 August 1955. INA asks the Tribunal to accept the amount of its initial investment in Shargh as the best available indicator of the value of the company as a going concern at the time of nationalization just over one year later.

The respondent government concedes that, in principle, the working of Article I of the nationalization law does, in appropriate cases, envisage the payment of compensation to private shareholders of nationalized insurance companies, but that this must be based on the "net book value" of the company.

It has long been acknowledged that expropriations for a public purpose and subject to conditions provided for by law—notably that category which can be characterized as "nationalizations"—are not *per se* unlawful. A lawful nationalization will, however, impose on the government concerned the obligation to pay compensation.

This case presents, in addition, a classic example of a formal and systematic nationalization by decree of an entire category of commercial enterprises considered of fundamental importance to the nation's economy. During the course of the post-Revolutionary economics restructuring in Iran.... The insurance companies, including Bimek Shargh, were nationalized by decree on 27 June 1979.... Such measures number among the risks which investors must be prepared to encounter.

In the event of such large-scale nationalizations of a lawful character, international law has undergone a gradual reappraisal, the effect of which may be to undermine the doctrinal value of any "full" or "adequate" (when used as identical to "full") compensation standard as proposed in the case.

However, the Tribunal is of the opinion that in a case such as the present, involving an investment of a rather small amount shortly before the nationalization, international law admits compensation in an amount equal to the fair market value of the investment.

Decision. The Iran–United States Claims Tribunal awarded INA Corporation the amount it sought plus simple interest at 8.5 percent per annum from the date of nationalization.

Most international tribunals, including most panels of the Iran–United States Claims Tribunal, adhere to the modern–traditional theory. But no less an authority than the *Restatement (Third) of Foreign Relations Law*—which ostensibly reflects the consensus view—states that less than full compensation may be acceptable in "exceptional circumstances" such as agricultural land reform. Modern–traditional theory continues to be under attack.

LEVEL OF COMPENSATION. Once it has been determined that a taking was a "nationalization," sovereign rights advocates uniformly reject the modern–traditional formula of "prompt, adequate, and effective compensation." First, they often disavow the obligation to provide compensation at fair market value. With respect to the taking of lands or natural resources, for instance, they argue that the state already owns the resource and need pay only for the foreign owners' improvements to the land or resources.

If one scratches the surface of these arguments, one will uncover the practical point that the government that is taking the property cannot afford its fair market value. In the view of such a nation, if taking foreign property is necessary for effective political independence, this imperative overrides mere commercial considerations. Thus, a number of sovereign rights states have favored measures of compensation that bear only an attenuated relationship to fair value. One such measure is *net book value* of the nationalized asset. This value reflects the depreciated cost of assets (calculated using accounting conventions) without regard to whether there has in fact been depreciation in value. Many assets, for example, actually appreciate over time because of appreciation in the value of what they produce or because the business of which they are a part has a "going concern value" over and above the value of the asset in isolation.

Promptness of compensation is also a concern. Sovereign rights states generally insist on the right to schedule payment of the compensation over time. These installments sometimes are paid through devices such as the issuance of national bonds payable in the local currency.

In addition to bearing the risk of being paid less than market value, the victim of nationalization must bear the fluctuation risk associated with the local currency. As discussed in Chapter Eighteen, the value of a soft currency—and of a bond that promises to pay a certain number of units of that currency in the future—can change dramatically. Further, there is a substantial risk that the local country will not be able to repay its bonds. Many emerging nations have defaulted on their international debts. Because of these risks, such bonds might be transferable to others only at a massive discount, if at all.

CREEPING EXPROPRIATION. Short of outright expropriation, a foreign nation may impose regulations that gradually limit the exercise of ownership rights—so-called *creeping expropriation*. Creeping expropriation is the effect of laws and regulations that subject the investor to discriminatory taxes, legislative controls over management of the firm, price controls, forced employment of nationals, license cancellation, and, as discussed in Chapter Eighteen, restrictions on currency convertibility. Unlike straightforward expropriation, creeping expropriation requires a careful fact-based determination as to whether the sovereign has engaged in a taking or merely exercised its right to regulate industry. This ambiguity makes creeping expropriation even more dangerous to the foreign investor. The determination usually considers the economic impact, the extent of interference with reasonable investment-backed expectations, and the character of the government action.

Investors in emerging nations need also concern themselves with the business consequences of politically unstable environments. For example, the Indonesian government's refusal to comply with International Monetary Fund mandates caused an economic crisis that sparked the destructive Jakarta riots in the spring of 1998. Apart from causing widespread physical damage to business assets, such "political violence" interrupted the business of enterprises with operations in Indonesia. In many cases, the violence, and subsequent government countermeasures, forced firms to abandon projects and sent employees racing out of the country for their lives. All of these occurrences are casualties against which the prudent business manager may wish to insure.

Guarding Against Political Risk

Prior to the recent resurgence of the sovereign rights theory in Latin America, the modern–traditional theory seemed to have permanently trumped the sovereign rights approach. Indeed, former communist nations turned so completely from the sovereign rights approach that they created procedures for compensating Western firms for nationalizations that occurred decades earlier. The U.S. Foreign Claims Compensation Commission, which resolves claims by U.S. citizens against countries that have nationalized their assets without adequate compensation, has aggressively pursued U.S. claims in the new democracies.

If economic conditions do not improve and populist governments gain a stronghold, today's modern–traditionalist might be tomorrow's nationalizing government. In March 2001, the South African government announced a plan to expropriate one-third of the nation's farmland to black ownership from white owners. This plan included land owned by foreign investors. The plan called for "adequate compensation" to the white owners, but this was redefined to mean something other than the land's current fair market value. The plan was enacted and the owners had their property effectively taken for modest compensation. In another example, in late 2003, the government of Argentina announced that it considered all bilateral investment treaties that agreed to "full, adequate, and effective" compensation in international arbitration to be unconstitutional and unenforceable. As noted earlier in this chapter, a handful of Latin American states are nationalizing or re-nationalizing key industries. Nations that in the 1990s led the way to privatization now seem to be considering selective re-nationalization.

The bottom line is that the U.S. investor in countries that once espoused the sovereign rights theory now is exposed to risk of loss from political action. Its investment can be taken for a fraction of its true value.

Political Risk Insurance

Having defined the problem, the investor must determine how to guard against it. He or she may do so either by purchasing insurance against an event before it happens or bringing legal action against the wrongdoer after it happens.

Entrepreneurs normally assume the risk that their business will fail because their product is unable to find an adequate market. However, the entrepreneurs will usually try to avoid the risk of failure caused by events beyond their control, such as fire, earthquake, or employee dishonesty. To cover those risks, they normally contract with an insurance company, which assumes this risk for a fee, called a *premium,* which is based on an actuarial assessment of the probability of loss among all of the company's insureds. The concept of insurance against political risk arose from this practice. Entrepreneurs who are unwilling to hazard the risk of a foreign government taking will pay a premium to a public or private insurance company.

Obviously, the cost of this insurance is a disincentive to investment abroad. In order for the U.S. or Western European investor to justify foreign investment, the anticipated increased marginal returns on the emerging market venture—as compared to a comparable U.S. or Western European investment—must be greater than the cost of the insurance. If political risk and the cost of insurance become too great, the emerging market investment becomes financially unjustifiable. Indeed, the historic commitment of the United States to protecting private property from public seizure—thereby eliminating political risk and the need to buy political risk insurance—is one of the qualities that make it one of the world's most attractive investment markets.

Political Risk Insurance from Government Agencies. A number of capital-exporting nations have established government corporations that provide political risk insurance, such as the United States' *Overseas Private Investment Corporation* (OPIC). National agencies like OPIC hope to promote exports to foreign countries by insuring domestic firms that do business abroad against expropriation (including creeping expropriation), nationalization, revolution, insurrections, and currency inconvertibility. These agencies' purpose is both good and bad for the U.S. investor. They provide insurance at rates that do not include a significant profit for the insurer. However, the availability of insurance is sometimes subject to politically motivated conditions that exclude many projects. For example, when India tested nuclear weapons in May 1998, OPIC funding for projects based in India immediately became unavailable.

OPIC investments must not adversely affect the U.S. balance of payments or U.S. employment. The host country must not impose performance regulations that are likely to reduce "positive trade benefits likely to accrue to the United States." A manufacturing joint venture that makes nothing but components for export back to the United States may not meet this requirement.

OPIC also gives preference to investments in countries with relatively low per capita annual income. This condition targets the insurance coverage to the poorest countries, which coincidentally also have the least viable infrastructure. These are countries where the commercial risk is often so high that it deters foreign investment irrespective of the political risk.

Finally, OPIC can operate only in a country with which the United States has concluded a bilateral investment agreement. Because most bilateral investment agreements require the host country to agree to waive its sovereign rights views on takings in disputes with the United States, some nations have not entered into them.

Other developed nations have similar public *export credit agencies* that promote investment from their own countries. These include Japan's Bank for International Cooperation, Germany's Hermes Kreditversicherung-AG, France's Compagnie francaise d'Assurance pour le commerce extérieur, and the Export Development Corporation of Canada. The conditions and limitations of these political risk programs are quite similar to those of OPIC. In some projects, a number of these national export credit agencies will pool their efforts.

A similar but internationally based investment insurance company is the *Multilateral Investment Guarantee Agency* (MIGA). Started in early 1988 as an independent affiliate of the World Bank, MIGA issues insurance guarantees to protect foreign investors from losses relating to currency transfer restrictions, expropriation, war, civil disturbance, and breach of contract. MIGA guarantees are granted for a fifteen-year term. To qualify, both the investor's home country and the country into which it is investing must be parties to the *MIGA Convention*.

PRIVATE POLITICAL RISK INSURANCE. In recent years, trends toward the modern–traditional theory and international investment treaties and codes have lowered the perceived risk of political risk insurance. The result has been an explosion in the availability of such insurance.

Two principal markets provide private political risk insurance. Lloyds of London insurance *syndicates*—pools of money provided by investors to insure specific projects—provide such insurance on a case-by-case basis. In this market, the U.S. investor engages a broker for a specific transaction, and the broker negotiates terms with heads of syndicates specializing in political risk insurance. The syndicate heads then obtain commitments from other syndicates in order to spread the risk exposure.

Alternatively, the investor can approach a lead underwriter of a group operating under a *reinsurance treaty*, which is an agreement among insurers whereby the underwriter leading the group spreads the risk among its members. Under the terms of the reinsurance treaty, the lead underwriter can commit the resources of the entire group after negotiating the transaction with the U.S. investor.

Private insurance has many advantages. First, private insurers have no political agendas and therefore have no special political prerequisites for issuing insurance. The host country need not be extremely poor and the foreign investor can hail from anywhere. In addition, the private insurance approval process can be faster than is the case with public agencies.

Private insurers, however, are in business for profit and their coverage can be quite expensive as compared to the government programs. Another issue is that many private syndicates will not enter particularly politically volatile areas without a public agency as a partner. A third problem is that the term of private insurance policies is generally limited to five to seven years, too short for an adequate return from larger capital-intensive construction projects.

Resolving Investment Disputes with Foreign Nations

Foreign investors must understand the risks associated with seeking relief from U.S. or international forums if their prospective investment is nationalized. The first alternative for a victim of nationalization is to seek relief in the courts of the country where the property was nationalized. In countries with well-developed traditions of an independent judiciary, this alternative is feasible. As German or Japanese investors in the United States will testify, however, even there the foreigner is at a disadvantage as a stranger in the other party's "home court." Even worse, the judiciaries of countries with significant political risk tend not to be as independent as those of developed nations. Finally, if a country happens to ascribe to sovereign right principles, recourse to its judiciary would be rather fruitless for the injured U.S. investor. Nevertheless, under traditional international law principles, an injured investor may need to exhaust local remedies before invoking diplomatic or international adjudication.

A second possibility would be for the investor to sue the host state in the United States. After all, most governments have assets in the United States that are subject to attachment by U.S. courts. For example, if a Boeing 747 owned by a state-owned airline was sitting on the tarmac at Chicago's O'Hare Airport, it could be attached to satisfy most types of judgments. But there are serious obstacles to this course of action. First, under the *Foreign Sovereign Immunities Act of 1976*, a federal court will not have jurisdiction over the foreign nation unless the court finds that the state's acts fall within a *commercial activity exemption* to immunity. Second, even if the court has jurisdiction over the foreign state, it might abstain from exercising it under principles of abstention referred to as the *Act of State Doctrine*. Finally, if the investor can get a U.S. court to hear the case, the investor should be prepared to rely on a treaty or powerful international law argument because U.S. courts will often decline to hear a case if most of the evidence is abroad. In light of these difficulties, the foreign investor may wish to bring its case before an international arbitration tribunal. To do this, however, the host nation must have consented to such dispute resolution in advance.

THE *FOREIGN SOVEREIGN IMMUNITIES ACT*. In 1976, Congress enacted the *Foreign Sovereign Immunities Act* (FSIA). Under FSIA, foreign states are generally immune from the jurisdiction of U.S. courts, save for seven exceptions: (1) the foreign state waives immunity; (2) the state's action constitutes "commercial activity" carried on by the state; (3) rights in property are taken in violation of international law; (4) rights in property are acquired through inheritance or gifts in the United States; (5) the suit involves noncommercial torts within the United States; (6) the suit involves maritime liens based on the foreign state's "commercial activity"; or (7) the suit involves certain types of counterclaims and the foreign state instituted the lawsuit against a U.S. citizen.

In light of the rising terrorist threat, Congress amended FSIA to allow a U.S. citizen to sue a foreign state in a U.S. court for damages resulting from a state-sponsored act of terrorism. The U.S. Supreme Court has held that these are the only exceptions to FSIA's grant of immunity and has interpreted these exceptions narrowly.

The most significant of these exceptions to FSIA is the "commercial activity" exception. In relevant part, the exception provides that "a foreign state shall not be immune from the jurisdiction of the United States or the states in any case ... in which the action is based ... upon an act outside the territory of the United States in connection with the commercial activity of the foreign state elsewhere and it causes a direct effect on the United States." This exception is principally aimed at situations in which the state enters into a commercial contract with an investor and is acting as a private commercial party. One of the most comprehensive analyses by the Supreme Court on what constitutes "commercial activity" under the FSIA is found in the *Saudi Arabia v. Nelson* case. Writing for a slim majority of the Court, Justice Souter was careful to contrast the actions charged against Saudi Arabia with the *Republic of Argentina v. Weltover, Inc.* case, where Argentina had clothed its actions in official enactments.

Saudi Arabia v. Nelson
507 U.S. 349 (1993)
United States Supreme Court

BACKGROUND AND FACTS

The Nelsons, a married couple, filed an action for damages against the Kingdom of Saudi Arabia, a Saudi hospital, and the hospital's purchasing agent in the United States. The purchasing agent had, at the direction of the Saudi government, recruited the husband through advertising in the United States to work at a hospital in Saudi Arabia. The plaintiffs alleged that, once in Saudi Arabia, the Saudis had unlawfully detained and tortured the husband. They also based their suit on the defendants' negligent failure to warn him of the possibility of severe retaliatory action if he attempted to report on-the-job hazards. The Court of Appeals found subject matter jurisdiction, concluding that the husband's recruitment and hiring were "commercial activities" that Saudi Arabia and the hospital carried on in the United States and that the Nelsons' action was "based upon" these activities within the meaning of the statute. There was, the Court of Appeals reasoned, a sufficient nexus between those commercial activities and the wrongful acts that had allegedly injured the Nelsons.

JUSTICE SOUTER

The Foreign Sovereign Immunities Act of 1976 entitles foreign states to immunity from the jurisdiction of courts in the United States ... subject to certain enumerated exceptions. One is that a foreign state shall not be immune in any case "in which the action is based upon a commercial activity carried on in the United States by the foreign state." ... The Act defines such activity as "commercial activity carried on by such state and having substantial contact with the United States" ... and provides that a commercial activity may be "either a regular course of commercial conduct or a particular commercial transaction or act," the "commercial character of [which] shall be determined by reference to its "nature," rather than its "purpose." ...

We begin our analysis by identifying the particular conduct on which the Nelsons' action is "based" for purposes of the Act.... In denoting conduct that forms the "basis," or "foundation," for a claim ... the phrase is read most naturally to mean those elements of a claim that, if proven, would entitle a plaintiff to relief under his theory of the case.... Earlier ... we noted that [the commercial activity exception] contains two clauses following the one at issue here. The second allows for jurisdiction where a suit "is based ... upon an act performed in the United States in connection with a commercial activity of the foreign state elsewhere," and the third speaks in like terms, allowing for jurisdiction where an action "is based ... upon an act outside the territory of the United States in connection with a commercial activity of the foreign state elsewhere and that act causes a direct effect in the United States."... Congress manifestly understood there to be a difference between a suit "based upon" commercial activity and one "based upon" acts performed "in connection with" such activity. The only reasonable reading of the former term calls for something more than a mere connection with, or relation to, commercial activity. (We do not mean to suggest that the first clause of [the exception] necessarily requires that each and every element of a claim be commercial activity by a foreign state, and we do not address the case where a claim consists of both commercial and sovereign elements. We do conclude, however, that where a claim rests entirely upon activities sovereign in character, as here, jurisdiction will not exist under that clause regardless of any connection the sovereign acts may have with commercial activity.)

In this case, the Nelsons have alleged that petitioners recruited Scott Nelson for work at the hospital, signed an employment contract with him, and subsequently employed him. While these activities led to the conduct that eventually injured the Nelsons, they are not the basis for the Nelsons' suit. Even taking each of the Nelsons' allegations about Scott Nelson's recruitment and employment as true, those facts alone entitle the Nelsons to nothing under their theory of the case. The Nelsons have not, after all, alleged breach of contract ... but personal injuries caused by petitioners' intentional wrongs and by petitioners' negligent failure to warn Scott Nelson that they might commit those wrongs. Those torts, and not the arguably commercial activities that preceded their commission, form the basis for the Nelsons' suit. Petitioners' tortious conduct itself fails to qualify as "commercial activity" within the meaning of the Act.... [T]he Act defines "commercial activity" as "either a regular course of commercial

continued

continued

conduct or a particular commercial transaction or act," and provides that "[t]he commercial character of an activity shall be determined by reference to the nature of the course of conduct or particular transaction or act, rather than by reference to its purpose." ... If this is a definition, it is one distinguished only by its diffidence; as we observed in our most recent case on the subject, it "leaves the critical term 'commercial' largely undefined." *Republic of Argentina v. Weltover, Inc.*... We do not, however, have the option to throw up our hands. The term has to be given some interpretation, and congressional diffidence necessarily results in judicial responsibility to determine what a "commercial activity" is for purposes of the Act.

We took up the task just last Term in *Weltover* ... which involved Argentina's unilateral refinancing of bonds it had issued under a plan to stabilize its currency. Bondholders sued Argentina in federal court, asserting jurisdiction under the third clause of [the exception]. In the course of holding the refinancing to be a commercial activity for purposes of the Act, we observed that the statute "largely codifies the so-called 'restrictive' theory of foreign sovereign immunity first endorsed by the State Department in 1952." We accordingly held that the meaning of "commercial" for purposes of the Act must be the meaning Congress understood the restrictive theory to require at the time it passed the statute.

Under the restrictive, as opposed to the "absolute," theory of foreign sovereign immunity, a state is immune from the jurisdiction of foreign courts as to its sovereign or public acts (jure imperii), but not as to those that are private or commercial in character (jure gestionis).... We explained in *Weltover* ... that a state engages in commercial activity under the restrictive theory where it exercises "only those powers that can also be exercised by private citizens," as distinct from those "powers peculiar to sovereigns." Put differently, a foreign state engages in commercial activity for purposes of the restrictive theory only where it acts "in the manner of a private player within" the market.... We emphasized in *Weltover* that whether a state acts "in the manner of" a private party is a question of behavior, not motivation:

> [B]ecause the Act provides that the commercial character of an act is to be determined by reference to its "nature" rather than its "purpose," the question is not whether the foreign government is acting with a profit motive or instead with the aim of fulfilling uniquely sovereign objectives. Rather, the issue is whether the particular actions that the foreign state performs (whatever the motive behind them) are the type of actions by which a private party engages in "trade and traffic or commerce."

We did not ignore the difficulty of distinguishing "purpose" (i.e., the reason why the foreign state engages in the activity) from "nature" (i.e., the outward form of the conduct that the foreign state performs or agrees to perform), but recognized that the Act "unmistakably commands" us to observe the distinction. Because Argentina had merely dealt in the bond market in the manner of a private player, we held, its refinancing of the bonds qualified as a commercial activity for purposes of the Act despite the apparent governmental motivation.

Unlike Argentina's activities that we considered in *Weltover,* the intentional conduct alleged here (the Saudi Government's wrongful arrest, imprisonment, and torture of Nelson) could not qualify as commercial under the restrictive theory. The conduct boils down to abuse of the power of its police by the Saudi Government, and however monstrous such abuse undoubtedly may be, a foreign state's exercise of the power of its police has long been understood for purposes of the restrictive theory as peculiarly sovereign in nature.... Exercise of the powers of police and penal officers is not the sort of action by which private parties can engage in commerce.

The Nelsons ... urge us to give significance to their assertion that the Saudi Government subjected Nelson to the abuse alleged as retaliation for his persistence in reporting hospital safety violations, and argue that the character of the mistreatment was consequently commercial.... But this argument does not alter the fact that the powers allegedly abused were those of police and penal officers. In any event, the argument is off the point, for it goes to purpose, the very fact the Act renders irrelevant to the question of an activity's commercial character. Whatever may have been the Saudi Government's motivation for its allegedly abusive treatment of Nelson, it remains the case that the Nelsons' action is based upon a sovereign activity immune from the subject-matter jurisdiction of United States courts under the Act.

In addition to the intentionally tortious conduct, the Nelsons claim a separate basis for recovery in petitioners' failure to warn Scott Nelson of the hidden dangers associated with his employment. The Nelsons allege that, at the time petitioners recruited Scott Nelson and thereafter, they failed to warn him

continued

continued

of the possibility of severe retaliatory action if he attempted to disclose any safety hazards he might discover on the job.... In other words, petitioners bore a duty to warn of their propensity for tortious conduct. But this is merely a semantic ploy. For aught we can see, a plaintiff could recast virtually any claim of intentional tort committed by sovereign act as a claim of failure to warn, simply by charging the defendant with an obligation to announce its own tortious propensity before indulging it. To give jurisdictional significance to this feint of language would effectively thwart the Act's manifest purpose to codify the restrictive theory of foreign sovereign immunity.

Decision. The Supreme Court reversed the judgment of the Court of Appeals, dismissing the case. This meant that the Nelsons could not bring suit in an American court over the alleged actions in Saudi Arabia.

In the wake of the terrorist attacks on September 11, 2001, the "state-sponsored terrorism" exception to the FSIA has received increased attention. This exception requires a plaintiff to satisfy a number of prerequisites. First, the plaintiff must seek money damages, not injunctive relief, for personal injury or death resulting from "an act of torture, extrajudicial killing, aircraft sabotage, hostage taking, or the provision of material support ... for such an act." Second, the plaintiff must be a U.S. national when the act of terrorism occurs. Third, the defendant sovereign nation must be designated a "state sponsor of terrorism" by the State Department at the time the act occurs. Finally, if the terrorism occurred in the defendant state's territory, the plaintiff must have first tried to seek an international arbitration. In *Cicippio-Pueblo v. Islamic Republic of Iran,* the District of Columbia Court of Appeals ruled in 2004 that while the "state sponsored terrorism" exception to the FSIA waives the immunity of a foreign state, this exception did not provide a cause of action directly against the foreign state itself. Instead, the court held that the exception only provides a private right of action for U.S. citizens against officials, employees, and agents of a foreign state in their individual capacity, not their official capacity. Such a ruling makes it much more difficult to sue a foreign government. Victims can still bring suit against foreign state sponsors of terrorism, and their agencies and instrumentalities, but they must do so under other statutes or the common law.

For a U.S. entrepreneur, the act becomes relevant if it is considering doing business, directly or indirectly, with a nation that is on the State Department's list of "state sponsors of terrorism." For example, there are over 6,000 claims against Cuba alone. If any of the claimants can show that the entrepreneur owes an account payable to such a "state sponsor of terrorism," it might find itself to be the recipient of an order of attachment, seizing funds ostensibly owed to the terrorist sponsor. Doing business in such nations has become very risky indeed.

ACT OF STATE DOCTRINE. If a court decides that, under the FSIA, it can hear the U.S. investor's case against the sovereign state, the investor must still persuade the court to exercise this jurisdictional power despite the *Act of State Doctrine*. The doctrine was historically referred to as a choice-of-law doctrine under which, for reasons of *comity* among nations—friendly relations marked by mutual recognition of laws—a U.S. court will refuse to inquire into the validity of any act of a foreign government. In a more recent case, however, the U.S. Supreme Court has narrowed the impact of the doctrine by abandoning the comity rationale.

The *Act of State Doctrine* is also inapplicable if the foreign state has entered into an investment treaty that effectively waives the policy as regards U.S. investors. Indeed, this principle permits U.S. agencies to rely on bilateral investment treaties to exert significant influence over foreign governments so that they will not take adverse political action against U.S. investment.

W.S. Kirkpatrick v. Environmental Tectronics Corp.
493 U.S. 400 (1990)
United States Supreme Court

BACKGROUND AND FACTS

The government of Nigeria awarded a military contract to W. S. Kirkpatrick & Co. The losing bidder, Environmental Tectronics Corporation (ETC), investigated the circumstances under which the contract had been awarded and learned that the winner had bribed key government officials who were responsible for making the award. Ultimately, the U.S. Department of Justice conducted an investigation that confirmed ETC's findings, and high Kirkpatrick officials pled guilty to violations of the *Foreign Corrupt Practices Act.* Thereafter, ETC brought a civil lawsuit against Kirkpatrick in the United States under the *Racketeer Influenced Corrupt Organizations Act* and U.S. antitrust laws. Kirkpatrick moved to dismiss the lawsuit on the basis that the *Act of State Doctrine* prohibited the federal court from considering the matter. The district court granted Kirkpatrick's motion, but the Court of Appeals reversed the district court.

JUSTICE SCALIA

This Court's description of the jurisprudential foundation for the act of state doctrine has undergone some evolution over the years. We once viewed the doctrine as an expression of international law, resting upon "the highest considerations of international comity and expediency." We have more recently described it, however, as a consequence of domestic separation of powers, reflecting "the strong sense of the Judicial Branch that its engagement in the task of passing on the validity of foreign acts of state may hinder" the conduct of foreign affairs....

We find [that] the factual predicate for application of the act of state doctrine does not exist. Nothing in the present suit requires the Court to declare invalid, and thus ineffective as "a rule of decision for the courts of this country," the official act of a foreign sovereign.

In every case in which we have held the act of state doctrine applicable, the relief sought or the defense interposed would have required a court in the United States to declare invalid the official act of a foreign sovereign performed within its own territory. In the present case, by contrast, neither the claim nor any asserted defense requires a determination that Nigeria's contract with Kirkpatrick International was, or was not effective. Petitioners point out, however, that the facts necessary to establish respondent's claim will also establish that the contract was unlawful. Specifically, they note that in order to prevail, respondent must prove that petitioner Kirkpatrick made, and Nigerian officials received, payments that violate Nigerian law, which would, they assert, support a finding that the contract is invalid under Nigerian law. Assuming that to be true, it still does not suffice. The act of state doctrine is not some vague doctrine of abstention but a "principle of decision binding on federal and state courts alike." "The act within its own boundaries of one sovereign State ... becomes ... a rule of decision for the courts of this country." Act of state issues only arise when a court must decide—that is, when the outcome of the case turns upon—the effect of official action by a foreign sovereign. When that question is not in the case, neither is the act of state doctrine. That is the situation here. Regardless of what the court's factual findings may suggest as to the legality of the Nigerian contract, its legality is simply not a question to be decided in the present suit, and there is thus no occasion to apply the rule of decision that the act of state doctrine requires.

Petitioners insist, however, that the policies underlying our act of state cases—international comity, respect for the sovereignty of foreign nations on their own territory, and the avoidance of embarrassment to the Executive Branch in its conduct of foreign relations—are implicated in the present case because, as the District Court found, a determination that Nigerian officials demanded and accepted a bribe "would impugn or question the nobility of a foreign nation's motivations," and would "result in embarrassment to the sovereign or constitute interference in the conduct of foreign polity of the United States." The United States, as amicus curiae, favors the same approach to the act of state doctrine, though disagreeing with petitioners as to the outcome it produces in the present case. We should not, the United States urges, "attach dispositive significance to the fact that this suit involves only the 'motivation' for, rather than the 'validity' of, a foreign sovereign act," and should eschew "any rigid formula for the resolution of act of state cases generally."

continued

continued

But what is appropriate in order to avoid unquestioning judicial acceptance of the acts of foreign sovereigns is not similarly appropriate for the quite opposite purpose of expanding judicial incapacities where such acts are not directly (or even indirectly) involved. It is one thing to suggest, as we have, that the policies underlying the act of state doctrine should be considered in deciding whether, despite the doctrine's technical availability, it should nonetheless not be invoked; it is something quite different to suggest that those underlying policies are a doctrine unto themselves, justifying expansion of the act of state doctrine (or, as the United States puts it, unspecific "related principles of abstention") into new and uncharted fields.

The short of the matter is this: Courts in the United States have the power, and ordinarily the obligation, to decide cases and controversies properly presented to them. The act of state doctrine does not establish an exception for cases and controversies that may embarrass foreign governments, but merely requires that, in the process of deciding, the acts of foreign sovereigns taken within their own jurisdictions shall be deemed valid. That doctrine has no application to the present case because the validity of no foreign sovereign act is at issue.

Decision. The U.S. Supreme Court affirmed the decision of the Court of Appeals, permitting ETC to proceed with its lawsuit against Kirkpatrick.

Justice Scalia suggested in the *Kirkpatrick* case that "some Justices have suggested" a possible exception to the *Act of State Doctrine* for commercial activity. He was referring, specifically, to the plurality opinion of Justice Byron White in *Alfred Dunhill of London, Inc. v. Cuba,* 425 U.S. 682 (1976). In 2002, Judge Garland of the District of Columbia Circuit, writing in *World Wide Minerals Ltd. v. Republic of Kazahkstan,* 296 F.3d 1154, 1166 (D.C. Cir. 2002), observed that this question had not yet been resolved. Other lower courts have split on the question of whether such an exception exists. Until the Supreme Court again addresses the issue, the matter will remain open.

International Adjudication. If it is too difficult to proceed in either the host country or the United States, the investor should look into the possibility of dispute resolution in an international tribunal, a subject addressed in Chapter Three. However, as pointed out there, arbitration is by nature a voluntary action. If one is concerned about a hostile sovereign act, the time to seek the host state's consent to arbitration is before the investment is made, not after it has been expropriated. A carefully drawn arbitration clause in a contract with a government agency can provide reasonable assurance that an expropriation will be adjudicated according to the prevailing principles of international law, which require full compensation.

When contracting with a government agency, the entrepreneur should not blindly rely on the arbitration provision in the contract (the *clause compromissoire*) because the government official agreeing to the provision might have no power to do so. In many nations, national legislation or the national constitution supersedes the contractual provisions that the arbitrator is called upon to interpret. In other cases, the arbitrator cannot pass judgment on the exercise of sovereign power or affect public institutions. In other cases, certain areas of law are excluded from coverage. For example, *Andean Pact Decision 24* once excluded foreign investment contracts and foreign transfer of technology contracts from the jurisdiction of any foreign court or arbitrator. Similarly, Article 100 of the Argentine Constitution prohibits the state from submitting to arbitration on issues arising out of remittance of capital or profits abroad. Under national legislation, relatively straightforward matters such as the payment of damages to an entrepreneur upon the state's breach of an agreement not to take property are generally deemed to be within an arbitrator's power.

The entrepreneur should also be on the alert for special procedural requirements imposed by national laws. Perhaps the most common of these in the context of arbitration is the requirement of a document (the *compromise*), signed by the parties to the *clause compromissoire,* which submits the specific dispute at issue to arbitration. The theory of the compromise is that the parties will begin to come together through the process of framing the dispute for the arbitrator. Obviously, a recalcitrant party can instead make this process the source of unnecessary delay.

These national procedural requirements are as diverse as nations themselves. In the following case, a foreign investor neglected to structure its contract with a government entity so as to ensure that its choice of an international arbitral tribunal would be honored under local law. The result was very bad for the foreign investor.

National Thermal Power Corp. v. The Singer Co.

1993 Y.B. Com. Arb. 403 (1992)

The Supreme Court of India

BACKGROUND AND FACTS

The National Thermal Power Corporation of India (NTPC) entered into a contract with The Singer Company (Singer), a British concern, to supply equipment and erect certain projects in India. A dispute arose and Singer sought arbitration under International Chamber of Commerce (ICC) rules in London, as provided in the contract. Singer won the arbitration and was granted an award by the ICC tribunal. Singer then sought to enforce the award in India under the *Indian Foreign Awards Act,* which limits the role of Indian courts to recognition and enforcement of the foreign arbitral award. NTPC argued against enforcement of the award, claiming that because the contract was governed by Indian law, it was not a "foreign award" under the *Foreign Awards Act.* Therefore, despite the contract's clear submission to ICC arbitration, the whole case should be retried in India under the *Indian Arbitration Act.* The Delhi High Court dismissed NTPC's application and NTPC appealed to the Supreme Court of India.

JUSTICE THOMMEN

The General Terms and Conditions of Contract ... are expressly incorporated in the agreements and they state: "the laws applicable to this Contract shall be the laws in force in India. The Courts of Delhi shall have exclusive jurisdiction in all matters arising under the contract." [Another clause] of the agreement deals with arbitration in respect of a foreign contractor. The latter provision says:

> In the event of foreign Contractor, the arbitration shall be conducted by three arbitrators ... all Rules of Conciliation and Arbitration of the International Chamber of Commerce shall apply to such arbitrations. The arbitration shall be conducted at such places as the arbitrators may determine.

The fundamental question is whether the arbitration agreement contained in the contract is governed by the law of India so as to save it from the ambit of the Foreign Awards Act and attract provisions of the Arbitration Act....

[Counsel for Singer contends] that while the main contract is governed by Indian law, as expressly stated by the parties, arbitration being a collateral contract and procedural in nature, it is not necessarily bound by the proper law of the contract.... London having been chosen in accordance with the ICC Rules to be the seat of arbitration, English law is the proper law of arbitration, and all proceedings connected with it are governed by that law....

[I]f the parties have specifically chosen the law governing the conduct and procedure of arbitration, the arbitration proceedings will be conducted in accordance with that law so long as it is not contrary to the public policy or the mandatory requirements of the law of the country in which the arbitration is held.... Where ... the parties have, as in the instant case, stipulated that the arbitration between them will be conducted in accordance with the ICC Rules, those rules, being in many respects self-contained or self-regulating and constituting a contractual code of procedure, will govern the conduct of the arbitration....

The proper law of the contract in the present case being expressly stipulated to be the laws in force in India and the exclusive jurisdiction of the courts in Delhi in all matters arising under the contract having been specifically accepted, ... the proper law governing the arbitration agreement is indeed the law in force in India, and the competent courts of this country must necessarily have jurisdiction over all matters concerning arbitration. Neither the rules of procedure for the conduct of arbitration contractually chosen by the parties (the ICC Rules) nor the mandatory

continued

continued

requirements of the procedure followed in the courts of the country in which the arbitration is held can in any manner supersede the overriding jurisdiction and control of the Indian law and the Indian courts. . . .

A "foreign award," as defined under the Foreign Awards Act means an award made . . . on differences arising between persons out of legal relationships . . . which are considered to be commercial under the law in force in India. To qualify as a foreign award under the Act, the award should have been made in pursuance of an agreement in writing for arbitration to be governed by the New York Convention or the Recognition and Enforcement of Foreign Arbitration Awards . . . and not to be governed by the law of India. . . . An award is "foreign" not merely because it is made in the territory of a foreign State, but because it is made in such a territory on an arbitration agreement not governed by the law of India. An award made on an arbitration agreement governed by the law of India, though rendered outside India, is . . . not treated in India as a "foreign award." . . .

Such an award necessarily falls under the Arbitration Act and is amenable to the jurisdiction of the Indian Courts and controlled by the Indian system of law just as in the case of any other domestic award. . . .

Decision. The Supreme Court of India set aside the judgment of the Delhi High Court and ordered a retrial of the entire case in India, effectively finding that if Indian law governs a contract, an international arbitration provision is void.

Many countries have agreed to arbitration in cases of investment disputes in *foreign investment codes*. Another source of consent to arbitration is by treaty. The United States has negotiated bilateral investment treaties with a large number of its trading partners under which the host countries consent to arbitration in case of dispute with U.S. investors. The arbitration agreement can provide for *ad hoc* arbitration, as under the United Nations' UNCITRAL Rules, or may refer to an arbitral institution. Perhaps the most significant arbitration agreement involving a government is the *Convention on the Settlement of Investment Disputes Between States and Nationals of Other States*, to which the United States is a party. The Convention provides a forum and a set of rules for the arbitration of disputes between U.S. citizens and signatory countries. Both the citizen and the host country agree that the Convention governs and that all disputes will be resolved by the *International Centre for the Settlement of Investment Disputes* (ICSID). As of May 2007, 156 countries had signed the Convention.

The growth of cross-border trade and investment has also led to a proliferation of bilateral investment treaties (BITs) from the 1980s through the first years of the twenty-first century. Each BIT is a treaty between two trading nations in which each agrees to provide the other's citizens specific investment protections. Typically, BITs offer foreign investors a set of substantive rights, such as national treatment, most-favored-nation treatment, fair and equitable treatment, and guarantees of compensation for expropriation. They also provide foreign investors with direct access to international arbitration to address violations of those substantive rights. At the end of the 1980s, there were approximately 385 BITs. By 2006, the number of BITS had ballooned to more than 2,500. Most BITs designate ICSID as a forum for arbitration, either exclusively or as an option. The principal focus of this network of treaty-enforced international adjudication is to protect investors against state action.

In light of the resurgence of sovereign rights theory in Latin America, it is not surprising that this adjudication system focuses on that area. Of the 112 pending cases before ICSID in July 2007, 61 were against Latin American countries. Developments there demand closer scrutiny.

Developments in International Adjudication, BITs, ICSID, and Latin America. Recent events in Latin America vividly illustrate that an international treaty does not provide assurance of protection against expropriation in the face of shifts in the host country's economic and political climate. The economic crisis in Argentina in 2001–2002 led the government dramatically to end both the official 1-to-1 ratio between the Argentine peso and U.S. dollar and the practice of periodically adjusting consumer electric energy prices according to foreign inflation indices. Foreign investors, who had financed and built electric facilities based on contractual assurances from the Argentine government that prices would be maintained in accordance with those indices, suffered heavy losses. Accordingly, these investors brought action under the U.S.–Argentina BIT at ICSID. Argentina advanced the "necessity" defense, claiming that the measures were necessary in order to avoid an imminent economic and social collapse. They maintained that if prices were allowed to rise, citizens would soon be unable to afford electricity, driving the nation into a downward spiral. In the 2005 ICSID decision in *CMS Gas Transmission Company v. Argentine Republic,* however, the tribunal rejected the necessity argument and entered a $133.2 million judgment against Argentina. Following the *CMS* ruling, Argentina was found to have violated BIT provisions in four other cases, with awards totaling well over $600 million. It did not help the cause of arbitration that, while all panels went against Argentina, one panel ruled that the period from 2001 to 2003 justified the necessity defense, while others found it did not. Thus, the tribunal decisions were irreconcilable and, because there is no substantive appeal in ICSID arbitration, there could be no definitive judicial ruling on the question. The apparent arbitrariness of the judgments—there was no consistent governing legal principle—further damaged the legitimacy of arbitration in Latin America. Latin critics of arbitration had a field day.

In this muddled context, Argentine domestic courts made a preemptive strike against the ICSID system. In *Jose Cartellone Construcciones Civiles SA v. Hidroelectrica Norpatagonica SA,* the Argentine Supreme Court held that it had the right to review arbitral awards if they were unconstitutional, illegal, or "unreasonable," even if the parties to the investment dispute had explicitly waived the right to appeal to national courts. The Court also held that a waiver of appeal to domestic courts cannot be construed to waive the right to appeal awards that are rendered against public policy. While the decision only addressed a domestic arbitral award under ICSID Rules, *Cartellone* served notice that if the awards against Argentina are not reversed, Argentine domestic courts might simply invalidate them as "unreasonable" or against public policy. Indeed, political leaders have said as much, and gone so far as to introduce legislation intending to limit international arbitral awards unless they are subject to appeal in Argentine courts.

Argentina is not the only place to experience the awakening of Calvo or sovereign rights theory. After nationalizing its oil and gas industry on May 1, 2006, Bolivia became the first country to ever withdraw from the ICSID Convention in anticipation of foreign investor arbitrations. Since that time, Bolivia has also moved toward nationalizing its railroad system and sections of the mining industry. But events in Bolivia are not all running in the direction of treaty repudiation: In May 2006, the Bolivian Constitutional Tribunal rendered *Judgment 0031/2006,* which found that Bolivian laws ratifying BITs are constitutional and that the BITs, once ratified by Bolivia, are not subject to review. Enforcement of arbitral awards, of course, should follow. Bolivia has signaled its intention to revise its BITs, most notably, to limit investor-state arbitration to domestic venues.

Since Venezuelans reelected President Hugo Chavez in 2000 and 2006 and international petroleum prices began to surge, Venezuela has embarked on a program of "oil socialism." In April of 2006, Venezuela seized oil fields operated by two multinational oil companies after they refused to convert their contracts into joint ventures with Venezuela. Another sixteen companies avoided such a takeover by agreeing to new contracts with Venezuela, ceding majority control over to the state oil company PDVSA. In May 2007, Venezuela seized the four major oil ventures in the Orinoco Belt. Because Venezuela has abundant oil revenues, it has generally been able to avoid arbitration by making financial settlements with foreign investors. The nationalizations have produced few arbitrations, because companies fear that any move against Venezuela in an international forum will seal their investment fate in Venezuela. Tellingly, the renegotiated joint venture agreements require foreign investors to submit all disputes to domestic Venezuelan arbitration. In mid-2007, oil giant Exxon-Mobil finally initiated an ICSID proceeding against Venezuela, which will test the ability of private investors to enforce BITs against expropriation. Exxon-Mobil proceeded to freeze over $14 billion of Venezuelan assets in pre-judgment actions in New York, London, and Zurich to ensure that any arbitral judgment ultimately rendered would be enforced. It is too early to declare the passing of sovereign rights theory.

Historical Development of Privatization

Although privatization is the opposite of nationalization, the two are historically intertwined. In the Middle Ages, the national monarch owned the great bulk of property. Indeed, the monarch's grant of fiefs in that property formed the basis for the feudal system. In due course, sovereigns saw that by permitting merchants to own property in exchange for taxes, they could generate substantial revenues and create an effective counterpoint to the nobility. The centralized nation-state soon followed. Not until the rise of the merchant and industrial classes did private property become important. It was at that time that Grotius, a good son of merchant burghers, shaped the limitations on the powers of a sovereign to "nationalize" the property of a foreign merchant.

Some sovereigns began to realize that if they, like feudal lords, transferred property to private parties who would better develop and manage it, they could realize tax revenues from otherwise valueless assets. One of the first "sovereigns" to do so extensively was the United States of America, a nation possessed of vast undeveloped natural resources. For example, American law favored the right of millers to dam a river over the rights of downstream property owners because the United States wanted to encourage the development effects of mills. Similarly, entrepreneurs were given concessions to build and collect tolls from canals they built, to encourage the building of canals. The *Homestead Acts* transferred government land to those who farmed it. Federal land management laws permitted private ranchers to graze on government land at low fees. A similar privatization trend was taking place throughout the world, particularly in Europe's colonial possessions. By the end of the nineteenth century, the bulk of the world's wealth was in private hands.

This trend was reversed by Marx's indictment of the excesses of capitalist economics. Marxist views were fully or partially accepted in Russia and other communist countries, newly independent African and Asian nations, and newly elected labor or other leftist governments in Western Europe and Latin America. These governments nationalized or expropriated all or large parts of the private sector, especially those parts of the private sector owned by foreigners.

But government's ability to develop property had not improved in the intervening centuries. Without the engine of the individual profit incentive, nationalized enterprises grew inefficient and flaccid. The nationalized enterprise gradually went from producing profits for the government to requiring subsidies from the government to cover its losses. The nationalization trend collapsed and privatization returned. In the late 1970s and the 1980s, Great Britain's Thatcher government began sales of government assets, reversing the nationalizations of industry effected by Labour governments decades earlier.

Mrs. Thatcher's ideas became fashionable in other developed nations and the privatization process took hold. Countries as diverse as France, Japan, and Argentina soon effected privatizations of their own industries. Upon the fall of the communist bloc in 1989, privatization expanded to transform the economies of former nonmarket economies. Even mainland China and Vietnam, the last major bastions of communism, developed business forms that transferred control of assets to private entrepreneurs, especially foreign investors. The recent trend away from privatization in some Latin countries has not affected the great bulk of privatizations.

Preparation for Privatization

The focus of this chapter now turns to the specifics of the structure of the privatization process.

Privatization takes many forms. Indeed, each combination of assets, sellers, and purchasers requires its own particular structure for privatization. Although in many ways privatization can be like acquiring a division of a private company, the steps that sellers take to prepare for privatization, the structure of those sales, and the legal concerns that they raise tend to be different from those of other asset transfers.

At the outset of the process, the industry to be privatized is a functioning unit of the national government. Whether it is a steel manufacturer or an individual power plant, its purpose is to further national interests, as defined by the government's political leaders. National interests typically dictate increasing the volume of the enterprise's output or the number of persons it employs. Profit is only incidentally one of these interests. (In fact, in many former communist countries the concept of profit was unknown.) The fact that the expenses associated with bloated employee numbers may overwhelm an enterprise's revenues is not of particular concern for the enterprise's managers. All revenues go into the state and all expenses are covered by the state. Government employees, whose purpose is public service, not private gain, staff the government enterprise. The enterprise's equipment may have been chosen to maximize employment, rather than to minimize unit cost. If the enterprise received free supplies or natural resources from other government divisions, those supplies may have been used in a wasteful manner.

If such an enterprise were put on the block "as is," it might not attract a buyer. In addition, the prospective purchaser would not have reliable financial information from which to make a risk assessment. This is why the privatizing government needs to prepare the asset for sale before privatizing it.

Similarly, the legal infrastructure for private investment must be created. International investors require a functioning commercial code. They require an understandable regulatory regime governing the newly privatized enterprise. They need to understand competitive requirements. Preparing national assets for privatization has become a critical part of the process. The process of preparing government assets for privatization has four standard steps, described below.

The Creation and Organization of an Independent Government Corporation

The privatization process typically begins with a functioning unit of the government, such as the national telecommunications ministry or the national steel manufacturing ministry. The assets that are necessary for the unit to function are segregated and transferred to a new corporate entity, the stock of which is wholly owned by the government. Thus, the Telecommunications Administration of the Ministry of Communication becomes Telco, Inc., a government-owned company.

This transfer is generally followed by a transitional period during which the new entity begins to operate as a private enterprise. It will record its expenses and its revenues separately from those of the government and develop financial statements that will permit potential purchasers to assess its performance. The framework of non–fair market value exchanges with other government units and lax accounting practices is disassembled. During this transitional period, the government continues to fund net capital needs of the fledgling enterprise. This process takes much of the guesswork out of privatization acquisitions, permitting the right investor to come into the company at the right price.

Preparation of a Legal System for Privatization

Before foreign investors acquire an interest in former government assets, they will want a solid legal infrastructure in place. This infrastructure creates clear rights of property and enforceability of contracts.

"Clearing" of Expropriation Claims. Before any transfer of assets to private hands can occur, the government must develop a property system that permits *clearing title* or eliminating combatting claims of ownership to such assets. Many assets owned by governments were once "nationalized" from private parties. The people who owned the assets before the government nationalized them may have a restitution claim against the government based on a wrongful nationalization or expropriation. Unless title is cleared, that claim might be available against the purchaser of the asset.

To solve this problem, governments frequently create a legal network whereby the victim of expropriation must either assert its claim within a specified period or waive it. If the period passes without a claim, the government can transfer the asset with clear title. If restitution claims are asserted, a system is put in place for prompt rulings.

If a quick sale is desired, the government may forego a title-clearing procedure and assume responsibility for possible adverse claims. For example, Germany's privatization trust, the Treuhand, issued an Investment Preference Decision (*Investitionsvorrangbescheid*) when it wished to promote investment in a priority sector. If an investor complies with the conditions of the decision—such as by making a specified level of investment—restitution claims are blocked. In *blocked claims,* the government often limits the expropriation victim to the proceeds of the sale of the asset if the sale is deemed to have been conducted under reasonable commercial terms.

The investor must be sure that it obtains approval of the transaction from whichever government office has the authority to waive these restitution liabilities. Frequently that office is different from the office actually selling the asset.

Property and Contract Law. In former communist countries, the state was the only legitimate repository of wealth. Expropriation and nationalization was so complete that there was no longer a legal concept of private property. The recognition of private property rights is essential to privatization. If the investor cannot obtain clear assurance of its right to own the property as it is developed, its incentive to invest is diminished.

A functioning system of private property requires establishment of laws governing the acquisition and transfer of title, filing registries for real property mortgages, systems for acquiring and recording chattel mortgages, and other unglamorous mechanisms. Russia, for example, passed a law on mortgages in 1991, but was very slow to establish the filing registries necessary to implement the law. Without the registries, mortgage financing—a bedrock of capital investment in the West—can operate only with great complexity, unnecessary expense, and substantial risk.

A free market maximizes value by permitting and enforcing voluntary exchanges between independent merchants. In capitalist economies, contract law performs this exchange function. Before launching privatization, therefore, a government must implement a modern contract law system.

Methods of Distribution

The final preparation for privatization is the development of a plan to distribute shares. Shares can be distributed in private or public equity placements, through a voucher system, or as debt-for-equity swaps.

Private and Public Equity Placements. The simplest transfer of ownership is to sell to a single group of investors. Typically, such an investment is part of a strategic entry into the local market or an acquisition of new manufacturing capacity. The deal is worked out in direct negotiations between government and investor groups and is made firm in a shareholders' agreement between them.

The government may also sell ownership interests to the passive investing public through the sale of part of the enterprise's stock on local stock exchanges and may sell another portion in foreign equity markets through American Depository Receipts or other similar securities.

Voucher Systems. Governments also occasionally transfer public assets to their citizens for free. The concept underlying these *voucher* systems is that in order for capitalism to take hold, stock ownership should be widespread among the national population. In populations in which the standard of living is low, most people do not have the resources to invest, so the objective of wide distribution can only be achieved through free distribution. Further, the theory continues, the people have paid for their shares through years of laboring for a state-owned system.

This type of distribution typically begins with the issuance of voucher coupon booklets that contain points for bidding on shares in state firms. These vouchers may be distributed to the entire population or to a portion of the population with a specific interest in the enterprise being privatized, such as its workers or citizens of a region greatly affected by the enterprise.

Often private citizens entrust their vouchers to large private investment funds that pool vouchers. These funds then bid against one another to acquire specific entities being privatized. After a fund or group of funds acquires the asset, they, as the owners of the enterprise, enter into transactions with foreign investors. With the financial assistance of multilateral banks, many of these funds actually finance and direct the process of preparing the former public entity for the subsequent transfer of interests to international investors. In this way, the investment funds effectively take the place of the government in privatizing the enterprise.

Voucher systems do not always work well. In Russia, private citizens—who lacked knowledge about capital markets and were often in dire need of cash—promptly sold their vouchers to unscrupulous individuals at low prices. Massive numbers of vouchers were soon concentrated in the hands of people with few entrepreneurial credentials. Similar experiences led subsequent voucher programs, such as Poland's National Investment Fund program, to require eligible members of the public to make a modest payment for the vouchers. In Hungary, the government permits citizens to pay off the modest sum over a number of years and does not transfer the vouchers until final payment is made. Other nations make the vouchers nontransferable during the transitional period.

Debt-for-Equity Swaps. A popular mechanism in selling state assets is the *debt-for-equity swap*. One popular type of debt swap involves the exchange of external sovereign debt for internal equity. In essence, the government permits foreign investors to pay for the government's equity in the entity to be privatized with debt instruments of that government.

The debt of many governments, of course, is in default and may be purchased at a substantial discount from current holders. If the investor can purchase a government's debt for twenty cents on the dollar, it can buy $1 million of the government's debt for only $200,000, thereby conserving its hard currency. By pursuing such a strategy in its many privatizations, the Argentine government drastically slashed the national debt.

In a second type of swap, local investors exchange external debt for internal debt. Host country investors obtain debt instruments of the host country government being traded abroad at a discount with their hard currency assets, convert them into local currency–denominated debt, and resell them in the host country as internal debt. This latter approach has the positive side effect of reversing capital flight from the host country. By allowing residents to use assets abroad to purchase external debt and convert it to domestic debt, privatization of a company actually improves the nation's balance of payments.

Models of Privatization

Privatizations can be organized into four groups or "models" to facilitate one's understanding of the various important characteristics. Few real-world transactions will be "pure" examples of any one of the models. Most will include elements of more than one model.

Sale of a Noncontrolling Interest

The least radical type of privatization involves the sale of a substantial but *noncontrolling interest* in the enterprise to private investors. The predominant feature of this model is that control remains in the hands of the government employees who formerly managed the asset for the government, and the government retains a substantial equity interest in the new enterprise (see Exhibit 19.2).

A noncontrolling interest is often sold to a single strategic investor. In such cases, the purchaser can try to ameliorate the downside of continued government control through the terms of an agreement between the government (in its capacity as public shareholder) and the private shareholder. Such shareholder agreements lay out the terms under which the private shareholder takes the stock. The agreement normally gives it specified rights and protections greater than those of a typical minority investor. Of course, when governments are replaced, they can sometimes be unfaithful to such promises.

If the sale does not involve a strategic investor, the privatization of a minority holding will not bring in new expertise. The passive investor, after all, wants to pick a manager for its investment and then go looking for other investments. Private investors typically do not wish to put their money in an enterprise in which critical decisions affecting profit will be made by an entity that does not

Exhibit 19.2

Partial Sale

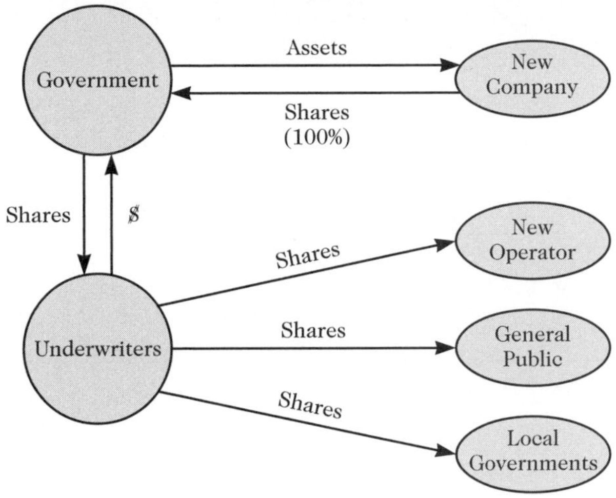

react to the profit motive. Such a sale does not, therefore, achieve the objective of injecting entrepreneurship into the entity and typically results in lower private investor interest and a smaller capital investment.

Some governments retain some control even after selling a majority interest in the enterprise by creating a stock interest called a *golden share.* The golden share gives no economic rights, but can limit the private investors' voting rights to a set threshold, place government appointees on the company board, or give the holder veto power over board decisions in certain specified areas. At times, this veto power is stated in general "wherever necessary to further national interest" terms. The government that uses this strategy does not wish to turn a significant source of national employment and manufacturing over to people outside its control. In short, it is reluctant to cede power.

Another way for the government to retain control while transferring a majority interest is to reserve a substantial portion of the shares for local or provincial governments or labor unions. Unless the private entrepreneur is well connected with the local polity, the local government can be expected to vote in a manner consistent with the national government, particularly on issues of employment reduction.

The Trade Sale

At the opposite end of the privatization spectrum is the *trade sale* model, the transfer of control of the unit's assets to a single private investor or group of investors. The distinguishing feature of this model is that the purchaser ultimately controls the use of the assets. It decides which of the former employees are kept and what capital plant improvements are to be made. The government may pursue the trade sale either as a stock sale or as a sale of assets (see Exhibit 19.3).

If the former government unit primarily provided services, the government may achieve privatization through *management contracts* whereby the government contracts with a private firm to perform services formerly provided by the government. Such services can range from maintenance of port facilities to trash pickup. Using management contracts may make it possible for the government to sell some state-owned assets. The government's participation is no longer needed now that the contractor is operating the enterprise.

A variation of this asset trade sale concept occurs when a private firm is sold a right, called a *concession,* to provide a service or infrastructure over which the state can exercise substantial

EXHIBIT 19.3

Trade Sale

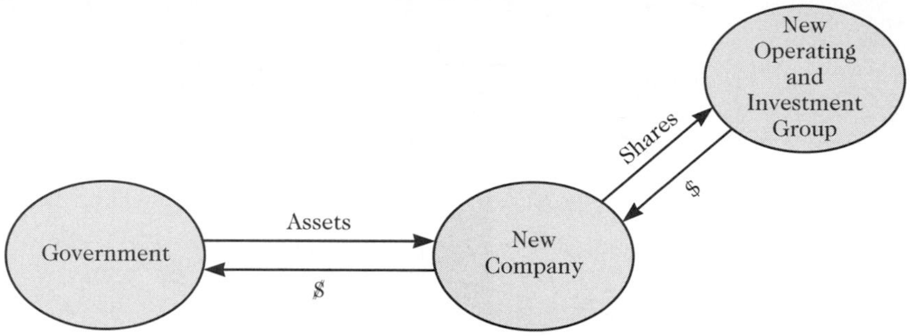

control. The concession is discussed in greater depth in the following section.

ADVANTAGES AND DISADVANTAGES OF THE TRADE SALE. A trade sale has many advantages. First, of course, it is the capitalist ideal of privatization. It brings assets into the hands of private entrepreneurs with a strong financial incentive to transform the former state entity into one that can function in a competitive market. Second, it is the speediest way to effect privatization and reduces the need for government interference during any transitional period. Third, it is an especially useful way to sell small companies for which demand is low in equity markets. In countries such as the Czech Republic, small shops were simply transferred to the individuals or families who had previously operated them for the state.

The trade sale also presents disadvantages. First, the complete takeover of a national company by a foreign entity can lead to backlash from the local population. When Spanish-owned Iberia Airlines acquired Aerolineas Argentinas, many Argentines condemned a "new Spanish colonialization." Such publicity was unhelpful to a firm such as Aerolineas Argentinas, an airline that relied primarily on the patronage of Argentines. To avoid this type of problem in a trade sale, the new entrepreneur group should consider including significant local participation.

Second, a trade sale also places a great deal of responsibility on private entrepreneurs who may not have the capital resources necessary to make the privatization succeed. In fact, some would-be privatizers have collapsed into bankruptcy soon after the sale. Thus, the government has a stake in carefully exploring the financial depth of the buyer in a trade sale.

The Sale to Employees

Privatization can also be structured as a transfer to the enterprise's former employees, without retention of control by the government. Under this model, existing management and employees become the new owners, most often in conjunction with a group of outside private investors (see Exhibit 19.4).

Within the private sector in developed economies, acquisitions of companies by their management and supporting investment groups are known as *leveraged buyouts* (LBOs). In that context, management enlists private investors to purchase a private company as majority partners. These investors give the members of management a minority equity stake because of the value they add to the assets of the company. This also gives management a financial incentive to make the enterprise succeed.

In the context of public enterprises, giving the current senior government employees an equity stake in the new enterprise serves the same objectives, as well as others peculiar to privatizations. First, privatizations are political transactions that require broad support within the government. Senior government officials who have a financial

Exhibit 19.4

Sale to Management or Employees

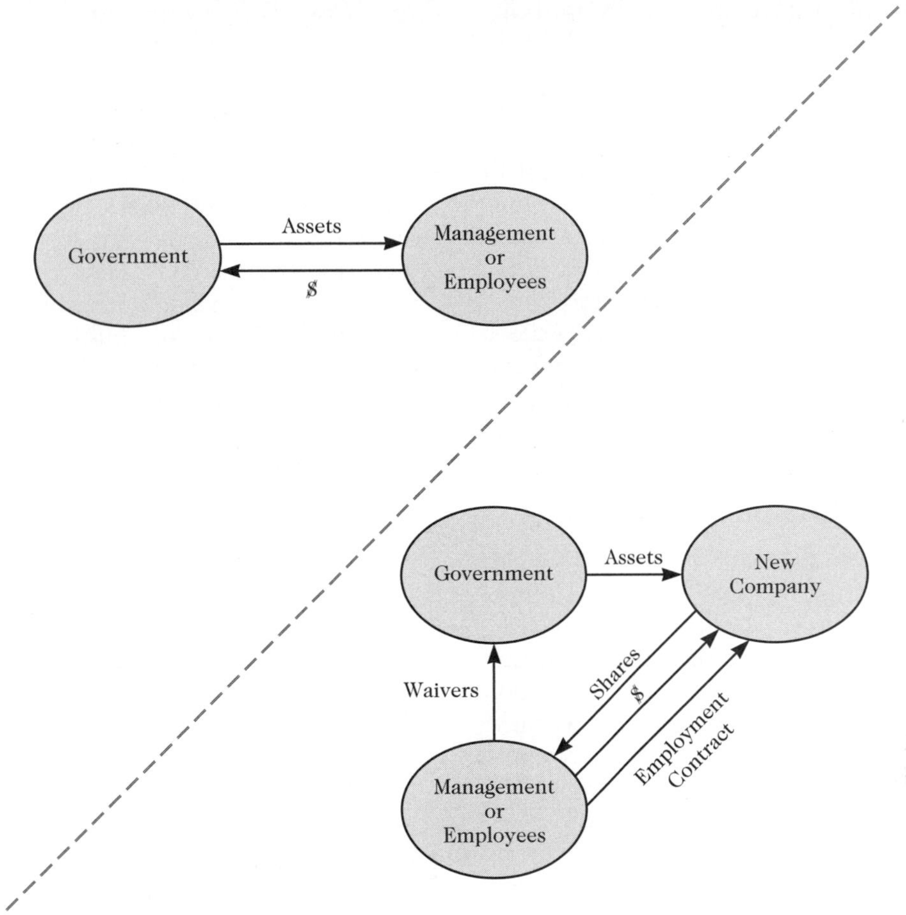

stake in privatization (as future shareholders) will favor it more readily than if they have no stake in its outcome. Second, lower-level employees will generally be asked to make wage, pension, and work rule concessions to the new private entity. Resistance from government employees is perhaps the greatest barrier to privatization. In many Latin American countries, for example, union representatives of these employees have used their considerable political influence to prevent or retard privatization. In such circumstances, including a significant employee ownership element in the privatization structure may be necessary to quell opposition from employee groups. Third, in the case of Eastern European nations, not all traces of socialist ideology have been erased from consciousness. The concept of excluding workers from ownership remains politically unattractive. Russian lawmakers have entertained legislation that called for leasing of state property to workers' collectives with a subsequent option to purchase. Similarly, the Czech and Slovak privatizations issued a percentage of shares to workers for free. In a privatization of a Polish chocolate waffle manufacturer by a Swiss concern, 20 percent of the new company's privatization order specifically provides for sale of equity to workers at half price.

This LBO model has occurred in a relatively pure form in some developed nations, such as in the privatization of British Telecomm. But in less-developed nations, it occurs principally as a facilitating element. Most government units are being privatized largely because they are poorly managed. Therefore, existing upper government officials are not viewed as adding significant value to the underlying assets. As for the rank and file, privatization is often a prelude to the dismissal of large segments of the bureaucracy under a regime in which expenses are incurred to generate revenues. Placing substantial numbers of shares in the hands of ex-employees makes little sense. Nonetheless, foreign investors can expect to issue a number of shares to employees of the old government unit as a necessary part of concluding the acquisition of privatized government assets.

Concessions: BOTs and BOOs

A different sort of privatization involves "conceding" to private parties the right to perform a function previously reserved to the government. The most common of these is the right to build different types of infrastructure—electric generation plants, ports, airports, highways, bridges, tunnels, mineral extraction facilities—and the accompanying right to collect revenues generated by the infrastructure. In contrast to other privatizations, the government is not transferring an existing asset. Instead, it is transferring a right to earn revenues in order to encourage the building of a new asset.

BOTs and BOOs. There are two basic types of concessions. In the more common concession, the government grants the right to collect revenues for a number of years. After the term of the concession, the right and the asset built by the concessionaire revert back to the state. Under this model, often referred to as a *Build-Operate-Transfer* (BOT) transaction, shown in Exhibit 19.5, the government obtains an infrastructure asset that promotes development of the economy without making any current capital expenditures.

The duration of the BOT concession is generally sufficient for the investor group to repay the debt it incurred and recoup its equity outlay with a profit. This period can vary widely depending upon the project. The period in the British Channel Tunnel is fifty years; the period in the Malaysian North/South Expressway is thirty years; power generation projects often have periods of ten to twenty-five years. At times, rather than a fixed term of years, the parties will use benchmarks, such as the repayment of debt financing.

In the second major type of concession, the government actually sells the concessionaire a "permanent" concession. These transactions, called *Build-Operate-Own* (BOO) deals, are common in infrastructure projects that involve particularly high risk and therefore require particularly high incentives. For example, the high risk normally associated with doing business in many less-developed African nations often requires that the BOO model be followed. Similarly, in countries with an emphatic history of state intervention in the economy, governments pursue BOO projects to give an added measure of assurance to the private investment community that the move to privatization is not a passing political phase.

The Concession and Anticompetitive Considerations. Because the government is granting a right to perform an activity in which it has a monopoly, the recipient of the right will expect to receive at least some part of the monopoly right for some period of time. For example, a concessionaire will not assume the risk of building a railroad line if the government is then free to use the roadbed that the concessionaire has graded to build a competing line.

Because infrastructure projects by their nature generally involve modifying the environment in a way that facilitates later competitive investment, such monopoly concessions are common. The concession to the company that built the English Channel Tunnel specified that England and France would not help finance, through public funds or public guarantees, any competing connection during the fifty-year term of the concession. Without such state help, any competitor would face a difficult road.

The government must take steps to prevent abuse of the economic power a monopoly implies. This includes not only pricing abuses, but asset maintenance and service issues as well. In the absence of a free market that ensures good service and safe equipment at fair prices, the

EXHIBIT 19.5

BOT Transaction

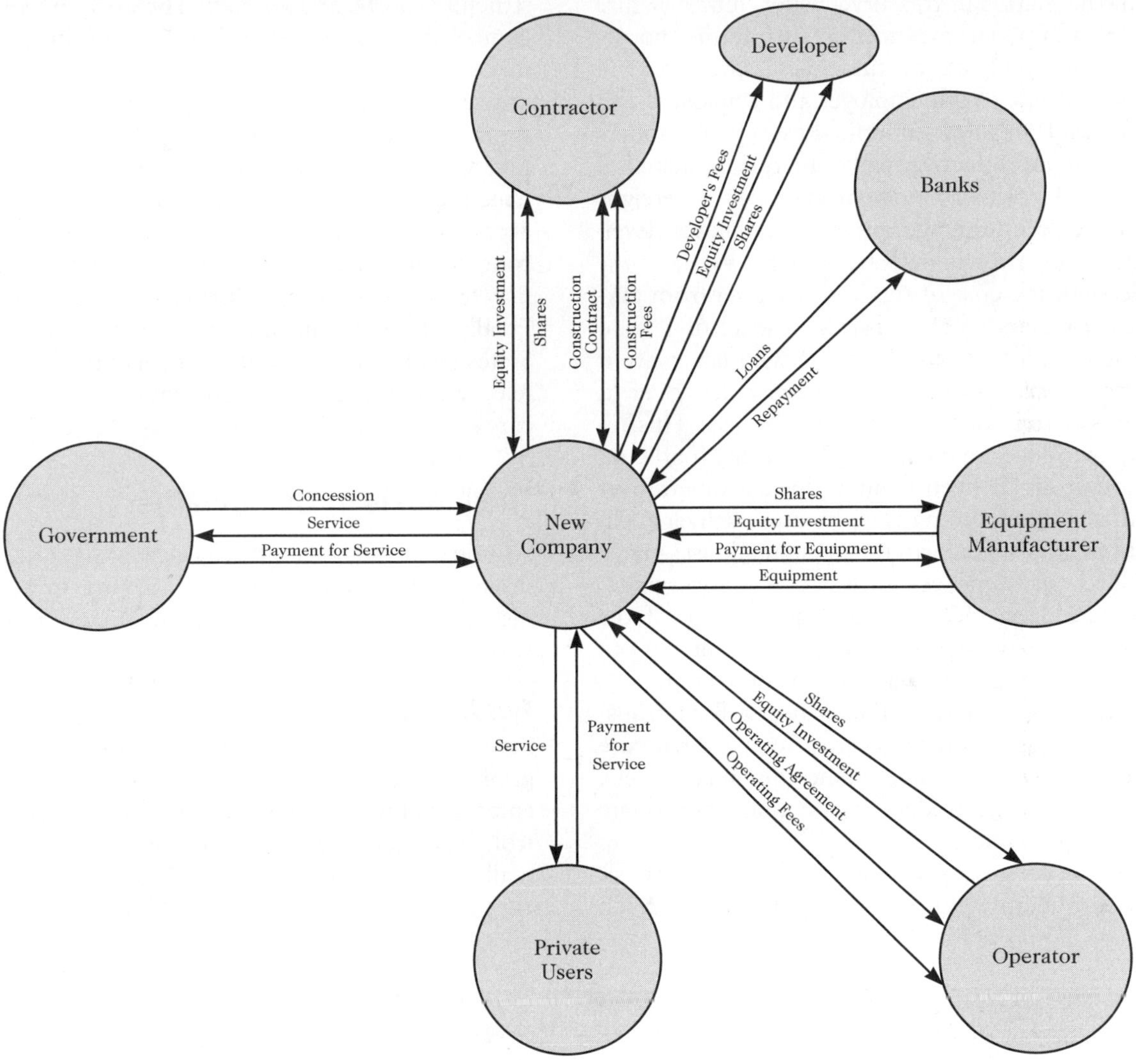

government must devise reasonable alternatives. These concerns are addressed through controls on the concessionaire's pricing, either through regulation or in the concession contract itself. For example, if the project suffers cost overruns due to the fault of the concessionaire, it must not be permitted to recover that overrun through price increases.

The best remedy to monopoly power is to end it. Accordingly, governments have been increasingly aggressive in limiting the term of monopoly rights to reasonable periods for the repayment of debt and return on investment.

ADVANTAGES AND DISADVANTAGES OF THE CONCESSION. In granting a concession, the government cedes control for the duration of the concession over a crucial aspect of the national economy—its infrastructure—to people who may not have the interests of the nation foremost in their minds.

There are, however, substantial advantages that counter the drawbacks.

First, the government adds an infrastructure asset to the nation without having to spend any sums from the national treasury. Better infrastructure attracts additional investment, which further boosts the economy. Each of these new investors will employ citizens. Both employer and employees will pay taxes. Instead of an outflow from public coffers to sustain unproductive public enterprises, there is a substantial positive inflow of taxes. As sovereigns discovered centuries ago, privatization moves development forward while the treasury grows.

Second, the cost of services is shifted from taxpayers to users of the services. Instead of a road that is paid for equally by those who never use it and those who routinely send semitrailers over it, there is a toll road that charges by use. This, in turn, introduces market discipline. If the road concessionaire is to keep winning his customers over from their free alternatives, he must deliver well-maintained roads worth the price of admission.

Third, in some transactions, the government may be able to negotiate an equity share of the project company. In such cases, the government can actually earn a profit from its own concession.

Fourth, at the end of the term of a BOT transaction, the government receives an infrastructure asset of substantial value. Some equipment assets, such as roads and bridges, may actually appreciate in value over time.

Finally, concessions enhance the nation's physical and human technological infrastructure. Such projects bring in and improve the use of modern technology and train local citizens in the use of such technology.

The government's loss of control over its infrastructure can be ameliorated. The government can control the central network that these infrastructure projects connect to. An independent electric power producer must generally sell all or a substantial portion of its output into the national grid. Likewise, a bridge services the national road system, and so on. By controlling the concessionaire's access, the government can maintain a measure of control over the concessionaire. The concession may also contain performance requirements. Finally, the government can do what the United States has historically done with its private utility, telecommunications, transportation, and health care sectors. It can regulate.

The Models in Combination

As noted at the outset, the models of privatization discussed here seldom occur in a pure form. For instructive purposes, a review of a few "impure" variations is helpful.

The Joint Venture Privatization. A government may compromise its desire for control enough to grant the investor group an even share of the new enterprise, but not enough to give it minority control. The resulting joint venture privatization is really a mix of the trade sale model and the non-controlling interest model (see Exhibit 19.6).

Exhibit 19.6

Joint Venture

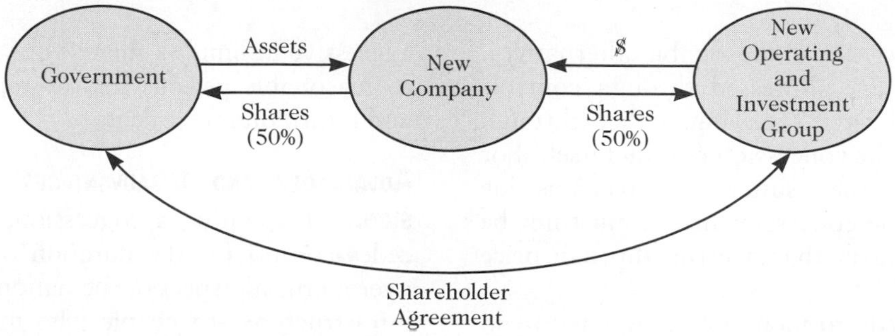

Because of the ensured equity deadlock in the joint venture structure, most of the important issues are addressed in the shareholders' agreement between the parties. In a typical government–foreign investor joint venture, such a shareholder agreement will grant the investor control over most day-to-day operating matters. The government maintains control over certain issues in which it has a special interest, such as minimum production or employment levels.

EXAMPLE OF PRIVATIZATION MIXING MODELS. Some privatization deals include a little of everything. The following model, outlined in Exhibit 19.7, addresses a number of issues.

The transaction begins with the government transferring public assets, including a concession, to a new company for 40 percent of the shares and a waiver of some pension and other rights from its former employees. Simultaneously, the private operator makes a significant capital contribution in the new firm in exchange for 50 percent of the new company. The employees enter into a labor contract with the new firm on more favorable terms than their former contract with the government and waive rights against the government in exchange for 10 percent of the new company.

To obtain cash for the national treasury immediately, the government sells three-fourths of its holding—30 percent of the new company—to underwriters for distribution to the general public. As a condition of the sale, the government requires the underwriters to resell a portion of the stock to the local national public on local stock exchanges. In addition to generating revenue for the public coffers, the offering gives a broad segment of the citizenry a stake in the venture. The government maintains a 10 percent interest in order to retain a voice in the affairs of the firm and to realize some of the long-term equity growth associated with a successful new venture.

EXHIBIT 19.7

Mixed Example

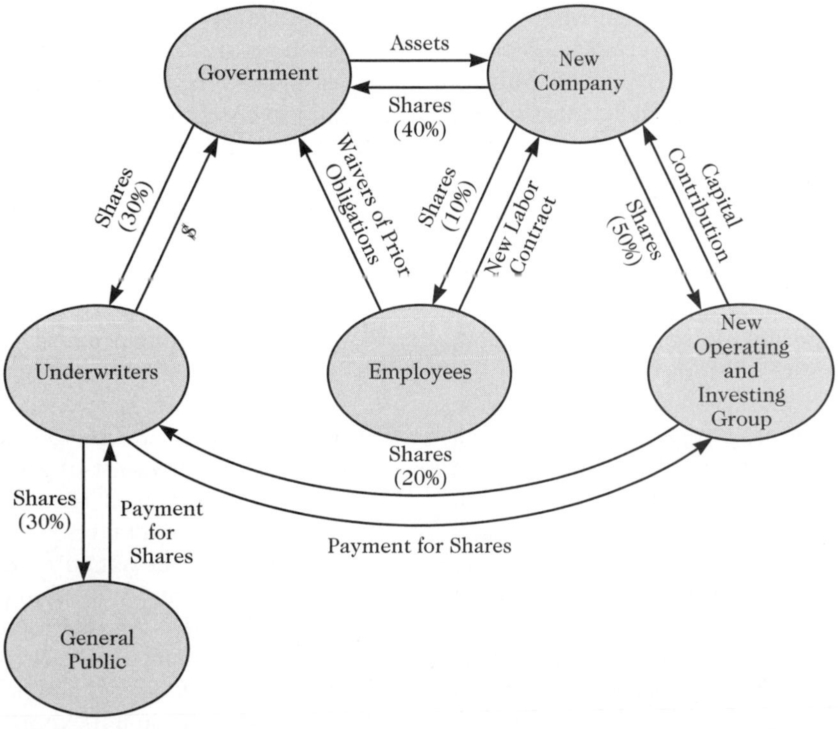

Similarly, the operator reduces its capital exposure by reselling part of its stake—20 percent of the new company—to the public in an underwritten offering. This sale on the international equity market ensures the highest possible return to the operator. The operator retains a 30 percent block, which is sufficient in light of how widely held the balance of the stock is. After the smoke clears, the passive investing public holds 50 percent of the stock, assuring the operator of continued effective control with its 30 percent block. The transaction is essentially a trade sale, but has broad elements of the employee purchase, noncontrolling interest, and concession financing models. In short, it is privatization soup.

As privatization has encompassed more and more industries, a real debate has arisen as to the proper limits of this technique. Are there any government activities that ought not to be run for profit? Should air traffic control be privatized? Police? Jails? This question continues to fuel the debate on the proper limits of privatization as it has encompassed more and more industries.

Conclusion

U.S. citizens who invest in sovereign rights countries—even those privatizing government assets or services—need to consider seriously the possibility that the foreign sovereign will take their investment. All such investors must decide whether they wish to assume the risk of litigating such a taking or whether they wish to obtain political risk insurance to cover it. Those investors who choose the former will wish to place themselves in the best position possible by having appropriate international arbitration or litigation provisions that both establish the measure of compensation due and identify the arbiter that will do the measuring. Arbitration or litigation is perhaps best done in a nation where the ground rules have been set by a bilateral investment treaty between the foreign nation and the United States. If the investors decide to obtain insurance covering political risk, they should avail themselves of the alternative that presents the best mixture of cost and flexibility. In making these decisions, investors should consider the fact that the law in this area is in a state of evolution. Risk is therefore exacerbated by the element of unpredictability.

The privatization of formerly state-run enterprises is the most important development in international corporate law in recent memory. Its dramatic rise has virtually eliminated nonmarket economies and has made the private corporation or partnership the most important economic factor in the international marketplace. With its rise, nations have lost direct control over labor and environmental issues and have turned to regulation as a way to curb capitalism's less attractive tendencies.

Chapter Summary

1. The modern–traditional theory recognizes the sovereign's right to nationalize foreign-owned property, but places conditions on the proper exercise of that right. The exercise of the right must be (1) for a public purpose; (2) nondiscriminatory (not directed specifically against a particular foreign person); and (3) accompanied by prompt, adequate, and effective compensation. To modern–traditional thinkers, "adequate" compensation meant fair market value as a going concern, including future earnings and intangibles; "prompt" meant as soon as reasonable, and "effective" meant cash or a commodity immediately available and freely convertible to cash.
2. In the first decade of the twenty-first century, the Latin American countries of Argentina, Bolivia, Venezuela, Nicaragua, and Ecuador have rejected the jurisdiction of international arbitral tribunals to adjudicate alleged nationalizations/expropriations and, in some cases, have re-nationalized assets of foreign investors.
3. An expropriation is a taking of an isolated item of property where the foreign investor is singled out as the target of governmental action. A nationalization is the taking of an entire industry or a natural resource as part of a plan to restructure the nation's economic system. In a nationalization, full compensation is not required under sovereign rights theories. Political risk insurance protects foreign investors against foreign takings and political violence.
4. A number of capital-exporting nations have established government corporations that

provide political risk insurance. Such insurance is also available through the internationally based Multilateral Investment Guarantee Agency, Lloyds of London syndicates, and groups operating under international reinsurance treaties. Private insurance is more expensive, but it is more easily and quickly available. All insurance programs avoid areas of active nationalizing governments.

5. If an investment is nationalized, a victim may seek relief in the courts of the country where the property was nationalized, in the courts of the investor's own nation, or in international arbitral tribunals.
6. Bringing a legal action in the United States has a number of hurdles. First, under the *Foreign Sovereign Immunities Act of 1976,* a federal court would not have jurisdiction over the foreign nation unless the state's acts fall within a commercial activity exemption to immunity. Second, a U.S. court might abstain from exercising jurisdiction under the Act of State Doctrine. Third, unless there is an applicable treaty, U.S. courts may decline to hear a case if most of the evidence is abroad.
7. The "commercial activity" exception provides that a foreign state will not be immune from U.S. jurisdiction if the action is based upon an act outside the United States in connection with the commercial activity of the foreign state and causes a direct effect on the United States, such as where the foreign state enters into a commercial contract with an investor and is acting as a private commercial party.
8. The act of state doctrine is a principle of decision binding on U.S. courts to the effect that when the outcome of a case turns on the effect of an official action by a foreign state, U.S. courts will deem the acts of foreign sovereigns taken within their own jurisdictions to be valid.
9. The most important arbitration agreement for claims against governments is the *Convention on the Settlement of Investment Disputes Between States and Nationals of Other States,* which provides a forum and a set of rules for the arbitration of disputes between foreign investors and signatory countries. If both the citizen and the host country agree in the investment documents that the Convention governs, disputes will be resolved by the International Centre for the Settlement of Investment Disputes (ICSID).
10. Privatization is the opposite of nationalization. The foreign government sells a government asset or right to provide a service to private parties.

Questions and Case Problems

1. Pursuant to Bulgaria's new joint venture program, Zasada, Inc., a U.S. firm, constructs a football helmet manufacturing facility in Sofia to produce helmets for export to the United States. Four years later, a change in the Russian Parliament leads to domestic policy reversals. Russia annexes Bulgaria as a member of its federation and takes possession of all Bulgarian factories that employ more than twenty-five people, including Zasada's helmet facility. Was this a nationalization or an expropriation? How would the *INA Corp.* tribunal assess the appropriate compensation to Zasada? How would a traditional theory court measure that compensation? How would a modern–traditional theory court measure that compensation? What do these decisions suggest about the development of compensation theory?
2. Economic development in the Republic of Costa Azul is perceived to be hindered by the ownership of all farmland by a few families and a few firms, some of which are U.S.-owned. A new government is democratically elected on a platform of land redistribution. The government, however, has no currency to buy such land and lacks the credit necessary to borrow significant sums. If Costa Azul cannot afford to pay "prompt and just" compensation for foreign private property, should it refrain from initiating social change? Does it make a difference if Costa Azul refrains from taking the land and instead increases property taxes on lots greater than twenty-five hectares by a factor of 100?
3. How should the FSIA apply if a government purchases private property as an embassy and violates local ordinances in its operation? What if

a government-owned airline sells a tour package to a private citizen, then detains her and refuses her entry into the country as an undesirable? What if the government retains a consulting firm to develop a national agricultural development plan and then refuses to pay the firm because the nation changes its agricultural policy?

4. Was the "confiscation" of all cigar manufacturers by the Cuban government in the early 1960s an expropriation or a nationalization? Was this confiscation commercial activity in which a private businessperson could engage? Was the Cuban government's assertion of rights to post-intervention sums paid for cigars a commercial act? Is the analysis any different with respect to pre-intervention shipments?
5. Maria Hartman, a U.S. investor, owns a toy assembly plant in the Kingdom of Fromage Vert. At a tennis match between a leading U.S. player and a star Fromagian, Maria irritates the king by cheering for the American. The next day, the king issues an edict taking Ms. Hartman's plant for the kingdom. Ms. Hartman sues Fromage Vert in U.S. District Court for the Southern District of New York, where the kingdom's airline owns an office. Would the U.S. court have jurisdiction in the absence of a treaty? Do you think the Fromagian taking of the toy assembly plant was a commercial activity? Was it an "act of state"?
6. Is privatization a recent phenomenon? Why has it become more prominent in recent years? What triggered the move to more privatization in Latin American countries? In former communist nations?
7. Briefly describe the partial sale model of privatization. What is the predominant characteristic of the partial sale? How can a minority private investor try to protect itself from abuse by the majority government owner?
8. Briefly describe the trade sale model of privatization. What is the distinguishing feature of the trade sale? How is privatization achieved through management contracts?
9. List three reasons why giving employees an equity share in the new private entity makes sense. Give a reason that is principally applicable in Eastern Europe. What are two disadvantages associated with transferring shares to employees? What are two types of consideration that employees can be asked to give in exchange for their shares?
10. Briefly describe the concession model of privatization. How long should the term of the concession be?
11. Name four types of adjustments to regulations that are often addressed in the context of privatizations. Explain how they may be addressed.
12. Ernesto Ortiz, famed American corporate raider, initiates a hostile takeover of Bundesbank Freidumia (BF), the largest commercial bank in Freidumia. In purchasing 70 percent of BF's shares, Ortiz pays a substantial premium for control. After he concludes the transaction, Freidumia outlaws any foreigner or person under foreign control from voting shares in a commercial bank corporation, thereby wresting control from Mr. Ortiz. Has a nationalization taken place? An expropriation?

Managerial Implications

Your firm, Lloyd Aviation Company, is a leading U.S. manufacturer of helicopters. While on a trip to Moscow, you met Gennady Tupolev, the head of the former Soviet Air Force division that once manufactured military helicopters. The Russian government has no funds to finance further operations for the Tupolev Division and he needs to privatize its operations. The Russian government is reluctant to cede control over an industry that is so central to its national security. However, its conversion to commercial production will require thorough control by Lloyd. The division has a strong research and development department. Many of the division's lower-level employees will need to be laid off if it is to be a commercially viable operation.

1. Prepare a memorandum to Lloyd's board of directors outlining your plan for privatizing the Tupolev Division.
2. What regulatory arrangements should Lloyd make with the Russian government?

For Internet Activities, Visit academic.cengage.com/blaw/schaffer.

CHAPTER 20
Labor and Employment Discrimination Law

Corporations are lifeless entities with one principal objective: maximizing profit for their stockholders. To be sure, many corporate leaders find it good business to be thoughtful of those who work for the firm. Unless government intervenes, however, corporations will often subordinate the interests of their workers to those of their stockholders. Accordingly, virtually all societies have enacted laws that protect workers from abusive or discriminatory practices.

This regulation varies widely from place to place. For example, the paternalistic protective framework that safeguards and enfranchises German workers is extremely different from the United States' emphasis on individual achievement by workers and on control by managers. This chapter examines different approaches in this important area and their effect on international business transactions.

General Directions of Labor Law Abroad

Any active investment, whether controlled by investors from the United States or from some other country, relies on employees and is thus influenced by the host country's labor laws. Because these laws are often different from those encountered in the United States, investors must review them and the attitudes they reflect. Although a more detailed study would reveal countless differences between U.S. and foreign labor laws, a review of three principal areas gives a general sense of the distinctions.

First, many nations' laws require employee consultation or participation in management decisions that Americans view as being central to the owner's prerogative. Second, many countries place legal constraints on employee dismissal that are completely unfamiliar to the U.S. investor. Third, when a U.S. investor acquires a foreign business, by operation of law, it may also be acquiring the foreign industry's labor arrangements.

Employee Participation in Strategic Decisions

A current controversy in managerial theory involves the level of discretion owners and management should have in making strategic decisions and whether labor should participate in such decisions. A nation's laws on these issues have historically been shaped by its sociopolitical traditions. For example, in the Scandinavian countries, the workers' participation in management decisions is solely through labor unions. France, Greece, Portugal, and Spain utilize both trade unions and a body elected by all employees to participate in management's decision making. Ireland and the United Kingdom do not permit trade unions this type of access. One of the interesting phenomena of modern labor law is how these approaches seem to be merging as the world's economies merge.

The U.S. View. Notwithstanding legislative initiatives such as the *Worker Adjustment, Retraining, and Notification Act*—which at times requires a company to give sixty days' notice of plans to close a plant with more than 100 employees—U.S. companies come from an environment that allows owners great flexibility. Traditionally, U.S. management, completely by itself and in secret, makes strategic decisions such as whether to close a plant or reduce manpower levels. In the United States, management decides and labor carries out those decisions at an agreed hourly rate.

U.S. law mirrors this perspective. The U.S. Supreme Court has squarely held that an employer need not bargain with its employees over whether to shut down part of its business. The Court viewed this prerogative as akin to the closing down of a business, where "an employer has the absolute right to terminate his entire business for any reason he pleases."

The German Approach. Europeans have traditionally viewed the role of workers quite differently. The law in many Continental countries grants workers a right of consultation about or notice before the implementation of decisions resulting in workforce reductions. German law illustrates these worker rights of participation. Each plant with more than five employees must have a *Betriebsrat* (works council) to represent that plant's interest. In contrast to their U.S. counterparts, these works councils are independent from trade unions. They represent the interests of plant employees as distinct from those of the employer or trade unions.

Under the *German Works Constitution Act*, the employer must fully inform the works council in "due time" of any plant changes that might result in "substantial disadvantages for employees" and consult with it on such proposals. In the course of that consultation, the employer solicits the works council's approval of the employer's method of selecting persons to be terminated as a result of the plant change. If the employer and the works council cannot resolve a dispute by this method, they then appear before an arbitration committee. In addition, the employer notifies the regional office of the Federal Employment Institute. If this office believes the plant change would strain local resources, it can delay the change until two months after notice is given. As these examples illustrate, U.S. companies can be confronted with a radically different labor situation once they go abroad.

Mandatory Employee Representation on Boards of Directors. A number of countries require substantial employee representation on the corporate board of directors. This is often accomplished by mandating a two-tiered board: a large supervisory board (in Germany, the *Aufsichtsrat*) and a management board (in Germany, the *Vorstand*). The *Aufsichtsrat* is responsible for representing shareholder interests, while the *Vorstand* manages the firm from day to day.

In Germany, the Netherlands, Austria, and Luxembourg, employees have direct representation in the *Aufsichtsrat*. Indeed, in Germany, companies that employ more than 2,000 workers must establish *Aufsichtsrat* representation that is 50 percent labor and 50 percent shareholders. In companies with more than 500 workers, one-third of the *Aufsichtsrat* must be composed of workers.

This focus on worker participation in corporate decisions has proved attractive to former communist nations that for half of the twentieth century emphasized the rights of workers. Laws in the Czech Republic and Poland, among others, have followed the German law model of worker boards.

The implications for U.S. investors are important. All significant strategic decisions in these countries require supervisory board approval. Thus, the *Vorstand* must present persuasive reasons for a strategic plan that involves workforce reductions. In short, the flexibility of management is not as great in German-model countries as in the United States.

The Japanese Approach. In Japan, management–labor strife is rare because of traditional and structural factors that blur distinctions between management and workers. Union leadership is a stepping-stone to management. Nearly 15 percent of union officials rise to serve as executives of the company. Consequently, union leaders have little incentive to take strident labor positions against those responsible for their advancement. Under Japanese tradition, the income differentiation between management and labor is not as great as in the West. There is less of a perceived need for labor–management confrontation and labor laws are generally inoffensive.

Impediments to Dismissal

Prevailing national norms also create different legal frameworks on the issue of employee dismissal.

National attitudes toward the proper relationship between manager and employee heavily color the content of national law.

Underlying Philosophical Foundations. People in the United States, perhaps the most capitalist of nations, do not commonly believe that anyone is entitled to a job. Once an individual ceases to be productive, his/her future employment is in jeopardy. Legally required severance pay is low and is viewed as a humane cushion to help the discharged until they can find new employment.

Europeans, on the other hand, tend to feel that employees acquire a property interest in their jobs over time. The more senior an employee is, the greater his or her property interest. Accordingly, severance pay is legally required as compensation for the taking of this substantial property, and it increases as the employee becomes more senior. For the most senior employees, severance pay can be so high as to strongly discourage involuntary dismissal. This system is often criticized as creating a very senior workforce with little incentive to perform.

The traditional Japanese view is that one's job is a central part of his or her place in society and that a job largely defines the person. An individual is expected to hold a job for the same company for a lifetime. In Japan, the focus is not on the conditions of dismissal but on the propriety of dismissal in the first place.

Other nations tend to fall within one of these models or between them.

Legal Frameworks Reflecting Philosophy. In the United States, employers historically have been able to terminate employees with little notice. Unless a collective bargaining agreement was in place, U.S. management had few limits on its employee termination options. This picture has changed somewhat as U.S. businesses have been influenced by European and Japanese practices. Relatively recent federal legislation now gives employees unpaid leave to care for family members, guarantees workers their jobs back after such leave, and requires a warning of plant closings. More and more U.S. managers now take a page from Japanese companies and seek ways of providing greater assurance of employment. Nonetheless, U.S. law gives entrepreneurs great flexibility to do as they wish with their employees. U.S. businesses face a very different legal world beyond these shores.

United Kingdom law mandates that an employer consult with the appropriate trade union before making a dismissal. If the workforce is to be reduced by ten or more employees, a consultation must take place sixty days prior to termination. Under German law, the works council must approve any dismissal. If it does not, the employer may appeal to a labor court. Indeed, the *Betriebsrat* can affirmatively call for the dismissal of employees even without a request from the employer.

Japan is perhaps the most interesting case. There the written law seems to permit relatively free dismissal of employees. However, tradition—embodied in decisional law—protects the employee.

A similar attitude was reflected in Japan's approach to plant closings. Japanese companies in financial stress seldom closed factories. Instead, plants were taken over by friendly affiliates in good financial condition, or workers were turned over to local successful firms. Again, the discretion implicit in Japanese labor law was interpreted to enforce these cultural traditions. U.S. companies, such as Procter & Gamble and Chase Manhattan Bank, have faced court proceedings from local unions challenging facility shutdowns in Japan as "unfair labor practices." This has occurred even when the U.S. firms offered the dismissed employees new jobs in different locations.

Just as U.S. employment practices are being influenced by those of Europe and Japan, the Japanese are being influenced by Westerners. During the long recession of the 1990s and early twenty-first century, giants such as Nippon Telephone & Telegraph, NKK Corporation, and Nissan Corporation all successfully implemented reductions in their workforces. These companies did not actually lay off employees, but effected the reductions through normal attrition, intracompany transfers, and transfers to subsidiaries. Because many employees rejected unattractive transfers and many of the subsidiaries went out of business, this shift proved to be significant. At the same time, surveys of Japanese executives indicated a broad consensus that the days of lifetime employment and strict seniority advancement systems were numbered. The differences between nations

Kochi Hoso (Broadcasting Co.)
Rokeisoku No. 937 (1977)
Supreme Court of Japan

BACKGROUND AND FACTS
Like all Japanese firms with more than ten employees, Kochi Hoso, a radio broadcasting company, was required to maintain rules of employment that specified the conditions under which an employee could be discharged. Kochi Hoso clearly specified that tardiness for a broadcast was cause for dismissal. No contractual provision excused such tardiness.

The plaintiff, a radio announcer, had failed twice to arrive at the studio in time for a news broadcast. After the second offense, Kochi Hoso discharged the plaintiff, pointing to the unambiguous rules. Plaintiff sought reinstatement, arguing that although the discharge was within the rules, it was unreasonable or contrary to public policy. The Supreme Court found no reasonable cause for termination.

PER CURIAM
Even when an employee's conduct constitutes a cause for a discharge, an employer may not always discharge the employee. It should be noted that when the said discharge is found to be significantly unreasonable under the specific situation so that it could be hardly approved as being appropriate in the light of the socially accepted view, such a discharge should be considered to be an abusive exercise of an employer's power to discharge employees and, thus, to be invalid.

Decision. The Supreme Court of Japan ordered that the radio announcer be reinstated in his job.

regarding the permanence of employment are still quite significant. However, they are becoming less profound over time.

Assumption of Employment Arrangements

To a far greater extent than in the United States, many nations—particularly in Europe—compel corporate acquirers to adhere to existing employment arrangements. In other words, when acquiring a manufacturing plant, one may be acquiring the collective bargaining agreement that the seller had negotiated with the trade union prior to the purchase of the company. A U.S. investor must assess this inheritable liability before acquiring a foreign company.

Employment Discrimination Outside the United States

The United States almost certainly has the world's most comprehensive set of laws against discrimination of all sorts in employment. Because most countries outside the Americas were created as the geographic homes of homogeneous ethnic groups, they have perceived relatively little need to develop antidiscriminatory schemes. Germany is the nation-state created by the ethnic Germans who lived in that area and the Japanese islands are those where ethnic Japanese live. In many countries, the overwhelming ethnic majority has not felt a need to protect against ethnic discrimination. Indeed, at the opposite extreme, the Baltic countries, formerly part of the Soviet Union, have passed laws mandating discrimination against the ethnic Russian minority.

The Common Market's goal of allowing people of all member nations to work in other member states has begun to introduce laws against ethnic discrimination to those economies. As Europe's declining populations require increasing numbers of immigrants from Africa and the Middle East, these issues are likely to expand.

The issue of discrimination against women has brought a new legal complexity to employment issues. However, all of these schemes are in formative stages. The principal employment discrimination issue for U.S. companies remains whether the comprehensive U.S. laws apply to their overseas operations.

The Extraterritorial Application of U.S. Employment Discrimination Law

There has been significant disagreement in Congress and the legal community concerning the extent to which U.S. discrimination laws apply abroad and how they can be enforced if they do. For instance, how can a U.S. company operate in Islamic countries that legally require discrimination against Christians and Jews if it has to treat everyone equally? In 1991, the U.S. Supreme Court first gave some direction in this area.

Soon after the Supreme Court spoke, Congress sought to overrule the *Aramco* case by partially extending U.S. employment law overseas. Congress expressly extended Title VII to firms operating outside the United States under the "control" of a U.S. entity. In addition, as the *Aramco* Court predicted, Congress made an exception for situations where compliance with Title VII would violate the law of the country where the firm is located.

Congress' action did not prove to be the last word. Since *Aramco,* courts have interpreted both the Age Discrimination in Employment Act (ADEA) and the Americans with Disabilities Act (ADA) to prohibit U.S. employers and foreign companies controlled by a U.S. employer

Equal Employment Opportunity Commission v. Arabian American Oil Co.
499 U.S. 244 (1991)
United States Supreme Court

BACKGROUND AND FACTS

The respondents are two Delaware corporations, Arabian American Oil Company (Aramco) and its subsidiary, Aramco Service Company (ASC). Aramco's principal place of business is Dhahran, Saudi Arabia, and it is licensed to do business in Texas.

In 1979, Boureslan was hired by ASC as a cost engineer in Houston. A year later he was transferred, at his request, to work for Aramco in Saudi Arabia. Boureslan remained with Aramco in Saudi Arabia until he was discharged in 1984. He instituted this suit in the United States District Court for the Southern District of Texas against Aramco and ASC. He sought relief under Title VII of the *Civil Rights Act* on the ground that he was harassed and ultimately discharged by respondents on account of his race, religion, and national origin.

CHIEF JUSTICE REHNQUIST

Both parties concede, as they must, that Congress has the authority to enforce its laws beyond the territorial boundaries of the United States. Whether Congress has in fact exercised that authority in this case is a matter of statutory construction. It is our task to determine whether Congress intended the protections of Title VII to apply to United States citizens employed by American employers outside of the United States.

It is a long-standing principle of American law "that legislation of Congress, unless a contrary intent appears, is meant to apply only within the territorial jurisdiction of the United States." It serves to protect against unintended clashes between our laws and those of other nations which could result in international discord.

Title VII prohibits various discriminatory employment practices based on an individual's race, color, religion, sex, or national origin. An employer is subject to Title VII if it is "engaged in an industry affecting commerce." "Commerce," in turn, is defined as "trade, traffic, commerce, transportation, transmission, or communication among the several States; or between a State and any place outside thereof." ...

Petitioners ... assert that since Title VII defines "States" to include States, the District of Columbia, and specified territories, the clause "between a State and any place outside thereof" must be referring to areas beyond the territorial limit of the United States. The language relied upon by petitioners—and it is they who must make the affirmative showing—is ambiguous, and does not speak directly to the question presented here. The intent of Congress as to the extraterritorial application of this statute must be

continued

continued

deduced by inference from boilerplate language which can be found in any number of congressional acts, none of which have ever been held to apply overseas.

If we were to permit possible, or even plausible interpretations of language such as that involved here to override the presumption against extraterritorial application, there would be little left of the presumption.

Petitioners argue that Title VII's "alien exemption provision ... clearly manifests an intention" by Congress to protect U.S. citizens with respect to their employment outside of the United States. The alien exemption provision says that "the statute" shall not apply to an employer with respect to the employment of aliens outside any State. Petitioners contend that from this language a negative inference should be drawn that Congress intended Title VII to cover United States citizens.

If petitioners are correct that the alien-exemption clause means that the statute applies to employers overseas, we see no way of distinguishing in its application between United States employers and foreign employers. Thus, a French employer of a United States citizen in France would be subject to Title VII—a result at which even petitioners balk. The EEOC assures us that in its view the term "employer" means only "American employer," but there is no such distinction in this statute.

It is also reasonable to conclude that had Congress intended Title VII to apply overseas, it would have addressed the subject of conflicts with foreign laws and procedures. In amending the Age Discrimination in Employment Act of 1967 to apply abroad, Congress specifically addressed potential conflicts with foreign law by providing that it is not unlawful for an employer to take any action prohibited by the ADEA "where such practices involve an employee in a workplace in a foreign country, and compliance with the ADEA would cause such employer ... to violate the laws of the country in which such workplace is located." Title VII, by contrast, fails to address conflicts with the laws of other nations.

Decision. Petitioners failed to present sufficient affirmative evidence that Congress intended Title VII to apply abroad. Accordingly, the judgment of the Court of Appeals was affirmed.

from discriminating in employment of U.S. citizens in other countries. Courts have found, however, that the same laws do not give rights to foreigners seeking work from U.S. entities.

In 2005, the U.S. Court of Appeals for the District of Columbia provided additional guidance on the limits of extraterritorial application of U.S. antidiscrimination laws in *Shekoyan v. Sibley Int'l*

Reyes-Gaona v. North Carolina Growers Ass'n, Inc.

250 F.3d 861 (2001)

United States Court of Appeals (4th Cir.)

BACKGROUND AND FACTS

Plaintiff Luis Reyes-Gaona was a Mexican national over the age of 40. Defendant North Carolina Growers Association (NCGA) was an American corporation that assisted agricultural businesses in North Carolina in securing farm labor through a legal federal program. Defendant Del-Al was an agent of NCGA that recruited workers for NCGA and its members. Reyes-Gaona went to a Del-Al office in Mexico and asked to be placed on a list of workers seeking employment in North Carolina. Del-Al told Reyes-Gaona that NCGA would not accept a worker over 40 years old unless that person had worked for NCGA before. With the support of the United States Equal Employment Opportunity Commission, Reyes-Gaona filed suit against NCGA and Del-Al, alleging age discrimination in violation of the *Age Discrimination in Employment Act.*

continued

continued

WILKINSON, CHIEF JUDGE

This case requires us to decide whether the *Age Discrimination in Employment Act* (ADEA) covers foreign nationals who apply in foreign countries for jobs in the United States. We hold that the Act does not cover such persons....

Plaintiff is a foreign national who applied in a foreign country for work in the United States. Accordingly, we begin, as we must, by acknowledging the "longstanding principle of American law 'that legislation of Congress, unless a contrary intent appears, is meant to apply only within the territorial jurisdiction of the United States.' " ... This interpretive canon is an especially important one as it "serves to protect against unintended clashes between our laws and those of other nations which could result in international discord." ... Thus, the presumption against extra-territorial application of a federal statute can be overcome only if there is an "affirmative intention of the Congress clearly expressed." ... Since this determination is necessarily "a matter of statutory construction," we begin with the text of the ADEA itself.

The ADEA makes it unlawful "for an employer" to "fail or refuse to hire" or "otherwise discriminate against any individual with respect to his compensation, terms, conditions, or privileges of employment, because of such individual's age." The term "employer" means any company "engaged in an industry affecting commerce who has twenty or more employees" and includes the agents of such companies.... The term "employee" means "an individual employed by any employer," and "includes any individual who is a citizen of the United States employed by an employer in a workplace in a foreign country." ... Prior to 1984, the ADEA did not contain the language regarding U.S. citizens employed in foreign workplaces. To the contrary, [the ADEA] adopted language from the Fair Labor Standards Act (FLSA) excluding from coverage any individual "whose services during the workweek are performed in a workplace within a foreign country."...

Based on the exclusionary language adopted from the FLSA, many courts held that, before 1984, the ADEA had a purely domestic focus and did not cover American citizens working for American companies in foreign countries.... The presumption against the extra-territorial application of American laws required this result because absent a clear statement from Congress, the scope of American law is limited to "the territorial jurisdiction of the United States." ... Thus the presumption prevented the ADEA from regulating events taking place in foreign countries even when they involved citizens of the United States. And the Act certainly could not have reached the even more attenuated situation of a foreign national applying in a foreign country for work in the United States.

In 1984, Congress partially closed this gap. Congress [amended] the ADEA to give it limited extra-territorial application. The definition of "employee" was amended to include "any individual who is a citizen of the United States employed by an employer in a workplace in a foreign country." ... This new statutory language explicitly expanded the ADEA to prohibit U.S. companies from discriminating against U.S. citizens employed in foreign countries. Congress also included an accompanying provision outlawing such discrimination by subsidiaries of U.S. corporations.... The language was "carefully worded to apply only to citizens of the United States" who worked for a U.S. company or its subsidiary because Congress recognized that the "well-established principle of sovereignty" prohibited the United States from imposing "its labor standards on another country."... These amendments demonstrated that "when it desires to do so, Congress knows how to" expand "the jurisdictional reach of a statute."... Notably missing from the 1984 amendments, however, is any provision regulating the conduct at issue here. Congress explicitly gave the ADEA extra-territorial application with respect to certain U.S. citizens while simultaneously declining to extend coverage to foreign nationals like Reyes-Gaona. Nothing in the amendments regulates age discrimination by U.S. corporations against foreign nationals in foreign countries. And the doctrine of *expressio unis est exclusio alterius* instructs that where a law expressly describes a particular situation to which it shall apply, what was omitted or excluded was intended to be omitted or excluded.... Thus, a faithful reading of the plain text of the statute, especially in light of the 1984 amendments, compels the conclusion that Reyes-Gaona's claim is not sustainable under the ADEA.

Reyes-Gaona and the EEOC disagree. They claim that this case does not require extra-territorial application of the ADEA because the job Reyes-Gaona applied for was in the United States. The crux of their argument is that when determining whether a suit requires extra-territorial application of the ADEA, courts always look to the place of employment rather

continued

continued

than the place where the decision was made. Because Reyes-Gaona applied for a job in the United States, they argue, the presumption against extra-territoriality is not implicated by this suit. In support they note that the ADEA itself contains the term "workplace." For example, "employee" is defined to include U.S. citizens employed "in a workplace in a foreign country." ... And the Act excepts from its reach employees "in a workplace in a foreign country" where compliance would conflict with the laws of the country "in which such workplace is located."

We are not persuaded. All of these statutory references come from the 1984 amendments to the ADEA which, as previously explained, do not cover Reyes-Gaona. Nothing in the ADEA provides that it shall apply anytime the workplace is in the United States regardless of the nationality of the applicant or the country in which the application was submitted. And the fact that the 1984 amendments refer to workplace does not mean that the Act focuses on work situs to the exclusion of the situs of the application or the nationality of the applicant....

The simple submission of a resume abroad does not confer the right to file an ADEA action. Indeed, such a broad reading of the Act could have staggering consequences for American companies. Expanding the ADEA to cover millions of foreign nationals who file an overseas application for U.S. employment could exponentially increase the number of suits filed and result in substantial litigation costs. If such a step is to be taken, it must be taken via a clear and unambiguous statement from Congress rather than by judicial fiat.

The Supreme Court has instructed the lower courts to take seriously the presumption against extra-territorial application of U.S. laws. In keeping with these instructions, many lower courts, including this one, held that the ADEA had no extra-territorial application prior to 1984. Congress responded by amending the Act to provide for limited extra-territorial reach. Since these amendments do not reach the case at bar, there remains nothing in the text of the ADEA to rebut the presumption against extending it to cover Reyes-Gaona. And the limited nature of the 1984 amendments indicates that foreign nationals in foreign countries are not covered by the ADEA, regardless of whether they are seeking employment in the United States or elsewhere.

Decision. The Fourth Circuit Court of Appeals affirmed the district court's dismissal of Mr. Reyes-Gaona's suit.

Corp., 217 F. Supp.2d 59, *aff'd*, 409 F.3d 414. In *Shekoyan*, the court excluded a permanent U.S. resident alien who worked abroad for a U.S. government contractor from the extraterritorial protection of Title VII and the ADEA. The *Shekoyan* court held that although the employee was a U.S. resident and his employment and training occurred in the United States, he was an alien and therefore was not protected by U.S. antidiscrimination laws when his job was solely located abroad.

There are other instances in which courts have declined to apply U.S. employment law abroad. In its opinion in *Ofori-Tenkorang v. American Intern. Group, Inc.*, 460 F.3d 296 (2006), the United States Court of Appeals for the Second Circuit held that the provisions against racial discrimination found at 42 U.S.C. §1981 did not apply outside of the United States. In addition, a number of other American laws by their terms have no extraterritorial application. These include the *National Labor Relations Act*, the *Employee Retirement Income Security Act of 1974*, the *Occupational Safety & Health Act*, the *Worker Adjustment & Retraining Notification Act*, the *Fair Labor Standards Act, the Equal Pay Act*, the *Family and Medical Leave Act*, the *Sarbanes-Oxley Act of 2002*, and state equal employment opportunity laws.

Defenses to U.S. Employment Law When Applied Extraterritorially

There are three principal defenses to U.S. challenges of employment decisions abroad. These are (1) the decision is made by "a foreign person not controlled by an American employer," (2) the U.S. equal employment opportunity law (EEO law) conflicts with a host country's laws, so that the employer faces "foreign compulsion" because to

Exhibit 20.1

Extension of Title VII to Foreign Operations of U.S. Firms
Civil Rights Act of 1991; Pub. L. No. 102–166, §109, 105 Stat. 1071, 1077–78 (1991)
Protection of Extraterritorial Employment

a. Definition of Employee. [The Civil Rights Act and the Americans with Disabilities Act] are each amended by adding to the end the following: "With respect to employment in a foreign country, such term includes an individual who is a citizen of the United States."...
b. "It shall not be unlawful under [the Civil Rights Act] for an employer (or a corporation controlled by an employer), ... to take any action otherwise prohibited ... with respect to an employee in a workplace in a foreign country if compliance with such section would cause such employer (or such corporation), ... to violate the law of the foreign country in which such workplace is located.
c. 1. If an employer controls a corporation whose place of incorporation is a foreign country, any practice prohibited by section 703 or 704 engaged in by such corporation shall be presumed to be engaged in by such employer.
   2. Sections 703 and 704 shall not apply with respect to the foreign operations of an employer that is a foreign person not controlled by an American employer.
   3. For purposes of this subsection, the determination of whether an employer controls a corporation shall be based on:
      A. the interrelation of operations;
      B. the common management;
      C. the centralized control of labor relations; and
      D. the common ownership or financial control of the employer and the corporation.

comply with U.S. law would violate the host country's laws, and (3) the performance of the job requires a trait such as a specific religion or gender, allowing the employer the "bona fide occupational qualification" defense. We will review each of these in turn.

Control by a Foreign Person

When Congress passed the ADEA amendments, it was generally possible to define clearly the nationality of a corporation's controlling person. However, because the stock of an international company may be simultaneously offered on many international exchanges—each of which allows people of all nationalities to purchase stock anonymously—it becomes virtually impossible to identify the nationality of owners in industrialized countries. Courts have, however, prevented the EEOC and U.S. citizens from bringing suit against "foreign" firms with very substantial U.S. operations.

The Foreign Compulsion Defense

Congress also intended to provide a "foreign compulsion" defense, permitting U.S. firms flexibility when the enforcement of U.S. employment laws overseas would result in a violation of foreign law. This defense does not apply to foreign employers who are charged with employment discrimination in the United States. As in all things legal, however, interesting questions arise in difficult cases. In the following case, the U.S. Court of Appeals for the District of Columbia found that where U.S. law would cause a U.S. firm to violate a foreign collective bargaining agreement—not a law, strictly speaking—the foreign compulsion defense nonetheless applied.

The Bona Fide Occupational Qualification Defense

The bona fide occupational qualification defense (BFOQ), both in Title VII and the ADEA, provides that an employer may engage in discrimination if it is "reasonably necessary to the normal operation of the particular business or enterprise." This is not much of a "safe harbor" for U.S. employers. What is "reasonably necessary" for one person may not be for another. For example, when an American hospital refused to send Jewish

Mahoney v. RFE/RL, Inc.

47 F.3d 447 (1995)

United States Court of Appeals for the District of Columbia Circuit

BACKGROUND AND FACTS

RFE/RL, Inc. is a Delaware nonprofit corporation that is funded but not controlled by the federal government. It is best known for its broadcast services, Radio Free Europe and Radio Liberty. RFE/RL's principal place of business is Munich, Germany. In 1982, the company entered into a collective bargaining agreement with unions representing its employees in Munich. One of the provisions of the labor contract, modeled after a nationwide agreement in the German broadcast industry, required employees to retire at age sixty-five.

After Congress amended the *Age Discrimination in Employment Act* (ADEA) to cover American citizens working for American corporations overseas, RFE/RL thought its American employees in Munich would no longer have to retire at the age of sixty-five, as the collective bargaining agreement provided, and could continue to work if they chose. In order to implement this understanding, the company applied to the Works Council for limited exemptions from its contractual obligation. Rejecting RFE/RL's requests, the Works Council determined that allowing only those employees who were American citizens to work past the age of sixty-five would violate not only the mandatory retirement provision, but also the collective bargaining agreement's provision forbidding discrimination based on nationality. RFE/RL appealed the Works Council's decisions with respect to the plaintiffs to the Munich Labor Court and lost. The Labor Court agreed with the Works Council that RFE/RL must uniformly enforce the mandatory retirement provisions because exemptions would unfairly discriminate against German workers. The Labor Court also held that the company's retaining employees over the age of sixty-five despite the collective bargaining agreement would be illegal. The company terminated plaintiff De Lon in 1987 and plaintiff Mahoney in 1988. Both plaintiffs were working for the company in Munich, both were U.S. citizens, and both were discharged pursuant to the labor contract because they had reached the age of sixty-five.

CIRCUIT JUDGE RANDOLPH

If an American corporation operating in a foreign country would have to "violate the laws" of that country in order to comply with the Age Discrimination in Employment Act, the company need not comply with the Act. The question here is whether this "foreign laws" exception ... applies when the overseas company, in order to comply with the Act, would have to breach a collective bargaining agreement that foreign unions....

The parties agree that RFE/RL thereby violated the ADEA unless the "foreign laws" exception applied. The Act prohibits employers from discriminating against employees on the basis of age. "Employee" includes "any individual who is a citizen of the United States employed by an employer in a workplace in a foreign country;" and it is common ground that the Act covers RFE/RL.

The "foreign laws" exception to the Act states: It shall not be unlawful for an employer, employment agency, or labor organization—(1) to take any action otherwise prohibited under subsections (a), (b), (c), or (e) of this section where ... such practices involve an employee in a workplace in a foreign country, and compliance with such subsections would cause such employer, or a corporation controlled by such employer, to violate the laws of the country in which such workplace is located. The district court held [the provision] inapplicable because the mandatory retirement provision is part of a contract between an employer and unions—both private entities—and has not in any way been mandated by the German government. Second, the provision does not have general application, as laws normally do, but binds only the parties to the contract....

If RFE/RL had not complied with the collective bargaining agreement in this case, if it had retained plaintiffs despite the mandatory retirement provision, the company would have violated the German laws standing behind such contracts, as well as the decisions of the Munich Labor Court. In the words of [the foreign compulsion defense], RFE/RL's "compliance with [the Act] would cause such employer ... to violate the laws of the country in which such workplace is located." Domestic employers of course would never face a comparable situation; the Supremacy Clause of the Constitution would force any applicable state laws to give way, and provisions in collective bargaining agreements contrary to the

continued

continued

Act would be superseded. Congressional legislation cannot, however, set aside the laws of foreign countries. When an overseas employer's obligations under foreign law collide with its obligations under the Age Discrimination in Employment Act, [the foreign compulsion defense] quite sensibly solves the dilemma by relieving the employer of liability under the Act....

We recognize that RFE/RL's collective bargaining agreement is legally enforceable, which necessarily means that breaching the agreement in order to comply with the Act would ... "cause" RFE/RL "to violate the laws of" Germany. Plaintiffs complain that RFE/RL could have bargained harder for a change in the labor contract. But application of [the foreign compulsion defense] does not depend on such considerations. The collective bargaining agreement here was valid and enforceable at the time of plaintiffs' terminations, and RFE/RL had a legal duty to comply with it. There is not, nor could there be, any suggestion that RFE/RL agreed to the mandatory retirement provision in order to evade the Age Discrimination in Employment Act. Such provisions are, the evidence showed, common throughout the Federal Republic of Germany, and RFE/RL entered into this particular agreement before Congress extended the Act beyond our borders.

Decision. The Court of Appeals reversed the District Court's opinion and remanded the case to the District Court with instructions to dismiss the matter.

anesthesiologists to Saudi Arabia, a court held that the BFOQ defense did not defeat a suit by a group of Jewish doctors. The court found that the employer had not made appropriate efforts to determine the Saudi Arabian policy regarding the entry of Jewish doctors into the country and that the Saudi government had never directed the employer that American Jews could not participate in the program. Another court found the BFOQ defense did not justify a refusal to promote a woman to a senior position at a U.S. company's Latin American office. The court found inadequate the company's reasoning that she would have to deal with men in Latin America, where, they argued, businesspeople believe that women belong in the home. The BFOQ defense might be useful to the litigator trying to defend a company's action after the fact, but it seems too uncertain to be a useful tool for business planning.

Antidiscrimination Laws Outside the United States

The history of the United States is peppered with successive immigrations by various ethnic groups, each seeking civic or economic freedom. Even the framers of the Constitution, who were virtually all of British ancestry, were products of four different migrations from different parts of Britain and came from distinctly different religious traditions. Not surprisingly, the United States has a highly developed legal system proscribing discrimination based on religion or national origin. As we have seen in the preceding section, this body of law has in turn given rise to related legal principles prohibiting discrimination based on other criteria that have become socially unacceptable bases for differentiation, such as race, age, and gender.

The multiethnic makeup of the United States has been relatively unusual. As F. Scott Fitzgerald elegantly noted, "France was a land, England was a people, but America having about it that quality of the idea, was harder to utter.... It was a willingness of the heart." Most Europeans and Asians lived in geographic regions inhabited by their ethnic brethren. The same has been true to a lesser extent in Africa, where traditional ethnic groups remain dominant in regions of multi-tribal nations created by European colonists. Even today, the competing desires of ethnic groups to dominate a geographically contiguous zone are a primary cause of civil strife in these continents. "Ethnic cleansing" in Bosnia and post-1999 "counter-cleansing" in Kosovo were efforts to create geographic regions where only one ethnic group resides. Although Latin Americans do not have the same tie to the land as do the peoples of the

Eastern Hemisphere, the dominance of the Spanish culture in Hispanic America and of the Portuguese culture in Brazil have prevented legal developments similar to those in the United States. As the result of these social conditions, these countries have few antidiscrimination laws.

The revolution in transport and communications, however, is ending ethnic homogeneity in the Old World. Ethnic North Africans work in Paris, ethnic Pakistanis in London, and ethnic Turks in Frankfurt. Women are not as willing to accept discrimination in the workplace. Moreover, as the population of Europe ages and declines, more and more companies are grappling with issues of an older workforce. In 2000, the European Union adopted *Council Directive 2000/78/EC,* which prohibits employment discrimination on the bases of religion or belief, disability, age, or sexual orientation. As member states have enacted legislation or regulations to incorporate this directive's general framework, more U.S. employers are likely to see more claims brought by their European-based employees.

Globalization of trade and finance has had ramifications in the area of employment as well. For the past fifteen years, most of the trade agreements that the U.S. has signed have included labor standards, even though these are typically aspirational and without any true monitoring or enforcement mechanism. Financing entities, including the World Bank's International Finance Corporation, are incorporating labor standards as a condition of their loans. Friendship, Commerce, and Navigation treaties between the United States and other nations, which allow a foreign employer to choose its own executives and experts to run its operations in the other signatory nations, have come under greater scrutiny as to which levels and positions the foreign executives can occupy. Other nations, like Japan and China, are reforming their equal employment opportunity laws to provide greater protections against discrimination in employment.

Laws Favoring Discrimination Based on National Origin or Religion. Despite these movements, some nations still permit discrimination based upon their historical and cultural backgrounds. In many countries, the law actually requires discrimination based on religion or national origin. When a country is synonymous with an ethnic group, that ethnic group sometimes justifies preservation of ethnic identity by methodically excluding those outside it. Estonia has created citizenship laws, the plain intent of which is to deny citizenship to ethnic Russians who arrived during the seventy years of Soviet rule. Because Estonia confers employment and other benefits on the basis of citizenship, its citizenship law is a device for favoring ethnic Estonians over ethnic Russians in employment opportunities. Dominant ethnic groups in small, wealthy nations threatened by large numbers of industrious ethnic outsiders often enact laws to prevent those outsiders from holding certain types of jobs. For example, ethnic Kuwaitis and Jordanians have excluded Palestinian co-religionists from key jobs and properties. Likewise, when a nation does not distinguish between religion and the state, the law often calls for discrimination against infidels. Pro-discrimination laws are most frequently found in Middle Eastern Islamic countries such as Pakistan, Iran, and Saudi Arabia. One may also encounter such pro-discrimination statutes in countries where atheism is the state "religion," such as Cuba and North Korea.

There are no such pro-discrimination laws in the United States. Nonetheless, the U.S. investor must take such laws into account in staffing foreign operations. Because they are rooted in deep cultural or political fear of outside influence, violations of their terms generally lead to adverse action by the local government.

Non–U.S. Laws Prohibiting Discrimination Based on National Origin or Religion. The U.S. investor must understand foreign laws prohibiting ethnic discrimination. They are both similar to and different from their U.S. counterparts. Articles 7, 48, 52, and 59 of the *European Union Treaty* forbid different types of discrimination within the Union based on nationality. The motivating principle behind these provisions is that nationals from each member state should be free to pursue their economic interests anywhere within the unified European economy without fear of differential treatment. The following case demonstrates the Community's commitment to protect even the oldest of professions.

In the past, EU antidiscrimination law has not prohibited discrimination against ethnic individuals

Bezguia Adoui v. Belgian State & City of Liège; Cornuaille v. Belgian State

1982 E.C.R. 1665

Court of Justice of the European Communities

BACKGROUND AND FACTS

On June 3, 1980, Miss Adoui, a French national, submitted an application to the City of Liège for a permit to reside in Belgium. The Minister of Justice denied her application and ordered her to leave the country because her personal conduct made her residence undesirable. This order was based on the Minister's finding that she worked in a bar in which waitresses displayed themselves in the window and were able to be alone with their clients for sexual encounters. Such conduct was contrary to the laws of Liège. She was not actually found to have so displayed herself, however.

Miss Adoui refused to comply with the expulsion order, asserting that she was the victim of discrimination based on national origin. In essence, Miss Adoui took the position that no similar action was taken against Belgian women merely suspected of engaging in display activities in furtherance of the business of prostitution. She sought relief from a court with jurisdiction over the Minister of Justice, the Tribunal de Premiere Instance at Liège.

Miss Cornuaille, another French national, was similarly accused of being a waitress of questionable moral character who "in scant dress display[ed] herself to clients" for purposes of prostitution. The Committee of Aliens Office issued an opinion recommending her expulsion, without having taken account of the matters which had been the subject of the complaint to the criminal authorities. Like Ms. Adoui, Miss Cornuaille summoned the Committee to the Liège Tribunal, alleging discrimination on the basis of national origin.

The President of the Liège Tribunal stayed the proceedings in both cases. Pursuant to Article 177 of the *Treaty of Rome*, he asked the Court of Justice for a preliminary ruling to determine whether a foreign national could be expelled based on conduct for which a citizen was not normally reprimanded.

J. MERTEN DE WILMARS, PRESIDENT; G. BOSCO AND A. TOUFFAIT, PRESIDENTS OF CHAMBERS; P. PESCATORE, LORD MACKENZIE STUART, A. O'KEEFE, T. KOOPMANS, U. EVERLING, AND A. CHLOROS, JUDGES

The questions were raised in actions brought against the Belgian State by the Plaintiffs in the main proceedings, who are of French nationality, in connection with the refusal by the administrative authority to issue a permit enabling them to reside in Belgian territory, on the ground that their conduct was considered to be contrary to public policy by virtue of the fact that they were waitresses in a bar which was suspect from the point of view of morals.

The *Belgian Law of 21 August 1948* terminating official regulation of prostitution prohibits soliciting, incitement to debauchery, exploitation of prostitution, the keeping of a disorderly house or brothel, and living on immoral earnings. The *police regulation of the City of Liège of 25 March 1957* and subsequent orders provide that persons engaged in prostitution may not display themselves to passers-by, that the doors and windows of the premises where they pursue their activity are to be closed and covered so that it is impossible to see inside, and that those persons may not stand in the street near such premises.

[The questions referred to the Court] are essentially concerned with the question whether a Member State may, by virtue of the reservations contained in Articles 48 and 56 of the EEC Treaty, expel from its territory a national of another Member State or deny him access to that territory by reason of activities which, when attributable to the former State's own nationals, do not give rise to repressive measures.

Those questions are motivated by the fact that prostitution as such is not prohibited by Belgian legislation, although the Law does prohibit certain incidental activities, which are particularly harmful.

The reservations contained in Articles 48 and 56 of the EEC Treaty permit Member States to adopt, with respect to the nationals of other Member States measures which they cannot apply to their own nationals, inasmuch as they have no authority to expel the latter from the national territory or to deny them access thereto. Although that difference of treatment, which bears upon the nature of the measures available, must therefore be allowed, it must nevertheless be stressed that, in a Member State, the authority empowered to adopt such measures must not base the exercise of its powers on assessments of certain conduct which would have the effect of

continued

continued

applying an arbitrary distinction to the detriment of nationals of other Member States.

Although Community law does not impose upon the Member States a uniform scale of values as regards the assessment of conduct which may be considered as contrary to public policy, it should nevertheless be stated that conduct may not be considered as being of a sufficiently serious nature to justify restrictions on the admission to or residence within the territory of a Member State or a national of another Member State in a case where the former Member State does not adopt, with respect to the same conduct on the part of its own nationals, repressive measures or other genuine and effective measures intended to combat such conduct.

The answer to [the questions referred to the Court] should therefore be that a Member State may not, by virtue of the reservation relating to public policy contained in Articles 48 and 56 of the Treaty, expel a national of another Member State from its territory or refuse him access to its territory by reason of conduct which, when attributable to the former State's own nationals, does not give rise to repressive measures or other genuine and effective measures intended to combat such conduct.

Decision. On those grounds, the court, in answer to the questions referred to it by the President of the Tribunal de Premiere Instance, Liège, ruled that

> [A] Member State may not, by virtue of the reservation relating to public policy contained in Articles 48 and 56 of the Treaty, expel a national of another Member State from its territory or refuse him access to its territory by reason of conduct which, when attributable to the former State's own nationals, does not give rise to repressive measures or other genuine and effective measures intended to combat such conduct.

The court further found that notification of the grounds relied upon to justify an expulsion measure or a refusal to issue a residence permit must be sufficiently detailed and precise to enable the person concerned to defend his or her interests.

The person concerned must be entitled to put forward to the competent authority his arguments in defense and to be assisted or represented in such conditions as to procedure as are provided for by domestic legislation. Those conditions must not be less favorable to the person concerned than the conditions applicable to proceedings before other national authorities of the same type.

who are not Member State nationals. But this is changing. The EU's Group on Treaty Amendment and Community Competence has in recent years noted that measures prohibiting racism and xenophobia should become part of the EU's discussion on EU treaty amendments. Among the measures discussed have been granting legal status to resident non–EU citizens and granting third-country nationals EU–citizen status upon completion of a five-year lawful residency requirement in one of the Member States.

Discrimination Based on Gender. The movement to abolish discrimination based on gender is relatively new. Until the twentieth century, few nations even granted women the right of suffrage. The great majority of nations imposed many restrictions on work outside the home.

During the twentieth century, women's legal status changed radically. Gender discrimination laws were largely replaced with antidiscrimination provisions. Legal restrictions on women's roles in the workplace are now principally limited to a few Islamic nations. In fact, in 2005, the International Labor Organization (ILO) reported that 56.6 percent of the workforce worldwide is female. The highest rates are in North America (71.1 percent) and the lowest are in the Middle East (32 percent).

Notwithstanding these legal advances, some level of gender discrimination remains almost universal in the twenty-first century. In Japan, women earn only 63 percent of what men earn. In the United States, the figure is 74 percent. Pay rates in Northern European nations are among the most equal. In Sweden and Denmark, the figures are 87 and 88 percent, respectively. However, in other countries, women's pay is dramatically less equal. Chile's booming economy has done little to improve the pay ratio of 54 cents for women to every dollar men make. Discriminatory access to educational opportunity is not the explanation.

In Latin America, on the average, a woman needs fifteen years of education to make the same amount of money as a man with eleven years of education. Similarly, a 2003 study of gender discrimination in the Ukraine found widespread discrimination against women in all employment sectors despite broad legal guarantees of equal protection. The discrimination included job announcements that specified male applicants only and job announcements requiring an attractive appearance for female applicants. In addition, the study found discrimination against unmarried women and women with small children.

Lawmakers have particularly focused on the issue of maternity leave. An EU directive now provides for a minimum of fourteen weeks' maternity leave and an allowance of at least 75 or 80 percent of net salary. It further stipulates that pregnant workers cannot be fired. In Hong Kong, a new law provides for ten weeks' maternity leave at two-thirds of the woman's latest salary. India requires six weeks' leave at full pay. The Ukraine allows ten weeks' pre-birth and eight weeks' post-birth salaried maternity leave, as well as additional unpaid leave until the child reaches age three. The up-to-age-three leave allows the mother to collect benefits from the state.

There has also been change in the area of equal pay for equal work. Article 119 of the *EU treaty* and *Community Directives 75/117 and 76/207* require equal pay for equal work and equality in access to employment. As noted in the *Bilka-Kaufhaus* case, compliance with these principles is determined through a practical "effect-oriented" test.

Bilka-Kaufhaus GmbH v. Karin Weber von Hartz
1986 E.C.R. 1607
Court of Justice of the European Communities

BACKGROUND AND FACTS

By order of June 5, 1984, the Bundesarbeitsgericht (German Federal Labour Court) referred the following question to the Court of Justice of the European Communities for a preliminary ruling: Is there an infringement of Article 19 of the *EEC Treaty* in the form of "direct discrimination" where a department store that employs predominantly women excludes part-time employees from benefits under its pension plan, although such exclusion affects disproportionately more women than men?

LORD MACKENZIE STUART, CHIEF JUDGE; KOOPMANS, EVERLING, BAHLMANN, AND JOLIET, PPC; BOSCO, DUE, GALMOT, AND KAKOURIS, JUDGES

By order of 5 June 1984, received by the Court on 2 July 1984, the Bundesarbeitsgericht (Federal Labour Court) requested a preliminary ruling pursuant to Article 177 of the EEC Treaty ... concerning the interpretation of Article 119 of the Treaty.

The questions have arisen in the context of an action brought against Bilka Kaufhaus GmbH (Bilka) by its previous employee, Karin Weber von Hartz, concerning her entitlement to a retirement pension under the supplementary pension scheme set up by Bilka for its employees.

It appears from the file that Bilka has for several years had a supplementary pension scheme (occupational pension) for its employees.... According to the version in force from 26 October 1973, part-time employees qualify under the scheme only if they have been in full-time employment for fifteen years out of a total of twenty.

Mrs. Weber was employed by Bilka as a sales assistant from 1961 to 1976. After working full-time, she opted to work part-time from 1 October 1972 up to the date when her contract of employment came to an end. As she had not worked a minimum of fifteen years full-time Bilka refused her an occupational pension.

Mrs. Weber challenged the legality of Bilka's refusal in the German labour courts on the ground, inter alia, that the occupational pension scheme was in breach of the principle of equal pay for men and women, enshrined in Article 119 of the EEC Treaty. On this point Mrs. Weber argued that the requirement, for receiving an occupational pension, of a

continued

continued

minimum period of full-time employment is to the detriment of female workers who, in order to be able to take care of their family and children, are more likely to be induced to choose part-time work than their male colleagues.

Bilka, on the other hand, maintained that it could not be accused of violating the principle of equal pay because the decision to exclude part-time employees from the occupational pension scheme was based on objectively justified economic grounds. In this connection it emphasized that the employment of full-time workers, by comparison with part-time workers, involves fewer ancillary costs and permits staff to be used for the whole period during which stores are open.

In the first question on which it seeks a preliminary ruling, the national court asked whether the staff policy of a department store company, consisting in excluding part-time employees from an occupational pension scheme, constitutes discrimination prohibited by Article 119 if the exclusion affects far more female workers than males.

For a reply to this question, reference should be made to the judgment of 31 March 1981. In that judgment the Court considered the question whether a pay practice consisting in fixing a lower hourly rate of pay for part-time work than for full-time work is compatible with Article 119. A practice of this kind is comparable to that referred to by the national court in the present case because, although Bilka makes no distinction in relation to hourly pay as between part-time or full-time employees, it grants an occupational pension only to employees in the latter category. As an occupational pension is within the definition of pay given by paragraph 2 of Article 119, as shown above, it follows that the global pay given by Bilka to full-time employees is higher than that for part-time employees, assuming an equal number of hours worked.

It follows that, if it were found that a considerably smaller percentage of women than men work full-time, the exclusion of part-time workers from the occupational pension scheme would be contrary to Article 119 of the Treaty if, taking account of the difficulties encountered by women arranging matters so as to be able to work full-time, this measure cannot be explained by factors excluding discrimination based on sex.

However, if the enterprise is able to show that its pay practice can be explained by objectively justified factors which are unrelated to discrimination based on sex, it would not be possible to find a breach of Article 119. Therefore the reply to the first question by the national court should be that Article 119 of the EEC Treaty is infringed by a department store company which excludes part-time employees from its occupational pension scheme where that exclusion affects a much greater number of women than men, unless the enterprise shows that the exclusion is based on objectively justified factors which are unrelated to any discrimination based on sex.

In the second question the national court aims in substance to establish whether the reasons put forward by Bilka to explain its pay policy can be considered "objectively justified economic reasons" within the meaning of the judgment of 31 March 1981, when reasons of commercial expediency in the department store sector do not necessitate such a policy.

It falls to the national court, which alone is competent to assess the facts, to decide whether, and if so to what extent, the grounds put forward by an employer to explain the adoption of a pay practice which applies irrespective of the employee's sex, but which in fact affects more women than men, can be considered to be objectively justified for economic reasons. If the national court finds that the means chosen by Bilka meet a genuine need of the enterprise, that they are suitable for attaining the objective pursued by the enterprise and are necessary for that purpose, the fact that the measures in question affect a much greater number of women than men is not sufficient to conclude that they involve a breach of Article 119.

Therefore the answer to question 2(a) should be that, according to Article 119, a department store company may justify the adoption of a pay policy involving the exclusion of part-time employees from its occupational pension scheme, regardless of sex, by contending that it seeks to employ as few workers of this kind as possible, if it is found that the means chosen to attain this objective meet a genuine need of the enterprise, are suitable for attaining the objective in question and are necessary for that purpose.

Finally the national court, in question 2(b), asks whether the employer is compelled, pursuant to Article 119 of the Treaty, to organize the occupational pension scheme for employees in such a way as to take account of the fact that the family commitments

continued

continued

of female employees prevent them from fulfilling the conditions for entitlement to a pension.

It should be observed that the ambit of Article 119 is limited to the problem of discrimination in pay between men and women. On the other hand, problems connected with other conditions of work and employment are envisaged generally by other provisions of Community law, particularly Article 117 and 118 of the Treaty, with a view to harmonization of the social systems of Member States and approximation of their legislation in this field.

This imposition of an obligation of the kind described by the national court in its question goes beyond the ambit of Article 119 and has no other basis in Community law as it stands at present.

Therefore the reply to question 2(b) must be that Article 119 does not have the effect of compelling an employer to organize the occupational pension scheme for employees in such a way as to take account of the special difficulties encountered by employees with family commitments in fulfilling the conditions entitling them to such as pension.

Decision. The Court of Justice remanded the case to the German Federal Labor Court for proceedings consistent with the foregoing rulings.

Gender discrimination cases have found only mixed success in Japan. In July 1990, a Tokyo district court ruled for the first time that female employees had been improperly denied promotions due to gender discrimination. Although the court awarded eighteen women $640,000, consistent with Japan's respect for the integrity of the workplace, the court declined to direct promotions because such action would interfere with personnel decisions. However, in November 2003, the Tokyo District Court found that different, lower pay for women was acceptable. Notwithstanding occasional setbacks, movement on gender discrimination issues seems consistent throughout the world.

Foreign Laws Permitting Difficult Work Conditions

One of the principal reasons for locating a plant abroad is relative cost advantage. Particularly in low-skill manufacturing, one's dollars, marks, or yen go farther paying salaries in an economy with a weak currency and a low cost of living. Many Third World countries lack burdensome work rules that add costs.

Other nations boast smooth labor–management relations that avoid expensive disputes. In some cases, cost savings are attributable to work conditions that, while lawful in the host country, are not legal in industrialized Western nations. In fact, these labor practices may not even be legal under local law. U.S. companies seldom directly engage in illegal employment practices. Instead, they often place orders for a product or a component with a foreign buying agent that submits a low bid. These agents procure foreign suppliers to assemble the products or components in accordance with the U.S. company's specifications. These suppliers in turn subcontract parts of the product to smaller shops. Typically, the worst abuses occur in low-cost small shops that are several steps removed from the U.S. purchaser.

A U.S. firm, even if operating legally within the host country, must concern itself with whether those practices violate nonbinding standards issued by the ILO and other international standards. If a business is unaware of dubious labor practices but uses foreign buying agents, it should conduct due diligence to satisfy itself that such practices are not in use. As will be seen, a failure to do so can have adverse consequences in the U.S. firm's target markets.

Unsafe Labor Conditions

In developed countries, government agencies similar to the U.S. Occupational Safety and Health Administration regulate conditions in the workplace. In many emerging nations, there is no such legal framework and working conditions can be quite hazardous. One of the more common and dangerous of these practices is the blocking and locking of all exits in manufacturing facilities as a low-cost measure to prevent pilfering. This practice has caused thousands of workers to be trapped and burned alive when fire broke out in such buildings. For example, a fire in a locked toy factory near Bangkok killed more than 240 workers and injured hundreds of others. In a separate incident, a fire in a locked facility killed eighty young women in Dongguan, China. The lack of ventilation in such factories also increases the incidence of tuberculosis and sinusitis among workers.

A second common safety issue is the use of antiquated and poorly maintained equipment, which causes the rate of work injuries to balloon. Indeed, in many emerging nations where such equipment predominates, work-related injuries have doubled in the last five years.

Harsh work rules, which are legal in many developing nations, are a third major concern. For instance, in order to maximize output per worker and thereby reduce cost per unit, some manufacturers permit assembly line workers to use the restroom only three times in a twelve-hour day. This practice not only subjects workers to great physical discomfort, but it increases the incidence of urinary tract infections. Harsh work rules also involve very long work hours. In China's Guandong Province, factories with 130-hour work weeks—with dormitory rent deducted from wages—have been reported.

Prison Labor

Prison labor exists to some extent in virtually all countries. State prisoners manufacture most of the license plates in the United States. However, in a few nations—including China—it is legal for prisoners to work in traditionally commercial forms of manufacturing. If developed nations have difficulty competing with low-cost labor in underdeveloped countries, they have even less chance of competing with free, involuntary labor from such nations. The use of such labor is unacceptable to Western governments.

Because China has close relations between government and business, the practice of prison labor became particularly prevalent in the late 1980s. In 1992, the United States stepped up the pressure on China to exclude prison labor products from exports to the United States. The result was the diplomatic Memorandum of Understanding.

As is often the case in matters of international trade, the matter did not end with the signing of this agreement. The United States continues to receive reports of prison labor generating exports to the United States. The United States threatened trade sanctions to enforce the Memorandum before concluding a new agreement with China in 1994. Under the 1994 agreement, the United States is allowed to inspect "labor reform camps." However, the United States has complained that it has received only modest cooperation in implementing the agreements.

Child Labor

Because wages for children tend to be quite low, child labor is common, if illegal, in "low-cost" nations. For instance, although work during school hours is illegal for anyone under fourteen years of age in Sri Lanka, Zambia, and Mexico, 500,000 children under fourteen work in Sri Lanka, 700,000 work in Zambia, and millions work in Mexico. Children are the labor foundation of Bangladesh's garment industry and India's oriental carpet industry. In 2002, the ILO reported that 211 million children under 15—out of 1.2 billion worldwide—were engaged in some form of child labor.

Children who are employed cannot attend school or otherwise receive formal education. They also get sick: children in unsanitary environments are not as resistant to disease as adults are. Children working in Indian carpet shops, for example, have a high incidence of tuberculosis, worm infestation, skin disease, and enlarged lymph glands.

Consequences of Participation in Illegal or Harsh Work Conditions

Participating in illegal or harsh work conditions might ultimately raise more than an ethical dilemma. The U.S. investor might have to see the workers on the other end of a summons in the United States. Since the U.S. Supreme Court's decision in *Sosa v. Alvarez-Machain,* 542 U.S. 692 (2004), U.S. employers in foreign countries have begun to face lawsuits filed by their foreign employees. In *Sosa,* Justice Souter interpreted the *Alien Tort Statute* (ATS) to permit non–U.S. citizens to bring private causes of action in U.S. courts based upon torts (such as piracy) that violate norms of international law that are as widely accepted and definite as those recognized by Congress when the ATS was passed in 1789. Since *Sosa,* federal courts have struggled to define what qualifies as a norm of international law for jurisdictional purposes under the ATS, as reflected in the following case.

Sarei v. Rio Tinto, PLC

487 F.3d 1193 (2007)

United States Court of Appeals (9th Cir.)

BACKGROUND AND FACTS

Rio Tinto is an international mining group headquartered in London. It operated a mine in Bougainville, Papua New Guinea from 1972 to 1989. Plaintiffs are former or current residents of Bougainville who alleged damages as a result of the mine's operations and a ten-year civil war that erupted following an uprising at the mine. Plaintiffs claim that ever since the mine opened, Rio Tinto's practices there polluted Bougainville's waterways and negatively affected the residents' physical and mental health, causing residents, particularly children, to suffer devastating illnesses such as upper respiratory disease. Moreover, workers at the mine were supposedly subjected to "slave-like" working conditions and racially discriminatory wages. In November 1988, residents sabotaged the mine, forcing it to close. Rio Tinto obtained the assistance of the national army to quell the uprising, which it did on February 14, 1990. This resulted in the death of many civilians. Bougainville subsequently called for its secession from Papua New Guinea, and a ten-year civil war began. During the war, the army committed war crimes and human rights abuses "at the behest of Rio Tinto, including a blockade, aerial bombardment of civilian targets, burning of villages, rape and pillage."

CIRCUIT JUDGE BYBEE

Plaintiffs filed suit under the ATS against Rio Tinto for its alleged commission of war crimes, human rights abuses and racial discrimination. The Ninth Circuit analyzed the Plaintiffs' appeal of dismissal of their claims below, determining whether it had subject matter jurisdiction under ATS. Relying upon *Sosa,* the Court found that "so long as plaintiffs alleged a nonfrivolous claim by an alien for a tort in violation of international law," the Court had proper subject matter jurisdiction. The Court found that the Plaintiffs alleged violations of "specific, universal, and obligatory norm[s] of international law" when they claimed that Rio Tinto directed and aided the national army in carrying out its war crimes and human rights abuses against the residents of Bougainville, in addition to directly discriminating against residents based upon their race.

Decision. The plaintiffs could bring claims against the U.S. defendant for violations of international law norms under the ATS.

In the *Rio Tinto* litigation, one of the plaintiff's burdens was to prove that there are international norms that may be prosecuted under the ATS. While it should be relatively easy to show norms in an international compact against war crimes, it might prove more difficult to prove that there is international consensus on racial discrimination. Under the ATS, of course, the plaintiff may not rely on U.S. antidiscrimination law. The following case further illustrates the difficulty of proving the existence of such international norms.

John Roe I v. Bridgestone Corporation

492 F. Supp.2d 988 (2007)

United States District Court for the Southern District of Indiana

BACKGROUND AND FACTS

Adults and children who work on the Firestone Rubber Plantation near Harbel, Liberia brought suit against Bridgestone Corporation, an entity headquartered in Japan; five of its U.S. subsidiaries; one Liberian subsidiary; and two individuals who respectively head subsidiaries of Bridgestone in America and Liberia. The plaintiffs sought relief under the ATS, as well as other federal and state laws, based upon claims of forced labor, forced child labor, poor working conditions, and low wages.

DISTRICT JUDGE HAMILTON

Counts One and Two assert claims under the law of nations and invoke the court's subject matter jurisdiction under the federal Alien Tort Statute ("ATS"), which provides: "The district courts shall have original jurisdiction of any civil action by an alien for a tort only, committed in violation of the law of nations or a treaty of the United States." 28 U.S.C. §1350. The defendants have moved to dismiss the ATS claims for lack of subject matter jurisdiction and for failure to state a claim upon which relief can be granted.

On the motion to dismiss the ATS claims, defendants' central argument is that the Complaint does not actually allege violations of international law standards that are sufficiently specific, universal, and obligatory to support relief under the ATS. See *Sosa v. Alvarez-Machain,* 542 U.S. 692, 732, 124 S.Ct. 2739, 159 L.Ed.2d 718 (2004) ("[F]ederal courts should not recognize private claims under federal common law for violations of any international law norm with less definite content and acceptance among civilized nations than the historical paradigms familiar when §1350 was enacted"); *Sarei v. Rio Tinto, PLC,* 487 F.3d 1193, 1202 (9th Cir. 2007) (noting that Sosa accepted the requirement of a "specific, universal and obligatory norm of international law" for an ATS claim).

[A] complaint ordinarily must set forth only a colorable or arguable claim arising under federal law to establish federal question subject matter jurisdiction.... The doubtful validity or even invalidity of such a claim does not undermine the court's subject matter jurisdiction. Although there is conflicting authority on the question, the court finds that the same standard applies to international law claims asserted under the Alien Tort Statute. Because plaintiffs have alleged claims arising under international law that are at least colorable and arguable, the court has subject matter jurisdiction over Counts One and Two under the ATS....

When deciding a motion to dismiss ... the issue is not whether plaintiffs have submitted "competent proof" or even are likely to prevail upon the evidence. The focus is on the sufficiency of the pleading in the Complaint....

The ATS was enacted in 1789 by the First Congress, but it was used only rarely before 1980....

In 2004, the Supreme Court gave its first detailed consideration to the scope of the ATS in Sosa v. Alvarez-Machain.... The Supreme Court unanimously concluded that the ATS "enabled federal courts to hear claims in a very limited category defined by the law of nations and recognized at common law," but that "the limited, implicit sanction to entertain the handful of international law cum common law claims understood in 1789...."

Plaintiffs cite several pre-Sosa federal cases holding or stating that "forced labor" violates the law of nations. Those cases show that some forms of forced labor violate the law of nations, but the facts in those cases are so different from the plaintiffs' allegations in this case as to show that the label "forced labor" adds little to the needed analysis.

In *Iwanowa v. Ford Motor Co.,* ... the plaintiff alleged that during World War II, she was literally sold from her home in Russia and transported by Nazi troops to Germany to work for the German subsidiary of Ford under inhuman conditions and without compensation.... In *In re World War II Era Japanese Forced Labor Litigation* ... the court also dismissed all claims as time-barred but stated it was inclined to agree with the *Iwanowa* conclusion that forced labor violates the law of nations....

The Complaint in this case uses the same powerful label "forced labor." That conclusory label is not decisive. The court need not take at face value the legal conclusions in a complaint.... This case lies at a point on a continuum far from the forced labor of Nazi Germany, Japanese labor camps, or the workers

continued

continued

rounded up more recently by the Burmese military. Even if the adult plaintiffs' factual allegations are credited, as the court must, these plaintiffs have not alleged violations of a specific, universal, and obligatory norm of international law.

The adult plaintiffs in this case rely on several international agreements to show that their working conditions violate international law. The first is ILO Forced Labour Convention (No. 29), ... ILO Convention 29 entered into force on May 1, 1932. Liberia and Japan have ratified ILO Convention 29, but the United States has not. Article 2 of ILO Convention 29 defines forced labor to mean "all work or service which is exacted from any person under the menace of any penalty and for which the said person has not offered himself voluntarily." In ILO Convention 29, the ratifying members of the ILO agreed to end some forms of forced labor and to impose certain minimum standards for working conditions and wages in cases in which forced labor was permitted. Prohibited forms of forced labor include forced labor "for the benefit of private individuals, companies or associations." Art. 4. This prohibition would apply to forced labor for the benefit of private corporations like the defendants in this case, at least if plaintiffs could allege and prove true forced labor and if ILO Convention 29 were deemed to apply in the United States....

The question here is what is "forced labor," keeping in mind that international norms are actionable under the ATS only if they are as specific, universal, and obligatory as Blackstone's three 18th century archetypes—piracy, wrongs against ambassadors, and violations of safe conducts.

Plaintiffs have submitted a 2005 report by the Director General of the ILO entitled "A global alliance against forced labour" that reports on the ILO Declaration on Fundamental Principles and Rights at Work.... The report tackled the problem of definition in terms that help illuminate the parties' arguments in this case:

> "Yet the very concept of forced labour, as set out in the ILO standards on the subject, is still not well understood. In many quarters the term continues to be associated mainly with the forced labour practices of totalitarian regimes: the flagrant abuses of Hitler's Germany, Stalin's Soviet Union or Pol Pot's Cambodia. At the other end of the spectrum, such terms as "modern slavery", "slavery-like practices" and "forced labour" can be used rather loosely to refer to poor or insalubrious working conditions, including very low wages. Indeed, some national legislation has identified the late payment of wages, or remuneration below the legal minimum wage, as at least one element of a forced labour situation." ...

Forced labour cannot be equated simply with low wages or poor working conditions. Nor does it cover situations of pure economic necessity, as when a worker feels unable to leave a job because of the real or perceived absence of employment alternatives. Forced labour represents a severe violation of human rights and restriction of human freedom, as defined in the ILO Conventions on the subject and in other related international instruments on slavery, practices similar to slavery, debt bondage or serfdom....

Plaintiffs in this case do not allege that any of these indicators of involuntary work apply to the current generation of adult Plantation workers. The plaintiffs allege that their grandparents and great-grandparents were abducted, kidnapped, and/or physically threatened when the Plantation was established in the 1920s, but plaintiffs are not in a position to assert claims for money damages today based on the mistreatment of their ancestors. Plaintiffs allege that they have nothing left after they spend their wages at company stores and other company facilities (such as schools), but they do not allege induced indebtedness. Plaintiffs allege that they are physically isolated at the Plantation, but they do not allege that Firestone keeps them physically confined there. To the extent plaintiffs allege psychological compulsion, they are clearly alleging what the ILO report calls "pure economic necessity, as when a worker feels unable to leave a job because of the real or perceived absence of employment alternatives," which is not forced labor under international law....

Count Two also seeks relief under the ATS, asserting that work done by the child plaintiffs on the Plantation violates international law. The Complaint alleges that the Firestone supervisors on the Plantation encourage and even require the adult latex tappers to put their children to work to help meet the production quotas... Plaintiffs allege that children apply fertilizers and pesticides by hand, without protective equipment.... Plaintiffs also allege that children as young as six years old work at the Firestone Plantation.... The defendants deny these allegations, but the court must accept these factual allegations for purposes of the motion to dismiss...

The circumstances alleged here include at least some practices that could therefore fall within the

continued

continued

"worst forms of child labor" addressed in [International Labour Organization ["ILO"], Worst Forms of Child Labour Convention (No. 182)]. The conditions of work alleged by plaintiffs (and reported by the UN investigators) are likely to harm the health and safety of at least the very youngest of the child plaintiffs in this case.

As noted above, and as Firestone has argued, national child labor laws and international conventions on child labor are often written to allow even very young children to help out on family farms. Those special accommodations for family farms have no application here. Plaintiffs do not challenge labor practices on subsistence farms. They challenge the practices of a huge multinational corporate family that hires the children's parents and then (allegedly) encourages the parents to require their young children to do much of the work. Plaintiffs allege that defendants have set the daily production quotas so high that use of child labor is both necessary and inevitable, and that defendants take advantage of the parents in this situation. …

The court recognizes that international legal standards for child labor do not always establish bright lines, though there are some. That is also the case with forced labor, as discussed above. Just as some practices that might be described by some as "forced labor" might not violate international law, some practices that could be described as "child labor" also do not violate international law. One must look more closely at the particular circumstances, as shown by the pleadings and later by the evidence.

At least some of the practices alleged with regard to the labor of very young children at the Firestone Plantation in Liberia may violate specific, universal, and obligatory standards of international law, such that Count Two should not be dismissed on the pleadings. In light of ILO Convention 182, the court believes that the allegations of child labor in Count Two meet the Sosa standard for ATS claims. It would not require great "judicial creativity" to find that even paid labor of very young children in these heavy and hazardous jobs would violate international norms. Those international norms are not inconsistent with Liberian law. Those norms also are stated in an international convention that both the United States and Liberia have ratified. On this record, there is no indication that this lawsuit threatens to cause friction with the foreign policy of the United States. … Plaintiffs may face other daunting challenges in pursuing their case, and the court will address those issues as they are raised.

Decision. The court denied the defendants' motion to dismiss all claims for lack of subject matter jurisdiction. It granted the defendants' motion to dismiss for failure to state a claim as to Count One alleging "forced labor" and denied the motion as to Count Two, the child labor claim under international law.

U.S. companies must carefully consider the working conditions that their operations in foreign countries support. As litigation under the ATS increases, more and more companies will consider taking a closer look at the foreign-based operations for any exposure to these types of lawsuits.

U.S. companies whose foreign operations use such practices may also face consumer boycotts in their markets. Labor organizations and other increasingly active opponents of dubious labor practices are identifying and targeting companies involved—directly or indirectly—in such practices. The threat of such protests has proved a potent incentive for investors to avoid them.

The developed nations are attempting to stop these labor practices through international trade treaties. Under these proposals, non-enforcement of employment standards would be a violation of international trade agreements, just as are dumping or subsidies discussed in Chapter Ten. The United States has proposed amendments to the WTO trade rules that tie labor standards to international trade. These amendments were stalled and the delegates decided that labor issues should instead be discussed in the context of the ILO, where discussion has not been particularly effective. In its effort, the United States has focused on providing a tool for enforcing ILO conventions on unsafe working conditions, minimum age for child labor, and forced labor, without addressing any issues on minimum wages. Developing nations cried foul, asserting that such standards would be misused by the developed world to bar their products from developed markets. Although this matter remains under intense negotiation, some nations have agreed to combat trade practices like child labor in order to secure trade deals with the United States.

The U.S. Congress has reacted to the stalled effort to tie labor standards to international trade by entertaining a unilateral expansion of its own trade laws. Under a proposed revision of Section 301 of the *Trade Act of 1974*—discussed in Chapter Eleven—the harsh Section 301 sanctions and retaliatory measures would be available if a U.S. firm could prove that an importer is violating an established set of labor standards. Because such a measure is not addressed in the global trade rules, however, the law, if passed, might be deemed a violation of the international trade agreement.

In October 1997, Congress passed the Sanders Amendment, which bans the import of any product made by forced child labor. In addition, Congress established the Child Labor Command Center, located at U.S. Customs headquarters, which acts as a clearinghouse for information and provides 24-hour "hotline" telephone service to a wide variety of audiences in order to provide a venue for allegations about prohibited importations. The initiative increases foreign staffing by assigning three additional special agents to areas where forced child labor is the most common. In addition, Customs is to engage in outreach programs with trade, government, and nongovernmental organizations to achieve successful enforcement of the Sanders Amendment.

A private initiative is also making significant progress. Some U.S. firms—of which Levi Strauss & Co. is particularly prominent—have instituted global "sourcing guidelines" to determine with whom they will do business. Levi Strauss requires a certification from suppliers that they are in compliance with the guidelines. If Levi Strauss has reason to believe that a supplier or its subcontractors have violated one of these guidelines, it will investigate the matter. If it finds a violation, it will terminate its contract with the supplier. As a result of this program, Levi Strauss stopped manufacturing jeans in China in 1993.

By April 1998, China had made sufficient concessions to human rights to permit Levi Strauss to return. Such a guidelines approach, if adopted by more firms, would go a long way toward eradicating questionable working conditions.

Conclusion

Labor law poses particular difficulties for the U.S. investor because of markedly different attitudes toward employer–employee relations in other nations. Especially surprising are laws that require employee input into strategic decisions, prescribe employee representation on boards of directors, and place impediments upon dismissals. The investor must also familiarize itself with different countries' approaches to employment discrimination and coordinate such approaches with U.S. requirements for such operations. Finally, the U.S. investor abroad should avoid companies that permit types of harsh work conditions that are illegal in the West. Such practices may come back to haunt the investor in his home jurisdiction through personal injury lawsuits and consumer boycotts.

Chapter Summary

1. Different nations approach worker participation in corporate decision making differently. U.S. law gives great discretion to the owner of the enterprise, with no input from workers. Most European nations formally require worker input on corporate decisions and representation on boards of directors. In Japan's more collective system, there is not as much distinction between management and labor, because union officials are often promoted into management ranks.
2. Different countries have varying legal approaches to employee dismissal. In the United States, in the absence of a collective bargaining agreement or an employment agreement, company owners have near-total discretion to terminate employees. In Europe, dismissal of employees typically requires consultation with a works council or some employee group. In Japan, it can be very difficult to terminate an employee at all. With globalization of business, however, the approaches have tended to merge toward one another.
3. Employment discrimination law in many countries is less developed than that of the

United States. Indeed, the greatest employment discrimination problem faced by U.S. firms operating in some foreign countries is that many countries, by custom, require employment discrimination. Thus, U.S. firms must determine when U.S. law might make illegal their compliance with foreign discriminatory norms.

4. Congress has provided that Title VII of the *Civil Rights Act* does not apply where it would violate the law of the country where the firm is located. However, courts have since interpreted both the *Age Discrimination in Employment Act* and the *Americans with Disabilities Act* to prohibit U.S. employers and foreign companies controlled by a U.S. employer from discriminating in employment of U.S. citizens in other countries. Courts have found, however, that the same laws do not give rights to foreigners seeking work from U.S. entities. In other cases, discrimination laws have been found inapplicable to U.S. residents hired to work exclusively abroad. The law is unsettled in this area.
5. Courts have found and Congress has now provided that quite a number of other U.S. antidiscrimination laws do not apply outside the United States. These laws include the *National Labor Relations Act,* the *Occupational Safety & Health Act,* the *Fair Labor Standards Act,* the *Equal Pay Act,* the *Family and Medical Leave Act,* and other federal and state laws.
6. The three principal defenses to U.S. challenges of employment decisions are that (1) the decision is made by "a foreign person not controlled by an American employer;" (2) the U.S. law conflicts with a host country's laws, and therefore the employer faces "foreign compulsion" because to comply with U.S. law would violate the host country's laws; and (3) the performance of the job requires a trait such as a specific religion or gender, allowing the employer the "bona fide occupational qualification" defense.
7. The European Union now has a significant body of law prohibiting discrimination based on age, gender, and (as to nationals of other Member States) national origin or ethnicity. Despite some study groups on the question, however, there is not yet Community-wide protection for immigrants from other nations.
8. Unsafe working conditions, harsh work rules, forced/prison labor, and child labor are commonplace in less developed countries. Because these practices create cost advantages and usually occur several levels away from the purchasers of these products in developed countries, they have not historically been a cause for private enterprise concern. Most advances in this area have resulted from government-to-government pressure.
9. In the *Sosa* case, the United States Supreme Court held that a party could bring a suit under the *Alien Tort Statute* for violations of "specific, universal, and obligatory norm[s] of international law." This means that foreign parties wronged by an American firm's use of proscribed practices in child labor, unduly harsh work rules, and the like can win a judgment in a U.S. court if they can prove the existence and violation of an applicable international norm. This showing can be quite difficult to make, but creates a significant issue for any international enterprise with significant operations in the United States.
10. Faced with the prospect of adverse publicity, potential liability, and dubious ethics, international companies are increasingly investigating their supply chains to ensure that their products or product components are not being manufactured through the use of ethically questionable practices.

Questions and Case Problems

1. Would a U.S. court override an employer's contractual rights (as the Supreme Court of Japan did) because of a countervailing "socially accepted view"? What if the employment contract was between a drug lord and his "trigger man"? Do you think that the relative homogeneity of a national

culture affects the breadth of issues on which there is a "socially accepted view"?

2. Susan Currie is a U.S. manufacturer of tear gas, which she sells to various governments for crowd control. To reduce transportation costs to the interested governments, Ms. Currie is considering building a new plant in Germany. The plant will employ 2,500 people. What foreign labor law considerations should she take into account?

Managerial Implications

Your firm is Crystallina, a U.S. mineral water producer and distributor. A strong market for mineral water is South Moravia, a nation dominated by a fundamentalist state religion that prohibits drinking any alcohol or carbonated beverages. Market studies indicate that if Crystallina established offices in South Moravia, it would reap rich profits. If employees of a company like Crystallina violate South Moravian religious law, however, the company is liable for severe fines.

1. South Moravian religious law prohibits women from engaging in gainful employment. Accordingly, if Crystallina establishes an office there, it will not be able to offer any of its women executives an opportunity to work there. What U.S. legal issues are raised for Crystallina? Should Crystallina establish an office in South Moravia?
2. Now assume that South Moravian religious law permits women to work, but strictly prohibits homosexual behavior of any kind. Accordingly, if Crystallina establishes an office there, it will not be able to offer any of its gay executives an opportunity to work there. Does this raise any U.S. legal issues for Crystallina? Should Crystallina establish an office in South Moravia?
3. Now assume that South Moravian religious law permits women to work and has no particular concern about private homosexual behavior, but strictly prohibits Christian worship of any kind. Because Roman Catholics recognize a duty to worship on Sundays and holy days, if Crystallina establishes an office in South Moravia, it will not be able to offer any of its Catholic executives an opportunity to work there. What U.S. legal issues are raised for Crystallina? Should Crystallina establish an office in South Moravia?

For Internet Activities, Visit academic.cengage.com/blaw/schaffer.

CHAPTER 21
Environmental Law

Laws protecting the environment once deserved only brief mention in a book about laws affecting foreign investments. In recent years, however, there has been extraordinary activity in international environmental law. There have been large-scale international environmental disasters, and concern over global warming has greatly intensified. "Green" political parties have formed around environmental issues. In some important nations they have become part of governing coalitions. Consequently, nations have been furiously enacting legislation, investing in the development of alternative energy, and entering into treaties concerning the environment. Although this body of international law is not yet as well developed as other centuries-old legal canons, its impact on commercial activity has become noteworthy.

Consideration of Varying Environmental Requirements

Virtually all human activity alters the environment in some way. The central problem of environmental law is determining which activities alter the environment to an unacceptable degree. Those determinations, like all human judgments, vary depending on the circumstances of the person making them. Cutting down huge forests is as acceptable to Brazilian pioneers as it was to the North American pioneers—such as Abraham Lincoln—who turned the virgin forests of Illinois and Indiana into the heart of the grain belt. In the twenty-first century, most North Americans find Brazilian tree cutting unacceptable, even though none have proposed a reforestation of Peoria.

All things being equal, most people favor a clean and aesthetic environment. But all things are not equal. Poorer nations tend to oppose extensive international environmental regulation because it impairs their ability to profit from less-sophisticated production procedures. Wealthy countries tend to favor environmental protection, not only because they can afford to, but also because they profit from it. Citizens of wealthy nations design and manufacture the sophisticated equipment that makes production pollution-free. Wealthy nations sometimes use environmental and health issues as a pretext for keeping price-competitive foreign competition at bay.

Understanding the reasons for differences in environmental views between nations is critical to understanding the dynamics of traditional and emerging legal remedies.

Differences in Regulatory Schemes

Differences in nations' circumstances and views lead to differences in their environmental laws. First, the cost–benefit analysis as to any environmental modification often varies from country to country. A country with an opportunity to profit from a sulphur-belching power plant is more likely to think that the plant's modification of the environment is acceptable than a neighbor nation, which does not profit from the plant but suffers from its acid rain. Second, countries that are happy with the economic status quo are more inclined to favor environmental measures. Wealthy nations tend to have more laws to reduce pollution from industrial processes than countries plagued with malnutrition. Third, some nations lack the technological infrastructure to produce goods without pollution. In a strict economic sense, enacting a regulatory scheme that mandates buying such infrastructure greatly benefits wealthier nations, which manufacture and sell such equipment, and hampers less-developed nations that must spend scarce resources to purchase it. Finally, some governments permit officials to profit from environmental modifications. Thus, a nation may be lax in regulating hazardous waste disposal if the families of government officials greatly profit from the activity.

Obviously, many of these factors tend to place the wealthier, more-developed democracies on the side of international environmental regulation and the less-developed nations in opposition to such regulation. This dichotomy between the rich "North" and the poor "South" forms the principal dividing line in virtually all issues relating to international environmental law.

For foreign investors, these differences mean they may prefer to locate their facilities in countries with fewer environmental restrictions. A steel factory will cost millions less to build in South Korea than in the United States, where sophisticated antipollution equipment is required. A hazardous waste dump is easier to locate in Ghana than in Germany because Germany has a more comprehensive legal framework protecting groundwater from such waste.

These incentives have not been lost on countries pursuing conservation. First, because nature does not recognize political boundaries, European nations' compliance with international global warming will not reverse the upward trend in temperatures if China and India vastly increase their productive capacity. Canada's laws against acid rain are not fully effective if its populous southern neighbor does not enact similar laws. Second, the environmental regulations of the conservation-minded nations will make their products more expensive, placing them at a competitive disadvantage vis-à-vis countries less concerned about the environment. To level the playing field, conservationists have sought legal relief through international dispute resolution, import bans, and multilateral treaties.

Foreign investors must consider the risk that the host country's less-restrictive environmental laws will be changed through international action. This risk can be substantial. Installing anti-pollution devices after a plant is built, for example, can be vastly more expensive than including them during construction. In many circumstances, the better choice for the risk-averse investor is to build on the assumption that local environmental laws will evolve to First World standards.

Environmental Law as an Anticompetitive Tool

"Environmentally responsible" nations are not without sin. Such nations often enact strict local environmental laws not so much to save the environment as to prevent foreign competition.

The EU has been accused of doing this to protect its meat and dairy products industries, which have been battered by foreign competition. In 1993, the EU traced an outbreak of hoof and mouth disease in Italian livestock to Croatia. Rather than banning Italian meat or Croatian meat, the Union banned meat from the entire former Eastern bloc. Needless to say, the arbitrariness of banning meat from half a continent on the basis of a disease outbreak in a region of one small nation, especially while not banning meat from the only country where the disease had actually occurred, struck many producers as unfair. Eastern bloc meat was, however, cheaper. Similarly, members of the EU banned U.S. beef because many U.S. producers enhanced their livestock through bovine growth hormones. No proof that the hormones had any adverse effect on the meat has yet been offered. U.S. meat was, however, demonstrably less expensive and more popular among European consumers.

The United States has also been accused of using environmentally disguised trade barriers. The EU has complained of a variety of U.S. taxes and fines that they assert are disproportionately directed at European auto imports. In the mid-1990s, the United States enacted Corporate Average Fuel Efficiency (CAFE) standards and "gas-guzzler" surtaxes. These measures were ostensibly enacted to encourage fuel conservation and reduce air pollution. At the same time, the United States enacted a luxury tax on certain high-priced vehicles. The taxes nominally apply to domestic cars as well as European autos. Interestingly, European automakers pay about 90 percent of the combined gas-guzzler taxes, luxury taxes, and CAFE fines, although they hold only about 4 percent of the U.S. automobile market.

Another instance of U.S. discrimination may be seen in the *Standards for Reformulated and Conventional Gasoline* case later in this chapter.

An amusing example of alleged "environmental" anticompetitive behavior occurred in the French resort town of Grenoble. The city's leaders banned Bermuda shorts in public pools and encouraged bathers to wear bikinis and other skimpy traditional French bathing suits. They argued that the added material in the Bermuda shorts polluted their pools. Interestingly, all Bermuda shorts were foreign made.

TRADITIONAL INTERNATIONAL REMEDIES

The Polluter Pays: Responsibility for Pollution

In the absence of an agreement, the only way a country may address its neighbor's environmental pollution is through the dispute resolution mechanisms available under international law. Binding adjudication has not been common because in the absence of treaties such as those recently implemented with Europe, the alleged polluter would not consent to jurisdiction in such cases. An instance in which the polluter did consent to arbitration involved a Canadian smelter that was sending fumes into the United States in

The Trail Smelter Arbitration
3 R. Int'l Arb. Awards 1938 (1941)
Trail Smelter Arbitral Tribunal

MESSRS. HASTIE, GREENSHIELDS, AND WARREN

This Tribunal is constituted under, and its powers are derived from and limited by, the Convention between the United States of America and the Dominion of Canada signed at Ottawa, April 15, 1935.... The controversy is between two governments involving damage occurring or having occurred, in the territory of one of them (the United States of America) and alleged to be due to an agency situated in the territory of the other (the Dominion of Canada). As between the two countries involved, each has an equal interest that if a nuisance is proved, the indemnity to damaged parties for proven damage shall be just and adequate and each has also an equal interest that unproven or unwarranted claims shall not be allowed. For, while the United States' interests may now be claimed to be injured by the operations of a Canadian corporation, it is equally possible that at some time in the future Canadian interests might be claimed to be injured by an American corporation. The Columbia River has its source in the Dominion of Canada. At a place in British Columbia named Trail, it flows past a smelter located in a gorge, where zinc and lead are smelted in large quantities. From Trail, its course is easterly and then it swings in a long curve to the international boundary line, at which point it is running in a southwesterly direction; and its course south of the boundary continues in that general direction. The distance from Trail to the boundary line is about seven miles as the crow flies or about eleven miles, following the course of the river....

In 1906, a smelter was started under American auspices near the locality known as Trail, B.C. In 1936, the Consolidated Mining and Smelting Company of Canada, Limited, obtained a charter of incorporation from the Canadian authorities, and that company acquired the smelter plant at Trail as it then existed. Since that time, the Canadian company, without interruption, has operated the smelter, and from time to time has greatly added to the plant until it has become one of the best and largest equipped smelting plants on the American continent.... This increased production resulted in more sulphur dioxide fumes and higher concentrations being emitted into the air.

From 1925, at least, to 1937, damage occurred in the State of Washington resulting from sulphur

continued

continued

dioxide emitted from the Trail Smelter [by adversely affecting agricultural activities]. The second question under Article III of the Convention is as follows:

> In the event of the answer to the first part of the preceding question being affirmative, whether the Trail Smelter should be required to refrain from causing damage in the State of Washington in the future, and, if so, to what extent?

Damage has occurred since January 1, 1932, as fully set forth in the previous decision. To that extent, the first part of the preceding question has thus been answered in the affirmative.

As Professor Eagleton puts it ... "A state owes at all times a duty to protect other states against injurious acts by individuals from within its jurisdiction." ... But the real difficulty arises rather when it comes to determine what, *pro subjecta materie,* is deemed to constitute an injurious act.

The Tribunal ... finds that, under the principles of international law ... no state has the right to use or permit the use of its territory in such a manner as to cause injury by fumes or in the territory of another or the properties or persons therein, when the case is of serious consequence and the injury is established by clear and convincing evidence.

Considering the circumstances of the case, the Tribunal holds that the Dominion of Canada is responsible in international law for the conduct of the Trail Smelter. Apart from the undertakings in the Convention, it is, therefore, the duty of the government of the Dominion of Canada to see to it that this conduct should be in conformity with the obligation of the Dominion under international law as herein determined.

Decision. The Tribunal held that so long as the existing conditions in the Columbia River Valley prevailed, the Trail Smelter would be required to refrain from causing any damage through fumes in the State of Washington. It further found that the indemnity for such damage should be fixed in such manner as was agreed upon by the governments, acting under the Convention.

the 1930s. The case remains one of the more complete statements of the environmental obligations between nations.

Regulation of Products that Violate Environmental Objectives

Because international binding arbitration of environmental disputes such as in the *Trail Smelter* case is rare, a more frequent method for counterattack is for the conservation-minded nation to enact domestic legislation outlawing import of the offending product. These regulations are imposed against a product for two reasons: because the product itself violates environmental norms in the regulating country, or because it is manufactured through a process that is environmentally objectionable.

This type of domestic counterattack is somewhat restricted by the *General Agreement on Tariffs and Trade* (GATT), but GATT restrictions do not prevent nations from excluding products that are environmentally offensive by their very nature. Thus, if meat or a bathing suit poses a health or other environmental threat under local standards, and local standards are applied in a nondiscriminatory way, GATT presents no difficulty. In the following case, the United States was able to keep out Canadian lobsters because they did not meet U.S. minimum size requirements designed to protect the lobster population. This "nondiscriminatory internal regulation" was upheld although lobsters that reside in colder Canadian waters are by nature smaller and therefore disproportionately affected by the regulation. One should especially focus on the tribunal's explanation of GATT restrictions and how the United States avoided them. The minority view is also instructive because it points out gray areas in these GATT restrictions.

As the *Canadian Lobster* case demonstrates, states have a great deal of flexibility in excluding products that are by their own nature contrary to local environmental standards. In fact, the flexibility is so great that nations at times misuse

Lobsters from Canada

1990 WL 299945

United States–Canada Free Trade Agreement Binational Panel

BACKGROUND AND FACTS

The American lobster is only found in U.S. and Canadian waters in the western Atlantic Ocean. It grows by shedding its external shell, a process called "molting." American lobsters molt about twenty to twenty-five times between birth and sexual maturity. Water temperature affects how often lobsters molt. In cold waters, it may take a lobster up to ten years to reach sexual maturity; in warm waters, lobsters reach sexual maturity in as little as five years. Canadian waters tend to be colder than U.S. waters.

In 1989, the U.S. Congress passed an "environmental" amendment to the *Magnuson Fishery Conservation and Management Act* that prohibited the transport of whole live lobsters smaller than a certain minimum size. Canada sought relief against the United States before the Free Trade Agreement Binational Panel, alleging that the amended *Magnuson Act* was actually a restriction on importation of lobsters from Canada, in violation of Article XI of GATT. The United States argued that the amendment was not a "restriction on importation" but an "internal measure" subject only to GATT Article III. The United States further argued that even if Article XI applied, the *Magnuson Act* fell within an exception to Article XI found in Article XX(g), which permits restrictions on importation if they relate to conservation of an exhaustible natural resource.

CHAIRMAN NORWOOD, MESSRS. CLINGAN, LATIMER, AND POLLER, AND MS. WEST

The Majority View. The pertinent part of Article XI . . . reads:

> No prohibitions or restrictions other than duties, taxes or other charges . . . shall be instituted or maintained by any contracting party on the importation of any product of the territory of any other contracting party. . . .

Article III, in summary, prohibits the use of any form of [nontariff barrier] (NTB) to afford protection to domestic production. . . . Article III sets forth the principle of nondiscrimination or equal treatment or, more precisely, "national treatment" between imported and domestic products[:]

> The products of the territory of any contracting party imported into the territory of any other contracting party shall be accorded treatment no less favorable than accorded to like products of national origin in respect of all laws, regulations and requirements affecting their internal sale, offering for sale, purchase, transportation, distribution or use.

Article XI is the principle GATT Article containing the general ban against the use of QRs [qualitative restrictions] to limit importation. The Article itself contains exceptions, such as that for certain QRs on agricultural and fisheries products.

Article III is the principal GATT Article limiting the use of "border" and "internal" measures on imported goods. The rule of "national" treatment that it specifies to carry out the competition principle noted earlier bars a country from extending internal measures to imported goods in a way that bears more onerously on the imported products than on the like domestic products. . . .

As between Articles XI and III . . . [t]he trade effects on Canadian lobsters will not differ if the U.S. measures are determined to fall under one of these Articles rather than the other. Whether as Article XI measures on importation or as Article III measures on internal marketing, the U.S. limits on Canadian lobsters will have identical effects: imports of sub-sized lobsters will be zero.

The import counterpart of some of these measures would presumably be permitted by one of the general exceptions listed in Article XX, for example, any that could be justified as necessary to protect human, animal, or plant life or health. But many such prohibitions or restrictions affecting imported goods clearly would not. The internal marketing counterparts of these measures therefore would not be permissible under GATT if they were to fall under Article XI. Article III, on the other hand, was structured to permit governments to impose internal regulatory measures, subject to the national treatment standard, whether or not such measures met the specific exceptions of Article XX.

The Panel concluded that the appropriate principle to be used in determining whether the U.S. measures were covered by Article III was the nonprotection principle of . . . that Article.

The Panel determined that the U.S. measures imposed on live U.S. and Canadian lobsters were

continued

continued

covered by Article III and not by Article XI. In particular, they considered that the measures, as now applied in the U.S. internal market, or as they might be imposed at the border, came within the scope of "laws, regulations requirements affecting the internal sale, offering for sale, purchase, transportation, distribution or use of products."

The Minority View: That Article XI Is Applicable. Some members of the Panel concluded that [w]hat is determinative is the practical effect of the measure.... Measures couched in terms leading the reader to Article III may in truth and substance and effect be measures which the GATT signatories intended to prohibit by Article XI.... In any event, it is one thing to make an exporter's competition in the importing country's market prohibitively expensive, by discriminatory requirements, but it is quite another to bar entry into the market; the 1989 amendment fits into the latter category.

In view of the effect of the 1989 amendment (effect which is exactly the intent of those drafting it: to exclude Canadian sub-sized lobsters from the American market), and in view of the language of Article XI and of the analysis of GATT Panel precedents, some members of the Panel concluded that the 1989 amendment is prohibited by Article XI. It is a prohibition or restriction on international commerce, in effect on importation. Its intended and practical effect is to deny to Canadian, and some domestic, sub-sized lobsters the access they had to the American market until January of 1990. Taking all this into consideration, the members of the Panel who concluded that the U.S. measures were in conflict with Article XI were able to conclude only that the objectives of the 1989 amendment were both of a conservation nature and a trade restriction. Due to the fact that there was no persuasive evidence to support the assertion that the amendment's primary objective was conservation, and the limited discussion of alternatives, these members were unable to draw a conclusion that the amendment was "primarily aimed at" conservation. The United States, for example, did not address the reasons for which its conservation objectives could not be met by special marking of Canadian small lobsters, requirements that lobsters be sorted by size prior to importation into the United States, particular documentary requirements as to sub-sized lobsters of Canadian origin, increased penalties for the possession of sub-sized lobsters, more vigilant enforcement efforts, or possibly other requirements.

Decision. The majority ruled that the U.S. lobster size regulations were "internal measures" and therefore did not violate GATT's prohibition against restrictions that apply only to imports. The United States was permitted to continue applying its minimum-size rules.

facially neutral standards—such as "no baggy swimsuits"—to give preference to local products. But if nothing is wrong with the product itself, a country will have more difficulty excluding the product on an environmental basis.

Regulation of Products with Environmentally Objectionable Production Processes

The *Canadian Lobster* case is an example of a trade restriction based on a threat to the environment inherent in a product itself—the sale of premature lobsters. The environment is more frequently injured, however, by the process used to make a particular product. Nothing about finished steel is environmentally harmful. But if the plant that manufactures the steel has no pollution-control devices, the plant will destroy the ecosystems in bodies of water surrounding it, darken the atmosphere, and contribute to acid rain. In *Canadian Lobsters,* Articles III and XI of GATT were interpreted to allow highly discriminatory restrictions if a foreign product threatened the environment. Ironically, these articles have also been interpreted to *forbid* discriminatory restrictions if they target an environmentally offensive process used to create the product, unless the proscribing party is flexible in the application of standards.

As the *Shrimp* case makes clear, the WTO Appellate Body is quite tolerant of a nation that attempts to force foreign producers to comply with the same environmentally conscious procedures as are required within the nation, so long as the

United States—Import Prohibition of Certain Shrimp and Shrimp Products
Recourse to Article 21.5 of the DSU by Malaysia; WT/DS58/AB/RW (Oct. 21, 2001)
WTO Appellate Body

BACKGROUND AND FACTS

To protect endangered sea turtle populations from further decline by reducing their incidental mortality in commercial shrimp trawling, U.S. commercial shrimp trawlers are required to use Turtle Excluder Devices (TEDs) approved in accordance with standards established by the United States National Marine Fisheries Service. In 1989, the U.S. Congress enacted Section 609 of Public Law 101–162, under which the Department of State was to certify whether nations that export shrimp to the United States had adopted programs to reduce the incidental capture of sea turtles in their shrimp fisheries that were comparable to the program in effect in the United States. If the State Department did not certify a nation, that nation would be banned from exporting shrimp to the United States. In practice, the State Department effectively required that other countries adopt a TEDs requirement. In 1998, the WTO Appellate Body found the U.S. measure to be a forbidden prohibition on imports that was not justified under Article XX(b)'s exception for measures taken to protect animal life "not applied in a manner which would constitute a means of arbitrary or unjustifiable discrimination between countries." In essence, the Appellate Body found that the United States' de facto insistence on a U.S. excluder device was "unjustifiable discrimination" and therefore recommended that the United States bring Section 609 into conformity with the GATT.

Congress did nothing to the law, but the State Department revised the guidelines it used in enforcing the law. Where the government of a harvesting country requested certification based on its having adopted a program based on TEDs, the Department of State was to issue it so long as the program included a requirement that commercial shrimp trawlers use TEDs "comparable in effectiveness" to those used in the United States. The program also had to include a credible enforcement effort that included monitoring for compliance.

In May 1998, the State Department certified that sixteen nations had indeed adopted such programs. It also certified that the fishing environments in twenty-three other countries did not pose a threat of the incidental taking of sea turtles protected under Section 609. Under Section 609, shrimp imports from any nation not certified were prohibited effective May 1, 1998.

Malaysia was not certified and challenged the revised procedure. The WTO panel ruled that, as enforced under the revised State Department guidelines, Section 609 no longer constituted an "unjustified discrimination." Malaysia appealed to the WTO Appellate Body.

CHAIRMAN BACCHUS AND MESSRS. GANESAN AND LACARTE-MURÓ

In 2000, Malaysia informed the [WTO Dispute Settlement Body] DSB that it was not satisfied that the United States had complied with the recommendations and rulings of the DSB, and announced that it wished to seek recourse to a panel ...

[In this appeal, the] issue was whether the Panel had erred in finding that the measure at issue was now applied in a manner that no longer constituted a means of "arbitrary or unjustifiable discrimination between countries where the same conditions prevail" and was, therefore, within the scope of measures permitted under Article XX of the GATT 1994. To answer this question, the Appellate Body analyzed (1) the nature and extent of the duty of the United States to pursue international cooperation in the protection and conservation of sea turtles and (2) the flexibility of the Revised Guidelines. Regarding the issue of international cooperation, the Panel reached the conclusion that the United States had an obligation to make serious good faith efforts to reach an agreement before resorting to the type of unilateral measure currently in place.

> whereas subject to the requirement that such measures are not applied in a manner which would constitute a means of arbitrary or unjustifiable discrimination between countries where the same conditions prevail, or a disguised restriction on international trade, nothing in this Agreement shall be construed to prevent the adoption or enforcement by any contracting party of measures: [...]

continued

continued

The Appellate Body also mentioned its conclusion in the *United States—Shrimp* case that the United States had to provide all exporting countries "similar opportunities to negotiate" an international agreement to avoid "arbitrary or unjustifiable discrimination." ... With respect to that measure, the United States could conceivably respect that obligation, and the conclusion of an international agreement might nevertheless not be possible despite the serious, good faith efforts of the United States. Requiring that a multilateral agreement be concluded by the United States in order to avoid "arbitrary or unjustifiable discrimination" in applying its measure would mean that any country party to the negotiations with the United States, whether a WTO Member or not, would have, in effect, a veto over whether the United States could fulfill its WTO obligations. Such a requirement would not be reasonable. The Appellate Body concluded that the United States could not be held to have engaged in "arbitrary or unjustifiable discrimination" under Article XX solely because one international negotiation resulted in an agreement while another did not. The Appellate Body upholds the Panel's finding....

Afterwards, the Appellate Body turned to the analysis of the next issue, the flexibility of the Revised Guidelines. Malaysia claimed that the United States unilaterally imposed its domestic standards on exporters. Moreover, Malaysia disagreed with the Panel that a measure could meet the requirements of the chapeau of Article XX if it would be flexible enough, both in design and application, to permit certification of an exporting country with a sea turtle protection and conservation programme comparable to that of the United States. The Appellate Body stated that "conditioning access to a Member's domestic market on whether exporting Members comply with, or adopt, a policy or policies unilaterally prescribed by the importing Member may, to some degree, be a common aspect of measures falling within the scope of one or another of the exceptions (a) to (j) of Article XX." However, a separate question arises, when examining under the chapeau of Article XX, a measure that provides for access to the market of one WTO Member for a product of other WTO Members conditionally.

In *United States—Shrimp,* the Appellate Body concluded that the measure at issue there did not meet the requirements of the chapeau of Article XX relating to "arbitrary or unjustifiable discrimination" because, through the application of the measure, the exporting members were faced with "a single, rigid and unbending requirement to adopt essentially the same policies and enforcement practices as those applied to, and enforced on, domestic shrimp trawlers in the United States." In this dispute, on the other hand, the Panel found that the new measure is more flexible than the original measure and had been applied more flexibly than was the original measure. The new measure, in design and application, did not condition access to the United States market on the adoption by an exporting Member of a regulatory programme aimed at the protection and the conservation of sea turtles that was essentially the same as that of the United States.

The Appellate Body noted that the Revised Guidelines contained provisions that permitted the United States authorities to take into account the specific conditions of Malaysian shrimp production, and of the Malaysian sea turtle conservation programme, should Malaysia decide to apply for certification. It concluded that the provisions of the Revised Guidelines, on their face, permitted a degree of flexibility that would enable the United States to consider the particular conditions prevailing in Malaysia if, and when, Malaysia applied for certification.

Decision. The Appellate Body upheld the finding of the Panel and therefore made no recommendations to the DSB with respect to Section 609.

importing nation is flexible in accepting other nations' approaches to achieving the same environmental objective. But when a nation attempts to create different standards for foreign parties—as in the *Reformulated and Conventional Gasoline* case—the WTO can be very demanding.

Litigation Against Polluters in an Affected Country

If the polluting foreign investor is subject to the jurisdiction of the conservationist nation's courts, it might be haled into court there. This scenario is

United States—Standards for Reformulated and Conventional Gasoline

WT/DS2/AB/R (Apr. 29, 1996)

WTO Appellate Body

BACKGROUND AND FACTS

The *Clean Air Act* of 1990 (the CAA) established two programs to control pollution from gasoline combustion. The first program created large metropolitan ozone "nonattainment areas" that had experienced the worst summertime ozone pollution. All gasoline sold to consumers in these nonattainment areas had to be "reformulated." The second program concerned "conventional" gasoline, which could be sold to consumers in the rest of the United States. The sale of conventional gasoline in nonattainment areas was not allowed.

The U.S. Environmental Protection Agency (EPA) enacted the "Gasoline Rule" to implement these programs, which relied heavily on the use of 1990 baselines as a means of determining compliance. Baselines could be either individual (established by the entity itself) or statutory (established by the EPA and intended to reflect average 1990 United States gasoline quality), depending on the nature of the entity concerned. The Gasoline Rule did not provide individual baselines for foreign refiners. It did not impose the statutory baseline requirement on domestic refiners. In short, foreign refiners had to comply with industry averages, while domestic refiners could, if they chose, look to their individual circumstances.

Venezuela challenged the Gasoline Rule as an "arbitrary or unjustifiable discrimination" under the chapeau of GATT Article XX. A WTO Panel ruled in favor of Venezuela and the United States appealed.

CHAIRMAN FELICIANO AND MESSRS. BEEBY AND MATSUSHITA

[The Appellate Body] came to the question of whether [the Gasoline] rules would also meet the requirements of the chapeau of Article XX. The Appellate Body stated that the chapeau was animated by the principle that while the exceptions of Article XX may be invoked as a matter of legal right, they should not be so applied as to frustrate or defeat the legal obligations of the holder of the right under the substantive rules of the [GATT]. Put otherwise, if those exceptions were not to be abused or misused the measures falling within the particular exceptions must be applied reasonably, with due regard both to the legal duties of the party claiming the exception and the legal rights of the other parties concerned.

The Appellate Body noted that there was more than one alternative course of action available to the United States in promulgation regulations implementing the CAA. These included the imposition of statutory baselines without differentiation as between domestic and imported gasoline. Such an approach, if properly implemented, could have avoided any discrimination at all. Moreover, the United States could have made available individual baselines to foreign refiners as well as domestic refiners.

In explaining why individual baselines for foreign refiners had not been put in place, the United States laid heavy stress upon the difficulties related to anticipated administrative problems that individual baselines for foreign refiners would have generated which the EPA would have had to face. The Appellate Body, following the reasoning of the Panel, denied these arguments. It acknowledged that the anticipated difficulties concerning verification and subsequent enforcement would be doubtless real to some degree, but they viewed them as insufficient to justify the denial to foreign refiners of individual baselines permitted to domestic refiners. There are established techniques for checking, verification, assessment and enforcement of data relating to imported goods, techniques which in many contexts are accepted as adequate to permit international trade—trade between territorial sovereigns—to go on and grow.

The United States also explained why the statutory baseline requirement was not imposed on domestic refiners as well. The United States concluded that the application of the statutory baseline to domestic producers of reformulated and conventional gasoline in 1995 would have been physically and financially impossible because of the magnitude of the changes required in almost all United States refiners. As the Appellate Body noted, while the United States counted the costs of its domestic refiners of statuary baselines, there was nothing in the record to indicate that it did other than disregard that kind of consideration when it came to foreign refiners.

continued

continued

The Appellate Body found that the resulting discrimination must have been foreseen, and was not merely inadvertent or unavoidable.

Decision. The Appellate Body concluded that the baseline establishment rules in the Gasoline Rule, in their application, constitute "unjustifiable discrimination" and a "disguised restriction on international trade." It thus held that the baseline establishment rules, although within the terms of Article XX(g), were not entitled to the justifying protection afforded by Article XX as a whole. The Appellate Body recommended that the Dispute Settlement Body request the United States to bring the baseline establishment rule into conformity with its obligations under the General Agreement.

quite possible where the pollution directly affects the territory of the conservationist nation.

An interesting example involves international emissions from a nuclear plant. The Supreme Court of Austria held that Austrian landowners could sue the former Czechoslovakia in Austrian courts for the environmental effects of such emissions. Note especially the court's reliance on the absence of a valid claim under Czech law.

Judgment of February 23, 1988

39 Österreichische Zeitschrift für Öffentliches Recht und Völkerrecht 360

Supreme Court of Austria

BACKGROUND AND FACTS

The plaintiff, an owner of real estate in Austria near the former Czechoslovakia, brought action in Austrian courts seeking to prevent the construction of a nuclear power plant 115 kilometers away in Czechoslovakia. The plaintiff alleged that the plant had not been properly licensed and that the effects of radionuclides generated during the plant's normal operation, as well as those that would be released in a nuclear accident, threatened his real estate. The plaintiff alleged that the plant could not operate without emitting radioactive-contaminated water vapor and excessive warmth.

The Court of First Instance denied plaintiff's claim, holding that it lacked *jurisdiction ratione loci*—geographic jurisdiction over the matter. On appeal, the Court of Second Instance affirmed the lower court decision. The Oberste Gerichtshof (Supreme Court) of Austria, however, disagreed with the courts below.

PER CURIAM

The Court of First Instance—affirmed by the Court of Second Instance—has disavowed its [own] *jurisdiction ratione loci* ... but the Supreme Court is of the opinion that [the statute governing venue of claims related to real estate] also provides *jurisdiction ratione loci* for Austrian courts over claims ... of real estate owners affected by emissions [of a foreign state]. No treaty rules exist in the case in question with respect to Czechoslovakia.

It is unreasonable to require the claimant to pursue legal proceedings in Czechoslovakia, which obviously are not possible because there the problem under consideration is treated as a public law problem and acts *jure imperii* [official acts] cannot give rise to civil law obligations. This view is not consistent with Austrian law [under which] foreign states can be sued for acts *jure gestionis* [commercial activity] before courts [of another state]; and the question whether acts of the state are acts *jure imperii* or *jure gestionis* is not to be determined by the national law in question but according to general international law. Under such international law, the construction and the operation of a ... plant for the generation of electricity are not within the scope of *jure imperii*, but are *jure gestionis* and therefore not excluded from the national [Austrian] jurisdiction....

continued

continued

It cannot be said that legal proceedings in Austria would only lead to a judgment which is not enforceable and therefore would only have academic, and not protective, importance; although in the absence of a treaty on execution of judgments with the state in question, an execution of the judgment would presumably not be possible in Czechoslovakia, the pecuniary penalties imposed to enforce the claim ... could probably be enforced in Austria and a violation by the defendant of the restraining order of a court could be a legal ground for possible claims of damages by the plaintiff.

As all conditions for Austrian jurisdiction exist but the *jurisdiction ratione loci* has been rejected by the court which would have been competent according to [Austrian law], the Supreme Court ... is competent to designate a Court of First Instance as the court having *jurisdiction ratione loci* in this case.

Decision. The Supreme Court of Austria reversed the finding of the Court of Second Instance that Austrian courts lacked jurisdiction over the plaintiff's claim. It remanded the matter to the trial court where the plaintiff's real estate was situated for further litigation.

Litigation Against Polluters in Polluter's Home

Another traditional approach to obtaining relief against a polluter is to sue it in its home jurisdiction. In many countries, this approach is not practical. The local judges would be disinclined to rule against a significant local enterprise. Even in a neutral forum, however, such a suit can run into significant difficulties. In *Aguinda v. Texaco, Inc.*, a U.S. court found that the victims of environmental misdeeds abroad could sue in the United States to seek legal redress. However, obtaining such a ruling required a demonstration that significant activities had occurred in the United States. While reading the *Aguinda* case, note that, as in the *Judgment of February 23, 1988,* the court focuses on the availability of a remedy in the Ecuadorian court system.

Aguinda v. Texaco, Inc.
1994 WL 142006
United States District Court (S.D.N.Y.)

BACKGROUND AND FACTS
Plaintiffs were Ecuadoran citizens residing in the tropical rain forest of Eastern Ecuador. They sought to represent a class of 30,000 Ecuadorans against Texaco, Inc., alleging that Texaco had engaged in environmental abuse for decades until 1990. The alleged misdeeds included large-scale disposal of inadequately treated hazardous wastes and destruction of tropical rain forest habitats. These activities, the plaintiffs asserted, caused harm to indigenous peoples living in the rain forest, to their property, and to the stability of Amazon basin habitats. The plaintiffs sought damages for their injuries and an injunction preventing the defendant from continuing or renewing its polluting activities.

Texaco moved to dismiss the case, arguing that courts of the United States were an inconvenient forum for adjudicating the claims and that some of the counts should be thrown out in any case.

JUDGE BRODERICK
Pursuit of individualized monetary relief for a large class of persons in a foreign country growing out of events implemented abroad presents substantial difficulties, even though those events were partially initiated in the United States. These difficulties are sufficient to make a forum in New York inconvenient, and to cause litigation of such claims here to run counter to the goal of "just, speedy and inexpensive" judicial administration ... provided necessary steps are taken to assure availability of an alternate forum for such claims in Ecuador. Disputes over class membership, determinations of individualized or common damages, and the need for large amounts of

continued

continued

testimony with interpreters, perhaps often in local dialects, would make effective adjudication in New York problematic at best. Most [factors] appear to favor resolution of damage claims in Ecuador. These include access to proof, availability of witnesses, possible viewing of sites, local interest, administrative difficulties, problems of choice of law and application of foreign law.

Appropriate caution in making any final determination requires that prior to dismissal of any part of this case on *forum non conveniens* or other grounds raised by Texaco, Texaco must:

a. Execute a binding acceptance of personal jurisdiction over it in Ecuadoran courts and
b. Provide binding acceptance of such jurisdiction by any Texaco subsidiaries having assets derived from the operations in Ecuador at issue, or waiver of the corporate veil by Texaco, or
c. Post an adequate bond to cover any liability imposed by the Ecuadoran courts.

If these requisites are met, consideration may be given to (a) absolute dismissal of plaintiffs' individualized monetary and class action claims or (b) stay of litigation of such claims in this court to permit their pursuit in Ecuador.

Many of the factors discussed above which may favor dismissal of plaintiffs' individual and class action damage claims on *forum non conveniens* grounds are less applicable insofar as injunctive relief is concerned, particularly if the demand for such relief is based on allegedly initiatory events in the United States. There is no known currently ongoing litigation between the parties in Ecuador, nor is there supervision of any entity located in Ecuador, nor is there [anything] which would be disrupted were jurisdiction over such equitable claims ... to be exercised by this court.

The existence or nonexistence of events in this country which may be related to alleged injury in Ecuador may be explored based on documents or other information received in or sent from this country, minutes or recollections of consultations conducted with management in the United States, and evidentiary support from U.S. sources for types of conduct challenged by plaintiffs....

In *Sequihua v. Texaco* ... the court dismissed environmental pollution claims against Texaco also involving Ecuador on grounds of comity and *forum non conveniens*. That case differs from the one at bar as set forth in plaintiffs' complaint ... in that in *Sequihua* the "challenged activity ... occurred entirely in Ecuador," the "enforcement ... of any judgment" was assumed to be required to be pursued in Ecuador, and relevant witnesses were expected to be solely those located in Ecuador. By contrast, decision making on the part of the defendant in the United States may or may not turn out to support some or all of plaintiffs' claims in the present case....

Texaco moves to dismiss several claims as based on the "local action" doctrine under which actions involving specific real property ... must be tried where the land is located.

Further information is necessary to determine whether or not the current case falls within this category. If any injury caused by defendant's conduct is confined to specifiable real estate, the core concerns underlying the local action doctrine would be applicable. Large-scale industrial pollution in liquid form by contrast, may spread in widening circles not limited to any specific properties.... If discovery indicates that actionable steps were initiated in the United States, the local action concept might be inapplicable....

Texaco moves to dismiss count VIII alleging violation of the Alien Tort statute ... which was originally enacted in 1789 and by its terms is applicable to private as well as governmental actors. The Alien Tort statute provides:

> The district courts shall have original jurisdiction of any civil action by an alien for a tort only, committed in violation of the law of nations or a treaty of the United States.

Plaintiffs rely on the Alien Tort statute as a source of substantive law. Ordinarily governmental abuses such as official torture are the subject of suits under the Act, but the absence of such a limitation was explicitly noted as significant in *Argentine Republic v. Hess*.... No violation of a treaty has been alleged. The law of nations is, by contrast, customary in nature, to be defined by the usages, solemn commitments and clearly articulated principles of the international community. Participation of the United States in formulation of such usages, commitments and principles is, of course, of particular importance—and may indeed be necessary—where the courts of the United States are asked to enforce them.

Non-treaty international law may be treated as the "sober second thought of the community" upon which, as stated by [Justice] Harlan F. Stone, ... all law ultimately rests. No single document can create it, but the unanimity of view as well as consistency with domestic law and its objectives are highly relevant....

continued

continued

Although many authorities are relevant, perhaps the most pertinent in the present case is the Rio Declaration on Environment and Development (1992). Principle 2 on the first page of the document recognizes that states have "the sovereign right to exploit their own resources pursuant to their own environmental and developmental policies," but also have "the responsibility to ensure that activities within their jurisdiction or control do not cause damage to the environment of other States or areas beyond the limits of national jurisdiction." The Rio Declaration may be declaratory of what it treated as pre-existing principles just as was the Declaration of Independence.

Environmental damage is recognized in the domestic law of the United States as subject to legal restrictions. See among numerous other provisions, the National Environmental Policy Act [and] Endangered Species Act.... Indeed, an entire title of the United States Code (Title 16) is devoted explicitly to conservation. The totality of these enactments bespeak an overall commitment to responsible stewardship toward the environment....

Decision concerning the possible applicability of [U.S. law] to this case must await additional information after further discovery focusing on events, if any, initiated or assisted in the United States which might violate international law....

Decision. The court reserved judgment on each of Texaco's motions, pending the results of discovery on the extent to which events giving rise to the harm occurred in the United States or were carried out in response to directives issued in the United States. Texaco did not immediately agree to Ecuadoran jurisdiction, so the damages case proceeded, pending discovery, in the United States.

An approach centered on the jurisdiction of U.S. courts may be effective against U.S. companies, but it seems ultimately doomed to be ineffective because it cannot provide relief if none of the acts relating to environmentally suspect behavior occurred in the United States. A U.S. investor could, for example, ensure that all discussion relating to a specific polluting project take place in the country with the most forgiving environmental laws. For an approach to be effective in furthering conservation, therefore, it needs to be multinational in scope.

Inadequacies of the Traditional International Pollution-Control System

Existing international remedies can be effective in specific instances, but they are unlikely to be effective in transforming the international environmental legal system. International arbitration can proceed only if both parties have consented. Such consent is infrequent in the environmental context, because a nation usually does not voluntarily subject itself to a proceeding about pollution generated on its own territory.

As we have seen, trade sanctions must be couched in product defects. However, most environmental damage is caused by manufacturing processes and, as illustrated in the *Import Prohibition of Certain Shrimp and Shrimp Products* decision, such processes are largely exempt from regulation under GATT. Litigation in the affected conservationist nation can be effective against investors, but the affected nation must be sufficiently close to suffer a direct physical adverse effect. Litigation in the polluter's home country can be circumvented by having all actions and decisions occur in the less conscientious nation. Accordingly, new approaches are being pursued to address the problem of global pollution.

Emerging Problems and Solutions

In light of the perceived shortcomings of traditional legal methodologies for addressing environmental controversies, environmentalists have been developing regional and global solutions. We now will survey a representative group of the more important of these approaches.

Regional Approaches

The most regional approach to environmental protection is in national environmental regulations of exports. Even if GATT constrains a nation from excluding imports created in environmentally suspect ways, the nation can regulate its exports. The U.S. law relating to the export of environmentally hazardous materials is an excellent case in point.

National Constraints on Exports. The cornerstone of U.S. environmental regulation of the export of hazardous materials is the principle of prior informed consent (PIC). The export of pesticides, for example, is regulated by the U.S. Environmental Protection Agency (EPA) under the *Federal Insecticide, Fungicide, and Rodenticide Act* (FIFRA). FIFRA requires that before a U.S. seller can export pesticides that are not registered for use in the United States, it must obtain the PIC of the purchaser and give notice to the appropriate official in the receiving country. The restrictions of the *Resource Conservation and Recovery Act* (RCRA) are even more demanding on the export of hazardous waste. RCRA requires the exporter to provide notice to the EPA of any forthcoming shipment. Then, the government of the receiving country must expressly accept the shipment and provide written notice to the EPA of that consent. Special manifest requirements apply to the shipment, and the exporter has annual reporting obligations to the EPA.

U.S. legislation also seeks to ensure that the foreign government's consent is thoroughly informed. The *Toxic Substances Control Act* (TSCA) imposes reporting and record keeping requirements on all chemical substances. In international transactions, TSCA requires exporters to notify the EPA of the export of any chemical or article containing a chemical that is or has been subject to testing under the statute. The EPA must then notify the foreign government of the EPA action with respect to the chemical.

The United States has many laws regulating pesticide use within the United States, but no law exists that forbids manufacturers from exporting banned pesticides to countries with less stringent or poorly enforced laws. This creates the so-called "Circle of Poison." U.S.–banned pesticides are exported to the Third World and are used on crops, which are then exported back to the United States. These pesticides then reenter the United States as residues on food products.

Because it dramatized the inherent inadequacy of domestic legislation, the "Circle of Poison" problem motivated the developed world to seek global solutions to the international distribution of toxins. As discussed later, nations are now turning to international treaties.

In certain substantive areas, national legislation—even in a nation as large as the United States—has virtually no effect. For most environmental issues, global and regional problems require multinational solutions.

North American Environmental Treaties. In North America, progress toward common environmental standards has been made through bilateral treaties and the *North American Free Trade Agreement* (NAFTA). NAFTA's *Environmental Side Agreements* established the North American Commission for Environmental Cooperation (CEC), headquartered in Montreal. Although the North American Free Trade Commission normally considers all trade disputes, including disputes with environmental implications, the CEC determines whether any party to NAFTA has shown a "persistent pattern of failure" to "effectively enforce its environmental law." The CEC indicates these findings in Factual Records. In 2007, the CEC released a Factual Record on allegations that Canada was failing in its enforcement of pollution provisions of the Fisheries Act and provisions of the Pulp Paper Effluent Regulations (PPER). A finding of a pattern of failure can result in a broad range of sanctions, including suspension of NAFTA benefits. Thus, nongovernmental organizations now have an international forum to challenge the anti-conservation activities of the three signatory governments (Canada, Mexico, and the United States). The following case discusses the requirements in one such challenge.

Under the NAFTA Treaty, the United States, Canada, and Mexico also agreed to finance jointly a variety of border wastewater and water pollution projects. Further, NAFTA creates permanent

Hudson River Audubon Society of Westchester, Inc. & Save Our Sanctuary Committee: United States

Determination of Submission SEM 00-003 (Apr. 12, 2000)

Secretariat of the Commission for Environmental Cooperation

BACKGROUND AND FACTS

The Submitters, Hudson River Audubon Society of Westchester, Inc. and Save Our Sanctuary Committee, filed a submission on enforcement matters pursuant to Article 14 of the *North American Agreement on Environmental Cooperation* ("NAAEC" or "Agreement") with the Secretariat of the North American Commission for Environmental Cooperation. They alleged that the United States Department of Interior–National Park Service was failing to enforce and proposing to violate: (1) the *Migratory Bird Treaty Act* (MBTA), a U.S. statute that prohibits the killing of migratory birds without a permit from the U.S. Fish and Wildlife Service; and (2) the *Endangered Species Act of 1973* (ESA), which prohibits the taking of endangered and threatened species, requires the protection of such species "whether by protection of habitat and food supply," and requires the designation of "critical habitat." The Department of Interior was alleged to be doing this by proposing to construct a paved, multipurpose bicycle path through the Jamaica Bay Wildlife Refuge, which is part of the Gateway National Recreational Area located in Queens, New York. The Submitters asserted that the construction of this pathway through the Jamaica Bay Wildlife Refuge would destroy critical habitat for endangered and threatened species, would result in the taking of migratory birds (including nests), and would therefore be in violation of both the MBTA and the ESA.

DIRECTOR MARKELL

A. OVERVIEW

Article 14 of the NAAEC directs the Secretariat to consider a submission from any non-governmental organization or person asserting that a Party to the NAAEC is failing to effectively enforce its environmental law. When the Secretariat determines that a submission meets the Article 14(1) requirements, it then determines whether the submission merits requesting a response from the Party named in the submission based upon the factors contained in Article 14(2)....

The Secretariat ... has determined that the submission does not presently meet the criteria in Article 14 for further consideration.

B. THE GOVERNING LEGAL FRAMEWORK

The opening sentence of Article 14(1) authorizes the Secretariat to consider a submission "from any non-governmental organization or person asserting that a Party is failing to effectively enforce its environmental law...." Following this first sentence, Article 14 (1) lists six specific criteria relevant to the Secretariat's consideration of submissions. The Secretariat must find that a submission:

a. is in writing in a language designated by that Party in a notification to the Secretariat;
b. clearly identifies the person or organization making the submission;
c. provides sufficient information to allow the Secretariat to review the submission, including any documentary evidence on which the submission may be based;
d. appears to be aimed at promoting enforcement rather than at harassing industry;
e. indicates that the matter has been communicated in writing to the relevant authorities of the Party and indicates the Party's response, if any; and
f. is filed by a person or organization residing or established in the territory of a Party.

C. APPLICATION OF THE GOVERNING LEGAL FRAMEWORK

As noted above, the opening sentence of Article 14 (1) authorizes the Secretariat to consider a submission "from any non-governmental organization or person asserting that a Party is failing to effectively enforce its environmental law...." The submission, filed by the Hudson River Audubon Society of Westchester, Inc. (Hudson River) and Save Our Sanctuary Committee, meets the requirement in the opening sentence of Article 14(1) that it be filed by a "non-governmental organization." It also meets the requirement that it focus on an asserted failure to enforce a Party's environmental laws, rather than on a deficiency in the law itself. Further, both the Endangered Species Act and the Migratory Bird Treaty Act qualify as environmental laws. The submission, however, does not meet the requirement in the first sentence that the assertion focus on an alleged ongoing failure to enforce.

continued

continued

Article 14(1) requires that a submission allege that a Party "is failing" to effectively enforce its environmental law. The process presupposes in a case such as this one, where the submission identifies a particular government action as the source of the alleged enforcement failure, that the Party involved actually has taken the action at issue or made some final decision. Absent such a final action or decision, any allegation of a failure to effectively enforce is based on speculation.

Although the submission alleges that the National Park Service "is failing to enforce" the MBTA and the ESA, it also alleges that the NPS is "proposing to violate" these statutes. Based on the Secretariat's understanding of the status of the potential bicycle path project that is the focus of the submission, it appears that the submission focuses on a prospective rather than on an ongoing asserted failure to effectively enforce. It therefore fails to comply with Article 14(1)'s requirement that the submission assert that a Party "is failing" to effectively enforce its environmental laws. . . .

The information supplied in the submission and the attachments to it do not reflect that the NPS has made a final decision to construct a bicycle path through the Refuge in any particular form or location. Indeed, the information provided with the submission suggests that the government is currently engaged in evaluating the appropriate location and other details of such a bicycle path. . . . Because the submission does not identify a final government decision on the bicycle path, the assertion that the content of that decision constitutes a failure to effectively enforce is premature.

Further, . . . the submission . . . does not meet the requirement in Article 14(1)(c) of the NAAEC that a submission provide sufficient information to allow the Secretariat to review the submission, including any documentary evidence on which the submission may be based. The activity that allegedly constitutes a failure to enforce both the MBTA and the ESA involves construction of a bicycle path that, according to attachments to the submission, is tentatively planned to be 10 feet wide with one-foot shoulders. The submission does little to support its assertion that construction of the path "will destroy critical habitat" for endangered and threatened species and thereby violate the ESA. The submission, for example, does not indicate what endangered or threatened species are found within the Refuge. It similarly does not indicate where "critical habitat" exists within the Refuge or the portion of such habitat (if any) which purportedly will be destroyed by the proposed bicycle path. Concerning the Migratory Bird Treaty Act, the submission alleges that construction of the path will result in the taking of migratory birds (including nests). It adds that the construction and resulting recreational use of the path will disrupt nesting and feeding of migratory birds and destroy nests and feeding areas in violation of the MBTA.

The Submitters cite to recent CEC publications that identify the Refuge as a key conservation site and an important bird area. The submission, however, does not provide support for its assertion that the path, in light of its location and other details, will cause disruption or destruction that violates the MBTA. Absent further information to support the existence of a connection between construction of the bicycle path and the types of impacts that would violate the ESA and/or the MBTA, the submission fails to satisfy Article 14(1)(c). . . .

Decision. The Secretariat terminated the Article 14 process with respect to this submission, effectively finding that the Submitters did not have a right to be heard under the Agreement.

committees for Standards-Related Measures and for Sanitary and Phytosanitary Measures to harmonize the environmental laws of the three nations. The objectives of these efforts, together with the CEC, are to convert such regulation into acceptable standards in NAFTA countries and ultimately to remove such standards as an impediment to trade.

In addition to resolving enforcement disputes, the CEC has conducted studies of proposed developments in border areas. For example, in 2007, the CEC hosted symposia focused on environmental technology, including a symposium featuring experts on green building and architecture. Research presented at the symposium evaluated how governments can encourage green and carbon-neutral building through zoning regulations, tax incentives, and government-supported research and development. The Commission has supported similar small "eco-projects."

The work of the CEC has been more that of a development agency than of an environmental cop. For example, at its annual meeting in 2003, the CEC Council discussed conserving biodiversity, managing freshwater, sound management and tracking of hazardous waste, and promoting cooperation in environmental enforcement. Other topics included the promotion of public–private partnerships to encourage voluntary initiatives to attain higher levels of environmental protection and the enhancement of "the availability of financially relevant environmental information" to explore voluntary mechanisms through which environmental information can be made available to financial investors. The emphasis is on voluntary action even though most effective compliance is achieved through involuntary means.

NAFTA mechanisms still do not permit the United States and Canada to impose their policies on less-developed Mexico. In fact, the Commission has broadly declared it has no right to investigate actions by legislatures of NAFTA countries even if those actions effectively nullify other laws. The lure of free trade was effectively employed to persuade Mexico to make its laws more protective of the environment and, for the first time, a multinational structure was created to enforce environmental standards. Through a variety of actions before the Commission, non-governmental organizations have tried to make enforcement of this new legal scheme in Mexico more satisfactory.

European Union Environmental Initiatives. In 1985, the *Single European Act* made the environment an official responsibility of the EU, amending Section 13 of the *Treaty of Rome* with a new Title VII on the environment. In 1987, the European Council enacted a comprehensive environmental action program. In all, the Council of Ministers of the European Communities has adopted more than 200 different directives on environmental protection that the member states are obliged to implement through national legislation. Further, the European Commission has pursued hundreds of infringement procedures against member nations to compel implementation of these directives. Because of this aggressive approach, EU members generally go beyond the United States in thoroughness of environmental protection schemes. The Commission may further intensify its approach through a directive, proposed in 2007, requiring member states to provide criminal sanctions for noncompliance with specific offenses.

The European Commission has also issued a number of "Green Papers" in its attempt to advance Union-wide environmental standards. First, it proposed a uniform system of civil liability for damage to the environment. The proposal would standardize the principles under which firms have to pay to repair environmental damage. It specifies situations under which strict liability concepts apply and compensation mechanisms for cases in which the responsible party cannot be identified. In 2003, the European Parliament issued a directive that established an emissions trading scheme for the energy sector and large industrial installations. The scheme ensures that the greenhouse gas emissions from the energy and industry sectors covered are cut at least cost to the economy and meet emission commitments under the *Kyoto Protocol*. The Commission made an initial assessment of National Allocation Plans (NAPs) in November 2006 in which it established emission caps from 2008–2012 for each member state. The Commission has also introduced legislation on the *Registration Evaluation Authorization and Restriction of Chemicals* (REACH), which entered into force in 2007. The REACH legislation creates the European Chemicals Agency, which is responsible for implementing requirements and publishing guidance documents to protect human health and the environment from the EU's chemical industry while keeping the industry competitive. On environmental issues, the Commission is increasingly in the position of clearinghouse and arbiter for policy differences within the EU.

In 2003, the European Parliament issued a directive to ensure that, on environmental matters, the public has full access to whatever information it needs to petition the Commission on these policy matters. The legislation creates an inherent public right to such information and a presumption that disclosure of information is the general rule. By creating this unusual right to information, the directive seeks to achieve greater awareness of environmental matters, a free exchange of views, and more effective participation by the public in environmental decision making in all the nations of the European Union. The Commission will be pressed to continue in its efforts.

REGIONAL MARINE TREATIES. Nations sharing bodies of water have cooperated significantly on environmental issues. Marine environmental protection was pioneered in 1972 by the *London Convention for the Prevention of Marine Pollution by Dumping from Ships and Aircraft*, which prohibited the dumping of specified hazardous wastes from ships at sea and required permits for the dumping of others. The *Helsinki Convention on the Protection of the Marine Environment of the Baltic Sea Area* improved on the *London Convention* by providing for an effective international inspection and enforcement network. The *Barcelona Convention for the Protection of the Mediterranean Sea from Pollution* took matters further by enlarging the *London Convention's* list of prohibited substances. In November 2003, the environment ministers of the Mediterranean countries signed a declaration "to speed up the eradication of the at-risk single hull vessels which travel to and across the Mediterranean." Similar convention arrangements have been concluded for the Red Sea and the Gulf of Aden, the Caribbean, the Southeast Pacific, and the South Pacific. In 2007, twenty-five shipping states within the UN's International Maritime Organization (IMO) enacted legislation that bans the use of tributyltin (TBT). TBT is a compound, found in many anti-fouling paints on ships, which kills algae and barnacles and is toxic to many other marine organisms. The depopulation of commercial oysters in the 1970s near France and the UK is linked to TBT contamination. The ban was considered a victory for the IMO.

DEVELOPMENTS IN SOUTH ASIA AND THE SOUTH PACIFIC. Countries in South Asia and the South Pacific are not renowned for vigilant enforcement of environmental policy. Nations in this region have emphasized industrial development rather than reduction of environmentally adverse byproducts of that development. Indeed, as discussed later, China and India lead the emerging world's resistance to global attempts to outlaw technologies believed to deplete the ozone layer and cause global warming. Other nations in the region have made efforts at regional environmental cooperation.

A number of countries in the region have entered into the *ASEAN Agreement on the Conservation of Nature and Natural Resources*, under which each of the parties recognize "the responsibility of ensuring that activities under their jurisdiction or control do not cause damage to the environment or the natural resources under the jurisdiction" of other nations. In addition, a number of regional environmental programs have been established to coordinate policy. These include the South Asia Cooperative Environment Program (Afghanistan, Bangladesh, India, Iran, Maldives, Nepal, Pakistan, and Sri Lanka); ASEAN (Singapore, Thailand, and Brunei); and the South Pacific Regional Environment Program (comprising twenty-one South Pacific island nations).

Following the 2004 tsunami, several environmental issues emerged in the South Asia and South Pacific region. The tsunami was caused by an Indian Ocean earthquake measuring approximately 9.0 on the Richter scale and caused the deaths of 200,000 people. The disaster affected 12 countries, reduced 400,000 homes to rubble, and caused around $10 billion worth of damage. Among the many structures destroyed was the infrastructure for solid and liquid waste and industrial chemicals. Drinking water and soil were contaminated. The *United Nations Environment Programme* (UNEP) established an Asian Tsunami Disaster Task Force at the request of the affected countries. The Task Force assessed damage, mobilized recovery assistance, and worked to ensure that the environment was part of national recovery agendas.

Some of the nations most devastated by the tsunami had experienced warning signs through rising sea levels. Losses of life and property were particularly high in areas with major erosion problems and in areas where mangrove forests had been logged and cleared for agricultural use or for fish farming. The UNEP has instituted rehabilitation and protection of natural ecosystems, including mangrove forests and coral reefs, as part of its effort to mitigate major destruction in future natural disasters.

Developments in Eastern Europe and Central Asia. During Eastern Europe's communist years, it was the most environmentally devastated region in Europe. The corruption and poverty of the communist system did not leave funds to protect the environment. In the first years after the fall of the Berlin Wall, Eastern Europe was preoccupied with economic recovery and did not expend significant resources on environmental compliance and monitoring. Now, finally, Eastern Europe has joined the "green" movement.

In 2003, the Czech Republic, Hungary, Montenegro, Poland, Romania, Serbia, Slovakia, and the Ukraine adopted the *Convention on Environment Protection and Sustainable Development of the Carpathians*. The *Carpathian Convention* creates treaty obligations among the signatories to protect, maintain, and sustainably manage the natural resources of that mountain region. The Treaty specifically adopts (1) the precaution and prevention principles, (2) the "polluter pays" principle, articulated in the *Trail Smelter* case, and (3) public participation and stakeholder involvement in development initiatives in each country, ending the "race to the bottom" among these emerging European economic participants. By creating a multinational approach to the problem, the Carpathian nations seek to restore their collective environment. At the Pan-European Ministers' Conference, the environment ministers of the region's countries expressed their support of the Carpathian effort, noting their intent to contribute to improving environmental conditions by strengthening the efforts of these countries in environmental protection and by facilitating partnership and cooperation between these countries and other European countries.

At the Kyiv Conference in 2003, twenty-two European countries, including eleven nations formerly in the Eastern bloc, signed the *Protocol on Civil Liability and Damage Caused by the Transboundary Effects of Industrial Accidents*. The Protocol arose from the accident at a dam at Baia Mare (Romania) in January 2000, which sent 100,000 tons of wastewater infused with highly toxic pollutants, including cyanide, into rivers in Hungary, Yugoslavia, and Romania. This Protocol gives affected individuals a legal claim for compensation and fills in the major gap in remedies reflected in the *Judgment of February 23, 1988*. A wronged party in one signatory nation can now make the polluter pay in another nation. Memories are long, however. The Czech Republic, target of the *Judgment of February 23, 1988,* did not sign the Protocol.

Middle East and Africa. The Middle East and Africa face a number of environmental challenges. In particular, several countries in this region face water scarcity, land and coastal degradation, and desertification. Additionally, the Middle East and Africa enjoy large natural resource endowments but are plagued by civil unrest, both which can contribute to environmental degradation. In recent years, countries in this region have begun to develop and coordinate policies to maintain and improve the environment.

For example, in February 2006, several North African national and local governments convened in Rabat, Morocco to establish a regional network for environmental issues. The nations formed the Network for Environmental Compliance and Enforcement in the Maghreb (NECEMA). Morocco and Tunisia were co-chairs of the network. At the Conference and in the following months, NECEMA participants discussed countries' current environmental compliance and enforcement programs, analyzed examples of international experience, and developed a set of best practices for country assessment.

In 2007, representatives of forty-two African countries gathered in Kigali, Rwanda at the African Regional Conference to address desertification and climate change in Africa. This gathering was convened in preparation for a conference of the parties to the *United Nations Convention to Combat Desertification* (CCD). The CCD entered into force in 1996 and has 191 parties.

Several countries in attendance at the African Regional Conference had launched Green Belt initiatives in the late 1980s and throughout the 1990s. The Green Belt movement focused on tree planting to conserve the environment and stem the effects of deforestation and desertification. In 2004, Kenyan national Wangari Maathai received the Nobel Peace Prize in recognition of her efforts to promote ecologically viable development and her activities with the Green Belt movement.

Initiatives by Multilateral Agencies. Multilateral agencies have advanced the effort by applying uniform environmental standards to projects that they finance. The World Bank, for example, has published a 460-page volume of environmental guidelines for its personnel to use in evaluating the adequacy and effectiveness of pollution control measures for industrial projects. If a country wishes to obtain financing for its projects from the World Bank or its private project finance affiliate, the International Finance Corporation (IFC), the characteristics of the project must fall within accepted world environmental standards. In light of the importance of these financing sources in the Third World, the impact of these guidelines on both public and private projects has been very substantial.

Global Solutions

The United Nations began its work in the environmental arena in 1972 when it adopted the *Stockholm Declaration on the Human Environment* and founded the United Nations Environmental Programme (UNEP). UNEP has now been the catalyst for the formulation and adoption of almost thirty binding multilateral instruments and ten sets of nonbinding environmental guidelines and principles.

THE WORLD TRADE ORGANIZATION. As demonstrated in the *Reformulated Gasoline* and *Shrimp* cases, GATT affirmatively prevents a conservationist nation from imposing its environmental policies on others through trade law. Environmentalists are working hard to reverse this.

As with other international environmental initiatives, most developed nations favor the creation of a permanent trade and environment committee to advance and implement pro-environment proposals, while less-developed countries resist the concept strongly. Most proposals likely to come out of an environmental committee would, in their view, adversely affect their exports into the developed world. Some structure seems inevitable, but years of discussion have created little more than commissions to study the possibility further.

One proposal advanced is to impose an additional *ad valorem* tax on all imports. This would promote environment-friendly development in poorer nations. This proposal addresses the inability of the Third World to pay for the technology necessary to implement a cleaner environment. However, poor countries are not enthusiastic about the proposal. First, imposing a tax on their exports would make them less competitive with domestic products in developed countries. Second, the funds would ultimately find their way back to the richer countries that manufacture the antipollution infrastructure.

During debate on the *Convention on Biological Biodiversity*, the less-developed countries offered their own suggestion: that the richer nations simply make "green" technology available for no charge. This triggered strong opposition from the United States, the home of most inventors and manufacturers of that equipment. The less-developed world also was willing to ensure that species important to biomedical research would be kept alive. However, in return, the owners of intellectual property would have to share that information for free. Not surprisingly, the United States, the home country of most firms with important biomedical intellectual property, did not support that portion of the Convention either. The crafting of provisions that left some of the more difficult questions open for another day allowed the United States to join in the Convention.

Another set of proposals focuses on establishing uniform WTO-accepted standards for labeling and packaging. The objective is to establish standards that protect the environment but prevent nations from using such standards as a trade barrier. During the Ministerial Conferences in Doha (2001) and Cancún (2003), the Ministers instructed the Committee on Trade and Environment to give attention to the impact of eco-labeling on trade and to examine whether existing WTO rules stand in the way of eco-labeling policies.

Environmentalists were quite active among the groups that rioted at the 1999 WTO ministerial meetings in Seattle, Washington. The protests had relatively little impact on the trade-oriented group, but they did reflect long-term pressure from "green" constituencies that the WTO is taking into account. The continuing North–South conflict on these questions has prevented significant progress to date in that forum. More heartening news has come from other global gatherings.

Finally, at the Ministerial Conference in Cancún, the Ministers agreed to launch negotiations on how WTO rules are to apply to WTO members that are parties to environmental agreements. Today, about 20 out of approximately 200 multilateral environmental agreements contain trade provisions. According to the Ministers, the objective of the new negotiations will be a clarification of the relationship between trade measures taken under the environmental agreements and WTO rules. The Ministers also agreed to negotiations on the reductions or elimination of tariff and non-tariff barriers to environmental goods and services.

THE INTERNATIONAL COURT OF JUSTICE. Another forum for addressing environmental disputes may be the International Court of Justice (ICJ). The ICJ, seated in The Hague, Netherlands, is the principal judicial organ of the United Nations and is charged with resolving disputes between sovereign states. Despite the fact that the ICJ set up a standing Chamber for Environmental Matters in 1993, the Argentina–Uruguay dispute, filed in 2006 and described below, is the first environmental matter to come before the ICJ.

The Uruguay–Argentina matter has not yet been resolved. The ICJ's failure to act for "lack of a risk of prejudice" cannot give other parties much incentive to use the ICJ in future disputes. It may

Pulp Mills on the River Uruguay (Argentina v. Uruguay)

46 I.L.M. 314 (March 2007)

International Court of Justice

BACKGROUND AND FACTS

On May 4, 2006, Argentina brought a complaint against Uruguay before the ICJ. Argentina alleged that Uruguay breached obligations to provide notice to and consult with the Administrative Commission for the River Uruguay (CARU) before authorizing the construction of paper mills on the banks of the river. CARU is the body charged with regulating and coordinating bilateral issues affecting the river, including pollution prevention, and has an equal number of experts from Uruguay and Argentina. The reporting obligations and the duties of CARU are embodied in the *Statute of the River Uruguay*, a 1975 treaty between the two parties that has the goals of utilizing, conserving, and preventing pollution of the River Uruguay.

As a basis for the ICJ's jurisdiction, Argentina cited Article 60 of the 1975 treaty, which allows submission to the ICJ if the parties fail to settle the dispute through negotiations. Discussions between the presidents of the two countries and among members of a technical group failed to resolve the issue in 2006.

Argentina alleged that the paper mills would release toxic air and liquid, resulting in damage to the ecosystem of the River Uruguay and risks to the health of more than 300,000 Argentine inhabitants. Furthermore, Argentina claimed that the mills would cause material injury to the local Argentine economy, particularly to fisheries and tourism, because the mills were proposed to be located 25 kilometers from the Argentine tourist resort of Gualeguaychú.

Uruguay contended that, based on its environmental impact assessments, the proposed mills would not meet the threshold level of emissions to trigger notification requirements under the 1975 statute. The plan would consist of two greenfield eucalyptus pulp mills that would produce air-dried pulp for use in paper products. Uruguary conceded that the production process would rely on "elemental" chlorine-free technology, which, unlike totally chlorine-free technology, results in the emission of some dioxins. Uruguay argued this emission was immaterial.

Argentina disputed Uruguay's factual contentions and petitioned the Court for provisional measures—in common law terminology, an injunction—to ensure that Uruguay suspend authorization for the construction of the mills, suspend building work, refrain from any further action with respect to the construction of the mills, and refrain from any action that could aggravate or extend the dispute or render settlement more difficult. These temporary injunctions were to maintain the status quo while the ICJ decided the merits of the case.

Uruguay responded with its own request for provisional measures in response to blockades of key roads by Argentine protesters. Uruguay claimed that the blockades deprived Uruguay of tourism revenues and requested that the ICJ order Argentina to take steps to prevent the interruption of transit between

continued

continued

Uruguay and Argentina and enforce its laws prohibiting the blockade of roads and bridges.

Decision. Although the court had the power to indicate provisional measures in this particular case under Article 41 of the *Statute of the Court,* it declined to exercise such measures. The standard for exercising provisional measures was that there be an urgent necessity to prevent irreparable prejudice to a party's rights before the court rendered its final decision. The court found no risk of prejudice to the rights claimed by the parties and declined to exercise provisional measures.

Instead, the ICJ called on the parties to implement, in good faith, the consultation and cooperation procedures provided for in the 1975 *Statute of the River Uruguay* while it considered the merits of the parties' positions.

well have been appropriate to decline Argentina's request for a temporary injunction based on lack of likelihood of success on the merits. Requests to stop construction are frequently denied on such grounds in domestic litigation. There can be little question, however, that once the paper mills are built, it would tremendously prejudice Uruguay to disassemble them or make material structural modifications to them. As a practical matter, it would be much more difficult to reach an environmentally friendly solution in the future. Although the ICJ may have avoided criticism though its decision, it is unlikely to have protected the environment if, indeed, it needed protection.

Global Ban on Toxic Substances. As noted earlier, domestic legislation such as TSCA has banned certain toxic substances domestically, and somewhat limited their circulation abroad. But so long as developing nations permit the use of these substances, their adverse effect is felt throughout the world. Beginning in 1998, nations began to discuss global solutions to the issue of proliferation of toxins.

These negotiations did not go easily. The environmental effects of toxins in the developed world are alarming. Because toxins drain into the world's waters, effects are often contracted through the eating of fish. American researchers have documented learning and behavioral problems in children exposed prenatally to PCBs through mothers who ate Great Lakes fish. In Japan, high dioxin levels have been found in whale and dolphin meat sold there. Research has detected toxins in animals thousands of miles from where the pollutant is used. However, toxins are often effective in controlling pests. Their use permits crops to grow more abundantly in areas where food is otherwise scarce. In light of its recurring history of famine, it is understandable that Ethiopia has 250 sites of dangerous pesticides, including 1,500 tons of aldrin, chlordane, and DDT.

In 2000, negotiators from 122 countries signed the first global ban on the use of specified chemical compounds. The banned substances were the acknowledged "dirty dozen" of chemical contamination, linked to birth defects and genetic abnormalities: PCBs, DDT, dioxins, and furans. The industrialized nations agreed to pay poor countries $150 million annually to help them find alternatives and permitted the limited use of DDT for public health reasons, such as malaria control.

The *Basel* Convention. One of the best examples of multinational cooperation in environmental matters is the *Basel Convention on Transboundary Movements of Hazardous Wastes and Their Disposal,* which was adopted by 170 nations under the auspices of UNEP. The Basel system is not as stringent as the U.S. law on movement of hazardous waste discussed previously, but is broader in scope.

As the volume of waste ballooned in the 1980s, a substantial trade developed in the transport of wastes from the United States and Western European countries to developing nations. Because there were strict environmental restrictions on disposal in the developed countries, and few or no restrictions in developing nations, waste generators could dispose of hazardous waste at a much lower cost by sending it on a barge to a less-developed country. For example, Guinea Bissau entered into contracts valued at more than $600 million over five years—about the size of its entire gross national product—to receive U.S. and European garbage. The downside of this system, of course, is that unremediated hazardous wastes enter the world's ecosystem just as surely whether they are dumped in Bissau, Guinea Bissau, or Champaign, Illinois. The emerging countries, which were realizing substantial revenues, were reluctant to change the arrangement.

The *Basel Convention* regulates the transport of wastes that display certain "hazardous characteristics." Transport is prohibited unless the disposer notifies the governments of the receiving and transit nations of the nature and amount of wastes in a shipment. These governments must then authorize the shipment. The receiving nation must also confirm that arrangements are in place for the "environmentally sound management of the wastes in question." During shipment, the refuse must be clearly marked with the contents of the shipment. Upon completion of disposal, the exporter must notify the receiving nation. If completion does not happen, the exporting nation must accept a return of the wastes. And to prevent the development of "waste outlaw" nations, all signatories are prohibited from permitting the transport of wastes to nonsignatories.

The *Basel Convention* is hampered by a lack of consensus on a number of critical definitions. There is no widely accepted definition of what is "hazardous." Nor is there universal agreement on what management is sufficient to *remediate* wastes (i.e., render them harmless to the environment). The difficulties in these areas are exacerbated by the substantial incentive that officials in receiving nations have to allow unrestricted transport of refuse. This can make them less demanding than officials in developed nations. If the governing elites in the receiving countries—many of which are not democratic—are unenthusiastic about enforcement, the *Basel Convention* does not work well. UNEP and others continue to work on these difficult definitional and enforcement issues.

THE *CONVENTION ON INTERNATIONAL TRADE IN ENDANGERED SPECIES*. The *Convention on International Trade in Endangered Species of Wild Fauna and Flora* (CITES), which was enacted about two decades ago and is now in force in 172 nations, is an example of how well a treaty can work when it has broad political support. CITES created a system for identifying and listing endangered and threatened species. It forbids the import or export of such species unless a "scientific authority" finds that the import or export will not aggravate the species' situation. It currently governs trade in more than 30,000 protected plant and animal species.

Noncompliant nations—whether parties or nonparties to the Convention—face potentially severe multilateral trade sanctions for violations. For example, CITES has identified certain species of Caspian Sea sturgeon as endangered. Unless leading exporters such as Russia and Iran demonstrate that the caviar trade is not detrimental to sturgeon, their caviar exports to all markets would be banned under CITES. Because of the broad support for CITES in both developed and most less-developed nations, the treaty is generally judged to be effective. The former outlaw nations have been brought to heel by overwhelming political pressure.

THE *MONTREAL PROTOCOL*. UNEP has sponsored a particularly comprehensive example of a global solution to a global environmental problem in the *Montreal Protocol on Substances That Deplete the Ozone Layer*. The *Montreal Protocol* called for a gradual reduction of substances feared to damage the ozone layer by imposing a freeze on consumption; a 10 percent limit on increases in production beginning in 1990; a 20 percent reduction in both consumption and production by 1993; and a further 30 percent reduction in production by 1998. The Protocol used the same sanction as used in CITES against violators: all signatories to the Protocol pledge to impose trade sanctions against violators.

The *Montreal Protocol* assuaged the concerns of the less-developed countries by permitting them greater flexibility in compliance than the more-developed countries. In other words, the developed countries were required to reduce their chlorofluorocarbon (CFC) levels before the emerging countries. For a period, factories in the emerging countries had to meet less demanding standards than those in other nations. The idea was that, over time, the production levels of chlorofluorocarbons (CFCs) in the developed world would move toward parity with those in the less-developed world, and eventually, all would decline.

This inequality in treatment created a significant political issue in the United States. As manufacturers and workers discovered the difficulties of competing with foreign-based firms that could use less expensive, dirtier equipment and processes, they objected loudly to the disparity in treatment. In fact, many U.S. corporations in affected industries have moved manufacturing facilities to such lower-cost nations, a trend which still continues. This has triggered adverse reactions from organized labor and increasing political backlash from politicians whom labor supports. The future of the *Montreal Protocol* may rest with how industrialized nations cope with this transitional period of inequality.

THE *CLIMATE CONTROL CONVENTION*. Difficult as resolving the issues of the ozone layer has proved to be, agreement is even more difficult in the context of "global warming," addressed in the *U.N. Framework Convention on Climate Change*. Chlorofluorocarbons (CFCs) and halons make life somewhat easier—they facilitate the functioning of certain appliances and machines—but are not critical to industrial development. However, if the earth really is experiencing a global warming, resolution of such a problem requires a substantial reduction in thermal energy use. Fossil fuels are the main source of thermal energy in the United States. They are used both in the internal combustion engines of automobiles and lawn mowers and in electric power generation. Most electric power used in the United States is generated from the burning of fossil fuels.

Because energy use is central to economic growth, the less-developed countries are not likely to agree quickly to any limitations that could restrict their economic development. And the less-developed world is not alone in its opposition. The United States, Canada, and the United Kingdom, all of which rely heavily on fossil fuels for their energy needs, have steadfastly—through both liberal and conservative administrations—opposed proposed quantitative or temporal goals for carbon dioxide emissions. Arrayed against this alliance are the "green-influenced" governments of continental Europe and Japan, which rely on carbon dioxide–free nuclear power. The latter nations are impatient to push for hard restrictions, especially on the United States.

To complicate matters further, global warming would not affect all nations in the same way. A rise in the ocean levels from arctic ice melt may flood much of Southeast Asia while causing drought in some currently fertile areas. On balance, however, a warmer, moister climate would provide longer, frost-free growing seasons. According to a UNEP study, a temperature increase of 1.5 Celsius degrees in the Central European section of the former Soviet Union would result in a 30 percent increase in its wheat yield.

Finally, some scientists continue to disagree about whether the thickening blanket of greenhouse gases is, in fact, increasing world temperatures. Various theories as to the circulation of air in the atmosphere and the cooling effect of other synthetic airborne materials—such as sulfate particles that impede sunlight's penetration of the atmosphere—support the arguments of those nations that oppose a global warming treaty.

At the 1992 United Nations Rio Conference on Environment and Development, the world community took its first tentative step toward a multilateral resolution of this problem with the *Framework Convention on Climate Change*. The Convention did not resolve any of the foregoing disputes or require any measures from its parties. Rather, it established a framework for later discussions leading to more specific treaties on the issue. The Convention identified two areas to address in the future: harmonization of national regulation and disguised discrimination against imports. In 1997, the *Kyoto Protocol* to the Convention went a step further, setting quantitative targets for the reduction of greenhouse gases to 5 percent below 1990 levels. The EU agreed to reduce emissions by 8 percent, the United States by 7 percent, and Japan by 6 percent.

Then, from 1998 through 2000, officials from all corners of the globe fought over how to measure such reductions. The United States and Canada argued that they should be allowed to purchase "pollution credits" from countries with low emissions rather than meeting the goals immediately. They also argued that they should be allowed to deduct from their emission totals "carbon sinks"—areas such as forests and farmlands that absorb carbon compounds. In late 2000, the

EU rejected these arguments, accusing the North Americans of evading their Kyoto commitments. There matters stood as the George W. Bush administration took power in the United States. In 2001, the administration quickly took the position that the carbon dioxide commitments were not enforceable against the United States in the absence of a pollution credit scheme.

Little progress has occurred since then. In late 2003, nations again met to confer on the *Convention on Climate Change*. While the Ministers passed a resolution "that climate change remains the most important global challenge to humanity and that its adverse effects are already a reality in all parts of the world," there was no further agreement on enforcement apparatus. Instead, two funds were developed to support developing countries' efforts in the area, the Special Climate Change Fund and the Least Developed Countries Fund. These funds support technology transfer, adaptation projects, and other activities. Several countries renewed an earlier pledge to contribute US$410 million annually to developing countries. Obviously, in light of the magnitude of the problem, this is not very much money.

The parties continue to make efforts to arrive at a resolution, but are stymied by the same roadblocks. In 2005, Canada hosted over 180 countries at the first meeting of the Parties to the *Kyoto Protocol* and the eleventh session of the Conference of the Parties to the Climate Change Convention. The meetings included a mandate to approve twenty-one decisions to implement the Protocol, including establishment of an enforcement branch relating to compliance procedures. The parties also developed the *Montreal Plan of Action* to shape commitments for developed and developing countries beyond the expiration of the *Montreal Protocol*'s first commitment period in 2012. Two major emitters, the United States and Australia, did not ratify the *Protocol,* and major developing countries did not meet their emission/stabilization commitments in the first commitment period. The discussions did not lead to new commitments.

Alternative Energy Movement. Spurred by soaring fossil fuel prices more than environmental concerns, many nations are intensifying their focus on the development of biofuels as a source of energy. These technologies are not new, as both the United States and Europe first developed biofuel industries in the early twentieth century. Until recent technological developments and spikes in energy prices, however, these fuels were prohibitively expensive relative to traditional fuels.

The fuels are made from plant matter such as corn or sugar cane stalks and when combined with petroleum in liquid, gaseous, or solid form, they can produce electricity and heat. *Ethanol* (ethyl alcohol) is one of the more popular biofuels and is mixed with petroleum at varying ratios.

Several countries have adopted incentive programs for biofuel. The U.S. Department of Energy has established a Renewable Energy Biomass Program to encourage the development and improvement of technology for biofuel. Producers currently enjoy an excise tax exemption and an earned income tax credit. The government increased regulation of producers in the *Energy Policy Act of 2005 (EPACT)*. The Act established minimum requirements for ethanol and biodiesel fuel usage in automotive fuels through 2012.

Brazil is a pioneer in the field of biofuel. Its ethanol fuel program, which uses sugar cane, has been in use for over twenty-nine years. More recently, the Brazilian Parliament passed *Law 10438* to create the Program of Incentives for Alternative Energy Sources (PROINFA) in 2002. The Brazilian government requires that all gasoline contain a minimum of 20 percent ethanol, and on average, fuel for transportation includes more than 40 percent ethanol. Brazil is also beginning to export ethanol to other markets, including Japan and other Asian countries.

Even here, however, national protectionism can overshadow environmental concerns. Ethanol produced with sugar cane in Brazil is far less expensive to produce than corn-based ethanol. In reaction, the United States has thrown up trade barriers to protect its corn-based ethanol industry, needlessly making all biofuels in the United States more expensive and retarding the development of a renewable alternative to petroleum. Environmentalism has not yet overcome baser economic concerns.

The European Union is also encouraging the development of alternative energy. The EU has set a target: fuels should contain 5.75 percent biofuels by 2010. To meet this target, member states are offering tax rebates to producers. For example, France offered a rebate for production of 80,000 tonnes of biodiesel and 320,000 tons of ethanol by the end of 2007. France, like other European countries, typically produces ethanol from sugar beets or cereals and produces biodiesel from rapeseed. Germany is Europe's leading biodiesel producer, accounting for 80 percent of production, while Spain is the leading ethanol producer.

Like the United States, however, the EU has high biofuel production costs relative to fossil fuels. This overall higher cost for biofuel has impeded market-based expansion in the United States and the EU. Brazil's lower cost of production has allowed biofuel to penetrate the market more easily.

General Prospects for Global Environmental Solutions. In a world where emerging public opinion strongly favors environmental protection, one should not underestimate the potential for global solutions. A relatively short time ago, for example, the differences between whaling nations and environmentalists in nonwhaling nations were thought to be irreconcilable. The force of public opinion in the whalers' own countries led to an agreement to permit international regulation. Today, commercial hunting of whales is regulated by the International Whaling Commission, which meets periodically to determine how much, if any, whaling is to be allowed. From 1986 through 1992, the commission effectively banned whaling. This allowed whale stocks to replenish. The threatened mammal has come back from the edge of extinction to the point where limited hunting has begun again.

For "First World" investors, agreements like the *Montreal Protocol*—if it stays in force despite political pressure—mean that their Third World manufacturing plants will need to comply with international standards at some point in the future. Further, because the Protocol also prohibits trade in CFCs between parties to the Protocol and nonparties, foreign investors that manufacture products in the less-developed world for export to the developed world must expect that those export markets are likely to be closed to them if their plants are located in a country that is not a party to the agreement. The bottom line for foreign investors is that differences in environmental regulations are becoming increasingly difficult to exploit.

Conclusion

Environmental law is an area of rapidly increasing regulation as conservationism becomes an accepted goal of groups across the political spectrum. As this trend is internationalized through bilateral and multilateral treaties, the investor who seeks to avoid environmental protection laws runs the risk of being trapped abroad with an unusable investment.

Chapter Summary

1. Nations may enact domestic legislation outlawing import of a product because the product itself violates environmental norms in the regulating country or because it is manufactured through a process that is environmentally objectionable.
2. According to WTO rules a nation may require foreign producers to comply with the same environmental standards that are required by domestic firms, but may not subject foreign firms to more rigorous standards.
3. Victims of environmental misdeeds abroad can sometimes sue the foreign investor polluter in its home country, but such a ruling often depends on the demonstration that significant activities to the pollution had occurred in the home country.
4. NAFTA established the North American Commission for Environmental Cooperation to determine whether any party to NAFTA has shown a "persistent pattern of failure" to "effectively enforce its environmental law." The Commission has declared it has no right to investigate actions by legislatures of NAFTA countries even if those actions effectively nullify other laws.
5. The Council of Ministers of the European Communities has adopted more than 200 different directives on environmental protection that the member states must implement through national legislation. The European

Commission has pursued hundreds of infringement procedures against member nations to compel implementation of these directives. EU countries now have the most rigorous environmental laws in the world.

6. The *London Convention for the Prevention of Marine Pollution by Dumping from Ships and Aircraft* prohibits the dumping of specified hazardous wastes from ships at sea and requires permits for the dumping of others.
7. If a country wishes to obtain financing for its projects from the World Bank or its private finance affiliate, the International Finance Corporation, the characteristics of the project must fall within accepted world environmental standards articulated in the World Bank's publications.
8. The *Basel Convention* regulates the transport of wastes that display certain hazardous characteristics. Transport is prohibited unless the disposer notifies the governments of the receiving and transit nations of the nature and amount of wastes in a shipment and confirms that arrangements are in place for environmentally sound management of the wastes.
9. The *Convention on International Trade in Endangered Species of Wild Fauna and Flora,* ratified by 172 nations, created a system for identifying and listing endangered and threatened species. It forbids the import or export of more than 30,000 protected plant and animal species unless a scientific authority finds that the import or export will not aggravate the species' situation.
10. The *Montreal Protocol* has gradually reduced substances feared to damage the ozone layer by imposing first a freeze on consumption, then staged reductions in consumption and production. All signatories to the Protocol are pledged to impose trade sanctions against violators.
11. The *Framework Convention on Climate Change* did not resolve any of the disputes as to numerical deadlines for reduction of carbon dioxide emissions. Rather, it established a framework for later discussions leading to more specific treaties on the issue. The *Kyoto Protocol* set quantitative targets for the reduction of greenhouse gases, but was not approved by the United States and places no constraints on China or India.

Questions and Case Problems

1. In the *Judgment of February 23, 1988,* what would the Austrian Supreme Court have done if a private cause of action had been available in Czechoslovakia? How do you think the court would handle complaints about a nuclear accident such as Chernobyl?
2. How would an Austrian judgment for money damages against the Czechoslovak government be enforced? What type of injunctive relief would be possible?
3. If a U.S. company is presented with the opportunity to build a plant in a former communist country with less stringent laws on carbon dioxide emissions, what factors should it take into consideration before proceeding with the project? To what extent should they consider the long-term investment interest of the company's shareholders? Are any other issues relevant to management's consideration? Would the company's president, who bypassed this low-risk opportunity to realize profit for the shareholders because of personal political views, have fulfilled management's fiduciary obligations to the shareholders?
4. Assume that a democratically elected government, after a favorable vote in a popular referendum, launches a program to clear 150,000 acres of tropical rain forest in order to promote economic development. To carry out the will of the people, the government issues a request for proposals to international engineering firms for a contract to help clear the acreage. A number of international firms have indicated that they will bid on the project. Prepare a memo to your U.S. firm expressing your views on whether the firm should submit a bid.
5. Despite the *Montreal Protocol,* the nation of Livy continues to produce CFC-emitting refrigerators and to export them to nations throughout the world. A number of governments object to Livy's practices and ban its exports pursuant to the Protocol. Livy brings an action under GATT, alleging that under the principles stated in the *Shrimp Excluded Devices* case, this is an attempt to impose

conservationist policies on Livy. How should the GATT panel rule?

6. The Kingdom of Carolinium has a strong commitment to the preservation of wild horse herds. The neighboring Republic of Giles Run is a major dog food manufacturer and regularly uses wild horse meat in its products. These products are exported to and marketed in Carolinium. In accordance with its principles, Carolinium enacted the Horse Conservation and Health Act (HCHA) banning the use of all horse meat in any animal or human food products. Carolinium justified the HCHA on conservationist and health grounds. The evidence for any health hazard from horse meat is limited to a few scattered cases of botulism. The Carolinium ban effectively terminated all dog food exports from Giles Run. In response, Giles Run called for the creation of a GATT panel to consider the HCHA violation of GATT. How should the GATT panel rule?

Managerial Implications

Your employer, Ortiz-Hartman Steel Limited, is a specialty U.S. steel manufacturer. Over the past several years, Ortiz-Hartman has been underpriced in its specialty steel submarket by a manufacturer from the Bishopric of Saul, a nation that has virtually no environmental laws. Steel plants in Saul spew pollutants into the air and the rivers. Some of the pollutants damage the property and health of Saul subjects, but no cause of action in Saul affords them relief. Other pollutants damage the environment in neighboring countries. Faced with crippling competition, some members of Ortiz-Hartman management recommend that Ortiz-Hartman build a plant in Saul and take advantage of the more forgiving pollution laws.

1. Your employer asks you to prepare a memorandum summarizing the potential liability to Ortiz-Hartman associated with building a plant in Saul under current law. In your assessment, address all possible sources of liability, even those that you consider to be unlikely. Explain the detailed reasoning for your assessments.
2. Prepare a memorandum summarizing long-term risk in light of emerging international environmental legal standards.

For Internet Activities, Visit academic.cengage.com/blaw/schaffer.

CHAPTER 22
Regulating the Competitive Environment

An enterprise with great market power must be concerned with the limits that antitrust or competition laws place on extensions of that power. Such extensions include not only the introduction of products but also franchise and licensing arrangements.

Unlike other bodies of law reviewed in Part Four of this book, the general substance of competition laws is markedly similar from nation to nation. The way in which that law is implemented, however, differs significantly from place to place.

Historical Development of International Competition Law

Antitrust law has been important in the United States since the end of the nineteenth century. At that time, Congress passed the *Sherman Antitrust Act* and the *Clayton Act* to permit government "trust-busters" to break up a number of "trusts" and cartels that used their size to crush their competition. These laws, which had strong populist support and developed independently in American courts, are the foundation of an economic system that relies on maximizing competition to permit free-market forces to operate.

After the Second World War, the European equivalent of antitrust law—*competition law*—developed rapidly. Under Articles 81 (formerly 85) and 82 (formerly 86) of the *Treaty of Rome,* the members of the European Union pledged to regulate anticompetitive actions within the Union and outlaw the abuse of dominant market power. These articles, now implemented by the Commission of the European Communities, form the bedrock upon which the highly sophisticated competition law of the EU is based. In recent years, the Commission's Directorate-General COMP (DG-COMP)—the EU's version of a combination of the Federal Trade Commission and the U.S. Department of Justice, which regulate antitrust matters in the United States—has prepared numerous regulations for adoption by the European Council of Ministers and issued a host of decisions and exemptions.

Competition law has also become an important focus for the European Court of Justice, which hears appeals of Commission decisions and referrals from the courts of the EU member states on competition law issues. The European approach, however, puts less confidence in market forces and is more fearful of unrestrained competition. The Europeans are more willing to rely on direct government action and less willing to count on litigation, although individual countries within Europe are beginning to emerge as more "litigation friendly."

More than seventy other nations around the world now have enacted competition policy–based national merger notification and review regimes. From South Korea to Brazil to the Czech Republic, all nations are concerned with private domination of sectors of the national economy.

Even as competition laws multiply, their content becomes more diverse. Some nations follow the U.S. model, some follow the EU model, some combine those approaches, and some opt for new ideas. The U.S. Attorney General's International Competition Policy Advisory Committee initially sought to promote substantive convergence among competition law schemes and procedural "best practices," but concluded that "... agreement on specific substantive rules is unlikely in the foreseeable future" and that "[c]omplete harmonization will be achieved only in the long run, if ever." Antitrust scholars agree that harmonization in the near future is highly unlikely, though the discord generated from divergent results on the two sides of the Atlantic in the same or similar cases will likely maintain pressure for harmonization.

Thus, businesses today face conflicting trends in competition law. To understand how these trends affect businesses, this chapter begins with a review of the basic structure of antitrust/competition law.

Basic Regulatory Framework

The form of antitrust laws differs somewhat from nation to nation. The German competition legislation—the *Gesetzgegen Wettbewerbsbeschrankungen*—is highly detailed and addresses many issues in advance. This limits the discretion of the administering agency and the courts to define and develop the law. In stark contrast, but consistent with its reliance on government policy implementation, the Korean *Monopoly Regulation and Fair Trade Act* is drafted in more general terms. Administrative regulations contain the specifics of what is prohibited and how it is prohibited. The Japanese *Antimonopoly Law* facially resembles the U.S. law from which it is largely drawn, but is administered by the Japanese Fair Trade Commission and works more like EU law. Consistent with its litigious tradition, antitrust laws in the United States are stated in general terms. The details are worked out in court.

Despite these differences in form and enforcement, the substance of competition law is remarkably similar in its focus on two types of activity. First, competition laws tend to prohibit agreements between competitors that restrict competition. From this general principle flows a whole range of specific prohibitions against anticompetitive clauses in licensing, franchising, and other types of agreements. Second, such laws prohibit the abuse of a dominant market position. From this general principle come a variety of concepts such as bans against predatory pricing and refusals to deal.

Prohibitions Against Agreements to Restrict Competition

Article 81 of the *Treaty of Rome* and Section 1 of the *Sherman Act* both prohibit concerted anticompetitive conduct. The *Sherman Act* does so in broad, unspecific language. Article 81(1) of the *Treaty of Rome* flatly prohibits "all agreements between undertakings [firms], decisions by associations of undertakings and concerted practices which may affect trade between the Member States and which have as their object or effect the prevention, restriction, or distortion of competition within the Common Market." Article 81(2) automatically voids all agreements that violate Article 81(1), and Article 81(3) authorizes the European Commission to grant exemptions from this prohibition. Similar regulatory schemes may be found in competition law provisions of other nations.

Prohibitions against agreements that restrict competition are ordinarily the most relevant to international transactions. As noted in Chapter Seventeen (Licensing Agreements and the Protection of Intellectual Property Rights), a principal objective of every licensor is to prevent its licensee from competing with it. Left to its own devices, the licensor would seek pledges of eternal noncompetition throughout the Milky Way. However, the licensor must moderate its demands so they are consistent with local competition law.

This principle is implemented differently under different systems. Some nations require governmental review of virtually all such "vertical" arrangements between firms and their distributors, customers, or suppliers. For example, Chile generally prohibits the establishment of exclusive distribution systems that restrict trade. Because exclusive distribution agreements always restrict trade, this prohibition means that one must review all such arrangements with officials from the *Fiscalía Nacional Económica,* the Chilean competition law enforcer, to obtain discretionary preclearance.

The United States characteristically looks at such arrangements in the context of determining whether they enhance or inhibit the workings of a competitive marketplace. The regulators and courts will allow vertical restraints if a reasonable case can be made that they foster better service and hence enhance interbrand competition;

encourage innovation; or do not foreclose a substantial part of the market to others.

In the EU, the Commission is more likely to intervene to prevent vertical restraints. In the area of patent licensing, DG-COMP is forgiving of some anticompetitive restrictions but not as forgiving as U.S. authorities would be, particularly with respect to products that include both patented and unpatented components. U.S. policy tends to accept a patent holder's restrictions in the hope of giving greater encouragement to innovation.

A significant difference exists between the ways that the EU and the United States analyze competition issues raised by patent licenses. U.S. antitrust experts tend to view enhanced profit for the patent holder as a desirable incentive to innovation. By contrast, the Europeans increasingly view the monopoly inherent in a patent as a danger to competition that should be minimized as much as possible.

The European Commission is more flexible with respect to know-how transfer agreements than patent licenses. The rationale is that because the owner of know-how does not have any legally cognizable right to its knowledge, it can rely only on secrecy. The only way to protect secrecy is through restrictive provisions that prohibit the licensee from competing against the licensor or from disclosing the know-how to any third party. If the Commission could not give the potential licensor of know-how confidence that its know-how would be kept secret, the licensor would be left with little incentive to enter into any agreement. The result would be anticompetitive because no one but the licensor would have the know-how.

The EU and other competition authorities also show flexibility in reviewing franchise agreements. Franchise agreements involve peculiar considerations because the franchiser must have substantial control over the franchisee. Like other licensors, the franchiser must protect its know-how. In addition, the franchiser must ensure that the franchisee is producing and marketing the product in a manner consistent with the franchiser's good name. Uniformity is important to most franchise businesses. One franchisee's poor performance can have adverse effects on the franchiser's operations internationally. In addition, the franchiser may wish to prevent the franchisee from charging prices that are inconsistent with the pricing practices of other franchisees. The European Court of Justice has considered these unusual attributes of the franchiser–franchisee relationship and, in general, has given franchisers and franchisees great flexibility in structuring their relationships.

Japan's consensus-oriented tradition has historically encouraged collaboration rather than competition among its major corporations. Consistent with this tradition, Japan permitted development of tightly wound *keiretsu* networks of suppliers and distributors. Although these networks competed against one another in Japan, their control over the means of distribution, exercised through highly restrictive distribution agreements, effectively prevented foreign firms from entering the Japanese market. In fact, when they could enter the market at all, foreign companies were compelled to enter into a single, exclusive distributorship agreement for all of Japan. Obviously, the single distributor was able to exact quite favorable terms, and the Japanese consumer was confronted with relatively high prices. In 1990, the Japan Fair Trade Commission ruled that companies with at least a 25 percent share of the Japanese market were prohibited from signing exclusive import distribution contracts. Enforcement of these restrictions has not been aggressive, however.

Abuse of Dominant Market Position

Article 82 of the *Treaty of Rome,* Section 2 of the *Sherman Act,* and their counterparts in other national competition statutes address the problem of monopolies and the abuse of monopoly power. To be in violation of such monopoly provisions, a company must have a dominant market position, which is defined differently in different countries and in different industries. In addition, the dominant party must be found to have abused this position.

In smaller countries where, by definition, fewer entities can survive in the relevant markets, market domination tends to be more widely tolerated. Thus, in Canada, where industry is considerably more concentrated than in the United States, optimal levels of industrial concentration are likely to be relatively higher than in the United States. Moreover, cultural and historical factors are also of considerable importance. For instance, in

Germany and France, refusals to deal (*refus de vente*) are closely proscribed, even if the refuser has a relatively low level of market dominance.

In the following case involving Microsoft, the European Commission took a decidedly different approach than the United States when addressing abuse of a dominant market position. Its more aggressive position was generally upheld by the European Court of First Instance in the following 2007 decision.

Microsoft Corp. v. Commission of the European Communities

Case T-201/04, 5 C.M.L.R. 11 (2007); Available at 2007 WL 2693858

European Court of Justice Court of First Instance—Grand Chamber BB

BACKGROUND AND FACTS

Microsoft Corp., a U.S. company, designs, develops, and markets software products, including operating systems for client personal computers (client PCs), operating systems for work group servers, and streaming media players. In December 1998, Sun Microsystems, Inc., another U.S. company, lodged a complaint with the European Commission alleging that Microsoft had refused to give Sun the information and technology necessary to allow Sun's work group server operating systems to interoperate with the Windows client PC operating system. In 2000, the Commission launched an investigation of Microsoft's Windows 2000 generation of client PC and work group server operating systems and Microsoft's integration of its Windows Media Player in its client PC operating system. That investigation concluded in August 2001, when the Commission sent Microsoft a statement of objections about client/server interoperability. The statement also raised questions relating to interoperability between work group servers and the integration of Windows Media Player in Microsoft's client PC operating system. Microsoft responded in late 2001. Between April and June 2003, the Commission conducted a market survey, sending a series of requests for information to a number of companies and associations. This resulted in the Commission proposing another set of objections and remedies against Microsoft.

Finally, after a hearing and additional briefing, in March 2004, the Commission entered a decision finding Microsoft guilty of two abuses of dominant position, violating Articles 82 and 54. As a result, the Commission ordered it to (1) make its operating system more accessible to competitors, (2) offer client PC systems that did not bundle the Windows Media Player, and (3) set up and pay for an independent monitoring trustee to ensure Microsoft did not violate the order. Microsoft was ruled to have had a dominant position in the client PC operating systems market since at least 1996 and in the work group server operating systems market since 2002. To support its finding of dominance in the client PC operating systems market, the Commission found that: Microsoft's market share was consistently over 90 percent. It also found that there were significant barriers to market entry, because users like platforms on which they can use a large number of applications and software designers write applications for the client PC operating systems that are the most popular among users. The Commission based its finding that Microsoft had a dominant position in the work group server operating systems market on the fact that Microsoft's market share is at least 60 percent. No other competitor in the work group market had a share greater than 25 percent. Further, the Commission found that there were close commercial and technological links between the PC and work group markets.

The Commission found that, in light of Microsoft's dominant position, it was abusive for Microsoft to (1) refuse to share interoperability information and (2) make the availability of the Windows client PC operating system conditional on the simultaneous acquisition of the Windows Media Player software. The Commission thus imposed a fine and a number of remedies on Microsoft. Microsoft appealed the decision to the Court of First Instance in June 2004. Because of its importance, the matter was ultimately referred to the Grand Chamber of that Court.

PRESIDENT VESTERDORF AND JUDGES JAEGER, PIRRUNG, GARCÍA-VALDECASAS, TIILI, AZIZI, COOKE, MEIJ, FORWOOD, MARTINS RIBEIRO, WISZNIEWSKA-BIAŁECKA, VADAPALAS AND I. LABUCKA

PRELIMINARY ISSUES

[T]he Commission raises a number of issues relating to the extent of review by the Community Courts....

continued

continued

The Commission claims that the contested decision rests on a number of considerations involving complex technical and economic assessments. It submits that, according to the case-law, the Community Courts can carry out only a limited review of such assessments.... The Court observes that it follows from consistent case-law that, although as a general rule the Community Courts undertake a comprehensive review of the question as to whether or not the conditions for the application of the competition rules are met, their review of complex economic appraisals made by the Commission is necessarily limited to checking whether the relevant rules on procedure and on stating reasons have been complied with, whether the facts have been accurately stated and whether there has been any manifest error of assessment or a misuse of powers. Likewise, in so far as the Commission's decision is the result of complex technical appraisals, those appraisals are in principle subject to only limited review by the Court, which means that the Community Courts cannot substitute their own assessment of matters of fact for the Commission's. However, while the Community Courts recognise that the Commission has a margin of appreciation in economic or technical matters, that does not mean that they must decline to review the Commission's interpretation of economic or technical data. The Community Courts must not only establish whether the evidence put forward is factually accurate, reliable and consistent but must also determine whether that evidence contains all the relevant data that must be taken into consideration in appraising a complex situation and whether it is capable of substantiating the conclusions drawn from it.

THE CRITERIA ON WHICH AN UNDERTAKING IN A DOMINANT POSITION MAY BE COMPELLED TO GRANT A LICENCE, AS DEFINED BY THE COMMUNITY JUDICATURE, ARE NOT SATISFIED IN THE PRESENT CASE

It follows from [the facts presented to the Court] that ... Windows work group networks rely on an 'architecture' of both client/server and server/server interconnections and interactions and that that 'architecture'—which the Commission characterises as 'Windows domain architecture'—ensures 'transparent access' to the main services provided by work group servers. Those various factors also show that ... those interconnections and interactions are closely interlinked. In other words, the proper functioning of the Windows work group networks relies both on client/server communication protocols—which, by their nature, are implemented both in Windows client PC operating systems and in Windows work group server operating systems—and on server/server communication protocols. [F]or numerous tasks, server/server communication protocols appear, in fact, as 'extensions' of the client/server communication protocols. In certain cases, a server acts as a client PC vis-à-vis another server.... The Court therefore finds that the Commission is quite correct to conclude that 'the common ability to be part of [the Windows domain architecture] is a feature of compatibility between Windows client PCs and Windows work group servers'....

The first abusive conduct in which Microsoft is found to have engaged is its refusal to supply the interoperability information to its competitors and to allow its use for the purpose of developing and distributing work group server operating system products....

By way of remedy for that refusal, the Commission ordered Microsoft, ... to do the following:

> 'make the interoperability information available to any undertaking having an interest in developing and distributing work group server operating system products and shall, on reasonable and non-discriminatory terms, allow the use of the interoperability information by such undertakings for the purpose of developing and distributing work group server operating system products[.]'

It must be borne in mind that Microsoft's argument is that its refusal to supply interoperability information cannot constitute an abuse of a dominant position within the meaning of Article 82 EC because, first, the information is protected by intellectual property rights (or constitutes trade secrets) and, second, the criteria established in the case-law which determine when an undertaking in a dominant position can be required to grant a licence to a third party are not satisfied in this case. [T]he Commission contends that there is no need to decide whether Microsoft's conduct constitutes a refusal to license intellectual property rights to a third party, or whether trade secrets merit the same degree of protection as intellectual property rights, since the strict criteria against which such a refusal may be found to constitute an abuse of a dominant position within the meaning of Article 82 EC are in any event satisfied in the present case.... While Microsoft and the Commission are thus agreed that the refusal at issue may be assessed under Article 82 EC on the assumption

continued

continued

that it constitutes a refusal to license intellectual property rights, they disagree as to the criteria established in the case-law that are applicable in such a situation.... The Commission ... maintains that, in order to determine whether such a refusal is abusive, it must take into consideration all the particular circumstances surrounding that refusal.... Thus it explains ... that '[t]he case-law of the European Courts ... suggests that the Commission must analyse the entirety of the circumstances surrounding a specific instance of a refusal to supply and must take its decision [on the basis of] the results of such a comprehensive examination'.... At the hearing, the Commission, questioned on this issue by the Court, confirmed that it had considered in the contested decision that Microsoft's conduct presented three characteristics which allowed it to be characterised as abusive. The first consists in the fact that the information which Microsoft refuses to disclose to its competitors relates to interoperability in the software industry, a matter to which the Community legislature attaches particular importance. The second characteristic lies in the fact that Microsoft uses its extraordinary power on the client PC operating systems market to eliminate competition on the adjacent work group server operating systems market. The third characteristic is that the conduct in question involves disruption of previous levels of supply....

In response to those various arguments, the Court observes that ... although undertakings are, as a rule, free to choose their business partners, in certain circumstances a refusal to supply on the part of a dominant undertaking may constitute an abuse of a dominant position within the meaning of Article 82 EC unless it is objectively justified. The Court of Justice thus considered that a company in a dominant position on the market in raw materials which, with the aim of reserving such raw materials for the purpose of manufacturing its own derivatives, refused to supply a customer which was itself a manufacturer of those derivatives, and was therefore likely to eliminate all competition on the part of that customer, abused its dominant position within the meaning of Article 82 EC. In [a another case], the Court of Justice was asked whether the refusal by a car manufacturer which was the proprietor of a design right covering car body panels to license third parties to supply products incorporating the protected design must be considered to be an abuse of a dominant position within the meaning of Article 82 EC. In its judgment, the Court of Justice emphasised that the right of a proprietor of a protected design to prevent third parties from manufacturing and selling or importing, without his consent, products incorporating the design constitutes the very subject-matter of his exclusive right. The Court of Justice concluded ... that 'an obligation imposed upon the proprietor of a protected design to grant to third parties, even in return for a reasonable royalty, a licence for the supply of products incorporating the design would lead to the proprietor thereof being deprived of the substance of his exclusive right, and that a refusal to grant such a licence cannot in itself constitute an abuse of a dominant position'. The Court of Justice added, however, that 'the exercise of an exclusive right by the proprietor of a registered design in respect of car body panels [might] be prohibited by Article [82 EC] if it involve[d], on the part of an undertaking holding a dominant position, certain abusive conduct such as the arbitrary refusal to supply spare parts to independent repairers, the fixing of prices for spare parts at an unfair level or a decision no longer to produce spare parts for a particular model even though many cars of that model [were] still in circulation, provided that such conduct [was] liable to affect trade between Member States.' ... It follows from the case-law cited above that the refusal by an undertaking holding a dominant position to license a third party to use a product covered by an intellectual property right cannot in itself constitute an abuse of a dominant position within the meaning of Article 82 EC. It is only in exceptional circumstances that the exercise of the exclusive right by the owner of the intellectual property right may give rise to such an abuse.

It also follows from that case-law that the following circumstances, in particular, must be considered to be exceptional:

- in the first place, the refusal relates to a product or service indispensable to the exercise of a particular activity on a neighbouring market;
- in the second place, the refusal is of such a kind as to exclude any effective competition on that neighbouring market;
- in the third place, the refusal prevents the appearance of a new product for which there is potential consumer demand.

Once it is established that such circumstances are present, the refusal by the holder of a dominant

continued

continued

position to grant a licence may infringe Article 82 EC unless the refusal is objectively justified....

In the light of the foregoing factors, the Court considers that it is appropriate, first of all, to decide whether the [exceptional] circumstances ... are also present in this case.

The Court observed, in particular, that ... in order to be able to compete viably with Windows work group server operating systems, competitors' operating systems must be able to interoperate with the Windows domain architecture on an equal footing with those Windows systems.... The Court has held that interoperability ... had two indissociable components, client/server interoperability and server/server interoperability and that it implied in particular that a server running a non-Microsoft work group server operating system could act as domain controller within a Windows domain using Active Directory and, consequently, would be able to participate in the multimaster replication mechanism with the other domain controllers.... It must be emphasised that the Commission's analysis of that question in the contested decision is based on complex economic assessments and that, accordingly, it is subject to only limited review by the Court.... It follows from the considerations set out below that Microsoft has not demonstrated that the Commission's analysis is manifestly incorrect.

Microsoft's dominant position on the client PC operating systems market exhibits ... 'extraordinary features,' since, notably, its market shares on that market are more than 90% ... and since Windows represents the 'quasi-standard' for those operating systems.... As the Windows operating system is thus present on virtually all client PCs installed within organisations, non-Windows work group server operating systems cannot continue to be marketed if they are incapable of achieving a high degree of interoperability with Windows.

More specifically, the Commission considers that, in order to be able to be viably marketed, non-Windows work group server operating systems must be capable of participating in the Windows domain architecture—which consists of an 'architecture' of both client/server and server/server interconnections and interactions, closely interlinked ... on an equal footing with Windows work group server operating systems. That means, in particular, that a server running a non-Microsoft work group server operating system is able to act as domain controller within a Windows domain using Active Directory and, consequently, is capable of participating in the multimaster replication mechanism with the other domain controllers.

It follows from all of the foregoing considerations that Microsoft has not established that the Commission made a manifest error when it considered that non-Microsoft work group server operating systems must be capable of interoperating with the Windows domain architecture on an equal footing with Windows work group server operating systems if they were to be marketed viably on the market. The Court also concludes from those considerations that the absence of such interoperability with the Windows domain architecture has the effect of reinforcing Microsoft's competitive position on the work group server operating systems market, particularly because it induces consumers to use its work group server operating system in preference to its competitors', although its competitors' operating systems offer features to which consumers attach great importance.

THE BUNDLING OF WINDOWS MEDIA PLAYER WITH THE WINDOWS CLIENT PC OPERATING SYSTEM

Article 6 of the contested decision orders Microsoft, inter alia, to offer, within 90 days of notification of the decision, a full-functioning version of its Windows client PC operating system which does not incorporate Windows Media Player, although Microsoft is to retain the right to offer a bundle of the Windows client PC operating system and Windows Media Player....

[T]he Commission clearly demonstrated ... that the fact that from May 1999 Microsoft offered OEMs, for pre-installation on client PCs, only the version of Windows bundled with Windows Media Player had the inevitable consequence of affecting relations on the market between Microsoft, OEMs and suppliers of third-party media players by appreciably altering the balance of competition in favour of Microsoft and to the detriment of the other operators. [N]o third-party media player could achieve such a level of market penetration without having the advantage in terms of distribution that Windows Media Player enjoys as a result of Microsoft's use of its Windows client PC operating system.... The Court considers that the Commission was correct to find ... that it was on the basis of the percentages of installation and use of media players that content providers and software developers chose the technology for which they would develop their own

continued

continued

products.... The Commission correctly stated, first, that those operators tended primarily to use Windows Media Player as that allowed them to reach the very large majority of client PC users in the world and, second, that the transmission of content and applications compatible with a given media player was in itself a significant competitive factor, since it increased the popularity of that media player, and, in turn, favoured the use of the underlying media technology, including codecs, formats....

It must be borne in mind, as a preliminary point, that although the burden of proof of the existence of the circumstances that constitute an infringement of Article 82 EC is borne by the Commission, it is for the dominant undertaking concerned, and not for the Commission, before the end of the administrative procedure, to raise any plea of objective justification and to support it with arguments and evidence. It then falls to the Commission, where it proposes to make a finding of an abuse of a dominant position, to show that the arguments and evidence relied on by the undertaking cannot prevail.... Microsoft has not demonstrated the existence of any objective justification for the abusive bundling of Windows Media Player with the Windows client PC operating system.

THE INDEPENDENT MONITORING TRUSTEE

Article 7 of the contested decision ... provides for the establishment of a suitable mechanism to assist the Commission in monitoring Microsoft's compliance with the contested decision and including, in particular, the appointment of an independent monitoring trustee. [T]he Commission states that the monitoring trustee's 'primary responsibility' is to issue opinions, and to do so upon application by a third party or by the Commission, or on his own initiative, on 'whether Microsoft has, in a specific instance, failed to comply with [the contested decision], or on any issue that may be of interest with respect to the effective enforcement of [that decision]'.

Microsoft seeks annulment of Article 7 of the contested decision on the ground that, by unlawfully delegating its powers of investigation and enforcement to a third party, the Commission exceeded its powers under Article 82 EC and Regulation No 17.... The Court considers that by establishing a monitoring mechanism involving the appointment of an independent monitoring trustee as referred to in Article 7 of the contested decision, and charged with the functions set out, in ... that decision, the Commission went far beyond the situation in which it retains its own external expert to provide advice....

It follows from all of the foregoing considerations that Article 7 of the contested decision has no legal basis in [EC Regulations] ... and therefore exceeds the Commission's powers of investigation and enforcement ... in so far as it orders Microsoft to submit a proposal for the establishment of a mechanism which must include the appointment of an independent monitoring trustee empowered to access, independently of the Commission, Microsoft's assistance, information, documents, premises and employees and also the source code of its relevant products ...

Decision. The Court of First Instance annulled the portion of the Commission Decision that ordered Microsoft to submit a proposal for the establishment of a mechanism that was to include a monitoring trustee empowered to have access, independently of the Commission, to Microsoft's assistance, information, documents, premises, and employees and to the source code of the relevant Microsoft products. It also annulled the requirement that Microsoft pay for the monitoring trustee. The Court upheld all other aspects of the Commission's decision.

The *EC Merger Regulation*

The foregoing commentary describes traditional enforcement mechanisms that are familiar to U.S. businesspeople. In these mechanisms, the parties act and the authorities react. Some exceptions will be discussed in the following section. In 1990, however, the Council of the European Communities' *Regulation 4064/89*—the *EC Merger Regulation*—became effective. Under the *Merger Regulation,* parties to all mergers, acquisitions, joint ventures, and other business combinations having a *community dimension* must provide pre-transaction notification to the Commission. Then, in 2004, the European Council made the most substantial amendments to the *Merger Regulation* since its enactment, when it formally adopted *Regulation 139/2004*. The new *Merger Regulation* affects both procedural review and the substantive test for merger prohibition.

The *EC Merger Regulation* had historically been administered by the Commission's Merger Task Force in rapid-fire fashion. Reorganization of DG-COMP in recent years has allowed for more sector-specific review of mergers. Under the Regulation, deals "notified" to the Commission automatically begin a five-week Phase 1 merger inquiry. During the five-week period, the Task Force intensively studies the competitive effects of the proposed transaction. It also entertains the views of third parties if they can demonstrate a sufficient interest in the proposed merger. The Task Force then renders a Phase 1 decision in which it determines whether the merger "raises serious doubts as to its compatibility with the common market." It will extend the ruling if the parties offer proposed undertakings in the hope of settlement. If no serious doubts result, the merger is cleared. If serious doubts arise, the merger review enters Phase II, a four-and-one-half–month review that can be extended. Phase II includes a meeting with the parties involved, often another meeting including third parties, a Statement of Objections describing the Commission's concerns, a reply by the parties involved, a formal hearing, and proposed undertakings to settle the case.

The Commission begins with an analysis of the materials submitted by the parties seeking approval. It also has broad investigative powers under the *Merger Regulation,* including the ability to request information, to examine business records, to ask "for oral explanations on the spot," and to conduct on-site investigations. The Commission has broad powers to levy fines for noncompliance or failure to cooperate during the investigative process.

In any inquiry, the Commission first attempts to determine "community dimension" in cases of any dispute on the issue. Such a dimension exists when either: (1) the aggregate worldwide sales of all the firms being combined exceed 5 billion European currency units (*euros*), and (2) the aggregate sales of each of two or more of the firms within the Union exceeds 250 million euros; *or* (1) the aggregate worldwide sales of all the firms being combined exceeds 2.5 billion euros; (2) in at least three member states the aggregate sales of the firms exceeds 100 million euros; (3) in each of those three member states the aggregate sales of at least two of the firms exceeds 25 million euros; and (4) the aggregate sales within the Union of each of at least two of the firms exceeds 100 million euros. (The value of the euro varies widely against the U.S. dollar, and by late 2007, one euro was worth nearly 1.4 dollars.) Even if either of these tests are satisfied, a concentration does not have a community dimension if more than two-thirds of the aggregate community-wide profit is in only one member state. If the proposed concentration has a "community dimension," then only the Commission is to examine the transaction; member states cannot interfere with or contradict the Commission's findings.

Once the Task Force determines that the transaction has a community dimension, it then determines whether the concentration is compatible with the common market. Under the test prior to the adoption of Regulation 139/2004, a concentration that created or strengthened a dominant position so as to "significantly impede" effective competition within the Union was "incompatible" with the common market. Under the new substantive test, the Task Force asks whether a merger "would significantly impede effective competition, in particular as a result of the creation or strengthening of a dominant position." While the two tests appear facially similar, under the new test, dominance is the primary but not sole impediment to "effective competition." In great part, the EC intended the modification to the existing language to prohibit unilateral effects on the relevant market, such as where major competitors merge to form a large firm, but the resulting entity is still not the dominant firm. The EC envisions that the new test will "catch" those cases where the merged entity would not be the leader within the defined market, but nevertheless would maintain a substantial market share. Dominance is meant to remain the staple of the test, and therefore, to ensure continuity with previous case law. Further, the new merger test moves closer to an effects-based test by explicitly providing in Recital 29 to the Regulation that it "is possible that the efficiencies brought about by the concentration counteract the effects on competition, and in particular the potential harm to consumers, that it might otherwise have and that, as a consequence, the concentration would not significantly impede effective competition."

The criteria employed in assessing compatibility include market share (compatibility is presumed if joint market share in the common market does not exceed 25 percent); legal or practical barriers to entry; notice of supply and demand in relevant markets; competition from firms outside the Union; and the structure of the markets.

In essence, the Commission undertakes a two-step analysis to determine whether an "undertaking" in a merger creates or strengthens a dominant position. First, it defines the "relevant markets" affected by the merger in terms of both product line and geography. Second, the Commission determines the effect of the merger on the market so defined by the new test noted above.

If a proposed transaction does not have a community dimension, it is jointly regulated by the Commission and member state enforcement authorities. The boundary between regulation under the *Merger Regulation* and "normal" DG-COMP review under Articles 81 and 82 is hazy. If a proposed joint venture is "concentrative"—if it will "independently and permanently perform all of the functions of an autonomous economic entity," without "coordination of the competitive behavior of the parties amongst themselves or between them and the joint venture,"—it is deemed to be subject to review under the *Merger Regulation.* If, on the other hand, it is merely "cooperative," regular review is appropriate.

Airtours v. Comm

Case T-342/99 2002 E.C.R. II-2585

European Court of First Instance

BACKGROUND AND FACTS

A UK–based travel company, Airtours (now MyTravel) sought to purchase a travel agency known as First Choice. It announced its planned merger to EC authorities in early 1999. Later that year, the Merger Task Force blocked that proposed merger, asserting that such a proposed combination of travel powerhouses would necessarily create a "collective dominant" position in the UK market for so-called short-haul travel vacations. The Merger Task Force asserted that this would lead to higher prices for consumers as well as the elimination of smaller, less visible agencies. Airtours appealed to the Court of First Instance.

PRESIDENT JUDGE LINDH

The prospective analysis which the Commission has to carry out in its review of concentrations involving collective dominance calls for close examination in particular of the circumstances which, in each individual case, are relevant for assessing the effects of the concentration on competition in the reference market.... [W]here the Commission takes the view that a merger should be prohibited because it will create a situation of collective dominance, it is incumbent upon it to produce convincing evidence thereof. The evidence must concern, in particular, factors playing a significant role in the assessment of whether a situation of collective dominance exists, such as, for example, the lack of effective competition between the operators alleged to be members of the dominant oligopoly and the weakness of any competitive pressure that might be exerted by other operators....

Finally, contrary to the Commission's contention ... the fact that to some extent (30 to 40% of the shares) the same institutional investors are found in Airtours, First Choice and Thomson cannot be regarded as evidence that there is already a tendency to collective dominance in the industry. It is sufficient to point out in that regard that ... there is no suggestion in the Decision that the group of institutional shareholders forms a united body controlling those quoted companies or providing a mechanism for exchange of information between the three undertakings. Furthermore, the Commission cannot contend that those shareholders are a further force for cautious capacity management, unless it has examined to what extent they are involved in the management of the companies concerned. Finally, even assuming that it were proved they are capable of exercising some influence on the management of the undertakings, since the concerns of the common institutional investors with respect to growth (and thus capacity) merely reflect a characteristic inherent in the relevant market, the Commission would still have to establish that the fact that institutional investors hold shares in three of the four leading tour operators amounts to evidence that there is already a tendency to collective dominance....

It is apparent from the foregoing that, since it did not deny that the market was competitive, the Commission was not entitled to treat the cautious

continued

continued

capacity planning characteristic of the market in normal circumstances as evidence substantiating its proposition that there was already a tendency to collective dominance in the industry. . . .

In the light of all of the foregoing, the Court concludes that the Decision, far from basing its prospective analysis on cogent evidence, is vitiated by a series of errors of assessment as to factors fundamental to any assessment of whether a collective dominant position might be created. It follows that the Commission prohibited the transaction without having proved to the requisite legal standard that the concentration would give rise to a collective dominant position of the three major tour operators, of such a kind as significantly to impede effective competition in the relevant market.

Decision. The CFI annulled the Merger Task Force's decision prohibiting the merger. This was the first time that the CFI had overruled such a merger ban by the EC.

A trio of cases decided in 2002 by the European Court of First Instance (CFI) in Luxembourg ushered in a more hospitable climate for mergers within the European Community. In often scathing language, the CFI vetoed the Merger Task Force's decisions blocking the unions. Altogether, the three cases suggest that, by 2003, EC regulatory power over mergers had been severely curtailed, and that any Merger Task Force rejection of a proposed merger will be held to a stringent standard of proof. Thus, any companies undergoing a merger review should expect a more thorough and intense review.

In *Airtours*, the CFI frequently criticizes the Merger Task Force for not meeting the requisite standard of proof, affording the EC none of the deference normally accorded an administrative agency's decision. Indeed, the CFI stated that the Task Force did "not give the slightest indication that there is no competition between the main tour operators." Such harsh criticism was particularly damning when one considers that, under the *Merger Regulation's* scheme, businesses do not take the risk of going forward without the agency's approval.

The *Airtours* CFI did agree that the so-called "collective dominance" test was the proper analytic framework for analyzing mergers, but it redefined the test to make it more difficult to stop mergers. Specifically, it stated that mergers must have "the direct and immediate effect of creating or strengthening a position of [collective dominance], which is significantly and lastingly to impede competition in the relevant market." The CFI emphasized that if no competitive effects were immediately created, then the merger must be allowed.

Airtours was only the first part of a run of bad news for the Merger Task Force. In the *Schneider* decision, the CFI annulled an EC decision because it had not followed its own procedural rules. This CFI decision served notice that it was henceforth going to require strict compliance with procedural safeguards in the preapproval process.

Schneider Elec. SA v. Comm'n

Case T-77/02, 2002 E.C.R. II-04201

European Court of First Instance

BACKGROUND AND FACTS

Schneider Electric SA (Schneider), a company incorporated under French law, is the parent company of a group engaged in the manufacture and sale of products and systems in the electrical distribution, industrial control, and automation sectors. Incorporated under French law, Legrand SA is a company that specializes in the manufacture and sale of electrical equipment for low-voltage installations. Schneider launched its bid to acquire Legrand in a

continued

continued

$6.43 billion purchase offer in January 2001. In accordance with the requirements in the Merger Regulation, Legrand notified the Commission of Schneider's proposal to make a public exchange offer for all shares of Legrand held by the public. Due to French merger rules, Schneider proceeded with its purchase of Legrand before the Merger Task Force ruled on the propriety of the merger. In August 2001 the Commission decided that the transaction would create an anticompetitive dominant position in a number of key markets. The CFI then considered the Schneider case under new fast-track provisions designed to hasten judicial review of such merger decisions.

PRESIDENT JUDGE VESTERDORF

The Court considers ... the claim that Schneider's rights of defence have been infringed in that the Commission included in the Decision a specific objection which was not clearly expressed in the statement of objections....

According to well-established case-law, the Decision need not necessarily replicate the statement of objections. Thus, it is permissible to supplement the statement of objections in the light of the parties' response, whose arguments show that they have actually been able to exercise their rights of defence. The Commission may also, in the light of the administrative procedure, revise or supplement its arguments of fact or law in support of its objections....

Nonetheless, the statement of objections must contain an account of the objections cast in sufficiently clear terms to achieve the objective ascribed to it by the Community regulations, namely to provide all the information the undertakings need to defend themselves properly before the Commission adopts a final decision....

In addition, in the procedures for reviewing concentrations, the statement of objections is not solely intended to spell out the complaints and give the undertaking to which it is addressed the opportunity to submit comments in response. It is also intended to give the notifying parties the chance to suggest corrective measures and, in particular, proposals for divestiture and sufficient time, given the requirement for speed which characterises the general scheme of Regulation No 4064/89, to ascertain the extent to which divestiture is necessary with a view to rendering the transaction compatible with the common market in good time....

The Commission was consequently required to explain all the more clearly the competition problems raised by the proposed merger, in order to allow the notifying parties to put forward, properly and in good time, proposals for divestiture capable, if need be, of rendering the concentration compatible with the common market.

It is not apparent on reading the statement of objections that it dealt with sufficient clarity or precision with the strengthening of Schneider's position vis-à-vis French distributors of low-voltage electrical equipment as a result not only of the addition of Legrand's sales on the markets for switchboard components and panel-board components but also of Legrand's leading position in the segments for ultra-terminal electrical equipment. The Court observes in particular that the general conclusion in the statement of objections lists the various national sectoral markets affected by the concentration, without demonstrating that the position of one of the notifying parties on a given product market would in any way buttress the position of the other party on another sectoral market....

Competitive overlap is conceivable only within a single national sectoral market and is thus different in nature from the mutual support provided at distribution level where two undertakings hold leading positions in one country in two distinct but complementary sectoral markets.

It follows that the statement of objections did not permit Schneider to assess the full extent of the competition problems to which the Commission claimed the concentration would give rise at distributor level on the French market for low-voltage electrical equipment.

Decision. The CFI annulled the Merger Task Force's prohibition on the merger because of the Force's defective procedural handling of the case.

In addition to noting this procedural error, the CFI specifically criticized the finding that the merged entity's dominance in France would necessarily imply dominance in other countries. Indeed, the court suggested that the Merger Task Force likely inflated the merged entity's probable strength.

The ultimate blow for the Task Force in the autumn of 2002 was the *Tetra Laval* case, reproduced in this chapter. There, the CFI rejected the Force's factual analysis of the likely negative horizontal and vertical impacts of the merger at issue. Further, in the CFI's first comment on the leveraging analysis adopted by the Merger Task Force, it redefined the "leveraging" theory of concentration, making it virtually useless.

The CFI noted that the leveraging theory, while still viable, was speculative in its actual impact. Notably, the CFI elsewhere criticized the Merger Task Force for failing to presume that the merged firm would at least attempt to behave in a legal fashion (because the prospect of being branded a criminal would be a strong deterrent on the merged entity's leadership). The CFI reasoned that although a conglomerate may have the ability to leverage its dominance, this is not tantamount to having a realistic incentive for doing so. In considering a "leveraging" theory, the Commission was to consider the extent to which the incentive to act illegally would be reduced due to the illegality of the conduct in question, the likelihood of its detection, the action taken by the competent authorities, and the financial penalties that could result. Today, leveraging as a concept remains a viable force in merger review, but the CFI signaled that the Merger Task Force will have to come up with more tangible proof regarding such leveraged effects. Specifically, "the proof of anti-competitive conglomerate effects of such a merger calls for a precise examination, supported by convincing evidence, of the circumstances which allegedly produce those effects."

In 2005, the ECJ upheld the CFI's major findings in *Tetra Laval*. On appeal, the Commission argued that the CFI had exceeded its authority in reviewing the merger decision by looking beyond purely legal grounds for reversal toward the Commission's economic and fact assessments. The Commission believed the CFI failed to give appropriate discretion to the CFI by requiring "convincing evidence" of conglomerate effects. The ECJ, while recognizing that the Commission does have a degree of discretion in making economic assessments, upheld the CFI's review of that assessment and stated that "[n]ot only must the Community Courts ... establish whether the evidence relied on is factually accurate, reliable and consistent but also whether that evidence contains all the information which must be taken into account in order to assess a complex situation and whether it is capable of substantiating the conclusions drawn from it. Such a review is all the more necessary in the case of a prospective analysis required when examining a planned merger with conglomerate effect." In addition, the ECJ held that it was appropriate for the CFI to require a more thorough consideration by the Commission of the firm's behavioral commitments, which may prevent the emergence of a dominant position.

In line with the CFI's and the ECJ's decisions in *Tetra Laval*, the Commission's analysis of conglomerate effects took another harsh blow from the CFI merger decision issued in 2005, involving General Electric and Honeywell. In 2000, General Electric and Honeywell had announced their intention to merge. The U.S. Department of Justice indicated that it would allow the merger, but in 2001, the Commission decided to block the merger. While the Commission's decision to block the merger was eventually upheld due to significant horizontal effects, the Commission's conglomerate effects analysis was dismantled. The CFI reaffirmed that in order to substantiate a merger prohibition based on conglomerate or vertical effects likely to harm competition, the Commission must have "convincing evidence" of the chain of events leading to that harm.

Together, the 2005 decisions in *Tetra Laval* and *GE/Honeywell* suggest that using a conglomerate effects analysis to prohibit a merger will be viewed with great suspicion unless there is a detailed showing of a high probability of anticompetitive effects. Further, these opinions also indicate that the European analysis, as noted, has shifted in the direction of the analysis undertaken in the United States. Nonetheless, divergent merger decisions on either side of the Atlantic, as General Electric and Honeywell can attest to, pose a serious risk for companies considering a merger.

This string of decisions resulted in suggestions that the European Union should abandon the present model of endowing the investigatory EC Merger Task Force with enforcement powers in favor of the U.S. antitrust regulatory model, which requires a court judgment to block a merger. As a result of such pressures, the EC adopted a set of fundamental reforms regarding mergers, as noted above. The reform package includes a more flexible time frame regarding merger investigations; guidelines regarding horizontal mergers; guidance regarding key concepts such as how to analyze anticompetitive behavior; and greater fact-finding powers for the Merger Task Force. The number of mergers notified to the Commission under the new regime reached a record level of 356 in 2006. When considering the new regime, the EC explored the merits of both the "dominance" test and the "substantial lessening of competition" (SLC) test for assessing anticompetitive effects, but settled on the "significant impediment to effective competition" (SIEC) test outlined above. In the future, the investigatory watchdog's powers will be split among the antitrust units of the EC's general competition directorate.

Tetra Laval BV v. Comm'n

Case T-5/02 2002 E.C.R. II-4381 and Case T-80/02 2002 E.C.R. II -4519

European Court of First Instance

BACKGROUND AND FACTS

Tetra Laval, a Swedish company that is the world's largest carton packaging manufacturer, decided to expand into the field of plastic bottle plugs. It sought to buy the French company Sidel, which makes the equipment that blows plastic plugs into milk and soft drink bottles, commonly known as PET technology. The proposed deal was valued at 1.7 billion euros. Tetra purchased Sidel prior to EC approval. The EC Merger Task Force later prohibited the merger on the grounds that the union would be able to "leverage" its dominance in carton packaging to also become dominant in the PET packaging equipment market, thus reducing competition horizontally and vertically. This so-called "leveraging" theory had been used earlier by the Merger Task Force to reject the highly controversial GE/Honeywell merger, despite the fact that the United States does not utilize the concept in antitrust review.

PRESIDENT JUDGE VESTERDORFF

Whilst it is true that the modified merger would enable Sidel, through Tetra's presence in the market for plastic bottle capping systems, to offer almost totally integrated PET lines, it is obvious that the vertical effects of Sidel's entry into that market through the merged entity, and Sidel's concomitant disappearance as a potential customer of the other operators active on that market, would be minimal in the light of the relatively weak position held by Tetra on that market. In addition, the global capacity of the merged entity, compared with Sidel's current capacity, to offer such integrated PET lines would not be strengthened by the modified merger, because Tetra would divest itself of its PET preforms activities. The Sidel annual report shows that sales of those lines accounted for only around 20% of Sidel's SBM machine sales in 2001, despite the alleged exponential growth of 30% between 1999 and 2000 to which the Commission refers in its defence.

As for the alleged effects on the EBM machines market, the contested decision expressly acknowledges that, in the light of Tetra's reply of 1 October 2001 to the supplemental statement of objections, the position of other players allayed concerns about dominance in a potential market for machines producing aseptic HDPE bottles with handles.... It is thus clear that the modified merger would not have significant negative effects on the position of converters active in the HDPE market. That market would, post-merger, remain a highly competitive market.

Consequently, it has not been shown that the modified merger would result in sizeable or, at the very least, significant vertical effects on the relevant market for PET packaging equipment. In those circumstances, the Court finds that the Commission made a manifest error of assessment in so far as it relied on the vertical effects of the modified merger to support its finding that a dominant position on those PET markets would be created for the merged entity through leveraging....

It follows from the foregoing that the Commission committed manifest errors of assessment in relying on the horizontal and vertical effects of the modified merger to support its analysis of the creation of a dominant position on the relevant PET markets.

Decision. The CFI rejected the Merger Task Force's decision. Its decision was based on a lack of evidence.

Distinctions of Non–U.S. Competition Law

Foreign competition law is similar to U.S. law in substance, but it is enforced quite differently. The most obvious distinction—and the primary reason for the absence of much competition law litigation outside the United States—is in the sanctions for violating the law.

Private Causes of Action for Damages and Criminal Prosecution

Although the Department of Justice has brought marquee cases such as *United States v. Microsoft*, 87 F.Supp.2d 30 (D.D.C. 2000), U.S. law is enforced principally by "private attorneys general," meaning private parties ostensibly injured by the antitrust violation. Such plaintiffs are encouraged by the United States' recognition of a private cause of action for violations of antitrust rules and the award of treble damages to successful litigants. With this large pot of gold at the end of the litigation rainbow, and relatively little downside exposure (U.S. litigants need not pay the other side's lawyer's fees if they lose), plaintiffs are encouraged to take their shot. Similarly, risk-averse defendants are encouraged to settle out of court before trial.

In Europe, EU competition laws may be enforced only in national courts. A private party may not go to the pan-European forums of the EU. Thus, a private party must generally play in the alleged violator's "home court," where the judiciary might be inclined to favor local interests. There is no equivalent to the U.S. federal court system.

Notably, there has been a recent push from the European Union's Competition Commissioner to enhance private enforcement of competition laws within the European national courts. The Commission adopted The Green Paper on damages actions for breach of the EU antitrust rules in 2005 in order to assess how private causes of action can be pursued more successfully in Europe. In Japan, for example, there are few remedies available to plaintiffs, and local courts are very reluctant to rule against large enterprises.

In countries outside the United States, if the plaintiff loses, it must pay the defendant's attorneys' fees, which are substantial. Further, outside the United States, treble-damage awards are generally unavailable. Thus, plaintiffs have much greater risk, less probability of success, and less reward if they succeed. The result is drastically less litigation.

In fact, many countries provide no private cause of action at all. In Germany, enforcement of competition law is in the hands of the *Bundeskartellamt* (Federal Cartel Office). In Korea, the Minister for the Economic Planning Board enforces the act. In the European Union, Article 81(2) declares void any agreement that violates the terms of Article 81(1), but does not provide for a private cause of action for damages.

United States antitrust law also poses the possibility of criminal liability, which is not possible under the European or Japanese models. This is not an idle threat: In 2000, the Department of Justice reported that it had no fewer than thirty pending grand jury investigations involving alleged international cartels. In a thirty-month stretch from January 2004 through August 2006, the Department of Justice collected over $1 billion in fines and brought criminal cases against nearly seventy firms. Those who approach the U.S. market have to tread gingerly in anticompetitive activity.

U.S. antitrust lawyers might be somewhat bemused by the punishment meted out in South Korea. When the three largest Korean manufacturers of color televisions were conclusively found to have engaged in a price-fixing scheme, they were ordered to end the scheme and to offer a public apology to the Korean people. The manufacturers appealed!

Article 81(3) and the Rule of Reason

The analytical framework established by U.S. antitrust law distinguishes between actions that are *per se* wrong and actions to which the *rule of reason* applies. Per se violations are those that no amount of explanation can make legal, while actions subject to the rule of reason can be legal if, upon analysis, they are found not to be anticompetitive. In 2007, the Supreme Court of the United States further entrenched the rule of reason analysis in a 5–4 decision in *Leegin Creative Leather*

Products, Inc. v. PSKS, Inc. In *Leegin,* the Court overruled a 96-year-old precedent by holding that vertical agreements between manufacturers and distributors to fix minimum resale prices are to now be judged by the rule of reason rather than a per se rule.

A dispute surrounds the issue of whether the rule of reason is an appropriate mode of analysis under EU competition laws. The language of Article 81(2) does not lend itself to the suggestion that some literally restrictive agreements may nonetheless be valid because of overarching procompetitive effects. Nonetheless, the Commission flirted with that interpretation of the language and included elements of the analysis in some of its decisions.

Previously, however, the Commission could, under Article 81(3), exempt agreements that violated the terms of Article 81(1) in advance by issuing a "comfort letter," an individual exemption, or a negative clearance.

An *individual exemption* allowed performance of an agreement that would otherwise violate Article 81 because it had favorable economic effects overall. For example, an individual exemption might have been granted if the proposed agreement improved the production of goods or promoted technological economic progress, imposed only restrictions indispensable to such product improvement, and did not eliminate competition as to a substantial part of the products in question. This concept of weighing public benefit against public loss from anticompetitive activity has been adopted in the antitrust laws of each of the formerly Communist nations of Central and Eastern Europe.

A *negative clearance,* on the other hand, was a confirmation that the proposed agreement did not fall within Article 81(1) at all. It required the Commission's analysis of whether, in fact, the proposed agreement would impair competition. The disadvantage of the negative clearance was that, if the facts as to competition turned out to be different from those represented on the application, the parties could nonetheless be fined.

The Commission would on occasion also issue "comfort letters" that told companies that their anticipated transaction, if implemented as represented, was not likely to infringe competition rules.

The Commission's actions in these processes functioned much like the rule of reason analysis. Employing a similar analysis, the Commission today grants *block exemptions* to entire classes of contracts. Under the terms of the block exemption, the Commission identifies the type of agreement eligible for exemptions and the types of anticompetitive provisions permitted in such agreements. In considering each provision to be included in a block-exemption contract, the Commission weighs the European Union's interest in promoting productive cooperation between parties against the costs of somewhat reduced competition. Three existing block exemptions are in place for exclusive distribution, exclusive purchasing (including special arrangements for beer), and oil-and-gas franchising.

As the discussion below will make clear, while the block exemption remains a possibility, the issuance of other preapproval exemptions and comfort letters has been almost entirely discontinued under the new EC competition law regime.

Preapproval Procedures Versus Litigation

The preceding examination of non–U.S. antitrust laws reveals another difference between the U.S. system and various foreign systems. In their exemption system and the EU Merger Regulation, Europeans traditionally structured their system to provide for a resolution of competition law issues prior to the transaction taking place, typically through administrative action. The parties to the request could generally rely on the European Commission's negative clearance. Other non–U.S. systems have similar preclearance procedures on which parties can rely. They significantly reduce the amount of private litigation brought to enforce competition law outside the United States.

If the European Commission had to clear every potentially anticompetitive action in Europe, however, it would need more people than are in DG-COMP. It tried to ameliorate this problem through its *de minimis* exceptions and by granting block exemptions. The *de minimis* exception essentially provides that Article 81(1) is not violated if (1) the parties to the agreement in question have combined gross annual revenues of less than

200 million euros, and (2) the products covered by the agreement do not account for more than 5 percent of the volume in the relevant market. And as noted previously, the *EU Merger Regulation* has a much higher "community dimension" threshold. Thus, with the *de minimis* exception, the majority of agreements within the European Union are not considered to be anticompetitive. The Commission issues block exemptions applicable to entire industries or types of agreements. The broad number of subject areas permits companies to proceed with confidence in not violating Article 81(1) as long as they follow the highly specific instructions of the Commission when forming their agreements. Parties whose agreements fall into these categories and precisely follow the wording approved by the Commission do not need to seek approval from the Commission in order to have their transaction considered exempt.

The great benefit of the preapproval approach traditionally pursued by the European Union and many other governments is that the parties can consummate the transaction without risk of subsequent nullification and fines. The preapproval approach, however, has costs of its own. First, even with block exemptions, *de minimis* rules, and comfort letters to reduce the flow of work, the Commission became overwhelmed. Over time, an enormous backlog developed at the Commission. Disposition of pending requests became notoriously slow. In contexts where the passage of time would kill the commercial objective of the transaction, firms would go forward and take their chances on a rule of reason analysis. Additionally, the block exemption approach effectively prohibits virtually everything, then exempts large areas. Businesses are burdened by the need to write agreements that fit the rigid categories of the exemptions. Such an approach greatly hinders innovation in fashioning contractual arrangements, and restricts the flexibility of entrepreneurs. This is a substantial cost. One of the engines of capitalism is the ability of parties to invent mutually beneficial arrangements that permit them to serve customers better. All efforts to address these problems in the Commission preapproval system have been widely judged insufficient.

In 2000, the Commission effectively proposed an end to its preapproval system. In 2004, that proposal became an operating reality. *Regulation 1/2003*, adopted by the EU Council of Ministers in 2002, became effective in 2004. Under the new regulation, the Commission has eliminated the requirement that transactions be notified to the Commission in advance. Instead, parties, as in the United States, decide for themselves, based on Commission law and precedent, whether an arrangement violates competition law or is subject to an exemption. Unless an agreement falls within a block exemption, companies will now face more uncertainty. DG-COMP now must use its scarce resources to police serious infringements, especially in the area of cartel enforcement. In that enforcement, DG-COMP now has broader investigative powers, which include the ability to conduct unannounced "dawn raids," to apply stiffer penalties for violations, and to take oral statements from staff of the companies under investigation. National competition enforcement authorities now play an integral part in antitrust enforcement.

Under the new regime, national courts and national competition authorities (NCAs) have increased responsibility for enforcement of Articles 81 and 82. When a transaction affects trade between member states, the national authorities must apply Articles 81 and 82, even if national law is also applied. To facilitate the new regime, a network of competition authorities has been established so that the Commission and NCAs can collaborate in enforcement activities. The Commission has abandoned the prior preapproval model in favor of an after-the-fact, decentralized enforcement regime whereby companies decide in advance whether they are violating Article 81(1), and if so, whether they are potentially exempted from coverage by Article 81(3).

The United States does not have a preapproval system. The closest mechanism to preapproval is the review process created by the *Hart–Scott–Rodino Act*, under which certain mergers, joint venture agreements, and similar transactions must be brought before the Department of Justice before they are concluded. Even if the DOJ gives the parties permission to conclude the transaction, the DOJ may later bring litigation relating to it. Neither does the *Hart–Scott–Rodino Act* prevent any private party from bringing such a suit. In fact, in *California v. American Stores Co.*, 495 U.S. 271 (1990), the U.S. Supreme Court held that private parties and state authorities may sue in federal court for divestiture of a merger even after it has been approved by the DOJ or the Federal Trade Commission. Overall, antitrust policy in the United States has developed in the courts.

Another area in which the United States differs from European Union countries is the extent to which statutes are given extraterritorial application. This difference has engendered such international hostility that it deserves separate treatment.

Extraterritorial Effect of Competition Laws

In an increasingly interdependent world, no country or continent operates in isolation. Anticompetitive behavior in Costa Rica may well have an adverse effect on the price of bananas in the United States. The basic question is whether U.S. law can or should do anything to prevent Costa Rican monopolistic action. Though the trend is now changing somewhat, Europeans have historically been reluctant to apply their competition law outside the Common Market. Conversely, Americans have tended to apply their antitrust law to every corner of the globe.

The U.S. Effects Test

The United States started with a limited concept of extraterritorial jurisdiction, but has since developed it in a way that accords U.S. antitrust law a substantial extraterritorial effect. The issue was first examined in *American Banana Co. v. United Fruit Co.*, 213 U.S. 347 (1909), by the great Justice Oliver Wendell Holmes. This case was resolved in a fashion with which most Europeans would feel comfortable.

In *American Banana*, the plaintiff, a U.S. corporation, alleged that a rival U.S. corporation had caused the Costa Rican government to seize the plaintiff's banana plantation and prevent the completion of the plaintiff's railway. The plaintiff argued that these acts prevented it from competing in the production and sale of bananas for export to the United States and therefore violated the *Sherman Antitrust Act*. Justice Holmes dismissed the complaint, interpreting the *Sherman Act* "as intended to be confined in its operation and effect to the territorial limits over which the lawmaker has general and legitimate powers." Because the United States could not control what happened in Costa Rica, Justice Holmes reasoned that Congress did not intend to regulate what happened there.

United States v. Aluminum Co. of America
148 F.2d 416 (1948)
United States Court of Appeals (2d Cir.)

BACKGROUND AND FACTS

In 1931, a group of aluminum producers, one French, two German, one Swiss, one British, and one Canadian, formed a Swiss corporation named "Alliance." Each of the producers was a shareholder of Alliance.

In 1936, the shareholders instituted a system of royalties centered around Alliance. Each shareholder was to have a fixed production quota for every share it held, but when its production exceeded the sum of its quotas, it was to pay a royalty, graduated in proportion to the excess, to Alliance. Alliance then distributed the royalties as dividends to the shareholders in proportion to their shares. The effect was to create a cartel that controlled aluminum supplies and therefore kept prices high. Imports into the United States were included in the quotas.

The cartel ended in 1939 when the German shareholders became enemies of the French, British, and Canadian shareholders.

JUDGE LEARNED HAND

Did the agreement . . . of 1936 violate Section 1 of the [Sherman] Act? [W]e are concerned only with whether Congress chose to attach liability to the conduct outside the United States of persons not in allegiance to it. That being so, the only question open is

continued

continued

whether Congress intended to impose the liability, and whether our own Constitution permitted it to do so: as a court of the United States, we cannot look beyond our own law. Nevertheless, it is quite true that we are not to read general words, such as those in this act without regard to the limitations customarily observed by nations upon the exercise of their powers; limitations which generally correspond to those fixed by the "Conflict of Laws." ... We should not impute to Congress an intent to punish all whom its courts can catch, for conduct which has no consequences within the United States. On the other hand, it is settled law ... that any state may impose liabilities, even upon persons not within its allegiance, for conduct outside its borders that has consequences within its borders which the state reprehends; and these liabilities other states will ordinarily recognize. It may be argued that this act extends further. Two situations are possible. There may be agreements made beyond our borders not intended to affect imports, which do affect them, or which affect exports. Almost any limitation of the supply of goods in Europe, for example, or in South America, may have repercussions in the United States if there is trade between the two. Yet when one considers the international complications likely to arise from an effort in this country to treat such agreements as unlawful, it is safe to assume that Congress certainly did not intend to act to cover them. Such agreements may on the other hand intend to include imports into the United States, and yet it may appear that they have had no effect upon them. That situation might be thought to fall within the doctrine that intent may be a substitute for performance in the case of a contract made within the United States; or it might be thought to fall within the doctrine that a statute should not be interpreted to cover acts abroad which have no consequence here. We shall not choose between these alternatives; but for argument we shall assume that the act does not cover agreements, even though intended to affect imports or exports, unless its performance is shown actually to have had some effect upon them. [The agreement] would clearly have been unlawful, had [it] been made within the United States; and it follows from what we have just said that [it was] unlawful, though made abroad, if [it was] intended to affect imports and did affect them.... [T]he change made in 1936 was deliberate and was expressly made to accomplish [a restraint on exportation of aluminum to the United States for sale in competition with Alcoa].... The first of the conditions which we mentioned was therefore satisfied; the intent was to set up a quota system for imports.

[A] depressant upon production which applies generally may be assumed ... to distribute its effect evenly upon all markets. Again, when the [shareholders of Alliance] took the trouble specifically to make the depressant apply to a given market, there is reason to suppose that they expected that it would have some effect, which it could have only by lessening what would otherwise have been imported....

There remains only the question whether this assumed restriction had any influence upon prices.... [A]n agreement to withdraw any substantial part of the supply from a market would, if carried out, have some effect upon prices, and was as unlawful as an agreement expressly to fix prices. The underlying doctrine was that all factors which contribute to determine prices, must be kept free to operate unhampered by agreements. For these reasons we think that the agreement of 1936 violated Section 1 of the [Sherman Antitrust] Act.

Decision. The U.S. Court of Appeals for the Second Circuit reversed the District Court's decision and remanded the case to it for further proceedings consistent with its opinion.

Justice Holmes's elegant prose was not long the law in the United States. Court decisions after *American Banana* tended to acknowledge it and its reasoning, but applied the ruling in odd ways. In time, ignoring the importance of the decision rendered it a nullity and opened the way for a new interpretation of the intent of Congress in the *Sherman Act,* thus creating the so-called U.S. *effects doctrine,* which was developed in the landmark case of *United States v. Aluminum Co. of America*.

Although careful to require consequences in the United States, Judge Hand in *Alcoa* pushed the reach of U.S. antitrust law farther toward extraterritoriality than Justice Holmes. In subsequent cases, this trend intensified. U.S. courts interpreted the *Sherman Act* to require an ever-decreasing "effect" on the United States before it was applicable. Other courts soon turned to the question of whether actions by Americans affecting foreign markets could somehow satisfy the "effects" test.

Perhaps the crowning touch in this expansion came in *Joseph Muller Corp., Zurich v. Societe Anonyme De Gerance Et D'Armament,* 508 F.2d 814 (2d Cir. 1974), when a Swiss corporation sued a French corporation in the United States claiming a violation of U.S. antitrust laws, even though no U.S. companies or consumers were directly affected by any of the acts in question. In fact, a Franco–Swiss treaty required that any suits between French and Swiss citizens were to be brought in the defendant's country. Nevertheless, the U.S. trial court found the requisite effects for jurisdiction over the dispute. U.S. courts, in applying the "effects" test of *Alcoa*, effectively displaced foreign treaties and laws on the basis of minimal U.S. connections.

By the 1970s, some federal courts of appeal had grown disenchanted with the *Alcoa* test because of its failure to take into account the legitimate interests of foreign nations. These courts developed a *jurisdictional rule of reason* that took into account (1) whether the action had some effect on U.S. commerce, (2) whether the restraint was of a type and magnitude to be considered a violation of the U.S. antitrust laws, and (3) the comity (goodwill) interests of the foreign nation against the interests of the United States in antitrust enforcement. Courts did not universally accept this approach, however, and U.S. court intervention continued to spark international friction. Thus, in 1982, the U.S. Congress finally clarified the intent of the *Sherman Act* by adopting a strict version of the "effects" test in the *Foreign Trade Antitrust Improvements Act*. That statute provides that U.S. antitrust law does not apply to conduct unless such conduct has a "direct, substantial, and reasonably foreseeable effect on United States commerce or on the business of a person engaged in exporting goods from the United States to foreign nations."

The *Foreign Trade Antitrust Improvements Act* did not end disagreement. As the following case makes clear, five of the members of the U.S. Supreme Court had a rather sweeping view of the scope of the *Sherman Act's* applicability. This case remains the law of the United States.

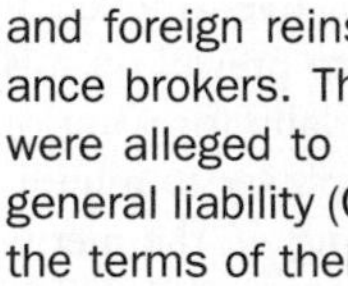

Hartford Fire Insurance Co. v. California
509 U.S. 764 (1993)
United States Supreme Court

BACKGROUND AND FACTS

Nineteen states and numerous private parties brought antitrust suits against U.S. insurers, U.S. and foreign reinsurers based in London, and insurance brokers. The insurers, reinsurers, and brokers were alleged to have agreed to boycott commercial general liability (CGL) insurers that refused to change the terms of their standard domestic CGL insurance policies to conform to the policies the defendant insurers wanted to sell. The plaintiff states asserted that as a practical matter, the policies that the defendant insurers wanted to sell would (1) make occurrence CGL coverage unavailable for many risks; (2) make pollution liability coverage almost entirely unavailable for the vast majority of casualty insurance purchasers; and (3) limit coverage of seepage, pollution, and property contamination risks.

The U.S. District Court for the Northern District of California dismissed the suits because it refused to exercise *Sherman Act* jurisdiction over foreign reinsurers under principles of international comity. The Court of Appeals for the Ninth Circuit reversed this decision of the District Court.

JUSTICE SOUTER

[W]e take up the question ... whether certain claims against the London reinsurers should have been dismissed as improper applications of the Sherman Act to foreign conduct....

continued

continued

At the outset, we note that the District Court undoubtedly had jurisdiction of these Sherman Act claims.... Although the proposition was perhaps not always free from doubt, see *American Banana Co. v. United Fruit Co.,* ... it is well established by now that the Sherman Act applies to foreign conduct that was meant to produce and did in fact produce some substantial effect in the United States.... Such is the conduct alleged here: that the London reinsurers engaged in unlawful conspiracies to affect the market for insurance in the United States and that their conduct in fact produced substantial effect.... According to the London reinsurers, the District Court should have declined to exercise such jurisdiction under the principle of international comity. The Court of Appeals agreed that courts should look to that principle in deciding whether to exercise jurisdiction under the Sherman Act.... But other factors, in the court's view, including the London reinsurers' express purpose to affect United States commerce and the substantial nature of the effect produced, outweighed the supposed conflict and required the exercise of jurisdiction in this case....

When it enacted the *Foreign Trade Antitrust Improvements Act of 1982* ... Congress expressed no view on the question whether a court with Sherman Act jurisdiction should ever decline to exercise such jurisdiction on grounds of international comity....

We need not decide that question here, however, for even assuming that in a proper case a court may decline to exercise Sherman Act jurisdiction over foreign conduct (or, as Justice Scalia would put it, may conclude by the employment of comity analysis in the first instance that there is no jurisdiction), international comity would not counsel against exercising jurisdiction in the circumstances alleged here.

The only substantial question in this case is whether "there is in fact a true conflict between domestic and foreign law." ... The London reinsurers contend that applying the Act to their conduct would conflict significantly with British law, and the British Government, appearing before us as *amicus curiae,* concurs.... They assert that Parliament has established a comprehensive regulatory regime over the London reinsurance market and that the conduct alleged here was perfectly consistent with British law and policy. But this is not to state a conflict. "[T]he fact that conduct is lawful in the state in which it took place will not, of itself, bar application of the United States antitrust laws," even where the foreign state has a strong policy to permit or encourage such conduct.... No conflict exists, for these purposes, "where a person subject to regulation by two states can comply with the laws of both." ... Since the London reinsurers do not argue that British law requires them to act in some fashion prohibited by the law of the United States ... or claim that their compliance with the laws of both countries is otherwise impossible, we see no conflict with British law.... We have no need in this case to address other considerations that might inform a decision to refrain from the exercise of jurisdiction on grounds of international comity.

JUSTICE SCALIA, DISSENTING

I dissent from the Court's ruling concerning the extraterritorial application of the Sherman Act....

[V]arious British corporations and other British subjects argue that certain of the claims against them constitute an inappropriate extraterritorial application of the Sherman Act. It is important to distinguish two distinct questions raised by this petition: whether the District Court had jurisdiction, and whether the Sherman Act reaches the extraterritorial conduct alleged here.

On the first question, I believe that the District Court had subject-matter jurisdiction over the Sherman Act claims against all the defendants.... The respondents asserted nonfrivolous claims under the Sherman Act, and [the U.S. judicial code] vests district courts with subject-matter jurisdiction over cases "arising under" federal statutes....

The second question—the extraterritorial reach of the Sherman Act—has nothing to do with the jurisdiction of the courts. It is a question of substantive law turning on whether, in enacting the Sherman Act, Congress asserted regulatory power over the challenged conduct.... If a plaintiff fails to prevail on this issue, the court does not dismiss the claim for want of subject-matter jurisdiction—want of power to adjudicate; rather, it decides the claim, ruling on the merits that the plaintiff has failed to state a cause of action under the relevant statute. See ... *American Banana Co. v. United Fruit Co.*

There is, however, a type of "jurisdiction" relevant to determining the extraterritorial reach of a statute; it is known as "legislative jurisdiction," ... or "jurisdiction to prescribe." ... This refers to "the

continued

continued

authority of a state to make its law applicable to persons or activities," and is quite a separate matter from "jurisdiction to adjudicate." ... There is no doubt, of course, that Congress possesses legislative jurisdiction over the acts alleged in this complaint: Congress has broad power under [the Constitution] "[t]o regulate Commerce with foreign Nations," and this Court has repeatedly upheld its power to make laws applicable to persons or activities beyond our territorial boundaries where United States interests are affected.... But the question in this case is whether, and to what extent, Congress has exercised that undoubted legislative jurisdiction in enacting the Sherman Act.

Two canons of statutory construction are relevant in this inquiry. The first is the "long-standing principle of American law 'that legislation of Congress, unless a contrary intent appears, is meant to apply only within the territorial jurisdiction of the United States.'" ... We have, however, found the presumption to be overcome with respect to our antitrust laws; it is now well established that the Sherman Act applies extraterritorially. See ... *United States v. Aluminum Co. of America*....

But if the presumption against extraterritoriality has been overcome or is otherwise inapplicable, a second canon of statutory construction becomes relevant: "[A]n act of Congress ought never to be construed to violate the law of nations if any other possible construction remains." ... Though it clearly has constitutional authority to do so, Congress is generally presumed not to have exceeded those customary international-law limits on jurisdiction to prescribe.

Consistent with that presumption, this and other courts have frequently recognized that, even where the presumption against extraterritoriality does not apply, statutes should not be interpreted to regulate foreign persons or conduct if that regulation would conflict with principles of international law.... "The controlling considerations" in this choice-of-law analysis were "the interacting interests of the United States and of foreign countries." ...

The solution ... adopted [by the Court in a maritime personal injury case] was to construe the statute "to apply only to areas and transactions in which American law would be considered operative under prevalent doctrines of international law." ... [T]he principle was expressed in *United States v. Aluminum Co. of America* ... the decision that established the extraterritorial reach of the Sherman Act....

The "comity" [authorities] refer to is not the comity of courts, whereby judges decline to exercise jurisdiction over matters more appropriately adjudged elsewhere, but rather what might be termed "prescriptive comity": the respect sovereign nations afford each other by limiting the reach of their laws. That comity is exercised by legislatures when they enact laws, and courts assume it has been exercised when they come to interpreting the scope of laws their legislatures have enacted.... Comity in this sense includes the choice-of-law principles that, "in the absence of contrary congressional direction," are assumed to be incorporated into our substantive laws having extraterritorial reach.... Considering comity in this way is just part of determining whether the Sherman Act prohibits the conduct at issue....

Under the Restatement [of Foreign Relations Law], a nation having some "basis" for jurisdiction to prescribe law should nonetheless refrain from exercising that jurisdiction "with respect to a person or activity having connections with another state when the exercise of such jurisdiction is unreasonable." ... The 'reasonableness' inquiry turns on a number of factors including, but not limited to: "the extent to which the activity takes place within the territory [of the regulating state], ... the connections, such as nationality, residence, or economic activity, between the regulating state and the person principally responsible for the activity to be regulated, ... the character of the activity to be regulated, the importance of regulation to the regulating state, the extent to which other states regulate such activities, and the degree to which the desirability of such regulation is generally accepted, ... the extent to which another state may have an interest in regulating the activity, ... [and] the likelihood of conflict with regulation by another state." ...

Rarely would these factors point more clearly against application of United States law. The activity relevant to the counts at issue here took place primarily in the United Kingdom, and the defendants in these counts are British corporations and British subjects having their principal place of business or residence outside the United States. Great Britain has established a comprehensive regulatory scheme governing the London reinsurance markets, and clearly has a heavy "interest in regulating the activity." ...

continued

continued

Finally, section 2(b) of the McCarran-Ferguson Act allows state regulatory statutes to override the Sherman Act in the insurance field, subject only to [a] narrow "boycott" exception ... suggesting that "the importance of regulation to the [United States]" ... is slight. Considering these factors, I think it unimaginable that an assertion of legislative jurisdiction by the United States would be considered reasonable, and therefore it is inappropriate to assume, in the absence of statutory indication to the contrary, that Congress has made such an assertion....

If one erroneously chooses, as the Court does, to make adjudicative jurisdiction (or, more precisely, abstention) the vehicle for taking account of the needs of prescriptive comity, the Court still gets it wrong. It concludes that no "true conflict" counseling nonapplication of United States law (or rather, as it thinks, United States judicial jurisdiction) exists unless compliance with United States law would constitute a violation of another country's law.... That breathtakingly broad proposition ... will bring the Sherman Act and other laws into sharp and unnecessary conflict with the legitimate interests of other countries—particularly our closest trading partners.

[T]here is clearly a conflict in this case.

Decision. The Supreme Court affirmed that part of the judgment of the Court of Appeals that reversed the District Court's refusal to exercise jurisdiction over foreign reinsurers.

As the operations and investments of U.S. and foreign businesses have become increasingly enmeshed, the DOJ and the Federal Trade Commission have been obliged to develop enforcement guidelines so that businesspeople would have a better sense of when they might expect prosecution. In 1995, they revised these Antitrust Enforcement Guidelines for International Operations, expressing a great "interest in international cooperation," and set forth fourteen illustrative examples. Despite these protestations, however, the agencies showed that they intend to be aggressive. The 1995 Guidelines cite the *Hartford Fire* holding to support the U.S. government view that interest balancing is a discretionary matter of comity.

U.S. courts similarly continue to be aggressive in the assertion of their jurisdiction over transactions concluded in foreign nations. In 1995, a federal judge ruled that a Danish company doing business in Great Britain could sue a British company in the United States for alleged anticompetitive conduct in Great Britain because the British company's activity would prevent the Danish company from exporting goods to the United States. However, in 2004, the U.S. Supreme Court, in *F. Hoffman-La Roche Ltd. v. Empagran S. A.*, clarified in a class action suit by vitamin purchasers that "[where] [t]he price-fixing conduct significantly and adversely affects both customers outside the United States and customers within the United States, but the adverse foreign effect is independent of any adverse domestic effect ... the FTAIA exception does not apply (and thus the Sherman Act does not apply)...."

The European "Implementation" Test

Most nations take a more restrained approach to extraterritorial antitrust jurisdiction than the United States. Under the *territorial* theory of jurisdiction, which is widely accepted throughout the world, a nation may clearly assert jurisdiction over a merger involving a firm based in its territory. Thus, the People's Republic of Mozambique would be within its internationally recognized rights in asserting jurisdiction over a merger between a Mozambique company and a Canadian firm.

A more controversial situation arises when a subsidiary of a foreign-based company seeks to engage in a transaction within the host country's jurisdiction. Although this situation does not involve questions as to jurisdiction over the subsidiary under the territorial theory, if the host country cannot also obtain authority over the foreign parent, that parent could evade the host country's competition laws merely by conducting all of its activities in the host country through a controlled subsidiary. Faced with this difficulty, the European Court of Justice devised the *single*

Eskofot A/S v. Du Pont (U.K.) Ltd.

872 F. Supp. 81 (1995)

United States District Court (S.D.N.Y.)

BACKGROUND AND FACTS

Eskofot A/S (Eskofot), a Danish company, was a large producer of equipment for the graphic arts and printing industry. It had average annual sales of approximately $75 million, $12 million of which was derived from sales in the United States. Du Pont UK was an English corporation with a printing and graphic arts division in England, more than 90 percent of whose total sales were in Britain. Du Pont UK conducted no business in the United States; had no office, employees, bank accounts, books, or records there; and was not licensed to do business in the United States. Howson-Algraphy Division of Vickers PLC (Howson) was the indirect predecessor of Du Pont UK.

Eskofot and Howson began work on a new printing system in 1987 and formalized their relationship in a written agreement later that year. In 1989, Howson was sold to E.I. Du Pont De Nemours & Company (Du Pont), a U.S. corporation, and its name was changed to Du Pont-Howson Limited (DPH). DPH accepted the assignment of Eskofot's contract and executed two additional agreements with Eskofot relating to materials for the development of platemaking systems.

In 1992, Du Pont UK acquired DPH, and in June 1992, Du Pont UK notified Eskofot that it wanted to cancel the agreements. Eskofot alleged that Du Pont retained full control of the plates, processors, and chemicals, and that the defendants intensified their worldwide sales and marketing efforts for the printing systems. In 1993, Eskofot instituted an action against Du Pont UK in England (the "English action") for breach of its agreement and for damages stemming from Du Pont's alleged abuse of its dominant market position, pursuant to Article 82 of the *Treaty of Rome*.

Four months after bringing the English action, Eskofot brought an action in New York under the *Sherman Act* against Du Pont and Du Pont UK. Eskofot alleged that the defendants had monopolized the domestic and international market for certain printing equipment and materials. It further alleged that the defendants had engaged in systematic, intentional conduct in restraint of trade.

JUDGE LEISURE

Defendants maintain that the Court's jurisdiction to hear antitrust claims brought by foreign competitors derives from the Foreign Trade Antitrust Improvements Act, 15 U.S.C. S §6a (the "FTAIA"). Defendants note that the FTAIA was intended to exempt from U.S. antitrust law conduct that lacks the necessary level of domestic effect.... Defendants contend that Eskofot's complaint pleads no facts from which the Court can conclude that defendants' conduct had a direct, substantial, and reasonably foreseeable effect in the United States.... Plaintiff argues that the FTAIA does not apply to a claim that trade, involving foreign nations, has affected the import commerce of the United States.... Eskofot further argues that the instant dispute relates directly to import commerce. Consequently, Eskofot concludes, this case should not be considered under the FTAIA "direct, substantial and reasonably foreseeable" standard....

This Court notes that the FTAIA, by its own terms, clearly states that the provisions of the Sherman Act do not apply to conduct involving trade or commerce, "other than import trade or import commerce," with foreign nations. The implication that the Sherman Act provisions continue to apply to import trade and import commerce is unmistakable. Plaintiff contends that defendants' actions have precluded it from exporting goods into the United States. Consequently, plaintiff's pleading alleges an impact on import trade and import commerce into the United States.

Rather than the FTAIA's "direct, substantial and reasonably foreseeable" standard, the Court must determine whether the challenged conduct has, or is intended to have, any anti-competitive effect upon United States commerce.... Eskofot alleges that defendants' actions have had a significant anti-competitive effect upon United States commerce. Moreover, Eskofot alleges facts which, if true, amply support its contention. As a result, this Court has subject matter jurisdiction.

Eskofot alleges that both it and Du Pont always planned to market and sell, respectively, the Proff Print and Silverlith systems and their component

continued

continued

parts in the United States. Eskofot further asserts that it would have sold its Proff Print system in the United States if it were not for defendants' conduct, and that defendants still intend to market their Silverlith system in the United States. Defendants dispute these assertions and contend that they are merely conclusory allegations that should be accorded little weight in determining whether to apply American antitrust laws.

The Court notes that, in the present posture of this action, factual questions must be resolved in favor of plaintiff. The instant allegations, for example, require a careful investigation of the records of the various parties before they can be resolved.... Certainly Eskofot and defendants have the capacity to sell their systems in the United States, and both Du Pont and Eskofot currently sell a certain percentage of their products in the United States. Whether Du Pont or Du Pont U.K. has sold, developed plans to sell, or harbors ambitions of selling the Silverlith system in the United States are questions of fact. Resolving these questions and other factual questions in favor of the plaintiff, this Court finds that plaintiff has sufficiently demonstrated that defendants' conduct impacted the import trade of the United States....

In sum, plaintiff has alleged that: its sale of the Proff Print system in the United States was precluded by defendants' actions, defendants intend to sell Silverlith in the United States, defendants have already initiated marketing activities in the United States to facilitate future sales, and that consumers in the United States will be negatively affected by the higher prices and reduced output that flow from the emergence of a monopoly....

[T]his Court cannot even conclude that the conduct alleged by plaintiff has not had a direct, actual, and foreseeable effect in the United States.

Decision. The Court denied the defendants' motion to dismiss the lawsuit and permitted the case to proceed in the United States.

economic unit concept, under which the court imputes the behavior of a controlled subsidiary to the parent. This concept also permits the court to consider the parent's level of market dominance in determining whether the subsidiary's actions are monopolistic. The court expanded this concept in the *Philip Morris* judgment (*BAT Reynolds v. Commission,* 1987 E.C.R. 4487), to find jurisdiction not only when actual voting control is acquired, but also when the foreign acquirer would achieve "material influence" over an erstwhile European competitor.

The farthest reach of the accepted territorial jurisdiction doctrine is the principle of *objective territoriality.* Under this principle, a state may exercise jurisdiction over conduct commenced outside its territory when the act or effect of the act is physically completed inside its territory. However, many nations have vigorously resisted the extension of this effects test beyond physical effects in the host country to mere consequences that result in a nation, such as the effects from anticompetitive conduct.

The more restricted European effects test has meant that companies can conspire to limit competition in exports to a nation without that nation being able to claim jurisdiction over the conspiracy. For example, in Germany, each *exportkartell* unifies the marketing power of German corporations in a single industry for potent export activity outside the Common Market.

As Europeans have begun to develop their own massive multinational market, they have become more flexible in defining what constitutes a "physical completion" of an act within a territory. In the following case, commonly referred to as the *Wood Pulp* case, the European Court of Justice found that the European Commission could assert jurisdiction over foreign companies that have no presence in the Union but that export to the Union through independent distributors. The court justified jurisdiction on the basis that the firms had engaged in price-fixing activity that was "implemented" within the Union.

The court in the *Wood Pulp* decision expressly declined to adopt the U.S. effects test, setting forth a new "implementation within the Community" test. The *EU Merger Regulation* literally applies to companies outside the EU. Its definition of "community dimension" measures aggregate worldwide sales of the merged entities, not whether the assets are located inside the EU. If two large U.S. firms with significant sales to European distributors merge in the United States, must they comply with the regulation? While it would be a logical extension of *Wood Pulp,* such an exercise of jurisdiction would convert the "implementation" test into a thinly veiled European "effects test."

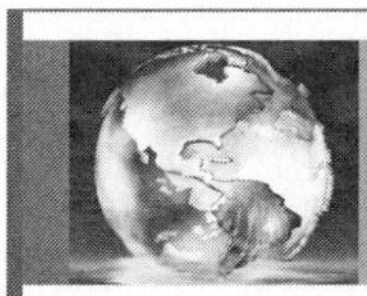

A. Ahlstrom Osakeyhtio v. Comm'n

1987–88 Tfr. Binder Common Mkt. Rep. (CCH) 14,491 (1988)

Court of Justice of the European Communities

BACKGROUND AND FACTS

Wood pulp is the principal raw material used in production of paper and paperboard. In 1988, the EU member states produced only a small fraction of their requirements for wood pulp. Virtually all of the product purchased in the Union originated from producers in countries that were then not members of the Union: Finland, Sweden, Canada, and the United States.

Many of these wood pulp producers had no presence in the Union. They sold their products to independent distributors and users located in the Union.

In each of these countries, the wood pulp producers organized into associations for export. In the United States, this group was the Pulp, Paper, and Paper Board Export Association of the United States (known as KEA), formed under the *Webb-Pomerene Act,* which exempts associations of U.S. exporters from U.S. antitrust laws. Each of these associations engaged in discussions on pricing policy regarding exports to the Union.

The European Commission brought an action against the members of the associations under the *Treaty of Rome,* found them guilty of anticompetitive activity under Article 81 of the Treaty, and imposed fines on them. The associations appealed to the Court of Justice, asserting that the Commission lacked jurisdiction over them.

PRESIDENT LORD MACKENZIE STUART

All the applicants that made submissions regarding jurisdiction maintain first of all that by applying the competition rules of the Treaty to them the Commission has misconstrued the territorial scope of Article 81. They note that ... the Court of Justice did not adopt the "effects doctrine" but emphasized that the case involved conduct restricting competition within the Common Market because of the activities of subsidiaries that could be imputed to the parent companies. The applicants add that even if there is a basis in [Union] law for applying Article 81 to them, the action of applying the rule interpreted in that way would be contrary to public international law, which precludes any claim by the [Union] to regulate conduct restricting competition adopted outside the territory of the [Union] merely by reason of the economic repercussions which that conduct produces within the [Union].

The applicants which are members of the KEA further submit that the application of [Union] competition rules to them is contrary to public international law insofar as it is in breach of the principle of noninterference. They maintain that in this case the application of Article 81 harmed the interest of the United States in promoting exports by United States undertakings as recognized in the Webb–Pomerene Act of 1918, under which export associations, like the KEA, are exempt from United States antitrust laws.

Insofar as the submission concerning the infringement of Article 81 of the Treaty itself is concerned, it should be recalled that under that provision all agreements between undertakings and concerted practices which may affect trade between Member States and which have as their object or effect the restriction of competition within the Common Market are prohibited.

It should be noted that the main sources of supply of wood pulp are outside the [Union]—in Canada, the United States, Sweden, and Finland—and that the market therefore has global dimensions. Where wood pulp producers established in those countries sell directly to purchasers established in the [Union] and engage in price competition in order to win orders from those customers, that constitutes competition within the Common Market.

It follows that where those producers concert on the prices to be charged to their customers in the [Union] and put that concentration into effect by selling at prices that are actually coordinated, they are

continued

continued

taking part in concentation that has the object and effect of restricting competition with the Common Market within the meaning of Article 81 of the Treaty.

Accordingly, it must be concluded that by applying the competition rules in the Treaty in the circumstances of this case to undertakings whose registered offices are situated outside the [Union], the Commission has not made an incorrect assessment of the territorial scope of Article 81. The applicants have submitted that the decision is incompatible with public international law on the grounds that the application of the competition rules in this case was founded exclusively on the economic repercussions within the Common Market of conduct restricting competition which was adopted outside the [Union].

It should be observed that an infringement of Article 81, such as the conclusion of an agreement that has had the effect of restricting competition within the Common Market, consists of conduct made up of two elements: the formation of the agreement, decision, or concerted practice and the implementation thereof. If the applicability of prohibitions laid down under the competition law were made to depend on the place where the agreement, decision, or concerted practice was formed, the result would obviously be to give undertakings an easy means of evading those prohibitions. The decisive factor therefore is the place where it is implemented.

The producers in this case implemented their pricing agreement within the Common Market. It is immaterial in that respect whether or not they had recourse to subsidiaries, agents, sub-agents, or branches within the [Union] in order to make their contacts with purchasers within the [Union].

Accordingly, the [Union's] jurisdiction to apply its competition rules to such conduct is covered by the territoriality principle as universally recognized in public international law.

As regards the argument based on the infringement of the principle of non-interference, it should be pointed out that the applicants who are members of KEA have referred to a rule and the effect of those rules is that a person finds himself subject to contradictory orders as to the conduct he must adopt, each State is obliged to exercise its jurisdiction with moderation.

There is not, in this case, any contradiction between the conduct required by the United States and that required by the [Union] since the Webb–Pomerene Act merely exempts the conclusion of export cartels from the application of United States antitrust laws but does not require such cartels to be concluded.

Decision. The Court of Justice affirmed the Commission's imposition of fines on the foreign companies that had coordinated their pricing policies.

Blocking Legislation

A necessary upshot of the U.S. effects doctrine is that the U.S. litigation system and pro-competition policies are carried into many foreign nations. The United States is by far the world's largest market. In addition, as noted earlier, both the U.S. system of litigation and the U.S. pro-competition policies are inconsistent with the systems and policies in other nations. The clash triggered a rash of dueling legislation. In an antitrust action brought by the Justice Department against the uranium production industry, an American producer alleged that uranium producers outside the United States had formed a cartel to raise the price of uranium. As the producer sought discovery against foreign producers to document its charges, foreign nations cried foul. They asserted that the uranium litigation was an attempt by the United States to enforce its economic policies abroad.

In short order, Canada, Australia, France, the Netherlands, New Zealand, Switzerland, Germany, and the United Kingdom enacted *blocking legislation*—statutes containing provisions that block the discovery of documents located in their countries and bar the enforcement of foreign judgments there. In addition, some contain *clawback provisions* under which the foreign companies can sue in their own country to recover against local U.S. assets all or part of the amount of an antitrust judgment rendered in the United States.

These blocking laws are tantamount to international legal warfare. However, blocking legislation is still a useful tool in other contexts. For example, many nations reacted against the *Cuban Democracy Act of 1992*, a U.S. law that prohibits foreign subsidiaries of U.S. corporations from doing business in Cuba, by forbidding those subsidiaries from obeying the act. Blocking legislation again appeared when the Clinton Administration set forth its somewhat more aggressive international antitrust stance.

China Begins to Regulate the Competitive Environment

After more than a decade of deliberations, in 2007 China passed the *Anti-Monopoly Law of the People's Republic of China* (AML). The new law takes effect on August 1, 2008. While China previously had numerous antitrust laws, they were not codified in one place and were generally seen as ineffective. The new law, based in great part on European competition law, targets anticompetitive monopoly agreements, abuse of dominant market positions, and concentrations viewed as likely to eliminate or restrict competition. It remains to be seen how the new law will interact with the previous laws, who will enforce the new law, how enforcement will work, and how the courts and enforcement agencies will interact in the new regime. Like laws in many other countries, China's new AML lays out a basic regulatory framework, but leaves the details of implementation open-ended.

Conclusion

One of the prices of business success is regulation by antitrust laws. In recent years, antitrust/competition law, which had its roots in the United States, has spread around the world. This has created a new area for American entrepreneurs to be careful of when engaging in business activities.

Chapter Summary

1. Competition law, referred to in the United States as antitrust law, prohibits agreements between competitors that restrict competition. It also prohibits a firm from abusing a dominant market position through predatory pricing and refusals to deal.
2. Some nations require governmental review of virtually all "vertical" arrangements between firms and their distributors, customers, or suppliers. In the United States, regulators allow vertical restraints if a reasonable case can be made that they foster better service and hence foster inter-brand competition, encourage innovation, or do not foreclose a substantial part of the market to others. In the EU, the Commission is more likely to intervene to prevent vertical restraints.
3. The European Commission is more flexible with respect to know-how transfer agreements than patent licenses. The rationale is that because the owner of know-how does not have any legally cognizable right to its knowledge, it can rely only on secrecy.
4. Competition authorities also show flexibility in reviewing franchise agreements because the franchiser must protect its know-how and the franchiser must ensure that the franchisee is producing and marketing the product in a manner consistent with the franchiser's good name. Poor performance by one franchisee can have adverse effects on the franchiser's reputation and operations internationally.
5. To be in violation of abuse of monopoly power provisions, a company must have abused its dominant market position, which is defined differently in different countries and in different industries.
6. In 1990, the *Council of the European Communities' Regulation 4064/89—the EC Merger Regulation*—became effective. Under the merger regulation, parties to all mergers, acquisitions, joint ventures, and other business combinations that have a community dimension must provide pre-transaction notification to the commission. In 2004, the European Council put into effect substantial amendments to the merger regulation that strengthened EU competition laws.
7. In the United States, private parties harmed by anticompetitive activity may bring damage actions in federal court against a firm violating U.S. antitrust laws. In Europe, EU competition laws may be enforced only in national courts; a private party may not go to the pan-European forums of the EU. There has been a recent push from the EU's Competition Commissioner to

enhance private enforcement of competition laws within the European national courts.

8. *Per se* competition law violations are those that no amount of explanation can make legal, while actions subject to the rule of reason can be legal if, upon analysis, they are found not to be anticompetitive. In 2007, the Supreme Court of the United States overruled a 96-year-old precedent by holding that vertical agreements between manufacturers and distributors to fix minimum resale prices are to now be judged by the rule of reason rather than a *per se* rule. A dispute surrounds the issue of whether the rule of reason is an appropriate mode of analysis under EU competition laws.
9. Under the U.S. Supreme Court case of *F. Hoffman-La Roche Ltd. v. Empagran S.A.*, where "[t]he price-fixing conduct significantly and adversely affects both customers outside the United States and customers within the United States, but the adverse foreign effect is independent of any adverse domestic effect ... the Sherman Act does not apply." Europe and most other nations have a more restricted view of anticompetitive conduct jurisdictions. Under the principle of objective territoriality, a nation may exercise jurisdiction over conduct commenced outside its territory when the act or effect of the act is physically completed inside its territory.

Questions and Case Problems

1. The Slobovian Confederation's five producers control 95 percent of the world's supply of "goom," the key ingredient in the production of goomey bears. To maximize the Slobovian standard of living, the government passed a law creating a cartel among the five producers and forbidding access to Slobovian goom by any other entity. The price of goomey bears skyrocketed in the United States. Giggles Consolidated, a U.S. candy manufacturer, attempted to purchase a goom mine in Slobovia but was rejected by the cartel. As a result, Giggles brought an antitrust action against the cartel members in federal district court. Does U.S. law apply? If the U.S. court finds for Giggles, how can U.S. courts enforce such a judgment?
2. In the case in Question 1, if a U.S. court sought to enforce U.S. laws on Slobovia's leading export, how would U.S.–Slobovian relations be affected? What if a key U.S. naval base was located in Slobovia? How well equipped are courts to conduct such relations?
3. In *Alcoa,* Judge Hand points out that even agreements to restrict trade only in Europe and South America would have anticompetitive repercussions in the United States. What additional element did he require before giving U.S. antitrust law extraterritorial effect?
4. If Judge Hand had written his decision in December 1941, at the beginning of World War II, rather than in 1945, at its successful end, would he have handed down a judgment against the national aluminum company of a principal ally of the United States? Should a decision affecting the nation's relations with an ally reflect such considerations? Do you think the U.S. role in that war affected judges' perceptions of the relative importance of U.S. law?
5. Why would a British company bring a competition lawsuit under U.S. antitrust laws rather than EU competition law? What advantages does a company have in alleging an antitrust conspiracy? Describe the differences between U.S. law and EU law in the areas of pretrial discovery, attorneys' fees, and potential damage awards.
6. As Sir Donaldson pointed out, English courts have no authority to interpret treaties, whereas U.S. courts do. What arguments suggest that the English approach is preferable? What arguments indicate that the U.S. approach is better?
7. U.S. antitrust law reflects U.S. economic policy. If U.S. antitrust law resolves an economic dispute among British companies, has U.S. economic policy been extended to Britain? What are the implications of the United Kingdom's requirement that British companies use its own policy in resolving such disputes?

MANAGERIAL IMPLICATIONS

Your firm, Ellis Pets Consolidated, has developed a state-of-the-art process for producing see-through plastic hamster cages. The plastic is thin, so it does not distort the pet owner's view of the hamster, yet hard enough to resist the hamster's gnawing, and is quite inexpensive in a market with great price elasticity. The Ellis process is strictly know-how. On advice of patent counsel, Ellis has not sought any patent protection. Ellis has achieved a dominant share in the U.S. market with its line of see-through hamster cages. Now, a large international plastics manufacturer headquartered in Lyon, France—Vivian Plastique, S.A.—wishes to license the process from Ellis to apply it to other uses.

1. Vivian sees the process as so valuable that it is willing to agree never to use the process for applications within the pet industry anywhere in the world. In fact, Vivian is willing to agree never to enter the pet industry in any way. Analyze for Ellis the enforceability of these proposed agreements by Vivian. Include in your analysis alternatives that would be preferable for Ellis.
2. The hamster cage manufacturers of Europe suddenly become aware of the threat posed by Ellis. They agree to apply concerted pressure on pet stores throughout Europe to shut Ellis out. Ellis brings an antitrust action in the U.S. District Court for the Southern District of Florida. Does the court have jurisdiction over the European hamster cage manufacturers? Will Ellis be able to enforce discovery requests in Europe?

FOR INTERNET ACTIVITIES, VISIT ACADEMIC.CENGAGE.COM/BLAW/SCHAFFER.

Appendix A

United Nations Convention on Contracts for the International Sale of Goods[1]

The States Parties to this Convention,

Bearing in mind the broad objectives in the resolutions adopted by the sixth special session of the General Assembly of the United Nations on the establishment of a New International Economic Order,

Considering that the development of international trade on the basis of equality and mutual benefit is an important element in promoting friendly relations among States,

Being of the opinion that the adoption of uniform rules which govern contracts for the international sale of goods and take into account the different social, economic and legal systems would contribute to the removal of legal barriers in international trade and promote the development of international trade,

Have agreed as follows:

Part One: Sphere of Application and General Provisions

Chapter I. Sphere of Application

Article I

(1) This Convention applies to contracts of sale of goods between parties whose places of business are in different States:
  (a) when the States are Contracting States; or
  (b) when the rules of private international law lead to the application of the law of a Contracting State.

(2) The fact that the parties have their places of business in different States is to be disregarded whenever this fact does not appear either from the contract or from any dealings between, or from information disclosed by, the parties at any time or at the conclusion of the contract.

(3) Neither the nationality of the parties nor the civil or commercial character of the parties or of the contract is to be taken into consideration in determining the application of this Convention.

Article 2

This Convention does not apply to sales:
  (a) of goods bought for personal, family or household use, unless the seller, at any time before or at the conclusion of the contract, neither knew nor ought to have known that the goods were bought for any such use:
  (b) by auction;
  (c) on execution or otherwise by authority of law;
  (d) of stocks, shares, investment securities, negotiable instruments or money;
  (e) of ships, vessels, hovercraft or aircraft.
  (f) of electricity.

Article 3

(1) Contracts for the supply of goods to be manufactured or produced are to be considered sales unless the party who orders the goods undertakes to supply a substantial part of the materials necessary for such manufacture or production.

(2) This Convention does not apply to contracts in which the preponderant part of the obligations of the party who furnishes the goods consists in the supply of labour or other services.

Article 4

This Convention governs only the formation of the contract of sale and the rights and obligations of the seller and the buyer arising from such a contract. In particular, except as otherwise expressly provided in this Convention, it is not concerned with:
  (a) the validity of the contract or of any of its provisions or of any usage;
  (b) the effect which the contract may have on the property in the goods sold.

Article 5

This Convention does not apply to the liability of the seller for death or personal injury caused by the goods to any person.

Article 6

The parties may exclude the application of this Convention or, subject to article 12, derogate from or vary the effect of any of its provisions.

Chapter 2. General Provisions

Article 7

(1) In the interpretation of this Convention, regard is to be had to its international character and to the need to

[1]Source of text: U.N. Document A/CONF.97/18, Annex I, English version reprinted in 52 Fed. Reg. 6264 (1987) and in 19 I.L.M.

promote uniformity in its application and the observance of good faith in international trade.

(2) Questions concerning matters governed by this Convention which are not expressly settled in it are to be settled in conformity with the general principles on which it is based or, in the absence of such principles, in conformity with the law applicable by virtue of the rules of private international law.

Article 8

(1) For the purposes of this Convention statements made by and other conduct of a party are to be interpreted according to his intent where the other party knew or could not have been unaware what that intent was.

(2) If the preceding paragraph is not applicable, statements made by and other conduct of a party are to be interpreted according to the understanding that a reasonable person of the same kind as the other party would have had in the same circumstances.

(3) In determining the intent of a party or the understanding a reasonable person would have had, due consideration is to be given to all relevant circumstances of the case including the negotiations, any practices which the parties have established between themselves, usages and any subsequent conduct of the parties.

Article 9

(1) The parties are bound by any usage to which they have agreed and by any practices which they have established between themselves.

(2) The parties are considered, unless otherwise agreed, to have impliedly made applicable to their contract or its formation a usage of which the parties knew or ought to have known and which in international trade is widely known to, and regularly observed by, parties to contracts of the type involved in the particular trade concerned.

Article 10

For the purposes of this Convention:

(a) if a party has more than one place of business, the place of business is that which has the closest relationship to the contract and its performance, having regard to the circumstances known to or contemplated by the parties at any time before or at the conclusion of the contract;

(b) if a party does not have a place of business, reference is to be made to his habitual residence.

Article 11

A contract of sale need not be concluded in or evidence by writing and is not subject to any other requirements as to form. It may be proved by any means, including witnesses.

Article 12

Any provision of article 11, article 29 or Part II of this Convention that allows a contract of sale or its modification or termination by agreement or any offer, acceptance or other indication of intention to be made in any form other than in writing does not apply where any party has his place of business in a Contracting State which has made a declaration under article 96 of this Convention. The parties may not derogate from or vary the effect of this article.

Article 13

For the purposes of this Convention 'writing' includes telegram and telex.

Part Two: Formation of the Contract

Article 14

(1) A proposal for concluding a contract addressed to one or more specific persons constitutes an offer if it is sufficiently definite and indicates the intention of the offeror to be bound in case of acceptance. A proposal is sufficiently definite if it indicates the goods and expressly or implicitly fixes or makes provision for determining the quantity and the price.

(2) A proposal other than one addressed to one or more specific persons is to be considered merely as an invitation to make offers, unless the contrary is clearly indicated by the person making the proposal.

Article 15

(1) An offer becomes effective when it reaches the offeree.

(2) An offer, even if it is irrevocable, may be withdrawn if the withdrawal reaches the offeree before or at the same time as the offer.

Article 16

(1) Until a contract is concluded an offer may be revoked if the revocation reaches the offeree before he has dispatched an acceptance.

(2) However, an offer cannot be revoked:

(a) if it indicates, whether by stating a fixed time for acceptance or otherwise, that it is irrevocable; or

(b) if it was reasonable for the offeree to rely on the offer as being irrevocable and the offeree has acted in reliance on the offer.

Article 17

An offer, even if it is irrevocable, is terminated when a rejection reaches the offeror.

Article 18

(1) A statement made by or other conduct of the offeree indicating assent to an offer is an acceptance. Silence or inactivity does not in itself amount to acceptance.

(2) An acceptance of an offer becomes effective at the moment the indication of assent reaches the offeror. An acceptance is not effective if the indication of assent does not reach the offeror within the time he has fixed or, if no time is fixed, within a reasonable time, due account being

taken of the circumstances of the transaction, including the rapidity of the means of communication employed by the offeror. An oral offer must be accepted immediately unless the circumstances indicate otherwise.

(3) However, if, by virtue of the offer or as a result of practices which the parties have established between themselves or of usage, the offeree may indicate assent by performing an act, such as one relating to the dispatch of the goods or payment of the price, without notice to the offeror, the acceptance is effective at the moment the act is performed, provided that the act is performed within the period of time laid down in the preceding paragraph.

Article 19

(1) A reply to an offer which purports to be an acceptance but contains additions, limitations or other modifications is a rejection of the offer and constitutes a counter-offer.

(2) However, a reply to an offer which purports to be an acceptance but contains additional or different terms which do not materially alter the terms of the offer constitutes an acceptance, unless the offeror, without undue delay, objects orally to the discrepancy or dispatches a notice to that effect. If he does not so object, the terms of the contract are the terms of the offer with the modifications contained in the acceptance.

(3) Additional or different terms relating, among other things, to the price, payment, quality and quantity of the goods, place and time of delivery, extent of one party's liability to the other or the settlement of disputes are considered to alter the terms of the offer materially.

Article 20

(1) A period of time for acceptance fixed by the offeror in a telegram or a letter begins to run from the moment the telegram is handed in for dispatch or from the date shown on the letter or, if no such date is shown, from the date shown on the envelope. A period of time for acceptance fixed by the offeror by telephone, telex or other means of instantaneous communication, begins to run from the moment that the offer reaches the offeree.

(2) Official holidays or non-business days occurring during the period for acceptance are included in calculating the period. However, if a notice of acceptance cannot be delivered at the address of the offeror on the last day of the period because that day falls on an official holiday or a non-business day at the place of business of the offeror, the period is extended until the first business day which follows.

Article 21

(1) A late acceptance is nevertheless effective as an acceptance if without delay the offeror orally so informs the offeree or dispatches a notice to that effect.

(2) If a letter or other writing containing a late acceptance shows that it has been sent in such circumstances that if its transmission had been normal it would have reached the offeror in due time, the late acceptance is effective as an acceptance unless, without delay, the offeror orally informs the offeree that he considers his offer as having lapsed or dispatches a notice to that effect.

Article 22

An acceptance may be withdrawn if the withdrawal reaches the offeror before or at the same time as the acceptance would have become effective.

Article 23

A contract is concluded at the moment when an acceptance of an offer becomes effective in accordance with the provisions of this Convention.

Article 24

For the purposes of the Part of the Convention, an offer, declaration of acceptance or any other indication of intention 'reaches' the addressee when it is made orally to him or delivered by any other means to him personally, to his place of business or mailing address or, if he does not have a place of business or mailing address, to his habitual residence.

Part Three: Sale of Goods

Chapter 1. General Provisions

Article 25

A breach of contract committed by one of the parties is fundamental if it results in such detriment to the other party as substantially to deprive him of what he is entitled to expect under the contract, unless the party in breach did not foresee and a reasonable person of the same kind in the same circumstances would not have foreseen such a result.

Article 26

A declaration of avoidance of the contract is effective only if made by notice to the other party.

Article 27

Unless otherwise expressly provided in this Part of the Convention, if any notice, request or other communication is given or made by a party in accordance with this Part and by means appropriate in the circumstances, a delay of error in the transmission of the communication or its failure to arrive does not deprive that party of the right to rely on the communication.

Article 28

If, in accordance with the provisions of this Convention, one party is entitled to require performance of any obligation by the other party, a court is not bound to enter a judgement for specific performance unless the court would do so under its own law in respect of similar contracts of sale not governed by this Convention.

Article 29

(1) A contract may be modified or terminated by the mere agreement of the parties.

(2) A contract in writing which contains a provision requiring any modification or termination by agreement to be in writing may not be otherwise modified or terminated by agreement. However, a party may be precluded by his conduct from asserting such a provision to the extent that the other party has relied on that conduct.

Chapter 2. Obligations of the Seller

Article 30

The seller must deliver the goods, hand over any documents relating to them and transfer the property in the goods, as required by the contract and this Convention.

Section I. Delivery of the Goods and Handing over of Documents

Article 31

If the seller is not bound to deliver the goods at any other particular place, his obligation to deliver consists:

(a) if the contract of sale involves carriage of the goods —in handing the goods over to the first carrier for transmission to the buyer;

(b) if, in cases, not within the preceding subparagraph, the contract relates to specific goods, or unidentified goods to be drawn from a specific stock or to be manufactured or produced, and at the time of the conclusion of the contract the parties knew that the goods were at, or were to be manufactured or produced at, a particular place—in placing the goods at the buyer's disposal at that place;

(c) in other cases—in placing the goods at the buyer's disposal at the place where the seller had his place of business at the time of the conclusion of the contract.

Article 32

(1) If the seller, in accordance with the contract or this Convention, hands the goods over to a carrier and if the goods are not clearly identified to the contract by markings on the goods, by shipping documents or otherwise, the seller must give the buyer notice of the consignment specifying the goods.

(2) If the seller is bound to arrange for carriage of the goods, he must make such contracts as are necessary for carriage to the place fixed by means of transportation appropriate in the circumstances and according to the usual terms for such transportation.

(3) If the seller is not bound to effect insurance in respect of the carriage of the goods, he must, at the buyer's request, provide him with all valuable information necessary to enable him to effect such insurance.

Article 33

The seller must deliver the goods:

(a) if a date is fixed by or determinable from the contract, on that date;

(b) if a period of time is fixed by or determinable from the contract, at any time within that period unless circumstances indicate that the buyer is to choose a date; or

(c) in any other case, within a reasonable time after the conclusion of the contract.

Article 34

If the seller is bound to hand over documents relating to the goods, he must hand them over at the time and place and in the form required by the contract. If the seller has handed over documents before that time, he may, up to that time, cure any lack of conformity in the documents, if the exercise of this right does not cause the buyer unreasonable inconvenience or unreasonable expense. However, the buyer retains any right to claim damages as provided for in this Convention.

Section II. Conformity of the Goods and Third Party Claims

Article 35

(1) The seller must deliver goods which are of the quantity, quality and description required by the contract and which are contained or packaged in the manner required by the contract.

(2) Except where the parties have agreed otherwise, the goods do not conform with the contract unless they:

(a) are fit for the purposes for which goods of the same description would ordinarily be used;

(b) are fit for any particular purpose expressly or impliedly made known to the seller at the time of the conclusion of the contract, except where the circumstances show that the buyer did not rely, or that it was unreasonable for him to rely, on the seller's skill and judgement;

(c) possess the qualities of goods which the seller has held out to the buyer as a sample or model;

(d) are contained or packaged in the manner usual for such goods or, where there is no such manner, in a manner adequate to preserve and protect the goods.

(3) The seller is not liable under subparagraphs (a) to (d) of the preceding paragraph for any lack of conformity of the goods if at the time of the conclusion of the contract the buyer knew or could not have been unaware of such lack of conformity.

Article 36

(1) The seller is liable in accordance with the contract and this Convention for any lack of conformity which exists at the time when the risk passes to the buyer, even though the lack of conformity becomes apparent only after that time.

(2) The seller is also liable for any lack of conformity which occurs after the time indicated in the preceding paragraph and which is due to a breach of any of his obligations, including a breach of any guarantee that for a period of time the goods will remain fit for their ordinary purpose or for some particular purpose or will retain specified qualities or characteristics.

Article 37

If the seller has delivered goods before the date for delivery, he may, up to that date, deliver any missing part or make up any deficiency in the quantity of the goods delivered, or deliver goods in replacement of any nonconforming goods delivered or remedy any lack of conformity in the goods delivered, provided that the exercise of this right does not cause the buyer unreasonable inconvenience or unreasonable expense. However, the buyer retains any right to claim damages as provided for in this Convention.

Article 38

(1) The buyer must examine the goods, or cause them to be examined, within as short a period as is practicable in the circumstances.
(2) If the contract involves carriage of the goods, examination may be deferred until after the goods have arrived at their destination.
(3) If the goods are redirected in transit or redispatched by the buyer without a reasonable opportunity for examination by him and at the time of the conclusion of the contract the seller knew or ought to have known of the possibility of such redirection or redispatch, examination may be deferred until after the goods have arrived at the new destination.

Article 39

(1) The buyer loses the right to rely on a lack of conformity of the goods if he does not give notice to the seller specifying the nature of the lack of conformity within a reasonable time after he has discovered it or ought to have discovered it.
(2) In any event, the buyer loses the right to rely on a lack of conformity of the goods if he does not give the seller notice thereof at the latest within a period of two years from the date on which the goods were actually handed over to the buyer, unless this time-limit is inconsistent with a contractual period of guarantee.

Article 40

The seller is not entitled to rely on the provisions of articles 38 and 39 if the lack of conformity relates to facts of which he knew or could not have been unaware and which he did not disclose to the buyer.

Article 41

The seller must deliver goods which are free from any right or claim of a third party, unless the buyer agreed to take the goods subject to that right or claim. However, if such right or claim is based on industrial property or other intellectual property, the seller's obligation is governed by article 42.

Article 42

(1) The seller must deliver goods which are free from any right or claim of a third party based on industrial property or other intellectual property, of which at the time of the conclusion of the contract the seller knew or could not have been unaware, provided that the right or claim is based on industrial property or other intellectual property:
    (a) under the law of the State where the goods will be resold or otherwise used, if it was contemplated by the parties at the time of the conclusion of the contract that the goods would be resold or otherwise used in that State; or
    (b) in any other case, under the law of the State where the buyer has his place of business.
(2) The obligation of the seller under the preceding paragraph does not extend to cases where:
    (a) at the time of the conclusion of the contract the buyer knew or could not have been unaware of the right or claim; or
    (b) the right or claim results from the seller's compliance with technical drawings, designs, formulae or other such specifications furnished by the buyer.

Article 43

(1) The buyer loses the right to rely on the provisions of article 41 or article 42 if he does not give notice to the seller specifying the nature of the right or claim of the third party within a reasonable time after he has become aware or ought to have become aware of the right or claim.
(2) The seller is not entitled to rely on the provisions of the preceding paragraph if he knew of the right or claim of the third party and the nature of it.

Article 44

Notwithstanding the provisions of paragraph (1) of article 39 and paragraph (1) of article 43, the buyer may reduce the price in accordance with article 50 or claim damages, except for loss of profit, if he has a reasonable excuse for his failure to give the required notice.

Section III. Remedies for Breach of Contract by the Seller

Article 45

(1) If the seller fails to perform any of his obligations under the contract or this Convention, the buyer may:
    (a) exercise the rights provided in articles 46 to 52;
    (b) claim damages as provided in articles 74 to 77.
(2) The buyer is not deprived of any right he may have to claim damages by exercising his right to other remedies.
(3) No period of grace may be granted to the seller by a court or arbitral tribunal when the buyer resorts to a remedy for breach of contract.

Article 46

(1) The buyer may require performance by the seller of his obligations unless the buyer has resorted to a remedy which is inconsistent with this requirement.

(2) If the goods do not conform with the contract, the buyer may require delivery of substitute goods only if the lack of conformity constitutes a fundamental breach of contract and a request for substitute goods is made either in conjunction with notice given under article 39 or within a reasonable time thereafter.

(3) If the goods do not conform with the contract, the buyer may require the seller to remedy the lack of conformity by repair, unless this is unreasonable having regard to all the circumstances. A request for repair must be made either in conjunction with notice given under article 39 or within a reasonable time thereafter.

Article 47

(1) The buyer may fix an additional period of time of reasonable length for performance by the seller of his obligations.

(2) Unless the buyer has received notice from the seller that he will not perform within the period so fixed, the buyer may not, during that period, resort to any remedy for breach of contract. However, the buyer is not deprived thereby of any right he may have to claim damages for delay in performance.

Article 48

(1) Subject to article 49, the seller may, even after the date for delivery, remedy at his own expense any failure to perform his obligations, if he can do so without unreasonable delay and without causing the buyer unreasonable inconvenience or uncertainty of reimbursement by the seller of expenses advanced by the buyer. However, the buyer retains any right to claim damages as provided for in this Convention.

(2) If the seller requests the buyer to make known whether he will accept performance and the buyer does not comply with the request within a reasonable time, the seller may perform within the time indicated in his request. The buyer may not, during that period of time, resort to any remedy which is inconsistent with performance by the seller.

(3) A notice by the seller that he will perform within a specified period of time is assumed to include a request, under the preceding paragraph, that the buyer make known his decision.

(4) A request or notice by the seller under paragraph (2) or (3) of this article is not effective unless received by the buyer.

Article 49

(1) The buyer may declare the contract avoided:
   (a) if the failure by the seller to perform any of his obligations under the contract or this Convention amounts to a fundamental breach of contract; or
   (b) in case of non-delivery, if the seller does not deliver the goods within the additional period of time fixed by the buyer in accordance with paragraph (1) or article 47 or declares that he will not deliver within the period so fixed.

(2) However, in cases where the seller has delivered the goods, the buyer loses the right to declare the contract avoided unless he does so:
   (a) in respect of late delivery, within a reasonable time after he has become aware that delivery has been made;
   (b) in respect of any breach other than late delivery, within a reasonable time:
      (i) after he knew or ought to have known of the breach;
      (ii) after the expiration of any additional period of time fixed by the buyer in accordance with paragraph (1) of article 47, or after the seller has declared that he will not perform his obligations within such an additional period; or
      (iii) after the expiration of any additional period of time indicated by the seller in accordance with paragraph (2) of article 48, or after the buyer has declared that he will not accept performance.

Article 50

If the goods do not conform with the contract and whether or not the price has already been paid, the buyer may reduce the price in the same proportion as the value that the goods actually delivered had at the time of the delivery bears to the value that conforming goods would have had at that time. However, if the seller remedies any failure to perform his obligations in accordance with article 37 or article 48 or if the buyer refuses to accept performance by the seller in accordance with those articles, the buyer may not reduce the price.

Article 51

(1) If the seller delivers only a part of the goods or if only a part of the goods delivered is in conformity with the contract, articles 46 to 50 apply in respect of the part which is missing or which does not conform.

(2) The buyer may declare the contract avoided in its entirety only if the failure to make delivery completely or in conformity with the contract amounts to a fundamental breach of the contract.

Article 52

(1) If the seller delivers the goods before the date fixed, the buyer may take delivery or refuse to take delivery.

(2) If the seller delivers a quantity of goods greater than that provided for in the contract, the buyer may take delivery or refuse to take delivery of the excess quantity. If the buyer takes delivery of all or part of the excess quantity, he must pay for it at the contract rate.

Chapter 3. Obligations of the Buyer

Article 53
The buyer must pay the price for the goods and take delivery of them as required by the contract and this Convention.

Section I. Payment of the Price

Article 54
The buyer's obligation to pay the price includes taking such steps and complying with such formalities as may be required under the contract or any laws and regulations to enable payment to be made.

Article 55
Where a contract has been validly concluded but does not expressly or implicitly fix or make provision for determining the price, the parties are considered, in the absence of any indication to the contrary, to have impliedly made reference to the price generally charged at the time of the conclusion of the contract for such goods sold under comparable circumstances in the trade concerned.

Article 56
If the price is fixed according to the weight of the goods, in case of doubt it is to be determined by the net weight.

Article 57
(1) If the buyer is not bound to pay the price at any other particular place, he must pay it to the seller:
  (a) at the seller's place of business; or
  (b) if the payment is to be made against the handing over of the goods or of documents, at the place where the handing over takes place.
(2) The seller must bear any increase in the expenses incidental to payment which is caused by a change in his place of business subsequent to the conclusion of the contract.

Article 58
(1) If the buyer is not bound to pay the price at any other specific time, he must pay it when the seller places either the goods or documents controlling their disposition at the buyer's disposal in accordance with the contract and this Convention. The seller may make such payment a condition for handing over the goods or documents.
(2) If the contract involves carriage of the goods, the seller may dispatch the goods on terms whereby the goods, or documents controlling their disposition, will not be handed over to the buyer except against payment of the price.
(3) The buyer is not bound to pay the price until he has had an opportunity to examine the goods, unless the procedures for delivery or payment agreed upon by the parties are inconsistent with his having such an opportunity.

Article 59
The buyer must pay the price on the date fixed by or determinable from the contract and this Convention without the need for any request or compliance with any formality on the part of the seller.

Section II. Taking Delivery

Article 60
The buyer's obligation to take delivery consists:
  (a) in doing all the acts which could reasonably be expected of him in order to enable the seller to make delivery; and
  (b) in taking over the goods.

Section III. Remedies for Breach of Contract by the Buyer

Article 61
(1) If the buyer fails to perform any of his obligations under the contract or this Convention, the seller may:
  (a) exercise the rights provided in articles 62 to 65;
  (b) claim damages as provided in articles 74 to 77.
(2) The seller is not deprived of any right he may have to claim damages by exercising his right to other remedies.
(3) No period of grace may be granted to the buyer by a court or arbitral tribunal when the seller resorts to a remedy for breach of contract.

Article 62
The seller may require the buyer to pay the price, take delivery or perform his other obligations, unless the seller has resorted to a remedy which is inconsistent with this requirement.

Article 63
(1) The seller may fix an additional period of time of reasonable length for performance by the buyer of his obligations.
(2) Unless the seller has received notice from the buyer that he will not perform within the period so fixed, the seller may not, during that period, resort to any remedy for breach of contract. However, the seller is not deprived thereby of any right he may have to claim damages for delay in performance.

Article 64
(1) The seller may declare the contract avoided:
  (a) if the failure by the buyer to perform any of his obligations under the contract or this Convention amounts to a fundamental breach of contract; or
  (b) if the buyer does not, within the additional period of time fixed by the seller in accordance with paragraph (1) of article 63, perform his obligation to pay the price or take delivery of the goods, or if he declares that he will not do so within the period so fixed.

(2) However, in cases where the buyer has paid the price, the seller loses the right to declare the contract avoided unless he does so:
   (a) in respect of late performance by the buyer, before the seller has become aware that performance has been rendered; or
   (b) in respect of any breach other than late performance by the buyer, within a reasonable time:
      (i) after the seller knew or ought to have known of the breach; or
      (ii) after the expiration of any additional period of time fixed by the seller in accordance with paragraph (1) of article 63, or after the buyer has declared that he will not perform his obligations within such an additional period.

Article 65

(1) If under the contract the buyer is to specify the form, measurement or other features of the goods and he fails to make such specification either on the date agreed upon or within a reasonable time after receipt of a request from the seller, the seller may, without prejudice to any other rights he may have, make the specification himself in accordance with the requirements of the buyer that may be known to him.

(2) If the seller makes the specification himself, he must inform the buyer of the details thereof and must fix a reasonable time within which the buyer may make a different specification. If, after receipt of such a communication, the buyer fails to do so within the time so fixed, the specification made by the seller is binding.

Chapter 4. Passing of Risk

Article 66

Loss of or damage to the goods after the risk has passed to the buyer does not discharge him from his obligation to pay the price, unless the loss or damage is due to an act or omission of the seller.

Article 67

(1) If the contract of sale involves carriage of the goods and the seller is not bound to hand them over at a particular place, the risk passes to the buyer when the goods are handed over to the first carrier for transmission to the buyer in accordance with the contract of sale. If the seller is bound to hand the goods over to a carrier at a particular place, the risk does not pass to the buyer until the goods are handed over to the carrier at that place. The fact that the seller is authorized to retain documents controlling the disposition of the goods does not affect the passage of the risk.

(2) Nevertheless, the risk does not pass to the buyer until the goods are clearly identified to the contract, whether by markings on the goods, by shipping documents, by notice given to the buyer or otherwise.

Article 68

The risk in respect of goods sold in transit passes to the buyer from the time of the conclusion of the contract. However, if the circumstances so indicate, the risk is assumed by the buyer from the time the goods were handed over to the carrier who issued the documents embodying the contract of carriage. Nevertheless, if at the time of the conclusion of the contract of sale the seller knew or ought to have known that the goods had been lost or damaged and did not disclose this to the buyer, the loss or damage is at the risk of the seller.

Article 69

(1) In cases not within articles 67 and 68, the risk passes to the buyer when he takes over the goods or, if he does not do so in due time, from the time when the goods are placed at his disposal and he commits a breach of contract by failing to take delivery.

(2) However, if the buyer is bound to take over the goods at a place other than a place of business of the seller, the risk passes when delivery is due and the buyer is aware of the fact that the goods are placed at his disposal at that place.

(3) If the contract relates to goods not then identified, the goods are considered not to be placed at the disposal of the buyer until they are clearly identified to the contract.

Article 70

If the seller has committed a fundamental breach of contract, articles 67, 68 and 69 do not impair the remedies available to the buyer on account of the breach.

Chapter 5. Provisions Common to the Obligations of the Seller and of the Buyer

Section I. Anticipatory Breach and Installment Contracts

Article 71

(1) A party may suspend the performance of his obligations if, after the conclusion of the contract, it becomes apparent that the other party will not perform a substantial part of his obligations as a result of:
   (a) a serious deficiency in his ability to perform or in his creditworthiness; or
   (b) his conduct in preparing to perform or in performing the contract.

(2) If the seller has already dispatched the goods before the grounds described in the preceding paragraph become evident, he may prevent the handing over of the goods to the buyer even though the buyer holds a document which entitles him to obtain them. The present paragraph relates only to the rights in the goods as between the buyer and the seller.

(3) A party suspending performance, whether before or after dispatch of the goods, must immediately give notice of the suspension to the other party and must continue with performance if the other party provides adequate assurance of his performance.

Article 72

(1) If prior to the date for performance of the contract it is clear that one of the parties will commit a fundamental breach of contract, the other party may declare the contract avoided.
(2) If time allows, the party intending to declare the contract avoided must give reasonable notice to the other party in order to permit him to provide adequate assurance of his performance.
(3) The requirements of the preceding paragraph do not apply if the other party has declared that he will not perform his obligations.

Article 73

(1) In the case of a contract for delivery of goods by instalments, if the failure of one party to perform any of his obligations in respect of any instalment constitutes a fundamental breach of contract with respect to that installment, the other party may declare the contract avoided with respect to that instalment.
(2) If one party's failure to perform any of his obligations in respect of any instalment gives the other party good grounds to conclude that a fundamental breach of contract will occur with respect to future instalments, he may declare the contract avoided for the future, provided that he does so within a reasonable time.
(3) A buyer who declares the contract avoided in respect of any delivery may, at the same time, declare it avoided in respect of deliveries already made or of future deliveries if, by reason of their interdependence, those deliveries could not be used for the purpose contemplated by the parties at the time of the conclusion of the contract.

Section II. Damages

Article 74

Damages for breach of contract by one party consist of a sum equal to the loss, including loss of profit, suffered by the other party as a consequence of the breach. Such damages may not exceed the loss which the party in breach foresaw or ought to have foreseen at the time of the conclusion of the contract, in the light of the facts and matters of which he then knew or ought to have known, as a possible consequence of the breach of contract.

Article 75

If the contract is avoided and if, in a reasonable manner and within a reasonable time after avoidance, the buyer has bought goods in replacement or the seller has resold the goods, the party claiming damages may recover the difference between the contract price and the price in the substitute transaction as well as any further damages recoverable under article 74.

Article 76

(1) If the contract is avoided and there is a current price for the goods, the party claiming damages may, if he has not made a purchase or resale under article 75, recover the difference between the price fixed by the contract and the current price at the time of avoidance as well as any further damages recoverable under article 74. If, however, the party claiming damages has avoided the contract after taking over the goods, the current price at the time of such taking over shall be applied instead of the current price at the time of avoidance.
(2) For the purposes of the preceding paragraph, the current price is the price prevailing at the place where delivery of the goods should have been made or, if there is no current price at that place, the price at such other place as serves as a reasonable substitute, making due allowance for differences in the cost of transporting the goods.

Article 77

A party who relies on a breach of contract must take such measures as are reasonable in the circumstances to mitigate the loss, including loss of profit, resulting from the breach. If he fails to take such measures, the party in breach may claim a reduction in the damages in the amount by which the loss should have been mitigated.

Section III. Interest

Article 78

If a party fails to pay the price or any other sum that is in arrears, the other party is entitled to interest on it, without prejudice to any claim for damages recoverable under article 74.

Section IV. Exemptions

Article 79

(1) A party is not liable for a failure to perform any of his obligations if he proves that the failure was due to an impediment beyond his control and that he could not reasonably be expected to have taken the impediment into account at the time of the conclusion of the contract or to have avoided or overcome it or its consequences.
(2) If the party's failure is due to the failure by a third person whom he has engaged to perform the whole or a part of the contract, that party is exempt from liability only if:
  (a) he is exempt under the preceding paragraph; and
  (b) the person whom he has so engaged would be so exempt if the provisions of that paragraph were applied to him.
(3) The exemption provided by this article has effect for the period during which the impediment exists.
(4) The party who fails to perform must give notice to the other party of the impediment and its effect on his ability

to perform. If the notice is not received by the other party within a reasonable time after the party who fails to perform knew or ought to have known of the impediment, he is liable for damages resulting from such nonreceipt.

(5) Nothing in this article prevents either party from exercising any right other than to claim damages under this Convention.

Article 80

A party may not rely on a failure of the other party to perform, to the extent that such failure was caused by the first party's act or omission.

Section V. Effects of Avoidance

Article 81

(1) Avoidance of the contract releases both parties from their obligations under it, subject to any damages which may be due. Avoidance does not affect any provision of the contract for the settlement of disputes or any other provision of the contract governing the rights and obligations of the parties consequent upon the avoidance of the contract.

(2) A party who has performed the contract either wholly or in part may claim restitution from the other party of whatever the first party has supplied or paid under the contract. If both parties are bound to make restitution, they must do so concurrently.

Article 82

(1) The buyer loses the right to declare the contract avoided or to require the seller to deliver substitute goods if it is impossible for him to make restitution of the goods substantially in the condition in which he received them.

(2) The preceding paragraph does not apply:

(a) if the impossibility of making restitution of the goods or of making restitution of the goods substantially in the condition in which the buyer received them is not due to his act or omission;

(b) if the goods or part of the goods have perished or deteriorated as a result of the examination provided for in article 38; or

(c) if the goods or part of the goods have been sold in the normal course of business or have been consumed or transformed by the buyer in the course of normal use before he discovered or ought to have discovered the lack of conformity.

Article 83

A buyer who has lost the right to declare the contract avoided or to require the seller to deliver substitute goods in accordance with article 82 retains all other remedies under the contract and this Convention.

Article 84

(1) If the seller is bound to refund the price, he must also pay interest on it, from the date on which the price was paid.

(2) The buyer must account to the seller for all benefits which he has derived from the goods or part of them:

(a) if he must make restitution of the goods or part of them; or

(b) if it is impossible for him to make restitution of all or part of the goods or to make restitution of all or part of the goods substantially in the condition in which he received them, but he has nevertheless declared the contract avoided or required the seller to deliver substitute goods.

Section VI. Preservation of the Goods

Article 85

If the buyer is in delay in taking delivery of the goods or, where payment of the price and delivery of the goods are to be made concurrently, if he fails to pay the price, and the seller is either in possession of the goods or otherwise able to control their disposition, the seller must take such steps as are reasonable in the circumstances to preserve them. He is entitled to retain them until he has been reimbursed his reasonable expenses by the buyer.

Article 86

(1) If the buyer has received the goods and intends to exercise any right under the contract or this Convention to reject them, he must take such steps to preserve them as are reasonable in the circumstances. He is entitled to retain them until he has been reimbursed his reasonable expenses by the seller.

(2) If goods dispatched to the buyer have been placed at his disposal at their destination and he exercises the right to reject them, he must take possession of them on behalf of the seller, provided that this can be done without payment of the price and without unreasonable inconvenience or unreasonable expense. This provision does not apply if the seller or a person authorized to take charge of the goods on his behalf is present at the destination. If the buyer takes possession of the goods under this paragraph, his rights and obligations are governed by the preceding paragraph.

Article 87

A party who is bound to take steps to preserve the goods may deposit them in a warehouse of a third person at the expense of the other party provided that the expense incurred is not unreasonable.

Article 88

(1) A party who is bound to preserve the goods in accordance with article 85 or 86 may sell them by any appropriate means if there has been an unreasonable delay by the other party in taking possession of the goods or in taking them back or in paying the price or the cost of preservation,

provided that reasonable notice of the intention to sell has been given to the other party.

(2) If the goods are subject to rapid deterioration or their preservation would involve unreasonable expense, a party who is bound to preserve the goods in accordance with article 85 or 86 must take reasonable measures to sell them. To the extent possible he must give notice to the other party of his intention to sell.

(3) A party selling the goods has the right to retain out of the proceeds of sale an amount equal to the reasonable expenses of preserving the goods and of selling them. He must account to the other party for the balance.

PART FOUR: FINAL PROVISIONS

Article 89

The Secretary-General of the United Nations is hereby designated as the depositary for this Convention.

Article 90

This Convention does not prevail over any international agreement which has already been or may be entered into and which contains provisions concerning the matters governed by this Convention, provided that the parties have their places of business in States parties to such agreement.

Article 91

(1) This Convention is open for signature at the concluding meeting of the United Nations Conference on Contracts for the International Sale of Goods and will remain open for signature by all States at the Headquarters of the United Nations, New York until 30 September 1981.

(2) This Convention is subject to ratification, acceptance or approval by the signatory States.

(3) This Convention is open for accession by all States which are not signatory States as from the date it is open for signature.

(4) Instruments of ratification, acceptance, approval and accession are to be deposited with the Secretary-General of the United Nations.

Article 92

(1) A Contracting State may declare at the time of signature, ratification, acceptance, approval or accession that it will not be bound by Part II of this Convention or that it will not be bound by Part III of this Convention.

(2) A Contracting State which makes a declaration in accordance with the preceding paragraph in respect of Part II or Part III of this Convention is not to be considered a Contracting State within paragraph (1) of article 1 of this Convention in respect of matters governed by the Part to which the declaration applies.

Article 93

(1) If a Contracting State has two or more territorial units in which, according to its constitution, different systems of law are applicable in relation to the matters dealt with in this Convention, it may, at the time of signature, ratification, acceptance, approval or accession, declare that this Convention is to extend to all its territorial units or only to one or more of them, and may amend its declaration by submitting another declaration at any time.

(2) These declarations are to be notified to the depositary and are to state expressly the territorial units to which the Convention extends.

(3) If, by virtue of a declaration under this article, this Convention extends to one or more but not all of the territorial units of a Contracting State, and if the place of business of a party is located in that State, this place of business, for the purposes of this Convention, is considered not to be in a Contracting State, unless it is in a territorial unit to which the Convention extends.

(4) If a Contracting State makes no declaration under paragraph (1) of this article, the Convention is to extend to all territorial units of that State.

Article 94

(1) Two or more Contracting States which have the same or closely related legal rules on matters governed by this Convention may at any time declare that the Convention is not to apply to contracts of sale or to their formation where the parties have their places of business in those States. Such declarations may be made jointly or by reciprocal unilateral declarations.

(2) A Contracting State which has the same or closely related legal rules on matters governed by this Convention as one or more non-Contracting States may at any time declare that the Convention is not to apply to contracts of sale or to their formation where the parties have their place of business in those States.

(3) If a State which is the object of a declaration under the preceding paragraph subsequently becomes a Contracting State, the declaration made will, as from the date on which the Convention enters into force in respect of the new Contracting State, have the effect of a declaration made under paragraph (1), provided that the new Contracting State joins in such declaration or makes a reciprocal unilateral declaration.

Article 95

Any State may declare at the time of the deposit of its instrument of ratification, acceptance, approval or accession that it will not be bound by subparagraph (1)(b) of article 1 of this Convention.

Article 96

A Contracting State whose legislation requires contracts of sale to be concluded in or evidenced by writing may at any time make a declaration in accordance with article 12 that any provision of article 11, article 29, or Part II of this Convention, that allows a contract sale or its modification or termination by agreement or any offer, acceptance, or other indication of intention to be made in any form other than in writing, does not apply where any party has his place of business in that State.

Article 97

(1) Declarations made under this Convention at the time of signature are subject to confirmation upon ratification, acceptance or approval.

(2) Declarations and confirmations of declarations are to be in writing and be formally notified to the depositary.

(3) A declaration takes effect simultaneously with the entry into force of this Convention in respect of the State concerned. However, a declaration of which the depositary receives formal notification after such entry into force takes effect on the first day of the month following the expiration of six months after the date of its receipt by the depositary. Reciprocal unilateral declarations under article 94 takes effect on the first day of the month following the expiration of six months after the receipt of the latest declaration by the depositary.

(4) Any State which makes a declaration under this Convention may withdraw it at any time by a formal notification in writing addressed to the depositary. Such withdrawal is to take effect on the first day of the month following the expiration of six months after the date of the receipt of the notification by the depositary.

(5) A withdrawal of a declaration made under article 94 renders inoperative, as from the date on which the withdrawal takes effect, any reciprocal declaration made by another State under that article.

Article 98

No reservations are permitted except those expressly authorized in this Convention.

Article 99

(1) This Convention enters into force, subject to the provisions of paragraph (6) of this article, on the first day of the month following the expiration of twelve months after the date of deposit of the tenth instrument of ratification, acceptance, approval or accession, including an instrument which contains a declaration made under article 92.

(2) When a State ratifies, accepts, approves or accedes to this Convention after the deposit of the tenth instrument of ratification, acceptance, approval or accession, this Convention, with the exception of the Part excluded, enters into force in respect of that State, subject to the provisions of paragraph (6) of this article, on the first day of the month following the expiration of twelve months after the date of the deposit of its instrument of ratification, acceptance, approval or accession.

(3) A State which ratifies, accepts, approves or accedes to this Convention and is a party to either or both the Convention relating to a Uniform Law on the Formation of Contracts for the International Sale of Goods done at The Hague on 1 July 1964 (1964 Hague Formation Convention) and the Convention relating to a Uniform Law on the International Sale of Goods done at The Hague on 1 July 1964 (1964 Hague Sales Convention) shall at the same time denounce, as the case may be, either or both the 1964 Hague Sales Convention and the 1964 Hague Formation Convention by notifying the Government of the Netherlands to that effect.

(4) A State party to the 1964 Hague Sales Convention which ratifies, accepts, approves or accedes to the present Convention and declares or has declared under article 92 that it will not be bound by Part II of this Convention shall at the time of ratification, acceptance, approval or accession denounce the 1964 Hague Sales Convention by notifying the Government of the Netherlands to that effect.

(5) A State party to the 1964 Hague Formation Convention which ratifies, accepts, approves or accedes to the present Convention and declares or has declared under article 92 that it will not be bound by Part III of this Convention shall at the time of ratification, acceptance, approval or accession denounce the 1964 Hague Formation Convention by notifying the Government of the Netherlands to that effect.

(6) For the purpose of this article, ratifications, acceptances, approvals and accessions in respect of this Convention by States parties to the 1964 Hague Formation Convention or to the 1964 Hague Sales Convention shall not be effective until such denunciations as may be required on the part of those States in respect of the latter two Conventions have themselves become effective. The depositary of this Convention shall consult with the Government of the Netherlands, as the depositary of the 1964 Conventions, so as to ensure necessary coordination in this respect.

Article 100

(1) This Convention applies to the formation of a contract only when the proposal for concluding the contract is made on or after the date when the Convention enters into force in respect of the Contracting States referred to in subparagraph (1)(a) or the Contracting State referred to in subparagraph (1)(b) of article 1.

(2) This Convention applies only to contracts concluded on or after the date when the Convention enters into force in respect of the Contracting States referred to in subparagraph (1)(a) or the Contracting State referred to in subparagraph (1)(b) of article 1.

Article 101

(1) A Contracting State may denounce this Convention, or Part II or Part III of the Convention, by a formal notification in writing addressed to the depositary.

(2) The denunciation takes effect on the first day of the month following the expiration of twelve months after the notification is received by the depositary. Where a longer period for the denunciation to take effect is specified in the notification, the denunciation takes effect upon the expiration of such longer period after the notification is received by the depositary.

DONE at Vienna, this day of eleventh day of April, one thousand nine hundred and eighty, in a single original, of which the Arabic, Chinese, English, French, Russian and Spanish texts are equally authentic.

IN WITNESS WHEREOF the undersigned plenipotentiaries, being duly authorized by their respective Governments, have signed this Convention.

INDEX

For listings of specific statutes, treaties and cases, see also Tables on pages xix–xxx

List of Frequently Used Acronyms

AD or ADD	Antidumping Duty
ADRs	American Depository Receipts
AECA	Arms Export Control Act
AGOA	African Growth and Opportunity Act
AGP	Agreement on Government Procurement (WTO)
AID	Agency for International Development
APEC	Asia Pacific Economic Cooperation
ASEAN	Association of Southeast Asian Nations
ATPA	Andean Trade Preference Act
ATS	Alien Tort Statute
BEA	Bureau of Economic Analysis, U.S. Department of Commerce
BIS	Bureau of Industry and Security (U.S. DOC)
BIT	Bilateral Investment Treaty
BOP	Balance of Payments
BOT	Balance of Trade
CACM	Central American Common Market
CAFTA-DR	Central American Free Trade Agreement
CAP	Common Agricultural Policy of the European Union
CARICOM	Caribbean Common Market
CBERA	Caribbean Basin Economic Recovery Act
CBI	Caribbean Basin Initiative
CBP	Bureau of Customs and Border Protection (U.S. DHS)
CBSA	Canadian Border Services Agency
CCC	Customs Cooperation Council
CCJ	Caribbean Court of Justice
CCL	Commerce Control List
CE	Conformité Européene
CE	Mark Conformite Européene
CET	Common External Tariff (or CXT)
CFI	European Court of the First Instance
CIS	Commonwealth of Independent States
CISG	Convention on Contracts for the International Sale of Goods
CIT	Court of International Trade
CITES	Convention on International Trade in Endangered Species of Wild Fauna and Flora
CITT	Canadian International Trade Tribunal
CMI	Comite Maritime International
CO	Certificate of Origin
CODEX	Codex Alimentarius Commission
COE	Council of Europe
COGSA	Carriage of Goods by Sea Act
CVD	Countervailing Duty
D/A	Documents Against Acceptance
D/P	Documents Against Payment
DFAIT	Department of Foreign Affairs and International Trade (Canada)
DG-COMP	European Commission Directorate General for Competition
DOC	Department of Commerce
DSB	Dispute Settlement Body (WTO)
DSU	Dispute Settlement Understanding (WTO)
EAR	Export Administration Regulations
EBRD	European Bank for Reconstruction and Development
EC	European Community
ECCN	Export Control Classification Number
ECJ	European Court of Justice
EDI	Electronic Data Interchange
EEA	European Economic Area
EFTA	European Free Trade Association
EIB	European Investment Bank
EMC	Export Management Company
EOTC	European Organization for Testing and Clarification
EPO	European Patent Office
ERM	Exchange Rate Mechanism
ETC	Export Trading Company
EU	European Union
EXIMBANK	Export-Import Bank of the U.S.
FCIA	Foreign Credit Insurance Association
FCN	Friendship, Commerce, and Navigation treaties
FCPA	Foreign Corrupt Practices Act
FCTC	World Health Organization's Framework Convention on Tobacco Control
FDI	Foreign Direct Investment
FMC	Federal Maritime Commission
FPA	Free of Particular Average
FSC	Foreign Sales Corporation
FSIA	Foreign Sovereign Immunities Act
FTA	Free Trade Agreement or Area
FTAA	Free Trade Area of the Americas
FTZ	Foreign Trade Zone
GATS	General Agreement on Trade in Services
GATT	General Agreement on Tariffs and Trade